Ubuntu® Linux® Bible

Third Edition

Ubuntu® Linux® Bible

Third Edition

Featuring Ubuntu 10.04 LTS

William von Hagen

WILEY

Wiley Publishing, Inc.

Ubuntu® Linux® Bible: Featuring Ubuntu 10.04 LTS, Third Edition

Published by
Wiley Publishing, Inc.
10475 Crosspoint Boulevard
Indianapolis, IN 46256
www.wiley.com

Copyright © 2010 by Wiley Publishing, Inc., Indianapolis, Indiana

Published simultaneously in Canada

ISBN: 978-0-470-60450-2

Manufactured in the United States of America

10 9 8 7 6 5 4 3 2 1

For general information on our other products and services please contact our Customer Care Department within the United States at (877) 762-2974, outside the United States at (317) 572-3993 or fax (317) 572-4002.

Wiley also publishes its books in a variety of electronic formats. Some content that appears in print may not be available in electronic books.

Library of Congress Control Number: 2010926822

To Dorothy, for more than words can say...

Quidquid latine dictum sit, altum sonatur.

About the Author

William von Hagen (Bill) has been a UNIX system administrator for more than 20 years, and a Linux fanatic since the early 1990s. He has worked as a Linux product manager, systems programmer, system administrator, writer, application developer, drummer, and content manager. Bill has written or co-written books on such topics as Linux server hacks, GCC, Xen virtualization, Linux filesystems, SUSE Linux, Red Hat Linux, SGML, Mac OS X, and hacking the TiVo. He has also written numerous articles on Linux, embedded computing, Mac OS X, UNIX, and various open source topics. An avid computer collector specializing in workstations, he owns more than 200 computer systems but is not compulsive at all. You can reach him at wvh@vonhagen.org.

Credits

Executive Editor
Carol Long

Project Editor
Tom Dinse

Technical Editor
Timothy Boronczyk

Production Editor
Kathleen Wisor

Copy Editor
Catherine Caffrey

Editorial Director
Robyn B. Siesky

Editorial Manager
Mary Beth Wakefield

Marketing Manager
Ashley Zurcher

Production Manager
Tim Tate

Vice President and Executive Group Publisher
Richard Swadley

Vice President and Executive Publisher
Barry Pruett

Associate Publisher
Jim Minatel

Project Coordinator, Cover
Lynsey Stanford

Compositor
Maureen Forys,
Happenstance Type-O-Rama

Proofreaders
Nancy Carrasco
Sheilah Ledwidge, Word One
Louise Watson, Word One

Indexer
Robert Swanson

Cover Image
Joyce Haughey

Cover Designer
Michael E. Trent

Acknowledgments

Nothing I have ever written would have been possible without the love, support, and infinite patience of Dorothy Fisher, my wife and best friend. Dorth believed in me from day one, removed several thousand commas from my earliest writing, and has accepted "I can't do that now—come back in 15 minutes or 6 hours" as an excuse more times than anyone should ever be expected to. I am similarly lucky to have great friends like Jeff "Sunshine" Kaminski, Gregg Kostelich, Dr. Joe O'Lear, Jim Morgan, Larry Rippel, and Kim Walter in my life. I heard once that a good friend will come and bail you out of jail, but a true friend will be sitting in jail with you saying, "Man! That was fun!" Luckily, we haven't had to test that, but I'm sure we'd all look great in orange.

I would also like to thank Carol Long, Tom Dinse, and others at Wiley who enabled me to do a new edition of this book and supported me during its creation. Similarly, Tim Boronczyk did a great job as the technical editor for this edition of the book, catching old errors that remained undetected and new ones that I introduced, as well as making some great suggestions. All errors are mine alone, but this would be a much weaker book without all of your contributions. I quite literally wouldn't have been able to do it without you.

Finally, this book wouldn't exist without Linus Torvalds; Mark Shuttleworth; the Ubuntu folk in general; the Debian, GNOME, and KDE Projects; Richard Stallman; the FSF; and the millions of contributors to the cornucopia that is GNU/Linux.

Contents at a Glance

Introduction xxxiii

Part I: Getting Started With Ubuntu 1
Chapter 1: The Ubuntu Linux Project 3
Chapter 2: Installing Ubuntu 31
Chapter 3: Installing Ubuntu on Special-Purpose Systems 61

Part II: Ubuntu for Desktop Users. 103
Chapter 4: Basic Linux System Concepts 105
Chapter 5: Using the GNOME Desktop 129
Chapter 6: Using the Compiz Window Manager 189
Chapter 7: Managing E-Mail and Personal Information with Evolution 221
Chapter 8: Surfing the Web with Firefox 281
Chapter 9: Migrating from Windows Systems 319
Chapter 10: Sending and Receiving Instant Messages 355
Chapter 11: Using Command-Line Tools 391
Chapter 12: Working with Text Files 427
Chapter 13: Creating and Publishing Documents 461
Chapter 14: Other Office Software: Spreadsheets and Presentations 499
Chapter 15: Working with Graphics 531
Chapter 16: Working with Multimedia 559
Chapter 17: Would You Like to Play a Game? 617
Chapter 18: Consumer Electronics and Ubuntu 641
Chapter 19: Adding, Removing, and Updating Software 667
Chapter 20: Adding Hardware and Attaching Peripherals 721
Chapter 21: Network Configuration and Security 763
Chapter 22: Going Wireless 799
Chapter 23: Software Development on Ubuntu 819
Chapter 24: Using Virtual Machines and Emulators 857
Chapter 25: Connecting to Other Systems 905
Chapter 26: File Transfer and Sharing...925

Contents at a Glance

Part III: Ubuntu for System Administrators 953

Chapter 27: Managing Users, Groups, and Authentication..955

Chapter 28: Backing Up and Restoring Files..985

Chapter 29: Setting Up a Web Server...1023

Chapter 30: Setting Up a Mail Server...1035

Chapter 31: Setting Up a DHCP Server..1059

Chapter 32: Setting Up a DNS Server..1075

Chapter 33: Setting Up a Print Server..1095

Chapter 34: Setting Up an NFS Server...1105

Chapter 35: Setting Up a Samba Server...1125

Appendix: What's on the CD-ROM?..1137

Index...1141

Contents

Introduction . . . . **xxxiii**

Part I: Getting Started With Ubuntu   **1**

Chapter 1: The Ubuntu Linux Project 3

Background 4
    Why Use Linux? 4
    What Is a Linux Distribution? 5
Introducing Ubuntu Linux 7
    The Ubuntu Manifesto 8
    Ubuntu Release Schedule 10
    Ubuntu Update and Maintenance Commitments 11
    Ubuntu and the Debian Project 11
Why Choose Ubuntu? 12
What Versions of Ubuntu Are Available? 14
    Desktop and Laptop Users 14
    Netbook/MID Users 18
    Server Users 18
Installation Requirements 19
    Supported System Types 19
    Hardware Requirements 20
    Time Requirements 21
Ubuntu CDs 21
Support for Ubuntu 22
    Community Support and Information 23
        Blogs 23
        Ubuntu Forums 23
        IRC 25
        Mailing Lists 25
        What's on the Fridge? 26
    Documentation 26
    Commercial Support for Ubuntu Linux 27
        Paid Support from Canonical, Ltd. 27
        The Ubuntu Marketplace 28
Getting More Information about Ubuntu 28
Summary 29

Contents

Chapter 2: Installing Ubuntu **31**

Getting a 64-Bit Desktop CD...32
Booting from a Desktop CD 32
Installing Ubuntu from a Desktop CD...37
  Booting Ubuntu...45
  Booting Ubuntu on Dual-Boot Systems 45
  The First Time You Boot Ubuntu...46
Test-Driving Ubuntu Linux 47
  Exploring the Desktop CD's Examples Folder 47
  Accessing Your Hard Drive from the Desktop CD 49
    Accessing Existing Partitions from a Desktop CD....................49
  Copying Files to Other Machines over a Network 51
  Using Desktop CD Persistence...52
Wubi: Installing Ubuntu on Windows 56
Summary..59

Chapter 3: Installing Ubuntu on Special-Purpose Systems **61**

Getting a Different Install CD..62
Booting from a Server or Alternate Install CD 62
Install Options on the Server Install CD 63
  Installing an Ubuntu Server...65
  Manually Specifying Your Partition Layout...................................81
  Booting Your Server for the First Time 90
Installing an Ubuntu Enterprise Cloud 91
Install Options on the Alternate Install CD.....................................95
  Installing a Desktop System in Text Mode 97
  Installing in OEM Mode 98
  Installing a Command-Line System 100
  Installing an LTSP Server..100
Summary..101

Part II: Ubuntu for Desktop Users   103

Chapter 4: Basic Linux System Concepts **105**

Working with Files and Directories..106
  Standard Linux Directories..107
  Other Common Directories on Linux Systems 108
Introduction to Linux Filesystems...108
  Disks, Partitions, and Mountpoints 109
  Introducing Logical Volumes..110
  Local Filesystems: Standard and Journaling................................112
  Network Filesystems...114
Working with Partitions and Filesystems...115
  Mounting Filesystems...115
  Automatically Mounting Filesystems at Boot Time....................118
  Automatically Mounting Removable Media Filesystems 121

Contents

Understanding Linux Permissions 122
   Basic Concepts: Users and Groups 122
   File and Directory Permissions under Linux 124
   Performing Privileged Operations in Ubuntu 125
Summary 126

Chapter 5: Using the GNOME Desktop 129

What's a Desktop? Graphical Environments for Linux 130
Using the Mouse 132
GNOME Desktop Overview 133
GNOME Application Windows 135
Menus in GNOME 136
   Panel Menus 137
      The Application Menu 138
      The Places Menu 139
      The System Menu 139
   Context-Sensitive Menus 140
   Customizing GNOME Menus 141
Customizing Your Desktop 146
   Customizing Mouse Behavior 146
   Configuring Screen Resolution 148
   Customizing Panels 149
      Customizing Panel Properties 151
      Customizing Panel Contents 152
   Configuring the Screensaver 155
   Configuring Power Management 157
   Changing Desktop Backgrounds 162
   Switching Themes 163
   Assistive Technologies for Using GNOME 165
GNOME Keyboard Shortcuts 166
Introducing the Nautilus File Manager 167
   Basic Operations in Nautilus 168
   Examples of Using Nautilus 169
      Exploring the Filesystem 170
      Copying Files or Directories 170
      Selecting Multiple Files and Directories 171
      Moving Files or Directories 171
      Renaming a File or Directory 171
      Creating a Directory 172
   Getting More Information about Nautilus 173
Using the Tracker Desktop Search Application 173
   Searching with Tracker 174
   Configuring Tracker 176
   Using the GNOME Deskbar Applet 179
Using a Window Manager 181
Summary 186

Contents

Chapter 6: Using the Compiz Window Manager **189**

What Is Compositing? Why All the Fuss?..190

Compiz History: Compiz, Emerald, Beryl, and Friends 191

Enabling Special Effects in Compiz...193

    Using the Appearance Preferences Application..193

    Detailed Compiz Configuration 196

        Configuring Compiz Using GNOME Configuration Tools...................196

        Installing and Using CompizConfig Settings Manager........................202

Other Useful Packages for Compiz...209

    Installing and Using the Avant Window Navigator..209

    Other Dock Software for Ubuntu Systems 214

    Using Emerald and the Emerald Theme Manager...216

Summary...219

Chapter 7: Managing E-Mail and Personal Information with Evolution . . . **221**

Starting Evolution..222

Using the Evolution Setup Assistant..223

Sending and Receiving Mail 232

    Sending Mail in Evolution 235

    Setting Evolution Preferences for Sending and Viewing Mail.........................236

    Undeleting Mail Messages..240

    Creating and Using Mail Folders 240

    Using Search Folders 242

Filtering Incoming Mail...244

    Automatically Processing Incoming Mail...245

    Automatically Checking for Junk Mail..248

Accessing Free and Web-Based E-Mail...249

    Reading Gmail from a Desktop Mail Client 249

        Selecting a Transport Protocol in Gmail 250

        Accessing Gmail Using POP..252

        Accessing Gmail Using IMAP 253

    Reading Mail from Other Web-Based Mail Providers 254

        Installing and Using FreePOPs! 255

        Creating POP Accounts for Use with FreePOPs! 256

Managing Contacts..257

    Configuring Evolution's Contact Support 257

        Configuring Contact/E-Mail Interaction...257

        Accessing Remote Contact Information via LDAP 260

    Adding and Editing Contact Information 262

    Defining Mailing Lists 265

Managing Your Calendar...267

    Basic Calendar Configuration 267

        Defining Your Work Day and Work Hours 268

        Setting Event Granularity on Your Calendar.......................................268

    Creating and Editing Personal Calendar Entries...269

Contents

Creating and Editing Meetings 272
Integrating Online Calendars 274
Publishing Your Free/Busy Information 276
Additional Sources of Information about Evolution 278
Summary 279

Chapter 8: Surfing the Web with Firefox 281

A Quick History of Firefox 281
Starting Firefox 283
The Firefox User Interface 284
Standard Parts of a Firefox Window 285
Using the Mouse in Firefox 286
Special and Not-So-Special Firefox Features 287
Configuring Firefox 290
Setting Your Home Page 291
Controlling Pop-Ups, JavaScript, and More 292
Configuring Your Privacy Settings 293
Working with Bookmarks 297
Creating Bookmarks in Firefox 298
Managing Your Bookmarks 300
Creating Live Bookmarks 303
Enhancing Firefox 306
Registering for Add-Ons 306
Viewing Installed Firefox Add-Ons, Themes, and Personas 307
Adding Firefox Add-Ons, Themes, and Personas 309
Adding New Firefox Plug-Ins 315
Summary 317

Chapter 9: Migrating from Windows Systems 319

Overview of Migration Scenarios 320
Backing Up Your Personal Data 322
Migrating E-Mail to Linux 323
Migrating Mail via Thunderbird 324
Where Thunderbird Stores Its Mail 326
Installing or Updating Thunderbird 327
Importing Mail into Thunderbird: New Users 327
Importing Mail into Thunderbird: Existing Users 328
Importing Thunderbird Mail into Evolution 332
Manually Migrating Mail 335
Migrating Outlook Express Mail with readdbx 336
Migrating Outlook Mail with readpst 337
Migrating Web/Browser Settings to Linux 339
Migrating from Firefox to Firefox 340
Checking Your Ubuntu System First 341
Migrating an Existing Profile 342
Troubleshooting Profile Migration 343

Contents

Migrating from Internet Explorer/Safari to Firefox 343
Migrating Just Your Bookmarks 345
    Exporting Internet Explorer Bookmarks 346
    Exporting Safari Bookmarks 349
    Importing Bookmarks into Firefox 350
Working with Windows Application Data 351
Summary 353

Chapter 10: Sending and Receiving Instant Messages 355

Instant Messaging Overview 356
Getting an Instant Messaging Account 358
Instant Messaging on Ubuntu with Empathy 361
    Starting Empathy 361
    Configuring Instant Messaging Accounts in Empathy 362
        Importing Pidgin Accounts 363
        Defining Existing Accounts Manually 363
        Creating a New Account 365
        Seeing People Online Nearby 366
        Adding and Removing Empathy Accounts 367
    Using Empathy 369
        Adding Contacts in Empathy 370
        Reviewing Past Conversations 372
        Exiting Empathy 372
    Getting More Information about Empathy 373
Instant Messaging on Ubuntu with Pidgin 373
    Configuring Instant Messaging Accounts in Pidgin 374
    Using Pidgin 376
        Connecting to Your IM Accounts in Pidgin 379
        Adding Buddies in Pidgin 380
        Organizing Buddies in Pidgin 382
        Viewing Buddies in Pidgin 383
        Logging Your Conversations 383
        Exiting Pidgin 384
    Getting More Information about Pidgin 385
Using IRC 386
    Using IRC in Empathy 387
    Getting More Information about IRC 388
Other Instant Messaging Packages 388
Resolving IM Communication Problems 389
Summary 390

Chapter 11: Using Command-Line Tools 391

Why Use the Command Line? 392
Executing Commands from the Command Line 393
What's a Shell? 399

Contents

Getting to a Shell 401

    Using the GNOME Terminal Application 401

    Using the X Window System Terminal Application 403

Popular Command-Line Commands 406

    Moving Around in the Linux Filesystem 407

    Copying, Moving, Renaming, and Deleting Files and Directories 408

    Changing File and Directory Permissions 412

    Finding Commands That Do Specific Things 415

Working with the Bash Shell 415

    Using Command History 416

    Using Command and Filename Completion 417

    Using Wildcards 418

    Pipes and Input and Output Re-Direction 420

    Introducing Job Control 421

    Exploring the Bash Configuration File 423

    Using Environment Variables 424

    Defining and Using Aliases 426

Summary 426

Chapter 12: Working with Text Files 427

Introduction to Linux Text Editors 428

Using vi 430

    Starting and Exiting vi 431

    Inserting Text in vi 432

    Moving Around in vi 432

    Deleting and Changing Text in vi 434

    Cutting, Copying, and Pasting in vi 435

    Searching for and Replacing Text in vi 436

    Undoing Changes in vi 437

    Using Multiple Windows in vi 438

    Customizing vim 439

    Graphical Versions of vi 441

    More Information about vi and vim 442

Using Emacs 442

    A Few Words about Emacs Commands 446

    Emacs Terminology 447

    Starting and Exiting Emacs 448

    Moving Around in Emacs 451

    Cutting, Copying, and Pasting in Emacs 452

    Searching for and Replacing Text in Emacs 452

    Working with Multiple Windows and Buffers in Emacs 453

    Customizing Emacs 453

        Changing Key Bindings 453

        Setting Variables 454

        Specifying Modes...454

Contents

Changing File Associations...455
Defining Your Own Functions..455
Getting More Information about Emacs....................................456
Using gedit...456
Other Text Editors for Linux Systems..458
Summary..459

Chapter 13: Creating and Publishing Documents **461**

Using Document Markup Languages..462
Using TeX and LaTeX...462
More Information about TeX and LaTeX......................................465
Word Processing with OpenOffice.org Writer...............................466
Installing Files for Writer...468
Taking a Quick Tour of Writer...469
Personalizing Writer..472
Using Wizards to Create Documents..473
Modifying Document Styles and Layout.....................................477
Creating and Using Templates...480
Importing Documents from Other Word Processors..................483
More Information about Writer..485
Desktop Publishing with Scribus..486
Installing Scribus..487
A Quick Scribus Tutorial..487
More Information about Scribus..497
Other Word Processors and Office Suites.......................................497
Summary..498

Chapter 14: Other Office Software: Spreadsheets and Presentations . . **499**

Introduction to Spreadsheets..500
Using OpenOffice.org Calc..501
Starting Calc...501
Taking a Quick Tour of Calc..502
A Quick Calc Tutorial...503
Invoking Functions in Calc..514
Specifying the Type of Data in a Cell..515
Importing Existing Spreadsheets into Calc.................................517
Supported Import Formats..518
Importing Spreadsheets Using the Document Converter.....519
Creating and Using OpenOffice.org Presentations.....................522
Starting Impress...522
Using the Presentation Wizard..522
Taking a Quick Tour of Impress..525
Creating a Presentation..526
Importing Existing Presentations...528
Summary..530

Contents

Chapter 15: Working with Graphics **531**

Overview of Digital Graphics Terminology 532

Using GIMP 536

    Starting GIMP 537

    A Quick Tour of GIMP 538

    Sample GIMP Tasks 539

        Taking Screenshots Using GIMP 541

        Converting and Reducing Images Using GIMP 544

    More Information about GIMP 548

Photo Editing Overview 548

Using OpenOffice.org Draw 551

    Starting Draw 551

    A Quick Tour of Draw 552

    More Information about OpenOffice.org Draw 553

Vector Graphics Tools for Linux 553

    Using Inkscape 554

        Starting Inkscape 555

        A Quick Tour of Inkscape 555

        More Information about Inkscape 556

Other Graphics Applications 557

Summary 558

Chapter 16: Working with Multimedia **559**

Overview of Digital Audio and Video Terminology 560

Configuring Sound Devices, Levels, and System Sounds 566

    Specifying and Testing Sound Devices 566

    Setting System Sound Levels 568

    Testing and Customizing System Sounds 568

    Getting Detailed Information about Your Sound Hardware 569

    Setting Blank CD and DVD Preferences 570

Exploring the Linux Multimedia Stack 573

    Introducing Drivers, Servers, and Frameworks 573

        Linux Sound APIs 573

        Linux Sound Servers 573

        Linux Multimedia Frameworks 574

        What Should You Care About? 574

    Configuring the GStreamer Framework and Plug-Ins 575

    Configuring PulseAudio 577

Playing CDs and DVDs 579

    Playing Audio CDs Using Rhythmbox 580

    Installing Software to Play Encrypted DVDs 581

    Playing DVDs with Totem 581

Ripping Audio CDs 583

    Ripping Audio CDs Using Rhythmbox 583

    Ripping Audio CDs Using k3b 585

    Backing Up DVDs from the Command Line 589

Contents

Creating CDs and DVDs..590

    Burning CDs Using Brasero..590

        Creating Audio CDs with Brasero 590

        Burning CD and DVD Images Using Brasero 595

    Burning Data CDs and DVDs Using Nautilus 596

    Burning CDs and DVDs Using k3b...599

        Burning an Audio CD Using k3b 600

        Burning an ISO Image to CD or DVD with k3b...............................602

        Copying a CD or DVD with k3b...603

Working with Other Audio Sources 606

    Playing Audio Files and Internet Radio Using Rhythmbox....................606

        Creating Playlists 609

        Playing and Adding Internet Radio Stations 609

        Adding and Playing Podcasts...610

    Converting Audio File Formats...613

Summary..616

Chapter 17: Would You Like to Play a Game? 617

GNOME Games on Ubuntu 618

    Card Games..618

        AisleRiot Solitaire 619

        Tali 619

    Board Games 619

        Chess 620

        Five or More 620

        gbrainy 620

        Iagno...620

        Klotski...621

        Lights Off 621

        Mahjongg..621

        Mines 621

        Sudoku..621

        Tetravex 622

    Video Games..622

        Four-in-a-Row..622

        Nibbles..622

        Quadrapassel 623

        Robots...623

        Swell Foop 623

Other Popular Games...624

    Billions and Billions of Versions of Chess 624

    Go...627

    Monopoly Clones...629

    Scrabble Clones 633

    Unique Arcade Games for Linux 635

        Atomic Tanks 635

        DOOM 636

Contents

Frozen Bubble 636

Metal Blob Solid 637

Tux Racer 638

More Great Arcade Games 639

Summary 640

Chapter 18: Consumer Electronics and Ubuntu **641**

Configuring Your System for Consumer Electronics Devices 642

Default Actions 643

Customizing Digital Device Recognition 645

Working with Your Digital Camera 648

Working with iPods and Other Digital Audio Players 654

Digital Audio Players and Rhythmbox on Ubuntu 656

Playing Music 657

Copying Music to an Audio Player 658

Copying Music from an Audio Player 658

Removing Music from an Audio Player 658

Creating, Renaming, and Editing Playlists 658

Disconnecting Your Audio Player 659

Working with an iPod Using gtkpod 659

Attaching Your iPod 660

Using gtkpod 660

Writing Changes to Your iPod 664

Safely Disconnecting Your iPod 664

Working with CompactFlash and SD Cards 665

Summary 665

Chapter 19: Adding, Removing, and Updating Software **667**

Installing Software with the Ubuntu Software Center 669

Package Management Software Overview 670

Ubuntu Repositories and Components 672

Enabling Additional Repository Components 674

Other Repositories of Interest 676

Enabling Additional Repository Sources Using the Software Sources Tool 676

Problems Adding or Accessing Nonstandard Repositories 681

Exploring Your System Using dpkg and Friends 682

Listing the Packages That Are Installed on Your System 682

Listing the Packages That Are Available for Your System 683

Listing Information about a Package 687

Listing the Contents of a Package 687

Determining What Package Provides an Existing File 688

Determining What Package Provides a Missing File 690

Using apt-get to Add and Remove Software 690

Upgrading Your System Using apt-get 692

Smart System Upgrades Using apt-get 692

Retrieving Package Source Code Using apt-get 693

Satisfying Build Dependencies Using apt-get 694

Contents

Using aptitude to Add and Remove Software..695
    Tips and Tricks for Using the aptitude User Interface.............................696
    Using aptitude to Install Recommended Software 698
    Advantages of Using aptitude to Install and Remove Software 699
Using Synaptic to Add and Remove Software 700
    Configuring Synaptic Preferences..702
    Searching for Software in Synaptic 704
    Installing Packages in Synaptic..706
    Removing Packages in Synaptic 711
Using the Ubuntu Update Manager 713
Converting Packages from Other Package Formats 714
Keeping Your System Lean, Mean, and Pristine...717
Summary...718

Chapter 20: Adding Hardware and Attaching Peripherals 721
Adding a Printer...722
    Configuring an Existing Printer 724
    Manually Defining a New Printer 725
Using a Scanner..731
    Using Simple Scan 732
    Using XSane 734
Adding Internal Disks and CD/DVD Drives...739
    Adding EIDE/PATA Drives 740
    Adding SATA Drives...742
    Adding SCSI Drives 742
    Troubleshooting Boot Problems After Adding New Drives 743
        Changes to BIOS Hard Disk and Boot Device Priority Settings....................743
        Problems After Adding IDE Drives to a SATA System 744
        Problems Related to SATA Drive Name Changes 744
        Temporarily Changing GRUB Boot Loader Information 745
        Problems After Adding PATA/SATA Drives to an SCSI System 746
    Locating, Partitioning, and Formatting New Drives 746
        Using the GNOME Partition Editor to Examine and Format Drives.............747
        Using Command-Line Tools to Identify Drives and Partitions.....................752
        Using Command-Line Utilities to Partition and Format Drives....................753
Using PCMCIA Cards...758
Adding PCI Cards 759
Examining and Troubleshooting Devices Graphically...................................760
Summary...761

Chapter 21: Network Configuration and Security 763
Networking 101...764
Configuring Your Network Hardware 768
    Using the Network Manager 769
        Configuring Wired Connections...770

Configuring Wireless Connections...773
Configuring a VPN Connection..777
Configuration Files for Network Interfaces...783
Network Testing with Network Tools...786
Tips for Securing Your System..789
Installing a Firewall...790
Overview of Linux Firewalling and Packet Filtering.............................791
Installing and Configuring a Firewall...793
Summary..797

Chapter 22: Going Wireless 799
Overview of Wireless Technologies..799
Using Wicd..803
Installing Wicd..803
Using Wicd..804
Configuring Wicd..807
Command-Line Tools for Wireless Networking 811
Installing and Using Windows Networking Drivers..813
Installing NDIS Wrapper and Friends...814
Installing Microsoft Windows Drivers...814
NDIS Wrapper Tips and Tricks...817
Summary..818

Chapter 23: Software Development on Ubuntu 819
Installing and Using Development Software...820
Installing GCC Compilers, make, and Friends.......................................820
GCC Compiler Overview..821
Using GCC's C Compiler 822
Creating Simple Makefiles 823
Using an Integrated Development Environment...825
Popular IDEs for Linux...825
Installing Eclipse..827
Using Eclipse for C Application Development 827
Starting Eclipse...827
Getting Add-Ons and Updates..829
Creating a New Source Project in Eclipse 831
Importing an Existing Source Project into Eclipse 838
Getting More Information about Eclipse...845
Source Code Control Software 845
The Concurrent Versioning System (CVS) 846
Installing and Using Subversion...847
Installing Subversion 847
Setting Up a Subversion Repository 848
Importing Projects into a Subversion Repository 849
Setting Up a Subversion Server 850

Contents

Checking Files Out of a Subversion Repository 853
Committing Changes to a Subversion Repository 854
Getting More Information about Subversion 854
Summary 855

Chapter 24: Using Virtual Machines and Emulators 857

Overview of Virtualization and Emulation 858
Why Virtualize? 858
Types of Virtual Machines 860
What Kinds of Virtualization Can I Use? 862
Selecting a Virtualization Technology 863
Popular Emulation Software for Linux 863
Managing Virtual and Emulated Machines 864
Getting More Information about Virtualization 865
Installing and Using VirtualBox 866
VirtualBox Overview 867
Installing VirtualBox 868
Creating a Virtual Machine in VirtualBox 869
Installing an Operating System in a Virtual Machine 877
Installing VirtualBox Guest Additions 881
Starting and Stopping Virtual Machines 881
Networking and VirtualBox 884
Fixing Virtual Machine Boot/Installation Problems 890
Installing and Using KVM 891
Installing KVM and Related Packages 892
Creating a Disk for a KVM Virtual Machine 892
Installing an Operating System in a Virtual Machine 893
Starting a KVM Virtual Machine 896
Networking for KVM 896
Using KVM with User Networking 897
Using KVM with a Virtual Bridge 899
Installing and Using QEMU 901
Summary 903

Chapter 25: Connecting to Other Systems 905

Establishing Secure Connections to Other Systems...905
Logging In to Remote Systems Using ssh 906
Enabling Incoming SSH Connections to Your System.....................................908
Connecting to Other Systems Using VNC 909
Configuring a VNC Server...910
Enabling and Configuring Ubuntu's Vino VNC Server 910
VNC Client and Server Software for Other Systems 912
VNC Servers and Clients for Mac OS X 912
VNC Clients and Servers for Windows 913
Using Ubuntu's Remote Desktop Viewer..913

Contents

Connecting to Remote Windows Terminal Servers 917
    Using rdesktop for Terminal Server Connections 918
    Using Ubuntu's tsclient for Terminal Server Connections 921
Using Other Remote Connection Software 923
Summary 923

Chapter 26: File Transfer and Sharing 925

Transferring Files to Other Systems 926
    Using FTP 928
        Connecting to an FTP Server from the GNOME Desktop 928
        Connecting to an FTP Server from the Command Line 931
        Connecting to an FTP Server Using Graphical Clients 935
    Accessing Shares on Windows Systems 937
        Locating Windows Shares 938
        Mounting Windows Shares at Boot Time 939
        Connecting to Windows Shares from the GNOME Desktop 940
        Connecting to Windows Shares from the Command Line 942
    Accessing NFS Directories from Linux Systems 943
Peer-to-Peer File Sharing on Ubuntu 944
    Installing and Using gtk-gnutella 945
        Installing gtk-gnutella 946
        Using gtk-gnutella 946
    Using BitTorrent 948
        Using Transmission on Ubuntu Systems 949
        Finding Torrents 951
        Getting More Information about BitTorrent 951
Summary 952

Part III: Ubuntu for System Administrators   953

Chapter 27: Managing Users, Groups, and Authentication 955

Creating and Managing Users and Groups 956
    Managing Users and Groups on Ubuntu Systems 957
        Creating New Users 957
        Managing Existing Users 960
        Creating New Groups 960
        Managing Existing Groups 962
PAMs and the Linux Authentication Process 963
    PAM Configuration Files for Applications and Services 964
    Example: PAMs Used by the Login Process 965
    Configuration Files for Various PAMs 969
    What if PAM Configuration Files Are Missing? 970
Customizing the sudo Command 971
Configuring Kerberos Authentication 975
    Installing Kerberos Client and Server Commands 975

Contents

Configuring NTP on Servers and Clients..976
    Configuring an NTP Server 977
    Configuring an NTP Client..977
Setting Up a Kerberos Server 978
Setting Up a Kerberos Client..981
Summary..982

Chapter 28: Backing Up and Restoring Files.......................985

Backups 101 986
    Why Do Backups?..986
    Different Types of Backups 988
    Verifying and Testing Backups 991
    Deciding What to Back Up 992
Backup Software for Linux 992
    Local Backup and Restore Software for Linux 994
    Network-Oriented Backup Software for Linux 996
Backing Up Files to Local, Removable Media 998
    Archiving and Restoring Files Using tar 998
    Making an Up-to-Date Copy of a Local Directory Using cp...................1000
    Making an Up-to-Date Copy of a Remote Directory Using rsync.........................1001
Installing and Using BackupPC 1003
    Installing and Configuring BackupPC 1005
    Identifying Hosts to Back Up..1007
    Defining a Backup Using rsyncd.......................................1008
    Defining a Backup Using SMB 1011
    Starting Backups in BackupPC 1013
    Restoring from Backups in BackupPC 1014
Backing Up and Mirroring to the Cloud with Ubuntu One.........................1017
Linux Time Machines...1019
Summary...1021

Chapter 29: Setting Up a Web Server...........................1023

World Wide Web 101 1024
Introduction to Web Servers and Apache 1025
Installing Apache...1027
Apache 2 File Locations..1027
Configuring Apache 1029
Troubleshooting 1033
More Information...1034
Summary...1034

Chapter 30: Setting Up a Mail Server...........................1035

Introduction to Mail Servers...1036
    Popular Linux Mail Transfer Agents 1037
        exim..1037
        Postfix..1037

qmail..1037

Sendmail...1038

Why Run Your Own Mail Server?...1039

Installing Postfix and Friends..1040

Packages to Install 1040

Built-In Postfix Configuration Models 1041

Configuring Postfix 1043

Postfix Configuration Files 1044

Identifying Trusted Hosts and Domains..1047

Rewriting Addresses in Outgoing Mail..1047

Accepting Mail for an Entire Domain...1048

Activating Qpopper for POP/POP3 Support 1048

Adding Spam Filtering and Virus Scanning to Postfix...............................1050

Greylisting via Postgrey 1051

Adding Postfix Parameters to Reject Bogus Mail..............................1051

Integrating MailScanner, SpamAssassin, and ClamAV with Postfix 1054

More Information 1056

Summary..1057

Chapter 31: Setting Up a DHCP Server **1059**

Overview of DHCP..1060

Installing a DHCP Server...1062

Managing a DHCP Server from the Command Line..................................1063

Creating DHCP Configuration Files Using a Text Editor 1064

Specifying Additional DHCP Server Configuration File Entries 1066

Managing a DHCP Server Graphically..1067

Troubleshooting DHCP 1072

Summary..1073

Chapter 32: Setting Up a DNS Server **1075**

Overview of DNS and BIND..1077

Installing a DNS Server 1079

Overview of BIND Configuration Files..1080

Creating DNS Zone and Reverse Lookup Files..1082

Using Common Entries for Zone and Reverse Lookup Files: SOA and $TTL 1082

Creating Zone Files...1085

Creating Reverse Lookup Files...1087

Incorporating Zone and Reverse Lookup Files with BIND 1088

Restarting and Testing Your Name Server 1089

Troubleshooting DNS 1091

Getting More Information about DNS and BIND...1094

Summary..1094

Chapter 33: Setting Up a Print Server **1095**

Linux and UNIX Printing History...1096

Enabling Remote Hosts to Access Your CUPS Print Server........................1097

Enabling Remote Printing on Ubuntu Systems.................................1097

Contents

Troubleshooting Remote Printing..1100
    Checking the CUPS Log Files..1100
    Accessing Controls for Portions of the CUPS Web Interface..............1101
    Handling Preformatted Print Jobs..1102
Getting More Information About CUPS..1102
Summary...1103

Chapter 34: Setting Up an NFS Server 1105

Overview of the Network File System..1106
    How NFS Works...1107
    Comparing Different Versions of NFS..1109
Installing an NFS Server..1111
Configuring an NFS Server 1112
    Configuring Common NFS Options...1112
    Configuring NFS Kernel Server Options..1113
    Setting Up the Pseudo-Filesystem and Exported Directories.............1114
    Defining Exported Directories in /etc/exports..................................1115
Mounting NFS Directories on Clients..1117
Debugging NFS Problems..1119
    Verifying RPC Services 1119
    Verifying Filesystem Export 1121
    Debugging NFS Operations...1121
Getting More Information about NFS..1122
Summary...1122

Chapter 35: Setting Up a Samba Server 1125

Overview of Microsoft Windows File Sharing.....................................1125
Introducing Samba...1127
Installing the Samba Server and Friends..1128
Samba Server Configuration Essentials...1128
    Identifying Your Workgroup or Domain..1129
    Configuring Samba Authentication 1131
    Sharing Printers and Home Directories Using Samba.......................1131
    Verifying the Samba Configuration File..1133
    Testing Samba Availability and Services..1134
Sharing Other Directories via Samba..1135
Getting More Information about Samba...1135
Summary...1136

Appendix: What's on the CD-ROM? 1137

Index 1141

Introduction

A *Linux distribution* is basically the sum of the things that you need to run Linux on your computer. There are many different Linux distributions, each with its own target audience, set of features, administrative tools, and fan club—the latter of which is more properly known as a *user community*. Putting aside the downright fanatics, most of the members of the user community for any Linux distribution are people who just happen to find themselves using that particular distribution for one reason or another. These reasons range from what they've heard from friends, what CD or DVD came with a Linux magazine they bought, or which Linux book they happened to buy.

Ubuntu Linux is the most exciting Linux distribution in years. Ironically, while Ubuntu itself is indeed new, it also comes with a respectable Linux pedigree. Ubuntu has direct roots in one of the oldest and best-known Linux distributions available, the Debian GNU/Linux distribution. The folks who initially created and supported Ubuntu, Canonical Ltd., started out as Debian fans who wanted a faster-moving, more up-to-date distribution than Debian provided. So, in the spirit of Linux and the open source movement, they made their own distribution, Ubuntu Linux, by incorporating the best of Debian, other Linux distributions, and open source applications, and added their own special sauce.

Ubuntu means "humanity to others" in Zulu. For the people who use and bring you Ubuntu Linux, this is not just a name with touchy-feely overtones. The special sauce in Ubuntu is a social and business commitment to Ubuntu users everywhere. Ubuntu releases occur regularly, every six months, and support and updates for any Ubuntu release are available for a minimum of 18 months after that. More about that in the first chapter, where you'll read more about Ubuntu, its philosophy, its community, and why the sum of those makes Ubuntu different from any other Linux distribution.

In a nutshell, Ubuntu is a Linux distribution for people. While reading this book, you'll see that there are plenty of excellent technical reasons for using Ubuntu, even if you're a hardcore Linux propeller head. However, that's not the point of Ubuntu—Ubuntu is for people who want to use their computers and need a solid software foundation for doing so. Whether your focus is on writing code or surfing the Web, sending and receiving electronic mail, working with your digital photographs, watching DVDs, listening to music, or whatever, Ubuntu offers the software that you need to do what you want to do.

Like any Linux distribution, you can freely download and install Ubuntu, but it gets even better. If you don't have access to a CD burner or simply don't have the time, the Ubuntu folks will send you CDs that you can use either to install Ubuntu or to run Ubuntu on your current computer system, without changing anything. That's more than free—it's revolutionary!

Who Should Read This Book

If you're reading this in a bookstore and are unsure about which Linux distribution to get started with, or whether to use Linux at all, this book is for you. Ubuntu is a complete, visually friendly, and community-oriented distribution that makes it easy for you to get started using Linux. Ubuntu is designed to be a distribution for users, but as you'll see throughout this book, you can do anything that you want with it—from running your desktop to running servers and network services for the enterprise—thanks to the inherent power of Linux. Ubuntu comes with a tremendous selection of up-to-date software, and plenty more can be quickly downloaded and installed, thanks to easy-to-use administrative tools. Ubuntu is frequently updated, and there is no such thing as a user-level Linux virus or "accidentally installed spyware." Linux is inherently secure.

The rich Ubuntu user community is a big win for new and existing users. There are places to ask questions and actually get answers. People seem to want to help. The Ubuntu forums and mailing lists are live, constant demonstrations of the philosophical and social aspects of Ubuntu, which are discussed in Chapter 1. In a nutshell, every Linux distribution has fans, devotees, forums, and mailing lists, but Ubuntu's is the most exciting, usable, and useful that I've ever seen in my years of using Linux. You can feel the excitement. Ubuntu also brings the promise of internationalization alive—you can get versions of Ubuntu for many languages and character sets, and more are actively on the way.

If you're already using Ubuntu, this book should be equally useful to you because it explains how to use the standard applications provided with these distributions, how to do common system configuration and system administration tasks, and the like. If you're already using Ubuntu on your desktop and want to do more with it, this book clearly explains how to install common servers for file-sharing, electronic mail handling, Web servers, and much more.

How This Book Is Organized

The *Ubuntu Linux Bible, Third Edition,* is organized into three parts.

Part I: Getting Started with Ubuntu

The first part of this book provides background information about Ubuntu Linux, including instructions on installing it on your machine or simply taking it for a test drive from a Live CD. Chapter 1 introduces Ubuntu and the Ubuntu philosophy, and explores the Ubuntu community and the various web sites where you can get information and assistance in using and configuring your system (if you need help *now*, rather than simply reading this book). Chapter 1 also discusses some of the main reasons why Ubuntu is the right Linux distribution to use. Chapter 2 explains how to install Ubuntu as your only operating system, or as an alternate operating system on an existing computer system if you can't live without whatever you're already using. Chapter 3 explains how to experiment with Ubuntu even if you don't have a computer system or disk space to spare, and also discusses alternate CDs that you can download to install Ubuntu on systems that don't meet the standard installation requirements, on systems that you are reselling as an OEM, or as a server operating system.

Part II: Ubuntu for Desktop Users

Part II explores the rich set of applications that are available for Ubuntu systems and explains how to use them to accomplish the kinds of things that people use modern personal computers for—reading and sending e-mail; surfing the Web; creating documents and spreadsheets; playing games; and playing and managing audio CDs, online music files, and DVD movies. Chapter 4 provides a basic discussion of Linux and UNIX fundamentals if you are curious about how Linux systems are organized or about using a command line. Chapters 5 and 6 give you an overview of the graphical user interface provided by Ubuntu and explore its window manager in detail. If you're migrating to Ubuntu from a Microsoft Windows system, Chapter 9 explains how to move all of your existing e-mail, Internet Explorer Favorites, and other data to your new (and superior) operating system and applications. The rest of the chapters in Part II are task-oriented discussions of common tasks, such as editing files, reading and sending mail, surfing the Web, sending instant messages, printing things, working with multimedia, creating spreadsheets and presentations, sharing and transferring files to other computer systems that are on your local network or anywhere on the Internet, working with your iPod or other MP3 player, adding hardware to your system, application development on Ubuntu, and using virtual machines.

Part III: Ubuntu for System Administrators

Anyone who sets up his or her computer to connect to a network, enable users to log in, and so on is an official junior system administrator as far as I'm concerned. This part explains how to do all of the system administration tasks that any home user will want to do, but also explores all of the system administration tasks that you or any other administrator will need to do when using Ubuntu in a business setting. Chapters in this section discuss basic system administration; network security; and how to set up a Web server, select and configure a mail server, use your Ubuntu system as a centralized print server, provide basic file sharing and print services to Microsoft Windows and Mac OS X systems on your network, and set up servers for popular acronyms such as DNS, DHCP, and NFS.

There are many different organizational and typographical features throughout this book designed to help you get the most out of the information.

Conventions Used in This Book

Tips, Notes, and Cautions

Whenever I want to bring something important to your attention, the information will appear in a Caution, Tip, or Note.

Tip

Tips generally are used to provide information that can make your work easier—special shortcuts or methods for doing something more easily than the norm. ■

Note

Notes provide additional, ancillary information that is helpful, but somewhat outside of the current presentation of information. ■

Caution

This information is important and is set off in a separate paragraph with a special icon. Cautions provide information about things to watch out for, whether they are simply inconvenient or potentially hazardous to your data or systems. ■

Ubuntu® Linux® Bible

Third Edition

Part I

Getting Started With Ubuntu

IN THIS PART

Chapter 1
The Ubuntu Linux Project

Chapter 2
Installing Ubuntu

Chapter 3
Installing Ubuntu on Special-Purpose Systems

The Ubuntu Linux Project

IN THIS CHAPTER

Introducing Ubuntu Linux

Choosing Ubuntu

Reviewing hardware and software requirements

Using Ubuntu CDs

Getting help with Ubuntu Linux

Getting more information about Ubuntu

Personal computers and their operating systems have come a long way since the late 1970s, when the first home computer hit the market. At that time, you could only toggle in a program by flipping switches on the front of the machine, and the machine could then run that program and only that program until you manually loaded another, at which time the first program was kicked off the system. Today's personal computers provide powerful graphics and a rich user interface that make it easy to select and run a wide variety of software concurrently.

The first home computer users were a community of interested people who just wanted to do something with these early machines. They formed computer clubs and published newsletters to share their interests and knowledge — and often the software that they wrote for and used on their machines. Sensing opportunities and a growing market, thousands of computer companies sprang up to write and sell specific applications for the computer systems of the day. This software ranged from applications such as word processors, spreadsheets, and games, to operating systems that made it easier to manage, load, and execute different programs.

Although the power and capabilities of today's personal computers are light-years beyond the capabilities of those early machines, the idea of writing software and freely sharing it with others never went away. While it never got much press because nobody was making money from it, free software (and often its source code) has continued to be available from computer clubs, bulletin board systems, and computer networks such as today's Internet. The free software movement finally blossomed with three seminal events:

- The creation of the GNU Project (www.gnu.org) by Richard Stallman in 1983, a project dedicated to developing software whose source code would always be freely available
- The announcement of the Free Software Foundation (FSF) (www.fsf.org), initially dedicated to fundraising for the GNU project
- The introduction of a free operating system project in 1991 that came to be known as *Linux*, by a Finnish computer software student named Linus Torvalds

The book that you hold in your hands wouldn't exist without these three events, the resulting shockwave of independence and empowerment, and the perpetuation of the community spirit throughout the computer industry that these events (and many related ones) caused. Sometimes, if you're lucky, the more things change, the more they stay the same.

The operating system and applications discussed in this book are free, and their source code is freely available. Anyone who wants to can build, install, and run them. A huge online community of users has sprung up around them, including specialized groups who create easily installed sets of this software, known as *Linux distributions*. This chapter explores the philosophy, community, and history behind one of the newest, and arguably the best, of these easily obtained, easily installed, and easy-to-use free software environments, known as the *Ubuntu Linux distribution*.

Background

The emergence of Linux, a freely available operating system, is a landmark event in modern personal computing. Today, Linux is arguably the most popular operating system in use for server environments and is quickly gaining significant numbers of users as a personal computer operating system for home use. The following two sections provide some background on Linux if you're just considering adopting it or are unfamiliar with some standard Linux terms such as the idea of a Linux distribution. If you're already familiar with Linux and are interested in Ubuntu as your Linux distribution of choice, you can skip this section and go directly to "Introducing Ubuntu Linux."

Why Use Linux?

Presumably, you've bought this book because you want to use Linux. But if you're just reading to find out why you might want to do so, some common reasons for using Linux are the following:

- **Powerful, modern design:** Linux was designed from the ground up to enable you to run multiple programs at the same time and to provide services that your computer and others can use. Most other desktop computer operating systems, such as Microsoft Windows, started out as small operating systems that could run only one program at a time, and they have been trying to catch up ever since.

- **Freely available source code means no lock-in to a single vendor:** Regardless of the operating system that you're currently using, you may have encountered problems with applications or the way things worked. However, if you're using an off-the-shelf operating system from Microsoft or Apple, you can get fixes and updates only from Microsoft or Apple, because they're the only vendor of their particular operating system. Linux is open and free, so if you don't like the way that Red Hat's Linux works, how much it costs, or the type of customer support that's available, you can always switch to Novell's SUSE Linux, Mandriva Linux, or (preferably) to Ubuntu Linux—but you'll still be running Linux.

- **Thousands of free, powerful applications:** Need a word processor? Download and install OpenOffice Writer, AbiWord, or dozens of others. Need a database? Download and install MySQL, PostgreSQL, or many others. Need to create graphics or manipulate digital photographs? It doesn't get much better than GIMP (GNU Image Manipulation Program). If anything, a problem with Linux can be that you have too many choices, none of which costs money.

- **Support for standards:** Linux and Linux applications are designed to support standards, because standards are the language of free intellectual commerce. Linux applications support modern application and data formats for audio, multimedia, document formatting, spreadsheet data, and many more. Because Linux is open and free, there can be no such thing as a proprietary Linux data or application format. This not only fosters data exchange between Linux applications, but also guarantees that you'll always be able to get to your data.

- **Lower total cost of ownership:** If you want to use Linux on your desktop or throughout your business, it's free to obtain, and there are legions of Linux wizards available who can help you do whatever you want with it. There are no licensing fees—if you need to pay for something, you can pay for support from the vendor of your Linux distribution.

- **Stable, powerful, and virus-free:** *Linux* is a mature, multi-user system that is dependable, stable, has built-in security, and is immune to viruses except through system administration slipups.

It used to be the case that using Linux required some amount of special knowledge, but that's basically not the case any longer. Linux distributions such as Ubuntu make Linux easy—or, more properly, they make Linux invisible. As you'll see throughout the rest of this book, Ubuntu Linux provides an easy-to-use operating system and all of the applications that you need to do almost anything. The goal of this book is to explore Ubuntu Linux, explain how to have fun and get work done with it, and to provide any special details, insights, or knowledge that you might need. Shhh! Your grandmother doesn't have to know that she's running Linux.

What Is a Linux Distribution?

If you've been curious about Linux for a while, you've probably noticed that a bewildering number of different versions of it seem to be available. Computer magazines and Linux-related web sites discuss Red Hat Linux, SUSE Linux, the Novell Linux Desktop, Fedora Core Linux, and many other things ending in *Linux*, each available from a different company or organization. Understanding exactly what people mean when they say "Linux" is the key to understanding how so many different versions of the same thing can be available, but that requires a little insight into how personal computers actually work in terms of software.

When you install an operating system such as Linux, Microsoft Windows, or Apple's Mac OS X on your computer system, you're installing some amount of software that is invisible to any regular user because it runs behind the scenes. This software handles scheduling, starting, and stopping different programs; communicating with your computer's hardware; handling communications with peripherals such as your printer; and so on. This is generally known as *system software* because regular users don't directly interact with it, but it needs to be present and running to provide the services that application software relies on. The core piece of this system software is usually referred to as a *kernel* because it is the central piece of the operating system and everything else builds on the fundamental services that it provides.

By itself, a kernel isn't very interesting—people don't actually want to run a kernel; they want to run applications. These applications depend on services that are provided both by the kernel and by other system software. For example, if you want to print a file, whatever application you're using needs to create a version of your file that is formatted in a way that your printer understands, and then schedule that file for printing. Another piece of software handles sending the formatted file to the printer, making sure that the file prints correctly, and so on.

In popular usage, *Linux* is the collective name for an operating system kernel and its associated applications. In reality, *Linux* is technically the name of just the kernel—most of the applications that anyone uses with Linux come from other free software projects. A *Linux distribution* is the correct term for a Linux kernel, a set of applications that can run on top of it (regardless of where they come from), and a tool to install everything and configure your system. Each company or organization that provides a Linux distribution is taking advantage of the open source nature of the Linux kernel and the applications that run on top of it by putting together the "right" version of the Linux kernel with what they view as the "right" collection of core applications that anyone would want to run on top of it.

Note

Because many of the key applications that systems running the Linux kernel depend on have their roots in the GNU project, the historically proper way of referring to a Linux distribution is as a *GNU/Linux distribution*. However, given the number of other projects that have made huge contributions to today's Linux distributions, this book simply refers to the term as *Linux distributions*, rather than as "GNU/GNOME/KDE/TeX/*your-favorite-project-here*/" Linux distributions. This in no way minimizes the fundamental and huge contributions that the GNU projects and the FSF have made to modern computing. I'm an FSF member and strongly suggest that you should become one, too. See www.fsf.org/associate for details. It's always a good idea to support the things that you believe in (and depend on). ∎

Of course, getting a CD or DVD that just contains a bunch of software would be next to useless without some easy way of installing it and configuring it so that it works with your particular computer system (identifying peripherals, setting it up to communicate over your network or with your ISP, creating user accounts, etc.). Therefore, anyone who puts together a Linux distribution also provides a tool for installing and configuring the system, which is generally what runs when you boot from a Linux CD or DVD for the first time. This installation and configuration tool generally leverages a package management system that makes it easy to add or remove sets of related applications, identifying dependencies between different software components to ensure that the applications that you install will actually execute correctly.

Linux distributions are the key to understanding how Linux can be free and sold at the same time. The source code for the Linux kernel and open source applications is, indeed, freely available from thousands of sites on the Internet. Anyone who wants it can get it, but putting it all together in an easily installable, usable form is another thing entirely. When people sell a Linux distribution, they are basically just charging you for the media that it comes on, the time and effort that they invested in putting it all together, and (in some cases) "charging in advance" for any customer support that you might need if you encounter installation or initial configuration problems.

Developing Linux distributions and making them widely available have been critical to the adoption of Linux as an operating system because these distributions have made it possible for people to actually install and use Linux, the GNU utilities, and so on.

Introducing Ubuntu Linux

Ubuntu Linux is a Linux distribution founded in 2004. Originally focused on the needs of desktop and laptop users, Ubuntu has branched out since then and now also offers distributions focused on the needs of commercial users with its Ubuntu Server distribution, Ubuntu JeOS for virtualization platforms, and Ubuntu Mobile for mobile and embedded devices such as smartphones, Internet tablets, and so on. All of these flavors of Ubuntu Linux are products of the Ubuntu project sponsored by Canonical, Ltd. (www.canonical.com), a company founded by Mark Shuttleworth, a successful South African entrepreneur, long-time Debian Linux developer, and general open source advocate. *Ubuntu* is a Debian-based Linux distribution (more about that later in this chapter) that uses a graphical user interface known as *GNOME* as its desktop environment. (GNOME is discussed in detail in Chapter 5, "Using the GNOME Desktop.") Sister projects (officially known as *Ubuntu Editions*) to Desktop Ubuntu include:

- **Kubuntu:** A version of Ubuntu that uses the KDE desktop environment instead of GNOME
- **Xubuntu:** A version of Ubuntu that uses the lighter-weight Xfce desktop
- **Gobuntu:** A version of Ubuntu that uses completely open source software
- **Edubuntu:** A version of Ubuntu that focuses on educational applications and popularizing the use of Linux in schools

Note

All of the versions of Ubuntu are built and distributed in the same way and simply target different groups of users. Aside from their target audience, the only real differences between them are how they are installed, the set of applications that they provide when they are first installed, and how the Linux operating system itself is preconfigured for each. For more information about these different editions of Ubuntu and what differentiates them from each other, see the section later in this chapter entitled, "What Versions of Ubuntu Are Available?" ■

Everything has to have a name, but what is the *Ubuntu* in *Ubuntu Linux*? Not too surprisingly, the Ubuntu Linux web site puts it best:

> *Ubuntu is an ancient African word, meaning "humanity to others." Ubuntu also means "I am what I am because of who we all are." The Ubuntu Linux distribution brings the spirit of Ubuntu to the software world.*

Although that may be a bit touchy-feely for some, it's hard to argue with success and commitment. In 2005, its first year of availability, Ubuntu Linux received awards such as the *Linux Journal*'s Reader's Choice award, *Tux Magazine*'s Reader's Choice 2005 for Favorite Linux Distribution award, Ars Technica's Best Distribution award, the UK Linux & Open Source Industry's Best Distribution award, and the Linux World Expo's Best Debian Derivative Distribution award. Not too shabby for the new distribution on the block! Since 2005, Ubuntu has almost always been the most popular Linux distribution listed on the central Linux distribution site www.distrowatch.org. Ubuntu's popularity with users extends to computer vendors as well—computer hardware vendors such as Dell Computer have selected Ubuntu as their distribution of choice to ship with new hardware. Ironically, Ubuntu has also benefited from the business decisions of other Linux distributions such as Red Hat, who have shifted their focus to Enterprise computing and abandoned the desktop.

Aside from its technical excellence and usability (and some good funding thanks to Mark Shuttleworth), much of the success to date of Ubuntu Linux grows from the fact that its creators and proponents are not just the traditional Linux fanatics, but are genuinely committed to creating and promoting a usable and easily managed Linux distribution for end users all over the world.

The Ubuntu Manifesto

The *Ubuntu Manifesto* is a mission statement phrased in the classic manifesto form much beloved of artistic and political movements. The Ubuntu Manifesto is summarized online as the Philosophy section of the Ubuntu web site (www.ubuntulinux.org/ubuntu/philosophy). Its core ideas are as follows:

- Every computer user should have the freedom to run, copy, distribute, study, share, change, and improve his software for any purpose, without paying licensing fees.
- Every computer user should be able to use her software in the language of her choice.
- Every computer user should be given every opportunity to use software, even if the user works under a disability.

The first bullet is largely a clear restatement of the goals of open source software in general, but the second and third bullets are two of the big drivers for the success of Ubuntu.

Internationalization is the term for producing software that is capable of displaying all prompts, dialogs, system messages, and so on, in any user's native language and any specific character set used with that language. The term *internationalization* is such a mouthful that it is frequently referred to as *i18n* because the word *internationalization* consists of the letter *i* followed by 18 letters and ends with an *n*. The two aspects of i18n are *translation*, ensuring that versions of the operating system and application messages and text are available in other languages; and *localization*, which ensures that messages and text can be displayed in a language's native character set(s). Amusingly, *localization* is often referred to as *l10n*.

Linux and its applications have been focused on i18n for years, thanks to initiatives such as the Linux Internationalization Initiative (www.li18nux.net/, known as *Li18nux*) and the Free Standards Group's Open Internationalization Initiative (www.openi18n.org/). These initiatives focus on ensuring that open source applications take i18n into account when developing, maintaining, and enhancing code. Many of the structural enhancements to the last few releases of desktop environments such as GNOME and KDE have been related to making sure that these environments and their applications support different languages and character sets.

The key to successful internationalization is two-fold — not only do applications and graphical environments need to support multiple languages and character sets, but also the translations of prompts, dialogs, and system messages have to be available. Ubuntu's focus on a truly usable Linux distribution for an international audience has helped it become a hub for translation and localization work in Linux (www.ubuntulinux.org/community/participate#l10n) and GNOME (its primary graphical environment — more about that later) through an online translation system known as *Rosetta* (https://launchpad.net/rosetta), documentation translation efforts, active mailing lists, and other resources.

Tip

For additional information about Linux internationalization, see additional web resources through a simple Web search for "Linux internationalization", which will turn up great documents such as the Linux Internationalization HOWTO, available online at sites such as http://folk.no.net/davidjo/i18n.php. ■

Although many of the structural enhancements to the last few releases of desktop environments such as GNOME and KDE have been related to internationalization, a great deal of work has also been done to make Linux graphical environments easier to use by people with disabilities. Ensuring that graphical applications provide keyboard or gesture shortcuts for all menu commands and dialog interaction has been a growing focus for GNOME, KDE, and graphical application development. Ubuntu's emphasis on usability is a boon to all computer users, regardless of whether or not they have a physical disability.

Tip

For additional information about Linux accessibility projects and usability awareness, see additional web resources such as the Linux Accessibility HOWTO (www.tldp.org/HOWTO/Accessibility-HOWTO/), the Linux Developers Accessibility HOWTO (www.faqs.org/docs/Linux-HOWTO/Accessibility-HOWTO.html), and the Linux Accessibility Resource Site (http://larswiki.atrc.utoronto.ca/wiki). ■

Ubuntu Release Schedule

Given the pace of open source software development, it's important for anyone who depends on a Linux distribution to be able to get the latest and greatest kernels and versions of software packages. Kernel and associated device driver improvements provide low-level security fixes, facilitate the use of the latest hardware, and often provide performance improvements in the handling of existing devices and protocols. The latest versions of software packages typically provide improvements in both capabilities and usability. Because the open source community model virtually guarantees that thousands of improvements are in progress at any given moment, delivering an integrated and tested version of the latest and greatest Linux kernel and supported software packages is a complex task, but is one that is extremely important to the success and widespread adoption of any Linux distribution.

The Ubuntu folks deliver a fresh Ubuntu release every six months. These regular releases provide an up-to-date and tested kernel and a well-tested, integrated set of user software including the X Window System release from X.Org, the latest stable GNOME desktop, and core Linux and GNOME applications including Ubuntu-specific applications and customizations.

A regular release schedule is something that is unique in the Linux space and has led to a unique approach to version numbering for Ubuntu releases. Traditional software releases are numbered according to major and minor release numbers, where the major release number is essentially arbitrary and generally indicates some major upgrade in functionality. For example, in traditional release numbering, *version 4.2* is the minor release of version 4 of the software that follows version 4.1. Ubuntu, however, uses major release numbers that identify the *year* in which the software was released, and what appears to be the minor numbers actually represents the *month* in which the release was made. Therefore, *version 8.04* is the Ubuntu release from the fourth month of 2008. In typical, lighthearted Linux fashion, each Ubuntu release also has a nickname. The following are the Ubuntu releases to date:

- **4.10:** Warty Warthog
- **5.04:** Hoary Hedgehog
- **5.10:** Breezy Badger
- **6.06 LTS:** Dapper Drake Long Term Support release
- **6.10:** Edgy Eft
- **7.04:** Feisty Fawn
- **7.10:** Gutsy Gibbon
- **8.04 LTS:** Hardy Heron Long Term Support release
- **8.10:** Intrepid Ibex
- **9.04:** Jaunty Jackalope
- **9.10:** Karmic Koala
- **10.04:** Lucid Lynx Long Term Support release
- **10.10:** Maverick Meerkat

This is a refreshing approach to version numbering, especially in the open source space where software is essentially under continuous development. Not only does it make it possible for users and system administrators to predict and schedule system updates to their systems, but it also makes it easy to identify the vintage of existing, installed systems without consulting a reference text or the Web.

Ubuntu Update and Maintenance Commitments

The frequency with which a distribution is released is important to any user in order to guarantee that they have access to the latest and greatest system and application software. However, for any business that is interested in the power, cost savings, and flexibility of Linux, the period of time in which a release will be updated and maintained is even more important. Many businesses have hundreds or thousands of computer systems. Businesses with substantial infrastructure on top of deployed systems need to spend significant time testing updates and new releases before they can even think about rolling them out to all of their computer systems. Once testing is complete, the physical act of updating deployed systems takes significant time, which literally translates into money in terms of MIS and IT personnel.

By default, security updates for each Ubuntu release are issued for 18 months after the release date — after that date, existing security updates are still available, but there is no guarantee that new updates for that release will be provided. To address the longer-term requirements of commercial Ubuntu users, Mark Shuttleworth and Canonical, Ltd., the founders and sponsors of Ubuntu Linux, formed and funded the Ubuntu Foundation in mid-2005. The Ubuntu Foundation employs some of the core Ubuntu community members to help guarantee the success and continuity of the Ubuntu development and release process. One aspect of the Ubuntu Foundation is an increased commitment to maintenance and updates. Ubuntu version 6.06 was the first Ubuntu Linux release to benefit from this when the Ubuntu Foundation announced that Ubuntu version 6.06 would be supported for three years on the desktop and five years on the server, doubling the standard 18-month support commitment that is a backbone of Ubuntu. The acronym *LTS*, for "Long Term Support," was added to its release number to highlight that fact. Long-term support commitments are valuable to any Ubuntu user because they guarantee that both support and updates will be available for an extended period of time, but are especially important for business users, who need to select a stable and long-lived platform to satisfy their enterprise computing requirements.

Given the pace of hardware and open source software development, Ubuntu's regular release schedule and long maintenance commitment help ensure that Ubuntu users always have stable, secure, and up-to-date versions of the software that they depend on. Ubuntu also provides a firm update and support commitment that is mandatory for its successful commercial adoption of Ubuntu.

Ubuntu and the Debian Project

Debian is one of the longest-lived Linux distributions available and is the Linux distribution that is the conceptual parent of Ubuntu Linux. Debian is pronounced *Deb'-ian*, with a soft *e*, and is a contraction of the names of the founders of the Debian Project, Debra and Ian Murdock.

The Debian Project (www.debian.org) was founded in 1993 and has been delivering quality GNU/Linux distributions ever since. Debian is well known for stable releases based on a huge collection of thoroughly tested and completely integrated software packages. Unfortunately, the downside of balancing testing and integration with keeping up with the pace of open source development has led to a painfully slow release history — there have literally been years between official Debian releases. To be fair, three versions of the current Debian release are always available: stable (the released version), testing (the candidate for the next release), and unstable (the development version). However, many businesses (and users) are uncomfortable depending on something labeled *testing* or *unstable*. Providing a faster release process, focusing on specific core technologies such as the GNOME desktop interface, and providing a better structured mechanism to deliver software updates and notify users of their availability are the key reasons why the Ubuntu Project was born.

Some of the key ways in which the Debian and Ubuntu Linux distributions interact are the following:

- Ubuntu shares the software packaging format used by Debian (known as *DEB packages*) and also relies on the excellent and impressive technologies that were pioneered by Debian for identifying and resolving dependencies and relationships between different open source software packages.

- Ubuntu developers feed their changes and enhancements to open source packages back to the open source community, but also provide them directly to the Debian developers responsible for that package and even record patch information directly into the Debian bug-tracking system. Bug fixes and related enhancements made by Ubuntu developers are delivered as they are made during the Ubuntu release and testing process, not in a Big Bang fashion once an Ubuntu release is complete. This is better for everyone.

- The Debian and Ubuntu distributions are based on a slightly different selection of open source packages but follow the same general organization of those packages into separate domains, as explained in Chapter 19, "Adding, Removing, and Updating Software."

The Debian and Ubuntu Linux distributions are closely linked, complementary distributions with different goals. Ubuntu would not exist without the pioneering efforts and contributions of the Debian distribution but provides a more predictable distribution with better support channels for many users and enterprise computing environments.

Why Choose Ubuntu?

As mentioned earlier in this chapter in any recent computer magazine, and if you've ever picked up a Linux magazine or looked at the Linux section in your local bookstore, there are zillions of different Linux distributions. After all, it's free, so why not? Techies aside, most of the users of any Linux distribution are people who have heard that they should be using a specific Linux distribution, got a free Linux CD for some distribution in a Linux magazine that they bought, or happened to buy a book about a specific Linux distribution.

Ubuntu means "humanity to others," but the title bar on the Ubuntu web pages has often stated "Linux for People," and that's what Ubuntu is really about — a Linux distribution for people who want to get work done with a minimum of fuss and bother. Never mind that it's also a technically sophisticated Linux distribution with up-to-date software. Does it do what I want it to do?

The answer is unquestionably "Yes!" However, if you're unconvinced or find yourself in a discussion about Linux at a cocktail party, you may want more empirical data. Here are a few of the attributes of Ubuntu Linux that make it an attractive distribution to just about anyone:

- **Regular, up-to-date releases:** The Linux kernel and the thousands of software packages that make up the Linux user and administrative environment are constantly being updated. As discussed earlier in this chapter, providing the latest and greatest kernel and application software on a regular schedule is a fundamental principle of Ubuntu Linux.

- **Commitment to quality:** The quality of a Linux distribution hinges on two things: how good it is in the first place, and the distributing vendor's degree of commitment to fixing problems that arise. In both cases, Ubuntu shines. Each release goes through extensive internal testing by the Ubuntu team and extensive public testing of release candidates. Once a release occurs, updates for that release are delivered for a minimum of 18 months (as needed, of course).

- **Community and commercial support:** Much of the support for any Linux distribution comes from its user community, and it's hard to beat the passion and commitment of the Ubuntu community. However, just as no business can afford to depend on an operating system without a reasonable maintenance commitment, no business can afford to depend on an operating system without some chance of guaranteed support. As discussed later in this chapter, a complete spectrum of commercial and community support is readily available for Ubuntu Linux.

- **Easy retrieval and application of updates:** The previous bullets have stressed the importance of being able to keep installed Linux systems up-to-date. Ubuntu provides great tools that notify users when updates are available and makes them easy to obtain and install. Ubuntu's graphical Update Manager and Synaptic Package Manager tools (discussed in Chapter 19) are the best examples of such tools that I have ever used.

- **Focus on usability:** Ubuntu defines itself as "Linux for People" and provides custom graphics, window decorations, and color schemes designed to provide an attractive, usable desktop environment for real people for personal use and to get work done. Like any other Linux distribution, you can customize this extensively, even switching to any of a variety of other window managers or desktop environments that are easily retrieved and installed through tools such as the Synaptic Package Manager. Ubuntu uses the GNOME desktop environment by default, which is well known for its support of and sensitivity toward accessibility requirements such as keyboard equivalents for menus and menu commands.

- **Focus on internationalization:** Ubuntu is extremely focused on supporting translation efforts and providing a Linux distribution that people anywhere on the planet can use in their native language, with their native character sets.

- **Active and involved community:** As I'll discuss in the next section, it is hard to conceive of a more active, dynamic, and involved user community than that which surrounds Ubuntu. An active and involved community translates into more places to ask questions, a better chance of getting answers, and a more friendly experience when doing so.

As you can see from this list, Ubuntu Linux distributions focus on solving many of the issues that plague other distributions or that make it difficult for new users to adopt Linux as their operating system of choice. Most general-purpose Linux distributions would claim that they address the same sorts of issues, but in my experience, Ubuntu is exceptional in terms of delivering on them.

What Versions of Ubuntu Are Available?

As discussed earlier in this chapter, several different versions of Ubuntu are available directly from the folks at Canonical or from the distribution sites for sister projects. In addition to Ubuntu's "official" sister projects, a number of other Linux distributions are available that are based on Ubuntu, taking advantage of the rich set of packages that are supported by Canonical and the Ubuntu build infrastructure and distribution tools, just as Ubuntu itself leveraged the Debian Linux distribution to create the first Ubuntu distributions. The free and open source nature of most Linux code and applications makes it easy (well, relatively easy) to create different Linux distributions that are tailored to the needs and personal tastes of different types of users.

The standard Ubuntu Desktop distribution, using GNOME as its desktop environment, is my personal favorite for desktops and modern laptops and is the one that I recommend for most people. It's hard to argue with success. On the other hand, other versions of Ubuntu may be better for you depending on your goals and personal tastes. This section discusses the different Ubuntu and Ubuntu-based distributions to help you decide which of these best suits your tastes and requirements, dividing these distributions based on the audience and type of user that they target.

Note

This book focuses on the GNOME-based Ubuntu Desktop and Ubuntu Server distributions. If you decide to use one of the other Ubuntu or Ubuntu-based distributions that are covered in the next few sections, the discussions of using various desktop applications, server applications, and the GNOME desktop will still be valuable to you. Unfortunately, there is no discussion of the applications and tools that are specific to other distributions. Finishing this book in my lifetime was a requirement from the publisher. ■

Desktop and Laptop Users

By "desktop and laptop computer users," I mean end users (like myself) who are typically looking for a Linux distribution that is stable and easy to maintain and that provides a rich set of available applications. End users typically want to have some fun and get some work done. This isn't limited to home computing and includes office, development, and educational environments. The following lists the complete Ubuntu-based distributions for desktop users that I am most familiar with, what differentiates them from other flavors of Ubuntu, and where to get them:

- **Edubuntu:** An official edition of Ubuntu that focuses on educational applications and popularizing the use of Linux in schools. Edubuntu uses GNOME as its default desktop environment and provides several different desktop themes that are designed to be attractive (and useful) for users of different age groups. Edubuntu provides an incredibly rich set of educational applications, such as the KDE Edutainment suite (education and entertainment, get it?), GCompris for kindergarten users, Tux4Kids (paint, math, and typing applications), and the OpenOffice suite of desktop applications. You can find out more about Edubuntu or download a copy from the Edubuntu web site at www.edubuntu.org. A Live CD version of Edubuntu is available if you want to experiment with it before permanently installing an Ubuntu distribution.

- **Fluxbuntu:** An extremely lightweight Linux distribution that is based on Ubuntu and targets machines with limited amounts of memory, relatively small disks, and so on. It refers to itself as an *LPAE* (Lightweight, Productive, Agile, Efficient) Linux distribution, which is both accurate and a fine addition to your collection of computer-related abbreviations. Fluxbuntu's official memory requirements are less than 64 MB, and its disk requirements are under 1.5 GB, making it ideal for older or inexpensive machines that you don't want to invest in additional hardware for. Fluxbuntu isn't limited to older or low-power hardware — for example, a 64-bit version of Fluxbuntu is available. Fluxbuntu uses the Fluxbox window manager as its default graphical environment and includes AbiWord as its primary word-processing application, Gnumeric as its default spreadsheet application, and lightweight web applications such as Kazehakase (Web browser, http://kazehakase.sourceforge.jp), Claws (e-mail client, www.claws-mail.org), and Pidgin (instant messaging, discussed later in this book). Like any Ubuntu-based distribution, many other packages are available. You can find out more about Fluxbuntu or download a copy from the Fluxbuntu web site at www.fluxbuntu.org.

- **Geubuntu:** Another lightweight Linux distribution that is based on Ubuntu. Unlike Fluxbuntu, Geubuntu uses E17, which is the window manager formerly known as *Enlightenment* (www.enlightenment.org), which now includes various desktop features and the Xcompmgr compositing manager. Enlightenment has always been known as one of the most attractive and configurable window managers, and this Ubuntu-based distribution is an excellent choice for use on lower-power machines or on systems for which you prefer to devote as much of your CPU and memory as possible to the processes you're running versus the desktop environment. The founder of the Geubuntu effort is an Italian designer, so the aesthetics of Geubuntu are attractive and compelling. Geubuntu is available both as a live/install CD and via a script that enables you to add its packages to an existing Ubuntu installation. For more information about Geubuntu or to download a copy, see the Geubuntu web site at http://geubuntu.intilinux.com/Home.html.

- **Gobuntu:** An official edition of Ubuntu that uses completely open source software with no restrictions on use or re-distribution. The primary goal of Gobuntu is to provide a powerful and usable Ubuntu-based distribution that adheres to the Free Software

Foundation's four freedoms (`www.fsf.org/licensing/essays/free-sw.html`). Gobuntu therefore does not include any firmware, drivers, applications, or other content for which the complete source code is not available and whose license does not provide the right to use, study, modify, and re-distribute the body of work. Gobuntu is the most philosophically pure Ubuntu-based distribution available. However, because of the restrictive licensing terms that are greedily imposed on device drivers and much audio, video, and other multimedia software, you may find it hard to use Gobuntu on certain hardware or to play certain types of audio or video files on Gobuntu. If this isn't critical to you and you are more philosophically pure than I am, you can find out more about Gobuntu or download a copy from the Ubuntu site at `www.ubuntu.com/products/whatisubuntu/gobuntu`.

- **Kubuntu:** An official edition of Ubuntu that uses the KDE desktop environment instead of GNOME. The KDE desktop environment is a powerful, extremely usable desktop environment for modern UNIX and UNIX-like computer systems that pre-dates the GNOME desktop and has a large and fanatical following for good reason. Many people prefer KDE to GNOME, and the discussions/arguments about selecting one desktop interface over the other have consumed just as much time and disk space as any other type of religious argument. Kubuntu combines the traditional ease-of-use of KDE with the stability and power of Ubuntu. Old and new Linux distributions such as Ark, Corel, Linspire, Mandrake, Mandriva, Mepis, OpenSUSE, Sabayon, SUSE, and Xandros use KDE as their default desktop environment. If you are already a user of one of these distributions or simply like what you've heard about KDE, Kubuntu may be the distribution for you. For more information about KDE, see the official KDE web site at `www.kde.org`. You can find out more about Kubuntu or download a copy from their web site at `www.kubuntu.org`. A Live CD version of Kubuntu is available if you want to experiment with Kubuntu.

- **Mythbuntu:** A version of Ubuntu that is customized for use with the MythTV personal video recorder software. If you don't own a TiVo, MythTV is an impressive package. See `www.mythbuntu.org` for more information, including supported hardware, download links, and installation instructions.

- **Sabily:** A version of Ubuntu that has been augmented by adding Islamic software such as Islamiccal (an Islamic calendar), content-filtering packages (DansGuardian and Tinyproxy, preconfigured to filter many offensive web sites), Minibar (an application that identifies daily prayer times), and Zekr (a *Qur'an* study tool). Sabily was previously known as *Ubuntu Muslim Edition*. Beyond simply addressing some of the requirements of Muslim computer users, this distribution also demonstrates the tremendous range of available software for Linux and how easy it is to customize Ubuntu to address the requirements of a specific audience. This distribution is currently available only for the 32-bit x86 systems. The Islamic software packages used by Sabily can also be installed on any existing Ubuntu distribution by downloading and executing a script that installs them on your current system. For more information about Sabily or to download a copy, see its web site at `www.sabily.org`. A Live CD version of Sabily is available if you want to experiment with it before permanently installing an Ubuntu distribution.

- **Ubuntu Studio:** A version of Ubuntu that targets creating and editing multimedia. Ubuntu Studio is a relatively young Ubuntu-based distribution that was first available in late 2007. If you routinely work with graphics, audio, or other types of multimedia, Ubuntu Studio is well worth a look. It includes standard graphics applications such as GIMP and Inkscape, but also includes Ardour 2, an audio recording and editing application much like traditional audio applications such as ProTools and Blender, for modeling and rendering three-dimensional graphics and animations; PiTiVi, Kino, and Cinepaint, for video creation and editing; and much more. I have the graphics skills of a block of wood and, music-wise, used to play the drums, but anyone with artistic ability who is interested in using open source software should definitely investigate Ubuntu Studio. You can get more information about Ubuntu Studio or download a copy from the Ubuntu Studio web site at `www.ubuntustudio.org`.

- **Xubuntu:** An official edition of Ubuntu that uses the Xfce desktop rather than GNOME or KDE. Xfce is a much lighter-weight desktop environment than GNOME or KDE that doesn't spare power or usability. Using Xfce makes Xubuntu a good choice for use on older or less-powerful systems where you still want to use a desktop environment rather than simply a window manager such as that provided by Fluxbuntu. (Desktop environments support capabilities such as drag-and-drop and other forms of application interaction rather than simply managing applications on the desktop — for more information about the differences between window managers and desktop environments, see the "What's a Desktop? Graphical Environments for Linux" section in Chapter 5. Xubuntu includes applications such as Thundar (a lightweight file manager), the GIMP image editor, the AbiWord word processor, the Firefox Web browser, and many popular GNOME applications. For more information about Xubuntu or to download a copy, see the Xubuntu web site at `www.xubuntu.org`. A Live CD version of Xubuntu is available if you want to experiment with it before permanently installing an Ubuntu distribution.

Note

Canonical's Launchpad web site (`http://launchpad.net`) provides a Web-based software development, source code control, and build system that hosts many other Ubuntu-based distributions, such as Elbuntu (Ubuntu with the Enlightenment window manager as its primary GUI, `http://launchpad.net/elbuntu`), Mint (focused on producing an elegant desktop, `http://launchpad.net/linuxmint`), and many more. ■

Other Ubuntu-based distributions are available, but weren't listed here because I haven't actually had the chance to experiment with them or because they don't seem to be supported any longer. This list also doesn't include complete distributions such as Freespire (the community version of Linspire, `www.freespire.org`), Linspire (`www.linspire.com`), MEPIS (`www.mepis.org`), Sabayon (`www.sabayonlinux.org`), and others that are based on the Ubuntu packages but that are independent distributions in their own right. I also didn't list "distributions" such as Medibuntu (`http://medibuntu.org`) that only add specific sets of packages to an existing Ubuntu installation. (Medibuntu adds popular multimedia packages with various licensing encumbrances.) If I've missed an installable, ready-to-run, Ubuntu-based distribution that you enjoy, please let me know. I'm always happy to learn, too.

Netbook/MID Users

Netbooks are probably the hottest computing platforms around, offering an impressive combination of low cost, sufficient power to be useable, and network-readiness. A similar platform that is growing in popularity and availability is mobile Internet device (MID) systems, which are wireless, handheld devices that typically feature a touchscreen rather than a keyboard. Several complete Ubuntu-based distributions targeting these types of systems are available, all optimized for their smaller screens, network orientation, and audio/video capabilities:

- **EasyPeasy:** An Ubuntu-based distribution that was originally focused on the Asus EeePC netbooks, but which now supports a wide range of netbooks. See `www.geteasypeasy.com` for more information, including links to download and installation instructions.

- **Kubuntu Netbook Edition:** A Kubuntu-based distribution that brings the power of the latest KDE 4 desktop to the netbook platform. See `https://wiki.kubuntu.org/Kubuntu/Netbook` for more information, including links to download and installation instructions.

- **Ubuntu Mobile Internet Device (MID) Edition:** An Ubuntu-based distribution that was originally developed by Canonical in partnership with Intel, Ubuntu Mobile seems to have largely faded on Intel MIDs in favor of the Moblin Project (`www.moblin.org`), a Linux Foundation Project that is now working directly with Intel. See `www.ubuntu.com/products/mobile` for more information about Ubuntu Mobile. Canonical's MID focus has largely shifted to Ubuntu Netbook Remix for Intel-based netbooks and MIDs and Ubuntu Desktop Edition for ARM (`www.ubuntu.com/products/whatisubuntu/arm`) for netbooks and MIDs that use ARM processors (`www.arm.com`).

- **Ubuntu Netbook Remix (UNR):** An official edition of Ubuntu from Canonical that provides a customized user interface that is optimized for the smaller screens of netbooks, UNR is my favorite netbook-oriented, Ubuntu-based distribution. See `www.canonical.com/projects/ubuntu/unr` for more information, including links to download and installation instructions.

Portable, network-aware, and small-footprint systems are still increasing in popularity, and I'm sure that many other Ubuntu-based distributions will emerge for these types of systems.

Server Users

While it is quite possible to run server applications such as mail systems, Web servers, DNS servers, print servers, and file servers on a desktop Linux system, this is often the wrong thing to do in enterprise or academic environments. Many server systems are lean and mean, command-line-oriented machines that devote all available cycles to the server processes that they are running, rather than "wasting" them by running a GUI (at least by default). For server systems, Canonical offers the Ubuntu Server Edition, a version of Ubuntu that brings the power, stability, and easy management of Ubuntu Linux to the server room. By default, Ubuntu Server Edition provides a basic, secure system with no open network ports, but you can install other fundamental configurations such as a LAMP (Linux, Apache, MySQL, and Perl) system in which these key server components are preconfigured to work together, minimizing your installation and administrative efforts. The Server Edition also provides out-of-the-box support for LTSP (Linux Terminal Server Project), which supports thin clients and enables one server system to satisfy the storage and application requirements of many lightweight desktop systems. Ubuntu Server Edition does not install a graphical user interface by default, but the standard GNOME desktop (or the X Window System window manager of your choice) is available as a package that can be manually installed. For more information about the Ubuntu Server Edition or to download a copy, see `www.ubuntu.com/products/whatisubuntu/serveredition`.

Canonical formerly offered a version of Ubuntu Server Edition, known as *JeOS*, that targeted servers intended to run virtual machines, aka virtual appliances. JeOS stands for "Just Enough Operating System," meaning that JeOS is optimized for a small disk and memory footprint and minimal resource consumption, leaving as much of your server hardware as possible available for use by virtual machines. JeOS is now an optimized kernel that is bundled with the Ubuntu Server Edition distributions. For more information about JeOS, see `www.ubuntu.com/products/whatisubuntu/serveredition/jeos`. For more information about virtualization on Ubuntu, see Chapter 24.

Installation Requirements

As Linux distributions have moved to the 2.6 kernel and Linux is becoming more and more popular, the chances of your having hardware that is not supported by Ubuntu Linux grow less and less. This section outlines the types of systems on which Ubuntu is supported and the general hardware requirements for a usable system.

Note

One of the best things about Linux is the wide range of system types upon which it is supported. Most Linux distributions, including Ubuntu, will run on older systems that would probably otherwise be discarded or used as doorstops. However (and feel free to repeat this quote), *software runs slower on slower hardware.* When running on older systems, you will probably want to use the command-line interface or a lighter-weight graphical environment than the default GNOME (or KDE for Kubuntu) desktops. Desktops such as Xfce or window managers such as Fluxbox and IceWM are popular and powerful alternatives to GNOME and KDE. See more about these in the "What's a Desktop? Graphical Environments for Linux" section in Chapter 5. ■

Supported System Types

Ubuntu is supported on any of the following types of systems:

- i386 or compatible processors from Intel, AMD, and so on
- ARM-based systems. ARM processors are low-power, high-performance CPUs that are very popular in embedded systems, including netbooks from various vendors. See `www.ubuntu.com/products/whatisubuntu/arm` for detailed information about specific platforms.

- 64-bit AMD, INtel 64, and EM64T processors (which include Athlon 64, Opteron, and Xeon EM64T)

Note

Ubuntu was officially supported by Canonical on PowerPC (PPC) processors, such as those used on many Macintosh computer systems, through the Ubuntu 6.10 release. Similarly, Ubuntu was also officially supported by Canonical on UltraSPARC platforms from the Ubuntu 6.10 through 7.10 distributions. Subsequently, the PPC and UltraSPARC versions of Ubuntu became community-supported distributions. This means that Canonical may still produce them, but that PPC- or SPARC-specific problems will not hold up an official Ubuntu release, and versions of Ubuntu for these platforms may not be available from all Ubuntu download sites. See the Ubuntu PowerPC FAQ at `https://wiki.ubuntu.com/PowerPCFAQ` **for more information about Ubuntu distributions for the PPC. ∎**

Hardware Requirements

As with any computer software, you'll have a better experience if you install and use Ubuntu on the most powerful system that you have available, but Ubuntu will technically still run fine (although slowly) on your dusty 25 MHz i386. However, the American national slogan is eminently true here: "More is better." Taking off my Linux evangelist hat for a moment, you shouldn't really bother trying to install and run Ubuntu on a system with a processor that runs slower than 166 MHz or that has less than 96 MB of memory. I use a system with exactly those characteristics for testing purposes (an old IBM ThinkPad 380XD that I just can't bear to part with), and GNOME is excruciating on that system. If you really need to run Ubuntu on such a system, see the note earlier in this section about alternate graphical environments for low-speed or low-memory systems.

The minimum hardware requirements for installing Ubuntu and having a reasonable user experience are as follows:

- 700 MHz or better processor
- 384 MB of memory
- CD-ROM drive
- Ethernet interface
- VGA graphics interface capable of 1024 ??768 resolution
- 8 GB of available disk space

Note

If you want to use Ubuntu's compositing and advanced visual effects capabilities, you should have at least a 1.2 GHz processor and a recent ATI, Intel, or nVidia graphics card. ∎

If your system satisfies or exceeds these requirements, you're good to go. Customized distributions for specific platforms such as netbooks and MID devices have different requirements, such as a USB drive rather than a CD-ROM drive. You can certainly install Ubuntu on slower systems or systems with less memory, but that's like putting racing slicks on a Hyundai — you're not really going to get the most out of the experience.

Time Requirements

The amount of time that it takes to install Ubuntu depends on the speed of your system, how you are configuring that system, and the type of distribution that you're installing. Installing Ubuntu on a laptop that already runs Microsoft Windows, Solaris, or even Mac OS X and that you want to set up as a dual-boot machine may take an hour or two. Installing any version of Ubuntu on a new machine can take less than an hour. In general, you should plan on spending an hour or two installing Ubuntu — I'm assuming that you're not going to complain if it takes less time than that.

Ubuntu CDs

The disk that is included with this book is the Ubuntu Desktop CD, which enables you to test-drive Ubuntu on an existing computer system without changing anything and which also provides a simple, easy-to-use installer that enables you to install Ubuntu on that system permanently. Three different CDs are available for Ubuntu. These CDs and the capabilities that they provide are as follows:

- **Desktop CD:** The CD that is included with this book provides a bootable version of Ubuntu Linux that enables you to run and experiment with Ubuntu without changing anything on your existing computer system. This CD, known as a *Live DVD*, also includes an easy-to-use graphical installer that makes it easy for you to permanently install Ubuntu on your computer system. Finally, this CD includes a special installer that you can use to install and use Ubuntu on a system running Microsoft Windows without re-partitioning the disk. For information about using this CD, see Chapter 2.

Note

When you are running a program from a live CD, any work that you do, files that you create, and so on, will be lost when you reboot your computer system unless you save it to another system over the network or to removable storage such as a USB stick, removable hard drive, and the like. See the section of Chapter 2 entitled "Using Desktop CD Persistence" for information on using a USB stick or other removable media to automatically save and restore any changes that you make while running Ubuntu from the Ubuntu Desktop DVD, or see the sections "Accessing Your Hard Drive from the Desktop CD" and "Copying Files to Other Machines Over a Network" in Chapter 2 for information about manually saving any work that you do while you are running Ubuntu from the Ubuntu Desktop CD. ■

- **Server Install CD:** This CD enables you to install versions of Ubuntu Linux targeted to machines that are being used as servers. You can choose to install a generic server and add the server software of your choice, or you can install a LAMP (Linux, Apache, MySQL, Perl) server where the traditional packages required for a Linux Web server will be preinstalled. None of the versions of Ubuntu installed from this CD include a graphical user interface, although you can always add one subsequently. For more information about obtaining this CD and installing from it, see the section, "Install Options on the Server Install CD," in Chapter 3.

- **Alternate Install CD:** This CD enables you to install Ubuntu on systems with certain hardware characteristics or in specialized configurations. These include creating pre-configured systems for re-distribution by Original Equipment Manufacturers (OEM), upgrading existing systems without network access, and setting up automated Ubuntu installations for multiple systems. Hardware-wise, the install options on this disk enable you to install Ubuntu on systems that use Logical Volume Management (LVM), systems that use Redundant Arrays of Inexpensive Disks (RAID), where you want to install GRUB in a location other than the Master Boot Record (MBR), or on systems with limited amounts of memory (i.e., less than 192 MB of RAM). For more information about obtaining this CD and installing from it, see the section, "Install Options on the Alternate Install CD," in Chapter 3.

The Desktop CD included with this book is the one that most people use to install Ubuntu. However, depending on the type of system that you want to create, you may want to download and burn a copy of another installation CD. The Ubuntu web site provides freely downloadable ISO images of all of the available Ubuntu CDs, for all supported platforms, at `http://us.releases.ubuntu.com/releases`. (*ISO images* are files that contain an image of a CD in International Standards Organization CD format, which you can download and then burn to a CD yourself.) Pick the directory associated with the latest release, select the appropriate ISO image, download it, and burn a copy — or you can request that the folks at Ubuntu ship you a set of CDs. To do this, go to the page at `https://shipit.ubuntu.com`, create an account by entering your e-mail address and a password, and request Ubuntu CDs for the current release. You can even order free CDs for multiple system types at the same time. The Ship-It site is cool for getting copies of Ubuntu to turn on your friends, but is not a good personal alternative if you're into instant gratification because shipping and delivery can take a few weeks.

Support for Ubuntu

By its nature, computer software occasionally requires that you ask questions about how to use it or ask for help with resolving specific problems. This is especially true of software such as Linux, where you are installing not only a zillion applications, but also the operating system that they depend on. The primary advantage of off-the-shelf operating systems from a single commercial source, such as Microsoft Windows and Apple's Mac OS X, is that you can presumably contact the vendor if you're having problems installing, configuring, or using it. However, in reality, just try contacting Microsoft if you're having a problem using Windows. (Let me know how that goes.) In general, books like this one provide a central resource for installation, configuration, and general "How do I..." questions, but there are always specific questions that I can't anticipate. So how do you get your questions answered or find help when you need it?

Ubuntu offers an impressive array of support opportunities, ranging from community resources to paid support from Ubuntu's sponsor company, Canonical, Ltd., and several other companies located all over the world. The next few sections highlight the various ways in which you can ask questions, get answers, request paid support, and even hire experts to help with custom Ubuntu programming and support tasks.

Community Support and Information

Because Linux software depends on the community development model, getting timely, free help for problems often relies on a similar community approach. This is one of the areas in which Ubuntu truly shines, hosting mailing lists, blogs, and interactive forums that are all excellent sources of up-to-date information about Ubuntu. Forums and mailing lists enable you to post specific questions and receive responses from other Ubuntu users who have already solved the issue that you're experiencing. These online resources also serve as excellent feeder sites for the Ubuntu project, helping the project identify issues and common problems that should be addressed in future Ubuntu releases.

Blogs

Blog (from the term *Web log*) is a popular buzzword, and it often seems as though almost everyone has one. The Ubuntu blog, known as *Planet Ubuntu* (`http://planet.ubuntulinux.org`), is a bit different because it's not a continuous stream of consciousness from a single individual. Instead, Planet Ubuntu is a place where Ubuntu developers and community members can share various musings, insights, complaints, and successes.

If you're enough of a blog or Ubuntu fan to want to subscribe to it rather than simply visit its web page, Planet Ubuntu is also available in the following popular RDF (Resource Description Framework) and general markup formats:

- **FOAF:** Friend of a Friend, available at `http://planet.ubuntulinux.org/foafroll.xml`

- **OPML:** Outline Processor Markup Language, available at `http://planet.ubuntulinux.org/opml.xml`

- **RSS:** Really Simple Syndication or Rich Site Summary, depending on whom you ask. Planet Ubuntu feeds are available in RSS 1.0 (`http://planet.ubuntulinux.org/rss10.xml`) or RSS 2.0 (`http://planet.ubuntulinux.org/rss20.xml`) formats. You should use the appropriate format for your RSS reader.

Ubuntu Forums

Forums are the latest generation of what used to be known as bulletin board systems, and are an attractive alternative to mailing lists if you have the time to visit the web site that hosts them. Ubuntu's forums are hosted at `www.ubuntuforums.org`. This site provides a huge selection of well-organized forums that you can easily search to find specific information, where you can post questions, or where you can simply chat with or see the posts of other Ubuntu users, dipping your toe into the waters of the Ubuntu community if you're not already an active member. You don't have to be a member of the forums to read them, but you do need to be a member to post there. Registration is free and easy—just go to www.ubuntuforums.org/register.php, and read and accept the Ubuntu Forum rules. You can then specify the username that you want to use on the forums, enter a password, and provide your e-mail address and some minimal personal information.

The forums index page at www.ubuntuforums.org/index.php displays the categories into which the Ubuntu forums are organized, as follows:

- **Absolute Beginner Talk:** A forum section where anyone can ask questions about computers, Linux, UNIX, and Ubuntu. If you were ever afraid to ask a question because it might be too basic, this forum is for you!

- **Main Support Categories:** A forum section that provides a number of different forums dedicated to various support topics for any release of any official Ubuntu/Kubuntu/Xubuntu/Edubuntu distribution. Specific forums include Apple Intel Users, Apple PPC Users, Desktop Environments, Desktop Effects & Customization, General Help, Hardware & Laptops, Installation & Upgrades, Multimedia & Video, Multimedia Production, Networking & Wireless, Sun Sparc Users, System76 Support, Dell Ubuntu Support, and x86 64-bit Users.

- **Other Community Discussions:** A forum section that provides various forums dedicated to general topics, Ubuntu and community announcements, available Ubuntu projects, co-location and development teams, and much more. Specific forums include 3rd Party Projects, Accessibility Discussions, Art & Design, Community Announcements & News, Gaming & Leisure, Ubuntu Gamers Arena (an offsite link), Education & Science, Servers & Security, Tutorials & Tips, Ubuntu LoCo Team Forums, Ubuntu Testimonials & Experiences, Ubuntu Weekly Newsletter, Development & Programming, Virtualization, and WINE.

- **Forum Community Discussions:** A set of forums dedicated to general discussions and topics about the forums themselves. Specific forums include Community Cafe, Community Cafe Games, Community Market, Forum Feedback & Help, Forum Council Agenda, Other OS Talk, The Fridge Discussions, and the Ubuntu Forum Teams.

Although other distributions have similar forum sites (such as Fedora Core's www.fedoraforum.org site), the Ubuntu forums embrace and reflect Ubuntu's commitment to users of the current Ubuntu release and previous Ubuntu releases that are still supported, which is truly unique.

In addition to the English-language forums discussed previously, Ubuntu forums are also available in many other languages, reflecting the commitment of Ubuntu and Ubuntu users to provide a truly international Linux distribution. These are not just translated, native character set versions of the English-language forums—in many cases, different native language sites host their own forums and organize those forums differently. You can find pointers to these forums on the page at www.ubuntulinux.org/community/forums. At the time of this writing, specialized Chinese, Dutch, Finnish, French, German, Italian, Polish, and Portuguese forum sites are hosting forums in those languages, using any associated character sets. Ubuntu is truly an international effort!

IRC

Internet Relay Chat (IRC) is a popular mechanism for interactive online discussions of just about anything. The English-language Ubuntu IRC channel is named *#ubuntu* and is available through the IRC site at `http://irc.freenode.net`. IRC channels for other versions of Ubuntu are available at #kubuntu, #edubuntu, and #xubuntu. Non-English IRC channels are also available, including Chinese (#ubuntu-zh), Dutch (#ubuntu-nl), German (#ubuntu-de), Hebrew and Arabic (#ubuntu-il), Italian (#ubuntu-it), Portuguese (#ubuntu-pt), Russian (#ubuntu-ru), and Spanish (#ubuntu-es), at the time of this writing. For a complete list of Ubuntu-related IRC channels, see `https://help.ubuntu.com/community/InternetRelayChat`.

An IRC channel is a great, real-time mechanism for asking about current problems and getting online help to resolve them (assuming that your problem isn't related to getting online in the first place). The Empathy instant messaging client is installed by default as a basic part of Ubuntu Linux and also can be used for IRC communication, as can Pidgin, the instant messaging client used on Ubuntu systems up to Ubuntu 9.10. Providing IRC support by default makes it easy to connect and take advantage of IRC as a support and community resource. For more information, see Chapter 10, "Sending and Receiving Instant Messages."

Mailing Lists

Mailing lists are a great *push* format, meaning that questions and posts are delivered (pushed) directly to you, unlike forums, which are generally referred to as a *pull* format, because you have to connect to the web site that hosts them and locate new posts and information yourself.

There are a huge number of Ubuntu mailing lists, many of which are quite specialized, and listing them all here would simply waste paper because you have to subscribe to them online in the first place. The standard Ubuntu mailing lists, as listed at `www.ubuntulinux.org/community/lists`, include the following:

- **Ubuntu Announcement list (ubuntu-announce):** This list has very few e-mails (less than one a month, usually) and will keep you up-to-date on new releases of Ubuntu and significant new developments.

- **Ubuntu Development list (ubuntu-devel):** This list is intended for highly technical discussions and implementation details regarding current Ubuntu development.

- **Ubuntu Security Announcement list (ubuntu-security-announce):** This is a read-only mailing list to which announcements of security updates to Ubuntu releases are posted. This list is extremely useful for Ubuntu system administrators or anyone who wants to make sure that they know about the latest security-related Ubuntu package updates.

- **Ubuntu Users list (ubuntu-users):** This is an extremely high-traffic mailing list for technical support discussions and to which Ubuntu users can post new feature requests and wish lists.

- **Ubuntu Women list (ubuntu-women):** This list is intended as a mailing list for all Ubuntu users, volunteers, developers, and others who wish to involve more women in the Ubuntu community.

There are many more lists, of course — these are just some of the highlights. You can find a complete, up-to-date list of available Ubuntu mailing lists at `http://lists.ubuntu.com`, which will take you to `http://lists.ubuntu.com/mailman/listinfo`. The Ubuntu mailing lists are managed using the popular Mailman mailing list management package.

Tip

For Usenet fans, the Ubuntu mailing lists are also available as Usenet news groups thanks to the folks at Gmane (`www.gmane.org`). The Ubuntu-related mailing lists available as news groups are listed at `http://news.gmane.org/index.php?prefix=gmane.linux.ubuntu`. ■

What's on the Fridge?

Remember how your parents would post your latest accomplishments on their refrigerator? Let's hope they've stopped now, but the Ubuntu web site provides a software implementation of the same concept. The Fridge (`http://fridge.ubuntu.com`) provides a central location where Ubuntu users can find out what's truly new in the Ubuntu community. It features summaries of upcoming Ubuntu-related events, recent information about Ubuntu on the Web and in print media, status messages from various Ubuntu teams and projects, and newsletters such as the *Ubuntu Desktop News* and *Ubuntu Documentation News*.

Documentation

Traditional software products provide printed or online documentation to help anticipate and answer users' questions. However, as both a writer and long-time computer user, I've always appreciated and evangelized for good documentation. It doesn't matter how good software or an operating system is if you can't figure out how to use it. Linux documentation is an interesting issue because most Linux distributions are freely downloadable. There are few Linux distributions that you can actually buy off-the-shelf at a computer retailer, and even these provide relatively little printed documentation. Given the speed at which Linux distributions evolve and the tremendous variety of hardware upon which Linux can be installed, complete printed documentation is difficult to produce in a timely fashion and is even harder to maintain. Novell's SUSE Linux is famous for the quality and bulk of the printed documentation that accompanies its boxed products.

Ubuntu has a large and well-organized documentation team that is focused on producing quality, user-oriented documentation that is just as easy to use as Ubuntu itself. Ubuntu documentation is available at two primary locations:

- `http://help.ubuntu.com`: The source for all of the official documentation that has been developed by the Ubuntu documentation team. By default, this page displays the documentation for the current Ubuntu release, but documentation for older releases is available through tabs that you can select in the upper-right corner of the page.

- `https://wiki.ubuntu.com/UserDocumentation`: A hierarchical collection of resources in wiki format that makes it easy to find documentation on specific topics.

Much information on Ubuntu Linux and other Ubuntu-based distributions such as Fluxbuntu and Mint is available at the Ubuntu Documentation Storage facility at `http://doc.gwos.org/doku.php`.

The Ubuntu documentation team produces quality documentation that is well-organized and adheres to a single style guide to provide the sort of consistency that you'd expect from an organized documentation effort. The home page for the Ubuntu Documentation Project is at `http://doc.ubuntu.com`, where you can find pointers to both current documents and works in progress. All communication between documentation team members is done online, using IRC and mailing lists described at `https://wiki.ubuntu.com/DocteamCommunications`. If you're interested in contributing to the Ubuntu documentation effort, a list of current and planned projects is available at `https://wiki.ubuntu.com/DocteamProjects`. Documentation that is contributed by the Ubuntu community in general is available at `https://help.ubuntu.com/community`.

Commercial Support for Ubuntu Linux

As discussed earlier, it's especially important for companies that are planning on adopting an enterprise-wide Linux solution to have a source from which they can get guaranteed support. Although you can typically find answers to most of your questions and solutions to most problems by simply searching the Web, most CEOs and IT managers won't accept, "I'm googling it," as a suitable status message when an entire business is offline or some of their employees are unproductive because of a software or operating system problem. In business situations, it's important to have specific resources that you can depend on to solve problems in a timely fashion.

Although the majority of this chapter has stressed the scope and usability of the Ubuntu community and related resources in terms of helping you solve problems, commercial support is also available for Ubuntu from a variety of sources, as described in the next two sections.

Paid Support from Canonical, Ltd.

Canonical, Ltd. the sponsor of the Ubuntu Linux Project, offers two levels of paid support for Ubuntu Linux, known as *9x5 support* and *24x7 support*, which reflect the hours during which you can expect to get responses to your support questions. These support packages and their current pricing are described at `www.ubuntu.com/support/paid`. These support levels are available for three different types of production systems: desktop, server, and thin client/cluster systems, each of which has different costs depending on the hours of support that you're interested in.

The software packages that Canonical supports depend on the portion of the Ubuntu software repository in which those packages are located. As described in detail in Chapter 19, the software in the Ubuntu repository is grouped into several different classes, essentially depending on the license(s) under which a software package has been released. Ubuntu support agreements include full support for packages in the *main* class, partial support for packages in the *restricted* class, and no support for software in the *universe* and *multiverse* classes.

The Ubuntu Marketplace

The Ubuntu Marketplace is a portion of the Ubuntu web site that lists the network of companies that provide support for desktop and server systems running Ubuntu Linux. The main page for the Ubuntu marketplace is `www.ubuntu.com/support/supportoptions/marketplace`, which provides centralized access to lists of companies all over the world that support Ubuntu, organized into separate pages listing such companies in Africa, Asia, Europe, Latin America, North America, and Oceania. (A related URL is the Community Market forum at `www.ubuntuforums.org`, which was mentioned earlier, although that contains much more information than the actual Ubuntu Marketplace.)

Providing a centralized clearinghouse for companies that can help you or your firm with support problems is a tremendous advantage for companies that are just moving to Linux and would like to engage with a support organization that is geographically close to your physical location.

At the time of this writing, there are no specific certification requirements to have your company listed in the Ubuntu Marketplace — you simply fill out a form that is linked to from the Marketplace page.

Getting More Information about Ubuntu

Ubuntu Linux is increasing in popularity faster than any other Linux distribution that I have previously encountered. Technical excellence aside, much of the credit for its increasing popularity lies in the excellent organization and breadth of coverage provided on the main Ubuntu web site. However, let's face it — the Ubuntu web site is largely blowing its own horn. What do other people say? Are there locations other than the mother ship where you can go for information about and help with Ubuntu?

The answer to these questions is a definite "Yes!" There are a huge number of sites that provide information about Ubuntu beyond simple software reviews. In addition to the support and general web resources listed previously in this chapter, some of my favorite Ubuntu-related sites are as follows:

- **DistroWatch** (`http://distrowatch.com/table.php?distribution=ubuntu`): This site provides summary information about the contents of most Linux distributions, including Ubuntu. Their Ubuntu page provides high-level information about the contents of the various Ubuntu releases, but more importantly provides links to many Ubuntu-related web sites, reviews of the various Ubuntu releases, and much more. If you're not already familiar with DistroWatch, it's an essential Linux site for finding out almost anything about any Linux distribution.

- **Ubuntu Blog** (`http://embraceubuntu.com/`): This is a blog about Ubuntu that provides a great selection of entries about general Ubuntu tasks organized into categories such as administration, office, servers, and so on. It also features links to other sites and great task-specific articles such as the best instructions for getting the MythTV package working on an Ubuntu system.

- **UbuntuGuide** (`http://ubuntuguide.org`): This site is an Ubuntu "Getting Started" guide that is an excellent information resource, although it may not always reflect the latest Ubuntu release. This site provides a great deal of very detailed information about how to do specific tasks on Ubuntu Linux, and is well worth a look.

- **Ubuntu Women** (`www.ubuntu-women.org`): This site provides FAQs, a wiki, a blog, and mentoring programs, and is focused on getting more women involved in Ubuntu and FLOSS (Free/Libre/Open-Source Software) in general. This is a great site with a great message and purpose, through which we all win.

- **Ubuntux** (`www.ubuntux.org`): This site is a community of Ubuntu users that provides a variety of forums, blogs, links to recent articles about Debian and Ubuntu, and a variety of other resources designed to help users work with Ubuntu. The forums are especially nice, covering the spectrum of topics from getting started with Ubuntu to specific customization and optimization topics. Ubuntux also features forums targeted toward Ubuntu-based distributions such as Kubuntu, Edubuntu, and Ubuntu Lite, as well as a forum on the Ubuntu Server distribution. The Ubuntux site also offers an RSS feed to help you keep up-to-date with the latest Ubuntu-related happenings.

There are many other Ubuntu-related sites on the Web, with more appearing every day. The DistroWatch site provides a good collection of Links to Ubuntu-related sites and reviews, but as with anything on the Internet, your favorite search engine is your friend and will quickly help you find hundreds of other sites to search for answers to specific questions or simply to see what others think and say about Ubuntu.

Summary

Ubuntu is the fastest growing Linux distribution in recent memory and is one of the finest examples of the power of open source and community that I've ever seen. After providing some general information about Linux, this chapter provided an overview of the philosophy behind Ubuntu Linux and the goals of the distribution. As discussed in this chapter, much of the success of Ubuntu to date beyond its technical excellence and ease-of-use is rooted in a rich, fast-growing user community and a well-organized web site that provides easy access to various Ubuntu-related resources.

Installing Ubuntu

This chapter discusses how to install or simply experiment with Ubuntu Linux on a new or existing 32-bit or 64-bit PC system. This book includes an Ubuntu 10.04 Desktop CD from which you can either install permanently on your system or simply test-drive Ubuntu 10.04 without making any changes to your current system. Test-driving Ubuntu provides a great way to experiment with a preconfigured Ubuntu installation without actually modifying your hard drive or going through the installation process. You can also use a Live CD as a portable Ubuntu installation that you can take with you, temporarily converting other computer systems to Ubuntu Linux systems regardless of whether the machine is currently running Microsoft Windows or another Linux distribution. The Live CDs also offer an impressive Live CD Persistence function that enables you to save work and system configuration done while using the Desktop CD to removable media that you can then reuse the next time you boot from the Live CD. In most cases, you can also access your existing disk storage after booting from the Ubuntu Desktop CD, so that you can even do real work while using the Live CDs and save it on a USB stick or to the disk storage used by your existing operating system(s).

The Ubuntu Desktop CD takes the traditional Live CD concept one step further by also enabling you to quickly install Ubuntu Linux using an easy-to-use installer that is available by clicking an icon on the desktop that you see after booting from the Live CD. The Ubuntu installer can automatically reduce the size of existing Microsoft Windows or Linux partitions to free up space in which you can install Ubuntu (assuming that your existing partitions aren't full, of course).

But wait, there's more! Inserting the Live CD into a system that is running Microsoft Windows enables you to use a package known as Wubi (Windows-based Ubuntu Installer) to install Ubuntu on your Windows

IN THIS CHAPTER

Booting a Desktop CD

Installing Ubuntu

Test-driving Ubuntu

Accessing existing partitions from a Desktop CD

Creating bootable USB drives

Installing Ubuntu without partitioning

system without modifying that system in any way, except for adding an option to boot Ubuntu when you turn it on (and, of course, using some of your existing disk space to store the Ubuntu boot image). More about that later!

If you're using a 32-bit x86 system and want to run or experiment with Ubuntu Linux, the Ubuntu Desktop CD provided with this book is for you. If not, this chapter explains how to get the Ubuntu Live CD that's appropriate for the system you're using.

Note
In late 2009, Canonical announced support for the ARM platform, extending Ubuntu's availability to newer netbooks that use ARM processors. To obtain a version of Ubuntu for ARM, see www.ubuntu .com/products/whatisubuntu/arm. Versions of Ubuntu are also available for the PowerPC (PPC) and UltraSPARC platforms, but these are no longer officially supported by Canonical. Ubuntu for PPC is a community-supported project that is still quite active, while Ubuntu for UltraSPARC systems seems to have faded away. You can see what community-supported versions of Ubuntu are available and download CD images of them from the URL http://cdimage.ubuntu.com/ports/releases/VERSION/release, where VERSION is the name of a standard Ubuntu release, such as Karmic, Lucid, and so on. ∎

Getting a 64-Bit Desktop CD

The Ubuntu Desktop CD provided with this book will boot on any x86 PC system. If you want to install or experiment with Ubuntu on a 64-bit computer system, you will need to obtain a different, but equivalent, Desktop CD. If you have a reasonably fast Internet connection (or plenty of time) and a CD burner, the easiest way to get a different Desktop CD is to download an ISO image. (An *ISO image* is a file containing an exact copy of a CD-ROM or DVD that is in the format mandated by the International Standards Organization 9660 specification.) To get a 64-bit Ubuntu Desktop CD, go to Ubuntu's web page at www.ubuntu.com/download, select the version of Ubuntu that you want a CD for, select a mirror site in your country or one that's closest to you in general, and select an ISO image of the 64-bit Desktop CD. Save the downloaded ISO image to a file, burn that ISO image to a CD once the download completes, and you're ready to go!

If you have a slow Internet connection or do not have a CD burner, don't panic! As mentioned in the Introduction for this book, the Ubuntu folks will even ship you Ubuntu CDs, although they take a few weeks because they're shipped from the Netherlands. This isn't the right solution for those of us who are into instant gratification, but it might work for you. To request CDs directly from Ubuntu, go to the Ubuntu web page at https://shipit.ubuntu.com, create an account by entering your e-mail address and a password, and request one or more sets of Ubuntu CDs for the current release. You can even order free CDs for multiple system types at the same time.

Booting from a Desktop CD

Booting from an Ubuntu Desktop CD is as easy as inserting the appropriate Desktop CD into your system's CD drive, restarting your system, and making sure that the system boots from the CD drive before booting from a hard disk partition.

Caution

If your PC boots from the hard drive even if the correct Desktop CD is present in your CD drive, you'll need to modify the *boot order* in your BIOS settings. The boot order is the sequence in which available devices are searched for bootable disks when your system is powered on. To do this, turn your computer on and press the key on your keyboard that gives you access to the BIOS. This is typically either the Delete or F2 key on most modern systems — if not, the key that you'll need to press is usually identified at the bottom of your screen when you turn on your computer and it first starts up.

Depending on the type of BIOS your computer uses, boot order settings are usually stored in an Advanced Settings or Boot screen, which you can navigate to using the arrow keys on your keyboard. Press Return to display this screen once its name is highlighted. Once this screen displays, use the down-arrow key to navigate to the First Boot Device or CD Drive entry, and see the help messages at the right side of the screen for information about how to make your CD Drive the first boot device. You can then press the Esc (Escape) key to exit this screen, and press F10 to save the new settings, exit the BIOS settings screen, and reboot. ■

When you boot from the Ubuntu Desktop CD, you'll initially see a screen like the one shown in Figure 2-1.

FIGURE 2-1

The initial boot screen on the Desktop CD

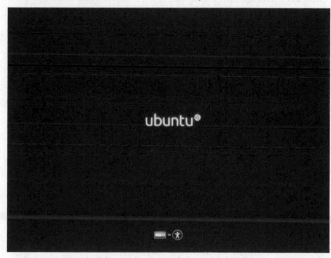

If you do nothing when you see this screen, your system will continue booting from the Desktop CD and will eventually display the screen shown in Figure 2-2.

FIGURE 2-2

The default Desktop CD try/install screen

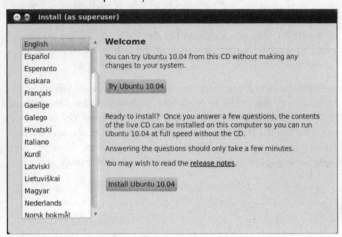

Once you see this screen, you can optionally use the scrollable list at left to change the language that the Ubuntu Live CD or the Ubuntu installer uses. You can then either:

- Click "Try Ubuntu 10.04" to boot into Ubuntu Linux without making any changes to your computer system. This allows you to experiment with Ubuntu without making any changes to your system (generally referred to as *test-driving*). The Live CD desktop is shown in Figure 2-5, later in this section. Experimenting with Linux after booting from a Desktop CD is described in the section, "Test-Driving Ubuntu Linux," later in this chapter. Skip ahead to that section for more information.

- Click "Install Ubuntu 10.04" to install Ubuntu Linux on your system. Installing Ubuntu on your system is described in the next section, entitled "Installing Ubuntu Linux from a Desktop CD". Skip ahead to that section for more information.

Tip

If the screen shown in Figure 2-2 displays a link that says "update this installer", you may want to click that link to ensure that you have the latest version of the installer. If you do not update the installer, the installation process will still work correctly, but may offer slightly different installation options than those that are discussed in this section. Similarly, updating the installer may introduce dialogs that are slightly different than those discussed in this section, but which should still provide the same capabilities. ■

If you press any key on your keyboard while the screen shown in Figure 2-1 is visible, the screen shown in Figure 2-3 displays.

This screen enables you to specify the language that you want to use when booting or installing Ubuntu from the Desktop CD. This highlights one of the great features of Ubuntu — it is truly designed for and committed to an international audience.

FIGURE 2-3

Specifying a language when booting the Desktop CD

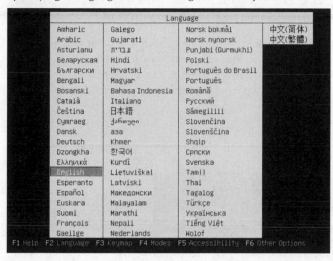

To continue, use the cursor keys to select your language and press Return. If you do not select a language within 30 seconds, English will be used as the default language. The traditional boot menu for the Live CD displays, as shown in Figure 2-4.

FIGURE 2-4

Boot options from the Ubuntu Desktop CD

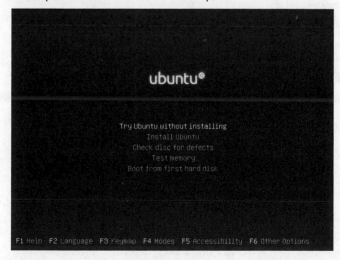

This screen is similar to the boot screens for the Ubuntu Server/Alternate CDs (discussed in Chapter 3) and older versions of the Ubuntu Desktop CD. This screen enables you to select whether you want to boot from the Desktop CD to try Ubuntu, install Ubuntu, test the CD for defects, test your system's memory, or ignore the Desktop CD and boot from the system's first hard drive.

To boot Ubuntu Linux on your system so that you can experiment with it without making any changes to your system (generally referred to as *test-driving*), press Return or wait 30 seconds, at which point your system will automatically boot from the Desktop CD. If you're booting from an Ubuntu Desktop CD, the standard Ubuntu Desktop displays, as shown in Figure 2-5.

FIGURE 2-5

The standard Ubuntu desktop from the Desktop CD

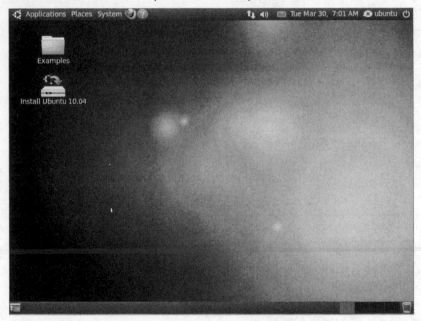

Once you're running Ubuntu from the Desktop CD, you can:

- Install the distribution from the Desktop CD as described in the next section.
- Test-drive Ubuntu using the menus that are available in the upper-left corner of the screen and the sample files provided in the Examples folder.

Experimenting with Linux after booting from a Desktop CD is described in the section, "Test-Driving Ubuntu Linux," later in this chapter. When test-driving Ubuntu, you can practice running specific applications and even experiment with installing and configuring the software that is discussed in the remainder of this book.

Installing Ubuntu from a Desktop CD

There are several ways to use a Desktop CD to install Ubuntu on a computer system:

- Boot from the CD, wait until the screen shown in Figure 2-2 displays, and click "Install Ubuntu 10.04."

- Boot from the CD, press a key while the boot screen shown in Figure 2-1 displays, set your language, use the arrow keys to select the "Install Ubuntu" option, and press Return or Enter on your keyboard.

- Boot from the CD, press a key while the boot screen shown in Figure 2-1 displays, set your language, and press Return or Enter on your keyboard to boot using the "Try Ubuntu without any change to your computer" option. Once your system boots using the Desktop CD, double-click the Install Ubuntu 10.04 icon on the desktop.

These two mechanisms run the same installer to permanently install Ubuntu on your computer system. The instructions in this section describe how to install the Desktop, or end-user, version of Ubuntu from an Ubuntu Desktop CD, such as the Ubuntu Desktop CD that is included with this book. See Chapter 3, "Installing Ubuntu on Special-Purpose Systems," for information about installing other versions of Ubuntu Linux, such as the Ubuntu Server or OEM distributions, which require that you obtain a different installation CD from the Ubuntu web site. For an overview of the different Ubuntu CDs, see the section of Chapter 1, "The Ubuntu Linux Project," entitled "Ubuntu CDs."

Caution

If you are installing Ubuntu onto a system on which another operating system is already installed, make sure that you have backed up any data that you want to preserve to removable media such as a CDROM, DVD, USB flash drive, and so on. If you want to continue using that operating system, the Ubuntu installer does a great job of automatically re-partitioning your disk so that you can boot your computer system into either your existing operating system or Ubuntu, but nothing is perfect, and "soft" is a big part of "software." It is completely impossible to have too many backups of your critical data. If your computer system already has another operating system installed on its hard drive(s) that you want to preserve, the Ubuntu installer will automatically offer to resize the existing operating system partitions and install Ubuntu as an alternate operating system on your machine. ■

You'll need to supply a few pieces of information during the installation process so that Ubuntu is correctly configured for your system, language, and geographic location. The installation process is as follows:

1. The dialog shown in Figure 2-6 prompts you to specify the location and associated time zone where you will be using your computer. This value is used to further customize the language that you specified in the previous screen by using the appropriate date and time formats, numerical conventions, and currency values for your geographic location. If the time zone that is initially displayed is incorrect, click the map in your approximate location, or select a time zone or city from the Zone pop-up menu. Once you've selected an appropriate time zone or city, click Forward or press Return to proceed to the next screen.

FIGURE 2-6

Specifying your geographic location

2. The dialog shown in Figure 2-7 prompts you to specify the type of keyboard attached to your computer. The default value is based on your settings on previous screens—if this is incorrect, click "Choose your own" and select your keyboard type from the full list of supported keyboard types. You can enter sample text into the text area at the bottom of the screen to verify that the correct symbols are being displayed as you type. Once you are sure that the correct keyboard is set, click Forward to proceed.

FIGURE 2-7

Specifying your keyboard type

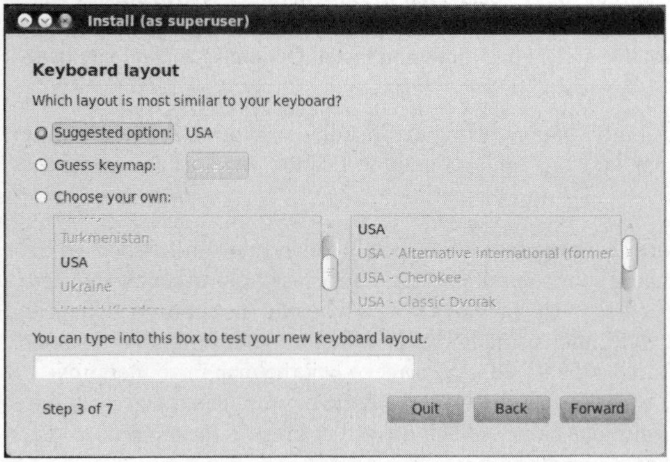

3. The dialog shown in Figure 2-8 enables you to select where you want to install Ubuntu. This dialog looks different and provides different options depending on how the disks in your system are currently configured and what partitions they already contain (if any). Figure 2-8 shows the screen that you would see if you were installing Ubuntu on a system where no operating system is currently installed.

FIGURE 2-8

Specifying where you want to install Ubuntu

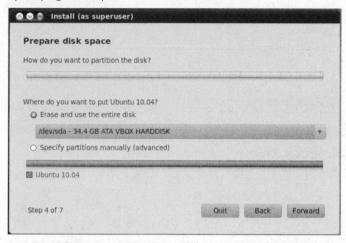

The option that you want to select on this screen therefore depends on the current state of your system's hard drive(s), how many hard drives are present in the system, and where you want to install Ubuntu. Your options are as follows:

● If you are installing on a new computer system or hard drive, the "Erase and use the entire disk" option will be selected, as shown in Figure 2-8.

● If you are installing Ubuntu on an x86 or 64-bit PC system on which an operating system is already installed and do not have unallocated space on your disk, the "Install them side by side, choosing between them each startup" option will be selected, as shown in Figure 2-9.

● If your system already contains an operating system but you do not want to preserve it, you can select the "Erase and use the entire disk" option to erase your existing operating system and install Ubuntu on the entire disk on which it was located. The image of your disk at the bottom of the screen will be updated to illustrate that you will be using the entire disk, as shown in Figure 2-10.

● If your system contains multiple hard drives, they will all be listed in this dialog. Select the disk upon which you want to install Ubuntu.

FIGURE 2-9

Suggested partition resizing in order to install Ubuntu

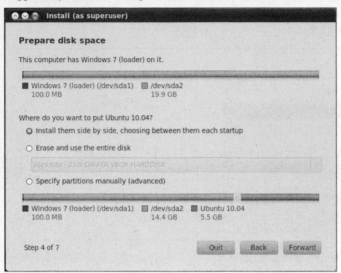

FIGURE 2-10

Deleting an existing operating system in order to install Ubuntu

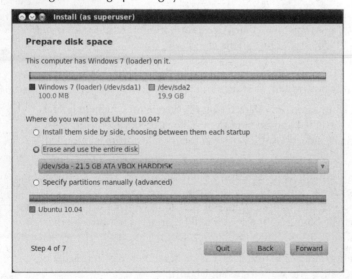

- If you have unallocated space on your disk that is large enough for your Ubuntu installation, select the "Use the largest contiguous free space" option.

- If you are an experienced Linux user and want to manually specify how to partition your disk, select the "Specify partitions manually (advanced)" option, and see the sidebar entitled "Manually Partitioning a Disk" for additional information about using the manual partitioning tools provided by the Ubuntu installer.

Once you have selected the appropriate option for your system, click Forward to continue. if you are resizing an existing operating system in order to install Ubuntu on your system as a dual-boot system, you may see a dialog notifying you that changes have to be written to your disk. Click Continue to proceed.

4. The dialog shown in Figure 2-11 enables you to provide personal information that will be used to create your account during the installation process. This account will have the ability to execute privileged commands on the system, as explained in the section of Chapter 4, "Basic Linux System Concepts," entitled "Performing Privileged Operations in Ubuntu."

FIGURE 2-11

Specifying information about your account

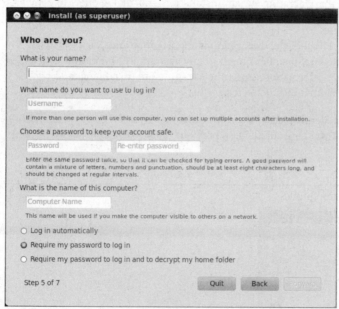

The three options at the bottom of this dialog enable you to specify how your system will start up. Depending on the resolution of the monitor on the system where you are installing Ubuntu, you may need to scroll down to see all of these options:

- **Log in automatically:** Your system will start and automatically use the account that you specify on this dialog to log in and display your default desktop

- **Require my password to log in:** Your system will display a generic login screen on which you must select or enter the name of the user that you want to log in as. Once you enter that user's login name and password, the system will log you in and display your default desktop.

- **Require my password to log in and to decrypt my home folder:** Your system will display a generic login screen on which you must select or enter the name of the user that you want to log in as. Once you enter that user's login name and password, the system will log you in and display your default desktop. The difference between this and the previous option is that your home directory will be stored in an encrypted fashion while you are not logged in, so that no other users can possibly view its contents without your password.

After you have filled out all of the fields on this form, click Forward to proceed.

5. A special intermediate screen displays if another Linux operating system was detected on your system and you are preserving that operating system. You will not see this screen if you are installing Ubuntu on a new system or are installing on a system where you are deleting any previously installed operating systems.

   If any customized account information, such as e-mail settings, browser bookmarks, and so on, was found in that operating system installation, this dialog offers to copy it to the new installation that you are creating.

   If no custom settings were found, the dialog simply reports this, and you can click Forward to proceed to the final installer screen. If any account information was detected and you want to copy that information, select the account(s) in this dialog, and click Forward to proceed to the final installer screen.

6. The Ubuntu Desktop installer displays the screen shown in Figure 2-12, which summarizes the information that you have supplied on previous dialogs. Click Install to proceed.

FIGURE 2-12

The summary dialog for starting the installation process

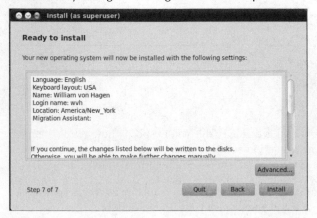

Manually Partitioning a Disk

If you are an experienced Linux user and have a specific reason to do so, you may want to manually specify how you want to divide up the space on your hard disk (or unallocated space on a dual-boot system). If you do not manually partition your disks, Ubuntu provides reasonable default values for the different partitions that it creates automatically (a swap partition whose size is a multiple of the amount of memory in your system and a single large root partition). However, you may want to further divide the disk space on your system and/or allocate it differently. For general information about disks and partitions, see the section of Chapter 4 entitled "Disks, Partitions, and Mountpoints" for more information.

If you are installing Ubuntu on a new disk and select the Manual option on the dialogs shown in Figures 2-8, 2-9, or 2-10, a dialog like the one shown in the following figure displays after you click Forward.

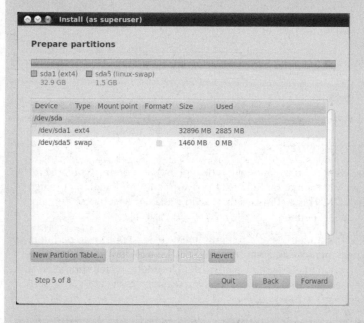

If any existing partitions are present on the selected disk, they will be shown in this dialog. If you are installing Ubuntu on a new disk, you will be prompted to create a new partition table on the disk. Click Continue to proceed.

If your disk contains existing partitions and you want to delete any or all of them on your disk, select each partition that you want to delete and click "Delete partition" to remove it and return the space associated with that partition to the pool of free space that is available on your disk. Be careful — deleting a partition permanently removes any information that it contains. Next, select the free space on your disk and click New to define a new partition. The dialog shown in the following figure displays:

continued

continued

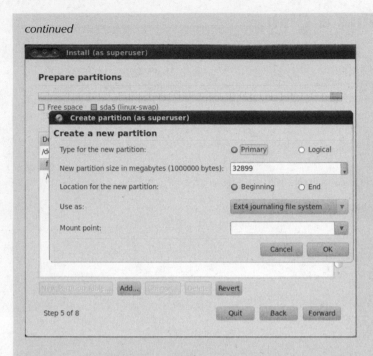

Enter the size of the partition that you want to create and verify the type of partition that you are creating (physical or extended), along with its format (usually ext4 or swap) and the location at which you want to mount that partition; click OK. This re-displays the previous dialog, which now contains information about the partition that you just defined.

Repeat this step for every partition that you want to create. You must create at least one swap partition, which Ubuntu will use to support virtual memory and whose size should be a multiple of the amount of memory in your system, and one partition to hold your system's root filesystem, which should be at least 6 GB in size. Once you have defined all of the partitions that you want to create and you're sure that these settings are correct, click Forward to proceed.

7. The installer displays several progress dialogs as it formats the partitions on your hard disk, installs Ubuntu Linux to your system, creates accounts and other system configuration information, and so on. Once the installation completes, a dialog like the one shown in Figure 2-13 displays.

FIGURE 2-13

The final installation dialog

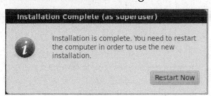

This completes the Ubuntu Desktop installation process — the next time that you boot your system (after removing the Desktop CD), you're ready to run Ubuntu Linux from your system's hard drive(s). Congratulations!

Booting Ubuntu

If you installed Ubuntu as the only operating system on a new or existing computer, you will see a simple graphical screen known as a splash screen that changes slightly during the boot process to confirm that your system is actually booting. If you want to manually interact with the boot loader that is used by Ubuntu (known as GRUB, the Grand Unified Boot Loader), you can press the Esc key during the first five seconds of the boot process to display the GRUB boot menu. The GRUB boot menu enables you to boot different kernels (if more than one kernel is installed on your system), boot any available kernel in different modes, boot other operating systems, or test system memory. For more information about GRUB and its menus, see www .gnu.org/software/grub.

Booting Ubuntu on Dual-Boot Systems

If you installed Ubuntu on a system on which another operating system is also installed, the GRUB (Grand Unified Boot Loader) boot loader menu displays automatically to let you use the arrow keys on your system to select the operating system that you want to boot. By default, your dual-boot system will boot Ubuntu after 30 seconds. On an x86 system, this screen looks like the one shown in Figure 2-14.

FIGURE 2-14

Selecting an operating system on a dual-boot x86 system

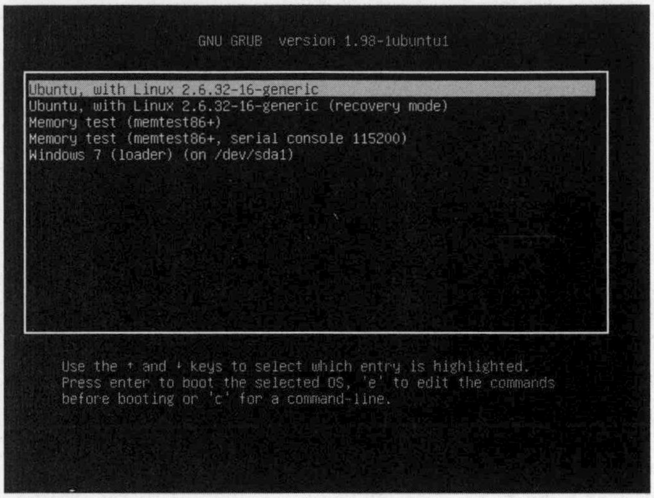

The First Time You Boot Ubuntu

The first time that you boot Ubuntu, you will want to update your system. This ensures that you have the latest and best versions of all of the standard Ubuntu software, which provides security-related fixes, bug fixes, and general enhancements. After any first-time boot screens (as discussed in the remainder of this section), the Ubuntu Update Manager should run automatically and display an icon alerting you that updates are available in the top-right portion of the panel on an Ubuntu system, or a dialog to the same effect on your main screen. For information about updating an Ubuntu system, see the section of Chapter 19, "Adding, Removing, and Updating Software," entitled "Using the Ubuntu Update Manager."

If you selected the "Require my password to log in and to decrypt my home folder" option on the screen shown in Figure 2-11 when you were installing Ubuntu, you will see an information dialog about recording your encryption passphrase. This dialog offers to run an application that enables you to specify a passphrase as a backup mechanism for you to manually decrypt your home directory. Ubuntu's automatic directory encryption mechanism normally uses your password to decrypt an encrypted directory, but also supports a passphrase as an alternate decryption mechanism. When this dialog displays, click "Run this action now" to proceed.

A standard terminal window opens, displaying a "Passphrase:" prompt. Enter a word or series of words that you will remember, and press Return. The information dialog re-displays, at which point you can click Close to terminate that dialog and begin using your new Ubuntu system. If you ever want to change the passphrase for your encrypted directory, you can use the `encryptfs-unwrap-passphrase` command from the command line to do so.

Note

If you are using an encrypted directory as your home directory, you will notice that an entry for your home directory shows up in the output of commands, such as the df command, that list mounted directories. Your home directory is actually stored as encrypted files in the central system directory /home/.encryptfs/ USERNAME/.Private, where USERNAME is your login, and that directory is mounted on your home directory when you log in. ■

Test-Driving Ubuntu Linux

Figure 2-5 shows the standard Ubuntu desktop displayed after you boot from the Ubuntu Desktop CD that is provided with this book. From this desktop, you can experiment with any of the applications provided on the Desktop CD, including audio-, video-, and network-oriented applications.

Although you can experiment on your own with any of the applications that are provided on the Desktop CD, the Ubuntu Desktop CD also provides a folder of sample documents, graphics files, and so on that simplifies experimenting with different types of applications by giving you some actual documents to experiment with. The Examples entry on the desktop of an Ubuntu Desktop CD is a symbolic link to the /usr/share/example-content directory.

Desktop CDs are complete Ubuntu systems, and you can follow the instructions in any of the chapters of this book to experiment with Ubuntu without ever installing it to your hard drive. The down side of this type of experimentation is that any files that you create or software that you configure will usually be lost when you reboot your system.

This section discusses the contents of the Examples folder provided on the Ubuntu Desktop CD and the applications associated with each of the files that it contains. It also explains a variety of ways that you can save any data that you create, ranging from manually saving it to an existing filesystem or networked system to using a USB stick to create a truly portable, persistent system based on the Ubuntu Desktop CD.

Exploring the Desktop CD's Examples Folder

All Ubuntu Desktop CDs, including the one that is provided with this book, include a folder of sample documents, graphics files, and so on that makes it easy for you to experiment with different Linux applications by giving you some actual files to open, edit, save, and generally play with. The example files not only serve to demonstrate various applications, but also provide you with a convenient source of marketing literature for Ubuntu. You should feel free to circulate documents such as the PDF case studies to your non-Ubuntu friends.

The documents and other files in the Examples folder are as follows. All of the PDF files in this folder open in the Evince PDF viewer; the description of other types of files explains the application in which they open if you click on them:

- case_Contact.pdf: A case study of the adoption of Ubuntu by Contact Air Gmbh, a division of the German airline Lufthansa

- `case_howard_county_library.pdf`: A case study of the adoption of Ubuntu by the Howard County Library

- `case_KRUU.pdf`: A case study of the adoption of Ubuntu by KRUU, a non-profit radio station

- `case_OaklandUniversity.pdf`: A case study of the adoption of Ubuntu by the University of Oakland

- `case_oxford_archaeology.pdf`: A case study of the adoption of Ubuntu by Oxford Archaeology, an English excavation and heritage management firm

- `case_Skegness.pdf`: A case study of the adoption of Ubuntu by the Skegness Grammar School

- `case_ubuntu_johnshopkins_v2.pdf`: A case study of the adoption of Ubuntu by Johns Hopkins University

- `case_ubuntu_locatrix_v1.pdf`: A case study of the adoption of Ubuntu by Locatrix Communications

- `case_Wellcome.pdf`: A case study of the adoption of Ubuntu by the Wellcome Trust Sanger Institute

- `fables-01_01_aesop.spx`: A sample Speex audio file (an open source audio compression format) in Ogg container format. Double-clicking this item opens and plays it using the Totem video player application.

- `gimp-ubuntu-splash.xcf`: A sample Ubuntu splash screen in the native open source XCF format used by the GIMP imagine manipulation program. Double-clicking this item opens it in the GIMP graphics editor.

- `kubuntu-leaflet.png`: A sample Kubuntu document in the Portable Network Graphics (PNG) format. Double-clicking this item opens it in the GIMP graphics editor.

- `logos`: A folder containing sample Ubuntu and Kubuntu logos in PNG format. Double-clicking either of these items opens it in the GIMP graphics editor.

- `oo-about-these-files.odt`: A sample OpenOffice.org document that provides information about the files in the Examples folder. Double-clicking this item opens it in OpenOffice Writer.

- `oo-about-ubuntu-ru.rtf`: A sample Russian document in Microsoft's Rich Text Format (RTF) markup. Double-clicking this item opens it in OpenOffice Writer.

- `oo-derivatives.doc`: A sample document in Microsoft Office/Word document format that discusses derivatives of the Ubuntu Linux distribution, such as Edubuntu, Kubuntu, and Xubuntu. Double-clicking this item opens it in OpenOffice Writer.

- `oo-maxwell.odt`: A sample OpenOffice.org document that shows the mathematical capabilities of OpenOffice.org Writer by discussing Maxwell's equations. Double-clicking this item opens it in OpenOffice Writer.

- `oo-payment-schedule.ods`: A sample OpenOffice.org spreadsheet that shows calculations and other capabilities. Double-clicking this item opens it in OpenOffice Calc.

- `oo-presenting-kubuntu.odp`: A sample OpenOffice.org presentation that discusses Kubuntu. Double-clicking this item opens it in OpenOffice Impress.

- `oo-presenting-ubuntu.odp`: A sample OpenOffice.org presentation that discusses Ubuntu. Double-clicking this item opens it in OpenOffice Impress.

- `oo-trig.xls`: A sample Microsoft Office/Excel document that shows calculations and the graphical display of results. Double-clicking this item opens it in OpenOffice Calc.

- `oo-welcome.odt`: A sample OpenOffice.org document that contains embedded graphics and provides an introduction to Ubuntu Linux. Double-clicking this item opens it in OpenOffice Writer.

- `Ubuntu_Free_Culture_Showcase`: A folder containing the winning audio and video files from the Ubuntu Free Culture Showcase (`https://wiki.ubuntu.com/UbuntuFreeCultureShowcase`), which sought media files that were released under a Creative Commons Attribution ShareAlike license (`https://wiki.ubuntu.com/ShareAlike`) to use when demonstrating (i.e., showing off) a new Ubuntu system. Double-clicking the OGA or OGV file in this directory plays it in the Totem audio/video player.

Double-clicking on these sample documents and files gives you the opportunity to experiment with the associated software package without having to start from scratch. You cannot modify these documents in place because they are loaded from the CD. To modify any of them, copy the document or file to the login directory and make it writable. For information about changing Linux file permissions, see the section of Chapter 4 entitled "Understanding Linux Permissions."

Accessing Your Hard Drive from the Desktop CD

Booting a Desktop version of Ubuntu on your Microsoft Windows or other Linux system is fun, but if you do any real work while in "Desktop CD mode," you may actually want to save it for future reuse. Because the Ubuntu Desktop CD runs from an in-memory filesystem (known as a *RAM disk*), the key to saving data that you've created when running Ubuntu from a Desktop CD is being able to access the existing filesystems on your hard drive(s) and saving your data there, or using an external persistent storage device as explained later in this chapter in the section entitled "Using Desktop CD Persistence." To access the filesystems on your local disk drives, you have to explicitly make them available (mount them) when running Ubuntu, and this requires that you use a few special utilities — and, as always, you have your choice of graphical or command-line utilities.

The next sections explain how to mount and access your existing filesystems from different types of Desktop CDs so that you can preserve files that you've created when running Ubuntu from a Desktop CD.

Accessing Existing Partitions from a Desktop CD

Microsoft Windows systems use either the NTFS (NT File System) or the older FAT32 (32-bit File Allocation Table) filesystems. Luckily, Linux provides complete support for both of these types of filesystems, so once you've booted from an Ubuntu Desktop CD, it's easy to mount the filesystems that are already present on your system's hard drive so that you can access your existing files or save any files that you have created while running from a Desktop CD:

1. After booting from the Desktop CD, select the Places ➪ Computer menu item. A Nautilus File Manager window displays, showing all of the available disk partitions in the right-hand pane and also listing them in the Places list in the left-hand pane, as shown in Figure 2-15.

FIGURE 2-15

Available disk partitions in Nautilus

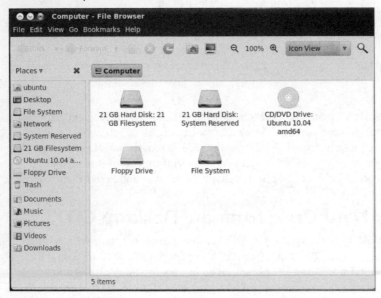

Figure 2-16 shows a mountable partition that is 21 GB in size. The CD/DVD drive contains the Ubuntu Desktop CD, and the File System entry represents the in-memory RAM disk that contains the root filesystem that is created when you boot from a Desktop CD.

2. To mount any of the partitions from your hard disk, left-click on the name of the partition in the Places list in the left pane. An icon for the partition displays on your desktop, and the contents of that partition display in the right pane of the Nautilus window, as shown in Figure 2-16.

FIGURE 2-16

Viewing a Windows partition in Nautilus

You should be able to identify the partition and type of partition that you've mounted by examining the files that it contains. For example, the partition shown in Figure 2-16 is clearly a Microsoft Windows partition given that it contains directories such as `Windows`, `Program Files`, and `My Music`.

Once you've mounted a partition, a graphical arrow displays to the right of its name in the Places list, showing that it is currently mounted. After dragging and dropping any files or directories that you want to save from your Live CD session to that partition in Nautilus, you can left-click on that arrow to unmount the partition. As a general rule, it's a good idea to unmount any of your hard disk partitions that you've mounted before shutting down or rebooting from the Live CD.

Copying Files to Other Machines over a Network

If you create or modify files while running from a Desktop CD and want to save that work, but don't want to save it to any of your system's hard disk partitions (as described earlier in this chapter), you can still save those files by copying them over the network to another machine.

Linux provides several ways to enable copying files to other systems over the network. Two of the most common and popular of these are as follows:

- The `ftp` (file transfer protocol) utility, which establishes a connection to another machine and enables you to interactively transfer files in either direction

- The `scp` (secure copy) utility, which enables you to quickly transfer files to other machines over a secure, encrypted connection

These commands are explained in detail in Chapter 25, "Connecting to Other Systems." They're summarized here so that you know that there are ways to save any work that you've done from an Ubuntu Desktop CD that don't involve local storage. This can be very useful if, for example, you are using an Ubuntu Desktop CD to recover data from a crashed system or one that can't boot on its own for some reason.

Using Desktop CD Persistence

Live CDs like the Ubuntu Desktop CD provide an easy way to temporarily turn any compatible computer system into an Ubuntu Linux system. However, the fact that most Live CDs don't provide any sort of persistent storage for configuration data, custom applications, and so on (other than manually copying files to other local or networked storage) traditionally limited the practical usability of Live CDs to simple demonstrations, one-time experimentation, and general system repair and recovery efforts. Luckily, things are better now — thanks to some really clever people, it's fairly easy to automatically save changes that you make when running from the equivalent of an Ubuntu Desktop CD — and without having to deal with manually mounting and unmounting filesystems, saving your work there, and so on.

Earlier Ubuntu releases introduced a mechanism for associating persistent storage with the Live CD boot process. This mechanism enabled you to format an external storage device with a special name (`caspar-rw`) and use that at boot time (in conjunction with the Desktop CD), adding a special kernel boot option (*persistent*) to tell the boot process to use the contents of that device to restore desktop settings, personal data, and even installed applications. This approach had a few problems, the most significant of which was that it required both an external storage device (typically a USB flash memory stick) and an Ubuntu Desktop CD. Aside from the hassle of carrying around both of these, my particular complaint was that my Desktop CDs kept breaking when I put them in my back pocket and then sat on them.

Luckily, improvements in flash drive size, price reductions for flash drives, and software improvements have made being able to do real work from an Ubuntu Desktop CD even easier. Ubuntu systems include an easy-to-use command for creating a bootable USB flash drive (generally referred to as a *stick*) that works like the Desktop CD but provides persistent storage when booting using the "Try Ubuntu without any change to your computer" option. This gives you a portable Ubuntu system from which you can either run Ubuntu or install it on another computer system without requiring the use of a CD drive. All you need nowadays for this type of portable Ubuntu system is a USB flash drive that is at least 2 GB in size.

Caution

If you want to create a bootable USB flash drive manually, the folks at PenDriveLinux.com (www.pendrivelinux.com) have some truly useful tutorials that will walk you through the process of manually creating a bootable Ubuntu system on a USB stick and just about anything else that you could conceivably boot from a USB stick. Their tutorials are clearly explained and eminently readable, and also often include scripts and configuration files that you can download from their site to make things even easier for you. ■

Flash drives are great — they are fast, use far less energy than hard drives, don't generate heat, don't make noise, and have no moving parts that can stop moving when you drop them down a flight of stairs. On the down side, they do have one potential limitation that you'll hear people talk about — you can only write to each underlying storage unit a certain number of times. (Flash storage units are usually referred to as *cells* or *address blocks*, and are analogous to the sectors on a standard hard drive.) Luckily, most flash drives use a technique known as *wear-leveling* to evenly distribute writes across the drive, so that no single area on the drive gets written to more frequently than another. The longevity of a modern flash drive is usually predicted to be at least 5 or 10 years. If you're still running Ubuntu off the same flash drive 5 years from now, it might be time to finally consider an upgrade. You are backing up your "real work" anyway, right?

Note

In order to use the bootable USB flash drives discussed in this section, your computer system must be able to boot from a USB device. Most modern PCs support this, but you should certainly check before bothering to create a bootable USB stick that you can't use. Booting from USB devices is usually a standard BIOS boot option, but some systems also require that you manually enable USB BIOS support before you can boot from a USB device. ■

As mentioned previously, the Ubuntu Desktop provides an easy, graphical mechanism for creating a bootable USB flash drive that works much like the Desktop CD, but that also provides persistent storage so that any system settings that you configure, applications that you install, and files that you create are preserved across reboots. This application will try to reuse any FAT32 partition that you have on your USB stick, so if you have formatted your USB stick to use another type of filesystem or have created multiple partitions on your USB stick, you may want to see the sidebar on "Reformatting a USB Flash Drive," later in this chapter.

To use this application, do the following after booting from an Ubuntu Desktop CD using the "Try Ubuntu" option:

1. Select the System ⇨ Administration ⇨ Startup Disk Creator menu option. A dialog like the one shown in Figure 2-17 displays.

2. Verify that the mountpoint for your Ubuntu Desktop CD is listed and highlighted in the Source disk image (.iso) or CD area at the top of the dialog. If not, click Other and browse to the correct location.

FIGURE 2-17

Creating a USB startup disk

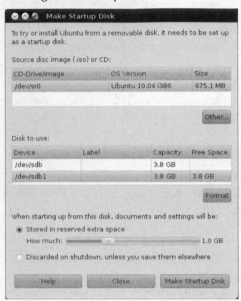

3. Verify that the USB disk partition upon which you want to create a bootable Ubuntu system is listed and highlighted in the USB disk to use area in the middle of the dialog. The line below the USB disk list identifies whether the selected USB partition has sufficient space for installing a bootable system. If the USB stick that you are using is not formatted, click Format to format it. Once formatting completes, you should see two entries in the "Disk to use" section — one for the stick itself, and one that ends with a number, identifying a specific partition on that stick. Make sure that the entry that ends in a number is selected.

4. To create a bootable USB stick that supports the persistent storage of applications that you install, files and directories that you create, and applications and system configuration information, make sure that the "Stored in reserved extra space" radio button is selected at the bottom of the dialog shown in Figure 2-17. Drag the slider below this radio button to identify the amount of space that you want to allocate on the selected partition for storing persistent data.

If you do not want to create any persistent storage, click the "Discarded on shutdown" radio button. If you select this radio button, your bootable USB stick will behave exactly like an Ubuntu Desktop CD. Any files or directories that you create, applications that you install, and application and system configuration information that you modify will not be preserved when you shut down a system that you have booted from the USB stick.

Reformatting a USB Flash Drive

The Ubuntu "Create a USB startup disk" application will try to reuse any existing FAT32 (VFAT) partition on your USB stick. If you've reformatted the USB stick to contain multiple partitions, changed the filesystem type of any of your existing partitions, or already have multiple partitions on the stick but don't need to use them, this sidebar explains how to reformat your flash drive so that it contains a single FAT32 partition that the "Create a USB startup disk" option can make the most of. As you might expect, this will delete any information that is currently present on the USB stick, so make sure that you've copied anything that you ever want to see again elsewhere before following the instructions in this sidebar.

To reformat a USB stick, do the following:

1. Select the Applications ⇨ Accessories ⇨ Terminal menu command to start a GNOME terminal.

2. Enter the **sudo -s** command and your password to become the root user.

3. Use the `df` command to see the mounted partitions on your system. If any of the partitions from your USB stick are mounted, unmount each of them using the `umount` command.

4. Execute the `fdisk` command with the name of the device corresponding to your USB stick as an argument. You must specify the name of the device, not a partition on that device. For example, if your USB stick were `/dev/sdb`, you would execute the command `fdisk /dev/sdb`.

5. Type **p** and press Enter/Return to see a list of all of the partitions on the USB stick. Use the `d number` command to delete each of these, where `number` is the number of the partition as listed in the device names in the first column of the output displayed by the p command. When you're done, type the **p** command again to list the partition table—you should not see any partitions listed.

6. Use the `n` command to begin creating a new partition on the flash drive. Enter **p** to create this as a primary partition, and enter **1** as the partition number. Press Return when prompted for the starting block of the new partition to accept the default value of 1. When prompted for the end of the partition, press Enter/Return again to use the entire disk.

7. Type **t** and press Enter/Return to begin changing the type of the first partition on the drive. Enter **1** to identify the partition that you want to change, and enter **c** (Windows 95 FAT32 LBA) as the type of the partition.

8. Type **a** and press Enter/Return to set your new partition as *active* (i.e., bootable). When prompted for the partition number, enter **1** and press Enter/Return.

9. Type **w** to write your updated partition table to the USB stick. Type **q** to exit from the `fdisk` application.

After re-partitioning your USB stick, you must remove and reattach it to your system to cause the system to read the new partition table. After re-attaching the drive, use the `dmesg` command to display the last few kernel messages, one of which should identify the device name and available partitions on the USB stick that you just reattached. You can use the `fdisk -l /dev/DEVICE` command to list the partitions on the device named `DEVICE` to verify that you know the device name of the re-attached drive—it is

continued

continued

not necessarily the same device name that it had before. Once you are absolutely sure that you know the device name of the re-attached USB stick, you can format it using a command like the following:

```
mkfs.vfat -F 32 -n NAME /dev/PARTITION
```

Replace *NAME* with the name that you want to assign to your USB stick, and replace *PARTITION* with the name of the partition on the device, which would be something like sdb1, sdc1, and so on. You're now ready to create a bootable Ubuntu system on your USB stick.

5. Click "Make Startup Disk" to begin creating the bootable USB stick. This process takes a few minutes. A dialog displays when the bootable system has been successfully created in the selected USB device partition. Click OK to close this dialog and the startup disk creation application.

At this point, you can remove the USB stick from your system and test it on another system, or you can reboot your current system to test rebooting from the USB stick. Make sure that you have activated booting from USB devices in the BIOS of any system that you use to test the USB stick, and that the USB boot device has a higher priority than your system's CD, DVD, or hard drives.

Wubi: Installing Ubuntu on Windows

Versions of the Ubuntu Desktop CD prior to version 8.04 provided a variety of open source software packages that were compiled for Microsoft Windows systems, enabling Windows users to try out some of the amazing software that they could see and use after booting from the Desktop CDs in Live CD mode. These packages included Mozilla Firefox, Mozilla Thunderbird, the GIMP image creation and editing package, and several others.

Versions 8.04 and later of the Ubuntu Desktop CDs stopped offering the Windows versions of these packages, providing an even better option for Windows users: the option to install Ubuntu onto any existing Windows system without re-partitioning your existing disk, adding a boot option to your Windows system that enables you to boot into either Ubuntu or your existing Windows system. This capability is provided by an impressive package called Wubi (Windows-based Ubuntu Installer — http://wubi-installer.org). Installing Ubuntu onto an existing Windows system requires a minimum of 4 GB of disk space (5 GB or better is recommended), but gives you a complete Ubuntu system that is installed into a new directory on your Windows system. On the Windows side, a Wubi-based installation looks like any other Windows application and can even be removed using the traditional "Add/Remove Applications" Control Panel application.

A Wubi installation works by creating an Ubuntu directory at the top level of your system's hard drive and populating that with the files that Wubi requires to boot Ubuntu, including a filesystem image for that distribution. The installation process adds an Ubuntu option to your Windows boot menu (which you may never have even seen before if your system only ran Windows), and then installs the boot loader (wubildr — the Wubi loader) that it uses to mount and access the filesystem image as the application that is executed when the Ubuntu boot option is selected.

To take advantage of this installation option, insert an Ubuntu Desktop CD into the CD/DVD drive of an existing Windows system. After any dialogs that your Windows system uses to confirm that you want to run the Wubi.exe software from the CD, the dialog shown in Figure 2-18 displays.

FIGURE 2-18

Ubuntu dialog on a Microsoft Windows system

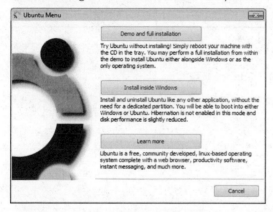

To install Ubuntu on your existing Windows system, click "Install Inside Windows." The dialog shown in Figure 2-19 displays.

FIGURE 2-19

Beginning the Ubuntu installation process on Windows

By default, the Username field shows the name of the Windows user that is currently logged in. If you want to use a different user when logging into your Wubi-based Ubuntu installation, enter the username that you want to use.

Next, enter the password that you want this user to have on your Wubi-based Ubuntu installation, verifying that you haven't made a typo by entering the password twice.

Finally, if you have any special Accessibility requirements, click Accessibility to display a dialog like the one shown in Figure 2-20. After setting any accessibility options that you want to use, click Next to return to the main installation dialog.

FIGURE 2-20

Accessibility settings for a Wubi-based installation on Windows

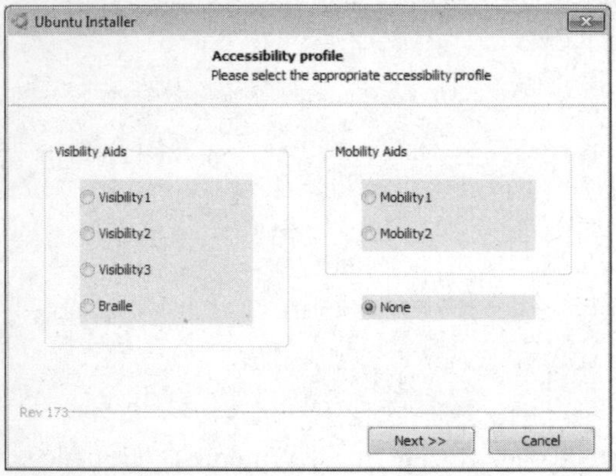

To begin the installation process, click Install. You will see a progress dialog as Wubi verifies the checksums of the files and directories that it is installing, installs Ubuntu into the filesystem image, and so on. A summary dialog displays when the installation completes, offering you the option to reboot now or later to start using your new Wubi-based Ubuntu installation.

After installing Ubuntu and Wubi, you will see a screen like that shown in Figure 2-21 the next time you boot your Windows system.

To boot into your existing Windows installation, simply press Enter/Return on your keyboard. To boot into Ubuntu, use the arrow keys to select that boot option and press Enter/Return.

Wubi is another shining example of the creativity of the open source community; it provides yet another way for Windows users to experience the power of Ubuntu Linux.

FIGURE 2-21

A Wubi boot screen on Windows 7

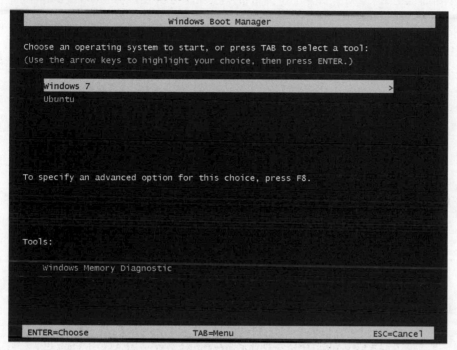

```
                        Windows Boot Manager

Choose an operating system to start, or press TAB to select a tool:
(Use the arrow keys to highlight your choice, then press ENTER.)

    Windows 7                                                    >
    Ubuntu




To specify an advanced option for this choice, press F8.




Tools:

    Windows Memory Diagnostic



ENTER=Choose               TAB=Menu                    ESC=Cancel
```

Summary

This chapter explained how you can take Ubuntu Linux for a test drive or even permanently install it after booting from the Ubuntu Desktop CD that is appropriate for the type of personal computer that you're currently using. (This book includes an Ubuntu Desktop CD for x86 systems.) Although I hope that you've installed Ubuntu Linux permanently on your computer system, this chapter also discussed various ways of experimenting with Ubuntu and saving your data if you're not yet ready to install it permanently on your computer.

If you're not ready to completely commit yourself to Ubuntu Linux, the Ubuntu Desktop CD also enables you to install Ubuntu on an existing Windows system as a dual-boot system, or within an existing Windows partition without re-partitioning or making any significant changes to your existing Windows system (aside from adding a boot option and using up some disk space, that is). The latest generation of the Ubuntu Desktop CD makes it easier than ever before to experience the power, flexibility, and freedom provided by the Ubuntu Linux distributions.

The next chapter discusses other ways of installing Ubuntu Linux using CDs other than the Desktop CD that this chapter focused on. These include CDs that enable you to install Ubuntu on systems with less than 512 MB of memory or in OEM scenarios by using a text-based installer, and the Ubuntu Server CD, which makes it easy to install Ubuntu for server systems and provides some default configurations to help you get up and running with Ubuntu as a core component of your SOHO (Small Office/Home Office) or enterprise infrastructure.

Installing Ubuntu on Special-Purpose Systems

The previous chapter discussed using the graphical installer that is provided as part of the Ubuntu Desktop disk, which is the CD that is included with this book. Using this disk and its installer is the standard way to install an Ubuntu Desktop system. However, as discussed in the section "Ubuntu CDs" in Chapter 1, "The Ubuntu Linux Project," other CDs are also available from the Ubuntu folks. These are the Ubuntu Server Install CD and the Ubuntu Alternate Install CD:

- **Ubuntu Server Install CD:** The Ubuntu Server CD installs Ubuntu without a GUI for server systems.

- **Ubuntu Alternate Install CD:** The Ubuntu Alternate CD installs Ubuntu using a quasi-graphical installer that enables you to install Ubuntu on systems without sufficient memory to run the traditional graphical installer found on the Ubuntu Desktop CDs, or on which you are using an unrecognized graphics card (the latter is quite rare).

IN THIS CHAPTER

Getting other Ubuntu CDs

Installing Ubuntu Server

Installing an Ubuntu Enterprise Cloud

Resolving installation problems

Installing from an alternative CD

This chapter discusses how to obtain these CDs and how to use the installation alternatives that each of them provides.

The Ubuntu Desktop CD's graphical installer differs from the quasi-graphical, Debian-based installers used on the Server and Alternate Install CDs. Before providing a graphical installer on the Desktop CDs, the Debian-based installers used by Ubuntu received their share of the criticism traditionally aimed at the Debian installer — "It's not fancy enough," "It looks like something from 1985," "It doesn't use all of the whizzy features of my five-dimensional, accelerated graphics card," and so on. These are all true, and for good reasons.

Although it's nice to have a fancy, mouse-oriented, graphical installation program, an installer is something that you use once per system and then forget about. An installer therefore has to be rock-solid, easy-to-understand, and easy-to-use. It also has to work on any computer system from the most wretched, low-resolution VGA system to the high-end gaming systems of today, which provide stunning resolution and visual nuances that many people can't even detect. Server systems often run headless (i.e., without a graphical console), and therefore an installer that works on those types of systems is fairly important.

Getting a Different Install CD

Ubuntu disks aren't available in stores, which is fine because a CD suitable for test drives and installation is provided with this book, and the other Ubuntu installation CDs are readily available over the Internet. If you have a reasonably fast Internet connection and a CD or DVD burner, the easiest way to get a different install CD from the one provided in this book is to download an ISO image for that CD. (An *ISO image* is a file containing an image of a CD-ROM or DVD that is in the format mandated by the International Standard Organization 9660 specification.) See the section "Ubuntu CDs" in Chapter 1 for more information about the Ubuntu disks that are available other than the one provided in this book. Once you've decided which CD meets your needs, go to the page at `www.ubuntu.com/download` to get other Ubuntu CDs, select a mirror site in your country or a site that's closest to you in general, and select the Install CD that is associated with your platform and the type of system that you want to install. Save the downloaded ISO image to a file, burn that ISO image to a CD once the download completes, and you're ready to go!

If you have a slow Internet connection or do not have a CD burner, don't panic! As mentioned in the front matter for this book, the Ubuntu folks will even ship you CDs, although they take a few weeks to arrive depending on your geographic location. This isn't the right solution for those of us who need instant gratification, but it may work for you. To request CDs from the Ubuntu folks, go to `https://shipit.ubuntu.com`, create an account by entering your e-mail address and a password, and request the Ubuntu CDs for the current release. You will then have to haunt your mailbox until they actually arrive.

Booting from a Server or Alternate Install CD

Booting from an Ubuntu Server or Ubuntu Alternate Install CD is as easy as inserting the appropriate CD into your system's CD drive, restarting your system, and telling the system to boot from the CD drive instead of booting from a hard disk partition. On PC systems, this is done using BIOS settings.

Tip

If your x86 system boots from the hard drive even if the correct Ubuntu install CD is present in your CD drive, you'll need to modify the *boot order* in your BIOS settings. The *boot order* is the sequence in which available devices are searched for bootable disks when your system is powered on. To do this, turn your computer on, and press the key on your keyboard that gives you access to the BIOS. This is typically the Delete or F2 key for most modern systems, but the key that you'll need to press is usually identified at the bottom left of your screen when you turn on your computer and it first starts up.

Depending on the type of BIOS your computer uses, boot order settings are usually stored in an Advanced Settings or Boot screen, which you can navigate to using the arrow keys on your keyboard. Press Return to display this screen once its name is highlighted. Once this screen displays, use the down-arrow key to navigate to the "First Boot Device or CD Drive" entry, and see the Help messages at the right side of the screen for information about how to make your CD drive the first boot device. You can then press the Esc (Escape) key to exit this screen, and press F10 to save the new settings, exit the BIOS settings screen, and reboot. ■

Once your system begins booting from an Ubuntu Server or Alternate Install CD, you'll supply some basic information to help the installer correctly configure your system, install the correct internationalization and location software, and set up an initial user account. The next two sections discuss your install options from the Server and Alternate Install CDs, which share the same quasi-graphical installer discussed in the introduction to this chapter, and walk you through the installation process.

Install Options on the Server Install CD

As you might guess, the Ubuntu Server Install CD is intended for use in installing Ubuntu on a system that will be used as a server. Because many server systems are rack-mounted systems that use a system console rather than a graphical monitor, Ubuntu Server installations do not include a graphical user interface such as an X Window System window manager or desktop such as GNOME. Not installing these graphics-related packages by default reduces the amount of disk space required for a basic installation and also reduces the amount of software that you have to keep up-to-date.

Tip

You can always add a graphical interface to server systems later if you want to have a graphical interface available on your server system to support specific tools or for your general convenience. For example, you can add the `xubuntu-desktop` package to add the Xfce desktop system, the `ubuntu-desktop` package to add the complete GNOME desktop, the `kubuntu-desktop` package to add the complete KDE desktop, or add the `xserver-xorg` package, the window manager of your choice, and specific graphical tools. Adding software packages is discussed in detail in Chapter 19, "Adding, Removing, and Updating Software." ■

Figure 3-1 shows the initial screen that is displayed when you boot your system from an Ubuntu Server Install CD, after selecting your language from the menus that are initially displayed.

The Boot menu on the Ubuntu Server Install CD

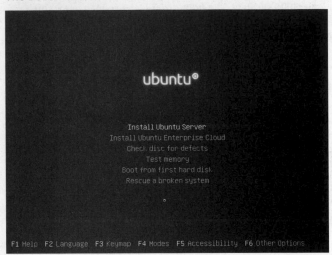

The options on the Server Install CD's Boot menu are as follows:

- **Install Ubuntu Server:** Installs a basic Ubuntu Server system to your hard drive(s) using Ubuntu's quasi-graphical installer. Installing an Ubuntu Server using this installer is discussed in detail in the next section, "Installing an Ubuntu Server."

- **Install Ubuntu Enterprise Cloud:** Installs an Ubuntu Server that is powered by Eucalyptus (www.eucalyptus.com) and enables you to experiment with (or deploy) cloud computing within your own IT environment. Installing an Ubuntu Cloud Server using this installer is discussed in detail later in this chapter, in the section entitled "Installing an Ubuntu Enterprise Cloud."

- **Check disc for defects:** Tests the integrity of the CD or DVD that is currently inserted in your system and verifies its contents.

- **Test memory:** Performs several memory tests to verify your system's memory and associated cache. You can press the letter *C* to display a configuration menu that enables you to run or rerun specific tests. Once you are finished testing your system's memory, press Esc to reboot your system and return to the Ubuntu Server Install CD boot menu.

- **Boot from first hard disk:** Bypasses booting from the Ubuntu Server Install CD and boots from your system's hard drive. This is the option to use if you accidentally left the Ubuntu Server Install CD in the CD drive of a system upon which you did not intend to install Ubuntu or perform the available system tests.

- **Rescue a broken system:** Prompts for a few pieces of information such as the language that you want messages to be displayed in and your geographic location, and then boots a diskless version of Ubuntu Linux that runs from the CD and that you can use to repair corrupted disks, correct or reinstall your GRUB boot loader's configuration, and so on.

Tip

If you have problems entering Rescue mode, booting from the Ubuntu Desktop CD included with this book provides the same capabilities as a Rescue mode installation, but with a whizzy graphical interface. ∎

Selecting the default "Install Ubuntu Server" Boot menu option will install an Ubuntu Linux Server system on your hard drive(s). The next section walks you through the process of installing an Ubuntu Server after selecting this menu option.

Installing an Ubuntu Server

Depending on the speed of your system and your Internet connection, installing Ubuntu can take a little while. However, the wait is worth it. Insert the Ubuntu install CD in your CD drive, and boot from it. Now do the following:

1. After booting from the CD and selecting your language from an initial set of menus, the screen shown in Figure 3-1 displays. Beyond selecting whether you want to install a standard Ubuntu Server or an Ubuntu Enterprise Cloud, the Server Install CD has four more detailed installation options, which you can display by pressing F4, which displays the pop-up menu shown in Figure 3-2. These options are as follows:

FIGURE 3-2

Available configurations on the Ubuntu Server Install CD

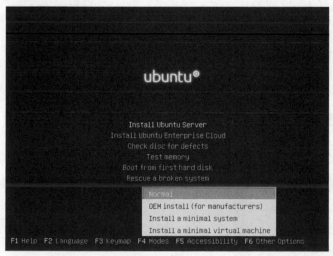

- **Normal:** Install a standard Ubuntu Server system.
- **OEM Install (for manufacturers):** Install an Ubuntu Server that is designed for OEM use and that therefore enables additional customization before actual deployment.

- **Install a minimal system:** Install an Ubuntu Server system with the minimum number of packages required to boot and run. You should select this option if you want to configure your server manually, installing only the specific packages (and their dependencies) that you are interested in.

- **Install a minimal virtual machine:** Install an Ubuntu Server system using the Ubuntu JeOS (Just Enough Operating System) configuration. (See the section of Chapter 1 entitled "Server Users" or www.ubuntu.com/products/whatisubuntu/serveredition/jeos for more information on JeOS.) Like the "Install a minimal system" option, this option installs an Ubuntu Server system with a minimum number of packages, but further reduces the list of installed packages and installed hardware drivers to create a truly minimal system that is suitable for use as a virtual machine installation.

To proceed, select any of these options or simply press Return to leave the Normal option selected. The screen shown in Figure 3-1 re-displays. Make sure that the "Install Ubuntu Server" option is still selected, and press Return to continue with the installation process for the selected server distribution. (For information about installing Ubuntu Enterprise Cloud, see the section entitled "Installing an Ubuntu Enterprise Cloud," later in this chapter.)

2. The screen shown in Figure 3-3 displays, prompting you to select the language in which you would like system messages and dialogs to be displayed during the remainder of the installation process and on the installed system. You can either press Return to accept the default value of English, or use the arrow keys to scroll up and down in the list of supported languages until you find your native language, and then press Return to continue.

FIGURE 3-3

Specifying your language

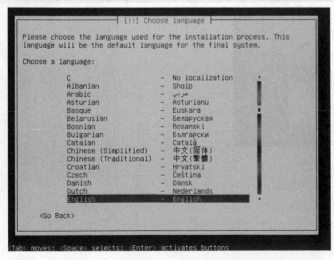

3. The screen shown in Figure 3-4 prompts you to specify the location where you are using your computer. This value is used to further customize the language that you specified in the previous screen by using the appropriate date and time formats, numerical conventions, and currency values for your geographic location.

FIGURE 3-4

Specifying your geographic location

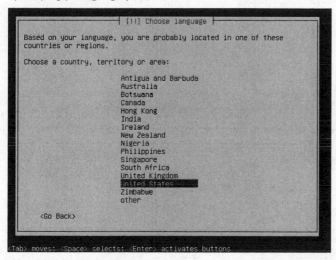

4. The screen shown in Figure 3-5 prompts you as to whether you want to try to automatically detect or manually specify the type of keyboard that you are using:

   - Pressing Return to accept the default value of No, displays two dialogs that contain lists from which you can verify or modify the type of keyboard that you are using.

   - Pressing Tab twice, selecting Yes, and pressing Return displays a few additional screens that prompt you to press specific keys on your keyboard or ask if certain keys exist on your system.

   In most cases, you should accept the default value of No and select your keyboard from the subsequent screens. The first screen lets you identify the country of origin of your keyboard; the second enables you to specify the layout of your keyboard. If your keyboard is not listed on these dialogs or you can't determine the type of keyboard to select, you can always select "Go Back" on the list of dialogs to return to the screen shown in Figure 3-5 and use the installer's keyboard layout detection dialogs to try to determine your keyboard type and layout based on the keys that are available on your keyboard.

FIGURE 3-5

Specifying your keyboard type

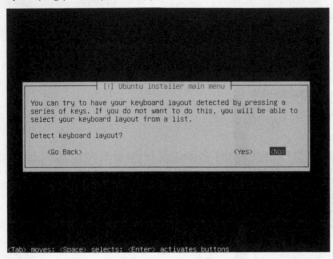

After selecting the country of origin and layout of your keyboard, a few screens display as the Ubuntu Server installer looks for your CD-ROM drive, probes your system's hardware, retrieves some fundamental packages for the installation, and identifies and configures your network interface. These screens are not interactive.

Tip
If the installer has problems automatically configuring your network interface and you see an error dialog at this point, see the sidebar "Resolving Installation Problems" later in this chapter for more information. ■

5. The screen shown in Figure 3-6 prompts you to enter a name for this machine. This is a one-word entry (without any domain name) that can be used to uniquely identify this system on your local network. You can accept the default name *ubuntu*, or you can enter a name for your machine (as I have in Figure 3-6), and then press Return to continue.

6. The server installation process next attempts to retrieve the current time from a time server on the Internet and then displays the screen shown in Figure 3-7, which configures your system's clock by suggesting a default time zone for your system. If this is correct, press Return to continue. If this is incorrect, press tab to select No, and press return. This displays an additional screen on which you can use the arrow keys to select the appropriate time zone for your home location, and press Return to continue.

FIGURE 3-6

Specifying a name for your Ubuntu Server

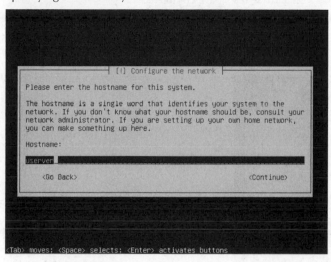

FIGURE 3-7

The time zone screen

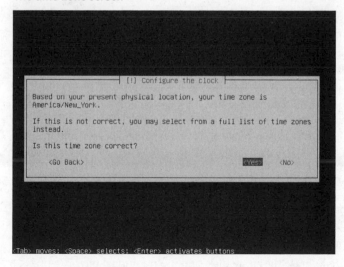

7. The installer displays several informative screens as it probes and identifies your system's hard disks and verifies the contents of the install CD. The partitioning screen shown in Figure 3-8 displays once these tests have completed.

The standard Ubuntu Server Partitioner screen

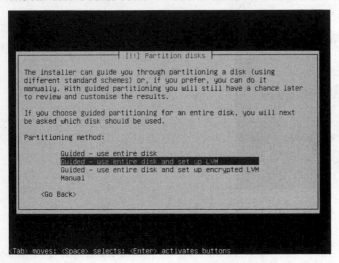

8. The partitioning screen shown in Figure 3-8 is really the only potentially complex portion of the Ubuntu installation process. If you are installing the Ubuntu Server on a system with a single disk and you want to devote that entire disk to Ubuntu, the installation screen should look much like the screen in Figure 3-8 except for differences in device names and sizes. This screen provides a few options:

- **Guided - resize partition and use freed space:** This option only displays if you are installing Ubuntu Server on a computer system whose disk(s) already contain filesystems. Selecting this option enables you to resize an existing partition and install Ubuntu Server in the newly freed space, which would give you a dual-boot system that can boot into either the operating system that is already on the disk or Ubuntu Server. It is extremely rare to want to install a server system as part of a dual-boot setup, because servers are servers, and thus typically only boot one operating system in order to provide certain services. However, this option is available if you do indeed want to do this, as in the case where you have limited hardware resources and are simply experimenting with the latest release of Ubuntu Server.

- **Guided - use entire disk:** Erase the entire disk, and use traditional physical partitions.

- **Guided - use entire disk and set up LVM:** Erase the entire disk, and create logical volumes from the physical space that is available on your disk. This is the default option and makes it easy for you to subsequently add additional storage to the system and expand the size of your logical volumes as required by your server applications or the way in which you are using the system.

- **Guided - use entire disk and set up encrypted LVM:** This is equivalent to the previous option, except that the logical volumes that are created will be encrypted and will be decrypted when mounted and used. You may want to select this option if you will be shipping the server to other locations or generally want an additional level of security for your data.

- **Manual:** Specify the partition layout for your system. If you want to manually partition your system, see the section later in this chapter entitled "Manually Specifying Your Partition Layout," and then return here once you've finished partitioning.

The advantage of using logical volumes is that if you run out of space on your existing system, you can always add another disk drive and add the space that it provides to existing logical volumes. (You can accomplish the same sort of thing with physical disk partitions through the creative use of symbolic links, but this makes administering and maintaining your system more complex.) The advantage of using encrypted logical volumes is that your data will be secure if someone steals your machine and sells it on eBay, although anyone with physical access to the server while it is running and who can log in on it will be able to bypass this encryption, since it will be transparent once the volumes are mounted.

In most cases, you will either want to use the default "entire disk - LVM" or "entire disk" (physical partitions) options. Make sure that the partitioning option that you want to use is selected, and press Return to proceed.

9. The Partitioner displays an additional screen that requests confirmation of the disk that you want to partition for use as the system disk for your Ubuntu Server installation. If your system contains multiple disks, make sure that the right one is selected. Press Return to proceed. If the disk that you have selected for partitioning already contains partitions or logical volumes, an additional confirmation screen displays that gives you a final chance to avoid formatting the wrong disk by requiring confirmation before proceeding. If the correct disk is selected and you do, indeed, want to remove any existing data that it contains, press Return to proceed.

10. The Ubuntu Partitioner's summary screen displays, requesting confirmation of the partitioning scheme that you want to use, as shown in Figure 3-9. As the screen says, this operation cannot be undone. Double-check the displayed values. To accept the values that it displays, press the Tab key to select the Yes value on the screen, and press Return to continue. To make changes to the suggested partitioning scheme, make sure that the No value is highlighted, and press Return. You will be returned to the manual partitioning screens discussed later in this chapter in the section "Manually Specifying Your

Partition Layout." In that case, please see that section for more information, and then return to this point of the installation process.

FIGURE 3-9

The partitioning summary screen

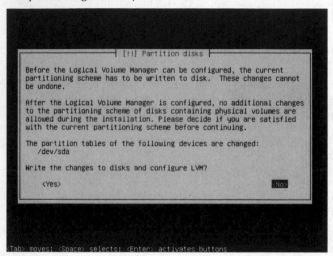

```
┌──────────┤ [!!] Partition disks ├──────────┐

Before the Logical Volume Manager can be configured, the current
partitioning scheme has to be written to disk.  These changes cannot
be undone.

After the Logical Volume Manager is configured, no additional changes
to the partitioning scheme of disks containing physical volumes are
allowed during the installation. Please decide if you are satisfied
with the current partitioning scheme before continuing.

The partition tables of the following devices are changed:
   /dev/sda

Write the changes to disks and configure LVM?

    <Yes>                                          <No>
```

<Tab> moves; <Space> selects; <Enter> activates buttons

If you selected either of the logical volume partitioning mechanisms, a dialog displays that enables you to specify the amount of disk space that you want to initially devote to those logical volumes. You may not want to initially use the entire disk for your server installation, which will enable you to subsequently create other logical volumes in any unused space without having to reduce the size of the volumes used by your server installation.

If you do not want to use the entire disk for logical volumes at the moment, reduce the amount of disk space shown in this dialog and press Return to continue; otherwise, simply press Return to continue.

If you are using logical volumes, a final confirmation dialog displays, identifying the names of the volume groups that will be used and the partitions that will be formatted to accommodate them. If you are sure that you want to use these values, press Tab to select Yes and press Return to accept these values and proceed; otherwise, press Returns while the No value is selected to return to the main partitioning screen shown in Figure 3-9 to modify your partitioning selections.

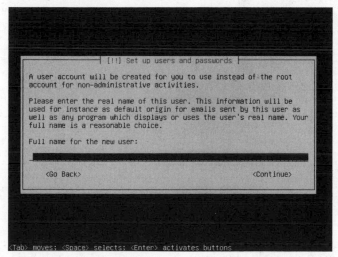

11. After partitioning and basic package installation complete, the screen shown in Figure 3-10 displays, prompting you for the full name of a user to create on your system. As discussed in Chapter 4, "Basic Linux System Concepts," Ubuntu uses a special permissions scheme to give a single user (by default) the ability to perform administrative tasks on your machine. The name of the user that you enter here will have those administrative abilities, so this should almost always be your name or a name associated with a generic system administration user. For server installations, it is generally best to use a generic name like *System Administrator* so that you don't build the name of a specific individual into all of your Ubuntu Servers. (After all, people do occasionally change jobs.) Enter an appropriate full name and press Return to proceed.

FIGURE 3-10

Creating the default user account

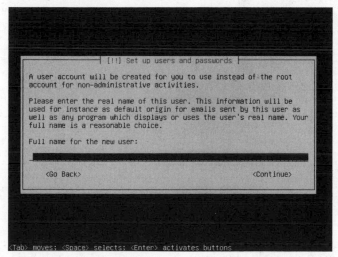

12. The screen shown in Figure 3-11 displays. You must enter the login name for the user whose name you specified in the previous step. This screen initially displays a suggested login name based on the full name that you specified in the previous step. If you want to change this, use the Backspace key to delete the default suggestion and enter the login name that you want to use. To proceed with the default or with a custom username, press Return to continue.

FIGURE 3-11

Creating the default login name

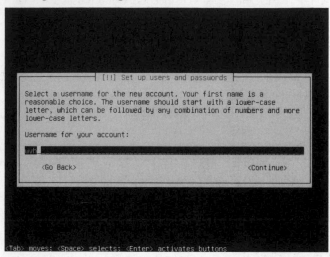

13. The screen shown in Figure 3-12 displays. Enter the password for the user that you are creating, following good password rules such as using a password that contains a mixture of uppercase and lowercase letters and one or more numbers, and *not* using the name or birthday of your spouse, children, yourself, or traditional but deprecated administrative passwords such as *god*, *qwerty*, or *letmein*. Press Return to continue.

FIGURE 3-12

Specifying a password

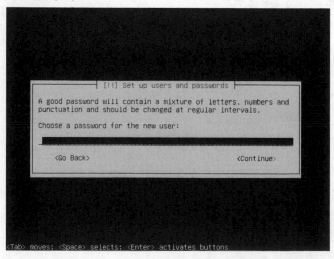

14. After entering your password for the first time, a second password confirmation screen displays (see Figure 3-13). Enter the same password that you entered on the previous screen, and press Return to continue.

FIGURE 3-13

Confirming a password

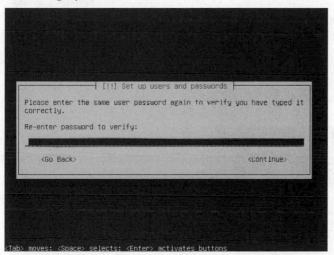

15. The dialog shown in Figure 3-14 displays, asking if you want to encrypt the home directory for the specified user.

FIGURE 3-14

Optionally creating a private, encrypted volume

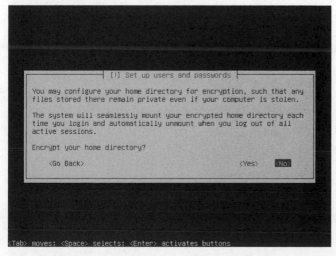

This option is rarely necessary on a server installation, since the system should be physically secure and the object of this option is to protect the administrative account from access by other users of the system (which should be none on a server system). To create this secure file volume, press Tab twice to select Yes, and then press Return. To skip creating an encrypted home directory for the specified user, make sure that the default value of No is selected, and press Return.

16. The dialog shown in Figure 3-15 prompts you as to the location of any HTTP proxy that you need to use in order to access the Internet to download packages. If you need to use an HTTP proxy, enter its URL in this dialog. If you do not need to use an HTTP proxy, leave this field empty and press Return to proceed.

FIGURE 3-15

Identifying an optional HTTP proxy

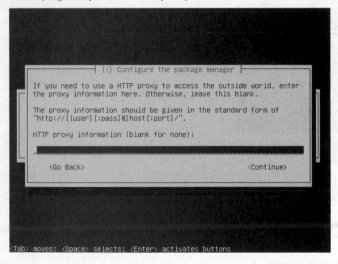

17. The installer installs and configures several packages based on your selections up to this point. Next, the dialog shown in Figure 3-16 displays, which enables you to specify whether the system should not download updates automatically, should download updates automatically, or should use Landscape to manage the system. (*Landscape* is a Web-based system management and monitoring system that is available from Canonical. For more information about Landscape, see `www.canonical.com/projects/landscape`.)

I typically leave this set to the default value, No automatic updates, because it's good policy to only update servers when necessary — it's more important to know exactly what's running on your servers than to always be up-to-date (though it's equally good practice to check for security-related updates frequently).

FIGURE 3-16

Specifying an update mechanism

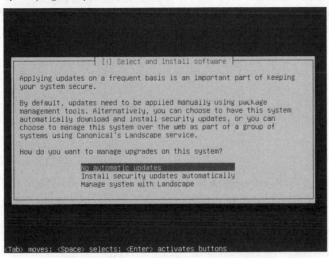

Make your selection on this screen and press Return to proceed.

18. The dialog shown in Figure 3-17 displays, which enables you to select a variety of server-related packages for installation along with the base system.

FIGURE 3-17

Selecting server software for installation

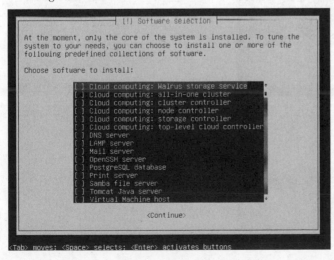

Select any packages that you want to install as part of your initial installation by using the arrow keys to select their names and pressing the spacebar to select the highlighted package. When done, press Tab to select "Continue," and press Return to proceed.

19. At this point, the installer begins copying files from the CD to the hard disk, installing the default packages and any that you selected from the dialog shown in Figure 3-17. If you selected any additional packages in Figure 3-17, the installation process will display any dialogs that are necessary for their configuration.

Note

See the bonus chapters on the book's web site for information about the configuration requirements of many of these server packages. ■

Tip

If you see an error message about the Ubuntu repositories during the installation process, see the sidebar "Resolving Installation Problems" later in this section for more information. This is a nonfatal error, but it is something that you'll want to correct. ■

20. If you are installing an Ubuntu Server on a dual-boot system (which is absolutely not recommended unless you're just experimenting with Ubuntu Server), the screen shown in Figure 3-18 displays after the package installation process completes. The default location to which GRUB, the Linux boot loader used by Ubuntu, is installed is to the master boot record on the primary hard drive. To install GRUB to this location, press Return to proceed to the next step of the installation process.

FIGURE 3-18

The GRUB boot loader location screen for dual-boot systems

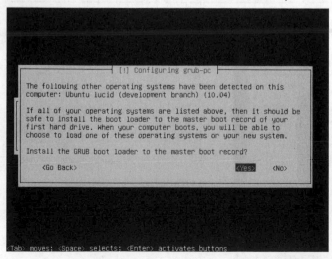

If you want to install GRUB to a different location, use the Tab key to select "No" and press Return. The screen shown in Figure 3-19 displays, in which you can specify where you want to install GRUB. Select the location where you want to install GRUB, and press Return to continue.

The GRUB boot loader installation screen

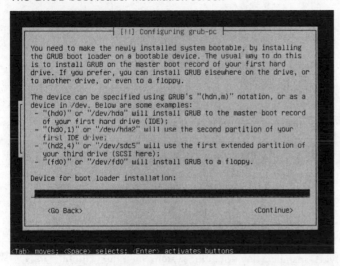

21. If you are installing Ubuntu Server on a dual-boot system, a dialog displays asking whether your system uses UTC (Coordinated Universal Time, formerly Greenwich Mean Time, a time standard based on the time at Greenwich, England). The alternative is that it is set to your local time. if you see this dialog, select Yes or No, and press Return to proceed. This dialog always appears in some other Ubuntu installation scenarios—you can see this dialog later in this chapter in Figure 3-39.

22. After some additional package configuration, the screen shown in Figure 3-20 displays.

Once you see the screen in Figure 3-20, remove the install CD and press Return to reboot your computer into your newly installed Ubuntu Linux Server system! Skip ahead to the section, "Booting Your Server for the First Time," later in this chapter, for more information.

FIGURE 3-20

The final installer screen

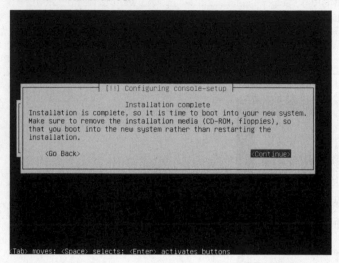

Resolving Installation Problems

Most of the problems that you encounter when installing any operating system, including Ubuntu Linux, are fatal. Problems encountered when reading from the installation media; accessing, partitioning, and formatting your system's hard drives; and other hardware-related problems must be resolved before you can successfully install Ubuntu Linux. However, you may encounter two fairly common problems when installing Ubuntu Linux that can easily be corrected. The first is a problem with automatic network configuration; the second is a problem accessing Ubuntu's online repositories and correctly configuring the Ubuntu software update system.

If the Ubuntu installer cannot automatically configure the network, you will see a screen stating that automatic network configuration failed and asking you if you want to configure the network manually. If this occurs, select Continue or press Return to display a manual network configuration screen.

This screen enables you to retry automatic network configuration via DHCP broadcasts, retry automatic network configuration via DHCP by querying a specific host, configure your network manually, or skip network configuration altogether. Before doing anything else, check your network cabling to make sure that the machine you are installing Ubuntu on is correctly attached to the network, especially if your network is actually running a DHCP server.

You can select any of the available options, but I suggest that you select the "Configure network manually" option to provide your Ubuntu Server with a static IP address and related networking information. In my experience, few servers have dynamic IP addresses because this makes it more challenging to contact them remotely if a problem occurs, because you aren't guaranteed to know their IP address.

If you select the "Configure network manually" option, the installer displays four additional network configuration screens that respectively prompt you for the server's IP address, the netmask for that IP address, the IP address of your network gateway, and the name server(s) on your network. (If you want to enter multiple name servers, separate them by a space, not a comma.) Once these screens are displayed, the system's network interface is configured, and you are returned to the installer.

Another common problem you may encounter when installing Ubuntu Linux is in contacting and verifying all of the default Ubuntu Linux repositories, which are sites on the Internet that provide new and updated software packages for different Ubuntu releases. If problems occur when contacting the Ubuntu repositories, a dialog about this failure may display during the installation process, and certain repositories may be disabled temporarily.

If you see a message along these lines, you shouldn't be concerned. This is usually a transient, network connectivity or load problem. After you reboot, you will need to uncomment any repositories that were identified in this dialog. (Most of these problems occur when contacting the security repositories.) To uncomment these, use your favorite text editor via a command such as `sudo vi /etc/apt/sources.list`. Remove the hash mark at the beginning of each of the lines associated with the specified repositories, save the modified file, and execute the command `sudo apt-get update` to verify that the new repositories can be contacted successfully. See Chapter 19 for more information about the Ubuntu repositories and software package management utilities.

Manually Specifying Your Partition Layout

Manually specifying the layout of the partitions on your system can be useful, but it is also time-consuming and requires some understanding of the Linux filesystem. Manually partitioning your system enables you to put specific directories from the Linux filesystem on their own partitions, which can improve performance, minimize the size of backups for your system (because backups are usually done on a per-filesystem or per-directory basis), and simplify future upgrades and system reconfiguration.

Note

By default, the Ubuntu installer automatically creates a reasonable partitioning scheme for you, which means that it creates one large partition for user and system files and another, smaller, partition to use as swap space to support virtual memory on your Ubuntu system. This section describes an alternative to the quasi-graphical Ubuntu installer's automatic partitioning scheme. If you're reading this book chapter-to-chapter, you can skip over this section if you've already installed your system.

If you are installing Ubuntu for the first time or are relatively unfamiliar with Linux, I'd suggest letting the Ubuntu installer automatically partition your disk for you. Automatic partitioning will get you up and running much more quickly, and doesn't require that you understand the content and use of various directories on your Linux system. As you become more familiar with Ubuntu and Linux, you can always subsequently back up your user account to another machine, and then reinstall Ubuntu using manual partitioning. ■

The following are common directories in the Linux filesystem that are often put into their own partitions:

- `/`: The top level of the Linux filesystem. A partition must always be available through the `/` directory in order for a Linux system to boot.
- `/boot`: The directory that holds the Linux kernel and other associated system files used during the boot process
- `/home`: The directory where user files and accounts are located
- `/opt`: A directory where optional programs and related files are typically installed
- `/tmp`: A directory used to hold temporary files created by user and system processes
- `/usr`: A directory that holds applications, system files, and libraries used by the standard Linux system. On Ubuntu systems, the `/usr` directory requires up to 1.25 GB of disk space, depending on the packages that you have selected for installation.
- `/usr/local`: A directory that holds applications, system files, and libraries used by a particular Linux system, but that may not be present on all Linux systems

Most Linux systems that do not use a single partition to hold the entire filesystem create separate partitions for `/`, `/boot`, and `/home`. For more information about these directories and the structure of the Linux filesystem in general, see Chapter 4.

Linux partitions can be grouped into two general types: *swap partitions*, which are used internally by the system to support virtual memory; and *data partitions*, in which files and other directories are located. A Linux system must have at least one area to swap to in order to function correctly — this is usually a dedicated partition, although you can also swap to a file in the filesystem if you are desperate. (See Chapter 4 for more information about partitions and virtual memory.) In this section, you will create a few basic data partitions and a single swap partition to illustrate manual partitioning — how you actually decide to partition your system is up to you.

Manually partitioning your disk involves steps like the following:

1. In the screen shown in Figure 3-8, select the Manual option. The screen shown in Figure 3-21 displays.
2. Use the arrow key to select the pool of available space on the disk drive that you want to partition, and press Return to continue. The screen shown in Figure 3-22 displays.

FIGURE 3-21

The screen for manually partitioning disks

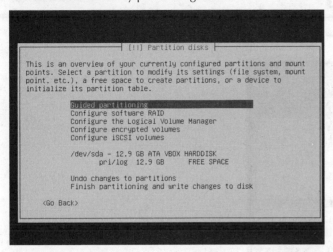

FIGURE 3-22

Beginning to define a new partition

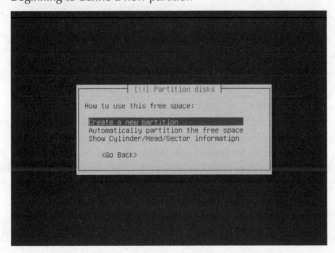

3. Select the "Create a new partition" entry, and press Return to continue. The screen shown in Figure 3-23 displays.

Specifying the size of your new partition

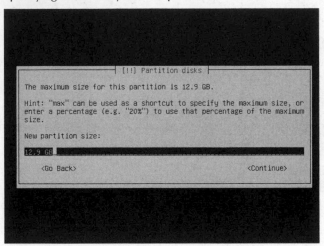

4. Enter the size that you want your new partition to have. The amount of unallocated disk space is displayed as a default value. You can specify the size of your new partition as an absolute value, such as 100 MB; specify it as a percentage of the available space, such as 10 percent; or use the max keyword to create a partition of the maximum size available based on existing free space. After entering this value, press Return to continue. The screen shown in Figure 3-24 displays.

5. Select the type of partition that you want to create. Disks can contain up to four physical partitions — any partitions beyond that number must be logical partitions. *Logical partitions* can contain other partitions, whereas *physical partitions* are just that — physical portions of your disk drive that cannot be further subdivided. Unless you plan to create more than four partitions, use the arrow keys to ensure that the physical entry is selected, and press Return to continue. The screen shown in Figure 3-25 displays.

FIGURE 3-24

Specifying the type of your new partition

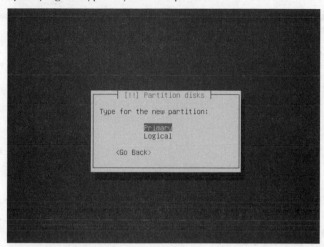

FIGURE 3-25

Specifying the location of your new partition

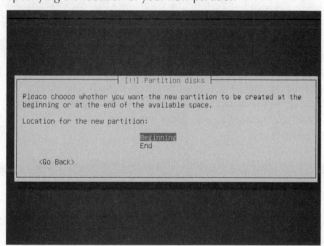

6. Unless you have a specific reason to position the new partition on a special portion of your disk, accept the default value Beginning and press Return to continue. The screen shown in Figure 3-26 displays.

Specifying the type and mountpoint of your new partition

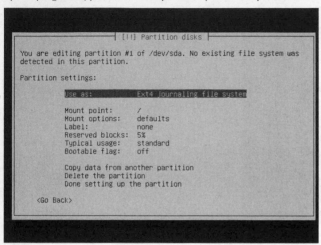

7. The highlighted entry on this screen enables you to specify the type of filesystem used on the partition that you are creating, which is essentially how the data is organized and managed on the partition that you are creating. Linux systems support many different types of filesystems, each of which has certain characteristics that are explained in more detail in Chapter 4. In this example, we'll be creating a partition to be mounted at /boot, which is a data partition, and the Linux ext4 filesystem is the default (and most popular) format for data partitions. Unless you have a specific reason to do so, you should not change the default value.

   However, if you want to specify another type of filesystem, press Return. The screen shown in Figure 3-27 displays, showing the list of available filesystem types. After selecting the type of filesystem that you want to use, press Return to continue. The screen shown in Figure 3-26 re-displays.

8. The *mountpoint* for a partition is the directory through which the contents of that partition are made available to your system. (See Chapter 4 for more information about Linux directories and mountpoints.) A list of common partitions and associated mountpoints was given at the beginning of this section. The only mandatory filesystem and associated mountpoint on a Linux system is /, the root directory of the Linux filesystem, which is shown as the default value on the screen shown in Figure 3-26. Use the arrow keys to select the "Mount Point" menu item, and press Return to continue. The screen shown in Figure 3-28 displays.

FIGURE 3-27

Specifying the partition type

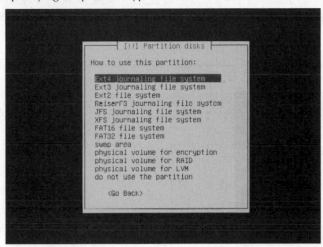

FIGURE 3-28

Specifying the mountpoint for your new partition

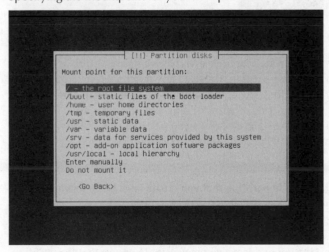

In this example, you'll mount your new partition at /boot, which is the directory that holds the Linux kernel and associated system files. Use the arrow keys to select the entry for /boot, and press Return to continue. The screen shown in Figure 3-26 re-displays.

9. Use the arrow keys to scroll down and select the "Done setting up the partition" option. A screen like the one shown in Figure 3-21 re-displays, showing the new partition that you have just defined and the remaining free space for the drive. Figure 3-29 shows the updated version of this screen.

FIGURE 3-29

Manual disk partitioning with one partition defined

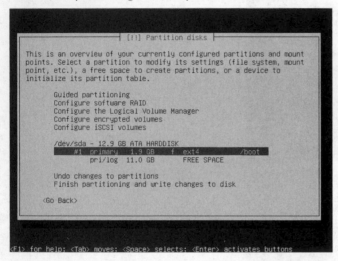

10. Repeat Steps 2 through 9 to create additional partitions. As discussed in the previous section, filesystems that are often created on their own partitions are /boot (used in this example), /, /home, and a swap partition. Creating any other filesystem partitions follows exactly the same process as described previously. To create a swap partition, follow the same process as when creating other partitions, but select the swap area entry from the screen shown in Figure 3-27. The size of a swap partition should be approximately the same size as the amount of memory in your computer system.

Caution

If you plan to create more than four partitions, the fourth partition that you create must be an Extended partition, in which the other partitions that you want to use can then be created. ■

Tip

To help guarantee that you do not encounter installation problems, you may want to ensure that the partition that you mount at / is at least 3 GB in size. Following this rule should guarantee that your Ubuntu system will install correctly unless you have defined other partitions such as /usr with insufficient space to hold the files that are installed under that directory when it is used as a mountpoint. ■

11. Once you have allocated all of the available free space on your system to partitions, your screen should look something like the one shown in Figure 3-30. This screen displays a summary of the partitions that you have defined for use on your system. Remember that there must be one partition mounted at / and one swap partition. To accept the values shown on this screen, use the arrow keys to select the "Finish partitioning and write changes to disk" option, and press Return to display the screen shown in Figure 3-31.

FIGURE 3-30

The partition summary screen

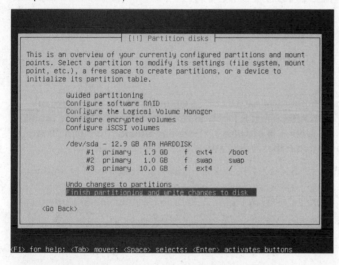

FIGURE 3-31

The final partition confirmation screen

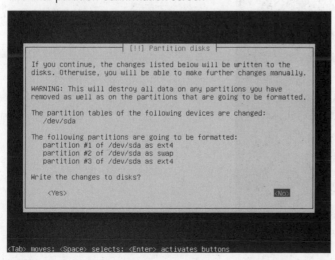

12. Because disk partitioning cannot be undone, the screen shown in Figure 3-31 requests final confirmation of your manual partitioning selections. To accept these values and continue with the installation process, use the Tab key to select "Yes," and press Return to continue.

You can now return to Step 11 of the Ubuntu Server installation process in the previous section. And congratulations — you're now at least a Linux wizard in training!

Booting Your Server for the First Time

Once the server installation process completes, the screen shown in Figure 3-20 displays. Remove the install CD and press Return to reboot your system into your newly installed Ubuntu Linux Server!

Note

The Ubuntu boot process differs depending on whether you have installed Ubuntu as a dual-boot system or as the only operating system on your computer. Although it is highly unlikely that you would have installed an Ubuntu Server on a dual-boot system, see the section in Chapter 2, "Installing Ubuntu," entitled "Booting Ubuntu on Dual-Boot Systems" for more information if that is the case. ■

As Ubuntu boots, you will see many text messages displayed to the screen as it probes and initializes your hardware and related system software. When the boot process is complete, you will see a command-line login screen like that shown in Figure 3-32. You can now log in using the username and password that you defined during the installation process.

FIGURE 3-32

The Ubuntu Server login screen

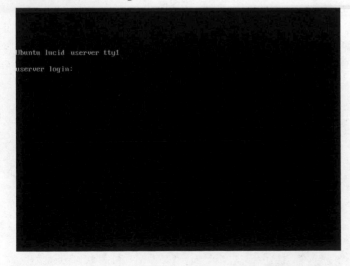

Congratulations — you're running an Ubuntu Linux Server! For more basic information about Linux, see Chapter 4. Depending on the server applications that you installed, see the later chapters of this book for information about configuring and fine-tuning a specific server application to meet the needs of your computing environment.

Installing an Ubuntu Enterprise Cloud

Cloud computing is one of today's most popular computing models because it leverages the power of network connectivity to create powerful and flexible storage, processing, and software execution infrastructure. A cloud installation typically delivers virtualized storage and computing (through virtual machines) in response to administrative and user requests. Traditionally viewed as a pay-as-you-go-model supported by a variety of Internet software and infrastructure vendors, cloud computing can also be installed and supported in a local network environment to deliver those same capabilities without relying on third-party vendors. The Ubuntu Enterprise Cloud (UEC) installation that is supported on the Ubuntu Server installation CDs enables you to set up and configure a cloud computing environment on your own systems thanks to Eucalyptus, an open source cloud computing package.

Cloud computing is a topic that deserves, and already has, many books dedicated to its concepts and configuration. This section highlights the differences between installing a traditional Ubuntu Server and a UEC Server, but does not provide a detailed discussion of all of the components of a Eucalyptus-based cloud. Links to more detailed information, including user and administrator guides, are provided at the end of this section.

A minimal Eucalyptus cloud installation typically involves at least two systems, a front-end system that runs cloud-related server processes such as the cloud controller, cluster controller, the network-based storage service manager (known as *Walrus*), and the storage controller; and another system that runs a node controller, functions as a node within the cloud, and delivers virtual machine instances.

As a server installation that provides cloud services and virtual machine instances in an entire computing environment, the suggested installation requirements for a UEC installation are much larger than those of a standard Ubuntu Server. Recommendations are:

- **Front-end system:** Multi-core or multiple processors at 1.7 GHz or better, 2 GB or more of system memory, 200 GB or more of disk space (depending on the number of virtual machine images you will be supporting), Gigabit Ethernet

- **Node:** 64-bit, multi-core processor with hardware virtualization support (Intel VT or AMD-V), 4 GB or more of system memory, 100 GB or more of disk space (depending on the number of virtual machine images that will be running at one time on each node), Gigabit Ethernet

The installation process for an Ubuntu Enterprise Cloud Server is very similar to that of a standard Ubuntu Server, with the exception of some screens that are specific to configuring Eucalyptus. When installing an Ubuntu Enterprise Cloud Server, the following screens display after the screen shown in Figure 3-6, which prompts for the name of your server system:

1. Figure 3-33 shows the initial Cloud Installation Mode dialog that prompts you for the network address of the system that is running the Eucalyptus cloud controller package. This system coordinates activities between all systems that are members of a single Eucalyptus cloud. If this is your first Ubuntu Enterprise Cloud installation (and you are not already running Eucalyptus in your environment), you will not have an existing cloud controller, and you should leave the address field empty (which implies that the system that you are installing will be the cloud controller). If you already have a system serving as a Eucalyptus cloud controller in your environment, enter its IP address. Press return to continue.

FIGURE 3-33

Identifying any existing cloud controller

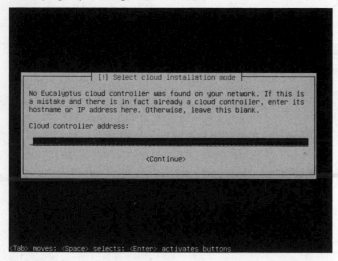

2. The second Cloud Installation Mode dialog shown in Figure 3-34 displays if you did not identify the IP address of a cloud controller in the screen shown in Figure 3-33 — in other words, if you are installing a UEC system that will function as a cloud controller. As mentioned earlier in this section, a minimal cloud installation requires at least two systems, so this screen identifies the processes that should be running on a cloud controller if you did not identify an existing system that functions as a cloud controller. If you did specify the IP address of a cloud controller system, the screen that displays

is very similar to the screen shown in Figure 3-34, except that only the Node controller entry is highlighted.

FIGURE 3-34

Identifying cloud-related server processes to install

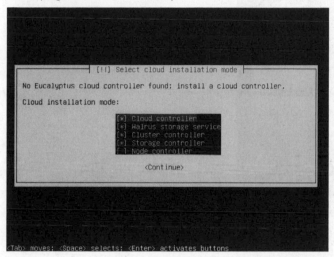

At this point, the normal server installation process resumes with the screen shown in Figure 3-7, as discussed in the section entitled "Installing an Ubuntu Server." The only significant differences between the remainder of the Ubuntu Enterprise Cloud and standard Ubuntu Server installation processes are the following:

- The cloud controller system in an Ubuntu Enterprise Cloud installation automatically installs the Postfix Mail Server. The installation process will therefore display the standard Postfix configuration dialogs, which are discussed in Chapter 30, "Setting Up a Mail Server."

- The dialog shown in Figure 3-35 displays, prompting you for the name of the Ubuntu Enterprise Cloud that you are installing. Enter a logical name for the cloud, and press Return to continue.

- The dialog shown in Figure 3-36 displays, prompting you for a pool of IP addresses that can be used as the publicly visible IP addresses of virtual machines that will be created and made available in the cloud. Enter a range of IP addresses that are not already in use or are already available through a DHCP server in your computing environment, and press Return to continue.

FIGURE 3-35

Specifying the name of your Ubuntu Enterprise Cloud

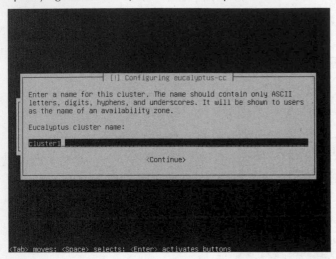

FIGURE 3-36

Specifying IP addresses for virtual machines in your Ubuntu Enterprise Cloud

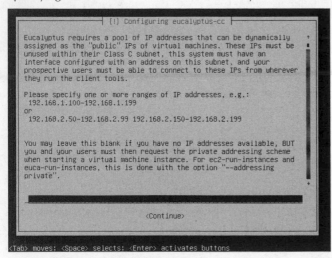

For general information about the Ubuntu Enterprise Cloud and comparisons with third-party cloud computing environments, see www.ubuntu.com/cloud. For more detailed information about UEC, the topology and configuration of a Eucalyptus cloud, and the processes that control the behavior of a Eucalyptus-based cloud, see https://help.ubuntu.com/community/UEC. For specific information about Eucalyptus, see www.eucalyptus.com, the commercial arm of Eucalyptus, or http://open.eucalyptus.com, the Eucalyptus open source site where you can find extensive documentation including guides for administrators and users.

Install Options on the Alternate Install CD

Figure 3-37 shows the menu that is displayed when you boot your system from an Ubuntu Alternate Install CD.

FIGURE 3-37

The Boot menu on the Ubuntu Alternate Install CD

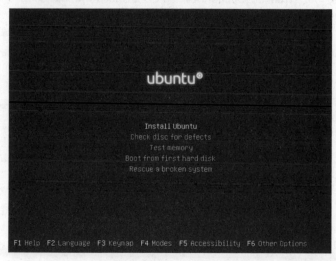

The options on an Alternate Install CD's Boot menu are as follows:

- **Install Ubuntu:** Installs a basic Ubuntu Desktop system to your hard drive(s) using a quasi-graphical installer. Installing an Ubuntu Desktop system using this installer is very similar to installing an Ubuntu Server system, as discussed in detail earlier in this chapter. The differences between using the standard and quasi-graphical installers to install an Ubuntu Desktop system are discussed in the next section, "Installing a Desktop System in Text Mode."

- **Check disc for defects:** Tests the integrity of the CD or DVD that is currently inserted in your system and verifies its contents.

- **Test memory:** Performs several memory tests to verify your system's memory and associated cache. You can press the letter *c* to display a configuration menu that enables you to run or rerun specific tests. Once you are finished testing your system's memory, press Esc to reboot your system and return to the Alternate Install CD Boot menu.

- **Boot from first hard disk:** Bypasses booting from the Alternate Install CD and boots from your system's hard drive. This is the option to use if you accidentally left an Alternate Install CD in the CD drive of a system on which you did not intend to install Ubuntu or perform the available system tests.

- **Rescue a broken system:** Prompts for a few pieces of information such as the language that you want messages to be displayed in and your geographic location, and then boots a diskless version of Linux that runs from the CD and that you can use to repair corrupted disks, correct or reinstall your GRUB boot loader's configuration, and so on.

Tip

If you have problems entering Rescue mode, booting from the Ubuntu Desktop CD included with this book provides the same capabilities as a Rescue mode installation, but with a whizzy graphical interface. ■

The Alternate Install CDs actually have additional installation options that you can display by pressing F4, which displays the pop-up menu shown in Figure 3-38. These options are as follows:

- **Normal:** Installs a standard Desktop system using the quasi-graphical installer.

- **OEM Install (for manufacturers):** Installs an Ubuntu Desktop system to your hard drive(s) using Ubuntu's quasi-graphical installer. Unlike the standard installations, the OEM-mode install defines an OEM user that you can use to customize the system so that you can distribute it to end users. After customizing the system, OEMs then run a simple command to remove the OEM user and define a standard Ubuntu privileged user. Installing an OEM system is discussed in the section, "Installing in OEM Mode."

- **Install a command-line system:** Installs a basic Ubuntu system to your hard drive(s) using the quasi-graphical installer. The installed system has no graphical capabilities (these can always be added later, if desired). Installing a command-line system using this installer is discussed in detail later in this chapter, in the section, "Installing a Command-Line System."

- **Install an LTSP server:** Only available on the Ubuntu Alternate Install CD, this option installs a Linux Terminal Server Project (LTSP) server system and a good selection of applications for use by clients of that server. Installing an LTSP Server using this installer is discussed in detail later in this chapter, in the section, "Installing an LTSP Server."

To proceed, select any of these options, or simply press Return to leave the Normal option selected. The screen shown in Figure 3-38 re-displays. Make sure that the "Install Ubuntu" entry is still selected, and press Return to continue with the installation process.

FIGURE 3-38

Installation options for the Ubuntu Alternate Install CD

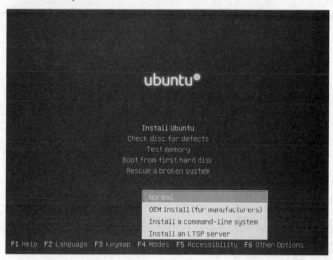

The next sections explain each of these options and highlight the differences between the Text-mode installers used by these options and the quasi-graphical installer described earlier in this chapter in the section, "Installing an Ubuntu Server."

Installing a Desktop System in Text Mode

Selecting "Install Ubuntu" from the Ubuntu Alternate Install CD's Boot menu enables you to install an Ubuntu Desktop system using the Text-mode installer. This menu option is useful in various scenarios, such as the following:

- You are having problems getting the appropriate Desktop CD to boot on your system because of conflicts or problems with your graphics hardware.

- You want to install the Ubuntu Desktop system but use logical volumes rather than physical partitions to hold your filesystem(s).

- You want to install the Ubuntu Desktop system but want to install GRUB to a location other than the master boot record of your primary hard drive.

As with the other quasi-graphical Ubuntu installers, the text-mode Desktop install follows the same series of prompts and steps as discussed in the section, "Installing an Ubuntu Server," earlier in this chapter. Installing a desktop system from the Alternate Install CD simply installs a somewhat expanded set of packages to your system compared to the server install. This expanded set of packages is equivalent to those installed from the standard Desktop CD, and therefore includes the GNOME Desktop, the X Window System, graphical tools, and so on.

The only difference between a text-mode desktop install and the server install process that was discussed earlier occurs near the very end of the installation process, where, before ejecting the CD and suggesting that you reboot your system, the desktop installer prompts you for information about whether you would like the system clock to be set to Coordinated Universal Time (UTC) or local time. This screen is shown in Figure 3-39.

Note
Coordinated Universal Time, **or** *Universal Coordinated Time,* **(UTC) is Greenwich Mean Time, the time at the Royal Observatory in Greenwich, London, United Kingdom;** *local time* **is the actual time at your physical location.** ■

FIGURE 3-39

Specifying system clock settings

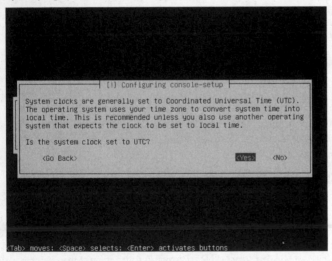

When you see this screen, press Return to use UTC, or press Tab and then Return to use local time and continue with the installation process. After this screen, the standard installation procedure continues, eventually ejecting the CD and prompting you to reboot into your new, graphical Ubuntu Desktop system.

Installing in OEM Mode

Selecting "OEM install for manufacturers" from an Alternate Install CD's Modes menu (shown in Figure 3-38) enables you to install an Ubuntu Desktop system using the Text-mode installer, but installs the system with a temporary privileged user (OEM). This enables OEMs to perform additional configuration on this system using this privileged user, installing custom software, installing additional packages, and removing packages as necessary, and then to re-distribute the system to their customers. To turn this system into a standard Ubuntu Desktop installation with a customer-specific privileged user after completing its configuration, the OEM should execute the sudo oem-prepare command, which will delete the OEM user and will prompt the customer to enter customer-specific user and other configuration questions the next time the system boots.

Throughout the OEM installation process, a banner in the upper-left corner of the screen identifies the fact that you are doing an OEM-mode installation. As with the other quasi-graphical installers, the quasi-graphical OEM installer follows much the same series of prompts and steps as discussed earlier in this chapter in the section, "Installing a Desktop System in Text Mode." Because an OEM system is installed with a specific privileged user (OEM), the install process does not prompt you for a username and login, but only for a password for the OEM user. The OEM-mode installer then continues with the standard text-mode installation and configuration process.

Just before the final installation summary screen, the OEM-mode installer displays a screen that summarizes how OEM mode is to be used, as shown in Figure 3-40.

OEM mode process summary

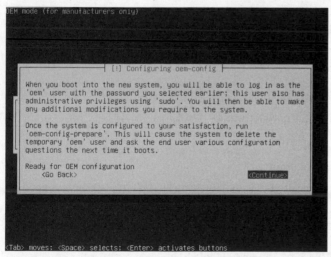

After this screen, the standard installation procedure continues, eventually ejecting the CD and prompting you to reboot into your new, graphical Ubuntu OEM mode system to complete its configuration before distribution to the OEM's customers.

Installing a Command-Line System

Selecting "Install a command-line system" from the Alternate Install CD's Modes menu (shown in Figure 3-38) enables you to install an Ubuntu Desktop system that does not contain any of the packages required for any graphical, X Window System application. This provides a small-footprint installation to which you can subsequently add any graphical packages that you are interested in. This installation option provides a great starting point for creating a small, highly customized, and highly personalized Ubuntu-based system. The installation process for installing a command-line Ubuntu Desktop system from the Alternate Install CD is exactly the same as installing a standard Ubuntu desktop system in text-mode, as described in the section of this chapter entitled "Installing a Desktop System in Text Mode," except for the fact that a smaller number of packages are installed.

Installing an LTSP Server

The Linux Terminal Server Project (LTSP; `www.ltsp.org`) is one of the most excellent Linux development efforts ever. The LTSP enables you to configure a system to act as a central server for large numbers of lightweight Linux clients, much like a Microsoft Windows Terminal Server except for the price differential. As you might expect, Windows Terminal Server and its associated per-client access licenses (CALs) cost a tremendous amount of money, whereas the LTSP is free for both servers and any number of clients. The LTSP is extremely popular in schools, libraries, and any other institution that needs to maximize its computing power but may have a tragically limited budget.

Selecting "Install an LTSP Server" from the Ubuntu Alternate Install CD's Options menu enables you to install what is essentially an Ubuntu Desktop system with all of the LTSP server software built-in.

For more information about the LTSP, see:

- `www.ltsp.org`: The home page for the LTSP project, which is the same as its SourceForge page at `http://ltsp.sourceforge.net`. Documentation for the latest LTSP releases is available at `http://sourceforge.net/apps/mediawiki/ltsp/index.php?title=Ltsp_Documentation`.

- `http://en.wikipedia.org/wiki/Linux_Terminal_Server_Project`: A good overview of the LTSP from Wikipedia

- `http://k12ltsp.org/mediawiki/index.php/Main_Page`: The home page for the K12 on Linux Project, an excellent LTSP implementation that has unfortunately chosen CentOS rather than Ubuntu as the foundation of its LTSP

Summary

This chapter covered a lot of ground, explaining some basic concepts required to successfully install Ubuntu Linux as a server operating system on an existing machine or as the only operating system on a system using various specialized installation configurations via the quasi-graphical Debian installer. Regardless of the type of system that you installed or are using, by the end of this chapter, you have Ubuntu Linux installed and running on your computer system.

Chapter 4 discusses basic Linux concepts that may be new to you if this is the first Linux or UNIX-like system that you have used. Chapters 5 and 6 discuss the basics of using Ubuntu with its standard graphical interface (GNOME) and window manager (Compiz), respectively.

Part II

Ubuntu for Desktop Users

IN THIS PART

Chapter 4
Basic Linux System Concepts

Chapter 5
Using the GNOME Desktop

Chapter 6
Using the Compiz Window
Manager

Chapter 7
Managing E-mail and Personal
Information with Evolution

Chapter 8
Surfing the Web with Firefox

Chapter 9
Migrating from Windows Systems

Chapter 10
Sending and Receiving Instant
Messages

Chapter 11
Using Command-Line Tools

Chapter 12
Working with Text Files

Chapter 13
Creating and Publishing
Documents

Chapter 14
Other Office Software:
Spreadsheets and Presentations

Chapter 15
Working with Graphics

Chapter 16
Working with Multimedia

Chapter 17
Would You Like to Play a Game?

Chapter 18
Consumer Electronics and Ubuntu

Chapter 19
Adding, Removing, and Updating
Software

Chapter 20
Adding Hardware and Attaching
Peripherals

Chapter 21
Network Configuration and
Security

Chapter 22
Going Wireless

Chapter 23
Software Development on
Ubuntu

Chapter 24
Using Virtual Machines and
Emulators

Chapter 25
Connecting to Other Systems

Chapter 26
File Transfer and Sharing

Basic Linux System Concepts

This chapter explains basic Linux system concepts, focusing on how data is stored and organized on all Linux systems and how the Linux operating system controls access to that data and to privileged operations. Aside from specific sections on how Ubuntu deals with and grants high-level permissions, the information in this chapter applies to any Linux system and to most other UNIX-like systems.

In this chapter, I err on the side of caution. As impossible as it now sounds, I had never used a computer before deciding to study computer science at university. (I can be excused for this to some extent because this was a zillion years ago, just as personal computers were starting to become popular and long before DOS, Microsoft Windows, Apple Macintosh, and so on.) At any rate, I remember sitting in my first computer science class while the professor said things such as, "Once you write your program, save it to a file," and thinking, "What the heck is he talking about?"

This chapter therefore contains some sections, such as "Working with Files and Directories" that you might find insulting in their simplicity and exploration of basic concepts that "everybody knows," which is fine with me. Everybody who knows that stuff can skip over it, but the people who just got their Ubuntu Linux boxes at the local electronics shop or from well-meaning friends or relatives can secretly read these sections, and think, "Oh, I get it!" and we'll all be happier.

IN THIS CHAPTER

Understanding files and directories

Understanding disks and disk partitions

Understanding logical volumes

Understanding Linux filesystems

Introducing users and groups

Understanding privileged operations on Ubuntu systems

Working with Files and Directories

A *file* is nothing more than a collection of information that programs and your operating system can locate and deal with as a single unit. Files are containers for some sort of data, whether they contain a letter to your mother or parole board, a copy of one of your favorite songs (legitimate, of course), a digital photograph, or the data used by a spreadsheet to calculate the health of your personal finances. Providing the general concept of a *file* as a container for related data makes it easy for applications and Linux to locate and use that information — hence the File menu that is present in most graphical applications today. This menu contains the commands that you use to open existing files, create new ones, and save changes that you have made to any file that you are working with.

Files are mandatory on a computer system — the operating system has to have a way to identify and access your data, the applications that it needs to run, any configuration files used by those applications, and so on. Similarly, when you turn it on, your computer system needs to know how to find the operating system and related configuration information that it requires to boot. However, as more and more files were required, used for different purposes, and created by different users, it didn't take long for users to look for an intermediate mechanism for organizing files, which led to the introduction of directories. *Directories* are simply containers for groups of related files, and they can also contain directories (or *subdirectories*). This is what is known as a hierarchical collection of files — the location of any specific file is described by identifying the series of directories that eventually contains the file that you're looking for. The directory that all searches start with on Linux systems is known as the *root directory* because it is the starting point for the description of how to navigate to any file that is stored locally (i.e., on your computer).

The standard analogy for files and directories is a filing cabinet — you can find any file in the filing cabinet by following a process like this: Start at the filing cabinet, open the first drawer, open the hanging file labeled Personnel, select the manila folder with your name on it, and check your healthcare enrollment form. On a computer, the process for finding the location of an analogous file might be something like this: Go to the root of the filesystem (/), go to the home directory, go to the wvh directory (my login name), and look for the file named health_enrollment.txt.

Linux systems use the "/" character as both the name of the top-level directory on your system and to separate file and directory names, so this is often more simply expressed as, "Get the file /home/wvh/health_enrollment.txt." The series of directories leading to a given file is often referred to as the *path* to that file.

Linux systems that provide a graphical user interface, such as GNOME, provide graphical ways of navigating through directories, typically by clicking on them to open them and opening a window that displays graphical icons corresponding to the files that they contain. As explained in more detail in Chapter 11, "Using Command-Line Tools," any Linux command-line environment uses a command known as cd (which stands for "change directory") to navigate through a sequence of directories. You can change to each directory in a series of directories (paths) one at a time, or you can simply cd to a specific target directory. In other words, the following two sequences of commands are equivalent:

```
cd /
cd home
cd wvh
```

and

```
cd /home/wvh
```

Linux systems also provide a variety of tools to list the contents of directories and provide detailed information about specific files and directories. I explain these in detail in Chapter 11. For now, I'll focus on describing how things are organized on a Linux system.

Standard Linux Directories

All Linux systems provide a standard set of core directories. The following directories are used to hold programs that must run when you are booting your Linux system, configuration files for those programs, libraries used by those programs, temporary files created by running programs, and so on:

- /: As the top-level directory of a Linux system, this directory must exist so that other directories can be located within it.
- /bin: A directory that holds core applications used by a Linux system
- /dev: A directory that holds special files, known as *device nodes*, which are used to access any devices that are attached to your Linux system
- /etc: A directory that holds system configuration information, contains the files that explain the sequence of applications that execute on a Linux system as part of its boot process, and stores configuration files for some of the applications that are executed by a Linux system
- /lib: A directory that holds libraries of functions that can be called by other applications
- /proc: A directory in which the Linux kernel tracks active processes and general status information
- /sbin: A directory containing applications that are usually executed only by the superuser
- /sys: A directory in which the Linux kernel tracks the status of system hardware and related hardware interfaces
- /tmp: A directory that holds temporary files created by various applications on a running system

You will find these standard directories on most Linux systems, regardless of the type of distribution or the size of the disk they are using.

Other Common Directories on Linux Systems

Depending on the number of files you've installed on your system and its layout, you will probably find several other directories on any Linux system. Some other commonly used directories on Linux systems are as follows:

- /home: A directory that holds the subdirectories where different users store their files. For example, most (if not all) of the files owned by the user wvh are stored in the /home/wvh directory (or subdirectories of that directory). The directories used by individual users to store their personal files are known as their *home directories* — this name led to user directories being stored in /home, not the other way around. On older UNIX and UNIX-like systems, users' home directories were stored under /usr (pronounced "slash user"), but are now created under /home to simplify system upgrades.

- /opt: A directory typically used when installing third-party software. This directory takes its name from the idea that it contains "optional" (i.e., non-system) software that may differ across different machines.

- /usr: A directory hierarchy that contains files meant to be used by normal users as they use a Linux system. The directory /usr/bin contains applications that users may need to execute, /usr/lib contains libraries used by those programs, and so on.

- /var: A directory that holds other directories with variable content. For example, the directory /var/log contains log files for system applications and events. These log files are created while a system is running, and can grow very large over time.

As you can see, a Linux system provides a large, hierarchical collection of files and directories that are organized to simplify locating certain types of files such as executables, libraries, configuration files, system status information, and so on. Now, let's look at how Linux uses various types of storage devices to store and deliver all of this information.

Tip
The directories listed in this section are fairly standard across most Linux systems, but their exact contents differ slightly from distribution to distribution. The Linux Standard Base project (LSB) was formed with the mission of standardizing directories and their contents across Linux distributions. For more information about this project, see the LSB web site at www.linuxbase.org. ∎

Introduction to Linux Filesystems

The directories discussed in the previous section provide a standard way of organizing the files and directories required for a Linux system to boot, run standard applications, and so on. You'll note that the path to all of these directories begins with the / symbol. This doesn't necessarily mean that they're all located on the same hard drive or other storage device. Unlike Windows systems, which refer to different disk drives or disk partitions by using unique drive letters (C:, D:, etc.), or Mac OS X systems, which represent different disk drives or disk partitions as different volumes on the desktop, Linux systems provide what is known as a *single namespace* for all of the storage devices and partitions that it can access.

This section discusses how Linux systems manage and access disks, what disk partitions are, and how disk partitions are integrated into the hierarchy of directories that you can access on a Linux system. The hierarchy of files and directories on a Linux machine is generally referred to as the *Linux filesystem*, although, as I'll discuss in the next few sections, the term *filesystem* is also used to refer to the way that data is organized on a specific disk partition. This section also introduces *logical volumes*, which provide a more flexible mechanism of allocating and using disk storage than simply using disk partitions, but which are most commonly only used on server systems or other systems with huge storage requirements.

Disks, Partitions, and Mountpoints

The bottom line of any computer system is storing, retrieving, manipulating, and saving information. As a writer and computer systems administrator, I'm always amazed when friends who are generally computer savvy say to me, "Your laptop is so slow. Why don't you upgrade?" Frankly, if I could type faster than my primary laptop's 1.4 GHz Pentium processor could handle, I'd be posing for "Ripley's Believe It or Not!" ads or touring with the circus instead of writing books. On the other hand, if it took five minutes for me to save a chapter of whatever I'm working on or if I could never find the space to save a modified file without deleting something else, I'd drop-kick my current laptop into the river in a heartbeat and buy the newest, brightest, shiniest Linux-capable laptop available today. For what I do, being able to reliably and quickly read and write data is far more important than blazing CPU speed.

Every computer system includes some sort of storage devices such as hard disks, SSD (Solid-State Drive) disks, DVD and CD drives, CompactFlash cards, and so on, which store the operating system and your applications, and also provide some space that you can use to store the files and directories that you create. One of my favorite bits of technical writing ever is the following quote from a Hewlett-Packard manual shipped with one of their UNIX (HP-UX) workstations in the mid-1980s:

> "On a clear disk, you can seek forever."

In geek-speak, this means that without imposing some organization on the devices used to store your data, your operating system would have no idea where to look for specific files, directories, or anything else. To store data on a disk and access that data afterward, a disk has to be prepared in a way that your operating system and associated applications can read, write, and interact with. This preparation usually consists of two steps:

1. Dividing the disk into one or more sections that can be uniquely located by the operating system. Each section of a disk is known as a *partition*.

2. Formatting the partitions, referred to as *creating a filesystem*, in such a way that your operating system can access each partition and create files and directories there

Disk drives are partitioned for several reasons:

- To reduce the amount of time required to locate a specific piece of data on the drive. It simply takes less time (and less location information) to find a specific piece of data in a smaller pool of information.

- To limit the amount of data that can be lost or damaged if a disk or partition becomes corrupted

- To speed up administrative operations such as defragmentation, consistency checking, and repair (when necessary)

- To simplify administrative operations, such as backups. It's simpler to back up partitions that will fit on a single tape or other backup media because no operator intervention is required (such as switching tapes). Multiple partitions also enable you to install system files and applications on different partitions from where you store your user data. You can then back up the partition containing user data relatively frequently, without accidentally backing up a vast amount of relatively unchanging executables, system files, and so on.

As mentioned in the previous section, the term *filesystem* is often used colloquially to refer to the entire hierarchy of files and directories that make up a Linux system. In this section, I'm using *filesystem* in its more specific sense, which refers to the way in which a disk partition is formatted so that you can store data there and even retrieve it.

Once you format a partition and create a filesystem on it, you need to be able to make that disk partition available to your system. This is known as *mounting* that filesystem, which simply attaches that filesystem to some part of the Linux directory structure so that you can use the storage it provides. Linux systems mount filesystems on a directory so that they become a part of the standard Linux filesystem namespace, which I discuss in more detail in the section on "Mounting Filesystems," later in this chapter. Any Linux directory can act as a mountpoint for a filesystem, and many of the standard directories discussed in the previous section are actually mountpoints for separate filesystems that hold the contents of those directories. The standard Linux /mnt directory generally contains special-purpose subdirectories that are used as mountpoints for filesystems that you are planning to use temporarily.

Note

The discussion of disks in this chapter focuses on larger storage devices, such as hard drives and SSD disks. See the section of Chapter 18, "Consumer Electronics and Ubuntu," entitled "Working with CompactFlash and SD Cards" for detailed information about using these types of small, removable storage devices. ■

Introducing Logical Volumes

Today's disk drives are larger and faster than ever before, and both of these trends are likely to continue. However, one insurmountable problem with physical storage is that any filesystem that you create on a physical disk partition can grow no larger than the size of that partition. Although needing a partition greater than 100 GB or so might be difficult to conceive of for the casual home user, placing constraints on volume size can be a serious problem for computers used in the enterprise, academic, and research communities. Identifying the largest partition that you can create at the moment is as easy as reading the label on your hard drive. Unfortunately, identifying the size of the largest partition you'll ever need is a philosophical problem that has no answer. Although utilities are available for most modern filesystems that enable you to increase or decrease the size of a filesystem, you are still constrained by the size of the physical device upon which those filesystems are located.

Logical volumes are a solution to the finite size of physical storage devices and disk partitions. A *logical volume* is created out of a pool of storage space, known as a *volume group*, that comprises partitions (known as *physical volumes*) from one or more hard drives, or entire hard drives themselves. You create a filesystem on a logical volume in exactly the same way that you create a filesystem on a physical partition. Figure 4-1 shows the relationships between physical storage and logical volumes.

FIGURE 4-1

Physical disk space and logical volumes

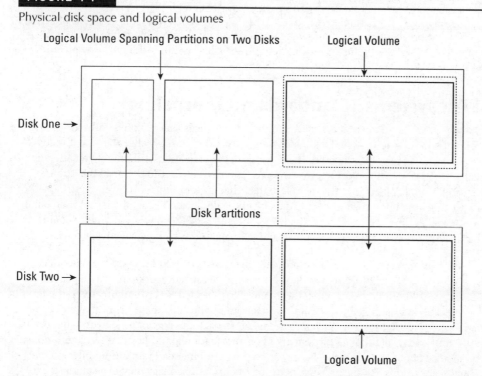

The key benefit of logical volumes appears when you run out of space on a filesystem that is contained in a logical volume. Because a logical volume is a logical entity rather than a physical one, you can easily increase its size by allocating additional storage to it from the volume group. You can then use the administrative utilities for your filesystem to increase the size of that filesystem so that it uses all of the newly added space in the logical volume. If no free space is available in the volume group, you can easily add new partitions or disks (physical volumes) to that volume's group, and then allocate some or all of that additional storage from the volume group to your logical volume. Rinse, lather, repeat.

Good examples of when you might need to increase filesystem size are simulation and image analysis projects or my research into backing up my entire CD collection onto my computer system. Without logical volumes, you could still add new disk storage to your system by formatting new disks and partitions and mounting them at various locations in your existing filesystem, but your system would quickly become an unmanageable administrative nightmare of mountpoints attaching storage all over the place. With logical volumes, you simply add new disks to your system, add them to the appropriate volume group, and increase the size of the logical volume and the filesystem that it contains, solving the problem quickly and easily.

The standard Ubuntu Desktop installation CD does not support creating logical volumes during installation. Creating physical volumes, volume groups, and logical volumes on your disk(s) during installation is supported only if you are installing Desktop Ubuntu from their alternate Desktop installation CDs or if you are installing the Ubuntu Server.

For more information about creating and using physical volumes, volume groups, and logical volumes after you have initially installed your system, see Chapter 20, "Adding Hardware and Attaching Peripherals."

Local Filesystems: Standard and Journaling

Local filesystems are filesystems that are located on storage devices that are physically connected to your computer. Access to data on local filesystems is therefore fast because they are directly connected to your machine. On the other hand, local filesystems are useful only if you and any other users who need access to the data that they contain can connect to the machine upon which they are located. When you need access to data that is stored in a local filesystem, connecting to the machine upon which specific data is physically located generally isn't a problem in today's networked environments — you can always open an SSH (Secure Shell) or telnet connection to that machine, as long as that specific machine is up and working correctly, of course.

The most common type of filesystem used on Linux systems is the ext2 filesystem (Extended Filesystem, Version 2). I'll call this a "standard filesystem" because it works the way most vanilla filesystems work. When you update a file, the changes to that file are written directly to the target filesystem. If your system goes down at that exact point, your changes may or may not have been made to the target filesystem. As your system comes back up, part of its startup sequence is to check the consistency of all of its filesystems. (For information about how your system knows what filesystems it should use and check, see the section "Automatically Mounting Filesystems at Boot Time," later in this chapter.) The utility used to check the consistency of a standard ext2 filesystem is known as `fsck` ("file system consistency check"). The `fsck` utility traverses all of the data structures within a filesystem to make sure that all of the data in the filesystem is correctly associated with files and directories.

Running the `fsck` utility (known as *fscking* a filesystem) can take quite a bit of time on large partitions, which means that it takes longer for your system to become available to users. To help minimize system restart time by eliminating the need to run `fsck` (or by reducing the type of work that `fsck` has to do), a newer type of filesystem known as a *journaling filesystem* has been developed. In *journaling filesystems*, changes made to any file in the filesystem are initially written to a special part of the filesystem known as the *journal* (sometimes referred to as the *log*) in the form of a transaction. The changes recorded in the journal are then applied to the filesystem asynchronously and transactionally. The record of these changes stays in the filesystem log until they have completed successfully, at which point the records associated with that transaction are removed.

Journaling filesystems improve system restart time because a filesystem can always be made consistent by playing any pending transactions against the filesystem. Therefore, running the `fsck` utility generally consists, at most, of executing any pending changes that are recorded in the filesystem log. Journaling filesystems can also improve overall filesystem performance because the filesystem doesn't have to wait until a file update completes successfully, as standard (i.e., non-journaled) filesystems do. Once changes are written to the log, normal filesystem operations can continue and the filesystem can be updated asynchronously. Because the log is usually stored in a special, high-performance portion of the filesystem that uses a special format, log updates can be substantially faster than updates to the actual filesystem. Obviously, changes to any file must be completed before that file can be modified again, so it is necessary to check whether there are pending updates to a file before modifying it.

The most common journaling Linux filesystem in use today is the ext3 filesystem, which is basically the ext2 filesystem with journaling capabilities. This type of filesystem is quite popular because ext2 filesystems can be converted into ext3 filesystems with a simple change, and all filesystem repair, debugging, and analysis software written for the ext2 filesystem automatically works with the ext3 filesystem. Other popular types of journaling filesystems are ReiserFS and Reiser4 (both written by Hans Reiser and friends from namesys.com), the JFS filesystem (originally written by IBM for OS/2 and AIX, and released by IBM as an open source project; `http://jfs.sourceforge.net/`), and XFS (originally written by SGI for IRIX and released by SGI as an open source project; `http://oss.sgi.com/projects/xfs/`).

For a bit of humor, here is the man page for the `fsck` utility for the XFS journaling filesystem:

```
fsck.xfs(8)                                             fsck.xfs(8)
NAME
        fsck.xfs - do nothing, successfully

SYNOPSIS
        fsck.xfs [ ...]

DESCRIPTION
        fsck.xfs is called by the generic Linux fsck(8) program at
        startup to check and repair an XFS filesystem.  XFS is a
        journaling  filesystem  and  performs recovery at mount(8)
        time if necessary, so fsck.xfs simply exits  with  a  zero
        exit status.

FILES
```

```
                    /etc/fstab

SEE ALSO
          fsck(8), fstab(5), xfs(5).
```

Well, that certainly cuts down on `fsck` and restart time!

Ubuntu 9.10 introduced the ext4 filesystem, which, surprisingly, is a new and improved filesystem that incorporates the improvements to ext2 made by ext3, and which also adds many new features — such as larger over-all filesystem size up to 1 EB (1 exabyte = 1 billion gigabytes) per filesystem and up to 16 TB per file within an ext4 filesystem], support for extents (simultaneous allocation of large numbers of filesystem blocks), faster fsck times — and supports defragmentation. The ext4 filesystem is the default filesystem used for Ubuntu 9.10 and later installations.

Network Filesystems

Network filesystems are filesystems that are stored on remote systems (usually known as *file servers*) and can be mounted on your local machine just like a local filesystem. Networked filesystems provide users with the freedom to access their information from any system on which they can log in and that has access to those networked resources.

Network filesystems offer several advantages over local filesystems:

- They reduce the chance that the failure of a single machine will prevent you from accessing your data. Most networked filesystems enable you to log in on multiple machines and access your data in exactly the same way.

- They provide central locations for data that must or should be shared among all users.

- They simplify accessing existing data from faster systems. Suppose that you have written an application to test CPU and memory performance, or that your work or research depends on CPU- and memory-intensive calculations. Running your application on a faster, more powerful machine is as simple as logging in on that machine and running the application from the networked filesystem.

- They provide the opportunity to centralize administrative operations such as backups.

- They promote interoperability and flexibility. You can usually access networked filesystems from systems running Linux, Microsoft Windows, Mac OS X, and so on. This makes it easy for you to use the software and hardware that are best suited to your desktop requirements and still access the same data on the networked filesystem.

A number of networked filesystems are available for Linux. The most popular of these is NFS, the Network File System originally written by Sun Microsystems and subsequently supported on almost every other UNIX-like system since the dawn of the workstation. NFS is actively supported by Apple's Mac OS X, and NFS clients (and servers) are even available for Microsoft Windows systems. The other most commonly used network filesystem is, ironically, Microsoft's SMB (Server Message Block) filesystem, which has been renamed CIFS (Common Internet File

System) to make it sound more platform-independent and modern. SMB/CIFS is supported on Linux systems by a suite of client and server software known as *Samba* (www.samba.org). Samba clients enable Linux systems to mount and access SMB/CIFS filesystems exported by Microsoft Windows systems. Samba servers enable Linux systems to export their filesystems so that they can be mounted and accessed from machines running different versions of Microsoft Windows. Linux systems also support connectivity to Novell Netware filesystems through the Linux NCP (Novell Core Protocol) utilities (www.novell.com/coolsolutions/feature/15350.html) and pre-OS X MacOS Apple filesystems via the Linux netatalk and afpfs utilities (http://netatalk.sourceforge.net/ or, historically, www.anders.com/projects/netatalk/).

Working with Partitions and Filesystems

Like Ubuntu, most Linux systems automatically identify the disks in your system and propose a reasonable partitioning scheme as part of the installation process. Similarly, when you attach a new disk to your system or add one internally, Ubuntu displays a dialog box asking if you want to configure that disk. Partitioning during the installation process is explained in Chapter 2, "Installing Ubuntu"; using graphical partitioning utilities after your system is already running is explained in detail in Chapter 20, "Adding Hardware and Attaching Peripherals."

Even after you partition and mount a disk, or you attach an existing disk that has already been partitioned and formatted, your system can't access it until you mount it somewhere. This section discusses how to temporarily mount a disk using the Linux mount command, the most popular options that are available for that command, and how to mount a specific disk as part of your system's startup process by adding it to your system's filesystem configuration file, /etc/fstab.

Mounting Filesystems

Once you've attached a disk, you can always query the filesystems that it contains by using the Linux fdisk utility's l (list) option, as in the following example:

```
$ sudo fdisk -l

Disk /dev/sda: 250.0 GB, 250059350016 bytes
255 heads, 63 sectors/track, 30401 cylinders
Units = cylinders of 16065 * 512 = 8225280 bytes

   Device Boot      Start         End      Blocks   Id  System
/dev/sda1               1        1306    10490413+  83  Linux
/dev/sda2            1307        2090     6297480   82  Linux swap
/dev/sda3   *        2091        2122      257040   83  Linux
/dev/sda4            2123       30399   227135002+   f  W95 Ext'd (LB
/dev/sda5            2123        2645     4200966   83  Linux
/dev/sda6            2646        6562    31463271   83  Linux
/dev/sda7            6563       10478    31455238+  83  Linux
/dev/sda8           10479       30399   160015401   83  Linux

Disk /dev/hde: 250.0 GB, 250059350016 bytes
```

```
255 heads, 63 sectors/track, 30401 cylinders
Units = cylinders of 16065 * 512 = 8225280 bytes

   Device Boot      Start         End      Blocks   Id  System
/dev/hde1                1       30401   244196001   83  Linux

Disk /dev/hdf: 250.0 GB, 250059350016 bytes
255 heads, 63 sectors/track, 30401 cylinders
Units = cylinders of 16065 * 512 = 8225280 bytes

   Device Boot      Start         End      Blocks   Id  System
/dev/hdf1                1       30401   244196001   83  Linux
```

By default, the fdisk command lists all partitions on all disks that it can detect in your system. You can also use the fdisk command to list the partitions on a specific device, as in the following example:

```
$ sudo fdisk -l /dev/sda

Disk /dev/sda: 250.0 GB, 250059350016 bytes
255 heads, 63 sectors/track, 30401 cylinders
Units = cylinders of 16065 * 512 = 8225280 bytes

   Device Boot      Start         End      Blocks   Id  System
/dev/sda1                1        1306    10490413+  83  Linux
/dev/sda2             1307        2090     6297480   82  Linux swap
/dev/sda3    *        2091        2122      257040   83  Linux
/dev/sda4             2123       30399   227135002+   f  W95 Ext'd (LB
/dev/sda5             2123        2645     4200966   83  Linux
/dev/sda6             2646        6562    31463271   83  Linux
/dev/sda7             6563       10478    31455238+  83  Linux
/dev/sda8            10479       30399   160015401   83  Linux
```

Note that the primary argument to this command is the base name of the disk that you want to query, not the name of a specific partition. You can get similar information, although in a slightly less usable form, by examining the file /proc/partitions, which a running system uses to track all disks and partitions that are currently in use on your system. The contents of this file are the following on the same system from which the previous example was taken:

```
$ cat /proc/partitions
major minor  #blocks  name
   8     0  244198584 sda
   8     1   10490413 sda1
   8     2    6297480 sda2
   8     3     257040 sda3
   8     4          1 sda4
   8     5    4200966 sda5
   8     6   31463271 sda6
   8     7   31455238 sda7
```

```
   8     8  160015401 sda8
  33     0  244198584 hde
  33     1  244196001 hde1
  33    64  244198584 hdf
  33    65  244196001 hdf1
```

Once you've identified the partitions on your new disk (and presumably know which ones you want to use), mounting them using the mount command is easy. You will always need to explicitly mount filesystems that aren't listed in the file /etc/fstab (explained in more detail in the next section).

For example, the following command mounts the partition /dev/sda5 on the mountpoint /mnt/tmp (which must already exist):

```
$ sudo mount /dev/sda5 /mnt/tmp
```

If you're mounting a partition that contains a type of filesystem that your system can autodetect, you don't need to specify the type of filesystem that the partition/device uses. If it is something nonstandard, you will have to identify the type of filesystem using the mount command's -t option, followed by the name of that type of filesystem, as in the following example, which mounts the XFS filesystem on /dev/sda6 on the mountpoint /mnt/xfs:

```
$ sudo mount -t xfs /dev/sda6 /mnt/xfs
```

The -t option actually causes the mount command to first look for a special, filesystem-specific mount command, /sbin/mount.type, where type is the name of that type of filesystem. These filesystem-specific commands are usually installed along with the other administrative utilities for different types of filesystems using the Synaptic Package Manager, aptitude, or apt-get, as explained in Chapter 19, "Adding, Removing, and Updating Software."

Supported types of filesystems that you can specify using the -t option are adfs, affs, autofs, cifs, coda, coherent, cramfs, debugfs, devpts, efs, ext, ext2, ext3, ext4, hfs, hfsplus, hpfs, iso9660, jfs, minix, msdos, ncpfs, nfs, nfs4, ntfs, proc, qnx4, ramfs, reiserfs, romfs, smbfs, sysv, tmpfs, udf, ufs, umsdos, usbfs, vfat, xenix, xfs, and xiafs.

Some filesystems require additional options, such as NFS filesystems, SMB/CIFS filesystems, and so on. These options are highly filesystem-specific, so I won't bore you with all of them here. Instead, I'll focus on the options for a SMB/CIFS filesystem because that is probably the most common networked filesystem that you'll want to mount. Some other mount options that are commonly used in the filesystem/mount configuration file are discussed in the next section.

When mounting a networked SMB/CIFS filesystem, you will need to specify the name of the Windows user that you want to access the filesystem as, your Windows password, and also the identity of the Linux user who should appear to own the files in the filesystem, so that you write to the remote filesystem as needed. The following is an example of specifying these in a mount command:

```
//192.168.6.66/share /mnt/terastation
```

This command mounts the smbfs filesystem called `share` on the host `192.168.6.66` on the Linux directory `/mnt/terastation`, using the Windows username of `wvh` and whose password is `mypassword`. The mounted filesystem will appear to be owned by the user `wvh`, which means that I'll have the ability to write anywhere on that filesystem that isn't protected by Windows ACLs or some similar mechanism.

Automatically Mounting Filesystems at Boot Time

When your Ubuntu system boots, the boot block on your primary disk identifies the filesystem that contains the second-stage boot loader, which uses a configuration file to determine what kernels and associated boot options are available on your system. Older Linux systems used a boot loader called *LiLo* (Linux Loader), while Ubuntu and most other modern Linux systems use a boot loader called *GRUB* (Grand Unified Boot Loader).

During the boot process, the root filesystem is initially mounted read-only for standard processes so that its consistency can be verified. Once this is done, it is remounted in read-write mode, and your system verifies the existence and consistency of any other filesystems that it will be using. The list of filesystems that are available to your system is contained in the file `/etc/fstab` (File System Table).

Each line in the `/etc/fstab` file provides information about one of the filesystems that should be available to your system. To add a new filesystem so that it will always be mounted when your system boots, or to customize how your system interacts with a specific type of device, you need only add or customize an entry for that filesystem in the `/etc/fstab` file. A sample section of the `/etc/fstab` file on one of my systems looks like the following (this file will be different on your system):

```
$ cat /etc/fstab
LABEL=/       /            ext4          noatime,acl,user_xattr 1 1
/dev/sda3     /boot        ext3          acl,user_xattr         1 2
/dev/sda8     /home        ext4          noatime,acl,user_xattr 1 2
/dev/sda5     /tmp         ext4          acl,user_xattr         1 2
/dev/sda6     /usr         ext4          noatime,acl,user_xattr 1 2
/dev/sda7     /usr/local   ext4          noatime,acl,user_xattr 1 2
/dev/sda2     swap         swap          sw                     0 0
/dev/hde1     /opt2        ext4          noatime,acl,user_xattr 0 0
devpts        /dev/pts     devpts        mode=0620,gid=5        0 0
proc          /proc        proc          defaults              0 0
sysfs         /sys         sysfs         noauto                0 0
/dev/hdd      /media/cdrom0 udf,iso9660  user,noauto           0 0
/dev/fd0      /media/floppy0 auto        rw,user,noauto        0 0
```

The fields in each `/etc/fstab` entry (i.e., each line) are as follows:

- The first field is the device or remote filesystem to be mounted. This is usually the Linux device file for the partition that is to be mounted, but can also be an entry of the form `hostname:directory` for networked filesystems such as NFS. Any ext2, ext3, and ext4 filesystems can also be identified by the name that they were assigned in the file-system volume label when the filesystem was created. For example, the entry LABEL=/ in the example /etc/fstab file could be replaced with /dev/sda1 because that is the disk partition where my root filesystem actually lives. However, using labels is more flexible than using specific partition device files because the device file associated with a specific partition may change if the disk containing that partition is moved to another system or if other disks are added to an existing system.

- The second field is the directory upon which the specified filesystem should be mounted. For special types of partitions that should not be mounted, such as swap partitions, this field should contain the entry none.

- The third field identifies the type of filesystem. Common entries in this field are ext2 (the generic Linux local filesystem type), ext3 (the journaling version of ext2), ext4 (an improved, higher-performance, and high-capacity version of ext3), vfat (a 32-bit Windows FAT partition), iso9660 (the standard CD-ROM filesystem), nfs (networked filesystems using Sun's NFS protocol), and swap (swap space). If a filesystem is not currently used but you want to keep an entry for it in /etc/fstab, you can put the word ignore in this field, and that filesystem will not be mounted, checked for consistency, and so on.

The types of filesystems that are compiled into your kernel are listed in the file /proc/filesystems, but this can be misleading. Your kernel usually also supports other types of filesystems, but as loadable kernel modules rather than being hardwired into the kernel. For example, the /proc/filesystems file on my main system contains the following entries:

```
nodev   sysfs
nodev   rootfs
nodev   bdev
nodev   proc
nodev   cgroup
nodev   cpuset
nodev   debugfs
nodev   securityfs
nodev   sockfs
nodev   usbfs
nodev   pipefs
nodev   anon_inodefs
nodev   tmpfs
nodev   inotifyfs
nodev   devpts
        ext3
        ext2
        ext4
nodev   ramfs
nodev   hugetlbfs
nodev   ecryptfs
nodev   fuse
```

119

```
        fuseblk
nodev   fusectl
nodev   mqueue
nodev   rpc_pipefs
nodev   nfs
nodev   nfs4
nodev   nfsd
nodev   cifs
nodev   binfmt_misc
```

- Filesystems whose types are prefaced by a `nodev` entry are not associated with physical devices, but are used internally by applications and the operating system.

- The fourth field contains a comma-separated list of any options to the `mount` command that should be used when the filesystem is mounted. Many mount options are filesystem-specific, but some common ones are the following:

  - `async`: Writes to the filesystem should be done asynchronously.

  - `auto`: The filesystem should be automatically mounted when detected or when a command such as `mount -a` is executed.

  - `defaults`: The default options `-async`, `auto`, `dev`, `exec`, `nouser`, `rw`, and `suid` are used.

  - `dev`: The character or block device containing the filesystem is local to the system.

  - `exec`: You can execute programs, scripts, or anything else whose permissions indicate that it is executable — from that filesystem.

  - `gid=value`: Set the group ID of the mounted filesystem to the specified numeric group ID when the filesystem is mounted.

  - `noatime`: Do not update file timestamps in the inode for a file when the file is simply being accessed. Not updating this timestamp can provide significant performance improvements.

  - `noauto`: Don't automatically mount when a filesystem is detected or when the command `mount -a` is issued. Usually used with removable media such as floppies and CD-ROMs.

  - `nouser`: You must be `root` to mount the filesystem — the filesystem can't be mounted by any non-`root` user.

  - `owner`: The ownership of the filesystem is set to the user who mounted it — usually `root` if the filesystem is automatically mounted by the system.

  - `ro`: Mount the filesystem read-only.

  - `rw`: Mount the filesystem read-write.

  - `suid`: Allow programs on the filesystem to change the user's user or group ID when they are executed if their permission bits indicate that they should do this. Be very careful when using this option with imported filesystems that you don't actually administer because running a program that sets the UID to `root` is a common way of hacking into a system.

- `uid=value`: Set the user ID of the mounted filesystem to the specified numeric user ID when the filesystem is mounted.

For more information on generic options available to the `mount` command, see the man page for the `mount` command in Section 8 of the online Linux manual (by using the `man 8 mount` command).

- The fifth field is used by the `dump` command, a standard Linux/UNIX filesystem backup command, to identify filesystems that should be backed up when the `dump` command is executed. If the fifth field contains a 0 (or is missing), the `dump` command assumes that the filesystem associated with that `/etc/fstab` entry does not need to be backed up.

- The sixth field is used by the Linux/UNIX filesystem consistency checker discussed earlier in this chapter in the section entitled "Local Filesystems: Standard and Journaling.") to identify filesystems whose consistency should be verified when the system is rebooted, and the order in which the consistency of those filesystems should be checked. If the sixth field contains a 0 (or is missing), the `fsck` program assumes that the filesystem associated with that `/etc/fstab` entry does not need to be checked.

The contents of this file may seem complex at first, but over time you'll get used to creating and editing them. Many of the graphical utilities provided for manipulating disk partitions automatically create these entries for you — or you can always do what I do, which is to copy an existing, but similar, entry and then modify it as needed for the partition(s) I'm adding.

Automatically Mounting Removable Media Filesystems

Beyond the entries in your `/etc/fstab` file, Ubuntu also provides special support to simplify interacting with removable media on your system. Although discussed in more detail elsewhere in this book, it is worth mentioning this here to complete this section's overview of storage device handling on Ubuntu systems.

Ubuntu's automatic recognition of removable media is done via the `gnome-volume-manager` application, which is configured using the `gnome-volume-properties` application. You can start this configuration application by selecting "Removable Drives and Media" from the System menu's Preferences submenu.

Once configured, the `gnome-volume-manager` makes it easy for your system to automatically recognize CDs, DVDs, CompactFlash cards, and other common removable media, and automatically mount them for you in appropriate mountpoints under your system's `/media` directory. Using and customizing the `gnome-volume-manager`'s recognition and handling of these types of media is discussed in detail in Chapter 19.

The `gnome-volume-manager`'s support for devices that are often attached to your system while it is running extends beyond just storage devices — it includes peripherals such as printers, mice, keyboards, tablets, and so on. It also makes it easy for your system to automatically recognize consumer electronics devices such as digital cameras and personal digital assistants (PDAs) so that you can easily transfer files back and forth to the storage media that these devices use. This aspect of the gnome-volume-manager is discussed in detail in Chapter 18.

Understanding Linux Permissions

If you're sharing your Ubuntu system with other users, it's useful to understand how Linux systems protect files and directories so that they can be accessed by only the people that you want to have access to them. Similarly, if you have installed your own Ubuntu system and are therefore responsible for taking care of it ("system administration" in geek-speak), you need to know how Ubuntu systems ensure that only specific, authorized users can perform privileged tasks. For example, it would be potentially inconvenient if random users could format disk drives, reconfigure your system's connection to networks such as the Internet, and so on. Although you'd hope that no one would do these sorts of things maliciously, it's easy enough to accidentally click OK when you are exploring system configuration applications, thinking perhaps that this would simply exit from the application.

Linux supports the traditional permission model used by all UNIX-like systems, users, and groups, with a few interesting twists that have been introduced to foster Ubuntu's goals of usability and user-friendliness. If you've used other Linux systems in the past, it's easy enough to adapt to doing things the Ubuntu way, and if you're new to Linux, you'll find the Ubuntu model for privileged commands to be quite easy to understand, configure, and use.

Note

Ubuntu provides an easy-to-use graphical application for creating and managing the users on your Ubuntu systems. This section focuses on the underlying concepts of Ubuntu permissions — using Ubuntu's graphical application for creating and managing Ubuntu users and groups is discussed in detail in Chapter 27, "Managing Users, Groups, and Authentication." ■

Basic Concepts: Users and Groups

All Linux systems provide two basic administrative entities that are used to determine who has access to what files and who can perform specific, privileged operations. Each person who can log in on a Linux system does so via a *user* account, which consists of a name and password, and which has a specific home directory that contains that user's configuration data as well as any files that they create. The file /etc/passwd (known as the *password file*, but why type a few extra letters if you don't have to?) contains a list of every user who has an account on that specific machine.

All Linux users belong to one or more groups. A *group* is an administrative entity that makes it easier for multiple users to access the same sets of files. Information about the groups that are defined on your Ubuntu system and the users who belong to those groups is stored in the file /etc/group, which is a text file with easy-to-understand entries. As explained later in this section, file and directory permissions can be set such that users who are members of a specified group can read and/or write files in shared directories, which other users on the system still cannot access. This makes it easy to set up collaborative projects or to simply share information with selected other users on your systems.

Note

Most Linux systems use the local /etc/passwd and /etc/group files for authentication and group membership information, but systems that use networked authentication mechanisms can get these types of information from other systems on your network. For example, systems that use NIS, the Network Information Service that is used in many NFS-based Linux environments, can contain entries in the password and group files that tell your system to check NIS for user, group, and authentication information. Linux also supports PAMs (Pluggable Authentication Modules), which enable the system to contact networked sources of these types of information such as LDAP (Lightweight Directory Access Protocol) servers, Kerberos servers, and even Microsoft Windows authentication servers. PAMs aren't discussed here because they are very special, advanced cases, and this section is only intended as an introduction to Ubuntu and basic Linux security. ■

My entry in the /etc/passwd file on one of my Ubuntu systems is as follows:

```
wvh:x:1000:1000:William von Hagen,,,:/home/wvh:/bin/bash
```

The fields in this entry are as follows:

- My login name
- The password field. In this case, an x means that password information is actually stored in the file /etc/shadow.
- My user ID, which is the numerical value associated with my login name
- The numeric group ID of the default group of which I am a member
- A field containing my full name and other text information such as office location and office and home phone numbers
- My home directory
- The application that runs when I log in, in this case a shell

A few sample entries from the /etc/group file on that same system are as follows:

```
adm:x:4:wvh,juser
cdrom:x:24:hal,wvh,juser
lpadmin:x:106:wvh,juser
admin:x:112:wvh,juser
wvh:x:1000:
```

Each entry in the /etc/group file begins with the name of the group, a password field (in these examples indicating that any group passwords are stored in the file /etc/shadow), the numeric identifier associated with that group, and the list of users who belong to that group.

As you can see from these examples, it is common for users to belong to multiple groups, each of which provides access to a specific resource such as files, directories, or administrative capabilities. You can list the groups that you belong to by executing the `groups` command at any Linux command-line prompt.

When you create user accounts on an Ubuntu system (including during the installation process), a default group is created for each of those users. This group is the group of which that user is a default member when he or she logs in on your system. Most applications that use group membership to indicate administrative privileges will automatically check the `/etc/group` file when they first execute. To access shared directories, you may have to change the group that you are actively a member of. You can do this using the `newgrp` command at any Linux command-line prompt.

Ubuntu systems reserve group numbers less than 1000 for administrative purposes. The different applications that use these groups, generally referred to as *system groups*, automatically check group memberships when they execute. There's no need to memorize the default groups used by different system applications on Ubuntu because the administrative applications that require them typically add you to the right group. See the section "Performing Privileged Operations in Ubuntu" later in this chapter, for details.

File and Directory Permissions under Linux

This section provides an introduction to how file and directory permissions are displayed and used on Linux systems. Although discussed in more detail in Chapter 11, it makes sense to introduce this topic here to illustrate how user and group identities can provide shared access to files, directories, and other resources, and how to manipulate those settings.

The easiest command to use to view the permissions on a file or directory is the Linux `ls` (list) command, which displays information about the files and directories in a specified location.

For example, the command `ls -ld /home/wvh` provides a long listing of my home directory, which includes information about the current permissions on that directory:

```
drwxr-xr-x  145 wvh wvh 7728 2009-03-05 10:54 /home/wvh
```

I'll focus on the first field, which shows the current permissions on my directory — see Chapter 11 for detailed information about all of these fields, options to the `ls` command, and the `ls` command itself.

The permissions field of `ls` output can be broken down into four sections:

- The first character, which identifies the type of object you're looking at. The most common of these is a - (a dash) if the thing you're listing is a regular file, a d if it's a directory, a c if it's a device node that can be accessed as a stream of characters, or a b if it's a device node that can be accessed as a block device.
- Three sets of three characters, which represent the permissions that the owner, the group owner, and all others have on the file or directory

The most common values for each position in the three permissions sections are r, which means that the file or directory can be read; w, which means that the file or directory can be written to; and x, which (for a file) means that the file can be executed or (for a directory) means that the directory can be searched for other files or directories. If any of these permissions is not set, its position is represented by a dash. In addition, the user and group execution bits can be set to s, which means "set user or group ID upon execution." In other words, executing that file is done as though it were being done by the owner and/or group of the specified file. This is commonly done to execute a command as though it were being executed by another, more privileged user on your system.

Performing Privileged Operations in Ubuntu

Aside from your own username and numeric ID, the most important username on a Linux system is the user named root, whose user ID and group ID are both 0 and who is often known as the *superuser*.

On most Linux systems, privileged operations are often done by using the su (substitute user ID) command to become the root user. However, Ubuntu does things slightly differently. Ubuntu uses the sudo (substitute user ID do) command to perform all privileged operations. The sudo command uses the text-format configuration file /etc/sudoers to determine which users can perform privileged operations as the superuser. On Ubuntu systems, any member of the admin group can perform privileged operations as the root user. You can use the sudo command on any Linux system, but you cannot use the su command on an Ubuntu system.

The difference between using the su and sudo commands is subtle but significant:

- When using the su command to perform a privileged operation, you execute the su command and supply the root user's password in response to the password prompt, which then starts a subshell with root privileges. You then execute whatever privileged commands you want within the context of that shell. They are all therefore executed as the superuser. When you are done, you can either exit from that shell or suspend it for subsequent reuse.

- When using the sudo command, you execute the sudo command, followed by the name and arguments to the command that you want to execute.

Note

The su and sudo commands are not restricted to executing commands as the root user. You can become any user using the sudo command by specifying that user's name after the su command and providing that user's password in response to the password prompt. Similarly, you can use the sudo command's -u option to specify the name of the user that you want to execute a command as. As always, the su command requires that you know a specific user's password, while the sudo command requires only that you provide *your* password. ∎

Let's look at a few examples to compare using these commands. The following is an example of using the su command to display the partitions available on a disk:

```
$ su
Password: <enter-root-password>
```

```
#  fdisk -l /dev/sda
[output]
#  exit
$
```

To do the same thing using the `sudo` command, you would do the following:

```
$ sudo fdisk -l /dev/sda
Password: <enter-your-password>
[output]
$
```

On Linux systems other than Ubuntu, you could also use the `su` command's `-c` option (execute a single command) to do something similar, as in the following example:

```
$ su -c fdisk -l /dev/sda
Password: <enter-root-password>
[output]
$
```

The key difference between the `su` and `sudo` commands is whether the command prompts you for the `root` password or your personal password. However, Ubuntu's focus on using the `sudo` command has a few basic advantages:

- The system is harder to attack because an attacker first has to discover the identity of a privileged user on the system before they can attempt to break in.

- Users have to remember only their personal passwords to perform privileged operations if they are permitted to do so. There is no need to set and secure the system's `root` password separately.

Tip

If you want to execute several privileged commands in a row on an Ubuntu system, you have two alternatives. First, you can execute the `sudo -s` command to execute a shell as the `root` user. Second, you can do the same thing by running the `sudo /bin/bash` command. In both of these cases, you have to remember to explicitly exit from the root shell once you're done running the commands that you want to execute. ∎

Summary

This chapter covered some of the basic concepts of Linux and Ubuntu. The chapter began by introducing files and directories and explaining the directories that are commonly used on Ubuntu systems. It then discussed how Ubuntu uses disks and partitions them into separate filesystems. I covered the different types of filesystems that you can use on partitions or on Ubuntu systems in general, and how to make those filesystems available for use on your system. The last few sections introduced basic Linux administrative concepts such as managing users, working with groups and file permissions, and executing privileged commands on the Ubuntu system.

This chapter provided the basic knowledge that you'll need to understand these concepts when you encounter them elsewhere in this book.

The next chapter introduces the graphical user interface, GNOME, that is installed by default with the Ubuntu desktop system. It discusses how to use the different mouse buttons to interact with GNOME and graphical applications, how to use the GNOME menus to start applications, and how to interact with panel applications (the GNOME equivalent of desk accessories), and helps you start to actually use your newly installed Ubuntu Linux system.

Using the GNOME Desktop

IN THIS CHAPTER

Using the mouse

Learning GNOME basics

Using the desktop

Personalizing the desktop

Using the Nautilus File Manager

Desktop searching on Ubuntu

Using a window manager

Although many curmudgeons and long-time UNIX users reject any sort of graphical interface, let's face it — most people today want (and expect) one. The graphical environment used on Ubuntu systems, the GNOME desktop, provides a stable and usable environment for running your graphical applications and interacting with your system graphically. Most of the Linux utilities used for system administration and configuration provide graphical interfaces to simplify formerly complex tasks and are easily accessed from one of the primary menus provided by the GNOME desktop.

This chapter begins by providing some background information on the graphical environment used on all Linux systems, such as explaining exactly what the word *desktop* means, and what graphical alternatives exist on Linux systems. This information provides a good foundation for understanding how graphical interfaces work on Linux systems, regardless of the specific graphical environment that you choose to use. The majority of the chapter focuses on the organization and use of the GNOME desktop provided on standard Ubuntu Desktop systems. GNOME is a powerful graphical interface with all of the features that you'd expect in a modern graphical user interface (GUI) — once you know where to find them. The final section explains how you can further customize GNOME by replacing the software that it uses internally to manage window placement, movement, and so on.

What's a Desktop? Graphical Environments for Linux

Almost all of the high-resolution support for interacting with any Linux system is handled by a graphics package called the *X Window System*, known to its friends as *X11.*, or simply *X*. The X Window System is one of the most attractive aspects of Linux and almost any operating system running on modern bitmapped graphics workstations. *X* is a network-aware graphics windowing system that provides a similar set of capabilities for creating and working with applications as do the graphical environments used on Microsoft Windows and Mac OS X systems. The X Window System was designed to provide a common windowing environment on multi-processing, networked computer systems and is the industry standard windowing system for computers running different versions of Linux, any other UNIX-like operating system, and even computers that are still running Compaq's VMS operating system. Versions of the X Window System are also available for all releases of Windows greater than 3.1, and for any version of Mac OS X—these run X Window System applications in the context of the native windowing systems for those platforms.

The X Window System was originally developed at the Massachusetts Institute of Technology (MIT), was under the custodianship of the Open Group (`www.opengroup.org`) for a while, and is now stewarded by the X.org Foundation (`www.x.org`). A previous implementation of the X Window System for Linux systems, known as *XFree86*, is no longer used on Linux systems—the official source of the X implementation for Linux systems is now `x.org`.

The X Window System enables you to run multiple applications on a bitmapped display screen, each of which displays its own window(s), graphics, dialog boxes, and so on in one or more separately controllable windows on the screen. An X Window System window manager is an application that also runs on a bitmapped display screen, but its job is to manage the individual windows that are created and used by other applications. The window manager is the application that enables you to move windows around on the screen and raise and lower windows. The window manager displays the window borders that enable you to move applications; displays the menus that pop up when you click on a part of the screen that is not occupied by a window; displays the window controls that enable you to minimize, maximize, and close separate windows; and so on. Popular window managers include After Step, Black Box, Compiz, Fluxbox, FVWM, ICEwm, KWin, Metacity, twm, vtwm, and Window Maker. All of these provide the same basic functionality, although they differ in terms of how and where they manage minimized applications, how the window manager is configured, how applications are bound to menus and/or graphical areas on your screen, how they support alternate fonts and display styles, and so on.

Tip

One great feature of the X Window System is that, because it was designed to work across multiple hardware platforms, you can start X Window System client applications on one system but have them display on the bitmapped screen of another system (assuming that this capability is not blocked by a firewall or system configuration setting). This is done by setting an environment variable called DISPLAY and then starting the application that you want to display remotely. The DISPLAY environment variable has the following form:

```
host:display.screen
```

Here, *host* specifies the name or IP address of the system that you want to display the window on, and is followed by a colon. After the colon, the first number identifies the graphics *display* upon which the window should be displayed, followed by a period, and the number followed by a colon, followed by the number of the physical screen attached to that card. In most cases, both *display* and *screen* are 0.

See the section of Chapter 11, "Using Command-Line Tools," entitled "Using Environment Variables" for more information about setting environment variables. In many cases, you can also start an X Window System application on a remote screen by starting the application from the command line and specifying the `-display host:display.screen` argument. ∎

After window managers, the next step in the evolution of the X Window System desktop experience is the desktop manager. Desktop managers, colloquially referred to simply as *desktops*, always run a window manager under the covers, but also provide additional capabilities such as the following:

- Drag-and-drop
- A file manager of some sort to simplify graphically browsing files and directories
- Easy, flexible ways to tie applications to buttons, icons, and menu items
- A centralized mechanism for configuring the appearance of your screen and the windows that it displays, generally referred to as applying a *theme*
- Support for running lightweight applications (known as *applets*) within the context of the window manager to support certain types of tasks

The most common desktops for Linux systems are GNOME (GNU Network Object Model Environment; www.gnome.org), KDE (K Development Environment; www.kde.org), ROX (http://roscidus.com/desktop/), and Xfce (www.xfce.org). Both GNOME and KDE are rich, robust desktop environments that provide their own window managers (on Ubuntu systems, GNOME uses Compiz, while KDE uses KWin) and primarily differ in terms of default mouse and key bindings, menu organization, and the underlying graphical toolkit. (GNOME uses a widget toolkit known as GTK, while KDE uses one called QT.) Both ROX and Xfce are lightweight desktops, which means that they attempt to strike a balance between the heavy resource requirements and corresponding power of rich desktop environments such as GNOME and KDE, and the much lighter requirements but more limited capabilities of traditional window managers. You can find a great introduction to most of the X Window System window managers and desktop environments available for Linux at http://xwinman.org. Versions of Ubuntu prior to the 7.10 (Gutsy Gibbon) release used the Metacity window manager with GNOME, but versions 7.10 and later use the Compiz window manager. For detailed information about the Compiz window manager, see Chapter 6, "Using the Compiz Window Manager."

The rest of this chapter primarily focuses on GNOME, which is the desktop environment that is used on Ubuntu systems and which starts automatically the first time you log in to an Ubuntu system. Although you can change the window manager used by GNOME, switch to KDE, or even switch your Ubuntu experience to using a window manager rather than using its default GNOME configuration, those are all advanced tasks. First things first—let's explore how things work on a standard Ubuntu Desktop system just in case your goal is getting your work done rather than tweaking your Ubuntu system. There's plenty of time in the future to trick out your graphical environment, which I'll discuss in the section entitled "Using a Window Manager" later in this chapter.

Favorite desktop environments are like opinions—everybody has one. Even those of us who have used many different window managers and desktops over the years, and are therefore reasonably agnostic, have our own favorites.

Using the Mouse

Interacting with a graphical user interface of any kind traditionally requires the use of a mouse and keyboard to control the cursor, to select and move items, access menus, and enter data within applications. As you'll see throughout this book, the actions associated with the different mouse buttons do different things depending on the portion of the screen or application in which you use them. This is known as being *context-sensitive*, and is one of the keys to performing many different types of actions using only three little buttons.

By default, the mouse in GNOME is configured for a right-handed user, with the different mouse buttons assigned to the following actions:

- **Left button:** Single-clicking selects an icon, menu, menu item, or object within an application. Double-clicking on a desktop icon opens the item associated with that icon. Holding down the left button and dragging the cursor in an application or on the desktop selects multiple icons or objects within that application. Holding down the left button and dragging a selected object moves that object. These operations can be (and often are) combined. For example, in a word-processing program, you frequently left-click once to position the cursor, hold down the left button and drag the cursor to select a block of text, and then left-click, hold down the mouse button, and drag the selected text to a new location in your text.

- **Middle button:** Single-clicking pastes text or objects that have been cut or copied, or moves a selected window behind other windows that are currently displayed on the screen. Middle-clicking on a desktop icon and dragging it to a new location displays the Move menu, which enables you to move or copy icons to new locations without actually relocating the icon until you confirm your intentions. If you only have two buttons on your mouse or laptop, you can typically configure clicking both buttons together to function as a middle mouse click.

- **Right button:** Displays any context-sensitive menu that is available at the current cursor position

You can configure how reactive the mouse is, what your mouse cursor looks like, and what the various mouse buttons do using the Mouse Preferences application, which is explained later in this chapter in the section "Customizing Mouse Behavior." For example, if you are not right-handed and haven't been beaten into submission so that you use the mouse with your right hand, you can configure the mouse for left-handed use (which reverses the meaning of the various buttons) using this application.

Note

If you have trouble seeing the screen or using a mouse or keyboard because of a physical condition, don't worry—the GNOME and Ubuntu folks are sensitive to your needs. See the section "Assistive Technologies for Using GNOME" later in this chapter for more information. ■

GNOME Desktop Overview

Figure 5-1 shows the default GNOME desktop on an Ubuntu Linux system the first time you log in. This figure also displays a single application window as an example — you won't see that unless you explicitly select the Applications ⇨ Accessories ⇨ Terminal menu command, but I wanted to be able to explain the window controls that are available in any GNOME application window. The Ubuntu folks have gone through a lot of effort to create an attractive, eye-pleasing background, set of fonts, window decorations, and control buttons for any applications that you start on your Ubuntu system. These window decorations and controls are known as a *theme*, which you can easily customize yourself, as explained later in this chapter.

FIGURE 5-1

The default GNOME desktop in Ubuntu Linux

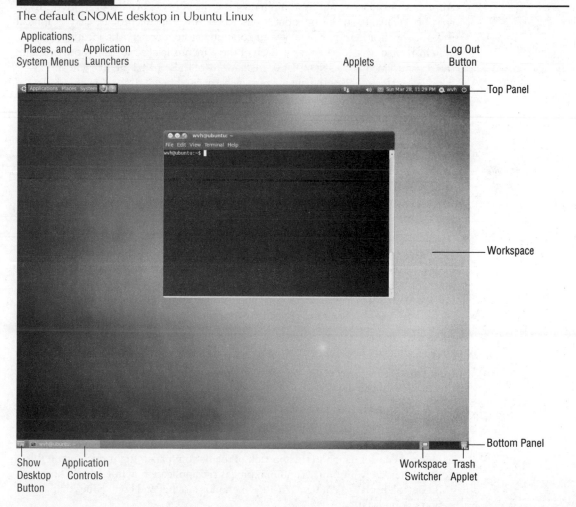

133

Note

Figure 5-1 shows the default desktop — in other full-screen screenshots, I've changed the background to a solid color to make things easier to see. Changing the default background is discussed in the section "Changing Desktop Backgrounds," later in this chapter. ■

Figure 5-1 identifies the various portions of the default GNOME desktop. The following describes them in more detail:

- **Top panel:** A *panel* is a special portion of your desktop, controlled by the `gnome-panel` application, which provides access to various ways of interacting with the desktop and launching different types of applications. GNOME can display panels along any edge of the screen, but the default GNOME configuration displays panels at the top and bottom of the screen. By default, the top panel contains the following items:

  - **Applications, Places, and System menus:** A *menu* consists of a list of shortcuts to specific commands, tasks, or applications. These three menus provide easy, graphical access to applications, portions of your computer system or network locations, and system-related tasks, respectively. Each of these menus is described in more detail in the section, "Menus in GNOME." To display any of these panel menus, you simply left-click on the name of the menu, and the associated menu drops down and displays on your screen. To close the menu, simply left-click elsewhere on the screen.

  - **Application launchers:** These icons start specific applications for you when you left-click on them.

  - **Notification area:** A portion of the panel where applications and applets display icons in response to specific events, such as receiving mail, low-power conditions, and so on. One especially important icon that can be displayed in this area is the Updates icon, which alerts you that updates to your system or the packages that you've installed are available.

  - **Applets:** These icons launch lightweight applications that provide various capabilities. Adding and configuring applets is discussed later in this chapter in the section entitled "Customizing Panels." The default applets installed with Ubuntu enable you to interact with the Empathy Instant Messaging client or the Evolution Mail client, display the current data and time and interact with a calendar, configure your instant messaging status, and control the current login session.

- **Workspace:** This is the portion of the screen in which applications execute and display associated windows and dialogs.

- **Bottom panel:** This panel is displayed at the bottom of the screen and contains the following items by default:

  - **Show Desktop button:** This button minimizes all windows and dialogs that are currently displayed on the screen, revealing the current desktop.

  - **Window list:** Each application that is active on your current workspace displays an associated control region in this portion of the bottom panel. Right-clicking on this control alternately minimizes and maximizes the application, while left-clicking on this control displays a context-sensitive menu for moving and controlling that application's window(s).

- **Workspace Switcher:** This is a special applet that enables you to manage multiple workspaces and provides a miniature display of each active workspace. Workspaces are essentially separate virtual screens that are provided by the GNOME desktop. You can run applications on different workspaces, move applications between workspaces, and so on. Multiple workspaces provide a convenient way of running different types of applications on different virtual screens without them being visible until you actually switch to the workspace where they are displayed. This is useful, for example, when you're at work and want to play a game — you can start the game on a different workspace from the one where you're actually working, and switch to it when no one is looking.

- **Trash applet:** This is a special applet that provides access to the Trash Can, which is a special portion of the GNOME desktop to which you can drag files to subsequently delete them.

As you'll see throughout the rest of this chapter, GNOME is extremely configurable — the chances are that no two users' GNOME desktops will look the same, which is completely fine. How you configure and use your computer system is up to you and should reflect your interests and the types of things that you want to do. The job of desktops like GNOME is to make it as easy and as comfortable as possible to accomplish whatever task you are trying to do.

GNOME Application Windows

The GNOME application window shown in Figure 5-1 provides several window controls that enable you to move the window around on the screen, control its size, and so on. The window manager that you are using determines the location of these controls, the number of controls displayed, and the capabilities provided by these controls. These window controls are shown in the top part of the frame around the application window (typically known as the *title bar*) in most window managers.

Left-clicking anywhere on the title bar of any window displays a menu of window control commands. The contents of this menu depend on the window manager and theme that you are using. The Window Control menu displayed by the default window manager used by GNOME on Ubuntu systems, Compiz, is shown in Figure 5-2.

The three window controls at the left of the title bar in Figure 5-2 do the following, from left to right:

- Minimize the current window. (This control is a down-arrow.)
- Switch between a full-screen or a user-specified window size. (This control is an up-arrow or square, depending on whether the window is currently a user-specified size or full-screen.)
- Close the current window, terminating any processes that it is running. (This control is an 'X', and is red.)

FIGURE 5-2

The Compiz window manager's Window Control menu

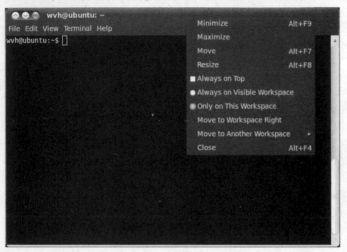

All of these window controls are fairly standard and are found in the window decoration and title bar layouts used by most modern window managers. However, they are often found in different portions of the title bar and look very different. Ubutnu 10.04 introduced a new theme called Ambiance, which replaced the traditional brown Human theme that was used by all previous versions of Ubuntu. The Human theme features the window controls that are disucssed in this section in the more traditional upper-right portion of the title bar. Regardless of how you feel about them, you can always move the controls back to the right by executing the following command from a GNOME Terminal or other command-line application:

```
gconftool-2 --set /apps/metacity/general/button_layout \
        --type string menu:minimize,maximize,close
```

You can put them back to their default position in the Ubuntu 10.04 Ambiance theme by reversing the command, as in the following example:

```
gconftool-2 --set /apps/metacity/general/button_layout \
        --type string minimize,maximize,close:
```

Menus in GNOME

As discussed earlier in this chapter, GNOME provides two different types of menus: menus located in a panel, which provide easy access to different applications, locations, and capabilities on your system; and context-sensitive menus that provide access to different capabilities depending on the context (application, desktop, etc.) in which you've activated them. This section provides a more detailed discussion of these different types of menus — how to display them and how to customize them, and the types of actions that they provide access to.

Panel Menus

Menus are displayed in the panels when you left-click on the menu name in the panel. Menus either contain entries for specific tasks or locations on your system, or contain other menus. Menus located on other menus are known as *submenus*. As an example, Figure 5-3 shows the default contents of the Application menu's Internet submenu, which I discuss later in this section.

FIGURE 5-3

Menus and submenus in GNOME

The next few sections describe the standard panel menus and their contents in more detail.

The Application Menu

The Application menu makes it easy to launch different types of GNOME applications, grouping them into submenus that display when you move the cursor over each menu entry. The Application menu provides the following groups:

- **Accessories:** Contains a general category for small, commonly used applications such as a calculator, dictionary, text editor, and command-line terminal

- **Games:** Contains exactly what you'd expect. Ubuntu is designed for people, so it naturally includes a good selection of games as part of its default installation. For more information about games on Ubuntu Linux, see Chapter 17, "Would You Like to Play a Game?"

- **Graphics:** Provides access to several applications for creating graphics and capturing and manipulating images off the screen or from a scanner, and a small, lightweight image viewer for previewing existing graphics files. See Chapter 15, "Working with Graphics," for more information about graphics software on Ubuntu Linux systems.

- **Internet:** Contains entries for accessing information sources found on the Internet, such as a Voice-Over-IP telephone system, the Evolution e-mail client (discussed in Chapter 7, "Managing E-Mail and Personal Information with Evolution"), the Firefox Web browser (discussed in Chapter 8, "Surfing the Web with Firefox"), instant messaging and IRC clients, and so on

- **Office:** Lists the standard business applications available on your system. By default, this menu includes an entry only for the Evolution e-mail client, but you can easily add entries for your favorite word processors (see Chapter 13, "Creating and Publishing Documents"), spreadsheet and presentation software (see Chapter 14, "Other Office Software: Spreadsheets and Presentations"), and any other Linux software that you use as part of your daily activities.

- **Sound & Video:** Provides easy access to audio and video applications, including applications for recording sounds, converting your (officially purchased) audio CDs to online format, and playing online audio and video, as well as sophisticated applications for creating different types of CDs, VCDs, and DVDs. See Chapter 16, "Working with Multimedia," for more information about working with different types of multimedia files and mediums on Ubuntu Linux systems.

In addition, the Applications menu provides an "Ubuntu Software Center" entry that makes it easy to add applications to the menu. As discussed in Chapter 19, the Ubuntu Software Center application is seamlessly integrated with Ubuntu's package update mechanism — if you add an application that is not already installed on your system but is available from the Ubuntu repositories, the application will be downloaded and installed as part of the menu update. Pretty cool!

The Places Menu

The Places menu provides quick access to files, directories, and storage-related activities. Selecting a location or storage device on the Places menu opens the Nautilus File Manager, displaying the contents of the selected location. The Places menu also provides convenient access to storage-related actions, such as writing to a CD or DVD, connecting to a file server, and searching for or revisiting specific files and directories. For more information about the Nautilus File Manager, see the section later in this chapter entitled "Introducing the Nautilus File Manager."

Note

The contents of the Places menu on your system will change as you add and remove external storage devices to your system, visit remote file servers, and so on. ■

Aside from shortcuts to specific locations on your system, the Places menu provides a Recent Documents submenu, which contains a list of the 10 files or desktop objects that you've most recently opened. This menu makes it easy for you to continue working on the same documents each time you log in on your Ubuntu Linux system.

The System Menu

The System menu provides access to commands for interacting with GNOME and your Ubuntu system, such as setting personal preferences for how the GNOME desktop looks and behaves, performing system administration tasks such as configuring hardware, updating your system, and configuring network services, getting help, and logging out of or shutting down your Ubuntu system.

The System menu contains the following items:

- **Preferences:** Provides access to a large number of applications that enable you to configure how you interact with GNOME, your Ubuntu system, and any networks that you have access to (such as the Internet or a home network). If you don't like the way that something works on your Ubuntu system, check the items on the Preferences menu for something that seems appropriate, start any applications that appear to be relevant, and explore a bit. The section "Customizing Your Desktop," later in this chapter, explains how to perform many of the most common GNOME and Ubuntu configuration tasks using commands from this menu.

- **Administration:** Provides access to applications that enable you to configure the software installed on your Ubuntu system, the devices attached to your Ubuntu system, the services that your system runs, and core system information such as the time, the date, the list of users who are authorized to access your system, and so on

- **Help and Support:** Provides different types of help for using your system. This menu provides access to the online documentation installed on your Ubuntu system, a shortcut to the Ubuntu documentation team's web site on the Internet, and even a shortcut to the Ubuntu Marketplace (discussed in Chapter 1, "The Ubuntu Linux Project"), where you can identify firms that may be able to help you with any tough problems or configuration issues that I may have missed in this book.

- **About GNOME:** Displays information about the specific version of GNOME that you are running, as well as general information about the many wizards who have contributed to the GNOME project in one way or another. You will probably need to provide GNOME version information if you post problem reports or questions, or if you contact any of the Ubuntu vendors in the Ubuntu Marketplace.

- **About Ubuntu:** Displays online documentation for the Ubuntu Project, which includes information about the specific version of Ubuntu Linux that you are using. As with GNOME version information, you will probably need to provide Ubuntu version information if you post problem reports or questions, or if you contact any of the Ubuntu vendors in the Ubuntu Marketplace.

Context-Sensitive Menus

The menus discussed in the previous section always display when you left-click on a specific menu heading or submenu, regardless of what else is happening on your Ubuntu Linux system. Context-sensitive menus display when you right-click on something on your Ubuntu Linux screen, but their contents depend on what you've right-clicked on. Because their contents differ based on the context in which you've right-clicked, these right-click menus are referred to as *context-sensitive menus*. Figure 5-4 shows the context-sensitive menu that you see when you right-click on any portion of the background for your Ubuntu desktop.

FIGURE 5-4

The GNOME desktop's context-sensitive menu

To show how application-specific these different context-sensitive menus can be, Figure 5-5 shows the context-sensitive menu that displays when you right-click within the main window for the Firefox Web browser.

The contents of context-sensitive menus are application-specific, which means that you can't directly customize them. However, these menus can be customized by installing additional applications or applets, or (in the case of extensible applications such as Firefox or Nautilus) by installing extensions or plug-ins that add new capabilities and therefore provide associated menu items.

FIGURE 5-5

A context-sensitive menu in the Firefox Web browser

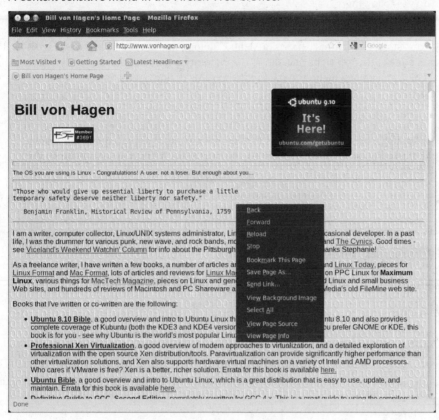

Customizing GNOME Menus

Ubuntu Linux provides you with two ways to customize the contents of the basic GNOME menus. The Ubuntu Software Center item at the bottom of the Applications menu makes it easy for you to add new applications to any of the preexisting sections defined on the Applications menu by installing those applications and creating their menu entries as part of the installation process. Using the Ubuntu Software Center menu item is discussed in the section of Chapter 19, "Adding, Removing, and Updating Software," entitled "Installing Software with the Ubuntu Software Center." This menu item is extremely convenient if you want to add some popular application to the Applications menu, but isn't much use if you want to add your own menus or create custom menu entries for specific applications. To do this, you'll need to use the System ➪ Preferences submenu's Main Menu application. Selecting this menu item starts the Alacarte Menu Editor, which makes it easy for you to add almost anything (including custom submenus) to any existing GNOME menu.

For example, suppose you wanted to create your own submenu called *Favorites* and begin adding entries for your favorite applications to it. To do this (adding the Emacs text editor to this menu as an example), do the following:

1. Select System ➪ Preferences ➪ Main Menu to start the Menu Editor. This Menu Editor dialog consists of two primary panes: a Menu Catalog pane at the left and a Menu Contents pane at the top right that shows the current contents of the currently selected menu. The Applications menu is expanded when this dialog opens, as shown in Figure 5-6.

Tip

You'll notice that the Menu Catalog pane lists many menus that are not currently displayed on your system. This is because they are not marked to be shown (via the Show column) in the Menu Contents pane on the right, as shown in Figure 5-6. ■

Editing menus on your Ubuntu system

2. Click the "New Menu" button. A dialog like the one shown in Figure 5-7 displays (with no entries in the text fields).

142

FIGURE 5-7

Adding a new menu

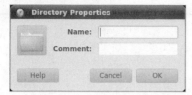

3. Enter the name of the new menu that you want to create (I'm using *Favorites* in this example), add an optional comment that will be used as the tool tip for this menu, and click OK. The new menu will be added to the Applications menu, and the Applications menu entry in the Menu Catalog pane will expand to show the current contents of that menu (which should be identical to the list in the Menu dialog at the top right). Select the name of your new menu in the Menu Catalog pane. The contents of the new menu (i.e., nothing) display in the Menu Contents pane at the top right, as shown in Figure 5-8.

FIGURE 5-8

Viewing the new menu

4. Click the New Item button. A dialog like the one shown in Figure 5-9 displays.

Adding a new entry to a menu

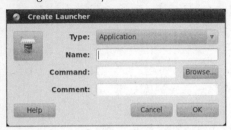

5. Enter the information about your new entry (in this case, the Emacs text editor) and click OK. The dialog closes, and the new entry on your Favorites menu displays, as shown in Figure 5-10.

Tip

If you don't know exactly where the application that you want to add is located, you can click Browse to display a Browse dialog that lets you navigate to and select the application for which you want to create a new menu entry. ■

Your new menu entry in the Menu Editor

6. Select the Applications menu in the Menu Catalog pane at the left, and make sure that the checkbox in the Show column for your new menu is selected in the Menu Listing pane at the top right, as shown in Figure 5-11. This entry is required so that the menu is listed in the Applications menu once you exit from the Menu Editor.

FIGURE 5-11

Making sure that the new menu is visible

7. Click Close to exit from the Menu Editor and add your changes to the Applications menu. The Applications menu is updated, and your new menu and entry are now available, as shown in Figure 5-12.

FIGURE 5-12

Your new entries on the GNOME Applications menu

If you decide not to save your changes, you can click the Revert button to undo your current changes, and then click Close.

The flexibility provided in the dialog shown in Figure 5-9 makes it easy for you to create menu entries for applications that you have manually compiled and installed yourself, such as in corporate or academic environments, and also to add your own favorite command-line parameters to new or existing menu entries.

Tip

You can also add menus in GNOME using the Nautilus File Manager, but I find that using applications designed for editing menus is easier to understand. For information about using Nautilus to create menus and menu items, see the online *GNOME Users Guide*, available through the System menu's Help menu. ■

Customizing Your Desktop

As explained earlier in this chapter, GNOME makes it easy to customize its menus and the sections and applications that they contain. Luckily, every part of the GNOME desktop is similarly configurable. This section highlights how to do some of the most common customizations that most people do to make their systems easier to use and generally personalize them. Many other customizations are available, but discussing all of them could make this book impossible to lift. Let's focus on the highlights!

Customizing Mouse Behavior

One of the most common customizations that people want to do is to change how responsive the mouse is, in one way or another. Available customizations include:

- Whether the mouse is configured for left-handed or right-handed users. The latter is the default, but may not suit you if you use your left hand to control the mouse.

- The speed at which the cursor moves and the amount of screen real estate the mouse covers in relation to your moving the mouse

- The period of time that can elapse between two mouse clicks to consider them as a double-click (which opens the target) rather than simply two single clicks (which simply selects something). If you have difficulty double-clicking, you can increase the double-click time period.

All of these customizations are controlled by the System ➪ Preferences menu's Mouse application, which is shown in Figure 5-13.

This application provides two tabs that enable you to configure different aspects of the mouse: the General tab, where you can specify the behavior of the buttons and the speed and sensitivity of mouse motion, and the Accessibility tab, where you can configure the mouse to perform special actions to simplify the use of a mouse by people who may have difficulty using a mouse in a traditional fashion. The General tab is shown in Figure 5-13. To switch between different tabs, simply select the appropriate tab in the Mouse Preferences application.

FIGURE 5-13

The Mouse Preferences dialog

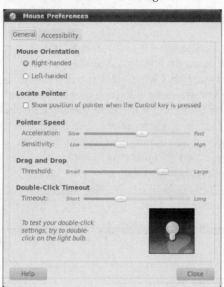

The configuration items on the General tab that control the motion and sensitivity of the mouse require some explanation. The entries on this tab include the following:

- **Pointer Speed - Acceleration:** This option controls how far the cursor moves on the screen in response to your moving the mouse, and is controlled by a slider. Being able to change this ratio guarantees that you don't need a mouse pad the size of your computer monitor — acceleration enables the cursor to cover larger distances as you move the mouse continuously. Slower values mean that cursor movement is closer to the actual distance that you're moving the mouse; faster values mean that the cursor moves proportionately farther distances as you continue to move the mouse — in other words, the cursor starts out moving slowly and accelerates as you continue to move the mouse. To change your settings, click and hold the button on the slider using the left mouse button and drag it to the new value that you want to use.

- **Pointer Speed - Sensitivity:** This option determines how sensitive the cursor is to any movement of the mouse. If you have set Acceleration to be very fast, you may find that the cursor jumps when you simply touch the mouse. In this case, you could decrease the sensitivity of the mouse, while still retaining fast acceleration.

- **Drag and Drop - Threshold:** This option controls the distance that the mouse must cover when you have selected a desktop object in order for the motion to be considered a drag-and-drop action. For example, when double-clicking, you may find that you move the mouse slightly between the two clicks. If the drag-and-drop threshold is set very low, GNOME will interpret this as a drag-and-drop or move operation rather than a double-click operation. In this case, you would want to increase the threshold value.

Changes to your mouse preferences take effect immediately, so it's easy for you to experiment with the set of values that gives you the control and behavior that you want on your system.

Configuring Screen Resolution

The Ubuntu installer does a good job of guessing the resolutions that it can use with your current monitor and selecting an initial value that is somewhere in the middle. Unfortunately, display resolution is a matter of personal taste — it really makes sense only when you can see what different resolutions actually look like. Consequently, even if you are using a 30-inch monitor and the sexiest video card in the universe, you may find that your Ubuntu Linux system initially displays everything at a resolution such as 1024×768, where each of the icons on your screen is approximately the size of a grapefruit. This is probably not what you had in mind, and is certainly not the best use of your hardware or screen real estate. This section explains how to correct that problem by selecting a higher screen resolution. Internally, this means that your screen displays more pixels, but the visual effect is that things on the screen are both smaller and sharper. In the computer industry, this is known as "the right thing™."

Screen resolution in GNOME is controlled by the System ➪ Preferences menu's Monitors Preferences application, which is shown in Figure 5-14.

FIGURE 5-14

The Monitor Preferences application

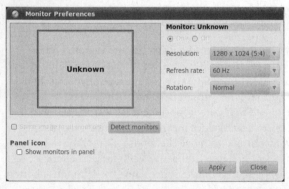

Once this application displays, you can see the list of available screen resolutions by left-clicking the Resolution button. A pop-up list displays, as shown in Figure 5-15.

After selecting another screen resolution, click Apply to try out the new resolution. GNOME will change your screen to the new resolution and display the dialog shown in Figure 5-16, asking if you want to keep the new screen resolution or permanently switch to the new resolution.

Note

Because it's possible to select a resolution that may not actually work correctly, your screen will automatically revert to its former resolution in 20 seconds. No need to panic if your screen goes haywire for a little while! ■

FIGURE 5-15

Selecting other screen resolutions

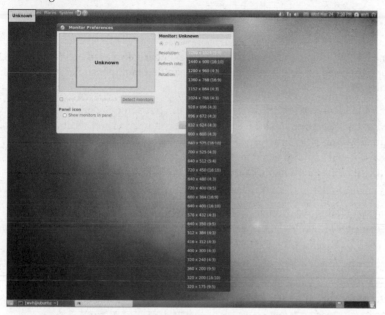

FIGURE 5-16

Confirming screen resolution changes

If you're happy with the new resolution, click "Keep Resolution." The dialog will close, your screen will remain at the new resolution, and it will be the default screen resolution used whenever you log in to your Ubuntu system.

If the new resolution looks odd or is simply too small for your taste, click "Use Previous Resolution." You can then experiment with other resolutions, clicking Apply to test out any newly selected resolution until you find one that you're happy with.

Customizing Panels

As discussed earlier in the chapter, *panels* are regions on your desktop that are displayed by the gnome-panel application and provide access to various ways of interacting with the desktop and launching different types of applications. The gnome-panel application can display panels along any edge of the screen, but the default Ubuntu configuration displays panels at the top and bottom of the screen.

Note

A single instance of the gnome-panel application controls all of the panels that are displayed on your system. The fact that multiple panels are displayed on your screen does not mean that multiple copies of the gnome-panel application are running. ■

By default, the GNOME panels displayed at the top and bottom of your screen contain the menus and other items discussed in the "GNOME Desktop Overview" section earlier in this chapter. Not only can you configure how and where the panels are displayed on your screen and how many panels are displayed, but you can also extensively customize the contents of each. Ubuntu's default installation of GNOME comes with many other applets, buttons, and controls that you can install in the panels on your system.

Right-clicking on any existing panel displays that panel's context-sensitive menu, as shown in Figure 5-17.

FIGURE 5-17

The gnome-panel application's context-sensitive menu

Along with standard entries to display online help and get information about the version of the application, the context-sensitive menu for the gnome-panel application displays the following configuration-related entries:

- **Add to Panel:** Enables you to add a new applet, button, or other supported object to any panel that is currently displayed on your screen. See the section, "Customizing Panel Contents," for details on adding objects to an existing panel.

- **Properties:** Displays a panel properties dialog that enables you to set certain properties for the currently selected panel. See the next section, "Customizing Panel Properties," for details on the types of things that you can customize for an existing panel.

- **Delete this Panel:** Deletes the currently selected panel from the screen and removes all information about its current configuration from the system

- **New Panel:** Creates a new panel on the next available edge of the screen. You can create an essentially infinite number of panels — each new panel will simply start on the next edge of your screen, adjacent to any existing panel that is already associated with that edge. I find two panels to be the right number, but you may feel differently.

- **Help:** Displays online help for the gnome-panel application
- **About Panels:** Displays author, contributor, and copyright information about the gnome-panel application

The next two sections explain how to modify the properties of the existing panels on your screen; add other applets, buttons, and controls to those panels; and highlight some of the most fun and useful of these that are provided with Ubuntu Linux.

Customizing Panel Properties

Selecting the Properties entry on any panel's context-sensitive menu displays the dialog shown in Figure 5-18.

FIGURE 5-18

The gnome-panel application's "Panel Properties" dialog

This dialog contains two tabs: a Background tab, which enables you to control the color and transparency of the current panel or select an existing image to use for its background; and the General tab, shown in Figure 5-18, which enables you to control the location and behavior of that panel. The properties that you can configure on this tab are as follows:

- **Orientation:** Enables you to specify the edge of the screen at which the currently selected panel should display. Selecting another value immediately moves the currently selected panel to the specified edge.

Tip

You can also move an existing panel to another edge of your screen by left-clicking on its background, holding down the left mouse button, and dragging it to the new edge. ∎

- **Size:** Enables you to specify the height (or width, depending on the panel's orientation) in pixels of the currently selected panel

- **Expand:** Selecting or deselecting this toggle checkbox determines whether the panel occupies the entire edge of the screen or whether it takes up only that portion of the edge that is required to display the objects that it currently holds.

- **Autohide:** Selecting or deselecting this toggle checkbox determines whether the panel is displayed only when the cursor is moved to the edge of the screen that the currently selected panel is associated with. If this property is selected, the panel is not displayed when the cursor is located over any other portion of the screen.

- **Show hide buttons:** Selecting or deselecting this toggle checkbox determines whether buttons for collapsing or expanding the currently selected panel are displayed at each end of that panel. Selecting this checkbox also activates the "Arrows on hide buttons" option, which simply determines whether the icons at either end of the panel display arrows to highlight the direction in which the panel will expand or contract if they are selected.

Changes that you make to the properties of any panel take effect immediately. To close the "Panel Properties" dialog, click Close.

Customizing Panel Contents

Selecting "Add to Panel" from any panel's context-sensitive menu displays the "Add to Panel" dialog, as shown in Figure 5-19.

FIGURE 5-19

The "Add to Panel" dialog

This dialog enables you to add application launchers, buttons, and common applets to any panel that is currently displayed on your screen. All of the currently available buttons and applets are displayed in this scrollable dialog. To add any of these to any panel that is currently visible on the screen, left-click on that applet, hold down the left mouse button, and drag the applet to the location on the panel where you want it to be displayed. Releasing the mouse button positions the selected applet at that location in the panel.

Tip

After adding any applet to any panel, you can move most applets by right-clicking on the applet and selecting Move from its context-sensitive menu. (If the "Lock to Panel" item is selected on the context-sensitive menu, you will have to deselect this first in order to move the applet. You can then reselect it once you've moved the applet.) After selecting the Move menu item, the applet will follow the current cursor position — once you have moved the applet to its new location, left-click to position it at the new location. Applets can be moved to any other panel that is currently displayed on the screen. ∎

The applets displayed in the "Add to Panel" dialog are organized alphabetically and provide capabilities ranging from user-oriented features such as monitoring the weather and the ability to insert special characters into the documents and other files that you are working with, to system-oriented features such as CPU frequency and system status monitoring. Some of my personal favorite applets are as follows:

- **Deskbar applet:** Located in the Accessories section, this applet makes it easy to perform a single search of multiple Internet and filesystem locations, query the Tracker desktop search application, query online dictionaries, and even perform specific system actions based on your keywords.

- **Drawer:** Located in the "Desktop & Windows" section, a drawer is a convenient way of adding multiple applets or buttons to a panel without consuming all available panel real estate. A *drawer* is essentially just an extension of a panel that can hold other panel objects. Clicking on a drawer causes it to expand, showing the panel objects that it contains, which you can then select just as if they were directly located on a panel. If you're really into applets but don't want to use too many panels, drawers can be a big convenience.

- **Sticky Notes:** Located in the Accessories section, this applet enables you to create and manage multiple onscreen sticky notes that are analogous to the Post-Its that festoon everyone's monitors and physical desktops nowadays. This applet provides a simple alternative to Ubuntu's Tomboy Notes application, which is located on the Applications ➪ Accessories menu, and for which a separate applet is available.

- **System Monitor:** Located in the "System & Hardware" section, this applet can be configured to display graphical and associated tool tips that provide information about processor, memory, network, swap space, and hard drive usage, as well as general system load information.

- **Volume Control:** Located in the "System & Hardware" section, this applet provides an easy way of increasing (or occasionally decreasing) your sound card's volume. (This applet is installed by default in the top panel on Ubuntu systems.)

- **Weather Report:** Located in the Accessories section, this applet displays information about the temperature and general weather conditions in any specified location. Because many of us don't have windows in our offices (or perhaps offices at all), this can be very handy when you're thinking about going outside. It's sad how often I find this applet to be useful — "Oh, it's snowing outside?"

Application launchers are panel entries that execute a specific application for you, and mirror the entries found on Ubuntu's Applications and System menus. To add one of these predefined application launchers, select the "Application Launcher" entry in the "Add to Panel" dialog and click forward, or simply double-click on that entry. The "Application Launcher" dialog displays, as shown in Figure 5-20.

FIGURE 5-20

Adding a predefined application launcher to a panel

To add a predefined application launcher, use the plus signs to the left of each submenu entry to navigate to the application launcher that you want to add to the panel, and double-click that entry to add it to the panel from which you started the Add to Panel application, or select and drag it to the location on any panel where you want it to be displayed. To return to the main "Add to Panel" dialog, click Back.

Tip

Each panel applet has its own configuration opportunities — for example, the Weather Report applet requires that you identify your location to be able to display accurate information about the local weather, but that information isn't really germane to any other applet. To configure any panel applet, right-click on its panel icon and select the Preferences item from the context-sensitive menu that displays. The configuration dialog for that applet displays, showing any configurable properties of that applet. ∎

The Add to Panel application also enables you to add custom application launchers that you can define yourself. This enables you to create panel entries that will launch your favorite applications with your own favorite command-line options. To define a custom application launcher, click the "Custom Application Launcher" button in the "Add to Panel" dialog. The "Create Launcher" dialog displays, as shown in Figure 5-21.

FIGURE 5-21

Defining a custom application launcher

The "Create Launcher" dialog enables you to set various characteristics of the launcher that you are defining, the application that it starts, and how that launcher displays in the panel. After providing that information, click OK to create the new launcher. By default, the new launcher is displayed in the panel from which you started the Add to Panel application.

Once you're finished customizing and fine-tuning the applets, buttons, and launchers that are displayed in your system's panels, click Close to close the "Add to Panel" dialog and get back to work.

Tip

To remove an applet from any of your panels, right-click its name and select the "Remove from Panel" command from its context-sensitive menu. ∎

Configuring the Screensaver

There was a time when computer monitors were quite sensitive to displaying the same characters for long periods of time. Monitors that showed the same applications in the same locations for long periods of time would end up damaging the phosphors on the inside of the monitor, which therefore displayed a ghostly outline of that application on the screen. (This was known as *screen burn* or *video burn*.) To eliminate or, at least, reduce this problem, many companies developed applications known as *screensavers*, which would start automatically after a computer system had been unused for a specified period of time and would display random patterns or images on the screen, preventing the burn-in of default images.

Today's monitors are much more sophisticated than the monitors of old, and are therefore less susceptible to image burn-in. Today, screensavers are typically used because they look nice or for security purposes, so that unauthorized users can't see what is displayed on the screen of your computer while you're at lunch.

By default, your Ubuntu system comes configured to blank the screen after 10 minutes of keyboard and mouse inactivity. You can select a specific screensaver for your system to use (there are hundreds), configure the period of time after which a screensaver is activated, or disable the screensaver on your system entirely. All of these are done through the System ⇨ Preferences menu's Screensaver Preferences application, which is shown in Figure 5-22.

FIGURE 5-22

Configuring your system's screensaver

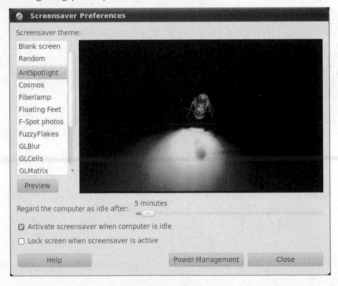

Once this dialog displays, you can explore all of the other screensavers that are available on your system by selecting them from the scrollable Screensaver theme list at the left of the dialog. A preview of the appearance and behavior of the currently selected screensaver displays in the preview pane to the right of the screensaver list.

Once you select the screensaver that you want to use, the "Screensaver Preferences" dialog also enables you to set some general characteristics of your system's use of that screensaver. To change the period of time after which the screensaver is activated, drag this dialog's slider to reflect the new time period. To deactivate the screensaver entirely, clear the "Activate screensaver when computer is idle" checkbox.

Ordinarily, moving the mouse or pressing any key on your keyboard causes the screensaver to stop displaying its default image and reset its inactivity timer. To combine the screensaver with a dialog that requires that you provide your password to stop displaying the screensaver and regain access to your keyboard and screen, select the "Lock screen when screensaver is active" checkbox. You will need to supply your password to re-display your normal desktop.

The "Screensaver Preferences" dialog also provides a "Power Management" button that starts the Power Management Preferences application, which you can also execute by selecting the System ⇨ Preferences ⇨ Power Management menu item. This dialog enables you to configure how your system reacts to longer periods of inactivity than those covered by the screensaver. Configuring power management is discussed in the next section.

Once you are finished configuring the screensaver, click Close to terminate the Screensaver Preferences application.

Configuring Power Management

As mentioned in the previous section, the "Screensaver Preferences" dialog also provides a "Power Management" button that starts the Power Management Preferences application. A more common (and more intuitive) way of configuring power management and related activities is by selecting the System ⇨ Preferences ⇨ Power Management menu item. Selecting either of these displays the dialog shown in Figure 5-23.

FIGURE 5-23

Configuring power management on your system

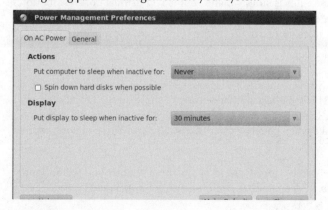

The "Power Management Preferences" dialog provides two or three tabs: the On AC Power tab, which enables you to configure how your system behaves after significant periods of inactivity when it is running from AC power (i.e., when it is plugged in, which should be always for a desktop or server system but occasionally for a laptop or netbook); On Battery Power, which is displayed only on laptop systems and which enables you to configure how your system behaves after significant periods of inactivity when it is running from battery power; and the General tab, which enables you to configure how your system reacts when the Power or Suspend buttons are pressed, and whether a power management icon is displayed in the notification area at the upper right of the top GNOME panel.

The On AC Power tab displays when you first start the Power Management Preferences application:

- **Put computer to sleep when inactive for:** A dropdown list that enables you to configure your system to go to sleep if it has been inactive for a specified period. (For an explanation of what "putting your computer to sleep" means, see the discussion of Suspend mode later in this section.) The default setting for this option is "Never," which means that your system will never go to sleep, regardless of how long it has been inactive. If you do not need to access your system remotely (via a network connection or modem), you should probably set this to a lower value by selecting an appropriate value from the list. If you need to access your system remotely and will be accessing it over a network, you can still safely set this to a lower value if your system has a BIOS configuration option that tells it to wake up if network activity to the machine is detected. Otherwise, if you need to be able to access your system remotely, you should leave this setting at its default value so that it is always awake and available for access.

- **Spin down hard disks when possible:** A checkbox that instructs the power management system to spin down the disks whenever no activity has been detected for 60 seconds

- **Put display to sleep when inactive for:** A dropdown list that enables you to configure your system to put your monitor into a low-power mode if it has been inactive for a specified period. To resume regular use (known as *waking* your monitor), you can simply move your mouse or press any key on your keyboard. Putting your monitor to sleep is very different from simply blanking your monitor, as the default GNOME screensaver does. In the latter case, the monitor is simply blank, but is still using a normal amount of power. In sleep mode, the monitor is actually consuming less power. The default setting for this option is 30 minutes, but something like 10 minutes is probably a better selection in most cases.

The On Battery Power tab displays only if you are using a laptop, netbook, or other portable computer that can run on battery power. This tab offers similar settings to those on the On AC Power tab, adding options that are specific to battery-powered systems with integrated screens, such as the actions that your system should take when battery power is critically low. These options are the following:

- **Put computer to sleep when active for:** A dropdown list that enables you to configure your laptop or netbook to go to sleep if it has been inactive for a specified period. See the explanation of this option on the AC Power tab, earlier in this section, for more information.

- **When battery power is critically low:** A dropdown list that enables you to configure how a laptop or netbook system reacts when battery power is almost exhausted. Possible values are Hibernate (the default), Sleep, Shutdown, and Ask Me. The latter simply displays a warning on your screen and prompts you for the action to take, while Shutdown terminates all processes and turns off your system. See the discussion of Suspend and Hibernate later in this section for detailed information about the differences between them.

- **Spin down hard disks when possible:** A checkbox that instructs the power management system to spin down the disks whenever no activity has been detected for 60 seconds. This can be extremely valuable on laptop systems.

- **Put display to sleep when inactive for:** A dropdown list that enables you to configure your system to put your monitor into a low-power mode if it has been inactive for a specified period. See the explanation of this option on the AC Power tab, earlier in this section, for more information. The default value for this option is 10 minutes when on battery power, as opposed to 30 minutes for desktop systems.

- **Reduce backlight brightness:** A checkbox that enables you to configure the screen to automatically reduce brightness after being inactive for 60 seconds

The most interesting settings on the General tab are in the Actions area, which defines how your system reacts when you press the Power or Suspend buttons on your system. (All systems have a Power button; not all systems have a Suspend button.) Your choices for the Power button are "Ask me" (the default), which displays a dialog that prompts you to ask what you want to do, "Hibernate," and "Shutdown." Your choices for the Suspend button are Hibernate and Suspend. The differences between suspending, hibernating, and shutting down your computer are as follows:

- **Suspend** (also known as *sleep* mode) is a reduced-power mode in which all active applications, associated documents, and the current state of the kernel are saved to RAM, which enables the system to power down most of the devices on your system (such as the hard drive, display, network interfaces, etc.) while waiting for some activity. Your system's processor and memory are still using power while your system is in sleep mode, but these use substantially less power than your system normally does. Be careful when using this mode for an extended period of time on laptop computers. If you are using suspend mode on a laptop without being connected to AC power, you will still lose any unsaved work when your battery is depleted.

- **Hibernate** mode saves all active applications, associated documents, and the current state of your kernel to your hard drive and then actually shuts down the system. When you power the system back on, the system detects the saved state information on your hard drive and restores it to memory, enabling you to pick up exactly where you left off. No power is consumed while the computer is hibernating because it is actually turned off, but restoring the system from the hard disk (known as *resuming* the system) requires that a large file be read and restored to memory, which takes longer than waking up from suspend mode. By default, system images are saved to swap space, so the amount of swap space available on your system should be equivalent to the amount of memory on your system. See the /etc/acpi/hibernate.sh script for detailed information about what happens when your system hibernates.

- **Shutdown** terminates all active applications, unmounts all filesystems, and turns your system off. Restarting your system takes longer than waking from suspend mode or resuming from hibernation mode because your system must go through the entire startup process, check your filesystems for consistency, and so on.

You can use the Notification Area preferences in the Power Management Preferences application to configure whether a power management icon is always shown in the Notification Area or whether it is never displayed. Normally, the power management icon is displayed only when your system is running on battery power.

After changing any of these values, click Close to save the new settings and close the Power Management Preferences application.

Tip

Always save any modified files if you know that you are going to be away from your computer for an extended period of time. While the suspend and hibernate modes usually work correctly, you shouldn't take the chance that they do not restore in-progress documents correctly. Your boss, publisher, or thesis advisor probably will not accept "Suspend mode ate my homework" as a valid excuse for being late or losing critical data. As a public service, I have personally tested this excuse for you, and it does not work. ■

Debugging Power Management Problems

Power management problems can be difficult to troubleshoot because they involve changing the state of your system. In some cases, requesting a suspend or hibernate operation can cause an error that will terminate your current session without any chance to see the error message. If you are experiencing problems getting your system to suspend or hibernate, here are a few things to try:

1. Verify that your kernel actually supports suspend/hibernate. You can do this with the lshal command, which queries your system's hardware abstraction layer to identify various capabilities, as in the following example:

```
$ lshal | egrep 'can_suspend|can_hibernate'
  power_management.can_hibernate = true  (bool)
  power_management.can_suspend = true  (bool)
  power_management.can_suspend_hybrid = false  (bool)
```

This shows that the kernel supports both suspending to RAM (suspend) and suspending to disk (hibernate). These capabilities are enabled by default in official Ubuntu kernels, but if you have built your own kernel, you will want to verify that they are enabled (and enable them and rebuild the kernel if they are not).

2. Verify that the ability to suspend and hibernate is still active in your GNOME environment, as in the following example:

```
$ gconftool-2 -R /apps/gnome-power-manager | grep can
  can_suspend = true
  can_hibernate = true
```

This shows that the `gnome-power-manager` application believes that the system can both suspend and hibernate.

3. If you are only having problems hibernating, make sure that the amount of swap space on your system matches or exceeds the amount of memory in your system. By default, the system image file that is created before your system can hibernate is saved to a contiguous portion of your system's swap space. If you do not have sufficient swap space, you can either increase it (and do so contiguously) or try using another of the hibernation methods that are available for Ubuntu such as those in the `hibernate`, `suspend2`, and `uswsusp` packages. Increasing swap space involves booting without it, resizing the swap and following partitions on your hard drive, reformatting the swap area, and rebooting with the new swap space.

4. Verify that your ACPI settings are correct by examining the file `/etc/default/acpi-support`. This file sets environment variables used by the ACPI scripts and may help identify problems. Make sure that both the ACPI_SLEEP and ACPI_HIBERNATE options are set to true. Depending on your hardware, you may need to modify settings such as ACPI_SLEEP_MODE, DOUBLE_CONSOLE_SWITCH, and RESET_DRIVE to get the suspend/hibernate operations to work correctly on your system.

5. If suspend and hibernate both look as though they should work, the next step is to try to run the suspend and/or hibernate scripts manually to see any error message(s) that they display. This is difficult to do on the machine that you are trying to suspend or hibernate, but is easy to do if you connect to that machine from another via the network using `ssh` or `telnet` commands, and then run the script manually. The scripts that you want to run are those in `/etc/acpi/suspend.d` when suspending your system, and the single script `/etc/acpi/hibernate.sh` when hibernating your system. If you are trying to suspend your system, you would run those scripts from your network connection using a command like the following:

```
$ for SCRIPT in /etc/acpi/suspend.d/*.sh; do \
    sh -x $SCRIPT \
done
```

Using `sh -x` runs all of the scripts in verbose mode to ensure that you see each command that the scripts try to execute, to make it easier to identify problems.

If the machine on which you are working isn't on a local network or you don't have another machine that you can use to connect to that machine, you can try using the script command or re-directing the output of the script into a file to capture any error messages that may be displayed.

Changing Desktop Backgrounds

GNOME also makes it easy for you to change the background displayed on your system's desktops. The background is a solid color or image that is displayed on your screen and over which all other application windows are displayed. To do this, select the System ➪ Preferences menu's Appearance menu entry. The Appearance Preferences application displays. To change your desktop background, select the Background tab, as shown in Figure 5-24.

FIGURE 5-24

Configuring your desktop background

Changing the background of your desktop is one of the more common configuration tasks when personalizing your system. To customize your desktop, you can select a solid background color, select an existing graphics image from the default list given in the "Desktop Wallpaper" dialog, or click Add to navigate to the location of a specific graphics file that you may want to use as your background. (I tend to use vacation or other scenic photos.)

Once you've selected an image, the Style value determines how that image is used as the background. Your options are as follows:

- **Center:** The selected wallpaper is displayed in the center of your screen at its original resolution.
- **Scale:** The selected wallpaper is scaled to fit your screen without changing its aspect ratio.
- **Stretch:** The selected wallpaper is increased in size as needed to completely fill the background of your screen. This does not preserve the aspect ratio of your original image.

- **Tile:** The selected wallpaper, at its original size, is repeated multiple times across your screen as needed to fill the background.

- **Zoom:** The selected wallpaper is increased in size so that it completely fills your screen. If the image is not exactly the right size, some portions of the image may be clipped so that the image completely fills the screen.

As you select different wallpaper and style options, the background changes instantly to reflect the current selections. Once you're happy with your new background, click Close to close the Appearance application.

Switching Themes

The word *theme* is the term for the combination of window and dialog controls, a color scheme, and a set of icons that gives your desktop and the windows that it displays a specific look and feel. Many themes also come with a specific desktop background to complete the visual experience that their author was trying to achieve. Experimenting with different themes can be a lot of fun, and can also be extremely useful to make it easier to read window titles and generally adjust contrast on your screen.

To change or configure the theme used on your Ubuntu system, select the System ⇨ Preferences menu's Appearance menu item. This application displays the Theme tab when it starts, as shown in Figure 5-25.

FIGURE 5-25

Specifying theme preferences

Ubuntu's GNOME desktop comes with many attractive themes. By default, Ubuntu uses a theme that is designed to be attractive, easy on the eyes, and easy to use. To switch to another of the themes provided with Ubuntu Linux, select it from the scrollable Theme pane in the center of the dialog. Even though the Theme pane includes preview images of each available theme, the new theme takes effect immediately so that you can see what it will actually look like. Figure 5-26, for example, shows the Theme tab after selecting the old Human theme. You should be able to see the differences in the window decoration, font placement, highlighting, window controls, dialog button shapes, and so on.

FIGURE 5-26

Selecting a different window theme

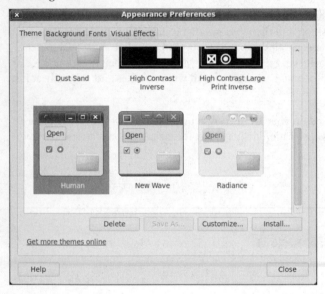

Once you've selected the theme that you like best at the moment, click Close to close the "Appearance Preferences" dialog. Your new theme will be used each time you log in, until you change it.

Tip
Although Ubuntu provides a large collection of nice themes, artistically inclined users are always creating new ones. Many excellent (or just plain interesting) themes are available at a variety of web sites. My favorites are the GNOME Art site (http://art.gnome.org), GNOME-Look.org (www.gnome-look.org), and Freshmeat (http://themes.freshmeat.net). A quick Web search for *GNOME themes* with your favorite search engine will turn up many more sites. To add any of these themes, simply select the "Install Theme" button after downloading the theme, and navigate to its location on your system. The new theme is added to the scrollable Themes list, and can be selected like any other theme. Somewhere out there is the perfect theme for you! ■

Assistive Technologies for Using GNOME

If you have trouble seeing the screen or using a keyboard or mouse, the GNOME and Ubuntu folks are sensitive to your needs and offer various assistive technologies that do things such as providing onscreen keyboard support and supporting screen magnification and audio output from portions of the screen. These features are installed by default as part of all Ubuntu desktop installations, but are not activated by default.

You can activate the capabilities of these packages by selecting the System ⇨ Preferences ⇨ Assistive Technologies menu item, which displays the dialog shown in Figure 5-27. You can then use the "Preferred Applications" button to select the tools that you want to use, whether these applications should always be used, and whether password dialogs should be treated as normal windows. (You may not want Orca to read your password as you type it, for example.) You must then log out and log back in to activate them. Separate Keyboard and Mouse Accessibility items provide shortcuts to the Accessibility tabs on the Keyboard and Mouse Preferences dialogs.

FIGURE 5-27

Enabling assistive technologies in GNOME

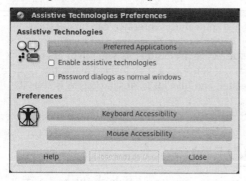

Clicking the "Preferred Applications" button displays a dialog, shown in Figure 5-28, that enables you to define the applications to invoke for screen reading and magnification via the Orca application (http://live.gnome.org/Orca) and a rapid text-entry system known as *Dasher* (www.inference.phy.cam.ac.uk/dasher) to help simplify text entry when a standard keyboard cannot be used easily.

These applications aren't perfect, but are actively under development to guarantee that anyone can take advantage of the power of Ubuntu Linux. For more information about assistive technologies and GNOME, see http://projects.gnome.org/accessibility.

Customizing accessibility in GNOME

Tip

The GNOME accessibility tools are quite good, but the value of a graphical user interface can be questionable for people with different types of accessibility issues. If you have visual or device control issues, you may find that a command-line system and a package like emacspeak are preferable. As you might guess, the emacspeak package is a screen reader that works with Emacs. If you start a shell inside Emacs, the emacspeak package will also serve as a great command-line reader, and (like all Emacs packages) is almost infinitely configurable. ∎

GNOME Keyboard Shortcuts

If you have problems controlling a mouse or simply prefer to keep your hands on the keyboard at all times, GNOME provides several special key sequences that enable you to perform most traditionally mouse-driven desktop activities using only the keyboard. These are commonly referred to as *keyboard shortcuts*. To activate these, press and hold down the first key in the sequence while pressing the second. The most popular keyboard shortcuts for the GNOME desktop are as follows:

- **Alt+F1:** Displays the Applications menu
- **Alt+F2:** Displays the "Run Applications" dialog, in which you can enter the name of a specific application that you want to execute
- **Alt+F4:** Closes the window that is currently selected

- **Alt+F5:** Reduces the size of the current window if it is maximized

- **Alt+F7:** Enables you to move the window that is currently selected. After pressing this key combination, use the arrow keys or mouse to move the window to a new location, and press any other key on the keyboard to complete the move operation

- **Alt+F8:** Enables you to resize the window that is currently selected. After pressing this key combination, use the arrow keys or mouse to increase or decrease the size of the window, and press any other key on the keyboard to complete the resize operation.

- **Alt+F9:** Minimizes the window that is currently selected

- **Alt+F10:** Maximizes the window that is currently selected

- **Alt+Tab:** Cycles through all of the windows and dialogs that are currently displayed on the screen, highlighting each in turn (known as *giving the focus* to that window) until you find the one that you're interested in

- **Alt+spacebar:** Displays any context-sensitive menu associated with the window that is currently selected

- **Ctrl+L:** When browsing for a file in any File ➪ Open dialog, displays a pop-up box in which you can type the full pathname of the directory containing the files that you are looking for, saving you many clicks if you need to drill down to a deeply nested directory. This dialog does automatic directory-name completion as you type, and is one of my favorite GNOME features.

GNOME supports several other keyboard shortcuts, most of which perform standard actions within various applications. For a complete list of available keyboard shortcuts, see the *GNOME Accessibility Guide*, available by selecting the System ➪ Help ➪ System Documentation menu item.

Introducing the Nautilus File Manager

The Nautilus File Manager, known to its friends simply as *Nautilus*, is a convenient application for computer users who are used to graphically displaying, examining, and moving around in files and directories on their computer systems. Nautilus is GNOME's equivalent of the Microsoft Windows Explorer or the Mac OS X Finder, and makes it similarly easy to work with and modify your files and directories. Figure 5-29 shows Nautilus exploring the contents of my home directory on one of my systems.

As mentioned earlier in this chapter, the Places menu in the top panel on the default GNOME desktop shipped with Ubuntu systems is actually a collection of shortcuts to using Nautilus to explore different portions of your system or network. For example, I selected "Home Folder" from the top panel's Places menu to display my home directory in Nautilus, as shown in Figure 5-29.

FIGURE 5-29

Exploring my home directory in Nautilus

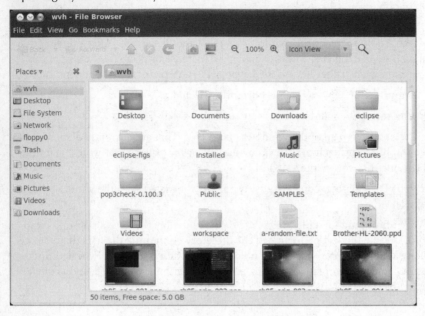

Basic Operations in Nautilus

Like other graphical file managers, Nautilus makes it easy to manage and manipulate files and directories. Most of the commands related to working with files and directories are located on the Edit menu, and are also accessible from the context-sensitive menu displayed when you right-click on any object in the Nautilus Display pane. Figure 5-30 shows the context-sensitive menu displayed when right-clicking on a file with the .txt extension in my home directory.

As you can see, this menu provides the standard actions that you'd expect to find in any file manager, enabling you to do the following:

- Open the file with the default application associated with that type of file.

- Open the file with other applications associated with that type of file.

- Cut or copy the file, enabling you to paste the file (or a copy of it) into another location to move or copy the file.

- Create a symbolic link to or rename the selected file.

- Rename the file.

- Copy the file to a specific location (only available in the version of GNOME used in Ubuntu 10.04 and later).

FIGURE 5-30

A context-sensitive menu in Nautilus

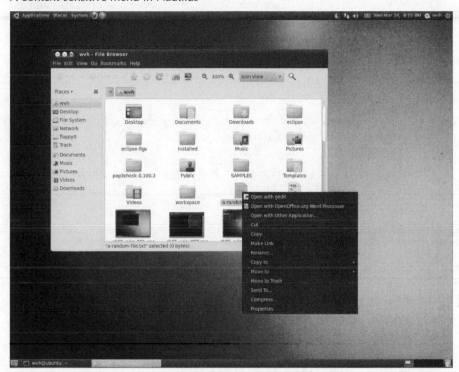

- Move the file to a specific location, removing it from its original location (only available in the version of GNOME used in Ubuntu 10.04 and later).

- Delete the file by moving it to the Trash Can, which is a temporary repository for files before they are actually purged from your system.

- Send the file to a specified device or create an archive file in compressed tar format containing that file. (See Chapter 28, "Backing Up and Restoring Files," for information about Linux archive file formats.)

- Examine or modify the properties of the file, including its name, permissions, and how it is displayed in Nautilus.

Examples of Using Nautilus

The previous section described the most common operations that you can do in Nautilus; this section provides a few examples of such operations to get you started working with Nautilus if you haven't used graphical file managers before.

Exploring the Filesystem

The GNOME desktop's Places menu contains several preconfigured shortcuts to various locations on your system and on your local network. If you're lucky, the directory or network location that you want to explore will be listed there. If not, you can navigate to any location on your system in Nautilus by doing the following:

1. Open Nautilus in a predefined location by selecting it from the Places menu.

2. Drill down into subdirectories of the selected location, and double-click on the icon for that folder.

3. Move up a level to the directory that contains the directory you are currently viewing, and click the Up button in the Nautilus toolbar.

Moving around between different files and directories in Nautilus is easy once you get the hang of it, and will soon become second nature to you.

Tip

You can start Nautilus and instantly display the contents of any accessible directory by starting Nautilus from the command line and specifying the name of that directory as an argument. For more information about using the command line, see Chapter 11. ■

Copying Files or Directories

To copy a file or directory in Nautilus, do the following:

1. Navigate to the directory that contains the file or directory that you want to copy.

2. Left-click on the icon for that file or directory to select it.

3. Select the Copy command from the Edit menu or right-click on the selected icon and select Copy from the context-sensitive menu.

4. Navigate to the directory where you want to place the copy of the selected file or directory.

5. Select the Paste command from the Edit menu or right-click on the background of the current directory in Nautilus and select Paste from the context-sensitive menu.

At this point, the icons for the files and directories that you had selected for copying display in the current Nautilus window, and the copy operation is complete. Copying directories that contain many files may take a bit of time.

Don't worry about accidentally overwriting files with the same name — if the directory to which you are copying files already contains files or directories with the same names as the files or directories that you are copying, the duplicate file will have the word *(copy)* added to its name to uniquely identify it.

Selecting Multiple Files and Directories

As you work with Nautilus, you may find that you want to move or copy multiple files and directories at the same time. This is easy enough to do as long as you select all of the icons associated with those files and directories before performing a copy or cut operation. You can select multiple items in Nautilus in a variety of different ways as follows:

- To select multiple files and directory icons, hold down the Ctrl key on your keyboard while selecting each of the icons for those files and directories.

- To select all of the files and directories that are alphabetically between two files and directories, select one icon, hold down either Shift key, and select the icon at the end of the range of files that you want to select.

- To graphically select multiple files that are next to each other in the Nautilus display windows, left-click the Nautilus background beside any of those files, hold down the left mouse button, and drag the mouse cursor to display a rectangle that contains all of the files that you want to select.

You can also combine these selection operations. For example, you could select a range of files graphically by using the Shift key and then holding down the Ctrl key to add other files or directory icons to the current selection.

Moving Files or Directories

To move a file or directory in Nautilus, do the following:

1. Navigate to the directory that contains the file or directory that you want to move.

2. Left-click on the icon for that file or directory to select it.

3. Select the Cut command from the Edit menu, or right-click on the selected icon and select Cut from the context-sensitive menu. The icons for the selected file or directory are removed from the current Nautilus window.

4. Navigate to the directory where you want to place the selected file or directory.

5. Select the Paste command from the Edit menu, or right-click on the background of the current directory in Nautilus and select Paste from the context-sensitive menu.

At this point, the icons for the files and directories that you removed from the first directory will display in the current Nautilus window, and the copy operation is complete. Copying directories that contain many files may take a bit of time.

Renaming a File or Directory

To rename a file or directory in Nautilus, do the following:

1. Navigate to the directory that contains the file or directory that you want to rename.

2. Right-click on the selected icon and select Rename from the context-sensitive menu. The name of the file will be selected in Nautilus.

3. Enter the new name of the selected file or directory and press Return. The updated name displays in Nautilus.

Creating a Directory

Creating a file is usually done by starting the application associated with that type of file and saving your work with the name of the file that you want to create. Creating directories can either be done from the command line, as explained in Chapter 11, or quickly and easily within Nautilus.

To create a directory in Nautilus, do the following:

1. Navigate to the directory where you want to create the new directory.

2. Right-click on the background of that directory as shown in Nautilus and select "Create Folder" from the context-sensitive menu, or select File ⇨ New Folder from the Nautilus menus. A new folder with the default name *untitled folder* displays in the Nautilus window, as shown in Figure 5-31.

3. Note that the name of the new folder is highlighted when that folder is created. To give the new folder a specific name, you can simply type that name or rename the directory as explained in the previous section.

FIGURE 5-31

Creating a new folder in Nautilus

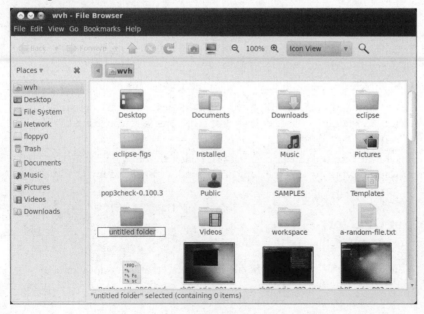

172

Getting More Information about Nautilus

Nautilus includes extensive and excellent documentation that is available by selecting Contents from its Help menu. Because it is so similar to the types of file managers used on other systems, you should find Nautilus extremely easy to use and master.

Using the Tracker Desktop Search Application

As disks and other local storage media get larger and larger, the amount of data that people save and keep around for an extended period of time gets equally large. Although this anecdote will date me, the first hard drive that I ever bought was a whopping 30 MB, and I remember thinking, "That should last a lifetime! How can I ever fill that up?" It actually didn't take very long to fill the drive, and I remember having to clean up after myself frequently, writing files that I didn't really need to back up media so that I could free up space on my hard drive. Nowadays, some of my data files are larger than that entire drive, and the fact that my desktop system has access to several terabytes of storage means that I'm less likely to clean up after myself anytime soon. It's simply easier to keep everything online (with off-site backups of truly critical data, of course). This is convenient when I want to consult an article about a defunct Linux distribution that I wrote a decade ago, but is not so convenient when I remember writing something a long time ago but have no idea what file or directory it's in.

Just as search engines make it possible to find information on specific topics regardless of where the information is located on the Internet, *desktop search applications* make it easy to find information that is located somewhere on your desktop computer. Online search engines and desktop search applications actually work in a very similar way—they crawl the information that they are responsible for and create an index of that information against which you can submit queries.

GNOME-based Linux distributions have provided a desktop search application called *Beagle* (http://beagle-project.org/Main Page), a desktop search application that was written in C# and uses Novell's Mono project to enable it to run on Linux systems. Beagle can index many different types of files and is nicely designed for integration—and while older versions of Beagle had a much-deserved reputation for being CPU-intensive while indexing files, the latest versions of Beagle are quite reasonable.

While Beagle was being paper-trained, other desktop search engines were being developed. My favorite is a desktop search application called *Tracker* (www.tracker-project.org). Tracker can index text, HTML, PDF, Microsoft Office, and Open Office documents, and can index a variety of audio and video files based on their MIME type.

Note
MIME (Multipurpose Internet Mail Extensions) is an Internet standard for identifying file formats, and is associated with mail systems because the need to identify files types was most commonly recognized when people began to attach files to their e-mail messages. ∎

In addition to its speed and search capabilities, Tracker provides some cool features such as the ability to tag files so that you can later find them by searching for the tag, and provides some automatic capabilities to expand your searches using the root(s) of your search term(s) (known as *stemming*), increasing the chance of finding what you're looking for.

Note

If you don't like Tracker or Beagle, you still have plenty of options. Recoll is another excellent package (www.recoll.org) that is both powerful and relatively easy on CPU resources. Strigi (http://strigi .sourceforge.net/) is a well-known desktop search application that is used on many KDE systems. The folks at Google are not asleep at the wheel, either — they offer DEB packages for the Linux version of their Desktop Search application as part of their Google Desktop package, available at http://desktop .google.com/linux. ■

Tracker is written in C, and consists of a daemon that indexes your files, a graphical configuration application, and several command-line and graphical utilities that make it easy to query and monitor the Tracker daemon and its index. The easiest way to query Tracker is by installing its desktop applet and then selecting the Magnifying Glass icon in the upper GNOME panel, as discussed in more detail later in this section. (See the section earlier in this chapter entitled "Customizing Panel Contents" for information on installing this applet.) Tracker can also be queried from the command line, which makes it handy for use in scripts.

Because of the number of desktop search solutions available, none of these packages is installed by default on an Ubuntu system. I suggest that you give Tracker a try by installing both the `tracker-search-tool` package (which installs Tracker and a GNOME front end) and the `tracker-utils` package (which installs command-line tools for accessing Tracker).

Searching with Tracker

After installing the Tracker packages, the Tracker daemon, `trackerd`, is automatically started as part of each Ubuntu user's GNOME login session. By default, Tracker automatically searches and indexes all of the files in your home directory. Once Tracker completes its initial scan of your files and directories, you can search the Tracker index in one of four basic ways:

- From the Tracker panel applet, which starts the Tracker Search Tool
- From the `tracker-search-tool` application, which you can start from the command line, or by selecting the Accessories menu's "Tracker Search Tool" menu option, or by creating a desktop launcher for this application
- From the command line by using the `tracker-search` command. This tool is part of the `tracker-utils` package.
- As part of the Deskbar applet panel tool

Tracker provides its own panel applet that starts once the Tracker daemon is running. You can click its icon, a magnifying glass, to start the Tracker Search Tool, as shown in Figure 5-32.

However, the Deskbar panel applet, discussed in the a later section, is the easiest way to submit a query to Tracker and other search sources at the same time.

FIGURE 5-32

Initiating a search in the Tracker panel applet

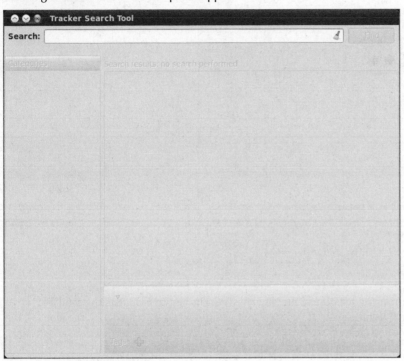

Pressing Return then automatically starts the graphical Tracker Search Tool application with these as the search terms, as shown in Figure 5-33.

As you can see from Figure 5-33, a Tracker search locates items whose filenames, pathnames, or content match the phrase that you're searching for. Double-clicking on any of the search results shown in the Tracker Search Tool window will open that result in the application with which files of that type are associated.

FIGURE 5-33

Search results in the Tracker Search Tool

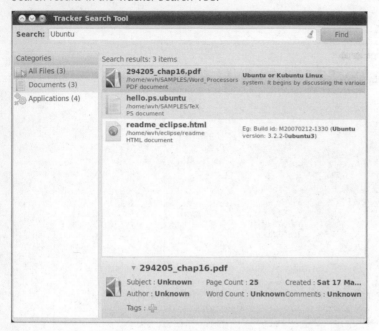

The summary line above the list of matching items shown in Figure 5-33 lists the available matches for the search term *Ubuntu*. If you have a large number of search results, the icons in the Categories section of the Tracker Search Tools can help you determine where various results are located, helping you find the "right" search result. Default categories include: All Files, Folders (a view of the folders in which search results were found), Documents (PDF, HTML, TeX, text, and related files), Images (image files in various formats that match your query), Music (audio files in various formats that match your query), Text (text files only), and Development (source code in various languages, Makefiles, etc.).

Once started as part of your GNOME login session, the Tracker daemon automatically runs in the background, continuously checking for new files in the directories that it is monitoring, indexing new files as they appear, and updating the index entries for existing files when you modify them.

Configuring Tracker

Tracker is a very powerful and flexible desktop search application whose behavior can be configured using the Tracker Preferences application. Per-user configuration information for Tracker is stored in the file ~/.config/tracker/tracker.cfg, which can be edited (carefully) using a text editor, or automatically by using the Tracker Preferences application. You can start the Tracker Preferences application from the command line (by executing the `tracker-preferences` command) or by selecting the System ⇨ Preferences ⇨ Search and Indexing menu item. (This menu option is only available after you have installed the Tracker packages.) Figure 5-34 shows the initial dialog that displays when you start the application.

Configuring the Tracker Search Tool

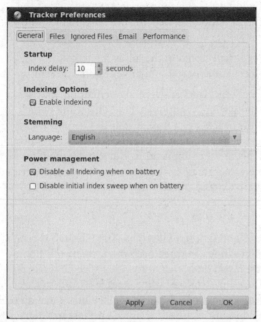

The different tabs in the Tracker Preferences application enable you to configure different aspects of how the Tracker daemon interacts with your system. These tabs are as follows:

- **General:** Enables/disables indexing and the delay after which indexing begins once you log in. This tab also enables you to set the language used when *stemming*, which is a mechanism for locating related words by identifying common roots, and enables you to configure how the Tracker daemon behaves on laptops that are running on battery power.

- **Files:** Lets you configure the directories that are indexed by the Tracker. This consists of two sets of directories — those that are indexed by the Tracker daemon and are actively monitored for changes, and those that are simply indexed once and are not subsequently checked for changes. The settings on this tab also enable you to config-ure whether the Tracker daemon indexes file contents in addition to filenames (both of these are enabled by default), whether the Tracker daemon generates a thumbnail image for each file that it indexes (disabled by default), and whether the Tracker daemon will cross mountpoints to index directories that are mounted under a directory that it is indexing or watching.

- **Ignored Files:** Enables you to identify directories and wildcard patterns for filenames that it will not index. For example, you can disable indexing anything under your music directory by entering **/home/*username*/music** in the "Ignored Paths" text area (you would, of course, replace *username* with your login name), and you can disable indexing all MP3 files by entering ***.mp3** in the "Ignored File Patterns" textbox. To add a new path or file pattern to ignore, click Add beside the appropriate text area, enter the path of the file pattern, and press Return. To remove an existing one, highlight it in the appropriate text area and click Remove.

- **Email:** Enables you to specify indexing of e-mail stored in the mbox mailbox format used by mail clients such as Evolution, but which is not located under your home directory.

- **Performance:** Enables you to configure how the Tracker daemon operates on your system in order to minimize its impact on the system. Options include Throttling (which lets you reduce the amount of CPU that the Tracker can use), Resource Usage (the amount of memory that the Tracker daemon uses — reduced memory use causes slower indexing but leaves more memory available to other applications), and Indexing Limits (per file) (how the Tracker daemon handles merging existing indexes with index entries for new files, and the maximum amount of text and number of words that should be indexed in each file).

The most commonly used of these tabs are the Files and Ignored Files tabs. The Files tab is especially useful if you store information that you want to index in directories other than your home directory. The Ignored Files tab is especially useful if you do not want to index specific types of files or files in certain directories. For example, I use a network-attached storage (NAS) device at home to archive old files that I want to be able to access from multiple systems, which I can do by mounting its filesystem on any given machine. Aside from archived personal and research data, I also store my music collection on this system. I therefore add the mountpoint for this device to the Files tab's list of directories that I want to index and watch, and add the music subdirectory of this mountpoint to the Ignored Files tab's list of Ignored Paths. I could also do the latter by adding the file extensions for the file formats in which I store music (*.ogg, *.flac, *.shn, and *.mp3) to the Ignored Files tab's "Ignored File Patterns" list, but this would prevent me from locating any music files that are in any other directories (such as on a specific system), which I personally don't want to do.

As you can see, the configuration options provided by the Tracker Preferences tool give you a lot of control over Tracker's performance and behavior. All in all, I find Tracker to be the best of the desktop search applications. However, one of the reasons for this is that Tracker is nicely complemented by other search mechanisms that are provided as part of the GNOME desktop in the GNOME Deskbar applet, which is described in the next section.

Tip

In addition to the Tracker-related applications discussed in this section, the `tracker-utils` package provides some other useful utilities, such as the `tracker-stats` and `tracker-status` utilities that provide information about the searches that Tracker has performed, how Tracker is performing in general, and so on. ∎

Using the GNOME Deskbar Applet

Deskbar applet, how do I love thee? Let me count the ways. I love thee when I forget the name of the file in which I've stored the great American novel or my mother's recipe for dilly beans, or when I need to look up a word in a dictionary or thesaurus, or when I want to search the Web. And most of all, I love thee when I don't want to have to start specific applications for each of these different, but related, tasks.

The Deskbar applet is a one-stop shopping applet for any search task that I can think of, including searching for non-file-related data such as specific applications and windows. The Deskbar applet even includes some useful hooks for performing common system tasks, such as logging out, suspending your system, and even shutting it down.

The Deskbar applet is not installed by default on an Ubuntu system, but can easily be installed by installing the `deskbar-applet` package using your favorite package management tool. If you want to use the Deskbar applet with Tracker (and who wouldn't?), you must also install the `libdeskbar-tracker` package.

Once installed and added to the GNOME panel, the Deskbar applet is accessed by clicking on its "magnifying glass and more" icon. Figure 5-35 shows the Deskbar applet dialog, which displays after clicking on this icon. (This looks slightly different on different Ubuntu releases, but the functionality is the same.)

FIGURE 5-35

The initial Deskbar applet dialog

Figure 5-36 shows the default results of a search for the word *Ubuntu* on one of my systems. As you can see from the position of the elevator button in the scrollbar at the right of this dialog, these results are only the tip of the iceberg—there are many more possible results.

Search results in the default configuration of the Deskbar applet are organized into various sections, including Actions (programs that you can execute whose name matches your search term), Documents that match your search term, Files with unrecognizable extensions, or MIME types whose path or filenames match your search terms, and so on.

A search for *Ubuntu* in the Deskbar applet

Simply pressing Return will execute the first item in the list, or you can click on a specific result to perform the associated action, whether it's opening a file or performing a Web search for your search terms. Empty sections are not displayed — for example, if no video file matches your search terms, there won't be a Videos section. However, as you can see, there's a whole lotta searching going on, and all of it available through this single applet. Personally, that's too much data for me — I prefer to reduce the overwhelming number of possible locations that are offered in response to a Deskbar applet search by configuring it to search only some of my favorites. To configure the locations that the Deskbar applet will query (or offer as additional query locations), right-click on its icon in the panel and select the Preferences menu option to display the "Deskbar Preferences configuration" dialog shown in Figure 5-37.

Configuring search locations for the Deskbar applet

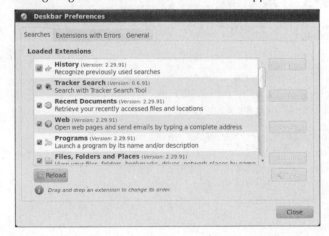

The Search tab in this dialog enables you to configure both the locations that will be queried for your search terms and the order in which those locations will be queried. Search options that are enabled are preceded by a check mark, and they are searched in the order that they appear. To enable or disable a search option, click on the checkbox. You can also change the order in which search options appear by selecting the name of a search option and dragging or dropping it to a new position in the list, or by using the Top/Up/Down/Bottom buttons to change its position.

Everyone's idea of what and where to search are different, but I typically reconfigure the Deskbar applet to use the following search options, in the following order:

- **Tracker Search:** I'm often looking for data in a file that is somewhere on my system, so putting this option first is a good complement to my Web search options.

- **Dictionary:** Believe it or not, I am occasionally at a loss for words (or at least the right one), so it's useful to be able to look up words in an online dictionary.

- **Google Search:** Submit my search terms to the Google search engine. I put this third because it offers more possible actions than the first two.

- **History:** Makes it easy to reuse previous searches, in case I want to pursue some subject in more detail, find a specific file again, and so on

As you can see, the Deskbar applet is a great complement to the Tracker family of desktop search applications. It's extremely convenient to be able to initiate a search for something from a single location, and it's sufficiently configurable to enable you to tailor your search preferences to the locations and types of searches that you typically want to perform.

Using a Window Manager

The first section of this chapter, "What's a Desktop? Graphical Environments for Linux," discussed the differences between window managers and desktops, and hinted at the fact that more X Window System window managers are available than you could shake a stick at. Popular window managers include AfterStep, Blackbox, Compiz, Enlightenment, Fluxbox, FVWM, IceWM, KWin, Metacity, twm, VTWM, and Window Maker, but there are many, many more.

After you experiment with GNOME for a while, you may be curious about what these window managers look like and how they work. Half the fun of a flexible computing environment such as Linux and the X11 Window system is experimenting with new software "because it's there." You might be especially interested in window managers if you are running Ubuntu on a slow system or a system with a limited amount of memory, such as many older laptops, because window managers require far less memory and other system resources than complete desktop environments like GNOME do.

As you might hope, it is extremely easy to temporarily switch between using GNOME and a specific window manager. First, you have to install one or more window managers using any of the software update tools that are also discussed in Chapter 19. After installing window managers and logging out, you can start any installed window manager by selecting the name of the user that you want to log in as to display the session configuration options at the bottom of the login screen. Click the down-arrow to the right of the Sessions option to see the list of available session managers. Figure 5-38 shows a sample Sessions menu on an Ubuntu system where a few window managers (FVWM, IceWM, and Fluxbox) have been installed.

FIGURE 5-38

The GNOME login screen's Sessions menu

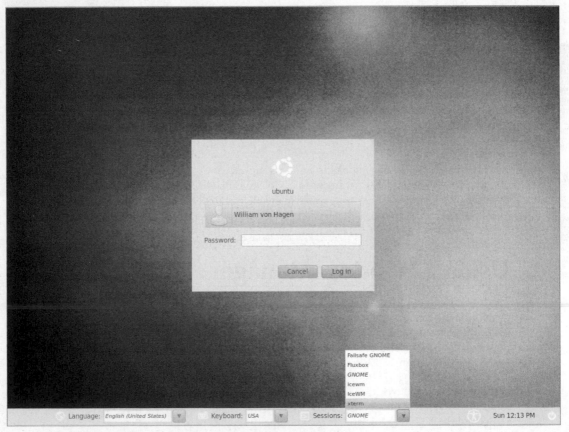

Select the window manager that you want to start, enter your password in the login dialog, and press Return or click Log in. As an example, selecting "IceWM" would start the IceWM window maanager, as shown in Figure 5-39.

FIGURE 5-39

The IceWM window manager on an Ubuntu system

 You can permanently customize the window manager that is started when you log in by using the System ⇨ Administration ⇨ Login Screen menu command. After selecting this menu item, clicking Unlock to make changes, and entering your password, you can select the window manager that you want to start from the Select drop-down list at the bottom of the dialog shown in Figure 5-40.

You can also change the window manager that your Ubuntu system starts by using a text editor to create a file called .xsession in your home directory, which contains a line like the following:

```
exec /usr/bin/icewm
```

FIGURE 5-40

Permanently changing Login Screen preferences

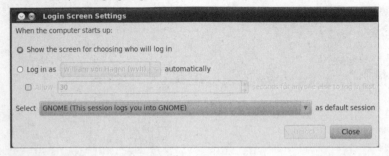

Make the file executable (`chmod 755 ~/.xsession`), and the next time that you log in on your system, the system will automatically start the IceWM window manager (in this example) instead of the GNOME desktop. For compatibility with other ways of starting the X Window System, you should also create a symbolic link to this file called `.xinitrc`, also in your home directory. You would do this with a command like the following:

```
ln -s ~/.xsession ~/.xinitrc
```

Experimenting with different window managers is fun because each represents someone's idea of how you "should" interact with a graphical system, start applications, and so on. I've been using the X Window System since version 10, and thus have burned more time than I could ever calculate in experimenting with, configuring, and customizing many of the window managers that have been written in the last 20+ years. But it's been fun.

Tip

On low-memory, low-resource systems such as older laptops, you may want to start Linux without a graphical interface — if you do this, you can always start the X Window System using a command such as `startx` or `xinit`, which will also pick up the X11 startup file and symbolic link that you just created, and will therefore start your window manager for you. ∎

The previous instructions changed whether your Ubuntu system runs GNOME or a window manager. However, as mentioned earlier, all Linux desktop systems run a window manager under the covers. By default, GNOME on Ubuntu runs Compiz, KDE runs KWin, and so on. If you still want to run GNOME but are interested in changing the window manager that it runs underneath, you must run another window manager that conforms to the *Inter-Client Communication*

Conventions Manual (ICCCM) 2.0 standard (`http://en.wikipedia.org/wiki/ICCCM`) published by the X Consortium, and also to the EWMH (Extended Window Manager Hints) guidelines. The former is an official specification for how X Window System clients running on the same server should interact, while the latter is an unofficial set of extensions to ICCCM 2.0 that were defined by the FreeDesktop.org folks to specify additional window manager, window, and utility interaction mechanisms. Window managers that conform to these specifications are often simply referred to as *GNOME-compliant*. Some GNOME-compliant window managers are After Step, Compiz, Enlightenment, Fvwm2, IceWM, Metacity, and Window Maker. Figure 5-41 shows GNOME using the IceWM window manager.

GNOME uses a variety of ways to change the window manager, some more complex than others. The simplest, which is something of a hack, is to modify your ~/.xsession or ~/.gnomerc file so that it first starts the window manager that you want to use, and then starts GNOME. The following is a sample ~/.xsession or ~/.gnomerc file that starts the IceWM window manager, and then starts GNOME:

```
/usr/bin/icewm&
exec gnome-session
```

This is a hack because it relies on the fact that only one window manager can be active at a time. By starting IceWM before starting GNOME, the Compiz window manager cannot start, and thus GNOME continues to run using IceWM.

You should actually be able to change your window manager by simply putting a line like the following in your ~/.gnomerc file:

```
export WINDOW_MANAGER=/usr/bin/icewm
```

Unfortunately, this doesn't work for me. If you search the Web, you'll find many other suggestions, such as modifying your gconf (GNOME configuration) database (using database entries that are explicitly unsupported in the latest GNOME releases), modifying GNOME window manager startup scripts (such as gnome-wm), modifying your session control file to reference the GNOME window manager scripts, and many combinations of these. In general, I'm a fan of things that "just work," so I prefer my "solution."

FIGURE 5-41

GNOME running with the IceWM window manager

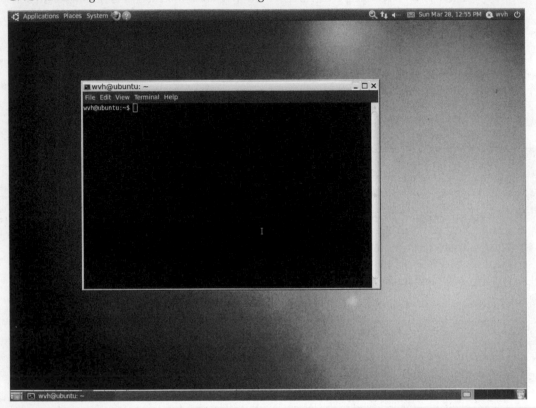

Summary

This chapter introduced the graphical user interfaces used on Linux systems, focusing on the GNOME desktop that is the default user interface provided on desktop Ubuntu Linux systems. After discussing the general organization of the GNOME desktop, the majority of the chapter focused on explaining how to customize and extend the default configuration of the GNOME desktop as installed on your Ubuntu system. Personalizing your computer system's desktop is one of the first steps to making it truly yours. GNOME provides the same types of customization and supports the same level of personalization as provided by other operating systems, such as Microsoft Windows or Mac OS X — it just doesn't cost as much. If you are using GNOME and are interested in customizing the Compiz window manager that is used by GNOME on Ubuntu desktop systems, see Chapter 6.

If you're interested in learning about underlying Linux commands and using the Linux command line, Chapter 11 complements the exploration of the graphical power of GNOME, Compiz, and the X Window System in general by exploring the power of the Linux command line. The fact that many Linux commands are command-line-oriented is one of the reasons that many hard-core Microsoft Windows users disparage Linux, which is just plain silly, because Linux gives you both a powerful graphical interface *and* a powerful command-line interface. Newer versions of Windows, such as Vista and Windows 7, have even added a *power shell* to enable Windows users to more easily perform various tasks from the command line. You don't have to look any further than Mac OS X, with its UNIX underpinnings and Terminal window, to see just how empowering the marriage of a great GUI and a powerful set of command-line tools can be in a commercial product. Ubuntu gives you this same power, if not more, but at no cost.

Using the Compiz Window Manager

IN THIS CHAPTER

What is compositing?

Compiz history

Enabling special effects

Dock software for Compiz

Among the most exciting recent developments in Linux graphics has been the advent of better-performing, open source graphics subsystems for the accelerated two-dimensional (2D) and three-dimensional (3D) graphics now provided by most modern graphics cards. Traditionally, only the specific X Window System graphics drivers that were delivered with more powerful video cards enabled users to take advantage of the high-end capabilities of these cards, and many graphics vendors didn't provide Linux drivers. Even when they did, the drivers themselves were typically precompiled and proprietary, and their source code was not freely available.

Today, however, life is better for users of more powerful graphics hardware under Linux. The use and popularization of standards such as OpenGL make it possible for open source systems to benefit from the capabilities of modern graphics cards, even with proprietary drivers. OpenGL (Open Graphics Library) is a standard that defines a cross-language, cross-platform API for writing graphical applications, providing hundreds of function calls in a standard API that can be used to draw complex 2D and 3D graphics. With the introduction of drivers that adhere to this standard, even proprietary video drivers that are available only in a binary format can be accessed and used from open source graphics applications and servers. Even better, the trend toward open source graphics drivers is accelerating, with open source drivers either being provided directly from graphics hardware vendors or developed by the open source community.

This chapter discusses the Compiz compositing window manager that has been installed by default on Ubuntu systems beginning with Ubuntu 7.10. After providing background information on exactly what *compositing* means and how compositing window managers work, this chapter explains how to configure and customize Compiz Fusion to provide sexy, high-performance graphics on your Ubuntu system.

189

What Is Compositing? Why All the Fuss?

Most current graphics cards provide at least 128 MB of onboard video RAM, while most of the video controllers integrated into today's motherboards enable you to allocate at least a similar amount of system memory to the graphics controller. Having a significant amount of memory available enables the video cards themselves to do substantial amounts of onboard graphics processing. Not only do today's video cards provide high-performance, built-in graphics processors, but offloading graphics calculations from the CPU and window manager to the video card improves overall system performance and responsiveness.

As discussed in Chapter 5, "Using the GNOME Desktop," Linux systems use the X Window System (also known as *X11*, or simply *X*) to provide the graphical framework that underlies most Linux desktop environments and window managers. A window manager handles creating, moving, and managing windows shown on high-resolution monitors that are managed by an X Window server, and they can be used either stand-alone or as components of a desktop environment that provides higher-level capabilities such as drag-and-drop. The X Window System uses high resolution monitors as a bitmapped display, which means that every bit (pixel) on the screen is actually mapped to a memory location. This enables fast graphics operations to be done by manipulating memory, and the result of that manipulation is immediately displayed on your monitor.

The term *compositing* refers to the combination of graphical or visual elements from separate sources into single images. On Linux systems, a compositing manager is an X Window System client that re-directs windows and other parts of the bitmapped display to video memory, tracks changes to that off-screen memory, and handles merging the updated images into the system's bitmapped display when changes occur and the screen has to be redrawn. An X Window System compositing window manager is therefore a unified window manager and compositing system that performs conventional window management functions while integrating and displaying high-quality, high-performance graphics being created and manipulated in your system's video memory, including special effects such as transparency and translucency. Traditional window managers (discussed in the "Using a Window Manager" section at the end of Chapter 5) are typically referred to as tiling or stacking window managers — tiling window managers display windows side-by-side with no overlap, while stacking window managers display windows on top of or overlapping one another, with no transparency. Compositing adds transparency and translucency to the standard stacking window manager model by taking advantage of modern graphics hardware.

Tip

Although the terms *transparency* and *translucency* are often used interchangeably, they actually have subtly different meanings for truly hardcore graphics fans. A *transparent* physical material shows objects that are behind it and doesn't reflect light off its surface. A *translucent* physical material shows objects that are behind it, but those objects are partially obscured because the translucent material reflects some of the light that hits it. See the OpenGL FAQ (www.opengl.org/resources/faq/technical/transparency.htm) for a more verbose explanation. ■

Modern compositing window managers like Compiz use separate applications to handle window decorations (window borders, buttons, frames, etc.), while the window manager focuses on managing window placement, movement, and special effects. This provides a flexible environment that follows the traditional UNIX philosophy of writing smaller applications that do one thing, do it well, and can work together to perform complex tasks.

Compiz, which is all the rage in Linux circles nowadays, provides a nice blend of making the best possible use of high-performance graphics hardware, providing attractive window effects for fans of eye candy and a flexible window management environment that is easily modified and extended.

Compiz History: Compiz, Emerald, Beryl, and Friends

This section discusses the history of compositing window managers on Linux and the window managers that led to Compiz and Compiz Fusion today. Not everyone wants a history lesson, so if you're not interested, feel free to skip ahead. However, this section will provide a handy reference after you've heard terms such as *Beryl*, *Emerald*, *Compiz*, and *Compiz Fusion* over and over and wonder what they mean.

Like almost all graphics components on Linux systems, compositing window managers depend on the capabilities of the underlying X Window System. To provide high-performance special effects, compositing window managers require especially tight integration between graphics drivers and the window manager. Compiz is not the first compositing window manager — compositing has been supported for a while in window managers such as Metacity, the window manager that was traditionally associated with GNOME 2.2 (and used on Ubuntu releases prior to 7.10), and Xfvwm, the window manager used by the Xfce desktop (`http://xfce.org`).

Tip

If you find that Compiz is too resource-intensive for your tastes, or if you simply want to run another window manager, you may want to experiment with running the Xcompmgr composition manager with that window manager. Xcompmgr is designed to provide the graphical eye candy associated with compositing for any X window manager. To experiment with this tool, install the `xcompmgr` package, switch to your favorite window manager, and then start Xcompmgr. If you like it, you can add it to your standard startup applications after customizing your system to start a window manager other than Compiz, as explained in the section of Chapter 5 entitled "Using a Window Manager." ∎

Regardless of the fact that Metacity, Xfvwm, and some lesser-known window managers pioneered built-in support for compositing, Compiz was the first widely available window manager that was designed from the ground up to support compositing via OpenGL. The efficient support of OpenGL requests between an X Window server is handled using one of two technologies, depending on the X Window System server in use:

- X Window servers such as Xgl require extremely tight communication between the X Window server and the graphics hardware, providing impressive performance on a more limited range of graphics cards from vendors such as ATI, Intel, and NVIDIA.

- X servers such as the standard X.Org server (as of release 7.1) use a more device-independent mechanism known as *AIGLX* (Accelerated Indirect GLX) that enables them to work with a wider range of graphics hardware.

Ubuntu systems use the standard X.Org window manager and thus use the AIGLX approach.

Tip

I've found that some systems with ATI or NVIDIA graphics chips work better with the Xgl server than with the standard X.Org server. This is especially true for laptop computers, which often use ATI or NVIDIA chips that require proprietary or highly specialized drivers. If you have problems getting Compiz working with the standard X server on a system with ATI or NVIDIA chips, it's worth trying the Xgl server. ∎

Compiz was designed to provide a flexible window management framework to which plug-ins could easily be added to provide additional capabilities and effects without the need to reinstall the entire window manager. Compiz and Xgl were both originally developed at Novell, and thus Compiz originally required Xgl. Thanks to AIGLX and lots of hard work, Compiz now also works with the standard X.Org server, and the AIGLX development effort has been merged directly into X.Org.

One of the reasons behind the foundation of the AIGLX effort was that some people felt that too much of the development of Xgl was local to Novell and didn't invite enough community discussion. Similarly, the Beryl project emerged as a fork of Compiz when people felt that the development of Compiz was moving too slowly. Beryl was previously known as the *Quinnstorm* version of Compiz, but as the codebases diverged, it seemed more reasonable to maintain two separate projects.

As mentioned in the previous section, one of the core ideas of Compiz is to use separate applications to handle window decorations. Compiz provides the `gtk-window-decorator` to customize window decorations in the GNOME environment, which can even use standard Metacity themes). Beryl's primary window decorator is Emerald, although window decorators named *Heliodor* and *Aquamarine* were available at one time.

Beryl racked up a tremendous set of plug-ins and whizzy features, while Compiz moved to AIGLX and became more open. Duplication of effort is rarely a good thing, and in 2007, the people working on the Beryl project merged with the folks who were developing Compiz plug-ins, resulting in the Compiz Fusion project. The goal of this project is to improve the usability and functionality of Compiz by porting most of the whizzy things that were done for Beryl to Compiz, and to continue to develop additional libraries, plug-ins, and tools that make Compiz both a fun and functional graphical environment. The Compiz Fusion folks have even ported Emerald to work with Compiz, to ensure that you will always have an impressive (and sometimes bewildering) smorgasbord of graphical choices. Today's Compiz comes with a core set of plug-ins, but the plug-ins and tools provided by Compiz Fusion make the whole far greater than the sum of its parts.

Tip

If you are having problems running Compiz or its performance seems sluggish, consult the Compiz Fusion web site (`http://wiki.compiz-fusion.org/Troubleshooting`) for good information on identifying and resolving such problems. ■

Enabling Special Effects in Compiz

As mentioned in the previous section, Compiz provides a flexible and easily extended compositing window management environment. Much of the functionality that people lump together as Compiz is actually provided by plug-ins that work within the framework provided by Compiz. Similarly, Compiz enables you to run separate window decorator applications to provide more granular control over such decorations, as well as over window controls and themes.

Note

When switching to Compiz, you may find some of the terminology confusing, particularly *workspace*, *virtual desktops*, and *viewports*. A *workspace* is a shared area that one or more applications can access — in the case of a window manager, think of it as a distinct graphical region upon which windows can be displayed. Workspaces are independent of one another and have their own graphical coordinate systems. A *viewport* is a view of a graphical region on the screen. Traditionally, GNOME and its window managers used multiple workspaces to support virtual desktops; each virtual desktop was its own workspace. In Compiz, each *virtual desktop* is a viewport into a shared workspace, and the use of a viewport improves performance and simplifies various graphical operations. For example, when you are using workspaces, each window should exist within only a single workspace. When you are using viewports, windows can be visible in multiple viewports, which provides for smoother graphics transitions from one virtual desktop to another and also simplifies implementing edge resistance, fast virtual desktop rotation and switching, and so on. ■

Tip

If you believe that your system should be able to run Compiz but attempting to enable Normal or Extra visual effects results in a dialog that says that your system does not support compositing, you can try overriding Compiz's internal capabilities checks by adding the line `SKIP_CHECKS=yes` to the file `~/.config/compiz/compiz-manager`. Log out, log back in, and try enabling visual effects again. This has worked for me on various laptops that use older ATI and NVIDIA graphics chips. ■

Using the Appearance Preferences Application

By default, when Compiz is installed, a basic set of plug-ins is activated. The most basic configuration utility for controlling the special effects associated with Compiz is the Appearance Preferences application, which you can start by selecting "Appearance" from the Preferences menu. After starting this application, select the Visual Effects tab, which displays the configuration options shown in Figure 6-1.

FIGURE 6-1

Basic effects management via Appearance Preferences

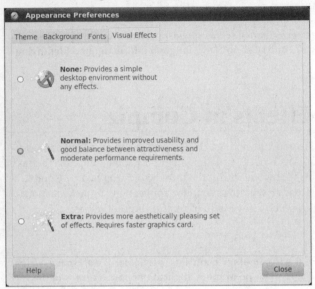

The following are the three basic Appearance Preferences settings:

- **None:** Selecting this option disables any special effects associated with Compiz and Compiz Fusion plug-ins, providing a Compiz desktop experience that is as near as possible to the Metacity desktop experience provided on Ubuntu releases prior to version 7.10.

Tip

As noted, selecting "None" will disable Compiz and Compiz Fusion plug-ins. You will not be able to enable or use these plug-ins, even if you manually enable them using one of the Compiz configuration utilities discussed in the next section. If you are having difficulty getting any Compiz or Compiz Fusion plug-ins to work correctly, first check that you have not accidentally disabled plug-ins by selecting this Appearance Preferences option. ■

- **Normal:** Selecting this option, which is the default setting if compositing could be enabled during installation, activates a small but useful set of Compiz and Compiz Fusion plug-ins. If your system could not enable compositing during installation (which depends on your video hardware), selecting this option may require that your system search for new video drivers. Once this option is active, several Compiz visual effects are automatically enabled. In my opinion, the most interesting of these are the following:
  - **Animations:** Provides graphical effects when performing window operations such as minimizing and maximizing applications, starting and terminating applications, and so on

- **Desktop Wall:** Provides a smooth virtual desktop/viewport-switching application
- **Expo:** Displays reduced-size images of all of your windows on the screen so that you can quickly select a specific window
- **Move Window:** Provides mouse and keyboard shortcuts for moving windows, which can be handy if the title bar is not easily selectable
- **Resize Info:** Provides a shaded preview when resizing windows and displays numeric information about the current size of the new window as you move the mouse
- **Snapping Windows:** Enables you to move a window to other desktops by dragging a window to the edge of the screen, and lets you configure how quickly this happens to prevent you from moving windows to other desktops accidentally
- **Static Application Switcher:** Provides a more attractive Alt+Tab interface (for switching between open applications), advanced image loading, and text-rendering effects
- **Window Decorations:** Additional window decoration features such as shadowing (required for some window decorators, such as Emerald)

The Normal setting also enables several other plug-ins, most of which perform internal functions or are not bound to specific keys by default.

- **Extra:** Selecting this option activates the plug-ins associated with the Normal Appearance Preferences settings and activates other plug-ins, the most interesting of which are the following:
  - **Shift Switcher:** An enhanced version of the Application Switcher, this plug-in displays available windows as minimized, angled previews that you can switch between using the Super+Tab key sequence rather than the traditional Alt+Tab sequence.
  - **Wobbly Windows:** One of the best-known Compiz effects, this plug-in causes the window borders to jiggle as you move a window, making it look as if your window is made out of JELL-O as it's being moved (fun!).

Tip

Most Compiz plug-ins are associated with specific actions, key combinations (known as keyboard shortcuts), and/or mouse movements. While these are configurable, most of the default key combinations require the use of the Super key on your keyboard, which is usually the key with the Windows or other graphical logo that is positioned between the Ctrl and Alt keys on most newer keyboards. If your current keyboard doesn't provide this key, I suggest getting a new keyboard that does (unless, of course, you are using an older laptop). You can always change the keys used to perform various actions (known as "remapping" those keys), but investing in a new keyboard is generally preferable to investing the amount of time it would take you to change everything. ■

As you can see, the default sets of Compiz and Compiz Fusion plug-ins provided by the Normal and Extra Appearance Preferences sets provide a good deal of functionality in a graphically attractive fashion. However, Compiz and Compiz Fusion provide many other plug-ins, some of which are alternatives to the ones that are already provided by the Normal and Extra configurations, and others that provide additional capabilities. The list of Compiz and Compiz Fusion plug-ins is always expanding, so it is impossible to give you a complete list here. The sidebar "These Are a Few of My Favorite Things," later in this chapter, lists some other plug-ins that I find useful and that I think you might also find useful and enjoyable. For a complete listing of available Compiz and Compiz Fusion plug-ins and information on their configuration, see `http://wiki.compiz-fusion.org/Plugins`.

Detailed Compiz Configuration

The configuration mechanisms discussed in the next two sections enable you to activate, customize, and deactivate Compiz and Compiz Fusion plug-ins, giving you access to the complete list of plug-ins that are currently installed on your system and all of their configuration settings.

On Ubuntu systems, you can configure Compiz, the Compiz plug-ins, and the Compiz Fusion plug-ins by using the standard GNOME configuration utilities or by using the CompizConfig Settings Manager. Other Compiz configuration utilities are also available, but GConf and CompizConfig are the two biggies. Of these two configuration mechanisms, I strongly recommend installing and using the CompizConfig Settings Manager, but the standard GNOME utilities will work just as well if you're a fan of the command line or already intimately familiar with the graphical GNOME Configuration Editor. However, I'll discuss both approaches to help you make your decision.

Configuring Compiz Using GNOME Configuration Tools

On Ubuntu systems, Compiz, the Compiz plug-ins, and the Compiz Fusion plug-ins can be configured using the standard GNOME configuration utilities without requiring that you install any special tools. GNOME systems provide two primary configuration utilities for manipulating the GConf (GNOME Configuration Editor) repository: `gconftool-2`, a command-line utility, and `gconf-editor`, a graphical application. You should run these utilities as yourself, without using `sudo`, because they manipulate GNOME configuration information stored in each user's personal GConf repository. If you ran these utilities via `sudo`, you'd edit the GConf repository for the root user.

Tip

The CompizConfig Settings Manager, discussed in the next section, is a much easier tool for configuring Compiz. This section is here for command-line fans and for completeness' sake. Most people — myself included — always use the CompizConfig Settings Manager. ■

Information in the GConf repository is stored as key/value pairs that are organized into various hierarchical sections, much like the information in the Microsoft Windows Registry. Information about Compiz is stored in the `/apps/compiz` hierarchy. Information about specific plug-ins is hierarchically organized under `/apps/compiz/plugins` and the name of each plug-in.

`gconftool-2` is a command-line line application that enables you to examine all or a portion of the GConf registry and set specific values by passing repository keys and new values on the command line. For example, the following command examines the settings for the Compiz Wobbly Windows plug-in:

```
$ gconftool-2 -R /apps/compiz/plugins/wobbly
/apps/compiz/plugins/wobbly:
 /apps/compiz/plugins/wobbly/allscreens:
  /apps/compiz/plugins/wobbly/allscreens/options:
  shiver = false
  snap_key = <Shift>
  snap_inverted = false
/apps/compiz/plugins/wobbly/screen0:
 /apps/compiz/plugins/wobbly/screen0/options:
  spring_k = 8
  map_effect = 0
  map_window_match = Splash | DropdownMenu | PopupMenu | \
      Tooltip | Notification | Combo | Dnd | Unknown
  focus_window_match =
  friction = 3
  focus_effect = 0
  maximize_effect = true
  grab_window_match =
  min_grid_size = 8
  grid_resolution = 8
  move_window_match = Toolbar | Menu | Utility | Dialog | \
      Normal | Unknown
```

The -R option tells gconftool-2 to recursively retrieve hierarchical settings below the specified repository key. Information about whether a given plug-in is enabled is stored in the /apps/compiz/general/allscreens/options/active_plugins repository entry, as shown in this example:

```
$ gconftool-2 -g /apps/compiz/general/allscreens/options/active_plugins
[svg,imgjpeg,text,place,png,neg,workarounds,dbus,video,regex,\
resize,core,vpswitch,move,resizeinfo,shift,extrawm,decoration,\
wall,animation,expo,ezoom,switcher,fade,scale,scaleaddon,scalefilter]
```

Note

As with all examples of command-line utilities in this book, the \ character is used at the end of text lines that are too long to be correctly displayed in the running text of this book. You would not see this character in actual output, and you should not use this character, the subsequent newline, or any spaces at the beginning of the next line when actually typing commands, as shown in the examples. ∎

The -g option retrieves the value of the specified repository key. The output from this command shows that the Wobbly Windows plug-in is not currently enabled.

To activate the Wobbly Windows plug-in from the command line, you would use the -s option, which lets you set the specified repository key to a specified value. The -s option must be used with the --type option to identify the type of the value that you are setting. Valid options for the

--type option are bool (Boolean), float (floating point numeric value), int (integer), list (a list of values of types bool, float, int, or string), pair (two distinct values), or string (a string of text). Identifying the type of value being set is required so that gconftool-2 can determine, for example, whether the value true is the string *true* or a Boolean value.

The command to set the active_plugins repository key to a value that activates the Wobbly Windows plug-in is something like the following:

```
$ gconftool-2 -s /apps/compiz/general/allscreens/options/active_plugins \
'[svg,imgjpeg,text,place,png,neg,workarounds,dbus,video,regex,resize,\
 core,vpswitch,move,resizeinfo,shift,extrawm,decoration,wall,animation,\
 expo,ezoom,switcher,fade,scale,scaleaddon,scalefilter,wobbly]' \
 --type list --list-type string
```

You must begin and end lists with the characters *[* and *]* in order to delimit the lists. Once you execute this command, reexamining the value of the active_plugins key shows that the Wobbly Windows plug-in is now in the list of active plug-ins:

```
$ gconftool-2 -g /apps/compiz/general/allscreens/options/active_plugins
[svg,imgjpeg,text,place,png,neg,workarounds,dbus,video,regex,resize,\
 core,vpswitch,move,resizeinfo,shift,extrawm,decoration,wall,animation,\
 expo,ezoom,switcher,fade,scale,scaleaddon,scalefilter,wobbly]
```

You can also confirm that this plug-in is enabled by using your mouse to grab the title bar of any window and move that window. There's always room for JELL-O!

gconftool-2 can be very useful for quickly querying and manipulating GConf settings from the command line. However, gconftool-2 is probably not the right tool for setting the "right" GConf keys, identifying possible values, and iterating through multiple settings and values until you get the effect that you're looking for. I'm a big fan of command-line tools, but I'm no purist — in most cases, graphical tools are more usable than command-line tools, especially when you need to perform a number of change and test cycles when experimenting with configuration values.

GNOME's graphical tool for examining and editing the GConf repository, gconf-editor, is installed by default on GNOME-based Ubuntu systems. You can start the gconf-editor tool from any command-line environment. As with gconftool-2, you want to start gconf-editor as yourself, not via sudo, so that you are editing only the contents of your personal GNOME repository.

Figure 6-2 shows gconf-editor when it's first started. To locate a specific repository key, click the Edit ➪ Find command to display the dialog shown in Figure 6-3.

FIGURE 6-2

The graphical GNOME configuration editor

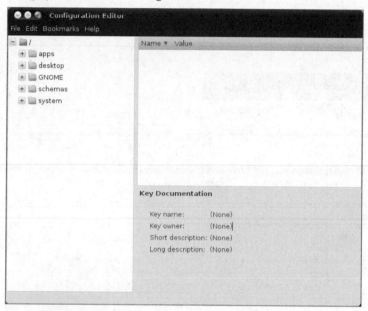

FIGURE 6-3

Searching for a repository key

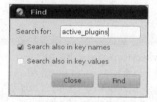

Enter the name of the key that you want to search for (active_plugins in the figure), and select the "Search also in key names" option to expand the types and places that are being searched for the specified key. By default, `gconf-editor` looks for only the search string you specify in key values. In this case, you want to search key names because the list of active plug-ins is stored as the value of the `/apps/compiz/general/allscreens/options/active_plugins`. After you click Find, you'll see a screen like the one in Figure 6-4, in which the matching keys are listed in the bottom pane. Select the `/apps/compiz/general/allscreens/options/active_plugins` key to display the view shown in Figure 6-4.

FIGURE 6-4

Repository matches for a search

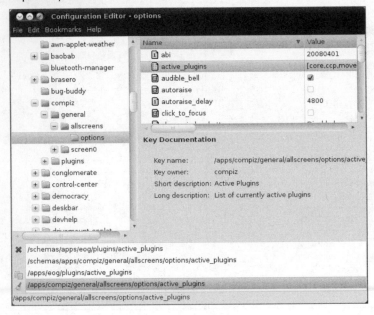

To edit an existing key, right-click on the name of that key, and select "Edit key" from the pop-up menu. You'll see the dialog shown in Figure 6-5.

As you can see from Figure 6-5 (and from the examples earlier in this section), the value of the `/apps/compiz/general/allscreens/options/active_plugins` key is a list of plug-in names. If the Wobbly Windows plug-in is not present in this list (which it is not by default, but you may have added it earlier in this section if you're following along), right-click in the key list pane and select "Edit Key" from the pop-up menu. Click Add to display the "Add New List Entry" dialog shown in Figure 6-6.

FIGURE 6-5

Editing a key value

FIGURE 6-6

Adding a new entry to a key value list

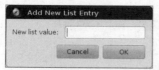

Enter **wobbly** as the new list value and click OK. The Wobbly Windows plug-in will be active at this point. You can then select File ⇨ Quit to close the `gconf-editor` application.

Both the `gconftool-2` and `gconf-editor` tools provide a generic interface to the GNOME configuration registry. While these tools provide a completely functional mechanism for examining, adding, and modifying repository key values, they simply see the repository as a hierarchical set of key/value pairs and thus see every configuration task as being essentially equivalent.

Unlike these standard GNOME registry configuration tools, the tool discussed in the next section was designed for manipulating Compiz and Compiz Fusion plug-ins, and can therefore make use of plug-in–specific information to provide an easier-to-use, smarter plug-in configuration tool.

Installing and Using CompizConfig Settings Manager

The CompizConfig Settings Manager, sometimes referred to as *CCSM* by fans of abbreviations, is a Compiz configuration utility created by the Compiz Fusion project (`http://wiki`
`.compiz-fusion.org/CCSM`). Why this configuration utility isn't installed by default with Compiz on Ubuntu systems is a mystery to me, because it provides an excellent interface that simplifies activating, configuring, and deactivating both Compiz and Compiz Fusion plug-ins. CompizConfig was designed solely for the purpose of configuring Compiz plug-ins. It is able to make use of some information about the internals of Compiz plug-ins and the capabilities that they provide and can therefore identify both dependencies and potential conflicts between plug-ins.

You can install CompizConfig by using your favorite package management tool (described in Chapter 19, "Adding, Removing, and Updating Software") to install the `compizconfig-settings-manager` package. This package is located in the Universe repository, so that repository must be enabled in your `/etc/apt/sources.list` file before you can install the package. (By default, the Universe repository is enabled in this file, but you may have disabled it for some reason.) Once you've installed the CompizConfig package, you can start the CompizConfig Settings Manager by selecting Preferences ➪ Advanced Desktop Effects Settings. Figure 6-7 shows the CompizConfig Settings Manager when you first start it.

FIGURE 6-7

The CompizConfig Settings Manager

Most configuration utilities make it incredibly easy for you to iteratively change too many options, to the point where you don't know how to restore things to their original values (or at least know what those original values were). The CompizConfig interface provides a nice, consistent solution to this problem by providing a small icon that looks like a whisk broom to the right of each individual configuration setting. Clicking this icon at any time restores the associated configuration option to its original, default value.

To enable any plug-in but use its default configuration, click the checkbox to the left of the icon and name for that plug-in, as shown in Figure 6-7. To configure any Compiz or Compiz Fusion plug-in, click on the name or icon of that plug-in. This displays the configuration panel for that plug-in, an example of which is shown in Figure 6-8. You can also enable or disable the plug-in after configuring it by selecting or deselecting the checkbox below the "Use This Plugin" label in the left-hand pane of a configuration panel such as the one shown in Figure 6-8. You can return to the top-level CompizConfig panel by clicking the Back button shown in the lower-left corner.

FIGURE 6-8

Configuring a specific plug-in in CompizConfig

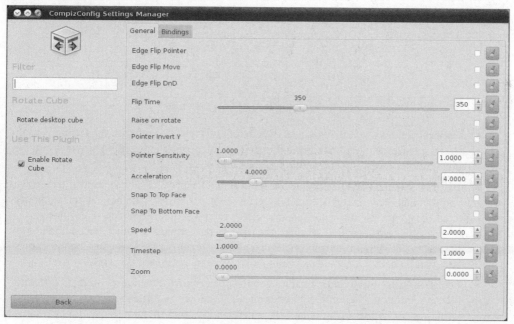

The "General Options" group at the top of the CompizConfig screen (refer to Figure 6-7) enables you to configure options for Compiz itself, and doing so may affect multiple (or all) plug-ins. The Commands, GNOME Compatibility, and KDE Compatibility groups enable you to define basic key/command mappings and fine-tune Compiz's emulation of the GNOME and KDE desktops. These are less commonly used, so I'll focus on the General Options group in this section.

After selecting the General Options group, five tabs display, as shown in Figure 6-9.

Setting "General Options" in CompizConfig

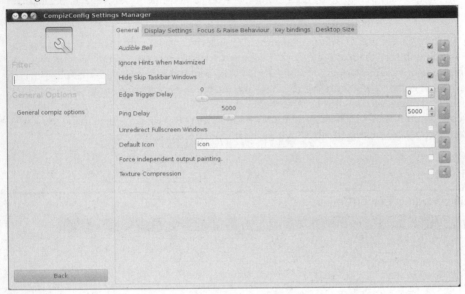

Each of these tabs contains multiple configuration options, such as:

- **General:** Enables you to configure the cursor and its size, configure the terminal application for use with command-line functions, control whether Compiz provides audible notification of warning and error messages, and so on

- **Display Settings:** Enables you to configure general aspects of how Compiz interacts with your display: how finely the screen displays surface textures, whether Compiz attempts to automatically identify your screen's refresh rate, whether the screen or a window dims as it is transformed (Lighting), the screen's refresh rate, whether screen updates are limited to taking place during vertical blanking, the output devices that Compiz knows about and whether it should attempt to identify them automatically, and so on

- **Focus & Raise Behaviour:** Enables you to specify how your mouse interacts with and selects windows: whether you have to click a window to set the focus to it, whether windows rise to the top automatically when you position the mouse over them (and how long it takes for this to happen), whether clicking anywhere in a window brings that window to the top, and which windows will not automatically steal the focus when they appear. (The last of these requires that the Regex Matching plug-in be enabled, as does any plug-in that needs to be able to identify specific windows or types of windows.)

- **Key Bindings:** Enables you to define the key bindings, mouse actions, or screen regions associated with common window operations (General section), as well as the commands to run when specific `run_command` functions are invoked (the Commands section). The commands on this tab also enable you to map keys, mouse actions, or screen regions to the Increase Opacity and Decrease Opacity operations.

- **Desktop Size:** Enables you to set the number of viewports that are supported by Compiz for each desktop, and their horizontal and vertical organization. As I'll discuss later in this section, the horizontal virtual size must be set to 4 if you are to use the Desktop Cube plug-in.

As an example of using CompizConfig, let's enable the Rotate Cube plug-in, which is one of the best-known Compiz plug-ins. When completely configured (along with some related plug-ins), this plug-in displays your active viewports as the four sides of a cube that you can quickly rotate to cycle through the available viewports. You can also rotate the cube in three dimensions to expose its top and bottom, which you can decorate with images. Why have an incredibly powerful graphics card if you're not going to make the most of it? To activate the Rotate Cube plug-in, follow these steps:

1. Configure your desktop so that four viewports are available.

2. As mentioned earlier in this section, you must use the General Options' Desktop Size tab to set the Horizontal Virtual Size of your desktop to 4 in order to provide four viewports that you can use as the four sides of your desktop cube, as shown in Figure 6-10. (The default value is 2, which is confusing.) To do this, select the General Options section of CompizConfig, select the Desktop Size tab, and either enter the new value of 4 or use the up arrow to increase the default value of 2 for the Horizontal Virtual Size parameter.

FIGURE 6-10

Increasing the horizontal viewports on your system

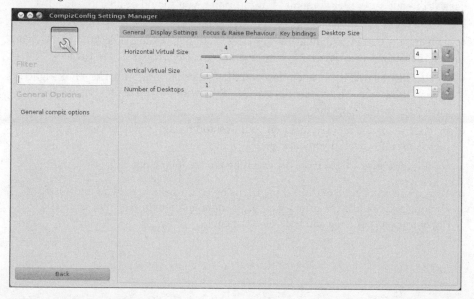

When you're finished, your screen should look like that shown in Figure 6-10. Click the Back button to return to the main CompizConfig screen.

3. Activate the Desktop Cube plug-in by clicking the X to the left of its icon and name. If you have made no previous configuration changes, you will see a warning dialog like the one shown in Figure 6-11.

FIGURE 6-11

Identifying potential plug-in conflicts

Dialogs of this type are one of the advantages of using application-specific configuration applications like CompizConfig instead of a generic configuration application like gconf-editor. Because the CompizConfig Setting Manager knows more about plug-ins than simply how to manipulate the GNOME registry, it can detect feature conflicts and offer to disable active plug-ins that might cause them to fail when you enable new plug-ins. In this case, click "Disable Desktop Wall," which will disable the enhanced, but linear, viewport scroller and will enable the Desktop Cube plug-in, as requested.

4. Select the checkmark beside the Rotate Cube plug-in, which is the plug-in that actually rotates the cube. (The Desktop Cube simply maps viewports to the sides of a cube but doesn't provide any whizzy graphics.) At this point, you should be able to rotate the faces of your new desktop cube in one of three basic ways:

- By using the Ctrl+Alt+Right arrow key combination to rotate the desktop to the right and the Ctrl+Alt+Left arrow key combination to rotate the desktop to the left

- By clicking the title bar of a window and dragging that window to the left or right edge of the screen. The cube will rotate, and the window you're moving will be moved to the new viewport.

- By positioning the mouse cursor on your desktop background and moving the mouse's scroll wheel (if you have one)

Pretty impressive, no? Even more eye-catching are the following:

- You can spin the cube in three dimensions by holding down the Ctrl and Alt keys, clicking and holding the primary mouse button, and moving the mouse up and down to expose the top and bottom of the cube.

- You can unfold the cube (flattening it to a single screen) by pressing the Ctrl+Alt+ Down arrow keys, and you can then scroll left or right by using the appropriate arrow keys. This makes it easy to locate the viewport that contains the applications you're looking for. Once the viewport that you're looking for displays in the center of the screen, release the Ctrl, Alt, and arrow keys to display it full-size.

Now that you've had some fun with this plug-in, you may want to consider tweaking it even further. Some fun suggestions are:

- Use the Desktop Cube's Appearance tab to add custom images to the top and/or bottom of the desktop cube by specifying image files in the "Cube Caps" section.

- Use the Desktop Cube's Appearance tab to specify a background image or gradient for the space "behind" the 3D rotating cube by selecting a gradient start and end color or specifying image files in the Skydome section.

- Set the cube to be transparent using the Desktop Cube's Transparent Cube tab, and then activate the Cube Gears plug-in to display a rotating set of gears inside the cube as it rotates. Figure 6-12 shows a transparent cube running the Cube Gears plug-in in the process of being rotated.

FIGURE 6-12

Rotating a transparent cube while using the Cube Gears plug-in

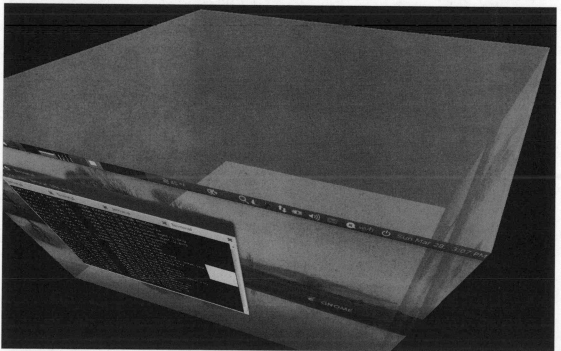

These suggestions show the fun you can have with Compiz and its plug-ins and the incredible range and power of the graphical capabilities it provides. Given the number of potential settings you can configure and the bells and whistles that Compiz provides, you may never get around to doing real work again!

Tip

A common Compiz problem is that the title bars of newly created windows display under the GNOME panel at the top of the screen. If this occurs, first make sure that the Place Windows plug-in is enabled. This plug-in uses a *smarter* algorithm that takes window title bars into account when placing new windows on the screen. You can also simply move such windows so that their title bars are visible by holding down the Alt key and clicking and holding the left mouse button in the window that you want to move. The standard window move icon displays, and you can then drag the window such that its title bar is visible. ∎

These Are a Few of My Favorite Things

Some of the plug-ins that I typically activate beyond the default set are as follows:

- **Desktop Cube/Rotate Cube:** Discussed in the previous section, quickly cycling through available viewports and rotating a cube with those viewports on its sides is not only attractive but also eminently useful.

- **Cube Gears:** Although I realize I'm using more of the CPU's resources, this is such a cool effect that I can't resist activating it.

- **Ring Switcher:** This plug-in adds the Super+Tab command to display available windows in a circular ring that spins as you tab through them, with the title of the selected window displayed in the center. It's similar to the standard Alt+Tab application switcher but much more fun.

- **Water Effect:** Sure to amuse the kids and amaze the neighbors, this plug-in lets you toggle onscreen raindrops with Shift+F9. This wastes computing power only when the raindrops are active, but it's quite visually impressive when you're showing Compiz to someone.

- **Wobbly Windows:** Discussed in the section of this chapter on using the GNOME configuration tools to configure Compiz effects, Wobbly Windows provide a jiggly, gelatinous view as you move windows. Like the Desktop Cube/Rotate Cube plug-ins, this plug-in provides one of the classic Compiz effects.

As mentioned earlier in this chapter, see `http://wiki.compiz-fusion.org/Plugins` for a complete listing of available Compiz and Compiz Fusion plug-ins and their configuration. The Compiz plug-ins page at `www.compiz.org/Plugins` lists the default plug-ins that are bundled with Compiz and also provides links to some additional, external plug-ins that you may find useful.

Other Useful Packages for Compiz

As the previous section showed, some extremely useful Compiz-related software is available in the Ubuntu repositories but is not installed by default on Ubuntu systems. The previous section discussed the CompizConfig Settings Manager; this section and its subsections discuss some other very interesting packages that you can install for use with Compiz (and which actually work in any compositing environment, including Xcompmgr).

Installing and Using the Avant Window Navigator

If you've ever seen or used Mac OS X, you're probably familiar with its dock, which is the panel-like application that runs at the bottom of the screen (by default), and in which you see icons for your favorite applications as well as icons representing running applications and the Trash Can. Although GNOME has its Panels and Microsoft Windows has its Taskbar, it's hard to deny that the Mac OS X Dock is the most attractive of any these entities with similar functionality. Perhaps until now. The Avant Window Navigator (AWN) is an open source dock application for compositing window managers that provides an attractive, powerful, extensible, and fully customizable dock for use with Compiz. The Avant Window Navigator was developed by Neil Patel and currently has its home page at the Ubuntu Launchpad site at `https://launchpad.net/awn`. Figure 6-13 shows the default appearance of an Ubuntu desktop running both the Avant Window Navigator and its configuration utility, the Awn Manager.

The Avant Window Navigator is not installed by default on Ubuntu systems, but you can easily install it using your favorite package management utility, as explained in Chapter 19. Installing the Avant Window Navigator will also install the library that it uses, some Python modules that it required, and its configuration manager.

Tip
To get the latest version of the Avant Window Navigator and its plug-ins, you should add `http://ppa .launchpad.net/awn-testing/ppa/ubuntu` to the sources listed in `/etc/apt/sources.list`. See Chapter 19 for information about enabling other sources for use with Ubuntu's package management tools. ■

After installing AWN, you can start it manually from any command-line application, such as an xterm or the GNOME Terminal. To configure AWN to start automatically when you log in, you can either enable it in the Awn Settings application (discussed later in this section) or add it to your standard startup application settings. To do the latter, select the System ➪ Preferences ➪ Startup Applications tool. On the Startup Programs tab, click Add, and enter information about the Avant Window Navigator, as shown in Figure 6-14.

FIGURE 6-13

The Avant Window Navigator and its administrative application

FIGURE 6-14

Configuring the Avant Window Navigator to start automatically at login

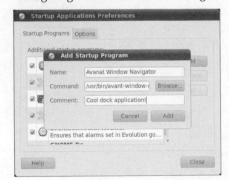

On Ubuntu systems, I prefer to eliminate the bottom panel and add the useful applets that it normally contains (most notably the WorkSpace Switcher) to the top panel, as shown in Figure 6-13. Using AWN at the bottom of the screen and the standard GNOME panel at the top gives me the best of both worlds.

Once you've installed and started AWN, you can start the Awn Settings application by selecting System ⇨ Preferences ⇨ Awn manager. This displays the application shown in Figure 6-13, which enables you to customize how icons in the dock are displayed; configure whether the dock is automatically hidden when not in use; configure the appearance of the bar underneath the dock; and add applets, launchers, and themes to customize the dock's behavior and appearance. Figure 6-15 shows AWN with the following customizations enabled:

- **Preferences ⇨ Behavior ⇨ Intellihide:** This one is actually hard to show because it causes the dock to disappear below the bottom of the screen when it is not in use. To re-display the dock, move the cursor to the bottom of the screen.

- **Preferences ⇨ Icon Effects ⇨ Spotlight:** Selecting Spotlight as the icon effect causes any icon to flash when you position the cursor over that icon in the dock

- **Preferences ⇨ Style ⇨ 3d:** Instead of the standard 2D dock background, activating this option causes AWN to use the tapering background shown in Figure 6-15. Compare this with the default flat bar shown in Figure 6-13.

By default, AWN displays only icons for running applications. Two of the nicest features of AWN are the capability to install applets that perform specific functions and the ability to install new themes to customize the appearance of the dock itself. A good selection of AWN applets is provided with Ubuntu, but you can see the list of available applets (and learn how to build and install them yourself) at `http://wiki.awn-project.org/Applets` and `http://wiki.awn-project .org/Awn-extras`.

Tip

AWN plug-ins enable you to improve the interaction between certain application and their icons in AWN. Plug-ins for audio applications such as Amarok, Audacious, Banshee, and Rhythmbox, and for online chat and instant messaging applications such as Pidgin and XChat, are available at `http://wiki.awn-project .org/Plugins.` ∎

AWN themes, which enable you to perform additional configuration of the dock's appearance, are much easier to install and use. A large number of custom themes can be downloaded from `http://wiki.awn-project.org/Themes`. One of my favorites, Transparent 3D, is not available there, but you can download it from `www.queervisions.com/arch/2007/10/ awn_avantwindow.html`.

FIGURE 6-15

The Avant Window Navigator after customization

Once you download an AWN theme, you install it by selecting the Awn Manager's Themes tab, clicking Add, and navigating to the location where your themes are stored. (I tend to keep them in ~/ART/AWN so that I know where to look for them if I want to use them on other systems.) You then select the compressed tar archive file that contains your theme and click Open. Once a theme has been added, the Themes tab looks like that shown in Figure 6-16.

FIGURE 6-16

The Awn Manager after adding a theme

You can then select the theme you want to use and click Apply to have it take effect. Figure 6-17 shows AWN with a theme called Frosted Glass enabled.

As AWN (and Compiz itself) becomes more popular, more and more applets, application launchers, and themes should become available. Look forward to hours of customization fun. For additional information about AWN, see the Avant Window Navigator Wiki at http://wiki .awn-project.org.

Tip

I've been using AWN for quite a while now, and have seen it crash a few times, at which point all of its icons disappear, although the dock itself is still visible. To cause AWN to redraw all of its icons, simply start any other graphical application. All of your icons will reappear. ■

FIGURE 6-17

The Avant Window Navigator with the Frosted Glass theme

Other Dock Software for Ubuntu Systems

If you like the idea of having a dock but aren't happy with the look and feel of the Avant Window Navigator, several other packages are available that provide a dock. This is Linux, after all — choice is never a problem. My favorite other docks are the following:

- **Cairo-Dock:** An excellent and highly customizable dock package that provides a large number of interesting plug-ins. Like other docks, Cairo-Dock is not installed by default on Ubuntu systems. To experiment with Cairo-Dock, you should install both the `cairo-dock` and `cairo-dock-plugins` packages to make the most of Cairo-Dock. Figure 6-18 shows a highly customized instance of Cairo-Dock running at the bottom of the screen as a replacement for the bottom panel.

FIGURE 6-18

A customized Cairo-Dock installation

- **Gnome Do:** A popular GNOME application launcher that also provides integrated search capabilities, GNOME Do also offers a fast, lightweight dock known as *Docky* that you can enable by selecting Docky as the "Selected Theme" on the GNOME Do Preferences application's Appearance tab. Like other docks, GNOME Do is not installed by default on Ubuntu systems — you must install the gnome-do package to experiment with GNOME Do. Figure 6-19 shows a customized version of Docky running at the bottom of the screen as a replacement for the bottom panel.

FIGURE 6-19

GNOME Do in Docky mode

If you decide that you like these alternate dock packages, you can configure whichever one you like to start automatically when you log in using the System ➪ Preferences ➪ Startup Applications tool. Activate the checkbox to the left of the dock that you want to use, make sure that no other dock package is also set to start automatically, and click Close to save your changes.

Using Emerald and the Emerald Theme Manager

The Emerald window decorator, discussed earlier in this chapter in the section "Compiz History," was originally designed for use with the Beryl compositing window manager. Once the Beryl and Compiz folks began working together, the Compiz Fusion project was formed to port many of the cool features and plug-ins that were created for Beryl so that they would work with Compiz. Luckily for all of us, one item they opted to port and update was Emerald, the window decorator used by Beryl.

As discussed earlier, compositing window managers such as Compiz and Beryl focus on standard window management tasks and compositing, using a separate application to handle window decoration tasks. This division of labor provides a flexible, easily extended desktop environment by enabling different window decorators to be used with a single compositing window manager. By default, GNOME-based Ubuntu systems running Compiz use the gtk-window-decorator window decorator. The purpose of this window decorator is to reimplement the look and feel of the traditional GNOME (Metacity) desktop and default window manager in the Compiz environment. Emerald provides an alternative to these that works in either desktop environment. It provides a substantially richer graphical desktop environment because its focus is on creating something new, not preserving a traditional look.

Emerald is not installed by default as a part of Compiz, but you can easily install it using any of the package management utilities that are discussed in Chapter 19. Installing Emerald will also install the library that it uses and the Emerald Theme Manager, a utility that makes it easy for you to configure general aspects of Emerald, as well as to retrieve, install, and use different Emerald themes. When installing Emerald, you should also install the Subversion source code control systems because this software is used by the Emerald Theme Manager to retrieve Emerald themes from remote theme repositories.

Once Emerald has been installed, before you can configure it you must enable the Compiz Window Decorator plug-in (using CompizConfig) and then start the Emerald window decorator by executing the following command:

```
emerald --replace &
```

This starts Emerald and tells it to replace any window decorator that is currently running. After executing this command, you will notice that the default controls on any open windows on your screen change to use Emerald's default theme. You can now start the Emerald Theme Manager by selecting System ⇨ Preferences ⇨ Emerald Theme Manager. The Emerald Theme Manager is shown in Figure 6-20, which also shows that the program thinks of itself as the *Emerald Themer*, which is how I'll refer to it from this point on.

The initial dialog displayed by the Emerald Themer isn't very interesting, primarily because no themes are provided by default. Figure 6-20 shows this dialog after two themes have been downloaded. To download and install default sets of themes, use your favorite Web browser to visit sites such as the following and look for themes labeled *Emerald Theme* or *Beryl Emerald Theme*:

- www.compiz-themes.org
- http://compizfusion.blogspot.com/2008/01/
  compiz-fusion-emerald-themes.html

You may need to click on the name of a theme that you're interested in so that you can see its Download button. Once you've downloaded any themes that you're interested in, you can load them into the Emerald Themer by clicking Import and navigating to the location where you downloaded the theme(s). Emerald themes typically have the .emerald file extension. After selecting an .emerald file, click Open to add that theme to the list in the Emerald Themer. Figure 6-20 shows the Emerald Themer with several new themes loaded, but still using its default theme.

FIGURE 6-20

The Emerald Theme Manager, aka the Emerald Themer

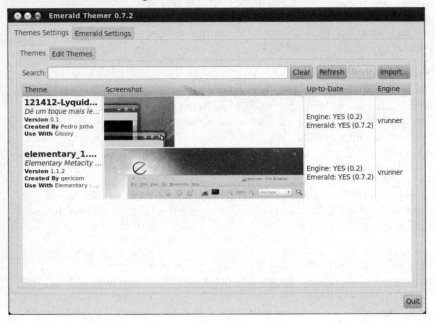

Experimenting with themes is fun. Selecting a theme that appeals to you can help make your computer system reflect your personality and aesthetics. My personal favorite this week is SolidSlateModified, and I forget what it was last month.

If none of the default themes that you've downloaded are "just right" and you are artistically inclined, you can even create (and optionally publish) your own themes by following the instructions provided at http://wiki.compiz-fusion.org/Decorators/Emerald.

Summary

Compositing window managers, specifically the Compiz window manager, have been the dar-lings of the Linux world for a while now. Compiz is now the default window manager installed and started on GNOME-based Ubuntu systems. This chapter explained the basic concepts behind compositing window managers and provided a quick history of compositing on Linux and of Compiz itself. The chapter then explained how to configure Compiz, locate and install plug-ins to improve its capabilities, and install and use various Compiz-related utilities such as the CompizConfig Settings Manager, the Avant Window Navigator, other popular dock utilities, and the Emerald window decorator.

The next chapter discusses Evolution, the popular GNOME e-mail client that supports stan-dard POP and IMAP mailers, as well as providing impressive interoperability with Microsoft's Exchange mail server, including calendaring and other office-related features that are almost mandatory for using a Linux system in a business environment.

Managing E-Mail and Personal Information with Evolution

After Web browsers, e-mail is the Internet's killer application. Like Web browsers, there are many different client applications for sending and receiving e-mail, especially in the open source community. In addition (and unfortunately unlike Web browsing, which basically uses HTML everywhere), there are many different protocols used to receive e-mail. Your choice of an e-mail client can therefore depend to some extent on whether it supports the protocols that your Internet service provider (ISP), business, or academic institution uses to send, store, and deliver e-mail.

The easiest solution to the "which protocol, which client" problem is to use a single e-mail client that speaks every modern e-mail protocol known to humanity. Ubuntu includes an e-mail client known as *Evolution*, which lives up to this promise. Evolution is a GNOME-based mailer that was originally developed by a company called Ximian. Oddly enough, Ximian was eventually acquired by Novell, whose SUSE Linux product is largely KDE-centric, but it's at least clear that Novell knows good software when they see it.

Evolution can receive mail from mail servers that speak all of the popular e-mail protocols including POP, IMAP, IMAP4rev1, Microsoft Exchange, Novell GroupWise, and a few that would require a Google search to figure out who uses them (and why). For outgoing mail, Evolution can communicate with any Simple Mail Transport Protocol (SMTP) server or any server that is compatible with the standard Linux/UNIX Sendmail application.

Beyond all this, Evolution is much more than just a multi-protocol e-mail client—it is actually more of a Personal Information Management

IN THIS CHAPTER

Setting up your e-mail client

Sending and receiving mail

Organizing your e-mail

Filing e-mail

Dealing with spam

Accessing webmail

Managing contacts

Managing your calendar

(PIM) package, of which sending and receiving e-mail is just one aspect. Evolution also provides integrated support for PIM capabilities including the following:

- Managing contacts stored locally or on Lightweight Directory Access Protocol (LDAP) or Microsoft Exchange servers
- Managing task lists stored locally or on a Microsoft Exchange Server
- Managing local calendars, Web-based calendars, or Microsoft Exchange calendars

By now, you may see something of a thread in this introduction — compatibility with Microsoft Exchange Servers and the services that they provide. Like it or not, many businesses depend on Microsoft Exchange to satisfy groupware requirements such as scheduling meetings, checking and sharing coworkers' calendars, and so on. The e-mail server portion of an Exchange Server is just a special type of IMAP mail server, but the calendaring and scheduling portions of Exchange are largely Microsoft-only. Evolution's support for complete interoperation with a Microsoft Exchange environment is truly impressive.

This chapter explains how to configure and use Evolution as a mail client, contact manager, and calendaring system. The chapter begins by discussing how to create your initial mail accounts and how to read, send, organize, and filter mail; and it discusses the powerful Virtual Folders feature that is unique to Evolution. It explains how to use Evolution to access popular webmail systems such as Gmail, Yahoo!, and Microsoft Hotmail/Live. It then discusses how to configure and use the contact and calendar management portions of Evolution. For even more information on Evolution's capabilities, see the section "Additional Sources of Information about Evolution" at the end of this chapter.

Starting Evolution

You can start Evolution in a variety of different ways:

- Select the envelope icon in the GNOME toolbar at the top of the screen (shown in Figure 7-1) and select Mail from the drop-down menu. This is the easiest and most common way to start Evolution.
- Select "Evolution Mail and Calendar" from the Applications ⇨ Office menu.
- Type the **evolution** command in a GNOME Terminal or xterm window, and press Return.

FIGURE 7-1

The Evolution icon on your GNOME desktop

Evolution icon

Ubuntu's GNOME desktop is also preconfigured to start Evolution for you if you click on a Uniform Resource Locater (URL) that is designed to send an e-mail message (known as a *mailto* URL) in a Web browser or other Internet-aware application.

The next section discusses the Evolution Setup Assistant, which walks you through the process of creating your first e-mail account in Evolution.

Using the Evolution Setup Assistant

When Evolution actually starts up for the first time, the "Welcome" window of the Evolution Setup Assistant displays and begins walking you through the process of creating your first e-mail account in Evolution.

A slight clarification here, just to be on the safe side — the Evolution Setup Assistant configures Evolution to send and receive e-mail for an existing e-mail account somewhere; it doesn't actually create the account. For example, even though I use my Ubuntu machines to send and receive mail, my e-mail account is actually located at the ISP that hosts my domain. The Evolution Setup Assistant lets me tell Evolution about where it should look to retrieve my incoming e-mail and the mail server through which it should send outgoing mail. In my case, the machine on which I'm running Evolution is separate from the machine through which I actually send and receive my e-mail.

Note
Of course, if you run your own mail server and it's running on the same machine where you're running Evolution, your Ubuntu account may well be your official e-mail account. I discuss this in more detail in Chapter 30, "Setting Up a Mail Server." ■

The idea of receiving e-mail can be confusing, so I generally think of this as the difference between *receiving* and *retrieving* — my actual e-mail account (at my ISP) receives my e-mail, and Evolution lets me retrieve my e-mail from there in order to read it, archive it locally or delete it, and so on. In official mailer-speak, this is the difference between a Mail Transfer Agent (MTA), a Mail Delivery Agent (MDA), and a Mail User Agent (MUA). The MDA at your ISP takes mail received by the MTA and puts it in your mailbox at your ISP. An MUA (in this case, Evolution) retrieves a piece of mail from your mailbox at your ISP and displays it on your local system. (For more detailed information about these terms, see Chapter 30.)

Once the Setup Assistant's Welcome window displays, click Forward to move to the next portion of the setup process. A window like the one shown in Figure 7-2 displays.

If you are already an Evolution user and have created an Evolution backup file on another system, you can import the contents of that file by clicking the "Restore Evolution from the backup file" checkbox and navigating to the location of your Evolution backup file using the navigation dialog that is displayed after clicking the "Please select an Evolution Archive to restore" button. You can create these backup files in recent versions of Evolution by selecting the File menu's Backup Settings command and specifying the name of the backup files that you want to create. These backup files are created as compressed tar files, with a default name of evolution-backup.tar.gz.

FIGURE 7-2

Restoring from backups

Migrating from Older Versions of Evolution

If you are already an Evolution user but are using a version of Evolution that does not provide the Backup Settings command, you can still migrate your existing Evolution configuration information by using the `tar` command to create a compressed tar file that contains the contents of the `.evolution` directory in your home directory (and its subdirectories). You could do this by using commands such as the following:

```
cd ~ ; tar czf evolution-backup.tar.gz .evolution
```

You can then transfer the file `evolution-backup.tar.gz` to your new Ubuntu system and restore it during the Evolution setup process. Do not delete your existing evolution information until you've verified that the backup file was successfully imported!

Older versions of Evolution used a directory called `evolution` in your home directory rather than the `.evolution` directory. If you're using a version of Evolution that uses the `evolution` directory, congratulations for being a long-time Evolution user, but your upgrade mechanism will be a bit more complex. You'll have to back up this directory to a file, copy that file to your new Ubuntu system, and extract its contents manually before beginning the Evolution setup process. If you haven't done this, exit the Evolution Setup Assistant now and do so. When you restart Evolution's setup process after restoring your old evolution directory, the Setup Assistant should detect this old directory and offer to migrate everything to the new `.evolution` directory.

If you are already an Evolution user and have an archive file, you can skip ahead to the "Sending and Receiving Mail" section of this chapter after restoring the backup file. No further configuration is necessary because the backup file contains both account information and archived e-mail.

If you are new to Ubuntu and Evolution and therefore don't have anything to restore, click Forward to proceed to the next dialog. A screen like the one shown in Figure 7-3 displays.

FIGURE 7-3

Specifying your name and primary e-mail address

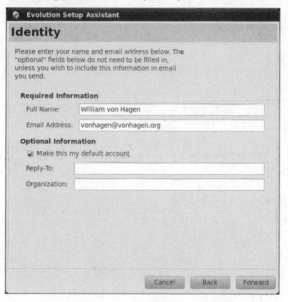

The "Full Name" field should already be filled out for you — Evolution grabs this information from the account from which you're running Evolution. You can change that name, of course, if you'd prefer to have the people who receive mail from you see a name that's more "clever" than your actual account name. The critical bit of information on this panel is in the "Email Address" field. This must be the e-mail address that you want to associate with this account. As mentioned previously, this is typically your e-mail address at your ISP or wherever else you get your e-mail.

The "Make this my default e-mail account" checkbox is selected by default in this dialog because Evolution starts the Setup Assistant only when it detects that you are starting Evolution for the first time. Your default account is simply the one that Evolution will continue to use unless you activate another account.

If you want people who receive e-mail from this account to actually reply to another, you can specify the e-mail address of that account in the "Reply-To" field, but this is usually unnecessary.

Similarly, if you want mail headers to announce that your mail is coming from a specific organization, you can specify the name of that organization in the Organization field. This is invisible to most recipients, but it can be handy for filtering e-mail messages (explained later in this chapter) if you use this field to uniquely identify that this mail is coming from a specific location. I typically put something like **Bill's Home Machine** in this field, so that I can tell that I actually sent a specific piece of mail from my machine at home, if necessary.

Once you've filled out this panel, click Forward to display the next panel in the Setup Assistant, shown in Figure 7-4.

FIGURE 7-4

Specifying incoming mail server (MTA) parameters

When you first see the panel shown in Figure 7-4, it will be largely empty and the "Server Type" field will display a default value. Click the "Server Type" field to display a list of the different types of mail servers that Evolution can talk to, and select the one that corresponds to the primary e-mail protocol supported by the mail server at the location that actually hosts your e-mail, which is typically your ISP. Most mail servers nowadays speak POP (Post Office Protocol) or a special version of POP known as POP3, which adds some extensions to the standard POP mail server capabilities. The second most popular protocol nowadays is IMAP, which also includes Microsoft Exchange mailers, because they speak a variant (of course) of IMAP.

A Quick Guide to POP versus IMAP

The key difference between the POP and IMAP e-mail protocols lies in where your e-mail is actually stored. POP mail clients typically download your e-mail from the POP server and store it on the machine where your mail client is running. This is extremely convenient for the operators of the mail server — they don't have to provide huge amounts of storage for e-mail because the storage requirements for POP mailers are transient. As people read their mail, it is downloaded to the client and then usually deleted from the server. IMAP servers, on the other hand, permanently store your mail on the server and only download the mail headers to your mail client when you first check your mail. These headers include the subject line, information about the sender, the date on which the message was sent, and so on. When you select a message to be read from an IMAP server, the mail is copied to your local system, but the master copy of the message remains on the IMAP server. The storage requirements for IMAP mailers therefore tend to increase over time, as more and more people accumulate larger collections of saved e-mail.

Each of these approaches has advantages and disadvantages. POP lets you keep all of your mail on your local machine, which is handy if you want to review your existing mail when you're not connected to the NET. The downside, of course, is that all of your mail lives on a single machine, and it's therefore tricky to read old mail from a machine other than the one where that mail is actually stored. IMAP mailers make it easy to access your old mail from any machine, anywhere, but require a network connection to that machine in order to do so. Most IMAP clients enable you to synchronize your local mailboxes with those stored on the IMAP server, so that you can easily access old mail while traveling without requiring a network connection. However, ISPs that use IMAP hate people like me, who have huge mail archives going back 10 years or so and therefore require significant storage on an IMAP server.

Most POP mail clients, including Evolution's POP support, provide a special option called "Leave mail on server." This enables you to configure multiple clients to read your POP mail, but only one of them (typically your home machine) actually downloads the mail and deletes it from the server. All POP clients remember the last message that they read, so they don't re-download all of your mail each time you check your mail — only those that they recognize as being new. This provides a nice compromise between the flexibility of IMAP and the local permanence of POP. For example, when I'm on the road, the copy of Evolution on my laptop lets me read my mail but doesn't delete it from the server — this only happens when I get back home and check mail from my primary machine. The downside of POP while traveling, of course, is that I don't have access to all of my old mail when I'm on the road, but if I'm really desperate, I can always connect to my home machine and either manually look through my mailboxes or run Evolution from that machine over the NET. Slow, but successful.

Once you select a specific type of server, the panel changes to reflect the particular types of settings that are associated with a mail server of that type, as shown in Figure 7-5, which shows the settings for a POP mailer.

On this panel, enter the name of your mail server and your username as far as the mailer is concerned. Note that your mailer's idea of your username may not actually be the same as your login name there — many POP mailers require a username of the form *login%domain.name* to guarantee the uniqueness of usernames on mailers that support multiple domains. For example, my login at my ISP is *vonhagen*, but my POP username is *vonhagen%vonhagen.org*.

FIGURE 7-5

Specifying parameters for an incoming mail server

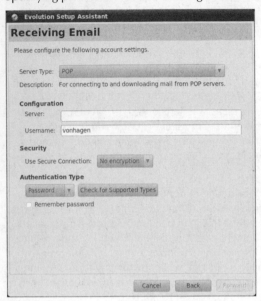

Next, specify the security settings required to log in on your mailer—whether or not to try to use a secure connection to retrieve your mail from the mail server, and the type of authentication required for connections to the server. Evolution provides a convenient "Check for Supported Types" button that you can click to probe your mail server to see what type(s) of authentication it supports. In most cases, you'll use Password authentication, but this option makes it easy to check whether your mailer supports more sophisticated types of authentication such as Kerberos or GSSAPI.

You can select the "Remember password" checkbox to optionally specify that Evolution remember the password to your incoming mail server, but I don't recommend that because this means that anyone who has access to your account will be able to read your mail.

Once you're finished specifying the options for receiving and retrieving incoming mail, click Forward to proceed to the next panel. A panel like the one shown in Figure 7-6 displays.

Panels like the one shown in Figure 7-6 enable you to configure the available options for how your mail client should interact with your incoming mail server. For all types of incoming mail servers, you can specify if, and how often, your mail client should automatically check for new e-mail. When configuring how Evolution interacts with an incoming POP mail server, you can also identify whether the copy of Evolution that you're configuring should remove the mail. As discussed in the sidebar "A Quick Guide to POP versus IMAP" earlier in this chapter, POP mailers typically provide short-term storage for mail, while other types of mailers, such as IMAP, provide long-term storage for your mail. This panel also lets you configure whether Evolution should pay attention to POP3 extensions, which are site-specific extensions that the administrator of the mail server may have implemented.

FIGURE 7-6

Options for handling incoming mail from a POP server

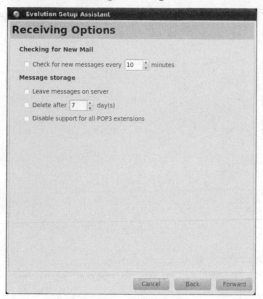

Many of the options for interacting with an incoming mail server are specific to the type of server that you're connecting to. For example, Figure 7-7 shows the configuration options available when communicating with an IMAP server.

There are many more options for configuring Evolution's interaction with an IMAP server than with a POP server. Because IMAP servers maintain a master repository for your e-mail, Evolution's IMAP Configuration panel offers options for how to connect to the server (such as through a custom command that provides a secure tunnel), how to interact with the mail folders on the IMAP server (both your personal folder and public ones to which you may have access), whether to synchronize your local mail folder with those on the server (giving you a local copy of all of your mail), and whether mail filters and general junk mail (spam) processing should occur against your master mailboxes or just locally. I'll discuss mail filters and junk mail handling in the section "Filtering Incoming Mail" later in this chapter. If you're configuring Evolution to interact with an IMAP server, I suggest activating both the "Apply filters" and "Check new messages" options for now. You can always turn them off later, and selecting these options initially will ensure that Mail Filters work as expected, and will also help get rid of some of the spam that plagues every e-mail user today.

After you configure how Evolution interacts with your incoming mail server when you read your mail, regardless of the type of incoming mail server you're using, you need to configure how Evolution actually sends mail. Click Forward to proceed to the panel shown in Figure 7-8.

FIGURE 7-7

Options for handling incoming mail from an IMAP server

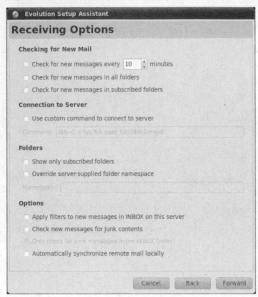

Previous configuration steps helped you configure how your system receives mail and the characteristics of your incoming mail server. The panel shown in Figure 7-8 enables you to specify the characteristics of the mail server you use to send outgoing mail. Your incoming and outgoing mail servers may be different machines or processes because the tasks involved with sending and receiving mail are very different.

The critical piece of information on this panel is the *type* of your incoming mail server. Evolution supports two types of outgoing mail servers — SMTP (Simple Mail Transport Protocol), which refers to any mail server that conforms to the SMTP standard; and Sendmail, which is the most popular mail server used on Linux and other UNIX-like systems and runs locally on most Ubuntu systems. Most people will want to select SMTP — if you are running your own mail server on your system (and plan to continue to do so), you can select Sendmail, but if you are using an ISP for mail handling, you'll want to select SMTP. (For more information about running your own mail server, see Chapter 30.)

If you select Sendmail, no additional configuration is required on this panel (because the server is running on the same machine as Evolution), but if you select SMTP, you'll need to specify the name of your outgoing mail server and provide information about how you authenticate to that server, if necessary. Most modern SMTP servers require authentication, so you need to check the "Server requires authentication" checkbox, specify that Evolution should use a secure connection whenever possible, and verify the type of authentication that your mail server supports by clicking the "Check for Supported Types" button, just as you did when providing similar information about your incoming mail server. As with the configuration of your incoming mail server, you can optionally specify that Evolution remember your password to the outgoing mail server, but I don't recommend that because this means that anyone who has access to your account will be able to send mail as you.

Options for sending mail

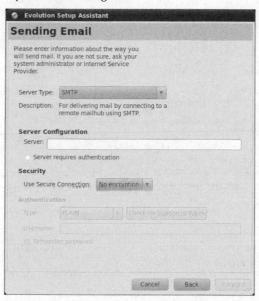

Once you've correctly configured Evolution's information about your outgoing mail server, click Forward to continue with the configuration process. Don't worry — you can always change these settings later if you discover that mail isn't working correctly, as explained in the "Setting Evolution Preferences for Sending and Viewing Mail" section later in this chapter. The panel shown in Figure 7-9 displays.

Almost there! The panel shown in Figure 7-9 simply requests a name for the e-mail account that you're configuring. This is the name that Evolution uses internally to identify this particular collection of e-mail settings, and is the name that you'll select in Evolution's Preferences dialog (discussed in the "Setting Evolution Preferences for Sending and Viewing Mail" section later in this chapter.) if you need to update or modify the settings for this e-mail account. By default, the name of a particular collection of settings is the same as the e-mail address for that account, which is what I typically use.

After making any desired changes to the name of this e-mail account, click Forward to continue. A final dialog displays, in which you can click Apply to save your new e-mail settings, or use the Back button to return to previous configuration screens if you want to change something.

FIGURE 7-9

Naming a configured e-mail account

Once you apply the current settings, you're ready to check your mail for the first time and begin using Evolution in general, as explained in the remainder of this chapter.

Tip

Unlike many e-mail clients, Evolution enables you to simultaneously send and receive mail for multiple e-mail accounts. Each e-mail account has a specific e-mail address, an associated server (and protocol) from which to read mail, and another through which to send outgoing mail. You can define other e-mail accounts using Evolution's Preferences dialog, which you can display by selecting the Preferences command from the Edit menu. One issue with Evolution's support for multiple POP e-mail accounts is that all addresses for which you retrieve and store mail in Evolution share the same set of local folders—each individual mail address doesn't have its own Inbox and set of folders. However, as I'll discuss later in this chapter, you can easily use mail filters or virtual folders to provide the appearance of having a per-address Inbox, which is the next best thing to having one. ■

Sending and Receiving Mail

Figure 7-10 shows the window that you'll see when starting Evolution (once you've gone through its Setup Wizard to create an initial account). Let's read mail!

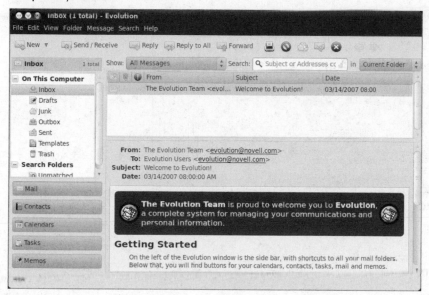

FIGURE 7-10

The primary Evolution window

To read your mail, click Send/Receive in the Evolution toolbar. Evolution prompts you for your password, contacts the remote mail server, and begins retrieving your mail. As it retrieves your mail (and sends any outgoing mail), Evolution displays a Progress and Status dialog.

Once Evolution retrieves your incoming e-mail and sends any queued outbound mail, the Progress dialog closes, and Evolution updates its internal information about the state of the various mail folders on your system. To read your new mail, select your Inbox from the navigation pane at the left, and select any of the new mail messages to display that message, as shown in Figure 7-11.

Any folder shown in bold in the pane at the left is a folder that contains a message that is currently identified as being unread. Notice that the Evolution title bar displays the number of unread messages in your Inbox, as does the number in parentheses beside the Inbox folder in the navigation pane at the left.

The options and buttons in the Evolution toolbar are your key to the most common functions in Evolution:

- **New:** Creates a new item of any of the types of items supported by Evolution: mail messages, contacts, calendar items, memos, tasks, and specialized versions of those items
- **Send/Receive:** Retrieves any new mail held at your incoming mail server and sends any pending mail that you've sent

FIGURE 7-11

Displaying a new message

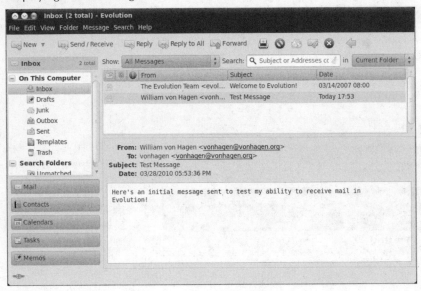

- **Reply:** Replies to the sender of the currently selected e-mail message

- **Reply to All:** Replies to the sender of the current message and sends a "carbon" copy (CC) of the mail message to anyone else who received a copy of that sender's message

- **Forward:** Lets you forward the current e-mail message to a new recipient

- **Print:** Opens a dialog that enables you to print the current message on any printer that has been configured on your system. (See Chapter 20, "Adding Hardware and Attaching Peripherals," for information on configuring printers.)

- **Delete:** Marks the current message for deletion, which removes the message from the list of active messages. To actually delete messages marked for deletion, select the File menu's Empty Trash command.

- **Junk:** Marks the current message as junk, reducing the chance that you'll receive similar messages in the future. For more information about junk mail handling, see the section "Automatically Checking for Junk Mail," later in this chapter.

- **Not Junk:** Enables you to identify a message that you had previously identified as junk as being acceptable. For more information about junk mail handling, see the section "Automatically Checking for Junk Mail," later in this chapter.

- **Cancel:** Cancels the current operation

- **Forward/backward arrows:** Provide a graphical way of going from one message to the next in the currently selected mail folder

The down arrow at the end of the Evolution toolbar indicates that other tool buttons are available, but that the Evolution window on my screen currently isn't wide enough to display them all. You can click on the down arrow to select these other commands (Previous and Next, by default) or simply resize the window to see these other tool buttons.

The buttons on the Evolution toolbar provide easy access to most of the commands that you'll ever need to work with your mail. However, Evolution is a large and powerful application with many bells, whistles, and knobs that you can turn, and deserves its own book. Luckily, Evolution also includes a great online manual that explains the ins and outs of using all of its capabilities. To access this online help, select Contents from the Evolution Help menu.

Because this is a book on Ubuntu, not Evolution, the focus of this chapter is on helping you get started with Evolution. Until a book dedicated to Evolution is published, Evolution's online help and various Evolution-related web sites are the ultimate source of information for this e-mail client. The next few sections provide some of my favorite tips for efficiently working with and managing your e-mail in Evolution. For additional information, see the web sites listed in "Additional Sources of Information about Evolution" later in this chapter.

Sending Mail in Evolution

You can begin composing a new message in Evolution in a variety of different ways, including:

- Click the New button when you are viewing e-mail.
- Press Ctrl+Shift+M on your keyboard.
- Select "Compose New Message" from the Message menu.

You can reply to a message that you are currently viewing by doing either of the following:

- Click the Reply button, press Ctrl+R on your keyboard, or select the Reply command from the Message menu.
- Click the "Reply to All" button, press Shift+Ctrl+R on your keyboard, or select the "Reply to All" command from the Message menu. This has the same effect as Reply if you are the sole recipient of the currently selected message.

Tip

If you are currently viewing a message that was sent to a mailing list to which you are a subscriber, you can press Ctrl+L or select the Message menu's "Reply to List" command to reply to the list rather than to the individual who posted that specific message. To follow the rules of good Netiquette, always trim as much of the message you're replying to as possible — especially if you're replying to a mailing list that you receive in digest form. ∎

Selecting any of these options displays Evolution's Compose Message window, as shown in Figure 7-12. If you are replying to an existing message, the contents of that message are displayed in the composition window in quoted form to provide some context for your response.

FIGURE 7-12

Composing a message in Evolution

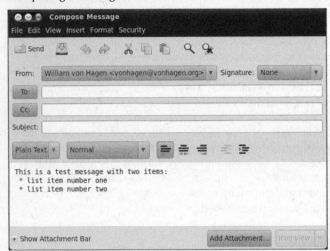

When you're composing e-mail, Evolution initially displays only the "From" and "To" fields in the message header to save space. In many cases, you'll want to send a copy of your mail to someone else (or perhaps to another e-mail address of yours). To display the fields of the mail header that support such additional recipients, click the View menu and select the other fields that you want to see such as CC (Carbon Copy), BCC (Blind Carbon Copy — one or more e-mail addresses that aren't listed in the mail that is actually sent to the other recipients), and so on.

Once you've finished composing your e-mail message, click Send to send the message. This queues the message to be sent, and you can continue working with your e-mail — while you're working, Evolution contacts the remote mail server in the background and sends the message as quickly as it can.

Setting Evolution Preferences for Sending and Viewing Mail

Evolution's Preferences dialog enables you to configure Evolution, and also to correct or change any of the basic information that you supplied when initially configuring Evolution. This section discusses one of the most common configuration changes, which is the format in which you send your e-mail.

Two basic types of encodings are used when composing and receiving e-mail. One is plaintext, which means that your messages display as standard text that might come out of a typewriter (if you remember what those are), with no special fonts or special formatting. The other is e-mail that is formatted as HTML, which lets you use different fonts, special characters for bullets, and so on. Many people prefer one or the other, and whether or not you can read mail delivered in HTML format is up to the e-mail client that you're using (although most can, nowadays—Evolution certainly can).

Note
Whether or not an e-mail client *can* send mail in HTML format is a different question from whether you *should* send e-mail formatted as HTML. Many people, some government and military sites, and many specific recipients such as mailing lists, do not want to receive or will not accept e-mail formatted as HTML. I'm not a fan, either—I always send text mail. ■

As shown in Figure 7-12, when you first compose messages in Evolution, it uses standard text format for your messages by default. If you want to switch to using HTML mail, you can do this in either of two ways:

- If you want to send just the current message in HTML format, select the HTML command from the Format menu in the window where you're composing your message. Figure 7-13 shows the same mail composition window as that in Figure 7-12, but displayed as HTML. Additional formatting buttons are active when sending an HTML message, enabling you to use different fonts, different justification formats for the paragraphs in your message, and so on.

- If you want to send all of your mail as HTML, you must set that as your preference in Evolution's Preferences dialog.

FIGURE 7-13

A message formatted as HTML

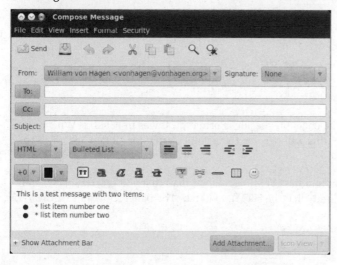

Evolution provides two Preferences panels for setting how it sends and interacts with incoming mail that is formatted as HTML. These are located on the Preferences dialog's Mail Preferences and Composer Preferences panels. To display Evolution's Preferences dialog, select the Edit menu's Preferences command.

To configure Evolution so that it always sends HTML mail, click "Composer Preferences" in the pane at the left. The panel shown in Figure 7-14 displays.

FIGURE 7-14

Specifying HTML as your default mail format

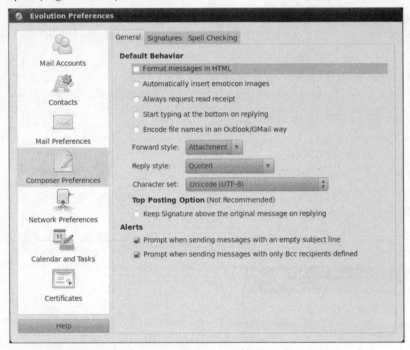

To always send HTML mail, click the checkbox beside "Format messages in HTML." When you close Evolution's Preferences dialog, this will become the default format for all new messages that you create.

To set the options for how Evolution handles HTML-formatted mail that you receive, click "Mail Preferences" in the pane at the left, and click the HTML Mail tab. The panel shown in Figure 7-15 displays.

FIGURE 7-15

Options for displaying incoming HTML mail

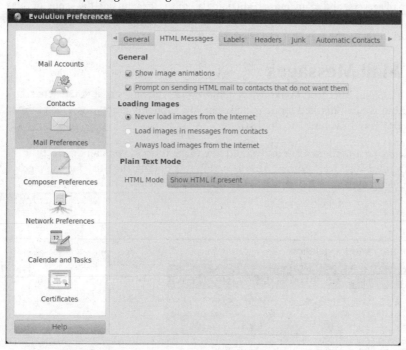

This panel provides several options for incoming HTML mail. For example, if you are occasionally checking your personal e-mail on a machine other than your primary home machine, you may want that to happen as fast as possible. In that case, you do not want to load images, because reading mail that contains images is slower than reading plain mail because images take some time (and network bandwidth) to download. To stop Evolution from downloading images at all, select the "Never load images from the Internet" radio button. If you want to download images only from people that you know (i.e., people who are in your contacts list), select the "Load images in mail from contacts" radio button. If you always want to load images, select the "Always load images from the Internet" radio button.

The panel shown in Figure 7-15 also provides a nice option for the benefit of those entities that do not want to receive HTML e-mail: the "Prompt when sending HTML messages to contacts that do not want them" option. This causes Evolution to display a confirmation dialog if you are sending HTML mail to a person or mailing list that identifies itself as not wanting to receive HTML e-mail.

Once you've finished setting Evolution's mail preferences, click Close to exit the Preferences dialog. Most of the preferences that you can set take effect immediately. Some may not take effect until the next time you start Evolution.

Tip

Evolution enables you to customize many other aspects of how it composes new messages, displays incoming e-mail, interacts with remote mail servers, and many more. Explaining all of these is outside the scope of this chapter, but I encourage you to explore the various panels and tabs available in Evolution's Preferences dialog to make sure that Evolution works exactly the way that you want it to. ■

Undeleting Mail Messages

Like files deleted on DOS and Microsoft Windows systems, e-mail messages that you delete aren't immediately purged, but are just marked for deletion when you explicitly empty the Trash or exit Evolution (if you've configured Evolution to do that).

If you accidentally delete an e-mail message and would like to get it back, you can deselect the View menu's "Hide Deleted Messages" option. After selecting this option, the titles for messages that are marked for deletion are shown with a line through them, as shown in Figure 7-16.

FIGURE 7-16

Showing mail messages that are marked for deletion

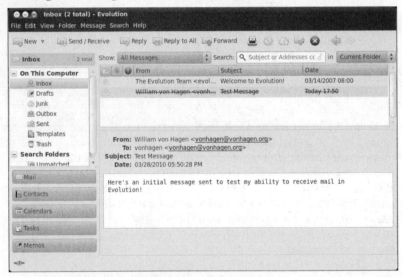

You can undelete any mail messages that are currently marked for deletion by selecting the message title and selecting the Edit menu's Undelete message command.

Creating and Using Mail Folders

After sending and receiving a fair amount of e-mail, your Inbox will become pretty cluttered, and you'll find it hard to locate a specific message even though Evolution provides some nice options for locating specific messages above the window where your Inbox is displayed. But why search for something if you can organize things better in the first place? The list of mail folders that Evolution provides by default is always displayed in the navigation pane at the left of your mail Evolution window, but Evolution also makes it easy for you to create your own custom folders to better (and permanently) organize your mail.

Evolution creates the following folders for you during its configuration process:

- **Inbox:** The folder in which incoming mail is deposited when read from your mail server
- **Drafts:** A folder in which you can put mail messages that you're working on but that have not yet been sent
- **Junk:** A folder that holds messages that have been identified as junk messages by Evolution's junk-mail scanner. For more information about this folder and junk mail in general, see the section "Automatically Checking for Junk Mail," later in this chapter.
- **Outbox:** A temporary location where mail that you have sent is stored before it is actually sent to your outgoing mail server
- **Sent:** A folder that is provided to hold copies of outgoing mail that you have sent, so that you have a record of their contents. Copies of sent messages will only be saved if you configure Evolution to do so using the Defaults tab in the Edit ⇨ Preferences dialog's Account Editor.
- **Templates:** A folder that stores templates for your mail messages. This enables you to create pre-formatted messages that you use for special purposes, such as a family news-letter, mail to specific groups of friends, and so on.
- **Trash:** A folder that contains messages slated for deletion when you explicitly empty the Trash or exit from Evolution (if you've configured your Evolution preferences to perform that action)

With the exception of your Inbox, mail folders are listed alphabetically. Your Inbox is always the top folder in Evolution's navigation pane so that it is always easy to find.

You can create a new mail folder by doing either of the following:

- Select New from the Folder menu.
- Right-click on the folder or location in which you want to create the new folder, and select "New Folder" from the pop-up menu.

After performing either of these actions, a dialog like the one shown in Figure 7-17 displays.

In this dialog, you can navigate to the location where you want to create the mail folder, enter the name of the new folder, and click Create.

Creating special-purpose mail folders makes it easy to organize your mail so that your Inbox contains only a minimum number of messages — often, only new ones. Mail folders can be hierarchical—in other words, the folder can also contain other folders. For example, I typically create a Friends folder with subfolders that correspond to each of the people with whom I regularly communicate. Once I've read or responded to a message, I put it in the appropriate folder. This makes it easy to review my correspondence with specific people without having to sift through many unrelated messages.

Creating a new mail folder

Using Search Folders

In addition to standard mail folders for organizing your mail, Evolution was the first mail client to introduce the idea of *search folders* for viewing related groups of mail messages. Standard mail folders actually hold mail messages—*search folders* are like an index or table of contents to a group of related messages that contains pointers to those messages rather than the messages themselves. This makes it easy to store your messages in explicit mail folders, but use virtual folders to give you alternate views of your mail folders. Search folders were known as *vfolders* or *virtual folders* in older releases of Evolution.

As an example, suppose that you subscribed to various mailing lists about different Linux distributions and types of Linux filesystems, and organized your incoming mail based on the name of the mailing list. Suppose that you also wanted to be able to examine all of the messages about a specific type of filesystem, regardless of which list they were posted on. You could always create a mail filter (as explained in the next section) to file the messages according to the mailing lists that they arrived on and copy them to a filesystem-specific folder, but that would eventually end up wasting a significant amount of space. Evolution's *search folder* concept to the rescue—it is easy to create a search folder that simply contains pointers to all of the matching messages without duplicating them.

Like most tasks in Evolution, there are a variety of ways to create a new search folder. These include the following:

- Right-click on the "Search Folders" item in the navigation pane, and select the "New Folder" command from the pop-up menu.

- Right-click on the heading on any sample message that satisfies the criteria for the search folder that you want to create, select the "Create Rule From Message" submenu, and select any of "Search Folder from Subject," "Search Folder from Sender," "Search Folder from Recipient," or "Search Folder from Mailing List." (The last displays only if you select a message that Evolution can recognize as having been sent to a mailing list.) Each of these menu commands creates an initial search folder based on searching the specified portion of that mail message, which you can retain as is or further customize.

- Select the Edit menu's "Search Folders" command and click Add to create a new search folder.

- While any sample message that satisfies the criteria for the search folder that you want to create is highlighted, select the Message menu's "Create Rule" submenu, and select any of "Search Folder from Subject," "Search Folder from Sender," "Search Folder from Recipients," or "Search Folder from Mailing List." (The last only displays if you select a message that Evolution can recognize as having been sent to a mailing list.) Each of these menu commands creates an initial search folder based on searching the specified portion of that mail message, which you can retain as is or further customize.

Performing any of these actions displays a dialog like the one shown in Figure 7-18 that contains any initial criteria implied by the command that you selected.

FIGURE 7-18

Creating a new search folder

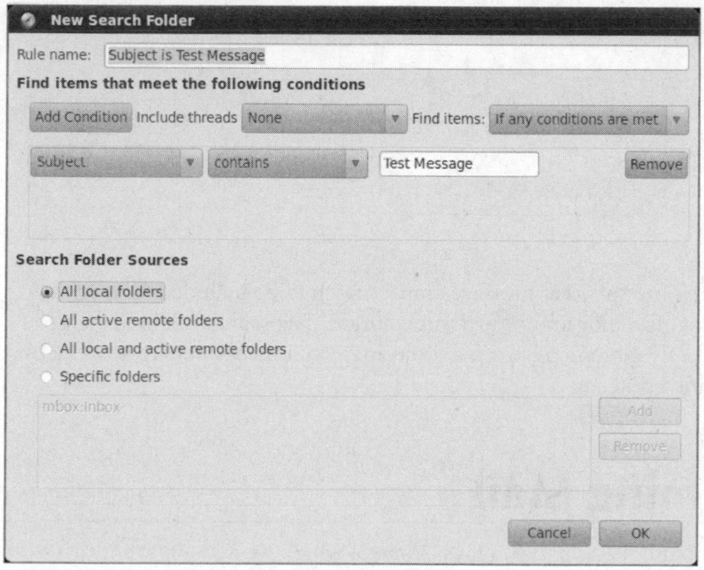

243

Once this dialog displays, you can specify a name for the search folder and add or refine the selection criteria for the search folder in the same way that you create filter rules for incoming mail, as explained in the next section. The primary difference between search folder and filter rule creation lies in the bottom half of the dialog shown in Figures 7-18 and 7-19, which (for search folders) identifies the location(s) that the folder should search for matching messages. You can specify that only certain folders be searched by clicking Add and selecting their names, or you can select "All local folders" to include messages from any folder, or "All local and active remote folders" to search the server-side, remote folders supported by mail protocols such as IMAP. Figure 7-19 shows a search folder that has been defined to search only a specific set of local folders.

FIGURE 7-19

A search rule associated with specific local folders

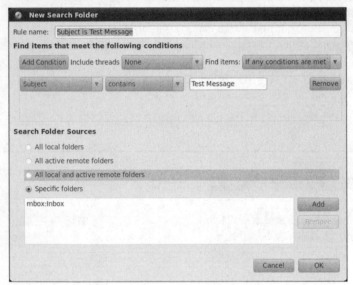

Once you're finished fine-tuning the rule that messages must match to be included in your new search folder, click OK to close this dialog and return to Evolution. The search folder is created under the Search Folder item in Evolution's navigation pane and contains pointers to any existing messages that match the specified criteria.

Filtering Incoming Mail

We all receive a significant amount of e-mail nowadays, some of which we actually want to receive. It's a sad fact of modern Internet life that all of us receive a significant amount of *spam* or *junk* mail. These are essentially equivalent terms for mail that we didn't ask for but that is either broadcast to collections of randomly generated e-mail addresses or perhaps sent to us directly if we were unlucky enough to get our e-mail addresses included on one of the lists that some companies, and certainly spammers, sell to each other.

Evolution provides two sophisticated features for automatically analyzing incoming mail and performing specific actions on mail messages that match these criteria. In the case of legitimate mail, Evolution enables you to create powerful filtering rules that can automatically file incoming mail in appropriate folders. Mail filters can also discard incoming messages from known spam sites, messages that contain words that only a spammer would use, or messages that match any other criteria that you define as spam.

In addition to making it easy for you to create powerful filtering rules, Evolution can also be integrated with other free Linux software that uses different approaches to identify spam and junk mail and automatically move it to your Junk folder. You can then quickly scan your Junk folder occasionally to see if all the mail in there is indeed junk, and, if so, you can easily delete it without having to read it.

The next two sections explain how to create your own filter rules and how to install the software required for junk mail processing in Evolution on Ubuntu systems.

Automatically Processing Incoming Mail

To expand on the definition of *filtering* given in the introduction to this section, *filtering* e-mail means to analyze its contents based on various criteria and to use the results of that examination to perform some action regarding that message. Message filters are typically applied to incoming messages that are stored locally — if you want to apply message filters to messages stored in a remote folder (such as your Inbox on an IMAP server), you must specify that as an option when creating your account, as shown in Figures 7-6 or 7-7.

As with most tasks in Evolution, there are several ways to create a new mail filter. These include the following:

- Right-click on the heading on any sample message that satisfies the criteria for the message filter that you want to create, select the "Create Rule From Message" submenu, and select "Filter on Subject," "Filter on Sender," "Filter on Recipients," or "Filter on Mailing List." (The last displays only if you select a message that Evolution can recognize as having been sent to a mailing list.) Each of these menu commands creates an initial message filter based on the specified portion of that mail message, which you can retain as is or further customize.

- Select the Edit menu's "Message Filters" command, and click Add to create a new message filter.

- While any sample message that satisfies the criteria for the search folder that you want to create is highlighted, select the Message menu's "Create Rule" submenu, and select any of "Filter on Subject," "Filter on Sender," "Filter on Recipients," or "Filter on Mailing List." (The last displays only if you select a message that Evolution can recognize as having been sent to a mailing list.) Each of these menu commands creates an initial message filter based on the specified portion of that mail message, which you can retain as is or further customize.

Performing any of these actions displays a dialog like the one shown in Figure 7-20 that contains any initial criteria implied by the command that you selected.

Creating or editing a message filter

When creating a message filter, the default action to perform on matching messages is to move that message to a specified folder. To identify that folder, click "<click here to select a folder>" and locate the target folder in the navigation dialog that displays.

Evolution provides a very sophisticated set of possible ways of matching messages in a message filter. The following are the portions of the message that you can match and the comparison operators that you can use. These correspond to the contents of the dropdown menus you see when clicking on the first two buttons when creating or editing a rule:

- **You can examine the following portions of a mail message when creating a rule:** Attachments, Date Received, Date Sent, Expression, Follow Up, Junk Test, Label, Match All, Message Body, Mailing List, Pipe to Program, Recipients, Regex Match, Score, Sender, Size (KB), Source Account, Specific Header, Status, and Subject.

- **You can analyze those portions of an e-mail message using the following comparison operators:** Contains, Does Not Contain, Does Not End With, Does Not Sound Like, Does Not Start With, Ends With, Is, Is After, Is Before, Is Greater Than, Is Less Than, Is Not, Returns Greater Than, Starts With, Sounds Like, And Starts With. Some of these operators can only be used when examining specific portions of a mail message. As an example, the "Is After" and "Is Before" operations can only be used with dates.

When creating a rule for matching a filter, you can select any of the items in the first and second columns, in any combination. Not all of the items in the second column are available for all types of match conditions—for example, options such as "is greater than" and "is less than" apply only when you are checking a match condition, such as Size, that has a numerical value.

As an example of using match conditions for filter rules, to create a rule that matches when a recipient of an e-mail message was ubuntu-users@lists.ubuntu.com, you would select "Recipients" from the first dropdown menu in the dialog shown in Figure 7-20, select "Is" from the second dropdown rule menu in that figure, and enter **ubuntu-users@lists.ubuntu.com** in the text area at the right to complete the rule.

Tip

When creating match rules, the most important control to set is whether a message must match only one (or more) of the specified criteria, or whether the associated operations will be performed only if the message matches *all* of the specified criteria. This can be the difference between a successful rule and one that doesn't work as you intended. This is controlled by the "Find Items" control, shown in the upper-right corner of any message filter dialog, which you can set to either "If any criteria are met" or "If all criteria are met." ■

Table 7-1 shows a list of the possible operations that you can perform on messages that match any (or all) of your filter conditions.

TABLE 7-1

Actions to Perform on Matching Messages

Operation	Action
Adjust Score	Select value from 3 to –3 or enter number to add.
Assign Color	Select color.
Assign Score	Select value from 3 to –3 or enter number.
Beep	N/A
Copy to Folder	Select folder.
Delete	N/A
Forward to	Specify an e-mail address to which to forward matching messages.
Move to Folder	Select folder.
Pipe to Program	Select program.
Play Sound	Select sound file.
Run Program	Select program.
Set Label	Specify a label that you want to associate with the message.
Set Status	Select from Replied to, Deleted, Draft, Important, Read, and Junk.
Stop Processing	N/A
Unset Status	Select from Replied to, Deleted, Draft, Important, Read, and Junk.

In Table 7-1, the first column is the operation that you want to perform, and the second column enables you to specify the value for that operation. For example, if you want to move a message to a specified folder after matching a filter rule, select the "Move to Folder" operation from the first dropdown menu in the "Then" portion of the rule, and click "<click here to select a folder>" to identify the target folder for that operation.

As an example of creating the "Then" portion of a filter rule, I'll continue with the example of messages whose recipients match ubuntu-users@lists.ubuntu.com. Assuming that I want to move such messages to their own folder, I would click "Move to Folder" from the dropdown menu in the first column and then navigate to the correct target folder. I could also add extra actions, such as Setting the status of the message to Read (otherwise the folder will show up in bold, indicating that it contains one or more unread messages), and conclude the rule with a "Stop Processing" instruction, which ensures that no other filter rules will be applied to the current message. This generally expedites message filtering because once a rule matches a message, no other analysis of that message is performed, and Evolution moves on to checking the next message.

Automatically Checking for Junk Mail

Evolution's ability to filter e-mail messages based on criteria that you can define is powerful but requires that you create a potentially huge number of rules to catch all of the spam and other junk mail that you may receive. Luckily, Evolution also supports the integration of external applications that can analyze messages and identify them as junk if that's the case. Popular examples of this sort of junk e-mail filter application are SpamAssassin (http://spamassassin.apache.org/) and Bogofilter (http://bogofilter.sourceforge.net/).

Evolution includes plug-ins for both SpamAssassin and Bogofilter, which will automatically execute the associated program and apply it to incoming mail. Bogofilter is installed by default on Ubuntu systems, so it's easiest to simply use that unless Bogofilter isn't working well enough for you. In my experience, SpamAssassin is more powerful and accurate than Bogofilter, but is also slower because it does many more SPAM checks than Bogofilter does.

Tip

If you want to install SpamAssassin on your system, you must use your favorite software installation tool to install SpamAssassin, as described in Chapter 19, "Adding, Removing, and Updating Software." You should then check Evolution's plug-in list to make sure that SpamAssassin integration is active. To do this, select Plugins from the Edit menu to display the "Plugin Manager" dialog. Once this dialog displays, scroll down to the SpamAssassin junk plug-in entry and make sure that it is enabled. Click OK after verifying this and enabling this plug-in, if necessary.

If you are having problems installing or using SpamAssassin, make sure that Evolution's Bogofilter plug-in is not enabled on the Edit ➪ Plugins dialog. This conflicts with SpamAssassin and can cause problems. ∎

Regardless of which SPAM filtering package you're using, clicking the Junk button in the Evolution toolbar will identify the currently selected message as junk and will move it to your Junk folder. Subsequent messages you receive that are conceptually similar to that message will automatically be identified as junk and also moved to the Junk folder. You should check the Junk folder periodically, verify that all of the messages that it contains are actually junk mail, and delete those messages. If you see messages classified as junk that are actually valid messages, select those messages and click the "Not Junk" button in the Evolution toolbar to make sure that similar messages are not categorized as junk. Over time, you will see that Evolution's support for junk mail filtering does a good job of identifying spam and other junk mail, saving you lots of time that would otherwise be spent examining such messages for criteria that you could use to manually filter out those e-mail messages.

Accessing Free and Web-Based E-Mail

The broadband or dial-up connection that you use to connect to the Internet from your home is generally supported by an academic or commercial Internet service provider (ISP) that also provides you with an e-mail address. Such e-mail addresses are inherently transient — once you finish with a class, graduate, and can't keep your .edu address, or change commercial ISPs, your e-mail account there is usually deleted. This may cause some of your more high-strung friends and family members, used to regularly exchanging mail with you as *bigdaddy@some-random-ISP. com*, to panic and begin sending sympathy cards to your wife, when all the while you simply have a new e-mail address.

As an alternative, companies such as AOL, Google, Microsoft, and Yahoo!, as well as hundreds of specialized web sites, provide free e-mail accounts that you can use regardless of your ISP and that you can access via any Web browser. Of course, these accounts are basically just free advertising for these companies, driving traffic to their web sites (gmail.com, hotmail.com, live .com, or yahoo.com, respectively), displaying advertisements in some cases, and so on.

With the exception of Gmail, you can read and send mail at these sites only by using a Web browser. This is a pain if you would like to use a single e-mail application, such as Evolution, to read and manage all of your e-mail. However, Gmail offers both POP and IMAP access, and you can at least read and archive your Web-based e-mail from any mailer that supports POP/POP3 mail by installing and configuring software such as FreePOPs. The next few sections explain each of these.

Tip

If you are interested in getting a free e-mail account, the EmailAddresses.com site (www.emailaddresses .com/guide_types.htm) is a good source of general information about the many different sites that provide free IMAP, POP3, and webmail accounts. ∎

Reading Gmail from a Desktop Mail Client

Google, providers of Gmail, is one of the few big-name, free e-mail providers that actually support POP and IMAP. This section explains how to configure Gmail to support either POP or IMAP. You could, of course, activate both to give yourself IMAP access to your account until you drain your e-mail with a POP client at some time, but I've never found that to be necessary.

The basic steps for reading Gmail using Evolution (or any other mail client) are as follows:

1. Configure Gmail to support the mail transport protocol that you want to use.

2. Create an account in your mail client that gives you access to your Gmail mail.

The next few sections provide the information that you'll need to do these steps for both POP and IMAP.

Selecting a Transport Protocol in Gmail

In order to access Gmail via POP or IMAP, you must first configure your Gmail account to be available via the protocol of your choice. To do this, log in to your Gmail account via Firefox — I mean, via your browser of choice — and select the Settings link in the upper-right portion of the screen. Next, select the Forwarding and POP/IMAP link in the header of the page that displays. This displays a screen like the one shown in Figure 7-21.

FIGURE 7-21

Configuring Gmail for POP/IMAP

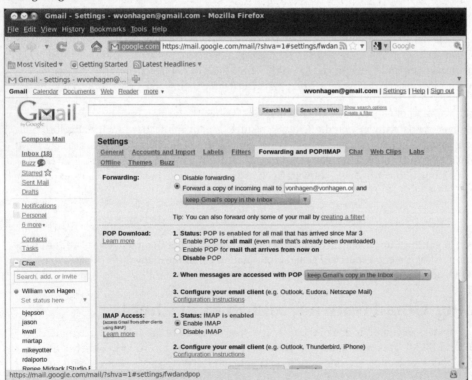

The bottom two settings on this screen enable you to activate POP and IMAP connectivity to your Gmail account. Personally, I tend to favor IMAP with Gmail because this guarantees that all of my Gmail mail is archived at Google and enables me to access it from anywhere, including any folders that I've set up in my Gmail account. Because I tend to use a variety of systems, this gives me a single view of my Gmail mail from anywhere. Your mileage may vary.

Tip

If you decide that you want to read Gmail via the Web only, you can also activate Forwarding, which will send a copy of any incoming Gmail mail to another e-mail address. To do this, click the "Forward a copy of incoming e-mail to" radio button, enter your other e-mail address, and make sure that the second configuration list says to keep Gmail's copy in the Inbox. This provides a nice notification mechanism for Gmail, which can be handy if your Gmail account is not your primary e-mail account. ∎

To activate IMAP access to your Gmail account, simply click the "Enable IMAP" radio button and click "Save Changes" at the bottom of the screen.

If you decide to use POP rather than IMAP, a few more configuration choices are available. First, you can either enable POP for all of your mail, or for all of the mail that arrives after the point at which you configured POP access. Which of these you want to use depends on how you want to use Gmail:

- If you want to personally archive all of your Gmail correspondence on one of your own systems, you'll probably want to select "Enable POP for all mail." The first time that you access your Gmail account with a mail client that is not configured to leave your mail on the server, all of the mail in your Inbox will be downloaded to your desktop system, and what happens to it in your Gmail account depends on how you set the "When messages are accessed with POP" configuration option (explained later in this section).

- If you use this option in the hopes of archiving all of your Gmail mail on one of your local systems, note that POP only deals with mail in the Inbox. Any mail that you've archived in folders that you created in your Gmail account will not be downloaded, only mail in the Inbox. If your goal is to archive everything locally, you'll have to copy or move the messages from your folder into your Inbox. Copying them will leave a copy in your Gmail account, but you won't be able to access those folders via POP.

- If you are simply using your mail client to check your Gmail mail and occasionally send messages but have configured your mail client to leave messages on the server, the first time that you check mail on any new system, you'll see a deluge of all of the mail that is still in the Inbox for your Gmail account. In this case, you should probably select the "Enable POP for all mail that arrives from now on" radio button.

There are plenty of other scenarios in which you may prefer one option over the other — these are just the most common cases. Personally, I like IMAP.

If you're still sold on POP, you can use the "When messages are accessed with POP" configuration item to fine-tune what happens to your Gmail mail when you read it via POP. These settings are as follows:

- **Keep Gmail's copy in the Inbox:** The default setting, this value enables you to read your Gmail mail over the Web but still access it via POP. This setting overrides whether your mail client wants to delete messages that it has downloaded and can protect you if you forget to tell your mail client to leave the messages on the server.

- **Delete Gmail's copy:** This value deletes mail from your Gmail Inbox once you've read it via POP and overrides the settings in your mail client. In other words, even if you've configured your mail client to leave messages on the server, any Gmail mail that you access via POP will be purged from your Gmail account.

- **Archive Gmail's copy:** This value deletes mail from your Gmail Inbox once you've read it via POP but leaves an archive copy of the mail on your Gmail account that you can still access via the "All Mail" link. This setting also overrides the settings in your mail client. In other words, even if you've configured your mail client to leave messages on the server, any Gmail mail that you access via POP will be purged from your Inbox but will still be available in the "All Mail" link.

After you have activated POP or IMAP on this screen, optionally enabled Forwarding, and specified any related configuration parameters, click "Save Changes" at the bottom of the screen. Your configuration changes will be saved, and your Inbox re-displays.

Accessing Gmail Using POP

To check and read your Gmail mail via POP, you must specify the following values when creating an account for receiving incoming mail:

- **E-mail Address:** *your-username*@gmail.com
- **Server Type:** POP
- **Server:** pop.gmail.com
- **Username:** *your-username*@gmail.com
- **Requires Security/Authentication:** Yes, SSL encryption
- **Port:** 995
- **Password:** *your-gmail-password*

Note

You should, of course, replace *your-username* and *your-gmail-password* with the appropriate values for your account when creating a new account in Evolution. ■

There are always plenty of other configuration options, such as whether you want messages to be stored on the server and for how long, whether you want to automatically check for messages and how often, whether checking mail at this account should be included in a default mail check, and so on. Different mail clients handle this information differently. For example, in Evolution, whether you check mail for an account by default depends on whether an e-mail account is enabled in Evolution's main Accounts dialog. You'll probably want to enable this option when first creating and configuring POP access to your Gmail account — you can always disable it after you're sure that everything is working correctly.

Sending outgoing Gmail mail is done via the SMTP protocol. To send your Gmail mail with your mail client, you must specify the following values when creating an account for sending mail:

- **Server Type:** SMTP
- **Server:** smtp.gmail.com
- **Port:** 587 or 465
- **Requires Security/Authentication:** Yes, TLS or STARTTLS. (If this option isn't available, try SSL encryption.)

Test your new account by using an existing e-mail account to send an e-mail message to your Gmail account, and clicking Send/Receive in Evolution. If you can successfully retrieve mail, you should then check that you can send mail using this account. To do this, create a new message using the icon or the File ⇨ New menu, selecting the menu item to send a new mail message.

To see the official Google explanation of how to configure POP access to your Gmail account, see http://mail.google.com/support/bin/answer.py?answer=13287. If you have any problems with the explanation provided in this section, you may want to check that site, just in case something has changed since this book was written.

Accessing Gmail Using IMAP

To check and read your Gmail mail via IMAP, you must specify the following values when creating an account for receiving incoming mail:

- **E-mail Address:** *your-username*@gmail.com
- **Server Type:** IMAP
- **Server:** imap.gmail.com
- **Username:** *your-username*@gmail.com
- **Requires Security/Authentication:** Yes, SSL encryption
- **Port:** 993
- **Password:** *your-gmail-password*

Note
You should, of course, replace *your-username* **and** *your-gmail-password* **with the appropriate values for your account when creating a new account in Evolution.** ■

There are always plenty of other configuration options, such as which folders to check mail in, whether you want to automatically check for messages and how often, whether checking mail at this account should be included in a default mail check, and so on. Different mailers handle this information differently. For example, in Evolution, whether you check mail for an account by default depends on whether an e-mail account is enabled in Evolution's main Accounts dialog. You'll probably want to enable this option when first creating and configuring POP access to your Gmail account — you can always disable it after you're sure that everything is working correctly.

Sending outgoing Gmail mail is done via the SMTP protocol. To send your Gmail mail with your mail client, you must specify the following values when creating an account for sending mail:

- **Server Type:** SMTP
- **Server:** smtp.gmail.com
- **Port:** 587 or 465
- **Requires Security/Authentication:** Yes, TLS or STARTTLS. (If this option isn't available, try SSL encryption.)

Test your new account by using an existing e-mail account to send an e-mail message to your Gmail account, and clicking Send/Receive in Evolution. If you can successfully retrieve mail, you should then check that you can send mail using this account. To do this, create a new message using the icon or the File ⇨ New menu, selecting the menu item to send a new mail message. Make sure that you specify that the identity of the sender is your Gmail account.

To see the official Google explanation of how to configure IMAP access to your Gmail account, see http://mail.google.com/support/bin/answer.py?answer=78799. If you have any problems with the explanation provided in this section, you may want to check that site, just in case something has changed since this book was written.

Reading Mail from Other Web-Based Mail Providers

Many free e-mail providers such as Hotmail and its successor, Microsoft Live, Yahoo!, mail.com, and so on provide free e-mail accounts that are designed to be accessed via webmail — in other words, via a browser-based interface. By default, these webmail-only e-mail accounts can therefore not be accessed via standard protocols such as POP or IMAP. Thanks to the cleverness and hard work of zillions of open source software developers everywhere, you can access these accounts via POP if you install and run a local software process that knows how to access these webmail sites, but provides a POP interface that you can talk to. I am a big fan of a package called FreePOPs! (www.freepops.org), which does exactly that. Many other open source and commercial packages provide similar functionality to FreePOPs!, but FreePOPs! is available in the Ubuntu repositories, is easy to set up, and has always worked for me. If you're interested in similar packages, you may want to look at YPOPs! (www.ypopsemail.com) or MrPostman (http://mrpostman.sourceforge.net/scripts.html). These are all generic solutions that provide a POP interface for your existing mail reader.

There are a variety of reasons why you may want to access a free webmail account from a local mail client such as Evolution. Some of my favorites are:

- It's nice to be able to use the same application for all of your e-mail.
- Using a POP client with a webmail account enables you to archive all of your mail on your local machine, which is reassuring for the paranoid among us.
- It's tricky (impossible) to access webmail when you're offline.
- You also don't have to worry about synchronizing address books using a directed graph that can end up looking like an M.C. Escher drawing if you have enough e-mail accounts.

Note that being able to access a webmail account via POP does not enable you to send mail through that account. As mentioned several times in this chapter, retrieving incoming mail is done via protocols such as POP and IMAP, while outgoing mail is either sent using a remote mail server that you communicate with using SMTP or by contacting a local mail server via a traditional UNIX/Linux Sendmail interface. You have a few choices for sending mail using your webmail account:

- Continue to use the webmail interface to send mail for this account (which is something of a pain).
- Send mail for your webmail account using an existing SMTP server to which you already have access.
- Follow the instructions provided in Chapter 30 on how to install, configure, and run your own mail server. It's really not that hard, and think how powerful you'll feel!

The next two sections explain how to install FreePOPs! and how to configure your mail client to access a free webmail account through it.

Note

Another alternative to using FreePOPs! or another, similar package, is to switch to a different mail reader such as Mozilla's Thunderbird, which provides support for webmail via its Webmail extension (http://webmail .mozdev.org/). As a long-time Evolution fan, that's not an option for me, but your mileage may vary.... ∎

Installing and Using FreePOPs!

The FreePOPs! package is available in Ubuntu's universe repository as the package freepops and can easily be installed using your favorite package management tools, as explained in Chapter 19. You should probably also install the freepopsdoc package, which will install the FreePOPs! documentation into /usr/share/doc/freepops-doc — you can't lose by having all of the documentation for a package.

Once you've installed the freepops package, the FreePOPs! startup file is installed as /etc/ init.d/freepops. The FreePOPs! server is not started by default. For testing purposes, you can start it manually by executing a command such as sudo /etc/init.d/freepops restart. (I use restart rather than start just in case a process is already running for some reason.) You should then add this startup script into your system's startup process, typically by creating a symbolic link to the FreePOPs! startup file in the /etc/rc2.d directory used to start processes under runlevel 2, which is the default runlevel for Ubuntu systems. You should also create an equivalent symlink for use when shutting down your system. These commands would look like the following:

```
sudo ln -s /etc/init.d/freepops /etc/rc2.d/S99freepops
sudo ln -s /etc/init.d/freepops /etc/rc2.d/K99freepops
```

After you've run the FreePOPs! startup script, the FreePOPs! daemon will be running on your system, which you should be able to see in a process listing. You are now ready to configure an e-mail account so that you can read your webmail via POP, as described in the next section. Even though I've been using this package for quite a while, I still find it incredibly cool that I'm able to do this. Thanks, Open Source Community!

Creating POP Accounts for Use with FreePOPs!

After installing FreePOPs!, you'll need to create accounts that enable you to access it. To check and read your webmail via POP, you must specify the following values when creating an account for receiving incoming mail:

- **E-mail Address:** *your-username@host.com*
- **Server Type:** POP
- **Server:** localhost
- **Username:** *your-username@host.com*
- **Requires Security/Authentication:** No
- **Port:** 2000
- **Password:** *your-password*

In these examples, replace *host* with *hotmail, live, mail, yahoo,* or whatever other domain name is used by your free webmail host. Similarly, you should replace *your-username* and *your-password* with the appropriate values for your account when creating a new account in Evolution.

If your mail client provides integrated incoming/outgoing accounts (as Evolution does), simply continue with the account definition process, specifying one of the SMTP servers discussed in the introductory text for the section entitled "Reading Mail from Other Web-Based Mail Providers." If your mail client stores information about incoming and outgoing mail messages separately (as Kontact does), save the current changes for POP access to your webmail account, and create an account for sending the mail associated with your webmail account.

Test your new account by using an existing e-mail account to send an e-mail message to your webmail account and clicking Send/Receive in Evolution. If you can successfully retrieve mail, you should then check that you can send mail using the outgoing mail server that you associated with this account. To do this, create a new message using the icon or the File ➪ New menu, selecting the menu item to send a new mail message. Make sure that you specify that the identity of the sender is your webmail account.

Note

POP/POP3 access to Yahoo! mail accounts is supposedly available to Yahoo! mail account holders in a non-USA Yahoo! domain. (I haven't verified this.) In the United States, you have to upgrade (and therefore pay money) for the Yahoo! Mail Plus package in order to get a send/receive POP e-mail account at Yahoo!. See http://mailplus.mail.yahoo.com for more information. ■

Tip

To ask questions about or make suggestions for FreePOPs!, see the FreePOPs! user forums at http://freepops.diludovico.it. ■

Managing Contacts

Contacts are the people with whom you often interact and exchange e-mail, and about whom you therefore want to maintain contact information: their full name; their surface address for snail mail; their e-mail address(es) at home, work, or both; their home page; any Instant Messaging addresses they have; their corporate or academic affiliation; their home, office, and mobile telephone numbers; and so on. Collections of Contact information are typically referred to as an *address book*.

Maintaining complete and easily accessed contact information is an important part of any PIM application. Evolution provides integrated support for managing local contact information, as well as the ability to contact networked address books via standard protocols. The next sections explain how to configure and use Contact information within Evolution.

Configuring Evolution's Contact Support

Evolution provides two basic levels of Contact customization: configuring how Evolution's mail composer interacts with the information in your Contact database(s) and configuring the source of your Contact information. Unless you're using Evolution in a commercial or academic environment, you probably won't care about remote sources of Contact information, so I'll focus on configuring contact/mail interaction first, and explain using Contact Information from remote LDAP servers second, for those of us who are lucky enough to be able to do so.

Configuring Contact/E-Mail Interaction

Evolution's Contacts doesn't require much independent configuration, but how an Evolution e-mail account interacts with a Contacts database, and which one it interacts with, can be configured in different areas of the standard Evolution Preferences dialog. Select Edit ⇨ Preferences (or press Shift+Ctrl+S) in Evolution to display this dialog.

By default, Evolution will automatically attempt to look up names and e-mail addresses from your default address book as you type them when composing mail, which is known as *autocompletion* because Evolution is automatically trying to provide complete names or e-mail addresses based on the characters that you have typed so far. When the characters that you have typed match one or more names or e-mail addresses in any of your address books, a list of all possible completions will be displayed in the appropriate field (To, CC, BCC) in Evolution's composition window. You can accept any of these potential completions by using the mouse to select that name or e-mail address, or continue typing to further refine the list of possible matches.

The default address book for Evolution is the Personal address book located on the computer that you are using to compose mail. If you have multiple address books, such as an LDAP address book that you can access via a network, you will have to activate these address books as other sources that Evolution should check when trying to automatically complete names and e-mail addresses. To do this, click the Autocompletion icon in the left pane of the Evolution Preferences dialog, which displays a dialog like the one shown in Figure 7-22.

Activating Autocompletion in available address books

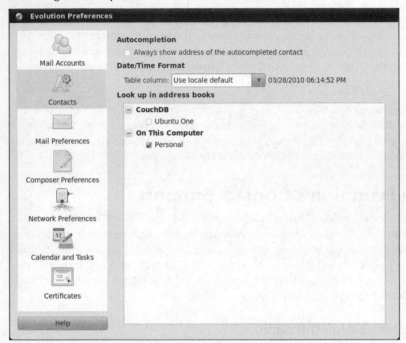

Address books that will be used for autocompletion are checked. To add another address book, simply select the checkbox to the left of its name. Once you're done making changes, click Close to close the Preferences dialog and return to Evolution, or click another icon to configure a different aspect of Evolution.

One of the features that I find most useful when building an address book is Evolution's ability to automatically create contacts based on the e-mail addresses in any messages that you respond to. Whenever I receive mail from an old (or new) friend, that friend is added as a Contact to my Personal address book automatically when I reply to the message. No more looking for a message from someone in order to figure out his or her e-mail address! Evolution simply does the right thing — once this configuration option is enabled, of course.

Activating automatic contact creation is done on the Mail Preferences pane of the Evolution Preferences application. To access related settings, first open the Preferences dialog by selecting Edit ➪ Preferences (or pressing Ctrl+Shift+S) in Evolution and clicking the Mail Preferences icon in the left pane of the Evolution Preferences dialog. Next, select the "Automatic Contacts" tab at the far right of the top of this dialog. This displays a screen like the one shown in Figure 7-23.

Configuring "Automatic Contact" creation and synchronization

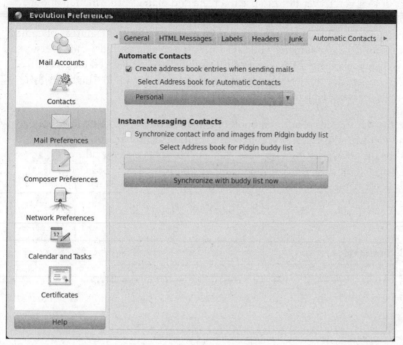

To automatically create contacts for any recipient of e-mail that you send, click the checkbox to the left of the aptly named "Create address book entries when sending mails" option. Once this checkbox is selected, you must also select the address book to which you want to add those entries. To add them to the address book on the computer that you are using to compose and send mail, click the "Select Address Book for automatic contacts" dropdown list and select Personal. If you have more than one local address book or have access to a networked LDAP address book, you can select any of these, but you can identify only a single address book to which contacts will be added automatically.

If you use Pidgin, one of the instant messaging clients discussed in Chapter 10, "Sending and Receiving Instant Messages," the dialog shown in Figure 7-23 also enables you to automatically pull contact information from your Pidgin buddy list. To activate this, click the checkbox to the left of the "Periodically synchronize" entry and click the dropdown list to select the Pidgin address book that you want to pull from. After selecting an address book, you can click the "Synchronize with buddy list now" button to extract current contact information from your Pidgin buddy list and copy it into Evolution. Don't worry—this information will still be available in Pidgin. This is strictly a non-destructive pull operation.

Accessing Remote Contact Information via LDAP

When using Ubuntu and Evolution on a home computer system, Evolution's local address book provides all of the power that you'll ever need to use to create and manage information about friends, family, and other contacts. However, Evolution's address book can also be seamlessly integrated with business or academic settings that maintain central, networked sources of contact information. If you work for a small company, you may know (or be able to figure out) everyone's e-mail address. When you work for IBM, that's a bit trickier, hence the need for centralized address books. Most networked address book information is provided by LDAP (Lightweight Directory Access Protocol) servers, which are well-supported in Evolution.

To add an LDAP server to the sources of address book information that are consulted when you compose mail and identify addressees, click New in Evolution's icon bar, and select "Address Book" from the dropdown list that appears. You can also create a new address book by right-clicking on any existing Address Book and using the menus by selecting the File ⇨ New ⇨ Address Book menu item. This displays the dialog shown in Figure 7-24.

FIGURE 7-24

Creating a new address book in Evolution

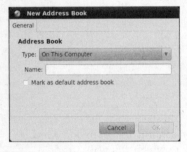

Once this dialog displays, click the Type dropdown list and select "On LDAP Servers." A dialog like the one shown in Figure 7-25 displays.

In the Name field, enter the name that you want to associate with the LDAP server that you want to contact and that you will see in the LDAP Servers list. (This does not need to be the hostname of the LDAP server.) Next, enter the hostname or IP address of the LDAP server in the Server field, and change the port if necessary ("port 389" is the default). Next, specify the type of security required to connect to and retrieve information from the LDAP server. This is either "No encryption," "TLS encryption" (Transport Layer Security), or "SSL encryption" (Secure Sockets Layer) connection. Finally, select the Login method required to authenticate to the server, which is one of "Anonymously," "Using email address," or "Using distinguished name" (DN). If you select one of the latter two, you must enter the appropriate information—either your e-mail address or your distinguished name in your LDAP domain, which is typically something like CN=vonhagen,OU=Users, DC=ldap,DC=vonhagen,DC=org (which means "the Users\vonhagen entry in the LDAP server running on the host ldap.vonhagen.org").

FIGURE 7-25

Creating an entry for an LDAP server

If searches for LDAP entries begin at a specific LDAP directory (such as users in the previous example), you can specify this by clicking the Details tab and entering the LDAP starting point in the Search base field.

Finally, click OK to save your LDAP address book definition. You should now be able to look up and retrieve e-mail addresses for people from the LDAP address book.

Tip

If Evolution does not display an error message but does not seem to retrieve remote contact info from your LDAP server, you may need to restart your evolution-data-server process. This is the Evolution process that communicates with remote services such as LDAP. To identify this process, execute a command such as the following:

```
$ ps ax | grep evolution
3014  ? Sl 5:34  evolution --component=mail
3021  ? Sl 0:02 /usr/lib/evolution/evolution-data-server
...
20031 ? Sl 0:00 /usr/lib/evolution/2.12/evolution-exchange...
```

In this case, you will need to restart process 3021, which you should be able to do with the command kill -HUP 3021. Worst case, terminate all of your evolution processes using the kill -9 PID command (where PID is the process ID of each process), and restart Evolution, which will restart all necessary processes. ■

Adding and Editing Contact Information

To view and edit your contacts, click the Contacts button in the lower-left corner of the main evolution window. A screen like the one shown in Figure 7-26 appears.

Your initial Contacts view

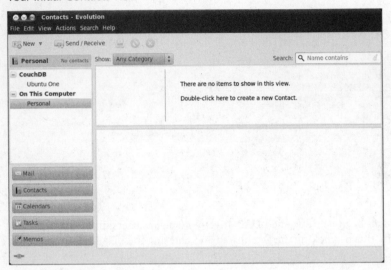

Unless you imported Contact information into Evolution during the Evolution setup process or have already sent mail in Evolution with the "Automatically add to addressbook" option active (described earlier in this chapter in the section, "Configuring Contact/E-Mail Interaction"), the first time that you view your contacts, you won't see any because you have not yet defined any. You can type Ctrl+N in the Contacts view to create a new contacts entry. This displays a dialog like the one shown in Figure 7-27.

This dialog enables you to enter all of the information that you can (or want to) about the contact that you are defining. The Contact tab, displayed by default when you first add a new contact or edit an existing one, contains name, e-mail address, phone, and instant messaging information for a contact. This dialog also provides two other tabs:

- **Personal Information:** Enables you to record information about a contact's Web presence (home page, online calendar, blog, etc.), professional information (such as their position, employer, manager, assistant, etc.), and personal information (such as the name of their significant other, their birthday, anniversary, etc.)

- **Mailing Address:** Enables you to enter a contact's personal and work e-mail addresses, and a spare address field for things such as the location of their beach house or hunting camp

FIGURE 7-27

Defining contact information

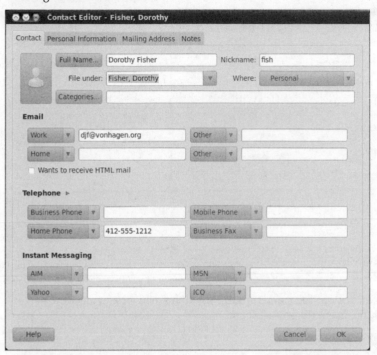

Once you've entered whatever information you want to record about this contact, click OK to close the "Contact Information" dialog and return to the general Contacts view. Once you've defined one or more contacts, the Contacts view will look something like Figure 7-28, with summary information about the currently selected contact displayed in the bottom half of the Contacts pane.

To see this summary information about any defined contact, select that contact from the Contacts list pane (above the summary information). You can scroll left to right through this list to locate any existing contact. Once you've accumulated a large number of contacts, you may find it more convenient to search for a contact by entering a portion of their name in the Search area above the contacts list and pressing Return to view any matches for that string. You can also click the icon at the left of the Search box to search by e-mail address or by the contents of any field in the contact information.

To edit or view detailed information about any existing contact, double-click on the entry for that contact to re-display the dialog shown in Figure 7-27, which enables you to correct or add information about that contact. If you were just checking information, click Cancel to close this dialog. If you have made changes, click OK to save the updated information.

FIGURE 7-28

Summary information about a selected contact

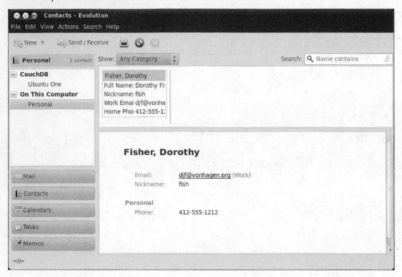

After viewing or editing information, you can return to Evolution's mail view at any time by clicking the Mail button in the list in the lower-left corner.

Working with vCards

VCards are text files with a .vcf file extension that contain contact information. The format of these files was designed to provide a standard method of exchanging contact information between users regardless of the e-mail client or computing platform that they use.

If you receive e-mail containing a vCard, you can easily import it into Evolution's contacts list by scrolling down in Evolution and clicking "Save in Address Book."

If Evolution doesn't give you this option for some reason, you can also save vCards to text files on your system by right-clicking the attachment and selecting "Save As." You can then use Evolution's File ⇨ ?Import command to import the vCard into your address book.

If you want to share your Evolution contact information with someone else as a vCard, you can create a vCard for a single contact or save all of your contacts to a single vCard file. To create a vCard file containing your selection(s), select one or more contacts and right-click on the selected items. Select "Save as vCard." A dialog displays that enables you to specify the name of the file to which you want to save your selection(s). To simply mail the vCard version of your selection(s), right-click on the selection(s) and select "Forward Contact." A new mail message opens in a composition window with a vCard containing your selection(s) as an attachment.

Defining Mailing Lists

Many of us belong to Internet mailing lists, Google groups, Yahoo! groups, and other focused e-mail discussions of our favorite topics, including perhaps the various Ubuntu mailing lists discussed in Chapter 1, "The Ubuntu Linux Project." These types of mailing lists are usually handled by specialized software packages such as Mailman (www.gnu.org/software/mailman), which handles things such as keeping the list members anonymous, providing a single e-mail address to send and respond to mail, and supporting online archives of mailing list traffic. While these requirements are almost mandatory for Internet-wide mailing lists, they are overkill for smaller mailing lists, such as your family, friends with a similar sense of humor, former colleagues from a previous employer, and so on. For most of us, having a simple way of associating multiple e-mail addresses with a single list name would suffice — which is exactly what Evolution provides.

Evolution makes it easy to set up your own mailing lists, known as *Contact Lists*, for personal communications by defining a Contact List name and then associating specific people from your Contacts address book with that list. You can then send mail to the name of the list, and Evolution handles sending that identical message to all of the people on that list.

You can create a new Contact List in various ways:

- Press Ctrl+Shift+L anywhere in Evolution.
- Select the File ⇨ New ⇨ Contacts List menu entry.
- Click the New button and select "Contacts List" from the dropdown menu.
- Right-click on the Contact List when in the Contacts view, and select "New Contact List" from the context-sensitive menu.

Performing any of these actions displays the dialog shown in Figure 7-29.

FIGURE 7-29

Creating a new Contact List

In the List name field, enter the name of the list that you want to create. You can then add e-mail addresses to the new list in any of the following ways:

- Click Select to display the dialog shown in Figure 7-30, in which you can select existing Contact entries and click Add to add them to the current Contact List. When you're done, you can click OK to return to the dialog shown in Figure 7-29.

FIGURE 7-30

Adding e-mail addresses to a Contact List

- Drag-and-drop contact entries into the Members area from the pane in which your contacts are listed.
- Manually enter e-mail addresses that you want to add to the list, pressing Return after each address.

Once you've created and populated a Contact List, you can configure whether or not the e-mail that you send to the list contains all of the e-mail addresses of its members. The "Hide addresses when sending mail to this list" checkbox is selected by default. When this checkbox is selected for a mailing list, the recipients of your messages will see *Undisclosed Recipients* as the name to which the message was sent and will not be able to reply to anyone other than to you (because the names of the other list members are hidden). If you deselect this checkbox, all of the e-mail addresses of the list members will be shown in the "To:" field of your mail message, and any recipient can therefore reply to every recipient by selecting the "Reply To All" command.

Note

Hiding the recipients of mail to a Contact List is done by putting their e-mail addresses in the BCC (Blind Carbon Copy) field. Evolution displays a warning message when sending a message that has no visible recipients, to which you can simply respond OK if you only wanted to send mail to list members without letting them know who else received the message. ■

To save your new Contact List and close the dialog shown in Figure 7-30, click OK. You can now send mail to the list by entering the name of the list in a new mail message, just as you would with a standard e-mail address. You can also send mail to the list by right-clicking on its name in your list of contacts in the Contacts view and selecting "Send Message to List" from the context-sensitive menu that displays.

Managing Your Calendar

After e mail and managing contact information, the last critical component of a Personal Information Management application is the ability to manage one's calendar. Evolution's Calendar component, accessed by clicking the Calendars button in the lower-left corner of the Evolution GUI, is both easy-to-use and powerful, making it quite easy for you to track and manage your personal calendar on your personal machine, creating custom reminders for the items on your calendar. By default, a local calendar named *Personal* is created in every Evolution installation.

Evolution's calendar support isn't limited to maintaining your calendar on your machine — you can publish information about your calendar to a web site for anyone to see, and you can also connect to remote calendaring resources via popular protocols like WebCal and CalDAV to know what others are doing or for group scheduling purposes. Because of this dual focus on individual and group calendaring items, Evolution's calendar module handles defining personal appointments and group meetings slightly differently.

The next few sections discuss the highlights of configuring your Evolution calendar and explain how to create local calendar entries with reminders, configure your Evolution calendar to integrate remote calendaring resources, and share your free/busy information with others.

Basic Calendar Configuration

You can configure a variety of aspects of the Evolution Calendar. To configure the Evolution Calendar, select the Edit menu's Preferences command, and select the "Calendars and Tasks" icon from the left pane of the Preferences dialog. This displays the dialog shown in Figure 7-31.

Evolution enables you to configure the time zone, time format (12 hour or 24 hour), the days of the week and hours of the day of your work week, the minimum size of a schedulable appointment, and many options having to do with how appointments, meetings, and alarms are displayed. Evolution's Calendar module provides a good set of default values, and many people do not need to customize the configuration of their calendar. However, I've tweaked a few things over the years, so I'll highlight those in the following subsections.

FIGURE 7-31

General Calendar configuration items in Evolution

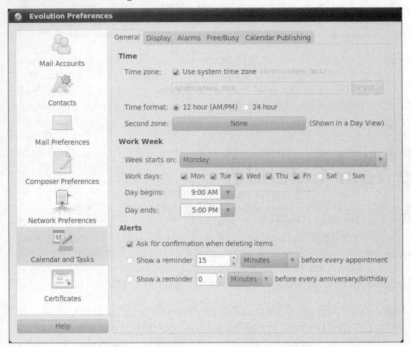

Defining Your Work Day and Work Hours

By default, Evolution assumes a work week of Monday through Friday, and working hours of 9 a.m. to 5 p.m. Not all of us are lucky enough to work those hours, so you may want to change this to reflect your actual schedule. You can do this from the screen shown in Figure 7-31 by selecting the days of the week that you work and selecting the hours at which your work day begins and ends from the appropriate dropdown lists.

Configuring your work week and hours doesn't affect Evolution's ability to schedule items at any time, but configuring the hours in your work day is necessary before you can print your calendar for a given day. By default, any single-day calendar that you print will contain only entries that fall within your workday.

After changing any values on this tab, click Close to close the Evolution Preferences dialog. The new work week and work hours that you selected will automatically be displayed on your calendar.

Setting Event Granularity on Your Calendar

Another commonly modified Evolution calendar setting is the time divisions that are shown on your calendar. Evolution's default calendar setting uses 30-minute time divisions, which means that you can't schedule an appointment for a time period less than 30 minutes. If, like me, you prefer to schedule things in 15-minute increments, you can change the time divisions by selecting the Display tab in the "Calendar and Tasks configuration" dialog, which is shown in Figure 7-32.

FIGURE 7-32

Configuring Calendar granularity and display in Evolution

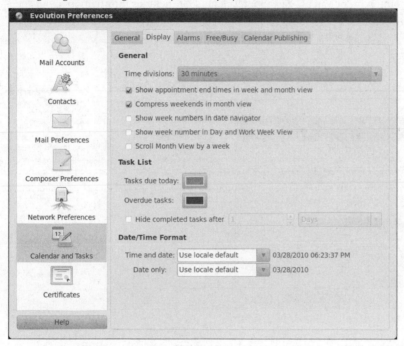

Once this dialog displays, you can select a different time division, such as 15 minutes, from the Time divisions dropdown list. After changing this value, click Close to close the Evolution Preferences dialog. The new time divisions that you selected will automatically be displayed on your calendar.

Creating and Editing Personal Calendar Entries

Evolution's Calendar module enables you to define two different types of events in your personal calendar: appointments that are scheduled for a specific day and time (and which can repeat), and "All Day Appointments" that are scheduled for a specific day. Like most things in Evolution, you can create these types of entries for your personal calendar in various ways:

- Press Ctrl+Shift+A anywhere in Evolution to create a personal appointment.

- Select the File ⇨ New ⇨ All Day Appointment or Appointment menu entries.

- Click the New button and select "All Day Appointment" or Appointment from the drop-down menu.

- Right-click on a calendar when in the Calendar view, and select "All Day Event" or Appointment from the context-sensitive menu.

Performing any of these actions displays a dialog like the one shown in Figure 7-33. This dialog is for defining an appointment, not an all-day appointment, so it includes information about the start and stop time for the appointment. The "All-Day Appointment" dialog is almost identical, except that it does not include a start and a stop time.

FIGURE 7-33

Defining a new appointment

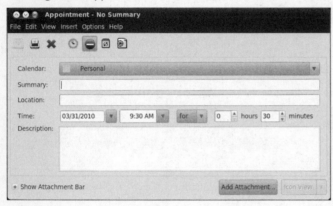

Enter the basic information about the appointment that you want to schedule by entering a *Summary*, which is the basic description of the appointment that will display on your Evolution Calendar. (Keep it brief but intuitive.) You can optionally enter a location for the appointment, and enter a more verbose description of the appointment (including meeting notes, phone numbers, etc.) in the Description field. You should also double-check the start and stop times for the appointment and correct them if necessary. (If you created your appointment by right-clicking on your calendar and selecting "New Appointment," the default start time for the meeting will reflect the time division in which the cursor was located when you selected that command.)

After filling in the details of your appointment, you may want to set an Alarm by clicking the Alarms icon in the Appointment dialog. This will cause a pop-up reminder dialog to display on your screen at the time for which the alarm was set.

Clicking the Alarms icon displays a dialog like the one shown in Figure 7-34.

Defining an alarm for an appointment

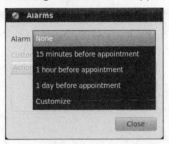

Click the Alarm field to show a dropdown menu of possible alarm times. After selecting an alarm, it is displayed in the Alarm list window. You can then click Close to close this dialog and return to the appointment dialog, or select Customize from the Alarm list to customize the text for the alarm that you selected.

When an alarm goes off, a dialog displays on your screen, reminding you of the upcoming appointment. You can either click Close to terminate the alarm, or click Snooze to dismiss the alarm for the specified period (the default is 5 minutes), after which the alarm dialog will re-display. If you need a bit more time, you can also customize the snooze period on the alarm dialog before clicking Snooze.

After defining an appointment and setting any alarms that you want to use as reminders, you can also configure this appointment to be a recurring appointment. This means that the appointment will be automatically added to your calendar based on the period that you specify for its recurrence. To configure an appointment as a recurring appointment, click the Recurrence icon in the toolbar for the appointment that you are defining. This displays a dialog like the one shown in Figure 7-35.

Once this dialog displays, click the "This appointment recurs" checkbox, and use the dropdown lists to specify when it re-occurs and for how long. If there are specific days on which you will not be having this appointment, such as on holidays, you can select those days on the Calendar previews and click Add to add them to the list of exceptions.

Once you have finished defining any recurrence of the appointment that you are creating, click Close to return to the Appointment dialog. You can then click Save to save the current state of this appointment and continue working on it, or click Close to close this dialog and return to Evolution's Calendar view.

After you have defined an appointment, you can edit it at any time by double-clicking on the appointment in Evolution's Calendar view.

FIGURE 7-35

Defining recurring appointments

Creating and Editing Meetings

Meetings differ from appointments and all-day appointments in that they involve multiple people. Entries for the meetings that you define will be sent to all of the participants that you define for the meeting and will show up on their calendars if they accept the invitation.

You can create a new meeting in various ways:

- Press Ctrl+Shift+E anywhere in Evolution.
- Select the File ➪ New ➪ Meeting menu entry.
- Click the New button, and select "Meeting" from the dropdown menu.
- Right-click in a calendar when in the Calendar view, and select "Meeting" from the context-sensitive menu.

Performing any of these actions displays the dialog shown in Figure 7-36.

Providing basic information about your meeting, setting alarms, and defining recurring meetings are all done as described in the previous section. The primary difference between creating an appointment and a meeting is that you will probably want to invite others to the meeting. You can add a single attendee by clicking Add and entering the name or e-mail address of that person. However, it is much easier to add other people to your meeting by clicking the Attendees button to display the dialog shown in Figure 7-37.

FIGURE 7-36

Creating a new meeting

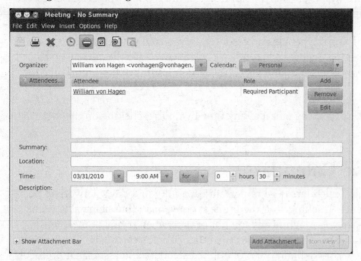

FIGURE 7-37

Adding attendees to a meeting

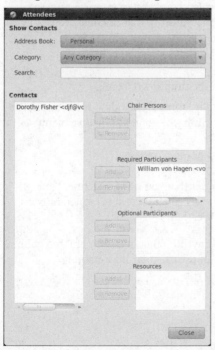

This dialog enables you to select a contact and then click Add beside the different dialogs that identify their role in the meeting: "Chair Persons," "Required Participants," and "Optional Participants." If your conference rooms are listed in an LDAP address book, you can also reserve them by adding them as resources.

Once you have finished identifying the people and resources associated with this meeting, click Close to return to the Meeting dialog. You can then click Save to save the current state of this meeting and continue working on it, or click Close to dismiss this dialog and return to Evolution's Calendar view.

After you have defined a meeting, you can edit it at any time by double-clicking on the meeting in Evolution's Calendar view.

Integrating Online Calendars

Being able to view other people's calendars is an important capability in today's networked business and academic environments. Tracking your own time is convenient, but being able to see other people's calendars can save you a significant amount of time when trying to meet with someone or simply track them down. To support viewing other people's calendar's, the Evolution Calendar module supports the most common types of online calendars and associated protocols that are in use today: Google Calendars, CalDAV, and WebCal. Evolution also supports weather calendars, which enable you to display current temperature and general weather condition information in Evolution's Calendar view.

Integrating an online calendar is done by creating a new calendar of the appropriate type in Evolution and filling in any information that is required to connect to that calendar. You can create a new calendar in Evolution in various ways:

- Select the File ⇨ New ⇨ Calendar menu entry.
- Click the New button, and select Calendar from the dropdown menu.
- Right-click on an existing calendar in the Calendar Summary window at the upper-left of the Calendar view, and select "New Calendar" from the context-sensitive menu.

Performing any of these actions displays the dialog shown in Figure 7-38.

Click the Type dropdown list, and select the type of calendar that you want to define. Your choices are Google, CalDAV, "On This Computer" (a new local calendar that is located only on your machine), "On The Web" (a WebCal calendar), and Weather.

Next, specify a name for this calendar. This name can be anything that is meaningful to you, but most people tend to use a name that identifies the source of the calendar information.

FIGURE 7-38

Creating a new calendar

Finally, depending on the type of calendar that you are creating, you will have to enter information so that Evolution's Calendar module knows how to contact the calendar. The information required for each type of calendar is as follows:

- **Google:** Enter your Google username. This provides read-only access to your Google calendar.

- **CalDAV:** Enter the URL of the calendar that you are contacting and the username to use when contacting the calendar, if necessary.

- **On This Computer:** No additional information is required, because this is simply a local calendar.

- **On The Web:** Enter the URL of the WebCal or iCal calendar that you want to access, whether or not a secure connection is required, and the username to use when contacting the calendar, if necessary.

- **Weather:** Click the location button to display a dialog that enables you to browse through available locations and select the one for which you want to display weather information. You can click Units to specify whether you want weather information in Celsius or Fahrenheit, and use the Refresh selector to specify how often you want to update the weather information.

Once you have entered the appropriate information for the type of calendar that you are creating, click OK to close the New Calendar dialog and save the configuration of your new calendar.

After having created a calendar, you can edit its settings at any time by right-clicking on its name in the Calendar Summary window at the upper left of the Calendar view, and selecting Properties from the context-sensitive menu.

Tip

A number of predefined WebCal calendars are available on the Web at sites such as `http://icalshare.com`. One of my favorites is the Pittsburgh Pirates season calendar at `webcal://sports.yahoo.com/mlb/teams/pit/ical.ics`. (Other teams are available from similar Yahoo! URLs, but I don't care about any of them.) ■

Publishing Your Free/Busy Information

The previous section discussed how to connect to remote calendars over a network. Google's online calendar is available from anywhere, and protocols such as iCal are fine if a business or academic site that you're involved with has a shared calendaring system that you can access from anywhere. However, even if you are only managing your own personal calendar, it can be quite useful to export your calendar and/or free/busy information so that others can access it directly.

Evolution makes it easy to publish your personal calendar in iCal or Free/Busy formats. I do this for my wife when I'm traveling on business so that she has some idea of what it is that I'm doing all day and when we may be able to actually talk rather than simply exchanging dueling e-mails. Publishing this information yourself simply writes this information to a file that others can then read to see your calendar information. I publish my calendar in iCal format to a file on my web site, which my wife then loads into Evolution in order to see my updated information.

Publishing your calendar is configured using the Evolution Preferences dialog, which you can display by selecting Edit ➪ Preferences. Once this dialog displays, click "Calendar and Tasks," and then click the Calendar Publishing tab. This displays a dialog like the one shown in Figure 7-39.

FIGURE 7-39

Configuring Calendar Publishing in Evolution

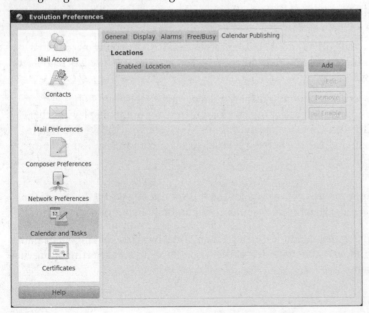

To define a publishing schedule and format for your calendar, click Add. This displays a dialog like the one shown in Figure 7-40.

FIGURE 7-40

Specifying publishing format and frequency for a calendar

Select the checkbox beside the name(s) of the calendar(s) that you want to publish, and select the format in which you want to publish your calendar by clicking the "Publish as" dropdown list and selecting either iCal or Free/Busy. The former provides a detailed listing of your calendar, while the latter simply shows when you are busy. Finally, select the frequency with which you want to publish your calendar information. The choices are Daily, Weekly, and Manually, by selecting the Actions menu's "Publish Calendar Information" command. Once you've made these selections, click the Publishing Location tab. The tab shown in Figure 7-41 displays.

Select the protocol that you want to use from the "Service Type" dropdown list. The supported protocols are SSH, Public FTP (no authentication required), FTP (with login), Windows Share (using the CIFS protocol), WebDAV and Secure WebDAV, and Custom (which enables you to specify a different protocol).

Next, enter the hostname or IP address of the server to which you want to publish your calendar, and the name of the file that you want to save it to. You can then enter an (optional) custom port number and any username and password that you need to use to connect to the remote site. Being able to enter a custom port is quite convenient because many sites move well-known services to different ports in order to try to hide them from hackers who expect to find specific services listening on specific, traditional ports.

After making these changes, click OK to save your calendar publishing information. You can then test whether you've configured everything correctly by selecting the Actions menu's "Publish Calendar Information" command, and then checking the remote location to make sure that a file containing your calendar information was correctly created there.

FIGURE 7-41

Specifying publishing connection and location information

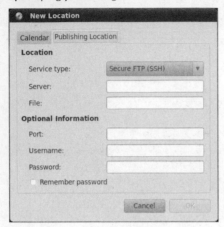

Additional Sources of Information about Evolution

Don't get your hopes up, Charles Darwin fans! This section discusses other sources of information about the Evolution PIM/e-mail application, not the theory of evolution.

Because the Evolution application is generally very popular and is the default e-mail application on most GNOME-based systems (such as Ubuntu), there are a good number of web sites that can provide you with additional information about using Evolution, as well as mailing lists that you can join to ask questions, file problem reports, and so on. Some of my favorites are as follows:

- **Evolution forums** (`http://nabble.com/Gnome---Evolution-f1297.html`): If you prefer to use a forum interface instead of a mailing list, Nabble provides a great collection of forums that present the various Evolution mailing lists in a user-friendly forum format. Messages posted to these forums go directly to the associated mailing list.

- **Evolution IRC Channel:** If you're a fan of Internet Relay Chat and have a client handy (such as the XChat-GNOME IRC client that is provided with Ubuntu), you can discuss developing and using Evolution in the #evolution channel on `irc.gimp.org`. You should lurk for a little while before broadcasting your questions, just to get a feel for the channel and to reduce your chances of being flamed if you ask "the wrong question" or one for which an answer is readily available in the documentation or elsewhere.

- **Evolution mailing lists:** You can subscribe to a general mailing list for Evolution users (known as the *evolution-list* — catchy, no?) at `http://mail.gnome.org/mailman/listinfo/evolution-list`, and you can also subscribe to a more advanced Evolution hackers list (evolution-hackers) at `http://mail.gnome.org/mailman/listinfo/evolution-hackers`. For general information about all GNOME-related mailing lists, see `http://mail.gnome.org/mailman/listinfo`.

- **Evolution Project home page** (`http://gnome.org/projects/evolution`): This is the home page of the Evolution project and, as such, is the definitive starting point for looking for additional information about Evolution, the source code for the latest version of Evolution, and so on.

- **Evolution wiki** (`www.go-evolution.org/Main_Page`): This is a great site for information about the current release of Evolution and for insights into (or making suggestions for) the capabilities that will be present in upcoming versions of Evolution.

Any reasonable Internet search engine will display many more sites with information about Evolution, but these are the primary official conduits for Evolution information.

Summary

This chapter explained how to configure and use Evolution, a powerful e-mail client and Personal Information Manager, focusing on the e-mail aspects of Evolution. Evolution is a great e-mail client that supports all popular e-mail protocols and provides unrivaled connectivity to specific types of mail servers such as Microsoft Exchange e-mail servers. Reading and sending e-mail is one of the most common tasks that anyone does with their personal computer nowadays. Equally common is surfing the Web, which is explained in the next chapter. To satisfy your Web surfing requirements, Ubuntu automatically installs the Firefox Web browser, the most powerful, extensible, and just plain fun Web browser available today.

Surfing the Web with Firefox

IN THIS CHAPTER

Reviewing the history of Firefox

Using Firefox

Configuring Firefox

Working with Bookmarks

Extending Firefox

As with other open source software, many Web browser options are available to Ubuntu users. Desktop systems such as GNOME and KDE both have multipurpose object browsers (Nautilus and Konqueror, respectively) that can also browse web pages and are fine for that purpose if you want to learn only one tool and use it for almost everything. However, Ubuntu installs the Mozilla project's Firefox browser as its default Web browser for a good reason — it's the best Web browser available on Linux systems (and on any other system, too, in my opinion). Firefox is the most popular open source browser available today, and it's the only browser in the past decade or so to have actually taken market share away from Microsoft's Internet Explorer. Many of the innovations that Windows users are looking forward to in upcoming releases of Internet Explorer were first introduced in Firefox and have been present for quite a few versions.

This chapter begins with a bit of history and explains what a long, strange trip it has been for Firefox. Then it discusses how to start, configure, use, and customize Firefox.

A Quick History of Firefox

Firefox has what is perhaps the best possible pedigree in Web browsing history — it is the latest descendant of the original Mosaic Web browser, the original graphical Web browser for UNIX systems. Mosaic was created in 1992 at the National Center for Supercomputing Applications (NCSA) at the University of Illinois at Urbana-Champaign.

Tip

For a quick history of the World Wide Web, see the section of Chapter 29, "Setting Up a Web Server," titled "World Wide Web 101." ∎

As the Internet boom unfolded around the Web and its killer application, the graphical Web browser, much of the team that developed Mosaic, including the leader of the team, Marc Andreessen, left the NCSA to found Mosaic Communications Corporation. Because of issues with NCSA over the Mosaic name, Mosaic Communications Corporation quickly became Netscape Communications Corporation, and the company's fledgling browser product became known as *Netscape Navigator*. Early versions of Netscape Navigator were available by mid-1994, with the first official release occurring near the end of that year.

Note

In one of the incestuous twists of fate that make hi-tech history interesting, a company named Spyglass, Inc. licensed the Mosaic technology and trademarks from the University of Illinois and used it to develop its own Web browser, Spyglass Mosaic, for personal computer systems running Microsoft Windows. Spyglass then eventually licensed the source code for Spyglass Mosaic to Microsoft, where it became the original basis for Microsoft's Internet Explorer. ∎

Netscape Navigator was merely a Web browser, and the growing legions of Internet devotees clamored for other Net-related applications. Demand for other Net-related applications, such as mail clients and web page composition tools, led Netscape to make Netscape Navigator a part of its new Netscape Communicator Suite.

Internet Explorer quickly began to take over the browser market from Netscape — after all, it came free straight from the mother ship on every Microsoft Windows desktop system, and its accompanying Web server product, Internet Information Server, which was included free with every Microsoft Windows server system. By 1998, Netscape Communications Corporation was essentially dead as a stand-alone entity, although it was acquired by America Online (AOL) for a surprising $4 billion.

Netscape's last gasp as a stand-alone entity was to found the open source Mozilla project, donate the Netscape Communicator source code, and create an accompanying Mozilla Organization. Both were chartered with stewarding the creation of the next-generation Internet suite for Netscape. *Mozilla* was the original code name for the Netscape browser throughout its creation, and an accompanying red dragon was a popular decoration at Netscape. The Mozilla project, often flamed for disorganization, eventually stabilized and modularized its code base to develop the last few versions of the Netscape browser, now discontinued.

Meanwhile, the Mozilla project began to create its own Web browser product. This browser was originally named *Phoenix* and then *Firebird*, both of which had naming conflicts with existing applications, so Mozilla eventually settled on the name *Firefox*.

Throughout its history, Firefox has introduced features that we all now take for granted, such as an integrated pop-up blocker, a customizable toolbar, a sidebar, integrated searches on the toolbar, graphical cookie management, a download manager, customizable themes, the ability to easily add external browser extensions, and tabbed browsing.

Note

Although Firefox and its sibling e-mail client, Thunderbird, are the primary products of the Mozilla Foundation, other related applications are still under development and available. The most interesting of these is the SeaMonkey project, a suite of Internet applications based on the original Mozilla Application Suite, the descendant of the Netscape Communicator. The SeaMonkey project includes a Web browser, an e-mail and newsgroup client, an IRC chat client, and a tool for composing HTML web pages. SeaMonkey is available at `www.seamonkey-project.org`. ■

Starting Firefox

Firefox is installed by default on standard GNOME-based Ubuntu desktop distributions and is one of the stellar examples of open source software quality and design.

You can start Firefox manually in a variety of ways on a standard Ubuntu system:

- By clicking the Firefox Web Browser icon in the GNOME toolbar at the top of the screen on Ubuntu desktop systems, as shown in Figure 8-1. This is the easiest, most common, and most intuitive way to start the browser.

FIGURE 8-1

The Firefox icon on your GNOME desktop

Firefox icon

- By selecting "Firefox Web browser" from the Applications ⇨ Internet menu
- By typing the `firefox` command in a GNOME Terminal or xterm window and pressing Return

Ubuntu's GNOME desktop is also preconfigured to start Firefox for you if you click on a Uniform Resource Locator (URL) in an e-mail reader or another Internet-aware application.

The first time you start Firefox on an Ubuntu system, it will automatically start its Add-on Manager and install two language packs — one for Firefox itself and a second for XULRunner, which is a runtime environment for Mozilla's XUL (XML User Interface Language) web applications. You can close this dialog for now — see the section titled "Enhancing Firefox" later in this chapter for more information about installing other extensions, themes, and plug-ins.

After you start Firefox for the first time, a screen such as the one in Figure 8-2 displays, showing the default home page, which displays a "Welcome" message and provides general information about the Ubuntu release that you're running. If you've started Firefox for the first time by clicking on a URL in another application, the web page corresponding to that URL displays.

FIGURE 8-2

Starting Firefox for the first time

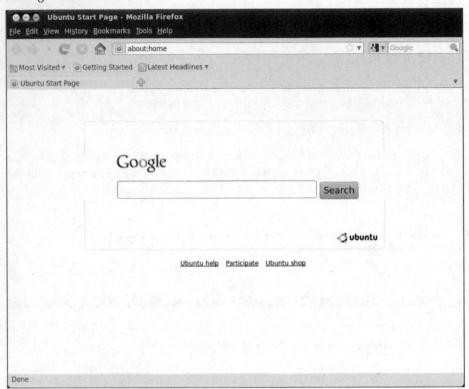

Most people configure Firefox (or any Web browser, for that matter) so that it starts up on a web page of their choosing, referred to as their *home page*. I'll explain how to configure that later in this chapter — for now, let's explore the Firefox user interface.

The Firefox User Interface

Although most Web browsers look and work approximately the same nowadays, this section provides an overview of the different portions of a Firefox window, just in case you're lucky enough to be running Ubuntu on your first computer. If you're already comfortable with Web browsers and graphical applications in general, feel free to skip this section entirely or skip ahead to the section titled "Special and Not-So-Special Firefox Features" to get an overview of some of the special capabilities available in Firefox that may not have been available in Web browsers that you've used previously.

Standard Parts of a Firefox Window

Figure 8-3 displays a sample Firefox screen, showing the different portions of a standard Firefox window.

Different portions of a Firefox window

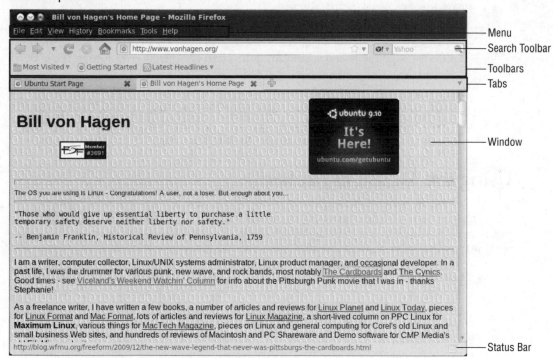

These different areas provide the following functionality:

- **Menus:** Displays a dropdown menu of related commands when you position the cursor over any of the items in this area and click on them

- **Navigation Toolbar:** Displays icons that control the web page displayed in the main Firefox window. By default, the Navigation toolbar also provides quick access to the Google search engine.

- **Bookmarks Toolbar:** Provides quick access to selected bookmarks that are more frequently visited than the standard bookmarks saved on the Bookmarks menu. The Bookmarks toolbar also includes a "Smart Bookmarks" item that provides quick access to recently visited sites (much like the History menu), sites that you visit often, sites that you've recently bookmarked, sites that you've tagged, and so on.

- **Tabs:** Represent different web pages that you are currently visiting. By default, this portion of the screen displays only if you are currently visiting more than one site, although this behavior is configurable.

- **Main Window:** Displays the contents of the web page that you are currently visiting

- **Search Toolbar:** Displays commands that enable you to search for specific text in the web page that you are currently visiting. This portion of the screen displays only if you have first executed a Search command.

- **Status Bar:** Provides summary information about Firefox's retrieval of the web page that you are currently visiting. Icons at the right end of this page display status information about that page if indexing is enabled, an RSS feed is available on that page, the page is retrieved through a secure connection, and so on.

As I explain later in this chapter, you can configure many of these items — what they contain (Navigation toolbar, Bookmarks toolbar), how they look (by using custom themes), and whether they display at all (Navigation toolbar, Bookmarks toolbar, status bar).

Using the Mouse in Firefox

There's nothing different about using the mouse in Firefox from using it in any other graphical application except for the contents of any menus that pop up in response to a right-click. However, if you're new to graphical applications, let's review. On a standard three-button mouse, clicking (pressing and releasing) a mouse button does the following:

- **Left button:** Selects something. Left-clicking on a menu displays that menu, and left-clicking on an item from that menu selects a command or submenu. Left-clicking on a button in the Navigation toolbar executes the command associated with that button or, in the case of the Google toolbar, positions the cursor so that you can specify what you want to search for. Left-clicking on a portion of a web page performs any action associated with that area — following a hyperlink, displaying a larger graphic, submitting a form, and so on.

- **Middle button:** Depending on where you click, middle-clicking can open a hyperlink in a new tab, paste selected text into a selected text area, and so on.

- **Right button:** Displays different menus depending on what you right-click on. These are known as context-sensitive menus for this reason. Figure 8-4 shows the context-sensitive menu that you see if you right-click on the background of the current web page.

You can customize context-sensitive menus such as those shown in Figure 8-4 by adding Firefox extensions that have associated menu items, as explained in the section, "Adding Firefox Add-Ons, Themes, and Personas," later in this chapter. You can even customize how the mouse behaves to some extent by adding Firefox extensions that tell Firefox to perform specific actions when specific types of mouse movements occur.

FIGURE 8-4

A context-sensitive menu in Firefox

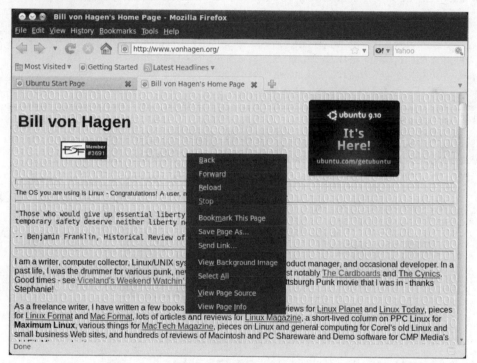

Special and Not-So-Special Firefox Features

You may be familiar with the vanilla Web browsers installed with other operating systems, such as Internet Explorer on Microsoft Windows, and Safari on Mac OS X. Firefox provides the same capabilities as those browsers and adds a few powerful, exciting new ones. Some of the most interesting features first added by Firefox and standard browser capabilities that aren't active by default in Firefox are as follows:

- **Tabbed browsing:** Enables you to open multiple web pages simultaneously without creating separate windows for each. Each web page that is currently open is represented by a separate tab, which displays above the portion of the screen that shows the current web page. You can quickly and easily switch between these web pages by clicking on the appropriate tab. This feature is so useful that it has been incorporated into most other modern browsers — for example, Microsoft added this capability in Internet Explorer 7, and this feature is also available in Mac OS X's Safari browser. To close a selected tab, click the red X icon at the top right of the Tab display area.

- **Sidebars:** Provide easy navigation through a given list of web pages. Firefox provides two different sidebars, one displaying your bookmarks and a second that provides a list of the web pages that you have visited recently (known as a *history* sidebar). These sidebars aren't turned on by default in Firefox, but you can easily activate whichever you prefer by selecting Bookmarks or History from the View ⇨ Sidebar menu. Figure 8-5 shows Firefox with the Bookmarks sidebar displayed. To close a sidebar, click the red X icon at the top right of the sidebar.

FIGURE 8-5

The Bookmarks sidebar in Firefox

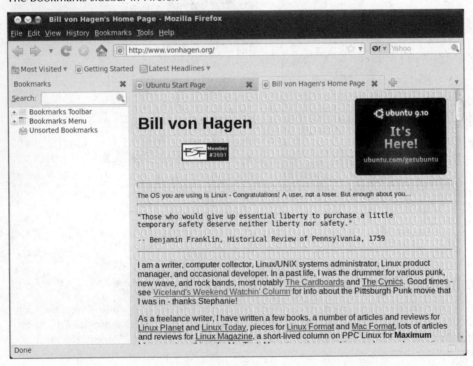

- **Missing plug-in detection:** Automatically identifies sites that provide content that requires that you install a special plug-in in order to view that content. Common examples of this are multimedia content types such as Adobe Flash content, Apple QuickTime content, and so on. Figure 8-6 shows the banner that displays (below the tabs) when Firefox identifies a missing plug-in. You can click the "Install Missing Plugins" button in this banner to have Firefox start its Plugin Finder Service, which will attempt to locate and enable you to install plug-ins that can handle the requested type of content. If this banner displays and you don't want to change anything, you can close it by clicking the red X icon at the right of this banner. See the section of this chapter titled "Adding New Firefox Plug-Ins" for more information about this service.

FIGURE 8-6

The missing plug-in banner in Firefox

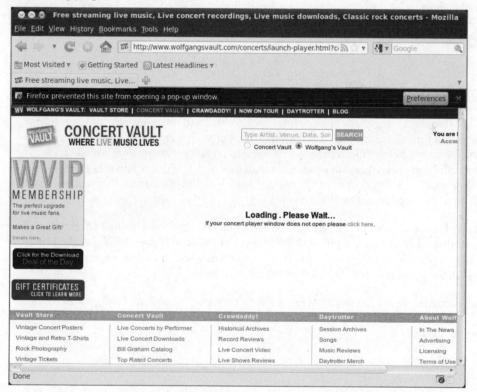

Done

289

- **Built-in pop-up blocking:** Prevents sites from displaying annoying pop-up windows unless you specifically authorize a site to display them (or you disable this feature entirely). You can click the Preferences button in this banner to customize how Firefox handles pop-ups from the current site, or in general. If this banner displays and you don't want to change anything, you can close it by clicking the red X icon at the right of this banner. Customizing how Firefox handles pop-ups is explained later in this chapter.

- **Live Bookmarks:** Provide a special type of bookmark that is dynamically constructed from an RSS feed provided by a specific site. Creating live bookmarks is explained later in this chapter.

Firefox is a powerful, flexible Web browser with all of the features that you'd expect in any modern Web browser, and then some. You could easily devote an entire book to exploring each and every menu and Firefox feature, but my publisher probably prefers that this not be that book. So I'll agree, and just encourage you to explore the various Firefox menus and the hundreds of available themes and extensions (some of which are discussed later in this chapter).

Configuring Firefox

Firefox is extremely configurable and provides enough knobs to turn that you could probably spend as much time tweaking your configuration and enhancing Firefox as you can in actually using the browser. Luckily, books such as this one and Firefox's own documentation can help make sure that you spend more time browsing than fine-tuning. Firefox provides great online help at www.mozilla.org/support/firefox/, which includes a tutorial that will walk you through its most popular configuration tasks.

Almost all of the permanently configurable aspects of Firefox are located in its Preferences dialog, which you display by selecting the Edit ➪ Preferences menu item. Figure 8-7 shows the Firefox Preferences panel in the version of Firefox that was current when this book was written. Yours may look slightly different, but the core contents are the same.

This section discusses the highlights of Firefox configuration, focusing on configuration options that you'll eventually want to know about, regardless of whether or not you want to customize them immediately.

FIGURE 8-7

The Preferences window in Firefox

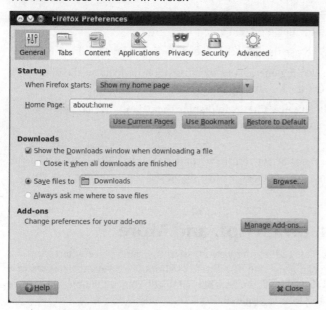

Setting Your Home Page

Your *home page* is the web page that displays when you first start Firefox (or any Web browser). Many people use a Web portal site of some sort, such as yahoo.com, msn.com, or aol.com, as their home page; others use news sites that are specific to their job or interests, and others use personally created web pages on Internet sites that they have created or are affiliated with. Regardless of what you use, setting your home page is one of the key aspects of personalizing your use of Firefox.

To set your home page in Firefox, first display the Preferences dialog. The Main pane should be displayed by default. If it is not, click the Main button at the top of the dialog to display the pane shown previously in Figure 8-7.

The Startup section at the top of this pane enables you to configure the page that displays when Firefox starts. Clicking the aptly named "When Firefox starts" dropdown gives you three general options:

- **Show my home page:** Displays a specific web page that you identify as your home page
- **Show a blank page:** Displays a blank page for faster startup
- **Show my windows and tabs from last time:** Displays the active page and all of the tabs that were visible the last time that you exited Firefox

I typically use a home page that lets me check for important news (and not-so-important news) before moving on to whatever specific sites that I want to browse. Firefox offers four options for setting your home page:

- Explicitly typing a URL into the Location text area
- Clicking "Use Current Page" to use the page that is currently displayed in Firefox
- Clicking "Use Bookmark," selecting one of your existing bookmarks from the dialog that displays, and clicking OK to close that dialog
- Clicking "Restore to Default" to cause Firefox to display the default "Welcome to Ubuntu" screen shown in Figure 8-2

Once you've chosen one of these options to select your new home page, click Close to dismiss the Preferences dialog. The home page that you specified will be displayed the next time you start Firefox.

Controlling Pop-Ups, JavaScript, and More

Firefox provides a single Preferences dialog for configuration, so in the same place where you selected your default home page, you can also configure Firefox's support for various features of modern web pages, and how these web features behave when enabled. You can enable, disable, or customize the behavior of the following from a single dialog:

- **Block Pop-up Windows:** Determines whether to block all remote sites from displaying pop-up windows, allow selected sites to display pop-ups, or allow all sites to display pop-ups on your system.
- **Load Images Automatically:** Determines whether to load all images on any web page, load images only from the site that actually hosts the web page (to block ads and graphics provided by other sites), and load images from a list of sites even if loading images is prohibited.
- **Enable Java:** Determines whether to support Java in Firefox so that remote sites can download Java applets that will execute locally on your machine.
- **Enable JavaScript:** Determines whether to support JavaScript, which enables programmatic content generation and window manipulation, and (if so) determines which specific features to support.

To enable, disable, or customize these content-related features, first display the Preferences dialog. Next, click the Content button at the top of the dialog to display the pane shown in Figure 8-8.

FIGURE 8-8

Enabling and customizing content in Firefox

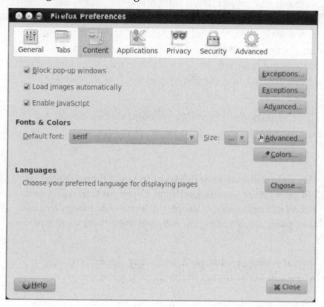

Once this pane displays, you can select the checkbox beside the feature you're interested in tuning to enable or disable that activity. For options that allow you to create lists of sites to be excluded from a specific setting, click the Exceptions button to the right of that option and enter the names of the sites that you want to exclude from that setting. Similarly, support for JavaScript is usually enabled by default in Firefox, but the dialog that displays after clicking the Advanced Settings button gives you very fine-tuned control over the sorts of things that JavaScript-enabled web pages can do on your system.

Once you've finished configuring these content-related features, click Close to dismiss the Preferences dialog. Changes to some settings will not take effect until you restart Firefox, so it's always a good idea to exit from and restart Firefox after changing content settings, just in case.

Configuring Your Privacy Settings

In the Privacy pane of the Preferences dialog, different sections enable you to customize groups of related privacy settings. This dialog enables you to customize privacy settings such as the following:

- **History:** Determines the period of time (in days) for which Firefox keeps a record of the URLs for the web sites that you've visited. This also includes a setting that determines whether Firefox keeps a list of the files that you have downloaded, and cookie-related settings. If you customize your history settings, you can configure more detailed browser history information, including cookie-related information. Cookies are encoded chunks of information that remote web sites can set in your browser to immediately recognize you the next time you visit. The cookie-related settings on this dialog determine whether or not Firefox accepts cookies in general, a list of sites excluded from this policy, and, if so, how long cookies are retained. You can also identify sites form which you do not want to accept cookies and manage the list of cookies that are currently stored on your system.

- **Location Bar:** Determines what suggestions, if any, Firefox makes when you begin typing a URL or search term in the location bar.

Note

If you've already been using Firefox for a while, this pane will look very different to you. Older versions of Firefox used a tabbed Privacy pane to control all of your privacy-related settings. Different tabs contained groups of related privacy settings. The current version of Firefox uses a simpler interface, dividing privacy-related settings into two separate panes: the Privacy pane, shown in Figure 8-9, and the Security pane, shown in Figure 8-10. ■

To enable, disable, or customize these privacy-related settings, first display the Preferences dialog. Next, click the Privacy button at the top of the dialog to display the pane shown in Figure 8-9.

Once this dialog displays, select Use custom settings for history (shown in Figure 8-9) if you want to significantly customize your browser history settings, including cooki-related settings. For example, if you are using a computer that you share with others, you may want to deselect options such as remembering browsing, download, and search and form history. Many people are also paranoid about cookies, which are used in both good and irritating ways. For example, cookies can store shopping cart information, which is very useful if you are buying something online and have to interrupt your session without making an actual purchase. On the other hand, many online sites and advertisers use cookies to track what you've looked at on their sites. This can be useful in terms of showing ads related to your buying and browsing decisions, but it also provides personal information that you may not want to share. In my opinion, browsing the Web without using cookies is a big hassle, so I always accept them, but I occasionally use the Show Cookies button on this Preferences pane to browse the list of cookies that are stored on my system and delete those cookies that are for sites that I don't recognize or care about anymore.

FIGURE 8-9

Customizing privacy settings in Firefox

After making any changes to the Privacy settings on this dialog, you can either click Close to save your changes and exit the Preferences dialog, or you may want to click the Security icon at the top of the Preferences pane to explore your Firefox security settings, which are certainly related to maintaining your privacy. Clicking the Security icon displays the pane shown in Figure 8-10.

The first few entries on this pane enable you to configure whether remote sites can install Firefox add-ons, whether Firefox will complain when you attempt to visit a site that is believed to contain spurious software, and whether Firefox will warn you if it believes that you are being re-directed to a site other than the one that you requested. The Passwords section determines whether or not Firefox stores username/password pairs that you've used to log in to different secure sites. This configuration item provides special dialogs for managing any login/password combinations that are currently saved. Clicking the Saved Passwords button displays the "Saved Passwords" dialog shown in Figure 8-11, which enables you to explore and manually delete any username/password pairs that are currently saved in Firefox.

FIGURE 8-10

Customizing security settings in Firefox

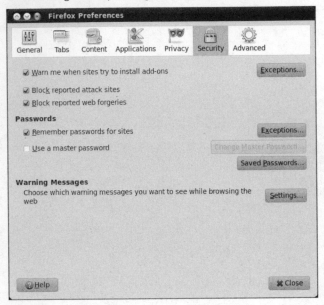

XFIGURE 8-11

Managing passwords saved in Firefox

To remove a saved username/password pair for a specific site, highlight that entry and click Remove at the bottom of the dialog (as my wife would probably like to do with my eBay login information). As with most graphical selections, you can hold down the Ctrl key while clicking on entries to select multiple username/password pairs, or select one item, hold down the Shift key, and click another to select those two items and all of the items between those two username/password pairs. Click Close to dismiss this dialog and return to the Privacy Settings pane when you're done.

Once you've finished configuring your privacy and security settings, click Close to dismiss the Preferences dialog. Changes to some settings will not take effect until you restart Firefox, so it's always a good idea to exit from and restart Firefox after changing privacy settings, just in case.

Working with Bookmarks

In a Web browser, a *bookmark* is a record of the Uniform Resource Locator (URL) for a web page that you've visited and you want to visit again. When you select a bookmark, Firefox goes directly to the page that it represents—no fuss, no muss.

Note
Bookmarks is the more common term for what Internet Explorer calls *Favorites*. ∎

Bookmarks are great things, just as they are in real books. Without a bookmark, you'd have to start searching a book at the beginning each time you picked it up. The same thing is true of bookmarks in terms of Web searches—once you've found somewhere that you want to return to on the Web, it's important to save a bookmark to that location so that you can easily return there. You certainly don't want to have to redo a complex Web search process or web page navigation sequence any more times than you have to—which should be once, if you've bookmarked a page.

Firefox provides two primary locations in which to save bookmarks: a hierarchical collection of bookmarks that you can access by selecting the Bookmarks menu, and the Bookmarks toolbar, which is displayed directly below the Navigation toolbar in the main Firefox window. The Bookmarks toolbar is designed to provide quick access to frequently visited bookmarks, while the Bookmarks menu provides access to everything. You can think of the Bookmarks toolbar as the bestsellers section of a bookstore, while the Bookmarks menu is the entire store.

Over time, most people tend to accumulate huge collections of bookmarks, which makes managing them—and being able to find the one you want when you want it—a very critical task for continued happiness through Web surfing. Firefox includes an excellent "Organize Bookmarks" dialog that simplifies both of these tasks. The next few sections explain how to create bookmarks in various ways; how to organize them using the "Organize Bookmarks" dialog; how to back up your bookmarks and even access them from other Web browsers; and how to use an exciting feature introduced by Firefox, known as *Live Bookmarks*, to automatically construct dynamic menus that provide an overview of selected web sites.

Creating Bookmarks in Firefox

Firefox provides three basic ways of creating a bookmark to the page that you're currently viewing:

- Click the star to the right of the web site's URL in the Firefox navigation bar. After doing so, you can click the star again (now yellow) to specify the location to which you want to save the bookmark, add tags, and so on.

- Press Ctrl+D on your keyboard (hold down the Ctrl key and press the letter *D*).

- Right-click on the background of the current page and select the Add Bookmark command from the pop-up menu.

- Select the Add Bookmark command from the Bookmarks menu.

You can also create a bookmark for a link on the page that you're viewing by right-clicking on the link and selecting the Bookmark This Link command from the pop-up menu.

Regardless of the method you use to create a bookmark, creating one displays the dialog shown in Figure 8-12. The top portion of the dialog shows the name that the bookmark will have. By default, this is the text under the link or the name of the current page, but you can change it to be something more memorable if you'd like.

FIGURE 8-12

The "Add Bookmark" dialog in Firefox

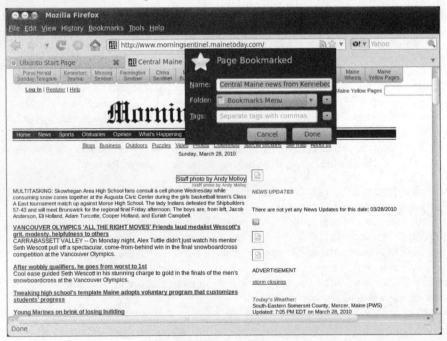

The Folder field of this dialog identifies where the bookmark will be saved. You can click on this entry to see a list of the folders that already exist in your bookmarks, or you can click the down arrow to the right of this dialog to display a browseable dialog that enables you to select a folder within those folders, as shown in Figure 8-13, or you can click on the New Folder button to create a new folder in which to store your new bookmark.

The dialog shown in Figure 8-12 also provides a field that enables you to add tags to your bookmarks. Tags are a type of metadata, which means "information about information." In this case, tags enable you to associate keywords with specific bookmarks so that later you can search for related items. To add tags to a bookmarked entry, enter them as comma-separated keywords in the Tags field on the bookmarks dialog, as shown in Figure 8-14.

FIGURE 8-13

Navigating folders when saving a bookmark

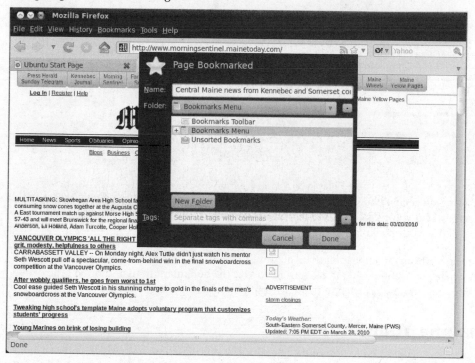

FIGURE 8-14

Adding tags when saving a bookmark

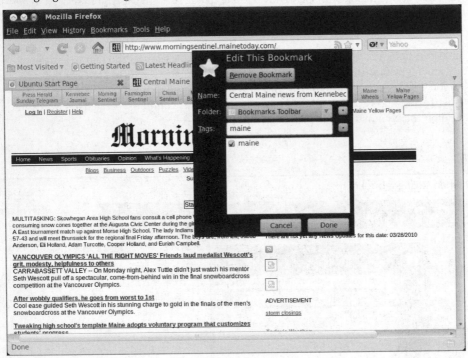

When adding subsequent bookmarks, you can click the down arrow to the right of the Tags field to see the tags that you've already used in other bookmarks. This can help you use a consistent set of tags across your bookmarks, simplifying future searches.

Once you've made any modification that you want to the name of the bookmark and selected the location where you want to store it, click Done to save the bookmark in that location. The dialog closes, and you can now easily go to that page again by selecting the bookmark.

Managing Your Bookmarks

Over time, most people tend to accumulate huge collections of bookmarks, which makes it harder and harder to find the right bookmark—which somewhat defeats the idea of having bookmarks in the first place. To solve this problem, Firefox includes an excellent bookmarks organizer that makes it easy to organize and search your valuable collection of bookmarks, known as your *Library*. The Library provides a central tool for managing your browsing history and bookmarks, generally referred to as *Places*. To display the Library, select Organize Bookmarks from the Bookmarks menu, and the dialog shown in Figure 8-15 displays.

FIGURE 8-15

The Library dialog in Firefox

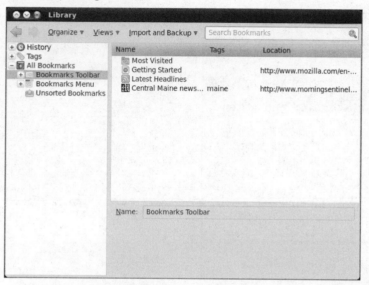

The panel on the left provides a hierarchical overview of how your bookmarks are currently organized, while the panel on the right provides a detailed view of the bookmarks in the folder that is currently selected. You can move bookmarks around by dragging and dropping them (left-clicking on the bookmark and dragging it to the new location) within either panel or even between the two. You can create new folders, new bookmarks, or new separators (the lines that appear in your bookmarks menu) by selecting the appropriate location in either panel and doing either of the following:

- Select the appropriate icon from the top of the Library dialog.
- Right-click and select the appropriate command from the pop-up menu.

Any changes that you make are immediately reflected on the Firefox Bookmarks menu and Bookmark toolbar.

The Library dialog also provides a convenient way to search your existing collection of bookmarks. You can search your bookmarks for text that appears in their name or URL, but you can also search your bookmarks based on any tags that you've applied to them. Figure 8-16 shows the result of a search for the tag "radio," which I generally apply to the bookmarks for local and Internet radio stations that I'm interested in.

FIGURE 8-16

Searching for bookmarks by tag

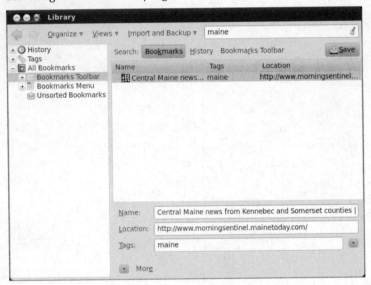

Once you're finished reorganizing or exploring your bookmarks, click the Close box (X) in the upper-right corner of the dialog to close the Library dialog.

Regardless of how you choose to organize your bookmarks, one traditional rule is to avoid having one huge list of bookmarks. You probably have specific interests, and can easily store your bookmarks in folders that represent those interests. This makes it easy to find a given bookmark, and also helps prevent you from accidentally bookmarking the same page 11 times because you couldn't find a specific bookmark when you were looking for it. Regardless of how well you organize your bookmarks, the Library dialog's search capability makes it easy for you to find specific bookmarks, but I don't feel that being able to search for something is an excuse for poor, or no, organization.

Backing Up Your Bookmarks

Because your evolving collection of bookmarks is one of the most precious things that you build up as you surf the Net, making sure that you don't accidentally lose them is critical. The Library dialog's Import and Backup dropdown menu provides both Export and Backup commands that enable you to save a copy of your current bookmarks in a separate file. This is especially important for the latest versions of Firefox, which store bookmarks and history in SQLite database files using an interface known as *Places*. Places is convenient for searching, but removes some of the ease-of-use of backing up bookmarks in previous versions of Firefox, where you could simply copy a flat HTML file called `bookmarks.html` from your personal preferences directory in the directory `~/.mozilla/firefox` in your home directory to back up your bookmarks. This file still exists but is only kept in sync with your SQLite bookmark files in certain cases, and there's no guarantee that this will continue in the future. Use the Library dialog's Export command to save an HTML copy of your bookmarks, or use the Backup command to save a copy of your bookmarks in JSON (JavaScript Object Notation) format.

When creating JSON backups, you can easily restore them using the Choose File command from the Restore menu on the Library's "Import and Backup" dropdown menu. This command enables you to restore a JSON backup file that you've saved manually. The Restore menu also lists dates for which internal Firefox backups are available.

I tend to save my bookmarks in HTML every week or two, giving them names containing the current date, like `bookmarks-27-Oct-06.html`, so that I can tell one from the other. This makes it easy to find a specific bookmark in one of these files if you've accidentally deleted the bookmark but have some idea of the last time that you saw it. JSON is a fine format, but it isn't supported in other browsers or in older versions of Firefox, and I also like to put a copy of recent bookmarks on my web site to help me find my favorite bookmarked locations even when I'm not in front of my primary machine.

Creating Live Bookmarks

The Live Bookmarks feature is one of the latest — and most useful — enhancements to Web surfing that have been introduced by the Firefox team. Live Bookmarks exploits a popular Web technology called *RSS*, which stands for "Really Simple Syndication," or "Rich Site Summary," depending on whom you ask. Many web sites today use RSS to publish a summary of recent changes to their site (known as an *RSS feed*), which other sites can read and display to provide links to those changes. A *live bookmark* to a site is essentially a special type of bookmark that points to the RSS feed on that site, made more usable by the fact that Live Bookmarks displays the headings in an RSS feed as menu items.

Sites that provide RSS feeds that can be used as Live Bookmarks in Firefox display a Live Bookmarks icon at the far right of their URLs in the Firefox Navigation toolbar, as shown in Figure 8-17.

To create a live bookmark, click on the Live Bookmarks icon in the URL for that site. The screen shown in Figure 8-18 displays.

FIGURE 8-17

The Live Bookmarks icon for a URL in Firefox

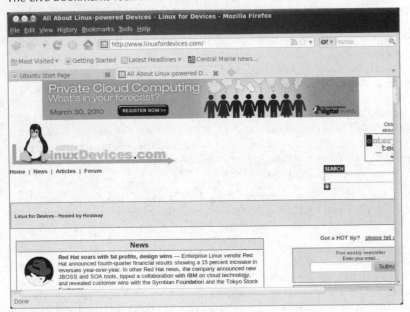

FIGURE 8-18

The Live Bookmarks subscription screen

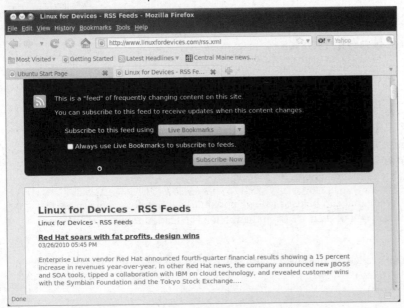

Click "Subscribe Now." The standard "Add Bookmark" dialog displays, enabling you to specify where you want to create the live bookmark. The "Add Bookmark" dialog closes, and the Live Bookmarks menu item displays. After a few seconds (the time it takes for Firefox to read the RSS feed and create the live bookmark), you can access the Live Bookmarks menu like any other menu in Firefox, as shown in Figure 8-19.

FIGURE 8-19

Λ Live Bookmarks menu in Firefox

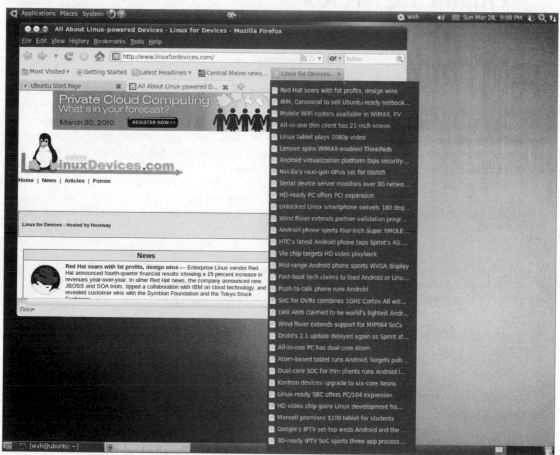

Tip

Your Bookmarks toolbar is a group of frequently used bookmarks that Firefox displays above the web page that you are viewing. This is the most common location for creating live bookmarks because they represent an up-to-date summary of a site that you're presumably very interested in. ∎

The live bookmark shown in Figure 8-19 is for the site that is currently shown in the main browser window in the same figure. If you look closely, you'll notice that the first item on the menu is the first heading on the page in the main browser window. As the site is updated, the Live Bookmarks menu will automatically update to reflect the changes to the site. What could be easier? Perhaps Firefox could also read each of those topics and tell me which ones I should actually care about — maybe in the next release?

Enhancing Firefox

This chapter has stressed the power and usability of Firefox as it comes "out-of-the-box." However, Firefox provides a final set of capabilities that make it even more interesting: You can easily add new Firefox capabilities (known as *add-ons* or *extensions*); new ways of displaying icons, windows, menus, backgrounds, and so on (traditionally known as *themes*, and supported in a lighter-weight fashion as *personas*, which were officially introduced in Firefox 3.6); and applets (known as *plug-ins*) that run within the Firefox framework and add support for specific types of multimedia files. This section explains how to add each of these items to further customize your Web surfing. In many cases, Firefox extensions provide extra capabilities that are worthy of being separate applications — but which Firefox smoothly integrates into your existing Web surfing experience. Similarly, everyone has their own idea of meaningful icons and appealing graphical design. Firefox themes and personas — much like the skins that you may be familiar with from popular audio applications such as Winamp or XMMS — enable you to customize the browser's appearance so that it is more attractive to you and quite possibly more usable for you.

Note

Old versions of Firefox used separate dialogs for retrieving, installing, and managing extensions and themes and didn't provide a centralized mechanism for retrieving and installing plug-ins. Firefox now provides a single menu command and dialog for performing all of these related tasks. ∎

Registering for Add-Ons

With versions of Firefox prior to 3.0, anyone could download and install any add-on, extension, or theme from their respective web sites. With Firefox 3.0, some extensions and themes are available only if you've registered with the Mozilla Add-ons site (`https://addons.mozilla.org/en-US/firefox/`). On the one hand, this is a pain and isn't going to help speed the adoption of Firefox; on the other hand, it's useful for the Mozilla Foundation and extension/theme developers to know how many people are using Firefox and which extensions and themes they're actually using.

You may not want to register until you run across an extension or theme that requires you to do so, but that didn't take me long. You can register with the Add-ons site by clicking the Register link in the upper-right corner of any page, or by going directly to `https://addons.mozilla.org/en-US/firefox/users/register`. After entering your e-mail address, a password, and a minimal amount of personal information, you'll be sent a confirmation message via e-mail. When you receive this, click the link in the message to confirm your subscription, and you're good to go. After registration, Firefox will also display a banner offering to save your login/password information. Even if you're paranoid about saving logins/passwords in browsers in general, saving this one in Firefox seems pretty benign (unless it's the same password you use everywhere, which would be a bad idea in general).

After registering and confirming your account, you can log in on the Add-ons web site at any time by clicking the "Log in" link in the upper-right corner of any page on that site. This will help make sure that you can download and install any extensions or themes that are available for your version of Firefox.

Viewing Installed Firefox Add-Ons, Themes, and Personas

The single dialog used in Firefox for themes/personas, extensions, and add-ons makes it easy to see which of these are currently installed in Firefox, which of those add-ons are currently enabled, and which theme is currently being used. While multiple extensions can be enabled at the same time, only one theme can be used at a time.

To see the add-ons that are currently installed in the version of Firefox that you're using, select the Add-ons command from the Tools menu. This displays the Add-ons dialog. Click the Extensions icon to display the pane shown in Figure 8-20, which shows a list of all of the currently installed extensions. This list will be almost empty initially, but we're going to fix that in the next section.

FIGURE 8-20

The Add-ons dialog in Firefox

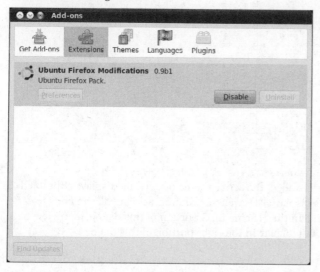

Note

If you have recently installed new extensions or themes, you will see a yellow banner identifying the number of new add-ons that have been installed. You can close this banner by clicking the button in the right of the banner. ∎

If an extension is active, you will see a Disable button that enables you to keep the extension installed but deactivate it. If any aspect of the extension is configurable, you will see a Preferences button that enables you to customize the behavior of that extension. If a disabled extension is compatible with your version of Firefox but is disabled, you will see an Enable button.

To see the themes that are currently installed in the version of Firefox that you're using, select the Add-ons command from the Tools menu if you are not already viewing the Add-ons dialog. Click the Themes icon to display the pane shown in Figure 8-21, which displays a list of all of the currently installed themes. As with the list of default Extensions, this list will be almost empty initially, but we'll also fix that in the next section.

FIGURE 8-21

The Themes dialog in Firefox

If you have multiple themes/personas installed, the active theme or persona displays a disabled "Use Theme" button. All other themes display a "Use Theme" button, which you can click to enable them. As you click on any theme in the "Theme List" portion of this dialog, a preview of the icons associated with that theme will display in the right portion of this dialog.

Adding Firefox Add-Ons, Themes, and Personas

Adding new add-ons and themes/personas to Firefox is easy because Firefox will automatically download and install them for you—but figuring out which ones you like best can be hard because there are so many to choose from. But that's what the hours between midnight and 6 a.m. are for anyway, right?

Note

Personas essentially replace themes in Firefox 3.6, providing a lighter-weight model for changing the browser's appearance, while also adding cool things like backgrounds for the toolbar and navigation bar. However, I'll simply refer to them as themes throughout the rest of this section, since that's what the buttons, icons, and menu commands still say. ■

To add new extensions or themes, first select the Add-ons command from the Tools menu. This displays the Add-ons dialog, which initially retrieves and displays a list of recommended add-ons that are not currently installed on your system, as shown in Figure 8-22.

FIGURE 8-22

Recommended Add-ons

Once this dialog displays, you can click the "Add to Firefox" button to install a selected add-on immediately, or you can use either of the links at the top right of the dialog to browse for available extensions ("Browse All Add-ons") or browse a list of add-ons that are recommended by the Ubuntu folks ("Get Ubuntu Extensions"). First, let's explore the huge set of add-ons that are available from Mozilla's Firefox Add-ons site. Click the "Browse All Add-ons" link to open a new Firefox tab that connects to Firefox headquarters at the Mozilla project and displays a page that shows all of the extensions that are currently available there, as shown in Figure 8-23.

The Categories menu at the left of the Firefox Add-ons page lists a number of topics into which available add-ons are organized, making it easier to find add-ons that are related to some specific task that you want to accomplish in Firefox. These categories can contain both extensions and themes, although there is a separate Themes category that I'll discuss in a moment.

FIGURE 8-23

Available extensions from Mozilla

The search dialogs enable you to search for one or more words in the titles and descriptions of available add-ons. You can restrict your search to a specific category by selecting that category from the dropdown category menu in the search bar. For example, Figure 8-24 shows a search for add-ons containing the word *Theme* in the "Themes" category. (I searched for the word *Theme* because this category also contains appearance-related extensions.)

FIGURE 8-24

Searching for a keyword in a category

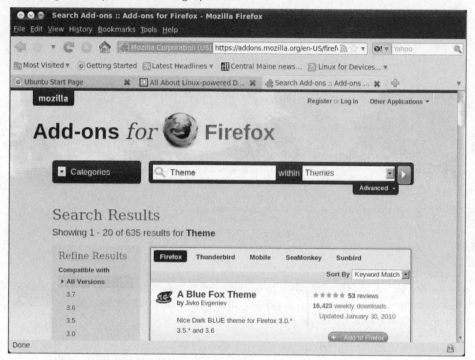

You can scroll through this list to see the available add-ons that match your search term. A deactivated button at the right displays if a given add-on is incompatible with your version of Firefox. A green "Add to Firefox" button displays to the right of any add-on that you can install in your version of Firefox. Figure 8-25 shows add-ons with each of these buttons (the one at the bottom is the green one).

FIGURE 8-25

Installable and uninstallable add-ons

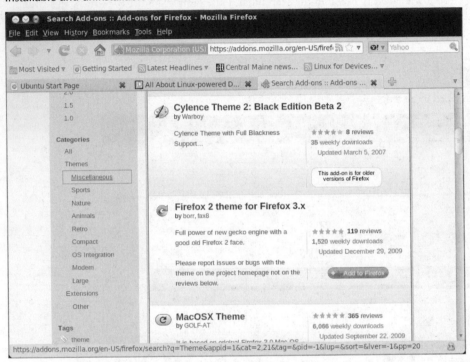

Once you've located an add-on that you want to install, click the "Add to Firefox" button to automatically download and install the selected add-on. After Firefox downloads the add-on, a dialog like the one shown in Figure 8-26 displays.

Click the Install Now button to install the requested add-on. Once you've downloaded and installed an add-on, an Installation button displays in the Add-ons dialog's toolbar, and the associated pane displays to list the new add-on(s) that you've installed, reflecting the fact that the new extension is installed but will not be active until after you restart Firefox, as shown in Figure 8-27.

FIGURE 8-26

Installing an add-on

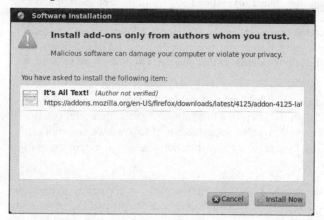

FIGURE 8-27

Newly installed add-ons

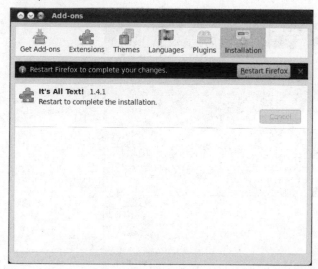

At this point, you can continue to browse for other themes and extensions at the Mozilla site and install any others that seem interesting. If you're installing more than one extension or theme, you can defer restarting Firefox until you've downloaded and installed all of them.

Tip

So many interesting extensions are available for Firefox that it's tempting to download and install a huge number of them at the same time, just to see which ones you like. I suggest that you try to control yourself and install only one or two at a time, for two reasons. First, some extensions may conflict with others, and this can cause problems with Firefox. Second, if you install too many extensions, it's hard to tell which one is responsible for which changes in Firefox. This can make it tough if you want to install the same set of extensions on multiple machines, because you may waste time installing extensions that you don't actually want or need. ∎

Some of these extensions are specific to Ubuntu (such as the Firefox Launchpad plug-in, if you're doing development or monitoring bugs, or the Ubuntu-it extension, if you're a member of the Italian Ubuntu community or speak Italian in general), while most are generally useful (such as AdBlock, for everyone, or Firebug or the Web Developers toolbar, if you're a web developer). Clicking on any extension in this list displays summary information about that extension in the bottom half of this pane.

After installing new extensions and themes and restarting Firefox, you can configure preferences for many of the extensions that you've installed. Some extensions, such as the AdBlock extension that helps block ads on web pages, automatically display a Preferences dialog when they are first started so that you can supply mandatory configuration information, as shown in Figure 8-28.

FIGURE 8-28

Setting preferences when an extension first starts

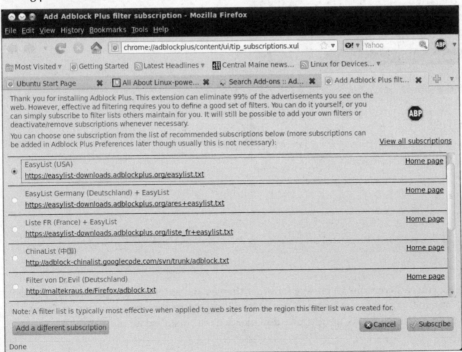

Most other extensions support some amount of configuration through preference settings. You can access the preferences dialogs for such extensions through entries for installed extensions on the Tools menu, or by searching for them in the extensions list and clicking the Preferences button in the entry for that extension. Figure 8-29 shows the preferences dialog for one of my favorite extensions, It's All Text!, which enables you to use the text editor of your choice to edit text areas on web pages.

This extension provides one of my favorite configuration items ever — the "Remove all bugs" checkbox! Sadly enough, this doesn't do exactly what it says, but instead activates verbose debugging so that the developer can diagnose and resolve problems. Maybe some day . . .

Tip

After experimenting with your new capabilities in Firefox, you can always uninstall an extension that you don't like or want by selecting the Add-ons command from the Tools menu, selecting the Extensions icon, highlighting the extension in question, and clicking Uninstall. The extension will be uninstalled the next time that you start Firefox. ■

FIGURE 8-29

Setting preferences for an extension through its preferences dialog

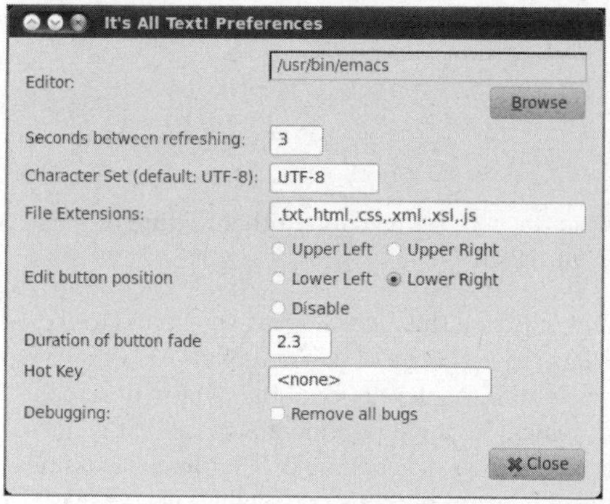

Adding New Firefox Plug-Ins

As mentioned at the beginning of the "Enhancing Firefox" section of this chapter, *plug-ins* are applets that work within the Firefox framework and provide support for playing different types of multimedia files within your browser. The standard Ubuntu installation of Firefox comes with several plug-ins that support popular multimedia file formats such as Flash (SWF), Microsoft's Direct Video Express (DivX), RealPlayer, QuickTime, Windows Media Player, and so on.

To see the plug-ins that are currently installed on your system, select the Add-ons command from the Tools menu, and click the Plugins icon. This displays the Plugins dialog, shown in Figure 8-30, which displays a list of all of the plug-ins that are currently installed on your system.

FIGURE 8-30

The Plugins dialog in Firefox

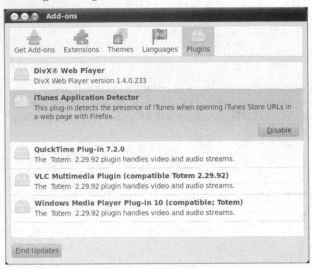

Generally, plug-ins are requested when you view a page containing content that requires a plug-in to play it, as shown earlier in this chapter in Figure 8-6.

When using Firefox on systems other than Ubuntu, clicking this button gives you access to the missing plug-in, enabling you to install it with a few mouse clicks (if you're lucky). You often have to install such plug-ins manually, depending on how well the developer of the plug-in designed and packaged it. Luckily, Ubuntu's ubufox package includes a Plugin Finder Service that is integrated with the GNOME Ubuntu package management tools, so clicking on the "Install Missing Plugins" button displays a page that displays a list of relevant plug-ins and enables you to select the one you want. After doing so, click Next, confirm the installation of the plugin, and the plugin will be installed.

Unlike extensions and themes, you can't remove plug-ins once they've been installed; you can only disable them. To disable an installed plug-in, click the Add-ons dialog's Plugins icon, and select the Disable button to the right of the entry for the plug-in that you want to disable. This enables you to install other plug-ins to handle a given type of content without losing track of the one(s) that you've already tried.

Summary

This chapter provided the highlights of configuring, using, and customizing Firefox, the most popular browser for Linux systems and one that is growing in popularity on other types of systems such as Microsoft Windows and Mac OS X. Firefox is the culmination of years of development and evolution in the Web browsing and open source communities. After using Firefox for a while on Ubuntu, you're sure to find that it's certainly worth installing and using on any other computer systems that you might have to use. You'll be happier because you'll have the same browser experience no matter what system you're using, and you're certainly not going to get any complaints from the open source community in general.

Migrating from Windows Systems

IN THIS CHAPTER

Introducing basic migration scenarios

Backing up

Migrating e-mail

Migrating web settings

Linux/Windows application equivalents

Whether you're currently investigating Ubuntu as an alternative operating system to run on the computers in your home or you're desperately looking for an alternative to operating system cost extortion, I hope that you'll eventually decide that switching to Ubuntu as your default operating system is the right thing to do. The political aspects of Linux are very important to many people (myself included), but most people simply want to be able to use their computers to get their work (or hobbies) done. Ubuntu does that. That it is stable, easy to upgrade, and largely virus-proof is just gravy.

Few people start out with Ubuntu as their first operating system and application environment. If you're moving to Ubuntu from another Linux distribution, you're in luck, because you can almost always find versions of the Linux applications that you're familiar with packaged for Ubuntu. However, if you're moving to Ubuntu from a computer that runs another operating system, switching to Linux is a bit more complex. After all, you've already configured your browser, e-mail, and networking. The computer that you're currently using is probably loaded with documents, spreadsheets, photographs, graphics, music, video files, and a lot of other data that you don't want to have to re-create (or simply may not be able to).

Moving existing files and personal data to your new Ubuntu system is discussed in the last section of this chapter. Copying files from one computer to another is easy, but sometimes copying isn't enough. Some of the most important data that any of us have is our e-mail, favorite web pages, and related configuration information. If you're coming from a traditional Microsoft Windows system, that data is locked into file formats and directory structures used by the applications that created it, such as Microsoft Outlook, Outlook Express, and Internet Explorer. Therefore, most of this chapter focuses on accessing your existing e-mail, browser favorites, cookies, and similar settings on your new Ubuntu system by converting that data into formats that are used by equivalent Ubuntu applications and then copying the converted data to your Ubuntu system.

This chapter focuses on migrating your data from a Microsoft Windows system to an Ubuntu Linux system. The same general concepts and tasks often apply if you're migrating from a Mac OS X system, but many of the details will differ. Although most of the examples in this chapter relate to different flavors of Windows, I will also provide tips that highlight Macintosh migration tasks without providing step-by-step instructions.

Overview of Migration Scenarios

Chapters 2, "Installing Ubuntu," and 3, "Installing Ubuntu on Special-Purpose Systems," discussed how to install Ubuntu, with a focus on installation on a new machine or on an existing machine where you can dedicate specific partitions to Ubuntu so that you can dual-boot. When migrating from a Windows system, you obviously need to be able to access the data from your Windows system. How you get to that information differs based on the type of Ubuntu installation that you're doing:

- **Installing Ubuntu on a new machine and leaving Windows on another:** This is the easiest migration scenario because you can copy file data from your Windows system to your Ubuntu system via a network connection or by copying your Windows data to a USB thumb drive. You can do any necessary file conversions on the Windows system, leaving your original data intact there, and then copy the converted data to your Ubuntu system to verify it.

- **Dual-booting an existing machine:** Still an easy scenario, you can mount your Windows partition(s) on your Ubuntu system and copy file data to Ubuntu. You may have to boot into Windows in order to convert some of your files, but you can copy the converted files directly from your Windows filesystem once you are running Ubuntu.

- **Converting a single system:** This is the trickiest scenario — you must use a backup of your Windows data as the location from which you can copy files. You must also do all necessary file conversions on the Windows system before you do the backup, or on the Linux system after you are running Ubuntu.

Both of the last two scenarios require making changes to your existing Windows system, so it is critical that you do a complete backup of your Windows system before installing Ubuntu. See the next section for details.

This chapter discusses various ways of migrating your existing Windows data to an Ubuntu system. Frankly, I hope that you'll never need to read some of the sections of this chapter, but they're here if you need them. I suggest the following sequence of events in order to smoothly migrate your data to your new Ubuntu system:

1. Start Outlook or Outlook Express and export your Address Book information in a generic format such as a CSV file. You may not need this, but it's always handy to have a spare copy of this information in an application-independent format such as a CSV file.

2. If you are using Outlook, export your tasks and calendar information so that you can refer to it later. If you're using Outlook 2007, you can save your calendar in iCalendar format, which you can use with Evolution and other popular Linux applications. Otherwise, you can at least save your tasks and calendar information in CSV format so that you can import that data in Evolution.

3. If you are using Outlook 2003 or later, use the File menu's Import and Export command to export your entire Personal Folders hierarchy (including subfolders) to a single PST file. This will provide a useful backup of all of your Contacts, Calendar entries, mail folders, and so on — just in case! Because this is an export operation to a file, Outlook will not track this file, as it normally does with PST archives. See the section "Migrating Outlook Mail with readpst" later in this chapter, for detailed information about using this file.

4. If you are using Outlook, have created PST archives of your mail in the past, and want to migrate the contents of those archives to your new Ubuntu system, create a new folder and restore those PST backups into it. (PST files are Microsoft Personal Folder Files used for backup purposes within Outlook.)

5. Install Thunderbird on your Windows system and allow it to import your existing mail and account information from Outlook or Outlook Express.

6. If you are using Outlook 2003 or later, create a new PST file in Windows 97–2002 format, and copy all of the mail folders from your existing mail folder there. Outlook 2003 introduced UTF-8 encoding in PST files, whereas previous versions of Outlook used ANSI-encoded PST files. You may not need this version of your existing PST file, but it's always handy to have a spare copy of this information in a standard format, just in case you ever need to access these files and don't have a Windows machine handy. See the section "Migrating Outlook Mail with readpst" later in this chapter for detailed information about doing this.

Note

If you use Thunderbird as part of your migration process, you can safely create this PST file after converting your mail with Thunderbird. Creating the new PST file before doing the conversion will cause Thunderbird to convert both of your PST files — not a big problem, but the duplication might be confusing. ■

7. Install Firefox on your Windows or Mac OS X system, and allow it to import your existing Favorites, saved passwords, cookies, and so on from Internet Explorer.

8. Export your Internet Explorer Favorites or Safari bookmarks to an HTML file. You may not need this, but it's always handy to have a spare copy of this information in an application-independent format such as HTML.

You will then want to back up all of the exported files that you created in the previous steps and your personal data (as described in the next section) from the Windows system to a CD, DVD, external drive, or network location, and verify that you can read the data that you've backed up on another computer system before proceeding.

Ready? Here we go…

Backing Up Your Personal Data

Backups are always a good idea. Few things are as frustrating as the realization that you've somehow lost years of e-mail, all your web settings, the great American novel, all of your tax returns for the last decade, your music collection, and the digital photographs and video for all of your vacations and special occasions. I hope that you're already doing backups, but if you're installing Ubuntu on a machine that is currently running Windows, this may be your last chance to preserve all of the personal data on your computer. I've never encountered a problem when setting up a computer to dual-boot Windows and Ubuntu, but there's always a first time. Back up your data before proceeding! If you're converting a system that is currently running Windows to an Ubuntu system, your existing disk will be erased, so back up your data before proceeding!

Note

This is not a Windows book, and I cannot guess all of the locations where you or various Windows applications may have stored important data. This section discusses some standard locations for personal information. I am not responsible if you miss some critical files. Your mileage may vary. Please make sure that your backups contain all of the files that you want to preserve before making any changes to your Windows system. ■

When backing up your Windows system with an eye toward migrating existing information to your new Ubuntu system, you must create your backups in a format that is accessible from an Ubuntu system. The easiest way to do this is by simply copying files and directories to a CD or thumb drive. You will need to back up at least the following directory on your Windows system, where *USERNAME* is your login name:

- On Windows XP and older Windows systems, the `C:\Documents and Settings\`*USERNAME* folder

- On Windows Vista and Windows 7 systems, the `C:\Users\`*USERNAME* folder

You should also back up any other directories from your local disk in which you have explicitly stored files that you've been working on. This can include project directories, personal directories that you've created on your C: drive, and so on.

When backing up your Windows system so that you can migrate existing data, do not use a PC backup program for which no Linux version exists. (That's pretty obvious, but it had to be said.) Frankly, even if you find a backup program that works on both Linux and Windows systems, I would not recommend using it for migration purposes. Backups that you can mount and access as standard ISO-9660 CDs and DVDs are easy to use and require no special software at any time. You can also easily test CD/DVD backups of files and directories on another system — do not assume that they will be readable from your new Ubuntu system without testing them. "Back up once, verify twice," as my grandfather used to say. You should verify that you can read the data that you've backed up on at least one other computer system before proceeding.

Migrating E-Mail to Linux

Because e-mail is one of the two killer applications for modern networked computing (the other being the Web browser), preserving your existing e-mail is a pretty important aspect of moving to a new computer. This is especially true if you're also moving to a new operating system such as Ubuntu. I'm pretty compulsive about saving e-mail — I still have messages that I exchanged with friends in the early 1990s. (I used some proprietary and academic mail systems before that, but I'm not 100% compulsive.) You may not be as much of an electronic pack rat as I am, but you still probably want to preserve any mail messages that you've bothered saving.

Migration is necessary when moving from one operating system and local mail client to another because different clients store your account settings and e-mail in different formats. (Migration is not necessary if your mail is stored elsewhere and accessed through a Web client — this section applies only to e-mail that is stored on your computer.) While there are many different mail clients for Windows systems, most people use either Microsoft Outlook Express, a free mail client that is typically included with Windows Internet Explorer downloads, or Microsoft Outlook, a commercial sibling that is part of the Microsoft Office Suite. The biggest thing that these two applications have in common is that they are both often described as virus propagation software disguised as an e-mail client, but their primary differences are core capabilities and the format in which they store mail. The DBX format used by Outlook Express is easy to migrate, as described in the next two sections. Migrating Outlook mail from PST files requires some special handling, which I'll discuss later in the section, "Migrating Outlook Mail with readpst." Most Linux mail clients use a format known as mbox (mailbox), which has been used by some Windows mailers (such as Eudora), and was also used by Mac OS X's Mail.app up to version 2.0, after which Apple switched to a proprietary mailbox format.

Note

Migrating your e-mail is necessary only if your e-mail account is a POP/POP3 mail account or you are using an IMAP account with Microsoft Outlook and have archived your mail on your local system. If your e-mail account is a standard IMAP account and you are either not using Microsoft Outlook or don't have any local archives, all of your saved mail is still on the IMAP server, and no migration is necessary. ■

The following is a quick overview of the pros and cons of the Outlook Express migration mechanisms discussed in the next two sections.

- **Migration via Thunderbird:** Convenient because your mail files and account settings are converted automatically. However, you have to download and install Thunderbird on your Windows system and do the conversion before you do your backups. You also have to search for the converted files when copying them to your Ubuntu system or reading them from your backups. Unless you continue to use Thunderbird on Ubuntu, you'll also have to import the converted files into Evolution format, one converted file at a time.

- **Manual migration:** Convenient because you can selectively convert individual mail files. However, if you are migrating Outlook Express mail, note that the readdbx application isn't provided on Ubuntu systems by default, so you have to compile it yourself, which also means that you have to install the GNU C compiler on your Ubuntu system. See Chapter 23, "Software Development on Ubuntu," for information about compiling applications. If you are migrating Outlook mail, the `readpst` utility is available in the Ubuntu repositories and can now read the PST files used by all versions of Outlook, including the 64-bit PST files created by Outlook 2003 and later. Regardless of whether you're migrating Outlook Express or Outlook mail, these utilities run only on your Ubuntu system, so you will then have to search for the files that you want to convert on your backups and convert them one at a time. Finally, you'll have to import the converted files into Evolution, one converted file at a time.

I suggest that you use Thunderbird for the migration. It's really much easier. However, if something goes wrong and you need to migrate e-mail from your backups when you no longer have a Windows system around, the `readdbx` and `readpst` mechanisms that are discussed later in this chapter can be lifesavers.

Migrating Mail via Thunderbird

Thunderbird is a popular mail client from the Mozilla Foundation (www.mozilla.com/thunderbird) that is available for the Microsoft Windows, Mac OS X, and Linux platforms. Like Firefox, Thunderbird supports plug-ins that make it easy to customize and extend its default behavior.

Aside from its excellence as a stand-alone mail client, Thunderbird can be very handy when migrating e-mail to Ubuntu from a Windows system. You can use Thunderbird to migrate your Outlook Express or Outlook mail in one of two ways:

- If you're already using Thunderbird on your Windows system and want to continue using Thunderbird on Ubuntu, you can install Thunderbird on Ubuntu, copy your existing Thunderbird profile to your new Ubuntu system, and everything will "just work."

- If you are using Outlook Express on your Windows system, you can install Thunderbird on your Windows system and let it convert your Outlook Express e-mail and account settings for you.

As you might expect, you must do these migrations on your Windows system, and you should probably do them before doing your final backups, so that both your original mail files and the converted versions are included on your backups.

You can download a copy of Thunderbird for Windows by clicking on the download link at www.mozilla.com/thunderbird. The last installation dialog offers to automatically start Thunderbird, which you should do. This displays the dialog shown in Figure 9-1, asking if you want to import your mail and account settings into Thunderbird.

FIGURE 9-1

Importing Outlook Express mail into Thunderbird

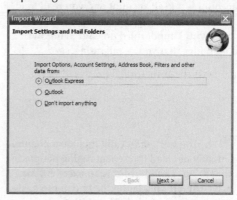

This dialog lists all Microsoft email applications that have been detected on your system. If Outlook Express is detected on your system, the Outlook Express radio button is selected by default — select the Outlook button if you want to migrate mail from Outlook instead. (You'll see the Outlook button only if Outlook is installed on your computer.) Click Next to proceed to a status dialog that reports the progress of importing your mail account settings, address book, and mail folders into Thunderbird. After displaying a final status dialog, Thunderbird will start on your system, displaying a dialog like the one shown in Figure 9-2.

FIGURE 9-2

The default client dialog in Thunderbird

Although you're migrating all of your mail to Ubuntu and will hopefully never need to read mail on Windows again, you may want to click OK with the E-Mail checkbox selected. This will modify your Windows mail application settings so that Windows will start Thunderbird, rather than Outlook or Outlook Express, if you accidentally click a link that causes you to read mail on your Windows system.

Note

Unless you are using IMAP, you should not read your mail on your Windows system using Outlook or Outlook Express after migrating your mail to Thunderbird. If your e-mail account is a POP account and you read mail, new mail will be downloaded to your Outlook or Outlook Express mail files, but will not be reflected in the Thunderbird mail files that you converted. Subsequently reading mail with Thunderbird on your Windows system is OK because your mail will be stored in the Thunderbird mail files that you're migrating. ■

At this point, you should create an external backup of at least the directories discussed in the section, "Backing Up Your Personal Data."

Note

After all this talk about Thunderbird, you're probably wondering, "Why the heck didn't Bill include a chapter on Thunderbird in this book?" I gave that serious thought, but eventually decided that encouraging people to use the mail clients provided in the Evolution PIM was the right thing to do. Thunderbird is an excellent mail client — many of my friends use and swear by Thunderbird, and I have used it on a laptop or two in the past. However, I think that most Ubuntu users will get much more long-term value out of sticking with Evolution. ■

Where Thunderbird Stores Its Mail

Thunderbird stores the mail for each user in the user's profile directory. On a Windows system, your profile directory is located in one of the the following directories (depending on the version of Windows that you are using), where *USERNAME* is your login name on the Windows machine (sometimes concatenated with the hostname of your Windows system):

```
C:\Documents and Settings\USERNAME\Application Data\Thunderbird\Profiles
C:\Usrs\USERNAME\Appdata\Roaming\Thunderbird\Profiles
```

You should be able to navigate to this folder using Windows Explorer. Thunderbird profile directories in this directory have names of the form *xxxxxxxx*.default, where *xxxxxxxx* is not an actual part of the name, but represents a unique sequence of eight characters that Thunderbird created for you the first time that you started Thunderbird. This directory contains all of your Thunderbird information, including a Mail subdirectory that contains all of your account information and mail files.

On Linux systems, mail is stored in a directory whose name has the same format, but its location depends on the version of Thunderbird that you're using:

- If you have downloaded, installed, and are using the official version of Thunderbird from the Mozilla project rather than using Synaptic or the Adept Manager, your profile directory and profile initialization file (profiles.ini) will be located in a directory called .thunderbird that is located in your home directory.

- If you have installed Thunderbird using Synaptic or the Adept Manager, your profile directory and profile initialization file (profiles.ini) will be located in a directory called .thunderbird that is located in your home directory. This was an older name for the directory that holds Thunderbird initialization files and has been preserved by the Ubuntu and Debian folks to guarantee compatibility with older Thunderbird installations.

In my opinion, it's unfortunate that Ubuntu and Debian have preserved the old name for the directory that holds Thunderbird initialization and profile information, but no one asked me.

Tip
On Mac OS X systems, your Thunderbird profile directory is stored in one of two locations, either `~/Library/Thunderbird/Profiles` **or** `~/Library/Application Support/Thunderbird/Profiles`. ∎

Installing or Updating Thunderbird

To migrate to a Ubuntu system upon which you plan to install and use Thunderbird, you'll need to install the Ubuntu version of Thunderbird, which you can find as the `thunderbird` package using any of the Package Management software discussed in Chapter 19, "Adding, Removing, and Updating Software." The related `.thunderbird` package is a compatibility package for users who are upgrading older systems and simply requires the `thunderbird` package.

How to proceed depends on whether you've just installed Thunderbird for the first time on your Ubuntu system, or whether you're already been using Thunderbird on your Ubuntu system for a while:

- If you have just installed Thunderbird for the first time, proceed to the next section ("Importing Mail into Thunderbird: New Users") for information on what files to copy from your Windows system, where to put them on your Ubuntu system, and how you'll need to modify the Thunderbird profile file.

- If you've installed and used Thunderbird on your Ubuntu system before, you'll want to preserve your old Thunderbird mail, and should therefore skip to the section, "Importing Mail into Thunderbird: Existing Users."

Importing Mail into Thunderbird: New Users

If you have never used Thunderbird on your Ubuntu system before, you can copy over the converted mail and profile initialization information from your Windows system and have Thunderbird use it immediately.

To do this, first create the directory `~/.thunderbird` before starting Thunderbird. Next, recursively copy the *xxxxxxxx*`.default` directory from your Windows backups to the `~/.thunderbird` directory that you just created in your Ubuntu home directory. You can do this by copying this directory from the CD, DVD, or network location to which you backed up the following directory (depending on the version of Windows that you were using):

```
C:\Documents and Settings\USERNAME\Application Data\Thunderbird\Profiles
C:\Usrs\USERNAME\Appdata\Roaming\Thunderbird\Profiles
```

Tip
If you are installing Ubuntu on a new machine, you can use Samba to mount a shared Windows drive on your Ubuntu system, and copy the files over the network. See Chapter 25, "Connecting to Other Systems," for information on mounting shared Windows drives on your Ubuntu system. ∎

You should also copy the following file from the backup of this directory from your Windows system into your ~/.thunderbird directory, depending on the version of Windows that you are using:

On Windows XP and earlier systems:

```
C:\Documents and Settings\USERNAME\Application Data\Thunderbird\profiles.ini
```

On Windows Vista and later systems:

```
C:\Usrs\USERNAME\Appdata\Roaming\Thunderbird\profiles.ini
```

When copied from a Windows system, this file will initially look something like the following:

```
[General]
StartWithLastProfile=1
[Profile0]
Name=default
IsRelative=1
Path=Profiles/hus5hy55.default
```

After copying it to your Ubuntu system, use a text editor to modify the version of this file that you copied from your Windows system and remove the Profiles directory from the Path variable. An updated version of this same file would look like the following:

```
[General]
StartWithLastProfile=1
[Profile0]
Name=default
IsRelative=1
Path=hus5hy55.default
```

When you start Thunderbird for the first time on Ubuntu, it will instantly use the Profile directory from your Windows system, and things should look exactly the same as they did there. If this is the case, congratulations! Your mail has been migrated successfully, and you can now resume your normal e-mail existence using Thunderbird as your default mail client.

Tip
If you subsequently want to switch to using Evolution, you can always import your Thunderbird mail into those applications as described later in the section, "Importing Thunderbird Mail into Evolution." ■

Importing Mail into Thunderbird: Existing Users
If you've already been using Thunderbird on Ubuntu and are simply migrating old mail from a Windows system, the directory ~/.thunderbird will already exist in your home directory on your Ubuntu system. That directory will already contain a default Profile directory named something like xxxxxxxx.default and your profile initialization file, profiles.ini.

In this case, you will want to use Thunderbird's import capability to import the Thunderbird mail from your Windows system into your existing Thunderbird mail files. You will therefore need access to the directory where Thunderbird stored the converted versions of your Windows mail. This should be located on the CD, DVD, external drive, or network location to which you backed up the `C:\Documents and Settings\`*USERNAME*`\Application Data\Thunderbird\Profiles` or `C:\Users\`*USERNAME*`\AppData\Roaming\Thunderbird\Profiles` directory.

Your Thunderbird mail is actually stored in a subdirectory of this directory, with a name like *xxxxxxxx*`.default/Mail/Local Folders`, where *xxxxxxxx* is a random string that was generated when you first started Thunderbird. This directory contains files that contain your mail and auxiliary files and directories used to store Thunderbird configuration information. To determine which files you need to import into Thunderbird, start an Ubuntu xterm or console window, change directory to the *xxxxxxxx*`.default/Mail/Local Folders` directory, and execute a command like the following:

```
$ find -not -empty | egrep -v '.msf$|.sbd$|.dat$|^.$'
./Personal Folders.sbd/Inbox
./Personal Folders.sbd/Personal
./Personal Folders.sbd/Writing
```

In this case, the files `Inbox`, `Personal`, and `Writing` are all non-zero in size (i.e., not empty) and thus contain mail that you will want to import. The `egrep` portion of the command filters out (in order) Thunderbird Mail Summary Files (MSF), empty Mail Subdirectories (SBD), and the DAT files in which Thunderbird stores registry and version data.

Once you've identified the files that contain the Windows mail that you want to import into your existing Thunderbird mail, you will need to copy these files to the directory in your existing Thunderbird profile so that you can access them from Thunderbird. You can do this in one of two ways:

- If you do not have Thunderbird message folders with the same name on your Ubuntu system, you can simply copy them with their existing names.

- If you already have Thunderbird message folders with the same names on your Ubuntu system, you will have to copy your Windows message folders and give them new names so that they don't overwrite the existing Thunderbird message folders with the same name.

For safety's sake, I always use the second approach because it's easy to overwrite folders with important names such as *Inbox*. After changing directory to the *xxxxxxxx*`.default/Mail/Local Folders` directory on your Windows backups, commands like the following would copy the mail folders that we previously identified to your Ubuntu installation, adding the `-imported` suffix to the copied folders:

```
cp "./Personal Folders.sbd/Inbox" \
   ~/.thunderbird/hf8dwpmj.default/Mail/Local\ Folders/Inbox-imported
./Personal Folders.sbd/Personal \
```

```
    ~/.thunderbird/hf8dwpmj.default/Mail/Local\ Folders/Personal-imported
  ./Personal Folders.sbd/Writing \
    ~/.thunderbird/hf8dwpmj.default/Mail/Local\ Folders/Writing-imported
```

That's extremely tedious to type for any more than one mailbox, so the following is a script that requires the -t argument to specify that you are migrating Thunderbird mail, takes the name of your profile directory as an argument, and does this for you:

```
#!/bin/bash

function usage {
    echo "Usage: import_thunderbird_mail.sh [-e] [-t profile-dir]"
    echo " -e : import Thunderbird mail into Evolution"
    echo " -t : import Thunderbird mail into Thunderbird"
    exit 1
}

if [ $# == 0 ] ; then
    usage
    exit
fi

while getopts ":t:e" opt
do
  case $opt in
    e  )
        TARGETDIR=~/.evolution/mail/local
        ;;
    t  )
        if [ $# != 1 ] ; then
          echo "No Thunderbird profile directory specified."
          exit 1
        fi
        TARGETDIR=~/.thunderbird/$1/Mail/Local\ Folders
        ;;
      \? ) usage
        exit 1;;
  esac
done
shift $(($OPTIND - 1))

find . -not -empty | egrep -v '.msf$|.sbd$|.dat$|^.$' | \
    while read mbox ; do
      newmbox='echo $mbox | sed -e 's;.*/;;' -e 's;$;-imported;'
      echo "Copying $mbox to $newmbox"
      cp "$mbox" $TARGETDIR/$newmbox
    done
```

Note

You can download this script and others in this book from my web site at www.vonhagen.org/Ubuntu/ **scripts. The name of this script is** import_thunderbird_mail.sh. ∎

You can find out the name of the Thunderbird profile directory by listing the directory ~/.thunderbird:

```
$ ls ~/.mozilla_thunderbird
hf8dwpmj.default    profiles.ini
```

In this case, your Profile directory is the directory hf8dwpmj.default. In this case, the command to run this script and the output from its execution would be the following:

```
$ import_thunderbird_mail.sh -t hf8dwpmj.default
Copying ./Personal Folders.sbd/Writing to Writing-imported
Copying ./Personal Folders.sbd/Inbox to Inbox-imported
Copying ./Personal Folders.sbd/Personal to Personal-imported
```

The next time that you start Thunderbird on Ubuntu, you should see the imported mailboxes, as shown in Figure 9-3.

FIGURE 9-3

Existing and imported mailboxes in Thunderbird

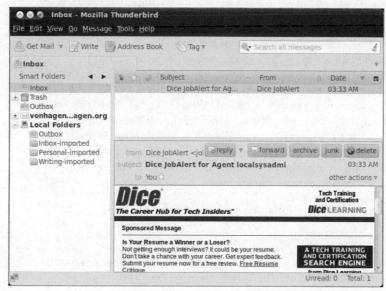

Congratulations! Your mail has been migrated successfully, and you can now copy messages from the imported folders into the folders that you are currently using in Thunderbird. You can also simply rename these folders, removing the `-imported` extension, if you want to preserve the familiar folder names that you used when you were a Windows user.

Importing Thunderbird Mail into Evolution

Letting Thunderbird convert your existing Outlook/Outlook Express e-mail (as described in the section, "Migrating Mail via Thunderbird") is an excellent first step for importing your Windows mail into Evolution, the GNOME PIM and mail client used by the standard Ubuntu desktop distribution. Both Thunderbird and Evolution store the mail for a mail folder in a file in the traditional UNIX mbox (mail box) format. This makes it extremely easy to import mail from Thunderbird into Evolution.

Evolution provides an Import Wizard that imports all mail from older Linux mailers (Netscape Navigator, etc.), and also lets you import single files in supported formats such as Berkeley Mailbox (mbox), Evolution CSV or Tab (.csv or .tab), Mozilla CSV or Tab (.csv or .tab), Outlook CSV or Tab (.csv or .tab), Vcard (.vcf or .gcrd), LDAP Data Interchange Format (.ldif), vCalendar (.vcf), and iCalendar (.icf). Using Evolution's Import Wizard to import single files is discussed later in this section, and makes sense if you are importing one or two files. However, single-file import can be tedious and time-consuming if you have a large number of mailbox files that you want to import. In the latter case, you can use the `import_thunderbird_mail.sh` script that was discussed in the previous section to import all of your mailboxes into Evolution, adding an `-imported` suffix to each of their names so that you can identify the imported mailboxes.

To run this script and import mailboxes that you created by importing your Outlook/Outlook Express mail into Thunderbird on a Windows system, first change directory to the CD, DVD, or network location to which you backed up the `C:\Documents and Settings\`*USERNAME*`\Application Data\Thunderbird\Profiles` or `C:\Users\`*USERNAME*`\AppData\Roaming\Thunderbird\Profiles` directory. Your Thunderbird mail is actually stored in a subdirectory of this directory, with a name like *xxxxxxxx*`.default/Mail/Local Folders`, where *xxxxxxxx* is a random string that was generated when you first started Thunderbird. This directory contains files that contain your mail and auxiliary files and directories used to store Thunderbird configuration information. Change directory to the *xxxxxxxx*`.default/Mail/Local Folders` directory and run the `import_thunderbird_mail.sh` script with the `-e` argument to state that you are migrating mail into Evolution.

The command to run this script and the output from its execution is as follows:

```
$ import_thunderbird_mail.sh -e
Copying ./Personal Folders.sbd/Inbox to Inbox-imported
Copying ./Personal Folders.sbd/Personal to Personal-imported
Copying ./Personal Folders.sbd/Writing to Writing-imported
```

The next time that you start Evolution, you will see the newly imported files, as shown in Figure 9-4.

Existing and Imported mailboxes in Evolution

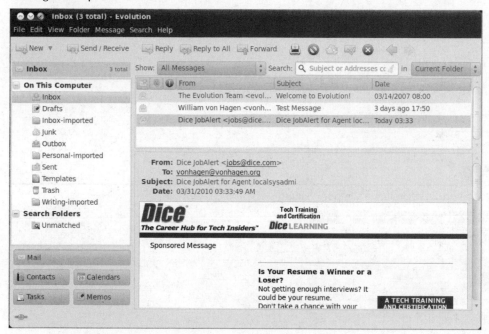

As mentioned previously, you can also import selected mailboxes into Evolution, which may be more convenient if you're uncomfortable at the command line or simply don't want to have to download and install my shell script. To use Evolution's Import Wizard, start Evolution and select the File menu's Import option. A Welcome dialog displays. Click Forward to proceed to the dialog shown in Figure 9-5, which enables you to identify whether you are importing data and settings from an older program, or whether you are importing a single file.

Select "Import a single file," and click Forward to proceed. The dialog shown in Figure 9-6 displays.

FIGURE 9-5

Identifying import type in Evolution's Import Wizard

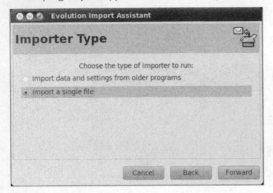

FIGURE 9-6

Locating the file to import in Evolution's Import Wizard

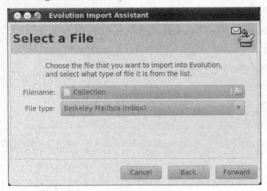

Click the Filename button to display a dialog that enables you to navigate to and select the file that you want to import. The mail files that you converted using Thunderbird should be located on the CD, DVD, external drive, or network location to which you backed up the C:\Documents and Settings*USERNAME*\Application Data\Thunderbird\Profiles or C:\Users\ *USERNAME*\AppData\Roaming\Thunderbird\Profiles directory. They will be located in a subdirectory of this directory that has a name like *xxxxxxxx*.default/Mail/Local Folders, where *xxxxxxxx* is a random string that was generated when you first started Thunderbird.

Click Open to close the navigation dialog and open the file that you want to import. The File type entry on the "Import a File" dialog should display "Berkeley Mailbox (mbox)" because this is the format of mail files that have been created by Thunderbird. (It is also the format of mail files used by Evolution.) Click Forward to proceed. The dialog shown in Figure 9-7 displays.

FIGURE 9-7

Specifying the Import Location in Evolution's Import Wizard

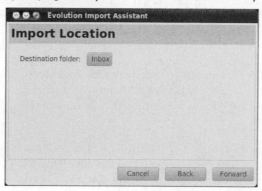

This dialog enables you to select the Evolution mail folder into which you want to import the messages in the mail file that you selected in the previous step. The default import location is your Inbox folder, but you can click the Destination folder button to navigate to and choose another folder into which you want to import your messages.

Tip

When importing mail for others, I sometimes create a new folder in Evolution named *IMPORT* **and use this as the folder into which I import messages. This makes it easy to differentiate between imported messages and messages that may already exist in a given folder. After finishing the import process and moving imported messages to other folders, I delete the IMPORT folder, and everything looks just as it did when I started (except for the number of messages in various folders).** ■

After selecting a folder, click Forward to proceed to the next dialog. A confirmation dialog displays. To proceed, click Import. Evolution displays a status dialog as it imports the messages. When this closes, congratulations! You've successfully imported mail from Thunderbird. You can now re-select the File ➪ Import command to import another mail folder, or begin filing and organizing the newly imported messages.

Manually Migrating Mail

The essentially automatic export mechanism that is provided by installing Thunderbird on a Windows system is extremely convenient and is also fairly bullet-proof because it uses Windows function calls that provide direct access to your Outlook Express mail. After importing your mail into Thunderbird, you can back up the directories in which Thunderbird stores its mail and use those to import your mail into Ubuntu's Evolution mail client. If you're lucky, you'll never need to see or use those backups again.

Unfortunately, not everyone is lucky. I've worked with clients who did their backups before using Thunderbird to generate portable versions of their mail files, managed to avoid exporting specific Outlook Express mail files into Thunderbird, or needed to restore mail from older Windows backups and import those restored folders. I don't even know how people manage to do some of these things, but these are all cases in which you can't use the traditional Thunderbird-to-Whatever mail migration method.

Luckily for us, the open source community is large enough that somebody has had to do these sorts of things before, and therefore has written tools to do these things. Migrating mail folders manually requires a bit more work than clicking a few buttons and letting Thunderbird do the heavy lifting, but it works just as well.

The next two sections describe how to use the command-line readdbx and readpst utilities to manually create mbox files from your DBX files (Outlook Express mail) and PST files (Outlook mail). I hope that you won't ever need this information, but better safe than really, really sorry.

Migrating Outlook Express Mail with readdbx

Outlook Express stores its mail folders in files that are in DBX format, a database format of sorts. Luckily, the libdbx package provides two utilities to help convert files in these formats to files in the standard mbox format. These are the readdbx utility, which converts single DBX files, and the readoe utility, which will take a directory of DBX files (such as the directory where Outlook Express stores your mail) and will convert all of the files in this directory into mbox-format files in another directory.

The libdbx project is actually a part of the ol2mbox (Outlook to mbox) project on SourceForge (http://sourceforge.net/projects/ol2mbox). There hasn't been a new release of libdbx for a while because, well, the current version "just works." (The libpst package for reading Outlook mail from PST files is a different story, as discussed in the next section.) For all of us Ubuntu users, the bad news is that the libdbx package is not available in the Ubuntu repositories, so you'll have to download the source code and build it yourself if you need to use it.

I won't go into the details of building and installing the package here — Chapter 23 explains how to install the tools necessary to compile source code that is written in the C programming language. Here's a quick overview:

1. Download the source code package from the SourceForge project web site by clicking the Download link and retrieving the libdbx_1.0.3.tgz compressed archive file.

2. Uncompress the archive using a command such as tar zxvf *filename*, where *filename* is the name of the file that you downloaded.

3. Change directory to the directory to which the software was extracted (probably libdbx_1.0.3), and configure the software using the command ./configure.

4. Use the make program to build and install the readdbx and readoe utilities by executing the command make install.

Once you've done all of these steps, you should be able to change directory to the directory that contains the DBX files that you want to convert. If you're working from backups of a Windows system, the *right* directory can be tricky to identify because it depends on the name of an internal identity that is created by Windows. The generic format of the name of this directory (located under your user directory) is as follows:

On Windows XP and earlier Windows systems:

```
Local Settings\Application Data\Identities\ID\Microsoft\Outlook Express
```

On Windows Vista and later Windows systems:

```
AppData\Local\Identities\ID\Microsoft\Outlook Express
```

In this example, you would change *ID* to some string that is your user identifier. You should be able to determine the "right" *ID* by exploring your backups.

To convert an entire directory of Outlook Express files to mbox format, the readoe utility must be run from the parent of this directory using commands such as the following:

```
cd ..
mkdir converted
readoe -i Outlook\ Express -o converted
```

All of the Outlook Express mailbox files in the Outlook Express directory will be converted to mbox-format files that will be created in the "converted" directory.

If you wanted to convert only a single DBX file (such as one that you've restored from backups), you'd execute a command like the following from the directory that contains your Outlook Express mail:

```
$ readdbx -f Personal.dbx -o personal.mbox
```

This command converts the contents of your Personal folder to the file personal.mbox. Once you've converted a mailbox, you can use your mail client's import capability to import the mbox file that you've created. Importing mail from mbox files was explained in the previous sections.

Migrating Outlook Mail with readpst

Microsoft Outlook stores its mail folders in files that are in PST format. PST stands for "Personal Storage Table," but are most often referred to as "Personal File Folder" files. The readpst utility, which is part of the libpst project and is available in the Ubuntu repositories, enables you to read PST files; extract the mail folders, contact information, calendar items, and other data that they contain; and create files that you can then import into Evolution.

The libpst project was originally a part of the ol2mbox (Outlook to mbox) project on SourceForge (http://sourceforge.net/projects/ol2mbox), just as the libdbx project is. The need for changes to libpst led to a new maintainer and home for libpst at `http://alioth.debian.org/projects/libpst` for some time, but the current home of the latest version of libpst is located at `www.five-ten-sg.com/libpst`. For Ubuntu users, the good news is that the `readpst` utility is also available in the Ubuntu repositories, so you can just install the `readpst` package using your favorite Package Management tool — no compilation required!

The latest versions of readpst (and the libpst project in general) can read both the 32-bit PST files produced by versions of Outlook prior to Outlook 2003, and the 64-bit PST files produced by Outlook 2003 and later.

Before you can use the `readpst` utility to extract Windows mail and other data from a PST, make sure that you know the location of the PST file(s) that you want to extract data from.

If you followed the suggestions in the section earlier in this chapter entitled, "Overview of Migration Scenarios," you will have a PST file produced by Outlook's Import and Export command that contains the entire hierarchy and subdirectories of your Personal Folders directory. If you're working from backups of a Windows system and are using standard PST files created using Outlook's Archive mechanism, the default location of the directory that contains your PST files (located under your user directory) is one of the following:

Windows XP and older systems:

```
Local Settings\Application Data\Microsoft\Windows\Outlook
```

Windows Vista and later systems:

```
AppData\Local\Microsoft\Outlook
```

Once you have located either type of PST file, create a directory to hold the files that you will be extracting, and execute the `readpst` command. An example command and related output for readpst looks like the following (using a directory called *Windows-Stuff* — which must already exist — as the location for the extracted files):

```
$ readpst -o Windows-Stuff 2007-export-backup.pst
Opening PST file and indexes...
Processing Folder "Deleted Items"
Processing Folder "Inbox"
Processing Folder "Outbox"
Processing Folder "Sent Items"
Processing Folder "Calendar"
Processing Folder "Contacts"
Processing Folder "Journal"
Processing Folder "Notes"
Processing Folder "Tasks"
Processing Folder "Drafts"
Processing Folder "RSS Feeds"
Processing Folder "Junk E-mail"
    "Personal Folders" - 12 items done, 0 items skipped.
```

```
    "Inbox" - 45 items done, 0 items skipped.
    "Contacts" - 3 items done, 0 items skipped.
Processing Folder "Popular Government Questions from USA.gov"
Processing Folder "USA.gov Updates: News and Features"
    "Tasks" - 0 items done, 1 items skipped.
Processing Folder "Microsoft at Home"
    "Popular Government Questions from USA.gov" - 0 items done,
        14 items skipped.
    "Calendar" - 1 items done, 0 items skipped.
    "Sent Items" - 2 items done, 0 items skipped.
    "USA.gov Updates: News and Features" - 0 items done,
        11 items skipped.
    "Microsoft at Home" - 0 items done, 57 items skipped.
Processing Folder "Microsoft at Work"
Processing Folder "MSNBC News"
    "RSS Feeds" - 5 items done, 0 items skipped.
    "Microsoft at Work" - 0 items done, 55 items skipped.
    "MSNBC News" - 0 items done, 24 items skipped.
```

This example shows data being extracted from an exported PST file that was created with Outlook 2007 and contains the entire hierarchy of a Personal Folders directory, including contact information (in VCARD format) and Calendar items (in ICS format). Note that the contents of RSS feeds are not extracted, since they are just pointers to web sites.

You can then import the converted files directly from the Windows-Stuff directory into Evolution using the Import command on Evolution's File menu, as discussed at the end of the section, "Importing Thunderbird Mail into Evolution," earlier in this chapter.

Migrating Web/Browser Settings to Linux

Chapter 8 of this book, "Surfing the Web with Firefox," discussed Firefox, the default Web browser provided on standard Ubuntu desktop systems. As a cross-platform browser that is officially supported on Linux, Windows, and Mac OS X systems, and available for Solaris, AIX, and other commercial UNIX distributions, Firefox is also a tremendous time-saver for when you have to use multiple operating systems but would like to standardize on one browser.

Like Thunderbird, Firefox is sponsored by the Mozilla Foundation, so it includes the same sort of excellent settings migration tools as Thunderbird. These enable you to install Firefox on a system and use a simple menu command to import settings from an existing browser. The goal of this command is, of course, to help you switch to Firefox on any given platform, but it is also a tremendous help when migrating from one operating system to another. The next two sections explain how to migrate existing Firefox configuration information from a Windows or Mac OS X system to an Ubuntu system, and how to migrate Internet Exploder settings from a Windows system to Firefox on an Ubuntu system. A final section explains how to export just your bookmarks if you want to start with a clean cache, set of cookies, and no saved passwords on an Ubuntu system, but don't want to lose all of the fun and useful bookmarks that you've created in Internet Exploder or Safari.

As mentioned in previous sections, I suggest that you install Firefox and export your bookmarks on your Windows or Mac OS X system before doing backups of those systems to CD, DVD, an external drive, or network storage. This gives you a permanent snapshot of the data that you are migrating (as well as the original web settings from your previous browser) just in case anything goes wrong and you no longer have your previous operating system to fall back on. The instructions here emphasize this by discussing things in terms of copying files from your backups, not from some other operating system. If you're dual-booting Ubuntu and another operating system, you can always copy files from that system.

For those who are new to Firefox, Table 9-1 shows the mappings between common Internet Explorer terms and the equivalent terms in Firefox.

TABLE 9-1

Common Internet Explorer Terms and Firefox Equivalents

Internet Explorer	Firefox
Address Bar	Location/Navigation Bar
Favorites	Bookmarks
Internet Options	Tools ⇨ Options
Links Bar	Bookmarks Toolbar
Refresh	Reload
Save Target As	Save Link As
Temporary Internet Files	Cache

As a final note, remember that the version of Firefox that is available for Ubuntu systems is Firefox 3, as discussed in Chapter 8. Because Firefox 3 stores bookmark and other data in a different format from previous versions of Firefox, you must make sure that the version of Firefox that you are migrating to can handle the Firefox settings data that you are migrating. If you are migrating Firefox configuration information from another system to an Ubuntu system, the version of Firefox running on your Windows or Mac OS X system must be less than or equal to the version of Firefox that is installed on your Ubuntu system.

Migrating from Firefox to Firefox

If you're already a Firefox user on the Windows or Mac OS X platform, congratulations on your excellent taste in Web browsers! You'll also be happy to know that it is extremely easy to migrate your existing Firefox settings (known as a *profile*) from any other operating system to Firefox on Ubuntu systems. After installing Firefox on a Windows or Mac OS X system, dialogs that offer to import the settings from your existing Web browser(s) are displayed automatically the first time that you start Firefox.

This section assumes that you imported the settings from your previous Web browser into Firefox when you first started Firefox and have not used Internet Explorer since then. If you want to make absolutely sure that you have gotten the latest favorites, cookies, saved passwords, and cache data from Internet Explorer, follow the instructions in the next section, "Migrating from Internet Explorer/Safari to Firefox," just to be on the safe side.

Migrating from Firefox on one operating system to Firefox on another is facilitated by the fact that Firefox on any platform stores all of its bookmarks, cookies, saved passwords, and cache data in exactly the same format on all supported systems. This information, which is unique to each user, is known as your *Firefox profile*. The location of this profile information differs on different systems:

- **Linux and UNIX systems:** `~/.mozilla/firefox`
- **Mac OS X:** `~/Library/Application Support/Firefox`
- **Windows 2000, XP, Server 2003:** `Documents and Settings\`*USERNAME*`\Application Data\Mozilla\Firefox`
- **Windows Vista, Server 2008, Windows 7:** `Users\`*USERNAME*`\AppData\Roaming\Mozilla\Firefox`

This directory typically contains a `Profiles` directory and a profile initialization file called `profiles.ini`. It may also contain a directory named *Crash Reports*, depending on the platform that you are using and whether Firefox has ever crashed on your system. (If the Crash Reports directory is present, you can safely delete it before doing your backups.)

Checking Your Ubuntu System First

Before migrating your existing Windows or Mac OS X Firefox profile to your new Ubuntu system, make sure that you do not need to preserve anything from any Firefox profile that you may already have on your Ubuntu system. If you aren't sure, try the following:

1. If you don't have a directory named `~/.mozilla/firefox` in your home directory, you don't have anything to preserve, so you can skip the rest of this list.

2. If the directory `~/.mozilla/firefox` exists in your directory, start Firefox on your Ubuntu system and examine the Bookmarks menu and the Bookmarks toolbar. If neither of these contains any entries that you created, you don't have any bookmarks to preserve. If these do contain bookmarks that you want to preserve, follow the instructions in the sidebar in Chapter 8 entitled, "Backing Up Your Bookmarks." Later in this section, I'll explain how to integrate your backups with the migrated Firefox settings.

341

Finding that you have bookmarks in an existing Firefox installation that you want to preserve is easy to accomplish by backing up/exporting those bookmarks in your current version of Firefox and then restoring/importing them in the version that you migrate from another system. (See the section, "Migrating Just Your Bookmarks," later in this chapter for detailed information.) However, finding cookies or saved passwords in an existing Firefox installation causes a problem. There is no easy way to merge cookie, saved passwords, saved forms, and other cross-session data between two profiles. If you have such data in a Firefox profile on a Windows/Mac OS X system and the same type of data in an existing Firefox profile on a Ubuntu system, you will essentially have to choose which Firefox profile you want to keep.

Migrating an Existing Profile

Assuming that you do not have an existing Firefox profile on your Ubuntu system or don't need to preserve anything that it contains, you can do the following to migrate your existing Windows or Mac OS X Firefox profile to your new Ubuntu system:

1. If you have a ~/.mozilla/firefox directory in your home directory, rename it using a command like the following from a GNOME Terminal or xterm window:

   ```
   mv ~/.mozilla/firefox ~/.mozilla/firefox.OLD
   ```

   You can delete this directory later, once you're sure that you didn't somehow lose anything important.

2. Create the directory ~/.mozilla/firefox in your home directory on your Ubuntu system, using a command like the following from a GNOME Terminal or xterm window:

   ```
   mkdir -p ~/.mozilla/firefox
   ```

3. Copy the contents of the Profile directory (identified in the location list in the previous section) from your backups to the ~/.mozilla/firefox directory in your home directory on your Ubuntu system. You can do this by dragging and dropping the contents of the Profile directory from your backups to the ~/.mozilla/firefox directory using a file manager such as Nautilus.

Tip

If you are using the Nautilus File Manager on a standard GNOME-based Ubuntu desktop system, you will have to press Ctrl+H to show hidden files and directories (those whose names begin with a period) in order to navigate to the .mozilla directory. ■

4. Start Firefox. You should see the same bookmarks, cookies, saved passwords, and so on, that you saw in the version of Firefox that you were running on your other operating system.

Troubleshooting Profile Migration

If you have a problem at this point, make sure that:

- The profiles.ini file was copied to your ~/.mozilla/firefox directory.
- The path statement in the profile.ini file identifies a directory that is also located in your ~/.mozilla/firefox directory. This is usually a directory with a name like *xxxxxxxx*.default, or a directory called Profile that contains a directory with a name like *xxxxxxxx*.default.
- The ~/.mozilla/firefox directory and all of its subdirectories are owned and are readable by you. You can ensure this by executing commands such as the following from a GNOME Terminal, Konsole, or xterm window:

```
sudo chown -Rv username ~/.mozilla/firefox
sudo chmod -R u+r ~/.mozilla/firefox
```

If either of the items in the first two bullets is missing, recopy the contents of your Windows or Mac OS X profile directory to your ~/.mozilla/firefox directory. Make sure that you copy the contents of your Windows or Mac OS X profile directory, and not the directory itself. Your ~/.mozilla/firefox directory must contain a profiles.ini file that identifies a valid directory where your personal profile data is located.

Migrating from Internet Explorer/Safari to Firefox

If you have not used Firefox on your Windows or Mac OS X system, you can take advantage of its configuration import and conversion capabilities to simplify migrate your Internet Explorer or Safari settings to Ubuntu. Firefox is a useful migration tool because the first time that you start it on a new system, it displays a series of dialogs that offer to import the settings from your existing Web browser(s). These settings are automatically converted into the formats used by Firefox. You can then follow the instructions given in the previous section for migrating Firefox settings from one system to another.

The first step in this process is, of course, downloading and installing Firefox on your Windows or Mac OS X system. You can get the latest official version of Firefox for Windows or Mac OS X from www.mozilla.com/en-US/firefox/all.html. Firefox for Windows downloads as a single executable, while Firefox for Mac OS X downloads as a disk image (.dmg) file that you must mount in order to find the installer.

Note

This section uses screen captures from a Windows system. The dialogs are essentially the same on a Mac OS X system. Any significant differences between dialogs and options are described in the text. ∎

Once you have downloaded Firefox, install it using your system's standard installation mechanism. The summary dialog at the end of the installation process provides a checkbox that enables you to start Firefox immediately. Click Finish to do so. If you are using a Windows systems, a dialog like the one shown in Figure 9-8 displays. If you are using a Mac OS X system, a similar dialog with different options displays.

FIGURE 9-8

Selecting the browser to import settings from

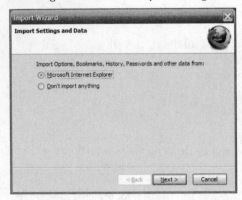

If you are using a Windows system, select the radio button beside Microsoft Internet Explorer and click Next. If you are using a Mac OS X system, select the radio button beside Safari and click Next. A dialog like the one shown in Figure 9-9 displays.

FIGURE 9-9

Specifying your Firefox home page

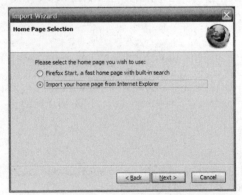

If you are happy with the home page that you've been using in Internet Explorer, click the radio button beside "Import your home page from Internet Explorer." If you would prefer to use a Firefox home page, make sure that the Firefox Start radio button is selected. Click Next to proceed. The import process begins. When it completes, a dialog like the one shown in Figure 9-10 displays.

FIGURE 9-10

The final import status dialog in Firefox

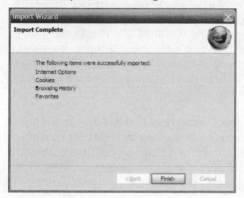

This dialog identifies all of the items that have been imported from Internet Explorer or Safari into Firefox. Click Finish to close this dialog and start Firefox. Favorites that have been imported from Internet Explorer will be listed on a menu called "From Internet Explorer," and bookmarks that have been imported from Safari will be located on a menu called "From Safari." Whichever of these menus you see will be located on Firefox's standard Bookmarks menu.

Once you have imported your browser settings from Internet Explorer or Safari into Firefox on a Windows or Mac OS X system, the remainder of the process of migrating that configuration data to Firefox on your new Ubuntu system is the same as that explained in the previous section of this chapter, "Migrating from Firefox to Firefox."

Migrating Just Your Bookmarks

The previous sections discussed ways of migrating all of your web settings from one computer system to another, primarily from Internet Explorer or Safari to Firefox on a Linux system. This can be done pretty easily using Firefox as a migration tool, as explained in the previous section. By default, migrating via Firefox preserves everything—favorites/bookmarks, cookies, saved passwords, and so on. However, you may not always want to preserve everything. Using a Web browser for a long time is like living in the same house for a long time—you tend to accumulate stuff and you may not even be aware of everything that you've accumulated. In a Web browser, this can mean that you have saved passwords to sites that you no longer visit, cached data that was useless long ago, collected cookies for sites that you last visited to purchase Y2K survival supplies, and so on. While you probably don't care about much of this stuff (and therefore won't miss it if you don't migrate it), one thing that you do care about and probably use is your collection of links to favorite sites, known as *favorites* to Internet Explorer users and as *bookmarks* to the rest of the universe.

This section explains how to save your Internet Explorer or Safari bookmarks to an HTML file that you can then import into the Firefox browser. As suggested in the previous paragraph, you may want to migrate only your bookmarks when moving to a new system as a sort of mandatory housekeeping exercise. However, being able to create HTML files containing your bookmarks can also be very useful if you need to use other computers and operating systems but want to have your familiar bookmarks there. Some businesses mandate using a specific operating system, and some web sites require specific browsers (sadly enough). In these cases, being able to export bookmarks from one browser and import them into another provides a usable, but somewhat crude, way of seeing the same bookmarks in multiple browsers.

A popular solution to the problem of seeing the same bookmarks from multiple browsers is to make your bookmarks available on the Web. You can do this by making an HTML file containing your bookmarks available on your web site (as I do), or by using various tools that enable you to store your bookmarks on specially designed web sites. For a huge list of Web-based bookmark management tools, see `www.dmoz.org/Computers/Internet/On_the_Web/` `Web_Applications/Bookmark_Managers`.

Regardless of why you want to do it, being able to save your current favorites/bookmarks to an HTML file is very convenient. Whether you're doing it for migration purposes, quick-and-dirty backups, personal convenience, or to share your favorite web time sinks with your friend, the next few sections explain how to export from and import to different popular browsers.

Tip

If you are using a browser other than the ones discussed in this section, see the MozillaZine web page on importing bookmarks, `http://kb.mozillazine.org/Import_bookmarks`. This page also discusses how to export bookmarks from several browsers other than IE or Safari. ∎

Exporting Internet Explorer Bookmarks

Both Internet Explorer 6 and 7 provide a convenient "Import and Export" dialog (shown in Figure 9-11) that makes it easy to export your favorites to a file that you can then import into other browsers on other systems — only the location of the command used to display this dialog has been changed to confuse the user.

To display this dialog in IE6, select the File menu's "Import and Export" menu item. To display this dialog in IE7 or IE8, click the "Add to Favorites" icon (second from left in your default toolbar), and select the "Import and Export" menu command. Click Next to proceed, which displays the dialog shown in Figure 9-12.

FIGURE 9-11

Internet Explorer's Import and Export Wizard

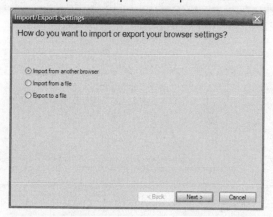

FIGURE 9-12

Selecting what to export from Internet Explorer

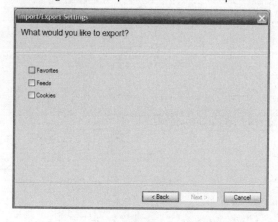

The dialog shown in Figure 9-12 enables you to select the type of information that you want to export from Internet Explorer: Favorites, Cookies, or RSS Feeds (the latter is only shown if you are exporting from IE7). To export your Favorites as an HTML file, select "Export Favorites" and click Next to proceed. The dialog shown in Figure 9-13 displays.

The dialog shown in Figure 9-13 enables you to select the Favorites folders that you want to export as HTML. To export your entire collection of Favorites, select the top-level Favorites folder, as shown in Figure 9-13. Click Next to proceed. The dialog shown in Figure 9-14 displays.

FIGURE 9-13

Selecting the Favorites folder(s) to export items from Internet Explorer

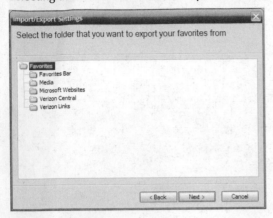

FIGURE 9-14

Selecting where to save exported items from Internet Explorer

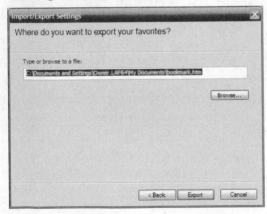

The dialog shown in Figure 9-14 enables you to specify the location in which the file containing your favorites (ironically called `bookmark.htm`) will be saved, or to optionally export them directly to another application. Because our goal is to save them to a file (which is the default action), leave the "Export to a File or Address" radio button selected and modify the name of the file if you want to use a name other than the default. Click Next to proceed.

A final dialog displays, which requires that you click Finish to begin the export process. A confirmation dialog displays when the export process is complete. Click OK to close the confirmation dialog, which will also close the "Import and Export" dialog.

Copy the file containing your favorites to the system where the browser to which you want to import them is running. If this system does not exist yet or is currently inaccessible, make sure that the file that you just created is saved to a location that will be included in the backups that you will be creating of your Windows system.

Exporting Safari Bookmarks

Strangely enough, the Safari browser that Apple provides for Mac OS X systems does not automatically provide the ability to save its bookmarks to an HTML. The good news is that Simone Manganelli has written an excellent (and free) application called the *Safari Bookmark Exporter* (`http://homepage.mac.com/simx/sbe.html`) that does just that. After downloading the disk image file for this application, you can either install it or run it directly from the image. A dialog like the one shown in Figure 9-15 (captured on a Mac OS X system) displays.

FIGURE 9-15

The initial "Safari Bookmark Exporter" dialog

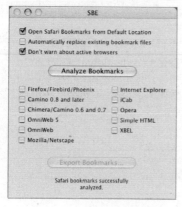

If Safari is currently running on your OS X system, click the "Don't warn about active browsers" button. Next, select an output target by clicking one of the browser/file format names below the Analyze Bookmarks button — your selection primarily determines where the Safari Bookmark Exporter will try to save the file containing your bookmarks. I typically select Firefox/Firebird/Phoenix just in case this option does anything special for Firefox, although Simple HTML is also a reasonable choice. Click "Export Bookmarks" to display a Finder dialog that enables you to identify where you want to save your bookmarks. If you selected Firefox/Firebird/Phoenix as your browser, the suggested location will be to save the output file to your Firefox profile directory, which you may not want to do because it will overwrite any file of the same name. I typically save these files to my home directory with a name like `safari-bookmarks-export.html`, which makes it pretty clear what the file contains.

Quick Hack for Saving Safari Bookmarks

If you don't want to download and install the Safari Bookmark Exporter application for a one-time effort, you can use some internal Safari hacks to save your Safari bookmarks to an HTML file. Because this is, indeed, a hack, it may not work in all newer versions of Safari, but it's worth a try:

1. Exit Safari and start the Terminal application.
2. Execute the following command in the Terminal window:

```
defaults write com.apple.Safari IncludeDebugMenu 1
```

3. Start Safari.
4. Select the new Debug menu's Export Bookmarks command and identify the location to which you want to save the Safari `Bookmarks.html` file.

You can then import this file into the Firefox browser, as described later in the chapter.

Importing Bookmarks into Firefox

To import an HTML file containing bookmarks into Firefox, first select the Bookmarks menu's "Organize Bookmarks" command to display the Library dialog. Once this dialog displays, click the "Import and Backup" menu to display the list of available commands, as shown in Figure 9-16.

FIGURE 9-16

Commands on the Library dialog's "Import and Backup" menu

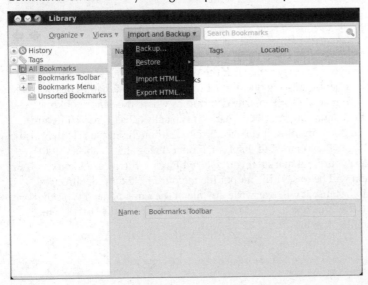

Select Import HTML from this menu to display the Firefox Import Wizard, as shown in Figure 9-17.

FIGURE 9-17

The Firefox Import Wizard

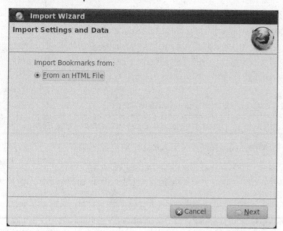

Click Next to proceed. A standard file navigation dialog displays, in which you can browse to and select the file containing the bookmarks that you want to import. Click Open to open that file. All of the bookmarks contained in that file will be added to the Bookmarks menu folder in Firefox. Click the Close box to dismiss the Library dialog and return to Firefox.

Working with Windows Application Data

The previous two sections of this chapter discussed how to migrate specific types of data — your e-mail and browser-related data — from another operating system to your new Ubuntu system. Although these are probably extremely important items for you, they're only the tip of the iceberg in terms of all of the data that you probably have on your previous computer system.

The general-purpose section, "Backing Up Your Personal Data," stressed the need for backing up all of your personal information, regardless of where it is located, from any computer that you are no longer planning to use — especially if you are planning on erasing or overwriting the disk on which your current data is located. In general, I suggest that you back up your data and preserve your existing disk whenever possible, until you are sure that you haven't accidentally left some critical files or directories out of your backups. This is easy to do in desktop systems because you can pull your old disk and replace it with a new one upon which you can install Ubuntu, but if that's not possible for one reason or another in your case, please verify your backups before proceeding.

Copying files and directories from CDs, DVDs, external drives, or network storage locations that contain your backups is a simple command-line or drag-and-drop operation once your Ubuntu system has mounted the CD, DVD, or networked storage device. CDs and DVDs should automount when inserted into your Ubuntu system unless you've disabled automounting, but you will probably have to use the command line or a graphical utility such as Ubuntu's Places ⇨ Connect to Server dialog to mount networked backups so that you can access them via Samba or NFS.

Copying files and directories is one thing — being able to actually work with them is another. Although I am a lifelong UNIX fanatic and have been a Ubuntu devotee since the first time I reviewed it years ago, here are the harsh truths about using any Linux system to work with files that have been created by Windows or Mac OS X applications. Depending on the type of file and the version of the application that created it, you may:

- Not be able to display, print, or edit your existing files in any way
- Not be able to do as good a job of displaying, printing, or editing your existing files
- Be able to do everything you could before, but using free Linux or Web-based applications
- Need to install your Windows software on your Linux system and run it using emulation, virtualization, or a similar solution

The first two of these are horror stories that can happen. The applications developed by most software vendors traditionally use their own data file formats. If that software vendor does not support Linux, whether or not Linux software exists that can read and write the data files produced by that vendor's applications depends on whether the data file format use by that application is well-known, open, or has been reverse-engineered. It also depends on whether the Linux developers of similar applications care enough to try to support reading and writing files in that format.

As much as it pains me to say it, if you are doing critical work in a Windows or Mac OS X application, you should use the Ubuntu Live CD or a scratch Ubuntu system to test if or how well you can work with your existing data files on a Linux system. Most of the chapters in the first part of this book are organized by common types of tasks and the Linux applications that you can use to accomplish them — writing documents, working with spreadsheets, creating presentations, and so on.

The following are a few commonly encountered types of files beyond those discussed in earlier chapters and the Linux applications that you can use to work with them:

- **AVI, MPG, SWF:** My favorite Linux player for all of these is the mplayer application, but applications such as Totem on Ubuntu are popular and improving with each release.
- **MP3 files:** You can use the EasyTAG application to edit the ID tags for MP3 files. The mpg123 and mpg321 applications are command-line utilities for playing MP3 files, which you can also play in graphical applications such as Rhythmbox and Helix Player under GNOME, and many more. You can encode various formats to MP3 using the graphical Sound Converter or command-line lame applications on Ubuntu.

- **DOC, XLS, PPT:** You can use the OpenOffice.org tools to open the files that are created by Microsoft Office applications. Microsoft's new XML-oriented DOCX, XSLX, and related formats are only supported by OpenOffice.org version 3.0 (and greater) tools.

- **PDF files:** Ubuntu provides the Evince application to display PDF files. This application does not enable you to edit PDF files, fill out PDf forms, and so on. Most Ubuntu applications enable you to create PDF files by selecting the "Print to File" option and specifying PDF output. The pdfedit application, which can be found in the Ubuntu repositories, can be used to edit existing PDF files.

As you can see, this list could go on forever. For a great summary of the Linux applications that are equivalent to popular Windows applications, see sites such as the following:

- **Linux Alternatives Project:** www.linuxalt.com

- **Linux Application Finder:** www.linuxappfinder.com/alternatives

- **Linux equivalents to Windows software:** www.linuxlinks.com/article/20070701111340544/Equivalents.html

- **Linux software equivalent to Windows software:** http://wiki.linuxquestions.org/wiki/Linux_software_equivalent_to_Windows_software

- **Table of Equivalents/Replacements/Analogs of Windows software in Linux:** www.linuxrsp.ru/win-lin-soft/table-eng.html

In addition to these Linux-specific sites, the Open Source Alternatives site (www.osalt.com) lists equivalent applications for Windows software that run on other open source operating systems (including Linux, of course).

For information about using emulation, virtualization, and similar techniques to enable you to run actual Windows software on your Ubuntu system, see Chapter 24, "Using Virtual Machines and Emulators." Yes, it can be done!

Summary

The wealth of software available for Linux makes it quite conceivable to make Ubuntu your *daily driver* operating system — the one where you get all of your work done. But what about all of the mail, browser favorites/bookmarks, and data files that you've accumulated on your existing Windows or Mac OS X systems? This chapter explained different ways of migrating e-mail and browser settings from a Microsoft Windows or Mac OS X system to an Ubuntu system, discussed good techniques for backing up your Windows or Mac OS X system to facilitate migration, identified some tasks that you should do before doing your final backups, and discussed critical directories where applications such as Internet Explorer, Outlook, and Outlook Express store their data. It also discussed other considerations for complete migration to an Ubuntu system, such as making sure that you can find applications that will enable you to work with your existing data files.

Constant connectivity and interaction is almost an expectation today, and even classic software such as e-mail is viewed as being too slow and not interactive enough for many people. The next chapter discusses instant messaging on Ubuntu, which enables you to hold virtual conversations with friends regardless of their location — just like texting from your desktop!

Sending and Receiving Instant Messages

IN THIS CHAPTER

Instant messaging history

Getting an IM account

Using Empathy on Ubuntu

Using Pidgin on Ubuntu

Using IRC

Other IM clients

Troubleshooting

E-mail has revolutionized how people communicate today. E-mail is the carrier of most business communications, replacing paper memos, faxes, and most information-sharing meetings, and enabling geographically disparate offices and personnel to keep in touch and know what each is doing. E-mail has revolutionized personal communications, too. Thanks to e-mail, I've been able to maintain friendships that would otherwise have atrophied because I'm not the best letter writer or snail mail user. I can send e-mail at any time, from any computer, and know that it will be waiting for the recipient after a very short time.

"Waiting for the recipient," however, identifies a key shortcoming of e-mail and a key advantage of instant messaging—the "instant" part. E-mail was designed as an asynchronous communications mechanism and does a great job at that. I can send you e-mail and you can respond at your convenience. Unfortunately, "at your convenience" isn't always good enough. If I have an extra ticket to a baseball game that starts in a few hours, I need to know whether you want it now. If you send an instant message to someone who is running an instant messaging client, they are usually alerted that a new message has come in—you don't have to wait for them to get around to checking their mail.

A related issue is that e-mail isn't really conversation-oriented. If I send e-mail with several questions, you can respond to my e-mail at the top or bottom, or intersperse your responses, but a back-and-forth exchange of conversational messages quickly gets hard to read, at best.

Instant messaging, in which you can open a direct connection between one or more people and either send a single message or have an online conversation, has been around for quite a while, but is still increasing in popularity as both a personal and business communication mechanism. This chapter provides a little background on instant messaging, explains what you need to do in order to participate in instant messaging, discusses the most popular instant messaging clients on Ubuntu systems (Empathy, the new one; and Pidgin, the former and still-popular one), discusses Internet Relay Chat, and provides some tips on resolving instant messaging problems.

Instant Messaging Overview

Believe it or not, people were actually online even before the Internet. Bulletin-board systems (commonly referred to as *BBSs*) were a popular early personal computing phenomenon, consisting of computers running specialized, multi-user software that users could connect to using a modem, and on which users could read and send both public and private messages using a terminal-based interface. (Many BBS systems also supported inter-BBS e-mail by forwarding messages from one system to another using modems and forwarding networks such as FidoNet.) Commercial dial-up/BBS services such as America Online (AOL), CompuServe, Prodigy, and many others provided centralized locations on which people could share resources and, more important, instantly communicate with each other in shared areas, commonly referred to as *chat rooms*, conferences, or echoes (FidoNet), or online forums. As the availability, popularity, and amount of content on the Internet increased in the early 1990s, the reason for these centralized services became less important — after all, once you can contact anyone anywhere via e-mail and have access to the entire Internet, why bother limiting yourself to a single online community? The entire planet is your potential community.

As discussed in the introduction to this chapter, e-mail is cool but is inherently message-oriented rather than conversation-oriented. UNIX and UNIX-like systems have always had real-time text communication software, starting with the `write` command in the original research edition of UNIX, which enabled you to immediately send a one-way message to another user on the terminal or other device that they were using. Enhanced versions of the `write` command, such as Orville Write — `http://unixpapa.com/write.html` — supported multi-user and multi-way communication, but were not part of the standard UNIX distribution.

Early UNIX distributions also provided the `talk` command, which enabled you to have real-time text conversations between two users by splitting your terminal window into two sections in which you could exchange messages back and forth. (I'm told that the first version intermingled text as both users typed, but I'm not quite that old.) I remember using the `talk` command in the early 1990s to help an acquaintance in Australia debug some problems he was having with one of his machines, while I sat in my office in Pittsburgh. Good times…

Outside the UNIX-only universe, the increased availability of the Internet led to the development of many cross-platform and admittedly friendlier instant communication mechanisms. The idea of a shared, instant communication area is always attractive for its immediacy. Modern Internet-based instant communication was born in 1988 with the creation of IRC (Internet Relay Chat), written by Jarkko Oikarinen (`www.ircnet.org/History/jarkko.html`). IRC, still in wide use today, enables instant communication between users by providing IRC channels (much like chat rooms) that users connect to, at which point their messages are seen by anyone on the channel. IRC is a client/server system, in which users connect to an IRC server in order to join an IRC channel that is supported by that server. While IRC enables user-to-user communications, it is primarily a user-to-channel message system reminiscent of chat rooms on bulletin-board systems. IRC was born on UNIX systems (big surprise), but clients quickly appeared for the Macintosh, Microsoft Windows, and DOS environments.

Note

Regardless of how well it fits the IM model, IRC is still popular, quite fun, and occasionally even useful. For example, the #ubuntu IRC channel is a great source of immediate help for Ubuntu (although there's also a lot of noise there). If you're using the standard GNOME-based Ubuntu Desktop, you can communicate via IRC using Empathy or Pidgin. Because IRC is somewhat different from instant messaging per se, it's discussed in a separate section later in this chapter. See the "Using IRC" for general information about IRC and specific information about using IRC on Ubuntu systems. ■

What most people think of as *instant messaging* today first appeared in 1996, when Mirabilis introduced its ICQ ("I Seek You") instant messaging software, which is still popular today (although now owned by Time Warner/AOL). ICQ is a client/server instant messaging system, wherein desktop users use ICQ client software to instantly exchange messages with other users through centralized ICQ servers. This is the same model used by most instant messaging software today.

ICQ was amazing when it first appeared and is still quite cool, although certain aspects of it show its age. All ICQ users are primarily identified by the User Identification Number (UIN), which is a bit kludgey nowadays. When's the last time you thought to yourself, "Wow, I've got to tell 481241598 about this!"? Although newer versions of ICQ allow identification via your e-mail address, most modern instant messaging systems let you create your own username, which must be unique within that system but can at least be reminiscent of your name or how you want yourself to be perceived online. My usernames are usually something reminiscent of my name, but identities such as *topdog* and *longdistancelover* are more attractive to others. Like any good technology, it's all up to you.

Most instant messaging applications provide core features such as the following:

- **Instant messages:** Exchange text messages with a friend who is online via a computer or cell phone.
- **Chat:** Have an electronic conversation with multiple people at the same time.
- **Exchange files:** Send audio, video, and other files to one or more contacts.

Some of the most modern clients like Empathy also provide support for Voice over IP (VoIP) and video chat.

Instant messaging is a lot of fun, and can even be useful in business communications. Many companies today rely on instant messaging for situations in which instant contact is important or simply to save you from having to keep walking over to someone else's desk and physically interrupting them (which can be tricky if you're in different parts of the country or the world).

As a general rule, people seem to be less verbose when sending instant messages, which is often a good thing if you just need a bit of info to get on with your work.

Tip

One important thing to remember when using instant messaging, especially for business purposes, is that the protocols used by many instant messaging services are not guaranteed to be secure. You may not want to send someone important business information, your credit card numbers, or your passwords via an IM client. ∎

Nowadays, you'll probably find some occasion to IM someone at some point. (As you can see, *instant messaging* is so popular that it's both a noun and a verb!) If you're not already registered with a system that supports instant messaging, see the next IM section for information about registering with one of the many free services that are available. If you already have an instant messaging account and just want to know how to join the IM scene from your desktop or laptop, skip ahead to the section of this chapter that discusses the standard instant messaging client for Ubuntu systems, either Empathy or Pidgin. Of course, many other IM clients are available for Ubuntu systems — the section, "Other Instant Messaging Packages," later in this chapter, provides an overview of some other popular IM clients for GNOME systems.

Tip

Fans of doing everything inside Emacs may want to see the article at www.instantmessagingplanet.com/ public/article.php/3742411, which describes how to do instant messaging (and tweeting) inside Emacs. Although I love Emacs like a brother, I'm not quite that dedicated, but your mileage may vary. ∎

Getting an Instant Messaging Account

To exchange instant messages with someone else, you need to be registered with some centralized system that supports instant messaging. You can get an instant messaging account by doing any of the following:

- Register with an instant messaging–focused service such as AIM, ICQ, or Jabber. (AIM will also toss in a free e-mail account, but their focus is still instant messaging. E-mail is just gravy.)

- Register with the instant messaging services provided by companies such as AOL, Google, Microsoft, Yahoo, and many others.

- Use a free Internet mail service such as AOL, Yahoo, Google, Microsoft Hotmail/Live, and so on, which also provide IM access.

One thing to consider when selecting or signing up for an IM service is what other IM services it can connect to, if any. You'd think that instant messaging providers such as AOL, Yahoo, Microsoft, and others would realize that it was useful for them to be able to support receiving instant messages from each other, but this is woefully not the case.

Most of the free instant messaging services focus on receiving messages from other members of the same service — compatibility between them is limited because all of these services use their own protocols to communicate between your desktop client and the instant messaging servers that are run by these companies. This isn't an issue for Linux users because Ubuntu IM clients such as Empathy and Pidgin are what is known as *multi-protocol clients*, meaning that they understand the protocols used to communicate with different IM services and thus enable you to exchange instant messages with almost anybody. Windows and Mac users aren't so lucky — although multi-protocol instant messaging clients are available for these platforms, the more traditional instant messaging clients for this platforms, such as MSN Messenger, Yahoo Messenger, Apple's iChat (AIM and Jabber), and others, primarily focus on communicating with other users of those IM services, although some offer limited interoperability. They all support some level of SMS (Short Message Service) compatibility so that they can send instant messages to cell phones.

Multi-Protocol IM Clients for Other Systems

You should encourage your Macintosh and Windows friends to install and use multi-protocol IM clients on their systems, so that they can exchange instant messages with anyone regardless of the IM service that they use.

- **Windows:** A version of the Pidgin IM client provided on Ubuntu systems is available for Windows (`www.pidgin.im/download`), and is therefore the package that I'd recommend. Another popular open source IM client for Windows is Miranda-IM (`www.miranda-im.org`). As far as proprietary, closed-source IM clients for Windows go, the most popular native multi-protocol IM client for Windows systems is probably Trillian (`www.ceruleanstudios.com`), which is also being ported to Mac OS X. Another popular multi-protocol client for Windows is Qnext (`www.qnext.com/universal_messenger.shtml`).

- **Mac OS X:** Alas, Pidgin is not available for Mac OS X except through a huge package called Fink (see `http://www.pidgin.im/download/mac/`), so Mac OS X users should get Adium X (`www.adiumx.com`), the most popular multi-protocol client on that platform.

For detailed and overwhelming information about IM clients, see the comparison of instant messaging clients on Wikipedia at `http://en.wikipedia.org/wiki/Comparison_of_instant_messaging_clients`.

If you're new to instant messaging, the big question is, "Whom should I sign up with?" The best answer to this question is, "Where are your friends?" Although multi-protocol clients such as Empathy and Pidgin enable you to send and receive instant messages from multiple services, you still have to be registered with those services for people to be able to send you instant messages through them. Microsoft and Yahoo enable their IM users to send instant messages to each other, but interoperability is still a relatively uncommon notion for instant messaging servers.

Although using a limited-protocol, closed-protocol site such as AIM, MSN Messenger, or Yahoo only encourages the persistence of proprietary protocols and associated tools, being able to talk to your friends is probably more important than philosophy. The good news is that because most instant messaging accounts are free, you can sign up with as many instant messaging services as you want and then use a multi-protocol client to communicate with all of your friends at any of them.

Note

If you're already using a free Internet mail service like AOL, Microsoft Live/Hotmail, Google, or Yahoo, you probably already have an instant messaging account through the same service. Log in to your webmail account and look for an FAQ (Frequently Asked Questions file) or general information about IM support. In most cases, your IM identify is the same as your e-mail address, without any domain information. For example, if your e-mail address is wvonhagen@yahoo.com, your Yahoo IM identity is almost certainly wvonhagen. ∎

The following is a list of some popular locations where you can sign up for free instant messaging accounts:

- **AIM:** AOL's acquisition of Mirabilis's ICQ software made AIM (AOL Instant Messenger) the original leader in the instant messaging space, and it's still one of the most popular IM sites around. You can get a free AIM identity (known as a *screen name* because of its roots in AOL) from www.aim.com, which comes with an equivalent aim.com e-mail account. Similarly, you can get an AIM account by registering for free e-mail with AOL (www.aol.com). The underlying communications protocol used by AIM is called *Oscar*.

- **Google:** Far be it from Google to miss out on any aspect of online life. Google Talk (www.google.com/talk) is Google's instant messaging platform, which you can access through the same Google account that you use for Gmail. If you do not have a Google account, launching Google Talk provides links through which you can create one. Not too surprisingly, Google Talk uses a browser interface for instant messaging and chats, so it works almost anywhere. Google Talk uses XMPP (Extensible Messaging and Presence Protocol) as its underlying protocol.

- **ICQ:** Although still focused on numeric IDs, ICQ popularized instant messaging and is still a popular site. You can register for an ICQ account at https://www.icq.com/register. Because AOL bought ICQ long ago, ICQ also uses Oscar as its underlying protocol.

- **Jabber:** Jabber is an open instant messaging platform where, as its PR material states, "... your messages are not monitored by a big company like AOL, Microsoft, or Yahoo." (Instead, it's monitored by a very tiny company.) Jabber uses the open XMPP (Extensible Messaging and Presence Protocol), which is also used by Google Talk. To register with Jabber, your IM client will automatically offer to create an account for you when you use any of the sites that use Jabber (see www.jabber.org/im-services for a list).

- **Microsoft:** Microsoft provides free Microsoft Live e-mail accounts (formerly *Hotmail*), which come with a free Windows Live Messenger (formerly known as *MSN Messenger*) account because all of your Microsoft accounts share the same identity. See http://login.live.com to sign up for an account. I know that you'll be surprised to learn that Microsoft uses its own, proprietary IM protocol for instant messaging.

- **Yahoo:** Yahoo has provided an instant messaging service for quite a while, and its Yahoo Messenger software is quite popular. You get instant messaging capabilities when you sign up for a Yahoo e-mail account (www.yahoo.com). Like Microsoft, Yahoo uses its own protocol for instant messaging.

These are just the big names in the IM space. See the subsequent sections of this chapter on Pidgin and Empathy for information about the protocols that are supported by each of these instant messaging clients.

Although I'll admit to being a little afraid of Googlezilla, if I were to suggest one of these sites for your own IM pleasure, I'd vote for Google Talk, simply because you can then use Gmail and the many other useful Google tools. Because it is open source software that uses a standard protocol, Jabber is a close second, especially if most of your IM friends are also Linux fans. If not, Yahoo and AIM are your best bets.

Instant Messaging on Ubuntu with Empathy

Empathy is the instant messaging client that is installed by default on the latest Ubuntu Desktop systems. Empathy replaces an older instant messaging client called *Pidgin*, which is still popular and is therefore discussed in the following section of this chapter. Open source software is all about choice, after all!

Empathy is a multi-protocol instant messaging client that enables you to send and receive instant messages from AIM, Facebook Chat, Google Talk, GroupWise, ICQ, IRC, Jabber, MSN, MySpace, SIP, Yahoo!, and many other instant messaging services. Empathy uses an underlying framework known as *Telepathy* that interfaces with standard, lower-level communication mechanisms used to exchange messages on Linux systems. For end users like you and me, this means that Empathy isn't limited to just instant messaging, but can also handle video chat and Voice Over IP (VoIP). Telepathy can also be extended to handle new communication mechanisms and associated protocols as they emerge from universities, the open source community, and tomorrow's hot startups.

Starting Empathy

Ubuntu provides two ways to interact with Empathy:

- By selecting the Applications ➪ Internet ➪ Empathy IM Client menu item to actually start Empathy
- By using the panel's MeMenu applet, shown in Figure 10-1. This applet enables you to configure your active instant messaging account(s) in Empathy, displays your current status, and watches for incoming conversations, displaying an OSD (On-Screen Display) notification when an instant message is received from any of your buddies on any active instant messaging account.

This applet only informs you about incoming messages—it doesn't start Empathy for you. The OSD notification displays both the message and the name of the buddy that initiated it. Once you start Empathy, any buddies from which incoming but unanswered messages have been received will be blinking in the Empathy "Contact List" dialog.

FIGURE 10-1

Ubuntu's MeMenu applet

Before you can actually use Empathy, you must configure at least one instant messaging account of some sort, as explained in the next section.

Tip

If you are currently using Pidgin on another system, you can import the accounts that are defined on that system into Empathy by creating an archive file of the directories that contain Pidgin account information, transferring that archive file to your new system, and extracting its contents before starting Empathy for the first time. To do this, execute the following command on a system upon which your Pidgin accounts have been defined:

```
cd ~ ; tar jcvf dot-pidgin-files.bz2 .gaim .purple
```

Transfer this file to the machine upon which you will be using Empathy, and extract its contents using a command like the following:

```
cd ~ ; tar jxvf dot-pidgin-files.bz2
```

The first time that you start Empathy on the system where you extracted the contents of this archive file, Empathy will detect the Pidgin configuration information and offer to import it.

If you didn't read this tip before starting Empathy for the first time, you can trigger Empathy's initial startup dialogs by terminating all processes with telepathy in their name, terminating the empathy process, and then recursively removing the ~/.mission-control directory (in your home directory), which is where Telepathy clients such as Empathy store account information. You can then start Empathy, and it will go through the initial account setup that is discussed in the next section. ■

Configuring Instant Messaging Accounts in Empathy

The first time that you start Empathy, it displays the dialog shown in Figure 10-2, which provides multiple ways for you to configure how you'll use Empathy:

- **Yes, import my account details from Pidgin:** Automatically imports account details from Pidgin account information. This option is only displayed if you are running Empathy for the first time on a system where you have previously used Pidgin.

- **Yes, I'll enter my account details now:** Displays a dialog in which you can manually enter information about one or more instant messaging accounts.

- **No, I want a new account:** Enables you to create a new instant messaging account on instant messaging services that support remote account creation. Currently, only Jabber enables remote account creation — instant messaging services like AIM, Yahoo, Google Talk, and so on require that you create an account via their web sites.

- **No, I just want to see people online nearby for now:** Enables you to define a *People Nearby* account, which is a local Empathy account that you can use to communicate with other people on your local network who are running Empathy and have this feature enabled.

FIGURE 10-2

Configuring Empathy accounts

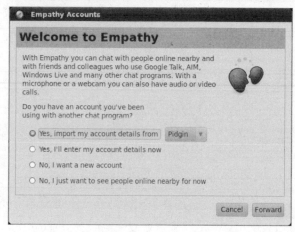

The next few sections explain the dialogs and procedures associated with each of these options.

Importing Pidgin Accounts

If the "Yes, import my account details from" option is available, make sure that its radio button is selected and click forward to proceed. A dialog like the one shown in Figure 10-3 displays.

Make sure that the checkbox to the right of each of the accounts that you want to import is selected, and click Forward to proceed. Skip ahead to the section entitled "Seeing People Online Nearby" to proceed.

Defining Existing Accounts Manually

If the "Yes, import my account details from" option shown in Figure 10-2 is not available or you do not want to import your Pidgin accounts and you already have instant messaging accounts with a service such as those discussed earlier in "Getting an Instant Messaging Account," make sure that the "Yes, I'll enter my account details now" option is selected, and click Forward to proceed. A dialog like the one shown in Figure 10-4 displays.

FIGURE 10-3

Importing accounts from Pidgin into Empathy

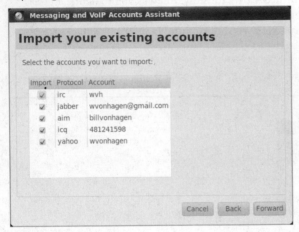

FIGURE 10-4

Defining an existing instant messaging account in Empathy

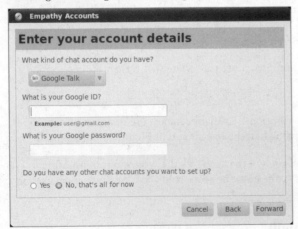

Select the type of instant messaging (chat) account that you have by clicking on the dropdown list at the top of this dialog. Enter the name or ID of your account and your password in the appropriate fields.

The "Do you have any other chat accounts that you want to set up?" radio buttons at the bottom of this dialog enable you to specify whether you want to configure Empathy to know about other instant messaging accounts that you may have, or if you simply want to continue the account setup process for Empathy. To supply information about another instant messaging account that you already have, make sure that the Yes radio button is selected. To continue configuring Empathy with only this account, select the "No, that's all for now" radio button. Click Forward to proceed.

Once you have finished defining all of your existing instant messaging accounts, skip ahead to the section, "Seeing People Online Nearby."

Creating a New Account

If you have no existing instant messaging accounts, you can use the "No, I want a new account" option on the dialog shown in Figure 10-2 to instantly create an instant messaging account. Make sure that the radio button to the left of this option is selected, and click Forward to proceed. The dialog shown in Figure 10-5 displays.

FIGURE 10-5

Creating a new instant messaging account in Empathy

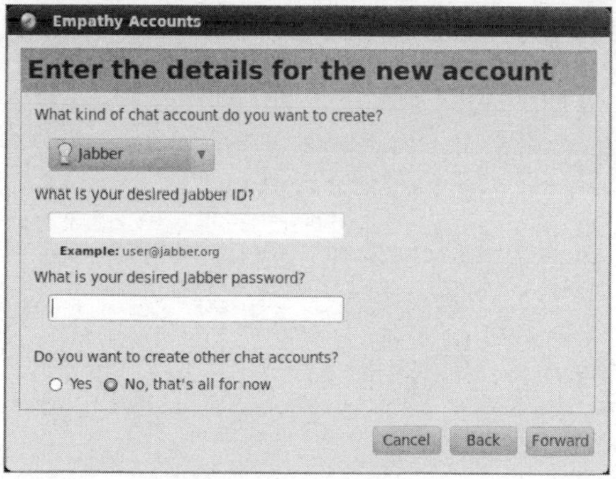

At the time that this book was updated, the only type of instant messaging account that you could create remotely (in other words, from within an application such as Empathy as opposed to going to the web site for the associated instant messaging service) was a Jabber account. When other types of instant messaging accounts are added, any accounts that you can create remotely will also be listed on the dropdown menu at the top of the dialog shown in Figure 10-5.

Select the type of instant messaging (chat) account that you want by clicking on the dropdown list at the top of this dialog. Enter the name or ID of the account that you want to create and the password that you want to use for that account in the appropriate fields.

The "Do you want to create other chat accounts?" radio buttons at the bottom of this dialog enable you to specify whether you want to create other instant messaging accounts, or if you simply want to continue the account setup process for Empathy. To create another instant messaging account, make sure that the Yes radio button is selected. To continue configuring Empathy with only this account, select the "No, that's all for now" radio button. Click Forward to proceed.

Once you have finished creating new instant messaging accounts, proceed to the next section, "Seeing People Online Nearby."

Seeing People Online Nearby

Empathy supports instant messaging between users on systems on a local network without requiring explicit instant messaging accounts with an external instant messaging service. To take advantage of this capability, you must set your name and nickname on the dialog shown in Figure 10-6.

FIGURE 10-6

Creating an instant messaging account for your local network

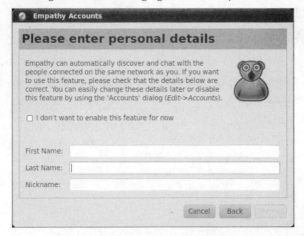

Empathy can discover other users who have activated this capability by broadcasting on your local network. This mechanism provides an extremely convenient way to use instant messaging on a local network without requiring an instant messaging server on your local network or the use of some external instant messaging server. This is especially convenient in business environments where you don't want to have to support an instant messaging server but also don't want your internal conversations and business information to be routed outside your company and through an external instant messaging server somewhere on the Internet.

If you don't want to enable this capability initially, select the "I don't want to enable this feature for now" checkbox. Otherwise, enter your first name, last name, and a nickname in the appropriate fields. Click Apply to complete Empathy's initial account setup process.

Adding and Removing Empathy Accounts

The previous sections described various ways of configuring new or existing instant messaging accounts the first time that you start Empathy. As you continue to use Empathy, you will probably want to add information about any new instant messaging accounts that you create. Instant messaging is a social activity, and keeping in touch with friends often requires creating new accounts at different instant messaging services so that you can communicate with friends who may use other instant messaging services than the ones at which you have existing accounts.

Adding, updating, and removing instant messaging accounts is done through Empathy's "Messaging and VoIP Accounts" dialog, shown in Figure 10-7. To display this dialog, select the Edit menu's Accounts menu item in Empathy's Contact List dialog, or simply press the F4 key on your keyboard while Empathy's Contact List window is selected.

FIGURE 10-7

Editing instant messaging accounts in Empathy

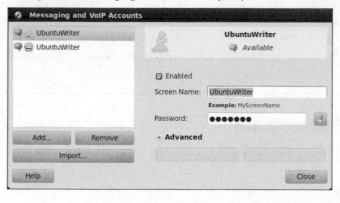

The dialog shown in Figure 10-7 contains the following information:

- The pane at left lists your existing instant messaging accounts. The icons to the left of the name of each account represent the status of that account (using an icon that looks like a comic strip's speech balloon) and the instant messaging service that is associated with that account. A dark speech balloon indicates that the account is disabled (inactive) in Empathy, while a green speech balloon indicates that account is enabled and ready for use.

- Action buttons below the left pane enable you to Add or Remove instant messaging accounts from Empathy. If you previously used Pidgin on your system, an Import button is also displayed, which enables you to import instant messaging accounts that you defined in Pidgin into Empathy. Clicking Help displays the online manual for Empathy.

- The pane at right provides detailed information about the instant messaging account that is selected in the left pane. Click the control to the left of the Advanced label to expose any detailed configuration settings that you can customize for this account. You will rarely need to change these, but they can be handy if you need to connect to a specific server, use a specific network port for your connection, and so on.

To enable or disable an account, select that account from this list and select or deselect the Enabled checkbox in the right pane. Disabling an instant messaging account only prevents it from being used in Empathy until it is re-enabled—it does not change any of the settings for your account with the instant messaging service that provided the account.

You may occasionally want to remove an instant messaging account that you no longer use, after you and your friends have all moved on to some different instant messaging service. To remove an instant messaging account, select that account in the left pane and click Remove. Much like enabling an account, removing an account only removes that account from your local Empathy configuration—it does not affect your account at the instant messaging service that provided the account. (Empathy displays a confirmation dialog that provides this information whenever you attempt to remove an existing instant messaging account from Empathy.)

Adding a new instant messaging account is the most common activity that you'll do from the dialog shown in Figure 10-7. To add a new account, click Add to display the dialog shown in Figure 10-8.

FIGURE 10-8

Adding a new instant messaging account

Select the instant messaging service that hosts your new account by selecting it from the drop-down Protocol list. Enter your login ID or name and password in the appropriate fields. To add the new account and connect to that service, click Login. (This button is only selectable when all of the information that is required to connect to the account has been specified.)

Any changes that you make to an existing account in the "Messaging and VoIP Accounts" dialog take effect immediately. Click Close to close this dialog and return to the "Contact List" dialog.

Using Empathy

Empathy's main dialog is the "Contact List" dialog, shown in Figure 10-9. From top to bottom, this dialog shows your current status, public entities that are supported by any of the instant messaging services that are associated with your accounts, and the status of any available contacts (generally known in IM-speak as *buddies*).

FIGURE 10-9

Status and available contacts in Empathy's Contact List

You can initiate a conversation with an existing contact in one of two ways:

- Double-click on that contact's name in the bottom portion of the "Contact List" dialog.
- Select the "Contact List" dialog's Chat ➪ New Conversation menu command, and enter the name of the contact that you want to converse with. This is the only way to initiate a conversation with a contact that you did not include in a group in the "Contact List" dialog.

Doing either of these displays a Conversation window like the one shown in Figure 10-10.

FIGURE 10-10

A Conversation window in Empathy

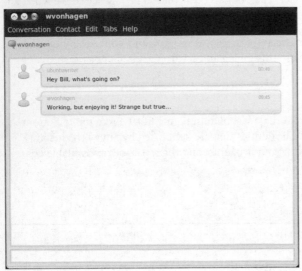

The name of this window is initially the name of your contact. If you start multiple conversations with different users at the same time, each of these appears in its own tab within the Conversation window.

The top portion of this window shows a record of your conversation, while the bottom field of this window is the area in which you type your message. Figure 10-10 shows an initial message and a response.

Once you've completed your conversation, select Conversation ⇨ Close in the Conversation window, or simply use the Close window control to close the Conversation window.

Adding Contacts in Empathy

Over time, you will probably want to exchange instant messages with more and more people. To simplify this, you'll want to add them as contacts (commonly referred to as *buddies*) so that they show up in the bottom portion of the "Contact List" dialog and you can easily initiate conversations (chats) with them.

To add a contact in Empathy, select the "Contact List" dialog's Chat ⇨ Add Contact menu command. This displays the dialog shown in Figure 10-11.

FIGURE 10-11

Adding a contact in Empathy

The top field of this dialog is a dropdown that enables you to identify which of your Empathy accounts is associated with the new contact. The instant messaging service (and associated protocol) must be the same as that used by the person that you want to contact. The Identifier field is the name of your contact's instant messaging account, and the Alias field enables you to specify a more memorable name for your contact. Any alias that you set will be the name that is shown for that contact in the "Contact List" dialog. For example, if you have problems remembering that the contact name for a college friend is *robotoverlord666*, you can enter your friend's real name as an alias, and you'll have an easier time distinguishing her from all your other contacts who have instant messaging accounts that begin with the string *robotoverlord*. If you don't specify an alias, Empathy will set the Alias to be the same as the Identifier for the account.

Once you enter the name of your new contact, the dialog shown in Figure 10-11 expands to look like the dialog shown in Figure 10-12.

This expanded dialog lets you specify which (if any) of the groups in your Contact List that the new contact will be added to. Groups are essentially section headings in the contact window that can be expanded or collapsed, and make it easy for you to organize your contacts. You can also define a new group by entering its name in the text area above the group list and clicking "Add Group." Being able to define your own groups makes it easy for you to organize your contacts into logical sets that have special meaning to you, like "Work Friends," "Poker Night," and "Family." On the other hand, you may not want to add someone with whom you rarely chat to a specific group, which will mean that their Identifier or Alias will not be displayed in the "Contact List" dialog. As described earlier, you can still initiate a conversation with unlisted contacts by using the "Contact List" dialog's Chat ⇨ New Conversation menu command and manually entering the name of the contact that you want to converse with.

FIGURE 10-12

Adding a contact to a group in Empathy

You can see detailed information about any of your contacts by moving the mouse over the name of that contact. This displays a pop-up dialog that lists the Empathy account associated with that contact, their account name, and any alias that you've specified for them.

Reviewing Past Conversations

Empathy automatically keeps a record of your conversations and provides a convenient calendar-driven dialog that enables you to locate previous conversations that you've had with any of your contacts, as shown in Figure 10-13.

To display this dialog, select the Conversation window's Contact ⇨ Past Conversations menu command. You can then select specific dates from the calendar at the upper left to see a record of any conversation that you had with that contact on the specified date. This can be especially convenient if you've made promises that you've forgotten or your contact is no longer speaking to you and you're wondering just what you said.

Exiting Empathy

To exit Empathy, select the "Contact List" dialog's Chat ⇨ Quit menu command or use the "Close Window" control to close the "Contact List" dialog.

FIGURE 10-13

Reviewing previous conversations in Empathy

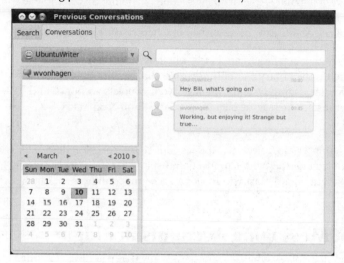

Getting More Information about Empathy

Empathy is a relatively young instant messaging client that is still expanding to take advantage of all of the capabilities of the underlying Telepathy framework that it uses. Some good sites for getting more information about these are the following:

- `http://live.gnome.org/Empathy`: The main Empathy site at the GNOME project
- `http://live.gnome.org/Empathy/FAQ`: Empathy's Frequently Asked Questions (FAQ) file
- `http://telepathy.freedesktop.org/wiki`: The main Telepathy web site

Instant Messaging on Ubuntu with Pidgin

Pidgin (`www.pidgin.im`) is the new name of a popular instant messaging application for Linux that was originally known as *GAIM* (GTK+ AOL Instant Messenger). This name was changed to *Gaim* due to pressure from AOL, which still wasn't good enough once AOL trademarked the term *AIM*, so there you go — *Pidgin* it is. The name is doubly clever, referring both to a simplified language used to communicate between groups who do not have an entire language in common (i.e., *Pidgin English*) and also referring to the *pigeon*, a bird that historically was used to send messages.

Until the arrival of Empathy, Pidgin was the most popular multi-protocol instant messaging client on GNOME-based systems and was installed as part of a default Ubuntu Desktop system.

Pidgin supports a huge number of instant messaging protocols, enables you to set up chat rooms for use by multiple users, and even supports file transfers. Although Empathy is now the default GNOME IM client, Pidgin is still very popular — the next few sections therefore discuss how to configure and use Pidgin. In order to use Pidgin, you must manually install the `pidgin` package using your favorite package management software, as described in Chapter 19.

Some terms that you'll encounter when using Pidgin are *Finch*, which is a terminal-oriented version of Pidgin, and *Purple*, which is the library (actually *libpurple*) that enables Pidgin and Finch to connect to multiple instant messaging systems, manages your contacts accounts, and so on. Purple is also used by other instant messaging clients, such as Adium X on Mac OS X, ScatterChat, Meebo, and so on.

To start Pidgin on an Ubuntu Desktop system, select the Applications ➪ Internet ➪ Pidgin Internet Messenger menu item. An icon for the Pidgin application displays in your panel's system tray/notification area, and either Pidgin's Buddy List window or an account configuration dialog displays on your screen.

Configuring Instant Messaging Accounts in Pidgin

The first time that you start Pidgin, it displays a dialog letting you know that you haven't configured any instant messaging accounts yet, and offering to let you configure your first one. Click Add to proceed. The "Add Account" dialog displays, as shown in Figure 10-14.

Note

If you have already defined an IM account in Pidgin and want to add another one, you can do so at any time from Pidgin's Accounts dialog, which you can display by selecting the Accounts ➪ Manage menu option from the Pidgin Buddy List window. Click Add to define a new Pidgin account from this dialog. This displays the same dialog shown in Figure 10-14. ∎

Click the Protocol dropdown menu to select the instant messaging protocol that you want to use, which essentially means the instant messaging service where you have an instant messaging account.

After selecting the protocol/service where you have an instant messaging account, enter your Screen Name (the name of your IM account at a given service), Password, and (optionally) a local alias that you want to use for this account. If your computer is secure, you can click the "Remember password" checkbox, which will prevent you from having to enter your password each time that you start Pidgin, but which will also store your password in plaintext in Pidgin's configuration file.

Next, you can optionally select the "New Mail notifications" checkbox to cause Pidgin to notify you whenever you have new e-mail (see Figure 10-15). You can also customize the icon that you want to associate with this account by selecting the "Use this buddy icon" checkbox and clicking on the icon to display a dialog that lets you navigate to a directory where the custom icons that you want to use are located.

FIGURE 10-14

Configuring an IM account in Pidgin

FIGURE 10-15

Pidgin's Accounts dialog

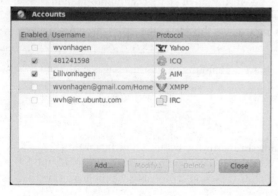

Caution

Pidgin's GAIM and Gaim predecessors showed distinct icons for users based on the protocol/service that they were using, but this default was dropped in Pidgin 2.0 because the developers felt that you were more interested in which people you were communicating with than the protocol that they were using. ■

When configuring a Pidgin account, you can select the Advanced tab if you need to do things such as communicating with a specific server, using a specific port for communication, or want to use a proxy server so that your friends won't know your IP address. (The last can be useful for business-related instant messaging when you're working from the golf course, the local Starbucks, and so on.) The options that are provided on the Advanced tab are specific to the protocol/service that you're using. In most cases, you won't need to set anything on this tab, but it's nice that Pidgin provides these sorts of advanced connectivity options if you do actually need them.

Once you've finished providing the details of your IM account, click Save to create the account in Pidgin. If this is the first time that you are configuring an IM account in Pidgin, Pidgin will display both the Buddy List window, shown in Figure 10-16, through which you can communicate with your IM friends; and the Accounts dialog, shown in Figure 10-15, from which you can add, modify, or delete IM accounts at any time. You can display the Accounts dialog at any time when you are running Pidgin by selecting the Accounts ➪ Manage menu option from the Buddy List window.

If you are done letting Pidgin know about your IM accounts, click Close in the Accounts window to close that window. Otherwise, you can click Add to define another IM account; select an existing account and click Modify to change its settings; or click Delete to delete that account. Deleting an IM account only removes Pidgin's information about that account — the account still exists at the remote service.

Tip

Because Pidgin uses the Purple library for communication and configuration, all of your Pidgin account and buddy information is stored in the directory ~/.purple. Specifically, all of your account information is stored in the file ~/.purple/accounts.xml. If you want to completely purge this information from your computer and reconfigure Pidgin from scratch, you can simply delete this file or the entire directory if you want a truly clean slate. ∎

Once you've configured Pidgin, you're ready to start exchanging instant messages with your friends.

Using Pidgin

Pidgin's "Buddy List" dialog is the primary dialog through which you initiate instant messages and manage the list(s) of people with whom you will communicate frequently. Figure 10-16 shows an empty Pidgin Buddy List window, which is what you'll probably see the first time that you start Pidgin if you're new to instant messaging.

The next few sections discuss how to define IM contacts (in other words, how to add users to your Buddy List), how to organize your buddies, and how to extend Pidgin's basic capabilities by adding plug-ins. However, the first thing that you may want to do with Pidgin is simply to send someone an instant message — Buddy Lists and other conveniences make Pidgin more convenient and more fun, but sending instant messages is what IM is really all about!

FIGURE 10-16

An empty "Buddy List" dialog in Pidgin

To send an instant message to someone, regardless of whether they're shown in your Buddy List window, you can always select the Buddies ➪ New Instant Message menu option. (Once someone is in your Buddy List, you can send them an instant message by double-clicking on their name in the Buddy List.) If you've defined multiple instant messaging accounts, the dialog shown in Figure 10-17 displays, in which you must identify both the person that you want to IM and the account that you want to use to do so. Once you do so, you'll see a dialog like the one shown in Figure 10-18. If you've only defined a single instant messaging account, you'll see a dialog like the one shown in Figure 10-18 immediately.

FIGURE 10-17

Initiating an instant message

FIGURE 10-18

An instant message dialog

The heading of this window identifies the user that you are sending an instant message to, and the icon and name of that user is also listed above the Conversation window. The Conversation window is the top field on this dialog and displays a record of your conversation as you send instant massages back and forth. The bottom portion of this dialog is where you type your messages. After typing a message to the user you identified, this dialog looks something like the one shown in Figure 10-19.

FIGURE 10-19

Sending a message in the Conversation dialog

Each message in an instant message dialog is preceded by the screen name or alias for the user that is sending the message. Once your friend responds, the instant message dialog will show your conversation to date, as shown in Figure 10-20.

Receiving a message in the instant message dialog

As you send messages back and forth, the last few messages will always be shown in the Conversation window. When you're done communicating with your friend, click the Close box, select the Conversation ⇨ Close menu option, or press Ctrl+W to close the Conversation dialog.

Welcome to IM! The next few sections explain how to make using Pidgin a bit easier by defining buddies and how to do some other common tasks in Pidgin.

Connecting to Your IM Accounts in Pidgin

I typically have the same instant messaging account defined on multiple computer systems, such as my primary desktop system at home and my laptop, so that I can stay in touch with friends and family wherever I am. This is one of the great advantages of defining buddies (explained in the next section) — your Buddy Lists are stored by the service that you're using, so you see the same contact whenever you log in to a given service.

Most instant messaging protocols only allow you to be logged in from a single instant messaging client at a time. This makes sense, because otherwise every system where you are running an IM client would display Chat and Instant Message windows, regardless of whether you were using that system or not. As mentioned in the previous section on defining IM accounts in Pidgin, you can set up those accounts to automatically log in whenever you start up Pidgin. This is usually a good idea for people with high-speed connections to the Internet, but the downside of this is that logging in from one computer system usually drops your connection to the same IM account from any other computer system. When this occurs, Pidgin displays a message about this at the bottom of the Buddy List window, as shown in Figure 10-21.

FIGURE 10-21

A multiple login message in Pidgin

To re-enable your account immediately when you get back to that computer, you can click the Re-enable button in the message. You can click the X in the upper-right corner of this message if you simply want to close this dialog and re-enable the account later.

Note
Some IM services, like AIM/AOL, don't automatically drop other connections, but instead display a dialog that enables you to select the connection that you want to drop. ■

If you need to re-enable an account manually, you can do so by selecting the Accounts menu's "Enable Account" submenu. This displays a list of all registered accounts that are not currently active — to re-enable one on your current computer system, simply select it from the dropdown list. If you are running a Pidgin client that supports that same account on any other machine, that account will be disconnected from the associated service on the other machine.

Adding Buddies in Pidgin

A *buddy* is the term for a person with whom you expect to communicate frequently via IM. As explained in the previous section, you don't actually have to add someone to your Buddy List in order to send them an instant message, but you'll probably want to add your friends to your Buddy List if you're going to communicate with them frequently (unless your memory is a lot better than mine is). When you first start using instant messaging, you may not have any predefined buddies, and your Buddy List may initially look like that shown in Figure 10-3.

To add a buddy, select the File ⇨ Add Buddy menu option to display the dialog shown in Figure 10-22.

FIGURE 10-22

Defining a buddy in Pidgin

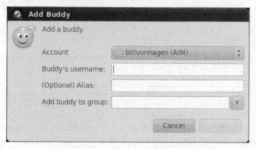

If you have defined multiple IM accounts in Pidgin, you'll first want to select the account that you want to use from the dropdown list at the top of this dialog. Next, enter the screen name of the person that you want to define as a buddy, an optional alias that you want to add them to, and (optionally, again) the group to which you want to add them. Groups provide a convenient way to organize your buddies so that you can easily recognize them as friends, family members, co-workers, and so on. This can be very useful as you accumulate more and more IM buddies — you may not immediately recognize the screen name of a person from whom you receive an instant message, so organizing them into groups will give you an immediate clue and should help clarify things. If you don't specify a group, your new buddy will be added to the default Buddies group.

After entering the screen name (and selecting an account, if necessary), click Add. The buddy that you have defined will immediately be listed in your Buddy List window.

Some instant messaging services, such as Yahoo, will automatically notify you when someone adds you to their Buddy List. This displays a field at the bottom of the Buddy List window, as shown in Figure 10-23.

Clicking Deny displays an "Authorization denied" message dialog that enables you to send someone an IM that explains why you don't want them to add you to their Buddy List. This is a message rather than a true rejection — you will still appear in their Buddy List, and they can subsequently send you a message to clarify why they wanted to add you.

FIGURE 10-23

Authorizing someone to add you as a buddy in Pidgin

If you click Authorize, Pidgin conveniently displays a dialog like the one shown in Figure 10-22 with the screen name of the person who is trying to contact you filled in, enabling you to easily add them to your Buddy List, too. After all, if you don't have a problem being on their Buddy List, you might as well have them on your list, too. If you click Add in this dialog, they'll see a dialog like the one shown in Figure 10-23, which essentially just confirms that you OK'd their request and added them to your Buddy List too.

As mentioned previously, once someone is in your Buddy List, you can easily send him/her an instant message by double-clicking on his or her name in the Buddy List window.

Organizing Buddies in Pidgin

As you accumulate more and more IM contacts, your Buddy List window will fill up and you'll have to scroll further and further to actually find someone whose screen name you don't remember offhand. As mentioned in the previous section, you can use groups in the Buddy List window to organize your contacts. This usually feels like overkill when you only have a few buddies, but once you have a few zillion of them, you'll wish you'd organized them into groups from the beginning. Luckily, you can organize existing buddies into groups almost as easily as you can add them to groups when defining them in the first place.

By default, Pidgin provides the following groups into which you can organize your buddies:

- Buddies
- Co-workers
- Family

- Friends
- Recent Buddies
- Top Level

To change the group that a buddy is located in, right-click on that buddy, select the "Move To" menu item, and select the group to which you want to move that buddy.

You can create custom groups by selecting the Buddies ⇨ Add Group command, which displays a dialog in which you can define the name of the new group. You can also rename an existing group by right-clicking on the name of that group and selecting the Rename command.

Viewing Buddies in Pidgin

By default, Pidgin only shows buddies who are online, which can be confusing after adding a buddy and then not seeing their name. You can change whether offline buddies are displayed in one of two ways:

- By selecting the Buddies ⇨ Show command and selecting Offline Buddies. This will display all of your buddies, regardless of whether they are online or offline. Offline buddies will be shown as grayed-out entries with the word *Offline* shown below their identities. If you are using the default icons for this buddy, the standard green circle (online) icon will be replaced by a circle with an "x" in the middle when they are offline.

- By right-clicking on the name of a specific buddy in the Buddy List window and selecting "Show when offline" from the context-sensitive menu that displays. This buddy will be shown in your Buddy List, regardless of their status or whether offline buddies are being displayed in general.

Using the Buddies ⇨ Show ⇨ Offline Buddies command can also be very handy if you aren't sure if you've added someone as a buddy or not, or when reorganizing your contacts into different groups. Selecting this command temporarily will enable you to see all of the buddies that you have defined so far and will also enable you to move existing buddies to other groups, as explained in the previous section.

Logging Your Conversations

Depending on how compulsive you are, you may want to save the conversations that you have with certain people over IM. This can be important if you're using IM to get detailed information that you will want to refer to later, or simply if you want to remember what you said to someone the last time that you exchanged messages with them.

You can keep a log of a specific conversation by selecting the Options ⇨ Log Messages menu option in a conversation window before entering the first message of a conversation with someone else.Selecting this menu option logs all subsequent messages in a conversation, so this is only convenient if you know beforehand that you want to keep a record of your conversation. Selecting this command displays a message in your Conversation window, confirming that logging has been enabled — the remote user doesn't see this message.

If you always want to keep a log of your conversations, you can configure Pidgin to do this by selecting the Tools ➪ Preferences menu option, and selecting the Logging tab in the Preferences dialog, shown in Figure 10-24.

FIGURE 10-24

Configuring logging preferences in Pidgin

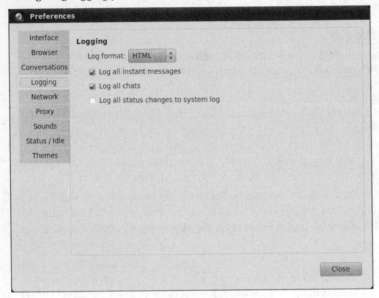

Select the "Log all instant messages" checkbox to log all instant messages to a text file. If you want to log messages in HTML format instead of text, click the "Log Format" dropdown, and select HTML. You can also log all chats by selecting the associated checkbox. Once you are finished configuring logging in Pidgin, click Close to close the Preferences dialog.

If you don't want to automatically log all of your chats, you can always disable logging and simply use the Conversation ➪ Save As menu option in a Chat window to save a specific chat to a file.

Exiting Pidgin

As mentioned earlier in this section, Pidgin creates an icon for itself in your panel's notification/system tray area when you start Pidgin. After closing the Buddy List window, Pidgin is still running and you can re-display the Buddy List window at any time by left-clicking on Pidgin's icon in the notification/system tray portion of the panel. Selecting Buddies ➪ Quit actually terminates Pidgin. The fact that Pidgin is still running will cause a slight performance glitch if you try to restart Pidgin from the Applications menu when it is actually still running in the system tray. An entry that says "Starting Pidgin" will appear in the Window List portion of the panel, but will eventually close without opening a Pidgin window on your screen.

Tip

If you do not want Pidgin to add an icon for itself in the system tray and continue running in the background once the Buddy List window is closed, select the Tools ➪ Preferences menu option to display the Preferences dialog, select the Interface tab, and select None from the "Show system tray icon" dropdown list. As a compromise, you can select "On unread message" to cause the notification area icon to continue to be displayed after closing the Buddy List window only if there are unread messages pending. ∎

To actually terminate Pidgin, you must right-click on the Pidgin icon in the notification portion of the GNOME panel (located at the far right of the top panel, by default) and select Quit from the content-sensitive menu that displays. If you select Quit while a Buddy List window is displayed on the screen, a Buddy List window will be displayed the next time that you start Pidgin. If you close the Buddy List window before selecting Quit from the Pidgin icon, whether the Buddy List window displays the next time that you start Pidgin depends on whether you've disabled the notification/system tray icon. If it is enabled (which is the default), only the notification/system tray icon is displayed the next time that you start Pidgin. If it is disabled, the Buddy List window will always display when you start Pidgin.

Getting More Information about Pidgin

As with all GNOME applications, you can get online help in multiple ways while using Pidgin:

- Pressing the F1 key or selecting the Help ➪ Online Help menu option takes you to the Pidgin FAQ on the Pidgin web site, which may already contain the answer to your question.

- Selecting the Help ➪ Get Help Online menu option takes you to the section of Ubuntu's Launchpad site that provides help for Pidgin in the release of Ubuntu that you're running. You can post a question there or review questions that others have already asked. This page also provides links to both the IRC channel where Ubuntu is discussed and to the Web-based Ubuntu forums. See the section of this chapter entitled "Using IRC" for more information about IRC.

As you might expect, the Pidgin web site, `www.pidgin.im`, also provides a good deal of information about Pidgin, primarily in the Support and Development section that is located at `http://developer.pidgin.im`.

Using IRC

As discussed in the "Instant Messaging Overview" section of this chapter, Internet Relay Chat (IRC) was the first cross-platform mechanism for real-time Internet communications. As mentioned earlier, IRC is a client/server. IRC users connect to an IRC server using a client application that runs on their systems. IRC servers are typically themselves organized into networks of servers that share information with each other. Hundreds, if not thousands, of IRC servers are publicly available and typically do not require a password in order to access them. (See www.irchelp.org/irchelp/networks for a good starting list of available IRC servers and networks.) The discussion areas on IRC are referred to as *channels*. Channel names are prefixed by a hash mark (#)—one of the most popular IRC channels for readers of this book should be the #ubuntu channel, which is a support channel for Ubuntu, a great place to ask Ubuntu-related questions at any level, and a generally useful resource. Most channels are accessible by anyone, but they can also be password-protected to provide private areas for communication between sets of users who know the password.

When you first connect to an IRC server, you define a nickname (generally referred to simply as a *nick*), which is how you are identified on any channel that you join. Once connected, you can use commands prefaced with a slash (/) character to interact with the server itself. The following are common IRC commands:

- /dcc chat nickname: Requests a direct, user-to-user chat session with the user who has the specified nickname.

- /help: Summarizes available IRC server commands. You can follow the /help command with the name of another command (without the /) to get specific information about that command.

- /join #channel: Enables you to connect to a specified channel. If the specified channel does not already exist, it will usually be created with you as its operator, but some IRC servers limit channel creation to specific users in order to cut down on the noise (and to prevent typos from automatically creating channels).

- /leave #channel: Leaves the specified channel.

- /list: Displays a list of available channels.

- /msg: Sends a private message to the user whose name you specify.

- /nick: Enables you to define a nickname for you in IRC, typically your username.

- /quit: Drops your connection to IRC, displaying a farewell (*signoff*) message.

- /who #channel: Lists the users that are currently connected to a specific channel.

Although the first IRC clients were for UNIX and UNIX-like systems, IRC clients have been available for other operating systems since shortly after the birth of IRC. Mac OS, Mac OS X, and Microsoft Windows systems all offer a wide selection of IRC clients. On the Windows platform, mIRC (www.mirc.com) is probably the most popular IRC client, although many others are available. The Miranda IM client for Windows (www.miranda-im.org) also supports IRC, as does Trillian (www.trillian.im). Macintosh users typically use IRC clients such as

Ircle (`www.ircle.com`), which has been popular on Macintosh systems forever; Adium X (`www.adiumx.com`), which provides both IM and IRC access; and Colloquy (`http://colloquy.info`), which is impressive on both the OS X desktop and on your iPhone.

The next two sections discuss how to connect to IRC using the Pidgin instant messaging client, and provide tips for getting more information about IRC.

Using IRC in Empathy

As discussed in the sections on Empathy and Pidgin, IRC is one of the messaging protocols that is built into both applications. This section focuses on Empathy because it is the default IM client on modern Ubuntu systems. Because most IRC servers are open, you can create an IRC account and connect to an IRC server without having to pre-register, but you must create an Empathy IRC account to do this. You create your Empathy IRC account like any other account, as explained in the section earlier in this chapter, "Adding and Removing Empathy Accounts." When creating an IRC account in Empathy, your nickname can be whatever you want it to be, but it must be unique on the IRC server that you're connecting to. Empathy offers a huge number of IRC servers in the Network dropdown, but if you're just getting started with IRC, the Ubuntu Servers entry is probably the best initial selection. This connects you to the IRC server `http://irc.ubuntu.com` (part of the freenode IRC network).

To join an IRC channel in Empathy, select the Contact List dialog's Room ⇨ Join menu command. The "Join Room" dialog displays. Select your IRC account as the account to use, and enter the name of a room that you want to connect to — #ubuntu is a good place to get started. A standard Empathy conversation window opens, and you'll see the ongoing public conversations between everyone else who's in that room (*channel* in IRC-speak). You can see a list of all of the channels available on the Ubuntu IRC server at `https://help.ubuntu.com/community/InternetRelayChat`.

At this point, you can enter other IRC commands in the text window at the bottom of the Pidgin screen, or simply enter text to send it to the channel. When you're done asking questions, answering questions, or simply watching the flow of communications, you can leave the channel by using the `/leave` command to leave a channel or the `/quit` command to close your connection to the IRC server.

Note

If you find IRC interesting, useful, or perhaps even both, you may want to investigate other Linux IRC clients. Although Empathy is fine for my purposes, the XChat program is a UNIX/Linux IRC client that has been around for a long time, is quite popular, and makes it very easy to connect to multiple channels and servers at the same time. XChat uses GTK, so it is well-suited for use on GNOME-based Ubuntu Desktop systems. XChat isn't installed by default, but is available in the default Ubuntu repositories. The latest version of XChat for Ubuntu systems is located in the `xchat-gnome` package, which you'll have to install using your favorite Package Management tool. ∎

Getting More Information about IRC

Regardless of how well it fits the IM model, IRC is still popular, quite fun, and occasionally even useful. When you first connect to IRC, you'll probably be doing so in order to connect to a specific channel, like #ubuntu. Most of the channels on the Ubuntu IRC servers are Ubuntu-related, but you may be interested in channels such as #new2irc, #newbies, or #newuser that are found on other IRC server and provide interesting starting points. If you'd like general information about IRC or have some specific questions, you may want to explore #irchelp. For information about available channels, use /list on the IRC server that you're connected to, or use a Web-based resource such as www.irchelp.org/irchelp/chanlist.

The following are some great sources of additional information about IRC, its culture, IRC servers, other IRC sites, and so on:

- **IRC.org** (www.irc.org): Known as the original home of IRC, this site provides news, help, IRC history and humor, information about ongoing developments in IRC, and a huge collection of useful links to many other IRC-related sites.

- **IRChelp.org** (www.irchelp.org): The Internet Relay Chat Help site provides a tremendous collection of IRC FAQs, primers, HOWTO guides, helper scripts, lists of active servers and supported channels, and so on.

- **Wikipedia** (http://en.wikipedia.org/wiki/Internet_Relay_Chat): In addition to the standard "online encyclopedia" info, the Wikipedia article on IRC provides good links to many other IRC-related sites — or at least it did at the time of this writing.

Other Instant Messaging Packages

Empathy and Pidgin provide all of the functionality that almost anyone needs in a multi-protocol IM client. However, Ubuntu is a Linux distribution, so you might suspect that there are a huge number of other IM applications out there. Some of my favorites are the following (listed in alphabetical order):

- **Google Talk** (www.google.com/talk): Google Talk is a Windows and Web-based client for Google's chat service, or any other XMPP-based chat service.

- **Licq** (www.licq.org): Licq is an ICQ client that uses the Qt desktop widgets. It is still actively under development. Plug-ins are available to enable Licq users to communicate with AIM and MSN users.

- **Meebo** (www.meebo.com): Meebo is a Web-based instant messaging service that supports its own accounts as well as providing access to other IM services that Meebo supports, such as AIM, GoogleTalk, ICQ, jabber, MSN, and Yahoo. A Firefox plug-in for Meebo is also available.

- **Psi** (http://psi-im.org): Also in Ubuntu repositories, Psi is a free Jabber/XMPP client that is available for Linux, Macintosh, and Windows systems and uses Qt for its graphical interface. Psi is a great Jabber client, but you can also use Psi to connect to other IM services by taking advantage of gateway/transport services such as those offered by the `im.flosoft.biz` Jabber server.

- **SamePlace** (`http://sameplace.cc`): SamePlace is a Web-based XMPP instant messaging system that provides Firefox, Flock, and Thunderbird plug-ins. You can also take advantage of its gateways to other services (known as *transports*, or *transport services*) to use SamePlace to communicate with other supported IM services.

- **ScatterChat** (`http://scatterchat.en.softonic.com`): ScatterChat is an encrypted, anonymous instant messaging application and is designed to provide a lifeboat of privacy in today's sea of online communication. ScatterChat is a product of the Hacktivismo project (`http://en.wikipedia.org/wiki/Hacktivismo`), which views access to information as a basic right. And right they are.

Many other IM clients are available in the open source universe, and I can't list them all here. Heck, I probably don't even know them all because I'm sure that one was just written yesterday. However, between the excellent and rich capabilities of Pidgin and Empathy and the packages listed in this section, I'm sure that you can find the instant messaging client that's just right for you.

Resolving IM Communication Problems

Both Pidgin and Empathy are popular applications that are used daily by many people. If you're having problems sending or receiving instant messages with either of these applications, the most common source of communication problems is that a firewall is blocking your connection to the instant messaging service that you're trying to reach. If you are experiencing communication problems and are running a firewall, make sure that the appropriate port(s) from the following list are not being blocked, re-directed, or used for something else:

- **AIM/ICQ:** Port 5190
- **Google Talk, Jabber, and XMPP in general:** Port 5222
- **IRC:** Port 6667
- **MSN:** Ports 443 (SSL) and 1863
- **Yahoo:** Port 5050

Blocking Internet-wide access to these ports is quite common at many businesses because of the possibility that random users on the NET could eavesdrop on business-related IM communications. Many companies offer enterprise IM solutions, but that's certainly outside the scope of this book.

If you are trying to use instant messaging on your personal computer and are not running a firewall, you may want to check with your ISP to make sure that they are not blocking these ports. That would be incredibly antisocial, but not completely surprising.

Summary

Instant messaging is a popular interpersonal communication mechanism for most Internet-connected people nowadays. This chapter provided some background and historical information on instant messaging and explained how to obtain an instant messaging account with various popular instant messaging services. The next two sections provided detailed configuration and usage information for the two most popular instant messaging clients that are commonly used on Ubuntu Desktop systems. The chapter also discussed Internet Relay Chat—a related multi-person communication mechanism—highlighted other instant messaging clients that are available for Linux systems, and concluded by providing some troubleshooting information that may help you if you are having problems communicating with your instant messaging service of choice.

Using Command-Line Tools

IN THIS CHAPTER

What is a shell?

Why use the command line?

Working with files and directories

Understanding Linux permissions

Getting help for Linux commands

How to configure the bash shell

Because Linux has its conceptual roots in the older UNIX operating system, many Linux applications are executed from a command line. A command line is the traditional interface found on older computer systems that may not have used the high-resolution, graphically oriented monitors that most people expect today. In the command-line model, the system runs a program, known as a *command-line interpreter*, which does just what its name suggests: It reads the commands that you type, locates the appropriate application on your system, and executes that application for you as instructed based on what you've typed. Once the command completes, the command interpreter displays a sequence of characters, known as a *prompt*, signifying that it is ready to accept another command.

Linux systems aren't reliant on the command-line approach simply out of historical interest — when a Linux system boots, it needs to be able to run several commands long before the graphical interface is available. On Linux systems, the graphical interface itself is started by a command-line utility, after which (of course) fancy graphics are available, expected, and used.

For most people, simply displaying a command-line prompt on a fancy graphical monitor powered by a multi-megabyte graphics card would be a waste of good hardware. However, Linux provides thousands of useful and extremely powerful command-line applications. Thus, graphical user interfaces (GUIs) such as GNOME, KDE, and X Window System window managers offer applications that display a command prompt in a separate window, giving you the best of both worlds. You can be running OpenOffice Writer or GIMP in separate windows, making the most of their graphical capabilities, while you can be simultaneously displaying a command prompt in another and executing command-line utilities there.

This chapter explains the basic ideas behind command-line utilities and the commands that execute them, discusses the primary Linux command-line interpreters, explains how to access them, and explores some of the most popular utilities for running command-line utilities on your Ubuntu Linux system.

Note

Most of the command-line examples given throughout this chapter begin with the character $, which is the default prompt used by Ubuntu's default Linux command interpreter. (A *prompt* is the character or characters that a command interpreter displays to signify that it is waiting for you to type something.) If you're following along, you should not type this character — you'll already see it (or some more complex prompt) at the beginning of your command line. ■

Why Use the Command Line?

Linux provides thousands of command-line utilities that range from simple programs for creating, examining, and modifying files and file permissions to complex utilities that enable you to fine-tune the performance of your hardware and low-level operating system capabilities, such as filesystems and networking. Many of these applications have graphical equivalents, especially user-level applications and system configuration utilities. For example, the System ⇨ Administration menu's Networking menu item starts the graphical `network-admin` application, which performs the same functions as the command-line `ifconfig` utility. Similarly, GNOME's Nautilus file manager is roughly equivalent to a Linux command-line interpreter in general because it enables you to examine and manipulate files and directories, execute other applications, and so on.

Using the command line isn't really an alien notion even to users of operating systems such as Microsoft Windows and Mac OS X (although it's newer to the latter). Many Windows users, especially system administrators, have always found a certain convenience in some of the command-line configuration utilities provided with Windows systems, especially those related to network configuration and status reporting such as `ipconfig`. The idea of a command line may be somewhat new to long-time Macintosh users because the command line was a serious alternative to the GUI when Apple introduced its UNIX-based Mac OS X.

Even if you don't specifically want to use the Linux command line, there is one case in which you may have to, which is if your Ubuntu system encounters major hardware or configuration problems during the boot process. If, for example, your system finds that its root filesystem is corrupted or inaccessible during the boot process, you'll see a command-line prompt faster than you can say, "Hmmm, I wonder if that's a major problem." All Linux systems fall back to the command line when major problems are identified during the boot sequence to give you access to the command-line applications that you'll need to use in order to correct the problem and re-enable the system to boot normally. The Linux boot process is a command-line process, executing the appropriate configuration utilities in the correct order, the last of which is the command that starts the X Window System and your GNOME desktop (or window manager, if you've customized things). Even if your computer's filesystems are in good shape and all of your hardware and associated system software runs correctly during the boot process, configuration problems with the X Window System are a common cause of seeing a command-line prompt instead of the graphical Ubuntu login screen when you boot your system.

Executing Commands from the Command Line

Applications that are designed to be executed from a Linux command line are typically referred to as *command-line utilities*. All command-line utilities have the same general organization — they begin with the name of the command that you want to execute and are optionally followed by information about the way in which you want the command to behave. Anything following the name of the command that you want to execute is known as an *argument* to that command. The arguments to each command-line utility differ based on the command that you want to execute. In an interesting example of recursion, the arguments to command-line utilities are generally referred to as *options*, each of which may take an argument.

Confused? If this is all new to you, don't worry. A few examples will help clear this up, and soon you'll be as comfortable at the command line as anyone. Let's use the Linux ls command as an example because it has more options than almost any other command and was also introduced in the section of Chapter 4, "Basic Linux System Concepts," entitled "Understanding Linux Permissions."

The ls command *lists* information about files and directories on your Ubuntu system. The Linux ls command is an updated version of a classic UNIX utility by the same name. In true UNIX fashion, no one was willing to type extra characters such as i and t, so the command was given the faster-to-type abbreviation of ls.

When used by itself on the command line, the ls command simply displays the contents of the current directory, as in the following example:

```
$ ls
boot_services.txt hello.c   hello.o  include_example.c    test
hello             hello.foo hello.s  include_example.out
```

You can also supply the name of a specific file or directory as an argument to the ls command, as in the following examples:

```
$ ls hello
hello
```

Using the ls command to list the name of a file that you already know is spectacularly uninteresting (although it can be very useful when combined with wildcards, which are discussed later in this chapter). However, listing a directory shows the contents of that directory, as in the following example:

```
$ ls test
libxml2  netdev  system
```

The output from this command shows that the test directory itself contains three other files or directories. I happened to know that test was a directory—if you're not sure what types of things are in the current directory, you can use the ls command's -F option to give you this information. For example, here's the current directory as shown using the ls -F command:

```
$ ls -F
boot_services.txt hello.c   hello.o  include_example.c   test/
hello*            hello.foo hello.s  include_example.out
```

The ls command's -F option decorates the names of the objects in the current directory with an extra character to identify any object that isn't simply a text file. An asterisk following the name of an object shows that this is an executable file, while a slash (/) following the name of an object shows that this is, indeed, a directory.

The ls command's -F option is very useful, but (in true Linux fashion) it isn't the only way to get detailed information about each of the objects in the current directory. You can also get this sort of information using other options to the ls command. For example, one of the most commonly used options to the ls command is the -l option, which means "display output in long format." Using this option gives a variety of additional information about the objects in the current directory, as in the following example:

```
$ ls -l
total 44
-rw-r--r--  1 wvh users  783 2010-03-15 06:36 boot_services.txt
-rwxr-xr-x  1 wvh users 9249 2010-03-15 06:37 hello
-rw-r--r--  1 wvh users   60 2010-03-15 06:37 hello.c
-rw-r--r--  1 wvh users   60 2010-03-15 06:37 hello.foo
-rw-r--r--  1 wvh users 2504 2010.03-15 06:37 hello.o
-rw-r--r--  1 wvh users  857 2010-03-15 06:37 hello.s
-rw-r--r--  1 wvh users  202 2010-03-15 06:37 include_example.c
-rw-r--r--  1 wvh users  736 2010-03-15 06:37 include_example.out
drwxr-xr-x  5 wvh users 4096 2010-03-15 06:37 test
```

As you can see, the long option displays more complete information about the files and directories in the current directory. From left to right, this information consists of the following: current permissions, the number of hard links to that file in the Linux filesystem (more about that later in this section), the owner and group, size, the date and time at which it was last modified, and the file or directory name.

As mentioned previously, you can combine options and arguments on the same command line to refine the behavior of most command-line utilities. For example, to get a long listing of the contents of the test directory, you would execute the following command:

```
$ ls -l test
total 0
drwxr-xr-x  2 wvh users 72 2010-03-15 06:37 libxml2
drwxr-xr-x  2 wvh users 80 2010-03-15 06:37 netdev
drwxr-xr-x  4 wvh users 96 2010-03-15 06:37 system
```

One other very popular option to the ls command is the -a option, which shows all of the objects in the current directory. By default, the ls command doesn't show objects whose names begin with a period (aka *full stop*) because all Linux directories contain two special entries that many people don't care about, but which are useful to traverse and support the hierarchical structure of a Linux filesystem. These are the "." entry, which always refers to the current directory, and the ".." entry, which always refers to the parent of the current directory. Using the ls -a command to look at the contents of the current directory shows the following:

```
$ ls -a
.                        hello.c       include_example.c    .run_me_now
..                       hello.foo     include_example.out
boot_services.txt        hello.o       test
hello                    hello.s       .my_music_directory
```

You'll note that the "." and ".." entries are listed in the first column. However, you'll also note that two new files have appeared in the directory. These are the files .my_music_directory and .run_me_now, which are listed in the directory listing based on the first alphanumeric character in their names because the ls command ignores leading periods when sorting filenames (unless, of course, the filename has no other characters, as is the case with the "." and ".." entries, which therefore appear first in the listing).

Tip

Because files beginning with periods aren't included in directory listings unless you use the -a option, using filenames that begin with a period has become a standard convention for "hiding" those files. Files and directories whose names begin with a period are most commonly used to hold configuration information used by various Linux commands. The most common example of this type of file is the .bashrc configuration file used by the bash shell, which I'll discuss later in this chapter. ■

You can combine multiple single-letter options after a single leading dash, and the ls command will perform all of the specified actions. For example, let's combine the -a and -F options to look at the current directory:

```
$ ls -aF
./                       hello.c       include_example.c    .run_me_now*
../                      hello.foo     include_example.out
boot_services.txt        hello.o       test/
hello*                   hello.s       .my_music_directory@
```

From the output of this command, you can see that the "." and ".." entries are both directories (actually, they are hard links to the current and parent directories), and the mysterious `.run_me_now` file is actually an executable command. The name of the `.my_music_directory` file is followed by an "at" symbol (@). What's up with that?

I've used the term *links* in passing previously, and this is a good time to explain the usage. Links are essentially just pointers to other files and directories in the Linux filesystem (much like short-cuts on Microsoft Windows systems or aliases on Mac OS X systems). Linux supports two types of links: *hard links*, which are actual connections to existing files or directories, and *symbolic links*, which contain the name of some other file or directory that you want to refer to. Because hard links are actual connections to an existing data structure, the thing that you're linking to must actually exist and must be within the same disk partition as the thing that you're hard-linking to. Because symbolic links, unlike hard links, just contain the name of something else, they can point to any file or directory on your machine. As you may now suspect, an @ symbol following the name of a file or directory indicates that this file or directory is just a symbolic link to another file or directory somewhere else on your system. Let's combine the `ls` command's `-a` and `-l` options to get some detailed information about everything in the current directory:

```
$ ls -al
total 45
drwxr-xr-x   3 wvh users  400 2010-03-16 06:20 .
drwxr-xr-x  13 wvh users 1376 2010-03-16 05:38 ..
-rw-r--r--   1 wvh users  783 2010-03-15 06:36 boot_services.txt
-rwxr-xr-x   1 wvh users 9249 2010-03-15 06:37 hello
-rw-r--r--   1 wvh users   60 2010-03-15 06:37 hello.c
-rw-r--r--   1 wvh users   60 2010-03-15 06:37 hello.foo
-rw-r--r--   1 wvh users 2504 2010-03-15 06:37 hello.o
-rw-r--r--   1 wvh users  857 2010-03-15 06:37 hello.s
-rw-r--r--   1 wvh users  202 2010-03-15 06:37 include_example.c
-rw-r--r--   1 wvh users  736 2010-03-15 06:37 include_example.out
drwxr-xr-x   5 wvh users  120 2010-03-15 06:37 test
lrwxrwxrwx   1 wvh users   11 2010-03-16 06:20 .my_music -> \
    /opt2/music
-rwxr-xr-x   1 wvh users  269 2010-03-16 05:47 .run_me_now
```

This actually shows you a fair amount of information about everything in this directory, especially in terms of links. Remember that the second column in a long directory listing identifies the number of hard links to each object. For example, the second column for the "." entry shows that there are three hard links to the current directory—these are the "." itself, its entry in the parent directory, and the hard link to "." that is present in the `test` subdirectory because the current directory is the parent of the `test` directory. The ".." entry, which is a hard link to the parent directory of the current directory, seems to be very popular because there are 13 hard links to it. This means that the parent directory of the current directory probably contains several other directories. Looking at the `.my_music` file, you can see that it is indeed a symbolic link because its name in the long listing actually shows the other object that it is a symbolic link to.

In this case, the file .my_music is a symbolic link to a directory that happens to live on another filesystem that is mounted on the /opt2/music directory on my system.

All of the command-line options I've discussed up to this point have begun with a single dash. This isn't always necessarily the case for all commands and their options. Some Linux commands with their conceptual roots in ancient versions of UNIX (such as the tar command) don't even require a leading dash before a single command-line option or a single group of command-line options. This antique command-line option convention is deprecated, which means that anyone who implements a command nowadays that doesn't require at least one dash before its options will be mocked and verbally abused via e-mail by the Linux and open source communities. (All UNIX commands that don't require a dash before their options have also been updated so that they can also handle finding a dash before their options.) Nowadays, command-line options always begin with a dash, but in an interesting usability twist, they can also begin with two dashes. The conventions for this are that single-letter options are preceded by a single dash, while multi-letter, "whole-word" options begin with two dashes. This is necessary for two reasons:

- Most command-line utilities support both styles of options: the traditional single-letter options and the newer whole-word options pioneered by the folks at the Free Software Foundation.

- Because you can combine multiple single-letter options into a single group of options (as you've seen throughout this section), unless you use two dashes to identify a whole-word option, the command that you're executing can't differentiate between the two.

To illustrate this, let's ask for help from the ls command:

```
$ ls -help
/bin/ls: invalid option -- e
Try '/bin/ls  --help' for more information.
```

Well, that was actually both illustrative and friendly. When preceded with a single dash, the ls command interprets each of the letters that follow as a single option and therefore complains because no option matches the letter e in the -help option. Let's try that again, correctly. Running the ls --help command displays the following output (truncated here because this is just an example):

```
$ ls  --help
Usage: /bin/ls [OPTION]... [FILE]...
List information about the FILEs (the current directory by
default). Sort entries alphabetically if none of -cftuSUX
nor -- sort.

Mandatory arguments to long options are mandatory for short
options too.
  -a,  -- all             do not ignore entries starting with .
  -A,  -- almost-all      do not list implied . and ..
[remaining output deleted]
```

Getting Information about Commands

As you can see from the final example in this section, many command-line utilities provide a `--help` option, which displays what is known as a *usage message*. A usage message is a short summary of how to use a command, summarizing available options and their meanings. Unfortunately, not all commands offer a `--help` option, and those that do can't display all possible information about those options. As discussed in Chapters 5, "Using the GNOME Desktop," and 6, "Using the Compiz Window Manager," the graphical user environments used on Ubuntu systems provide a huge assortment of online help that makes it easy for you to get information about how to use graphical commands. Luckily, the Ubuntu command-line environment also provides a similar amount of online help in the form of the `man` and `info` commands.

The `man` command is your best friend when using or simply experimenting with command-line programs. The `man` command displays online manual pages, formatted for your screen. In true Linux/UNIX fashion, the `man` command paginates its output using the Linux version of the familiar UNIX `more` command—known as `less`—to make it easy to scroll forward or backward in its output. Because the online reference information displayed by the `man` command is displayed a screen/page at a time and corresponds to the documentation you'd traditionally find in a printed reference manual, the documentation displayed by `man` is generally referred to as a *man page* or as *man pages*.

As an example of using the `man` command, you can type **man man** for additional information on the `man` command itself. The first part of this man page looks like the following:

```
man(1)                    Manual pager utils                    man(1)

NAME
       man - an interface to the on-line reference manuals

SYNOPSIS
       man  [-c|-w|-tZHT device]  [-adhu7V]  [-i|-I]
       [-m system[,....]] [-L locale] [-p string] [-M path]
       [-P pager] [-r prompt] [-S list]  [-e extension]
       [[section] page ...] ...
       man  -l  [-7] [-tZHT device] [-p string] [-P pager]
       [-r prompt] file ...
       man -k [apropos options] regexp ...
       man -f [whatis options] page ...

DESCRIPTION
       man is the system's manual pager. Each page argument given to
       man is normally  the  name  of  a  program,  utility or func-
       tion. The manual page associated with each of these arguments
       is  then found  and  displayed. A section, if  provided, will
       direct  man  to look only in that section of the manual.  The
       default  action  is to search  in  all  of  the  available sec-
       tions,  following  a  predefined order  and to  show only the
       first page found, even if page exists in several  sections.
[Additional output removed]
```

As you can see, the online man pages for Linux commands provide extensive information about available options, but also provide a significant amount of general information about using the commands themselves, usually including examples.

A more modern alternative to the man command, the info command provides similar usage and explanatory information about Linux commands. The info command uses Emacs to display its output and also provides more extensive and up-to-date command documentation than the traditional man command.

The GNU folks introduced the info command to provide a richer, more robust environment for displaying online help for command-line utilities. The text files that are used by the info command provide a very rich syntax for hyperlinking between different sections of info documentation, and the use of Emacs as the application for displaying info pages provides a much more flexible environment for moving around in the info that you're looking at. The info command can also display traditional Linux man pages, so you can even examine existing man pages using info — the info man command is perhaps the best example of that sort of recursion.

The Linux man and info commands will quickly become your new best friends when you are using or simply learning about command-line utilities.

What's a Shell?

A *shell* is the generic name given to any Linux command-line interpreter, and comes from UNIX, the conceptual parent of Linux. UNIX was one of the first operating systems to introduce the idea of using a command-line interpreter that was not built into the operating system and that had no special permissions to do mysterious operating system tasks. These ideas have been preserved in every conceptual descendant of UNIX and have proved handy for several reasons. The most interesting of these is that, because it is a separate, stand-alone executable, a Linux system can offer each user his or her choice of multiple shells, all of which can be upgraded independently from the operating system.

The original UNIX shell was written by Ken Thompson, one of the two primary creators of UNIX, and was extended by John Mashey, also at Bell Labs. These shells were somewhat primitive — the first shell that had the types of capabilities we have come to know and love today was the Bourne Shell, written by Stephen Bourne at Bell Labs in 1974. This shell, known to its friends as /bin/sh, is the shell that is used by default on most UNIX systems, and is the conceptual parent of the /bin/bash shell (which stands for "Bourne-Again Shell") that is used by default on most Linux systems today. As I'll explain in the next section, there are a variety of other shells to choose from on Linux systems. If you've come to Linux from a version of UNIX that features another shell, you'll be able to feel at home pretty quickly (and perhaps even bring over and reuse your existing shell configuration files).

Tip

A term that you will frequently hear when discussing shells, Linux, or UNIX in general is the term *shell script*. A shell script is a command file containing commands that are either internal to the shell (such as those for setting variables, conditional expressions, and looping constructs) or that reference other commands on your Linux system. The ability to write very sophisticated command files is a feature of the Linux/UNIX utility model, wherein each utility does one thing and does it well, and many different utilities can be linked together via pipes or temporary files to process each other's output. ■

For additional information about shells on UNIX systems, see:

```
www.softpanorama.org/People/Shell_giants/introduction.shtml

www.faqs.org/faqs/unix-faq/shell/shell-differences/

www.unix.org.ua/orelly/unix/ksh/ch01_03.htm
```

Available Shells for Linux Systems

A standard Ubuntu distribution installs only the standard GNU bash shell. However, other shells are available for installation through apt-get or the Synaptic Package Manager. The following shells are found on many Linux systems:

- /bin/ash: The Almquist shell, a small-footprint shell that began as a clone of the SYSV R4 version of the Bourne shell. The ash shell is often used on embedded systems or during the system startup and installation process on some Linux distributions.

- /bin/bash: The default, Bourne-Again shell inspired by /bin/sh and /bin/ksh. This is the default login shell installed and used by all users on Ubuntu systems.

- /bin/csh: If you install tcsh (see its description later in this list), a symbolic link from /bin/csh to /bin/tcsh is also created. This link is provided to support shell scripts that reference the traditional location of the C-shell, the standard shell used on Berkeley UNIX (BSD) systems and their descendants. The C-shell supports configuration commands that are reminiscent of C-language programming constructs and was originally written by Bill Joy, later a founder of Sun Microsystems.

- /bin/dash: The Debian Almquist shell, the Debian Linux distribution's version of the standard Almquist shell. This shell is used during the system boot process.

- /bin/ksh: If you install pdksh (see its description later in this list), a symbolic link from /bin/ksh to /bin/pdksh is also created. This link is provided to support shell scripts that reference the traditional location of the Korn shell, the standard shell used on later SYSV UNIX systems from AT&T and their descendants.

- /bin/nash: Another small-footprint shell used during the startup process on many Linux systems, specifically on Red Hat and Fedora Core Linux systems

- /bin/pdksh: An open source version of David Korn's Korn shell, written at AT&T and available with the SYSV R3 (as part of the "Experimental Toolchest") and R4 (as a completely supported utility) UNIX distributions. The Korn shell (and thus pdksh) is completely backward-compatible with the original Bourne shell. If you're interested in experimenting with this shell, it is available in the standard Ubuntu repository.

- /bin/sh: A symbolic link to /bin/dash, provided for compatibility with generic Linux and UNIX shell scripts

- /bin/tcsh: The TENEX C-shell, which is an advanced, open source version of the C-shell with command-line editing extensions that were originally introduced by the command interpreter used by DEC's TOPS-20 operating system for PDP-10 systems, which began life as BBN's TENEX (for the 10 in PDP-10) operating system and was therefore later mutated into TWENEX (for the 20 in TOPS-20) by the PDP-10 hacker community. If you're interested in experimenting with this shell, it is available in the standard Ubuntu repository.

- /bin/zsh: The Z shell is a powerful, tremendously extensible shell that provides many of the capabilities of bash and ksh, and much, much more. If you're interested in experimenting with this shell, it is available in the standard Ubuntu repository.

You can use the chsh command-line command to change the default shell used by your account if you decide that you want to use a shell other than the one that is currently listed in your /etc/passwd entry. However, you can't change your login shell to any random binary — all of the programs to which you can change your shell are listed in the text file /etc/shells on your Ubuntu system. If you want to be able to set some other application as a login shell using the chsh command, you must first add it to the file /etc/shells.

Getting to a Shell

Assuming that I've hyped the value of the Linux command line sufficiently and that your Ubuntu system boots correctly in graphical mode, you're probably wondering how to start a shell so that you can experiment a bit. Ubuntu provides two applications that are the most common mechanisms for starting a shell, one that is a standard part of the X Window System distribution, and another that is a standard part of any GNOME distribution. Both of these are referred to as *terminal applications*, not because they imply an end to life as we know it but because they are reminiscent of the user experience on systems without bitmapped graphical displays, when most users accessed their computer systems through *terminals* that couldn't do much more than display the input and output of a command interpreter.

Using the GNOME Terminal Application

The GNOME Terminal application is the most common way of starting a command-line shell on a graphical Ubuntu system. To start the GNOME Terminal, select the Terminal command from the Applications ⇨ Accessories menu. Figure 11-1 shows the default GNOME Terminal window.

FIGURE 11-1

The GNOME Terminal application

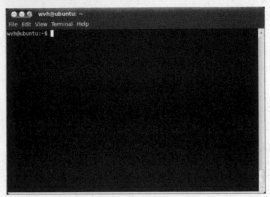

As with most GNOME applications, the GNOME Terminal provides extensive online help, which is available by selecting Help ⇨ Contents.

The GNOME Terminal application provides a variety of menus that make it easy to configure things such as the title of a GNOME Terminal window (Terminal ⇨ Set Title); configure the character set (Terminal ⇨ Set Character Encoding); and configure the size, fonts, colors, and other display attributes of the GNOME Terminal window (Edit ⇨ Current Profile). In my opinion, its most generally useful feature is its ability to open and manage multiple command-line sessions within a single Terminal window. To open a new tab, select the File ⇨ Open Tab command. A new tab displays, as shown in Figure 11-2.

FIGURE 11-2

Multiple tabs in the GNOME Terminal

Once multiple tabs are displayed, you can move between tabs by clicking on a specific tab or by using the appropriate command from the Tabs menu. If you want to have an existing tab display in its own window, you can select the Tabs ⇨ Detach Tab command. You can also start a new GNOME Terminal window by selecting the File ⇨ Open Terminal command.

Using the X Window System Terminal Application

Any X Window System distribution includes a lightweight terminal application known as xterm. The executable for the X Window System's terminal application, shown in Figure 11-3, is located in /usr/bin/xterm.

FIGURE 11-3

A traditional xterm

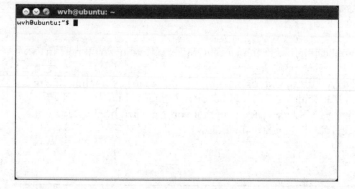

To start the xterm application, do any of the following:

- Add a menu item for the xterm application, as explained in "Customizing GNOME Menus" for GNOME in Chapter 5. You can then select that menu item to run the command.

- Create a launcher for the xterm application on your panel using the Run Application panel applet, and then select that panel applet. Adding items to a GNOME panel is explained in "Customizing Panel Contents" in Chapter 5.

- Create a desktop launcher for the xterm application by right-clicking on your desktop's background, selecting the Create Launcher command, and filling out the dialog shown in Figure 11-4. You can then start xterm by clicking on the desktop icon for the launcher.

- Execute the xterm command directly from the GNOME Terminal, which is somewhat recursive, but eminently doable.

FIGURE 11-4

Creating a desktop launcher for the xterm application

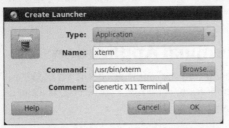

Many users who are new to Ubuntu but are already familiar with the xterm application find that they prefer xterm to GNOME Terminal. For complete details on all of the capabilities of the xterm application, see its man page — perhaps by starting xterm and executing the `man xterm` command in that window.

As a generic X Window System application rather than a GNOME application, you'll note in Figure 11-3 that an xterm window doesn't provide a menu or toolbar to provide easy access to configuration commands. Instead, you display xterm's configuration menus by holding down the Ctrl key on your keyboard and clicking the left, middle, or right mouse buttons on the background of the xterm window. Figure 11-5 shows the menu that you see when holding down the Ctrl key and left-clicking the background of an xterm window.

FIGURE 11-5

An xterm's Main Options menu

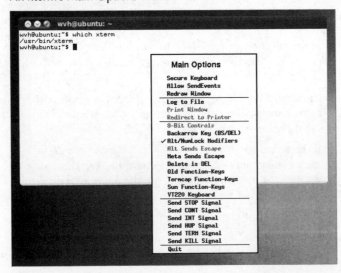

Each xterm configuration menu provides access to different xterm configuration commands:

- **Ctrl+left-click:** The Main Options menu, which primarily enables you to send various signals and special key sequences to the selected xterm

- **Ctrl+middle-click:** The VT Options enables you to set various characteristics of the terminal emulation provided by the selected xterm. The name *VT Options* comes from the name of the default type of terminal that is emulated by an xterm, which is a DEC VT-100. Figure 11-6 shows the VT Options menu. If you only have a two-button mouse, but it has a roller wheel, the roller wheel typically acts as a middle button if clicked. If you have a two-button mouse without a roller, pressing both buttons simultaneously usually emulates a middle-mouse click.

- **Ctrl+right-click:** The VT Fonts menu enables you to control the size of the fonts used in the selected xterm. Figure 11-7 shows the VT Fonts menu.

FIGURE 11-6

An xterm's VT Options menu

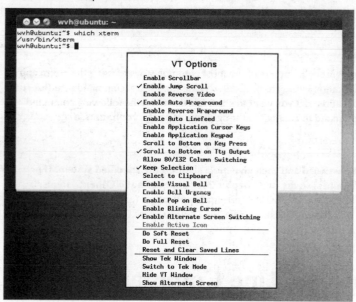

405

FIGURE 11-7

An xterm's VT Fonts menu

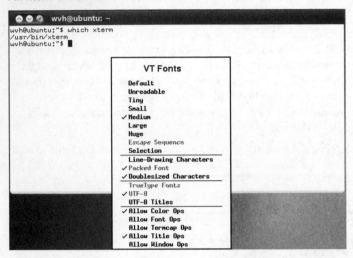

Tip

By default, an xterm starts a copy of your login shell, but one of the most common ways of using the xterm application is to automatically start another application in the xterm window using the xterm command's -e (execute) option and specifying the name of the application that you want to start. For example, the following command starts an xterm that is running the ssh command to connect to the system writing.vonhagen.org:

```
$ xterm -e ssh writing.vonhagen.org
```

This command would prompt for a login password and then give me a shell on the specified system. (For more information about connecting to remote systems, see Chapter 25, "Connecting to Other Systems.") Because xterm doesn't feature multiple tabs like the GNOME Terminal application (explained in the previous section), an xterm -e command is one of the most common ways for Ubuntu users to start a separate window that is running another nongraphical command. ■

Popular Command-Line Commands

The section of this chapter that introduced command-line utilities, options, and arguments used the standard Linux ls command as an example. Listing files and directories is one of the most common things that you'll want to do from a shell (or, at least, will find yourself doing). However, as explained in the previous section, your Ubuntu system provides hundreds of commands. I can't go into all of them here because that would mean that Wiley would need to put wheels on this book, but there are certainly some common tasks that you'll want to do from a shell. This section highlights some of the more common tasks you'll want to perform from the command line and concludes by discussing how to figure out which commands to use if you don't already know the cryptic name of the appropriate command-line utility.

Moving Around in the Linux Filesystem

Just as you do when you use a graphical user interface, you will want to organize your files and directories in some logical fashion if you're working from the command line. Once you've organized things that way, you'll need to use the cd ("change directory") command, which does exactly what you'd expect. In hard-core Linux terms, the cd command changes your current working directory to be the directory that you supply as an argument. For example, to change directory into a directory named test, you'd simply execute the following command:

```
$ cd test
```

Tip

If you're hanging around with hard-core Linux folks and want to fit in, refer to changing to another directory as *cd'ing* there. ■

If you don't know the name of the directory where you are currently working, that's somewhat scary, but you can use the pwd command (process working directory) to provide that information. The pwd command lists the full pathname of the directory in which the current process (in this case, your shell) is running, as in the following example:

```
$ pwd
/home/wvh/test
```

You can change to any directory on your Linux system by specifying its full pathname as the argument to the cd command, as in the following example:

```
$ cd /usr/local
$ pwd
/usr/local
```

As you can see, my shell is now working in the /usr/local directory, and any other commands that I execute will be performed in that directory. As a convenience, if you execute the cd command without any arguments, the cd command automatically changes directory to your home directory, which is probably where most of your files and directories are located in the first place. You can also execute the cd - command to take you to the previous directory that you were working from.

Tip

As you work at the command line, you may find that you often want to change to some other directory, do one or two things, and then return to the directory that you started in. When changing directories frequently, it's handy to let your shell keep track of things like "Where did I come from?" To save you time and mental energy, the bash shell provides built-in commands called pushd and popd to track this for you. The pushd command changes to a specified directory but remembers where you came from by pushing the name of the directory that you came from onto a list of previous locations known as a *stack*. Once you're done working there, you can type the popd command to return to the directory that you came from, which removes it from the stack (i.e., the list of previous working directory locations). If you're unfamiliar with the idea of a stack, the standard example of a stack is the spring-loaded stack of plates that you find at a cafeteria or your favorite local buffet. Pushing something onto the stack is analogous to putting a new plate on the top of the stack of available plates. Popping something off the stack is analogous to removing the top plate from the stack, which makes the next one available. ■

Copying, Moving, Renaming, and Deleting Files and Directories

Copying, moving, and renaming files are some of the most common actions that any computer user performs, regardless of whether you're using the command line or working with a graphical user interface. Whether you're cloning an existing file to use the former as a starting point for new work or reorganizing your files and directories to make things easier to find, copying and moving files and directories is just as easy to do from the command line as it is from a GUI, except for the fact that you have to type rather than point and click. In many cases, the zillions of options provided by many Linux command-line utilities give you much finer control over things than a generic graphical command ever could.

In continuing the Linux/UNIX tradition of "Why type more letters than necessary?" the Linux command to copy files and directories is the cp command. To copy one file to another, you simply execute the cp command, followed by the name of the existing file and the name that you want to have the copy. For example, to copy a file named file.txt to the new file new_file.txt, you would execute the command:

```
$ cp file.txt new_file.txt
```

Caution

Be very careful when specifying the name of the file that is the destination of a cp command. If a file with the same name as the file to which you are copying already exists, the cp command overwrites the existing file with the contents of the file that you are copying. If you're really paranoid about this, see the section later in this chapter on "Defining and Using Aliases" for information about how to permanently set up a safe version of the cp command. ■

By specifying the full pathnames of the source or destination file, the cp command can copy files anywhere in the Linux filesystem in which you have permission to create files. For example, to copy the file file.txt from my home directory to the file newfile.txt in the directory /tmp (where everyone can create files), I could execute the following command regardless of the file or directory in which I was currently working:

```
$ cp /home/wvh/file.txt /tmp/newfile.txt
```

You can also use the cp command to copy a file to different directories by specifying the name of a directory as the target of the cp operation. Continuing with the previous example, if I had wanted to copy the file file.txt from my home directory to /tmp, but have the copy retain the same name as the original file, I could have done so with the following command:

```
$ cp /home/wvh/file.txt /tmp
```

This command would create the file /tmp/file.txt as an exact copy of /home/wvh/file.txt.

The cp command doesn't require any special options when simply copying files. However, you can also copy directories using the cp command, by specifying its -r (recursive) option. For example, to copy the contents of a directory of mine called `include_test` to a new directory called `backup`, I would execute the following command:

```
$ cp -r include_test backup
```

After the command completed, the new backup directory would be an exact copy of the `include_test` directory. If you're from Missouri and need proof that the right thing is happening, you can add the `-v` (verbose) option to the `cp` command to list each part of the copy command. This command and its output would look like the following:

```
$ cp -rv include_test backup
'include_test' -> 'backup'
'include_test/libxml2' -> 'backup/libxml2'
'include_test/libxml2/xmlops.h' -> 'backup/libxml2/xmlops.h'
'include_test/netdev' -> 'backup/netdev'
'include_test/netdev/devname.h' -> 'backup/netdev/devname.h'
'include_test/system' -> 'backup/system'
'include_test/system/libxml2' -> 'backup/system/libxml2'
'include_test/system/libxml2/xmlops.h' -> \
    'backup/system/libxml2/xmlops.h'
'include_test/system/netdev' -> 'backup/system/netdev'
'include_test/system/netdev/devname.h' -> \
    'backup/system/netdev/devname.h'
```

As you'd hope, a recursive `cp` command also recursively copies all subdirectories and any files that they contain.

I mentioned earlier that specifying the name of a directory as the target when copying a file creates a file with the same name as the original in the target directory. The same is true when specifying the name of a directory as the target for a recursive `cp` command. This can initially be confusing if you're trying to copy a directory to a directory with a new name and a directory with that name already exists. In that case, the `cp` command creates a directory with the same name as your original directory as a subdirectory of the target directory.

Moving and renaming files from the command line is similarly easy. Linux systems don't actually provide a separate rename command—on a Linux system, the `mv` command both moves existing files and directories to a new location and also optionally renames them as part of the move operation. For example, to rename the file `file.txt` to the new name `newfile.txt`, you would do the following:

```
$ mv file.txt newfile.txt
```

The `mv` command follows the same conventions as the `cp` command in terms of specifying full pathnames and when specifying a directory as the name of the location to which you want to move a file. For example, the following command moves the file `/home/wvh/file.txt` to the `/tmp` directory and renames it `newfile.txt`:

```
$ mv /home/wvh/file.txt /tmp/newfile.txt
```

If you wanted to move the file to the /tmp directory and keep its original name, you would do so with the following command:

```
$ mv /home/wvh/file.txt /tmp
```

Unlike the cp command, the mv command doesn't need any special flags when moving or renaming directories. For example, to rename the directory test to backup, you would do the following;

```
$ mv test backup
```

As with the cp command, if the backup directory already existed, the mv command would move the test directory into the backup directory, retaining its original name. The mv command also provides a -v (verbose) option to show you what's going on during an mv operation, but this is somewhat less exciting when just renaming a directory, as you can see from the following example:

```
$ mv -v test backup
'test' -> 'backup'
```

In this case, the mv operation only needs to rename the directory. However, because of the way that Linux filesystems are created, moving directories across filesystems that live on different hard disk partitions requires that each file and subdirectory first be copied and then deleted by the mv command, as in the following example:

```
$ mv -v include_test /tmp/backup
'include_test' -> '/tmp/backup'
'include_test/libxml2' -> '/tmp/backup/libxml2'
'include_test/libxml2/xmlops.h' -> '/tmp/backup/libxml2/xmlops.h'
'include_test/netdev' -> '/tmp/backup/netdev'
'include_test/netdev/devname.h' -> '/tmp/backup/netdev/devname.h'
'include_test/system' -> '/tmp/backup/system'
'include_test/system/libxml2' -> '/tmp/backup/system/libxml2'
'include_test/system/libxml2/xmlops.h' -> \
    '/tmp/backup/system/libxml2/xmlops.h'
'include_test/system/netdev' -> '/tmp/backup/system/netdev'
'include_test/system/netdev/devname.h' -> \
    '/tmp/backup/system/netdev/devname.h'
'include_test/new_file' -> '/tmp/backup/new_file'
removed 'include_test/libxml2/xmlops.h'
removed directory: 'include_test/libxml2'
removed 'include_test/netdev/devname.h'
removed directory: 'include_test/netdev'
removed 'include_test/system/libxml2/xmlops.h'
removed directory: 'include_test/system/libxml2'
removed 'include_test/system/netdev/devname.h'
removed directory: 'include_test/system/netdev'
removed directory: 'include_test/system'
removed 'include_test/new_file'
removed directory: 'include_test'
```

As you can see, much of this output is very similar to that of the cp command. In this example, I first used the df command to demonstrate that my current directory (".") and the target directory (/tmp) are actually located on different filesystems. You can see the difference in the verbose output of the mv command.

Along with copying and moving files and directories, deleting files and directories is a similarly common operation. Whether you're deleting things to free up disk space for future projects, deleting backup copies of projects that you've finished, or deleting things that you don't want anyone else to see, it's quite easy to delete files from the command line. The key to doing so is the rm command, which continues the "the less typing, the better" philosophy and stands for *remove*.

To remove a single file on a Linux system, you simply type the rm command followed by the name of the file. For example, to delete the file file.txt, you would do the following:

```
$ rm file.txt
```

The file is gone. As with the cp command, the rm command provides an r (recursive) option to enable you to remove entire directories. For example, to permanently remove a directory named test, you would issue the following command:

```
$ rm -r test
```

Tip

You can remove empty directories using the rmdir command, but I don't find that to be a common scenario. I rarely have empty directories just sitting around because I usually create directories to store something in them. I generally use the rm -r command to delete any directory because that way I don't have to manually delete its contents first. Your mileage may vary. ■

If you've moved to Ubuntu from a Microsoft Windows system, you may be painfully aware that it is easy to recover files that you've deleted on a Windows system because it initially just erases the directory entry that identifies the file or folder that you're deleting. This is not the case on a Linux system. When you delete a file or directory on a Linux system using the command line or by emptying the Trash in a graphical environment, all of the disk storage associated with the file, directory, and the contents of that directory are returned to a general list of free space that is available on your system. Although deleted files and directories can still be recovered on a Linux system, it is much harder to do so and requires the assistance of someone who really knows the details of the filesystem.

The downside of this is that you can't easily recover any files that you've deleted by mistake unless you do so using a graphical utility such as a file manager. To help protect yourself from accidentally deleting files, see the section later in this chapter on "Defining and Using Aliases" for information about how to permanently set up a safe version of the rm command that will ask you for confirmation before it actually removes anything.

Tip

All of the cp, mv, and rm commands have many more options than I've covered here. To see all of the options available for any of these commands, use the man or info commands to see the online reference information for the command that you're interested in. ■

Changing File and Directory Permissions

Chapter 4 introduced the idea of Linux users and groups and also provided an initial explanation of how file and directory permissions are represented when listing the contents of files and directories. You saw the same thing earlier in this chapter when exploring the `ls` command's `-l` option. Being able to protect files so that only certain users or groups can examine or execute them is certainly handy, but it begs the question, "How do I do that?" You can easily change file and directory permissions from graphical file managers such as GNOME's Nautilus by right-clicking, selecting Properties, and selecting the Permissions tab, as shown in Nautilus in Figure 11-8. Fortunately, changing file and directory permissions from the command line is similarly easy, and may even be easier.

FIGURE 11-8

Setting permissions in Nautilus

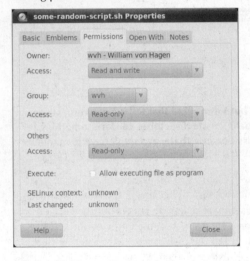

The `chmod` (change mode) command enables you to change any of the permissions associated with files and directories that you own. The `chmod` command supports two ways of setting permissions:

- Using octal values that actually represent the bits in the permission field of a file or directory

- Using friendly letters to represent permissions for the user who owns a file or directory (u), the group with which that file or directory is associated (g), other users on the system that are not in that group (o), or all users on the system (a), and using the plus and minus signs to add or subtract permissions. This is known as *changing permissions in symbolic mode*.

In this section, I'll focus on the second approach because many of us may be a bit rusty working in octal, and the symbolic mode is easier to visualize and use. I'll use as an example the file `hello.sh`, which happens to be a bash command file (shell script) that simply prints the string "Hello, World!" in the shell window from which it is executed. Let's first look at its default permissions:

```
$ ls -l hello.sh
-rw-r--r--   1 wvh wvh 36 2006.03-18 16:30 hello.sh
```

As explained in detail in Chapter 4, the characters at the left portion of the `ls` command's long output describe the current file permissions. These file permissions fall into four groups: the leading dash identifies the type of object that this is (a dash means that it's just a regular file), and the remaining three groups of three characters indicate the permissions that the owner of the file (wvh) has, the groups associated with that file (also named *wvh*), and the rights that all other users have to the file. Each of these groups of three characters can have the following values (in order):

- r: The file or directory can be read.
- w: The file or directory can be written to.
- x: The file can be executed or the directory can be searched for other files or directories.
- -: The permission is not granted.

The two instances of *wvh* in the `ls` output, from left to right, identify the owner of the file and the group that is associated with the file. In the sample `ls` output, we therefore can see that I (as the owner of the file) can both read and write to the file, but that other members of the group wvh can only read the file, and that all other users on the system can also only read the file.

Because this is a shell script, I presumably want to be able to execute it. To make the file executable by its owner (me), I would issue the following command:

```
$ chmod u+x hello.sh
```

Listing the file again, we can see that the file is now marked as being executable by its owner:

```
$ chmod u+x hello.sh
$ ls -al hello.sh
-rwxr--r--   1 wvh wvh 36 2006.03-18 16:30 hello.sh
```

If I want others in the group wvh and all other users on the system to be able to execute this shell script, I could issue the following commands to make those changes and verify them:

```
$ chmod g+x hello.sh
$ ls -al hello.sh
-rwxr-xr--   1 wvh users 36 2006.03-18 16:30 hello.sh
$ chmod a+x hello.sh
$ ls -al hello.sh
-rwxr-xr-x 1 wvh users 36 2006.03-18 16:30 hello.sh
```

That's a lot of typing for a repetitive series of operations! Luckily, the chmod command enables you to group multiple permission operations. Suppose I wanted to remove the ability for anyone other than myself to execute this script. I could do this with the following single command:

```
$ chmod go-x hello.sh
$ ls -l hello.sh
-rwxr--r--   1 wvh users 36 2006.03-18 16:30 hello.sh
```

Note that I used o, which means anyone who is not in the group wvh, rather than a, which means all users on the system, because all users on the system would include me.

You can add or remove read and write permissions for any supported permission group using the chmod command and similar options. Files and permissions have the same meanings for directories as they do for files, with the exception of the executable bit, which for directories grants permission to search that directory. For example, you can create a directory that no one but you can read, but still enable people to execute programs or shell scripts that it contains by removing read permission (r), but making sure that search permission (x) is still set. People won't be able to see what's in the directory, but they can execute scripts or programs that it contains if they know their exact names.

Tip

On a related subject, you can use the chown (change owner) and chgrp (change group) commands to change the owner and group of a file, but that's a privileged operation that you must do using sudo, and is a relatively rare task unless you're working as a system administrator. The online reference pages for these commands explain how to run them and provide a good number of examples. ∎

Default Permissions When Creating Files and Directories

A umask (user mask) is the classic UNIX mechanism for setting the default protections of files and directories that you create. By default, the umask is a four-digit octal number that is logically ANDed with the generic file protections of octal 0666 (ironically) when you create a file, or octal 0777 when you create a directory. These octal numbers are representations of the file/directory permission field that was discussed in Chapter 4. The default umask value on most Linux distributions is 0002, meaning that any file you create is created with the octal protection mode 0664 — both the owner and group can read and write to any file that you create, but randoms can only read the file. Similarly, any directory that you create is created with the octal protection mode 0775 — both the owner and group can create files in that directory, and anyone can list the contents of the directory and search for files in it. You find out a user's default umask setting by issuing the umask command from any Linux command-line prompt.

Most people set their umask to 0022 in their shell configuration command file (typically ~/.bashrc) to change their default file creation settings so that files can only be written by their owners (i.e., are created with an octal protection of 0644) and directories can only be written to by their owners (i.e., are created with an octal protection of 0755).

Finding Commands That Do Specific Things

The command line is a pretty friendly place to execute commands if you know what you're doing and know what command to do it with. Unfortunately, given the Linux tendency to avoid long command names by dropping extra characters from their names, it's often hard to figure out what command you want to use to do a specific task.

Luckily, the Linux online manual command, man, provides a truly convenient keyword search option (-k) that automatically searches for a specified keyword or phrase in the description fields of each man page. For example, suppose that you didn't know about the chmod command and wanted to see a list of commands that have something to do with file permissions. You could look for appropriate commands using the following command:

```
$ man -k permissions
chmod (1)                 - change file access permissions
```

Note that this can be tricky because just like a Web search, you have to look for the right phrase. However, at least the possibility is always there. You can search for single words or quoted strings to try to refine the list of commands that match what you're looking for.

If your man -k output lists a command but you can't seem to execute that command (you see the message "command not found" when you try to execute it), this means that the directory where that command is stored isn't one of the directories listed in your PATH variable. In that case, you can try using the whereis command to locate that command, as in the following example:

```
$ man -k "physical volume"
pvchange (8)          - change attributes of a physical volume
pvdisplay (8)         - display attributes of a physical volume
pvremove (8)          - remove a physical volume
pvs (8)               - report information about physical volumes
pvscan (8)            - scan all disks for physical volumes
vgextend (8)          - add physical volumes to a volume group

$ pvscan
bash: pvscan: command not found

$ whereis pvscan
pvscan: /sbin/pvscan /usr/share/man/man8/pvscan.8.gz
```

The whereis command tells you where the command is located (and where its documentation is found). You can then execute that command by specifying the full pathname of the executable, which in this case is /sbin/pvscan.

Working with the Bash Shell

Now that you've started a shell and learned some of the commands that you want to run from the command line, it's time to explore some of the cooler aspects of working with and configuring the bash shell. Obviously, you could simply type commands at the command prompt to your heart's content, but the bash shell provides many nice features that make it easy to use and are well worth taking advantage of. Some of these features can save a significant amount of time, typing, and typos when executing the same command over and over, when executing a group of similar commands, when typing the names of long commands or complex filenames as arguments to commands, and so on.

Using Command History

All Linux shells provide a history mechanism, which is a way of recalling and re-executing commands that you have previously executed. To see the list of recently executed commands, you can simply type history at any shell prompt, which displays something like the following:

```
$ history
231  make distclean
232  ../gcc/configure  -- enable-threads
233  make bootstrap
234  info -f gcc.info
235  export INFOPATH='pwd':$INFOPATH
236  vi ~/.bashrc
237  pushd ~/new
238  ls /mnt/terastation/CDs
239  pushd /mnt/terastation/CDs
240  find . -name "T*.txt"
241  find . -name "T*.txt" -exec rm {} \;
242 rar x ../United_Empire_Loyalists.rar
[much more output deleted]
```

You'll have to trust me that this list contains a recording of a certain number of the commands that I have executed on my system. The number of commands that the history mechanism records is identified by the HISTSIZE environment variable. (The section, "Using Environment Variables" later in this chapter provides information about setting and displaying the values of environment variables.)

You can recall or re-execute commands in several ways:

- Use the shell's built-in fc command.
- Use the shell's mechanism for interacting with the commands that you have typed (known as the *readline library*) to scroll backward through the history list from the command line.
- Use the exclamation point to identify the command that you want to display and re-execute.

I generally use one of the last two mechanisms, so I'll focus on those here.

You can re-display any recently executed command by typing the Ctrl+P command at any command prompt. Each time you type Ctrl+P, the shell displays the previous command in its history list. When you find the command that you want to re-execute, you can simply press Return to re-execute it or edit that command using Emacs commands (by default) such as Ctrl+B to move backward one character in that command, Ctrl+F to move forward in that command one character, the Backspace and Delete keys to delete the previous and current characters, and so on.

Obviously, if the command that you want to re-execute is far back in your command history list, scrolling back through a few hundred commands can be a bit tedious. In this case, you can use the exclamation point to identify a particular command from the history list in either of the following ways:

- **Identifying a command by its sequence number:** Each command in the history list is preceded by its sequence number in your command history. If you've displayed the history list and can see the command that you want to execute, you can re-execute a specific command by typing an exclamation mark followed by its sequence number. For example, using the history output displayed earlier in this section, the command !236 would re-execute the vi ~/.bashrc command.

- **Identifying a command by name:** You can re-execute the most recently executed command that begins with a certain command name by typing an exclamation mark followed by the name of the command that you want to re-execute. For example, using the history output displayed earlier in this section, the command !vi would re-execute the vi ~/.bashrc command.

Tip

If you want to re-display a previous command and edit it before re-executing it, you can use the history mechanism's :p modifier to simply print the command without executing it. You can then type Ctrl+P to re-display that command, edit it however you wish, and then press Return to execute the modified command. ■

If you've already executed several similar commands, you can narrow down the list of those shown by the history command by displaying only commands that contain a certain substring. For example, the command history | grep vi uses a pipe and the grep command to display only lines of output from the history command that contain the string vi. (See the section, "Pipes and Input and Output Re-direction" later in this chapter for more information about connecting different commands in this way.)

The bash shell's command-line history mechanism is extremely powerful, and this discussion only scratches the surface of the myriad ways that you can save yourself typing by recalling and updating previously executed commands. For all of the gory details on the shell's command-line history mechanism, use the info bash command to display the current online help for the bash command.

Using Command and Filename Completion

As you've seen throughout this chapter, the command line provides a very powerful, flexible mechanism for executing commands, but one of the goals of all UNIX and Linux developers seems to have been to allow users to type as few characters as possible in order to execute commands.

This has given us cryptic commands like `ls` and `pwd`, but has probably saved wear and tear on thousands of keyboards over the years.

This same "type as little as possible" philosophy extends to the shell in a variety of ways. One of the most useful is the use of the Tab key to help the shell match and display commands and filenames. Pressing the Tab key while typing the name of a command will cause the shell to expand the name of that command as uniquely as possible. For example, because I use the Emacs text editor for almost all activities related to text files (see Chapter 12, "Working with Text Files," for a discussion of my love affair with Emacs), I type commands like `emacs this_is_the_name_ of_a_file.txt` a few hundred times a day. In true Linux fashion, I can save myself a few characters of typing by typing **ema** on the command line and then pressing the Tab key. This displays the first matching command, which happens to be `emacs`, and I can then press a space and enter the name of the file that I want to edit.

But wait, there's more! The Tab key will also match and insert the names of filenames. For example, if I were indeed trying to edit a file called *this_is_the_name_of_a_file.txt*, I could type the first few characters of its name and press the Tab key to (hopefully) match and insert the complete filename so that all I'd have to do is press Return to begin editing the file. This is a more common use of the Tab key than completing the names of commands because, as we've seen throughout this chapter, the names of Linux commands tend to be short. On the other hand, they are cryptic, so if you don't remember the exact spelling of the command that you want to execute, the Tab key can often help you figure it out.

Pressing the Tab key matches as much of the name of a command or file as it can. If multiple commands or filenames match what you've typed before you press the Tab key, pressing Tab will have no effect because the shell can't tell which of the possible commands or filenames you mean. In this case, you can press the Tab key twice (quickly) to cause the shell to list all of the available matches. You can then type the additional few characters that are required to uniquely identify the command or filename that you're actually interested in.

Using Wildcards

Another example of the "type as little as possible" philosophy is the ability of the shell to identify groups of files whose names match certain patterns. The characters used to define those patterns are known as *wildcards* because they can match any single or multiple group of characters. The shell supports four primary types of wildcards:

- ? (question mark): Matches any single character
- * (asterisk): Matches any group of zero or more characters
- {string1, string2} (curly braces): Matches either string1 or string2
- [char1,char2,...] (square brackets): Matches any character or range of characters inside the square brackets

These wildcards can be extremely handy when working with directories containing multiple files with similar names. Consider the following directory containing several audio files in different formats:

```
$ ls
d1t01.flac   d1t04.flac   d1t07.flac   d1t10.flac   d2t02.flac
d1t01.mp3    d1t04.mp3    d1t07.mp3    d1t10.mp3    d2t02.mp3
d1t01.wav    d1t04.wav    d1t07.wav    d1t10.wav    d2t02.wav
d1t02.flac   d1t05.flac   d1t08.flac   d1t11.flac   d2t03.flac
d1t02.mp3    d1t05.mp3    d1t08.mp3    d1t11.mp3    d2t03.mp3
d1t02.wav    d1t05.wav    d1t08.wav    d1t11.wav    d2t03.wav
d1t03.flac   d1t06.flac   d1t09.flac   d2t01.flac   Horslips info.txt
d1t03.mp3    d1t06.mp3    d1t09.mp3    d2t01.mp3    playlist.m3u
d1t03.wav    d1t06.wav    d1t09.wav    d2t01.wav
```

You'll note that these filenames follow a certain convention, which in this case is disk <number> track <number>.format. To list just the MP3 files in this directory that are the first track on a given disk, you could type the following:

```
$ ls d?t01.mp3
d1t01.mp3   d2t01.mp3
```

This uses the question mark to represent the disk number, which is a single digit in my sample filenames.

Similarly, to list all of the MP3 files in this directory, you could use the asterisk to represent any matching filename with the .mp3 file extension, as in the following example:

```
$ ls *.mp3
d1t01.mp3   d1t04.mp3   d1t07.mp3   d1t10.mp3   d2t02.mp3
d1t02.mp3   d1t05.mp3   d1t08.mp3   d1t11.mp3   d2t03.mp3
d1t03.mp3   d1t06.mp3   d1t09.mp3   d2t01.mp3
```

Assume that you want to list just the files with extensions that are either flac or wav. You could do this using the curly brace wildcard in the following command:

```
$ ls *.{flac,wav}
d1t01.flac   d1t04.flac   d1t07.flac   d1t10.flac   d2t02.flac
d1t01.wav    d1t04.wav    d1t07.wav    d1t10.wav    d2t02.wav
d1t02.flac   d1t05.flac   d1t08.flac   d1t11.flac   d2t03.flac
d1t02.wav    d1t05.wav    d1t08.wav    d1t11.wav    d2t03.wav
d1t03.flac   d1t06.flac   d1t09.flac   d2t01.flac
d1t03.wav    d1t06.wav    d1t09.wav    d2t01.wav
```

Finally, suppose that you want to list all of the seventh and eighth songs in MP3 format from the first disk in this directory. You could do this using the square bracket wildcard, as in the following example:

```
$ ls d1t0[78].mp3
d1t07.mp3   d1t08.mp3
```

You can combine any of these wildcards to identify increasingly specific sets of files. For example, the following would identify just the seventh and eighth songs from the first disk that are in flac and wav format:

```
$ ls d1t0[78].{flac,wav}
d1t07.flac   d1t07.wav   d1t08.flac   d1t08.wav
```

The bash shell provides a very powerful wildcard mechanism. Wildcards such as these are especially useful when you want to move, copy, or delete specific groups of files.

Tip

If you're familiar with wildcards on other types of systems, be careful: Linux wildcards may not work exactly the same way. For example, on some systems, you can type something like ren *.txt *.foo to rename groups of files with the .txt extension to files with the same base filename but with the .foo extension. This will not work on a Linux system because wildcards are expended before the command is executed, and the *.foo portion of the command line wouldn't match anything because no files with that extension currently exist. ∎

Pipes and Input and Output Re-Direction

As discussed in Chapter 1, "The Ubuntu Linux Project," a core element of the basic philosophy of UNIX, and therefore Linux, is that utilities should do one thing and do it well. This obviates the need for a lot of duplicate code by enabling one command to process the output produced by another command. For example, you might want to find the number of files in a directory by listing the files in a directory, and then counting the number of outlines. One easy way to do this is to write the output of the ls command to a temporary file, and then count the number of lines in that temporary file using the Linux wc -l command. Linux makes it easy to write the output of a command to a file by using what is called *output re-direction*, which is represented on the command line by the greater-than symbol (>). As an example, the following command writes the output of the ls command to the temporary file /tmp/my_dir_list.txt:

```
$ ls > /tmp/my_dir_list.txt
```

I could then count the number of lines in that file using the wc -l command, as in the following example:

```
$ wc -l /tmp/my_dir_list.txt
8
```

There are apparently eight files in my current directory. However, using a temporary file requires some extra typing and also requires that you clean up after yourself. Luckily, Linux comes to the rescue again with the notion of using a special symbol, the vertical bar, to connect the output of one command to the input of another. This symbol (|) is known as a *pipe*. You could use a pipe to avoid the temporary file and get the same results by typing a command such as the following:

```
$ ls | wc -l
8
```

If you find yourself performing many command-line operations, you will find both the output re-direction and pipe concepts to be very convenient. Re-directing output is an easy way of keeping track of the contents of files and directories, recording system information, and so on.

An even more interesting use of output re-direction is its ability to append some amount of information to an existing file. In the previous example, using a single greater-than symbol creates a file if it doesn't exist, but overwrites the contents of that file if it already exists. You may want to append to an existing file rather than completely overwrite it, which you can easily do by using two greater-than signs rather than a single one, as in the following example:

```
$ ls > /tmp/my_dir_list.txt
$ ls >> /tmp/my_dir_list.txt
$ wc -l /tmp/my_dir_list.txt
16
```

As you can see, the temporary file now contains twice as many lines, which is what you'd expect because you wrote the same eight lines to it twice.

The bash shell also supports input re-direction, which is the ability to read data from a file and use that file as input to another command. For complete information on input re-direction and re-direction in general, see the online help for the bash shell. You'll find that you use output re-direction and pipes much more often than input re-direction, but you never know....

Introducing Job Control

Throughout this chapter, you've always executed commands at the shell prompt and then waited for them to finish. That's fine for commands that are relatively quick, but what about commands that run for a long time? The bash shell provides a nice solution for this sort of thing by enabling you to start commands but run them in what is known as the *background*. This enables you to type a command and indicate that it should run in the background, and that command will continue to execute even though the shell prompt is re-displayed in your current shell window. For example, suppose that you want to use the Emacs text editor to edit the file myfile.txt, but also want to be able to use your current xterm or GNOME Terminal window while Emacs is running in its own window on the screen. To start a command in the background, you simply follow its name with an ampersand (&), as in the following example:

```
$ emacs myfile.txt &
[1] 7539
```

Starting a command in the background is known in Linux-speak as starting a *background job* and causes the shell to display two bits of information:

- The job number (inside square brackets)
- The process ID of the process that was started to run your command

The job number is useful because it is possible to run multiple commands in the background at the same time. The job number therefore provides a unique way of identifying any particular background command. The *job number* is an identifier for that background job within the context of your current shell. The *process identifier* is a unique identifier for that process in terms of your entire Ubuntu system.

Tip

If you forget the ampersand while trying to start a command in the background, you can always suspend the command using the Ctrl-z key combination, and the using the bg (background) command to start it in the background. ■

Why care about identifying these processes? Primarily so that you can either terminate them or bring them to the foreground if something goes wrong. For example, suppose that you accidentally started a command in the background, but that command actually requires interactive input. To bring a background command back to the foreground (meaning that it is interactively running in the current shell), you can simply refer to it by using a percent symbol and its job number, as in the following example:

```
$ %1
```

This would bring the emacs command back to the foreground so that anything you type in the shell is actively sent to the command. Suppose, however, that you've lost your Emacs window on the screen and simply want to terminate the background job manually. You can do this by using the Linux kill command, providing the job number to identify the job that you want to terminate, as in the following example:

```
$ kill %1
```

Knowing not only the job number for a background process but its system-wide process identifier enables you to use the kill command to terminate a process from another shell. Because job numbers are unique to a specific shell, you can use the kill command to terminate a process-by-process ID from any shell or terminal session, as in the following example:

```
$ kill 7539
```

Being able to execute long-running commands in the background is very important in today's multi-windowed graphical environments because you usually want to be able to continue to use your current shell while the long-running command continues on its merry way.

As always, job control is much more flexible and powerful than the introduction given here describes. For complete information on job control, use the info command to see the online reference information for the bash shell.

Exploring the Bash Configuration File

When you start a bash shell on your Ubuntu system, it reads a certain amount of configuration information from various text files on your system. In the order they're read, these configuration files are the following:

- `/etc/profile` (login shells only)
- `/etc/bash.bashrc` (all bash shells)
- `~/.bash_profile` (login shells only)
- `~/.bashrc` (all bash shells)

Note

The ~ symbol is a bash shortcut for referring to any user's home directory. ~/.bashrc is the file .bashrc in my home directory; ~juser/.bashrc is a reference to the user called *juser*'s home directory. ■

The first two of these are shell initialization files that are read and incorporated when any user logs in on the system (`/etc/profile`) or starts a bash shell (`/etc/bash.bashrc`). The second two are personal configuration files that are stored in each user's home directory. As with the system-wide configuration files, the `~/.bash_profile` file is read by the user's login shell, while the `~/.bashrc` file is read by any shell that the user creates, such as in an xterm or GNOME Terminal window. Of these, the `.bashrc` file is most important for two reasons:

- The default `~/.bash_profile` on Ubuntu systems reads it even in the context of a login shell.
- Starting a bash shell is a much more common operation than logging in. A user only logs in once, although he or she may subsequently create many different xterm or GNOME Terminal windows.

The `.bashrc` file enables each user to customize various aspects of the bash shell, such as where it looks for commands, the prompt that it displays, the number of commands that it remembers in your command-line history, and many more things. The `.bashrc` file enables you to create your own shortcuts to specific Linux commands if you still feel that you're having to type too many characters and even enables you to create your custom shell commands. Lines in any bash configuration file (or shell script, for that matter) that begin with the hash mark (#) are considered to be comments and are not interpreted.

Tip

All Linux shells provide a command language and constructs for looping and support conditional expressions to make it easy to write shell scripts. Explaining shell programming is outside the scope of this book, but there are many excellent books and web sites on that topic. Two of my favorite web sites for this sort of information are the Linux Shell Scripting Tutorial at www.freeos.com/guides/lsst/ and the Linux Documentation project's *Advanced Shell Scripting Guide* at www.tldp.org/LDP/abs/html. ■

When a user account is created on your Ubuntu system, the default .bashrc and .bash_profile files are created by copying them from the templates with the same names that are stored in the directory /etc/skel. The following is the beginning of the default .bashrc file used for all Ubuntu user accounts:

```
# ~/.bashrc: executed by bash(1) for non-login shells.
#
# If not running interactively, don't do anything
[ -z "$PS1" ] && return
[much more text deleted]
```

The last statement in this example stops shells from reading the default .bashrc file if they are not running in interactive mode. It does this by using the [command to test the value of the PS1 environment variable, which defines the user's prompt, and returning to the parent shell if this variable is not set (which it would not be in the context of a shell used to run a shell script).

What's an *environment variable*? I'm glad you asked.

Using Environment Variables

Environment variables are variables that are defined in the context of a shell and that are read and used by applications on your system, including the shell itself. One of the most commonly used environment variables is the PATH environment variable, which contains a colon-separated list of directories that the shell searches (in order) to try to find commands. You can examine the environment variables that are defined in a shell using any of three mechanisms:

- Use the shell's built-in set command to display all shell variables that are currently defined.
- Use the printenv command to display a list of selected (or all) environment variables that are currently defined.
- Use the shell's built-in echo command to display the value of a specific environment variable.

Both the set and printenv commands produce large amounts of output, so the echo command is most commonly used to display the value of a single environment variable, as in the following example:

```
$ echo $PATH
/home/wvh/bin:/usr/local/Adobe/Acrobat7.0/bin:\
/usr/local/gcc_svn/bin:/home/wvh/BitTorrent/src/BitTorrent:\
/home/wvh/cxoffice/bin:/usr/lib/mit/bin:/usr/lib/mit/sbin:\
/usr/NX/bin:/usr/local/sbin:/usr/local/bin:/usr/sbin:/usr/bin:\
/sbin:/bin:/usr/bin/X11:/usr/games:
```

Note

The value of the PATH environment variable is a single string containing colon-separated directories. This example has been split across multiple lines for formatting purposes. ■

When using the echo command to display the value of an environment variable, you must refer to the environment variable by preceding its name with a dollar sign ($). This tells the shell to echo the value of a variable rather than simply echoing a string, which is what would happen if you simply typed the following:

```
$ echo PATH
PATH
```

This example of the PATH environment variable has been heavily customized. The default setting for the PATH environment variable on Ubuntu systems is actually the following:

```
/usr/local/sbin:/usr/local/bin:/usr/sbin:/usr/bin:/sbin:/bin:\
/usr/bin/X11:/usr/games
```

To add a directory to the list of directories that are searched for commands, you can execute something like the following from a shell prompt:

```
$ export PATH=/usr/wvh/bin:$PATH
```

This command sets the environment variable and exports it to the general shell environment. This example adds my personal bin directory as the first element of my PATH, so that the shell looks there first for any commands that I try to execute. To make this change permanent, I would add this line to the end of my ~/.bashrc file.

The echo command is useful for displaying the value of a single environment variable. You can also use the printenv command to do the same thing, as in the following example:

```
$ printenv PATH
/home/wvh/bin:/usr/local/Adobe/Acrobat7.0/bin:\
/usr/local/gcc_svn/bin:/home/wvh/BitTorrent/src/BitTorrent:\
/home/wvh/cxoffice/bin:/usr/lib/mit/bin:/usr/lib/mit/sbin:\
/usr/NX/bin:/usr/local/sbin:/usr/local/bin:/usr/sbin:/usr/bin:\
/sbin:/bin:/usr/bin/X11:/usr/games:
```

Because the printenv command is designed to display environment variables, you do not need to precede the name of the environment variable with a dollar sign.

The printenv and set commands are more commonly used to display the values of all environment variables that are currently defined. You can then search for a certain substring by piping their output to the grep command, as in the following example:

```
$ printenv | grep HIST
HISTCONTROL=ignoreboth
HISTFILE=/home/wvh/.bash_history
HISTFILESIZE=1000
HISTSIZE=1000
```

This sample command shows me the name and value of all environment variables that contain the string *HIST*, which are environment variables related to the shell's command-line history mechanism (discussed earlier in this chapter).

Defining and Using Aliases

Another interesting feature of the bash shell is its ability to enable you to define aliases for various commands. An *alias* is a string that the shell recognizes and expands into some other command. Some of the most common aliases used on Linux systems are those for the cp and rm commands that automatically execute those commands with their interactive option, which prevents you from accidentally overwriting or deleting files that you didn't want to overwrite or delete by prompting you to confirm each operation. These aliases are defined in the following way at the bash command line (or, permanently, in your ~/.bashrc file):

```
$ alias cp="cp -i"
$ alias rm="rm -i"
```

After defining these aliases, the shell automatically replaces either the cp or rm command with the command that it has been aliased to.

To simplify defining aliases (and to minimize the number of changes that you make to your ~/.bashrc file), the default ~/.bashrc file used on Ubuntu systems contains the following entries, which are initially commented out:

```
#if [ -f ~/.bash_aliases ]; then
#    . ~/.bash_aliases
#fi
```

If uncommented by removing the leading hash marks, this clause enables you to define all of your aliases in a file called ~/.bash_aliases, which would be located in your home directory.

Summary

This chapter introduced you to the Linux command line, the terminology used when discussing Linux command-line interpreters, and the basic capabilities of the bash shell, the command-line interpreter that is used by default on Ubuntu Linux systems. It discussed how to access a shell on your Ubuntu system and some of the more common commands that most people execute within a command-line environment. It concluded with an explanation of the configuration files used by the bash shell and some of the more common items that they contain.

Hand-in-hand with the idea of working from a command line is the notion of working with text files, which is discussed in the next chapter. Although many word processors now store their files in special binary formats, text files are alive and well on the Internet and on Linux systems. Documents written using markup languages such as HTML, SGML, and XML are all text files that are easily created and edited in a standard text editor. Most Linux servers, including those discussed in the last few chapters of this book, are configured by setting or changing operational parameters that are stored in text-format configuration files. For these reasons and many more, learning how to use a text editor is a fundamental Linux skill.

Working with Text Files

IN THIS CHAPTER

Using popular editors for UNIX-like systems

Using vi

Using Emacs

Using the graphical gedit editor

Using other editors for Linux systems

Most of us are used to working with files in various application-specific formats, often identified by their file extension or a special icon on our graphical desktops. We're all familiar with the doc files produced by graphical word processors such as Microsoft Word, xls files produced by spreadsheets such as Excel, fm files produced by FrameMaker, ppt files produced by PowerPoint, and so on. All of these files contain application data in a specific, often binary, format that lets the associated application make the best possible use of these files, but which often makes them hard to use with any application other than the one that created them.

At the other end of the spectrum from these application-specific files is the lowest-common-denominator file format known as *text files* or, to be a bit more specific, *ASCII text files*. The contents of these files consist of only the standard letters, numbers, punctuation, and symbols that you find on a computer keyboard. The nice thing about these types of files is that they are easy to read, easy to process, and easy to work with in general.

Regardless of what you use your Ubuntu Linux system for, you will almost certainly end up editing a text file one of these days. If you write code, it is almost certainly in standard text files because they provide a lowest-common-denominator format that can be processed by any compiler. If you're a writer, you may want to use text files because you can work with them on any system, with any editor or word processor — so you can work on them just as easily on your Ubuntu Linux system as you can on your Mac OS X system.

An even more critical point is that most system-level Linux utilities use one or more files to hold their configuration and initialization information. Even though most Linux utilities can also be configured using a graphical interface, editing a text file is often faster and simpler than locating and starting the right graphical tool, finding the correct tab or panel, and so on.

This chapter begins by briefly describing the history of editors on UNIX systems and the religious war over the "right" approach to editing text that still rages on in Linux/UNIX circles today. It then provides detailed information about using vi and Emacs, the two primary editors used on Linux systems. The chapter concludes by discussing gedit, a graphical text editor provided in the GNOME environment that walks the line between pure text and graphical editing, and provides an overview of other popular text editors for Linux systems, just in case you're not satisfied with the usual suspects.

Introduction to Linux Text Editors

The first versions of UNIX for the PDP-11 that were distributed by Bell Telephone Laboratories included a small, line-oriented text editor called *ed*, which was written by Ken Thompson (who is still out there, most recently working on the Go programming language at Google). Various people enhanced ed, most notably George Coulouris at Queen Mary College (QMC) in the United Kingdom, who added interactive support for editing single lines as part of his editor for mortals (em) editor, which he brought with him to the University of California at Berkeley (UCB) in 1976. At the same time, Ken Thompson had gone to UCB to teach for a year or so, and while there had begun working with Bill Joy and Chuck Haley on the UNIX enhancements that would eventually make up the original Berkeley Standard Distribution (BSD).

Haley and Joy hacked em for a while, revising it into en and then a bunch of other names, working their way through the alphabet until they arrived at ex, which was still line-oriented. In 1976, however, Joy created vi (which stands for "visual"), a screen-oriented editor that shared the ex command set, thanks to motivation provided by several ADM-3A terminals that were donated to UCB. The flexibility provided by vi in terms of using the entire screen, thanks to the /etc/ termcap (terminal capabilities) file, was a huge step in divorcing detailed knowledge about the hardware from an editor. Editing under UNIX has never been the same.

Around the same time, on the other side of the country, a bunch of Lisp and ITS/TOPS-20/ TWENEX hackers at the MIT Artificial Intelligence (AI) Lab were enhancing an aging line editor for their PDP-10 systems known as *Text Editor and Corrector* (TECO). With some inspiration from graphical editing work being done at Stanford's AI Lab, Richard Stallman (later of GNU and FSF fame) and Guy Steele collected and developed a version of TECO to which users could add their own commands. They also created and aggregated a set of TECO commands into a single package that provided support for screen-oriented editing using TECO. The TECO commands consisted of a set of macros (sequences of commands that execute together), so the set of macros became known as *Editing MACroS*, or more simply, *EMACS*.

This was all well and good if you happened to be using a DEC PDP-10, and Emacs would be an interesting footnote were it not for the efforts of Dave Conroy, who wrote a version of Emacs called *MicroEmacs* that ran on just about anything, and James Gosling (later of Java fame), who wrote a version of Emacs for UNIX systems in 1981. Unlike the Emacs macros that were their inspiration, these were actual compiled programs that ran directly on specific systems as compiled binaries. Gosling's version of Emacs, cleverly named *Gosling Emacs* or simply *gosmacs*, served as the original foundation for an open source version of Emacs for UNIX. Richard Stallman began writing GNU Emacs in 1984. For legal reasons, Stallman eventually replaced all of the Gosling Emacs code in GNU Emacs and replaced Gosling's MockLisp Emacs configuration language with a full-blown internal Lisp interpreter to parse configuration files and other startup data.

Note

Over the years, several alternative expansions of the EMACS acronym have been offered to replace the original "Editing MACroS." Some of my favorites are "Escape Meta Alt Control Shift," referring to the heavy dependence of Emacs on the Ctrl and Esc keys in its command set, and "Eight Megabytes And Constantly Swapping," which was funnier when 8 MB was a lot of memory for a computer, and referred to its large memory requirements (for the time). I think the garage door opener I use today has more than 8 MB of memory. ∎

Modal versus Modeless Editors

As mentioned earlier in this chapter, among Linux and UNIX users, there is no more entertaining or more long-running flame war than the debate over which editor is better — vi or Emacs. If all of the characters expended on this topic alone had been given instead to random simian typists, they would have, indeed, produced the works of Shakespeare. As a new Ubuntu fan, you'll eventually hear something about this, so this sidebar gives you a little background.

The basic difference between how you use vi and how you use Emacs boils down to the following: Emacs is what is known as a *modeless editor*, which means that any standard characters that you type are always inserted into whatever you're editing (which is therefore known as *insert mode*), whereas vi is what is known as a *modal editor* in which Insert mode is just one available mode. Both Emacs and vi are extremely configurable, although vi doesn't provide an internal implementation of Lisp to "simplify" creating your own functions. On the other hand, because vi doesn't provide an internal implementation of Lisp, it is much smaller and faster to execute than Emacs. Emacs is more powerful because it includes a mail client, newsgroup reader, and even a few games. On the other hand, you may just be looking for a text editor, not a one-stop-shopping computing environment.

People often complain that vi and Emacs are difficult for new users to learn. In my experience, it just depends where you want new users to get confused. In Emacs, the chances of figuring out that you hold down the Ctrl key and then press a particular two-key combination to save your file and exit are pretty small. However, vi rarely does anything useful until you enter Insert mode, and trying to get out of Insert mode and figuring out how to save your file has brought many a Linux/UNIX novice to tears.

Here's my take: I have used versions of Emacs since gosmacs, and I've written this book in Emacs. My fingers work that way. However, I use vi regularly when I'm performing most system tasks and especially when I'm sitting down at someone else's machine for the first time. Why? Because vi starts more quickly than Emacs, and because Emacs fans often extensively customize their Emacs key bindings. The key sequence that justifies a paragraph on my system might post a random snapshot to the alt.binaries newsgroup if I type it on your system. Your mileage may vary.

Using vi

Because the actual source code for the "real" version of vi is owned by AT&T, vi fans have completely rewritten vi from the ground up. Three popular vi clones are available today: elvis, nvi (new vi), and vim (vi improved). The version of vi used on most Linux systems is vim, but nvi is quite popular and is the default version of vi used on many open source BSD-like systems such as OpenBSD, FreeBSD, and so on. Elvis is also a fine clone of vi, supporting multi-file and multi-window editing, as well as X11 support. However, the discussion of vi in this book focuses on vim because that's what you get by default with an Ubuntu installation. Therefore, I'll generally refer to *vim* as *vi* throughout this section because it is indeed compatible with vi, and the package that installs vim on your Ubuntu system also installs an alias for vim called vi — and vim is, after all, just vi, *improved*. In any sections that are specific to vim and do not apply to vi in general, I'll refer to vim explicitly.

Tip

The default version of vim that is installed on Ubuntu systems is a small package called vim-tiny. After all, not everyone is a vi/vim fan! However, if you want to explore the full power of vim and work on your basic UNIX/Linux chops, you should install the vim package, which will also install another package called vim-runtime. Together, these packages provide many enhancements to vim. For example, the vim-runtime package includes an application called vimtutor, which starts vim with a copy of a tutorial on using vim. If you want to actually walk through many examples of using vi and get a feel for its command set, vimtutor is an excellent starting point. ∎

As discussed in the previous section, vi is a modal editor (which, if you skipped the previous section, means that the same keys do different things depending on the mode that you're in). The primary vi modes are as follows:

- **Normal:** vi is in Normal mode when you first start vi. In this mode you can enter all of the standard cursor movement and text deletion commands, but not enter text into the file that you are editing. This is the primary source of confusion for new vi users because most people expect to start an editor and begin editing text.

- **Insert:** In this mode, typing the standard alphanumeric and symbol keys on your keyboard enters those characters into the file that you are editing. Insert mode is the mode that most people expect to be in when you start a text editor. The fact that once in Insert mode you need to press a special key (the Esc key) to return to Command mode is the second primary source of confusion for new vi users who find themselves trapped in insert mode.

- **Command-Line:** In this mode, the cursor is positioned at the bottom line of your vi window, and you can enter a single line that is interpreted as a vi command, search request, or a request to invoke an external command on a portion of the file that you are editing (often referred to as a *filter* command).

The *modal editor* concept may initially seem confusing, but it makes vi a fast, extremely powerful editor. Once you learn how to get from one mode to another and work with vi for a while, you will find it to be an excellent editor. The fact that some version of vi is found on every UNIX-like system makes it well worth your time to learn.

One of the coolest features of vi is the ability to preface most vi commands with a numeric argument, movement, or scoping command, which executes that single command the specified number of times or the number of times specified by the movement command that you've specified, or applies a command to a specified portion of your file. I'll provide examples of this throughout the rest of this section, as well as some of my favorite vi tips and tricks that I've accumulated over the years.

Note

All of the examples in the vi portions of this chapter show vi in an xterm window rather than the GNOME Terminal to emphasize that vi is a command-line application that does not provide or use menus by default. For information on graphical versions of vi that do provide and use menus, see "Graphical Versions of vi" later in this chapter. ■

Starting and Exiting vi

The core tasks for any application are starting it and getting out of it. As mentioned previously, getting out of vi the first time can be tricky because of its modal nature, but after that, it becomes second nature.

Because vi is a command-line application, you usually start it by simply typing the vi command in a GNOME Terminal or xterm window. You can optionally provide the name of the file that you want to edit on the command line, and vi will automatically open and display that file for you. Figure 12-1 shows vi editing the text of this chapter in an xterm window.

FIGURE 12-1

A GNOME Terminal window showing the vi editor

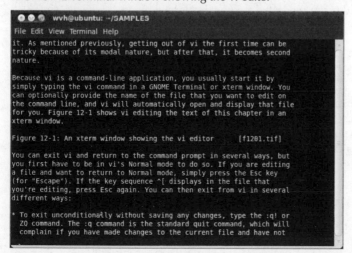

431

You can exit vi and return to the command prompt in several ways, but you first have to be in vi's Normal mode to do so. If you are editing a file and want to return to Normal mode, simply press the Esc key (for "Escape"). If the key sequence ^[displays in the file that you're editing, press Esc again. You can then exit from vi in several different ways:

- To exit unconditionally without saving any changes, type the :q! or ZQ command. The :q command is the standard quit commands, which will complain if you have made changes to the current file and have not saved them. The :q! command essentially means "Yes, I really want to quit, and I know what I'm doing."

- To save any changes that you've made to the current file and exit, type the :x or :wq command. The :x command is specific to vim, while the :wq command is the traditional vi exit mechanism (it stands for "write and then quit"). You can also write any changes to the current file and exit by typing the ZZ command (no colon required).

- To specify the name of the file that you want to save your changes to, type the :w filename command, where *filename* is the name of the file that you want to create. If the file already exists, you will have to use the :w! *filename* command, which, loosely translated, means "Yes, I really want to write this file, and I know what I'm doing."

Inserting Text in vi

Once you've started vi, you'll certainly want to start creating the program, letter, or other document that you're working on. As mentioned in the previous section, starting vi leaves you in Normal mode, where you can move the cursor and enter commands, but not actually enter text.

To begin inserting text, type the **i** command. This causes vi to enter Insert mode. Any characters that you type will be inserted into the file that you are editing until you exit from Insert mode. As a reminder, the easiest way to exit from Insert mode is by pressing the Esc key (Escape) on your keyboard. It's often useful to press the Escape key if you're not sure what mode you're in — if it doesn't beep, you've just exited Insert mode and are now in Normal mode. If it beeps, you're already (and still are) in Normal mode.

Note

All commands in vi and its clones are case-sensitive. ■

Using the **i** command begins inserting text at the current cursor position, which can be awkward. If you want to begin adding text immediately after the current cursor position, use the **a** command. To begin appending text after the end of the current line, use the **A** command. The **a** and **A** commands are just specialized commands for entering Insert mode at a specific point — to exit Insert mode after using these commands, press the Esc key.

Moving Around in vi

The vi editor is knee-deep in cursor movement commands. The most common are as follows:

- **h or left-arrow:** Move the cursor backward one character in the current line.

- **l or right-arrow:** Move the cursor forward one character in the current line.

- **j or down-arrow:** Move the cursor down one line, maintaining the current column position in the new line when possible.

- **k or up-arrow:** Move the cursor up one line, maintaining the current column position in the new line when possible.

Cursor movement commands such as h, j, k, and l may initially seem pretty strange or at least counterintuitive, but remember that vi was originally designed to be used on terminals, some of which didn't have the arrow keys. Ask your grandfather.

Note
When in Insert mode, the old-time vi cursor movement commands (h, j, k, and l) insert those letters rather than moving the cursor. (vi is a modal editor, remember?) However, the arrow cursor movement keys "do the right thing" when you're in Insert mode — they simply move the cursor but leave you in Insert mode. ■

As mentioned previously, you can repeat these simple cursor movement commands a specific number of times by prefacing them with a numeric argument. For example, you can move the cursor forward five letters by typing **5l**, up five lines by typing **5k**, and so on. This is handy, but requires that you count how far you want to move the cursor first. That's somewhat tedious when you really want to do things like move to the next word, move to the previous word, or (more commonly) go to some logical place in the current text. To simplify things, vi provides handy cursor movement commands like the following:

- **b:** Move backward one word.

- **w:** Move forward one word.

- **^:** Move to the beginning of the current line.

- **$:** Move to the end of the current line.

- **(:** Move to the beginning of the current sentence.

- **):** Move to the end of the current sentence.

- **{:** Move to the beginning of the current paragraph.

- **}:** Move to the end of the current paragraph.

- **1G:** Go to the first line in the current file.

- **0G:** Go to the last line of the current file. Just pressing **G** in vim does the same thing, but that may not work in all versions of vi.

The last two commands are actually examples of the standard vi commands to go to a specific line, and they highlight how nicely vi commands work with numeric arguments. For example, you could move to the 14th line in your file by typing the **14G** command. Similarly, you could move to the end of the third paragraph from your current position by typing the **3}** command.

In addition to these cursor movement commands, vi also provides several commands to enable you to scroll the screen without moving the current cursor position (unless you want to, of course). These screen movement commands are as follows:

- **Ctrl+d:** (Hold down the Ctrl key and press the letter *d*.) Scroll down one screen in the current file.
- **Ctrl+e:** (Hold down the Ctrl key and press the letter *e*.) Scroll down one line in the current file.
- **Ctrl+u:** (Hold down the Ctrl key and press the letter *u*.) Scroll up one screen in the current file.
- **Ctrl+y:** (Hold down the Ctrl key and press the letter *y*.) Scroll up one line in the current file.

The Ctrl+d and Ctrl+u commands scroll the screen but leave the cursor at the same position on the screen (although the text underneath the cursor has changed). The Ctrl+e and Ctrl+y commands keep the cursor at the same position in your text until that line scrolls off the screen, at which point the current position is preserved, but the text below it has changed.

Deleting and Changing Text in vi

As with most operations, you can delete text in vi with several different commands. To delete the character at the current cursor position, press the letter **x**. You can, of course, delete a specific number of characters by prefacing the x command with a numeric argument. For example, typing **14x** deletes 14 characters from the current character position.

Although the x command is handy when deleting a few characters, most people think of deletion in terms like "delete the current word," "delete everything to the end of the current line," or "delete the rest of the current paragraph." To perform these sorts of actions, you use the d command, followed by a cursor movement command that delimits the end of the area that should be affected by the delete operation. For example, the command dw deletes all of the text from the current cursor position to the end of the current word, d$ deletes everything from the current cursor position to the end of the current line, and d} deletes everything from the current cursor position to the end of the current paragraph. If you remember, the second character of each of these commands is one of the cursor movement commands described in the previous section.

When you're editing a file, it is common to delete some text and then immediately replace it with new text. You could do that with a combination of one of the delete commands, followed by an insert or append command. To save typing, vi provides the c (change) command to do both of these things (deleting a delimited portion of your text and entering Insert mode) at the same time. For example, you could use the cw command to change the text from the current cursor position to the end of the current word, the c$ command to change the text from the current cursor position to the end of the current line, and so on. When using vi's change command, you are placed in Insert mode, so you must use the Esc key to return to Normal mode when you're done entering text.

Cutting, Copying, and Pasting in vi

It's easy enough to cut-and-paste text using a graphical text editor because a mouse-aware text editor enables you to copy and cut text with a combination of the mouse and special keyboard commands. You can, of course, do the same thing in vi, but it requires a bit more knowledge of vi internals and visualization.

Cutting text is done using the delete command (explained in the previous section), which actually just puts the text in an internal storage area (known as a *buffer*) from which you can subsequently paste it back in. However, the vi editor also provides the y (yank) command to copy a specified region to a buffer so that you can subsequently paste it somewhere else. As with the delete command, you can delimit the area that you want to copy by following the y command with a cursor movement command. For example, y$ copies the text from the current cursor position to the end of the line into the buffer, while y} copies all of the text from the current cursor position to the end of the paragraph into the buffer. If you copy or delete anything more than a single line, the number of lines yanked into the buffer is displayed at the bottom of your vi window. Figure 12-2 shows the message displayed by vi running in an xterm window after copying the current paragraph (which is six lines long) into the buffer.

The vi editor displaying a yank status message

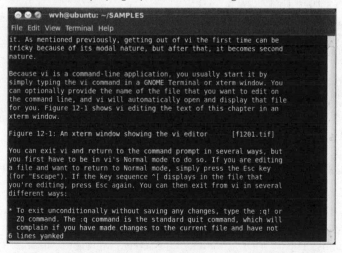

Of course, cutting or copying text isn't all that interesting unless you can paste it back in somewhere, for which vi provides the p and P commands. To paste a single line from the buffer back into your text at the current cursor position, use the p command. However, if you have copied multiple lines into the buffer, you should preface the p command with the number of lines that you want to paste back in. If you didn't happen to notice how many lines you yanked and you simply want to paste all of the text that you recently copied to the buffer, you can simply use the P command to paste it all back in at once.

Searching for and Replacing Text in vi

The vi editor provides separate commands for searching forward and backward in your file. Pressing the / command, followed by the case-sensitive sequence of characters that you want to search for, and pressing Return causes vi to search forward in the current file until (and if) it locates a matching sequence of characters. Figure 12-3 shows vi running in a GNOME Terminal window, getting ready to search for the string *Windows* in the text. If the string is found, vi adjusts the text display window and moves the cursor forward in the file to display the line of text containing the match. If no matching string is found in the text, vi displays a status message to that effect and does not move the cursor.

FIGURE 12-3

Searching for a string in vi

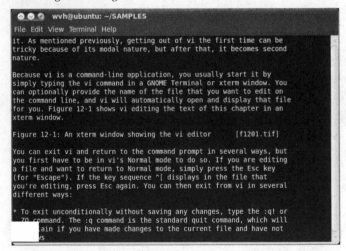

The ? command is the opposite of the / command, searching backward through the current file for a specified string. Both the / and ? commands are examples of vi's Command-Line mode, in which pressing a command positions the cursor at the bottom of the screen, waiting for subsequent information.

Once you've located a match for the characters you're looking for, you can press n to search for the next match, or N to search for the previous match.

The vi editor's Command-Line mode also provides a convenient case-sensitive text-substitution command to enable you to search for a string and either globally or conditionally replace it with another. This is the :%s/foo/bar/ command, which (in this case) would search for the next instance of *foo* and replace it with *bar*. You can follow the final / with other characters to indicate whether the replacement should automatically be done globally throughout the rest of the file (:%s/foo/bar/g), or whether vi should ask you for confirmation before performing each substitution (:%s/foo/bar/gc). Figure 12-4 shows a conditional replacement of the string *Linux* with *Ubuntu Linux*. Conditional replacements of this sort are often known as query/replace operations because they ask you for confirmation before doing each replacement.

FIGURE 12-4

A query/replace operation in vi

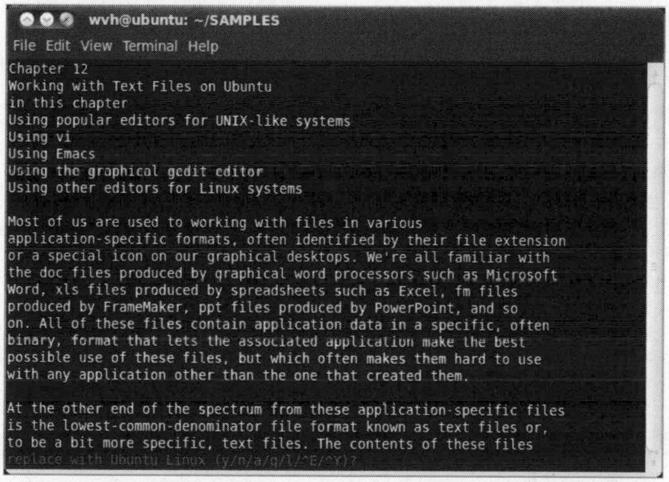

Note that the prompt at the bottom of the screen asks you to confirm (Y) or reject (N) each change, but also provides two cursor movement commands. The query/replace operation also supports the use of the Ctrl+E (scroll down one line) and Ctrl+Y (scroll up one line) commands to make it easier for you to see the context in which you're replacing the specified text.

Undoing Changes in vi

Unless you're a much better writer and programmer than I am, and therefore never make a mistake, you'll eventually find yourself making several changes to a file and then thinking, "Dang, I didn't want to do that." Luckily, vi remembers all of the commands that you executed in your current editing session and enables you to undo all of them, in order, until you get your file back to the state in which you wish you'd left it in the first place. To undo the last operation you performed in vi, use the u (undo) command. Each subsequent u command undoes one previous operation. Some complex operations, such as a global search/replace operation, are remembered (and therefore undone) as a single operation, but for the most part, you can use the u command to undo each single command until you return your file to the preferred state.

Using Multiple Windows in vi

One of the longest-running complaints about vi is that it doesn't support multiple windows. In terminal-oriented applications like vi, multiple windows are typically just views onto multiple files in the same application at the same time, with each having its own status bar. One of the oldest and choicest bits of vi folklore is that Bill Joy had apparently been working on a multi-windowed version of vi, but that the source code got lost, and thus vi never developed multiple windows until the advent of modern versions of vi, such as vim. In Joy's own words, as quoted from an interview in the August 1984 issue of *Unix Review* magazine:

> …What actually happened was that I was in the process of adding multi-windows to vi when we installed our VAX, which would have been in December of '78. We didn't have any backups and the tape drive broke. I continued to work even without being able to do backups. And then the source code got scrunched and I didn't have a complete listing. I had almost rewritten all of the display code for windows, and that was when I gave up. After that, I went back to the previous version and just documented the code, finished the manual and closed it off. If that scrunch had not happened, vi would have multiple windows, and I might have put in some programmability—but I don't know.…

Luckily, the vim folks have solved this problem by implementing several commands that enable you to split the current window, open another file in another part of your vim window, cycle between multiple files displayed in different windows, and so on. Figure 12-5 shows vim displaying two different files in separate windows within the same vim session.

FIGURE 12-5

Multiple windows in vim

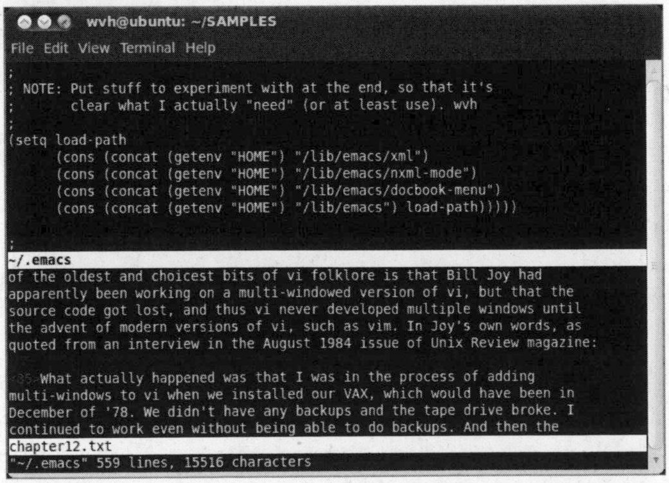

The primary command-line commands for manipulating multiple windows in vim are as follows:

- **:hide:** Close current window (works only when multiple windows are displayed).
- **:only:** Close all windows except for the current one.
- **:split** *filename*: Split window horizontally and load *filename* in the new window.
- **:sview** *filename*: Same as split, but displays *filename* in read-only mode.
- **:vsplit** *filename*: Split window vertically and load *filename* in the new window.

Tip

You can start vim in multi-window mode by using the ~o option and specifying multiple filenames on the command line, as in the following example:

```
$ vim -o file1.txt file2.txt file3.txt ■
```

Once you've created multiple windows, you can move between and manipulate them using the following commands:

- **Ctrl+W+up arrow:** Move cursor up a window.
- **Ctrl+W, Ctrl+W:** Move cursor to another window (cycle).
- **Ctrl+W_:** Maximize current window.
- **Ctrl+W=:** Make all equal size.
- **Ctrl+W+:** Increase window size by one line.

After a bit of experimentation (and training your fingers to use a few new commands), working with multiple windows in vim is just as easy as working with them in any other text editor.

Customizing vim

By default, vim reads three configuration files when you first start the editor. These are as follows:

- The system configuration file /etc/vimrc
- A per-user configuration file, located in each user's home directory and called .vimrc
- The traditional per-user configuration file used by vi, located in each user's home directory and called .exrc

It is not an error if any of these files do not exist, but together they provide a very flexible mechanism for customizing vim. Each of these files can contain any number of the following types of configuration commands:

- **autocmd:** Automatically execute specific commands based on the type of file that you are editing.

- **iab:** Define abbreviations that will be expanded into a specific sequence of characters when they are encountered as a word in the text that you are typing. This can function like the AutoCorrect feature in Microsoft Word.

- **map:** Map existing vim commands to a custom key or define your own vi commands.

- **set:** Set a vim variable to a value.

In addition to these specific commands, vim configuration files also support a rich set of conditionals that enable you to write your own functions and execute them in different contexts.

As an example of configuring or personalizing vim, my `.vimrc` file is as follows:

```
"
" wvh's .vimrc
"" Variable Settings
"" Don't use vi-compatibility mode
set nocompatible
" use the smart version of backspace
set backspace=2
" I don't like syntax highlighting
syntax off
" define the point at which lines wrap in vanilla mode
set wrapmargin=10
" always display row/column info
set ruler
" don't highlight all search terms, just find them
set nohls
" create backup files with a tilde extension
set backupext=~
set backup
"
" Abbreviations
"
" auto-correct a favorite typo
iab teh the
"
" special key mappings
"
" use F5 to reformat paragraphs
map <F5> !}fmt <CR>
"
" Specific settings for different types of files
"
" define some specific settings for when editing C files
au FileType c setlocal shiftwidth=4 softtabstop=4 expandtab
```

As you can see, lines that begin with a single double-quotation mark enable you to intersperse comments in your `.vimrc` file.

Note

As mentioned previously, the default version of vim that is installed on Ubuntu systems is a small package called `vim-tiny`. The `.vimrc` file given as an example uses several configuration settings that are only available if you have manually installed the vim package, which provides many enhancements to vim. ∎

- Unfortunately, a complete discussion of the possible contents of a `.vimrc` file would require its own book. And, not too surprisingly, several good books on vi are available that include this information.

Graphical Versions of vi

Many people, especially former users of systems such as Microsoft Windows and Mac OS X, expect applications to have a graphical user interface. This poses an interesting problem for applications like vi and Emacs that were originally designed for use with terminals back when a mouse was just a pesky rodent. To make people feel more at home with powerful tools such as vi (and to drag them, often kicking and screaming, into the Twenty-First Century), various graphical interfaces for vi have been developed over the years. Figure 12-6 shows GNOME vim, which is executed as the command gvim, and is a version of vim to which menu support has been added.

FIGURE 12-6

GNOME vim, a graphical version of vim

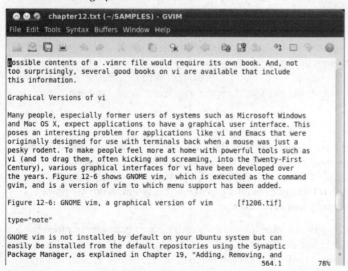

Note

GNOME vim is not installed by default on your Ubuntu system but can easily be installed from the default repositories using the Synaptic Package Manager, as explained in Chapter 19, "Adding, Removing, and Updating Software." GNOME vim is contained in the package `vim-gnome`. ∎

More Information about vi and vim

Because vi is one of the oldest text editors available for UNIX-like systems, you can find numerous sources of information about it on the Web, including many that are specific to vim. Some of my favorites are the following:

- **Vim home page:** `www.vim.org/`
- **Vi Lovers Home Page:** `www.thomer.com/vi/vi.html`
- **Introduction to Display Editing with vi (the original Bill Joy/Mark Horton paper):** `http://ex-vi.sourceforge.net/viin/paper.html`

A simple Internet search will turn up hundreds of other sites containing tips, tricks, and configuration settings for customizing your version of vim. However, remember that one of the primary advantages of using a vi-like editor is that it can be found on any Linux-like system and generally works the same way on all systems. If you customize your copy of vim to death and grow to depend on your customizations, you might as well be using Emacs.

Using Emacs

The history of Emacs was described earlier in this chapter — now, let's meet our new best friend. As I mentioned earlier, I am a long-time Emacs user and find it to be "the right editor" for me. Your mileage may vary, but no one can deny the power and flexibility of Emacs. Many of the old arguments against using Emacs, such as its memory requirements, simply don't matter anymore thanks to the generally increasing memory requirements of desktop systems and improvements in the type of hardware that most personal computer systems have today. As far as I'm concerned, the simple fact that Emacs is a modeless editor that starts up in Edit mode, enabling you to create files without having to do anything fancy, is a great argument for using Emacs.

Tip

For some unknown reason, the `emacs` package is not installed by default on Ubuntu systems. You will have to install it using any of the software update tools discussed in Chapter 19 before you can experiment and become one with Emacs. The `emacs` package is a meta-package that always depends on the latest `emacs` packages. Installing Emacs is the first thing that I do after installing any Ubuntu system. From my point of view, a Linux system without Emacs is a contradiction in terms. ∎

By default, the version of Emacs that is available for your Ubuntu system is integrated into the X Window System and therefore automatically starts up its own window, which provides both an extensive set of menus and a graphical toolbar to simplify selecting frequently used commands. Figure 12-7 shows an Emacs window, displaying a text file that represents the beginning of this chapter.

FIGURE 12-7

Emacs on an Ubuntu system

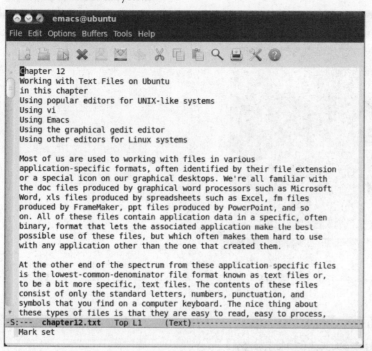

The Emacs editor can also be started in non-graphical mode, which can be handy if you simply want to do some quick editing or if you've connected to a remote machine and don't want to enable the remote system to create windows on your screen. To start Emacs in non-windowed mode, use the -nw command-line option when starting Emacs. Figure 12-8 shows Emacs editing the same file as that shown in Figure 12-7, but in the context of a GNOME Terminal window.

One of the best features of Emacs is its customizability, which extends to its graphical display. As an example, Figure 12-9 shows Emacs with the graphical customizations that I normally use, with the toolbar hidden and the scrollbar moved to the right of the Emacs window (as you can see, it's on the left in Figure 12-7).

FIGURE 12-8

Emacs in a GNOME Terminal xterm window on an Ubuntu system

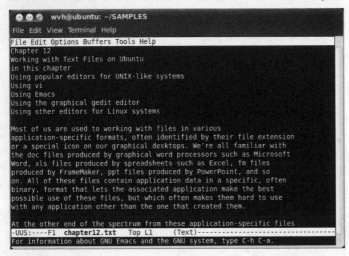

FIGURE 12-9

Emacs showing graphical customization

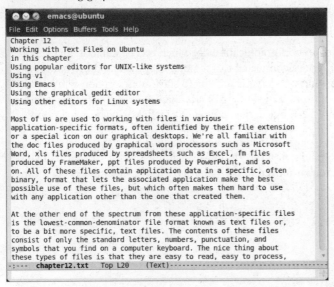

If you're a fan of graphical customization and are interested in being able to use a variety of fonts in your Emacs session, try a version of Emacs known as *XEmacs*. Figure 12-10 shows the default XEmacs startup window, which highlights the fact that XEmacs provides great support for multiple fonts, provides much more extensive toolbar and icon support, and even supports displaying graphical images within an XEmacs window.

FIGURE 12-10

The startup screen for XEmacs, the "other" Emacs

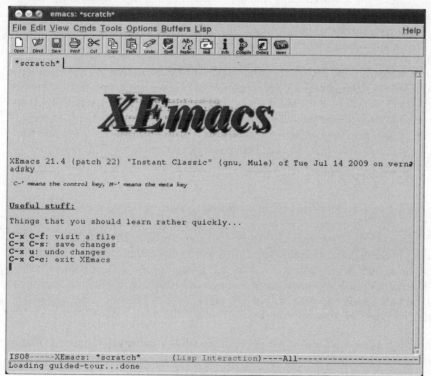

XEmacs was originally the work of the folks at Lucid, Inc., but is now an open source project that is hosted at www.xemacs.org. XEmacs was originally created to provide a more graphic — and mouse-aware — version of Emacs, primarily because the first release of GNU Emacs to intrinsically support the mouse in a meaningful way, Emacs 19, took forever to be released. Because of several legal issues that would numb my brain to discuss here, the XEmacs code has never been merged back into the official GNU Emacs, and it exists as a separate entity today. Regardless, XEmacs is a fantastic version of Emacs that many people find much more attractive and usable than GNU Emacs and is therefore well worth looking into. XEmacs is not officially supported by the Ubuntu folks but is provided in the Multiverse Repository. The primary XEmacs package at the time of writing is named *xemacs21*. You can install XEmacs using any of the mechanisms discussed in Chapter 19.

A Few Words about Emacs Commands

Before I tell you how to do anything in Emacs, it's important to have a quick discussion of Emacs commands, how they work, and how they're represented in this book.

Because Emacs is a modeless editor, typing any standard keyboard character actually inserts that character into the file that you're working on. That makes perfect sense in a graphical environment where you can use menu commands to perform most Emacs commands (as long as they're listed on a menu). However, because Emacs predates the use of graphical environments, and therefore menus, there has to be another way to issue basic Emacs commands.

All available Emacs commands are bound to a combination of keystrokes that use the modifier keys on your keyboard. These modifiers are keys such as Ctrl (known as *Control*), Esc (known as *Escape*), and the Alt and Shift keys. If you think about how a computer works, you'll realize that these keys, when combined with the standard alphanumeric and symbol keys, change the signal that is sent to your system when one of these standard keys is sent. Using the Ctrl, Esc, and Alt keys does exactly the same sort of thing as what happens when you press the Shift key when typing a letter or number key on your keyboard — it sends a different signal from what that key normally sends.

Emacs commands are therefore bound to key combinations that are represented as things like Ctrl+s, Esc+s, Alt+s, Ctrl+Shift+s, and so on. This is one of the things that the users of editors like to make fun of because watching someone type in Emacs can be quite amusing if they are executing a continuous mixture of text insertion keystrokes and Emacs commands. As an example of this, one of my old officemates described my typing as looking like an "epileptic spider." Of course, the fact that I don't touch-type didn't help me any, but his point was still both amusing and well taken, and I am clearly still amused (but have not changed). This has something to do with how different keyboard modifier keys work.

The Ctrl key works as a direct modifier by being held down while another key is pressed. This is usually represented as *Ctrl+s*, which means "hold down the Ctrl key, press the letter *s*, and then release the Ctrl key." The Ctrl key is much like the Shift key in this respect, except that there is no equivalent "Ctrl Lock" key to confuse and irritate people.

Tip

A printed sequence beginning with the caret symbol (^) is often used as a shortcut when referring to the Ctrl key. For example, ^s and Ctrl+s are two ways of representing the same thing. This simplifies having to continually type Ctrl+s, and also prevents anyone from being confused about whether to type the + (you don't). Some books also use Ctrl+s, Ctrl-s, or simply C-s as other shortcuts for Ctrl+s. In this book I'll stick with Ctrl+s. Emacs can be confusing enough without drowning in a sea of duplicate representations. ■

On the other hand, the Esc and Alt keys work as prefix keys. To use these keys, you press and release them once, and then press another letter. These are generally represented as Esc+s and Alt+s, and the keyboard interaction is very different. Commands associated with the Escape key are therefore often referred to as an *Escape sequence* to reinforce the notion that these are a *sequence* of key presses, not a simultaneous combination of multiple keys.

This would be pretty simple if Emacs commands were limited to a single Ctrl command, Escape sequence, and so on. However, this would limit Emacs to having a hundred or so possible commands, which is hardly sufficient. Therefore, most Emacs commands are combinations of Ctrl keys, Escape sequences, Alt sequences, and the Shift key. This gives you an essentially infinite number of available commands, which can be hard to remember, leads to derogatory comments like those of my old officemate, and amuses everyone with potential key sequence descriptions like Esc+S+Ctrl+Shift+S. However, I feel that this is a small price to pay for the power of a zillion possible commands.

Tip

One thing that confuses users who are familiar with text editors or word processors on other systems is that Emacs does not follow the traditional conventions for things such as cutting, copying, and pasting text. This is unfortunate, but the reason for this is because Emacs predates these conventions, and those key sequences are already used for other things in Emacs. Who would you rather tick off — thousands of Emacs users who are potentially unruly in the first place, or new users who are new to Emacs anyway? I thought so. . . . ■

Emacs Terminology

Because GNU Emacs is designed to interact with a graphical window manager, I have to use slightly different terminology to describe what you see on the screen. This section explains that terminology so that I can use it without guilt throughout the rest of this chapter.

Figure 12-11 shows two windows on an Ubuntu system, each running Emacs but displaying different files. Each Emacs window has its own menu bar and toolbar. The window in the foreground displays two different files, each in its own buffer. Each Emacs buffer has a mode line at the bottom, which provides information about the file being viewed in that buffer and its state. At the bottom of each Emacs window is a status line in which you interact with Emacs, or in which Emacs displays any messages displayed by a particular Emacs function.

Note

The term *window* has a different meaning in this section from the way in which I used it in the portions of this chapter that discussed vi and vim. This is because Emacs is natively aware of the X Window System and therefore can display multiple windows on the screen, whereas vi can only divide a terminal application screen into multiple sections. In the context of Emacs, a vi *window* is equivalent to an Emacs *buffer*. ■

FIGURE 12-11

Windowing terminology for GNU Emacs

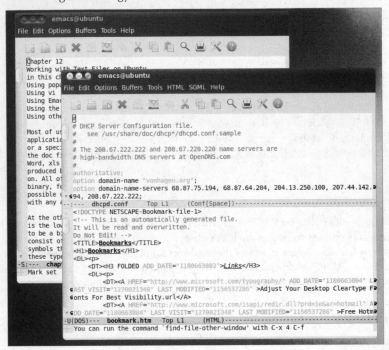

Starting and Exiting Emacs

As with vi, to begin editing a file in Emacs, you can do either of the following:

- Select the GNU Emacs command from the Applications ➪ Accessories menu.

- In any xterm or GNOME Terminal window, simply type the command **Emacs** filename, where *filename* is the name of the file that you want to edit. By default, starting Emacs from a terminal window on an Ubuntu system creates a new window for the Emacs application. As a result, you will probably want to follow the name of the file that you want to edit with an ampersand to start your Emacs session in the background and return control to the Terminal window so that you can type additional commands there while Emacs is running.

In either case, Emacs will create an initial window displaying any file that you are editing, as shown in Figure 12-7. If you start Emacs from the GNOME menus, Emacs displays an initial Welcome screen, as shown in Figure 12-12.

FIGURE 12-12

The startup screen for GNU Emacs

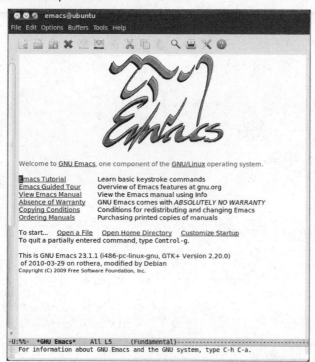

To exit Emacs, you can use either the Exit Emacs command on the File menu or type the Ctrl+x Ctrl+c (as a refresher, this means to hold down the Ctrl key and press the letter *x*, then press the letter *c*, and then release the Ctrl key) key combination.

If you have not modified any files while working with Emacs or have already saved all of the changes that you have made, Emacs exits immediately. However, if you attempt to exit from Emacs using menu commands and have not saved any of the changes to the file(s) that you've been editing, Emacs displays the confirmation dialog shown in Figure 12-13 for each file that contains unsaved changes.

To proceed without saving your changes, click No. To save your changes and proceed, click Yes. If you save your changes by selecting Yes, Emacs exits immediately once those changes have been saved for each modified file that you were working on. If you click No, Emacs displays yet another confirmation dialog, asking if you're really, really sure that you want to exit without saving your changes, as shown in Figure 12-14. Emacs doesn't quite beg you to save your files, but it makes every attempt to ensure that you know what you're doing and aren't accidentally exiting without saving the great American novel.

FIGURE 12-13

Changed file notification when exiting Emacs graphically

FIGURE 12-14

Final confirmation dialog when exiting Emacs graphically

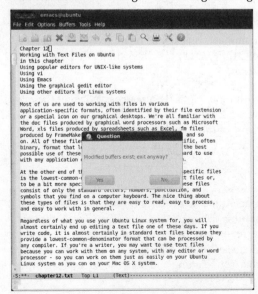

This same exchange occurs when you're attempting to exit Emacs using the equivalent command (Ctrl+x Ctrl+c), but it occurs in the Emacs message buffer instead of as a dialog, as shown in Figure 12-15.

FIGURE 12-15

Final confirmation prompt when exiting Emacs using the keyboard

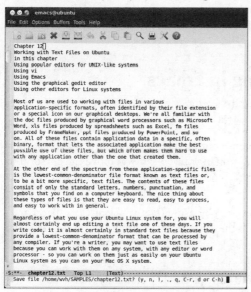

Moving Around in Emacs

There are many different keys for moving the insertion cursor in Emacs:

- **Ctrl+a:** Go to the beginning of the current line.
- **Ctrl+e:** Go to the end of the current line.
- **Ctrl+f:** Move forward one character.
- **Ctrl+b:** Move backward one character.
- **Ctrl+p:** Move to the previous line.
- **Ctrl+n:** Move to the next line.
- **Ctrl+v:** Scroll down one screen.
- **Esc+b:** Move backward one word.
- **Esc+f:** Move forward one word.
- **Esc+v:** Scroll up one screen.

- **Esc+<:** Go to the beginning of the current buffer.
- **Esc+>:** Go to the end of the current buffer.

These are the most common keyboard commands for moving the cursor around within the current window. When using Emacs in any graphical mode, you can also scroll the screen by clicking and dragging the button in the scrollbar, or simply move the cursor by pointing and clicking.

For information about the commands used to switch or move between multiple buffers that are displayed on the screen, see the section later in this chapter entitled "Working with Multiple Windows and Buffers in Emacs."

Cutting, Copying, and Pasting in Emacs

Because Emacs is aware of the X Window System and therefore supports moving the cursor using the mouse, there are two different ways to select the text that you want to copy or move:

- By positioning the cursor using the left mouse button, holding down the left mouse button, and dragging the cursor to select a portion of your text. If you move the cursor into the mode line of any Emacs buffer, Emacs will automatically scroll the text while continuing the selection operation.
- By setting a mark at the current cursor position by using the Ctrl+@ or Ctrl+spacebar commands, and then moving the cursor to the location that delimits the end of the text that you want to cut or copy.

Once you have identified the region that you want to copy or cut, you can copy that region to an internal paste buffer by pressing **Esc+w**, or cut the selected text to the paste buffer by pressing **Ctrl+w**. You can then move the cursor to the position where you want to paste the copied or deleted text, and press **Ctrl+y** to paste the text at the new location.

Tip
If you simply want to cut the text from the current cursor position to the end of the current line, you can press Ctrl+k to kill that text, and then press Ctrl+y to paste it back in elsewhere. ■

Searching for and Replacing Text in Emacs

By default, the Ctrl+s key is bound to an incremental search mode that is extremely convenient to use. After you press **Ctrl+s**, the message "I-Search:" displays in the Emacs message buffer, and Emacs searches forward in the current buffer for the text that you type there, finding the first match for whatever string you are currently typing. For example, if you are searching for the string *cantaloupe*, as you type each letter of that word, Emacs searches forward for the first instance of the letter *c*, then the first instance of the letters *ca*, the first instance of the letters *can*, and so on, much like the incremental search behavior in the Firefox Web browser. You can press **Ctrl+g** at any time to abort the search and return to the cursor position at which the search began. Typing any other Emacs command (with the exception of Ctrl+g, that is) terminates the search and leaves the cursor at the current location in the buffer.

Working with Multiple Windows and Buffers in Emacs

If you are using Emacs in graphical mode, switching between buffers or windows using the mouse is pretty easy — you just left-click the mouse in the window or buffer that you want, and voilà! However, if you're already working in a window that's been split into multiple buffers (or if you're using Emacs in no-window mode), it's useful to know how to switch between different buffers.

To switch to another buffer that is currently displayed on your Emacs screen, press the Ctrl+x Ctrl+o command. This command cycles through all of the buffers that are currently displayed on your screen.

If you want to switch to another buffer regardless of whether or not it is displayed on the screen, you can press Ctrl+x+b (Ctrl+x, and then the letter *b*) and enter the name of the buffer that you want to switch to at the prompt in the Emacs status line.

If you don't happen to remember the name of the other file that you were working on or are using a temporary name, you can press Ctrl+x Ctrl+b to list all available buffers, and then middle-click on the name of the buffer that you want to switch to.

Customizing Emacs

If you've ever used Emacs on another user's computer, you've probably noticed that it doesn't seem to work the same way as it does on your system. The reason for this is that Emacs is the most configurable editor in existence. Not only does Emacs provide a rich configuration language for changing the commands that different keys are associated with (known as *key bindings*), but also it includes a complete implementation of the Lisp programming language that makes it easy for serious Emacs users to write their own commands or modify the behavior of existing ones.

Most Linux systems store all per-user Emacs customization information in the file `.emacs` in the user's home directory. As mentioned throughout this chapter, Emacs's customizability and flexibility account for much of its popularity. The next few sections highlight the basic types of customizations that you can make in an Emacs configuration file, providing examples of each. Several excellent sites on the Web provide much more detailed information about customizing Emacs, such as `http://jeremy.zawodny.com/emacs/emacs-4.html` and `http://linuxplanet.com/linuxplanet/tutorials/3166/4/`.

Changing Key Bindings

Whenever you execute an Emacs command, you are actually executing a Lisp function. As explained earlier, Emacs is configured to execute specific commands in response to combinations of the Ctrl or Esc keys and the standard keys on your keyboard. These are known as *key bindings* because they associate (bind) a specific function with a specific key sequence. However, if you're already familiar with another editor that also uses commands consisting of combinations of the Ctrl or Esc keys and the standard keys on your keyboard, your fingers are probably used to pressing certain keys to execute certain commands. The most common customization made to Emacs is therefore to change the keys to which commonly used commands are associated.

Although Emacs enables you to change key bindings globally or within a specific mode, it is more common to customize a specific key binding so that it works regardless of the mode in which you are using Emacs. The Emacs configuration command to set a key binding globally is `global-set-binding`. For example, to set the key sequence Ctrl+z globally to a function that scrolls the current buffer up one line rather than attempting to suspend Emacs, you would put the following command in your ~/.emacs file:

```
(global-set-key "\C-Z" 'scroll-one-line-up)
```

In Lisp fashion, you must preface the name of the function that you are referring to with a single quotation mark (not the back quote). If you're interested, the `scroll-one-line-up` function is provided as an example in the section entitled "Defining Your Own Functions" later in this chapter.

Note

When you are specifying key bindings in an Emacs configuration file, the Ctrl key is usually represented by `\C-` and the Esc key is usually represented by `\M-`. ■

Setting Variables

Emacs uses several internal variables to control its behavior. You can modify these variables using the `setq` command. For example, to cause Emacs to scroll more smoothly in one-line increments, you could add the following line to your ~/.emacs file:

```
(setq scroll-step 1)
```

As another example, the default settings in Emacs cause it to automatically save your files each time you have typed or modified 300 characters. To decrease this value to every 100 changes, you could add the following line to your ~/.emacs file:

```
(setq auto-save-interval 100)
```

Specifying Modes

As discussed earlier, Emacs provides different key bindings and functions based on the types of files that you are using, known as *modes*. The default mode used by Emacs when you start Emacs without specifying the file that you want to edit is known as the *fundamental mode*. You may want to customize Emacs to always use a different mode by default, regardless of the name of the file. For example, to make text mode the default mode each time you start Emacs, you could add the following line to your ~/.emacs file:

```
(setq default-major-mode 'text-mode)
```

As you can see from this example, the name of the default mode in Emacs is defined through an Emacs variable, `default-major-mode`, which in this case requires the name of an Emacs function rather than a numeric value as shown in the examples in the previous section.

Each Emacs mode also enables you to specify other actions whenever you use that mode. For example, to turn on auto-fill (wrapping words to the next line when you reach a certain column on your screen), you could add the following line to your ~/.emacs file:

```
(add-hook 'text-mode-hook 'turn-on-auto-fill)
```

Changing File Associations

As discussed earlier, Emacs automatically enters specific modes when you open files with a specific extension, just as many GUIs do when you click on a specific type of file. You may occasionally want to have Emacs automatically enter a specific mode when you open files that the specified mode is not traditionally associated with. For example, Emacs automatically enters text mode when you edit files with the .txt or .text extensions. But what if you typically name text files with the .inf extension and want Emacs to automatically enter text mode when entering files of that type?

The file extensions associated with different Emacs modes are stored in a list consisting of extension/mode-name pairs. Therefore, to add the .inf extension to the list of extensions associated with text mode, you would simply append that extension to the list of extensions associated with text mode, as in the following example:

```
(setq auto-mode-alist
   (cons '(".inf" . text-mode) auto-mode-alist))
```

This example uses the Lisp `cons` function to append the pair .inf and `text-mode` to the list of automatic file associations, and then uses the `setq` function discussed earlier in this chapter to set the `auto- mode-alist` variable to the new, expanded list.

Defining Your Own Functions

The fact that Emacs includes an internal implementation of Lisp makes it relatively easy to define your own functions and provides a practical reason for learning Lisp if you've always wanted one. Lisp functions are defined using the `defun` command, which takes a list of five values as arguments. Without turning this into a Lisp tutorial, let's just quickly look at a sample function definition and examine its components.

The following Emacs Lisp code defines a simple function that scrolls the contents of the current window up some number of lines, with the default number being 1:

```
(defun scroll-one-line-up
   (&optional arg)
   "Scroll the selected window up one or N lines."
   (interactive "p")
   (scroll-up (or arg 1))
)
```

The name of the function that you are defining is the first argument to the `defun` command. The second argument is the list of arguments that are used by the function that you are defining. In this case, this list uses the `&optional` argument to state that this function can take one argument, but that the argument is optional. The third argument to the `defun` command is an informational message about the function, enclosed in double quotes. The fourth argument defines whether the function is interactive (p means "true" in Lisp). The fifth argument is the actual Lisp code for the function that you are defining, which in this case executes the built-in Emacs scroll-up function a single time or the number of times you specified as a numeric argument to the function.

This section won't exactly make you a Lisp wizard, but just knowing that Emacs includes a complete Lisp implementation can be quite empowering. As you can see from this example, defining simple functions is not all that complex. The power and flexibility of Emacs provide you with the chance to add that function you've always wished for in a text editor!

Getting More Information about Emacs

The Emacs editor contains its own tutorials and help files: Type **Esc+x help** to begin. These include a "learning by doing" tutorial. There are also plenty of Emacs tutorials out there, some of which are written from the beginner's point of view. The official GNU Emacs manual is available from `www.gnu.org/software/emacs/manual/`. It can also be purchased in book form. There is also an Emacs wiki at `www.emacswiki.org`.

Using gedit

Now that I've discussed the two classic UNIX/Linux text editors and their attendant philosophies, it's worth mentioning that Ubuntu also provides text editors that you can use without a class in UNIX history and pledging your undying allegiance to Richard Stallman or Bill Joy. For example, the standard Ubuntu desktop distribution installs an easy-to-use graphical text editor called *gedit*. Figure 12-16 shows gedit displaying the same file used to illustrate the vi and Emacs editors earlier in this chapter, namely, the text of this chapter as I was writing it.

The gedit editor is completely mouse- and menu-driven and follows the standard keyboard conventions for most graphical editors across platforms. These include the following:

- **Ctrl+c:** Copy selected text.
- **Ctrl+n:** Open a new file.
- **Ctrl+s:** Save the current file.
- **Ctrl+v:** Paste copied or cut text.
- **Ctrl+x:** Cut selected text.

As a graphical application, gedit provides convenient and more traditional dialogs for interacting with, moving around in, and selecting files and directories. It can also be customized to suit your specific editing needs by selecting the Edit menu's Preferences command, which displays the dialog shown in Figure 12-17.

FIGURE 12-16

The gedit text editor

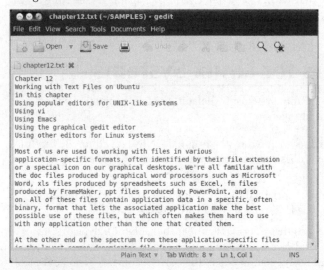

FIGURE 12-17

gedit's Preferences dialog

The tabs on this dialog provide access to different sets of configuration options so that you can make gedit work the way that you want it to. For example, word-wrapping is great for documents like this one, but you probably don't want to use it when you are writing programming code. The most interesting of the Preferences tabs is the Plugins tab, which enables you to activate or deactivate different features that are provided as extensions to the basic capabilities of gedit.

As with most GNOME applications, extensive online help for gedit is available by selecting the Help menu's Contents command.

Other Text Editors for Linux Systems

Several other editors are available for Ubuntu systems. By default, the following other editors are installed as part of a standard Ubuntu installation:

- **ed:** A simple, line-oriented editor inspired by the original UNIX text editor. Be careful when you start this, because it doesn't actually display a prompt. (The command to exit is the letter *q*.)

- **ex:** Invokes the vim editor in line-oriented mode. When using ex, you can instantly switch to vim's full-screen mode by typing the keyword **visual**.

- **nano:** An enhanced clone of pico that is available under the GPL (unlike pico). One of the nicest things about nano and pico is that the bottom of any window always provides a quick summary of the most useful commands in the current context. nano (and pico) is completely unaware of the X Window System, and must be executed within an xterm or GNOME Terminal window. Figure 12-18 shows nano editing the text file for this chapter.

- **pico:** A simple, screen-oriented text editor that was originally introduced by the Pine mail system on UNIX systems. On Ubuntu Linux systems, this is actually just a symbolic link to the nano editor, and thus looks exactly like the screen shown in Figure 12-18.

If you are new to Linux, you might be interested in two other popular editors that are not provided with Ubuntu but that you can compile or execute on your Ubuntu system:

- **jedit:** A popular, cross-platform editor for programmers. For more information, see www.jedit.org/index.php.

- **THE:** The Hessling Editor, a clone of the popular IBM mainframe editor XEDIT, THE includes support for various Linux versions of the associated REXX scripting language. See www.lightlink.com/hessling or http://hessling-editor.sourceforge.net for more information.

FIGURE 12-18

The nano text editor

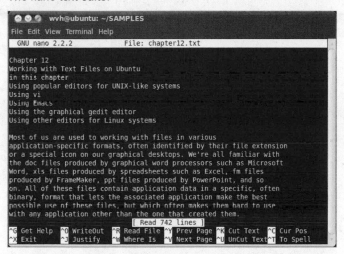

If you're looking for a Linux clone of a specific editor, check the web page at `http://texteditors.org`. This site lists many available editors for different operating systems (including Linux) and may help you find the exact editor that best meets your needs.

Summary

Your Ubuntu Linux system provides a variety of text editors that different types of users can quickly get comfortable with. If you are familiar with Linux or other UNIX-like systems, Ubuntu installs vim (a vi clone), and GNU Emacs is easily installed using the software update commands discussed in Chapter 19. This chapter discussed in detail how to use both vi and Emacs, how to accomplish the most common tasks you'll need to do in an editor, as well as how to customize each to suit your preferences. It then provided an introduction to gedit, a fast graphical editor that is installed as part of the GNOME desktop environment. The chapter concluded with information about other editors that are available on your Ubuntu system and provided suggestions for finding other editors that may be more to your liking.

The next chapter discusses how to create and edit documents, rather than simply text files. Document files are typically binary files that contain embedded information about the formatting of different aspects of the document, including font information, layout information, style information, and so on.

Creating and Publishing Documents

C hapter 12, "Working with Text Files on Ubuntu," discussed using
text editors on Linux systems. Text editors are fine for creating documents if the document you're creating is a shopping list, a To-Do
list, or a ransom note. For more sophisticated documents, most people
today expect a word processor, which is an application that enables you to
create documents that use multiple fonts and different styles within a font
(bold, italic, etc.); create bulleted and numbered lists automatically; and
provides basic support for page layout using advanced constructs such as
tables, multiple columns, and so on.

This chapter explains how to do various types of word processing on your
Ubuntu Linux system, focusing on OpenOffice.org Writer, which is the
word processing component of the powerful OpenOffice.org suite of applications that is featured throughout this book. OpenOffice.org is a fantastic
suite of office software, and this chapter's discussion of using OpenOffice
.org Writer should make even the most dyed-in-the-wool Microsoft Word,
Corel WordPerfect, or Mac OS X Nisus Writer user feel right at home.

Finally, this chapter discusses desktop publishing on Ubuntu, highlighting
the excellent Scribus application. When you have to do serious, hard-core
layout in your documents, a word processor is no longer the right tool
because it doesn't provide sufficiently granular control of page elements.
Desktop publishing software makes it easy to create documents that contain many different page elements, routing text from one to the other as
needed, and easily inserting and manipulating graphics to create documents that look exactly the way that you need them to. Scribus is a relatively young but incredibly impressive application. Adobe InDesign, Adobe
PageMaker, and Quark XPress users, hold on to your hats, but don't worry
about your wallets—Scribus is open source!

IN THIS CHAPTER?

Markup Languages: TeX and LaTeX

Using OpenOffice.org Writer

Using Scribus

Other word processors for Linux

Using Document Markup Languages

Long ago, when people just used terminals, "word processing" meant creating documents in a text editor and embedding special commands to tell some other application how to format your document for a specific target printer. The format in which these documents were created is known as a *markup language*, of which the most common example is HTML. Of course, HTML is designed to mark up documents that are targeted for use as web pages, but the same principles apply. Creating documents in markup languages is still popular in academic and publishing circles because many institutions and journals use text files in a markup language as the lowest common denominator for submissions. This enables them to combine documents from multiple sources into a single, stylistically consistent publication without worrying about what version of Word everyone used, what fonts they used, and so on.

Using TeX and LaTeX

TeX (pronounced *tech*) is a typesetting program and associated markup language that is designed to produce extremely high-quality output, especially for scientific and mathematical notation. The eminent computer scientist Donald Knuth wrote TeX in 1977, largely because he needed a suitably high-quality tool for producing the first three volumes of his *Art of Computer Programming* series.

Many different implementations of TeX are available today, all based on Knuth's original version, many converted into other languages, and all enhanced with the addition of extra capabilities. The source code for TeX is freely available, but in order for anything based on the TeX source code to call itself *TeX*, it must pass a TeX formatting torture test known as *TRIP*. The version of TeX provided in the Ubuntu repository (as on most Linux systems nowadays) is TeX Live, a complete TeX distribution for UNIX-like and Windows systems that is collaboratively developed by a number of TeX user groups. The home page for TeX Live is www.tug.org/texlive.

Because TeX isn't for everybody, it isn't installed by default on Ubuntu Linux systems. The Ubuntu repositories provide a huge number of TeX-related files, but the only one that you really need to install is the `texlive` package, which depends on many others and therefore guarantees that you'll get everything you need for a usable TeX formatting environment. You may also want to install the appropriate `texlive-doc` package for your national language, which, for English-speakers like me, would be the package `texlive-doc-en`. The `texlive-doc` packages provide FAQs, HOWTOs, tutorials, and many other documents about the TeX system.

TeX markup is quite primitive, er, simple, requiring many low-level commands to do basic text formatting. To simplify creating documents using TeX, a variety of macro packages have been developed, the best known of which is Leslie Lamport's LaTeX macro package. These macro packages support different types of documents, such as articles, manuals, letters, and so on, and provide easy-to-remember macros for the traditional components of those types of documents. For your convenience, the LaTeX macros package and associated applications are automatically installed when you install `texlive` on your Ubuntu system.

The following is a simple document in LaTeX:

```
\documentclass{article}
\begin{document}
\title{This is a Title}
\author{Bill von Hagen}
\date{\today}
\maketitle

\begin{abstract}
This example shows a simple examples of creating a document using
\LaTeX\ macros that identify the structural components of a document.
\end{abstract}
\section{Introduction}
This would be the text of an introduction...
\end{document}
```

To process this file using LaTeX, execute the command latex *filename*. Processing a file using LaTeX produces an output file in DVI (Device Independent) format. DVI output is an intermediate binary form that contains character positioning and font information in addition to the content of your document, and must be post-processed by another program that understands how to display this file on your screen or produce output in the specific format or printer control language used by your printer. Figure 13-1 shows a preview of the DVI file produced by processing this LaTeX document, shown in the xdvi DVI previewer.

FIGURE 13-1

Previewing output from the simple LaTeX example

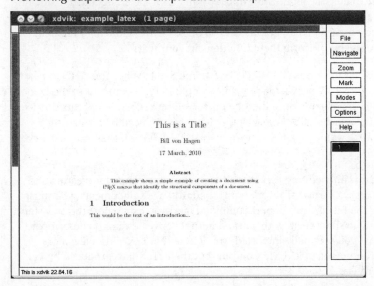

Most people who create documents using TeX actually use LaTeX today for the convenience of its macros and also because it supports the automatic creation of things such as a table of contents, lists of figures, an index, and other document constructs that are both important and useful. Discussing the details of creating LaTeX documents is outside the scope of this book, but many other people have already done that. For suggested sources of detailed information about creating LaTeX documents and using LaTeX, see "More Information about TeX and LaTeX" later in this chapter.

As much of this book shows, it's a graphical world nowadays, and Ubuntu Linux provides all of the graphical applications that any computer user expects to find. Although command-line utilities like TeX and LaTeX are easy to use and the text-based format of TeX and LaTeX files makes them easy to exchange with users of many other computer systems and applications, it's hard to beat the convenience of a graphical application, especially when you're doing something such as word processing.

It's a good thing that the folks in the world of open source have stepped up to provide graphical solutions for creating and working with documents in LaTeX format. These are the Lyx and GNU TeXmacs applications, all of which are available in the Ubuntu repositories. Like tex-live, these packages are not installed by default on your Ubuntu system, but are easy enough to locate and install using apt-get, aptitude, or the Synaptic Package Manager. (See Chapter 19, "Adding, Removing, and Updating Software," for more detailed information on installing applications using these tools.) Installing Lyx adds the Lyx Document Processor command to the Office menu. Installing TeXmacs doesn't add anything to your menus, so you will have to execute TeXmacs by running the texmacs command from a command line.

If you're writing LaTeX documents but prefer a GUI tool, it's hard to beat the convenience and usability of a graphical front-end, such as Lyx.

Lyx provides a great graphical interface for creating and working with LaTeX documents, including conveniences such as being able to select document elements and styles from dropdown menus and reformat selected characters, paragraphs, and so on, all without having to remember the low-level LaTeX commands that perform these functions in your text.

One of the coolest things about Lyx is its WYSIWYG ("What You See Is What You Get") display and editing environment. Figure 13-2 shows the previous sample LaTeX document in the Lyx document processor. You'll immediately notice that the on-screen representation of this document is almost identical to the appearance of the DVI file that was produced by formatting it using LaTeX. Maybe *quasi-WYG* would be a better term than *WYSIWYG*, but that term has never caught on.

To facilitate previewing and simplify editing, Lyx actually uses its own format for creating and storing documents, known as lyx format. To work with standard LaTeX documents, you must import them into Lyx using the File menu's Import command, and you can export them as standard LaTeX once you're ready to share them with your co-authors or reviewers. If you compare them with any LaTeX file that you originally imported, you'll note that Lyx adds a few more detailed LaTeX formatting commands to its LaTeX output, but the LaTeX files produced by Lyx are completely normal otherwise.

Editing a LaTeX document in Lyx

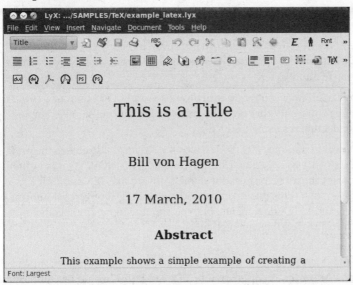

Lyx is an excellent tool and well worth experimenting with if you are working with LaTeX documents but want the convenience of a graphical application or simply can't remember all those pesky LaTeX commands. For more information about Lyx, see its home page at www.lyx.org.

Another alternative for working with LaTeX documents in a graphical form is the TeXmacs package, which is a graphical, LaTeX-aware package that is implemented on top of GNU Emacs. This enables you to use familiar Emacs commands while working with your LaTeX documents in a graphical fashion.

TeXmacs is convenient to use and provides several LaTeX-specific menus and icons that make it easy to apply LaTeX styles, create document elements, and even select and reformat portions of your documents. Unlike Lyx, you can use TeXmacs with TeX documents as well as LaTeX documents, and it is not necessary to import your LaTeX documents — TeXmacs will open your existing LaTeX files, but they may require a bit of tweaking to get them to display correctly. TeXmacs will also offer to save your LaTeX files in its own format, using the .tm file extension. For more information, see the TeXmacs home page at www.texmacs.org or consult the extensive online help that it provides.

More Information about TeX and LaTeX

Because TeX and LaTeX have been used for many years on a wide variety of systems, a tremendous amount of information about using them is available on the Web. A simple Internet search will turn up more hits than you could possibly want. As a timesaver, some of my favorite sites for information about TeX and LaTeX are as follows:

- Getting to Grips with LaTeX (`www.andy-roberts.net/misc/latex/index.html`) is a great series of tutorials on using LaTeX from Andrew Roberts.

- Introduction to LaTeX (`www.math.uiuc.edu/~hildebr/tex/course`) is a short course prepared at the University of Illinois Department of Mathematics that provides a nice, quick overview of TeX and LaTeX.

- Text Processing Using LaTeX (`www.eng.cam.ac.uk/help/tpl/textprocessing`) is a great site at Cambridge University that provides many online tutorials and examples of creating a variety of documents using LaTeX.

- The teTeX HOWTO (`www.tldp.org/HOWTO/TeTeX-HOWTO.html`) discusses the previous version of TeX/LaTeX that was used on Ubuntu systems. This HOWTO was written a few years ago, but one of the nice things about stable software like TeX and LaTeX is that things don't change much. This document provides a good deal of general information about creating TeX and LaTeX documents, but you should ignore any specific information about using the teTeX TeX implementation.

Several books dedicated to TeX and LaTeX are available, and a quick search at Amazon.com will provide an assortment of options. However, no discussion of TeX and LaTeX would be complete without identifying the two seminal texts for each of these:

- *TeXbook* by Donald E. Knuth (Addison-Wesley Professional, 1984, ISBN: 0201134489)
- *LaTeX: A Document Preparation System*, 2nd ed. by Leslie Lamport (Addison-Wesley Professional, 1994, ISBN: 0201529831)

As these books are by the authors of the respective systems, you can consider them definitive. Some changes have certainly been made to LaTeX since its creation by Lamport long ago, but these are still the bibles for both of these document preparation systems.

Word Processing with OpenOffice.org Writer

OpenOffice.org (`www.openoffice.org`) is a suite of office applications including a word processor (Writer), a spreadsheet (Calc), a drawing program (Draw), software for creating presentations (Impress), and a database program called *Base*, which keeps tagging along after the rest of OpenOffice. This section focuses on the word processing application — other chapters in this book discuss the OpenOffice.org spreadsheet, graphics, and presentation software. But first, a word from our sponsor.

OpenOffice.org is one of the most powerful and popular open source projects on the Web, and the people who are largely responsible for its existence are the folks at Oracle who were formerly part of Sun Microsystems. Scott McNealy, president of Sun Microsystems, has a long-standing rivalry with Microsoft, so it wasn't all that surprising when in 1999 Sun purchased StarDivision, the German vendor of a suite of office software called *StarOffice*. The purchase of StarOffice was originally seen as both a way to leverage Sun's Java offerings (because StarOffice and OpenOffice .org are both heavily dependent on Java) and to provide Sun users with an office suite that they could run natively on their workstations.

Sun then released the then-current source code for StarOffice into the open source community under the terms of Sun Industry Standards Source License (SISSL). Beginning with release 2.0 of the OpenOffice.org suite, all of the source code is now available under the GNU Lesser General Public License (LGPL). Sun still markets StarOffice, which is both supported and offers some capabilities beyond those provided by OpenOffice.org — but that's moot for us, because StarOffice doesn't run on Ubuntu Linux.

Aside from its power and the absence of cost, a truly compelling reason for using OpenOffice.org Writer is its use of the new OpenDocument Format (ODF) standard for storing and exchanging documents (www.oasis-open.org/committees/tc_home.php?wg_abbrev=office). Historically, all word processors used their own proprietary binary formats for storing documents, which made it a hassle when switching from one word processor to another or when simply trying to exchange documents with friends or coworkers who used a different word processor. The OpenDocument standard is designed to provide a published standard for storing documents in an XML format that can instantly be used in any other word processor that supports this format. This may seem like a minor thing, but get back to me after you try to open the WordStar files for your family history, short stories, or other documents that you may have written long ago but still want to be able to use.

Tip

If you are interested in document standards or read nerd news occasionally, you may be aware of the arm-wrestling contest between the ODF and Microsoft's OOXML (Open Office XML) standards regarding which of these gets to be the official open document standard. OOXML "won" this battle, but in my opinion you would be foolish to use OOXML. A standard that is more than 5,000 pages long (and that not even the Microsoft tools conform to at the time of this writing) isn't much of a standard as far as I'm concerned. Use ODF and reject this latest offering from Microsoft. It's one thing that their tools and operating system are bloatware — it's another to make bloat the standard. ∎

To avoid repeating the phrase *OpenOffice.org Writer* more times than necessary throughout the rest of this section, I'll typically refer to OpenOffice.org Writer simply as *Writer* (its name to its friends) or occasionally as `oowriter` (the name of the application that you must type to execute OpenOffice.org Writer from a command-line interface).

File Extensions for OpenOffice.org Documents

With the adoption of the OpenDocument format, OpenOffice.org Writer changed the names of its default file extensions to reflect the new formats. The following list shows the file extensions used by different OpenOffice.org versions:

- **odm:** OpenDocument Master Document
- **odt:** OpenDocument Document, OpenOffice.org 2.0 and greater
- **ott:** OpenDocument Document Template, OpenOffice.org 2.0 and greater
- **sxw:** Writer Document before OpenOffice.org 2.0
- **stw:** Writer Document Template before OpenOffice.org 2.0
- **sxg:** Writer Master Document before OpenOffice.org 2.0

The most common documents that you will see and create are those with the .odt and .ott file extensions. However, you may encounter the older .sxw format when exchanging documents with long-time OpenOffice.org users. SXW files are very interesting because they are actually zipped archives containing XML document files and associated metadata. You must use the Document Converter Wizard to import old-format SXW OpenOffice.org files into the new OpenOffice.org OpenDocument format, as explained in the section "Importing Documents from Other Word Processors" later in this chapter.

Installing Files for Writer

Writer is installed by default if you install Ubuntu from a Live CD, from an Alternate Install CD using the Text Mode installer, or from an Alternate Install CD using the OEM Mode installer. If you want to add Writer or the entire OpenOffice.org suite to a server system that has a graphical user interface, you can install them using any of the package management tools discussed in Chapter 19.

One thing that differentiates Ubuntu from other Linux distributions is their extreme dedication to the user, especially in terms of internationalization. If you are working in only a single language, the correct localization packages for your physical location are installed with your default Ubuntu installation. However, if you are installing Writer for use when creating documents in multiple languages, you may also want to search for and install the appropriate hyphenation, localization, and thesaurus packages for whatever other locales you are writing for. You can easily find these by looking for a string that represents the country code that you are looking for. For example, Figure 13-3 shows the specific German language support packages for OpenOffice.org that have been identified by searching for the string *-de* in a Package Management tool.

Tip

You can install complete language support for all applications (without translating the GNOME framework itself) by installing the appropriate language support meta-package for your target locale(s) — these packages have names of the form *language-support-country-code* (e.g., `language-support-de`) and include the dictionaries for the specified locale. To fully translate the GNOME interface and all internationalized applications, select the appropriate language pack. The names of the language packs are of the form *language-pack-country-code*. Once you've installed multiple dictionaries, and so on, you can set the default language for your documents in Open Office applications using the Tools ⇨ Options ⇨ Language Settings ⇨ Language dropdown list. You can also set the default language for various portions of your documents by using the commands on the Tools ⇨ Language menu. ■

FIGURE 13-3

Sample additional language packages for the OpenOffice.org suite

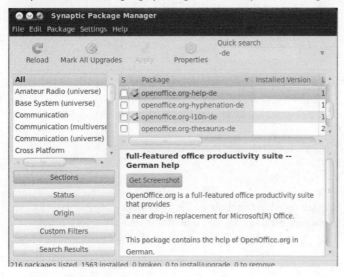

Taking a Quick Tour of Writer

You can start Writer from the command line by executing the `oowriter` command. More conveniently, a menu item for Writer is installed in the Applications ⇨ Office menu called "OpenOffice.org Word Processor." To start Writer from the menus, select this menu item. The application starts, displaying an empty document, as shown in Figure 13-4.

FIGURE 13-4

Starting Writer

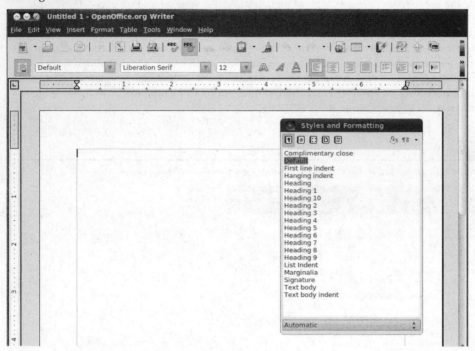

Writer provides excellent online help, as do all of the tools in the OpenOffice.org suite, so I won't bore you by walking you through each menu and entry that it contains. However, as a quick overview of the Writer interface, the callouts in Figure 13-4 highlight the following areas:

- **Menus:** The dropdown menus in Writer are organized much like the menus in Microsoft Word to provide a familiar user experience. Menu items with an arrow at their right edge lead to other, related submenus.

- **Toolbars:** By default, Writer displays the Standard and Formatting toolbars, which provide one-click access to specific commands when you click on the appropriate icon. You can modify the list of icons displayed on a toolbar by clicking on the control for that toolbar, located at the far right. You can display other toolbars or deactivate the default toolbar by selecting toolbars from the View ➪ Toolbars submenu.

- **Rulers:** These rulers display the horizontal and vertical location of the text insertion point in the current document. The grayed-out portions of each ruler reflect the page margins used in the current document. You can hide these rules by toggling the View ➪ Ruler menu command.

- **Styles and Formatting window:** Although it's not displayed by default, you can display this window at any time by selecting the Format ⇨ Styles and Formatting menu command. The Styles and Formatting window provides easy access to various sets of styles that are available for the current document and is especially convenient if you choose not to display the formatting toolbar. The dropdown menu enables you to display specific sets of styles in this window, such as Character Styles, List Styles, and so on. You can dock this window by holding down the Ctrl key and double-clicking on the gray portion of the window heading (beside the icons), making it a part of the default Writer interface rather than a floating window. Figure 13-5 shows Writer with the Styles and Formatting window docked. You can undock a docked window by repeating this process in the docked area.

FIGURE 13-5

Docking the Styles and Formatting window

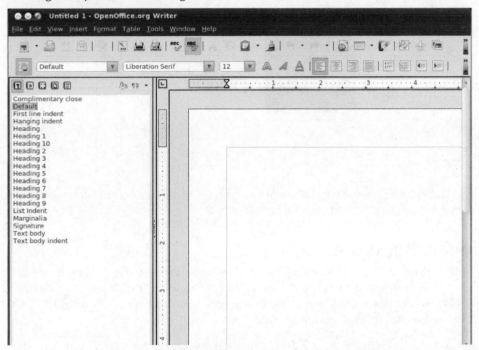

- **Context-sensitive menu:** Right-clicking on the background of any document that you are working on in Writer displays the context-sensitive menu shown in Figure 13-6. This menu provides quick access to several formatting and style-related submenus.

FIGURE 13-6

Writer's context-sensitive menu

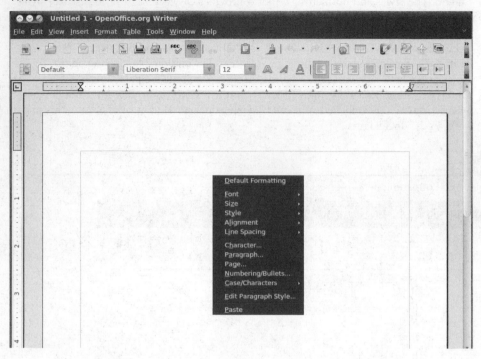

Writer provides extensive online help, available by selecting OpenOffice.org Help from the Help menu, or by pressing the F1 key on your keyboard at any time.

Personalizing Writer

The first thing that you'll want to do when getting started with Writer is to enter some information about yourself into its User data fields. This is primarily useful because Writer will use this information in various places when filling out fields in documents that you create using the OpenOffice.org Wizards (as explained in the next section).

Select the Tools ⇨ Options menu item to display the Options dialog's "User Data" form, as shown in Figure 13-7. Fill out the fields in this form and Click OK to return to Writer and your document.

FIGURE 13-7

Writer's "User Data" form

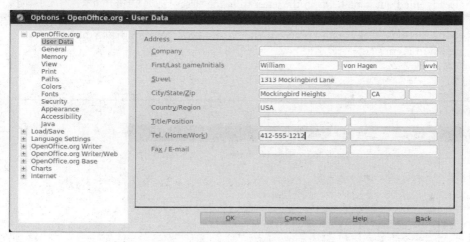

Using Wizards to Create Documents

The easiest way to create a document in Writer is to use one of the document wizards that it provides for many popular types of documents. This section provides an example of creating a letter in Writer using the Letter Wizard, but the process of using any wizard is quite similar regardless of the type of document you're creating—and the goal of these wizards is to be easy to use in the first place.

Tip

If you cannot start one of the Writer wizards, you should install the openoffice.org-java-common package. ■

To start the appropriate wizard for creating a new document, do the following:

1. Select File ➪ Wizards, and select the appropriate wizard for the type of document that you are creating. Writer provides wizards for creating letters, faxes, agenda, presentations, and web pages. For this example, I'll select the Letter Wizard. Writer creates a new letter document using its default and displays the first Letter Wizard dialog, as shown in Figure 13-8.

2. Select the radio button for the type of letter that you want to create: Business, Formal Personal, or Personal. Each type of letter provides some default page styles and decorations, which you can select from the Page Design dropdown list. The window behind

the Letter Wizard shows a preview of a letter with your current selections, so that you know what you're getting into. If you look closely, you'll see that the Letter Wizard has already filled out some fields in the letter from the "User Data" form that was discussed in the previous section. In this example, I'll select "Business Letter." Once you've made your selections, click Next to proceed. The second Letter Wizard dialog displays, as shown in Figure 13-9.

FIGURE 13-8

The first Letter Wizard dialog

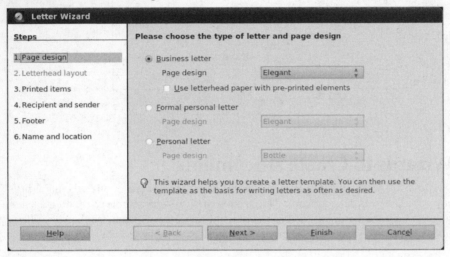

Tip

If you are creating a business letter and you are going to be printing it on your corporate letterhead, you can select the "Use letterhead paper with pre-printed elements" checkbox (shown in Figure 13-8). This removes any existing graphics from the letter preview and activates the Letterhead layout step in the Wizard, so that you can specify the dimensions of your letterhead stationery and thus avoid overprinting portions of it with your letter. ■

3. Select the Salutation or closing message for your letter. You can change these by selecting existing values from the dropdown menus or personalize them by selecting and replacing the default values shown for these. As you update these, the preview of your letter changes to reflect the new values. When you're done, click Next to proceed to the next screen. The Letter Wizard's Recipeient and sender dialog enables you to customize

your address and customize recipient information, such as specifying that the recipient information should come from a mail-merge database. Once you've made any changes that you want to make, click Next to proceed. Another Letter Wizard dialog displays, which enables you to customize the information in the footer of your letter. Once you've made any changes that you want to make, the Letter Wizard's final dialog displays, as shown in Figure 13-10.

FIGURE 13-9

The second Letter Wizard dialog

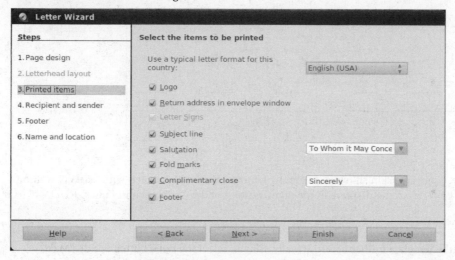

4. If you've made any changes to the default letter settings and are going to be reusing them, the final Letter Wizard dialog enables you to update the Wizard's default settings or save your modifications as a new template. To update your default settings, enter a name to associate with your new settings. If you want to create a new template from these settings and continue writing your letter, click the Browse button and enter a new filename for the new template. This file will still be used the next time you use the Letter Wizard, but you can easily create documents from different templates as described later in this chapter in the section "Creating and Using Templates."

FIGURE 13-10

The final Letter Wizard dialog

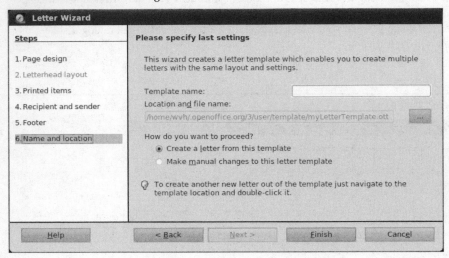

Once you're done, click Finish to terminate the Letter Wizard and proceed with actually writing your letter. Your new letter displays in the main Writer window, as shown in Figure 13-11.

Tip

If you'd rather tweak the template further before actually using it, select the radio button beside "Make manual changes to this letter template" (shown in Figure 13-10) and click Finish. This displays the template, at which point you can add or modify styles and page formatting, as described in the next section. ■

As you can see, Writer's wizards make it easy for you to create documents of certain predefined types. Writer's wizards leverage some of the predefined document templates that are provided with a default installation. If you want to create your own documents based on a template that is not supported by a wizard, Writer still makes it easy for you to define and use your own, specialized types of documents, as described later in this chapter in the section, "Creating and Using Templates."

Editing your new letter

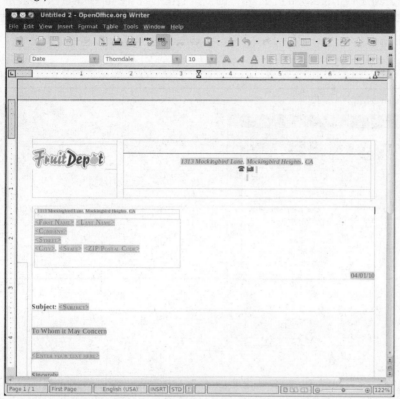

Modifying Document Styles and Layout

A *style* is the word processing term (borrowed from more advanced page layout programs like InDesign and PageMaker) for a set of formatting and display characteristics that are associated with a specific portion of your text, usually a paragraph. Once you're actually editing a document, you can apply any of the existing styles that have been defined for that document by selecting the name of a style from the dropdown list in the formatting window, or by selecting it from the Styles and Formatting window. To display the Styles and Formatting window, select the Format ⇨ Styles and Formatting menu command.

All of Writer's default document templates provide a default set of styles that enable you to format the different portions of your document. To apply a style to an existing paragraph, simply click anywhere inside it using the mouse, and select the style that you want to apply from the dropdown list or the Styles and Formatting window. I'm using the term *paragraph* here because, by default, a *paragraph* is any element in your document that ends with a hard return, even if it's empty.

To modify a single instance of a paragraph formatted with an existing style, position the cursor in that paragraph, right-click, and select Paragraph from the pop-up menu. This displays the dialog shown in Figure 13-12, which enables you to modify the style settings used in a single element in your document without changing them for other elements in your document that use the same style.

FIGURE 13-12

Modifying the style for a single paragraph

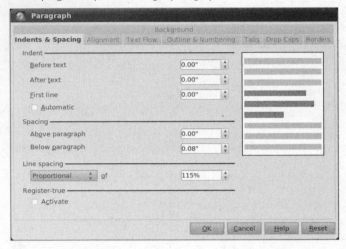

Although all OpenOffice.org documents come with a good set of default styles, everyone's tastes differ. To modify an existing style to reflect your personal tastes or corporate standards, right-click on any portion of your document that is currently formatted with that style, and select "Edit Paragraph Style" from the pop-up menu. A dialog like the one shown in Figure 13-13 displays.

Changing any of the settings in this dialog will change the style itself, which means that any other elements of your document that use this style will also be updated with your modified settings. You'll notice that the dialog shown in Figure 13-13 has many more options and tabs than the simple Paragraph formatting dialog shown in Figure 13-12. This is because the dialog in Figure 13-13 enables you to modify any aspect of the style, not just the formatting of a selected element.

Changing the default styles is fine, but may be the wrong thing to do if you want to modify only a few elements in your document that use a certain style. When the default styles aren't sufficient and it's a waste of time to tweak multiple paragraphs, the right thing to do is to create a new style, based on an existing one, that has slightly different characteristics.

FIGURE 13-13

Modifying the values for an existing style

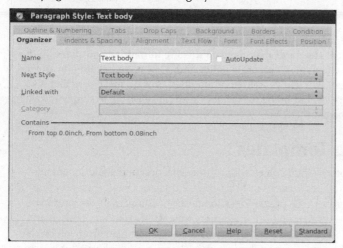

To create a new style based on an existing style, first make sure that the Styles and Formatting window is shown on your screen. Next, position the cursor in a paragraph formatted with the existing style, and click the "New Style from Selection" icon at the far right of the Styles and Formatting window toolbar. Select "New Style from Selection" from the dropdown menu to display the dialog shown in Figure 13-14.

FIGURE 13-14

Creating a new style from a selection

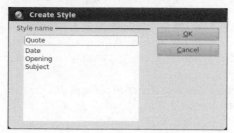

Enter the name that you want to associate with your new style, and click OK. Figure 13-14 shows me creating a style named *Quote*, which I use for indented quotations from other sources. Whatever value you enter, the name of your new style displays in the Styles and Formatting window, and the new style is associated with the currently selected element. You can then repeat the process for modifying an existing style, as described earlier in this section, to add the custom settings that you want to associate with your new style.

Tip

You should, of course, minimize the number of new styles that you create whenever possible. For example, you may be working with corporate document standards that mandate specific formatting and styles. In this case, adding new styles may be, at worst, a violation of corporate policy and, at best, an irritation to anyone who subsequently has to work on a document that you've written or modified. Always make sure that it's absolutely necessary before creating a new style, but doing so is almost always preferable to simply tweaking fonts and font sizes throughout your documents. ∎

Creating and Using Templates

As mentioned earlier in this chapter, Writer comes with a good selection of default document types, known as *templates*, and provides wizards to help you use them or even create new templates based on those document types. The previous section described how to create your own styles to further fine-tune the settings that you use in your documents. This is very convenient but only modifies the styles associated with a specific document — the template from which that document was created doesn't pick up the new styles, which makes it hard to share your stylistic insights with others. It also makes it hard for you to reuse them yourself, unless you subsequently create every new document by copying an existing document that has the new styles, and then replace its contents. At best, this is a pain in the anatomy, and at worst, it is almost completely inefficient. The right solution is to be able to easily create and manage your own document templates. You can then reuse your styles by starting new documents from your updated templates, and even share your Writer wizardry with other users simply by giving them copies of your templates.

Note

The process of creating a new template is initially the same as that for manually creating a new document (although without using a wizard). The primary differences are that you don't need to add much content (only representative elements for designing new styles) and that you save the new document as a template rather than as a document. Read on! ∎

To create a new template, do the following:

1. Select File ⇨ New ⇨ Templates and Documents from any Writer window to display the dialog shown in Figure 13-15.

2. Select the New Document icon at the left, and select Text Document as the type of document that you're creating. Click Open to begin modifying the new document, which displays as an empty document in a new Writer window. In this window, create any stylistic elements and layout settings that you want to provide through your new template. (The previous section explained how to create new styles from existing ones in existing documents.)

FIGURE 13-15

Creating a new template

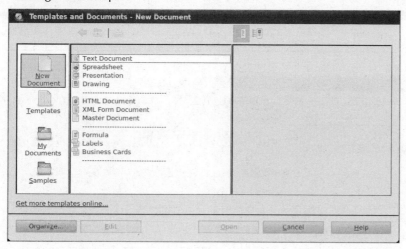

3. Make sure that your page settings are correct for the new style. Beyond creating new styles, one common change that you will want to make in your new template is to change the default page layout by selecting Format ➪ Page, selecting the Page tab, and modifying the page size, margins, and other settings in the dialog shown in Figure 13-16.

FIGURE 13-16

Modifying page type and layout settings

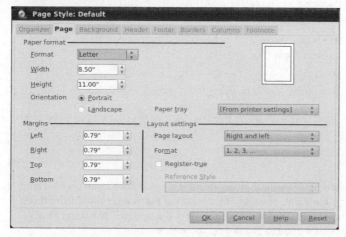

4. Once you've finished modifying your new template, you can save it as a template by selecting File ⇨ Templates ⇨ Save. A dialog like the one shown in Figure 13-17 displays.

Saving your new template

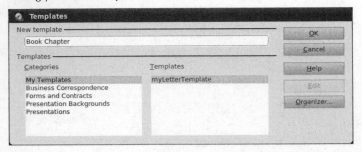

5. Enter the name for your new template and click OK. Figure 13-17 shows the creation of a new style called *Book Chapter*.

Congratulations, you've created a document template! Once you've created a template, you can easily create new documents based on that template by doing the following:

1. Select File ⇨ New ⇨ Templates and Documents to display the dialog shown in Figure 13-18.

2. To create a document from a specific template, click the Templates icon at the left and select the location where you saved the template (usually "My Templates"). You will see your templates listed in the window to the right of the icons. Figure 13-18 shows this dialog, which includes the template that I just created in the previous step.

3. Select the template that you want to use, and either click Open or double-click on its name to create a new document from this template.

Once you are finished editing your document, save it by using the standard File ⇨ Save As command.

Creating and using templates is a great way to standardize the documents that you or your organization is creating.

Tip

Modifying or otherwise updating a template does not mean that any documents that have been created from it are automatically updated. After updating a template, opening any document that was created from it will prompt you as to whether or not you want to update the document to reflect the updated template. That's usually a good idea, but it's nice that Writer is kind enough to ask you about it. ■

FIGURE 13-18

Creating a new document from a template

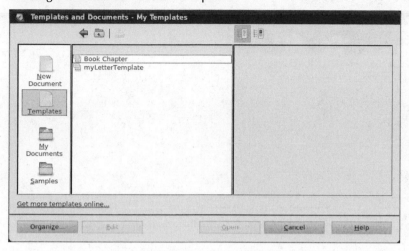

Importing Documents from Other Word Processors

Writer can open documents produced by many other word processors, especially those created by Microsoft Word or Corel WordPerfect, or documents stored in the intermediate Rich Text Format (RTF) document type. This is fine if you have only one or two documents that you want to update, but if you are moving all of your work to Ubuntu, you may find that you have hundreds of documents that you want to update to Writer format. It's a good thing that Writer provides a wizard for this that will not only import all of your documents, but also will import and convert any existing or attached style sheets that it detects.

To batch-import your existing Microsoft Word (or older OpenOffice.org) documents, do the following:

1. Select File ➪ Wizards ➪ Document Converter to display the dialog shown in Figure 13-19.

2. To import Microsoft Word files and style sheets, select the Microsoft Office radio button and select the "Word Documents" checkbox. To import existing SXW documents from StarOffice or a version of OpenOffice.org prior to 2.0, leave the StarOffice radio button selected. Click Next to proceed. The dialog shown in Figure 13-20 displays.

FIGURE 13-19

Specifying the input format when converting documents

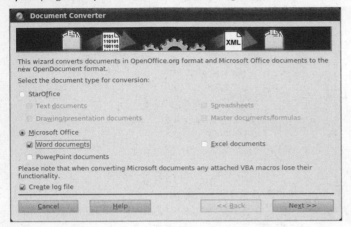

FIGURE 13-20

Specifying document and template locations when importing

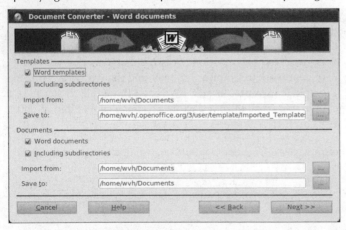

3. Specify the directories in which you want the wizard to search for the specified document types and the locations to which converted documents should be saved. You may want to update the location to which converted templates should be saved — I typically use my home directory, and subsequently move the files around manually. Once you've

checked the directory locations, click Next to proceed. A status dialog displays, summarizing the conversions that are about to take place. Click Convert to begin the conversion process. The dialog shown in Figure 13-21 displays as the conversion process progresses.

FIGURE 13-21

Monitoring the document conversion process

4. During the conversion process, the Conversion Wizard may display a character code confirmation dialog, asking you to select the character set, font, and language you want. This generally means that the Wizard encountered unknown characters in one of the documents. When the conversion process completes, the Close and Show log file buttons are displayed on the dialog shown in Figure 13-21.

Congratulations — the conversion process is complete! Your converted documents and templates are ready for use in Writer. Before clicking Close, it's a good idea to click the "Show log file" button. The log file for the conversion process lists successful conversions and also identifies any documents that should be fine-tuned or corrected before they can be used with Writer. This is often the case with Word DOT files, which may contain macros that are not completely compatible with anything other than Microsoft's own Visual Basic for Applications (VBA).

More Information about Writer

As mentioned earlier in this chapter, all OpenOffice.org applications provide complete, well-written online help. However, like most online help, this information is reference information, not HOWTO information.

If you are serious about using OpenOffice.org Writer for all of your documentation needs, the best site that I have seen on the Web for HOWTO information about using Writer is www .tutorialsforopenoffice.org. This site features great tutorials in PDF and OpenOffice. org formats, as well as links to a useful selection of other sites with useful, hands-on information about using Writer. Check it out — it's well worth your time! After you become an OpenOffice. org wizard, you may want to create a tutorial of your own and contribute it to the site.

Desktop Publishing with Scribus

The previous sections of this chapter discussed how to create different types of documents on Ubuntu systems using command-line and graphical word processors. These tools provide powerful styles to standardize the appearance of repeated elements in your documents. However, when the presentation and layout of your document are just as important as its content, you need a different sort of tool. *Word* and *text* processors do just that, formatting and organizing the content in your documents, usually providing little support for actual page layout beyond controlling the page margins, size of the print area, and the number of columns of text that are displayed on each page. To do actual, detailed document layout, you need an application that combines word processing capabilities with the layout and detailed formatting capabilities required by the publishing industry — in other words, a desktop publishing package. It's a good thing that the open source folks ran into that problem, too, and an excellent (and free) desktop publishing package for Linux, named *Scribus*, is easily installed on your Ubuntu system.

Scribus has been under development for a few years now and is an open source application that is available at no cost for Linux, Apple Mac OS X, and Microsoft Windows systems; it uses the QT graphical interface so that it looks and behaves the same way on all supported systems. The Scribus home page is www.scribus.net — check there for the latest Scribus information.

The basic concept in desktop publishing is the *frame*, which is conceptually similar to the idea of a *paragraph* in a word processing system. A frame is the key document element in desktop publishing. Desktop publishing documents are composed of many different frames, which can contain text, graphics, and so on. Dividing documents into these compositional elements makes it easy to move or resize them independently to suit changes in the document, its target layout, and so on. Text frames can be linked so that text flows from one frame to another, but they are still separately manageable document elements.

The next few sections explain how to install Scribus, how to create documents using the templates that it provides, and what basic steps are necessary to create new documents with the detailed page layout required by your most demanding publishing work. It's not quite Quark XPress, Adobe InDesign, or Adobe PageMaker, but you can't beat the price, and the quality is quite impressive. You can't import existing InDesign, PageMaker, or Quark files yet, although you can import OpenOffice and other open format documents as a starting point for your Scribus documents.

Installing Scribus

Because not everyone needs or wants a desktop publishing package, Scribus isn't installed by default on Ubuntu desktop systems. The primary package that you need to install in order to use Scribus is the `scribus` package, but you may also want to install the `scribus-doc` and `scribus-template` packages to help you make the most of Scribus. See Chapter 19 for more detailed information on installing applications using a variety of package management systems. Once the installation completes, you're ready to begin working with Scribus! Installing Scribus on your Ubuntu system installs a Scribus menu item on the Office menu that you can use to run the application.

A Quick Scribus Tutorial

Like OpenOffice.org Writer and most other publishing-related applications, Scribus comes complete with a few templates to get you started. When you first use a new application, it's often easiest to start with someone else's document and then modify it to suit your purposes. Once you get the hang of using the application, you can create your own documents, as explained in the next section. This section provides a whirlwind tour of the key features of Scribus to get you comfortable with the basics.

To start Scribus, select Applications ➪ Graphics ➪ Scribus. (This menu command may also be on the Office menu.) Scribus takes a little bit of time to start up as it examines your system's font resources (which are critical to a detailed, layout-oriented application). The first time you start Scribus, you will see a "New Document" dialog, as shown in Figure 13-22.

FIGURE 13-22

Selecting a document layout for a new document

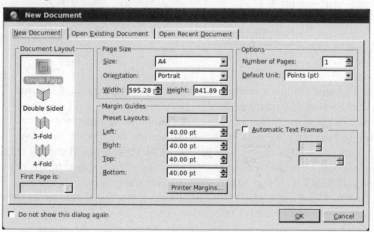

This dialog enables you to identify the document layout that you want to use when creating a new document. You can create a new document from a basic layout specification or using one of the templates provided with Scribus, as we'll do in this tutorial. To bypass this dialog for now, click Cancel. If you don't want to see this dialog the next time that you start Scribus, click the "Do not show this dialog again" checkbox before clicking Cancel.

Once Scribus starts, you can create a new document from one of its templates by doing the following:

1. Select the File ⇨ New from Template menu command to display the dialog shown in Figure 13-23.

FIGURE 13-23

Selecting a template as a starting point

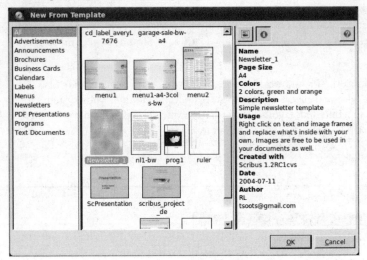

2. Select the template that you want to use for your new document and click OK. In this example, I'll use the Newsletter_1 template, which provides a working model for a newsletter that includes graphics. As Scribus opens the template, you may see one or more warning dialogs if the template uses fonts that are not installed on your system, followed by a summary dialog that suggests replacements for these fonts. If you see this dialog and want to use fonts that are available, select the "Make these substitutions permanent" checkbox and click OK. If you do not want to make these substitutions, click Cancel. You will have to locate and install the missing fonts if you don't want to see this dialog again the next time that you use the selected template.

3. Once font processing completes, the new document that is based on the selected template displays in the main Scribus window, as shown in Figure 13-24.

FIGURE 13-24

Scribus showing your working copy of a template

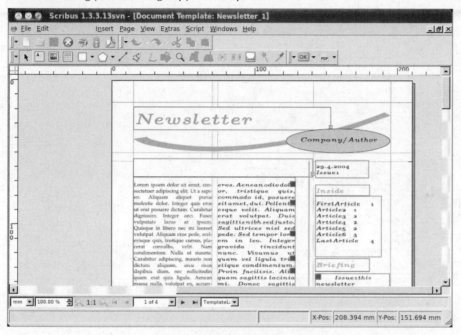

4. Now things get interesting. To work with or simply change the text in any frame, first select that frame. You can then select the "Edit Contents of Frame" button in the toolbar (this is the icon that shows a white letter *A* and a text cursor). After selecting this command, you can directly add or delete text in the current frame. However, for more detailed changes involving font and text changes, I tend to use the "Edit Text" dialog. To access this dialog, you can simply click the "Edit the text with the Story Editor" icon in the toolbar (the icon that looks like a pen and tablet computer). I tend to access this through the context-sensitive menus rather than the toolbar, so you can also right-click on that frame to display the pop-up menu shown in Figure 13-25.

5. To view the dialog used for low-level font changes, select the "Edit Text" menu item. A "Story Editor" dialog like the one shown in Figure 13-26 displays. The Story Editor is a small word processor, encapsulated within Scribus. Using the Story Editor, you can modify, replace, or add to the text in the frame using the lower window. The controls available in the Story Editor enable you to change justification within a frame, fonts, and font characteristics.

FIGURE 13-25

Editing options for frames in Scribus

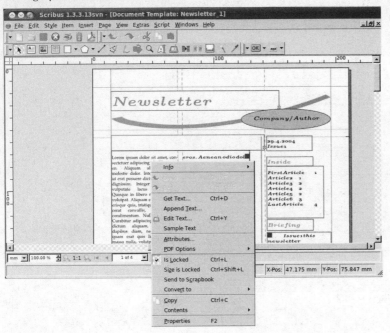

FIGURE 13-26

Modifying the text in a frame with the Story Editor

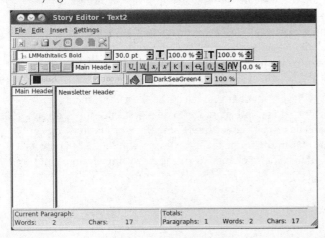

6. After modifying the frame text or its characteristics, click the checkmark icon or select the File ⇨ Update Text Frame and Exit command. In this case, I've changed the title of the newsletter from *Newsletter Header* to *Linux People and Pets*. An updated version of your document with the new information displays, as shown in Figure 13-27.

FIGURE 13-27

The updated version of the document

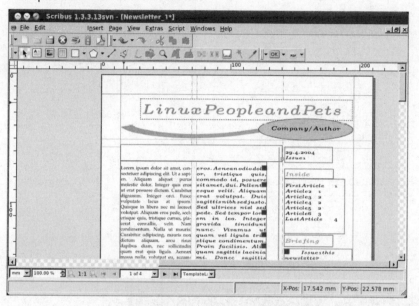

7. Working with graphical frames is similar but uses an external application (GIMP, which is discussed in Chapter 15, "Working with Graphics") to edit any existing image. For example, scroll down in Scribus until you see a figure on the right side of the second page. To replace this graphic, first right-click on its frame and deselect "Is Locked" from the context-sensitive menu to unlock the frame. This enables modifications to the frame. As you're working, you can lock any frame that you're happy with to prevent accidental modification.

8. To delete the existing image, right-click on the frame and select Contents ⇨ Clear. The document updates to reflect the absence of the graphic, as shown in Figure 13-28.

9. To select a new graphic for the frame, right-click on the frame and select the "Get Image" menu command. The dialog shown in Figure 13-29 displays, enabling you to navigate to, select, and preview any existing graphic on your system.

FIGURE 13-28

The newsletter after a graphic has been removed

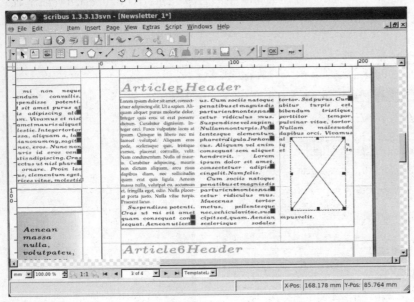

FIGURE 13-29

Selecting a new graphic for a frame

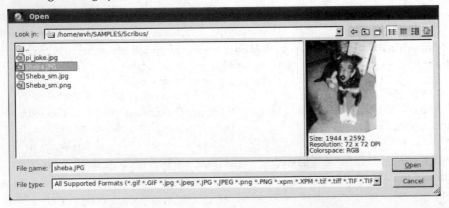

10. After selecting the new graphic, click Open to open the new graphic in the selected frame. The view of your newsletter updates to reflect the new graphic, as shown in Figure 13-30. Hmm, that doesn't actually look very good because the figure is supposed to show a picture of my dog.

FIGURE 13-30

The updated document showing the new graphic

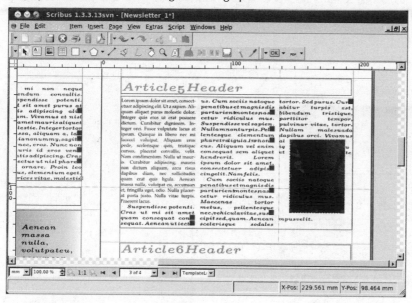

11. Because the graphic is a different size from the original frame, right-click on the graphic and select the Properties menu command to display the Properties dialog, as shown in Figure 13-31. Click Image to display the Image Properties tab.

FIGURE 13-31

The Properties dialog's Image tab

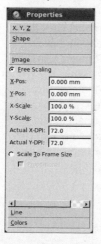

12. Select the "Scale To Frame Size" radio button to scale the image to fit the frame. To completely fill the frame, deselect the Proportional setting, which would otherwise preserve the original X and Y ratio of the image. Click the Close box in the upper-right corner of the Properties dialog to close it. Figure 13-32 shows the scaled image in the frame — much better!

FIGURE 13-32

The scaled image in the document

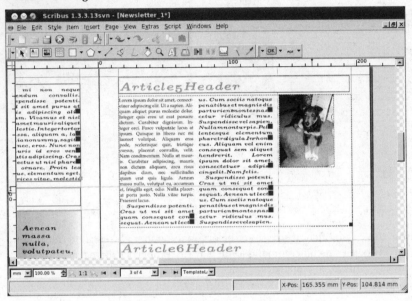

13. The extra space available in the document provides a good location for a new text frame. First, drag the image frame up by clicking and holding the left mouse button on the frame, and then dragging the frame to its new location. To add a new frame, click the "Insert Text Frame" icon from the toolbar (it looks like a small document) and click-and-drag to insert the new frame. For the purposes of this example, I'll insert some sample text into the frame by right-clicking on the frame and selecting "Sample Text" from the pop-up menu. Select the language for the sample text from the dialog that displays, and click OK. It may seem odd to have a command that inserts random text into a frame, but this is useful when laying out a document before the final content is ready, and it saves you the trouble of having to locate some random text, copy it to the Clipboard, and then paste it. Your document updates to reflect the new frame and its contents, as shown in Figure 13-33.

FIGURE 13-33

The updated document showing the new text frame

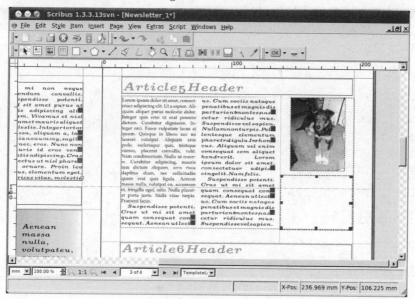

14. The final step in this quick tutorial is to link two text frames so that any text that overflows from the first goes into the second. You can link any two frames, but the frame that you are linking to must be empty. To clear the frame that you just added, right-click on it and select Content ⇨ Clear. (When clearing existing frames, you may first have to unlock their contents by deselecting "Is Locked" from the content-sensitive menu.)

15. Resize the frame to the left of the figure and frame that we just added. First, right-click on the frame and deselect "Is Locked." Red handles appear on the outline of the frame. Select the one in the middle of the right size of the frame, hold down the left mouse button, and drag the frame border to the right. The document should look something like that shown in Figure 13-34.

16. Because the frame is still selected, click the "Link Text Frames" button in the toolbar. (It shows two text frames with an arrow beside them, and is to the right of the "Edit the text with the Story Editor" button.) Left-click on the frame that you want to flow text to, which is the frame that we added earlier. An arrow displays on the screen, showing that the two paragraphs are now linked. The screen updates, flowing text from one frame to the other, as shown in Figure 13-35.

FIGURE 13-34

The updated document resizing a text frame

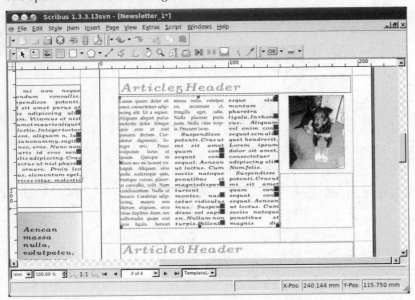

FIGURE 13-35

The updated document showing linked text frames

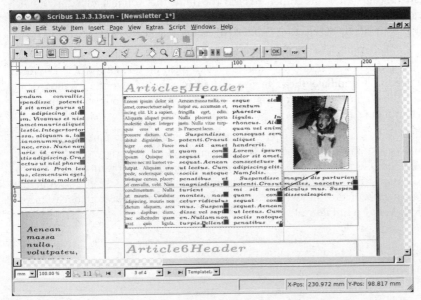

That's it for this tutorial. You can now save your document, or export it for printing by selecting the "Save the current document as PDF" icon (identified by the familiar PDF graphic).

Scribus is a powerful application with many features and deserves its own book some day. This tutorial guided you through the basics of creating, modifying, and linking text frames, as well as inserting and modifying graphics. Scribus is an impressive program that is a shining example of the power of the open source model and the skill and determination of a few developers who saw a need and filled it.

More Information about Scribus

Scribus is a relatively young application, but a significant and ever-increasing amount of information about it is already available on the Web, in various forums, and in different parts of the Scribus web site. My favorite locations for HOWTO information about Scribus are as follows:

- The Scribus Documentation Site (`http://docs.scribus.net`) provides a good deal of information about setting up and using Scribus, printing, color management in Scribus documents, and so on.

- Scribus Wiki (`http://wiki.scribus.net`) provides a great forum for discussing and documenting how to use Scribus.

- Tutorial: Getting Started with Scribus (`http://docs.scribus.net/index.php?lang=en&page=tutorials/freedomyug/scribustutorial`), although written for an older version of Scribus and thus slightly dated, is an excellent hands-on tutorial for getting started with Scribus. The sample files used in the tutorial are also available for download from this site.

Scribus is an open source project staffed by volunteers. If you become a Scribus fan and have something to contribute, I'm sure they'd be glad to hear from you.

Other Word Processors and Office Suites

This chapter focused on the most popular, open source command-line and graphical applications for word processing and page layout. There are certainly others — this is open source, after all, where anything worth doing is worth doing several times because of different perspectives on the task at hand. The following are two other popular word processors for Linux:

- AbiWord: The AbiWord word processor is part of the GNOME Office Suite (`http://live.gnome.org/GnomeOffice`). AbiWord is a powerful and popular word processor for Linux, with excellent capabilities for importing and working with existing documents in formats such as Microsoft Word. AbiWord is available in the Ubuntu repositories and can easily be installed on your Ubuntu system using the appropriate Package Manager for your system.

- Applixware: Applixware is an office suite that includes a powerful word processor, but has had an on-again, off-again relationship with Linux. Originally marked as an end-user package that was a direct competitor to StarDivision's original StarOffice Office Suite, Applixware has morphed into more of a toolkit for developing real-time and analytical applications. For more information about Applixware, see `www.vistasource.com/vs2/en/index.php`. For an article on installing Applixware on Ubuntu Linux, visit the Applixware group at `http://groups.google.com/group/Applixware` and search for Ubuntu.

Both of these word processors are quite easy to use and have their own circle of devotees. If you find something that you don't like about OpenOffice.org Writer, installing and experimenting with either of these is well worth your time.

Summary

This chapter explained how to do several word processing tasks on your Ubuntu system. It began by discussing TeX and LaTeX, the classic, command-line formatted document processors for Linux and UNIX systems, and even highlighted some of the graphical tools that are available for working with LaTeX documents. Next, the chapter covered OpenOffice.org Writer, the word processing component of the powerful OpenOffice.org office suite, and explained how to create documents and templates in Writer. The chapter also covered Scribus, a powerful desktop publishing application for Linux, which provides the layout and formatting power you need when appearance and detailed layout are just as important as content. The final section of the chapter listed a few other word processing packages that were not discussed in this chapter but that are also available for Ubuntu.

The document production software packages provided with Ubuntu Linux are great, but people do not live by documents alone. The next chapter explains how to use other office-related software on your Ubuntu system to create other popular types of files, such as spreadsheets and presentations.

Other Office Software: Spreadsheets and Presentations

IN THIS CHAPTER

Using spreadsheets: A tutorial

Using OpenOffice Calc

Creating presentations with Impress

The previous chapter discussed how to create documents on your Ubuntu systems. Along with surfing the Web and sending and receiving e-mail, writing letters, keeping To-Do lists, and working on your novel are probably the most common personal tasks that you'll find yourself doing on your new machine. Word processing is also a fairly critical business task because, although most companies live on e-mail at present, there's still always the need for the occasional memo, planning document, and so on.

This chapter discusses the other commonly used and office-related software that's available for your Ubuntu Linux system, namely, spreadsheets and presentation software. While few people actually need to give presentations on their home computer or to their family (maybe "Next Month's Budget — What It Means to You"?), spreadsheets are a crossover task that is often as important to home users as it is to office workers. If you are working from home or using Ubuntu on a laptop for business reasons, you may need to create both spreadsheets and presentations, and Ubuntu makes this easy (well, as easy as it is on any computer system). Ubuntu Linux Desktop, OEM, or Text-Mode installations automatically install the OpenOffice.org Calc spreadsheet application as part of the OpenOffice.org suite, and the OpenOffice.org Impress presentation application as part of the OpenOffice.org suite.

Note

To save repeating the phrases *OpenOffice.org Calc* and *OpenOffice.org Impress* (or *OpenOffice.org Presentation*, as it's known on the Ubuntu menus) more times than necessary throughout the rest of this section, I'll typically refer to OpenOffice.org Calc simply as *Calc* (its name among friends) and OpenOffice.org Impress (i.e., Presentation) simply as *Impress*. ∎

Introduction to Spreadsheets

This section provides background information on what a spreadsheet is, how it works, and how to use one. If you're already familiar with spreadsheets, you can skip this section. However, if you're not, this section is for you.

In paper terms, a *spreadsheet* is a sheet of paper divided into rows and columns that break down financial transactions into separate entities that a business person can examine and analyze. The first computerized spreadsheet was created for a mainframe computer system in the early 1960s by a professor named Richard Mattessich, then at the University of California at Berkeley. As a mainframe application, this had a somewhat limited audience — for you and me, spreadsheets were one of the original killer applications for personal computers, going all the way back to VisiCalc on misty dawn-of-time systems such as the Apple II. Then, like now, the power of the personal computer gave people the ability to enter and manipulate financial data on their own systems. Spreadsheets are not only good for calculations related to actual expenses and other financial transactions, but also provide an excellent mechanism for "what if" calculations. What if we bought a car now — could we afford the payments based on our monthly income? What if I paid something extra on my mortgage — how long before it would actually be paid off?

In a computer spreadsheet, each rectangle in the spreadsheet is referred to as a *cell*. Each *row* on a spreadsheet typically provides a variety of information about a specific transaction or other entity, while the *columns* are used to visually compare, mathematically summarize, or perform some other mathematical operation on the value for each row that appears in that column. The following is an example:

Meal	Cost	Tax	Tip
Breakfast	5.79	0.41	1.25
Lunch	8.48	0.60	1.75
Dinner	13.23	0.93	2.75

This simple table reflects my meals for a (fictitious) day. The first row is a set of headings that identify the meaning of the entries in each column. Each row provides the details of each of the meals for that day. It would be easy enough to find out the total cost for my meals that day in various ways — either by appending to the end a summary column that contains the total cost of each meal and then adding all of the values in that column together, or by inserting a new row that contains the totals of all of that type of item for the day, and then adding all of the value in that row together. I prefer the first approach, a summary column, so let's go with that approach for the remainder of this section. There's nothing preventing you from calculating your daily totals the other way if you prefer (or doing it both ways, for that matter) — the ability of spreadsheet applications to automatically perform these calculations is one of their coolest features.

Manually performing these calculations is fine if you don't have a computer or if you're far better at math than I am, but I prefer to use the appropriate tool whenever one is available — and spreadsheets come to the rescue in this case.

Using OpenOffice.org Calc

As mentioned in the introduction to this chapter, spreadsheets are often as important to home-computer users as they are to business users. This is especially true once a year for those of us in the United States, when tax time for anyone who itemizes deductions means trotting out all of your receipts for the past year, entering them into a spreadsheet, and totaling up everything that is legally deductible.

A recent poll by one of the Linux publications queried readers about what software they'd most like to see ported to Linux, and my vote went to TurboTax, because otherwise I'll have to have at least one Mac OS X machine around the house for the next 20 years or so. Until the TurboTax folks heed my plea (or, more likely, recognize Linux as a growing market opportunity), spreadsheets will have to do for tracking my personal business expenses. Fortunately, Linux provides some excellent spreadsheet packages.

The spreadsheet component of the OpenOffice.org package is called *OpenOffice.org Calc*, although you start it by selecting the OpenOffice.org Spreadsheet menu item. The OpenOffice.org Office suite is a set of applications that were designed together, share extensive amounts of code, have a similar look and feel, and invoke each other to satisfy certain requirements. For example, as I discuss later in this chapter, bulk-importing existing spreadsheets into Calc using its Document Converter Wizard produces a report of the results of the import process. This file is created in the OpenOffice.org document format used by OpenOffice.org Writer and can be displayed once the conversion process completes so that you can check for any errors or problems. You can't even select the Document Converter's Show log file button if OpenOffice.org Writer is not installed on your system. Fortunately, all of the OpenOffice.org Office suite is preinstalled on Ubuntu Desktop systems nowadays.

As companies such as Microsoft have discovered, there's a lot to be said for a set of consistent, related applications that know how to leverage each other's capabilities to perform many of the data-management tasks required in a modern, computer-oriented office. Unlike Microsoft Office, the OpenOffice.org suite is a high-quality, no-cost solution to your office software requirements.

Tip
See Chapter 13, "Creating and Publishing Documents" for information about installing alternate languages for both the OpenOffice.org tools and for GNOME itself. ∎

Starting Calc

You can start Calc from any command line by executing the command `oocalc`, but it is usually easier to start it from your GNOME menus. A menu item for Calc is provided in the Applications ⇨ Office menu. To start Calc, select the "OpenOffice.org Spreadsheet" menu item. The application starts, displaying an empty document, as shown in Figure 14-1.

FIGURE 14-1

Starting Calc

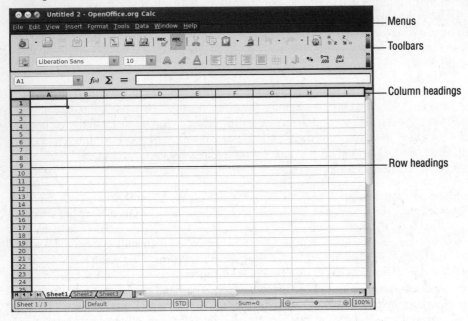

- Menus
- Toolbars
- Column headings
- Row headings

Taking a Quick Tour of Calc

OpenOffice.org Calc provides excellent online help, as do all of the tools in the OpenOffice.org suite, so I won't bore you by walking you through each menu and entry that it contains. However, as a quick overview of the Calc interface, the callouts in Figures 14-1 and 14-2 highlight the following areas:

- **Menus:** The dropdown menus in Calc are organized much like the menus in Microsoft Excel to provide a familiar user experience. Menu items with an arrow at their right edge lead to other, related submenus.

- **Toolbars:** By default, Calc displays the Standard and Formatting toolbars, which provide one-click access to specific commands when you click on the appropriate icon, and a Formula bar, in which you can view and edit any functions or formulas for selected cells. You can modify the list of icons displayed on a toolbar by clicking on the control for that toolbar, located at the far right. You can display other toolbars or deactivate the default toolbars by selecting the names of those toolbars from the View ➪ Toolbars submenu.

- **Row and column headings:** These headings identify the current row and column for the cells that you're viewing. They can be useful when manually entering cells or ranges in a formula.

- **Context-sensitive menu:** Right-clicking on any cell in a spreadsheet that you are working on in Calc displays the context-sensitive menu shown in Figure 14-2. This menu provides quick access to several cell-manipulation commands.

FIGURE 14-2

Calc's context-sensitive menu

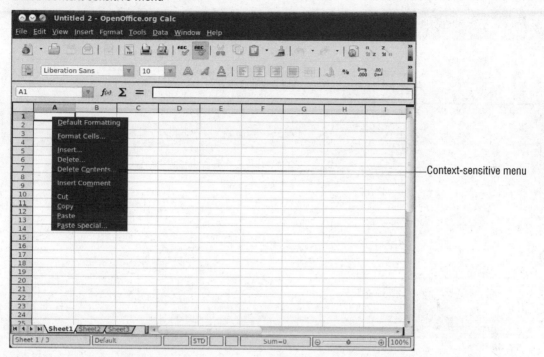

Calc provides extensive online help, available by selecting OpenOffice.org Help from the Help menu, or by pressing the F1 key on your keyboard at any time.

Tip

If you are having problems viewing the text for Calc's online help and OpenOffice.org Writer is not installed on your system for some reason, try installing Writer. This will force an update to the components that control online help in the OpenOffice.org suite and usually resolves the problem. ■

A Quick Calc Tutorial

This tutorial shows you how to create a working spreadhseet from the data provided earlier in the "Introduction to Spreadsheets" section. To do this, first start Calc, and then enter the values from the table shown in that section into the appropriate cells of the spreadsheet. (To enter a specific value in a cell in a spreadsheet, select that cell using the mouse or by using the arrow keys on your keyboard, and type the value.) Figure 14-3 shows the sample values after they've been entered into a Calc spreadsheet.

FIGURE 14-3

Sample values in a Calc spreadsheet

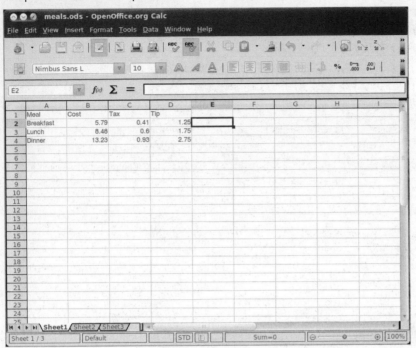

Now the fun begins! To create a cell that contains the sum of selected values from each row, click the cell where you want to create the value, and enter the value **=sum(**. The equals sign tells the spreadsheet that you are using a function, sum is the name of the function that you want to perform, and the opening parenthesis identifies the fact that this will be followed by a list of the cells that you want to be involved in the function. (You can also do this using the mouse, which I'll explain later, but typing the function operator is easier for the purposes of this example.) Figure 14-4 shows the sample spreadsheet at this point.

Note

As you enter this value in the cell, you will see the function that you are entering mirrored in the Formula bar, which is a toolbar above the spreadsheet that simplifies editing existing formulas. ■

FIGURE 14-4

Beginning to define a formula

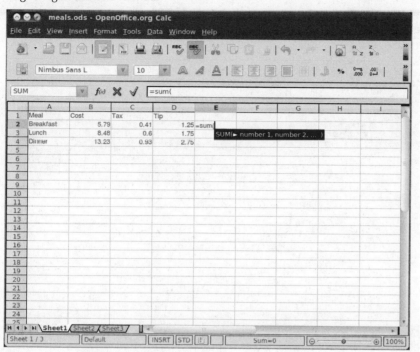

Next, identify the values that you want to summarize or perform an action on. This is most easily done using the mouse. To select the existing numerical values in a row, click the cell containing the cost value in the second column, and hold down the left mouse button while dragging the cursor to the right to encompass the other two numerical values in that row. This is known as selecting a *range* of cells. As you select a range of cells, a dotted rectangle outlines the cells that you've selected, and the identifiers for those cells are listed following the opening parenthesis in the formula, as shown in Figure 14-5. (This is often referred to as a *selection box*.) As you can see in this figure, the cells in a spreadsheet are identified by their column and row — for example, B2 refers to the cell in column B, row 2. When represented in a formula, a range of cells is identified by referring to the first cell and the last cell in the selected range, separating their names by a colon. In this example, *B2:D2* means "all cells between cells B2 and D2, including those two cells."

FIGURE 14-5

Selecting a range of cells for a formula to act on

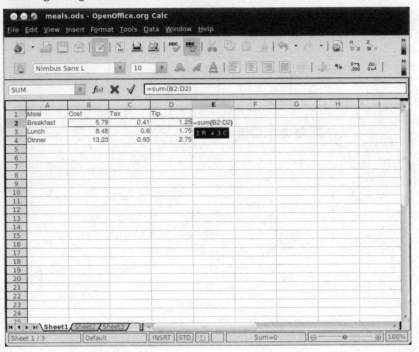

After selecting the cells for the function to act on, you can terminate the function by entering a closing parenthesis or simply pressing the Return/Enter key on your keyboard. Your spreadsheet calculates the value of the function that you've entered, displays that value, and moves the cursor to the next available cell, as shown in Figure 14-6. That was easy!

You could do the same thing in the next two rows, but there are easier ways to accomplish this that will help show some other basic spreadsheet capabilities. The easiest way to clone a calculated value to other cells in a column is to copy the contents of the first cell that contains the function and paste it into the other cells in that column. When you copy a calculated cell and paste it into multiple other cells at the same time, the spreadsheet figures out that you actually want to paste in a version of that function that applies to the rows in each column that you're pasting the function into. And people say that computer programs can't be smart!

To copy the function from the cell where you defined it, click on that cell and select the Edit menu's Copy command.

FIGURE 14-6

Displaying a calculated value

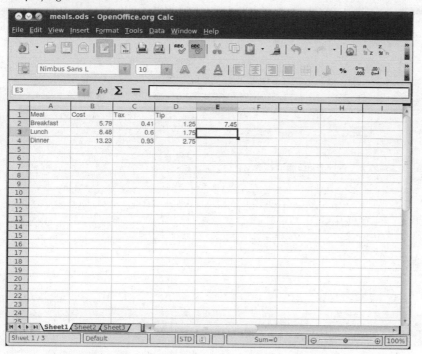

Next, select the range of cells that you want to paste that value into, in the same way that you selected a range of cells when defining your function. To do this, click on the cell below the one that currently contains the formula, and hold down the left mouse button while dragging the cursor down one row to encompass the same cell in the Dinner row, as shown in Figure 14-7.

Finally, select the Edit menu's Paste command to paste the function into the selected range of cells. Voilà! The function is pasted into each cell and automatically calculates the right value for each row, as shown in Figure 14-8.

FIGURE 14-7

Selecting the range of cells to paste the function into

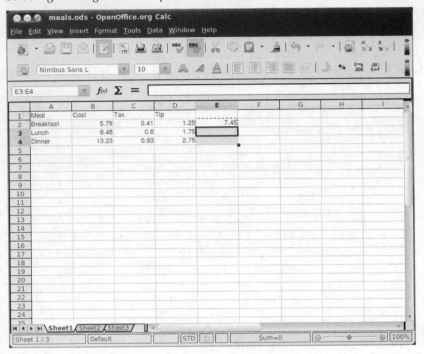

I love it when a plan comes together! The only numeric calculation that remains is to create another cell that summarizes the calculated values in the per-meal summary column. Adding a cell for a summary is easy enough to do, in exactly the same way as you did before, which I'll summarize:

1. Select the cell in which you want to invoke a function.

2. Type **=sum(** to start defining the function.

3. Click the left mouse button, hold it down, and drag the selection box to select the three cells in the column that you're summarizing.

4. Enter the closing parenthesis to conclude the function, and press Return to enter it and perform the calculation.

FIGURE 14-8

The updated spreadsheet with per-row calculations

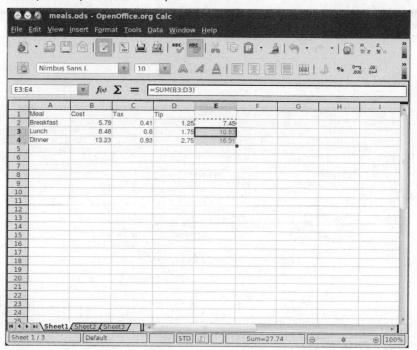

You can use any cell that you want. In my example, I skipped a row to make the summary cell stand out visually—your aesthetics and mine may differ. If all went according to plan, your spreadsheet should now look like the one shown in Figure 14-9. Congratulations—you've learned the basics of working with a spreadsheet!

Aside from the fact that you didn't have to do any of the math in this example (hooray!), one of the coolest things about a spreadsheet containing calculated values is that you can update any of the other cells that are involved in those calculations, and the spreadsheet will automatically update itself to reflect the new value in any cells that are based on the contents of the modified cell. Try it yourself—as all good software should do, *it just works*!

FIGURE 14-9

The sum of your previously calculated sums

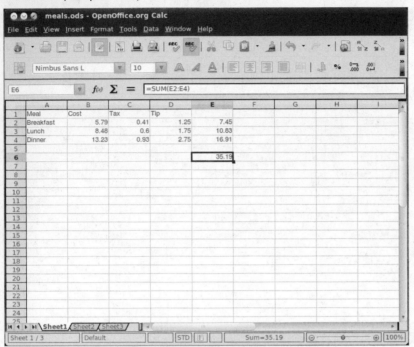

Once the basic calculations are complete, you can add some labels to clarify the meaning of the values in the different fields. You already have row and column headings, but nothing explains the cell that displays the daily total. To enter text in a cell of the spreadsheet, click on that cell to select it, and type whatever you want. Figure 14-10 shows the sample spreadsheet after I've entered the value "Daily Total" in cell D6.

Some of the columns in the spreadsheet are a bit wider than they need to be. To fix this, you can adjust the column width. To adjust the width of a column in a spreadsheet, left-click on the column heading (let's use column E as an example) to select it. Next, position the cursor over the line at the right edge of that column, hold down the left mouse button to select that edge, and drag it to the right to increase its size. As you drag the column edge, a tooltip appears that displays the current column width, as shown in Figure 14-11.

FIGURE 14-10

Adding a new text field to the spreadsheet

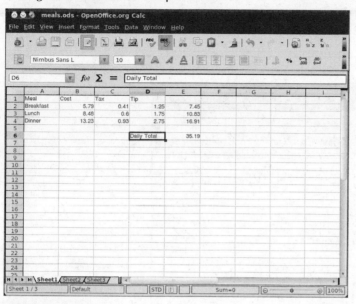

FIGURE 14-11

Resizing a column in the spreadsheet

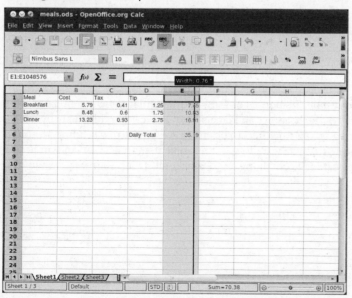

Once you've resized the column so that all of your text is visible, release the left mouse button to complete the resize operation. The column displays on the screen with its new width, as shown in Figure 14-12.

The resized column

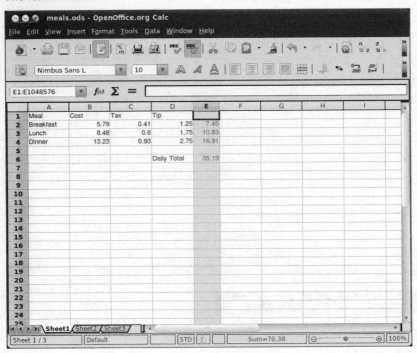

Next, let's clean up the formatting a bit. It's normal to want to differentiate labels from data values visually, so you can make all of the headings and labels bold. You can do this easily by multi-selecting all of them and applying bold formatting. To do this, click on the row heading for row 1, hold down the Ctrl key to indicate that you want to select multiple items, click the column heading for column A, and also select the cell containing the "Daily Total" label. Your screen should look like Figure 14-13.

FIGURE 14-13

Multi-selecting all labels in the spreadsheet

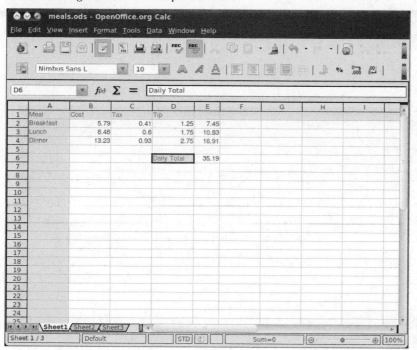

Next, click the Bold button in the formatting toolbar (the fat *A* icon). After you've applied the bold formatting, it may be easier to see the formatting if you select (click on) another cell first, so that the bold cells are no longer selected. All selected items are formatted in bold, and your screen should look like the spreadsheet shown in Figure 14-14.

The last thing to do after you've done any work is to save your file, which you can do by selecting the File ⇨ Save command. Because your spreadsheet has only a temporary name at this point, whatever spreadsheet you're using will display a dialog that enables you to specify a name for your spreadsheet (and optionally navigate to a specific directory location in which to save the spreadsheet).

Of course, there's much more to today's spreadsheets than the simple actions described in this tutorial, but this should be enough to get you started. All of the spreadsheets discussed in this chapter provide excellent online help, and plenty of books are available that explain how to use spreadsheets. Although few books are available on Linux-specific spreadsheets (yet), OpenOffice .org Calc is designed to be compatible with and similar to more common spreadsheets such as Microsoft Excel, so you should be able to get a lot of information out of almost any book on common spreadsheets.

FIGURE 14-14

Updated formatting in the spreadsheet

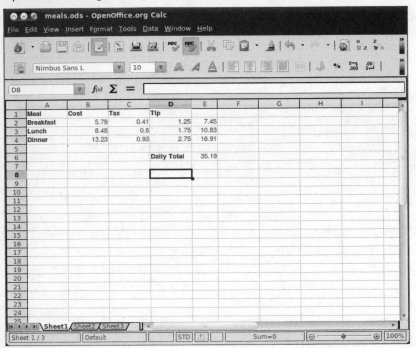

Invoking Functions in Calc

The tutorial in the previous section explained how to manually enter a function, which is fine if you are using a simple function that you happen to know the name of. Calc supports an extensive collection of predefined functions that you can easily select from the Insert ➪ Function dialog using the mouse. Figure 14-15 shows this dialog with the SUM function selected from the complete list of available formulas.

As you can see, selecting any function from the Function dialog displays abbreviated help for that function in the pane at the right of the dialog—in this case, "Returns the sum of all arguments."

FIGURE 14-15

Available functions in Calc

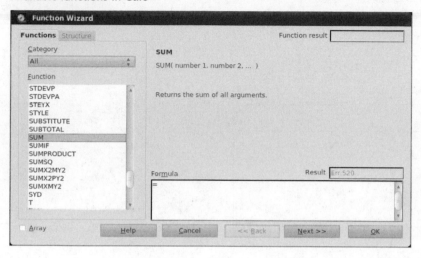

Specifying the Type of Data in a Cell

The spreadsheet tutorial in this section used fairly straightforward types of data that Calc could easily recognize — sequences of characters from the alphabet and spaces are probably words, whereas numbers and decimal points are probably numeric values. Knowing the type of data that is contained in a cell (generally referred to as its *data type* or *data format*) is fairly important, especially when you subsequently want to invoke functions that calculate values from the contents of various cells.

When you enter values in a spreadsheet without specifying their type, spreadsheets such as Calc assign them a general data format, which performs a best-guess of their data format based on the type of characters that they contain. However, you can also manually specify the format of any cell (or cells) by selecting those cells and using the commands on the Format ➪ Cells dialog, shown in Figure 14-16.

As an example, note that cell E6 in your example spreadsheet (most recently shown in Figure 14-11) doesn't display the traditional number of decimal places that you'd expect to see in a monetary value. This is because Calc's general data format recognized it as a decimal number but didn't have any way of knowing that this was a monetary value. To correct this, select that cell, select the Format ➪ Cells command, and click Currency in the pane at left. This displays a list of possible representations for that data format, as shown in Figure 14-17.

FIGURE 14-16

Specifying cell data formats in Calc

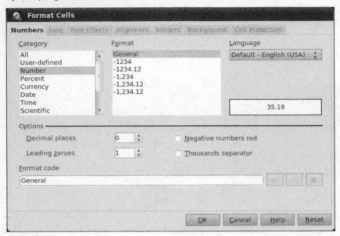

FIGURE 14-17

Specifying that a cell contains a currency value

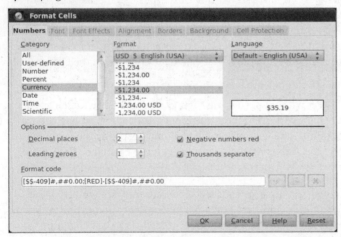

Note that two decimal places is the default for this data type, which is what you are trying to correct. Because this would do the trick, click OK to set cell E6 as a currency value and close the "Format Cells" dialog. This updates the spreadsheet, which now shows the correct number of decimal places for cell E6, as shown in Figure 14-18.

FIGURE 14-18

The updated spreadsheet showing the contents of cell E6 as a currency value (compare with Figure 14-11)

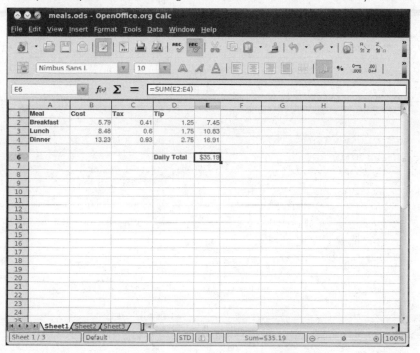

This is fine, except that Calc now recognizes that cell as a currency value but all other numeric cells are still general numeric values, which makes the spreadsheet look a bit odd. You can correct this by multi-selecting all of the numeric values in the spreadsheet (hold down the Ctrl key, click and hold the left mouse button on cell B2, drag the selection box to encompass all cells from B2 through E4, and then also click cell E6 before releasing the Ctrl key), displaying the "Format Cells" dialog again, selecting Currency, and clicking OK. Voilà! The cells in the spreadsheet are now consistent, as shown in Figure 14-19.

Importing Existing Spreadsheets into Calc

Linux folks like me tend to be Linux-centric, but that doesn't mean that we can completely ignore reality. When you're working with existing spreadsheets (and any other office-related documents), the chances are pretty good that you created them using more common software packages, such as Microsoft Excel, that run on other operating systems, such as Mac OS X and Microsoft Windows. The folks who wrote and support the OpenOffice.org suite and OpenOffice .org Calc couldn't ignore this reality either, so Calc provides built-in support for opening Microsoft Excel spreadsheets and workbooks.

FIGURE 14-19

The updated spreadsheet showing uniform currency values

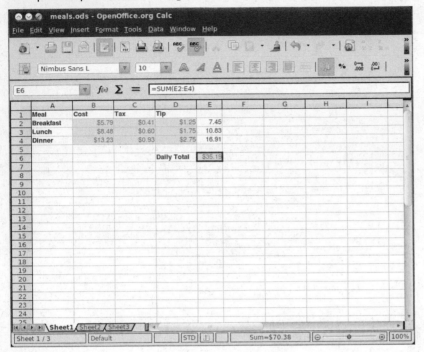

Note

If you have a lot of existing spreadsheets and are wondering how to transfer them to your new Ubuntu system, see Chapter 26, "File Transfer and Sharing," for detailed information on doing just that. Don't worry — it's really quite easy to do using a network connection or even a traditional mechanism such as a floppy drive (if you still have a floppy drive) or a flash drive, or burning a CD. ■

For example, to open an existing Excel spreadsheet, simply select the File ⇨ Open command. By default, the "File Selection" dialog that opens enables you to select files with any extension, including the .xls extension used by Microsoft Excel spreadsheets.

Supported Import Formats

The same mechanism described in the previous section can be used to open files in any other format supported by Calc. Calc can also open spreadsheets or other data files that have been saved in any of the following formats:

- **Comma-Separated Value (.csv):** A standard text-based interchange format, where each row appears on a single line and each field value is separated from the next by a comma.

This exchange format does not preserve the calculations required to produce cell values, only the values of the cells themselves.

- **Data Interchange Format (.dif):** Another standard text-based interchange format that does not preserve the calculations required to produce cell values, only the values of the cells themselves

- **Lotus 1-2-3 (.123, .wk1, .wks):** The spreadsheet formats used by various versions of Lotus 1-2-3 Spreadsheet

- **Microsoft Excel (.xls, .xlsx, .xlt, .xlw, .xml):** All of the common spreadsheet formats used by versions of Excel

- **Multiplan (.sylk):** The spreadsheet format used by the old Multiplan spreadsheet

- **Open/StarOffice Calc (.ods, .sdc):** The open document spreadsheet format used by Calc and other forward-thinking (i.e., open) spreadsheets

- **Quattro Pro (.wb1, wb2, .wb3):** The spreadsheet formats used by various versions of Borland's Quattro Pro spreadsheet

- **Pocket Excel (.pxl):** The spreadsheet format used by versions of Microsoft Excel for PDAs

- **Xbase (.dbf):** The database file format used by a variety of Dbase III–compatible applications such as Microsoft FoxPro, Dbase III and later, and so on

As you can see, the open source developers who are responsible for Calc have made a very significant effort to ensure that you can import any of your existing spreadsheet data files into Calc, so that you're not losing anything other than your dependence on your previous operating system.

Importing Spreadsheets Using the Document Converter

As you can see from the previous section, Calc can open spreadsheets produced by many other spreadsheet applications. It can also open spreadsheet files with Microsoft Excel extensions directly. After working on them, you can then save them directly in the new, open OpenDocument spreadsheet format (http://en.wikipedia.org/wiki/OpenDocument) that is used by Calc.

Tip

If you're actively sharing spreadsheets with people who are still using commercial spreadsheet applications like Excel, you'll want to use the File menu's "Save As" command to specify that you want to save them in their original format, such as Excel. ∎

Repeating this process is fine if you have only one or two spreadsheets that you want to update, but if you are moving all of your work to Ubuntu, you may find that you have hundreds of spreadsheets that you want to update to Calc format. Fortunately, Calc provides a Wizard for this that will not only import all of your Microsoft Excel spreadsheets, but also will import and convert any existing or attached templates that it detects.

To batch-import your existing Microsoft Excel (or older OpenOffice.org) documents, do the following:

1. Select File ▷ Wizards ▷ Document Converter. The dialog shown in Figure 14-20 displays.

FIGURE 14-20

Specifying the input format when converting documents

2. To batch-import Microsoft Excel files and templates, select the Microsoft Office radio button and the Excel Documents checkbox (grayed out in the figure, but if you select the Microsoft Office radio button, the Excel Documents checkbox will become available). Click Next to proceed. The dialog shown in Figure 14-21 displays.

3. Specify the directories in which you want the Wizard to search for the specified document types, and the locations to which converted documents should be saved. You may want to update the location to which converted templates should be saved — I typically use my home directory and subsequently move the files around manually. Once you've checked the directory locations, click Next to proceed. A Status dialog displays, summarizing the conversions that are about to take place. Click Convert to begin the conversion process. The dialog shown in Figure 14-22 displays as the conversion process progresses. When the conversion process completes, the Close and "Show log file" buttons are activated on the dialog.

Congratulations — the conversion process is complete! Your converted spreadsheets and templates are ready for use in Calc. Before clicking Close, it's a good idea to click the "Show log file" button, which opens the log file in OpenOffice.org Writer. (This button will not be selectable if OpenOffice.org Writer is not installed on your system.) The log file for the conversion process lists successful conversions and also identifies spreadsheets that should be fine-tuned or corrected before they can be used with Calc (if there are any). This is often the case with spreadsheet template files or spreadsheets containing complex macros, which may contain statements that are not completely compatible with anything other than Microsoft's own Visual Basic.

FIGURE 14-21

Specifying document and template locations when importing

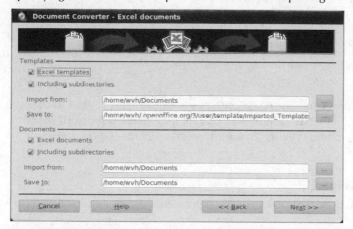

FIGURE 14-22

Monitoring the document conversion process

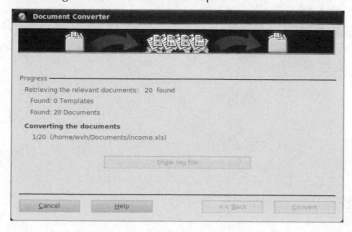

Creating and Using OpenOffice.org Presentations

The OpenOffice.org Office suite includes a powerful software package known as *Impress* for creating and editing presentations. As a tip of the hat to usability at the expense of confusion, the menu item for invoking this piece of software is labeled *OpenOffice.org Presentation*, which is what it creates. While you may not need to create presentations on your home computer, presentations are a fact of everyday life in business today, and no suite of office applications would be complete without this type of package. As mentioned earlier, I'll simply refer to OpenOffice.org Impress as *Impress* throughout the remainder of this section.

Starting Impress

You can start Impress from any command line by executing the command `ooimpress`, but it is usually easier to start it from your GNOME menus. A menu item for Impress is provided in the Applications ⇨ Office menu on Ubuntu systems. To start Impress, select the "OpenOffice.org Presentation" menu item.

Using the Presentation Wizard

When Impress starts, it runs a Wizard that walks you through creating a presentation. Let's follow along.

Figure 14-23 shows the initial screen of the Impress Presentation Wizard.

FIGURE 14-23

The first screen of the Impress Presentation Wizard

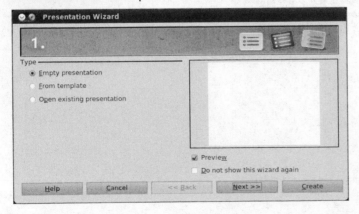

Assuming that you haven't opted out of the Presentation Wizard, click Next to begin creating your new presentation. The second Presentation Wizard screen displays, as shown in Figure 14-24.

Tip

When you start Impress and see the Presentation Wizard, you can opt out of the Presentation Wizard by selecting the "Open existing presentation" radio button. Selecting this button enables you to select an existing Impress or Microsoft PowerPoint presentation using the Open dialog that displays. If the presentation that you want to open is located in your home directory, you can double-click on its name to open it. If it is located in another directory, click Open to display a dialog that enables you to browse for the presentation that you want to open.

You can permanently opt out of starting Impress with the Wizard in the future by clicking "Do not show this wizard again" before you proceed. Impress will remember this setting and display a blank presentation the next time that you start Impress.

If you do not have any existing presentations that you want to open and simply want to open a new, blank presentation without using the Wizard, click the Create button while the "Empty presentation" radio button is selected. ■

FIGURE 14-24

Specifying a background in the Presentation Wizard

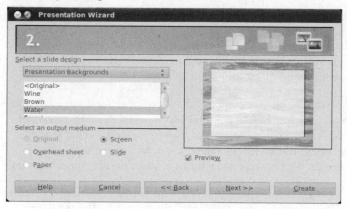

Select one of the available backgrounds for your presentation from the list (or keep the <Original> setting to continue without a background), and identify the output medium that you are targeting for this presentation: an onscreen presentation, overhead sheet, paper, photographic slides, and so on. Specifying the output medium modifies some internal settings to maximize the appearance and usable area in your presentation. Once you've made any desired changes to these settings (I selected the "Dark Blue with Orange" presentation background for this example), click Next to continue. The third Presentation Wizard dialog displays, as shown in Figure 14-25.

Providing presentation details in the Presentation Wizard

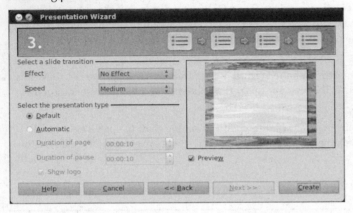

This screen enables you to select an effect that Impress should use when changing from one slide to the next. These include many different sweeping movements, rotations, and so on. Rather than try to describe them all here, I'll just suggest that you experiment with them. Selecting any effect from the list while the Preview checkbox is selected (which it is by default) shows a preview of the selected effect in the Preview window on this screen of the Wizard.

The other values on this Wizard screen enable you to specify the speed of any selected effect and the type of presentation that you are creating. *Default presentations* change slides only when you press a key or otherwise indicate that they should change. *Automatic presentations* change slides after a specified period of time and are intended for automated use in kiosks, perhaps at trade shows where one might want a regular, possibly repeating, series of slides to serve as an attractor.

Once you've changed any of the settings on this screen that you want to take advantage of, click Create to create your new presentation and complete the Presentation Wizard. The standard Impress screen displays, as shown in Figure 14-26.

FIGURE 14-26

The standard Impress screen displaying a new presentation

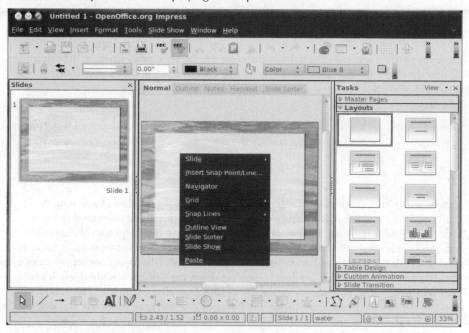

Taking a Quick Tour of Impress

Impress provides excellent online help, as do all of the tools in the OpenOffice.org suite, so I won't bore you by walking you through each menu and entry that it contains. However, as a quick overview of the Impress interface, the callouts in Figure 14-26 highlight the following areas:

- **Menus:** The dropdown menus in Impress are organized much like the menus in Microsoft PowerPoint to provide a familiar user experience. Menu items with an arrow at their right edge lead to other, related submenus.

- **Toolbars:** By default, Impress displays the Standard, Presentation, Drawing, and Line and Filling toolbars, which provide one-click access to specific commands when you click on the appropriate icon. You can modify the list of icons displayed on a toolbar by clicking on the control for that toolbar, located at the far right. You can display other toolbars or deactivate the default toolbars by selecting the names of those toolbars from the View ➪ Toolbars submenu.

- **Preview pane:** By default, the pane at the left displays a preview of all of the slides in the current presentation.

- **Edit pane:** By default, the central pane displays your working copy of the current slide. You can change the way in which this slide is displayed by selecting the other tabs at the top of this window.

- **Layouts pane:** By default, the pane at the right displays the predefined layouts that can be applied to the current slide. You can change the contents of this window by selecting other presentation-related tabs, such as Templates, Master Pages, Custom Animations, and Slide Transitions.

- **Context-sensitive menu:** Right-clicking on the slide that you are working on in Impress displays the context-sensitive menu shown in Figure 14-26. This menu provides quick access to several cell manipulation commands.

Tip

Although it's not displayed by default, you can display the Styles and Formatting window at any time by selecting the Format menu's Styles and Formatting menu command. (Select this menu command again to close this window.) The Styles and Formatting window provides easy access to the styles that are available in the current presentation, and is especially convenient if you choose not to display the formatting toolbar. Figure 14-26 shows Impress with the Styles and Formatting window displayed. Like most floating windows in OpenOffice.org applications, you can dock this window by holding down the Ctrl key and double-clicking on the gray portion of the window heading, making it a part of the default OpenOffice.org interface rather than a floating window. You can undock the window by clicking and dragging on the gray portion of the window heading, or by holding down the Ctrl key and double-clicking on the heading of the docked area. ∎

Impress provides extensive online help, available by selecting OpenOffice.org Help from the Help menu, or by pressing the F1 key on your keyboard at any time.

Tip

If you are having problems viewing the text for the online help in Impress and OpenOffice.org Writer is not installed on your system for some reason, try installing OpenOffice.org Writer. This will force an update to the components that control online Help in the OpenOffice.org suite and will usually resolve the problem. ∎

Creating a Presentation

Creating presentations in Impress is easy, although fine-tuning them can be as challenging as it is in any software for creating presentations.

To apply any of the available formats to the current slide, select the thumbnail for that format from the Layouts window. The selected layout is applied to the current slide. You can then click in any of the textboxes and enter the appropriate text for that region. Figure 14-27 shows a slide that uses the "Title Slide" layout at the upper right in the Layouts window.

Creating a title slide in Impress

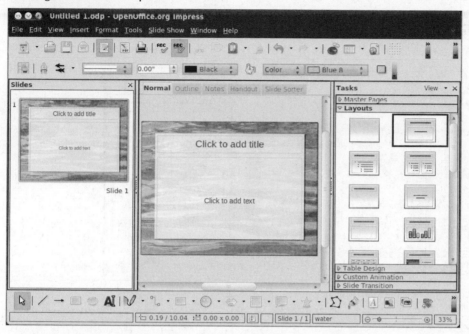

Impress provides many sample layouts, including title slides, slides that provide headings and text areas, slides that provide headings and areas for graphics, and so on. You can identify the intent behind any of the available layouts by positioning the cursor over the thumbnail for that layout and viewing the tooltip that displays.

Once you've entered your text or other content in the current slide, you can add a new slide by selecting the Insert ➪ Slide command. A new slide displays in the Editing window, and the Preview window is updated to display the new slide and any previous slides. You can then select the thumbnail for the format that you want to use on the new slide. For example, Figure 14-28 shows a new slide with the "Title, two Text Blocks" format applied, and a preview of the previous and current slides.

FIGURE 14-28

Adding a new slide in Impress

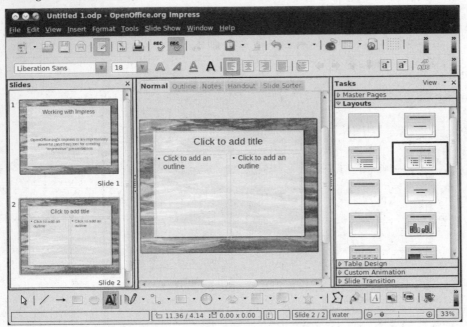

Once you've added a number of slides to your presentation, you should save it using the File ➪ Save command. If this is a new presentation, you will be prompted to supply a name for the presentation.

After saving your presentation, you will probably want to see what it looks like so far. To preview your actual presentation, select View ➪ Slide Show or press the F5 key on your keyboard. Your presentation displays on your screen, using any transition effects and timing that you specified when you created the presentation.

Tip

When you preview your presentation, the preview starts at the first slide selected in the Preview pane. To see your entire presentation, select the first slide in the presentation before requesting a preview. ■

Importing Existing Presentations

Impress can open existing presentations produced by Microsoft PowerPoint (and those produced by itself or StarOffice, of course). After working on these, you can then save them directly in the new, open OpenDocument presentation format that is used by Impress.

Repeating this process is fine if you have only one or two presentations that you want to update, but if you are moving all of your work to Ubuntu, you may find that you have many presentations that you want to update to Impress format. Fortunately, Impress provides a Wizard for this that will not only import all of your Microsoft PowerPoint presentations, but also will import and convert any existing or attached layout files and master documents that it detects. This Wizard is known as the *Document Converter*. You can start this Wizard by selecting the File ⇨ Wizards ⇨ Document Converter menu item.

The Document Converter used to convert presentations works identically to the Document Converter used to batch-import spreadsheets, as explained earlier in this chapter, so I won't waste space by repeating those instructions here. For information on using the Document Converter Wizard to batch-import documents of any supported type, see "Importing Spreadsheets Using the Document Converter" earlier in this chapter. The only real difference when importing presentations rather than spreadsheets (or word processing documents, as explained in Chapter 13) is that you must select "Microsoft Office and PowerPoint documents" on the initial screen of the Wizard, as shown in Figure 14-29.

FIGURE 14-29

Specifying the input format when converting presentations

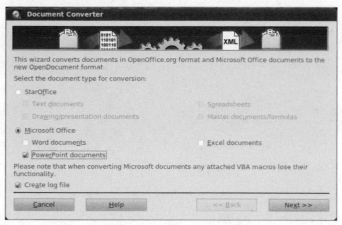

As shown in Figure 14-29, converting any Microsoft documents will make "any attached VBA macros lose their functionality." And that's a bad thing? You might also say that converting any Microsoft documents will cause them to lose much of their ability to carry and launch viruses. This seems like a selling point for using OpenOffice.org on all platforms, but your mileage may vary.

Summary

This chapter discussed common types of office software that you may need to use to complete your move to Ubuntu Linux. Linux often gets a bad rap in the press for not having a rich set of application software — as this book shows, that is entirely false. Not only is a good selection of powerful office software available for Linux, but the open source nature of Linux gives you many alternatives in terms of the packages that you want to use — and all at the same low, low price, which is $0.00 thanks to the hard work and time spent by the open source community and the folks who bring you Ubuntu Linux.

This chapter began by discussing OpenOffice.org Calc, the powerful spreadsheet component of the OpenOffice.org Office suite that is installed by default on Ubuntu desktop systems. The chapter concluded by discussing OpenOffice.org Impress, which is a powerful software package for creating, working with, and managing presentations, and is another part of the OpenOffice.org suite of office applications.

Now that we've explored creating documents, spreadsheets, and presentations, the next chapter discusses the software that enables you to create and convert various types of graphics files on Ubuntu desktop systems.

Working with Graphics

IN THIS CHAPTER

Introducing digital graphics

Working with images in GIMP

Introducing photo editing

Using OpenOffice.org Draw

Working with vector graphics

A s a writer, I've always somewhat resented the old saying "A picture is worth a thousand words." Can't I just do the thousand words and we can all move on?

I'm kidding, of course — there are many times when a picture is worth far more than any number of words, such as the screenshots in this book, photographs and artwork in advertising, or various publications that specialize in celebrating the human form. No one has ever described a text-heavy document as eye-catching, despite even the best efforts of typographers and the layout artists at *Wired*. Even if you're not a graphics artist, there are times when everyone needs software for editing graphics and creating drawings, whether you just want to remove the terminal case of red-eye from all of your vacation photographs or produce simple illustrations for a card, letter, or presentation.

If you've worked with graphics packages such as Adobe Photoshop, Adobe Illustrator, CorelDRAW, or Corel's Paint Shop Pro (formerly from JASC), you'll be happy to know that open source packages with the capabilities that you'll need to do the same sort of work are freely available for Ubuntu Linux. Some are preinstalled, and some are located in Ubuntu repositories and are therefore just a download away.

This chapter helps you make some sense out of the maze of abbreviations, acronyms, general terminology, and specialized jargon that aficionados use to describe digital graphics, and explains how to use the software available for Ubuntu Linux to create and edit drawings, images, and other types of computer graphics.

Tip

If you are creating graphics and need a starting point or some inspiration, you'll be happy to know that an open source library of clip art is available to complement the open source software that is discussed in this chapter. The aptly named "Open Clip Art Library" (`http://openclipart.org`) is a collection of user-contributed clip art that has been placed in the public domain according to the Creative Commons license for that purpose (`http://creativecommons.org/licenses/publicdomain`). To quote the license, this allows the graphics in this library to be "freely reproduced, distributed, transmitted, used, modified, built upon, or otherwise exploited by anyone for any purpose, commercial or non-commercial, and in any way, including by methods that have not yet been invented or conceived." There's a lot of nice stuff there—check it out! ∎

Overview of Digital Graphics Terminology

Even if you're not a graphics artist (and I certainly am not one), everyone with a web site or a digital camera has some familiarity with digital graphics. Terminology-wise, *digital graphics* is basically nothing more than storing images in files on your computer, regardless of whether these files contain pictures from your summer vacation, fancy buttons or other images that you're using on your web site, artwork and drawings that you've created using graphics software, pictures that you've used a scanner to capture, images captured directly from your computer screen, or just about anything else that you can store in a file and display in a graphics application.

The following provides a quick glossary of graphics terms that you may encounter as you start to work with online, digital graphics:

- **Anti-aliasing:** A technique used to reduce the jagged appearance of the edges of objects and text in graphical images. Anti-aliasing softens those edges by blending them with the colors or areas that appear beside them in an image.

- **Bitmap:** A graphical image that is composed of multiple picture elements known as *pixels*, each representing 1 bit of that image. Each pixel in a bitmap has its own color value, generally expressed as a combination of red, green, and blue (RGB) color values. Bitmaps are one of the two main formats for digital images—the other is vector graphics. Bitmaps are also referred to as *raster images*. The generic bitmap should not be confused with the common graphics format known as *bitmap*, or BMP.

- **BMP:** A graphics format originally developed by Microsoft that supports a variety of resolutions and color depths. A file in BMP format contains a single bitmap/raster image.

- **CMYK:** A color definition model that identifies the amount of **C**yan, **M**agenta, **Y**ellow, and Blac**K** in a given color. CMYK color designations are commonly used in printing because these are the four traditional ink colors used in commercial printing. Cyan, magenta, and yellow are referred to as *subtractive primary colors* because they are based on reflected light and thus begin with white light and subtract wavelengths to display specific colors. In the commercial (paper) print process, a separate printing plate is made for each of the CMYK colors. These are therefore often referred to as *process colors*.

- **Color depth:** The maximum number of colors contained in an image or that can be displayed by a given device or graphics card. Common color depths are 256 colors, 16-bit (65,535 colors), 32-bit (4,294,967,296 colors, generally simply referred to as *millions of colors*), and so on. The greater the color depth of an image, the greater its size, because the color of each pixel requires the associated number of bits to represent each of the red, green, and blue portions of its color. Color depth is often defined in *bits per pixel* (bpp). For example, high color uses 15 or 16 bpp: five bits for blue, five bits for red, and five or six bits for green.

- **Color space:** A model for representing color. RGB, CMYK, and HSV are common color spaces.

- **Dithering:** The process of displaying pixels of different colors in a portion of an image to give the visual impression of a single color. Dithering is often used to give a lower-resolution image the smoother appearance of a higher-resolution image.

- **GIF:** A popular lossless graphics format, Graphics Interchange Format (GIF) files were formerly quite popular on the Web because they produced relatively high-quality, small-file-size images through the use of a compression technique known as Lempel-Ziv-Welch (LZW) compression, which is patented by Unisys. Because of licensing issues, most web sites now use JPEG or PNG graphics. The primary advantage of the format is that a single GIF file can contain multiple images that can be configured to display in sequence. These multi-image GIF files are known as *animated GIFs*. To avoid patent and licensing issues, most animated web graphics today are created using file formats such as Flash, QuickTime, or Shockwave, or are created using Java-based animation techniques.

- **Grayscale:** An image that is composed of various shades of gray. The number of bits used to hold the color value for each pixel determines the number of shades of gray that the image can use. If the number of bits is 1, then the image is simply black and white, which is also known as *monochrome*. Grayscale is typically used in newspapers or books that are printed in black and white, where a halftone is used to print the different shades of gray.

- **Halftone:** The simulation of a continuous-tone image (shaded drawing, photograph) by using different-sized dots to make up different portions of the image. Smaller dots per print area are used for lighter areas, and larger dots are used for darker areas. Halftones are typically used for relatively high-resolution reproduction of black and white images in print, such as in a newspaper or magazine.

- **HSV:** A color definition model in which colors are represented by their hue (X axis), saturation (Y axis), and brightness (Z axis).

- **Jaggies:** The term for the staircase effect seen on the edges of bitmapped objects, also sometimes referred to as *aliasing*. This unpleasant visual effect can be mitigated by the use of techniques such as anti-aliasing.

- **JPEG:** A popular bitmapped image format consisting of 24-bit color and developed by the Joint Photographic Experts Group. JPEG is a lossy format, which is often used for graphics on web pages to provide a good balance of good image resolution and small file size.

- **Layers:** Most complex graphics files are internally composed of multiple image layers that are superimposed to create the final image. Working with different portions of an image (background, each component of an image, etc.) not only makes it easy to interact with each graphics element without disturbing others, but also makes it easy to build up complex graphics quickly by separating them into different logical elements that can be reused across similar graphics.

- **Lossless formats:** File formats that are not lossy, that is, file formats that provide all of the information that was present in the audio, graphics, or video information as it was originally recorded, drawn, or captured.

- **Lossy formats:** File formats that sacrifice image/audio quality to reduce file size. The term *lossy* refers to the data compression algorithm used to reduce file size, where some of the information that was present in the original file is actually eliminated to produce the smaller, compressed file, and therefore the original file can never be completely reconstructed from the compressed version. In the case of graphics, lossy images typically reduce both the available palette of colors and the number of pixels in the image. Lossy formats are quite common in graphics, audio, and video files because they can often reduce file size by eliminating information that is beyond the range of the human eye, the human ear (e.g., mp3 files), or both.

- **Metadata:** Data about other data. In graphics files, metadata typically provides information about file data elements, file attributes (name, size, location, color depth, data type, etc.), or free-form comments. Metadata simplifies the use and analysis of graphics files by providing a higher-level interface to the file than just the raw data itself.

- **Monochrome:** Images and text that are displayed using only black and white pixels. The term *monochrome* comes from the fact that there is only one chromatic (i.e., *color*) value used in the image: black is a pixel that is set to that color value, while white is a pixel that is not set to black.

- **Pantone colors:** A set of specific color designations created by Pantone, Inc. (`www.pantone.com`) that are used to provide definitive color values for various portions of an image. The set of these standardized colors is known as the *Pantone Matching System* (PMS). Pantone colors are identified by unique identification numbers in a color guide known as a *swatch book*. Pantone colors are used to identify spot colors in an image — in other words, portions of an image that do not blend with any other portions of the image.

- **PCL:** A Printer Control Language originally developed by Hewlett-Packard (HP) and now used in thousands of different printers. Files in PCL format can be printed directly on HP and compatible printers with no pre-processing.

- **Pixels:** The smallest graphical element in a digital image that can be displayed on your computer screen. Each pixel has its own color, generally expressed as a combination of red, green, and blue (RGB) color values. The term *pixel* stands for "picture element." Most graphical images, such as digital photographs, contain millions of pixels — hence the term *megapixels*. The more pixels an image contains, the more detail it provides and the higher its resolution.

- **PNG:** Portable Network Graphics, a graphics file format originally designed as an alternative to GIF and its attendant licensing problems. PNG files are lossless, supporting up to 48-bit color or 16-bit grayscale images without losing any detail during compression.

- **PostScript:** A printer control language developed by Adobe and used in thousands of high-quality laser printers. PostScript files support both bitmaps and drawing primitives (low-level commands that create graphics by drawing lines from point to point; generating geometric shapes using corner, center, perimeter coordinates; etc.), and therefore typically produce high-quality images. PostScript was inspired by an earlier printer control language called *InterPress*, which was developed at Xerox PARC, as were other handy things such as Ethernet, laser printers, bitmapped displays, and so on.

- **Prepress:** The process of preparing documents for printing. Nowadays, this generally refers to the use of computers to digitally prepare documents and illustrations for printing as opposed to the use of analog techniques in the past for such activities as the production of photographic negatives, manual page layout, manual typesetting, and the manual production of printing plates.

- **Raster graphics:** Another name for bitmap graphics. The term *raster* refers to a position in the grid of coordinates that make up a computer display.

- **Resolution:** The output quality of an image, defined in terms of dots, lines, pixels, or samples per inch, depending on your output device. PPI (pixels per inch) refers to screen resolution, DPI (dots per inch) refers to printer resolution, SPI (samples per inch) refers to the resolution at which images are obtained from a scanner, and LPI (lines per inch) refers to halftone resolution. High-resolution images contain 300 or more units per inch and are intended for printed output. Low-resolution images generally contain 100 or fewer units per inch and are generally intended for onscreen or Web-based display.

- **RGB:** A color definition model that identifies the amount of **R**ed, **G**reen, and **B**lue in a given color, typically represented as either three numbers from 0 to 255 or a series of six hexadecimal digits in which each pair of digits represents the intensity of each color. For example, **255 0 255** and **FF00FF** represent the same color, a bright purple comprising the maximum value of red, no green, and the maximum value of blue. All computer monitors use RGB colors. Red, green, and blue are added together to produce white and are therefore referred to as *additive primary colors*.

- **Stair-stepping:** Another term for jaggies.

- **TIFF:** Tagged Image File Format, a popular lossless graphics file format. Files in TIFF format often have the extensions .tif or .tiff. TIFF files are typically quite large and therefore are unsuited for display on web pages.

- **Vector graphics:** A digital graphics representation and associated file format that defines an image by identifying each object in that image and describing that object in terms of characteristics such as its outline, shape, color palette, associated text, gradients, patterns, and element grouping. Vector graphics are resolution-independent because they can be redrawn at the highest quality supported by a graphics application or display device.

For a general source of information about digital graphics, the best site I've found on the Web is About.com's Graphics Software section at `http://graphicssoft.about.com`. This site contains everything from a great dictionary of graphics terms to hundreds of useful tutorials, articles, and discussions. It's truly amazing! The only problem with this site is that it is focused on Windows and Macintosh software. Hey, what about the rest of us? Luckily, as you'll see throughout this chapter, the graphics tools available for free on your Ubuntu systems are more than sufficient for almost every graphics task.

Using GIMP

GIMP stands for "GNU Image Manipulation program," the premiere open source graphics package for Linux systems. *GIMP* originally stood for "General Image Manipulation Program" and was created by Spencer Kimball and Peter Mattis. From the beginning, GIMP was designed to be easily extendible by the addition of plug-ins that could be written, compiled, and maintained separately, but that would work seamlessly within the GIMP framework. Like any other open source package, GIMP has substantially benefited from the contributions of others, especially in terms of plug-in development. GIMP is a shining example of a powerful and successful open source package, having also been ported to Microsoft Windows and Apple's Mac OS X and used extensively on those platforms. For all of the details of GIMP history, see `www.gimp.org/about/ancient_history.html`.

Prior to Ubuntu 10.04, GIMP was automatically installed as part of a default Ubuntu desktop system installation. With Ubuntu 10.04, you will have to install the GIMP application yourself using any of the package management tools discussed in Chapter 19, "Adding, Removing, and Updating Software." The OpenOffice.org Draw package, discussed later in this chapter, is the default graphics application on an Ubuntu 10.04 system, but if you really want to do serious graphics work, you'll want to install GIMP.

GIMP is legendary among GNU software packages, especially as far as the GNOME desktop environment goes, because the toolkit upon which much of the GNOME user interface is based is GTK, the GIMP Tool Kit. Without restating everything on the GIMP Ancient History page, let's just say that GIMP started out using another X Window System toolkit, but its authors decided to create their own, which was full-featured enough to be adopted by many other projects. Biblically, GIMP begat GTK, which begat GTK+, which begat GNOME, which now supports GIMP. I hope that's clear — there will be a quiz later.

Note

People often refer to GIMP simply as *gimp* or *the gimp* (not to be confused with the character from Quentin Tarantino's *Pulp Fiction*), because that's the name of the command that you type at the command-line to start the program. Throughout this chapter, I'll use *GIMP* as a way of generally referring to the program, using `gimp` (lowercase) only when I'm specifically referring to the command-line command. ∎

Starting GIMP

Once GIMP is installed on your system, you can start it manually in a variety of different ways, the most basic of which are:

- By selecting GIMP Image Editor from the Applications ⇨ Graphics menu
- By typing the `gimp` command in a GNOME Terminal or xterm window and pressing Return

When you start GIMP for the first time, the default display that you see depends on the version of GIMP that you are running. If you've used GIMP before, the initial window layout may be different from what you're used to seeing. GIMP 2.6 introduced some basic simplifications of the user interface among its many other enhancements. Current versions of GIMP display a startup screen like the one shown in Figure 15-1.

FIGURE 15-1

Starting GIMP 2.6 for the first time

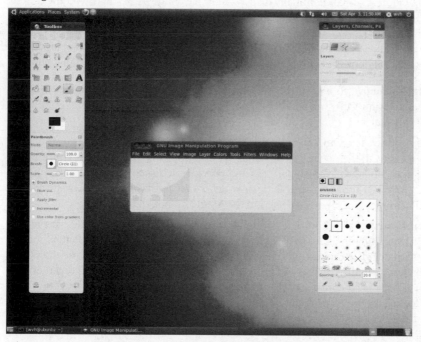

If you're used to older versions of GIMP, you'll still be able to locate and use your favorite GIMP commands — the primary change in GIMP 2.6 is that a new GIMP window replaces the Toolbox window as the primary GIMP window. The menus that were formerly located on the Toolbox window are now present on the main GIMP window, and have been re-designed to better organize sets of related commands. The main GIMP window serves as your primary image editing window, which was formerly done by separate edit windows. When you create or open a new graphic, it displays in the main GIMP window. Closing the last graphic that you're editing redisplays the generic GIMP window shown in Figure 15-1.

Note

If you're a long-time GIMP user, you may remember that GIMP formerly displayed a sequence of startup dialogs that enabled you to customize some aspects of GIMP's initial configuration. Because most people simply accepted all of the defaults, these introductory panels have been done away with. If this is your first time starting GIMP, things are simpler now. You can still configure GIMP to your heart's content by selecting the Edit ⇨ Preferences command, and explorihng the various configuration options that are available. ■

A Quick Tour of GIMP

The first thing that most people do when using GIMP is to customize the various panels and dialogs that display each time GIMP is launched.

As you can see from Figure 15-1, GIMP initially displays multiple windows. A single window can actually contain multiple dialogs that are combined into one dialog—such dialogs are known as *dockable dialogs*. To make things even more flexible, dialogs can be either docked together or combined as multiple tabs within a single dialog. The default screen shown in Figure 15-1 displays the following windows. Each window description includes a list of the dialogs contained in that window:

- **Main GIMP window:** Provides the GIMP menus and shows the first graphic or image that you are editing. Opening another graphic at the same time displays that graphic in a copy of this window.

- **Toolbox window:** The window at the left contains two dialogs: at the top, the Toolbox dialog and below it, the Tool Options dialog. The Toolbox dialog shows the editing or selection tool that is currently selected and provides access to all other editing and selection tools. The Tool Options dialog provides access to the configurable aspects of the GIMP tool that is currently selected in the Main Toolbox dialog.

- **Layers and Brushes window:** The window at the right contains two dialogs: at the top, the "Layers, Channels, and Paths" dialog; and below it, the "Brushes, Patterns, and Gradients" dialog. The interesting thing about this window is that each of the dialogs that it contains actually consists of multiple dialogs that have been docked together as tabs. The top dialog consists of the "Layers, Channels, and Paths" and the Undo dialogs docked together, while the bottom dialog consists of the Brushes, Palettes, and Gradients dialogs docked together.

Tip

GIMP's main window dialog must always be active in any version of GIMP, even if it is minimized—actually closing this dialog causes GIMP to exit. Similarly, most GIMP users find it extremely useful to always have the Layers dialog available so that they have easy access to the portions of an image that are contained on different layers. ■

Docking or undocking dialogs is a fairly simple process. To undock dialogs, select the header for that dialog (the header inside the window, not the title bar for the window itself), and drag it out of the window in which it is currently displayed. For example, to undock the "Toolbox Options" dialog from the Toolbox window, left-click and hold on the header of the "Toolbox Options" dialog (which initially says "Paintbrush" because the paintbrush is the tool that is initially selected when you first start GIMP), and drag the header out of the Toolbox window. An icon identifying that dialog follows the cursor (which changes into a hand), as shown in Figure 15-2, in which the "Tool Options" dialog header has been dragged out of the window shown at the left in Figure 15-1.

FIGURE 15-2

Undocking a GIMP dialog

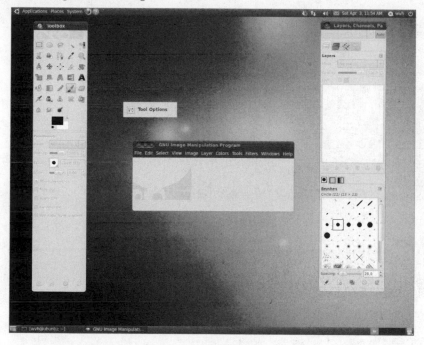

Releasing this icon on the screen at the point where you want the undocked dialog to appear results in a screen like that shown in Figure 15-3. The "Tool Options" dialog displays as a separate window, and the portion of the Main GIMP Toolbox window that it formerly occupied is now empty. You can resize the window that formerly contained this dialog to remove the empty space by selecting and dragging a corner.

Sample GIMP Tasks

As I acknowledged earlier, I am not a graphics artist. Many people who are serious artists have created extensive sets of tutorials on using GIMP, and I'd be insulting them (and you) by either parroting those or by trying to pretend that I have major graphics skills. That said, I do use GIMP regularly for a variety of common tasks that you may find useful, so I'll discuss some of those in the next two sections. For tutorials on using GIMP to do serious graphics work, see some of the URLs in the section "More Information about GIMP," later in this chapter.

FIGURE 15-3

The GIMP "Tool Options" dialog, undocked

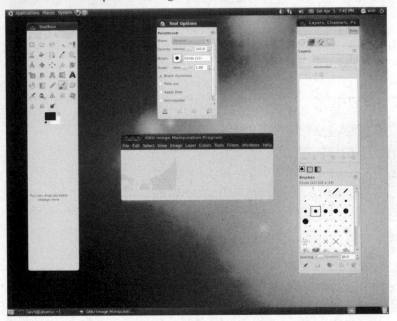

Color and GIMP

GIMP is often referred to as an Adobe Photoshop killer because it provides much of the functionality of Adobe Photoshop at no cost to the user. For most of us, this is probably true. However, professional graphics artists will probably either say, "What's GIMP?" or simply laugh when you say "artists of the world unite, and cast off your copies of Photoshop!" Two color-related issues prevent GIMP from serious commercial use: GIMP currently supports only 8-bit color specifications, and GIMP's color handling is fundamentally based on RGB colors, while professional printing relies on CMYK and Pantone color specifications. While work on 16-bit color support in GIMP is in progress (through the new GEGL rendering engine, www.gegl.org), it isn't available now, but the lack of built-in CMYK support is the real stumbling block to using GIMP for commercial illustrations that may end up in print publications. Newer versions of GIMP will show both the RGB and CMYK color values for any portion of an image, but GIMP saves only RGB color designations in its output. While most print shops can convert RGB to CMYK for you, this isn't an exact process, typically adding some black to an image when trying to match the colors. Not a good thing for professionals who expect their images to look like their original designs.

Fortunately, GIMP's plug-in architecture lends itself to addressing this sort of problem, and various GIMP plug-ins for CMYK support are available (although they are not installed with GIMP by default). The best known of these for the latest version of GIMP is the Separate+ plug-in by Yoshinori Yamakawa, which is available from http://cue.yellowmagic.info/softwares/separate.html. If you are a graphics artist, I'd love to hear whether this plug-in can crack the professional printing barrier for GIMP. Crossing fingers now…

Taking Screenshots Using GIMP

As you may have noticed so far, this book contains several screen captures that show the entire screen, specific windows, or certain portions of the screen. My graphics friends have finally convinced me that a picture is, indeed, worth a thousand words, or should at least accompany them. All of the screenshots in this book were done with GIMP, which is an excellent tool for screen and window captures. You may think that you'll never need to do a screen capture yourself, but that's not necessarily the case — screen captures are very useful when you're submitting problem reports and trying to share what you're seeing on your screen with a friend, and so on.

Tip

GIMP isn't the only screen capture software in town — after all, this is Linux. On Ubuntu systems, you can capture full-screen or single window images by selecting the Applications ➪ Accessories ➪ Take Screenshot menu command (or by running the gnome-screenshot command from any Terminal window). The Ubuntu repository includes other screen capture software, such as scrot (a command-line package) and shutter (an impressive graphical package), that focus on that task, and which you may want to experiment with. ■

Capturing a screenshot in GIMP is quite easy:

1. Select File ➪ Create ➪ Screen Shot from the main GIMP window (or the File ➪ Acquire ➪ Screen Shot menu command from the GIMP Toolbox window if you are using an earlier version of GIMP). The dialog shown in Figure 15-4 displays.

2. Select the radio button that identifies whether you want to capture a specific window or the entire screen.

FIGURE 15-4

The Screenshot dialog

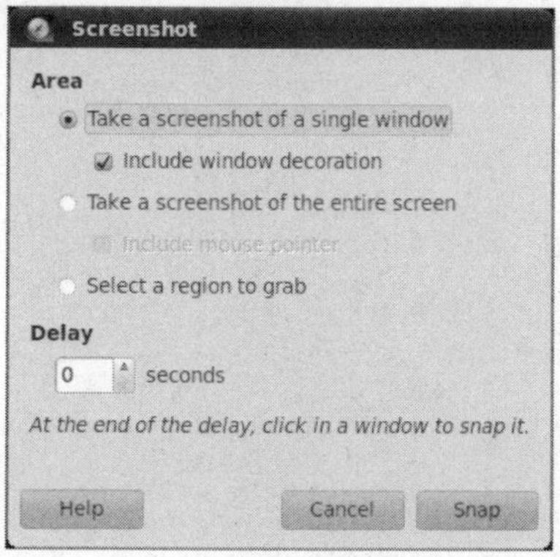

3. Select any delay that you want to take place before you capture a specific dialog or the entire screen. Specifying a delay enables you to pull down menus, set specific values, hide other dialogs, and so on — anything that you want to do to capture a screen or window shot that displays exactly what you want it to.

4. Click Snap to initiate the capture process. After any interval that you have specified elapses, the screen capture takes place. (If no delay was specified, it happens as soon as you click Snap.) If you specified that you wanted to capture a single window, the cursor turns into a set of crosshairs, and you must click on the window that you want to capture. Once the capture takes place, the result displays on the screen in its own GIMP window, as shown in Figure 15-5, which shows the entire screen capture for Figure 15-2.

FIGURE 15-5

A full screen capture in GIMP

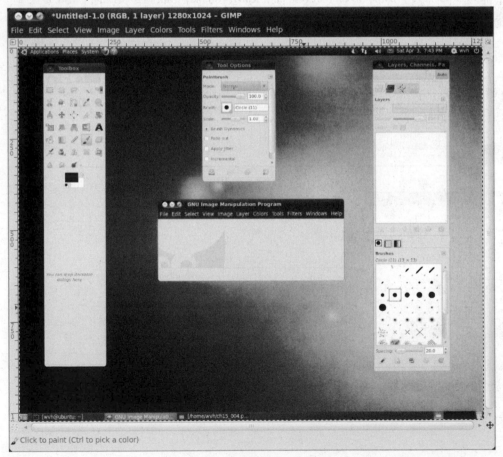

5. Once you have a full screen or window capture, the next step is to save it in a graphics format that you or someone else can use. To save the screen capture, right-click in the capture window and select File ➪ Save As. (You can also do this by pressing Ctrl+Shift+S, which is certainly my favorite method because of its brevity.) A dialog like the one shown in Figure 15-6 displays.

FIGURE 15-6

GIMP's first "Save Image" dialog

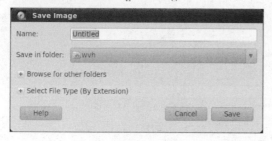

6. Dialogs like the one shown in Figure 15-6 enable you to save your screenshot in a specific graphics format, which is determined by the file extension. After entering the file name and the file extension that you want to use, click Save to display an additional, format-specific dialog, as shown in Figure 15-7.

Tip

By default, the file extension that you specify when saving a file in GIMP automatically identifies the graphics format in which you want the file to be saved. If you don't know the file extension that is associated with the graphics format in which you want to save your file, click the Select File Type control in the lower-left corner of the "Save Image" dialog to display a list of available graphics formats. Selecting a graphics format automatically adds the default file extension that is associated with the selected graphics format to the name of the file that you are saving. ■

7. The options associated with each graphics format differ, so the available options on dialogs like the one shown in Figure 15-7 are specific to your target file format. Once you have made any changes to the default values that GIMP associates with your target output format, click Save.

GIMP's format-specific Save dialog

GIMP not only supports a wide variety of output graphics formats, but it also makes it quite easy to capture high-quality screen images and fine-tune the characteristics of the files that you create.

Converting and Reducing Images Using GIMP

Most of us nowadays have a web page that we use to share information and pictures with our friends. Most digital cameras save images in JPEG format, which can provide a great balance between small file size (so that web pages containing images will load in our lifetimes) and good quality (so that you appear to know what you're doing with your digital camera). Regardless, there are going to be times when you have images in larger file sizes that you want to reduce in size and convert to other formats. For example, the TIFF files produced by most scanning software today are huge and shouldn't be displayed on a web page. Similarly, most digital cameras today capture photos in many megapixels, which are great for printing but are overkill on a web page.

Because GIMP supports so many different graphics file formats, it is an excellent tool for converting images to formats that you can use elsewhere (most notably on the Web), and for reducing file size without sacrificing too much quality. The sidebar "Graphics Formats Supported by GIMP" shows all of the graphics file formats and associated file extensions that are supported by GIMP.

The following are some tips on using GIMP to reduce the file size of your images so that you can easily put them on a web page or even mail them to loved ones:

- Save your files in a lossy format that supports compression. PNG files are an attractive choice because they support up to 48-bit color, but I've found JPEG files easiest to exchange with users of other types of computer systems (and they are also supported in all Web browsers — some older browsers don't support PNG graphics).

Tip
When saving files in a lossy format, make sure to save the modified files with a different name so that you still have your originals in case you want to print them or edit them in some other tool — as noted earlier, the original file can never be completely reconstructed from the compressed version. ∎

- When editing or converting JPEG images, experiment with reducing the quality level of your image. In most cases, you won't be able to tell the difference, and neither will your viewers. To reduce the quality level of a JPEG image, click File ⇨ Save As, enter the new, unique name, and click Save. The "Save As" JPEG dialog displays, as shown in Figure 15-8. By default, this dialog selects an image quality level of 85. Click the "Show preview in image window" checkbox, and experiment with dragging the slider to see how your image changes and how the file size changes with lower-quality images. Once you're happy with the new image, click Save.

FIGURE 15-8

Reducing JPEG quality when saving files

- For web graphics, reduce the size of your images by scaling them down from the physical size captured by your camera or scanner to a size that is better suited to viewing on a web page. To scale images in GIMP, select Image ⇨ Scale Image. The dialog shown in Figure 15-9 displays. Enter a new value in the Width field and press Return — the Height value will change automatically to preserve the current aspect ratio of your image. Click Scale to rescale the image and update the preview of your image.

Using these simple techniques, I've been able to reduce images from the (approximately) 500-KB size that my digital camera captures down to less than 50 KB, with no obvious loss of quality. Well, maybe someone with better eyesight than mine could notice a significant difference, but I certainly can't.

Tip

Ubuntu also provides several command-line tools that can quickly and easily manipulate images. One of my favorites is the `convert` utility, which reduces the color depth of an image. The `convert` utility is one of the graphics tools provided in the ImageMagick set of graphics tools that are installed by default on your Ubuntu system. For more information about the `convert` utility or ImageMagick in general, use the `man` command to see the online reference information for these commands. Another similarly useful set of tools for scripting graphics operations and transformations is the `netpbm` package, which is available in the Ubuntu repositories. For more information about netpbm, see `http://netpbm.sourceforge.net`. ■

Graphics and Archive Formats Supported by GIMP

GIMP enables you to read and save graphics files in the following formats, including archive file formats, each identified by one or more of the following associated file extensions:

- **Adobe Photoshop image:** .psd
- **Alias/Wavefront PIX image:** .pix, .mask, .matte, .alpha, .als
- **ASCII Art:** .txt, .ansi, .text
- **Autodesk FLIC animation:** .fli, .flc
- **Bzip archive:** .xcf, .bz2, .bz2, .xcfbz2
- **C source code:** .c
- **C source code header:** .h
- **Colored XHTML:** .xhtml
- **Digital Image and Communications in Medicine Image:** .dcm, .dicom
- **Encapsulated PostScript image:** .eps
- **Flexible Image Transport System:** .fit, .fits
- **GIF (Graphics Interchange Format) image:** .gif
- **GIMP Brush:** .gbr
- **GIMP Brush (animated):** .gih
- **GIMP Compressed XJT image:** .xjt, .xjtgz, .xjtbz2
- **GIMP pattern:** .pat
- **GIMP XCF image:** .xcf
- **Gzip archive:** .xcf.gz, .gz, .xcfgz
- **HTML table:** .html, .htm
- **JPEG (Joint Photographic Experts Group) image:** .jpg, .jpeg, .jpe
- **KISS CEL:** .cel

- **Microsoft Windows BMP image:** .bmp
- **Microsoft Windows icon:** .ico
- **MNG animation:** .mng
- **PBM (Portable BitMap) image:** .pbm
- **PGM (Portable GrayMap) image:** .pgm
- **PNG (Portable Network Graphics) image:** .png
- **PNM (Portable AnyMap) image:** .pnm
- **PostScript document:** .ps
- **PPM (Portable PixMap) image:** .ppm
- **Silicon Graphics IRIS image:** .sgi, .rgb, .bw, .icon
- **Sun Rasterfile image:** .im1, .im8, .im24, .im32, and so on
- **SVG (Scalable Vector Graphics) import/read only:** .svg
- **TarGA image:** .tga
- **TIFF (Tagged Image File Format) image:** .tif. tiff
- **X Bitmap image:** .xbm, .icon, .bitmap
- **X Pixmap image:** .xpm
- **X Window dump:** .xwd
- **Zsoft PCX image:** .pcx, .pcc

FIGURE 15-9

Scaling images for better web-page display

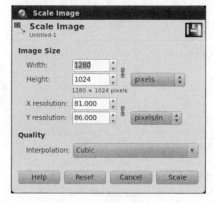

GIMP has many, many more great features and capabilities — this section has only scratched the surface to encourage you to experiment. See the next section for links to some great online sites that provide detailed information and tutorials about GIMP. Tutorials provide a great way to accomplish a specific task quickly and gain confidence in your growing proficiency.

Tip

GIMP provides several default keyboard shortcuts and also enables you to define your own shortcuts, as described in the "Pimp My GIMP" section of the GIMP documentation at `http://epierce.freeshell.org/gimp/gimp_ps.php`. If you're an Adobe Photoshop fan, you may be interested in the set of keyboard shortcuts by E Pierce as a starting point — although these are for older versions of GIMP and Photoshop, they still work in the current version of GIMP, for the most part. Actually, if you're an Adobe Photoshop user, you may be interested in GIMPshop (`http://plasticbugs.com/?page_id=294`), which is a version of GIMP in which the menus and dialogs have been reorganized to mimic the Photoshop interface — it's the same old GIMP under the covers. ■

More Information about GIMP

Hundreds of web sites provide information about using GIMP. The following are some of my favorites:

- `www.gimp.org`: The GIMP home page. Because this is the GIMP mother ship, it's a great starting point for checking the latest documentation, making sure that you have the latest version of GIMP, finding GIMP tutorials, and getting pointers to other online resources. All of the GIMP documentation is available at `http://docs.gimp.org`. A variety of GIMP tutorials are available at `www.gimp.org/tutorials`.

- `www.gimp.org/links`: Links ranging from the GIMP mother ship to interesting GIMP-related sites.

- `http://gimp-savvy.com/BOOK/index.html`: *Grokking the GIMP* is an excellent, although slightly older, book about GIMP that is available online. Although it doesn't have the latest and greatest GIMP information, it is still an excellent resource (and a book well worth having if you're going to be doing lots of work with GIMP).

- `http://gimps.de/en/tutorials/gimp/picture-photo-image/index.htm`: A great set of GIMP tutorials for photo retouching

Photo Editing Overview

Digital photography rules. Although many of us probably still have envelopes stuffed with old holiday and vacation photographs that have been glued together by time and humidity, it's been a long time since I've had to deal with film. I'm probably showing my age by mentioning it at all. I have a few generations of digital cameras with increasing resolution, my cell phone has a camera, my laptop has a camera, and even a digital watch that I bought during an eBay seizure a few years ago has one. Digital photography makes it incredibly easy to archive, catalog, and share your photos while also reducing the number of items that you can't find when you want them—they're all on your computer. (It also increases the number of items that you should back up!) Having all of your photos as digital images also makes it incredibly easy to "fix" problems ranging from red pupils and various forms of under- or overexposure, to Bolshevik-like purges of estranged relatives or insignificant others from the visual history of your life.

Although I use GIMP for editing all of my digital photographs, Ubuntu provides sophisticated software packages that make it easy for you to download images from a digital camera, store them as online albums, and clean up those images in zillions of ways. Google also offers Picasa, a free download that provides a nice solution for retrieving, archiving, and editing photos. (Picasa also runs on Microsoft Windows, in case that still matters to you.) These are discussed in more detail in the section of Chapter 18, "Consumer Electronics and Ubuntu," on "Working With Your Digital Camera," but I'll at least introduce them here. Ubuntu desktop systems install the F-Spot Photo Manager, shown in Figure 15-10, which is invoked by default when you attach a digital camera to your Ubuntu system, automatically extracts and archives photos, and provides some easy-to-use tools for cropping, removing red-eye, correcting colors, and much more.

FIGURE 15-10

Ubuntu's F-Spot Photo Manager

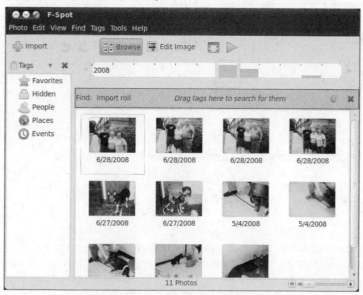

Everybody knows Google, and most people know that Google provides lots of free desktop and Web-based applications. Unfortunately, many of its desktop applications initially appear for Windows and are only later upgraded to run on Linux (which is somewhat ironic because Goggle is a huge Linux advocate and uses a homebrew Linux distribution on all of its servers). Picasa, Google's photo editing app, uses the software from the WINE project to run on Linux, which is somewhat disappointing but better than nothing. (*WINE* stands for "WINE is not an Emulator," and is an implementation of the Microsoft Windows API that runs on non-Windows systems.) If you like Picasa, you can also sign up for a Google Picasaweb account (`www.picasaweb.google .com`) to share your Picasa photo albums online. Like the other photo editing applications introduced in this section, Picasa is discussed in more detail in Chapter 18. Figure 15-11 shows Picasa running on an Ubuntu desktop system.

FIGURE 15-11

Google's Picasa photo management software

Applications such as GIMP, discussed earlier in this chapter, can largely eliminate most opportunities for Photoshop envy if you're moving to Linux from some other platform. However, if you simply must use Photoshop, you can always run it under WINE on Ubuntu desktop systems or run it inside a virtual machine. And there's more! Never one to leave a bandwagon un-jumped-upon, Adobe offers a version of Photoshop as an online photo editing tool known as *Adobe Photoshop Express* (`www.photoshop.com/express/landing.html`). Signing up for Photoshop

Express also gives you 2 GB of online storage for your images. On the down side, Photoshop Express requires Flash 9, and I generally dislike Flash on web sites in much the same way that I dislike cotton candy on the dinner plate. I'm also perfectly happy with the GIMP and F-Spot, and am wary of attempts to ensnare my digital content in online tools. Your mileage may vary.

Commercial photo editing software is also available for Linux — hooray! An excellent commercial photo editing package that's well worth checking out is Bibble (www.bibblelabs.com). Bibble comes in two versions, Lite and Professional, and also offers a trial version. Bibble is not included in your Ubuntu Linux installation because it is a commercial application, although it is still relatively inexpensive. Bibble is a great example of the growing amount of commercial software for Linux that makes it the equal of any other personal computer operating system.

Using OpenOffice.org Draw

As you may have heard before, *OpenOffice.org* (www.openoffice.org) is a suite of office applications including a word processor (Writer), a spreadsheet (Calc), a drawing program (Draw), software for creating presentations (Impress), and a database program called *BASE*. This section focuses on the drawing application — other chapters in this book discuss the OpenOffice.org word processor, spreadsheet, and presentation software. For some background about the OpenOffice.org suite in general, see the introductory section of "Word Processing with OpenOffice.org Writer" in Chapter 13, "Creating and Publishing Documents."

Draw is installed by default on desktop Ubuntu systems. Draw is primarily focused on creating drawings in OpenDocument Drawing (.odg) format. Like Inkscape (discussed later in this chapter), OpenOffice.org Draw enables you to create drawings in SVG format, although its ability to import existing SVG graphics is limited at the time of this writing. Stay tuned!

To avoid repeating the phrase "OpenOffice.org Draw" more times than necessary, I'll refer to it simply as *Draw* or as oodraw (the name of the application that you must type to execute OpenOffice.org Draw from a command-line interface) throughout the rest of this section.

Starting Draw

To start Draw on an Ubuntu system, select the Applications ⇨ Graphics ⇨ OpenOffice.org Drawing menu item. You can also start Draw by typing the oodraw command in a GNOME Terminal or xterm window and pressing Return.

When Draw starts, it displays an empty document, as shown in Figure 15-12.

FIGURE 15-12

Starting OpenOffice.org Draw

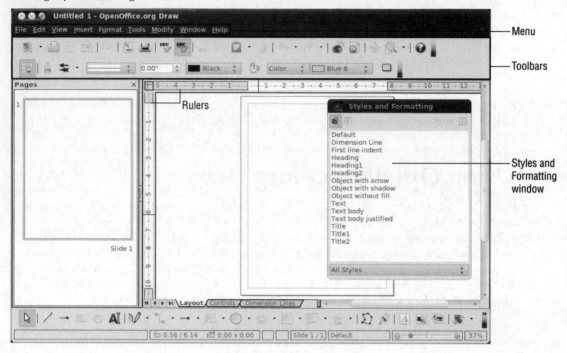

A Quick Tour of Draw

Draw provides excellent online help, as do all of the tools in the OpenOffice suite, so I won't bore you by walking through each menu and entry that it contains. However, as a quick overview of the Draw interface, the callouts in Figure 15-12 highlight the following areas:

- **Menus:** The dropdown menus in Draw are organized much like those in other drawing packages to provide a familiar user experience. Items on submenus with an arrow at their right edge lead to other, related submenus.

- **Toolbars:** By default, Draw displays the Standard, Line and Filling, and Drawing toolbars, which provide one-click access to specific commands when you click on the appropriate icon. You can modify the list of icons displayed on a toolbar by clicking on the control for that toolbar, located at the far right. You can display other toolbars or deactivate the default toolbar by selecting toolbars from the View ⇨ Toolbars submenu. Draw provides a great selection of drawing-oriented toolbars, such as a three-dimensional (3D) objects toolbar, so that you can quickly and easily create and modify the geometry of 3D images.

- **Rulers:** The rulers display the horizontal and vertical location of the cursor in the current drawing. The grayed-out portions of each ruler reflect the area outside the page margins used in the current document. You can hide these rulers by deselecting the View ⇨ Ruler menu command.

- **Styles and Formatting window:** This window is not displayed by default, but you can display it at any time by selecting the format menu's Styles and Formatting menu command. (Select this menu command again or simply click the close icon to close this window.)The Styles and Formatting window provides easy access to the styles that are available in the current drawing, and is especially convenient if you choose not to display the formatting toolbar. As with any floating window in OpenOffice, you can dock this window by double-clicking on the gray portion of the window heading, making it a part of the default OpenOffice interface rather than a floating window. You can undock a window by repeating this process in the docked area.

- **Context-sensitive menu:** Right-clicking on the background of any drawing that you are working on in OpenOffice.org Draw displays the context-sensitive menu shown in Figure 15-12. This menu provides quick access to several commonly used commands and submenus, including those for modifying the current page format, displaying a grid, and controlling snapping to grid points.

Draw provides extensive online help, available by selecting OpenOffice.org Help from the Help menu, or by pressing the F1 key on your keyboard at any time.

More Information about OpenOffice.org Draw

As the OpenOffice Suite continues to grow in popularity, more and more free resources are available for helping you with each of its components. The following are my favorite Draw-related sites on the Web:

- http://oooauthors.org/en/members/tutorials/draw/: Drawing tutorials and Frequently Asked Question (FAQ) files in a variety of languages

- http://openoffice.blogs.com/openoffice/draw/index.html: A blog by Solveig Haugland, author of the OpenOffice.org *Guidebook*. This portion of the blog contains a few tutorials, a variety of tips and tricks, and pointers to related information such as sources of clip art, templates, and more.

- www.openoffice.org: The OpenOffice mother ship, this site provides access to mailing lists, sample documents, FAQs, and much more.

Vector Graphics Tools for Linux

Standard document and graphics formats were less important before personal computers became the latest household appliance and the Internet provided a common platform for exchanging and presenting text and illustrations. Previous chapters stressed the importance and value of open standards for the written word such as HTML and the Open Document format. Similar standards are emerging in the area of graphics and illustration, where older formats such as GIF and JPEG are being complemented by the emergence of open raster graphics standards such as Portable Network Graphics (PNG) and an equally powerful, open standard for vector graphics such as the W3C standard Scalable Vector graphics (SVG) format. (For more information about the SVG standard, see www.w3.org/Graphics/SVG/.) Aside from being designed from the ground up as an open format, one of the primary advantages of SVG files is that they are, as the name suggests, scalable. Because SVG files consist of drawing and color information rather than actual images, they can be resized with no loss in image quality, as you would find in raster graphics formats such as PNG, JPEG, GIF, and the like.

Tip

Although OpenOffice.org Draw, discussed previously, can export images in SVG format and has some import capabilities, Inkscape and Karbon14 were designed for SVG graphics. The OpenDocument Drawing format used by Draw is an excellent format to use if your focus is on producing drawings for use with the other components of the OpenOffice.org suite, in documents, presentations, and so on. If your focus is on creating stand-alone artwork for web pages, I'd suggest that you use a program that was designed for vector graphics, such as Inkscape.

SVG graphic files are saved in XML format, which makes them highly portable and very flexible. As mentioned in the section of this chapter on GIMP, most professional printers require CMYK or Pantone color specifications. Inkscape provides some amount of support for CMYK color specifications, but integrated Pantone support is a legal swamp that no one wants to wade through. However, SVG's fill and stroke color attributes are natural places to attach tags that identify Pantone numbers. If you're going to try this, you should talk this over with your printer (the human, not the device) before simply assuming that they know about and will be able to use this information. ■

Using Inkscape

Inkscape is an open source application for creating and editing vector graphics and is similar to traditional applications such as Adobe Illustrator, Aldus (Adobe) Freehand, and CorelDraw. Inkscape can also import graphics in a variety of raster graphics formats that it can use as components of its SVG output. Inkscape can even export graphics in PNG format for compatibility with raster-only applications and older Web browsers. In addition to the standard elements of scalable vector graphics files, Inkscape also supports Web-oriented Creative Commons metadata and direct XML creation and editing.

Tip

When installing Inkscape, you may want to consider installing recommended programs such as Dia (a diagramming tool) and the Perl and Python XML extensions at the same time. These provide many import and export extensions for Inkscape, which you'll be glad to have if you ever need them. You can use aptitude's --with-recommends option, or select recommended tools from the Synaptic context-sensitive menu. ■

Because not everyone needs to create vector graphics images (and many people may have already decided to do so using OpenOffice), Inkscape isn't installed by default on Ubuntu Linux systems. Luckily, that's easy enough to fix, using the standard software installation tools discussed in Chapter 19.

Starting Inkscape

After installing Inkscape, you can start the program in a variety of different ways, the most basic of which are:

- On Ubuntu systems, by selecting Inkscape Vector Illustrator from the Applications ⇨ Graphics menu

- By typing the `inkscape` command in a GNOME Terminal or xterm window and pressing Return

The application starts, displaying an empty document, as shown in Figure 15-13.

FIGURE 15-13

Starting Inkscape

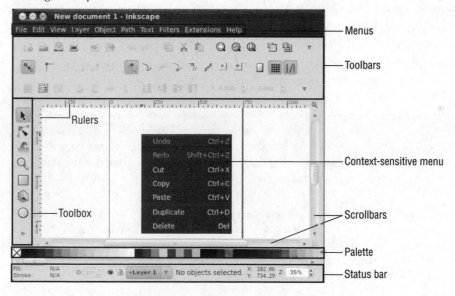

A Quick Tour of Inkscape

Inkscape provides great online help and even includes some tutorials that are available from its Help menu. The callouts in Figure 15-13 highlight the basic components of the Inkscape interface, which are as follows:

- **Menus:** The dropdown menus in Inkscape are organized to provide easy access to commands related to the basic elements of SVG drawings, such as Layer, Object, Path, and Text. The Inkscape designers have done a great job at minimizing the number of submenus used in the program—almost every command is directly available from a top-level menu.

- **Toolbars:** Inkscape provides two horizontal toolbars. The top toolbar, the Commands bar, provides access to some standard file and clipboard manipulation commands and also provides access to a variety of commands for zooming, copying, and grouping selected objects. The bottom toolbar, the Tool Controls bar, provides easy access to rotation, layer manipulation, and scaling commands. Clicking on the down arrow at the right of each of these toolbars displays additional, related commands for these toolbars.

- **Toolbox:** A vertical toolbox along the left side of the edit window. The toolbox contains icons for common creation and editing commands, such as those for selecting objects; zooming in and out; and creating squares, circles, 3D boxes, various sorts of lines, and so on.

- **Rulers:** These rulers display the horizontal and vertical location of the cursor in the current document.

- **Scrollbars:** Horizontal and vertical scrollbars shown at the bottom and right of an Inkscape window make it easy to move around in zoomed or otherwise large images. If the entire image can be viewed at once, the scrollbars do not appear.

- **Palette:** A horizontal palette at the bottom of an Inkscape window makes it easy to select new drawing and fill colors.

- **Status bar:** The status bar at the very bottom of an Inkscape window provides information about the current layer, selected fill color and stroke type, the current X and Y cursor position, the current zoom, and so on.

- **Context-sensitive menu:** Right-clicking on any component of a drawing that you are working on in Inkscape displays the context-sensitive menu that is also shown in Figure 15-13. This menu provides quick access to several commonly used commands and submenus, including those for duplicating a selected object, grouping and ungrouping, and undo operations, and a general object properties panel for the selected object.

You can hide (or subsequently reveal) all of these (except for the menus) by deselecting (or selecting) the associated items from Inkscape's View ➪ Show/Hide menu. You can also configure various Inkscape preferences by selecting the File ➪ Inkscape Preferences menu command. These preferences can be very handy for controlling cursor, scrolling, and selection granularity, which can be critical when doing detailed drawings in Inkscape.

More Information about Inkscape

I'm not the best graphics artist, so I'll leave the evangelizing to those who are. The following are some of my favorite Inkscape-related sites on the Web:

- www.inkscape.org: The home page of the Inkscape project, this page provides access to many Inkscape resources, such as mailing lists, articles, collections of images, and so on.

- www.inkscape.org/mailing_lists.php: Inkscape-specific mailing lists. The Inkscape-user list is a great place for asking questions and searching for solutions to whatever problem you're experiencing (with Inkscape, that is). The Inkscape-announce list is a low-traffic list, but is worth subscribing to so that you are notified of new major and patch releases of Inkscape.

- `http://tavmjong.free.fr/INKSCAPE/MANUAL/html/index.php`: Tavmjong Bah is writing a book about Inkscape that is freely available on the Web. This is a great book with a fantastic selection of information.

- `www.angelfire.com/mi/kevincharles/inkscape/index.html`: An unofficial (but extremely useful!) user manual for Inkscape written by Kevin Wixson

As with every popular open source package, more resources and sources of related information for Inkscape are probably appearing on the Web as I type this. If you find a great Inkscape resource that I've missed in this quick summary, please let me know. Inkscape is a great program!

Other Graphics Applications

Graphics programs seem to rank second to text editors and word processors in terms of the sheer number of available choices. Each has its own niche, fans, and detractors. Since I've already acknowledged that I'm not particularly good at graphics, I've covered only the graphics programs that I have actually used at one time or another and that I feel are the best applications for creating and editing various types of graphics on Linux systems. Some other good graphics applications are as follows (all of which are available in the Ubuntu repositories unless otherwise noted):

- **Blender** (`www.blender.org`): An impressive 3D graphics modeling, rendering, and animation package that has been used to make various animated films, video and desktop computer games, and so on. Blender is also a great tool for architectural or similar wire-frame drawings.

- **CinePaint** (`www.cinepaint.org`): An image-editing application that began life as a clone of an earlier version of GIMP, but which has had a significant amount of development since then, including adding support for 8-bit, 16-bit, and 32-bit color channels and high-quality image formats such as DPX, 16-bit TIFF, and OpenEXR. CinePaint has been used in many feature films (the "Harry Potter" films, *The Last Samurai*, the "Lord of the Rings" films, etc.), so it's impossible to dispute its quality or its business value.

Note
CinePaint is not available in the standard Ubuntu repositories but is included in the multimedia-oriented Ubuntu Studio Linux distribution (`http://ubuntustudio.org`). ∎

- **Dia** (`http://live.gnome.org/Dia`): A GNOME-based application for creating and editing diagrams and flowcharts on Linux systems, similar to and evocative of Microsoft's Visio application. Dia is not installed by default on Ubuntu systems.

- **GNU Paint** (`www.gnu.org/software/gpaint`): A simple, GNOME-based application for creating and editing graphics, GNU Paint has all of the attributes of XPaint (its ancestor), Microsoft Windows Paint, or MacPaint. GNU Paint is easy to use, but that's primarily because it doesn't do much when compared with the other graphics applications discussed in this chapter. GNU Paint is not available in the standard Ubuntu repositories. I'm primarily mentioning this here because you might have heard of it, not as a suggestion.

- **Xara Xtreme** (`www.xaraxtreme.org/about/`): A vector graphics application that was primarily developed for Microsoft Windows systems (and is still actively supported and under development there), Xara Xtreme was released as open source in 2006 and ported to Linux. This is an excellent, fast, and very usable graphics application that I've used numerous times. Its creators deserve significant kudos for releasing a commercial app as open source, but their efforts didn't capture the fancy of a substantial developer community (for both good reasons and bad). Xara Xtreme is not available in the standard Ubuntu repositories, but is available for download from `http://www.xaraxtreme.org`. Its web site hasn't been updated for a while, so I'm not sure how active its development is, but it's a great program!

This list, and the applications that were discussed at length in this chapter, should help you create and edit almost any type of graphical images or objects on an Ubuntu system. It's quite possible that I've missed some other excellent graphics applications for Linux—if you fall in love with some application that isn't mentioned here, please let me know. Inquiring minds want to know!

Summary

This chapter explored tools for creating and manipulating various types of graphics files on Linux systems. Linux has a great selection of powerful graphics tools that you can use to do real work that is constrained only by your artistic skills. (I am still waiting for a "mental image to graphics file" application, but that's my problem.) GIMP, OpenOffice.org Draw, and Inkscape are all shining examples of just how excellent and powerful open source software can be.

The next chapter explores how to work with audio and video on Ubuntu systems, with topics ranging from how to configure sound on your system, to how to work with CDs, DVDs, and the alphabet soup of digital audio and video file formats that one finds on the Web today.

Working with Multimedia

IN THIS CHAPTER

Understanding multimedia terminology

Configuring sound

Exploring the Linux multimedia stack

Playing, ripping, and burning CDs and DVDs

Working with audio files and Internet radio

MP3, WMA, OGG, FLAC, AAC, APE — this may look like a blast from a shotgun loaded with three-letter acronyms (TLAs), but it's really a list of the most popular formats for digital audio nowadays. The same is true of digital video, where acronyms such as MPG, MPEG, and VOB are king. There are also some really ugly acronyms such as MPAA and RIAA, which stand for groups of self-interested thugs trying to deny the rights of the consumer, but we won't go into that here.

The great thing about digital audio and video is that you no longer need specialized devices to play your music or watch a movie. You can listen to a music CD or play a video CD or DVD on your computer. Once you buy a CD or DVD, it should be completely legal for you to transfer its contents to your computer and listen to it or watch it there. This eliminates the need to carry around the original media, and you can safely leave them behind at home as backups in case your computer crashes. Digital Rights Management (DRM, also known as "ripping off the consumer") may prevent you from doing that, but the possibility exists unless it's actively subverted by the manufacturer of your CD or DVD.

This chapter helps you make some sense out of the maze of acronyms, general terminology, and specialized jargon that aficionados use to describe digital audio and video; and explains how to use the software available for Linux to listen to music, watch movies, and even create your own CDs and DVDs. I love being able to check into a hotel room and relax while listening to my favorite tunes because I've brought them along on my favorite modern multimedia device — a computer running Ubuntu Linux.

Overview of Digital Audio and Video Terminology

As mentioned in the introduction to this chapter, digital audio and video is an area in which the computer industry's tendency toward using jargon and three-letter acronyms makes many conversations and reference information almost incomprehensible to the novice. Although I've been a record collector, CD collector, and musician for years, I still encounter terms that I either have to look up or decrypt, and there is no single source of this sort of terminology outside of all-encompassing sites like Wikipedia.

This section, therefore, provides a basic glossary for the most common audio, video, and digital multimedia terminology and acronyms that I am familiar with and see often. It isn't necessarily easy reading, but it should be a great reference for the rest of the chapter, where these terms will be used.

- **AAC (Advanced Audio Coding):** A lossy codec (a codec that sacrifices sound quality for file size) originally developed by Dolby Laboratories that is similar to MP3 files in file size but provides slightly higher quality. AAC is now often, and incorrectly, referred to as the *Apple Audio Codec* because of Apple's use of a protected version of the AAC format to impose DRM on its iTunes customers.

- **ABR (average bit rate):** A type of encoding in which the user specifies the target bit rate for sampling and playback, and the encoder calculates the appropriate VBR (variable bit rate) values necessary to achieve the average

- **AIFF (Audio Interchange File Format):** A lossless audio codec (a codec that preserves sound quality but does so by using larger file sizes) originally developed by Apple Computer, and therefore commonly used on Macintosh systems

- **ALAC (Apple Lossless Audio Codec):** A proprietary lossless audio code developed by Apple Computer. This format is frequently confused with the M4A format, which is essentially a container file that can deliver files in ALAC and other formats.

- **APE:** The file extension for audio files encoded using the proprietary lossless Monkey's Audio codec. This codec provides slightly better compression (i.e., slightly smaller file sizes) than the FLAC or SHN codecs, but at the cost of slower encoding/decoding. APE files are primarily used on Microsoft Windows platforms because no official Linux port of the Monkey's Audio codec exists. For more information about the Monkey's Audio codec, see www.monkeysaudio.com.

- **bit rate:** The number of bits per time interval that make up an audio signal. The most common time interval used in bit rate calculations is 1 second (bits per second, BPS). High-speed data communication is often measured in Kbps (kilobits [thousands of bits] per second). This is overkill for digital audio.

- **BitTorrent:** A protocol for downloading and uploading digital data, including audio and video files. BitTorrent isn't really a multimedia term, except that it provides a common mechanism for sharing multimedia files, and I thought you might look for it here. See the section of Chapter 26, "File Transfer and Sharing," entitled "Using BitTorrent" for information on the applications that you can use to download and upload files with the BitTorrent protocol on Ubuntu systems.

- **Burn:** The term for writing data to recordable or rewritable CD or DVD media. The term *burn* comes from the fact that data is written to CDs and DVDs using a laser that inscribes miniscule pits on their surfaces to represent digital information.

- **CBR (constant bit rate):** A codec that uses a fixed number of bits per second as opposed to ABR or VBR codecs

- **CD (compact disc):** A storage device capable of holding approximately 650 MB of prerecorded/prewritten digital information

- **CD-R (compact disc/recordable):** A storage device capable of holding approximately 650 MB of digital information; each portion of the disc can be written to once by home computers with compatible drives. Writing a CD-R disc can be done in multiple sessions, where each session writes a different portion of the disc. Andy McFadden's CD-Recordable FAQ at www.cdrfaq.org is a tremendous resource with tons of detailed information about CD software. Web documents like these are true testimonials to the power of the Internet and the expertise and dedication of its users. Thanks, Andy!

- **CD-RW (compact disc/rewritable):** A storage device capable of holding approximately 650 MB of digital information, which can be written to multiple times by home computers with compatible drives. Only CD-RW drives can read CD-RW discs.

- **CDDA (Compact Disc Digital Audio):** The format used on most non-copy-protected audio CDs; sometimes also referred to as CDA because of Microsoft Windows's inability to use four-character file extensions

- **CDDB (CD Database):** A commercial, online database that provides identification information and track listings for commercial CDs

- **codec (compressor/decompressor):** An algorithm by which digital signals are compressed so as to lose a minimum amount of quality, and decompressed for playback

- **DAT (digital audio tape):** A digital recording tape medium used in recording studios and by audio professionals

- **DAE (digital audio extraction):** The process of cloning prerecorded digital media by directly copying it to files rather than by playing it, converting the resulting analog audio output and saving that information to a digital storage device

- **disc-at-once:** A CD/DVD burning mechanism that writes the entire surface of the CD or DVD disc rather than simply the amount of storage required to hold the information that you are recording

- **DMCA (Digital Millennium Copyright Act):** Legislation passed in the United States in which the supposed goal was to preserve copyrights for digital media but that has been used to squash reverse engineering, eliminate free-speech discussions of encryption technology, and rob users of the free reuse of legitimately purchased audio and video files; a good idea gone bad

- **DRM (Digital Rights Management):** A technique for denying legitimate users of audio and video files the ability to freely copy and use them

- **DSP (digital signal processing):** Using various algorithms to convert or modify digital audio and video signals. DSP can be done in hardware, software, or a combination of both.

- **DVD (digital video disc):** A storage device capable of holding approximately 4.7 GB of digital information

- **EQ (equalize):** A recording effect that increases or decreases the volume of different frequency ranges in an audio signal. Equalizing frequency ranges smoothes the audio signal by preventing extreme differences in volume across different frequency ranges.

- **FFP (FLAC footprint):** Checksum files that are typically distributed with FLAC-encoded files to enable you to verify their integrity. See the entry for MD5 in this glossary for more information about checksums.

- **FLAC (Free Lossless Audio Codec):** A lossless audio codec that typically achieves compression rates of 30 to 50 percent without any reduction in quality from the original recordings

- **Freedb (Free DB):** An open source alternative to CDDB that enables users to contribute information about CDs

- **ID3 tags:** 128-byte header information in MP3 files that is used to provide information about the audio file. ID3v1 tags provide album, artist, general comments, genre, and title information. ID3v2 tags provide this information and more in a more free-form fashion, permitting larger, user-defined tags that support all ID3v1 tags but can also include information such as lyrics and images.

- **ISO (International Standards Organization):** In the context of CDs and DVDs, ISO refers to the three-letter file extension added to CD and DVD images to show that the contents of the file conform to the ISO9660 specification, which defines CD and DVD formats. People often refer to conformant image files that contain complete CD or DVD images as ISOs.

- **Lossless formats:** File formats that are not lossy, that is, file formats that provide all of the information that was present in the audio, graphics, or video information as it was originally recorded, drawn, or captured

- **Lossy formats:** File formats that sacrifice quality to reduce file size. The term *lossy* refers to the data compression algorithm used to reduce file size, whereby some of the information that was present in the original file is actually eliminated to produce the smaller, compressed file, and therefore the original file can never be completely reconstructed from the compressed version. In the case of audio files, lossy images typically reduce both the bit rate and the frequency ranges at which audio is recorded, the theory being that the majority of this information is inaudible to most people.

- **M4A:** An audio file container format that can contain AAC or (more commonly) ALAC files. Protected versions of M4A files that have been subjected to Digital Rights Management are delivered as M4P files.

- **MD5:** An example of a popular mechanism, known as a *checksum*, used to verify the integrity of digital data files, especially lossless audio files. Files with this extension are plaintext files that typically contain unique 32-character ID numbers for one or more companion data files. An MD5 checksum value is unique to the data file that accompanies it, and therefore is often used to fingerprint (i.e., uniquely identify) that file and thus verify its integrity. If you generate an MD5 checksum (using a Linux application such as md5sum) and that checksum value matches the checksum value delivered with the file, the file has not been modified. MD5 is only one possible checksum mechanism—other popular checksum calculation algorithms, such as SHA, are also available.

- **MP3 (MPEG-1 Audio Layer 3):** The most popular audio format used today, MP3 is a proprietary lossy codec that produces relatively high-quality sound from relatively small audio files.

- **MP3 CD:** A compact disc that contains MP3 files rather than traditional CDDA audio. Because MP3 files are smaller than CDDA files, MP3 CDs can hold much more music than other CD formats and are quite popular nowadays even though they usually cannot be played in standard CD players.

- **MPAA (Motion Picture Association of America):** The motion picture industry's equivalent of the RIAA, a group of industry thugs bent on maximizing industry income at the expense of the end user and often the artist

- **MPEG (Motion Picture Experts Group):** An industry consortium responsible for defining standards for audio and video formats

- **MPEG-4:** The latest generation of MPEG standard at the time that this book was written, MPEG-4 is a standard file format for delivering audio, video, and other multimedia objects.

- **Noise reduction:** Audio processing techniques used to clean up audio files by removing, filtering, or equalizing specific frequency bands

- **Normalize:** An audio processing technique that identifies the loudest range of an audio file and then uses that as a baseline for the volume used when playing back the rest of the file. Normalizing audio data does not change relative volumes within a song, just the baseline volume.

- **OGG (Ogg Vorbis):** A popular, open source lossy codec and associated container format that provides a powerful, royalty-free alternative to lower-quality codecs such as MP3. Ogg Vorbis was developed by the Xiph.org foundation, a foundation dedicated to developing promotion-free, open source multimedia formats. (Ogg is the file format, while Vorbis is the actual codec, though files encoded using this codec typically have the .ogg file extension.) For more information about Ogg Vorbis, see www.xiph.org or www.vorbis.com. If your software or audio player does not support Ogg Vorbis, contact the manufacturer.

- **P2P (Peer-to-Peer):** A popular data exchange and delivery mechanism wherein each client (peer) identifies other peers and exchanges data with them without the use of a central server. Popular P2P applications are BitTorrent, GNUtella, LimeWire, and so on.

- **PCM (Pulse Code Modulation):** An audio and video data format that provides a true representation of the recorded signal by sampling it at regular intervals. PCM is the standard form for digital audio in computers, compact discs, and in digital video.

- **RealAudio:** A popular streaming audio format developed by Real.com and often used on the Web. For more information, see `www.real.com`.

- **RIAA (Recording Industry Association of America):** A group of industry thugs bent on maximizing industry income at the expense of the end user and often the artist

- **Rip:** The generic term used to describe the process of converting CD and DVD discs to files that can be used on a computer system

- **SHA (Secure Hash Algorithm):** A checksum mechanism similar to MD5. Multiple SHA functions, such as SHA-0, SHA-1, and SHA-2, are available. See the definition of MD5 for an explanation of checksums in general.

- **SHN (Shorten codec):** A popular, but older, lossless audio codec that is still frequently used for distributing authorized live recordings on the Internet. Shorten delivers slightly larger file sizes than FLAC, its primary competitor. Interestingly, the Shorten codec also offers a lossy mode, although I don't see why anyone would use that. For more information about the Shorten codec and Linux software for working with SHN files, a great resource is the SHN Resources page at `http://research.umbc.edu/~hamilton/shnlinks.html`. The Shorten codec is a commercial product of SoftSound Ltd. but has a user-friendly personal use license.

- **Skin:** An alternate user interface for graphical applications. New skins can be applied to an existing application without recompilation or any actual changes to the application other than its configuration information. Many audio players (such as XMMS and the venerable WinAmp for Microsoft Windows systems, which pioneered skinnable applications) are skinnable, which enables fans to easily customize their appearance.

- **Streaming:** A method of delivering digital content over a network such that an application (such as an audio player) receives information as it is needed without the need to store that data on the machine. The most common examples of streaming media players are the RealPlayer and RealOne applications from RealAudio. For more information, see `www.real.com`.

- **SVCD (Super Video CD):** The successor to Video CDs (VCDs), an SVCD contains MPEG-2 video and MPEG-1 or MPEG-2 audio recorded on a normal VCD. Most DVD players can also play SVCD discs because DVD players support the MPEG-2 codec required to decode the MPEG-2 video data.

- **Track-at-once:** A CD/DVD-burning mechanism that writes on a track of a CD or DVD disc but leaves the remainder of the CD or DVD available for further recording at a later stage

- **Transcode:** The process of converting from one encoding format to another, typically used when referring to converting a media file or object from one format to another, as is done when creating DVDs from MPEG files in other formats (or vice versa)

- **TTA (True Audio codec):** A free, lossless audio codec offering an average of 30 to 40 percent file size reduction without any loss of quality. I haven't encountered this codec much on the Web, but some people swear by it. For more information about the True Audio codec, see www.true-audio.com.

- **Torrent files:** The files that contain information about how to contact a BitTorrent server in order to upload or download digital files using the popular BitTorrent protocol. *Torrent files* isn't really a multimedia term, except that BitTorrent provides a common mechanism for sharing multimedia files and I thought you might look for it here. See the section of Chapter 26 entitled "Using BitTorrent" for information on the applications that you can use to download and upload files using the BitTorrent protocol on Ubuntu systems.

- **VBR (variable bit rate):** A type of encoding that attempts to reduce file size without sacrificing significant quality by varying the bit rate at which audio information is recorded. More complex audio is recorded at a higher bit rate, while simpler audio passages are recorded at a lower bit rate.

- **VCD (Video CD):** A storage device capable of holding approximately 650 MB of prerecorded/prewritten digital video and audio information that is encoded in MPEG-1 format. Most DVD and CD players can play VCDs because they support the MPEG-1 codec used to decode the video and audio data.

- **WAV:** A digital audio file format originally developed by Microsoft and IBM that has become the standard format for distributing lossless audio (waveform) files. WAV files consist of chunks of data that can actually be encoded using any codec but most commonly contain raw PCM (Pulse Code Modulation) audio data, which is lossless and therefore huge. WAV files are often used by audio professionals to ensure maximum quality and complete fidelity to the original recordings.

- **WavPack:** A free, lossless audio codec used primarily on Windows systems but also available for many different Linux distributions, architectures, and applications such as XMMS. I haven't encountered WavPack much outside of the Windows community, but your mileage may vary. WavPack is extremely quick at compressing and decompressing files with no loss of quality. For more information about WavPack, see www.wavpack.com.

- **WMA (Windows Media Audio):** A popular codec for Microsoft Windows users that is the default audio codec used by the Windows Media Player. Lossy, lossless, and DRM versions of the WMA codec are available. The most important thing that Linux users need to know about WMA is how to convert audio files encoded with this codec into more reasonable formats.

- **WMV (Windows Media Video):** A popular lossy codec for Microsoft Windows users that is the default video codec used by the Windows Media Player. The most important thing that Linux users need to know about WMV is how to convert video files encoded with this codec into more reasonable formats.

Unless you have plenty of free brain cells and nothing else to do with them, there's no need to memorize these terms — that's what books like this one are for. However, now that you have expanded your digital multimedia terminology, let's move on to something more important — configuring the sound devices on your system so that you can actually play audio and video on your Ubuntu system.

Configuring Sound Devices, Levels, and System Sounds

Most of the setup for your Ubuntu system's audio components is done automatically when you install your Ubuntu Linux system. Ubuntu's installer has excellent hardware detection capabilities and automatically installs and configures the ALSA (Advanced Linux Sound Architecture) and PulseAudio utilities, drivers, and libraries that Ubuntu uses to provide excellent, high-quality audio playback. The following sections enable you to specify and test the sound devices used by your system, set sound levels on your system, and customize the sounds that your system plays in response to various system events; they also tell you how to set preferences for CD and DVD handling.

Specifying and Testing Sound Devices

To verify that sound is working on your Ubuntu Linux system, first check the obvious things, such as whether your speakers are plugged into your sound card's audio out port (usually a light green socket — the central one — of the three sound ports on the back of your system or on your sound card), the speakers are turned on, and so on. Next, select the System ⇨ Preferences ⇨ Sound command. The Sound Preferences utility appears. Select the Hardware tab to display the screen shown in Figure 16-1.

FIGURE 16-1

Sound hardware settings in the Sound Preferences utility

This dialog lists all of the audio devices that were detected on your system, which will only be one device on most systems. Make sure that the profile for any audio device listed on this panel is set to something like "Analog Stereo Duplex" or "Analog Stereo Output." (You can use either of these as a starting point and select a more optimal profile once you get audio working on your system.)

Next, select the Output tab, which displays a screen like the one shown in Figure 16-2.

FIGURE 16-2

Sound output settings in the Sound Preferences utility

Select the output device that you want to use, and ensure that the Mute checkbox is not selected beside the Output volume slider at the top of the "Sound Preferences" dialog. To test the audio on your system, you can either start an audio application or use the sample alert sounds provided on the "Sound Preferences" application's Sound Effects tab (discussed later in this chapter in the section, "Testing and Customizing System Sounds"). You can double-click on any of these to produce the associated sound.

Tip

Most motherboards nowadays feature integrated audio hardware. Unless you've added a sound card to your system (in which case you probably know what it is), you can identify the primary audio device on your system by using the `lspci` **command, as in the following example:**

```
$ lspci | grep -i audio
00:1b.0 Audio device: Intel Corporation 82801H HD Audio...
```

Of course, you'll see a different audio device on your system, but the entry that is displayed should at least give you an idea of which of the available audio devices to try selecting first. To see device-level information about your sound hardware, see the section later in this chapter entitled "Getting Detailed Information about Your Sound Hardware." ■

Setting System Sound Levels

The section of Chapter 5, "Using the GNOME Desktop," entitled "Customizing Panel Contents" discusses how to add various applets to your GNOME desktop's panels. One of the more useful applets that is preinstalled for you in the upper panel on your Ubuntu desktop is the Volume Control applet, whose icon looks like a small speaker and is usually displayed in the notification area in the right portion of the top panel.

To customize your system's volume settings for the current session, right-click on this icon. A slider displays on your desktop, below the icon for the Volume Control applet. To change your current volume settings, drag the slider up or down to the value that you prefer.

Testing and Customizing System Sounds

By default, your system is configured to play a *welcome* sound when you log in. To configure (or disable) the sounds that your system plays in response to various events, select the Sound Preferences utility's Sound Effects tab. The dialog shown in Figure 16-3 displays.

FIGURE 16-3

Default system sound settings in the Sound Preferences utility

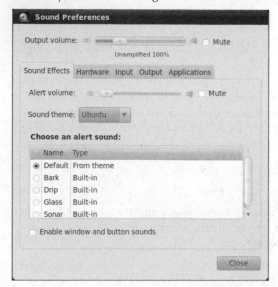

This tab in the Sound Preferences utility enables you to verify the system activities for which your system will play an associated sound, specify the sounds associated with system alerts, disable sound notification of system alerts, or disable system sounds entirely:

To disable sounds for system alerts (and only for system alerts), click the Mute checkbox to the right of the Alert volumes slider.

To disable sounds entirely on your system, click the down-arrow to the right of the Sound theme dropdown, and select "No sounds" from the list.

To disable sounds for window and button events, make sure that the checkbox to the left of the "Enable window and button sounds" field at the bottom of the tab shown in Figure 16-3 is disabled.

To customize the sounds associated with system alerts, first make sure that the Mute checkbox to the right of the Alert volumes slider is not set to Mute. Select the radio button to the right of one of the alternate sounds listed in the alert sounds list. (You can double-click on these entries themselves to preview the sounds that they make.)

Getting Detailed Information about Your Sound Hardware

If you've gotten to this point and sound still isn't working on your Ubuntu system, it may be time to explore your system's sound hardware to see if it is set up correctly and to give you the information that you need to ask for help. Information about your system's hardware, including your sound hardware, is available in Ubuntu's Device Manager application, which is not installed by default but can be quite handy when looking for detailed information about your system's hardware. To install this application, use any of the software installation tools discussed in Chapter 19, "Adding, Removing, and Updating Software," to install the `gnome-device-manager` package.

The GNOME Device Manager, which you can display by selecting the Applications ⇨ System Tools ⇨ Device Manager menu command or executing the `gnome-device-manager` command from any command line, is shown in Figure 16-4.

The entries in the Device Manager for your sound hardware will tell you whether Ubuntu has been able to identify the device, what it has identified it as, and whether valid entries for that device exist in the /sys filesystem, which is a virtual filesystem that provides direct access to various aspects of your system hardware.

Tip

If your system sounds play correctly but you can't play CDs, make sure that your CD player is correctly connected to your sound hardware. This connection typically consists of two or three pin cables that run from the back of your CD drive to your sound card or the sound hardware that is built into your motherboard. Some sound cards and motherboards support several input sound devices, and it's quite possible that your CD drive is connected to the wrong port or that the connector has become dislodged. ∎

FIGURE 16-4

Sound hardware entries in the Device Manager

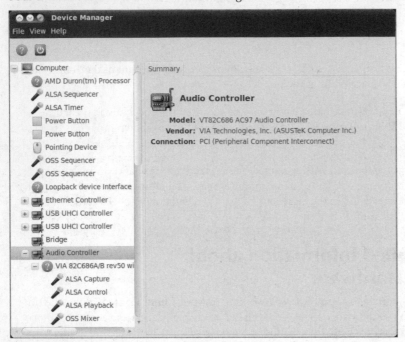

If the entries in the Device Manager appear to match your hardware, it's time to search the Web, starting with various Ubuntu resources listed in the section of Chapter 1, "The Ubuntu Linux Project," entitled "Support for Ubuntu." Paid support is always an option, but your best (and certainly cheapest) bet is to begin by searching the various forums for information about your sound hardware or the specific problem that you are seeing. If you don't find any relevant or helpful information, try posting to the Ubuntu Users mailing list. As emphasized throughout this book, one of the best aspects of Ubuntu Linux is its huge, helpful user community. You're also welcome to ask me, but my response time is certainly going to be slower than that of the thousands of continuous participants in the Ubuntu forums and mailing lists.

Setting Blank CD and DVD Preferences

Now that few people bother with floppy disks (or, perhaps, know what they are), CDs and DVDs are the most common examples of removable media that you'll use with your computer system. *Removable media* is the generic term for any media that contains digital data and that is not a mandatory part of your computer system. Removable disks, flash drives, and other devices that show up as disk drives (like an iPod) are not exactly the same things as far as Ubuntu is concerned, and are discussed in Chapter 18, "Consumer Electronics and Ubuntu," as well as in Chapter 20, "Adding Hardware and Attaching Peripherals." This section focuses on how you can configure what your system does when you insert a prerecorded or blank CD or DVD.

When you insert a blank CD or DVD in your Ubuntu system, the system does two things:

- Displays an appropriate icon on your desktop for the type of blank media that you have inserted.
- Displays a dialog asking what you would like to do with that media.

Figure 16-5 shows the icon and dialog displayed when you insert a blank CD-R or CD-RW disc in a compatible drive on your system. A very similar icon and dialog are displayed when you insert a blank DVD-R disc into a compatible drive on your system.

FIGURE 16-5

Dialog and icon for blank CD-R/RW insertion

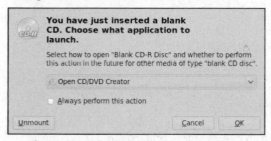

In either case, clicking Cancel closes the dialog without starting an application. Clicking OK opens Ubuntu's CD/DVD Creator application, which is the Nautilus File Manager in a special mode. I prefer to click on the dropdown menu and select Brasero, a specialized application for creating CDs and DVDs, which is discussed later in this chapter. If you always want to open Brasero when you insert a blank CD or DVD, you can select the "Always perform this action" checkbox before clicking OK.

How your system reacts when a blank CD or DVD is inserted, and the applications that are available in the dialog shown in Figure 16-5, are defined on the Nautilus Preferences dialog shown in Figure 16-6.

FIGURE 16-6

Setting preferences for blank CD/DVD or other media

To view this dialog, start Nautilus by clicking on an existing filesystem icon or by selecting an entry from the GNOME Desktop's Places menu. Select the Edit ⇨ Preferences menu item, and click the Media tab in the dialog that appears.

To prevent your system from displaying the dialogs shown in Figure 16-5, select "Blank CD disc" or "Blank DVD disc" from the dropdown Type menu in the "Other Media" section, and either select the "Do nothing" entry or select the application that you always want to open when blank media is inserted. You can specify a custom application by selecting the "Open with other application" menu entry and browsing for the location of the application that you want to use. (This is a great way to integrate my favorite CD/DVD burning application, k3b, into your Ubuntu system.)

How your Ubuntu system reacts when you insert a prerecorded CD or DVD depends on the Preferences settings for CD Audio and DVD Video on the same tab. To disable automatically starting a specified application, click on the dropdown menu beside the appropriate type of media and select "Do nothing." To change the application that starts automatically when prerecorded media is inserted, click on the dropdown menu beside the appropriate type of media, and either select one of the applications that is listed on the menu or select "Open with other application" and browse for the location of the application that you want to use.

For information about playing or burning CDs and DVDs, see the sections later in this chapter entitled "Working with CDs" and "Working with DVDs."

Exploring the Linux Multimedia Stack

Like related concepts such as disk access and displaying graphical output, your system must be able to play multiple audio streams at the same time, even for something as simple as playing the sound associated with a system event while also playing your favorite CD. The single-tasking approach, in which ancient audio applications seized sole control of an audio output device, simply isn't practical today. For this reason, most audio playback on Linux systems is handled by an intermediate layer or sound server, which can play and mix multiple audio streams at the same time.

Introducing Drivers, Servers, and Frameworks

I doubt that it will come as a surprise to hear that Linux distributions have taken several different approaches to supporting audio playback over the years. Hacking through the morass of acronyms that seems especially deep in the Linux multimedia space, the next few sections explain the core concepts in Linux Multimedia.

Linux Sound APIs

The primary sound APIs used on Linux systems (and UNIX systems, if anyone still cares) are OSS (Open Sound System) and ALSA (Advanced Linux Sound Architecture). These are the lower-level drivers that enable communication with sound devices. As the name suggests, ALSA is a Linux-only API, while OSS can be used on most UNIX-like systems.

OSS was the standard sound API on Linux systems through the 2.4 Linux kernel series, after which ALSA became the standard sound API. ALSA includes an OSS emulation mode for backward compatibility.

OSS is still being developed, although it has been marked as deprecated since development began on the 2.6 Linux kernel. It remains a more portable API if you are writing code that is intended to run on multiple UNIX-like systems, not just Linux systems.

Linux Sound Servers

Linux systems use sound servers (also called *sound daemons*) to enable the simultaneous playback of multiple output devices and to enable playing and controlling sound over a network. (ALSA audio drivers inherently support simultaneous playback and mixing, but most OSS drivers do not.)

Traditionally, the most common sound server on GNOME-based systems has been ESD (Enlightened Sound Daemon, also called *EsounD*; `www.tux.org/~ricdude/overview.html`). Since Ubuntu 8.04 (and in most other up-to-date GNOME-based Linux distributions), ESD has been replaced by PulseAudio (`www.pulseaudio.org`), although the transition was not necessarily a smooth one. Don't worry—subsequent sections discuss PulseAudio in more detail, but in my experience "it just works" on current Ubuntu systems.

Just to keep things confusing and infinitely flexible, several other, system-independent sound servers, such as the JACK Audio Connection Kit (`www.jackaudio.org`) and NAS (Network Audio System; `www.radscan.com/nas.html`), are also available and have been around for a while.

Linux Multimedia Frameworks

GStreamer (`www.gstreamer.net`) is a pipeline-based multimedia framework that can be used by applications to process the data afer it is read from ALSA drivers and before it is output, either directly or through a sound server. "Pipeline-based" means that GStreamer processes audio by passing it through a sequence, or pipeline, of multiple conversion steps. GStreamer uses a plug-in–based architecture that makes it easy to extend GStreamer to support new audio or video formats. Although originally developed for use on GNOME-based systems, GStreamer was designed to be platform-independent and is thus used on platforms that include Linux, Mac OS X, Microsoft Windows, and Solaris.

Some multimedia applications provide their own multimedia frameworks, which are therefore highly portable to other platforms and which can often be accessed by other applications. Good examples of this are the MPlayer Movie Player (`www.mplayerhq.hu`), VLC Media Player (`www.videolan.org/vlc`), and the xine Multimedia Player (`http://www.xine-project.org`).

What Should You Care About?

Having learned all of these acronyms, how do they affect you?

- If you simply want to play audio on your Ubuntu system, all you really need is ALSA (which is installed by default on Ubuntu systems).

- Ubuntu users who want to play MP3 files or watch DVDs, or who might ever encounter an audio or video format that is not completely open source, should install GStreamer plug-ins to expand the core GStreamer capabilities that are present on your system.

- If you need networked sound or want to be able to separately control the audio levels of different audio applications, you should also take advantage of PulseAudio on Ubuntu systems (which is installed by default).

Dealing with Proprietary Audio and Video Formats

The rest of this chapter provides detailed information about installing and configuring various packages and applications in order to enable you to work with various types of audio and video on your Ubuntu systems. This includes MP3 files that you've purchased, DVDs that you've purchased, and so on. You'd think that they would "just work" — but no! The music and motion picture industries and some bogons who have copyrighted various file formats impose many hurdles for the innocent Linux consumer to overcome in order to use legally purchased products. In order to be able to play many types of audio files, work with DVDs, and so on, you must install software packages on your Ubuntu system that the folks at Canonical cannot install by default for legal reasons. You can install these packages by installing the ubuntu-restricted-extras package on Ubuntu systems. These packages include a base set of GStreamer plug-ins (see the next section, "Configuring the GStreamer Framework and Plug-Ins," for more information about GStreamer) that will enable you to play most unencrypted audio and video formats.

Please note that I am not a lawyer and that installing the software that you need to use in order to play legitimately purchased audio and video data is completely your responsibility, regardless of how silly that may be. Installing these packages on your system may someday cause jackbooted enforcers from the RIAA and MPAA to kick down your door and drag you off to be forcibly reeducated. Hordes of winged monkeys with legal degrees may darken the skies over your home forever. You should probably never install the restricted-extras packages on a business system. For information about legally playing various proprietary audio format systems, see the "Getting Commercial GStreamer Plug-Ins" sidebar at the end of the next section.

Configuring the GStreamer Framework and Plug-Ins

As introduced in the previous section, most GNOME audio and video applications use an underlying open source multimedia framework called GStreamer (http://gstreamer.freedesktop .org or www.gstreamer.net). GStreamer makes it easy to integrate codecs by writing simple plug-ins that integrate with its framework. Most of the GNOME applications discussed in this chapter leverage the GStreamer framework for codec support via plug-ins. For this reason, you should use your favorite Package Management software (discussed in Chapter 19) to install the latest versions of GStreamer and associated sets of plug-ins before starting Rhythmbox, trying to play MP3 files, attempting to convert sound files, or attempting to play a DVD. If you don't, you may be extremely disappointed in Ubuntu's audio and video capabilities — at least, until you install the GStreamer plug-ins and try again.

As explained in Chapter 1, the Ubuntu folks are very strict about the legal and licensing requirements of the packages that they include in the default Ubuntu distribution. Because of copyright and licensing issues, many of the codecs that are commonly used by audio applications on other platforms are not installed by default on your Ubuntu Linux system. The best example of this is anything having to do with the MP3 audio format. Not everyone needs to play the most common audio file format found in the known universe, right? I can't blame them for this perspective, but in this case, it doesn't meet my needs.

To make GStreamer as full-featured as possible, use your favorite Package Management software from Chapter 19 to install the following packages (or to make sure that they're already installed):

- gstreamer0.10-fluendo-mp3
- gstreamer0.10-ffmpeg
- gstreamer0.10-plugins-bad
- gstreamer0.10-plugins-bad-multiverse
- gstreamer0.10-plugins-base
- gstreamer0.10-plugins-base-apps
- gstreamer0.10-plugins-good
- gstreamer0.10-plugins-ugly
- gstreamer0.10-plugins-ugly-multiverse
- gstreamer0.10-tools
- totem-gstreamer

Tip

You may not need all of these unless you are converting audio files from one format to another, and even in that case, the plug-ins that you need depend on the types of files that you're converting. I'm assuming that you would rather err on the side of caution—that is, installing a version of the GStreamer framework that is as full-featured as possible, at the expense of a bit of disk space. ■

GStreamer is a library that is used by many applications, not an application itself. The GStreamer library enables applications to access GStreamer plug-ins. Having installed the suggested GStreamer plug-ins, applications such as Rhythmbox and SoundConverter, discussed later in this chapter, will now be able to work with most types of audio files.

Tip

For up-to-date information on using GStreamer-based applications to play proprietary audio and video formats, see https://help.ubuntu.com/community/RestrictedFormats. ■

Getting Commercial GStreamer Plug-Ins

In September 2008, Canonical began to offer commercial codecs (actually just *DECs*, since they are only decoders) for various Microsoft Windows and Motion Picture Expert Group (MPEG) media formats through its online store (http://shop.canonical.com). These codecs, implemented as GStreamer plug-ins and thus intended for use on Ubuntu systems, are from Fluendo (www.fluendo.com), a Linux and UNIX multimedia firm that has already developed and released an open source MP3 codec. Two commercial packages are available:

- **Fluendo Windows Media and MP3 Playback Pack:** Provides codecs for Windows Media Audio (WMA files for Windows Media 7, 8, 9, 10, Pro, Lossless, and Speech), Windows Media Video

(WMV files for Windows Media 7, 8, 9, and VC1), Windows Media MMS, Windows Media ASF, and MP3 Audio.

- **Fluendo Complete Playback Pack:** Provides codecs for Windows Media Audio (WMA files for Windows Media 7, 8, 9, 10, Pro, Lossless, and Speech), Windows Media Video (WMV files for Windows Media 7, 8, 9, and VC1), Windows Media ASF, Windows Media MMS, MPEG2 Video, MPEG4 ISO and Part 2 (DivX version 4, 5, and 6) Video, H.264/AVC Video, MP3 Audio, and AAC Audio.

Needless to say, this caused the open source community to burst into flames, with pundits, open source purists, and Ubuntu fans turning on each other like members of the Donner party. Free GStreamer plug-ins that support most of these formats are already available but (as mentioned in the previous sections) cannot be used legally in many countries.

My take on this? Get over it! People who want to be able to replace Microsoft Windows installations with Ubuntu installations in commercial or off-the-shelf environments need these codecs. Just because no one likes the fact that certain audio and video formats are proprietary doesn't mean that one can ignore that fact in enterprise deployments. Similarly, no one is going to buy a netbook or mobile Internet device that can't play MP3s. Most of us don't have to buy these codecs, but having legally licensed versions available will spur the adoption of Ubuntu in business, academic, and preinstalled, off-the-shelf environments. That's a good thing for all of us.

Configuring PulseAudio

PulseAudio, introduced in the beginning of this section, is the latest sound server that is available for Ubuntu and most other GNOME-based Linux distributions. Originally called *Polypaudio*, the name was changed because *Polypaudio* sounded too much like something that you'd want to have surgically removed.

The PulseAudio server, a GStreamer plug-in for PulseAudio integration, and a startup item for integration between X Window System events and PulseAudio are all installed by default on current Ubuntu systems. The default PulseAudio installation provides several command-line utilities for configuring and monitoring PulseAudio. However, if you're like me, you'll probably want to install the padevchooser package, which provides graphical utilities such as the PulseAudio Device Chooser (padevchooser), PulseAudio Manager (paman), PulseAudio Preferences (paprefs), PulseAudio Volume Control (pavucontrol), and PulseAudio Volume Unit Meter (pavumeter) applications. Installing the padevchooser package using your favorite Package Management utility (discussed in Chapter 23, "Software Development on Ubuntu") creates the Applications ⇨ Sound & Video ⇨ PulseAudio Device Chooser menu item, which starts the PulseAudio Device Chooser as an applet in the notification area portion of the top panel. Its icon looks like an audio jack and a piece of audio cable. Left-clicking on this icon displays the menu shown in Figure 16-7.

The items on this menu provide access to the graphical PulseAudio utilities that were installed as part of the padevchooser package. For example, selecting the Volume Control menu item displays the PulseAudio Volume Control application, which provides a Playback tab where you can set the volume for any audio device that is currently playing audio. Figure 16-8 shows this tab when three different applications are all playing through PulseAudio at the same time.

FIGURE 16-7

The GNOME panel's PulseAudio Device Chooser menu

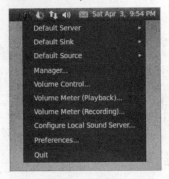

FIGURE 16-8

Separately adjusting the volume for audio applications in PulseAudio

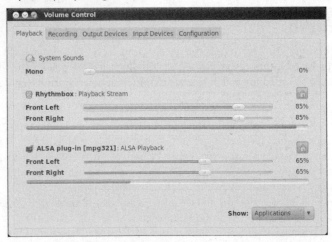

To adjust the volume of any of these, simply drag the slider for that application. You can also click the speaker icon beside the slider for any application to temporarily mute its audio stream. Very cool.

If you decide that you like the PulseAudio Device Chooser application (and what Ubuntu PulseAudio user wouldn't?), you can configure it to always start in any Ubuntu login session by selecting the PulseAudio Device Chooser's Preferences menu item to display the PulseAudio Preferences application, shown in Figure 16-9.

FIGURE 16-9

Setting PulseAudio preferences

Select the "Start applet on session login" checkbox to automatically start the PulseAudio Device Chooser each time that you log in on your Ubuntu system.

Playing CDs and DVDs

I still have a few friends who use Windows voluntarily, and one of their favorite rationales is the statement, "It just works!" Thanks to the efforts of all the contributors and testers who are associated with the Ubuntu project, playing music on those systems has this same mantra — I have never had a problem with an internal CD drive on any desktop or laptop system where I have installed Ubuntu Linux.

Unfortunately, playing DVDs is a little trickier. The only thing that could possibly make anyone nostalgic for videotapes is how badly the entertainment media is trying to screw DVD users. Region-specific DVDs. Video encryption. Licensed codecs. Suing young adults and prohibiting free speech for academicians just because both are smarter than their research staff. Need I say more?

For all of these reasons (and more), playing DVDs on a computer system isn't always an easy thing to do. However, Ubuntu provides a great DVD player called *Totem* that provides high-quality playback capabilities. Totem can either leverage the GStreamer framework that I discussed earlier in this chapter or leverage other multimedia back-ends such as xine.

Configuring how your system responds when you insert an audio or data CD, a prerecorded DVD, or a data DVD was discussed earlier in this chapter in the section, "Setting Blank CD and DVD Preferences." Ubuntu's default action is to display a pop-up dialog that enables you to select the application that you want to use to play your CD or DVD.

If no pop-up dialog displays when you insert a CD or DVD, you can select the application that you want to start from Ubuntu's Applications ➪ Sound and Video menu.

Playing Audio CDs Using Rhythmbox

Once Rhythmbox starts, you may need to select the entry in the Device section in the pane at the left to display information about the CD that you've inserted. This will initially try to look up any CD that you insert in the free online CD information database (freedb.org). If it finds a matching entry, it displays information about the CD and the tracks that it contains, as shown in Figure 16-10.

FIGURE 16-10

Information about a CD from FreeDB

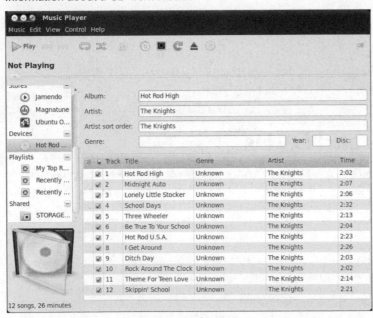

If the CD is not listed in FreeDB, Rhythmbox displays a similar screen, using a generic entry for the CD that says *Unknown Audio* and *Unknown* for both the Artist and Title in its Track Listing window, assigning each track a generic name such as *Track 1*, *Track 2*, and so on.

If you simply want to play the CD, click the Play icon in the toolbar to play the CD. It just works! If your CD was found in the FreeDB database, Rhythmbox will also display a miniature version of the

CD's cover art in the lower-left corner of the Rhythmbox window. As you might expect, you can play specific tracks by double-clicking on the track that you want to play.

Once you're done playing your CD, you can click the Eject icon in the toolbar to eject this CD and insert another. To exit Rhythmbox, select the Music ➪ Quit menu command. If you want to close the Rhythmbox window but continue to play the CD, you can either minimize the window, using the standard window controls, or select the Music ➪ Close menu item. In either case, the Rhythmbox icon (which looks like a speaker) will still be displayed in the system tray portion of the GNOME panel.

Installing Software to Play Encrypted DVDs

Installing the library necessary to read encrypted DVDs gives you the power to actually watch the DVDs that you've legally purchased, so let's install it now.

Caution

In my personal opinion, installing the CSS (http://en.wikipedia.org/wiki/Content_Scramble_System) software that enables you to play commercial DVDs on your Ubuntu Linux system is a right, not a privilege or a crime. However, I am not a lawyer. Installing this software on your system may some day cause Neanderthals from the MPAA to kick down your door and drag you off to be forcibly reeducated. You should make sure that you are comfortable with installing this software, and should probably never install it on a business system. ■

To install this library, you must first use your favorite Package Management software to install the libdvdread4 package. Once that package is installed, execute the following command from a GNOME Terminal or xterm command line:

```
$ sudo /usr/share/doc/libdvdread4/install-css.sh
```

As always, you'll be prompted for your password by the sudo command, which will then execute the specified shell script. The install-css.sh script will both retrieve the DeCSS library and install it on your system for you.

Congratulations! You can now watch your favorite DVDs in the privacy of your personal computer system.

Playing DVDs with Totem

The GNOME Totem application (http://projects.gnome.org/totem/) is a full-featured DVD and video file player that relies on underlying technologies such as GStreamer (the default) and xine (another video display and codec engine) for many of its low-level capabilities. Totem is preinstalled on Ubuntu Linux systems, as it is on all GNOME-based Linux distributions. To ensure that you use the standard gstreamer backend for totem, make sure that you install the totem-gstreamer package before using Totem. See "Configuring the GStreamer Framework and Plug-Ins" earlier in this chapter for more information about gstreamer.

Using Totem to play a DVD is easy. Because most prerecorded DVDs feature some sort of encryption, you should install the GStreamer framework and associated libraries before trying to play a DVD. For details on how to do this, see "Configuring the GStreamer Framework and Plug-Ins," earlier in this chapter.

As explained earlier in this chapter, Ubuntu's GNOME Desktop comes preconfigured to start Totem for you when it detects that you have inserted a prerecorded DVD. Therefore, if you haven't changed any of those settings, the only remaining step in playing a prerecorded DVD is the following: insert it into your DVD drive. GNOME starts Totem automatically for you, and you'll see a screen like that shown in Figure 16-11. (The DVD that is displayed will probably be different, of course.)

Tip

You can also start Totem manually at any time by selecting the Applications ➪ Sound & Video ➪ Movie Player menu command, or by typing `totem` in a GNOME Terminal or xterm Terminal session. ∎

FIGURE 16-11

A prerecorded DVD playing in Totem

Like most GNOME applications, Totem supports a variety of keyboard commands that make it easy for anyone to use. Some of the more common keyboard commands in Totem are the following:

- **B:** Skip back to the previous chapter or movie on the DVD.
- **F:** Switch to full-screen mode. In full-screen mode, Totem displays an icon in the upper-right corner of the screen that you can click on to return to the original display mode shown in Figure 16-11.

- **H:** Hide Totem's controls. Pressing H again re-displays them.
- **N:** Skip to the next chapter or movie on the DVD.
- **F9:** Hide Totem's Contents sidebar. Pressing F9 again re-displays the sidebar.
- **Page Up:** Increase the volume.
- **Page Down:** Decrease the volume.

Once you have watched a movie in Totem, you can select the Movie ➪ Eject menu command (or press Ctrl+E) to eject the current disk. If you choose to watch another, you can select the Movie ➪ DVD command to open and begin playing that DVD. If you do not want to watch another, you can exit from Totem by selecting the Movie ➪ Quit menu command.

Tip

Totem is still actively under development, and some versions have problems opening certain prerecorded DVDs when using the menu commands. If Totem complains about not being able to locate the codecs required to play a DVD in response to the Movie ➪ DVD command, exit Totem, eject the DVD, and let GNOME start Totem correctly for you when you reinsert the DVD. If you still have problems playing DVDs with Totem, try using one of the other DVD/Video players for Linux. VLC (VideoLAN Client, installable through the `vlc` package) and Xine (best installed through the `xine-ui` package) are both excellent DVD/Video players that provide their own multimedia frameworks. ■

Ripping Audio CDs

Ripping is the term that is used to describe the process of extracting the contents of audio CDs and converting them into audio files that you can play in other applications. It isn't necessary to rip a video DVD, because it just contains files in a certain order in certain directories, which you can copy from the command line or from any file manager. Audio CDs are different — they are constructed in a specific format and contain huge audio files in raw format.

The traditional UNIX philosophy has always been: "Write small applications that do one thing and do it well." That's a great philosophy for the command line, where you can string a series of applications together to do some amazing thing. That philosophy isn't as applicable or relevant for graphical applications that are designed for desktop use, which are somewhat self-contained by nature. Instead, graphical desktop applications are good examples of the philosophy of convergence, wherein single applications continue to gain related capabilities. As they grow, these convergent applications can overshadow other graphical applications by making it easier for users to perform a variety of related tasks within a single familiar application, set of menus, and so on. Convergence also makes life easier for the maintainers of a Linux distribution, who can focus on installing and maintaining a single application where two or more might have been required before.

Ripping Audio CDs Using Rhythmbox

Ripping CDs in Rhythmbox is almost exactly like playing them (as shown in Figure 16-10), with the exception that you click the Copy tracks to the library button rather than the Play button to start the process. While Rhythmbox is extracting the contents of an audio CD and converting each track to a file, it displays progress information in the lower-left corner of the Rhythmbox dialog.

Before ripping a CD, however, you may want to specify the format of the audio files that Rhythmbox creates, the location in which it creates them, and so on. This is done through Rhythmbox's Preferences dialog. To display this dialog, select the Edit ➪ Preferences menu command. To specify the location to which the audio files that you extract will be saved and the format in which they will be saved, click the Music tab, which is shown in Figure 16-12.

FIGURE 16-12

Rhythmbox preferences for ripping CDs

This dialog enables you to change the following settings:

- **Library Location:** Enables you to select the folder in which you want extracted audio to be stored. Although a folder named *Music* is automatically created for this purpose in each user's home directory, I tend to create a publicly writable directory called /home/music on my systems to make it easier for multiple users to access a centralized music collection. This also simplifies backups of all of the CDs that all users of your system have extracted. If you want to be really clever, you can either mount a shared network directory as /home/music using NFS or share a local /home/music directory via Samba so that users of all systems on your local network have access to your music. Ask your users not to copy music from this directory, lest the RIAA sue you for a few million dollars per song.

- **Library Structure:** Enables you to specify how the audio files that you extract from CDs will be organized in your music library. This section provides the following settings:

  - **Folder Hierarchy:** Enables you to specify the folder hierarchy in which Sound Juicer creates the audio files that it extracts. By default, the tracks of each CD are written in a folder with the name of the CD, which is itself a subdirectory of a folder with the artist's name.

  - **File Name:** Enables you to specify the format for the filename used for each audio track that you extract. The default value, "Number - Title," is a good setting to use, because this makes it easy for you to create playlists that follow the original track order of your CDs.

  - **Preferred Format:** Enables you to specify the file format in which extracted audio files are written. Your choices are "CD Quality, Lossless" (using the FLAC codec), "CD Quality, Lossy" (using the Ogg container format and Vorbis codec), "Voice, Lossless" (using the standard WAV file format), and "Voice, Lossy" (using the Ogg container format and Vorbis codec, but at a lower quality level).

I typically change the location of my music folder and, unfortunately, the Preferred format for any tracks that I extract from my audio CDs. You'll note that the default formats in which you can extract CD audio do not include MP3. This option will only be present if you have installed the `gstreamer0.10-plugins-ugly-multiverse` package, the `gstreamer0.10-fluendo-mp3` package, (or purchased and installed the commercial Fluendo codecs), as discussed in the Configuring the GStreamer Framework and Plug-Ins section of this chapter. If you see an entry for MP3 audio on this menu, thanks for following along earlier. If not, install any of the `gstreamer0.10-plugins-ugly-multiverse` package, the `gstreamer0.10-fluendo-mp3` package, or the commercial Fluendo codecs and restart Rhythmbox to see a menu entry for extracting audio files in MP3 format, which you will probably want to make your default if you want users of other operating systems to be able to play your extracted audio files. The OGG format is far superior to MP3 (and is free of licensing issues), but unfortunately, most people and portable music players can only deal with the MP3 format.

Once you've customized the location of your music files or the format in which they will be extracted, click Close to close the Preferences dialog. You can then click the Copy tracks to the library icon in the Rhythmbox toolbar to begin ripping a CD. While Rhythmbox is extracting the contents of an audio CD and converting each track to a file, it displays progress information in the Status bar at the bottom of the Rhythmbox dialog.

Ripping Audio CDs Using k3b

k3b is a KDE application that is simply great at doing most things with CDs and DVDs. I always install it on desktop Ubuntu systems, even though doing so requires that the basic KDE libraries and associated infrastructure are also installed. Disk space is cheap nowadays. To install k3b and the underlying packages that it requires, use your favorite Package Management software to install the `k3b` package, which will automatically install all of the necessary KDE packages.

k3b first tries to look up your CD in the freedb.org CD database. If more than one CDDB entry matches your CD or if there is no exact match, you'll see a dialog asking you to select the appropriate entry. k3b will then be populated and display the track listing based on your selection. If your CD can't be found in the database, k3b will use a generic name format such as *Track 01, Track 02*, and so on.

At this point, your k3b screen will look like the screen shown in Figure 16-13. (The track listing will be different unless you own a fairly obscure CD by the French band "Heldon.")

FIGURE 16-13

An audio CD listing in k3b

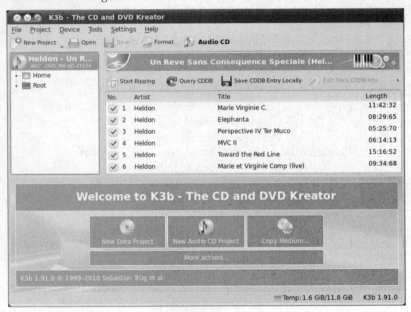

To proceed, click the "Start Ripping" button below the title of the CD. k3b displays a dialog that enables you to specify the format in which you want to save the extracted audio files and the directory to which you want to save them, as shown in Figure 16-14.

The audio file formats that are available through this dialog are Wave (raw, lossless PCM audio), MP3, and Ogg Vorbis. You can only save audio files in MP3 format if you have previously installed the lame (LAME Ain't an MP3 Encoder) package — the MP3 option is only displayed in the list of format choices if this package has already been installed.

Sadly, MP3 is probably the best format to use if you want to be able to clone your music to your iPod or other portable music player, play your audio files from computers running other operating systems, and so on.

FIGURE 16-14

k3b preferences for ripping CDs

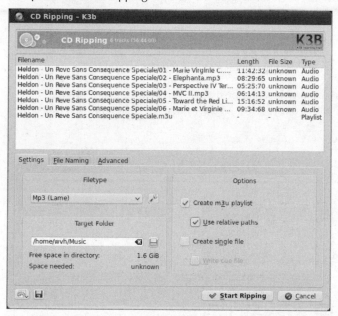

You will probably also want to customize the location to which the extracted audio files are saved, which is typically your ~/Music directory or some centralized music directory on a file server somewhere that is mounted locally.

Finally, I also usually select the "Create m3u playlist" and "Use relative paths" checkboxes. This will automatically create a playlist file for the extracted audio tracks, which is just a text file that lists the tracks in the order in which they appeared on the CD. Checking the "Use relative paths" checkbox causes the entries in the playlist file to list audio tracks relative to the directory where you stored your extracted audio tracks.

Tip

Note that the playlist files created by k3b are located in the directory where the directory that holds the extracted audio for a CD is located, not in the same directory with the extracted audio files. This can be confusing if you copy the files to another of your machines, since you may forget to copy the playlist file. Since the default filenames for each track of an extracted CD begin with the track numbers, I use a few shell aliases to enable me to quickly create playlist files for a CD. These aren't rocket science, but the ones I use are the following (in my ~/.bashrc file):

```
alias ftoc="ls *.[Ff][Ll][Aa][Cc] > playlist.m3u"
alias mtoc="ls *.[mM][pP]3 > playlist.m3u"
alias otoc="ls *.[Oo][Gg][Gg] > playlist.m3u"
alias stoc="ls *.[Ss][Hh][Nn] > playlist.m3u"
```

I can then create a playlist file (which I call *TOC*—Table of Contents—files) called `playlist.m3u` by changing the directory to the one that holds those files and running one of these aliases. The ftoc alias is for FLAC files, the mtoc alias is for MP3 files, the otoc alias is for Ogg Vorbis (OGG) files, and the stoc alias is for Shorten (SHN) files. ∎

You can also can change the format of the filenames that are associated with the extracted audio files by selecting the File Naming tab and modifying its contents, and you can use the Advanced tab to change some parameters if you are having trouble reading from an audio CD.

After making any changes that you want to make to the default k3b settings, click "Start Ripping" to begin extracting audio files from your CD. A status dialog is displayed, as shown in Figure 16-15.

FIGURE 16-15

---

k3b's status dialog while ripping CDs

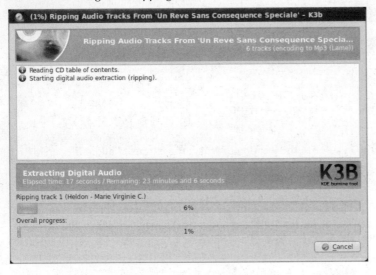

A small, general k3b status display dialog is also shown on your screen. This dialog remains on your screen even if you decide to minimize the other k3b dialogs, which is handy to see the status of any k3b task while you're working on something else. If you want to disable this other status dialog, you can do so from the Settings ➪ Configure K3b dialog by selecting the Misc icon, deselecting the "Show progress OSD (onscreen display)" checkbox, then clicking Apply or OK.

When all of the tracks from your CD have been extracted, a Close button displays on the k3b status dialog shown in Figure 16-15. Click Close to close this dialog and return to k3b. You can exit from k3b by clicking the Close box in the window decorations or selecting the File ➪ Quit menu command.

Getting More Information about k3b

I'm not the only fan of k3b — it's a very popular application with many advocates (not all of whom are purely KDE fanatics — case in point: me). Although I'll be using k3b in other sections of this chapter, it's such a great application that I wanted to provide some general pointers for additional information in case you're interested. Some of the better sites I've found for k3b information, tutorials, and tips and tricks are the following:

- www.k3b.org: The k3b application's home page, this site provides an FAQ and access to the latest and greatest releases, as well as the k3b subversion repository if you just can't wait for the next official release.

- www.novell.com/coolsolutions/feature/2746.html: A nice article from Novell entitled "CD Burning in Linux Made Easy with k3b," written by Jason Jones

- http://sourceforge.net/projects/k3b: The k3b Project's home page at SourceForge

- http://en.wikipedia.org/wiki/K3b: The k3b entry in the Wikipedia. Cool!

Backing Up DVDs from the Command Line

Ripping CDs is almost a necessity because most people want to be able to play their music files on portable music devices that don't have CD drives. Many fewer people want to extract the contents of DVDs, although anyone in his right mind would probably want to make backup copies of them. As a long-time UNIX/Linux geek and dog lover, my primary desire in copying DVDs is to back them up so that I still have a copy after our dogs finish using the original and its case as a chew toy.

Although a variety of different applications are available in the Ubuntu repositories and on the Internet to copy DVDs, most of them have a GUI and take a fair number of mouse clicks to simply copy the DVD. Therefore, my favorite command to back up most DVDs is the following:

```
$ dd if=/dev/dvd of=name_of_output_file.iso
```

Tip

You can clone a CD if you want to by executing a similar command, replacing /dev/dvd with /dev/cdrom, or whatever the appropriate device name is on your system. ■

This command is simple, works on every Linux and UNIX system in the known universe, and produces an output file that is an exact image of the original DVD. You can mount the output file just like an actual DVD if you're interested, using commands like the following:

```
$ sudo mkdir /mnt/dvd
$ sudo mount -o loop -t iso9660 name_of_output_file.iso /mnt/dvd
```

The first of these commands creates a directory upon which to mount the ISO image; the second actually mounts it and makes it available like any other mounted filesystem.

Once you create an ISO image of a DVD with the dd command, you can also immediately burn the image to a blank DVD-R, as explained later in this chapter.

Creating CDs and DVDs

This section concludes by discussing how to create audio and data CDs, copy CDs and DVDs, burn CDs and DVDs from image files, and assemble files on data or video DVDs. Although standard Ubuntu systems provide a very nice application called *Brasero* and also support data CD/DVD creation from within the Nautilus File Manager, I still personally do all of these things through k3b on desktop Ubuntu systems (although I certainly use Brasero and Nautilus on my laptops, where I want to minimize the amount of software that I install). Nothing personal to the authors of Brasero or Nautilus! Your mileage may vary, so the following sections discuss all of these applications.

Burning CDs Using Brasero

GNOME's Brasero application makes it easy to create audio CDs from selected audio files on your system or to create data CDs that contain copies of files and directories from your system for backup or portability purposes. This section focuses on creating audio — the steps for creating data CDs are much the same, although you must specify that you are creating a data CD using the Project ➪ New Project ➪ New Data Project menu item.

Creating Audio CDs with Brasero

Brasero is one of the application choices that Ubuntu provides in the dialog shown in Figure 16-5 when you insert a blank CD. If you don't see this dialog, you can start Brasero by right-clicking on the "Blank CD-R Disk" icon and selecting "Open with Brasero Disc Burning," or by selecting the Applications ➪ Sound & Video ➪ Brasero Disc Burning menu item.

Brasero initially displays a main screen that enables you to specify the type of audio or video CD project that you want to create. To create an audio CD, click "Audio project" (or select the Project ➪ New Project ➪ New Audio Project menu command). This displays the dialog shown in Figure 16-16.

To add files to your new audio CD project, click the Add icon (the plus sign) to display a browse dialog that enables you to navigate to the location where your audio files are stored. Once you display a directory containing audio files that you want to add to your audio CD, you can easily add them to the CD by selecting one or more files and clicking Add. As with most other graphical applications, you can select multiple tracks at one time using Ctrl+left-click or Ctrl+Shift to select a range of songs.

As you add tracks to your CD, Brasero checks each track to ensure that it knows how to convert a track in that format to the raw audio format that is used on CDs. If it doesn't recognize the format of a track or doesn't have a codec to handle that audio format, Brasero displays an error dialog that says that GStreamer doesn't know how to handle the specified file format, and displays another dialog that offers to look for a suitable codec for you, as shown in Figure 16-17. It doesn't get much more user-friendly than that!

FIGURE 16-16

Track selection when burning an audio CD

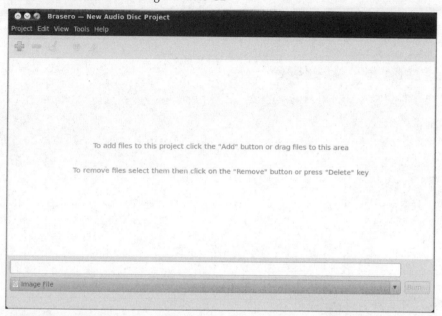

FIGURE 16-17

Ubuntu's initial codec finder dialog

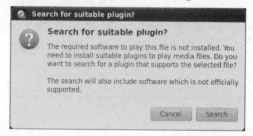

Tip

Seeing the "Find codec" dialog on your Ubuntu system generally means that you didn't install the `ubuntu-restricted-extras` package and all of the GStreamer plug-ins that I recommended earlier in this chapter. You may want to do that before proceeding, especially if you're trying to burn CDs from audio files in a variety of formats. ∎

Click Search to proceed to search for a relevant codec. If the system can find a suitable codec, it displays a dialog like the one shown in Figure 16-18.

FIGURE 16-18

Selecting a suitable codec for installation

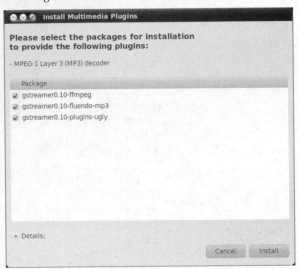

Note that the Install button can't currently be selected—in order to install the specified codec(s), you have to check the checkbox to the left of its name. Selecting this checkbox pops up another dialog, shown in Figure 16-19, that makes sure that you understand that greedy corporate morons have restricted your ability to convert audio files from one format to another in certain countries and explains the circumstances that would enable you to do so.

FIGURE 16-19

Verifying that it is legal for you to work with your data

After figuring out how one of these circumstances applies to you, click Confirm to indicate your grudging acceptance. The dialog shown in Figure 16-18 reappears, this time with the Install button enabled. Click Install to install the missing codec. Installing the missing codec is just like any other software installation process on your system — you'll have to enter your password in order for the package to be installed.

After installing any missing codecs and adding all the tracks that you want to put on your audio CD, the dialog shown in Figure 16-16 reappears, showing the tracks that you've added so far in the right pane of the Brasero window and displaying information about the remaining amount of time available on the CD below that window.

After adding contents to your CD or DVD, you may want to save the list of the contents of your CD or DVD as a Brasero project, which can be handy if you want to make another, identical CD or DVD at some point in the future. If you don't plan to make another copy, don't bother — but if you might, select the Project ⇨ Save menu command to display a dialog that enables you to specify the name and location of the saved project file. Brasero's project files are text-format XML files that list the contents of a CD or DVD — they do not actually contain the CD or DVD data.

When you're ready to burn your CD, select the Project ⇨ Burn menu command or click Burn in the lower-right corner of the Brasero dialog. The dialog shown in Figure 16-20 appears, requesting confirmation.

FIGURE 16-20

Confirmation request before burning a CD

Click Burn to proceed, and the CD burning operation proceeds. As the process proceeds, Brasero displays a status dialog, as shown in Figure 16-21.

FIGURE 16-21

The progress dialog when burning a CD

If you are burning an audio CD, Brasero first normalizes the tracks, which means that they will all be at approximately the same volume/equalization (EQ) level. This can be very useful if you are burning a CD that is composed of tracks from multiple sources, each of which probably has its own EQ level.

When writing your CD completes, Brasero ejects the disc and displays a dialog indicating whether writing the disc was successful or not, and giving you the option to create a cover for the CD, as shown in Figure 16-22.

FIGURE 16-22

The success dialog after burning an audio CD

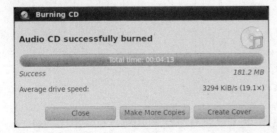

Click Close to close this dialog and return to Brasero. If you want to create a cover for your CD, click "Create cover" to display Brasero's Cover Editor, which lets you make simple text covers for your CDs, as shown in Figure 16-23.

FIGURE 16-23

Creating a cover for an audio CD

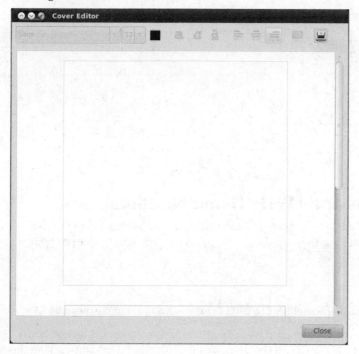

If you're finished creating CDs for the moment, you can select the Project ⇨ Quit menu command to close Brasero. If you haven't burned or saved a list of the set of files that you were working with as a Brasero project, you'll see a dialog asking if you want to do this before exiting from Brasero.

Burning CD and DVD Images Using Brasero

It's quite common to download the boot/live/install CDs for most Linux distributions as ISO (International Standards Organization) images, which means that these are CD or DVD images in a standard format. Brasero makes it easy to create physical CDs or DVDs from these image files. To do so, start Brasero and select the Project ⇨ New project ⇨ Burn Image menu command. The dialog shown in Figure 16-24 appears.

Use the Image browse button at the bottom of this dialog to locate the image that you want to burn to disc, and click Burn. Brasero displays a status dialog much like the one shown in Figure 16-21. When the entire image is written to disc, Brasero displays a Confirmation dialog. Click Close to close this dialog and return to Brasero. If you're done creating CDs or DVDs for the moment, you can select the Project ➪ Quit menu command to close Brasero.

FIGURE 16-24

Burning a CD or DVD image to disc

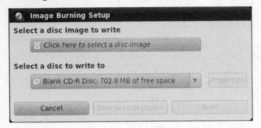

Burning Data CDs and DVDs Using Nautilus

GNOME's CD/DVD Creator application, which is just the Nautilus File Manager running in a special mode, is similarly easy to use to create data CDs and DVDs from selected files on your system.

Note

You can only create data CDs and DVDs using Nautilus's CD/DVD Creator — you cannot create audio CDs. ∎

The CD/DVD Creator is one of the application choices that Ubuntu provides in the dialog shown in Figure 16-7 when you insert a blank CD. (If you don't see this dialog, you can right-click on the Blank CD icon to see your choices.) The CD/DVD Creator's initial screen is shown in Figure 16-25, showing a special virtual folder that is used to track the files and directories that you want to add to your CD or DVD.

Once this screen displays, you can add files and directories to the CD or DVD by dragging and dropping them from any other location in Nautilus to the Blank CD-R Disc or Blank DVD Disc locations shown in the Places menu at the left side of the Nautilus display. You can take advantage of the support for tabs in Nautilus to simplify adding files and directories from multiple locations by visiting multiple directories in different tabs and incrementally adding files and directories from them (you can see the tabs in Figure 16-20).

When you're done adding files to your CD or DVD, select the Blank CD-R Disc or Blank DVD Disc location shown in the Places menu again to see the files and directories that you've added so far. An updated CD/DVD Creator Folder dialog is shown in Figure 16-26.

FIGURE 16-25

The initial CD/DVD Creator screen

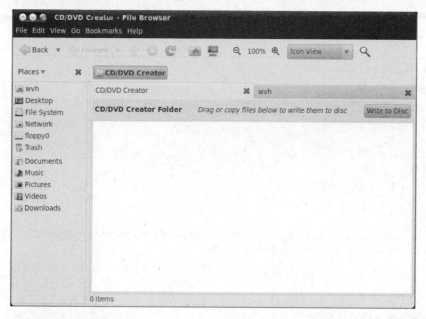

FIGURE 16-26

The CD/DVD Creator folder after adding directories

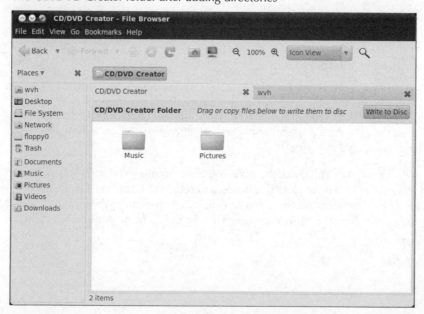

When you're ready to burn your CD, click "Write to Disc." The dialog shown in Figure 16-27 appears, requesting confirmation and enabling you to change default values such as the write speed, the name of the CD or DVD, and so on.

FIGURE 16-27

Confirmation request before burning a CD or DVD

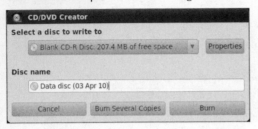

Click "Write to Disc" to proceed, and the burning operation proceeds. As the process proceeds, Nautilus displays a status dialog, as shown in Figure 16-28.

FIGURE 16-28

The progress dialog when burning a CD

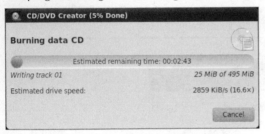

When writing your CD or DVD completes, Nautilus ejects the disc and updates this dialog, indicating whether writing the disc was successful or not and giving you the option to write another disc or close the dialog, as shown in Figure 16-29.

If you want to burn another CD or DVD with the same contents, simply insert a new blank disc and click "Write to Disc." Click Close to close this dialog and return to Nautilus. If you want to burn another audio CD with different contents, you can click Clear to remove the current track listing and start another one. If you're finished creating CDs for the moment, you can select the File ⇨ Quit menu command to close Nautilus.

The progress dialog when burning completes

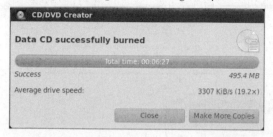

Burning CDs and DVDs Using k3b

k3b is the KDE tool of choice for burning CDs and DVDs on KDE-based systems such as Kubuntu, but is also a great package for use on GNOME-based Ubuntu systems. Once you've installed k3b, you can start it by selecting the Applications ➪ Sound & Video ➪ k3b menu command. As k3b starts and initializes, it displays a splash screen and then eventually displays the main k3b window, shown in Figure 16-30.

The initial k3b window

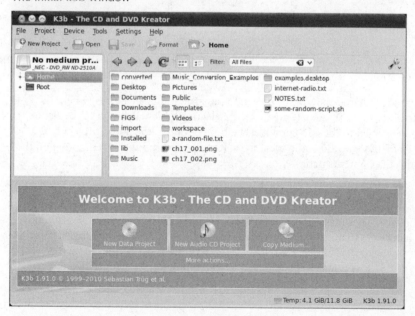

Burning an Audio CD Using k3b

To burn an audio CD from k3b, click the New Audio CD Project button from the main k3b dialog, or select the File ➪ New Project ➪ New Audio CD Project menu command. The dialog shown in Figure 16-31 appears.

FIGURE 16-31

The k3b dialog for an audio CD project

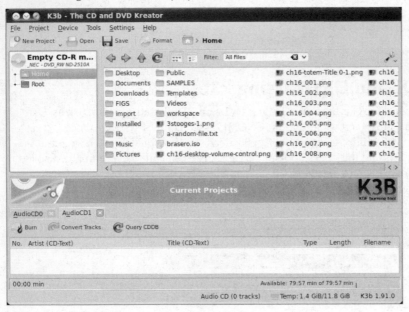

Use the Navigation pane at the top right of the screen to navigate to the location(s) where the files that you want to add to your audio CD are located. Selecting a file will add it to the list of files that is slated to be burned to the CD, shown at the bottom of the k3b audio project dialog, as shown in Figure 16-32. As you add audio files, the amount of time used and remaining on the CD displays below the CD Contents pane.

k3b is installed with several plug-ins that enable you to add audio files in a number of different audio formats to an audio CD — they will automatically be converted to the raw audio format used on audio CDs. These plug-ins support MP3, MPC, FLAC, OGG, WAV, WMA, and many other audio file formats thanks to plug-ins that leverage the codecs provided by the Sox (http://sox.sourceforge.net) and FFMPEG (http://ffmpeg.org) projects. If you attempt to add a file in a format that is not supported by a k3b plug-in, an error dialog appears that informs you that the file could not be added to the project.

FIGURE 16-32

Adding files to an audio CD project

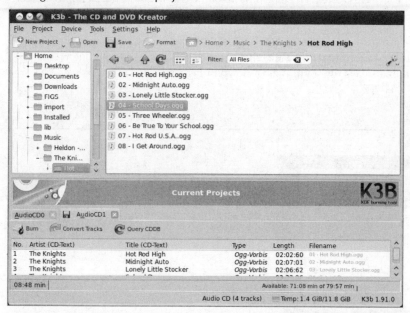

Once you have added all of the audio files that you want to add to your CD, click Burn to display a dialog that enables you to customize many aspects of the CD that you are creating, as shown in Figure 16-33.

FIGURE 16-33

Getting ready to burn an audio CD

The tabs of this dialog enable you to customize a disk image, add CD-TEXT to your CD, and do some other advanced customization. One option that I typically select is the Advanced tab's "Normalize Volume Levels" checkbox, which records all of the tracks on the CD at approximately the same volume equalization (EQ) level. (Checking this option requires that you install the `normalize-audio` package—it isn't installed by default.)

After making any customizations that you want, click Burn to begin writing your audio CD. As your CD is created, k3b displays the status dialog shown in Figure 16-34.

FIGURE 16-34

Burning an audio CD

Once writing completes, k3b displays a final status message. To return to the main k3b dialog, click Close. Eject your CD and have fun listening to the extracted versions of the music that it contains!

Burning an ISO Image to CD or DVD with k3b

To burn an iSO image to a CD or DVD after starting k3b, select the Tools ➪ Burn Image menu command. I'll use burning an iSO image to CD as an example in this section, and therefore the dialog shown in Figure 16-35 is displayed.

FIGURE 16-35

The k3b dialog for burning an ISO image

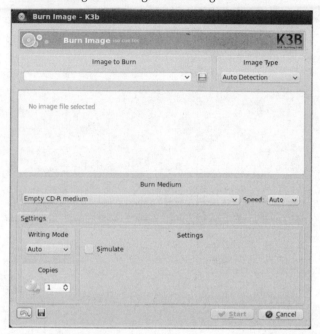

To navigate to the directory where your ISO image is located, click on the folder icon at the right of the "Image to Burn" textbox. A standard KDE navigation dialog appears, as shown in Figure 16-36. Once you've selected your ISO image, click OK to close the navigation dialog. k3b checks the integrity of the ISO image file and calculates an MD5 checksum to use when verifying the copy.

To begin writing the image to a CD, insert a blank, writable CD into the specified drive and click Start. A dialog like the one shown in Figure 16-37 appears as k3b fills its internal buffers and begins the write process.

Once writing completes, k3b displays a status message. To return to the main k3b dialog, click Close.

Copying a CD or DVD with k3b

The k3b CD or DVD copy process consists of several steps: k3b first creates an ISO image of the CD or DVD, ejects the original medium, requests a new CD or DVD, and then writes the ISO image to the new CD or DVD.

To copy a CD or DVD after starting k3b, select the Tools ➪ Copy Medium menu command. I'll use making a backup of a DVD as an example in this section, and therefore the dialog shown in Figure 16-38 is displayed.

FIGURE 16-36

Selecting a CD ISO image in k3b

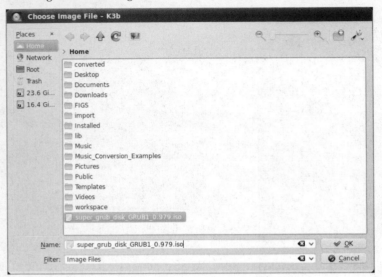

FIGURE 16-37

Status information while burning an ISO image to CD in k3b

Once you have added all of the audio files that you want to add to your CD, click Burn to display a dialog that enables you to customize many aspects of the CD that you are creating, as shown in Figure 16-33.

After verifying that the source and destination devices for reading and writing the DVD (respectively) are correct, click Start to begin the copy process. The dialog shown in Figure 16-39 is displayed.

FIGURE 16-38

The DVD Copy dialog in k3b

FIGURE 16-39

Status information while copying a DVD in k3b

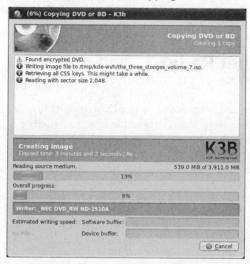

After k3b reads the disc and creates its ISO file, it will display a request for DVD insertion if the source and destination drives are the same, as shown in Figure 16-40.

A request for a blank disc when copying a DVD in k3b

Insert the new disc and wait a few seconds. The media request dialog closes, and k3b writes its ISO file to the blank DVD. Voilà, an exact copy!

Once writing completes, k3b displays a status message to that effect in the "Copy DVD" dialog. To return to the main k3b dialog, click Close.

Working with Other Audio Sources

Thanks to the Internet, portable music players, podcasting, and greater amounts of local disk space to devote to online audio files, playing audio on your computer isn't just about playing CDs anymore. A huge variety of alternate audio sources are available today, including streaming broadcasts over the Internet, downloaded podcasts (which are nothing more than MP3 files), and ripped audio files (so that you can store your original CDs safely away somewhere as backups). This section explains how to use Ubuntu's Rhythmbox application to play audio from other sources that it understands, and how to use Ubuntu's excellent Sound Converter application to convert audio files from their original formats into formats that you can more easily use on your computer system.

Playing Audio Files and Internet Radio Using Rhythmbox

Rhythmbox was discussed earlier in this chapter in the context of playing CDs, but it's really much more. Rhythmbox is oriented toward audio delivered in a variety of file formats, whether as a CD, a stream that you can read over the Internet, or a physical file that you downloaded or ripped, stored on your computer system, and subsequently want to play.

To start Rhythmbox, select the Applications ⇨ Sound & Video ⇨ Rhythmbox Music Player menu command.

Figure 16-41 shows the default Rhythmbox interface with no audio libraries, podcasts, or other audio sources specified.

FIGURE 16-41

Rhythmbox with no imported audio sources

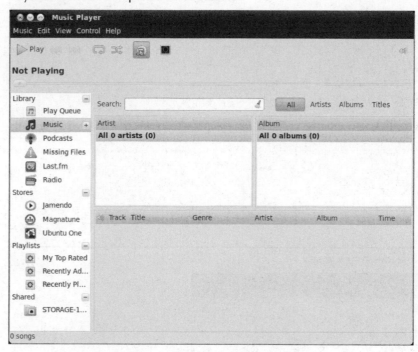

Next, you may want to add information about the location of your audio files if you haven't already done so when ripping CDs. To do this, select the Edit ➪ Preferences menu command. Click the Music tab of the dialog, which is shown in Figure 16-42.

To change the name of the directory in which Rhythmbox will look for your audio files, click the Library Location's Browse button and navigate to that folder in the resulting dialog.

Once you've specified the directory where your music files are located, select the "Watch my library for new files" checkbox to ensure that Rhythmbox notices any new audio files that you create or put in that directory, and click Close to exit the Preferences dialog. Rhythmbox begins the import process, updating its display as new files are added to its list of available music files. Any problems that Rhythmbox encounters during this process are displayed in a separate window so that you can examine them. In most cases, these are file corruption problems, but at least you can delete the offending files in your library and re-extract them from your original CDs. Figure 16-43 shows Rhythmbox after importing the contents of a subset of my music library.

FIGURE 16-42

Identifying the location of music files in Rhythmbox

FIGURE 16-43

Rhythmbox after loading music files from a library

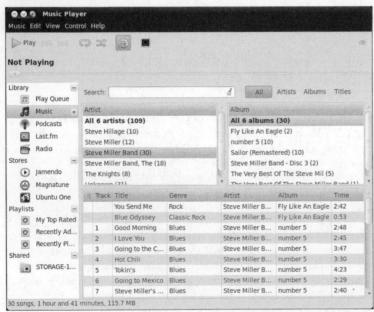

Once you've told Rhythmbox about your library, you can see that it creates summary entries for each artist across all of the directories in your library, and also creates per-directory listings that correspond to a playlist for each Album/CD in your library. To play a particular Album, select its name from the Album list and click Play. To see all of the Albums available from a specific artist, click on the name of that artist in the Artist window. You can then select the Album that you want to listen to and click Play. Once you're playing a specific Album, you can also skip from track to track by clicking on the name of the track that you want to play in the Track Listing.

Creating Playlists

If you're like me, you may own a lot of music but only truly love a few tracks on each album. Rhythmbox makes it easy for you to create your own "Greatest Hits" collections by making playlists that contain specific songs from any of the Albums in your library.

To create a new playlist and add songs to it, select the Music ⇨ Playlist ⇨ New Playlist menu command (or type Ctrl+N). A new playlist is displayed at the bottom of the Source pane at the left of the Rhythmbox window. To assign it a specific name, left-click on its blank name and enter the name that you want the new playlist to have. To change the name later, right-click on its name and select Rename from the pop-up menu. You can then type its name and press Return to give it the new name.

To add songs to a playlist, simply browse your library and drag-and-drop the tracks that you want to add to the name of the playlist that you want to add them to in the Sources window. Figure 16-44 shows the contents of a playlist containing my favorite tracks by the artist Kevin Ayers — my favorite tracks today, that is. One of the great things about creating your own playlists is that you can easily add and remove tracks from them to match your current mood or favorite tracks.

To remove a song from a playlist, right-click on its name and select Remove from the pop-up menu. This only removes the song from the playlist, not from your library — you can always add it to the playlist again if you want to hear it again.

Playing and Adding Internet Radio Stations

Internet radio is a revolutionary step for broadcast media because it enables people anywhere to listen to their favorite radio stations, regardless of whether they can physically receive the signal (or even have a radio, for that matter). Whether or not the RIAA will succeed in killing off music via Internet radio is still up in the air — but let's enjoy it while we can!

To listen to an Internet Radio station, you can simply click the Radio entry in the Rhythmbox Source pane and double-click on the name of the station that you want to listen to. To listen to a station that isn't present in Rhythmbox's default list of stations, right-click the Radio entry in the Rhythmbox Source pane, and select "New Internet Radio Station" from the pop-up menu. A dialog appears in which you can enter the URL of the Internet radio station that you're interested in. Click Add to add that station to your list of current radio stations, as shown in Figure 16-45.

FIGURE 16-44

A custom playlist in Rhythmbox

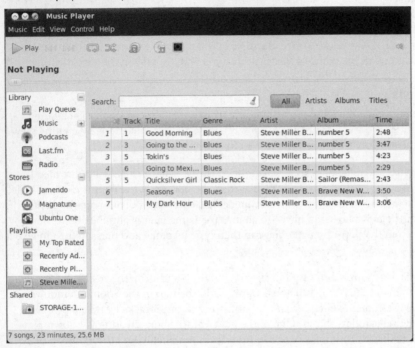

You can then click on the Radio entry to show all of your Internet radio stations, and listen to the station you're interested in by simply double-clicking on its name.

Tip

By default, radio stations identified by URL show up as URLs in the Radio Station list — you can right-click on an entry and select Properties from the pop-up menu to edit how the radio station appears in the Radio list. ■

Adding and Playing Podcasts

Podcasts are revolutionizing broadcast media because they give everyone the opportunity to share their opinions with anyone else. Podcasts make it easy for you to subscribe to certain shows and listen to them at your leisure. Podcasts are especially attractive for people on the move because they provide a great way for people anywhere to keep up with news, church sermons, and other audio presentations from their hometown.

FIGURE 16-45

Playing Internet radio in Rhythmbox

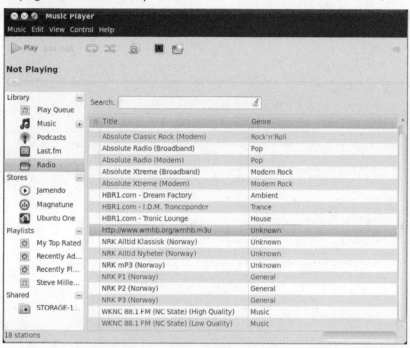

To subscribe to a podcast, right-click the Podcast entry in the Rhythmbox Source pane, and select "New Podcast feed" from the pop-up menu. A dialog appears in which you can enter the URL of the feed for a podcast you're interested in. Click Add to add that feed to your list of current Podcast feeds, as shown in Figure 16-46.

You can then click on the Podcast entry to show all of your Podcast feeds, and download any available podcast by right-clicking on an available podcast and clicking "Download episode" from the pop-up menu. Once a podcast has downloaded, you can listen to it by simply double-clicking on its name.

You can customize where your downloaded podcasts are stored and the frequency with which Rhythmbox looks for new podcasts by selecting the Edit ➪ Preferences menu command and clicking the Podcast tab. This displays the dialog shown in Figure 16-47, which enables you to update those settings.

FIGURE 16-46

Downloading and playing podcasts in Rhythmbox

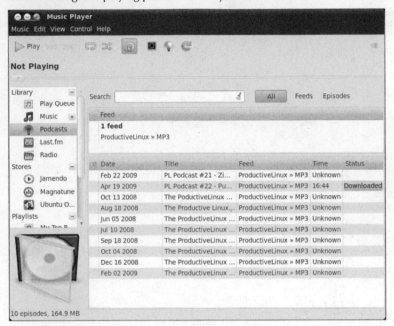

FIGURE 16-47

Customizing podcast settings in Rhythmbox

Converting Audio File Formats

It's almost inevitable that you'll eventually get some great music from free downloads, off the Internet, or after ripping it from your CDs, only to find that it isn't in "the right" format for some other purpose. The best examples of this are things like:

- Ripping CDs into Ogg Vorbis format and then wanting to play them on an iPod, which can't play OGG files

- Downloading live concert recordings in FLAC format, only to find that this format is not usable with today's iPod (and probably never will be because of the size of the FLAC files)

- Wanting to create a "greatest hits" CD for your car, only to find that you can't create a playable audio CD from MP3, OGG, or FLAC files

Regardless of which corner you find yourself in, it's irritating to have music that you can play on your desktop system but that you can't use in portable music players, to burn CDs, and so on. The problem that these examples expose is the fact that specific devices and types of media require specific audio formats. Apple's iPods can only play files in MP3 or Apple's own formats; audio CDs must contain WAV files; and so on. CD-burning applications such as Brasero and k3b will automatically convert files to the WAV format that is required when burning CDs, but they do so on the fly. What if you actually want to convert audio files that you already have so that you can permanently use them in some other format?

Luckily, Ubuntu provides a great solution to these sorts of problems through the Sound Converter application. As the name implies, this application's sole function is to convert digital audio files from one format to another.

Because not everyone will be using their Ubuntu system for serious audio work, Sound Converter isn't installed by default. You must install Sound Converter yourself from the soundconverter package, using your favorite Package Management application as discussed in Chapter 19.

Tip

Sound Converter uses the GStreamer framework discussed earlier in this chapter in the section on "Configuring the GStreamer Framework and Plug-Ins." You must follow the instructions in that section before trying to use Sound Converter — well, at least before trying to successfully use Sound Converter. ∎

Once you've installed Sound Converter, you can execute it by selecting the Applications ➪ Sound & Video ➪ Sound Converter menu command. Sound Converter's primary dialog displays, as shown in Figure 16-48.

To add the files that you want to convert, click "Add File" to display a dialog that enables you to navigate to and select the files that you want to convert to another format. Once you've selected those files, click Open to add the selected files to the list of files that you want to convert and close the Navigation dialog. The files that you selected display in the main Sound Converter dialog, as shown in Figure 16-49. (You can also click "Add Directory" to select and add an entire directory of files.)

FIGURE 16-48

Starting Sound Converter

FIGURE 16-49

Files slated for conversion

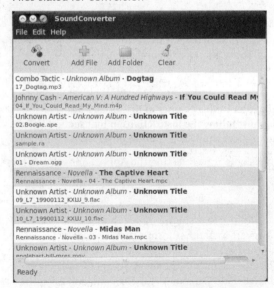

Next, specify your format conversion preferences. The files that I've selected in Figure 16-49 are in various file formats, but my goal is to be able to play all of these on my iPod, which requires MP3 files. Not a problem—I just need to specify MP3 as the target output format. To do this, select the Edit ➪ Preferences menu command to display the dialog shown in Figure 16-50.

FIGURE 16-50

Specifying format conversion preferences

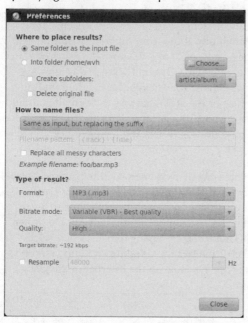

The "Where to place results?" section of Figure 16-50 determines where the converted output files are located. (I tend to leave them in the same directory so that I know what they are.) The "Type of Result?" section of this dialog shows that I am converting the files I selected to MP3 format, as desired. Click Close to exit the Preferences dialog. Once this dialog closes, you can click the Convert icon to begin the conversion process.

Once the format conversion is complete, the converted files are ready to be copied to your target device, or to do whatever else you want to do with them.

Tip

One of the few audio formats that isn't somehow supported by the GStreamer framework is Shorten (SHN), a free, lossless audio codec that is quite popular in live recording circles. To work with files of this type, you can use your favorite Package Management software to install the shntool package, a command-line utility that can convert them to WAV files so that Sound Converter can convert them to your favorite output format. ■

Summary

This chapter covered a lot of general audio and digital media ground to help you get the most out of your Ubuntu system. It began with a Rosetta Stone for the most common terms and acronyms associated with digital audio and video, whether stored on a CD or DVD, or in files on your computer. Subsequent sections explored how to configure the bleeps, boops, and boings your system can emit when various events occur, and explored the GStreamer framework that provides the underpinnings of all GNOME-based audio and video applications, explaining the packages that you'll want to install to deal with the zillions of audio file formats used on personal computer systems today. Other sections discussed the new audio systems used on Ubuntu systems; how to play, rip, and burn CDs and DVDs; how to play streaming audio from Internet radio stations; and how to play and convert online audio files. When I buy a CD or DVD nowadays, I rip it and toss the original in a box in the attic. Who wants to juggle CDs and DVDs all day anyway? Finding my online audio and video archives is always exponentially easier for me than finding the CD that I accidentally used as a coaster in my office or the DVD that was accidentally buried under a stack of magazines. This sucks up a lot of disk space, but as far as I'm concerned, disk space is cheap compared to my time — in terms of both finding things and trying to keep them organized.

Chapter 17, "Would You Like to Play a Game?," explores one of everyone's favorite pastimes, playing computer games. Sad to say, most game manufacturers don't release their wares for Linux platforms. Luckily, this doesn't mean that you can't play games on Linux systems, just that you may not be able to play the latest and hottest 3D shooters, version of Grand Theft Auto, or other games that fans of the Spanish Inquisition like Jack Thompson are trying to ban. A nice selection of classic card and board games is preinstalled on Ubuntu Linux desktop systems, as well as several clever (and fun) video games. Hundreds more are available on the Internet or are just a Package Manager session away.

Would You Like to Play a Game?

IN THIS CHAPTER

Default games for Ubuntu

Chess, Go, and Scrabble

Arcade games

Games on UNIX-like systems such as Linux have come a long way from "Hunt the Wumpus," a text-oriented adventure and exploration game that I spent many an hour playing in 1982 on a PDP-11 running primordial UNIX. Today, as you'd hope, Linux games are sophisticated graphical applications with plenty of performance and eye candy. One thing that you'll see in many of the games discussed in this chapter is that Linux games also have a sense of humor, which I always find refreshing. Losing and laughing is almost as good as winning (at least, that's what I tell myself).

As emphasized throughout this book, Ubuntu is a Linux distribution for people, and people are supposed to relax and have fun at times. Computer games are the aspect of desktop computer systems that give us all the opportunity to escape and relax without leaving our desks — hmmm, I'm not sure that this is exactly where I wanted to go when discussing relaxation, but *c'est le way it is*.

Ubuntu comes with a small number of games preinstalled as part of your basic desktop distribution, but you can easily install an even better selection by installing the gnome-games package. A huge number of other Linux games are available in the Ubuntu repositories and in source and package form on sites across the Internet. This chapter discusses a good selection of games that are available for Ubuntu, highlighting the fact that you can get work done and have fun with the exact same machine. The first section of the chapter explores the default games that are pre-installed on an Ubuntu system, plus those that are part of the gnome-games package; the second section discusses classic games such as Chess, Go, Scrabble, and Monopoly and how to play these (or similar games) on an Ubuntu system; and the last section discusses some great arcade-style games that you really shouldn't miss.

GNOME Games on Ubuntu

Figure 17-1 shows the games that are available on your Ubuntu system after installing the gnome-games package. This package plus the default games that are provided on an Ubuntu system gives you a variety of different games across the gaming spectrum, which I classify as board games, card games, and video games.

FIGURE 17-1

The Games menu in a default Ubuntu installation

As you can see from this figure, these games are organized into a single main menu and a submenu that contains logic-related games.

The rest of this section discusses the games shown on these menus, providing an overview of each game. I've organized these into logical sections rather than following the layout of the Games menu because most people tend to want to find a specific game or certain type of game — at least I do! Because these are all either part of a default Desktop installation or are easily installed as part of the gnome-games package, and everyone enjoys different types of games, you'll quickly be able to figure out which games appeal to you and try them out yourself.

Card Games

Who hasn't walked past the desk of a Windows user sometime during the past 20 years and seen the quick flash as a Solitaire window was being minimized? Nowadays, this same surreptitious time sink is completely cross-platform, as Ubuntu Linux comes with some great card games. Once you master these, many more are available in the Ubuntu repositories. The following sections provide an overview of the card games that come with a default Ubuntu Linux Desktop installation.

AisleRiot Solitaire

I've played Solitaire since I was a kid and somehow thought that there was only one Solitaire game — that being, of course, the one that I'd learned to play, which turned out to be Klondike. I became more enlightened recently when my wife asked me what other versions of Solitaire were available. A quick Internet search revealed that there were, indeed, a few zillion Solitaire games, so I bought her an analog data storage device that came preloaded with information about Solitaire — that is, a book on the subject.

I was similarly enlightened when I suggested that she play AisleRiot Solitaire, which sports a mean game of Klondike and is installed on her Ubuntu-based laptop. Unlike me, she read the online help, which immediately told her that AisleRiot Solitaire actually provides 81 different Solitaire games. (Ironically, this was a higher number than the ones discussed in the book I bought her.)

If you're a Solitaire aficionado who knows more than one game, you'll be happy to know that AisleRiot Solitaire provides the following games: Agnes, Athena, Auld Lang Syne, Aunt Mary, Backbone, Bakers Dozen, Bakers Game, Beleaguered Castle, Block Ten, Bristol, Camelot, Canfield, Carpet, Chessboard, Clock, Cover, Cruel, Diamond Mine, Doublets, Eagle Wing, Easthaven, Eight Off, Elevator, Escalator, First Law, Fortress, Fortunes, Fourteen, Freecell, Gaps, Gay Gordons, Glenwood, Golf, Gypsy, Helsinki, Hopscotch, Isabel, Jamestown, Jumbo, Kansas, King Albert, King's Audience, Klondike, Labyrinth, Lady Jane, Maze, Monte Carlo, Neighbor, Odessa, Osmosis, Peek, Pileon, Plait, Poker, Quatorze, Royal East, Saratoga, Scorpion, Scuffle, Seahaven, Sir Tommy, Spider, One Suit Spider, Two Suit Spider, Spiderette, Straight Up, Streets and Alleys, Ten Across, Thieves, Thirteen, Thumb and Pouch, Treize, Triple Peaks, Union Square, Valentine, Westhaven, Whitehead, Will o' the Wisp, Yield, Yukon, and Zebra.

If you're like me and just love Klondike, it's in there, and it's a great implementation of the classic game.

Tali

Tali is an online version of a dice game that essentially emulates a card game (poker). If you're familiar with a popular analog game called Yahtzee from Hasbro, Inc., Tali may not be a complete shock to you and may instead appear to be a familiar friend. By default, Tali is configured to enable one human player (you) to take on four computer-generated opponents, but you can easily configure your preferences to support multiple human players and reduce or eliminate the computer-generated opponents. I especially like the default prompt at the bottom of the screen when it's my turn: "Human! — You're up." Yes, Mr. Borg, sir!

Board Games

Board games have always been quite popular and don't have the sinful connotation that some people attach to card games. Although some of the games in this section are Linux implementations of existing computer games, I've defined *a board game* as any game that uses a grid or could conceivably be played on a board.

Chess

Chess is one of the oldest and most popular games on the planet, so it's no surprise that the Ubuntu folks provide a version of it as one of their default games. I'm not going to explain the rules of Chess here because there are thousands of books that are dedicated to doing that, plus it would quite simply take too long. The version of Chess that is installed by default on Ubuntu systems is a version of GNU Chess, which comes with a very clever Chess-playing engine that usually kicks my butt.

Beyond the game itself, one of the best things about Chess on Ubuntu systems is the number of different versions of Chess that are available. See the section later in this chapter entitled "Billions and Billions of Versions of Chess" for information about some of these, including those that enable you to play against real people online.

Five or More

Five or More, located on the Games menu's Logic submenu, is a GNOME version of a well-known Windows game called *Color Lines*. Like many good games, game play in Five or More is elegant in its simplicity. Each turn, three additional shapes appear on the screen in random locations. Your goal is to move existing shapes to try to arrange sequences of five matching disks, which removes them from the ever-more-crowded game field, somewhat like a slow-motion, nonlinear version of Tetris.

Unfortunately, Five or More is missing the "Boss Alert" key that was present in the Windows versions of this game, which was one of my favorite features. Pressing this key displayed a system utility screen that would make it look like you were doing real work while your boss was within range of your monitor. Fortunately, the game is just as addictive as Color Lines—you'll just have to hide the screen yourself when the boss approaches.

gbrainy

The gbrainy game is actually a collection of brain training puzzles and exercises that provide a fun way to while away a few minutes or a few hours. Icons across the top enable you to select between Logic, Calculation, Memory, and Verbal puzzles. As you test your skills, gbrainy tells you the correct answer to each puzzle (if you didn't already know it), keeps score, and displays a summary of how well you did when you complete each set of puzzles.

Iagno

Iagno is a disk-flipping game whose object is to flip as many of the other player's disks to your color, while protecting your own. You flip an opponent's disk by positioning two of your disks on either side of it. Iagno is a conceptual relative of the popular category of existing board games such as Othello and Reversi and offers much the same sort of game play.

Klotski

Klotski, the game with one of the least pleasant names I've ever heard, is another game that many Windows escapees will be familiar with, although it has its roots in analog games from France, Thailand, and most directly from Poland, where *Klocki* is the word for blocks.

Klotski, located on the Games menu's Logic submenu, is a strategy game in which the object is to maneuver a large square out of the enclosed area by moving the smaller squares that surround it. It's quite fun to play and comes with several pattern variants, each of which tells you in advance how many moves should be required.

Lights Off

Lights Off is the Linux version of a popular game in which the object of the game is to turn off all of the lights on a grid. Selecting a light causes it to turn off if it is on or turn on if it is off, and also changes the state of all of the cells that border the one that you selected. Multiple levels make it impossible to ever really finish this game, but you'll enjoy your new addiction.

Mahjongg

GNOME Mahjongg is a single-player version of the classic Chinese Mahjongg game, which was apparently developed as a combination of earlier Chinese games. Mahjongg was extremely popular in the United States and Great Britain in the early Twentieth Century and is still popular today. The object of the game is to remove tiles by matching pairs that display the same pattern. Mahjongg tile patterns are extremely intricate and can be quite beautiful, as they are in the graphics for this version of the game. The GNOME Mahjongg game is quite fun and addictive and also features a nice Hint button for use when your eyes blur after staring at too many intricately patterned, but very similar, tiles.

Mines

Mines, located on the Games menu's Logic submenu, is the GNOME version of the popular Microsoft Windows Minesweeper game. Clicking on a square reveals the number of mines in the area around that square. Once you identify a square as containing a mine, you mark it by planting a flag on that square. If you clear or mark all squares on the board without clicking on a mine, you win. You are then judged on the time that it took for you to reach the end.

I've never particularly understood why so many people find this game interesting, but I feel exactly the same way about the GNOME and Windows versions, so I suppose that this means that the GNOME version is quite faithful to the original.

Sudoku

If you aren't familiar with Sudoku, I envy you the rock that you must have been hiding under for the last few years. Hundreds of books of Sudoku games are available, many online sites provide daily Sudoku games, and I seem to see a new one of these every day in many of those daily paper things — oh, right, newspapers.

Sudoku, located on the Games menu's Logic submenu, is a number placement game, where the object of the game is to fill the game grid such that each column, each row, and each of the 3 × 3 block subsets of the game field contains each of the digits from 1 to 9 only once. Starting a game of Sudoku salts the game field with a starting set of numbers, and you supply the rest. Sudoku is incredibly popular and, although the craze seems to have peaked somewhat, it is still as sublimely addictive as any great game.

Tetravex

Tetravex is an interesting game in which you place squares with numerical values beside existing squares where the values on each edge match. I find Tetravex to be quite fun — and like the kindest GNOME games, its File menu provides a Hint key that hastens the learning process and lets you win early on, while you're still evolving your strategy.

Video Games

Video games have probably gotten more kids interested in computers than any other motivator. After all, it's not surprising to see a video game in a bar or grow up staring at your PlayStation and find yourself thinking, "I wish I could create something like that." This is a far more likely scenario than staring at a huge report in your father's or mother's briefcase and thinking, "I wish I could write a program that would produce neat reports like that!"

The GNOME Games pack installed on Ubuntu Linux Desktop systems has some great implementations and different takes on some classic video games, and many well-known games such as Quake are directly supported under Linux. For information about actually playing actual arcade classics on Linux using images of the original ROMs, see the information on MAME (Multi-Arcade Machine Emulator) in the "Popular Emulation Software for Linux" section of Chapter 24, "Using Virtual Machines and Emulators."

Four-in-a-Row

Four-in-a-Row is an interesting and addictive cross between tic-tac-toe and Tetris that should help keep you from doing real work for many hours. Your goal in Four-in-a-Row is to be the first to arrange a row of four pieces of your color, while preventing your opponent (or computer opponent) from doing so. You click in a row to drop and stack a piece in that row, adding to your sequence or blocking your opponent's.

Nibbles

Nibbles is a simple but classic game in which the user controls the movements of a snake that travels around the screen, eating diamonds of various colors and growing in length as the game progresses.

Each player has three lives, one of which is used up each time the snake hits a wall or itself. If you're playing by yourself, the game ends when you run out of lives.

Nibbles is interesting because it is also network-aware. The Game ➪ Network game menu command displays a dialog that enables you to identify and connect to a games server that enables you to play Nibbles against other users who also have access to that server. As you'll see later in this chapter, many of the classic board games such as Chess and Go also feature networked modes, but Nibbles is a simple and fun example of a game that you and your friends can play together over a network, each from the comfort of your own console.

Quadrapassel

Quadrapassel is a GNOME implementation of Tetris, probably the most famous computer game of all time after Pong. Invented in Russia, it has all of the elements of a great game — it's simple to grasp, easy to play, and when you lose you always find yourself thinking, "I was so close — I can beat this next time!"

The object of all Tetris-like games is to orient falling shapes so that they complete rows, which you then score points for as they disappear. The pace of the game accelerates as time passes, and once a shape reaches the top row of the screen without completing a row, the game is over. Simple, fun, fast, and addictive.

Robots

GNOME Robots is a graphical version of the many text-based hunt-and-kill games available on older UNIX systems. All of the robots in the game want to kill you, and your motivation is simple. First of all, you must survive, and second, you must trick the robots into destroying themselves, either by colliding with each other or by colliding with the wreckage left behind by a previous collision. This game can be surprisingly addictive.

Swell Foop

Swell Foop, located on the Games menu's Logic submenu, is a puzzle game that combines aspects of Tetris, Five or More, and similar games, in which you remove areas of similarly colored pieces on a grid by clicking on them, which causes the pieces around them to drop down or over, hopefully increasing the size of other similarly colored areas which you can then remove, and so on.

This is really a fun little game that can be surprisingly addictive. It's so simple that you'll continue to think, "I can beat this!" long after every other living creature in your house or apartment has fallen asleep.

Tip

If you have kids and find the standard Ubuntu games a bit too advanced, don't despair! There are lots of great Linux games that are designed for kids (and which may even be educational). The following web sites provide some great summaries, suggestions, and links:

    www.layhands.com/FreeGamesForKids/Linux.htm

    www.fanaticattack.com/2008/exceptional-linux-programs-for-kids.html

    www.makeuseof.com/tag/muo-games-10-open-source-online-games-for-kids

    www.happypenguin.org/list?sort=category&search=kids ∎

Other Popular Games

The games packs installed as part of a default Ubuntu Desktop installation are really just the tip of the iceberg as far as games on Ubuntu Linux are concerned. The Ubuntu repositories each offer many other games that are a package manager session away. Trying to describe each of these games would bloat this book far beyond its purpose of helping you to get up and running with all aspects of Ubuntu Linux, so this section focuses on how to find equivalents or clones of some well-known games that many people would enjoy playing on their systems if they only knew what they were called and how to use them. For information on installing packages, see Chapter 19, "Adding, Removing, and Updating Software." The remainder of this chapter focuses on explaining what to look for if you're interested in a specific game or type of game.

Billions and Billions of Versions of Chess

In the world of open source computing, Chess has two things going for it: It's incredibly popular, and nobody owns it. The fact that Chess and its ancestors have been popular for a few thousand years as a thought-provoking strategy game makes it no surprise that versions of computer Chess have existed since computers had enough memory to manage any sort of sophisticated game play. The fact that nobody owns the rights to the name *Chess* means that there are no royalty or licensing entanglements, so any computer Chess game can actually be called *Chess* without having to resort to camouflage names or slight changes to the rules to escape corporate greed.

A simple search for *Chess* against package names and descriptions in the Synaptic Package Manager shows 26 packages. These include local and network-enabled Chess games, Chess-playing engines that you can compete against, a Chess game that you can play inside Emacs, special fonts for typesetting Chess moves, and even boards that you can format using TeX and LaTeX (discussed in Chapter 13, "Creating and Publishing Documents"), and much, much more.

Tip

If you're a true Chess fan, your competition is no longer limited to friends, family, and neighbors, thanks to the Internet. You can find several Chess servers on the Internet, through which you can play remote opponents from the convenience of your own workstation. For more information, see web sites like the Free Internet Chess Server site at www.freechess.org and Tim Mann's great summary of worldwide Chess servers at www.tim-mann.org/ics.html. There are also a variety of Chess servers that require some sort of payment or subscription to use their services and play against their subscribers. ■

Figure 17-2 shows the version of Chess that is installed by default on Ubuntu desktop systems. This is GNU Chess, which is a version of Chess from the GNU folks that also includes a great Chess-playing engine that enables you to play against your computer long after all of the other humans in your house have turned you down or gone to sleep. The GNU Chess engine is probably the best-known local Chess engine for Linux (and most) systems because it is GNU software and therefore free.

FIGURE 17-2

The GNU Chess interface

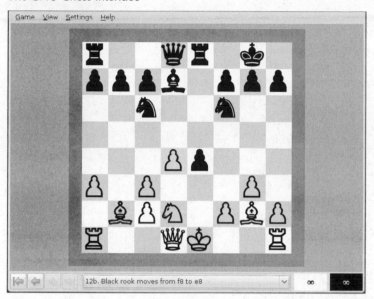

If you get angry at the GNU Chess engine for always kicking your butt or simply want to experiment with others, the alternative Fruit, Phalanx, and Sjeng Chess engines are also available in the Ubuntu repositories. Unfortunately, the default Ubuntu version of Chess can't be configured to use these other Chess-playing engines (it automatically uses its internal GNU Chess engine), so you'll have to install another Chess game that is a bit more social and therefore supports different Chess engines. On Ubuntu systems, a good candidate is XBoard, which is a generic interface for playing Chess against a variety of Chess engines. Installing the xboard package adds an entry for this game to the standard Applications ➪ Games menu.

After installing XBoard and the other Chess engines that you want to try, you start XBoard from a command line and use the -fcp (first Chess program) command-line option to specify the Chess engine that you want to play against. For example, the following command starts XBoard using the Phalanx Chess-playing engine:

```
/usr/games/xboard -fcp /usr/games/phalanx &
```

Figure 17-3 shows the screen that you would see after executing this command.

FIGURE 17-3

Using XBoard and a specific Chess engine

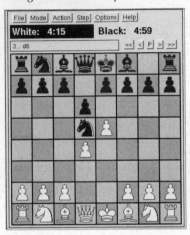

As you can see from Figure 17-3, the header identifies the players — in this case, me (wvh) against the Phalanx Chess engine. Playing against another Chess engine simply requires that you specify the path to the other Chess engine as the argument to the -fcp option. If you want to play an Internet opponent, you can use the -ics option to specify an Internet Chess engine to play against. (The -fcp and -ics options are mutually exclusive — you can only play one Chess entity at a time.)

Tip

Although the default version of Chess installed on Ubuntu systems is GNU Chess, the GNU Chess engine that applications like XBoard must use (gnuchessx) is not installed by default. To use XBoard with the GNU Chess engine, you should install the gnuchess and gnuchess-book packages, using your favorite package management software as described in Chapter 19. ■

Unless your screen is much larger than mine, you may want to use XBoard's -size option to specify the size of the game board that it displays when it starts. I typically use -size small when playing xboard, but you may prefer other sizes such as Medium, Moderate, or Average — see the main page for xboard for a complete list of available sizes.

Another popular Chess display application is eBoard, which is available in the Ubuntu repositories and displays a nice Help screen that explains how to configure eBoard for various Chess engines when you first start the application.

Of course, you may have already beaten Bobby Fisher or Big Blue or simply may be bored with standard Chess. For you, Ubuntu offers the 3dchess package (shown in Figure 17-4), which displays three chessboards and can automatically play against you if you start the game with the --play white|black argument, which specifies the color that you want the computer to play.

FIGURE 17-4

A 3D Chess game in progress

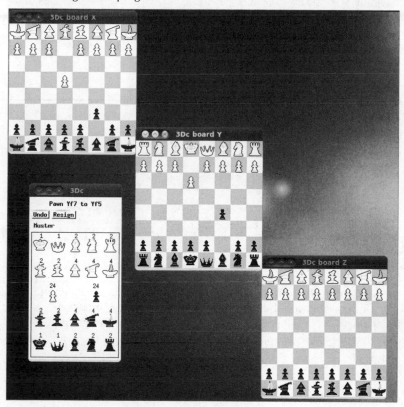

Unless you're already familiar with 3D Chess, you'll want to read the documentation in /usr/shared/doc/3dchess/3dc-rules.html so that you understand how this particular implementation of the game is played.

Tip

Fans of other versions of Chess such as Japanese Shogi, will be glad to know that you can install both the xshogi **display program and the** gnushogi **Shogi-playing engine from the Ubuntu repositories.** ■

Go

Besides Chess, one of the most historically popular strategy games in the known universe is Go, a game with a demonstrable history of several thousand years. Just like Chess, Go has the advantage of being wildly popular and free, so it matches Chess in the open source space in terms of the number of free front ends for displaying games, a clever GNU Go-playing engine (gnugo), and several free Go servers on the Internet that you can access to play Go any time of the night or day against opponents throughout the Internet universe. A simple search for *Go* against package names and descriptions in the Synaptic Package Manager shows many packages — the ones that I'll discuss in this section are cgoban (a playing interface) and gnugo (a Go-playing engine).

Figure 17-5 shows the startup screen shown by the cgoban graphical interface for Go.

FIGURE 17-5

Initial game selection and configuration in cgoban

This screen enables you to determine if you want to play against IGS (Internet Go Server), play against NNGS (No Name Go Server), or use the Go Modem protocol to play against the gnugo program or even another human if your ISP is down. Figure 17-6 shows how to use the "Go Modem" dialog to specify that one of the two players is human and the other is the /usr/games/ gnugo program.

FIGURE 17-6

Player specification in cgoban

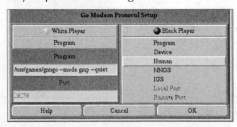

Figure 17-7 shows an actual game of Go in progress after filling out additional details about a local Go game in a per-game configuration dialog that enables you to specify rule sets, board size, per-player handicaps, and komi.

FIGURE 17-7

A Go game in progress against the gnugo engine

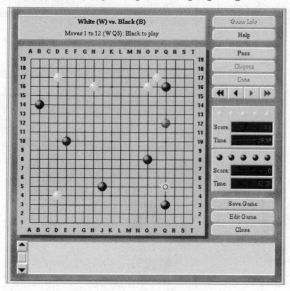

If you're interested in Go, the best site I've found for general information about Go is the British Go Association's (BGA) page at www.britgo.org/index.html, which provides information about applications, the history of the game, competitive Go, and a list of Internet Go servers. A great general site is the International Go federation's page at http://www.intergofed.org/aboutgo.htm, which I have never found as friendly as the BGA page, but it has a great set of pointers to Go sites all over the world. Sensei's Library of Go Servers at http://senseis.xmp.net/?GoServers also provides a fairly large list of online servers that speak various protocols.

Monopoly Clones

Like Chess and Go, Monopoly is a board game that is incredibly popular. Unfortunately for us, Monopoly is indeed owned by Hasbro (which bought Parker Brothers, Inc., which originally developed the game — see www.hasbro.com/monopoly), which has not seen fit to provide a Linux port of an online version of Monopoly. However, fear not, open source fans! An excellent Monopoly-like game called *Atlantik* is available in the Ubuntu repository, as is a game-playing engine that enables you to play Atlantik against other players over the network. Ubuntu users will want to install the gtkatlantik package from the resulting list. You will also want to install the monopd package if you ever want to actually host a game using your machine as a server (which you probably will).

Note

Atlantik is a network-aware game that can use a server, but it does not offer automated game play against a computer opponent. This means that you will either have to contact a remote opponent from a default Atlantik server or you will have to install the `monopd` package and enable users to connect to your server to play the game. ∎

After you install the appropriate packages, you can start Atlantik by selecting it from the Applications ⇨ Games menu on your Ubuntu system. Figure 17-8 shows Atlantik being played using the `gtkatlantik` interface.

FIGURE 17-8

A game of Atlantik in progress

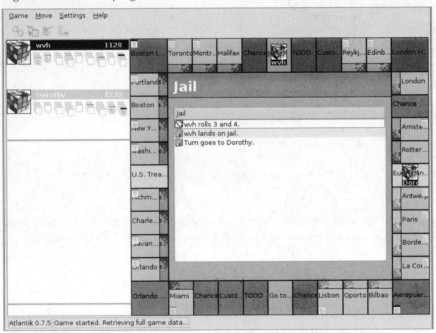

Atlantik normally plays its own version of Monopoly, but you can also play the traditional Monopoly game from within Atlantik. Figure 17-9 shows a game of Monopoly in progress using the `gtkatlantik` interface. There are few play-related differences between this and the Atlantik game shown in Figure 17-8. The primary difference is the game board used — the rules are identical by default, although you can customize them in Atlantik's Game Configuration screen, which is discussed later.

FIGURE 17-9

A game of Monopoly in progress using Atlantik

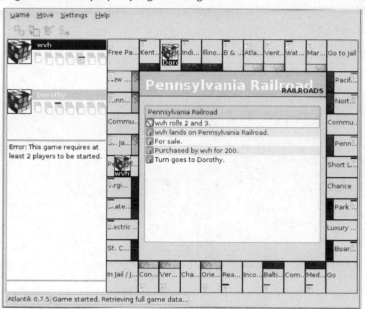

Getting to the point where you actually see a game screen can be slightly confusing. When you first start `gtlatlantik`, click Enter to get past the splash screen, and a game selection dialog such as the one shown in Figure 17-10 appears.

Enter the hostname or IP address of the `monopd` server that you want to contact in the "Another server" textbox. Click "Get games," and a list of the games available at that server is displayed. If one is available, select that game from the list, and click "CREATE/JOIN GAME," at which point the screen shown in Figure 17-8 or Figure 17-9 appears. The actual game that you see depends on the type of game(s) that the server is hosting and the one that you connected to.

If no game is available and you are running the `monopd` server, you will need to start one and wait for someone to connect to it. This is almost the same process as joining an existing game, except that you would select one of the "Create a new Monopoly game" or "Create a new Atlantik game" entries in the Game list. Your system will display a "Game Configuration" dialog until someone remotely connects to your game, at which point you will see the game board as the game begins.

FIGURE 17-10

Creating or joining a networked game of Atlantik

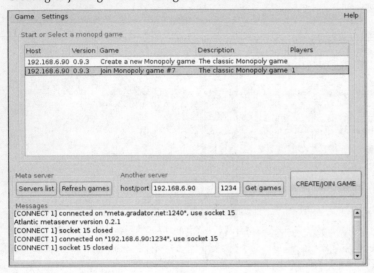

Tip

Installing the monopd **server package starts the** monopd **server on your system. If you cannot contact a remote** monopd **server or simply want to run your own, you can check its status using a command like** ps alxww | grep monopd. **If this doesn't show any** monopd **processes running, you can start one with a command like** sudo -u nobody /usr/sbin/monopd. ■

If you're a true Atlantik/Monopoly fan, a game board editor for Atlantik, called *Atlantik Designer*, is also available as a separately installable package. Figure 17-11 shows the initial Atlantik Designer screen with a blank board that you can customize, save, and use.

Using the Atlantik Designer in conjunction with Atlantik can be a lot of fun, because you can create your own game boards to reflect the streets and corporate landmarks in your own area. Who doesn't want to rule (or at least own) their neighborhood?

Atlantik is the easiest way to become a capitalist without actually crushing anyone under your boot heels, and it is great fun, just like the original Monopoly board game. Frankly, I wish that Hasbro would release an official Linux version because I believe in rewarding companies for fun games, but until then Atlantik is just all right with me.

FIGURE 17-11

Using the Atlantik Designer to create your own game board

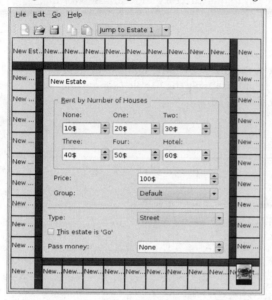

Scrabble Clones

Scrabble is another classic board game that is extremely popular but suffers from the same commercial ownership and corporate malaise as Monopoly. Scrabble is owned by Milton Bradley, which is also a wholly owned subsidiary of Hasbro. Microsoft Windows and Macintosh versions of Scrabble are available, but until Hasbro sees fit to release a Linux version, we'll just have to content ourselves with open source clones. Unfortunately, the unofficial Linux version (PyScrabble, written in Python) that is provided in the Ubuntu repositories requires that you play against an online Scrabble server, and no suitable servers are available on the NET at the time that this book was updated. You can also install and run your own PyScrabble server by installing and starting the pyscrabble-server package, but this will also install an older version of Python (2.4) and some of its associated dependencies, so it will require more disk space than you might want to devote to a game. However, if you're a true Scrabble fan, the sky may be the limit as far as disk space is concerned.

Another alternative exists for hard-core Scrabble fans. The Internet Scrabble Club (www.isc.ro) provides servers for its own application, WordBiz, which is a Scrabble clone that it written in Java and will therefore run on your Ubuntu system. Before downloading and installing this package, you should register with their site at www.isc.ro/en/registration.html. After doing so,

633

download the zip archive of their game from the URL `www.isc.ro/linux/WordBiz18linux`
`.zip` and extract its contents using the `unzip` command. This will create a directory named
`WordBiz`. Use the `cd` command to change directory to this directory and start the WordBiz
application using the following command:

```
java -jar wordbiz.jar
```

This will start the WordBiz application in its own window, shown in Figure 17-12, and will also
display an "Open connection" dialog in which you must supply the handle (login name) and
password that you registered on the Internet Scrabble Club site.

FIGURE 17-12

Playing the Internet Scrabble Clubs' WordBiz game

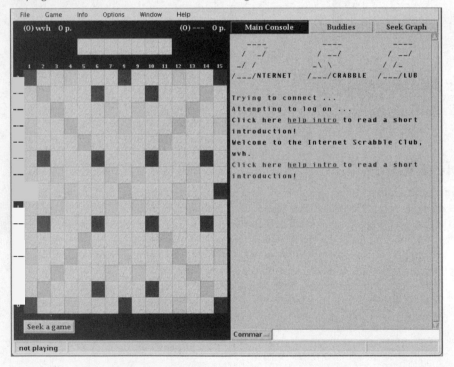

Once you have logged in, select the Game ⇨ Seek Game menu command to find another person
who wants to play Scrabble over the Internet, and away you go!

Tip

Other versions of Scrabble that actually provide a graphical interface are available for Linux systems, although not currently in a prepackaged form that can be easily installed on an Ubuntu system. You can get the tarballs for Xscrabble, an X11-based version of Scrabble, at ftp://ftp.ac-grenoble.fr/ge/educational_ games. A version of Scrabble called Quackle that provides its own game-playing engine is available from http://people.csail.mit.edu/jasonkb/quackle/. You may also want to look at a Java-based Scrabble game called JDuplicate, which is available at http://jduplicate.sourceforge.net. ∎

Unique Arcade Games for Linux

The previous sections primarily discussed GNOME games that are deeply inspired by classic arcade, board, and card games. While many of these are great fun to play, they just aren't always exciting to watch or all that unique. This section highlights a few games that feature good graphics, are genuinely fun, are largely unique, and (best of all) are still provided in the Ubuntu repositories. No visit to Best Buy, Wal-Mart, or Electronic Games is necessary — installing them is just a package management command away, and they are fun for the whole family.

Atomic Tanks

The Atomic Tanks arcade game is a tank fighting game that has good graphics and fun game play. You can install the Atomic Tanks game by using your favorite package management tool to install the atanks package. After installing this package, an entry for it is present on the Games menu on Ubuntu systems. Figure 17-13 shows a game of Atomic Tanks in progress on an Ubuntu system.

FIGURE 17-13

Playing Atomic Tanks

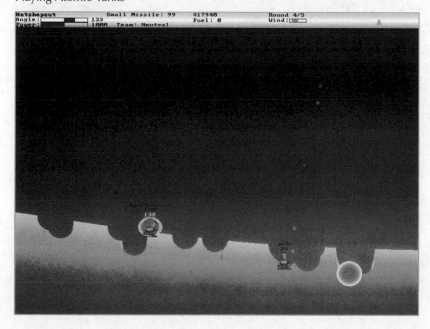

Atomic Tanks game play consists of taking turns shooting at another tank. You have a certain number of shields that you can use to protect your tank from actual hits, and missing the other tank (or hitting a shielded tank) blasts holes in the ground. As you move from level to level, you get money that you can spend on better shields and bigger weapons and great features like being able to teleport your tank to a new location.

For more information about Atomic Tanks, see its home page at `http://atanks .sourceforge.net`.

DOOM

DOOM is a classic first-person shooter game, in which you walk the halls of a military facility haunted by demons, aliens, and other opponents. The first rule of DOOM — shoot anything that moves. In addition to the commercial versions of DOOM from id Software (some of which run on Linux — see `http://zerowing.idsoftware.com/linux/doom`), open source versions of DOOM are instantly installable on your Ubuntu system by installing packages such as `prboom` or (my favorite) `lxdoom`, which installs Free Dm (Free Doom). Figure 17-14 shows a game of Free Doom in progress.

FIGURE 17-14

Playing Free Doom

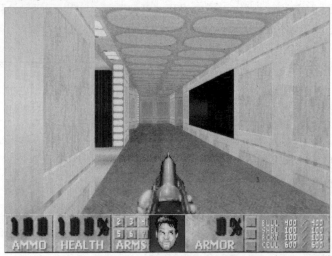

If you're into fast, pulse-pounding games, DOOM is, was, and will always be a classic. Playing Free Doom will capture both your cursor and your heart.

Frozen Bubble

Frozen Bubble is an open source bubble-popping game that you can play against the computer, against another local player in split-screen mode, or over a network against up to four other players. (Some of these features are only available for Linux systems, which is a pleasant change!) Your character is a penguin (Frozen Pingus) who shoots hanging balloons to form groups of balloons of the same color. Figure 17-15 shows a game of Frozen Bubble in progress.

FIGURE 17-15

Playing Frozen Bubble

Frozen Bubble was inspired by 1990s arcade games such as Bubble Bobble and Puzzle Bobble — if that means nothing to you, ask your parents. The game features excellent sound, graphics, and game play, and also includes a level editor so that you can create your own game levels. For more information about Frozen Bubble, see its home page at www.frozen-bubble.org.

Metal Blob Solid

Metal Blob Solid, or "Blob Wars" as it is affectionately known by its aficionados, is an impressive and original Linux arcade game. You install Metal Blob Solid by installing the blobwars package using your favorite package management software. After installing this package, an entry for it appears on the Games menu on Ubuntu systems.

After starting the game, you are the character Bob, a Blob freedom fighter who is fighting to free his Blob home world from aliens who have invaded it both to assimilate the population and to find four mysterious Crystals — Fire, Time, Space, and Reality (which is, coincidentally, the title of a song by the Moody Blues). When playing the game, your primary jobs are to rescue imprisoned compatriots, shoot aliens, and pick up treasures along the way. Figure 17-16 shows a game of Metal Blob Solid in progress.

FIGURE 17-16

Metal Blob Solid

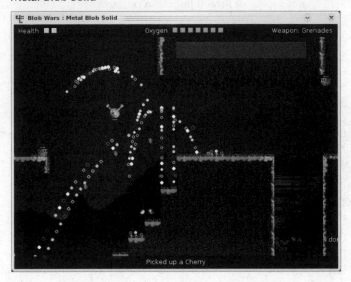

Metal Blob Solid is a truly fun game that could easily have sucked my pockets dry back in the heyday of arcade games. Given that it is free and available for my desktop, there is absolutely no reason to ever stop playing.

If you like Metal Blob Solid, you should investigate the other great Linux games that are available from the same folks at Parallel Realities (www.parallelrealities.co.uk). Project: Starfighter and Virus Killer are two of my personal favorites, but they're all great.

Tux Racer

Tux Racer is a 3D action game that features Tux, the penguin mascot of Linux, in various downhill racing scenarios, collecting herrings for extra points as he goes. You can increase Tux's speed by navigating so that you are sliding on ice, and you must avoid obstacles such as trees and rocks.

Tux Racer has an interesting history because it began life as GPL software, was marketed as a product containing closed-source enhancements, and then came back to life through multiple forks of the last versions of the original GPL code. For this reason, several different versions of Tux racer are available, including SuperTux (a 2D version, in the supertux package), Planet Penguin Racer (in the planetpenguin-racer package), and Extreme Tux racer (in the extremetuxracer package). Figure 17-17 shows a game of Extreme Tux Racer in progress.

Tux Racer is fast moving, attractive, and fun. The Extreme Tux Racer variant (www
.extremetuxracer.com) is the only version that is still actively being developed and supported.

FIGURE 17-17

Playing Extreme Tux Racer

More Great Arcade Games

In addition to the default games provided with Ubuntu systems and the few extra games highlighted in this section, a tremendous number of other open source games are available in the Ubuntu repositories. This chapter could go on forever—instead, I'll just highlight a few other games that I've had great fun playing. Some other popular games that you can install directly from the Ubuntu repositories are:

- **Armagetron** (www.armagetronad.net): A faithful implementation of the original Tron arcade game that puts simplified versions to shame. Install the armagetron package to play the local or networked versions of this game — It's great!

- **Battle for Wesnoth** (www.wesnoth.org): A fun, fantasy-based strategy game that features many different story lines. Fight to regain the throne of Wesnoth, ally yourself with Dwarves or Orcs to conquer the world, or be evil yourself and use your undead army to try to conquer the world. The game includes a tutorial to get you started, after which you begin to build an army of different fighters and proceed to conquer. You install this game by installing the wesnoth package.

- **Cube 2: Sauerbraten** (http://sauerbraten.org): A great first-person shooter in the DOOM tradition, but with great graphics and some interesting effects. Install this game by installing the sauerbraten package.

- **Torcs** (`http://torcs.sourceforge.net`): A fun 3D racing simulation that you can install by installing the `OpenGL` package
- **Wormux** (`www.wormux.org/wiki/en/index.php`): The mascots of various free software programs battle each other using dynamite, grenades, bazookas, and baseball bats. Wormux is a fun 2D game that you can install by installing the `wormux` package.

The games listed in this section are just the tip of the Linux iceberg. A quick Web search for something like *Linux Games* will show hundreds more. You may never do real work again!

Summary

Ubuntu desktop systems provide a great selection of computer games, ranging from classic card and board games to more modern video games. Beyond the default set installed with an Ubuntu desktop system, the Ubuntu repositories provide many, many more, including some very sophisticated, graphically oriented video games and simulations. Whether you want to play games like Go or Chess, which have been around for thousands of years, or you simply want to shoot aliens, Ubuntu can keep you occupied and happy until you finally have to give in to sleep deprivation or the need to go to work.

The next chapter discusses how to retrieve and install files on consumer electronics devices such as iPods and other music players, digital cameras, and PDAs. The types of consumer electronics devices are basic accessories for most people today, but they aren't very useful if you can't update their contents or, in the case of a digital camera, retrieve your current photos to free up space for capturing your next vacation or family get-together.

Consumer Electronics and Ubuntu

L inux is the embedded operating system of choice for many modern *embedded devices*. *Embedded devices* is the industry term for things that have computers or control systems running inside them. Twenty years ago, popular embedded devices were things like power plants, factories, assembly lines, and spacecraft. Today, the list still features those same technological chestnuts, but now also includes things like your car, your home gateway or router, your TiVo or other digital video recorder (DVR), your personal digital assistant (PDA), your MP3 or other digital audio player, and so on. Today, many consumer electronics devices contain a full-blown operating system to support their configuration and communication requirements.

Although the fact that Linux is the operating system of choice for most new embedded devices may not matter to you personally, it is very significant for you as a consumer and as a user of a desktop Linux distribution. There are a few major reasons for the popularity of Linux in the embedded world. The fact that Linux is free and, therefore, requires no payment of royalties or licensing costs is extremely important to embedded hardware vendors, who are planning on making a few million devices. First, if they had to pay some sort of royalties on the operating system they used, that cost would ordinarily be something that they would have to pass on to the consumer (you and me). Second, the flexibility of Linux makes it easy to adapt to a huge number of devices, which means that the support in Linux for the device drivers that control those devices and their peripherals continues to expand. And finally, the openness of Linux makes it easy for Linux to access files stored in almost any modern type of filesystem and communicate with just about any other operating system. This is good news if, for example, a company building a new digital audio player wants the freedom and power of Linux but needs its customers to be able to save and sync

IN THIS CHAPTER

Recognizing consumer electronics devices

Connecting to a digital camera

Working with iPods and other MP3 players

Working with CompactFlash and SD cards

their personal audio collections to it from their Mac OS X or Microsoft Windows systems. Read and write support for popular Windows filesystems? It's in there. Support for USB connections, wireless connections, or serial ports? Free. I think that you see where I'm going here....

The fact that you and I are using Linux on the desktop puts that same power and flexibility in our hands. As you'll see in this chapter, you can talk to just about anything from a Linux system because members of the Linux community provide drivers and connectivity software for just about anything. Users of other operating systems require that the makers of specific consumer electronics devices or third-party software vendors provide the software that enables an operating system to talk to a specific device. Microsoft Windows users would find their iPods to be nicely designed paperweights if Apple didn't provide iTunes for Windows. PDA users who use Mac and Windows boxes would find their digital assistants to be remarkably deaf and dumb if Apple, Palm, and various third parties didn't provide synchronization software for them. Sometimes this software is free, and sometimes it costs money—but never the latter for you and me.

As you'll see in this chapter, your Ubuntu Linux system can talk to, sync, and exchange files and data with almost anything. In the world of Linux, all it really takes is a motivated hacker with the latest widget from Spacely Sprockets, and sooner or later you'll be able to download and install a free `sprockinator` package that will make it easy for you to keep that widget in sync with your Ubuntu Linux system.

Configuring Your System for Consumer Electronics Devices

The section of Chapter 16, "Working with Multimedia," titled "Setting CD and DVD Preferences" explained how to configure your system's behavior when a blank, audio, or data CD or DVD is inserted. CDs and DVDs may be the type of removable media that you'll use most frequently with your computer system, but consumer electronics (CE) devices are probably a close second. This section discusses how to configure how your system handles digital cameras, PDAs, digital audio players, and so on. (How your system interacts with removable media such as flash drives (USB sticks) and external drives is discussed in detail in Chapter 20, "Adding Hardware and Attaching Peripherals.")

Digital devices such as music players, digital cameras, mobile Internet devices, and smart phones are a key element of today's culture. Although these devices are designed to work in isolation, they almost always require some sort of connection to a desktop or laptop to synchronize, update, or archive content. Each type of device has its own connection requirements. For digital music players, such as iPods and MP3 players, connecting to a laptop or desktop system enables you to synchronize libraries and playlists or simply to add new music. For digital cameras, you are usually downloading and archiving photos to free up space on the device. For smart phones and PDAs, you're usually synchronizing address books and archiving notes and other content.

Default Actions

When you attach a digital device such as a music player or digital camera to your Ubuntu system, it displays a dialog like the ones shown in Figure 18-1. These dialogs suggest a default action that Ubuntu believes is appropriate for that device—the dialog on the left is from a sample system to which I attached an MP3 player, whereas the dialog on the right was displayed after I attached a digital camera to the same system.

FIGURE 18-1

Prompt dialogs for music players and digital cameras

Prompt dialogs like the ones shown in Figure 18-1 suggest the default action of opening an application that is associated with the new media or device. These example dialogs suggest using the Rhythmbox application to access the files on a digital audio player and suggest using the F-Spot application to access the files on a digital camera. If you're comfortable with always being prompted for what to do when a specific type of media is attached to your system and want to use the suggested application, you can simply click OK to start that application. This doesn't change GNOME's default behavior when your system detects new media of that type—the next time you insert the same device or another device of that type, the same prompt will be displayed.

If you want to perform some other action for the new media or device but want to be prompted the next time you insert the same device or another device of that type, left-click on the drop-down list of possible actions to display a list like the one shown in Figure 18-2.

- **Do Nothing:** GNOME displays a desktop icon for the newly attached device, but does not open that device in the Nautilus File Manager or any other application.

- **Open Folder:** GNOME displays a desktop icon for the newly attached device and displays the contents of that device in the Nautilus File Manager.

- **Open Rhythmbox Music Player:** GNOME displays a desktop icon for the newly attached device and opens that device in the Rhythmbox Music Player application.

- **Open with other Application:** GNOME displays a desktop icon for the newly attached device and displays a dialog that enables you to select or browse for another application with which to open devices of this type, as shown in Figure 18-3.

FIGURE 18-2

Possible actions for a music player

FIGURE 18-3

Selecting another application to use with a music player

If you select "Open with other Application" to choose another application to associate with the current type of device, selecting an application from the dialog shown in Figure 18-3 doesn't actually open the device in the new application. Instead, it simply adds the selected application to the dropdown menu of possible options for that type of device. For example, Figure 18-4 shows the dropdown menu for digital audio devices after having selected xmms as another application to use with devices of that type.

FIGURE 18-4

Your new choices after selecting another application to use with a music player

Regardless of which of the items that you select from the dropdown menu in dialogs, such as those shown in Figure 18-1, you will see the same dialogs the next time that you attach the same devices. If you're comfortable with always being prompted for what to do when a specific type of media or device is attached to your system and simply want to start working with your device, you can skip ahead to the section of this chapter that discusses working with that type of device on an Ubuntu system. However, if you always want to use a specific application with a specific device or type of device, proceed to the next section for information about customizing the behavior of your system when a specific device or type of device is attached.

Customizing Digital Device Recognition

Many Linux distributions, including Ubuntu 8.04 and earlier, provided special configuration utilities that required you to uniquely configure how your system reacted when different types of consumer electronics devices were attached. For example, Ubuntu 8.04 and earlier provided the System ➪ Preferences ➪ Removable Drives and Media Preferences application. It was convenient to be able to use one application to do this, but it was still a pain because it didn't take advantage of common underlying features of these devices, such as the fact that almost all of them contain a filesystem that is stored on flash memory. You don't really need special applications to handle the devices themselves, just their content.

The latest versions of GNOME recognize this fraternity among digital devices. Configuring a specific application for use with various consumer electronics devices is now done by setting preferences in the Nautilus File Manager, in exactly the same way that you configure what happens when you insert a CD or DVD.

To configure how your Ubuntu system reacts when you attach an MP3 player, iPod, digital camera, or other type of device to your system, start Nautilus by clicking on an existing filesystem icon or by selecting any entry from the GNOME desktop's Places menu. Select the Edit ➪ Preferences menu item, and select the Media tab to display the pane shown in Figure 18-5.

Tip

You can also start GNOME's Preferences application from the command line by executing the `nautilus-file-management-properties` command. ∎

FIGURE 18-5

Default settings for consumer electronics devices in GNOME

This dialog enables you to customize what happens when different types of media are inserted into or attached to your system. As you can see from Figure 18-5, the default behavior of Nautilus is to prompt you for what to do when a DVD video is inserted into your system, when a music player is attached, when a device containing photos is attached, or when media containing installable software is attached. Figure 18-1 showed examples of these kinds of prompt dialogs.

To permanently change what happens when a specific type of device (Music Player) or media containing certain types of files (Photos, Software) is attached to your system, left-click on the dropdown list to the right of the appropriate label in Figure 18-5 to display the list of options for that device or the types of files that it contains. Figure 18-6 shows the list of choices for music players (i.e., portable audio devices).

FIGURE 18-6

Possible default actions for music players

This list is similar to the list that you see when clicking the dropdown menu on one of the prompt dialogs shown back in Figure 18-1, which was shown in Figure 18-2. However, the list shown in Figure 18-6 enables you to specify your system's default behavior, so it also includes an "Ask what to do" option. As you can see from Figure 18-6, you can specify the following default actions in response to attaching a digital audio player to your system:

- **Ask what to do:** GNOME displays a desktop icon for the newly attached device and displays a prompt dialog like the ones shown in Figure 18-1 that enables you to specify what to do for each device of this type.

- **Do Nothing:** GNOME displays a desktop icon for the newly attached device, but it does not open that device in the Nautilus File Manager or any other application.

- **Open Folder:** GNOME displays a desktop icon for the newly attached device and displays the contents of that device in the Nautilus File Manager.

- **Open Rhythmbox Music Player:** GNOME displays a desktop icon for the newly attached device and opens that device in the Rhythmbox Music Player application.

- **Open with other Application:** GNOME displays a desktop icon for the newly attached device and displays a dialog that enables you to select or browse for another application with which to open devices of this type.

Selecting any of these options changes how your system will respond to devices of a given type whenever one is attached in the future.

Changing your system's default behavior when a specific type of device is attached is a good idea if you always use a specific application to work with devices of that type. For example, if you always want to use F-Spot to extract and manage photos from your digital camera, then setting F-Spot as the default action for Photos is probably a good idea. Similarly, if you always want to use another application, such as Google's Picasa, to work with your photos, you may want to select "Open with other Application" and select that application from the list. If the application that you want to use isn't shown on the list, click "Use a custom command" and enter or browse for the location of the command that you want to use.

On the other hand, you will not want to change your system's default behavior if you use different devices of specific types and want to open each in a different application. For example, I'm a big fan of the gtkpod application for working with iPods, but I have a couple of more generic MP3 players that I use from time to time. I, therefore, don't set gtkpod as my default application for music players because it has no idea how to work with generic MP3 players. Instead, I use "Open with other Application" from the menu and dialog shown in Figure 18-2 to add gtkpod to the list of applications associated with music players, and then select the appropriate application from the prompt dialog whenever I attach an iPod or other MP3 player.

Working with Your Digital Camera

This section discusses F-Spot, the primary application that Ubuntu provides for working with your digital camera. This application was introduced in the "Photo Editing Overview" section of Chapter 15, "Working with Graphics" (which also lists some alternative digital camera related applications that are available for Ubuntu systems).

Prior to Ubuntu Hardy (8.04), Ubuntu systems used a shell script named gnome-volume-manager-gthumb to use the gThumb image viewer to import, organize, and display your photographs. In Ubuntu Hardy and later, this application and the associated script are still available, but the default application for importing, organizing, and displaying digital photographs is now F-Spot. If you want information about using gThumb, look for a PDF copy of the first edition of this book on thepiratebay.org—this section focuses on using F-Spot.

Tip
If you're upgrading an older Ubuntu system or have simply stored your existing digital photos in another directory, you can import them into F-Spot by using the Photo menu's Import command. ∎

When you attach your digital camera to a USB port on your Ubuntu system and turn on the camera, your Ubuntu system displays the dialog shown in Figure 18-7, identifying the fact that a device containing digital photos has been detected and asking how you want to proceed.

FIGURE 18-7

Your Ubuntu system detecting a digital camera

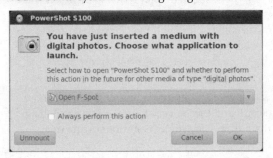

To use F-Spot, the recommended application, simply click OK. If you always want to automatically use F-Spot whenever any device containing digital photos is detected, you can select the "Always perform this action" checkbox before clicking OK. A dialog like the one shown in Figure 18-8 opens.

FIGURE 18-8

The F-Spot application preparing to import your photographs

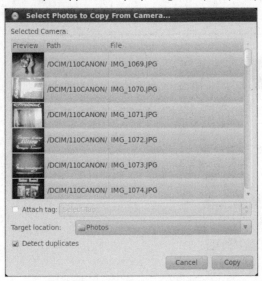

The dialog shown in Figure 18-8 provides two options that you may want to consider before importing the photographs from your camera:

- **Add Tag:** Add a customized tag to the set of photos that you are importing, which will make it easier to locate this set of photos in the future. Activating this checkbox enables you to select an existing tag to apply from a dropdown list, or to create your own. The predefined tags are Favorites, Hidden, People, Places, and Events. You can also select the "Create New Tag" option at the bottom of the list to display a dialog in which you can define your own tag, which I often do. This lets me use tags like "Mom's Birthday," "Luke's Graduation," or any other event-specific tag that will make it easy for me to find a related set of photos in the future. You can define top-level tags like the predefined ones, or define your own tags within one of the predefined tags to help organize your photos in the way that best suits you.

- **Detect Duplicates:** Analyze the photos that you are importing and only import those that are new. This option is active by default and can be very handy if you previously imported photos and did not remove them from your camera after importing them.

After making any changes to these settings that you want to use, click Copy to import your photos or click Cancel to close the dialog without importing your digital photographs. If you click Copy, an F-Spot dialog like the one shown in Figure 18-9 displays once your photos have been successfully imported. By default, photos are imported into subdirectories of the Photos directory, which itself is located in the Pictures directory in your home directory, based on the dates on which the photos were taken. For example, photos taken on February 1, 2010, would be stored in the directory ~/Pictures/Photos/2010/02/01. You can change this location using the Edit menu's Preferences dialog, which is discussed later in this section.

FIGURE 18-9

Imported photos in F-Spot

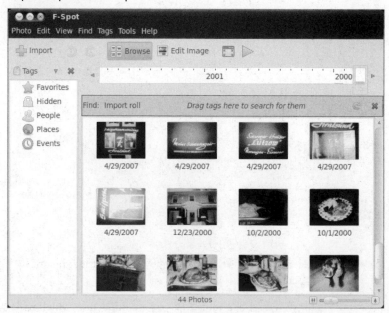

Tip

Many digital cameras automatically power down after a short period of time with no activity. This is great for saving battery life, but may cause import failures if the camera powers down while the F-Spot application is waiting for input. If you are importing photos and F-Spot creates files that do not contain your photos, try repeating the import process. ■

As shown in Figure 18-9, the primary F-Spot window consists of the following areas:

- **Left sidebar:** Lists the available tags if no photo is selected, and also provides details about any photo once you select one.

- **Right pane:** Initially displays thumbnails of your recently imported photos.

- **Find bar:** Located above the right pane, this bar enables you to display the sets of photos based on certain criteria. For example, if you selected or created a tag when importing a set of photos, you can select that tag in the left pane and drag it to the Find bar to display only photos that have that tag. The Find menu provides other selection criteria. For example, if you want to display photos with which no tags are associated, you can select the Find menu's "Untagged Photos" command. You can also use the Find menu's "By Rating," "By Date," or "By Import Roll" submenus to display photos by those criteria. ("Import Roll" essentially identifies a set of photos that you imported from your camera at the same time, using a single import session.)

- **Toolbar:** Provides easy access to common F-Spot commands.

- **Menus:** Provide easy access to all F-Spot commands.

Tip

F-Spot doesn't always display its initial dialog correctly. If you start F-Spot and don't see the left sidebar, you should see a slender bar with three horizontal lines in its center directly to the right of the left window border. Select this bar and drag it to the right to display the left sidebar. ■

After verifying that an import session worked correctly, you can purge the photos from your camera (or other media) by selecting the Edit menu's "Delete from Drive" command.

The Find bar is a very useful selection device. You'll find it useful to tag selected photos (and create your own tags) so that you can locate conceptually related sets of photos regardless of when you imported them. To locate photos by tag, simply select that tag in the left sidebar and drag it to the Find bar. (If you select the "Untagged Photos" menu command, you must deselect it before you can find photos by tag.) To undo a tag selection, you can either right-click on that tag in the Find bar and select "Remove from search" from the pop-up menu that opens, or select that tag in the Find bar and drag it out of the Find bar. If only one tag was specified, either of these actions also closes the Find bar. You can toggle whether the Find bar is displayed by pressing Ctrl+F at any time. Closing the Find bar removes any find criteria that you've currently specified from the Find bar. To refresh the selection of photos that are currently displayed in the right pane, click the "Refresh search" icon (the circular arrow). To close the Find bar, click the Close box at the right of the Find bar or press Ctrl+F.

By default, F-Spot imports your photographs into the Photos subdirectory in your home directory. You can change the location to which your photos are imported by selecting the Edit menu's Preferences command to display the dialog shown in Figure 18-10 and modifying the "Import Settings" section's Folder option.

FIGURE 18-10

F-Spot's Preferences dialog

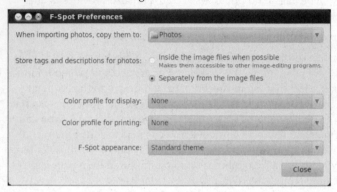

F-Spot is a great application with many features, all of which are discussed in detail in its online document, which you can display by selecting the Help menu's Contents menu option or pressing F1 while working in F-Spot. Some of my favorite F-Spot capabilities are the following:

- **Editing photos:** Selecting a photo and clicking the Toolbar's Edit button displays a list of edit options in the left sidebar. These provide common editing tasks like cropping, red-eye reduction, desaturation (decreasing the amount of a certain color in a photo), sepia toning, straightening (rotating the image to improve its alignment in the frame), Soft Focus, Auto Color (automatic color correction), and Adjust Colors. The Desaturate, Sepia Tone, and Auto Color edit options are applied immediately once they are selected. Selecting any of the other editing options displays associated controls for that type of edit in the left pane.

Tip

F-Spot does not have an Undo function. Instead, it saves multiple versions of your images. If you don't like a specific effect, you can switch to a previous version by selecting it from the Photo menu's Versions submenu. By default, the versions of a photo do not have specific names, but you can create a named version of a selected photo by selecting the Photo menu's "Create New Version" command, entering a name, and clicking OK in the pop-up dialog that appears. ∎

- **Exporting to online photo services:** Selecting some number of photos and selecting an option from the Photo menu's "Export to" submenu enables you to export photos from F-Spot to online photo sites like SmugMug, Picasa Web, Flickr, 23hq, and Zoomr. A dialog like the one shown in Figure 18-11 displays, explaining that F-Spot must be authorized in order to export photos to the specified online service (in this case, Flickr).

FIGURE 18-11

Exporting photos to Flickr using F-Spot

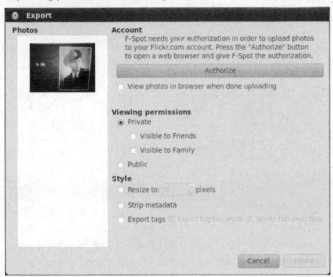

1. After specifying the access that you want other users on the remote site to have to your account, click Authorize to proceed, which will start your default Web browser so that you can log in to the specified service. Once you do this, your browser will display a screen like the one shown in Figure 18-12, which enables you to authorize F-Spot to access your account and upload your photos.

2. Once the upload completes, click Done to close the summary dialog and return to F-Spot.

FIGURE 18-12

Authorizing F-Spot's access to a Flickr account

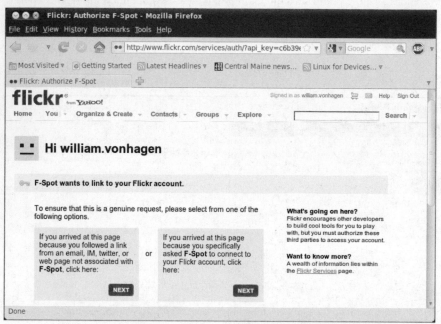

F-Spot is a great application for importing, managing, and exporting photos. Its support for tagging makes organizing and locating photos extremely easy, and its support for exporting photos to web galleries, other folders, CDs, and the online services discussed in the previous section is incredibly convenient.

Working with iPods and Other Digital Audio Players

Digital audio players of various sorts have largely replaced other portable music players such as cassette decks and CD players. Digital audio players don't skip, are extremely small, require little power, and are hard to damage because they have few moving parts. On the other hand, when those moving parts are a disk drive and the drive goes bad, that damage is usually fatal—which makes it all the more important to have backups of your digital audio collection on your desktop machine, where it is safer (and where, hopefully, you have more disk space).

You can't walk down the street today without seeing people who are listening to music using a digital audio player. Zillions of companies make them, the best known of which is Apple Computer—which could conceivably be just a footnote today were it not for Mac OS X and the runaway success of its iPod digital audio player and attendant iTunes applications and music store. The iPod is a great example of what happens when people who understand industrial design meet people who understand software and usability. In many households, the iPod has replaced the automobile as the device most likely to be buffed, polished, and accessorized.

If you use a digital audio player other than an iPod, the free, open applications that are available on Ubuntu systems provide complete support for downloading and managing the music on your device. However, if you're an iPod user (as I am), there is one big caveat. The iTunes application, which is the default software from Apple Computer that is used to manage music on an iPod, isn't available for Linux. The applications discussed in this section are an excellent replacement for iTunes as far as managing music on an iPod goes—but they don't enable you to buy music through iTunes. This is not a problem for me because I don't buy music there. I purchase and download MP3s from online sources that aren't tailored to a specific device, or I purchase CDs and rip them. Once you have MP3 files, you can play them on your desktop or put them on any digital audio player (including an iPod) using the applications discussed in the next few sections.

Tip

If you absolutely must use iTunes, you can actually install and run it on a Linux system using WINE, which is a software package that implements the Microsoft Windows API for Linux systems. I actually use this package when I have to run Microsoft Word, which it does a great job of. A version of WINE is available in the Ubuntu repositories, but I use a commercial version of WINE from CodeWeavers (www.codeweavers.com), who are the primary sponsors of the WINE project. You can also install and use iTunes in a Windows virtual machine, which is easy to set up and is discussed in Chapter 24, "Using Virtual Machines and Emulators." After all, why waste perfectly good hardware on Windows? ■

ID3 Tag Editing on Ubuntu

As discussed in Chapter 16, most of the popular audio file formats like MP3 and OGG support ID3 tags to provide information about file contents such as the artist, album title, song title, date recorded, and so on. All digital audio players can extract and display this information from supported audio file formats, and most use it to enable you to sort, search, and organize the files on a digital audio player. Before transferring audio files to your audio player, you should verify that they have valid ID3 tags, or else it may be hard to figure out exactly who performs Track03.mp3. You can usually verify the ID3 tag information by simply playing your audio files in a graphical audio application such as Rhythmbox or XMMS, because these applications automatically display ID3 information as they play each audio file.

Most CD-ripping applications will automatically fill out ID3 tag information during the ripping process, but you may occasionally encounter a CD that is not in the Internet CD databases, and for which you will therefore have to manually supply ID3 information. The Ubuntu repositories provide several applications for filling out or updating ID3 and ID3v2 tags. I have used id3, id3v2, and id3tool, all of which are command-line utilities, and EasyTAG, a great, graphical ID3 tag editor.

The next two sections explain how to work with different types of digital audio players on your Ubuntu systems. The first section discusses using the standard audio playback and management application used on Ubuntu (Rhythmbox) with iPods and other types of digital audio players. The following section discusses gtkpod, a GTK application for working with iPods that I've used for years, and highlights some specialized applications that are tailored for other types of digital audio players and that are available in the Ubuntu repositories.

Digital Audio Players and Rhythmbox on Ubuntu

Attaching an iPod or other digital audio player to your Ubuntu system with a USB or FireWire cable displays a dialog like the one shown at left in Figure 18-1 near the beginning of this chapter. The "Open Rhythmbox Music Player" option is selected by default. Click OK to proceed.

When the Rhythmbox Music Player opens (you may have to click its icon in the Notification Area in the top GNOME panel to actually display it on your screen), its left pane will contain a highlighted icon for your digital audio player in the Devices section, and the right pane will contain a list of all of the audio tracks that it contains. You can click on the arrow to the right of the menu item in the left pane to show all of the playlists that are currently present on that device, as shown in Figure 18-13, which lists the playlists on an iPod, but which also shows a Devices entry for a generic 4.1-GB audio player.

FIGURE 18-13

Playlists on an iPod in Rhythmbox

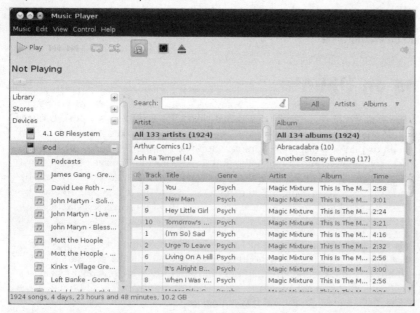

Playing Music

Rhythmbox will begin playing music immediately when some audio players are connected, while you must double-click a playlist or an audio track on others for them to begin playing. If you select a playlist, the tracks that it contains are listed in the right pane, as shown in Figure 18-14. If the Cover art plug-in is active in Rhythmbox and Rhythmbox can identify the album that contains the track that is playing, the cover art for that album will be displayed at the bottom of the left pane. You can enable or disable this plug-in by selecting the Edit menu's Plugins command and checking or unchecking its entry in the "Configure Plugins" dialog.

FIGURE 18-14

Playing a selected playlist

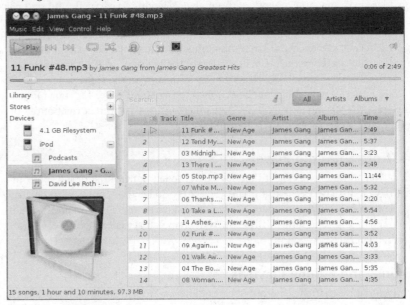

You can also play any specific song from your device by clicking the name of the device in the left pane to display all of the songs that it contains, and double-clicking a specific track to play it.

Tip

When copying or removing songs or creating and editing playlists as described in the next few sections, you can use the standard GNOME selection techniques to select multiple items at one time. To select non-contiguous entries from a list, you can hold down the Ctrl key while you select each individual entry. To select contiguous entries from a list, you can select the first entry in the range that you want to select, press the Shift key, and select the entry at the other end of the range to select those entries and all of the entries between them. ■

Copying Music to an Audio Player

To copy files to a digital audio player, select the music library or device in the left pane that contains the tracks that you want to copy. The list of the songs in that library or on that device displays in the right pane. Select the songs that you want to copy, drag them to the device to which you want to copy them, and release the left mouse button.

After you have dragged songs to your audio device, a progress bar that shows the status of the copy displays in the lower-right portion of the Rhythmbox window.

Copying Music from an Audio Player

Rhythmbox also makes it easy to copy files from your portable audio player to an existing library. This can be handy if you store your music collection on several different systems or want to listen to your audio files on a laptop or machine at work without always having to carry around and use a specific portable audio player.

To copy files from a portable audio player to a Rhythmbox music library on a desktop or laptop system, click the entry for that device in the Devices section of the left pane in Rhythmbox and select the tracks, artist, or album listing whose tracks you want to copy in the right pane. Left-click and hold the mouse button down, drag your selection(s) to the Music entry for your Library in the left pane, and release the left mouse button. A status message is displayed at the bottom of the Rhythmbox window as the files are copied to your library.

Removing Music from an Audio Player

To delete files from a digital audio player, select that device in the left pane. A list of the songs in that library or on that device displays in the right pane. Select the songs that you want to delete, and right-click to display a context-sensitive menu. Select the "Move to Trash" command, which will remove them from the listing. The songs will be purged when you actually disconnect your audio player, as described later in this section.

Creating, Renaming, and Editing Playlists

Playlists provide a convenient mechanism to group together and organize the songs that originally appeared together on a CD, or to simply create a list of songs that you like to hear together and in a certain order. In order to create a playlist on a digital audio player, the songs that you want to add to it must already be present on that device.

To create a playlist, right-click on the name of the digital audio player on which you want to create it, and select "New playlist" from the pop-up menu that displays. How you name a new playlist works slightly differently depending on the type of audio device that you are using:

- **On most MP3 players:** An empty playlist is displayed at the bottom of the list of available playlists. Enter the name that you want the new playlist to have—but enter it carefully because you cannot edit playlist names once you have created them on many generic digital audio players. To rename a playlist on most audio players, you have to create a new one with the correct name, copy the entries from the old playlist to the new one, and then delete the old playlist.

- **On iPods:** An empty playlist named *New playlist* is simply added to the end of list of available playlists on your iPod. This is fine, because you can edit the names of playlists on an iPod. To rename a playlist on an iPod, right-click on its name in the left pane and select Rename from the pop-up menu that displays. You can then edit the name of the playlist in the left pane and press Enter/Return on your keyboard or click elsewhere to save the new name.

Once you have created a new playlist, click the name of the device on which you created it to see the songs that it contains. You can drag songs to the playlist one by one, or use the techniques described in the tip earlier in this section to select and drag multiple songs at the same time.

Disconnecting Your Audio Player

You should not simply disconnect a digital audio player from your computer system. There should actually be no problem in doing so if you have not made any changes to its contents, but it's a good idea to get in the habit of always using the Rhythmbox Eject command before disconnecting a digital audio player. Don't worry, this doesn't actually shoot your iPod across the room — the *Eject* keyword is shared with devices that you actually do eject, such as CDs and DVDs. Using this command guarantees that all pending changes have been written to your digital audio device, including removing any tracks that you selected for deletion.

To eject a digital audio player in Rhythmbox, right-click on the name of the device in the left pane and select Eject from the context-sensitive menu that appears. If you have made recent changes to the device, you will see a notice in the lower-right corner of your GNOME desktop stating that data must be written to the device before you can remove it. When all data has been written to the device, another dialog opens stating that it is now safe to disconnect the device.

Working with an iPod Using gtkpod

You may be wondering why I'm even bothering to discuss a separate application for working with audio files on the iPod, when Rhythmbox already does a great job. This is simply because that wasn't always the case — iPod support is a fairly recent addition to Rhythmbox. Since gtkpod has been around for years and still offers some capabilities that Rhythmbox does not, I think it's a great application for working with an iPod, especially if you don't like Rhythmbox. So feel free to skip this section — or read on if you're interested in reading about an excellent alternative to working with your iPod using the "standard" Ubuntu audio applications.

Since Rhythmbox is installed by default and works with iPods, the gtkpod application is not installed by default on Ubuntu systems. In order to follow along in this section, you'll have to use your favorite Package Management software (as discussed in Chapter 19, "Adding, Removing, and Updating Software") to install the gtkpod package.

Tip

In order to use gtkpod with iPhones or the iPod touch, you will have to use your favorite Package Management software to install the `ifuse` package. You will also have to add yourself to the iFuse group on your system by using a command like `adduser` *USERNAME* `fuse`, where *USERNAME* is your login name. You will then have to log out and log back in for this to take effect. ■

Attaching Your iPod

Attaching an iPod to your Ubuntu system with a USB or FireWire cable displays a dialog like the ones shown in Figure 18-1. If you are just experimenting with gtkpod, you can select "Do Nothing" from the menu on this dialog. Your iPod will show up as a removable storage device, and a desktop icon for it will automatically be created. If you decide that you like gtkpod, you can always create a custom menu entry for it in the device recognition dialogs, as described in the section on customizing digital device recognition on Ubuntu systems, earlier in this chapter.

Caution

When you attach an iPod to your Linux system, the iPod's screen will display an international No symbol and a "Do not disconnect!" message. Believe it. Follow the instructions in the section called "Safely Disconnecting Your iPod," later in this section, to safely remove your iPod without risking damage to its disk and the files that it contains. ■

Using gtkpod

Installing `gtkpod` on an Ubuntu system creates the Applications ➪ Sound and Video ➪ gtkpod iPod Manager menu item. Selecting this menu item starts gtkpod. If your iPod was mounted and can be accessed successfully, it should be listed in the pane at the left of the gtkpod window. To see the actual contents of your iPod and begin working with it, select its name from this pane. The other gtkpod windows will update to show the contents of your iPod, as shown in Figure 18-15.

Tip

If you do not see your iPod listed in the left gtkpod pane, select the Edit menu's "Edit Preferences" command. In the dialog that appears, click "Set mountpoint or edit repository" options, and verify that the entry in the iPod Mount Point field is the directory where your iPod is actually mounted and change it if necessary. If you change this field, you will have to exit from and restart gtkpod to have it check the new mountpoint. You may also have to click the Read icon on the gtkpod toolbar to force the gtkpod application to read the database information from an iPod that is mounted in a new location. ■

The next few sections discuss how to do some common tasks with gtkpod. You can, of course, do much more — after all, there are entire books on iTunes — but the suggestions in the following sections will get you started and are the most common tasks that I do in gtkpod.

FIGURE 18-15

The contents of an iPod in gtkpod

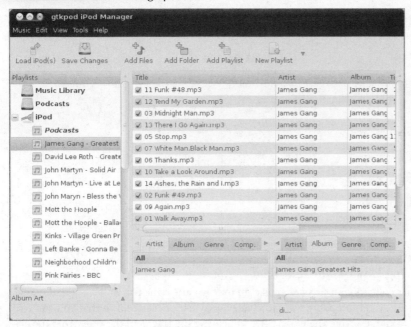

Adding Music to Your iPod

You can add MP3 files to your iPod in two different ways, either as individual files or by adding complete directories of MP3 files. To add individual files to your iPod, click the "Add Files" button in the gtkpod menu bar to display a standard browse dialog in which you can navigate to the directory containing the file(s) that you want to add, select them, and click Open. The file(s) that you selected will be added to your iPod, and the Artist and Album information will be added to the iPod (if it is present in ID3 tags in the audio file).

More commonly, you will want to add all of the audio files associated with a single album to your iPod at one time after you've ripped your latest CD acquisition. To do this, click the "Add Folder" button in the gtkpod menu bar to display the dialog, as shown in Figure 18-16.

Navigate to the directory that you want to add, and click Open to add that entire directory to your iPod. The main gtkpod window updates to reflect the addition of the new directory (entire album).

Even though the main gtkpod dialog shows the files and directories that you've added to your iPod, only the files have been copied there. The databases that your iPod uses to track file, song, and artist information aren't actually updated until you resynchronize the gtkpod database with the iPod's database by clicking Save Changes, as described in "Writing Changes to Your iPod" later in this section.

FIGURE 18-16

Adding directories of MP3 files to your iPod

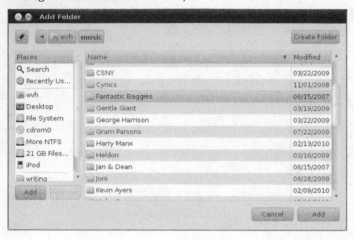

Creating and Editing Playlists on Your iPod

Creating playlists that contain your favorite music du jour is part of the fun of having and using an iPod. At a minimum, you'll probably want to create a playlist for each album that you add to your iPod, so that you can re-create the experience of hearing the tracks in the order that the artist intended.

The gtkpod application makes it easy to create many different types of playlists. There are also various ways of creating playlists, but you can access all of them from the Edit ➪ Create Playlists menu, shown in Figure 18-17.

For example, to create a playlist that contains all of the tracks associated with a certain album, navigate to that album in gtkpod and select all of the tracks that it contains. Once you've done that, select Edit ➪ Create Playlists ➪ Containing Selected Tracks. This displays a dialog that enables you to specify a meaningful name for the new playlist. (The default value is the catchy name *New Playlist*, which isn't all that memorable.) After entering a new name, click OK to save your playlist under its new name.

As you can see from Figure 18-17, gtkpod supports a wide variety of playlists. Once you've created a new playlist, its name is displayed in the leftmost pane in the main gtkpod dialog. (You may need to click on the entry for your iPod in order to see the playlists that it contains.) You can then select any playlist to show the sequence of tracks that it contains, as shown in Figure 18-18, which displays my newly created playlist for the ancient Steve Miller Band album, *Number 5*.

FIGURE 18-17

Different types of playlists in gtkpod

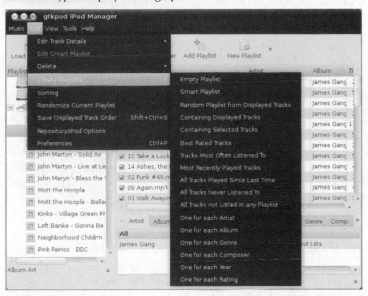

FIGURE 18-18

Examining a specific playlist

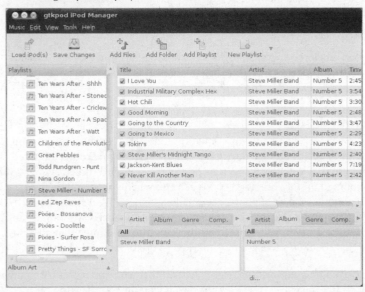

You can rename a playlist at any time by clicking its name in the left pane and entering a new name, or you can delete it and start over by selecting Edit ➪ Delete ➪ Selected playlist or right-clicking on the playlist and selecting "Delete but keep tracks" from the context-sensitive menu that displays. More often, you'll simply want to modify an existing playlist. To remove tracks from a selected playlist or otherwise manipulate the files that one contains, right-click on any entry in the playlist to display a context-sensitive menu. To remove a track from the playlist without removing the associated audio file from your iPod, select the "Delete From Playlist" command. To remove the selected track from both the playlist and the iPod, select the "Delete From iPod" command.

You can manipulate existing playlists in several other ways. For example, you can re-sort the playlist in different ways by clicking on any of the headings shown in the track-listing pane at the bottom of the gtkpod application. You can add other tracks to an existing playlist by navigating to those tracks and dragging them from the track-listing pane to the name of the playlist in the left pane. The gtkpod application provides a tremendous amount of control over playlists, making it easy for you to create playlists that enable you to hear what you want, when you want, in the order that you want.

Writing Changes to Your iPod

Once you've finished adding music to your iPod, creating and editing playlists, and so on, you will certainly want to save all of those changes to your iPod. Although files and directories of audio files, new playlists, and other new items are added to your iPod at the time that you create them, the database that your iPod uses to track these new and modified items isn't updated until you explicitly synchronize the information in gtkpod with those databases on your iPod. You should always synchronize gtkpod with your iPod after making any changes to ensure that those changes are not lost or saved in some incomplete, intermediate state. After all, updating playlists or adding new music to your iPod doesn't do you much good if you can't access the new information!

To synchronize this information, click the "Save Changes" button in the gtkpod toolbar. A dialog displays as the information is synchronized. Once this dialog closes, it is safe to disconnect your iPod from your Ubuntu system, as described in the next section.

Safely Disconnecting Your iPod

Simply writing your changes to your iPod and exiting from gtkpod doesn't disconnect your iPod from your Ubuntu Linux system. Like any storage device on a Linux system, an iPod is mounted as part of your Linux filesystem so that you can access it as part of the standard directory hierarchy. By default, iPods are mounted on the directory /media/ipod when you attach them to your system. Although it is mounted as a part of your system's filesystem, an iPod's screen will display an international No symbol and a "Do not disconnect!" message. To safely disconnect an iPod from the filesystem after using gtkpod, you must first unmount it to guarantee that all disk updates have been saved and that the iPod's filesystem is marked as up to date and clean.

If an icon for your iPod is displayed on your desktop, right-click on that icon and select Unmount from the context-sensitive menu that displays. If you do not see an icon on your desktop or selecting the menu command doesn't work for you, you can always resort to the command line. Linux provides the eject command to cleanly unmount a disk partition or mounted device. Before disconnecting your iPod from your system, you can execute the following command:

```
$ sudo eject /media/ipod
```

After you supply your password, this command will unmount the iPod filesystem, remove any desktop icons associated with the iPod, and will usually cause your iPod's screen to stop displaying the international No symbol and "Do not disconnect!" message. You can then disconnect it physically from your system.

Working with CompactFlash and SD Cards

Although Ubuntu systems can recognize a tremendous selection of digital audio players, digital cameras, and other devices, you may encounter a situation in which your system doesn't recognize a specific device or that device doesn't provide a USB or FireWire port to enable you to connect it to your Ubuntu system. Luckily, most of these devices provide removable storage such as CompactFlash or Secure Digital (SD) memory cards that can be accessed from your Ubuntu system using a generic USB media reader. These devices are quite common nowadays and can be purchased on eBay or at most camera stores. Using these devices with Ubuntu Linux is quite simple and makes it possible for you to copy your precious photos, files, or other information from just about anything to the safety of your Linux desktop computer system.

After ejecting the removable storage media from your camera or other device, insert it into the media reader, and attach that device to your system. If your system can identify the media as a storage device from a digital camera (in other words, if the flash card contains a directory called DCIM), it will give the same notification dialog that is used for digital cameras. In some cases, the notification dialog may simply offer to mount it because your system could not uniquely identify the storage device as having come from a camera. In that case, you can simply open the storage device in the suggested file manager and then copy the files off the media using that file manager. If the CompactFlash or SD card that you are exploring is from a digital camera, your photos will be located in subdirectories of the media's DCIM directory.

Once you are finished working with your removable media card, you should eject it by right-clicking on its desktop icon or file manager entry and selecting the Safely Unmount or Eject commands from the context-sensitive menu. These commands ensure that any pending changes are actually written to your storage card and that it is cleanly dismounted so that it can be safely disconnected from your system.

Summary

Portable consumer electronics devices like digital music players and digital cameras are essentially high-tech jewelry today. Almost everyone has at least one. Therefore, this chapter covered a lot of digital media ground, including how your system recognizes newly attached digital devices and how to customize the actions that it offers to perform, how to work with iPods and other digital audio players, and how to work with digital cameras or directly with removable CompactFlash or Secure Digital storage cards. Although I've been using Linux for more than a decade now, the quality, power, and even (nowadays) the ease-of-use of its application ecosystem still impresses me. After reading this chapter, I hope that you feel the same way.

The next chapter discusses how to add, remove, and update software on your Ubuntu system using both command-line and graphical utilities. It also explores how to use these tools to examine the software packages that are installed on your system, and how to locate, list, and explore the tremendous amount of additional software that is available for Ubuntu systems.

Adding, Removing, and Updating Software

I f you looked around before settling on Ubuntu Linux, one of the things that you were sure to notice is that hundreds of Linux distributions are available, each with its own installer; favorite desktop environment and/or X Window System window manager; set of core applications; and some way of updating, expanding, and maintaining the software that comes with the distribution. When you come right down to it, the last item is the most significant aspect of a Linux distribution aside from the size and involvement of its user and development communities. There's actually an interesting loop between ease-of-use/ease-of-maintenance and the size of the user community. A Linux distribution that makes it easy to keep existing software up-to-date, install new software, and figure out what's on your system in the first place is a Linux distribution that more people are apt to use. (This assumes that someone is actually keeping the distribution up-to-date.)

As discussed in Chapter 1, "The Ubuntu Linux Project," I find the Ubuntu Linux community the most exciting, dynamic, and energetic Linux community that I've ever encountered. The Ubuntu community is a committed community of both users and developers. A vast pool of software is available for easy download and installation at any time. The Ubuntu Software Center application, located at the bottom of the Applications menu, makes it easy to install new software from a preselected set of popular applications. If you want a bit more control or simply want to peek under the covers, the dpkg, apt-get, and aptitude tools make it easy to locate and install new software, and aptitude and the Synaptic Package Manager make it easy to search for software that's relevant to your interests. Who could ask for anything more?

Updates and corrections to existing software are frequent, which is a good thing, and access to updated software is similarly easy. Ubuntu systems automatically start an applet at system startup (and regularly thereafter)

IN THIS CHAPTER

One stop shopping at the Ubuntu Software Center

Overviewing package management

Using Ubuntu repositories

Finding things on your system

Using dpkg, apt-get, and aptitude

Using the Synaptic Package Manager

Using the Ubuntu Update Manager

Cleaning up your system

that automatically lets you know when updates are available to software that's installed on your system or the system software itself. Once you've been notified of updates, keeping your system up-to-date requires three or four mouse clicks. Not too shabby!

The key to all of this simplicity and ease-of-use is the excellent DEB (for Debian) package format, developed for the Debian Linux distribution and therefore inherited by Ubuntu. The DEB package format puts other software package formats, such as RPM, to shame — I personally would appreciate some electroshock therapy to forget the needless hours I've wasted trying to untangle twisty mazes of dependencies and requirements between various RPM packages. If you don't know what RPM is, you're lucky. Let's keep it that way.

Note

If you're familiar with RPM-based Linux distributions such as Fedora Core, Mandriva, Red Hat, or Centos, you're probably thinking, "Silly Human, yum solves most RPM problems!" Although this is probably true in a court of law, I don't feel that providing additional layers of syntactic sugar on top of a frustrating package management system like RPM is the "right thing" or an actual solution. I prefer using smarter package formats such as DEB and smarter utilities such as the ones discussed in this chapter that were designed to do the right thing in the first place. ■

Tip

If you must deal with packages that were created for other Linux distributions and are therefore in other package formats, see the section "Converting Packages from Other Package Formats" later in this chapter for information about converting packages. ■

The easiest way to install new software on an Ubuntu system is by using the Ubuntu Software Center menu item found at the bottom of the GNOME Applications menu. This application, which makes it easy to install new software from a preselected set of popular applications, is discussed in the first section of this chapter.

If you want more control over your system or will be doing system administration on multiple Ubuntu systems, you will want to know about the underlying Package Management utilities used on those systems. The second section of this chapter provides an overview of the *classic* Package Management utilities used on Ubuntu systems (and thus discussed in this chapter) so that you have a clear idea of "what does what" as you read through this chapter. The next section explains where the Ubuntu software that you can install on your system is located (in locations known as *repositories*) and how these repositories are organized, and provides some tips about other, unofficial repositories that you might find useful. After discussing repositories, the hands-on sections of this chapter begin by explaining how to find out what's on your system and what package-provided specific files are already on your system, and how to figure out what package you might want to install if you're looking for a specific file. This is most easily done from the command line, so that's our focus in this section.

Subsequent sections of this chapter focus on using the apt-get (command line), aptitude (terminal-oriented), and synaptic (graphical) tools to locate and install new packages on your system. The dpkg, apt-get, aptitude, and synaptic tools are knee-deep in online manual pages and web sites that explain every conceivable combination of command-line options, so I'm not going to bore you by repeating those in this chapter. This chapter explains how to do common tasks using these tools, focusing on helping you get your work done.

The last two sections discuss how to use the Ubuntu Update Manager to keep your system up-to-date and how to fine-tune your system by identifying and removing packages on your system that are no longer required because they were installed to satisfy dependency requirements for other packages that are no longer installed.

Installing Software with the Ubuntu Software Center

If you simply want to install a new software package on your Ubuntu desktop system, the easiest way to do so is by using the Ubuntu Software Center menu item at the bottom of Ubuntu's Applications menu. On Ubuntu systems, this menu item runs the `software-center` application. This menu item doesn't enable you to install every possible software package (for that, you will need to use tools such as `apt-get`, `aptitude`, or `synaptic`), but does make it easy to install the most commonly used and popular packages on an Ubuntu desktop system.

Selecting the Ubuntu Software Center item at the bottom of the Applications menu displays the main dialog for the `software-center` application, shown in Figure 19-1.

FIGURE 19-1

Starting the Ubuntu Software Center

669

The elements of the main Ubuntu Software Center window are as follows:

- **Search field:** Enables you to search for a specific application by name if you aren't sure which category it falls under

- **Software Category pane:** Enables you to switch between available software categories, either the list of Free Software that is available or a list of the Installed Software on your system

- **Departments/Applications List pane:** Lists all of the available groups (Departments) of software or shows the applications that are available in the currently selected department

- **Application description pane:** Displays a description of any currently selected software package

As an example, assume that you wanted to add the Gnumeric spreadsheet application to your Office menu. You would do the following:

1. Select the Ubuntu Software Center item from the Applications menu.

2. Select the Office Department in the Departments pane, and browse the Applications list pane for the Gnumeric application or enter **gnumeric** in the Search field and press Return.

3. Select "Gnumeric" in the Departments/Applications List pane. The Gnumeric entry expands displays a short definition of the package, a web site button that enables you to get more detailed information about the Gnumeric application from its web site, and an Install button.

4. Click Install to install the Gnumeric spreadsheet.

5. Enter your password in the "Administrative privileges" dialog that displays, and press Return.

The Ubuntu Software Center application automatically retrieves and installs the requested software and any associated packages required to satisfy its requirements. If the software package you've requested conflicts with any existing software, a dialog displays that identifies the conflict and offers you the option to remove the conflicting package.

Once the installation completes, the Install button in the Gnumeric entry in the Application List pane is replaced by a Remove button.

Package Management Software Overview

Ubuntu Linux installations provide several different utilities for managing and querying software packages, ranging from low-level command-line tools to tools with sophisticated graphical interfaces. The following are the basic user-level tools provided as part of a standard Ubuntu installation:

- `apt-get`: A command-line utility that provides subcommands, which enable you to install, remove, and manage packages on your system, both as individual packages and as components of a distribution

- `aptitude`: A terminal-oriented utility that serves as a front-end to lower-level utilities such as `apt-get` and `dpkg`. The `aptitude` utility provides both a quasi-graphical, menu- and screen-oriented user interface and the ability to install, remove, query, and manage packages from the command line. This is my preferred Package Management utility for all day-to-day package installation operations.

- `dpkg`: The basic command-line tool for installing, removing, querying, and generally managing packages. This utility uses even lower-level utilities, such as `dpkg-deb` — to perform package installation, removal, and manipulation — and `dpkg-query`, to search for packages, but these lower-level packages are not discussed in this chapter. Although handy to use directly 0.0001 percent of the time, the rest of the time I find it more convenient to think of the capabilities provided by these low-level utilities as functionality that is provided by the `dpkg` utility itself.

- `dselect`: A terminal-oriented front-end to the `dpkg` utility that provides quasi-graphical menus and an interactive display within the context of an xterm, GNOME Terminal, or other command-line environment. The `dselect` utility also accepts command-line options and arguments that you can use to initiate selected operations without selecting them from menus. This application isn't discussed in this chapter because its functionality is available in other tools.

- `software-center`: Discussed earlier in this chapter, this is a graphical application that is started when you select Ubuntu Software Center from the Applications menu on an Ubuntu system.

- `synaptic`: A graphical, X Window System tool for installing, removing, querying, and managing software packages on Ubuntu

- `update-manager`: A graphical, X Window System tool for identifying and installing updated versions of packages that are already installed on your Ubuntu Linux system

Note

The dpkg, apt-get, and aptitude utilities all use different databases to store information about installed packages and their state, and therefore all use different mechanisms for identifying and resolving conflicts and dependencies between software packages. (The synaptic and Adept utilities use the same database as the aptitude utility.) The dpkg utility stores its information about installed and available packages in files and directories under /var/lib/dpkg. The apt-get utility stores the information that it uses in files and directories under the directory /var/lib/apt. The aptitude utility stores the information that it uses in files and directories under the directory /var/lib/aptitude. When using either apt-get or aptitude, it is important that you run either the apt-get update or aptitude update commands in order to ensure that the package state and availability information used by these applications is up-to-date. Similarly, if you want to experiment with dselect after having installed packages using apt-get, aptitude, or synaptic, you must use the `dselect update` command before using `dselect`, to ensure that `dselect` (and therefore dpkg) is aware of the state of all installed and available software.

The `apt-get`, `aptitude`, and Synaptic Package Manager utilities also depend on the information about available repositories and associated packages maintained in a storage area that is generically known as the *apt cache*. The apt cache actually consists of several files that, by default, are located in the directory `/var/cache/apt` on your Ubuntu Linux system. ■

All of the automated aspects of the Package Management utilities available on Ubuntu systems rely on obtaining packages from the Ubuntu software repositories. The next section explains software repositories, how they are organized, the system configuration file that identifies them, and how to work with these files to ensure that your system has access to all of the latest and greatest software that is available for it.

Ubuntu Repositories and Components

A repository is exactly what the name suggests, a storage site for objects of some sort. In the case of the Ubuntu repositories, the objects stored therein are all of the source and binary packages that make up a variety of Ubuntu Linux distributions, including both the standard GNOME-based Ubuntu Linux and the command-line-oriented Ubuntu Server. When you download an ISO image (an image of a CD or DVD that conforms to the International Standards Organization 9660 standard for CD-ROM filesystems), the CD that you burn from this image and then use to install Ubuntu Linux provides the CD boot environment (known as *Isolinux*), an installer and the applications required to support it, a basic set of packages, and some documentation. As part of the install process, your system retrieves the majority of the Ubuntu Linux distributions from the Ubuntu repository over the Internet.

Making ISO images of Linux distributions available over the Internet is nothing new — it's the standard way of distributing most Linux distributions nowadays. Putting the Ubuntu repositories directly on the Internet has two primary advantages for Ubuntu fans:

- It keeps the installation media down to a single CD and ISO image.
- It makes every part of Ubuntu Linux instantly available to any computer that is connected to the Internet, anywhere, including the latest updates and additions.

To organize its repositories along lines that are important to the Ubuntu folks, to many individuals, and to many corporations, the Ubuntu repositories are organized into four components, which are basically ways of classifying Linux software along support and licensing guidelines. The Ubuntu repositories contain four basic components:

- **Main:** The main component contains binary packages (and source packages, in most cases) for Linux software that is officially supported by Canonical, Ltd., and can be freely re-distributed. This does not mean that everything in the main repository component is GPL — the main repository component can include software that is distributed in binary format, such as firmware and binary fonts. The main portion of the repository is designed to provide everything that most people will need for a fully functional Linux desktop or server system that is fully supportable by Canonical, Ltd.

- **Restricted:** The restricted component contains source and binary packages for commonly used software that is not available under a completely free license. Packages in the restricted repository component are not guaranteed to be completely supportable by Canonical, Ltd., but are provided because they are necessary to use Linux on certain hardware. For this reason, some items from the *restricted* repository are included on Ubuntu installer CDs in subdirectories of dists/dist-name/restricted and pool/restricted. Restricted items typically include drivers for specific network interface cards (NICs) and video cards.

- **Universe:** The universe repository component contains binary and source packages for the rest of the free and open source software that is commonly associated with Linux systems, but that is available under a variety of different licenses and is not guaranteed to be supported by Canonical, Ltd. There's simply too much software in the universe (pardon the expression) for Canonical to guarantee support for all of the software that it contains.

- **Multiverse:** The multiverse repository component contains binary and source packages for software that is not released under a license that meets the Ubuntu guidelines for free and open source software (www.ubuntu.com/ubuntu/licensing). This software is not supported by Canonical, Ltd., and it is your responsibility to verify that you satisfy the requirements imposed by software from the multiverse component.

Note

The official descriptions of the official Ubuntu repositories are located at www.ubuntu.com/ubuntu/components **— I've tried to distill them down to their essentials, but if you're a licensing fan, there's plenty of good reading there. ∎**

Two additional repository components also exist, known as the *backports* and *partner* repositories:

- **Backports:** The backports repository component contains updated or bleeding-edge versions of Linux software, including software that may already have an *official* version in one of the other repository components. Software in this repository component is not supported by Canonical but is provided because newer versions of existing software packages often provide some critical feature that users may require.

- **Partner:** The partner repository component contains software that is produced by various partners of Canonical. Software in this repository component is not supported by Canonical but is provided as a convenience to Ubuntu users who need access to software from Canonical's partner companies.

Tip

If you are curious about the packages that are installed or available in the Ubuntu repositories for different Ubuntu releases, see the web page at http://packages.ubuntu.com. **This page enables you to select the distribution that you are interested in and then view a list of all of the packages, organized into various logical categories. It also provides a search capability so that you can search for specific packages. ∎**

Enabling Additional Repository Components

The most common example of a situation in which you will want to access repository components other than the main and restricted components is when working with audio and video applications. The wide variety of codecs (compressor/decompressor modules) used to encode digital audio and video, the platform-specific roots of many of these codecs, and the hoops that many media companies make you jump through in order to actually play many digital audio and video formats on an Ubuntu Linux system make it necessary to push the boundaries of free software licensing.

By default, the main, restricted, universe, and multiverse components of the Ubuntu repositories are enabled when you install an Ubuntu Linux distribution. *Enabled* means that the online sources of these repository components are included in the default /etc/apt/sources.list file, which is the file that all of the package installation and management utilities discussed in this chapter consult when looking for new and updated software. This file is a text file containing entries that describe the locations and names of different online repositories and the repository components that are available there. The general format of an entry in the /etc/apt/sources.list file is as follows:

```
deb  URI distribution component-or-package(s)
```

The deb field identifies the package format; the URI is a universal resource identifier for the location where the repository can be found, and is typically an FTP or HTTP URL. The distribution field is typically the name of a standard Ubuntu distribution, but can be anything that is used to identify a subdirectory at the URI where associated packages can be found, and the component-or-package is one (or more) names of repository components or packages that are also used to navigate the directory tree at the URI and locate available packages. If multiple component-or-package names are provided, each identifies a different directory at the URI.

The entries in the /etc/apt/sources.list file for the main and restricted repository components of the 10.04 release of Ubuntu Linux, for example, are as follows:

```
deb http://archive.ubuntu.com/ubuntu/ lucid main restricted
deb-src http://archive.ubuntu.com/ubuntu/ lucid main restricted
```

The first of these identifies the source of binary packages, whereas the second identifies the source of source packages. A similar pair of entries provides access to updated versions of the packages in these repository components:

```
deb http://archive.ubuntu.com/ubuntu/ lucid-updates main \
    restricted
deb-src http://archive.ubuntu.com/ubuntu/ lucid-updates main \
    restricted
```

The latter two entries are broken across two lines for formatting purposes in this book; they appear on single lines in the actual /etc/apt/sources.list file.

Note

The examples in this section reflect the /etc/apt/sources.list settings for the Ubuntu 10.04 (Lucid) release. If you are working with a different release, you should replace the word *lucid* in these examples with the name of the Ubuntu release that you are using. You should not mix repository entries for different releases in an /etc/apt/sources.list file because the repositories for a newer release will typically provide the same software as the repositories for older releases and will be compiled against a set of system libraries that are found on the newer release. ∎

Finally, a similar pair of entries provides access to security fixes for the packages in these repository components:

```
deb http://security.ubuntu.com/ubuntu lucid-security main \
    restricted
deb src http://security.ubuntu.com/ubuntu lucid-security \
    main restricted
```

Lines beginning with a hash mark (#) in the /etc/apt/sources.list file are comments. If you look through the entries in the default /etc/apt/sources.list file on your system, you will note that entries for access to the partner repository are already present in this file, but are commented out. You can enable access to this repository by using sudo to edit this file in your favorite text editor. To do this, edit the /etc/apt/sources.list file with your favorite text editor, using a command like the following:

```
$ sudo emacs /etc/apt/sources.list
```

Remove the hash marks at the beginning of the lines that enable the partner repositories, and save the updated file. The updated entries in a sample sources.list file would look like the following:

```
deb http://archive.ubuntu.com/ubuntu/ lucid partner
deb-src http://archive.ubuntu.com/ubuntu/ lucid partner
```

You could, of course, simply add these entries to the ends of the lines that already provide access to the main, restricted, universe, or multiverse components of the Ubuntu repositories, but I prefer to keep them separate just for clarity regarding licensing differences — and because that stays closest to the original format of the default sources.list file.

Note

Just to be perfectly clear, installing software from the universe and multiverse repositories may add software to your system that has licensing requirements that you or the company that you work for find odious (such as MP3-related or video-related software), for which support is not guaranteed by the Ubuntu folks (even if you purchase support, there are no commitments to support it), and which may be difficult to get support for anywhere. If you are configuring systems for enterprise use, you should make sure that your firm is comfortable with the licenses provided with non-free software in the universe and multiverse repositories. I use all of the software discussed in this book and am therefore my very own test case for everything this book discusses, but your mileage (and your responsibilities) may vary. ∎

Other Repositories of Interest

As you can see from the examples in the previous section, the standard Ubuntu repositories are all hosted on systems that are in the ubuntu.com domain. This makes perfect sense because this is the only way that the Canonical folks can guarantee the integrity of their repository and the adherence of various components and their contents to the associated licensing guidelines. However, additional repositories of Ubuntu software are also available on the Internet (I know that's a surprise), maintained by various groups and individuals. These alternate repository sites may simply mirror the contents of the official Ubuntu repositories to "share the load," or may provide software that is not found in the official Ubuntu repositories. In the latter case, this software may provide even newer versions of popular software than is found in the backports repository component, or may provide up-to-date versions of locally maintained software. As mentioned earlier, if you are interested in working with audio and video on your Ubuntu system, you may find that these alternate repository sites provide versions of related software with bleeding-edge features that you need. In general, such sites will provide examples of the entries that you should add to your /etc/apt/sources.list file in order to be able to list and retrieve software from them. This is typically done by concatenating new entries to the end of this file using a text editor, but can also be done using the Software Sources tool, as discussed in the next section.

Unofficial, but useful software packages are one thing, but a more common need is to locate and install software with various licensing restrictions. A classic Linux problem is the fact that many of the codecs and much of the related software used to play CDs, audio files, DVDs, and video files is proprietary software that requires a software license, is unavailable for Linux systems, and sometimes both. This is not the fault of Linux, but is rather a side effect of greed and cluelessness in the software and audio/video media industries, as well as location-specific laws regarding software patents, copyrights, and intellectual property. Even though the last few Ubuntu releases have provided increasingly easy ways of retrieving problematic audio/video packages, you may still need to manually retrieve some of the packages that you need from unofficial (or certainly non-Canonical) repositories. One good site for information about such packages is the Medibuntu (Multimedia, Entertainment & Distractions In Ubuntu) site at www.medibuntu.org. The "Repository Howto" link there points to documentation on how to add repositories to your /etc/apt/sources.list file that will enable you to play your legally purchased audio and video CDs and DVDs on your Ubuntu system.

Enabling Additional Repository Sources Using the Software Sources Tool

Editing a text-format configuration file is pretty old-school Linux and is the sort of thing that you may not want to mention to your Windows or Mac OS X friends. (You'll still want to be able to do it, because it's fast and easy, but we'll keep that sort of thing our little Linux secret, OK?) For fans of graphical interfaces, Ubuntu provides a Software Sources tool that gives you a graphical view of the entries in your /etc/apt/sources.list file and makes it easy for you to enable, disable, or add entries with a few mouse clicks.

To start the Software Sources utility on a Ubuntu system, select the System ➪ Administration ➪ Software Sources menu item. After supplying your password to enable access to this administrative tool, the Software Sources tool's main dialog displays, as shown in Figure 19-2.

The main Software Sources dialog on Ubuntu

The main software preferences dialog displays all of the entries in your current /etc/apt/ sources.list file, regardless of whether they are commented out or not. Entries that are commented out in the /etc/apt/sources.list file are present, but the checkboxes beside their name are not selected. This gives you a convenient overview of all of the valid, standard repository entries in your /etc/apt/sources.list file.

The Software Sources dialog also makes it easy for you to add third-party repositories (often referred to as *custom* repositories) to the repositories that the Ubuntu software management tools will search for available and updated packages. This is done via the Software Sources application's Other Software tab, shown in Figure 19-3.)

To add a new repository or repository component to the list of repositories that your system will search for software packages, select the Third-Party Software tab and click Add. This displays the dialog shown in Figure 19-4.

FIGURE 19-3

Adding third-party repositories in the Software Sources tool

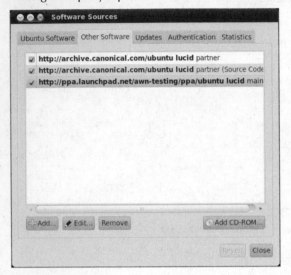

FIGURE 19-4

Adding a specific third-party repository

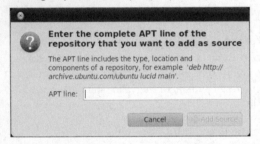

Although not particularly elegant, this dialog makes it easy for you to cut-and-paste a repository identification entry from a mail message or browser session where you found it, and automatically add it to your /etc/apt/sources.list file. To return to the dialog shown in Figure 19-3 without adding a custom repository entry, click Cancel. To save a new entry after typing it in or cutting and pasting, click "Add Source," which adds the new entry and returns you to the dialog shown in Figure 19-4.

In addition to the Ubuntu Software and Third-Party Software tabs, the Software Sources tool provides three other tabs that let you manage different aspects of your repositories and the update process. These tabs enable you to manage different aspects of system updates and how your system identifies valid repositories, and also enable you to provide some general statistical information about recent updates to your system to help the Ubuntu folks improve the repository configuration and software update tools.

Figure 19-5 shows the Software Sources tool's Updates tab, which enables you to specify when your system checks for updates and how it responds to any available updates that it detects.

The Updates tab in the Software Sources tool

By default, your system automatically checks for updates on a daily basis, displaying an "Available Updates" icon in the GNOME panel at the top of your screen when updates are available. If you are using a laptop or other system that only connects to the Internet infrequently, you may want to decrease the frequency with which your system checks for updates by selecting another value from the "Check for updates automatically" entry's dropdown menu, or disable this item entirely. If you disable this item, you can always check for updates manually using Ubuntu's Update Manager, which is discussed later in this chapter in the section, "Using the Ubuntu Update Manager." If you are performing regular checks for updates and are using a system that is often (or always) connected to the Internet, you may want to select the "Download updates in the background, but do not install them" option to make sure that packages are already available on your local system when you actually execute the update process. Similarly, you may want to select the "Install security updates without confirmation" option if you want to automatically retrieve security updates and install them so that your system is always secure against any known attacks or software exploits.

Figure 19-6 shows the Software Preferences tool's Authentication tab, which simplifies the process of importing identification keys for new repositories into the keyring used by Ubuntu's Package Management utilities.

The Authentication tab in the Software Sources tool

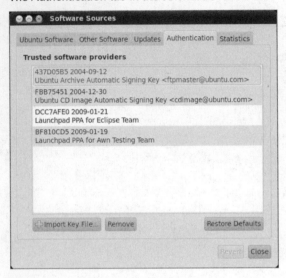

Each package in any repository is signed with the key for that repository to verify its authenticity and validity. The Ubuntu Package Management tools will not retrieve packages from unauthorized or unidentifiable repositories. Adding the authentication key that identifies a nonstandard repository as a valid package source requires several steps from the command line, using hard-to-remember options to the `gpg` command in conjunction with the `apt-key` utility. Clicking the "Import Key File" button enables you to navigate to and select any file that contains an ASCII representation of a PGP authentication key and import it for use by Ubuntu's Package Management tools.

After making any changes that you desire to the list of repositories available to your system, the way in which system updates are performed, or the Authentication keys available to the Ubuntu Package Management utilities, click Close to exit the Software Sources application. If you have made any changes, the Software Sources tool will display a dialog informing you that your channel (repository) information is out-of-date, as shown in Figure 19-7.

To automatically update the cache information used by the Ubuntu Package Management utilities, click Reload. To exit without updating the cache, click Close. If you exit without reloading the cache information, you will need to run the `apt-get update` or `aptitude update`, or use the Check button in Ubuntu's Update Manager or the Reload toolbar icon in the Synaptic Package Manager before you are guaranteed that your system is aware of all available packages in all valid repositories.

FIGURE 19-7

Change notification when exiting the Software Sources tool

Problems Adding or Accessing Nonstandard Repositories

After modifying your system's /etc/apt/sources.list file, you may find that packages from new repositories that you've added aren't actually showing up in the list of available packages. First, make sure that you've updated the list of available repositories and packages, as described at the end of the previous section. This should identify any inaccessible repositories and outright syntax errors in the sources.list file.

Next, when running apt-get update to update your system's idea of repository contents, seeing messages like the following means that your system does not have the right authentication keys to add packages from a specified repository to its cache:

```
Ign http://ftp.us.debian.org lenny Release
Ign http://ftp.us.debian.org unstable Release
```

Similarly, you may see messages at the end of the output from apt-get update. These are related to the previous messages, but are somewhat less subtle because they explicitly identify missing keys and associated repositories.

```
W: GPG error: http://ftp.us.debian.org testing Release: \
    The following signatures couldn't be verified because the \
    public key is not available: \
    NO_PUBKEY 010908312D190C5F
W: GPG error: http://ftp.us.debian.org unstable Release: \
    The following signatures couldn't be verified because the \
    public key is not available: \
    NO_PUBKEY 010908312D190C5F
```

In these cases, the associated entries in /etc/apt/sources.list point to repositories whose keys are not present in the keyring used by the Ubuntu Package Management utilities. See the man page for the apt-key application for information on retrieving and installing keys into this keyring.

Exploring Your System Using dpkg and Friends

Package Management software not only simplifies software installation, removal, and updates, but also provides great opportunities for asking questions about the software that is installed, or could be installed, on your system. Some of the command-line Package Management utilities that are installed on your system make it easy to find out exactly what software is installed on your system, what a specific package contains, what packages provided certain files, and so on. The next few sections describe how to answer some basic questions about existing files and available packages on your Ubuntu system.

Listing the Packages That Are Installed on Your System

The dpkg command's -l option provides the easiest way of listing the packages that are installed on your system. (This option can also be specified in verbose option format as --long.) You can execute this command with no other argument to produce a (long) listing of every package that is installed on your system, which looks something like the following:

```
$ dpkg -l
Desired=Unknown/Install/Remove/Purge/Hold
| Status=Not/Installed/Config-files/Unpacked/Failed-config/\
    Half-installed
|/ Err?=(none)/Hold/Reinst-required/X=both-problems \
    (Status,Err: uppercase=bad)
||/ Name          Version           Description
+++-=============-=================-===========================
ii  3dchess       0.8.1-11.1        3D chess for X11
ii  acpi          0.09-1            displays information on ACPI…
ii  acpi-support  0.84              a collection of useful apci events
ii  acpid         1.0.4-1ubuntu11   Utilities for ACPI power mgmnt
ii  adduser       3.80ubuntu2       Add and remove users and groups
[much more output deleted]
```

The first few lines above the actual package listing identify the meaning of the various fields on each line and the symbols that they contain. This information is provided in a fairly cryptic fashion that is mandated by the terminal-oriented output produced by the dpkg utility. The entries for package name, package version, and package description are pretty straightforward, but the first field requires some serious explanation. The characters in the first field have the following meaning and possible values:

- The first character in the first field indicates the desired status of the package, which is the state that the packaging system thinks the package should be in. Available indicators in this position are:

  - h: The package is marked as being on hold, and cannot be updated or removed.

- i: The package should be installed.

- p: The package and all associated configuration information is supposed to be purged.

- r: The package is supposed to be removed, but associated configuration files will be preserved.

- u: The package has never been installed on this system, so its state is unknown.

- The second character in the first field indicates the actual status of the package on your system. Available indicators in this position are:

  - c: The configuration files for the package are installed, but the package is not.

  - f: The script used to complete the configuration of this package, known as a post-installation script, failed for some reason, and the package is therefore not guaranteed to be correctly installed.

  - h: The package is partially installed because the installation process was interrupted.

  - i: The package is correctly installed.

  - n: The package is not installed.

  - u: The package was retrieved, unpacked, and is partially installed, but its post-installation script was not executed.

- The third character highlights any errors that are associated with the package. Available indicators in this position are:

  - A space: No errors, which looks remarkably like there is nothing in this position

  - H: The package has been marked as being on hold by the package management system itself, which usually means that other packages that this package requires are not installed.

  - R: Reinstallation is required.

  - X: The package both requires reinstallation and has been automatically put on hold by the package management system itself.

Now that I've explained what each character position in the first field of a package entry means, it's easy to see what the ASCII art in the dpkg output heading means. This is not exactly the same thing as being intuitive, but that's hard to do in the limited number of characters that you can display and easily use from the command line.

Listing the Packages That Are Available for Your System

The previous section explained how to figure out what packages are installed on your system. While that's interesting, perhaps a more interesting question is, "What packages are available for my system that I have not yet installed?" As mentioned in the previous section, the dpkg command's -l option with no other arguments shows the list of installed packages. You can supply an argument to this command to list available packages that match that argument, whether installed or uninstalled. For example, the dpkg -l emacs command should list all of the packages that have the string *emacs* in their package name. Let's try that:

```
$ dpkg -l emacs
No packages found matching emacs.
```

Well, that seems odd because I'm actually typing this in Emacs on my Ubuntu system. The problem is that any argument that you supply to dpkg is used as a pattern match, and there are apparently no packages installed on my system whose exact name is *emacs*. Let's try that again, using a standard Linux wildcard to say that you want to list any packages with a name that begins with *emacs*, as in the following example:

```
$ dpkg -l 'emacs*'
Desired=Unknown/Install/Remove/Purge/Hold
| Status=Not/Installed/Config-files/Unpacked/Failed-config/\
   Half-installed
|/ Err?=(none)/Hold/Reinst-required/X=both-problems \
   (Status,Err: uppercase=bad)
||/ Name                 Version          Description
+++-==================-===============-===========================
ii  emacs-chess          2.0b5-1          a client/library for Chess
ii  emacs-chess-pieces   2.0b5-1          XPM images of chess pieces
ii  emacs-goodies-el     26.4-1           Miscellaneous Emacs add-ons
un  emacs-goodies-extra-el  <none>        (no description available)
ii  emacs21              21.4a-3ubuntu2   The GNU Emacs editor
ii  emacs21-bin-common   21.4a-3ubuntu2   The GNU Emacs shared...
ii  emacs21-common       21.4a-3ubuntu2   The GNU Emacs shared...
un  emacs21-el           <none>           (no description available)
un  emacs21-nox          <none>           (no description available)
un  emacsen              <none>           (no description available)
ii  emacsen-common       1.4.17           Common facilities for…
```

That's more like it! Note that when using wildcards in a dpkg specification, you have to protect them from expansion on the command line by enclosing your dpkg wildcard specification within quotation marks of some sort.

The previous output showed some Emacs packages, but I could swear that there were others on my Ubuntu system. Let's try a more general wildcard that searches for packages that contain the string *emacs* anywhere in their names:

```
$ dpkg -l '*emacs*'
Desired=Unknown/Install/Remove/Purge/Hold
| Status=Not/Installed/Config-files/Unpacked/Failed-config/\
   Half-installed
|/ Err?=(none)/Hold/Reinst-required/X=both-problems \
   (Status,Err: uppercase=bad)
||/ Name                 Version          Description
```

```
+++-=================-===============-=====================
ii  emacs-chess            2.0b5-1        a client/library for Chess
ii  emacs-chess-pieces     2.0b5-1        XPM images of chess pieces
ii  emacs-goodies-el       26.4-1         Miscellaneous add-ons
un  emacs-goodies-extra-el <none>         (no description)
ii  emacs21                21.4a-3ubuntu2 The GNU Emacs editor
ii  emacs21-bin-common     21.4a-3ubuntu2 The GNU Emacs shared...
ii  emacs21-common         21.4a-3ubuntu2 The GNU Emacs shared...
un  emacs21-el             <none>         (no description available)
un  emacs21-nox            <none>         (no description available)
un  emacsen                <none>         (no description available)
ii  emacsen-common         1.4.17         Common emacsen facilities
un  xemacs                 <none>         (no description available)
un  xemacs support         <none>         (no description available)
un  xemacs-widget          <none>         (no description available)
ii  xemacs21               21.4.18-1ubuntu1 highly customizable editor
[additional output deleted]
```

Even better! Thanks to the explanation of the characters in the first field of your dpkg output (provided in the previous section of this chapter), it's clear that I need to install xemacs on this system.

Because this is a Linux system, you can pipe your dpkg output through other commands to answer questions like, "What packages are not yet installed on my system whose names contain the string *emacs* anywhere in their names?" which I can do using grep to look for lines that begin with the string *un*, as in the following example:

```
$ dpkg -l '*emacs*' | grep '^un'
un  emacs-goodies-extra-el <none>         (no description available)
un  emacs21-el             <none>         (no description available)
un  emacs21-nox            <none>         (no description available)
un  emacsen                <none>         (no description available)
un  xemacs                 <none>         (no description available)
un  xemacs-support         <none>         (no description available)
un  xemacs-widget          <none>         (no description available)
un  xemacs21-gnome-mule    <none>         (no description available)
un  xemacs21-gnome-mule... <none>         (no description available)
un  xemacs21-gnome-nomule  <none>         (no description available)
un  xemacs21-mule-canna-wnn <none>        (no description available)
un  xemacs21-nomule        <none>         (no description available)
un  xemacs21-supportel     <none>         (no description available)
```

Other Ubuntu Package Management utilities provide similar search features, particularly the aptitude utility. Although most commonly associated with its terminal-oriented, quasi-graphical interface (discussed later in this chapter in the section, "Using aptitude to Add and Remove Software," aptitude also provides a command-line mode with many powerful commands. To locate packages, aptitude provides a search keyword that enables you to specify a substring to search for (no wildcards necessary) and displays information about any installed or available package that is present in any repository listed in your /etc/apt/sources.list file. The following is sample output from a search for *emacs* using aptitude:

```
$ aptitude search emacs
p   acl2-emacs          - A Computational Logic for Applicative Comm
p   aleph-emacs         - The Aleph programming language - emacs mod
p   cxref-emacs         - Generates latex and HTML documentation for
p   emacs               - The GNU Emacs editor
i   emacs-chess         - a client and library for playing Chess fro
i   emacs-chess-pieces  - XPM images of chess pieces for emacs-chess
p   emacs-color-themes  - Color themes for Emacs
p   emacs-extra         - emacs configuration
i   emacs-goodies-el    - Miscellaneous add-ons for Emacs
i   emacs21             - The GNU Emacs editor
i   emacs21-bin-common  - The GNU Emacs editor's shared, architectur
i   emacs21-common      - The GNU Emacs editor's shared, architectur
[additional output deleted]
```

You'll notice that the aptitude utility finds more packages than the dpkg -l search command that was described earlier does.

Another very convenient application for searching for packages is the apt-cache utility, which is a command-line utility that provides subcommands that enable you to search and manipulate the cache of packages that are installed or available for installation on your system and the metadata that is associated with those packages. You must enable the universe repository in order to install the apt-cache utility. The apt-cache utility can also be used to search the packages in any repository that is active in your /etc/apt/sources.list file, and find even more matching packages because it searches within the package name and both the short and long descriptions of all available packages, whether installed or not. The following is sample output from an apt-cache search for our favorite string, *emacs*:

```
$ apt-cache search emacs
acl2-emacs - A Computational Logic for Applicative Common Lisp: emacs
    interface
ada-mode - Ada mode for GNU Emacs and XEmacs
af - An Emacs-like mail reader and composer
aleph-emacs - The Aleph programming language - emacs mode
anjsp - A major mode to edit JSP and PSP code with Emacs
anthy-el - A Japanese input method (elisp fronted)
apel - portable library for emacsen
aplus-fsf-el - XEmacs lisp for A+ development
artist - Emacs Lisp drawing package
asn1-mode - Emacs mode for editing ASN.1 specification files
bhl - Emacs mode for converting brut text to HTML and LaTeX
bigloo-ude - Bigloo Unified Development Environment for Emacs
biomode - [Biology] An Emacs mode to edit genetic data
[additional output deleted]
```

As you can see, the apt-cache and aptitude utilities are easiest to use when searching for packages and return the most verbose results.

Listing Information about a Package

Once you've found a package that you're interested in, there are an equivalent number of ways to get more detailed information about the package and its contents. However, because the apt-cache and aptitude utilities return the best search results, it makes sense to use them to display information about any packages that they've identified. For example, to find out detailed information about the xemacs21 package that was listed in the previous section, you could use either the apt-cache show xemacs21 or aptitude show xemacs21 commands, both of which return almost identical information. The following example shows the output from the aptitude show xemacs21 command, which is slightly more verbose:

```
$ aptitude show xemacs21
Package: xemacs21
New: yes
State: installed
Automatically installed: no
Version: 21.4.18-1ubuntu1
Priority: optional
Section: universe/editors
Maintainer: OHURA Makoto <ohura@debian.org>
Uncompressed Size: 49.2k
Depends: xemacs21-mule (= 21.4.18-1ubuntu1) | xemacs21-mule-canna-wnn
        (= 21.4.18-1ubuntu1) | xemacs21-nomule (= 21.4.18-1ubuntu1) |
        xemacs21-gnome-mule (= 21.4.18-1ubuntu1) |
        xemacs21-gnome-mule-canna-wnn (= 21.4.18-1ubuntu1) |
        xemacs21-gnome-nomule (= 21.4.18-1ubuntu1)
Conflicts: xemacs, xemacs-widget
Replaces: xemacs, xemacs-widget
Provided by: xemacs21-nomule, xemacs21-mule-canna-wnn,
        xemacs21-mule, xemacs21-gnome-nomule,
        xemacs21-gnome-mule-canna-wnn, xemacs21-gnome-mule
Description: highly customizable text editor
  XEmacs is a full fledged programming language with a mail reader,
news reader, info browser, Web browser, calendar, specialized editor
for more programming languages and other formats than most people
encounter in a lifetime, and much much more.
  This package exists to cause the installation of the real XEmacs
    packages.
```

This output probably provides more than you want to know about the specified package, but it's always better to err on the side of caution.

Listing the Contents of a Package

In some cases, you may want to list all of the files associated with a package that is installed on your system. To do this, you can use the dpkg command's -L option, followed by the name of the package whose contents you want to list. The following is sample output listing the contents of the emacs21 package on my Ubuntu system:

```
$ dpkg -L emacs21
/.
/usr
/usr/bin
/usr/bin/emacs21-x
/usr/share
/usr/share/emacs
/usr/share/emacs/21.4
/usr/share/emacs/21.4/etc
/usr/share/emacs/21.4/etc/DOC-21.4.1
/usr/share/applications
/usr/share/applications/emacs21.desktop
/usr/share/doc
/usr/share/doc/emacs21
/usr/share/doc/emacs21/README.Debian.gz
/usr/share/doc/emacs21/copyright
/usr/share/doc/emacs21/changelog.Debian.gz
/usr/lib
/usr/lib/emacs
/usr/lib/emacs/21.4
/usr/lib/emacs/21.4/i486-linux-gnu
/usr/lib/emacs/21.4/i486-linux-gnu/fns-21.4.1-x.el
/usr/lib/menu
```

Being able to identify the files provided by a package that is installed on your system can be handy if you are considering removing a package but want to make sure that doing so does not delete a file that you want to preserve. The next section describes how to find out what package does provide a specific file.

Tip
You can list the files that are provided by packages that are not yet installed by using the apt-file utility with a command such as apt-file list package, where package is the name of the package that you are interested in. The apt-file utility is described in more detail in "Determining What Package Provides a Missing File" later in this chapter. ∎

Determining What Package Provides an Existing File

After working with Ubuntu for a while and installing, updating, and removing some number of packages, you may be curious about which package provides a certain file on your system. This is easy enough to determine using the dpkg command's --search option, as in the following example, where I'm curious about which package provides the /usr/bin/ar archiving utility:

```
$ dpkg --search /usr/bin/ar
binutils: /usr/bin/ar
```

If you know that a utility that you're looking for is in your path but you don't want to have to determine the directory in which it is physically located, you can use the cool shell trick of using the output of an existing command as the input to another one, in this case combining the which command, to determine the full pathname of an application, and the dpkg --search command, which produces exactly the same output:

```
$ dpkg --search $(which ar)
binutils: /usr/bin/ar
```

When searching for files, the dpkg --search command can't find symbolic links that are created by package post-installation scripts. If you are trying to find a file that you know exists but cannot locate it, make sure that the file is not a symbolic link, and, if it is, search for the file that it actually points to. This can sometimes require a few tries, as in the following example:

```
$ dpkg --search /usr/bin/emacs
dpkg: /usr/bin/emacs not found.

$ ls -l /usr/bin/emacs
/usr/bin/emacs -> /etc/alternatives/emacs

$ dpkg --search /etc/alternatives/emacs
dpkg: /etc/alternatives/emacs not found.

$ ls -l /etc/alternatives/emacs
/etc/alternatives/emacs -> /usr/bin/emacs21-x

$ dpkg --search /usr/bin/emacs21-x
emacs21: /usr/bin/emacs21-x
```

Although sometimes tedious, symbolic links are usually not an actual part of a package, and you must therefore ferret out a file that actually is part of a package.

Tip

Another handy Package Management utility that you may want to use when determining what package provides a specific file is the dlocate utility. This utility is not installed on Ubuntu systems by default but can easily be installed using apt-get, aptitude, or Synaptic Package Manager. After installing this command, you can search for the package that provides a file using the dlocate -S command, as in the following example:

```
$ dlocate -S /usr/bin/emacs
emacs21-bin-common: /usr/bin/emacsclient.emacs21
emacs21: /usr/bin/emacs21-x
emacs21: /usr/bin/emacs21
```

The dlocate utility's -S option uses the string that you specify as a substring to search for and can therefore be a bit more helpful when looking for files on your system. ∎

Determining What Package Provides a Missing File

Identifying the package that provides a file that is not installed on your system is somewhat tricky, but is a common question when you are trying to build software whose source code requires an include file that is not present on your system, or you are trying to link software that requires a missing library. Unfortunately, the utility that performs this type of search, the `apt-file` utility, is not installed on Ubuntu systems by default, but it can easily be installed using `apt-get`, `aptitude`, or the Synaptic Package Manager. After installing this command, you must first update its idea of the available packages in the repositories that you are using by running the command `sudo apt-file update`.

Once this command completes, you can search for the package that provides a file, even if that file is not installed on your system, using the `apt-file search` command, as in the following example, which looks for the package associated with the libpowersave library:

```
$ ls -l /usr/lib/*power*
ls: /usr/lib/*power*: No such file or directory
$ apt-file search libpowersave.so
libpowersave-dev: usr/lib/libpowersave.so
libpowersave10: usr/lib/libpowersave.so.10
libpowersave10: usr/lib/libpowersave.so.10.0.3
```

Installing the `apt-file` utility can save you a tremendous amount of hair-pulling and general frustration when you are trying to build software and have no idea what package provides the missing include file or "the missing link." (Sorry, but I couldn't resist.)

Tip
You can also use the `apt-file` utility to list the contents of packages that are not yet installed by using the `apt-file list package` command, where `package` is the name of the package that you are interested in. ■

Using apt-get to Add and Remove Software

The `apt-get` command is the fundamental user-level command provided as part of the Ubuntu Package Management suite. The `apt-get` command is a command-line tool that is fast and easy to use.

Note
As with any system administrative utility on your Ubuntu system, running the `apt-get` command requires the use of the `sudo` command or an equivalent, such as running `apt-get` under a shell that itself has been executed using the `sudo` command. To simplify examples and the readability of the text, the examples and discussion of using the `apt-get` command throughout this section do not include the `sudo` command. ■

Much of the basic functionality provided by the `apt-get` command is quite straightforward. For example, you can install a package and any other packages that it requires using the `apt-get install package` command. Similarly, you can remove a package by using the `apt-get remove` `package` command, specifying the `--purge` option if you also want to remove any configuration files or other data associated with the package that you're removing. Before using `apt-get` to install new software or new versions of existing software, you should always first execute the `apt-get update` command to ensure that `apt-get` is aware of the latest software packages and versions of that software from all of the repositories listed in your `/etc/apt/sources.list` file.

When using the `apt-get` utility to install software, you may occasionally have to provide additional information during the installation process. In these cases, the `apt-get` utility displays a quasi-graphical screen in the terminal application from which you were running the `apt-get` utility, an example of which is shown in Figure 19-8.

Supplying configuration information during package installation

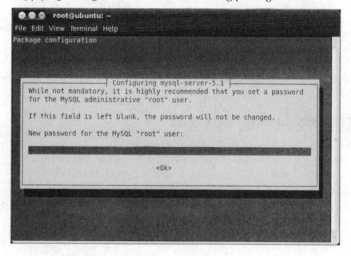

Whenever you see this sort of screen, you must answer any questions that it asks and supply any required information before the installation of your package can complete.

Tip

If you are using `apt-get` to install new software and the `apt-get` utility informs you that other packages are recommended or suggested for installation, you may want to consider using `aptitude`'s command-line interface to install these packages rather than `apt-get`. As explained later in this chapter in the section, "Using aptitude to Install Recommended Software," `aptitude` provides options that can automate installing recommended software when installing a new software package. ■

As mentioned throughout this book, I often use the graphical Synaptic tool to search for, install, and remove packages whenever possible. The `apt-get` tool provides these same capabilities, but also provides some powerful capabilities that are not duplicated in the Synaptic and Adept

Manager tools, or are at least much more easily done using apt-get from the command line. Even if you're a graphical utility fan, the next few sections explain how and when you still may want to use apt-get to perform these advanced functions.

Upgrading Your System Using apt-get

The apt-get upgrade command searches all of the repositories in your /etc/apt/sources.list file for new versions of packages that are currently installed on your system, and downloads and installs those new versions. Before using this command, you should always first execute the apt-get update command to ensure that apt-get is aware of the latest software packages and versions of that software from all of the repositories listed in your /etc/apt/sources.list file.

During the upgrade process, the apt-get upgrade command will not change the installation status of any other packages on your system. This is the installation status of a package, not the version of a package. If a new version of a package requires a newer version of another package that is already installed on your system, the apt-get upgrade command will also install the updated version of that other package. However, if a newer version of an existing package requires that new packages be installed or that existing packages be removed, the apt-get upgrade command will not install the newer version of the existing package. To do this, you will need to use the apt-get dist-upgrade command, as described in the next section.

Smart System Upgrades Using apt-get

The apt-get dist-upgrade command searches all of the repositories in your /etc/apt/sources.list file for new versions of packages that are currently installed on your system, and downloads and installs those new versions. Before running this command, you should always first execute the apt-get update command to ensure that apt-get is aware of the latest software packages and versions of that software from all of the repositories listed in your /etc/apt/sources.list file.

The difference between the apt-get upgrade and apt-get dist-upgrade commands is that the apt-get dist-upgrade command will do what is known as a *smart upgrade*. This means that it will do its best to handle any new package requirements or the removal of any existing packages that were mandated in order to install the latest versions of all of the software on your system. For example, if a new version of a package requires that a new package be installed on your system, the apt-get dist-upgrade command will install both of these, while the apt-get upgrade command would not have updated the original software package. Similarly, if installing a new version of an existing package requires the removal of any other package(s) that are currently installed on your system, the apt-get dist-upgrade command will remove those packages in order to install the new version of the existing package.

Even if you are a Synaptic fan, you may occasionally need to execute the apt-get dist-upgrade command in order to completely upgrade all of the packages on your system. Synaptic provides a *smart upgrade* preference that tries to do this sort of thing for you whenever possible, but the apt-get dist-upgrade command is still occasionally useful. When using Synaptic, you know you need to use the apt-get dist-upgrade command when packages are mysteriously identified as being held back and not updated—and, of course, the occasional pop-up message that explicitly tells you to run the apt-get dist-upgrade command. The Adept tools refresh your package lists more frequently than Synaptic seems to, and thus are less likely to require using apt-get to update things manually—but it's always handy to know how to do so, just in case.

Retrieving Package Source Code Using apt-get

Even in the wonderful world of constantly updated repositories with a rich collection of software, you may occasionally want to build your own versions of software packages for your system. The most common situation in which you'll want to do this is when you find patches to an existing software package that fix problems you're experiencing or add enhancements, and you just can't wait for them to appear in the official or backports repositories. You may also have your own ideas about changes that should be made to a package and want to test and work through your ideas. Linux and its ecosystem of utilities and other applications are open source, after all!

The apt-get command makes it remarkably easy to retrieve the source code for an installed package. The only requirement for this capability is that your /etc/apt/sources.list file include a deb-src entry for the repository from which you retrieved the binary version of that software. For example, if you want to retrieve the source for a package in which the binary version is located in the multiverse repository component, you must have entries like the following (or equivalent entries) in your /etc/apt/sources.list file:

```
deb http://archive.ubuntu.com/ubuntu/ intrepid multiverse
deb-src http://archive.ubuntu.com/ubuntu/ intrepid multiverse
```

Assuming that the right entries are present in your /etc/apt/sources.list file, retrieving the source code for a specified package is easy using the apt-get source command. The following example shows the retrieval of the source code for one of my favorite packages, the MythTV personal video recorder package:

```
$ apt-get source mythtv
Reading package lists... Done
Building dependency tree... Done
Need to get 9836kB of source archives.
Get: 1 http://.../multiverse mythtv 0.21.0+fixes18722-0ubuntu1...
Get: 2 http://... intrepid/multiverse mythtv 0.21.0. . .
Get: 3 http://... intrepid/multiverse mythtv 0.21.0. . .
Fetched 9836kB in 1m31s (107kB/s)
dpkg-source: extracting mythtv in mythtv-0.21.0
dpkg-source: unpacking mythtv_0.21.0.orig.tar.gz
dpkg-source: applying ./mythtv_0.21.0+fixes18722-0ubuntu1.diff.gz
```

When retrieving the source code for a package, the apt-get source utility actually retrieves multiple files. The extensions of these files are as follows:

- diff.gz: A compressed file containing any available patches to the standard source archive for the package

- DSC: A description file for the Ubuntu package that identifies the contents of the package, associated binary packages, any package dependencies for that package, and so on

- tar.gz: A compressed archive file containing the source code for the official version of this package

After retrieving these files, the apt-get source command unpacks the compressed source archive, creating a working directory for your development efforts, and automatically applies any patches that are available in the (optional) compressed patch file.

Chapter 23, "Software Development on Ubuntu," discusses how to install the basic packages required for software development on an Ubuntu system. If you are writing your own code or simply compiling existing applications on an Ubuntu system, that may be sufficient—except when you are building complex graphical software or when you are building your own DEB packages from the downloaded source for an Ubuntu package. In these cases, you will quickly encounter frustration from such facts as that today's graphical software has dependencies on libraries, include files, and utilities that you may not be familiar with or even have heard of before. Similarly, building DEB packages requires the use of billions and billions of utilities that may be new to you. Not to worry—you're not the first person to have encountered these issues, and the apt-get command provides a handy solution, as explained in the next section.

Satisfying Build Dependencies Using apt-get

Many of the software packages available for Linux have dependencies on other packages, which makes perfect sense—why reinvent the wheel when you can just link your code with it? However, if you decide to work on an existing Linux package, build-time dependencies can be frustrating. They're rarely well documented, so you tend to encounter them as an iterative set of errors when you try to compile and link the application you're trying to build. This is also true when you begin to work with software packages in the formats used by different package management systems. The DEB packages used on Ubuntu and Debian systems (and derivatives) eliminate the dependency mumbo-jumbo that you often encounter with other package formats (such as RPM), but require the presence of an entire ecosystem of related utilities in order to build and package them successfully. Getting started with these can be tricky—you don't know what you're missing until your build process goes up in flames.

The apt-get tool provides a great, automated solution for these sorts of problems through its build-dep command-line option. Using this command-line option, followed by the name of the package that you want to build, automatically identifies, retrieves, and installs all of the include files, libraries, and tools required to build the specified package. The following is an example of the output from this command when retrieving build dependencies for the MythTV package used as an example in the previous section:

```
$ sudo apt-get build-dep mythtv
Reading package lists... Done
Building dependency tree... Done
The following NEW packages will be installed
```

```
build-essential g++ g++-3.4 g++-4.0 libartsc0-dev libasound2-dev
libaudio-dev libdvb-dev libgl1-mesa-dev libglu1-mesa-dev
libjpeg62-dev liblame-dev liblcms1-dev liblircclient-dev
libmng-dev libmysqlclient14-dev libogg-dev libqt3-headers
libqt3-mt-dev libstdc++6-4.0-dev libstdc++6-dev libvorbis-dev
libxmu-dev libxmu-headers libxt-dev libxv-dev libxvmc-dev
libxxf86vm-dev mesa-common-dev qt3-dev-tools x11proto-video-dev
x11proto-xf86vidmode-dev
0 upgraded, 32 newly installed, 0 to remove and 0 not upgraded.
Need to get 14.2MB/17.9MB of archives.
After unpacking 63.4MB of additional disk space will be used.
Do you want to continue [Y/n]? Y
[much output deleted]
```

As you can see from this example, it would have taken me many, many iterative compilation attempts to retrieve all of the packages required to build MythTV. Identifying the packages that provide missing include files and libraries can also be time-consuming, even with the help of the apt-file application discussed earlier in this chapter in the section, "Determining What Package Provides a Missing File." The apt-get build-dep command eliminates these sorts of hassles, letting you focus on the software, not the infrastructure required for building it.

Using aptitude to Add and Remove Software

As mentioned earlier in this chapter, the dpkg utility provides the conceptual underpinnings of much of the Package Management software provided on Ubuntu (and Debian) systems. However powerful it may be, it is a command-line utility, and therefore doesn't provide any sort of graphical interface, so the dselect utility was developed in order to at least provide a quasi-graphical interface using terminal-oriented cursor-movement libraries such as curses (now ncurses, for "new curses"). However, dselect couldn't quite let go of its command-line roots and therefore also provides a command-line interface.

The apt-get application discussed earlier in this chapter provides a simpler, higher-level interface than that provided by the dpkg utility. However, apt-get is YACLU ("Yet Another Command-Line Utility") and therefore doesn't provide any sort of graphical interface either. The aptitude application was developed to solve this problem but couldn't quite let go of the command line either. Thus aptitude (like dselect before it) provides both a powerful command-line interface and a terminal-oriented, quasi-graphical interface.

Personally, I find terminal-oriented graphical interfaces quaint, at best. I prefer not to use them unless absolutely necessary, especially when they've been replaced by actual graphical user interfaces such as those provided by the Synaptic Package Manager.

Note

When using the `aptitude` utility to install software, you may occasionally have to provide additional, configuration-related information during the installation process. In these cases, the `aptitude` utility displays the same sort of information requests as those displayed by the `apt-get` utility and shown earlier in Figure 19-8. Whenever you see this sort of screen, you must answer any questions that it asks and supply any requested information before the installation of your package can complete. ∎

Software can easily be installed by `aptitude` using the command-line `aptitude install` command, and removed using the `aptitude remove` command. As discussed later in the section, "Using aptitude to Install Recommended Software," `aptitude` provides some convenient options that make it attractive to use `aptitude` from the command line in certain cases. Many people are also fans of the `aptitude` interface, primarily those who understand it. The next section discusses the absolute basics of the `aptitude` user interface, focusing on how to make it readable by mere mortals.

Tips and Tricks for Using the aptitude User Interface

Figure 19-9 shows the default `aptitude` interface that you see the first time that you start `aptitude` with no arguments in a GNOME Terminal.

FIGURE 19-9

The default aptitude interface in the GNOME Terminal

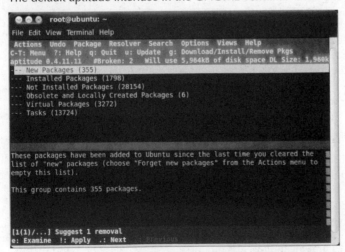

This interface looks essentially the same in an X Window System xterm or any other terminal application that supports color.

If you insist on using this interface but are having problems seeing the text or dealing with the color scheme, you're somewhat out of luck because the aptitude application doesn't offer command-line options for changing the color scheme. However, all is not lost — you can make the interface easier to read by changing your terminal application's underlying notion of the type of terminal in which you are running aptitude. A good choice for this is the value vt100, which is a classic terminal from the late Digital Equipment Corporation that only supported black and white. To make this change, exit aptitude by pressing **Q** and using the tab key to emphasize that you do actually want to exit from aptitude. Next, type the following command in your terminal application:

```
$ export TERM=vt100
```

After executing this command, you can then restart aptitude, which will look like the screen shown in Figure 19-10.

FIGURE 19-10

The aptitude interface in black and white

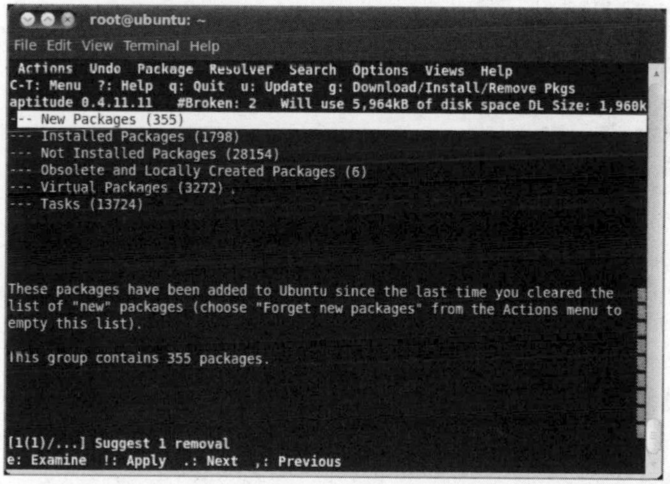

Changing the color scheme doesn't make the aptitude interface any more attractive, but (for me) it does at least make it more usable.

Once aptitude is running, the following are my favorite commands:

- **Q:** Enables you to exit aptitude
- **?:** Displays a panel containing summary information about using the aptitude interface
- **Ctrl+t:** Holding down the Ctrl key and pressing **T** displays aptitude's menus, which you can navigate through using the arrow keys or by pressing the highlighted key shortcut to execute a specific command.

Figure 19-11 displays a menu in `aptitude` using `aptitude`'s default color scheme. Need I say more? This is the sort of thing that gives Linux applications a bad name to people who are used to Macintosh (or even Windows) graphics.

FIGURE 19-11

A menu in the default aptitude interface

For more detailed (and less opinionated) information about using the `aptitude` user interface, see the online reference information for `aptitude` (`man aptitude`) or search the Web for relevant information.

Using aptitude to Install Recommended Software

If you have been using `apt-get` to install new software and the `apt-get` utility informs you that other packages are recommended or suggested for installation, you may want to consider using `aptitude`'s command-line interface rather than `apt-get`. The DEB packages used by Ubuntu identify various dependencies, divided into five different classes:

- **Conflicts:** Packages (or package versions) with which a package conflicts, and which cannot therefore be installed on a system when a specified package is being installed

- **Depends:** Packages that are mandatory for the correct operation of a package, and which therefore must also be installed when a given package is installed

- **Enhances:** Packages whose operation is improved or simplified as a result of installing a package, but between which there is no direct relationship

- **Pre-Depends:** Packages that must be completely installed on your system before you can install a given package

- **Recommends:** Packages that you should probably have, but which are not absolutely required for the correct operation of a given package
- **Suggests:** Packages that may be useful, and which are normally installed on systems where a given package is installed

Requirements marked as Pre-Depends (which are rarely used or necessary) must be satisfied before you can install a given package. Requirements marked as Depends are automatically installed along with a given package. The `aptitude` utility enables you to automatically install packages that are recommended for installation by including the `--with-recommends` command-line option on your `aptitude install` command line.

The `aptitude` utility is the only command-line package installation utility that enables you to automatically install recommended packages along with required packages. Specifying the `--with-recommends` command-line option when installing packages from the command line can be quite convenient and can save you search time in the future if you discover that you want to use a recommended package. A similar option to aptitude's `--with-recommends` option for `apt-get`, `--recommends`, and a related one for installing suggested packages, `--suggests`, have been "suggested" for `apt-get` for a long time, but are not available in any version of `apt-get` that I've ever seen. As I'll discuss in the section of this chapter on Synaptic, the Synaptic tool provides configuration options for considering recommended packages to be dependencies and automatically installing them; similarly, its interface provides a runtime option for manually selecting suggested packages and including them as part of the package installation process.

Advantages of Using aptitude to Install and Remove Software

Although I am not such a fan of the `aptitude` user interface, `aptitude` itself does provide some significantly useful capabilities. Its search capabilities, discussed earlier in this chapter in the section, "Listing the Packages That Are Available for Your System," are easy to use and quite powerful — exactly what you want in a utility. Similarly, the current version of `aptitude` has some other advantages when installing and, specifically, when removing packages. The most significant of these is the fact that `aptitude` remembers dependency information when installing packages. Every Ubuntu Package Management utility understands requirements when installing packages, but `aptitude` remembers this information and can therefore use if you decide to remove packages.

The following sample output shows an attempt to remove the PostgreSQL database system from one of my Ubuntu systems using `apt-get`:

```
$ sudo apt-get remove postgresql
Password:
Reading package lists... Done
Building dependency tree... Done
The following packages will be REMOVED
  postgresql
```

```
0 upgraded, 0 newly installed, 1 to remove and 0 not upgraded.
Need to get 0B of archives.
After unpacking 45.1kB disk space will be freed.
Do you want to continue [Y/n]? n
Abort.
```

Using aptitude to remove the same package is much more useful because it also offers to remove packages that were installed along with the postgresql package but that are no longer needed on that system if the postgresql package itself is removed, as in the following example:

```
$ sudo aptitude remove postgresql
Reading package lists... Done
Building dependency tree... Done
Reading extended state information
Initializing package states... Done
Building tag database... Done
The following packages are unused and will be REMOVED:
  postgresql-plperl-7.4 postgresql-plpython-7.4 postgresql-pltcl-7.4
The following packages will be REMOVED:
  postgresql
0 packages upgraded, 0 newly installed, 4 to remove \
  and 0 not upgraded.
Need to get 0B of archives. After unpacking 651kB will be freed.
Do you want to continue? [Y/n/?] Y
[much output deleted]
```

For me, this makes aptitude a much more attractive command-line package installation solution than apt-get. Note that aptitude only remembers dependency information for packages that it has installed, so I tend to use aptitude from the command line for both package installation and removal. Otherwise, if you actively install and remove large numbers of packages, your system tends to accumulate packages that you no longer need but that you're not aware of. For information about ways of checking for unneeded packages and removing them, see the last section of this chapter, "Keeping your System Lean, Mean, and Pristine."

Using Synaptic to Add and Remove Software

The Synaptic Package Manager is a graphical, GNOME application for installing, removing, and generally managing Ubuntu software packages. In the unlikely event that this is only the second sentence you have read in this book, you may not know that I recommend using the Synaptic Package Management utility for almost all package management tasks on Ubuntu systems. It's true. Synaptic is the type of administrative application that users of other Linux distributions and other personal computer operating systems wish they had.

Synaptic was originally developed by the folks at Connectiva Linux, a Latin American Linux distribution that was eventually acquired by Mandrake Linux, which then changed its name to Mandriva to highlight that it wasn't your father's Mandrake Linux distribution anymore. Synaptic was originally written using the WINGS toolkit used by the Window Maker X Window System window manager (`www.windowmaker.info`), which attempted to provide a look and feel familiar to users of NeXT computer systems. Today, Synaptic is built with the standard GTK+ toolkit used by GNOME. Interestingly, Connectiva was an RPM-based distribution, but Synaptic is now more commonly associated with the DEB packages used by distributions such as Ubuntu and Debian.

The Synaptic Package Management utility is installed by default as part of any Ubuntu installation. Select the System ➪ Administration ➪ Synaptic Package Manager menu item to start the Synaptic tool. As when trying to run any graphical administrative application on Ubuntu, you will be prompted for your administrative password before Synaptic actually starts. Figure 19-12 shows the dialog displayed when you first start Synaptic.

The startup dialog for the Synaptic utility

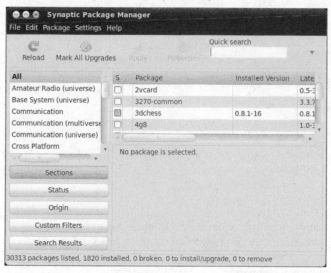

The left pane of the Synaptic dialog shown in Figure 19-12 shows the conceptual categories into which software is organized based on the default repositories enabled when you first install Ubuntu.

The basic package-related areas of Synaptic's main dialog are as follows:

- **Left pane:** Organizes available software into various conceptual categories based on the repositories listed in `/etc/apt/sources.list`

- **Upper-right pane:** Lists the software packages that are available in the category that is currently selected in the left pane. By default, the All category is selected in Synaptic's left pane, so that all available software packages are listed. As I discuss later in this chapter, performing a search in Synaptic creates a new category with the name of your search term(s) and hides all other default categories with the exception of the All category.

- **Bottom-right pane:** Displays the description of any package that is currently selected in the upper-right pane

Synaptic provides an excellent online manual, shown in Figure 19-13, that you can access by selecting the Help menu's Contents item.

FIGURE 19-13

The online manual for Synaptic

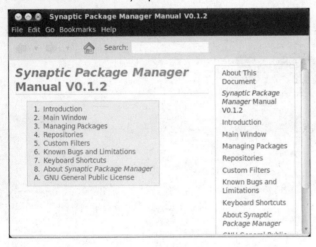

Because Synaptic includes thorough and up-to-date online help, I'm not going to bore you by repeating all of that. The next few sections focus on how to do common tasks in Synaptic, explaining how to configure Synaptic and how to perform basic package management tasks such as searching for and installing packages using Synaptic.

Configuring Synaptic Preferences

The entries on Synaptic's Settings menu enable you to set default values for using Synaptic, identify the repositories available to Synaptic, configure how searches work in Synaptic, configure how the icons are displayed in the Synaptic toolbar, and set internal variables used by Synaptic. Most of the settings that you will want to change are located on the Preferences dialog, which you can display by selecting the Settings menu's Preferences option. Figure 19-14 shows Synaptic's Preferences dialog.

FIGURE 19-14

The Synaptic Preferences dialog

The Synaptic preferences that you will most commonly want to change are all located on the General tab of Synaptic's Preferences dialog. These are the following:

- **Consider recommended packages as dependencies:** Selecting this checkbox causes Synaptic to always install any packages that are associated with a package that you are installing, but which are identified as recommended, but not required, for package installation. As discussed in more detail in this chapter in the section, "Using aptitude to Install Recommended Software," such recommended packages are ones that you will probably want to use with the package that you are installing.

- **System upgrade:** This item should always be set to "Smart Upgrade," which tries to identify other packages that must be installed, updated, or removed when installing or upgrading any package. Synaptic is much more conservative about this than other utilities such as `apt-get`.

  The `apt-get dist-upgrade` command is a more powerful equivalent for this Synaptic option. Even if you are a Synaptic fan, you will occasionally need to execute the `apt-get dist-upgrade` command in order to completely upgrade all of the packages on your system. When using Synaptic, you know you need to use the `apt-get dist-upgrade` command when packages are mysteriously identified as being held back and not updated — and, of course when you see the occasional pop-up message that explicitly tells you to run the `apt-get dist-upgrade` command.

- **Apply changes in a terminal window:** Selecting this option causes Synaptic to always display package installation/update status messages and results in a separate Terminal window. As mentioned when discussing installing software using the `apt-get` and `aptitude` utilities, you may occasionally have to provide additional, configuration-related information during the installation process. In these cases, the Synaptic utility displays the same sort of information requests as those displayed by the `apt-get` and `aptitude` utilities, as shown earlier in Figure 19-10. Whenever you see this sort of screen, you must answer any questions that it asks and supply any requested information before the installation of your package can complete. The Synaptic utility displays this information in the dialog that you see only when you expand the software installation status window, so it's a good idea to always monitor this window. If you choose not to and notice that Synaptic seems to have stopped installing things, expand this window to see if Synaptic is waiting for additional information.

Once you have changed any setting on any of the tabs in Synaptic's Preferences dialog, click Apply to make sure that your changes are saved, and then click OK to close the Preferences dialog and return to the main Synaptic dialog.

Searching for Software in Synaptic

One of Synaptic's most powerful capabilities is providing a powerful and usable package search capability that doesn't involve a command line. To locate packages that are relevant to one or more keywords, you can either use the "Quick Search" textbox in the main Synaptic dialog to search package descriptions and names, or click the down arrow to the right of the Quick Search area and select the Search button to display a more advanced search dialog that also enables you to specify what package fields to search, as shown in Figure 19-15.

FIGURE 19-15

Synaptic's Find dialog

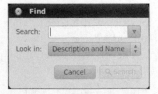

Most examples of installing software throughout this book have relied on Synaptic's search capabilities. To locate matching, available packages, you have to make sure that you're searching the right portion of the information that Synaptic has about packages. In almost all cases, you will want to make sure that the "Look in" value in Synaptic's Search dialog is set to "Description and Name" so that the search looks for matches for your keyword(s) in both package descriptions and package names. However, you may occasionally want to search other portions of the package information that is available via Synaptic. Other search possibilities are as follows:

- **Name:** Searches only package names for your keyword
- **Maintainer:** Looks for a package maintained by one of your favorite Ubuntu rock stars
- **Version:** Finds specific versions, which can be useful when looking for all packages that take their version number from higher-level packages, such as GNOME versions
- **Dependencies:** Identifies packages that depend on a given package
- **Provided Packages:** Identifies packages based on other packages that they also install

To search for packages in Synaptic, enter one or more keywords in Synaptic's "Quick Search" text area or Find dialog, and click Search (or press Return). Synaptic will create a new category in the left pane with the name of your search term(s) and hide all other default categories with the exception of the All category. Once the search completes, the new category is selected and any matching packages display in the upper-right pane. Figure 19-16 shows the results of a search for *window manager*.

FIGURE 19-16

Search results in Synaptic

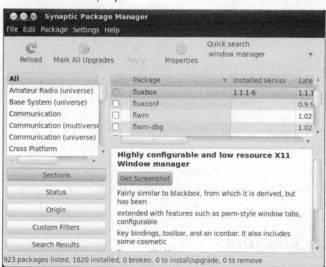

To select a package for installation, scroll down in the upper-right pane until you see the name of the package that you want to install. You can select the name of any package in the upper-right pane to see the description of that package, and can also click the Properties button in Synaptic's toolbar (or select the Properties item from the pop-up menu after right-clicking on its name) to display a Properties dialog that shows detailed information about the selected item. Figure 19-17 shows the Properties dialog for the package that provides the Fluxbox window manager, a lightweight window manager that I like to use on laptops.

FIGURE 19-17

A package Properties dialog in Synaptic

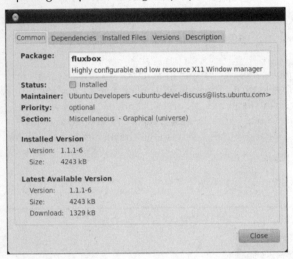

The Common tab, shown by default when you display a package Properties dialog, provides general information about the package. The Dependencies tab provides useful information about required, recommended, suggested, and conflicting packages. The Installed Files tab is also very useful, but only contains information on packages that are already installed. (To see information about the files that are included in a package that is not installed, you can use the apt-file application, which is discussed earlier in this chapter in the section, "Determining What Package Provides a Missing File.")

After examining any properties of a selected package, click Close to close the Properties dialog and return to the main Synaptic dialog.

Installing Packages in Synaptic

After locating a package that you want to install, right-click on its name in the upper-right pane and select "Mark for Installation" from the pop-up menu, as shown in Figure 19-18.

If installing the selected package requires that other packages be installed, Synaptic displays a dialog like that shown in Figure 19-19.

FIGURE 19-18

Marking a package for installation in Synaptic

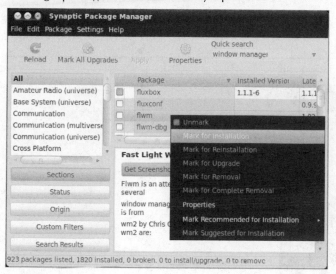

FIGURE 19-19

Identifying other packages required for installation

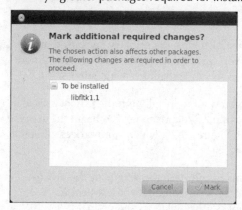

This dialog lists all packages whose installation is required by the package that you have selected. If you checked the "Consider recommended packages as dependencies" item in Synaptic's Preferences dialog, this list will also include any packages that are recommended, but not required, for installation. Click Mark to accept the installation of these other packages and close this dialog.

Next, right-click on the package name again, and check whether any packages are listed on a submenu of the "Mark Suggested for Installation" command at the bottom of Synaptic's pop-up menu, as shown in Figure 19-20.

FIGURE 19-20

FIGURE 19-20

Marking suggested packages for installation in Synaptic

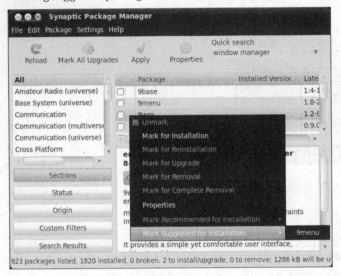

This submenu identifies packages that are normally installed with the primary package that you have selected for installation but that are not required or expected. You can select any of the additional packages listed on this menu (one by one) to also schedule them for installation.

Once you have selected any suggested packages that you want to install with the primary package that you have selected for installation, click Apply in the Synaptic toolbar to begin the actual installation process. This displays the dialog shown in Figure 19-21, which summarizes all of the activities associated with installing the selected package(s).

Once the download process completes, Synaptic begins installing and configuring the downloaded packages. If you did not select the "Apply changes" in a Terminal window item in Synaptic's Preferences dialog, Synaptic displays a simple status dialog, as shown in Figure 19-23.

FIGURE 19-21

A package installation summary in Synaptic

FIGURE 19-22

The download status dialog during Synaptic package installation

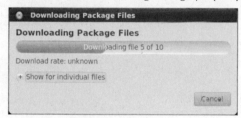

FIGURE 19-23

A simple installation and configuration status dialog in Synaptic

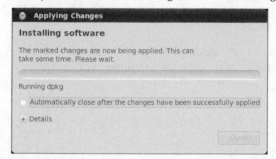

You can display a small Terminal window that lists the status of Synaptic's installation and configuration processes by clicking the arrow to the right of the Terminal option on this dialog. When the installation and configuration of your packages completes, the dialog shown in Figure 19-24 displays.

Tip

When using the Synaptic utility to install software without having configured Synaptic to always display configuration status in a Terminal window, it is useful to display a Terminal to see information about the status of software installation on your system. You may occasionally have to provide additional, configuration-related information during the installation process. In this case, the Synaptic utility displays the same sort of information requests as those displayed by the apt-get and aptitude utilities, as shown earlier in Figure 19-8. Whenever you see this sort of screen, you must answer any questions that it asks and supply any requested information before the installation of your package can complete. The Synaptic utility displays this information in the dialog that you see only when you expand the software installation Terminal window, so it's a good idea to always monitor this window. If you choose not to and notice that Synaptic seems to have stopped installing things, expand this window to see if Synaptic is waiting for additional information. ∎

FIGURE 19-24

A simple completion dialog in Synaptic

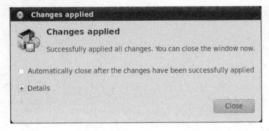

If you selected the "Apply changes" in a Terminal window item in Synaptic's Preferences dialog, Synaptic displays a single large Terminal window during its installation and configuration phases, shown in Figure 19-25, instead of the dialogs shown in Figures 19-23 and 19-24.

Regardless of which of the dialogs you see when package installation and configuration complete, click Close to close that dialog and return to Synaptic's main dialog.

Once you have finished installing any packages that you are interested in, you can exit from Synaptic by selecting the File menu's Quit command (or pressing the Ctrl+Q key sequence).

FIGURE 19-25

A Terminal window showing installation and configuration status

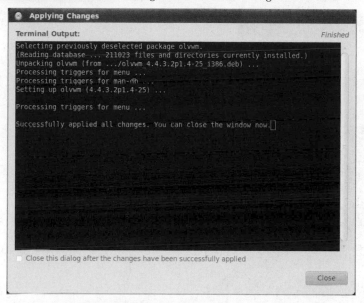

```
  Applying Changes

Terminal Output:                                                    Finished

Selecting previously deselected package olvwm.
(Reading database ... 211023 files and directories currently installed.)
Unpacking olvwm (from .../olvwm_4.4.3.2p1.4-25_i386.deb) ...
Processing triggers for menu ...
Processing triggers for man-db ...
Setting up olvwm (4.4.3.2p1.4-25) ...

Processing triggers for menu ...

Successfully applied all changes. You can close the window now.
```

☐ Close this dialog after the changes have been successfully applied

Close

Removing Packages in Synaptic

Removing software in Synaptic is very similar to the installation process. You must first locate the package(s) that you want to remove by selecting the appropriate category from Synaptic's left pane and scrolling through the package lists in the upper-right pane, or by searching for that package and then selecting it from the upper-right pane. Either way, once you have located the package that you want to remove, right-click on its name to display the pop-up menu shown in Figure 19-26.

Marking a package for complete removal removes the package and any configuration files for the application that you may have modified, while "Mark for Removal" removes the package but leaves the configuration files on your system.

Tip

Unfortunately, Synaptic does not automatically remove other packages that were required by a package that you are selecting for removal or that you installed as a result of their being suggested for installation. You must select all of these packages manually in order to remove them. You can also not worry about them and use the process described in the last section of this chapter, "Keeping your System Lean, Mean, and Pristine," to remove them at some point in the future. ■

FIGURE 19-26

Marking a package for complete removal in Synaptic

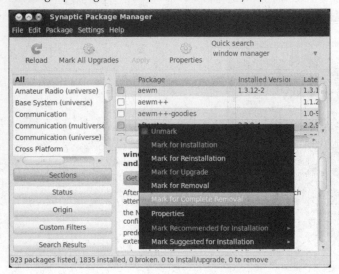

Once you have selected any packages that you want to remove and marked them for removal, click Apply to proceed with the installation process. This displays the Confirmation dialog shown in Figure 19-27.

FIGURE 19-27

The Confirmation dialog for package removal in Synaptic

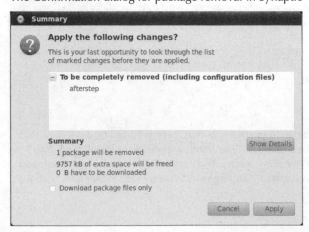

Click Apply to continue. As the removal process proceeds, the Synaptic dialog displays status dialogs similar to those shown during the package installation process, as described in the previous section. Once package removal completes, click Close to close the final status dialog and return to Synaptic's primary dialog.

Once you have finished removing packages from your system, you can exit from Synaptic by selecting the File menu's Quit command (or pressing the Ctrl+Q key sequence).

Using the Ubuntu Update Manager

Ubuntu's Update Manager checks the active repositories listed in your /etc/apt/sources.list file and notifies you if updates to any installed packages are available. The Update Manager uses an associated panel applet to let you know when updates are available by displaying a small orange icon and a pop-up dialog when updates are first found. If you see this icon, you can move the cursor over it at any time to display a tooltip that summarizes available updates.

Clicking on this icon starts the Update Manager itself, which is shown in Figure 19-28. You can also start the Update Manager manually at any time by selecting the System ➪ Administration ➪ Update Manager menu command.

FIGURE 19-28

The Ubuntu Update Manager

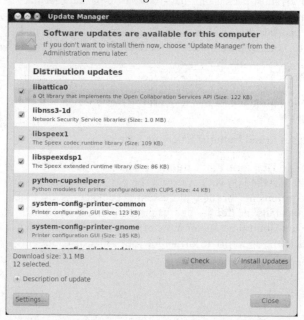

Using the Update Manager is simple — just click "Install Updates." The Update Manager then automatically retrieves, installs, and configures all available updated packages, displaying progress and status dialogs that are very similar to those used by the Synaptic Package Manager. When the update process completes, click Close to terminate the Update Manager and begin doing real work.

Tip

As when using the Synaptic utility, you should watch for configuration questions or requests for additional information that are required during the package update process. If the update process seems to have halted or is taking a long time, click the Terminal button in the Update Manager's status dialogs to see if any configuration questions are pending. ■

Converting Packages from Other Package Formats

Although the Ubuntu repositories contain most of the add-on software packages that anyone could ever want, there are cases when you must deal with prepacked software that is provided in the package formats used by distributions other than Ubuntu. This is often the case with commercial software whose Linux releases are distributed in formats such as RPM and LSB. Luckily, an easy solution to this sort of problem is provided by the `alien` application (`http://kitenet.net/~joey/code/alien`), which is a Perl script that can convert between different package formats. Most important, `alien` can convert most package formats to the DEB package format that is used by the Ubuntu and Debian installation and update tools that are discussed in this chapter. Depending on the format of the package that you are converting from, `alien` may need some additional software to be installed on your Ubuntu system — more about that in a second.

Tip

You must run `alien` as root (preferably using the `sudo` program) so that it can correctly set ownership and file permissions on the files in the converted package. ■

The `alien` application can convert packages to and from the following formats:

- **DEB:** When converting packages to DEB format, the `debhelper`, `dpkg`, `dpkg-dev`, `gcc`, and `make` packages must be installed on your system. (The `gcc`, `make`, and `dpkg-dev` packages are installed as requirements for the build-essential package, as discussed in Chapter 23. Installing `alien` installs the `debhelper` package.) If you're stuck with using some distribution other than Ubuntu on one or more of your systems, you can use `alien` to convert DEB packages to the appropriate format for your other distribution(s) until you can replace them.

- **LSB:** The package format used to distribute applications and entire distributions that are compliant with the Linux Standard Base (LSB) specification (`www.linuxfoundation.org/collaborate/workgroups/lsb`). Because the LSB specification mandates RPM packages, LSB packages are a superset of RPM packages. Therefore, the RPM Package Manager software must be installed on your Ubuntu system in order to convert LSB packages. (The RPM software is automatically installed for you when you install `alien` because it is listed as a requirement for the `alien` package.) If you are converting an LSB package that depends on other packages, the conversion process will correctly translate those dependencies, but will also introduce a new dependency on the `lsb` package, which is available in the Ubuntu repositories. You should also install the `lsb-rpm` package, which is suggested but not required by the `alien` package, if you are converting from LSB packages.

- **PKG:** The package format used by Solaris. Converting PKG files into other package formats requires Solaris-only tools such as `pkginfo` and `pkgtrans`. If you also install the RPM software from one of the Sun Free Software CDs, you can then use `alien` on your Solaris system to convert PKG packages into RPMs. This is probably useful only for packages composed of scripts, source code, or command files because you can't execute Solaris binaries on a Linux system.

- **RPM:** The package format used by distributions such as Red Hat, Fedora Core, Mandrake, Yellow Dog, and so on. To convert packages from the RPM format, the RPM Package Manager, formerly known as the Red Hat Package Manager, software must be installed on your Ubuntu system. (The RPM software is automatically installed for you when you install `alien` because it is listed as a requirement for the `alien` package.)

- **SLP:** The package format used by the extinct Stampede Linux distribution, which ceased development in 2002. I can't believe that this option is still actively supported, but because Stampede Linux is dead, I don't suppose much is changing in its package format.

- **TGZ:** The software distribution format used by most open source software projects and the Slackware Linux distribution, a TGZ file is a `tar` archive that has been compressed using the `gzip` compression tool, whether from the command line or by `tar` itself when creating the archive. Compressed `tar` archives are often simply referred to as *compressed tarballs*. Package files that are generated from TGZ files simply contain the same files as the compressed tarball, plus the package database information for the target package format.

Using `alien` to convert from one package format to another is easy. The `alien` application provides options such as `--to-deb`, `--to-lsb`, `--to-rpm`, and `--to-tgz` to specify the target output format. The following is an example of converting the RPM package for Adobe Acrobat Reader, which some of you may have heard of, to DEB format:

```
$ sudo alien --scripts --to-deb AdobeReader_enu-7.0.0-2.i386.rpm
Password:
adobereader-enu_7.0.0-3_i386.deb generated
```

Not much to see there, actually. The `--scripts` option tells `alien` to convert any pre- or post-installation scripts found in the package, although the validity of the converted scripts can't be guaranteed — you should watch carefully to make sure that nothing goes amiss when you install the converted package. The `--to-deb` option tells `alien` to generate a Debian package from the input package. If you want to see detailed output, you can add the `-v` option to the `alien` command line, but you're likely to see way more output than you actually care about.

Before installing a converted package, you can verify its integrity using `dpkg`, as in the following example:

```
$ dpkg --info adobereader-enu_7.0.0-3_i386.deb
 new debian package, version 2.0.
 size 37932742 bytes: control archive= 7436 bytes.
     484 bytes,    11 lines      control
   20061 bytes,   207 lines      md5sums
    1340 bytes,    60 lines   *  postinst              #!/bin/sh
     980 bytes,    45 lines   *  postrm                #!/bin/sh
     211 bytes,     7 lines      shlibs
 Package: adobereader-enu
 Version: 7.0.0-3
 Section: alien
 Priority: extra
 Architecture: i386
 Installed-Size: 91916
 Maintainer: root <root@vmdesktop>
 Description: Adobe Reader for Linux. An application that reads a
  PDF document. Adobe Reader 7.0.0 can read documents in PDF format.
  Adobe Reader also allows you to search within PDF files, search
  for PDF files on the internet and participate in collaborative
  document reviews.
  (Converted from a rpm package by alien version 8.64.)
```

This matches quite nicely with information about the original RPM package that was produced on one of my other systems:

```
$ rpm -q --info -v -p AdobeReader_enu-7.0.0-2.i386.rpm
Name        : AdobeReader_enu       Relocations: /usr/local/Adobe/Acrobat7.0
Version     : 7.0.0                 Vendor: Adobe Systems, Incorporated
Release     : 2                     Build Date: Mon 28 Mar 2005 06:34:42 AM EST
```

```
Install date: (not installed)          Build Host: acrolinux2.corp.adobe.com
Group        : Applications/Publishing  Source RPM: AdobeReader_cnu 7.0.0-2.
    src.rpm
Size         : 97613446                              License: Commercial
Signature    : (none)
Packager     : Adobe Systems, Incorporated
URL          : www.adobe.com
Summary      : Adobe Reader for Linux. An application that reads a PDF document.

Description :
Adobe Reader 7.0.0 can read documents in PDF format. Adobe Reader
also allows you to search within PDF files, search for PDF files on
the internet and participate in collaborative document reviews.
Distribution: (none)
```

For more information about the alien package, see its online reference information, which is available by typing the **man alien** command (after installing the package, of course).

Caution

You should never use alien in order to install packages containing low-level system utilities or system libraries. Although they may convert and install successfully, these packages will probably not work correctly on your Ubuntu system, and you risk reducing your Ubuntu system to a dysfunctional heap of slag that will not boot correctly. ■

Keeping Your System Lean, Mean, and Pristine

If you like to play with different software packages as much as I do, you'll find yourself installing lots of random packages on your system, playing with them for a while, and then forgetting about them unless they solve some major problem for you. You may occasionally even be thoughtful enough to remove packages that you aren't planning on using anymore. Unfortunately, this doesn't remove packages that were required, recommended, or suggested by the packages that you've removed (unless you use aptitude to both install and remove those packages).

Every now and then, it is therefore useful to run a utility that scans all of the packages that are installed on your system and looks for packages that are not used or required by any other package on your system, and that are also not a part of some system installation process. Good examples of programs that you can use to check your system in this way are the deborphan and debfoster packages. Neither of these packages is installed by default on an Ubuntu system, but you can easily install either of them using your favorite package installation utility.

The core difference between these two packages is that the `deborphan` utility simply produces a list of packages that are not used or referred to by any system package on your system, whereas the `debfoster` package builds its own database of the packages that are required, tries to be smart about things that you may not need, and also asks lots of questions the first time you run it. For all of these reasons, I prefer the `deborphan` package, but I suggest that you investigate both and see which utility best suits your needs and modus operandi.

As mentioned previously, the `deborphan` utility simply lists packages that are no longer required by or associated with any other package. To do something useful with this list, you can re-direct it into a file and use that file as the basis for a shell script that will remove the packages that you actually want to remove. Another solution, much more wizardly, is to feed this list to the `apt-get remove` command using the Linux `xargs` command, as in the following example:

```
$ sudo deborphan | xargs apt-get remove --purge -y
```

Before running this sort of command, you should examine the `deborphan` output to make sure that it isn't removing anything that you still want.

Running either the `deborphan` or `debfoster` command periodically will help you reduce the amount of software package detritus that tends to accumulate on any running system. Keeping your system as free of unneeded packages as possible can help guarantee that the maximum amount of free disk space is available on your system, which you can then devote to real work such as your online music archives or collection of artistic digital photographs.

Tip

Ubuntu 10.04 introduces a nice graphical utility called Computer janitor for locating orphaned packages. This application is installed by default on Ubuntu 10.04 systems, and can be executed by selecting the System ⇨ Administration ⇨ Computer janitor menu item. ■

Summary

Package management is a wonderful thing, enabling your system to identify installed packages and, with the help of excellent package formats such as DEB, identify and satisfy any requirements for successfully installing a completely functional software package. This chapter initially discussed the Ubuntu Software Center menu item and explained how to use the associated software (`software-center`) to locate and install specific software packages. This chapter then introduced the three basic package management utilities that are found on all Ubuntu systems (`dpkg`, `apt-get`, and `aptitude`) and explained how you can use these and related utilities to install and query packages, figure out other packages that you need, and many more interesting package management tricks.

The focus of the remainder of this chapter was on the graphical installation and automatic software update applications that are available on Ubuntu (Synaptic and Update Manager) systems. The chapter also discussed how to use the installation utilities to identify and install software packages and how to use the update utilities to keep your system up-to-date, by installing security fixes or enhanced versions of existing software whenever they are available.

Chapter 20, "Adding Hardware and Attaching Peripherals," discusses how to add various types of hardware to your Ubuntu system. Like most modern personal computer systems, Ubuntu systems do a great job of automatically recognizing and providing access to new printers, scanners, and removable storage such as USB sticks, USB hard drives, FireWire devices, and so on. Adding new internal drives requires a bit more work, but it is a key element of permanent system upgrades and is easy enough to master.

Adding Hardware and Attaching Peripherals

IN THIS CHAPTER

Adding printers

Adding and using scanners

Adding internal drives

Using PCMCIA cards

Adding PCI cards

Troubleshooting new devices

S upport for a tremendous variety of hardware is a key issue for any desktop computer system. As computer hardware becomes more and more of an end-user commodity, and as desktop computer users feel more and more comfortable adding cards and external peripherals to their computer systems, the extent to which an operating system supports all of this new hardware becomes increasingly important. An increasing number of devices that are designed as external plug-and-play devices using interfaces like USB and FireWire are available at the local Best Buy, CompUSA, or Stop-n-Go. People expect to buy these things, take them home, plug them in, and find that "they just work." And rightly so.

All hardware requires pieces of kernel software called *device drivers* in order to be accessed and correctly used by the operating system. This is true for the Microsoft Windows kernel, the Mac OS X kernel, and the Linux kernel. The fact that CDs labeled *Windows Drivers* fall out of their boxes containing almost every piece of modern hardware might make you think that you'll have a problem using this hardware with Linux. After all, there is no companion coaster labeled *Linux Drivers*. What gives?

Luckily, the answer is that the device drivers for most hardware are already available as part of the Linux kernel as installed on your Ubuntu system. Device drivers are usually either compiled into the kernel or are available as kernel modules that are loaded when specific hardware is detected (hence, the generic term for such on-demand drivers: *loadable kernel modules*). This is true for a vast amount of hardware — after all, in the open source world, all it takes is one motivated Linux user with driver development skills and a piece of hardware that "doesn't work quite right," and a working driver usually surfaces shortly thereafter.

Although I am a fan of Ubuntu and a general Linux advocate, I can't deny that the lack of device-specific drivers can sometimes be a problem. To get the absolute best performance out of some pieces of new hardware — most specifically, things like graphics and audio cards — you may need special drivers. Unfortunately, most hardware manufacturers are motivated by projected sales numbers based on market analysis, and the Windows market is currently at least 50 to a 100 times larger than the Linux market. This is why you get a *Windows Driver* coaster free with almost all new hardware. Open source support for these high-performance drivers may lag behind Windows support, although more and more hardware manufacturers are providing Linux drivers in one form or another, often only available for download from their web sites. Things are also getting better in that support for the Dynamic Kernel Module Support (DKMS) that was originally introduced by Dell is now present in the Linux kernel, which is a big step in the right direction because it can automatically download and update third-party drivers when you upgrade your kernel.

The good news is that, for the most part, drivers that are required for most new hardware come with your Ubuntu Linux distribution. Some specialized drivers that are not open source or that have licensing or other encumbrances are available as updates from portions of the Ubuntu repository such as the restricted, universe, or multiverse components, as discussed in Chapter 19. You may have to retrieve other drivers directly from a corporate web site. The bottom line is that, usually, things will indeed "just work" with Linux.

This chapter explores using different types of hardware devices with your Ubuntu Linux systems, focusing on the types of hardware that most desktop and laptop computer users will be interested in. Hardware detection and support under Ubuntu and Linux in general are constantly improving. Regardless, when researching or buying new hardware, it's always a good idea to spend a bit of time in your favorite search engine, looking for information about Linux support for your hardware. More information is always a good thing, regardless of what the U.S. Government says nowadays.

Adding a Printer

Most modern printers connect to your system via its USB interface, although some still connect to the classic parallel port. Regardless of the type of printer you are connecting to your system, the first things to do are to connect it to your system and turn it on. If it is a USB printer, you can verify that the printer is visible to your system by executing the lsusb (list USB) command, which provides information like the following:

```
# lsusb
Bus 007 Device 001: ID 1d6b:0001 Linux Foundation 1.1 root hub
Bus 006 Device 001: ID 1d6b:0001 Linux Foundation 1.1 root hub
Bus 005 Device 003: ID 04b8:0005 Seiko Epson Corp. Stylus D88+
Bus 005 Device 001: ID 1d6b:0001 Linux Foundation 1.1 root hub
Bus 003 Device 002: ID 0d8c:0001 C-Media Electronics, Inc. Audio Device
Bus 003 Device 001: ID 1d6b:0001 Linux Foundation 1.1 root hub
Bus 002 Device 001: ID 1d6b:0001 Linux Foundation 1.1 root hub
```

```
Bus 004 Device 001: ID 1d6b:0002 Linux Foundation 2.0 root hub
Bus 001 Device 003: ID 12c8:1f03
Bus 001 Device 001: ID 1d6b:0002 Linux Foundation 2.0 root hub
```

From this output, you can see that an Epson Stylus printer is attached to this system via USB.

Tip

If you have not purchased a printer yet and want to get information about Linux support for a specific printer, check out the LinuxPrinting.org site at www.linuxprinting.org. This site, which actually resolves to a site at the Linux Foundation (www.linuxfoundation.org/collaborate/workgroups/openprinting), provides an easy interface at www.openprinting.org/printers that enables you to get information about how well specific printers (or all of the printers from a specific manufacturer) work with the Linux printing system. For more information about printing on Linux, see Chapter 33, "Setting Up a Print Server." ■

Adding a locally attached printer has become incredibly simple thanks to the fact that most printers use USB interfaces nowadays rather than the classic Centronics parallel interface that many of us remember with varying degrees of fondness. Because attaching a USB device to your system causes a recognizable event that your system can detect, your system can also initiate its configuration. The next few sections discuss what happens when you attach a new printer to your Ubuntu system, and how you can create or customize that printer's configuration, if necessary.

Earlier releases of Ubuntu enabled you to configure what should happen when a new printer was detected by your system. This was friendly but largely a waste of time because the answer is almost always "Please configure the thing so that I can actually print on it." On modern Ubuntu systems, attaching a USB printer usually the printer being recognized automatically — it simply appears in the System ⇨ Administration ⇨ Printing dialog shown in Figure 20-1 — the printer is recognized, added, and configured, and your system is ready to use it.

FIGURE 20-1

An autodetected printer in the Ubuntu Printing utility

If the printer was recognized correctly, your new printer is automatically added to the list of printers that are available on your system, and you're ready to print! However, if your printer was not recognized correctly or if you simply want to test or further configure it, you can right-click the icon for the printer and select Properties to open the system-config-printer application, which is discussed in the next section.

Unfortunately, only USB printers and shared networked printers can be recognized automatically by your Ubuntu system. If you're adding a printer that uses the parallel port or need to define a networked printer that your system can't detect automatically, skip ahead to the section, "Manually Defining a New Printer."

Configuring an Existing Printer

You can fine-tune the settings for any printer on your system by selecting the System ➪ Administration ➪ Printing menu item, right-clicking the icon for the printer, and selecting Properties from the pop-up menu. This displays the configuration options that are available for a specific printer, as shown in Figure 20-2.

FIGURE 20-2

The Configuration dialog for a specific printer

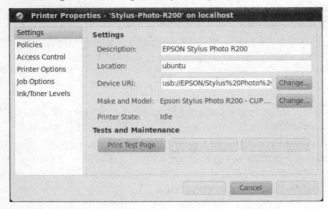

This dialog lists several different configuration options in its left pane. The Settings pane, which is selected by default, enables you to print a test page to verify that your printer is working correctly, identify how the printer is connected to your system, change the printer type if it was recognized incorrectly, and perform any printer-specific tasks that are available, such as cleaning the print heads on inkjet-style printers.

If your printer was recognized incorrectly or if you want to use drivers that have come with the printer, click Change beside the Make and Model field to display the "Change Driver" dialog. This dialog is identical to one of the dialogs used when configuring a new printer (shown in Figure 20-4 later in this chapter), which is discussed in the next section.

The other configuration options available in this dialog do the following:

- **Policies:** Enable you to control the state of the printer (is it enabled and accepting jobs, and is it shared so that other systems can access it?), general policies such as what happens if a printing error occurs, and banner options that enable you to print cover pages that can precede and follow each print job with various banners, including banners that identify print jobs as *Classified* or *Top Secret* so that any spies in your office will know which documents to steal

- **Access Control:** Enables you to configure who can print on that printer, either by disallowing printing by everyone but selected users, or by allowing printing by everyone except for selected users

- **Printer Options:** Lets you specify the paper size, type of paper being used, the paper tray from which to obtain paper (manual feed, paper tray, etc.), the level of print quality to use and the resolution in which to print, and so on. This dialog also enables you to specify whether you want the printer to print in grayscale or color and, if in color, which color model to use (RGB, CMYK, etc.). I know what you're thinking, but unfortunately this option cannot be used to enable you to print in color on a black-and-white or grayscale printer

- **Job Options:** Lets you set defaults for the number of copies of each document to print, the default font size and margins for generic text documents, the page orientation, number of pages per side, scaling, and so on

- **Ink/Toner Levels:** Provides access to messages that are available regarding printer ink or toner levels and general printer status

After changing any of these options, click OK to save your changes and close this dialog. The main printer configuration utility dialog, shown in Figure 20-3, will still be visible on your screen.

Manually Defining a New Printer

The dialog shown in Figure 20-3 enables you to configure existing printers or manually add new printers to your system, including shared printers. You can start this utility at any time by selecting the System ⇨ Administration ⇨ Printing menu command.

FIGURE 20-3

The Ubuntu Printers dialog

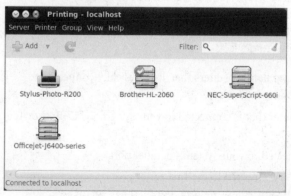

725

To begin manually defining a new printer, click the Add icon or select Server ⇨ New ⇨ Printer to start the Wizard that helps configure a new printer. After the `Printers` utility processes and parses its database of available printers, the first page of the "New Printer" dialog is displayed, as shown in Figure 20-4.

FIGURE 20-4

Specifying how a new printer is connected

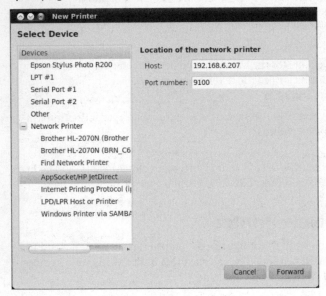

This dialog displays various choices for how your system will communicate with the new printer. Depending on the connection mechanism that you select, you should be able to obtain all of the necessary information from the documentation for your printer, from your local system adminis-trator, or by examining your system. The connection options are grouped into two sections, one for locally-attached devices, and one for network devices:

- **Devices:** This section enables you to define printers that are physically connected to your system through one of the following devices:
    - **Printer-Name:** Identifies a printer that is connected to your system via USB, showing the system's idea of the printer type
    - **LPT #1:** A printer that is connected to your system's parallel port
    - **Serial Port #1:** A printer that is connected to the first serial port on your system. Serial printers are extremely uncommon nowadays, but if you are using one, you

will need to provide information about your new printer. Enter the communication speed (*Baud rate*) that your new printer supports, and change the type of parity, the number of data bits, and the way in which the printer tells the system to start/stop sending data (*Flow Control*). The default values (8 data bits, no parity, and one stop bit) are usually the correct settings.

- **Serial Port #2:** A printer that is connected to the second serial port on your system
- **Other:** A local printer that you can access through a Universal Resource Identifier (URI) that uniquely identifies its connection mechanism

- **Network Printer:** Lists any existing network printers that can be located automatically, and provides several generic ways of communicating with a networked printer:

  - **AppSocket/HP JetDirect:** A printer that you can print directly with over the network by using a specific IP address and port. This is a common way of printing to modern stand-alone, network-aware printers from manufacturers such as Brother, HP, Epson, and so on. After selecting this option, you will need to provide information about your new printer. Enter the name or IP address of the printer in the Host field. You can leave the default port number (9100) unchanged unless you know that your printer uses a different port for JetDirect connections.

  - **Internet Printing Protocol (IPP):** A printer whose queue is managed by a specific host. IPP is a common alternative to JetDirect but supports capabilities such as authentication, access control, and host-side document formatting, and printer management. You will need to know the name or IP address of the host that manages the printer and the name of the queue for the specified printer on that host. You can use the "Find Queue" button to list all of the publicly available queues on a specified host.

  - **LPD/LPR host or printer:** A printer whose queue is managed by a specific host (including the local host) using the traditional UNIX Line Printer Damon (LPD) protocol. You will need to know the name or IP address of the host that manages the printer, and the name of the queue for the specified printer on that host. You can use the Probe button to list all of the publicly available queues on a specified host.

  - **Windows printer via SAMBA:** A printer that is managed by a host located on a Microsoft Windows network. Such hosts are typically Windows servers, but can also include Samba servers running on other UNIX or Linux systems on your network. You will need to know the name of your local workgroup or domain, the name or IP address of the host that manages the printer, and the name of the queue for the specified printer on that host. You can use the Browse button to navigate through your local workgroup/domain and hosts to locate the publicly available queues on a specified host.

Select the mechanism that your system uses to connect to the printer that you are adding, and specify any information that is required to communicate with the printer. Click Forward to proceed to the dialog shown in Figure 20-5.

FIGURE 20-5

Identifying your printer

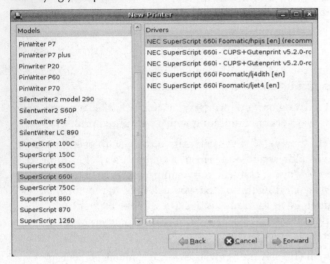

The dialog shown in Figure 20-5 enables you to provide your system with the information, known as a *driver*, that your system requires to format documents in the manner required by your new printer. This dialog provides three ways to identify your printer:

- **Select printer from database:** The default option, shown in Figure 20-5, this mechanism enables you to identify the driver(s) for your printer by identifying the vendor of your printer and then identifying its model number in a subsequent dialog. The combination of your printer vendor and model number enables the printer configuration tool to select (or create) an appropriate PostScript Printer Definition (PPD) file for your printer.

- **Provide PPD file:** PPD files are typically provided on a CD that accompanies your printer, and provide drivers and related information that describe how to print to your new printer. If you received a CD or other media with your printer, you should try this option first because the PPD files that are delivered with a printer typically provide the most up-to-date information about how to print to a specific printer. If you have trouble finding the PPD file for your printer, it may be located in the directory where Microsoft Windows printer driver(s) are located. Selecting this option displays the dialog shown in Figure 20-6.

- **Search for a print driver to download:** Selecting this option causes the printer configuration utility to search the www.openprinting.org site for an appropriate driver for your printer. If multiple possibilities are located, you can select among them from the dropdown Printer model list. Selecting this option displays the dialog shown in Figure 20-7.

FIGURE 20-6

Manually specifying a PPD file

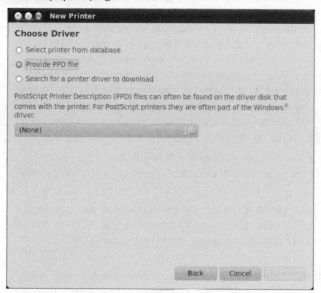

FIGURE 20-7

Downloading a PPD file

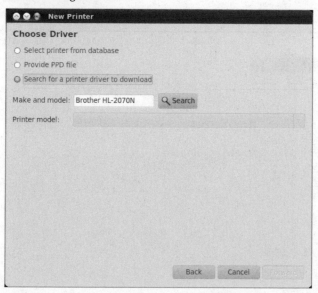

Different actions are required depending upon how you are locating the driver for your printer:

- **Select printer from database:** Select the maker of your printer, click Forward, and select the model of your printer from the pane that displays at right (or the model of the printer that is technically closest to yours). For example, I own a Brother HL-2070N printer, which was not listed at the time that I updated this book, but the driver for the Brother HL-2060 printer works fine with my printer. After locating and selecting the best printer driver for your printer, you may be able to select different drivers for that printer in the Driver list at the right of this dialog. The driver identified as recommended is usually the best one to use — you can always edit your printer (as described in the previous section) if the driver that you initially select doesn't work correctly for you. Click Forward to display the dialog shown in Figure 20-8.

- **Provide PPD file:** Click the Browse button to display a dialog that enables you to navigate to your PPD file. Click Open to use that PPD file and click Forward to display the dialog shown in Figure 20-8.

- **Search for a print driver to download:** Enter the make and model of your printer and click Search to locate available PPD files. Select the Printer Model that is closest to your your printer, and click Forward to display the dialog shown in Figure 20-8.

The dialog shown in Figure 20-8 enables you to provide some meaningful (but optional) information about your printer and to optionally change the name assigned to that printer. (You will certainly want to change the name of the printer if you have had to use the PPD file from a similar printer.) Once you are happy with the values on this screen, click Apply to complete the definition for your new printer.

FIGURE 20-8

Naming your printer

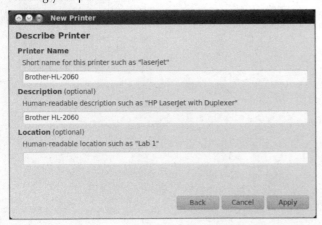

To verify that your printer definition is corect, a dialog that asks if you want to print a test page displays:

- To print a test page, click Yes. After attempting to print a test page, this displays the configuration dialog shown in Figure 20-3, which enables you to make changes if any are necessary. If the test page printed corectly, click Cancel to close this dialog. If the test page did not print correctly, change the configuration of your printer and try again. Once the test page prints correctly, click OK to save the updated configuration information for your printer.

- If you don't want to print a test page at the moment, click No.

The dialog shown earlier in Figure 20-3 displays, showing an icon for the new printer. The default printer for a system is indicated by a green checkmark on its icon. To change the default printer for your system, right-click its icon and select Set as Default from the pop-up menu. This displays a dialog asking if you want to make the selected printer the default printer for all users (the system-wide default), or your personal default printer.

To test a printer at any time, right-click its name, and select Properties from the pop-up menu. This displays a Properties dialog like the one shown in Figure 20-3. To verify that your printer is working correctly, click "Print a Test Page." This queues and prints a test page for your printer. If the test page does not print, use the other sections of the Properties dialog to verify that the correct connection settings are being used and that the right printer manufacturer and driver for your printer are specified. You should then be able to print a test page successfully.

Tip

If your printer is not automatically detected or cannot be made to print with any manual setting specified in the "Add printer" dialog, try rebooting your system with the printer connected and turned on. In some rare cases, Ubuntu's printer and device subsystems may not correctly detect a device unless it is present and active when you boot your system. ∎

Using a Scanner

Most modern scanners are USB devices and are well supported on Linux systems, as are older scanners that use a real SCSI (Small Computer System Interface) interface. Scanners are supported on Linux systems through the SANE (Scanner Access Now Easy) interface and associated front-end and back-end applications. The home of the SANE project is www.sane-project.org. If you are still shopping for a scanner or are interested in whether support for a specific scanner is available under Linux, see the page at www.sane-project.org/sane-supported-devices.html, which also provides access to an easy-to-use search engine application that provides data about specific scanners.

Ubuntu systems offer two main scanning packages, both of which use the SANE drivers:

- **Simple Scan:** as the name suggests, a fast, easy-to-use scanning package that is suitable for most basic scanning needs. This scanning package is automatically installed on Ubuntu systems.

- **XSane Image Scanner:** a more powerful, but more complex scanning package that supports a wide variety of scanner configuration options, and provides both quick preview scans for alignment purposes and final scans at a variety of scan resolutions. (Through the rest of this chapter, I refer to the *XSane Image Scanner* package simply as *XSane* to save a few words.) If you want to use this scanning package, you will have to install it manually using your favorite package management software, as discussed in Chapter 19.

These two scanning packages are discussed in the following two sections. For general information about SANE and scanners on Linux, see:

- **Linux Scanner HOWTO:** `http://tldp.org/HOWTO/Scanner-HOWTO/index.html`
- **SANE FAQ:** `www.xs4all.nl/~ljm/SANE-faq.html`
- **SANE Project Site:** `www.sane-project.org`

Note

This section is not a complete guide to every nuance of scanning software for Linux. The focus in this section is to introduce the software and common controls necessary to get a scanner working reasonably on your Ubuntu system. ∎

Using Simple Scan

Simple Scan is a relatively young package that is designed to do exactly what its name suggests — provide a fast, simple software package that makes it easy to quickly scan documents, photos, or anything else. Simple Scan is installed by default on Ubuntu systems.

To use Simple Scan, first attach a scanner to your system and turn it on. Next, select Applications ➪ Graphics ➪ Simple Scan. The dialog shown in Figure 20-9 displays.

FIGURE 20-9

Simple Scan's startup dialog

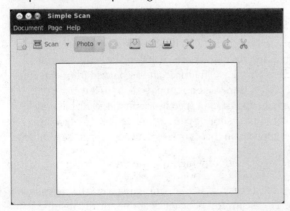

As you can see from Figure 20-9, Simple Scan's interface is quite easy to use. The icons at the top of the page enable you to control its operation without requiring advanced configuration. From left to right, these icons are the following:

- **New:** Discard any existing scanned image and create a blank document.
- **Scan:** Scan a single page or all documents that are located in the feeder of a multi-page scanner.
- **Scan Mode:** Enables you to specify whether you want to scan a document as text (black & white) or as a photo (higher resolution and in color, if supported by your scanner)
- **Stop:** Stops any in-progress scan
- **Save to File:** Displays a dialog that enables you to save the current scan to a file in any of the PDF, JPEG, or PNG formats
- **Email:** Starts your default e-mail client (Evolution by default) so that you can e-mail the scanned image to others
- **Print:** Enables you to print the current scanned image
- **Preferences:** Enables you to spefiy the scanner that you are using and the resolutions that it uses for text and photo-quality scans
- **Rotate Left:** Rotates the current image ninety degrees to the left
- **Rotate Right:** Rotates the current image ninety degress to the right
- **Crop:** Enables you to reduce the size of the current image so that it fits on a specified or custom page size. This option is best executed by selecting the target paper size from the Page ⇨ Crop menu. If you simply click the icon, Simple Scan arbitrarily selects a custom print area based on an internal analysis of image density.

Figure 20-10 shows a photo-quality scan of an old poster from my collection, Hard to imagine I was ever that young...

Simple Scan is an impressive piece of software that just does "the right thing" with little configuration and no hassle. Simple Scan is fine for 90% of my scanning needs, whether it's copying receipts or cloning photographs or old poster art. On the other hand, sometimes you may need a more powerful application that actually controls every nuance of your scanner, the dimensions and characteristics of the image that is being scanned, and so on. For these more complex needs, you'll want to install and use XSane, which is discussed in the next section.

FIGURE 20-10

A scanned poster in Simple Scan

Because Simple Scan (discussed in the previous section) is easy to use and sufficient for most people's scanning requirements, XSane is not installed by default on Ubuntu systems beginning with Ubuntu 10.04. You'll have to install it manually, using your favortie package management software, as discussed in Chapter 19.

Once you've installed XSane, you can start it by selecting Applications ➪ Graphics ➪ XSane Image Scanner. This displays an initial dialog as Xsane probes your system for available scanners and then displays a number of initial dialogs, as shown in Figure 20-11.

Using XSane

XSane has been the premiere scanning application for GNOME-based Linux systems for quite a while, but is a victim of its own success. As the definitive Linux scanning package, it has more bells, whistles, and knobs than many commercial scanning packages, and can therefore be somewhat complex to use. However, when you need to change something, chances are that XSane has a configuration mechanism for it.

To begin working with your scanner, click OK. Several dialogs are displayed on your system. You can close the Standard options and Histogram dialogs, leaving only the main XSane dialog (see Figure 20-12) and the Preview window (see Figure 20-13) on your screen.

FIGURE 20-11

The initial XSane dialog

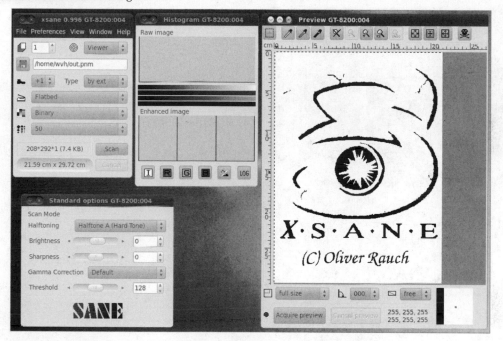

FIGURE 20-12

The primary XSane dialog

To get a *preview scan* (which is a low-resolution scan that is typically used to verify that your scanner is working, the document that you are scanning is correctly aligned, etc.), click "Acquire Preview" in the XSane Preview dialog. Your scanner should wake up, scan your document, and display a preview of that scan, as shown in Figure 20-13.

FIGURE 20-13

The XSane Preview window, showing a low-resolution, black-and-white preview

Don't panic at this point—so far, I've just used XSane's default resolution and scan settings, which are quite minimal. However, if the preview is acceptable, you can proceed to do a full scan of your document. In most cases, the preview will not be of sufficient quality, so you should return to the main XSane dialog shown in Figure 20-11 to set some common scanning configuration options. The most common settings that you will want to change are the following:

- **Scan Mode:** Enables you to select different scanning modes by clicking on a dropdown list. The icon for this option looks like black and white, grayscale, and color gradients beside each other. The available options are Binary (black and white, which is the default setting), Grayscale (many shades of gray, plus black and white), and Color (a full-color scan). Selecting either Grayscale or Color scan modes refreshes the main XSane dialog and shows additional configuration items that you can use to control brightness, contrast, colors, and so on.

- **Scan Resolution:** Enables you to control the resolution at which the image is scanned by selecting a numerical value from a dropdown list. The icon for this option looks like a number of pixels of different sizes. Possible values range from 50 DPI (dots per inch), the default value, to 3,200 DPI. The range of possible values depends on the capabilities of the scanner that you are using.

The combination of the scan mode and the scan resolution determines the size of the image file that will be produced by XSane when you do a final scan. For example, a black-and-white scan of a U.S. Letter-sized (8.25 × 11 inches) document at 50 DPI produces an image file that is 13 KB. A color scan at a resolution of 240 DPI increases the file size to 1.6 MB. Apparently, quality does, indeed, come at a price.

Once you have changed your settings, preview your image again by clicking "Acquire Preview" in the Preview window to display a new preview that should show a substantial improvement over your initial preview. Figure 20-14 shows an improved preview.

Wow, I can now even recognize myself in this ancient poster! Assuming that the new preview looks like it will be sufficient for your purposes, close the Preview window and click Scan in the main XSane dialog. The document will be scanned using the current settings. Once the scan completes, XSane displays the scan in its standard, full-screen View window, as shown in Figure 20-15.

FIGURE 20-14

A substantially improved preview in XSane

FIGURE 20-15

A final scan in the XSane viewer

Size 2008 x 2580 pixel, 8 bits/channel, 3 channels, 240 dpi x 240 dpi, 14.8 MB

You may want to iterate through several scans, adjusting things like contrast and brightness by using the controls on the main XSane dialog. When you get a scan that you are happy with, you can save the scanned image by clicking File ⇨ View, which displays a dialog that enables you to specify a filename and also the image format in which the scan will be saved.

Tip

If your Ubuntu system is having a problem locating your scanner or you need to know the name of the device node associated with your scanner, use your favorite Package Manager to install the `sane-utils` package, which provides a convenient utility called `sane-find-scanner` that does an excellent job of finding SCSI and USB scanners. Installing the package also installs man pages for `sane-scsi` and `sane-usb`, which provide a great selection of useful suggestions for resolving problems locating SCSI or USB scanners. ∎

Adding Internal Disks and CD/DVD Drives

Portable USB and FireWire hard drives are common today, as are USB flash/thumb drives (which look like small hard drives to your system). These portable, removable storage devices simplify backups, transporting large amounts of data and transferring large amounts of data from one system to another. For the most part, these removable devices are correctly identified by Ubuntu systems, which will either mount new devices or prompt you for the action to take, as described in the portions of Chapter 18 on digital device detection.

While portable, external devices are convenient, you may eventually want to add more storage to your system permanently, which usually means adding new drives to free connections that are available on your system. These interfaces are faster than the interfaces used for external storage and also keep the number of cables running to and from the exterior of your system to a minimum.

This section explains how to add new internal drives to your systems. The most common types of hard drives found in desktop and laptop PC systems today are EIDE/ATA (Enhanced Integrated Drive Electronics/Advanced Technology Attachment) and SATA (Serial Advanced Technology Attachment) drives. Because of the popularity of SATA drives, EIDE/ATA drives are also often known as PATA (Parallel Advanced Technology Attachment) drives, which highlights the basic difference between these two types of drives (parallel versus serial) and also delivers a nicely parallel acronym at the same time. SCSI (Small Computer System Interface) hard drives are another possibility, but are much less common in desktop systems, although they are still often used in server systems. Most CD and DVD drives are EIDE/ATA drives, using a standard referred to as *ATAPI*, although SCSI and SATA CD and DVD drives are also available.

To add any of these drives internally to your system, you will have to shut down the system and remove its side cover to give you access to the motherboard and to the portions of the case where hard drives can be mounted, which are usually referred to as *drive bays*.

The next few sections explain how to add extra drives of these various types to your system, describe how to identify the device nodes associated with those drives when you reboot your system, and provide an overview of partitioning and creating filesystems on these devices.

Tip

Before adding new internal disks to your system, you should modify the GRUB bootloader's configuration so that it gives you a chance to correct boot options in case something goes wrong. To do this, edit the file /etc/default/grub and comment out the following two lines (by putting a # character at the beginning of each line):

```
GRUB_HIDDEN_TIMEOUT=0
GRUB_HIDDEN_TIMEOUT_QUIET=true
```

Commenting out these lines causes GRUB to display a boot menu before showing its splash screen. If problems occur, you can edit the commands on this menu to boot your system, and then update your GRUB configuration to make your changes permanent.

After making these changes and saving the file, run the update-grub command to update the GRUB configuration files on your system. Once you've added the new drives and verified that your system boots correctly, you can un-comment these entries and rerun update-grub to hide the boot menus — until the next time that you need them, of course. ■

Adding EIDE/PATA Drives

Once your system is turned off and you have removed one of its side panels so that you have access to your motherboard, locate the IDE cables that are attached to the EIDE interfaces on your motherboard (or, in rare cases, to an IDE or EIDE controller card). IDE cables are flat, 40-pin ribbon cables with two flat, notched connectors near one end and a similar connector at the other end. Most PCs have two IDE interfaces, known as primary (IDE-1) and secondary (IDE-2). The cable from each IDE interface can be attached to a maximum of two hard or CD/DVD drives. If two drives are attached to a single cable, they must be configured as master and slave drives by connecting pins known as *jumpers* that are located on the back or bottom of the hard drive or CD-ROM drive. *Master* is the term used for the first drive on an IDE interface; *slave* is the term used for the second drive on the IDE interface.

To add a new drive to your system, you must set the jumper (or jumpers) on the new drive so that it does not conflict with any existing drive on a given IDE interface in your system. To do so, you must know how the current drives are connected. You can determine how the existing hard drive(s) and CD/DVD drive(s) are connected in one of two ways: automatically (by checking the BIOS settings on your system) or manually (by simply checking the connections and jumpers on the existing drives). Because you've (hopefully) already turned the PC off and the ways of collecting information from a PC BIOS differ depending on which BIOS your system uses, we'll focus on looking just at the cables and jumpers.

By tracing cables and examining jumpers, you can manually identify how the drives are connected. To do so, follow each of the IDE cables from your motherboard back to any hard drives or CD/DVD drives connected to them. The hard drive that your PC boots from is known as the *boot drive*, and it is usually connected as the master on the first IDE interface on your system. If your CD/DVD drive is connected to the same IDE cables as your hard drive, it is probably jumpered as the slave on the primary IDE interface (IDE-1). If your CD-ROM drive is connected to your other IDE cable (IDE-2), it is probably jumpered as the master on that interface.

Tip

If there are already two devices attached to an IDE interface and your PC was working correctly before, skip that IDE interface—it's already fully populated and correctly configured. ∎

Once you know how your current drives are connected, you can proceed to jumper your new drive so that it does not conflict with existing drives in your system. A guide to the jumpers on your hard drive that will cause the drive to be recognized as a master or slave drive is usually printed on the top of the hard drive.

Caution

Be careful when reading the jumper information; although it is usually written from left to right, just as the jumpers are physically located on the hard drive, some jumper settings are listed relative to a jumper key, which is a single pin on the left or right side of the hard drive jumpers. ∎

After you jumper your new drive, mount it in a drive bay, attach it to the selected IDE cable in your system, and provide power to the drive by connecting it to one of your system's power feeds. At this point, you can power up the system, boot into Linux, and then follow the instructions in the section later in this chapter entitled "Locating, Partitioning, and Formatting New Drives." Some common problems at this point are the following:

- If you have trouble booting your system after adding a new drive, see the section, "Troubleshooting Boot Problems after Adding New Drives," later in this chapter.

- The most common source of problems when adding a new EIDE/ATA drive to an existing system is jumpering it incorrectly. If a new drive is jumpered to be the same (master or slave) as an existing drive, your system will usually not be able to see either drive. You can verify that the new drive is jumpered, attached, and detected correctly by entering the BIOS immediately after rebooting the PC and examining the primary and secondary IDE interfaces.

- If you have problems finding the new drive after booting, reboot your system and press a key such as the F2 or Delete key to enter your system's BIOS setup screens. (A message that identifies the key that is required to access your system's BIOS is usually displayed when you boot your computer.) The Main or System section of these screens should enable you to probe your IDE or SATA drives to verify that your system can actually find them. If your system doesn't see the drive(s) at all, check the power and IDE/SATA connections to the drive.

You will not be able to use any new drive on your system until you have partitioned and formatted the drive. Some drives come pre-formatted with an NTFS filesystem, which is probably not a filesystem that you want to use on an internal drive on a Linux system. See the section later in this chapter entitled "Locating, Partitioning, and Formatting New Drives" for detailed information about partitioning and formatting your new drives.

Hard Drive Names on Linux Systems

The traditional IDE subsystem on Linux systems recognized EIDE/ATA hard drives as devices with names of the form /dev/hdX, where X was a letter that reflected the sequence in which drives were located on your system's IDE interfaces. SCSI hard drives used their driver subsystem, using names of the form /dev/sdX. SATA also used the SCSI subsystem and, therefore, followed the same naming convention as most removable Flash and USB drives. However, in 2007, the existing IDE subsystem in the kernel was replaced by a newer PATA subsystem, which uses the /dev/sdX naming convention. This is a superior subsystem, although it certainly confused many people when drives formerly known as /dev/hdX started showing up with names in the form /dev/sdX after a kernel upgrade, especially if their GRUB configuration file wasn't updated at the same time. This should all be water under the bridge now, but it's worth explaining because hard-drive naming conventions often confuse people in the first place, let alone after drives "rename themselves."

Adding SATA Drives

SATA drives are much easier to attach and use than EIDE/ATA or SCSI drives, primarily because no jumpering is required. SATA drives are automatically identified by your system based on the number of the SATA port that they are attached to. Most motherboards with SATA support have either two or four SATA ports that feature the small L-shaped SATA connector in their center. Stand-alone SATA controllers are also available that typically provide four SATA ports but can provide many more.

SATA has many advantages over traditional EIDE/ATA drives (which I'll call *PATA drives* in the rest of this section). First and foremost, each SATA drive has a separate cable connecting it to the controller, reducing the shared-cable, master/slave model used by PATA drives. Although performance is approximately the same between SATA II and PATA drives, the dedicated connection and controller for each SATA drive can provide higher overall throughput in disk-intensive environments. SATA cables can be up to 39 inches long, while PATA cables are supposed to be limited to 19 inches. The fact that SATA cables are much smaller than PATA ribbon cables makes them easier to route aesthetically within the tight confines of many computer cases. And finally, the biggest advantage of SATA over PATA drives is that SATA drives can be hot-swapped, which makes them eminently suitable for use in RAID or other environments with 24 × 7 availability requirements.

To add another SATA drive to your system, simply mount it in an available drive bay, connect it to an available SATA port, and provide power to the drive by connecting either a traditional power connector or a special SATA power connector, depending on the drive that you're using. At this point, you can power up the system, boot into Linux, and then follow the instructions in the section later in this chapter entitled "Locating, Partitioning, and Formatting New Drives." If you have problems booting your system after adding a new drive, see the section, "Troubleshooting Boot Problems after Adding New Drives," later in this chapter.

Tip

Some motherboards provide two different sets of SATA ports, one set for hardware RAID support and another set of normal SATA ports. Do not use the hardware RAID SATA ports unless you're sure that the hardware RAID controller is well supported under Linux and you're sure that you want to use hardware RAID. I usually prefer Linux software RAID to Linux hardware RAID because hardware RAID disk layouts are controller-specific. Using hardware RAID often means that if your motherboard fails, you will have to replace it with an identical motherboard or another with the same hardware RAID controller. In most cases, you will not be able to use your existing RAID drive(s) with a different hardware RAID controller. ∎

Adding SCSI Drives

Alas, poor SCSI, I knew thee well. SCSI drives have long been the traditional drive of choice for RAID boxes or in systems with 24 × 7 availability requirements. The primary reasons for this are high performance (SCSI drives are still faster than current SATA II drives), SCSI's traditional support for hot-swapping, and higher quality control (some manufacturers even offer longer warranties for SCSI drives for this reason). The downside is that SCSI drives are substantially more expensive than today's SATA II drives, which offer the same hot-swap capabilities. Some people would rather fight than switch—your call. Traditionally, only very high-end motherboards feature integrated SCSI controllers—SCSI controllers in most systems are stand-alone SCSI controller cards.

SCSI connectors and controllers vary according to the version of the SCSI standard that they conform to and the number of drives that they can support. Various types of SCSI connectors have evolved over the years, which are roughly associated with different versions of the SCSI standard and are specifically associated with different performance characteristics. The most common of connectors are Centronics-style parallel and IDC-50 connectors (typically associated with 8-bit SCSI-1 drives), DB-50 connectors (typically associated with 8-bit Fast SCSI-2 drives), and DB-68 connectors or SCA-80 (typically associated with 16-bit, Fast/Wide SCSI-3). SCSI-1 and SCSI-2 controllers support up to seven drives per controller, while SCSI-3 and later SCSI controllers support up to 15 drives per controller.

Each SCSI drive in a system must be uniquely identified by setting it to a unique ID number. In most cases, you must set one or more jumpers on the drive to indicate its ID, but if you have more money than I do and are using a multi-port SCSI controller, that controller may identify each drive based on the port that it is connected to. The last SCSI drive in a chain must also be terminated (i.e., drives that are installed sequentially, with each cabled to the next), although some drives and SCSI controllers do this automatically.

To add another SCSI drive to your system, set it to a unique ID if necessary, mount it in an available drive bay, connect it to your SCSI controller or to the next SCSI drive in a chain, and provide power to the drive by connecting a traditional power connector. Then you can power up the system, at which point you should see the BIOS on your SCSI controller identify the IDs on all connected SCSI drives. Once you boot into Linux, you can follow the instructions in the section later in this chapter entitled "Locating, Partitioning, and Formatting New Drives." If you have problems booting your system after adding a new drive, see the next section.

Troubleshooting Boot Problems After Adding New Drives

It is common that adding a new hard drive to your system will prevent it from booting immediately. Much of this has to do with settings in your computer's BIOS or other boot environment that enumerate the hard drives that are available and tell it in which order to try various disks and interfaces in order to boot. The next few sections discuss a few common problems and how to resolve them.

Changes to BIOS Hard Disk and Boot Device Priority Settings

Most BIOS menus feature a "Boot" or "Boot Settings" menu or screen that contains entries that lead to configuration screens for "Hard Disk Drives" and "Boot Device Priority." The "Hard Disk Drives" screen usually enumerates all of the hard drives in your system. Frequently, the first hard drive listed is the first that can be identified on the "Boot Device Priority" screen. Make sure that the first hard drive in this list is the drive that actually contains your operating system.

Next, make sure that the hard drive that contains your operating system is actually listed in the "Boot Device Priority" screen and that the entries on this screen appear in the right order. Many "Boot Device Priority" screens only provide three or four slots for possible boot devices, and I usually squander the first two of these for "Floppy Disk" and "CD-ROM" boot devices. Whatever boot device order you prefer, make sure that the hard drive that contains your operating system is present in this list and appears in the right sequence.

Problems After Adding IDE Drives to a SATA System

Most systems are configured to try to boot from IDE drives before SATA disks. If you have added IDE disks to a system that formerly only contained SATA drives, make sure that the sequence in which your system tries to boot from different disks is correct. I had a humorous experience a while ago when recycling some old IDE disks for use on one of my SATA systems, because I hadn't wiped the IDE disks. I'd forgotten that one of them contained an older Linux installation and was quite surprised when my Ubuntu system suddenly booted SUSE.

Problems Related to SATA Drive Name Changes

Adding SATA drives to an existing system can temporarily cause boot problems for various reasons, the most amusing of which is because of how SATA drives are detected and named. SATA disks not only use SCSI emulation (and thus have names beginning with /dev/sd), but the letter that follows /dev/sd in their names is assigned based on the sequence number of the specific SATA port that they are attached to. If whoever built your system was careful, your primary SATA disk will be attached to SATA port 1, and thus will always be assigned the name /dev/sda. If whoever built your system wasn't so careful and attached your boot drive to SATA port 4, your system will boot fine with a single drive, but adding another SATA drive will cause that drive to be assigned the name /dev/sda, and your existing SATA drive will be called /dev/sdb. Adding more than one new SATA drive will continue to demote the name of your original SATA disk. This generally confuses both the BIOS, as described in the previous paragraph, and certainly the boot loader used by Ubuntu systems, GRUB.

If you encounter this problem, there are two possible solutions:

- Open up your system again and connect your original drive to the first SATA port on your motherboard. This will guarantee that it will always be named /dev/sda. You may still have to change the BIOS settings, but you won't have to modify anything in your drive's boot configuration files.
- Change the boot settings used by the Linux GRUB boot loader to reflect the new name of your drive.

The first option is almost always preferable unless you have a very good reason for simply modifying the GRUB boot settings. If you insist on doing the second, and modifying GRUB, see the next section.

Temporarily Changing GRUB Boot Loader Information

If you need to change the GRUB boot loader's idea of the root partition on your system, first correct the boot order of the disks in your BIOS as described in the section earlier in the chapter entitled "Changes to BIOS Hard Disk and Boot Device Priority Settings." This will enable your system to begin to boot from your existing hard drive, which will almost certainly fail once GRUB tries to mount its root filesystem, which is probably identified with a name such as /dev/sda1; this is still the right partition but is now located on a disk with a different name. Ubuntu 10.04 uses UUIDs (Universal Unique Identifiers) to identify disk drives to help work around problems rated to changing drive names or ordering, but problems can still occur. The following instructions explain how to temporarily modify a boot entry in GRUB2, which is the version of GRUB used on newer Ubuntu systems.

To temporarily modify GRUB's boot settings to work around this problem, you must do the following:

1. Press Esc during the boot process to display the GRUB menu.

2. Press E to display the boot commands associated with your default boot entry.

3. Use the arrow keys to highlight the line beginning with the word *linux*.

4. Use the Backspace or Delete key to specify the name of the partition identified as the root partition (through the root= keyword). For example, if your disk was originally /dev/sda but is now /dev/sdd, the root partition is probably still identified as /dev/sda1. Change this to /dev/sdd1 and press Return to return to the Boot options screen.

Tip

If your system already had multiple disks and you were normally mounting partitions from all of them, your system may not come up in multi-user mode correctly because any partition names in your /etc/fstab file will be wrong. You may also want to temporarily add the word *single* to the end of the GRUB kernel entry to bring up the system in single-user mode so that you can correct the names of the partitions in /etc/fstab. ∎

5. Press *Ctrl-X* to boot using your modified GRUB boot options.

Once your system comes up correctly, you can use a text editor to permanently modify the file /etc/default/grub which is GRUB's configuration file. You should not only modify the boot settings for your default GRUB boot selection, but also modify the template values in this file that are used to prepare a new entry each time a new kernel is installed on your system.

You should also check the contents of the /etc/fstab file on your system and make sure that it reflects the current disk names in use on your system. It is not uncommon for a system to come up without swap space and identify its root partition incorrectly (in commands such as df) because entries in the /etc/fstab file are incorrect. During the boot process, the root partition is already mounted by the time the /etc/fstab file is used to mount other disks.

Tip

If you neglected to enable GRUB's boot menu as suggested at the beginning of this section, you can resolve boot problems by booting from an Ubuntu Desktop Live CD, manually mounting the partition that contains your system's /boot and /etc directories, and execute the chroot **command to temporarily make the directory where you mounted this partition into your root filesystem. You can then make the modifications suggested at the beginning of this section and run the** update-grub **command to update the system's boot files. You can then exit from the chroot shell, unmount the specified partition, and reboot your system. You should then see the GRUB menus, and be able to take advantage of the suggestions given in this section.** ■

Problems After Adding PATA/SATA Drives to an SCSI System

The last common problem that you may encounter occurs when adding SATA or PATA drives to a system that boots from SCSI disks. Both PATA and SATA drives now use the same naming convention as SCSI disks. PATA and SATA disks are also named before SCSI disks during the kernel boot process. The combination of these two facts means that adding one or more PATA/SATA disks will cause your SCSI disk to be renamed. For example, if your system was configured to boot from the real SCSI disk, /dev/sda, and you add two SATA drives, the name of your SCSI disk will now be /dev/sdc. This leads to the same sort of BIOS and GRUB boot loader problems discussed earlier in the "Problems Related to SATA Drive Name Changes" section, but you will have to solve them using the solution described in the section, "Temporarily Changing GRUB Boot Loader Information." See that section for an explanation of how to modify your GRUB settings and resolve this sort of problem.

Locating, Partitioning, and Formatting New Drives

After rebooting your system to locate new internal drives, you'll probably want to use the storage that those new disks provide. This requires that you identify the Linux device nodes associated with them, and then use various software packages to partition them and format those partitions using your filesystem of choice.

Note

As you might expect, there are some great command-line utilities for displaying information about the disks that are attached to your system, partitioning them, and formatting those partitions so that they contain a filesystem that you can mount in order to actually use the storage that they offer. Unfortunately, the story is not so good for graphical utilities that enable you to do the same sorts of things. Earlier releases of Ubuntu featured a graphical Disks utility on the System ➪ Administration menu (which you could execute from the command line as disk-admin**), but it is no longer provided on Ubuntu systems, and its most likely replacements, Disk Manager (**http://flomertens.free.fr/disk-manager/index.html **or** https://launchpad.net/disk-manager**, for the Ubuntu take on it) or GNOME Format (**http://live.gnome.org/gnome-format**), are not part of the Ubuntu distribution yet.** ■

The next three sections explain how to use the GNOME Partition Editor and command-line utilities to figure out what drives are attached to your system, the partitions they contain, how to partition or re-partition those drives, and how to format those partitions.

Note

Chapter 4, "Basic Linux System Concepts," provides an overview of Linux system concepts such as disk partitions, disk geometry, and related terms such as sectors and cylinders, filesystems, filesystem mountpoints, and so on. If you encounter unfamiliar terms in this section, refer to Chapter 4 for more information. ∎

Using the GNOME Partition Editor to Examine and Format Drives

The GNOME Partition Editor is a graphical front-end to the command-line parted tool, and is a great tool for use on Ubuntu systems of any type. This tool is not installed by default, but you can resolve that shortcoming by using your Package Management tool of choice, discussed in Chapter 19, to install the gparted package. Once installed, the GNOME Partition Editor provides a graphical view of all of the storage devices that are currently installed on your system and makes it easy for you to determine basic information about their capacity, any partitions that they contain, and the Linux device nodes associated with the device and each partition. It also enables you to add, remove, and format hard disk partitions.

On an Ubuntu system, you can start the GNOME Partition Editor by selecting System ➪ Administration ➪ GParted. After entering your administrative password, the dialog shown in Figure 20-16 appears.

FIGURE 20-16

Device information in the GNOME Partition Editor

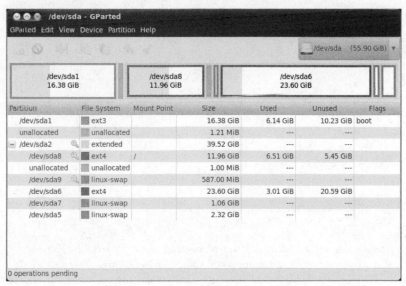

The panes display information about the storage device that is currently selected. The dropdown list in the upper-right corner lists all of the storage devices that are currently detected on your system, and provides information about the storage capacity of each device and the Linux device node through which that device can be accessed. Once a device is selected from the dropdown list, the pane at the bottom displays a summary of how that storage device is currently partitioned, as shown in Figure 20-16. The top pane shows a graphical view of the partitions on the selected disk, while the bottom pane identifies each partition, the device node through which it can be accessed, its format, and so on. For example, the partition list for the disk that is selected in Figure 20-15 shows that it is the boot disk for the current system, because one of its partitions is mounted as / and, therefore, contains the current system's root filesystem.

After adding a new disk to your system, select each device in the dropdown list to examine its current partitioning until you find the device that is associated with the new drive. Figure 20-17 shows the entry for a new disk that has not been partitioned.

FIGURE 20-17

Information about a new, unformatted disk

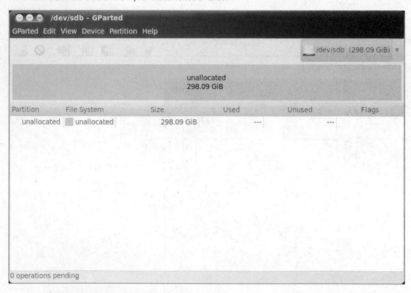

When working with a new, unformatted disk, you will first need to create a partition table so that you can subsequently create one or more partitions on the disk. To do this, select Device ➪ Create Partition Table. A dialog appears, warning you that creating a partition table on the device will erase all data on the disk (because doing so deletes any existing partitioning information that may currently be present on this disk).

After double- (and triple-) checking that you are, indeed, working with the correct disk, click Create to create a partition table on the device. Once the partition table has been created, a screen like the one shown in Figure 20-16 reappears. You're now ready to begin creating partitions on your new disk.

Note

By default, Linux systems use a partition table that is in the traditional MS-DOS format, which makes it possible to use disks that contain both Linux and MS-DOS/Windows partitions in a computer system that boots both Linux and Microsoft Windows. You can also create partition tables in different formats in the GNOME Partition Editor, which enable these disks to be used in systems that can boot both Linux and other operating systems, such as Solaris, AIX, and so on. To select one of these other partition table formats, click on the arrow beside the Advanced entry on the warning dialog displayed during the partition table creation process, and select one of the other partition table formats. Using a partition table format other than MS-DOS is extremely uncommon, but the option is available if you need it. ■

To create a partition on the current disk, first select the entry for the unallocated space on that disk in either the graphical or list portion of the dialog shown in Figure 20-15. Next, either right-click and select New from the context-sensitive menu that displays, or select the Partition ⇨ New menu item to display the dialog that enables you to specify the characteristics and size of that partition, as shown in Figure 20-18.

FIGURE 20-18

Creating a partition

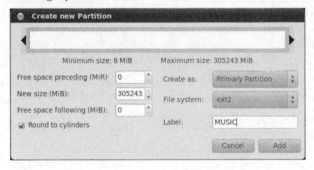

The dialog enables you to specify several different types of information about the partition:

- **Free Space Preceding:** Enables you to leave some free space on the disk before the partition that you are creating. Wanting to do this is uncommon, but it can be useful if you are formatting a disk upon which you subsequently want to install Microsoft Windows, which generally wants to be the first operating system on the disk (the big bully). Leaving free space before your new partition will leave unallocated space on the disk, which Windows can subsequently format and use.

- **New Size:** The size of the partition that you are creating. By default, the dialog assigns all available free space to any new partition. If you want to create multiple partitions on your disk, you need to reduce the number that is initially displayed to leave unallocated space in which you can create one or more other partitions. If you reduce the size of the partition that you are creating so that it does not use all of the unallocated space on the disk, the graphical display at the top of the dialog changes to reflect the size of the partition that you are creating and the amount of unallocated space that remains on the disk.

- **Free Space Following:** Enables you to leave some free space on the disk after the partition that you are creating. The number in this field is adjusted automatically if you do not allocate all of the available space in the unallocated space that you selected before beginning the process of creating a new partition.

- **Round to Cylinders:** Selected by default, this option causes the size of new partitions to be rounded to an appropriate number of disk cylinders to enable Linux to use your disk as efficiently as possible without wasting space.

- **Create as:** Enables you to specify the type of partition that you want to create. In most cases, you will be creating a primary partition, but if you are creating more than three partitions on your disk, you will need to create an extended partition in which you can subsequently create logical partitions.

- **Filesystem:** The type of filesystem that you want to create on the selected partition. Choices are ext2, ext3, fat16, jfs, linux-swap, ntfs, reiserfs, xfs, or unformatted. The default option is ext2, although you will probably want to select ext3 when creating a Linux filesystem to take advantage of some of the advanced features like journaling. To create a partition that you can access natively from a Microsoft Windows system, you will need to select either fat32 or ntfs. (fat16 filesystems can also be used by Windows, but they are tiny and antiquated — don't use them unless you have some specific reason to do so.) Selecting any entry other than unformatted causes the GNOME Partition Editor to format your new partition, creating a filesystem of the specified type in the new partition.

- **Label:** An optional text string that is used as the label for the partition. This can be handy if you use disk labels to identify partitions in your /etc/fstab file, as discussed in Chapter 4.

To create the new partition with the specified characteristics, click Add. The dialog shown in Figure 20-16 is re-displayed, but it has been updated to reflect the new partition that you have specified, as shown in Figure 20-19.

The pane at the bottom of Figure 20-19 lists scheduled operations for your disk, while the graphical and partition list information reflects what your disk will look like once those operations have been completed. In other words, your new partition is scheduled to be created, but it has not yet actually been created. This enables you to define multiple partitions and create them all at one. To proceed with any scheduled operations, click Apply. A confirmation dialog appears, asking if you're sure that you want to perform the specified operation(s). Click Apply to proceed. A progress dialog is displayed while the scheduled operations are being performed. Once the scheduled operations are completed, click Close to dismiss the progress dialog, and the GNOME Partition Editor dialog reappears, showing your new partition(s), as shown in Figure 20-20.

FIGURE 20-19

Partitions and planned operations in the GNOME Partition Editor

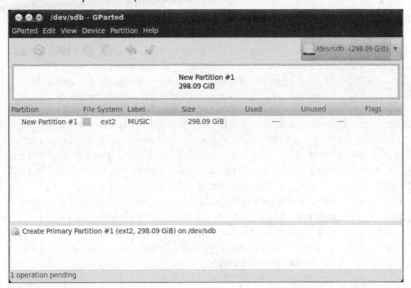

FIGURE 20-20

The GNOME Partition Editor after creating a new partition

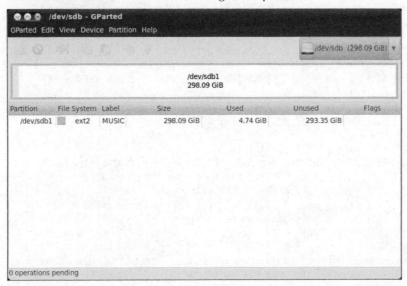

Using Command-Line Tools to Identify Drives and Partitions

The df command provides an easy way to examine all of the disk partitions and associated file-systems that are currently mounted and in use on your system. Unfortunately, commands like df don't provide information about devices that are newly attached to your system (and that therefore may not contain partitions yet) or devices that are attached to your system but whose filesystems are not mounted. Luckily, Linux provides some easy ways of finding all of the storage devices on your system, regardless of whether they're formatted, partitioned, mounted, or not. You'll have to put up with a small bit of cryptic command-line magic, but you're already at least an apprentice Linux wizard, right? After all, you just put a new drive in your system!

The easiest way to determine the device nodes associated with the storage devices in your system is to look through the kernel boot messages for patterns that match the strings associated with those devices. You can quickly look through the in-memory portion of these messages by using a command called dmesg. Because you know that IDE devices traditionally had names that began with *hd* and are followed by some other letter, that SATA and SCSI devices have names that begin with *sd* and are followed by some letter, and that that IDE devices on newer kernels follow the same naming convention as SATA and SCSI drives, you can use a pattern such as '[hs]d[a-z]: ' to see what messages match these device names. If you don't speak Linux regular expressions fluently, the string '[hs]d[a-z]: ' means, "match any sequence of characters that begins with an h or an s, followed by the letter d, followed by any character between a and z (inclusive), followed by a colon, followed by a space." That was easy, wasn't it?

The result of searching for this string in the output of the dmesg command on a sample system is pretty much exactly what you'd hope for, as the following example shows:

```
$ dmesg | grep 'hs]d[a-z]: '
[  846.564436] SCSI device sda: 234441648 512-byte hdwr sectors (120034 MB)
[  846.564453] SCSI device sda: drive cache: write back
[  846.564514] SCSI device sda: 234441648 512-byte hdwr sectors (120034 MB)
[  846.564526] SCSI device sda: drive cache: write back
[  846.564531]  sda: sda1 sda2
[  846.575071] SCSI device sdb: 156299375 512-byte hdwr sectors (80025 MB)
[  846.575086] SCSI device sdb: drive cache: write back
[  846.578550] SCSI device sdb: 156299375 512-byte hdwr sectors (80025 MB)
[  846.578826] SCSI device sdb: drive cache: write back
[  846.578830]  sdb: sdb1 sdb2 < sdb5 >
[  848.272430] hdc: DVDRW 16X16X, ATAPI CD/DVD-ROM drive
[  848.952828] hdc: ATAPI 48X DVD-ROM DVD-R CD-R/RW drive, 2048kB Cache
[  852.169148] SCSI device sdc: 8910423 512-byte hdwr sectors (4562 MB)
[  852.170635] SCSI device sdc: drive cache: write back
[  852.171452] SCSI device sdc: 8910423 512-byte hdwr sectors (4562 MB)
[  852.172941] SCSI device sdc: drive cache: write back
[  852.172943]  sdc: sdc1 sdc2
```

On this system, these messages tell you that three storage devices using SCSI device-naming conventions have been found, plus an old IDE/ATA CD/DVD-ROM drive that is available as /dev/hdc. The first storage device, /dev/sda, doesn't appear to contain any partitions. The second storage device, /dev/sdb, contains two physical partitions: /dev/sdb1 and /dev/sdb2, and a third virtual partition, /dev/sdb5. (This probably means that the partition /dev/sdb2 is an extended partition that contains the partition /dev/sdb5 — more about that in a moment.) The third storage device, /dev/sdc, contains two physical partitions: /dev/sdc1 and /dev/sdc2.

You can use the fdisk command and its -1 (list) option to get more detailed information about any of these storage devices. For example, fdisk provides the following information about the partitions on it:

```
$ sudo fdisk -1 /dev/sdb
Disk /dev/sdb: 80.0 GB, 80025280000 bytes
255 heads, 63 sectors/track, 9729 cylinders
Units = cylinders of 16065 * 512 = 8225280 bytes

   Device Boot     Start      End     Blocks    Id  System
/dev/sdb1    *         1     9566   76838863+   83  Linux
/dev/sdb2            956/     9729    1309297+    5  Extended
/dev/sdb5            9567     9729    1309266    82  Linux swap / Solaris
```

This shows that, as suspected, the partition /dev/sdb2 is an extended partition, which is a physical partition that can contain other, virtual partitions, and the partition /dev/sdb5 is a partition that was created inside that extended partition.

Your mind may be a bit numb after the preceding combination of arcane command-line syntax and kernel log messages, but this section has given you some extremely powerful insights into your system and the storage devices that it contains. Because one of these storage devices, the SATA drive /dev/sda in the first example in this section, didn't contain any partitions, it is still quite useless to your system. The next section explains how to partition and format a newly added disk from the command line.

Using Command-Line Utilities to Partition and Format Drives

Chapter 4 introduced basic computer system terms such as disks, partitions, and filesystems. As discussed in this chapter, you cannot use the storage on a disk until it has been partitioned and each of those partitions has been formatted for use, typically as a filesystem. This section explains how to actually do that using the command-line commands fdisk, mkfs, and (occasionally) mkswap. These commands do the following:

- fdisk: Creates and manipulates partitions on a specified disk. We all have our own ideas about what the *f* stands for, but it's probably *format*.
- mkfs: Creates a filesystem of a specified type on a specified partition
- mkswap: Formats a specified partition for use as a Linux swap partition, which is a special partition that your Ubuntu system can use as virtual memory

Once you've added a new disk to your system, the first thing that you'll want to do is partition it. The previous section used the fdisk command to simply list the available partitions on a specific storage device — now let's actually make it do some work. The following example creates two partitions on the disk /dev/sdb.

To partition a disk using fdisk, do the following:

1. Use the sudo command to start the fdisk command, supplying the name of the disk that you want to partition as an argument, as in the following example:

```
$ sudo fdisk /dev/sdb
The number of cylinders for this disk is set to 14593.
There is nothing wrong with that, but this is larger than 1024,
and could in certain setups cause problems with:
1) software that runs at boot time (e.g., old versions of LILO)
2) booting and partitioning software from other OSs
   (e.g., DOS FDISK, OS/2 FDISK)
Command (m for help):
```

The last line of the sample output is fdisk's command prompt, which shows that it is waiting for a command.

2. Use the p (print) command to display a list of any existing partitions that may already be on the disk. After all, you don't want to accidentally try to create partitions on the wrong disk or destroy any existing data. This command and its output look like the following:

```
Command (m for help): p
Disk /dev/sda: 120.0 GB, 120034123776 bytes
255 heads, 63 sectors/track, 14593 cylinders
Units = cylinders of 16065 * 512 = 8225280 bytes
   Device Boot      Start         End      Blocks   Id  System
Command (m for help):
```

Good. As the total lack of partitions shows, this disk does not currently contain any partitions.

3. Use the n (new) command to define a new partition:

```
Command (m for help): n
Command action
   e   extended
   p   primary partition (1-4)
```

4. Entering this command prompts you for the type of partition that you want to create, either e (extended) or p (physical). Use the p command to create a physical partition:

```
p
Partition number (1-4):
```

5. Specifying that you want to create a physical partition prompts you for the number of the partitions that you want to create. Linux disks can contain only four physical partitions, one of which can be an extended partition. Create partition number 1 by entering **1**, as in the following example:

```
1
First cylinder (1 14593, default 1):
```

6. Identifying the number of the physical partition that you want to create prompts you for the physical disk block at which the partition begins, and displays the range of possible values (1–14,593, in this case). Press Return to accept the default value of 1:

```
Using default value 1
Last cylinder or +size or +sizeM or +sizeK (1-14593, default 14593):
```

7. When creating partitions, you can define them in terms of the disk blocks at which they begin or end, or you can define them in terms of the blocks at which they begin and the size of the partition. Enter **+30G** to indicate that you want to create a 30-GB partition:

```
Last cylinder or +size or +sizeM or +sizeK (1-14593, default 14593): +30G
Command (m for help):
```

8. This completes the information required to create the partition, but doesn't tell you much about whether this actually succeeded. Use the p command again to list any partitions that are currently defined:

```
Command (m for help): p
Disk /dev/sda: 120.0 GB, 120034123776 bytes
255 heads, 63 sectors/track, 14593 cylinders

Units = cylinders of 16065 * 512 = 8225280 bytes
   Device Boot      Start         End      Blocks   Id  System
/dev/sda1               1        3648    29302528+  83  Linux
```

Sure enough, a 30-GB partition has been defined as the partition /dev/sda1, the first partition on your disk.

Tip

At this point, no physical changes to the partitioning of your disk have been made. Any proposed changes are only in memory and will be discarded unless you write your changes to disk before exiting the `fdisk` command. ∎

9. Repeat this process to create a second, smaller partition: no play-by-play this time. The complete sequence of prompts and commands used to do this is the following:

```
Command (m for help): n
```

```
Command action
   e   extended
   p   primary partition (1-4)
p
Partition number (1-4): 2
First cylinder (3649-14593, default 3649):
Using default value 3649
Last cylinder or +size or +sizeM or +sizeK (3649-14593, default 14593): +1G
```

10. This completes the information required to create the second partition, but again, doesn't tell you much about whether it actually succeeded. Use the p command again to list any partitions that are currently defined:

```
Command (m for help): p

Disk /dev/sda: 120.0 GB, 120034123776 bytes
255 heads, 63 sectors/track, 14593 cylinders
Units = cylinders of 16065 * 512 = 8225280 bytes

   Device Boot      Start         End      Blocks   Id  System
/dev/sda1               1        3648    29302528+  83  Linux
/dev/sda2            3649        3771      987997+  83  Linux
 Command (m for help):
```

Sure enough, you now have both a 30-GB partition and a second 1-GB partition.

11. Now, write these changes to disk and exit the fdisk command, because these examples are sufficient for my purposes in this section. You use the w (write) command to write partition changes to the disk and exit the fdisk command:

```
Command (m for help): w
The partition table has been altered!

Calling ioctl() to re-read partition table.
Syncing disks.
```

Congratulations, you've just manually partitioned a disk. Normally, I wouldn't have left unused space on this disk, but I'm only doing this as an example, and I can always rerun fdisk to create additional partitions in the remaining space.

The next step is to format each defined partition either as a filesystem or as additional swap space. Graphical utilities usually do this for you when creating partitions, but things aren't quite as user-friendly from the command line. To be honest, you'll very rarely create additional swap partitions after you've initially installed your system, but I want to make sure that you know how to do it just in case. 99.9 percent of the time, you'll be creating filesystems on the partitions of the disks that you add to your system, so that you can mount them to increase the amount of available storage on your system.

Creating a filesystem is done using the mkfs utility, which is actually just a wrapper for other commands that create different types of filesystems. On most Linux systems, you will probably be creating filesystems in any of the following formats: ext2, ext3, JFS, ReiserFS, Windows Virtual FAT (vfat), or XFS. These types of filesystems were explained in the section of Chapter 4 entitled "Local Filesystems: Standard and Journaling." To create any of these types of filesystems using the default options for that type of filesystem, you simply specify the type of filesystem that you want to create using the mkfs command's -t (type) option. The following example shows the command and output used to create an ext3 filesystem on the partition /dev/sda1:

```
$ sudo mkfs -t ext3 /dev/sda1
mke2fs 1.41.3 (12-Oct-2008)
Filesystem label=
OS type: Linux
Block size=4096 (log=2)
Fragment size=4096 (log=2)
3662848 inodes, 7325632 blocks
366281 blocks (5.00%) reserved for the super user
First data block=0
224 block groups
32768 blocks per group, 32768 fragments per group
16352 inodes per group
Superblock backups stored on blocks:
    32768, 98304, 163840, 229376, 294912, 819200, 884736, 1605632,
        2654208, 4096000
Writing inode tables:   224/224
Creating journal (32768 blocks): done
Writing superblocks and filesystem accounting information: done
This filesystem will be automatically checked every 25 mounts or
180 days, whichever comes first. Use tune2fs -c or -i to override.
```

That's all there is to it! You can now mount this partition temporarily by using the mount command, or permanently add it to the list of filesystems that will be mounted each time you boot your system. Both of these concepts were explained in Chapter 4.

The mkswap command enables you to format a specified partition in a special way so that it can be used as swap space for use by your system's virtual memory manager. As an example, the command used to create a swap partition on /dev/sda2 and the output from that command are the following:

```
# mkswap /dev/sda2
Setting up swapspace version 1, size = 1011703 kB
no label, UUID=731c0f53-bf25-4f91-9ac5-73a2b5bef1eb
```

You can begin using this swap space immediately by executing the command swapon /dev/sda2. To add this swap space to your system permanently, add it to your system's /etc/fstab file, as described in Chapter 4.

Using PCMCIA Cards

PCMCIA (Personal Computer Memory Card International Association) cards are the original mechanism designed to support removable and insertable interfaces in portable computer systems. PCMCIA cards are now often just called *PC Cards* because no one can ever remember what the acronym means (as suggested by the optional PCMCIA expansion, "People Can't Memorize Computer Industry Acronyms"). Thanks to the rise of USB, PCMCIA cards aren't as common as they once were, but it's still useful to talk about them in case you're installing Ubuntu on an older laptop.

PCMCIA cards are available that provide wired and wireless network interfaces, modems, SCSI, USB, and FireWire interfaces for computer systems that don't have them, and so on. With the 2.6 kernel, the traditional Linux PCMCIA support package was integrated into the hotplug system to support the creation of appropriate device nodes when PCMCIA cards are inserted.

The primary application to identify any PCMCIA cards inserted in your system is the pccardctl application (formerly known as *cardctl*). However, changes to how the kernel handles PCMCIA devices mean that this utility may not return detailed information about a PCMCIA card. To see what cards are present in your system and to display summary information about them, execute the pccardctl ident command. That will return something like the following:

```
$ pccardctl ident
Socket 0:
  no product info available
Socket 1:
  product info: " LEXAR ATA FLASH CARD    ", " STORM ", "TE01"
  manfid: 0x4e01, 0x0200
  function: 4 (fixed disk)
```

This shows that I have two PCMCIA cards inserted but that no information is available about the first one. Some of the other pccardctl commands may provide more information. The pccardctl ls command, for instance, displays the following:

```
$ sudo pccardctl ls
Socket 0 Bridge:       [yenta_cardbus]    (bus ID: 0000:02:03.0)
  CardBus card -- see "lspci" for more information
Socket 1 Bridge:       [yenta_cardbus]    (bus ID: 0000:02:03.1)
Socket 1 Device 0: [pata_pcmcia]   (bus ID:  1.0)
```

This shows that the PCMCIA network card in my first PCMCIA slot is being handled as a PCI card, while the compact flash card is being handled by the Parallel IDE (PATA) subsystem.

In most cases, the hotplug/udev subsystems will automatically create necessary device nodes, using the standard mechanisms to notify you when new PCMCIA storage devices are attached, when new PCMCIA wireless interfaces appear, and so on.

Adding PCI Cards

PCI cards are slightly different animals from most of the devices I've discussed elsewhere in this chapter, because they typically provide support for other devices, such as speakers (PCI sound cards) and storage devices (PCI USB, FireWire, or SCSI cards), or support for basic devices such as modems, additional serial or parallel ports, and so on. Your system must be turned off in order to add a PCI card, and discovering a new PCI card itself during the boot process isn't a notable event. The information that may appear in the kernel log related to new PCI cards is more commonly the discovery of devices that are attached to them, such as a modem, serial ports, disk drives, and so on.

If you have problems accessing newly-inserted PCI cards or accessing the devices attached to them, it is useful to be able to list the PCI devices found in your system in order to verify that the cards have been correctly inserted and identified by the system. The command used to do this is the `lspci` command, which displays output like the following:

```
$ lspci

0000:00:00.0 RAM memory: nVidia Corporation C51 Host Bridge (rev a2)
0000:00:00.1 RAM memory: nVidia Corporation C51 Memory Controller 0 (rev a2)
0000:00:00.2 RAM memory: nVidia Corporation C51 Memory Controller 1 (rev a2)
0000:00:00.3 RAM memory: nVidia Corporation C51 Memory Controller 5 (rev a2)
0000:00:00.4 RAM memory: nVidia Corporation C51 Memory Controller 4 (rev a2)
0000:00:00.5 RAM memory: nVidia Corporation C51 Host Bridge (rev a2)
0000:00:00.6 RAM memory: nVidia Corporation C51 Memory Controller 3 (rev a2)
0000:00:00.7 RAM memory: nVidia Corporation C51 Memory Controller 2 (rev a2)
0000:00:02.0 PCI bridge: nVidia Corporation C51 PCI Express Bridge (rev a1)
0000:00:03.0 PCI bridge: nVidia Corporation C51 PCI Express Bridge (rev a1)
0000:00:04.0 PCI bridge: nVidia Corporation C51 PCI Express Bridge (rev a1)
0000:00:05.0 VGA controller: nVidia Corporation C51 PCI Express Bridge
0000:00:09.0 RAM memory: nVidia Corporation MCP51 Host Bridge (rev a2)
0000:00:0a.0 ISA bridge: nVidia Corporation MCP51 LPC Bridge (rev a2)
0000:00:0a.1 SMBus: nVidia Corporation MCP51 SMBus (rev a2)
0000:00:0b.0 USB Controller: nVidia Corporation MCP51 USB Controller (rev a2)
0000:00:0b.1 USB Controller: nVidia Corporation MCP51 USB Controller (rev a2)
0000:00:0d.0 IDE interface: nVidia Corporation MCP51 IDE (rev a1)
0000:00:0e.0 IDE interface: nVidia Corporation MCP51 Serial ATA Controller
0000:00:0f.0 IDE interface: nVidia Corporation MCP51 Serial ATA Controller
0000:00:10.0 PCI bridge: nVidia Corporation MCP51 PCI Bridge (rev a2)
0000:00:10.1 0403: nVidia Corporation MCP51 High Definition Audio (rev a2)
0000:00:14.0 Bridge: nVidia Corporation MCP51 Ethernet Controller (rev a1)
0000:00:18.0 Host bridge: HyperTransport Technology Configuration
0000:00:18.1 Host bridge: [Athlon64/Opteron] Address Map
0000:00:18.2 Host bridge: [Athlon64/Opteron] DRAM Controller
0000:00:18.3 Host bridge: K8 [Athlon64/Opteron] Miscellaneous Control
0000:04:05.0 FireWire (IEEE 1394): VIA, Inc. IEEE 1394 Host Controller
0000:04:08.0 SCSI storage controller: LSI Logic / Symbios Logic 53c895
0000:04:09.0 Ethernet controller: 3Com Corporation 3c595 100BaseTX [Vortex]
```

Although this output is somewhat ugly, it is easy enough to scan to determine if your new card has been detected. If it has, you should proceed to the configuration utility associated with the capability or type of device that the PCI card provides.

Examining and Troubleshooting Devices Graphically

Ubuntu systems provide a great graphical utility called the *Device Manager* that enables you to browse, navigate through, and explore the hardware on your system from your system's point of view. This utility isn't installed by default, but you can install it using your favorite Package Management software (as discussed in Chapter 19) by installing the `gnome-device-manager` package on an Ubuntu system. Once it is installed, select Applications ➪ System Tools ➪ Device Manager on an Ubuntu system to start this tool, which displays the initial dialog shown in Figure 20-21.

FIGURE 20-21

Ubuntu's Device Manager

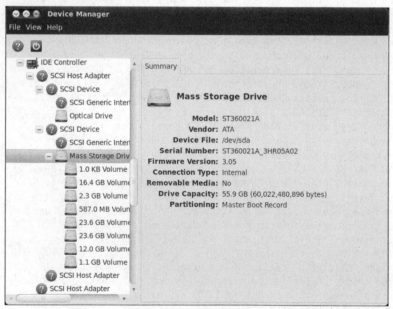

Once the Device Manager is displayed, you can use the pane at the left to scroll or drill down to examine any of the basic devices provided by your system or attached to any of its interfaces. As you select different devices, appropriate tabs display in the Device Manager's right pane. The right pane typically provides a general Device information tab and an Advanced tab, which provides additional details about a selected device or interface.

The information that this utility provides can be quite useful in determining how — or if — your system's hardware is being recognized, which can help you in terms of knowing where to start when trying to resolve problems with new hardware. Seeing how your system recognizes, organizes, and uses hardware is also just plain interesting to many of us.

Summary

This chapter explained how to add various types of hardware to your system, ranging from removable storage that you want to use only temporarily, to more permanently attached devices like printers, new internal hard drives, and scanners.

The next chapter explores how to secure your Ubuntu system. Although Linux is generally immune to most of the types of viruses, Trojans, and spyware that infest the Internet (and most Microsoft Windows systems), network security is as critical on a Linux system as it is on any other type of computer system that may be directly connected to the Internet. Hundreds of books are available that are dedicated to network and computer security, but the next chapter provides a basic explanation of the key concepts and concerns, explaining basic ways in which you may want to secure your system and highlighting areas that you may want to pursue further.

Network Configuration and Security

Almost from the very beginning of home computing in the 1970s, personal computers have reached out to touch other types of computer systems. Long before ISPs, and before the Internet even existed, home computer fans used modems to access bulletin board systems, remote mainframe or minicomputers, and ancient content providers like Compuserve and AOL, using various terminal emulation programs to communicate with each other, transfer files, and so on. Early store-and-forward mechanisms such as the Unix-to-Unix Calling Program (UUCP) and FidoNet provided great ways of disseminating files and other information across slow networks of computer systems that were *networks* only in the sense that they knew each other's phone numbers.

The conversion of the ARPANET to the Internet and its resultant commercialization gave birth to the notion of *ISPs*—commercial Internet service providers—who provided a mechanism for home computers to directly access the Internet, albeit through kludgey point-to-point solutions that still depended on a modem and thus provided Internet surfing speeds that were only guaranteed (supposedly) to be greater than zero. Regardless, the advent of the ISP ended the concept of the PC as an asynchronous island, making it a real participant in the Internet, even if slowly.

As ISPs surfaced and became a fundamental utility for many home computer users, networking and PC hardware costs continued to drop, approaching the commodity hardware pricing normally associated with toasters and refrigerators. The reality of more and more home computer users, even in the same homes, introduced the notion of the *home computer network*, often stand-alone or with a modem still connecting specific systems to the Internet by functioning as a 9,600- or 56-KB gateway to the Internet via an ISP.

IN THIS CHAPTER

Graphical tools for network configuration

Traditional network configuration files

Testing network interfaces

Tips for securing your network

Installing a firewall

Broadband Ethernet, even cheaper wired network hardware, and the explosive growth of wireless networking have made networking a true reality for many home computer users. Home computer systems may now have real IP addresses and functional connection speeds to the Internet and are also commonly members of home computer networks that share those connections to the Internet using mechanisms such as Native Address Translation (NAT). If you're new to networking, the first section of this chapter provides an overview of basic networking concepts and terminology.

Better networking and network access come at a price. Ubiquitous networking gives thousands of "randoms" access to your computer system through a real IP address or Web server and other network processes. Most of them could care less, some are simply curious, and others are downright malicious. The last set gives everyone else a bad name by actively trying to break into computer systems to exploit them in some fashion. I have no problem with hackers who are simply curious about what's out there — exploration has always been a fundamental part of the human condition. Real *hackers* are the electronic equivalent of the National Geographic Society or *Star Trek*, boldly going where no person has gone before. People who break into systems to damage or exploit them, however, are *crackers*, who give everyone else a bad name.

Unfortunately, there are plenty of unscrupulous crackers who would love to break into your machine and damage it or turn it into some sort of zombie system, either to supposedly demonstrate their cleverness or to somehow make a buck. Sigh. Ubiquitous networking begets the easy availability of tools that enable this sort of thing. The people that use them are often so-called *script kiddies*, who use existing tools to demonstrate cleverness in the same way that giving a child an Uzi demonstrates marksmanship.

The bottom line of ubiquitous networking is that security becomes everyone's job. If you live in a small town that considers taking two newspapers from the box on the corner a serious crime, locking your door at night may seem silly. Unfortunately, when you use a personal computer with network access, you are part of the big city known as the *Internet*. The administrators of enterprise and academic systems that require continuous access to the Internet have known this for a long time. Sadly enough, nowadays you, your parents, and even your grandmother have to worry about it, too. Security is more of a concern today than it has ever been before, and tomorrow will just be worse.

This chapter gives a basic introduction to networking, explains the tools that Ubuntu Linux provides to manually and graphically configure and test your network, and (most importantly) provides some general guidelines on how to secure your system to protect it as well as anyone can. There's an old saying in the IT business that the only truly secure system is one that isn't connected to anything. Although this is true, it's also impractical. There are easy rules to follow to minimize the chances that your system will be broken into. You're already running Ubuntu, which puts you miles ahead of the millions of vulnerable Microsoft Windows users out there.

Networking 101

Most modern computer systems can communicate with other systems and devices over a type of network called *Ethernet*, using the Transmission Control Protocol/Internet Protocol (TCP/IP) and

User Datagram Protocol (UDP) protocols. Ethernet and TCP/IP are the fundamental underpinnings of the Internet, which almost everyone wants (or needs) a connection to today.

Early home Internet connectivity was primarily done through dial-up connections, which emulated Ethernet, and unless you were a serious computer geek, developer, or researcher, a home network was somewhat rare, but the advent of broadband access to the Internet through cable and telephone providers changed all that. As mentioned in the introduction to this chapter, home networks are becoming more common, but most people have never needed to set one up before now. If you use a single PC, Mac, or workstation as your sole home machine, a straight connection to a cable or DSL modem works just fine. However, the instant you want to enable multiple machines to communicate over a home network, you may encounter unfamiliar terms like *hubs*, *switches*, *10-BaseT*, *RJ-45*, *crossover cables*, *uplink ports*, *packets*, *gateways*, *routers*, *Cat 5*, and a variety of others that pass for popular nouns among nerdier users. This section provides a quick overview of these terms. It tells you how to set up a simple home network and makes you comfortable with the network-related terms that are used throughout this book. For more detailed information, consult any of the hundreds of books available on home networking.

The basic element of a modern network connection is a standard Ethernet cable, which is just a length of multi-strand cable with connectors on either end that enable you to connect a network card in your personal computer (or whatever type) to another network device. The most common connectors used today are plastic connectors known as *RJ-45 connectors*, which are transparent plastic jacks that look like fatter versions of a standard telephone cable connector. Ethernet cables that use these connectors are often known as *10-BaseT*, *100-BaseT*, or even *1000-BaseT*, where the numerical portion of the name indicates the speed of your network — the cables are the same. 1000-BaseT is more commonly known as *Gigabit Ethernet*, and is the up-and-coming standard, because things tend to get faster. 10/100 Ethernet (10 Mb, megabit, or 100 Mb) is the current standard.

Note
You may also encounter the term *10-Base2* when researching network cards. This is an older type of 10-Mb Ethernet cabling that uses shielded Bayonet Neill-Concelman, or Baby N Connector (BNC), cables and is not supported by most networking hardware today. ∎

The best way to visualize the Internet or any Ethernet network is as an extremely long piece of cable to which several computers and network devices are attached. In the simplest case, you must use a device called a *hub*, *switch*, or *router* to attach multiple machines to an Ethernet. A *hub* is a device with multiple incoming connectors for attaching the Ethernet cables from different machines, with a single output connector that attaches it to another Ethernet device such as a cable modem, another hub, or a switch, router, or gateway. Network communications on any incoming port of the hub are broadcast to all other devices on the hub and are also forwarded through the outgoing connection. *Switches* are much like hubs on steroids because they keep track of how network connections between different machines are made and reserve dedicated internal circuitry for established connections. Switches are, therefore, typically both faster and more expensive than hubs because they do more.

Gateways and *routers* are similar to hubs and switches, but are designed to provide connectivity between different networks. If a machine that you are trying to connect to isn't immediately found on your local network, the request is forwarded through your gateway, which then sends it on. Network communication is done using discrete units of information that are known as *packets*. Packets contain the Internet Protocol (IP) address of the host that they are trying to contact. IP addresses are in the form of *NNN.NNN.NNN.NNN* and are the network equivalent of a Post Office box, uniquely identifying a specific machine. Packets for an unknown local host are sent through your gateway. *Routers* are expensive, sophisticated pieces of hardware that direct network communication between multiple networks, translate packets between different network communication protocols, and limit network traffic to relevant networks so that your request to retrieve a file from your local music server isn't broadcast to every machine on the Internet.

IP addresses use additional network configuration data, known as a *netmask*, to identify the portion of a network to which a given machine belongs. The netmask identifies the bits in your IP address that identify a network segment, and is typically 255.255.255.0 for a standard Class C IP address on a home network. The netmask 255.255.255.0 is 11111111.11111111.11111111 .00000000 in binary, which means that the last 24 bits in a binary IP address (i.e., the numbers after the final period in a standard IP address) are used to identify a specific machine. Some ISPs use more complex netmasks to divide their networks into subnets that provide better control over the IP addresses that they issue and the associated network traffic.

The most common way to connect machines on a home network is to use a hub or a home gateway that is connected to your cable or DSL modem. The difference between these is that a hub simply forwards packets through its outgoing connector (known as an *uplink port* because it simply links the network connections on that device with those on another, forwarding network packets to the other device, and is, therefore, wired differently). A home gateway may convert internal network addresses to addresses that are compatible with the outside world before sending the information on through its outgoing or uplink connector. If you're using a hub to connect your home network to your cable or DSL modem, each machine on your home network would require an IP address that is unique on the Internet. This can be expensive because most ISPs charge money for each unique host that can be connected to the Internet from your home at any given time. Home gateways provide a way around this because they enable your home network to use a special type of IP address, known as a *non-routable IP address*, to assign unique internal network addresses. As the name suggests, *non-routable IP addresses* are addresses that will not be forwarded (routed) by the networking devices that support the actual Internet. When using non-routable IP addresses, whatever gateway you (or your ISP) use to connect to the Internet internally translates these to valid external addresses whenever you try to connect to a machine on the Internet. The most common non-routable IP addresses are in the form of 192.168.*X.Y*, where *X* and *Y* are specific to how you've set up your network.

Tip

If you're really interested, you can get more information about non-routable IP addresses and address translation in the Internet RFCs (Requests for Comment) that defined them, 1597 and 1918. Use your favorite Internet search engine to find relevant information, or check out links such as `www.safety.net/sum1597 .html` **and** `www.howstuffworks.com/nat2.htm`. ■

IP addresses are assigned to computer systems in two basic ways, either statically or dynamically. *Static addresses* are unique to your home network and are always assigned to a particular machine. *Dynamic addresses* are addresses that are automatically assigned to a computer system or network device when you turn it on. Most ISPs use dynamic addresses because only a limited number of IP addresses are available on the Internet. Using dynamic IP addresses enables your ISP to recycle and reassign IP addresses as people turn their machines off and on. Most dynamic IP addresses nowadays are assigned using a protocol called *Dynamic Host Configuration Protocol* (DHCP), which fills out the network information for your system when it activates its network interface, including things like the IP address of a gateway system and the IP addresses of *Domain Name System* (DNS) servers that translate between hostnames and the IP addresses that they correspond to.

To use static addresses on your home network, you simply assign each network interface on each machine a unique, non-routable IP address from a given family of non-routable IP addresses. For example, most of my home machines have static addresses in the form of 192.168.6.Y. Because I use a home gateway, I've configured it to do address translation (more specifically known as *Network Address Translation*, NAT) to correctly translate between these addresses and the external IP address of my home gateway box.

Tip

Systems on which multiple Ethernet connections are available are quite common today. If you are using multiple Ethernet connections simultaneously, it usually only makes sense to have each interface connected to a different network, because network routing is somewhat confusing otherwise. Systems with multiple Ethernet connections where each of these connections is attached to a different network are known as *multi-homed* systems, because they have an identity (home) on each network. ■

If you want to use Dynamic IP addresses on a home network, one of the machines on your home network must be running a DHCP server. Most home gateways, such as those from DLink or Linksys, have built-in DHCP servers that you simply configure to hand out IP addresses from a specific range of addresses (192.168.6.200 through 192.168.6.250, in my case). Once you activate address translation on your home gateway, your gateway will route packets appropriately. Remember that your home gateway is probably getting its IP address by contacting your ISP's DHCP server, whereas hosts on your internal network will get their IP addresses from your DHCP server. Don't set up hosts on an internal network to contact your ISP's DHCP server unless you have only a single machine on your home network or want every one of your machines to be visible on the Internet. If you are using a home gateway that doesn't provide a DHCP server, want to have more control over what your DHCP server does, or are using Ubuntu Linux in an enterprise or commercial setting, you may want to set up your own DHCP server on an Ubuntu system, which is explained in Chapter 31, "Setting Up a DHCP Server."

A final aspect of networking is how your system identifies and locates specific computer systems on the Internet. This is typically done through the Domain Name System, which is explained in the introduction to Chapter 32, "Setting Up a DNS Server," and the section of that chapter entitled "Overview of DNS and BIND."

The overview in this section should have familiarized you with basic general and home-networking terms and concepts. As you might expect, the Internet is knee-deep in web sites that provide more general information about home networking. For truly detailed information about setting up and configuring a home network on a specific type of machine and operating system, see any of the hundreds of books on those topics at your local bookstore.

Configuring Your Network Hardware

Configuring the network hardware on your computer system is part of the Ubuntu installation process, which uses an automatic network configuration mechanism known as the *Network Manager* (`http://projects.gnome.org/NetworkManager`). However, things change. You may install new network hardware, change existing hardware from relying on DHCP to using static IP addresses on your network, or simply want to have a better understanding of how networking works or is configured on your system(s). The Network Manager is designed to autodetect networking hardware and network configuration changes, which can be especially handy when you're using a laptop and want to be able to connect your system to the Internet from your home, from random Wi-Fi hotspots, and perhaps even from work. The Network Manager interacts directly with your hardware using HAL, the Linux Hardware Availability Layer, and D-Bus, a message bus system that simplifies communication between applications regarding resources, system events, and so on. These provide a great deal of flexibility but can make it difficult to debug configuration problems, especially if you're used to the traditional network configuration mechanisms used on Debian-based distributions like Ubuntu.

The next two sections discuss how to use the standard Network Manager package that's installed by default on Ubuntu systems.

However, no matter how cool the Network Manager is, it doesn't work for everybody. Not to worry! The sections on the Network Manager are followed by a section that discusses how to configure your networking hardware using the traditional Debian/Ubuntu mechanism, which simply involves editing a text file. This may be the best approach for you if you have problems with the Network Manager or simply don't care about graphical tools for network configuration. As always, Linux has many options and alternatives, and the choice is yours.

Tip
This section provides information about using the graphical tools provided with Ubuntu systems for configuring both wired and wireless connections over Ethernet devices that use standard Linux device drivers. If you're having problems configuring your wireless connections using the Network Manager, see Chapter 22, "Going Wireless," for more detailed information about wireless networking and a discussion of other tools that you may find useful when configuring wireless networks. This includes command-line tools and a package called Wicd, an open source wired and wireless network manager that is an excellent (some say superior) alternative to the standard Network Manager. Chapter 22 also explains how to use Microsoft Windows drivers on your Ubuntu system if Linux does not yet support your Ethernet hardware. This is, unfortunately, somewhat common with wireless networking hardware—not all Ethernet hardware manufacturers have the same level of enlightenment. ∎

Using the Network Manager

By default, all interaction with network devices in Ubuntu is done through the Network Manager's GNOME panel applet, nm-applet. This applet is displayed in the Notification Area in the top right portion of the GNOME panel, using an icon that looks like a stylized view of two segments of cable and their connectors if you are connected to a wired network or a histogram if you are connected to a wireless network. (A red X is displayed at the bottom of the wired network icon if you are not currently connected to a network.) Left-clicking this icon displays a menu that lists the current status of all of the network connections that were detected on your system, as shown in Figure 21-1.

FIGURE 21-1

Dropdown status information from the Network Manager applet

The left portion of Figure 21-1 shows the Network Manager applet's dropdown menu on a system that has a single wired Ethernet interface that is automatically connected via the Ethernet device eth0. The selected radio button to the left of the name of that interface shows that it is currently active. The right portion of Figure 21-1 shows the Network Manager applet's dropdown menu on a system that has a single wired Ethernet interface that is currently disconnected (and is therefore represented by the grayed-out term *disconnected*), that also has a wireless Ethernet interface that is currently connected to the wireless network wvh, and has also detected the availability of three wireless networks. The bars to the right of each wireless network indicate the strength of the signal from an access point for that wireless network. The lock icon in the left portion of the available wireless networks indicates that these are secure networks that require authentication in order to access them, which the network named wvh does not.

To configure your network connections, you can either select the System ⇨ Preferences ⇨ Network Connections menu item or right-click on the Network Manager applet in the GNOME panel and select "Edit Connections" to display the dialog shown in Figure 21-2.

The "Network Connections" dialog displays your wired connections by default. Network connections that your system will try to automatically establish each time you restart the system are preceded by the word *Auto*.

FIGURE 21-2

The Network Manager applet's "Network Connections" dialog

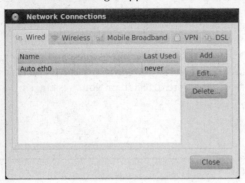

The next three sections explain how to configure wired, wireless, and VPN connections using the Network Manager applet on your Ubuntu system. Remember that the Network Manager is designed to automate enabling and configuring the network interfaces on your system. In most cases, you won't have to actually do anything for standard wired and wireless Ethernet connections—if you turn on your Ubuntu system and its network interface(s) come up automatically and correctly, you don't have to do any additional configuration and can just start reading mail, surfing the Web, listening to music, or any other activity that requires a network connection. However, if your interfaces didn't start automatically, use DHCP where you want to use a static IP address, you want to connect to a different wireless network, or if you want to create a connection to a virtual private network, read on.

Configuring Wired Connections

To examine or modify how a specific wired connection is configured, make sure that the Network Connections dialog's Wired tab is displayed, select the name of the connection that you want to configure, and click Edit. This displays a dialog like the one shown in Figure 21-3.

The "Connect automatically" option on this dialog is selected, showing that your system automatically tries to enable this connection each time it boots, and the "Available to all users" option identifies this network connection as a basic system setting rather than a user-configured setting—this network connection will be activated and available for all users of your system.

To see additional details for this network connection, select the IPv4 Settings tab to display the pane shown in Figure 21-4.

FIGURE 21-3

Information about a specific wired network connection

FIGURE 21-4

IP address configuration for a wired network connection

The selection in the Method dropdown list on this dialog identifies how your system obtains its IP address. The most common of these are Automatic (DHCP), the default, and Manual, which enables you to supply static IP address information. Static IP addresses are typically used for server systems, so that they can always be found at the same IP address — after all, you don't want the systems on your home network to have to search for your print server each time you print a file. It's much easier for Print and other servers to simply use a static IP address (although you can configure a DHCP server to deliver a specific address to a specific network card based on its MAC address, as explained in Chapter 31, "Setting Up a DHCP Server").

To manually specify an IP address, click the Method dropdown list and select Manual. This enables the other configuration options on this dialog, as shown in Figure 21-5.

FIGURE 21-5

Manually configuring a wired network connection

Click Add to specify the IP address for this network connection, and enter the IP address, netmask, and gateway for this connection. Next, enter the address for one or more DNS servers, separating each IP address from the next with a comma, and enter the name of the domain of which this machine is a member in the "Search domains" box.

Note

Because DNS servers are the usual source of information that map IP addresses to hostnames, you should enter only IP addresses in this dialog. If you specify a hostname, your system will need to use a DNS server to figure out the IP address associated with that DNS server, which would cause a nasty chicken-and-egg loop. ■

Once you have entered these values, click Apply to save and begin using your static network settings.

Configuring Wireless Connections

To examine or modify how a specific wireless connection is configured, or to create a new wireless connection, select the Wireless tab, which displays a pane like the one shown in Figure 21-6.

Tip

If you are connecting to a wireless network that uses WEP 40/128-bit Key, WEP 128-bit Passphrase, and no security (which are almost functionally equivalent nowadays), you can quickly define a new wireless network connection by right-clicking on the Network Manager applet and selecting the "Create New Wireless Network" menu option. This displays a dialog that prompts you for the name of the wireless network connection that you want to create; enables you to select between WEP 40/128-bit Key, WEP 128-bit Passphrase, and no security; and enables you to enter the key or passphrase for these two common WEP flavors. ∎

FIGURE 21-6

General information about wireless network connections

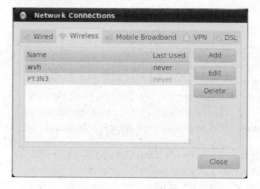

In this example, the Wireless pane shows two wireless network connections. To examine a specific connection, select the name of that connection and click Edit. To create a new wireless connection, click Add. Either of these actions displays a dialog like the one shown in Figure 21-7.

To make sure that your system automatically tries to enable this connection each time it boots, make sure that the "Connect automatically" option on this dialog is selected. You should not enable this option for wireless connections that you will only use in specific circumstances, such as when connecting to a wireless network at your office. Similarly, if the network connection that you are editing or defining is one that should be activated and available for all users of your system, make sure that the "Available to all users" option is selected to identify this network connection as a basic system setting rather than a user-specific setting. If this is a user-specific setting, make sure that the "Available to all users" option is not selected.

FIGURE 21-7

Information about a specific wireless network connection

Next, enter or verify the SSID (Service Set Identifier) for the wireless network you are connecting to. Make sure that the mode is set to Infrastructure unless you are establishing a direct connection between the wireless interfaces on two machines. Finally, setting the BSSID (Basic Service Set Identifier) or MAC address is only necessary if you want to make sure that your system only connects to a specific wireless access point and the wireless network with which it is associated.

To proceed with examining, modifying, or creating the definition of a wireless connection, click the Wireless Security tab. You can click the dropdown Security list to see your choices for the mechanism that your system will use to authenticate itself to the wireless network that is identified on the Wireless tab. If you are connecting to a wireless network that does not use security, select None. Otherwise, select one of the following options, each of which requires security information such as a key, passphrase, certificates, or username-and-password combination that you will need to obtain from the administrator of the wireless network that you want to connect to:

- **WEP 40/128-bit Key:** Enables you to enter an encrypted key that will be used to authenticate the computer to the wireless network. Although quite common, WEP (Wired Equivalent Privacy) keys can be cracked in a few minutes using popular open source packages such as Aircrack-ng (www.aircrack-ng.org/doku.php) and Kismet (www.kismetwireless.net/index.shtml). Nowadays, WEP is primarily used to indicate that you are interested in security as opposed to actually providing any, and is often the equivalent of painting a big target on your network.

- **WEP 128-bit Passphrase:** Enables you to enter a passphrase that will be used to generate WEP keys that will enable you to authenticate to the wireless network. 128-bit WEP security is much better than 40-bit WEP, requiring up to an hour to crack with the same open source tools. Ask the nearest fifth grader for more details.

- **LEAP:** Cisco's Lightweight Extensible Authentication Protocol (LEAP) supports username and password–based authentication between a wireless client and a RADIUS (Remote Authentication Dial-In User Service) server such as Cisco ACS or FreeRADIUS (http://freeradius.org).

- **Dynamic WEP (802.1x):** Automatically obtains up-to-date WEP keys from a key management service. This is a relatively uncommon, vendor-specific authentication mechanism.

- **WPA & WPA2 Personal:** Enables you to enter a passphrase that is used to authenticate yourself to the wireless network. Wi-Fi Protected Access (WPA and WPA2) provides improved security over the older, and simpler, WEP security. WPA Personal mode, also known as preshared key mode (PSK), is designed for home and small office networks that don't need a full-blown 802.1X authentication server — the passphrase is stored in the wireless access point.

- **WPA & WPA2 Enterprise:** Enables you to provide a username and password or identify user and certificate authority (CA) certificates and a key that was generated by the administrator of your wireless network. Certificates and keys are stored in files on your system and are used to authenticate you to an authentication server to provide access to the wireless access point. If you are using EAP or Protected EAP authentication, you will need to get a valid username-and-password combination from the administrator for the RADIUS server that you are accessing. WPA Enterprise mode supports additional EAP (Extensible Authentication Protocol) security mechanisms that have been certified by the Wi-Fi alliance and can also be used with the popular, free FreeRADIUS server (http://freeradius.org).

Figure 21-8 shows the fields that are associated with entering WPA/WPA2 Enterprise security information using TLS (Transport Layer Security) authentication information. Clicking the fields that initially say *None* displays a browse dialog that enables you to locate and identify the files that contain this information.

After selecting a security mechanism and providing the information that it requires, click the IPv4 Settings tab to display the dialog that was shown earlier in Figure 21-5. Follow the instructions earlier in this chapter if you want to specify a static IP address for your wireless host, which is an extremely rare circumstance. Wireless devices that use static IP addresses for security and monitoring purposes still typically retrieve them from a DHCP server that has been configured to deliver specific IP addresses to specific MAC addresses. See Chapter 31 for information about DHCP server configuration.

After entering all of the information required to access your wireless network, click Apply to save any changes that you have made to the configuration of your wireless network connection, or click Cancel to discard those changes.

FIGURE 21-8

Entering WPA & WPA2 Enterprise security information

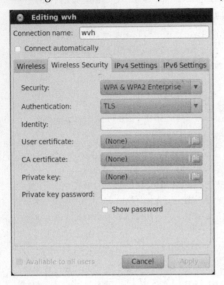

Tip

If configuration data such as wireless key information isn't being saved for a connection that is identified as a System setting, try deselecting and re-selecting the "Connect automatically" option. A little voodoo never hurts.... ■

After changing wireless network settings, the Network Manager will attempt to connect to any wireless connections that you have set as "Configure automatically." You can also initiate a wireless connection by left-clicking on the Network Manager applet and selecting the "Connect to Hidden Wireless Network" menu command. This displays a dialog from which you can select the network that you want to connect to, select its Wireless security settings, and click Connect to attempt to initiate a connection.

Tip

As mentioned earlier, if you are having problems getting your wireless connections to work using the Network Manager, see Chapter 22 for information about command-line tools to help with debugging, or for information about installing and using the Wicd package, which is a great replacement for the Network Manager that often does a better job of handling some types of wireless authentication. ■

Configuring a VPN Connection

Virtual private networks (VPNs) are essentially a mechanism for tunneling between two networks, enabling you to access a remote network as though it were local to your system (albeit with some slight decrease in access speed). VPNs are most commonly used when connecting to business or academic networks from home or laptop computer systems, making the home or laptop system a member of a business or academic network for the duration of the VPN connection, but they can also be used as a central corporate or academic resource by permanently connecting multiple locations as parts of a single network. Prior to the development of VPNs, institutions that needed multiple locations to interact on a single network did so by using dedicated connections, referred to as *leased lines*, that were provided by a telecommunications provider. VPNs provide an equivalent solution that is more cost-effective and flexible and does not require network administration by a third party such as a telecommunications carrier. VPN connections can be made from any location over an IP network, do not require purchasing or leasing dedicated network connections, and require no separate administration other than correctly configuring the VPN servers that remote clients contact in order to join the network.

As you might hope, Ubuntu's Network Manager applet makes it easy to set up VPN connections, using essentially the same mechanism that it provides for creating and editing wired and wireless network connections. The Network Manager supports OpenVPN, PPTP (Point-to-Point Tunneling Protocol), and VPNC (Cisco's VPN Concentrator) VPNs, each of which has its own configuration requirements.

Note

Although the Network Manager applet does, indeed, make it easy to set up VPN connections, you may want to initiate VPN connections manually. In that case, see the sidebar, "Setting Up and Using OpenVPN Manually," later in this chapter, for information on establishing a VPN connection to a remote network using OpenVPN, regardless of the state of the Network Manager. ■

Before starting to configure a VPN using the Network Manager applet, do the following:

1. Check with the administrator of the network that you want to access to determine the type of VPN that they are using at the remote end. Different VPNs require different Network Manager plug-ins.

2. Obtain the necessary security information from the administrator of the network that you want to access via a VPN. This security information can consist of certificate files, a key file and associated password, a username and password, or some combination of these.

3. Check with the administrator of the network that you want to access to verify how VPN clients obtain IP address, DNS, and domain information. The VPN server usually provides these automatically when you establish a connection, but it's a good idea to check. It is inconvenient at best to be sitting in a hotel room in East Nowhere and discovering that you need some missing bit of critical information such as the IP address of a DNS server for the remote network in order to actually use your VPN connection.

4. Install the Network Manager plug-in for the type of VPN that you are connecting to, using your favorite Package Management tool from those discussed in Chapter 19 "Adding, Removing, and Updating Software." Supported VPN frameworks and the packages that contain their associated plug-ins are Cisco AnyConnect (`network-manager-openconnect`), Cisco Compatible VPN (`network-manager-vpnc`), IPsec/IKEv2 strongwwan (`network-managerr-strongswan`), OpenVPN (`network-manager-openvpn`), and PPTP (`network-manager-pptp`).

Tip

If you are configuring a VPN connection on a laptop, it's a good idea to install all three of the VPN plug-ins. Although you'll probably only use one of these initially, it's convenient to already have them on your laptop if you are traveling and need to connect to a site that uses a different type of VPN software. ■

After completing these steps, you can begin configuring your end of the VPN by doing one of the following:

- Right-click the Network Manager applet in the Notification Area, select the "VPN Connections" menu, and select the "Configure VPN" menu item.

- Left-click the Network Manager applet, and select "Edit Connections" to display the "Network Connections" dialog shown in Figure 21-2. Click the VPN tab.

Doing either of these displays the "Network Connections" dialog's VPN pane. If the Add, Import, and Export buttons are not enabled, you neglected to install at least one of the plug-ins that the Network Manager uses to provide VPN access. See the final bullet in the "Before starting to configure a VPN using the Network Manager applet" list earlier in this section.

If the system administrator of the network to which you are connecting supplied you with a configuration file for VPN clients, you can click Import to display a dialog that enables you to browse for and open that configuration file. This will create a VPN connection for you that matches the settings required by the remote server, although you may still have to supply information that may not be in a generic configuration file, such as the location of your certificates and key, your username and password, and so on. You can then select the entry for that connection in the connection list and click Edit to customize it and supply any missing information.

If you do not have a configuration file to start with and therefore need to create a completely new VPN connection, click Add. A dialog appears that provides a dropdown list from which you can select the type of VPN connection that you want to create. Select the appropriate type of VPN connection, and click Create. A dialog like the one shown in Figure 21-9 appears. The contents of this dialog will differ based on the type of VPN connection that you are defining—the example in this section uses an OpenVPN connection as an example.

First, you'll probably want to change the name of your new connection to something more evocative than "VPN Connection N," which is the default name format for new VPN connections. I typically use names such as *Work* or *company-Consulting* that identify the target of the VPN, but you can use any name that you want.

FIGURE 21-9

Defining a connection to an OpenVPN VPN

Next, all types of VPN connections require that you identify a Gateway, which is the hostname (or IP address) of the system that is running the VPN server software and through which you connect to the remote network.

Finally, you probably want to make sure that neither the "Connect automatically" or "Systems setting" options are selected. You probably only want to connect to a VPN under certain circumstances, and you probably don't want other users to be able to see or attempt to use any VPN connections that you have configured.

After configuring these standard items, you need to supply the authentication information that is required to establish a connection to the remote network. This information differs for each type of VPN connection and also varies for the different authentication mechanisms that different types of VPN connections support. For OpenVPN connections, select the appropriate type of authentication from the Type dropdown, and then click to browse for the location of the files containing your certificates and key, enter password information if required, and so on.

After completing this dialog, you may want to click the IPv4 tab, shown in Figure 21-10, to verify that the mechanism by which your connection will get mandatory IP information matches the requirements of the remote system.

FIGURE 21-10

Verifying IP configuration for a connection to an OpenVPN VPN

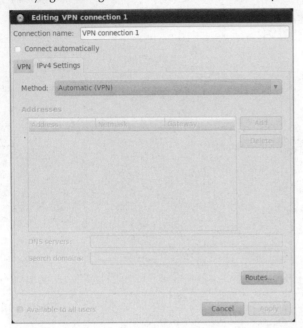

The default mechanism for obtaining IP information is Automatic (VPN), which means that the VPN server acts as a standard DHCP server, providing an IP address, the identity of at least one DNS server for the remote network, the domain name for hosts on the remote network, and so on. Some VPNs are configured to only provide an IP address and require that you identify a DNS server and supply the domain name for hosts on the remote network. Others only accept connections from specific IP addresses, which must therefore be manually configured.

Once you have supplied all of the information that is required for the type of VPN that you are connecting to, click Apply to save your new connection. You can then test it by right-clicking on the Network Manager applet, selecting the VPN Connections submenu, and selecting the entry for the VPN connection that you just configured from the list at the top of the submenu that appears. Depending on the type of VPN to which you are connecting and the information that you supplied in the VPN dialog like the one shown in Figure 21-9, you may be prompted for a username, password, or both in order to establish your connection. The icon for the Network manager applet will change to show a swirling globe and arrows as your system establishes your connection, and a status message will be displayed when the connection attempt completes.

If you get an error or connection failure message, edit and verify the settings for your connection and try connecting again. If you are still having problems connecting, your best bet is to search the Web using a query like *Ubuntu Network Manager VPN problem* to see if there are any known problems with the type of connection that you are trying to establish. You can also skip using the Network Manager and try to establish your VPN connection manually. The client-side server that your system must run in order to connect to a specific type of VPN was installed along with the Network Manager plug-in for that type of VPN and is usually integrated into the system boot process. However, connections will not be automatically started if you need to supply a password or other information during the connection process. See the sidebar "Setting Up and Using OpenVPN Manually" for an example of manually creating configuration files and establishing a connection to a remote OpenVPN VPN server.

Setting Up and Using OpenVPN Manually

If you don't use the Network Manager to set up your VPN connections (or aren't using the Network Manager), you will have to install and configure your VPN connections manually. The type of VPN connection that you set up depends on the type of VPN software that is running on the remote system through which you are establishing your OpenVPN connection. Although multiple VPN mechanisms are available for Ubuntu (eBox, OpenVPN, SecVPN, VPNC, etc.), OpenVPN is probably the most common of these, so this section focuses on its installation and configuration on your system. Sorry, CISCO fans!

OpenVPN is a free, open source VPN package that is released under the GPL and is one of the most popular VPN packages in use today. OpenVPN uses the OpenSSL library and SSL/TLS (Secure Sockets Layer/Transport Layer Security) for secure, encrypted communications, and uses preshared secret keys, certificates, or username/password combinations for authentication. Beyond its popularity on Linux systems, OpenVPN is also available for operating systems, including FreeBSD, Mac OS X, NetBSD, OpenBSD, Solaris, and Microsoft Windows 2000, XP, Vista, and 2008 Server.

Installing OpenVPN on your system can be done manually by installing the openvpn package, or automatically as a requirement for installing the network-manager-openvpn package that provides the Network Manager's support for creating and managing OpenVPN connections. As part of installing OpenVPN, it is integrated into your Ubuntu system's startup process. As part of its startup process, OpenVPN will try to automatically initiate any VPN connections for which configuration files are present in the directory /etc/openvpn. These configuration files can have any name, but must have the file extension *.conf*. Each configuration file identifies the OpenVPN parameters that are required to establish a VPN connection to a remote network, including the name and location of any certificate and key files that each connection requires. However, any connections that require specifying a password to unlock or verify a private key will fail during the boot process because OpenVPN does not support storing username and password information in configuration files unless it has been specially compiled to do so. Storing username and password information is usually not supported because storing this information in clear text in a configuration file is a huge potential security hole.

The following is a sample OpenVPN configuration file:

```
port 1194
dev tun
remote whereiwork.com
```

continued

continued

```
tls-client
ca ca.crt
cert vonhagen.crt
key vonhagen.key
mtu-test
tun-mtu 1500
tun-mtu-extra 32
mssfix 1450
pull
comp-lzo
verb 0
```

These remote, ca, cert, and key entries in OpenVPN configuration files will be different for each VPN connection. The remote keyword identifies the host that is running the OpenVPN server for a connection, the ca keyword identifies the file containing the root Certificate Authority certificate for the remote site, the cert keyword identifies the file containing the client's certificate, and the key keyword identifies the file containing the private key for the client. In this example, the latter two are user-specific, but they can also be sitewide to enable sitewide connections. User-specific key files are typically owned by the root user and are stored as mode 600 so that they can only be read by the root user.

The *key* issue in whether an OpenVPN connection can be automatically created at boot time is whether the private key file requires a password in order for it to be used. System administrators can create key files that do not require passwords using the -passin pass:*password* option (where *password* is a password that will be used automatically) when creating a key file using the openssl utility. Such key files can be used to automatically set up "always-on" VPN connections at boot time. VPN connections that use a key file that requires a password and for which all files are stored in /etc/openvpn can be initiated at any time by executing the following command from any command-line environment:

```
sudo /etc/init.d/openvpn restart
```

This command will temporarily stop all current OpenVPN connections and will then attempt to start all OpenVPN connections for which configuration files exist in /etc/openvpn, prompting you for any passwords that are required. A more elegant way of starting an individual OpenVPN connection without interrupting any existing connections is to execute a command like the following from any command-line environment:

```
sudo openvpn --cd /etc/openvpn --daemon --config configfile.conf
```

The --cd option specifies the directory in which any files without pathnames (such as those in the previous example) can be found, the --daemon option tells the openvpn daemon to detach from the command-line environment from which it was started if the daemon can start correctly, and the --config option specifies the name of the configuration file for the OpenVPN connection that you want to start. You will be prompted for the password for the key file identified in the configuration file, and the OpenVPN daemon will create the connection and put itself in the background in daemon mode. As you can see, this command also enables you to store user-specific OpenVPN configuration files in any directory by changing the value of the --cd option to the name of that directory.

OpenVPN connections that you started will persist after you log out, so you should terminate any user-specific OpenVPN connections by using the `ps` command to identify the process ID for the OpenVPN server that you started and using the `kill` command to kill that process, which will also remove any routing table entries for that OpenVPN connection. If you are only running a single instance of the `openvpn` process, you can simplify this by using a command like `kill -9 'pidof openvpn'` to shoot it down.

Configuration Files for Network Interfaces

Tools such as the Network Manager and `Wicd` (discussed in Chapter 22) are great if you want flexible, dynamically configured Ethernet interfaces on your system. But what if these don't work for you or if (gasp!) your system doesn't go anywhere or only uses one or two configurations? In these cases, you can eliminate the overhead that mechanisms such as the Network Manager and `Wicd` introduce by falling back to the original network configuration mechanism that was pioneered by the Debian Linux distribution and has therefore been inherited by its offspring such as Ubuntu systems: *text files*.

Network interfaces that rarely change can easily be configured by creating entries for them in the file `/etc/network/interfaces`, which is the core network configuration file used on Ubuntu systems. This file supports both wired and wireless interfaces, including security configuration for wireless interfaces. In order to configure your network interfaces using this file, you must first make sure that neither the Network Manager nor `Wicd` is running when you start your system. To remove either of these network configuration mechanisms from your system's startup sequence, you must remove the symbolic links `S28NetworkManager` or `S20wicd` from the directory `/etc/rc2.d`, which is the directory that contains the files that bring an Ubuntu system up to its default run level, run level 2. You can simply remove these links, but I typically like to remember what I've enabled and disabled on my systems. I, therefore, create a directory called `/etc/rc2.d/DISABLED` and move whichever of these symbolic links is present on my system into that directory. This will prevent those network configuration mechanisms from running the next time that you start your system.

Once you've disabled automatic network configuration mechanisms for your next reboot, you can create entries for your network interfaces in the file `/etc/network/interfaces` using your favorite text editor. This file will already contain an entry for the loopback interface on your system. The easiest type of entry in this file is an entry for an Ethernet interface that uses DHCP to obtain its IP address and other network configuration information. An entry that defines the Ethernet interface `eth0` as one that uses DHCP will look like the following:

```
auto eth0
iface eth0 inet dhcp
```

The `auto` line in this entry states that the interface `eth0` will be automatically enabled when the system starts. The `iface` line in this entry identifies the beginning of the interface definition for `eth0`, which is a TCP/IP (`inet`) device that uses `dhcp` to obtain its configuration information.

Entries that assign static IP addresses to specific interfaces are equally simple. For example, an entry that assigns a static IP address for the Ethernet interface eth0 will look like the following:

```
auto eth0
iface eth0 inet static
        address 192.168.6.64
        netmask 255.255.255.0
        gateway 192.168.6.1
```

The auto line in this entry states that the interface eth0 will be automatically enabled when the system starts. The iface line in this entry identifies the beginning of the interface definition for eth0, which is a TCP/IP (inet) device with static configuration. The next three lines define the IP address, netmask, and gateway for that Ethernet interface.

Manual DNS Configuration

If your network interfaces use static IP addresses, your system will not obtain general network configuration information such as DNS server addresses from a DHCP server. You should, therefore, manually create and populate the file /etc/resolv.conf that your system uses to identify its name servers. A sample /etc/resolv.conf file that uses open DNS servers from OpenDNS.org is the following:

```
domain vonhagen.org
nameserver 208.67.222.222
nameserver 208.67.220.220
```

The first line in this file identifies the default domain that your system should search for hosts that are specified without domain names. (You will probably use a default domain that is something other than my home domain.) You should add entries for any DNS servers that are provided by that default domain, which should appear before entries for the DNS servers from open services such as OpenDNS. When your system tries to find the IP address associated with a specific host, it will query the DNS servers in the order in which they are listed in this file.

For information about other DNS servers that are available to the general public, see www.dnsserverlist.org.

Wireless Ethernet interfaces are similarly easy to define in your /etc/network/interfaces file. For example, an entry that defines the Ethernet interface eth1 as one that uses DHCP and the wireless network with the ESSID wvh will look like the following:

```
auto eth1
iface eth1 inet dhcp
    wireless-essid wvh
```

The auto line in this entry states that the interface eth1 will be automatically enabled when the system starts. The iface line in this entry identifies the beginning of the interface definition for eth1, which is a TCP/IP (inet) device that uses dhcp to obtain its configuration information. The wireless-essid entry defines the name of the wireless network that this entry should connect to. You can use the keyword any instead of identifying a specific wireless-essid if you want to connect to any open wireless network that is available.

Entries such as this one are fine for open wireless networks. Entries associated with WEP wireless networks require at least one additional entry to specify the wireless key, as in the following example:

```
auto eth1
iface eth1 inet dhcp
    wireless-essid wvh
    wireless-key 0102030405
```

If the wireless network that you want to connect to uses WPA authentication, you will have to install and configure a package such as wpasupplicant and integrate that package into your wireless configuration entries. Describing how to install and configure this package is (unfortunately) outside the scope of this section. See the forum postings at http://ubuntuforums .org/showthread.php?t=202834 for more information about using wireless security mechanisms that are more powerful than WEP.

You can also define static IP addresses for wireless interfaces, as in the following example:

```
auto eth1
iface eth1 inet static
    address 192.168.6.42
    netmask 255.255.255.0
    gateway 192.168.6.1
    wireless-essid wvh
    wireless-key 0102030405
```

The file /etc/network/interfaces provides a simple, low-overhead mechanism for configuring network interfaces that are either fairly simple or don't change very often. The examples in this section have only scratched the surface of possible entries in this file, but have identified the most important ones. For complete information about the possible entries in this file for wired Ethernet interfaces, see the online man page for this file by typing the command **man 5 interfaces** from any command-line interface. The Web is the best resource for locating complete information about the keywords in this file that are related to wireless network configuration.

Configuring Modems and Dial-Up Connections

Although broadband Internet access is common nowadays, dial-up connections using protocols such as PPP (Point-to-Point Protocol) are still the way in which some people connect to the Internet. Depending on your geographic location, this may be your only option for connecting to the Internet. Unfortunately, many modern modems are so-called *Win-modems*, which saves hardware companies significant money by using Microsoft Windows device drivers and the operating system itself to do the MOdulation/DEModulation that gives modems their name. Unfortunately, such drivers are rarely provided for Linux. See `http://linmodems.org` for information on whether your modem is a Win-modem and, if there is software that may be able to make it work with Linux.

Using a modem to connect to the Web is rare nowadays, and, for that reason, Ubuntu systems don't install packages for modem configuration and connection setup by default. If you need to use a modem and have one that works on Linux systems, the graphical `gnome-ppp` and `kppp` packages can make it easy for you to configure and initiate modem-based network connections. Similarly, the `wvdial` package that is available in the Ubuntu repositories is a great command-line utility application to use to initiate a PPP or SLIP connection over your modem. See the man page for `wvdial`, its FAQ (`http://alumnit.ca/wiki/index.php?page=WvDialFAQ`), or its home page (`http://freshmeat.net/projects/wvdial`) for information on configuring and using this package. If you're reading this, I apologize for not discussing these packages in detail, but I don't have a dial-up account anymore (or enough phone lines to test with the stack of retired modems that are in my basement).

Network Testing with Network Tools

To maintain its tradition of easy graphical network tools, Ubuntu provides a convenient graphical tool that simplifies examining the current configuration of any of your network interfaces. Ubuntu provides GNOME's Network Tools application to give you a graphical display of network configuration information, as well as easy graphical access to a variety of network tools. Select the System ➪ Administration ➪ Network Tools menu item to start the Network Tools application. This displays a dialog like the one shown in Figure 21-11.

By default, the Network Tools application shows information about your system's loopback interface. To see information about a specific interface, click the Network Device dropdown menu and select the Ethernet interface that you're interested in. Figure 21-11 actually shows information about the primary physical Ethernet interface, `eth0`, on one of my test systems.

FIGURE 21-11

Information about eth0 in the Network Tools application

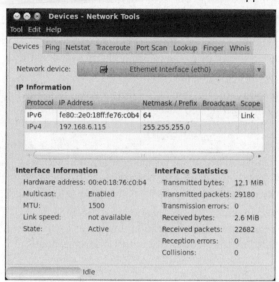

The easiest and fastest way to identify the current configuration of one of your Ethernet interfaces will probably always be to run the `ifconfig interface-name` command in an xterm or GNOME Terminal window, which will display output like the following:

```
$ ifconfig eth0
eth0      Link encap:Ethernet  HWaddr 00:16:EC:CA:AE:20
          inet addr:192.168.6.64  Bcast:192.168.6.255  Mask:255.255.255.0
          inet6 addr: fe80::216:ecff:feca:ae20/64 Scope:Link
          UP BROADCAST RUNNING MULTICAST  MTU:1500  Metric:1
          RX packets:32034 errors:0 dropped:0 overruns:0 frame:0
          TX packets:28776 errors:0 dropped:0 overruns:0 carrier:0
          collisions:0 txqueuelen:0
          RX bytes:12108607 (11.5 MiB)  TX bytes:4603767 (4.3 MiB)
```

As you can see, the text display of Ethernet interface information provided by the `ifconfig` command still requires a certain amount of interpretation when compared to the friendlier display of information shown in Figure 21-11.

In addition to a more readable display of basic network configuration information, the Network Tools application supports the graphical display of information produced by several standard network utilities, which traditionally operate only in Text mode. The tabs provided in the Network Tools application, along with the purpose of each tab, are the following from left to right:

- **Devices:** Displays configuration and traffic summary information for each available network interface on the system. This corresponds to the information provided by the traditional Linux/UNIX command-line ifconfig application.

- **Ping:** Displays connectivity and availability information by sending packets to a specified host or IP address, and displays elapsed time and success/failure information. This corresponds to the information provided by the traditional Linux/UNIX command-line ping application.

- **Netstat:** Displays status information about all active and available TCP and UDP network ports on the system. This corresponds to the information provided by the traditional Linux/UNIX command-line netstat application.

- **Traceroute:** Displays the systems through which communication to a specified host pass and the time required for each intersystem communication, known as a *hop*. This corresponds to the information provided by the traditional Linux/UNIX command-line traceroute application.

- **Port Scan:** Displays information about available ports and services on a specified remote machine. This roughly corresponds to the information provided by the traditional Linux/UNIX command-line nmap application.

- **Lookup:** Displays IP address information and available DNS aliases for a specified system. This roughly corresponds to the information provided by the traditional Linux/UNIX command-line nslookup or host applications.

- **Finger:** Displays any available personal information about a specific user or a specified host. This corresponds to the information provided by the traditional Linux/UNIX command-line finger application. Few hosts provide this information any longer.

- **Whois:** Displays information about the registrant and technical contact for a specified Internet domain. This corresponds to the information provided by the traditional Linux/UNIX command-line whois or bwhois applications.

As an example of the type of information and display provided by the Network Tools application, Figure 21-12 shows DNS hostname lookup information as shown on its Lookup tab for the host www.vivisimo.com.

FIGURE 21-12

Graphical display of DNS name lookup

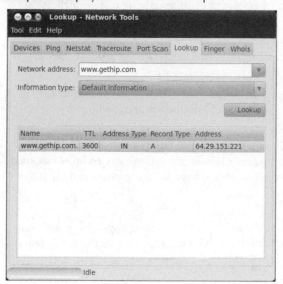

Tips for Securing Your System

System security is an open-ended topic because it has so many different aspects. These include physical security, login authentication, file and filesystem protections, and so on. Entire books have been written about security topics, and more are doubtless on the way. As mentioned in the introduction to this chapter, security in all forms will become an ever-increasing concern because of the increasing ubiquity of networking and the increasing availability of easy-to-use tools for probing, exploring, and breaking into remote machines.

The following are some specific suggestions for increasing the security of your system on a network. As you'd expect, these include some aspects of other security topics but also have their own unique concerns:

- If you are using an off-the-shelf home gateway, change the password before you put it into service. You should also change the name of the authenticated user if possible. If I had a nickel for how many systems have been broken into because people didn't change default passwords, I wouldn't even know how many nickels I had because most of these break-ins go unnoticed.

- Disable any unnecessary services on your system. You can use the Network Tools Port Scan tab to identify ports on your system that are listening for requests for services.

- Remove accounts for any users that are no longer using your system. This includes system accounts that were created for use by or with services that you are no longer running on your system.

- Always keep your system up-to-date using the Ubuntu Update Manager. Patches to system and application software are released for a (good) reason.

- Monitor important system log files regularly. The `/var/log/messages` and `/var/log/syslog` files can be an important source of information about who is trying to break into your system and how.

- Change your password regularly. Ubuntu's dependence on the `sudo` command rather than the traditional root account for system administration tasks is a useful obfuscation, but your dedicated cracker in Beijing often doesn't have anything better to do than try and try again.

As mentioned previously, security is your responsibility. Some interesting applications are available to test and probe your own system, which can be both educational and useful. My long-term favorites are:

- **chrootkit:** Checks for *root kits*, which is the term for precompiled sets of hacked applications that are often installed on systems that have been broken into. These root kits both make it easier for a cracker to get into your system again and also collect additional login/password information from a cracked system.

- **nmap:** Probes network connectivity on your machine and identifies potential problem points.

As you might expect, both of these applications are available in the Ubuntu repositories and can easily be installed on your system with any of the Package Management tools discussed in Chapter 19.

Installing a Firewall

Firewall is the term used to describe a system that sits between one or more computer systems and monitors and manages network traffic. Just like the firewall in your automobile, which prevents a fire in the engine compartment from proceeding into the passenger compartment and incinerating its occupants, a network firewall is intended to prevent malicious, spurious, or unnecessary network traffic from moving through it. Many firewalls serve multiple functions, also performing services such as Network Address Translation (NAT), but their primary purpose is to protect against network attacks and other unwelcome intrusions.

On modern Linux systems, firewalling is typically done using kernel modules that support a packet-filtering framework known as Netfilter, and an associated interface and user-space command known as iptables. *Packet filtering* refers to the ability to analyze network packets and perform various actions based on their source, destination, type, or other information that they contain. Because support for packet filtering is built into the Linux kernel, a Linux system that is directly connected to the Internet can serve as its own firewall, monitoring and managing network traffic before that traffic actually gets to any daemons or network-aware processes that it is running. Of course, a dedicated device or Linux system can also serve as a firewall, and many vendors sell prepackaged solutions that do just that. The fact that many of these off-the-shelf systems run Linux and use the Netfilter/iptables mechanism to implement their firewalling solutions is just proof of the power of the Linux kernel's built-in support for packet filtering.

Whether or not a Linux system actually requires a firewall is a hot debate topic among Linux fans. Standard Ubuntu Desktop installations do not expose any open ports to an outside network, so there are no network ports that need to be protected. This is not true, of course, for Ubuntu server systems that expose ports for services such as DNS, e-mail, SSH, a Web server, and so on, so a firewall is always a good idea for any server system.

Tip

If you are using your Ubuntu system in an environment that is already protected by a firewall, you probably do not need to set up a firewall on your system. You should, however, make sure that the firewall that your system is located behind is actually doing the right thing by checking with the manufacturer, your IT group in a business or academic environment, or your Internet service provider. Just because a box has *Firewall* printed on it doesn't mean that it is actually doing anything. ∎

As far as Ubuntu desktop systems go, you will probably find yourself opening up some ports on a desktop installation as you use your system over time, and a Netfilter/iptables firewall introduces very little overhead on a desktop system, so I suggest that you always install at least a simple firewall. This way, if you subsequently increase the exposure of your system by opening ports, the firewall will already be in place. You may want to revisit your initial firewall implementation in the future, but you will at least have some protection even if you neglect firewalling in your excitement to make some new service available from your Ubuntu system. Installing a simple firewall by default is also a good idea if you are setting up systems for friends, relatives, or small businesses, where you may not always have complete control over what they add to or activate on their systems.

Overview of Linux Firewalling and Packet Filtering

The packet-filtering mechanism used by the current Linux kernel (2.6.xx) is a combination of a loadable kernel module framework and API called *Netfilter*, and an interface and associated and user-space administrative command called iptables. The iptables interface is one of several kernel modules based on the Netfilter framework; others include a module that handles Network Address Translation (which enables multiple machines to share one public IP address) and the module that implements and supports connection tracking. Throughout the rest of this chapter,

I will collectively refer to this as `iptables`, because that is the interface that is most commonly associated with modern Linux firewalls and packet filtering.

The `iptables` interface and the Netfilter framework are actually the fourth generation of Linux packet-filtering solutions. The original Linux packet-filtering implementation `ipfw` was liberated from BSD-based systems and was introduced in Linux by Alan Cox in the Linux 1.1 kernel; it was designed to support the creation of simple IP firewalls and routers through packet inspection and filtering. The `iwfwadmin` tool and associated `ipfw` changes, which simplified creating `ipfw`-based firewalls, were added to the Linux 2.0 kernel and make up the second generation. The third generation of Linux packet filtering, consisting of a major rewrite of the entire Linux networking layer and introducing the user-space `ipchains` tool, was introduced in the 2.1 kernel series. The current Netfilter framework and `iptables` interface were introduced in the 2.4 kernel and have been the standard mechanism for packet filtering, network address and port translation, and general packet manipulation (often referred to as *packet mangling*) in the 2.6 series of Linux kernels.

Linux packet filtering works by inspecting incoming and outgoing packets and acting on them based on filtering rules that have been loaded into the Netfilter framework's filter table by the `iptables` command. By default, the `iptables` command supports three default sets of rules, known as *chains*, for filtering network packets using the information stored in the `iptables` filter table. These default chains are the INPUT, OUTPUT, and FORWARD chains. The rules in the INPUT chain are used to examine and process incoming packets intended for ports on the local machine. The rules in the OUTPUT chain are for examining and processing outgoing packets that are being sent from the local machine. And the rules in the FORWARD chain are used to examine and process packets that are being routed through the local machine.

Each of the default filtering-rule chains can have its own set of filtering rules. You can also define other sets of rules and use them for your own purposes. Many modern Linux and other UNIX-like systems come with predefined INPUT, OUTPUT, and FORWARD rule chains and automatically load them at boot time. As discussed later in this chapter, a variety of graphical and command-line software is available for all Linux distributions to make it easy to define your own packet-filtering rules.

Other Netfilter-based modules use packet-matching tables other than the filter table. The NAT module uses the NAT table, which contains three built-in rule chains: OUTPUT, POSTROUTING, and PREROUTING. Specialized packet manipulation operations use the mangle table, which contains prebuilt FORWARD, INPUT, OUTPUT, PREROUTING, and POSTROUTING chains. The connection tracking module uses the raw table, which contains preconfigured OUTPUT and PREROUTING chains.

You must have superuser privileges to examine, create, or modify any Netfilter-based rule chains. You can do this by putting `iptables` commands in a script that is executed as part of the system's boot process or by using a command such as `sudo` as a normal user to run the `iptables` commands with root privileges.

Installing and Configuring a Firewall

As mentioned in the previous section, many different software packages are available to help you configure and activate a firewall on your Ubuntu system. These packages include the default package that is installed on Ubuntu systems, ufw (the Uncomplicated Firewall), Lokkit, Firestarter, Fwbuilder, Guarddog, and many more.

The default firewall package for Ubuntu systems, ufw, is relatively easy to configure from the command line, but is even easier to configure using its associated graphical configuration utility, gufw. Unfortunately, this utility is not installed by default on Ubuntu systems. You will have to install it using your favorite Package Management tool, as discussed in Chapter 19. This graphical configuration tool is worth using unless you're a firewall wizard (in which case, I doubt you'd be reading this section), and therefore the rest of this section focuses on using the graphical gufw utility.

Installing the gufw graphical configuration utility adds the Firewall Configuration menu entry to the System ⇨? Administration menu on an Ubuntu system. Select this menu entry to begin configuring your firewall. After entering your password, the initial gufw dialog appears, as shown in Figure 21-13.

The initial gufw dialog

The first thing that you will want to do when configuring a firewall is to enable that firewall on your system. Click the "Firewall enabled" checkbox to do so. The shield graphic shown in Figure 21-13 will be displayed in green, helping you identify the fact that the firewall is now enabled and that your system is secure if you use the current configuration. The other configuration options on the gufw dialog will also be enabled, as shown in Figure 21-14.

FIGURE 21-14

Enabling your firewall

The gufw tool's Add button displays a dialog that makes it easy for you to create various types of rules without having to understand the syntax of the kernel's iptables rules. Click Add to display this dialog. Once you enable a firewall, all incoming traffic is disabled by default, which is secure but probably not what you want if you plan to support network services such as incoming SSH connections, incoming FTP, and so on. Note that you do not need to select the "Allow incoming" radio button shown in Figure 21-14 to enable incoming traffic. The radio buttons at the top left of the gufw dialog identify the default behavior of your system. Any rules that you subsequently define represent exceptions to that rule. For example, to quickly create a rule that allows incoming SSH connections, make sure that the Simple tab is selected in the "Add rule" dialog, enter **ssh** in the text entry field for this rule, and make sure that the first two fields display "Allow" and "In", respectively, as shown in Figure 21-15. Click Add to add the new rule. Once you add a rule, it displays in the main gufw dialog.

Click Add to add the new rule. The rule is added to the list of rules shown in the bottom of the gufw dialog, as shown in Figure 21-16, and your firewall will now allow both incoming and outbound SSH traffic.

FIGURE 21-15

Allowing inbound/outbound SSH connections through your firewall

FIGURE 21-16

Rules for allowing inbound SSH connections

The rules shown at the bottom of the `gufw` dialog refer to the ports associated with various services, which is not very user-friendly. If you aren't sure about the service that a rule is associated with, you can use the `grep` command to look up the port that it uses in the file `/etc/services`. For example, the following output shows how to look for the services associated with port 22 in this file:

```
$ grep -w 22 /etc/services
ssh                22/tcp          # SSH Remote Login Protocol
ssh                22/udp
```

The other tabs in the `gufw` utility's Add rule dialog make it easy to define other types of rules. The Preconfigured tab provides a drop-down menu with number of default rules that you can use to enable (or disable) external access to various programs and services. To create a rule associated with a service rather than a specific program, click Programs, and select Services from the drop-down menu that displays. You can then click the fourth field to display a list of services for which pre-defined rules exist, as shown in Figure 21-17.

Preconfigured rules for various services

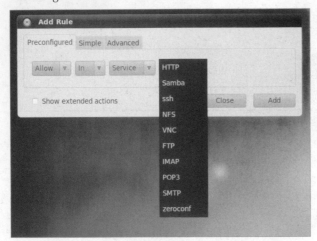

You can also use the Preconfigured tab to define other types of rules by selecting them from the Type dropdown menu at the left. For example, Figure 21-18 shows a rule that enables NFS traffic but also limits the bandwidth used by that service.

If you need more complex rules than the ones that can be created from the Simple or Preconfigured tabs, the Advanced tab, shown in Figure 21-19, provides a general mechanism for defining more sophisticated rules.

Enabling NFS access

FIGURE 21-19

Defining advanced rules

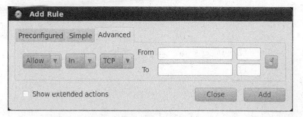

The Advanced rules tab makes it easy for you to add host or network-specific rules that enable traffic from specific hosts or networks to specific ports on your system, and vice versa.

Once you have finished defining the rules for the traffic that your firewall will allow or deny, click Close to save your rules and terminate the gufw utility. If you're curious, you can use the sudo iptables -L command to see what the rules that you have just created look like, which should make you eternally grateful for a tool like gufw.

Summary

This chapter explained the basics of setting up wired and wireless network connections on your Ubuntu system. Ubuntu systems provide easy-to-use graphical applets that simplify configuring these types of interfaces, eliminating the traditional command-line magic required when you are using the ifconfig command. This chapter also provided a basic discussion of securing your Ubuntu system and related networking hardware, and also discussed setting up a simple firewall on your Ubuntu system.

Chapter 22 discusses using wireless technologies on your Ubuntu system in more detail, providing a detailed explanation of setting up and using Wicd, an alternative to the Network Manager software that was discussed in this section. Chapter 22 also includes a detailed explanation of how to use Windows drivers on your Ubuntu system to make new or problematic Ethernet and other devices work with your new Linux system.

Going Wireless

Today's mandatory connectivity requirements would be a farce without the ubiquity of wireless connections, whether these are cell phones leveraging a distant tower, your cell phone or PDA syncing to your PC via Bluetooth or infrared, or your laptop using wireless network connections via an access point hidden in the linen closet in your hotel. It is incredibly liberating to be able to travel without carrying every cable and adapter that could possibly connect device A to device B, especially when airport security seems to frown on suitcases full of cables, power supplies, and connectivity hardware as last seen in the laboratory of Victor von Frankenstein (no relation to the author).

Like many other high-tech domains, wireless networking has its own vocabulary and a bewildering set of alphabetically similar but conceptually unique acronyms, protocols, and so on. The first section of this chapter provides a basic overview of wireless networking and associated terminology today. Subsequent sections of this chapter explain how to configure wireless devices that are directly supported by Linux, explain how to work with wireless devices that are not supported by Linux (an impressive trick), and provide tips and tricks for using Microsoft Windows drivers with your Ubuntu Linux system.

Overview of Wireless Technologies

Wireless networking is amazingly useful, both on the job (so that you never have to play rock/paper/scissors over a limited number of Ethernet cables in a conference room) and even more so when traveling, enabling you to connect laptops, phones, and PDAs to the Internet in libraries, coffee shops, hotels, and many other public places. Wireless networking also provides an excellent mechanism for connecting networks of computers that are located in inaccessible locations or in existing structures where running new or additional cabling is a problem. Excluding security concerns, wireless networks can prevent the need to drill additional holes through Mount Vernon, the Vatican, or the Louvre.

As used in this chapter, *wireless networking* refers to technology that enables a computer to communicate using standard network protocols, but without network cabling. Most commonly, *wireless networks* are local area networks (LANs) whose members use industry standards such as Institute of Electrical and Electronics Engineers (IEEE) 802.11 to communicate. The original 802.11 standard was released in 1997 and defines the frequencies, data rates, and media access methods used to communicate between the participants in a wireless network. Subsequent standards have defined a potentially bewildering variety of 802.11X standards, which I'll discuss a bit later in this section.

Regardless of the frequency and speed at which participants communicate, there are two basic types of wireless networks: ad hoc wireless networks and managed wireless networks. The characteristics of each (and their differences) are:

- **Ad hoc networks:** Also referred to as *peer-to-peer wireless networks*, these consist of some number of computers, each of which has a wireless networking interface card and communicate directly with all of the other wireless computers on that network. This enables them to share files and printers, but will not provide access to wired or Internet network resources unless one (or more) of the computers is also connected to those other network resources and is configured to serve as a gateway, bridge, or router to the other network(s). Acronym fans may see ad hoc networks referred to as *IBSS* (Independent Basic Service Sets).

- **Managed networks:** Also referred to as *infrastructure wireless networks*, these use an access point (sometimes also referred to as a *base station*) to manage communication between multiple wireless computers, acting much like a hub or switch for the wireless network. An access point is also typically connected to a wired network such as the Internet and serves as the bridge or gateway between the wireless and wired networks. Access points are traditionally dedicated hardware devices (sometimes referred to as a *HAP*, a hardware access point), such as Apple's Airports or devices from companies such as DLink, LinkSys, NetGear, Cisco, and others, but can also be software solutions (referred to as *SAPs*, software access points) that run on a computer that is equipped with both wired and wireless network connections. Acronym fans may see managed networks referred to as a *BSS* (Basic Service Set; N computers and one access point) or *ESS* (Extended Service Set; N access points and N computers forming one subnet).

Large areas that require wireless coverage can accomplish this by providing multiple access points and supporting roaming, which is the ability of a user's connection to transfer from one access point to another. This is usually invisible to the user, although some access points require passwords or other authentication when moving between access points. Many networking hardware vendors also provide specialized hardware known as *extension points* that amplify the signal and therefore extend the range of an existing access point. Whether or not hardware access points support roaming or extension points is dependent on the hardware manufacturer. As with most networking hardware, a good rule of thumb is that buying all of your network hardware from the same vendor increases your chances for compatibility.

Agreement between the low-level wireless networking standards that the computers in your wireless network use is the most important aspect of setting up a successful wireless network. If the computers and access points can't communicate in the first place, you aren't going to be setting up much of anything. Although IEEE 802.11 is a published standard for wireless communication, several different 802.11 protocols and associated standards exist, not all of which are compatible with each other. The following is a current list of popular 802.11 standards, communication speeds, and compatibility promises:

- **802.11a:** A standard for 802.11 communications using the regulated 5.0 GHz (GigaHertz) frequency, offering maximum communication speeds of 25 to 54 Mbps (megabits per second). It is not compatible with any other 802.11 standard.

- **802.11b:** A standard for 802.11 communications using the unregulated 2.4 GHz frequency, offering maximum communication speeds of 5 to 11 Mbps. The 802.11b standard is forward-compatible with the 802.11g and proposed 802.11n standards.

Tip

Some vendors offer wireless cards known as *dual-band* cards, which support both 802.11a and 802.11b, operating in the frequency range and with communications speeds dictated by the type of connection that they establish. ■

- **802.11g:** A standard for 802.11 communications using the unregulated 2.4 GHz frequency, offering maximum communication speeds of 25 to 54 Mbps. The 802.11g standard is backward-compatible with the 802.11b standard and forward-compatible with the proposed 802.11n standard.

- **802.11n:** A standard for 802.11 communications using the unregulated 2.4 GHz frequency, offering maximum communications speeds of 100 to 300 Mbps. The 802.11n standard is designed to be backward-compatible with the 802.11b and 802.11g standards.

Caution

Trying to get the jump on the competition, many hardware vendors released supposed "802.11n hardware"—you will see many wireless cards advertised as 802.11 Draft-N cards to recognize the fact that they adhere to an early version of the standard. If you have one of these "pre-standard" devices, a good rule of thumb for compatibility between supposed 802.11n devices is "buy everything from the same vendor." Most vendors' hardware will, after all, work with their other hardware. Worst case, you only have one vendor to complain to. ■

Many wireless cards are advertised as 802.11 b/g or 802.11 b/g/n cards because they can communicate with all of these networks. When using cards that support all of these standards, the speed of your connection is determined by the speed/type of the access point that they establish a connection with.

Wireless networks also support a variety of security solutions, ranging from network names to encryption mechanisms. The most common of these are the following:

- **MAC (Media Access Control) filtering:** A security mechanism that requires that access points be programmed with lists of the systems that can connect to them, identified by hardware Ethernet address. MAC security only prevents against unauthorized connections to an access point—it does not secure those communications, once established.

- **SSID (Service Set Identifier):** An SSID acts as a simple password by providing a unique identifier for a specific wireless network. Access points with a specific SSID can be configured to disallow access to anyone who does not provide that SSID when negotiating the initial connection. SSID security only prevents unauthorized connections to an access point—it does not secure those communications, once established. An *Extended Service Set Identifier* (ESSID) is just an SSID that is (or can be) used on multiple access points to identify the same network.

- **WEP (Wired Equivalent Privacy):** A security mechanism that requires supplying a 48-, 64-, or 128-bit security key when negotiating a connection to an access point. This key is used for encrypting and decrypting wireless communications. If this key is the same as that used by the access point, the two can communicate successfully. WEP security protects against unauthorized access and also provides secure wireless communication, because all communication packets are encrypted. Although still quite common, WEP keys can be cracked in a few minutes using popular open source packages such as Aircrack-ng (www.aircrack-ng.org/doku.php) and Kismet (www.kismetwireless .net/index.shtml).

- **WPA (Wi-Fi Protected Access):** A security mechanism that uses a Temporary Key Integrity Protocol to replace WEP and provides enhanced security on existing hardware. WPA uses a key server or pre-generated key set to encrypt communications on a per-packet basis. Multiple WPA standards exist: WPA, which was developed using a draft of the IEEE 802.11i security standard; WPA2, which was developed using an approved version of the 802.11i security standard; WPA Personal, which uses pre-shared key mode (PSK) and stores keys in access points; and WPA Enterprise, which uses a networked authentication server and supports a number of EAP (Extensible Authentication Protocol) security mechanisms.

All of these security measures can be used together, in any combination, or separately. Only WEP and WPA provide security for the packets that are being transmitted, but typing in a 128-bit key each time you configure a new wireless interface is both error-prone and incredibly tedious. Many sites, therefore, use MAC and SSID/ESSID security to establish connections, and then protect transmitted packets by using standard SSH tunneling or VPN technologies on top of the wireless communication layer.

The Linux kernel includes drivers for many popular PCI wireless cards, PCMCIA wireless adapters, and USB wireless adapters. On Ubuntu systems, wireless Ethernet interfaces are configured in the same way as wired Ethernet interfaces, which I'll explain in the next section.

If no Linux driver is available for your wireless card, all is not lost. Thanks to the cleverness of the folks in the open source community, a Linux kernel module and related utilities, called ndiswrapper, enables you to use the Microsoft Windows drivers for much of the networking hardware that is not yet natively supported by Linux. Installing these utilities, installing Windows drivers under Linux, and configuring your system to automatically start loading the kernel module are discussed later in this section.

Using systems that have both wired and wireless interfaces is quite common nowadays. Even though wireless specifications such as 802.11g and 802.11n provide high communication speeds, they can't match the speed of the high-speed wired connections such as Gigabit Ethernet connections. It's, therefore, a shame not to use your system's wired connection whenever possible. However, it's tough to travel and get work done while dragging along hundreds of miles of Ethernet cable — the convenience and flexibility of wireless network access far outweigh the slower performance that it provides. The Network Manager and the Ubuntu applet that simplifies configuring it make it relatively easy to use a wireless network interface from a variety of locations, and are discussed in detail in Chapter 21. However, we're talking about Linux here, so there are always alternatives. One extremely impressive alternative to the Network Manager is the wicd package, which is discussed in the next section.

Using Wicd

Wicd is an alternate Network Manager for Linux systems that makes it easy to establish connections to wired and wireless networks. Wicd is often easier to use and is frequently more successful at establishing connections to secure networks than the traditional Linux Network Manager. The Network Manager is a fine piece of software that usually works — however, when it doesn't, it is a total PITA (and I'm not referring to the popular Middle Eastern bread). As a replacement for the Network Manager and related applets, Wicd conflicts with the Network Manager, and only one of these network connection management packages can be installed on a system at a time. Luckily, as discussed in the next section, installing Wicd on a system where the Network Manager is installed will automatically purge the Network Manager for you. No fuss, no muss.

The next sections explain how to install, use, and configure Wicd to meet your needs. It's really a great application, which I use on all of my laptop systems (and any desktops with both wired and wireless network interfaces) rather than the Network Manager.

Installing Wicd

Ubuntu systems are currently committed to the Network Manager and related applets, so in order to install Wicd, you will first have to modify the list of sources that provide repositories from which your Ubuntu systems can install software. You can do this using Ubuntu's System ➪ Administration ➪ Software Sources application, or by directly modifying your /etc/apt/sources.list file. You will need to add the following entry in any of these locations:

```
deb http://apt.wicd.net lucid extras
```

If you are using a version of Ubuntu other than Lucid Lynx (10.04), you should replace *lucid* with the name of the version of Ubuntu that you are using (*karmic*, *jackalope*, *hardy*, etc.). If you are using Synaptic, it will automatically update the lists of available packages that it knows about. If you directly modified your /etc/apt/sources.list file, you will need to tell whatever package management software you are using to update its package lists. If you are using aptitude to install software, you can do this by executing the command sudo aptitude update from any command-line environment. If you have problems updating your package management application's list of available packages, see Chapter 19 for more information about updating package lists in whatever package manager you are using.

Before installing Wicd, you should also import its privacy key so that your package manager won't warn you about the dangers of installing software from unauthorized sources. You can import this key from any command-line environment by executing the following command:

```
wget -q http://apt.wicd.net/wicd.gpg -O- | sudo apt-key add -
```

After importing the Wicd key, you can use your favorite package management tool to install the wicd package. As a replacement for the Network Manager and its applet buddies, Wicd conflicts with the Network Manager, and only one of these network connection management packages can be installed on a system at a time. However, as mentioned previously, installing Wicd on a system where the Network Manager is installed will automatically purge the Network Manager and related applets for you. Installing Wicd will install both the Wicd daemon (/usr/bin/wicd) and a Python-based client application for your Ubuntu system's Notification Area. This client application will start automatically the next time that you log in on your system, but if it doesn't start automatically when you install Wicd, you can execute it manually by executing the command /usr/bin/wicd-client& from any command-line environment.

Using Wicd

To start the client portion of Wicd, click on its tray icon to display a screen like the one shown in Figure 22-1.

This initial dialog should show an entry for the wired connection on your system and any wireless networks that have been detected. The wireless networks that are listed depend on those that are detected in your location—if the screen that you see when you first start Wicd looks exactly like the one shown in Figure 22-1, then I'm flattered (and a little creeped out) that you're reading this book from somewhere in my house.

As you can see from Figure 22-1, Wicd initially identifies all available wired and wireless connections, but does not automatically connect to any of them by default. To connect to any of these, click the Connect button below that entry. If you attempt to connect to a network that requires authentication, you will immediately see a dialog like the one shown in Figure 22-2, which tells you that the connection requires encryption.

FIGURE 22-1

FIGURE 22-1

The Wicd Manager dialog

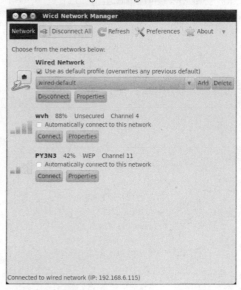

FIGURE 22-2

Attempting a connection that requires a password or key

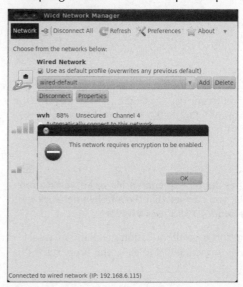

If you see the dialog shown in Figure 22-2, click OK to dismiss it, which automatically displays the dialog that is normally shown by clicking the Properties button below the name of the network that you were attempting to connect to. This dialog contains fields and dropdowns that you must use to define the encryption/authentication information that is required to establish a connection to that network, as shown in Figure 22-3.

FIGURE 22-3

Configuration options for a given wireless network

Make sure that the "Use Encryption" checkbox is selected, and click the dropdown list near the bottom of this dialog to display your encryption and authentication options. Select the mechanism that is used by the wireless network that you want to connect to, and enter the information that it requires in the fields that are displayed. For example, Figure 22-3 shows the area for entering a hexadecimal WEP key for a network that uses WEP.

Tip

Each wireless network shown in the dialog in Figure 22-1 identifies the type of encryption or authentication that it uses in the heading for that wireless network. For example, you can see that the wireless network wvh does not use authentication or encryption, while the wireless network PY3N3 uses WEP. ■

After entering the information required by the encryption or authentication mechanism associated with the wireless network that you want to connect to, click OK to close the Properties dialog and return to a screen like the one shown in Figure 22-1. If you want to try to connect to this wireless network each time you start your system, select the "Automatically connect to this network" option. Click Connect to connect to the specified wireless network. You will see status messages and a progress bar at the bottom of the Wicd Manager dialog, and the Wicd Manager will display a screen like the one shown in Figure 22-4 once the connection has been established successfully.

FIGURE 22-4

A successful connection to a wireless network

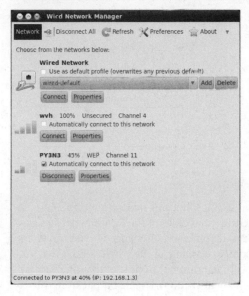

This dialog displays the IP address and transmission rate for your new connection at the bottom of the Wicd Manager window. You can now close the Wicd Manager dialog by clicking the Close box in its upper right-hand corner.

That's really all there is to it, except for some optional Wicd configuration that you may or may not want to do. Configuring Wicd is discussed in the next section.

Configuring Wicd

To configure Wicd, select the Preferences menu option from the Wicd Manager to display its Preferences dialog, as shown in Figure 22-5.

FIGURE 22-5

Setting preferences for Wicd

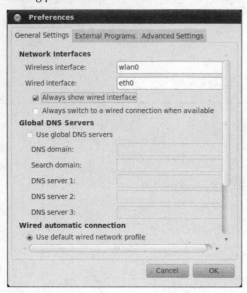

In most cases, you won't need to modify Wicd's basic settings, but this dialog provides some useful options. The handiest of these is the ability to identify the names of the Ethernet devices associated with wired and wireless devices on your system. If you insert or change wireless adapters while Wicd is running, you will probably need to modify the name of the wireless Ethernet device. After inserting a new wireless interface, you can determine the name of that interface by using the iwlist command, which is discussed in the next section. Sample output from this command looks like the following:

```
$ iwconfig
lo        no wireless extensions.

eth0      no wireless extensions.

irda0     no wireless extensions.

pan0      no wireless extensions.
```

```
wlan0      IEEE 802.11b+/g+  ESSID:"wvh"  Nickname:"acx v0.3.36"
           Mode:Managed  Frequency:2.437 GHz  Access Point: 00:06:25:/B:CE:3F
           Bit Rate:5.5 Mb/s   Tx-Power=15 dBm   Sensitivity=1/3
           Retry min limit:7   RTS thr:off
           Power Management:off
           Link Quality=31/100  Signal level=3/100  Noise level-0/100
           Rx invalid nwid:0  Rx invalid crypt:0  Rx invalid frag:0
           Tx excessive retries:0  Invalid misc:0  Missed beacon:0
```

In this case, the new wireless device on this system is wlan0, which you should then enter as the name of your wireless device in the dialog in Figure 22-5. If you change the name of your wireless (or wired) device, you can then click Close to close the Preferences dialog, and select the Refresh menu option in the Wicd Manager dialog to re-probe your networked environment and identify the wireless networks that can be detected using the new device.

The other option that I find useful in the dialog shown in Figure 22-5 is the "Always show wired interface" option, which should be selected to always list your system's wired interface in the main Wicd Manager dialog.

To see additional Wicd settings, click the External Programs tab to display the pane shown in Figure 22-6. Although you will rarely have to modify any of the settings on this dialog, doing so enables you to identify a specific application that you want to use as a DHCP client, to detect wireless links, to purge the routing table when switching network connections, and to display the password prompt when you attempt privileged operations such as network configuration.

Similarly, the Preference dialog's Advanced Settings tab provides other low-level configuration settings, as shown in Figure 22-7. Although you will rarely have to modify any of the settings on this dialog, you can select another application use to exchange authentication information. Doing so enables you to identify a specific driver for WPA authentication. If you are using the NDIS Wrapper application (discussed later in this chapter) to use Microsoft Windows network drivers on your Linux system, your system may automatically set the WPA Supplicant application to "ndiswrapper," which I usually have to change back to "wext" to get things working correctly. That and occasionally activating debugging when working with a stubborn wireless adapter (which writes detailed information to the Wicd log file in /var/log/wicd/wicd.log) are the only configuration changes that I've ever had to make on this dialog.

After making your changes or simply examining Wicd's current configuration, click OK to close the Preferences dialog and return to the Wicd Manager.

FIGURE 22-6

Setting external program preferences for Wicd

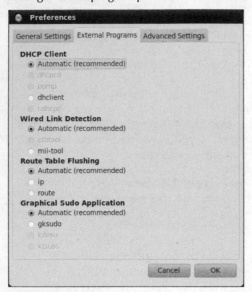

FIGURE 22-7

Configuring advanced settings for Wicd

Command-Line Tools for Wireless Networking

The wireless-tools package, which is installed on Ubuntu systems by default, provides several commands for probing and configuring wireless interfaces and networks. You can execute the man wireless command to get information about the wireless-tools package, learn how and where it is installed by various Linux distributions, and view a list of the commands that this package provides.

The wireless-tools commands that I find most valuable are the iwconfig and iwlist commands. The iwconfig command displays information much like the ifconfig command, providing information about the wireless status of all or specific Ethernet interfaces on a system. The following example shows the output of the iwconfig command, querying the wireless Ethernet interface that was installed in the previous section:

```
$ iwconfig wlan0
wlan0     IEEE 802.11b+/g+  ESSID:"wvh"  Nickname:"acx v0.3.36"
          Mode:Managed  Frequency:2.437 GHz  Access Point: 00:06:25:7B:CE:3F
          Bit Rate:5.5 Mb/s   Tx-Power=15 dBm   Sensitivity=1/3
          Retry min limit:7   RTS thr:off
          Power Management:off
          Link Quality=31/100  Signal level=3/100  Noise level=0/100
          Rx invalid nwid:0  Rx invalid crypt:0  Rx invalid frag:0
          Tx excessive retries:0  Invalid misc:0   Missed beacon:0
```

As you can see, this provides much of the same information as that provided by the ifconfig command, but it also includes wireless-specific information. The iwconfig command can also be used to set various wireless configuration options from the command line—see the online man page for iwconfig (using the command man iwconfig) for more information.

The iwlist command enables you to scan for wireless networks and examine various characteristics of a wireless interface. For example, scanning for wireless networks around my home using the iwlist wlan0 scan command displays the following information:

```
$ sudo iwlist wlan0 scanning
wlan0     Scan completed :
          Cell 01 - Address: 00:18:01:F4:0A:08
                    ESSID:"PY3N3"
                    Mode:Master
                    Frequency:2.462 GHz (Channel 11)
                    Quality=37/100  Signal level=12/100  Noise level=0/100
                    Encryption key:on
                    Bit Rates:1 Mb/s; 2 Mb/s; 5.5 Mb/s; 6 Mb/s; 9 Mb/s
                              11 Mb/s; 12 Mb/s; 18 Mb/s; 24 Mb/s; 36 Mb/s
                              48 Mb/s; 54 Mb/s
          Cell 02 - Address: 00:03:93:E9:89:22
```

```
                       ESSID:"wvh"
                       Mode:Master
                       Frequency:2.427 GHz (Channel 4)
                       Quality=52/100  Signal level=34/100  Noise level=0/100
                       Encryption key:off
                       Bit Rates:1 Mb/s; 2 Mb/s; 5.5 Mb/s; 6 Mb/s; 9 Mb/s
                                 11 Mb/s; 12 Mb/s; 18 Mb/s; 24 Mb/s; 36 Mb/s
                                 48 Mb/s; 54 Mb/s
             Cell 03 - Address: 00:06:25:7B:CE:3F
                       ESSID:"wvh"
                       Mode:Master
                       Frequency:2.437 GHz (Channel 6)
                       Quality=57/100  Signal level=40/100  Noise level=0/100
                       Encryption key:off
                       Bit Rates:1 Mb/s; 2 Mb/s; 5.5 Mb/s; 11 Mb/s
```

This command is useful for verifying that a wireless interface is actually working and that it can communicate with an access point. The information produced by the iwlist command is very useful in public areas, where you will usually detect more wireless networks, as in the following example from one of my laptops while I was on vacation:

```
$ sudo iwlist eth0 scan
Password:
eth0     Scan completed :
         Cell 01 - Address: 00:09:5B:36:22:38
                   ESSID:"Wireless"
                   Mode:Master
                   Frequency:2.412 GHz (Channel 1)
                   Signal level:20/153  Noise level:12/153
                   Encryption key:off
                   Bit Rates:1 Mb/s; 2 Mb/s; 5.5 Mb/s; 11 Mb/s
         Cell 02 - Address: 00:12:17:A6:E8:CC
                   ESSID:"linksys"
                   Mode:Master
                   Frequency:2.437 GHz (Channel 6)
                   Signal level:83/153  Noise level:13/153
                   Encryption key:off
                   Bit Rates:1 Mb/s; 2 Mb/s; 5.5 Mb/s; 11 Mb/s
         Cell 03 - Address: 00:12:17:A6:E8:CC
                   ESSID:"linksys"
                   Mode:Master
                   Frequency:2.437 GHz (Channel 6)
                   Signal level:81/153  Noise level:13/153
                   Encryption key:off
                   Bit Rates:1 Mb/s; 2 Mb/s; 5.5 Mb/s; 11 Mb/s
         Cell 04 - Address: 00:12:17:79:CF:D3
                   ESSID:"linksysR79cfd3"
                   Mode:Master
                   Frequency:2.437 GHz (Channel 6)
```

```
Signal level:49/153  Noise level:13/153
Encryption key:off
Bit Rates:1 Mb/s; 2 Mb/s; 5.5 Mb/s; 11 Mb/s; 18 Mb/s
             24 Mb/s; 36 Mb/s; 54 Mb/s
```

In this case, the information provided by the iwlist command was very useful in identifying available wireless access points, their names, and whether they were configured for authentication/encryption. The iwlist command can also query specific wireless configuration details—see the online man page for iwlist (using the command man iwlist) for more information.

Installing and Using Windows Networking Drivers

Device driver support is one of the few areas in which Linux lags behind Microsoft Windows. I hope that my making this statement doesn't induce Linus Torvalds to give me a call and demand the return of my official Linux Bigot decoder ring, but it's a fact. The reason that there are not Linux drivers for every piece of random hardware is not because of any problem or limitation in Linux, but rather because device manufacturers target their largest potential markets when writing device drivers for their hardware, and at the moment, the main market for random PC hardware is Microsoft Windows systems.

Clever folks in the open source community are writing new device drivers every day, and each new Linux kernel supports more hardware than ever before. However great that is, it doesn't help much when you need to use a specific Windows device today. Luckily, a Linux kernel module and related utilities, called ndiswrapper, enables you to use the Microsoft Windows drivers for much of the networking hardware that is not yet natively supported by Linux. How cool is that? Thanks to the ndiswrapper package, you can use Windows' own drivers on your superior Ubuntu Linux systems until a native Linux driver becomes available.

One obvious question is, "Why not just buy hardware that works with Linux in the first place?" To be honest, that's my general approach, but there are some very good reasons for wanting (or needing) to use hardware that is supposedly Windows-only. The most significant of these are the following:

- You already have a wireless network adapter that is not yet supported by Linux. Why buy another adapter if you don't have to?

- Dual-boot laptops may include built-in wireless hardware that is not supported by Linux. Similarly, if you are given a laptop as part of your job along with PCMCIA or USB network adapters that are not supported by Linux, using the Windows drivers with Ubuntu enables you to use a real operating system for work without requiring that you spend any money.

- Some wireless protocols, most specifically 802.11a, are poorly supported under Linux but are still used by many businesses. Because 802.11a is also largely extinct, I doubt that this will change. Using the Windows drivers for your 802.11a hardware enables you to run Linux at work, using existing hardware.

- There are a huge number of inexpensive wireless devices that only advertise support for Windows, even though you can use them with Linux by using the NDIS Wrapper package to leverage their existing Windows drivers.

The next few sections explain how to install this package and a handy graphical configuration utility, describe how to install a Windows driver on your Ubuntu system, and provide some tips and tricks for debugging problems and resolving problems using Windows drivers on your Ubuntu system.

Tip

Although primarily designed for use with Microsoft Windows drivers for network cards, the ndiswrapper package has been used with Windows drivers for many other devices, such as USB serial port devices, wired Ethernet cards, and so on. (For a complete list of devices that people have gotten to work with Windows drivers and the ndiswrapper package, see http://sourceforge.net/apps/mediawiki/ndiswrapper/index.php?mediawiki/index.php/List). If you have a device that came with Windows drivers that you can't get to work natively under Linux, the ndiswrapper package is certainly worth a try and is only a package management tool session install away. ■

Installing NDIS Wrapper and Friends

You will always want to install the ndiswrapper-modules package to get the Linux kernel module for the NDIS Wrapper software, but you'll probably also want to install some related utilities to simplify installing and configuring Microsoft Windows drivers. The ndisgtk package provides a graphical utility that simplifies installing and configuring Windows drivers; the ndiswrapper-utils package provides the underlying utilities that it uses, as well as a command-line utility that you can use to install Windows drivers if you're not a GUI fan. (The ndiswrapper-modules and ndiswrapper-utils packages will also have version numbers at the end of their names.) None of these packages are installed by default on Ubuntu systems because not everyone needs them, and why waste disk space if you don't have to?

See Chapter 19, "Adding, Removing, and Updating Software," for more detailed information on installing applications using a variety of package management tools.

Installing Microsoft Windows Drivers

This section explains how to install Microsoft Windows drivers using the graphical ndisgtk utility, which puts a friendly wrapper around the ndiswrapper utilities, kernel module, and Ubuntu network configuration. You can also install Windows drivers for use with the ndiswrapper kernel module by using the command sudo ndiswrapper -i name-of-INF-file from any command-line environment and then manually modifying some configuration files, but I prefer the graphical one-stop-shopping approach provided by the ndisgtk utility.

Note

Before installing Windows drivers, you must make sure that they are available on your Ubuntu system. This usually involves either putting the driver CD in your system so that it is available as /media/cdrom (or something similar, depending on the drives in your Ubuntu system) or copying a zip archive containing the drivers to your Ubuntu system and using the unzip command to extract the contents of that archive file into an Ubuntu directory. ■

Installing the ndisgtk package creates the System ➪ Administration ➪ Windows Wireless Drivers menu item on an Ubuntu System, which you can select to start the ndisgtk application. Figure 22-8 shows the initial driver installation dialog that is displayed when you first start this application.

FIGURE 22-8

The ndisgtk startup dialog

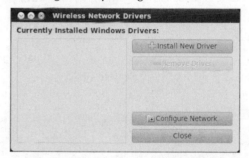

To install a driver, click "Install New Driver." This displays the dialog that enables you to select the INF file associated with a specific Windows driver, as shown in Figure 22-9. An INF file is a file with an .INF or .inf file extension that contains a description of a Windows driver, its installation options, associated files, and so on.

FIGURE 22-9

The INF file selection dialog for a Microsoft Windows driver

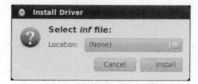

Click the Location button to display a standard file dialog that enables you to navigate to the directory containing the Windows driver and select the appropriate INF file. After navigating to and selecting the appropriate file, click Open to select that file and close the navigation dialog. The dialog shown in Figure 22-9 re-displays, showing the name of the selected INF file. (In this particular example, I'm installing the Windows drivers for an SMB W541C wireless adapter, although you wouldn't be able to guess that from the name of the driver or INF file.)

Click Install to install the driver and associated files for use by the ndiswrapper kernel module. The dialog shown in Figure 22-8 re-displays, now listing the driver that you've just installed and identifying if the hardware associated with that driver was located, as shown in Figure 22-10.

FIGURE 22-10

Loading the driver and detecting associated hardware

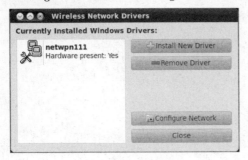

At this point, you can click Close to terminate the Windows driver installation process. Your network connection management software, whether Wicd or a Network Manager applet, should detect the new interface and offer options for using it.

To ensure that the ndiswrapper kernel module loads each time you restart your Ubuntu system, the ndiswrapper kernel module must be listed in the file that identifies modules that should be loaded at boot time, /etc/modules. This should have happened when you installed the package, but you may want to check. If you need to add an entry for this module, you can do so using your favorite text editor (which you must start using sudo so that you can edit this file), or via a command such as the following:

```
$ sudo echo "ndiswrapper" >> /etc/modules
```

Make sure that you use two angle brackets, not just one! If you accidentally use only one angle bracket, you will overwrite the contents of your existing /etc/modules file with a single line containing the name of the ndiswrapper module, which will probably certainly cause things like your mouse and printers to misbehave.

NDIS Wrapper Tips and Tricks

As you can see from the previous section, many Microsoft Windows drivers "just work" with the ndiswrapper kernel module when installed correctly. Unfortunately, some don't. I won't pretend to have tested every possible piece of wireless hardware and its associated Windows drivers (though I'd be happy to try if you would just send me a sample of the hardware that I can keep), but I have used many different ones with a wide selection of wireless hardware when configuring laptops for a variety of customers, coworkers, and friends.

For me, one of the most frustrating sets of experiences has been with a variety of LinkSys WPC54G wireless PCMCIA cards, all of which I've gotten working, but only after significant driver gymnastics, head scratching, Google searches, and commiseration with fellow Linux devotees. (I was originally planning to title this section "The LinkSys WPC54G, or How I Spent My Summer Vacation," but I am trying to generalize what I've learned rather than simply provide a single set of instructions.) By the way, these are great cards that support 802.11g (and therefore 802.11b), and because I typically find LinkSys hardware to be inexpensive and reliable, I often recommend them to friends. Unfortunately, a *huge* problem with these cards is that LinkSys has used a variety of wireless chips in them over the years, so they often use different drivers, each of which seems to require its own tweaks to get it to work with the ndiswrapper module.

One key item is to make sure that you have the right Windows drivers in the first place. For example, some of the 54G cards use a Realtek 8180 chipset, and, therefore, only work with these drivers. Others use a Texas Instruments ACX 1*xx* chipset, while others use the Broadcom BCM43*xx*, and some newer ones are rumored to use a Marvell chipset. If you can't identify the chipset by reading the product literature, you can usually identify it by using the lspci utility to list all of the PCI devices on your system and by scanning the lspci output for anything identified as a wireless controller.

As an example of driver and chipset weirdness, the Texas Instruments ACX 1*xx* chipset is directly supported under Linux, using the acx and acx_pci kernel modules (no ndiswrapper module required, although I prefer the ndiswrapper approach), but often requires that you play around with different versions of the microcode in /lib/firware/kernel-version/acx until you find the right version and name (see the Ubuntu Forums for some suggestions). If you want to use the ndiswrapper version of the 54G driver with ndiswrapper, you have to blacklist the standard Linux kernel modules by adding their names to /etc/modprobe.d/blacklist so that they are not loaded during the hardware detection phase of the boot process.

If you're sure that you have the right driver but still can't get it to work, use the Linux dmesg command to display recent kernel messages for error messages related to the ndiswrapper, the card that you're using, or any of the chipsets mentioned in the previous paragraph. This can help identify specific problems.

The WPC54G cards that use the Broadcom BCM43xx have a particularly interesting wrinkle—they require a specific microcode firmware driver that is bundled inside the Windows driver (bcmwl5.sys) but that must be provided as a stand-alone file in the /lib/firmware directory that the Linux kernel checks for firmware microcode. You must, therefore, use a utility called `bcm43xx-fwcutter` to extract the different firmware files from the driver and copy them into `/lib/firmware` before you can use this version of the card. If you have this version of the card, you can download the latest version of this utility from the page at `http://developer .berlios.de/project/showfiles.php?group_id=4547`.

As mentioned previously, these are examples of the types of problems that you may encounter when working with a random Windows driver, random wireless hardware, and the `ndiswrapper` package. Many people seem worried about the quality of open source code, but I think that the quality of Windows drivers is just as suspect. However, as my grandfather used to say, "A dysfunctional driver in the hand is worth several driver projects that are under development in the bush" (or something like that).

Tip

The `ndiswrapper` **developers provide as much online help as they can via the resources listed at** `http:// sourceforge.net/apps/mediawiki/ndiswrapper/index.php?support.html`**. If the people there can't solve your problem and you absolutely need to use a specific piece of "Windows-only" wireless hardware, a company called Linuxant (`www.linuxant.com`) provides an excellent piece of software called DriverLoader that is very similar to the** `ndiswrapper` **package. The Linuxant folks test their product on a huge selection of wireless hardware. They also offer Linux drivers for selected softmodem cards (modem cards that do everything in software, a traditional pain for Linux users). You can download a 30-day trial of the DriverLoader software to test it with your specific hardware, and also have the benefit of Linuxant's support personnel and extensive user community when diagnosing and resolving problems.** ◼

Summary

This chapter explored one of the most liberating and empowering features of computing today, wireless networking. Wireless networking is not only convenient from the standpoint of having fewer cables strewn around your house, but also enables people to do real work from their laptops, moving from conference room to conference room, office to office, and even city to city without having to plug their machines in and laboriously reconnect to and synchronize with a given network.

The next chapter moves into territory that is the traditional bugaboo of Linux systems—how to compile your own software on an Ubuntu system. Ubuntu systems do not include a compilation environment in their default installations because not everyone needs them, but more importantly, because the Ubuntu repositories provide such a great selection of software that you rarely have to do this unless you want to (or are a developer). The need to roll your own versions of applications on Linux systems is a traditional part of the FUD (Fear, Uncertainty, Doubt) that Linux detractors use to support their claims that Linux is hard to use and only for nerds. This is not true at all. Not only is building your own applications optional nowadays, but package management software like `apt-get`, `aptitude`, and `Synaptic` make it easy to install build tools and a powerful IDE if you need them.

Software Development on Ubuntu

As pointed out on the web site and throughout this book, Ubuntu is a distribution for everybody. And that includes developers! Just because Ubuntu is easy to use doesn't mean that serious, hard-core developers can't get real work done on an Ubuntu system — quite the contrary, actually. A good, recursive proof of this is the Ubuntu distribution itself, which is built by Ubuntu developers on Ubuntu systems. In addition, the fact that Ubuntu offers such a great user experience means that the time that you might ordinarily spend tweaking and fine-tuning your Linux desktop and installed software can be devoted to more productive pursuits, such as working on your personal code projects. The whole world may be waiting for your software!

Linux, in general, has a bad rep among many of the users of other platforms such as Microsoft Windows and Mac OS X, who often see Linux users as cave dwellers using VT100 terminals and living at the command line. Although there's a lot to be said for the command line, modern Linux distributions like Ubuntu strike just the right balance between providing graphical utilities for just about everything, with command-line access when and if you need it. The modern Linux model is strikingly similar to the user model provided by Mac OS X, and recent versions of Microsoft Windows include "new" tools that provide support for extensive use of the command line and sophisticated command-script support. Does any of that ring a bell?

This chapter explains how to install the packages that you'll need for most Linux software development projects, starting with the fundamentals of installing the world's most powerful compiler, gcc, the C compiler that is provided as part of the Free Software Foundation's GNU Compiler Collection (GCC)], related tools that you'll need to provide a complete software build environment on your Ubuntu system, and then branches out to

IN THIS CHAPTER

Installing a standard build environment

Using make to simplify recompilation

Installing and using the Eclipse IDE

Installing, configuring, and using Subversion

discuss other software packages that many people use when creating and maintaining software on Linux systems. These other packages include integrated development environments (IDEs) that put an easy-to-use face on modern software development, and source code control and management software so that you can easily track changes to your software.

Installing and Using Development Software

Ubuntu systems don't provide a software build environment out-of-the-box because many people don't want to do software development. After all, these distributions provide a great user solution and a tremendous selection of software packages, so many people will never need to build their own software. Providing the software that users need and providing it in an integrated, easy-to-install, and easy-to-manage way is what Linux distributions are all about in the first place.

For me, the most important part of the term *software* is the word *soft*. Software is flexible. Different people need different software packages to reflect their interests. When you're writing your own program to do "the right thing" that no one else seems to understand the need for, or simply want to use a special-purpose package that you can't live without from some random web site, you may need to compile software yourself.

The traditional Linux build environment is composed of several different software packages, providing compilers, a linker, an assembler, an archiver for building and working with libraries, a utility to simplify building complex software packages, and much more. As you'd expect, Ubuntu makes it easy to install all of these core components via one simple meta-package. As explained in the next section, installing this single package pulls together all of the basic ingredients of a Linux build environment, which you can subsequently augment with any other favorite tools that you've come to know and love when building software on your Linux system.

Installing GCC Compilers, make, and Friends

Ubuntu distributions include the basic gcc compiler and make utility as part of their default installation, primarily to facilitate building kernel modules for custom or virtualized hardware. However, these by themselves aren't enough to build end-user applications. The Ubuntu repositories make it especially easy to install the other elements of a basic Linux build environment by providing a package called build-essential that pulls in the GCC C++ compiler, the include files required for user-space C and C++ application development, and various build-related utilities used when building DEB packages. You install this package on your system using the Synaptic Package Manager, the Add/Remove Software menu item, or the command-line aptitude or apt-get commands as described in Chapter 19, "Adding, Removing, and Updating Software."

Depending on the build requirements of the software or package that you are compiling, you may find that you will subsequently need to install other packages. For example, configuration-related utilities such as autoconf and automake are not included in the build-essential package. Similarly, the build-essential package only provides the GCC C++ compiler in addition to the GCC C compiler that is installed by default—if you want to compile applications written in any of the other languages supported by GCC, you will have to install those compilers and any associated libraries separately. These additional packages can always be installed, as needed, in the same way as the build-essential package.

GCC Compiler Overview

In uppercase letters, *GCC* is an acronym for the "GNU Compiler Collection," formerly known as the *GNU Compiler Suite*. In lowercase letters, gcc is a specific compiler from the GNU Compiler Collection, the GNU C Compiler. GCC is a collection of compiler front-ends for a common back-end compilation engine. The list of compilers provided by GCC includes C (gcc), C++ (g++), Objective C (gcc with a special library), Fortran (gfortran), and Java (gcj). GCC also has front-ends for Google's Go, Pascal, Modula-3, and Ada 9x. The C compiler speaks several different dialects of C, including traditional and ANSI C. The C++ compiler is a true native C++ compiler — in other words, it does not first convert C++ code into an intermediate C representation before compiling it, as older C++ compilers did. GCC's C++ compiler, g++, creates native executable code directly from the C++ source code.

GCC is a GNU Project, which is directed by the Free Software Foundation (FSF). The FSF holds the copyright on the compilers and licenses the compilers under the terms of the GPL. Either individuals or the FSF hold the copyrights on other components, such as the runtime libraries and test suites, and these other components are licensed under a variety of free software licenses. The FSF also handles the legal concerns of the GCC project.

Retrieving Source Packages

Throughout this book, the information on installing software packages has always focused on retrieving and installing binary packages, which are the packages that contain executable programs, related precompiled libraries, and associated configuration data that may be either text or binary. Because this chapter discusses installing build tools, it seems reasonable to at least touch on how to retrieve the source code associated with any Ubuntu binary package. In a nutshell, there are essentially two steps to this, both of which are most easily done using the command-line apt-get utility:

1. Retrieve the source code for the package that you want to build.

2. Satisfy any dependencies on other software, libraries, and so on that are required to build a specific package.

To retrieve the source code for any Ubuntu package, use the apt-get source package command, where package is the name of the package that you want to build from source code. To install any other tools, libraries, header files, and so on that are required to actually build that package from its source, you use the apt-get build-dep package command, where package is the name of the package that you want to build.

See Chapter 19 for a more detailed discussion of satisfying build dependencies and retrieving package source code using the apt-get utility.

Using GCC's C Compiler

The gcc compiler supports a tremendous number of command-line options to control its behavior. It accepts both single-letter options, such as -o, and multi-letter options, such as -ansi. Because it accepts both types of options, you cannot group multiple single-letter options together, as you may be used to doing with many GNU and UNIX/Linux programs such as ps, ls, and so on. For example, the multi-letter option -pg is not the same as the two single-letter options -p -g. The -pg option creates extra code in the final binary that outputs profile information for the GNU code profiler, gprof. On the other hand, the -p -g options generate extra code in the resulting binary that produces profiling information for use by the prof code profiler (-p) and causes gcc to generate debugging information using the operating system's normal format (-g).

Despite its sensitivity to the grouping of multiple single-letter options, you can freely mix the order of options and compiler arguments on the gcc command line. The following two commands are identical in terms of what they tell gcc to do:

```
$ gcc -pg -fno-strength-reduce -g hello.c -o hello
$ gcc hello.c -o hello -g -fno-strength-reduce -pg
```

In most cases, the order of options and their arguments do not matter. In some situations, order does matter, especially if you use several options of the same kind or to avoid problems when passing those options to compiler components such as the linker. For example, the -I option specifies the directory or directories to search for include files. So, if you specify -I several times, gcc searches the listed directories in the order specified.

Compiling a single source file, hello.c, using gcc is easy — just invoke gcc, passing the name of the source file as the argument, as shown in the following example:

```
$ gcc hello.c
```

By default, the result is an executable file named a.out in the current directory, which you execute by typing ./a.out. (The name a.out is a historical artifact, and stands for "assembler output". To define the name of the output file that gcc produces, use the -o option, as in the following example:

```
$ gcc hello.c -o runme
```

If you are compiling multiple source files using gcc, you can specify them all on the gcc command line, as in the following example, which leaves the compiled executable in the file named showdate:

```
$ gcc showdate.c helper.c -o showdate
```

If you want to compile these files incrementally and eventually link them into a binary, you can use the -c option to halt compilation after producing an object file, which is an intermediate compiled file in which external references have not yet been resolved.. You can then use a single gcc command to link them all together and specify the name of the output file, as in the following example:

```
$ gcc -c showdate.c
$ gcc -c helper.c
$ gcc showdate.o helper.o -o showdate
```

It should be easy to see that a project consisting of more than a few source code files would quickly become exceedingly tedious to compile from the command line, especially after you start linking in external libraries, adding optimization commands, and providing other miscellaneous gcc options. The solution to this command-line tedium is the make utility, which is discussed in the next section.

Creating Simple Makefiles

Since just after the dawn of UNIX time, most UNIX applications have been built using a rule-driven application called *make*, which invokes the compilers and other utilities necessary to produce an executable from all the components of a program's source code. The make program also serves as the cornerstone for building C and C++ applications on Linux and all other UNIX-like systems. The make program does the following:

- It enables developers to identify relationships and dependencies between the source modules, include files, and libraries that are required for successful compilation.

- It specifies the sequence in which things must be compiled to build an application successfully.

- It avoids recompilation by limiting compilation to the portions of an application that are affected by any change to source code or statically linked libraries.

The make program was originally written by Stu Feldman at AT&T for an early version of UNIX. As a part of AT&T UNIX, the source code for the make program was not freely available, and it has therefore largely been replaced by the GNU make program. GNU make provides all of the features of the original make program and a few zillion others. Subsequent references to the make program throughout this chapter, therefore, refer to GNU make.

The rules used by any make program are stored in text files named *Makefile*, which contain dependency rules and the commands necessary to satisfy them. As you might expect, the Makefiles for complex applications can themselves be extremely complex as well as platform-specific, because they need to invoke platform-specific libraries and utilities that may be located in different directories or have different names on different systems. The simplest possible Makefile is the one for a simple application that is compiled from a single source code file, such as the legendary C language "Hello, World!" application. The Makefile for this application looks like this:

```
hello: hello.c
        gcc hello.c -o hello
```

The first line identifies the binary target (hello) that this Makefile builds, and the fact that this binary must be regenerated whenever the source file hello.c is modified. The second line (which begins with a tab) specifies the command necessary to produce that binary target. To invoke this Makefile, you simply execute the make command in the directory containing the Makefile. The make program automatically looks for a file named *Makefile* and follows any build rules that it contains.

Tip
The fact that all lines containing a build rule must begin with a tab is one of the most common problems with handcrafted Makefiles. ∎

Although this example shows the true basics of a Makefile, it is also a trivial example that doesn't show off any of the real benefits that Makefiles can provide in terms of simplifying and automating compilation and recompilation. Let's consider another example. In the previous section, one of the examples I used compiled a single binary from two object modules, using the following command lines:

```
$ gcc -c showdate.c
$ gcc -c helper.c
$ gcc showdate.o helper.o -o showdate
```

A Makefile for this application would look something like the following:

```
showdate: showdate.o helper.o
        gcc showdate.o helper.o -o showdate

showdate.o: showdate.c
        gcc -c showdate.c
helper.o: helper.c
        gcc -c helper.c
```

This example highlights how a Makefile can reduce the amount of recompilation necessary when you have only modified some of the files associated with a project. For example, this Makefile states that the showdate binary depends on the two object modules showdate.o and helper.o, and provides a rule for generating the binary by using gcc to link the two object files. It then continues to highlight that each of these object modules depends on its associated C language file, and provides a rule for using gcc to regenerate each of the object modules.

This sample Makefile can simplify recompilation if, for example, only one of the C files was modified. The Makefile would regenerate to the object module for only the C file that has been modified, and then relink the existing object file with the new object file to regenerate the binary.

As your projects become larger, you will want to take advantage of other Makefile features, such as defining and using variables, using some truly cryptic symbols to simplify make rules, and so on. Some good sources for more advanced information about the make program and Makefiles are the following:

- www.linuxdevcenter.com/pub/a/linux/2002/01/31/make_intro.html: A nice article on using make from O'Reilly & Associates Linux Development Center

- `www.tldp.org/HOWTO/Software-Building-HOWTO-3.html`: The section on using make from the Linux Documentation project's guide to Linux software development

- `www.gnu.org/software/make`: The home page for GNU make, which also includes links to the official make documentation

- `www.gnu.org/software/make/manual`: The official online home of the documentation for GNU make, which is available in various formats

Using an Integrated Development Environment

An *integrated development environment* (IDE) is a unified set of tools that typically provides an editing environment, compiler, build environment, and debugger that work together in a single framework. IDEs typically also provide infrastructure for creating and managing software projects composed of multiple source files, include files, and libraries. Most modern IDEs are graphical tools that work in desktop environments such as the X Window system, GNOME, KDE, Microsoft Windows, or Mac OS X. For this reason, many modern IDEs, therefore, also include tools for creating user interfaces and the other graphical elements of graphical desktop applications.

The key aspect of an IDE is the integration among the different tools that make up the development environment that it provides. Most IDEs give the impression of being a single tool, regardless of how many features and components they provide.

As I'll discuss in the next section, IDEs are traditionally oriented toward the requirements of developers working in a specific language or a set of related languages. Recently, general-purpose IDEs such as Eclipse have become more popular, because they provide a single framework that standardizes the developer experience regardless of the language in which a developer is working, and support a plug-in model that enables them to be extended easily.

Popular IDEs for Linux

As you might expect from an operating system that is used for the development of applications in a huge number of languages and one in which everyone has their own idea of how development should be done, Linux is knee-deep in IDEs. Ubuntu provides a large selection of IDEs for different languages in its repositories. Some of the more widely known IDEs provided in the Ubuntu repositories are the following:

- **Eclipse:** Eclipse is a multi-purpose IDE written in Java. Eclipse was originally developed as an IDE framework for developing Java applications, but has been extended to support development in other languages. The fact that Eclipse is written in Java makes it very portable and usable in a variety of different graphical environments and operating systems. For more information about Eclipse, see the rest of the discussion of IDEs in this chapter or the Eclipse home page at www.eclipse.org.

- **KDevelop:** A graphical IDE for C and C++ applications that is based on the KDE desktop environment. KDevelop is an extremely popular and easy-to-use IDE that provides wizards, which simplify creating standard command-line Linux applications, as well as graphical applications that use the Qt, GNOME, and KDE graphical environments. For more information about KDevelop, see its home page at www.kdevelop.org.

- **Motor:** The motor IDE is a text-based integrated development environment for C, C++, and Java applications that works well within any terminal application, such as an xterm or the GNOME Terminal. The motor IDE provides integrated support for various GCC compilers and the GNU debugger, gdb. For more detailed information about Motor, see its home page at http://konst.org.ua/motor.

- **NetBeans:** The NetBeans IDE is a complete IDE written in Java for developing applications in languages such as Java, C++, and Ruby. Because it is written in Java, it runs on many platforms including Microsoft Windows, Linux, Mac OS X, and Solaris, and is therefore a good choice for a cross-platform IDE alternative to Eclipse. For more detailed information on NetBeans, see its home page at http://netbeans.org.

- **Pida:** The Pida (Python Integrated Development Application) IDE is a GTK-based IDE for developing Text mode or graphical applications written in the Python scripting language. The Pida IDE is quite popular and supports easy integration of familiar development tools within its unified development framework. For more information about Pida, see its home page at http://pida.co.uk.

- **SBCL:** The SBCL (Steel Bank Common Lisp) IDE is a graphical development environment for applications written in the Lisp programming language. The SBCL IDE was originally based on the Common Lisp development environment provided by Carnegie Mellon University's CMU Common Lisp, but is actively being maintained and enhanced. The SBCL IDE features provide a native Lisp code compiler and a sophisticated debugger. For more information about SBCL, see its home page at http://sbcl.sourceforge.net.

This list is just a subset of the IDEs available in the Ubuntu repositories, but highlights the number of different IDEs available and the fact that many IDEs focus on specific programming languages. My favorite IDE is the Eclipse IDE, which was originally developed by IBM as an easily extended framework for Java development, but was released by IBM as open source and has soared in popularity since then. Eclipse is now released and supported by the Eclipse Foundation (www.eclipse.org), a not-for-profit organization dedicated to promoting Eclipse and helping guide its development and acceptance throughout the software development industry. Eclipse provides a plug-in-based framework that makes it easy to create, integrate, and support tools that provide specific functionality or target certain sets of developers. This plug-in model also gives developers the freedom to select and integrate plug-ins from different projects or commercial vendors and thereby assemble an IDE that does exactly what they need it to do. Eclipse is available for Linux, HP-UX, AIX, Solaris, QNX, Mac OS X, and Microsoft Windows systems.

As you might suspect from the previous paragraph, the rest of this part of the chapter focuses on installing and using the Eclipse IDE.

Installing Eclipse

To install Eclipse and related packages, use your favorite software installation tool to install the `eclipse` package, which installs a huge number of associated/required packages and provides everything you need to use the standard Eclipse IDE to develop Java applications, including plug-ins for Java and Python development, the `ant` utility for building Java applications, all required libraries, and so on.

See Chapter 19 for detailed information on installing applications on Ubuntu systems.

Note

If you have problems using or installing plugins and features in the version of Eclipse that is available through the Ubuntu repositories, you can always use your favorite package management tool to remove the eclipse package, and then download and install an "official" version of Eclipse from the eclipse.org web site (www.eclipse.org/downloads). The Eclipse downloads site offers preconfigured versions of Eclipse for Java EE developers, C/C++ developers, and so on. After downloading an archived tar files from the Eclipse site and extracting its contents, you can run the downloaded version of Eclipse by executing the file called eclipse" in the extracted directory. If you use this approach (which I often do to get the very latest versions of Eclipse), you will not get updates for Eclipse through the standard Ubuntu Update Manager, but you can keep these versions up-to-date by using the Help ⇨ Check for Updates menu item. Depending on the version that you download and install, you may still want to enable and install additional Eclipse features. ∎

Using Eclipse for C Application Development

This section provides two examples of using Eclipse: one that shows how to create a simple application from scratch, and one that shows how to import the source code for an existing software package into Eclipse to take advantage of its compilation, debugging, and usability features. Entire books are available about using Eclipse, and these introductory sections are hardly equivalent to those, but they should help you get a feeling for the power, capabilities, and ease-of-use of the Eclipse IDE.

Note

The examples in the next two sections are both C programs and therefore assume that you followed the instructions in the "Installing GCC Compilers, make, and Friends" section, and installed the build-essential package, which provides user-space include files that are typically required to build C applications. ∎

Starting Eclipse

Installing Eclipse on your Ubuntu system creates the Applications ⇨ Programming ⇨ Eclipse menu entry, which you can select to start the Eclipse IDE.

The first time that you start Eclipse, Eclipse displays a dialog that prompts you for a location in which to create a workspace, and then creates the workspace and `.eclipse` directories in the specified location (usually your home directory). Unless you have a good reason to use another location, accept the default suggestion and check the "use this as the default and do not ask again" checkbox so that you never have to bother with this question again.

Tip

Eclipse uses the workspace directory to store the projects that you create and uses the `.eclipse` directory to store information about your configuration settings, the organization of the Eclipse UI the last time you used it, features that you have installed, and so on. You can start Eclipse using a different workspace directory by using the `-data` command-line argument, followed by the full pathname of the workspace directory that you want to use. ■

After creating these directories and loading its initial execution environment, Eclipse then displays a Welcome screen that contains several strange graphical objects but nothing that resembles a code development tool.

The graphical objects on this Welcome screen are actually links to sources of information about working with Eclipse, such as tutorials, sample code, and so on. To close the Welcome screen, simply click the X in the Welcome tab. You can reopen it at any time by selecting Help ➪ Welcome.

After closing the Welcome screen, the standard Eclipse user interface displays, as shown in Figure 23-1.

At this point, the Eclipse environment is remarkably empty because you haven't created any projects. The next few sections explain how to fix that.

FIGURE 23-1

The standard Eclipse user interface

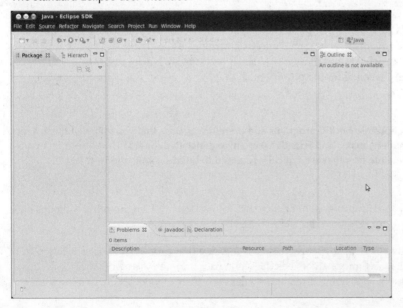

Eclipse Terminology

The Eclipse framework was originally developed by IBM, which seems to have also developed its own language to refer to the elements of the Eclipse user interface and framework. This shouldn't be much of a surprise to anyone who has worked with IBM in the past. The following are a few terms that you'll encounter when using Eclipse — like most languages, they make perfect sense once you have been assimilated, but they can be confusing at first:

- **editor:** A window that enables you to edit a specific type of file or other resources. The Eclipse toolbar and menus provide different options based on the editor that is currently active.

- **feature:** A packaged set of one or more plug-ins that make up a product

- **perspective:** A set of windows within the Eclipse GUI that are associated with a specific plug-in or task and that are organized in a specific way

- **plugin:** Code that performs a specific function or set of functions and can be integrated into the Eclipse framework

- **view:** A window within the Eclipse GUI that can support an editor or provide access to a certain type of resource. Each view has a title bar that provides tabs to select different resources that are open in that view, and also often provides its own menus and icons, which are available by right-clicking or selecting an icon in the title bar.

- **workbench:** One of the two key plug-ins provided with the Eclipse IDE, the workbench plug-in provides the basic user interface, menu structure, event notification mechanism, and mechanisms for creating new windows and views. This plug-in also provides the extension points that developers can use to create menus, menu items, events, editors, and views for their plug-ins. From the user's point of view, the workbench is simply the Eclipse user interface.

- **workspace:** The second of the two key plug-ins provided by the Eclipse IDE, the workspace plug-in enables you to interact with external resources such as project directories, files, and so on. The term *workspace* may also be used to describe a directory used by Eclipse to hold projects.

These are my interpretations of official *Eclipse-speak*. The online help for Eclipse provides the official definitions for these terms in its "Workbench User Guide" section.

Getting Add-Ons and Updates

Eclipse was designed as an IDE for Java developers, which is fine for Java developers but not for those of us who prefer other languages. Luckily, Eclipse was also designed as a flexible, plug-in-oriented IDE framework that makes it easy to add support for other languages, different types of projects, and external tools.

Zillions of tutorials on Java development in Eclipse are available on the Web, including a few that are provided by Eclipse itself, so rather than simply duplicating one of those, the tutorials in the next two sections show how to work with C applications in Eclipse. In order to do this, you have to add the Eclipse plug-ins that are available for C development, which are known as the *C Development Toolkit* (CDT). Eclipse makes it easy to get updates and add Eclipse-related software through its Help ⇨ Install New Software menu item, which displays the "Available Software" dialog shown in Figure 23-2.

FIGURE 23-2

The "Available Software" dialog in Eclipse

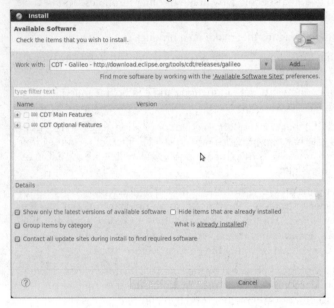

When this dialog first displays, it won't contain any update sites. To add the update site for CDT, click Add and enter **CDT** in the name field and the following URL as the location:

```
http://download.eclipse.org/tools/cdt/releases/galileo
```

The Galileo release of Eclipse was current when this book was updated; if your system displays the name of another release in the initial Eclipse splash screen, replace *galileo* with the name of your release of Eclipse. Click OK to save the new entry.

Tip

If Eclipse reports that the site could not be found or you see similar error messages, exit Eclipse and install the official Sun JDK so that you can use Sun's version of Java rather than the one provided by OpenJDK, which is the default Java JDK that is used on Ubuntu. To install Sun's JDK, you must first enable the partner repository in the System ⇨ Administration ⇨ Software Sources application. You can then install the `sun-java6-jdk` package, and use the `update-alternatives --config java` command to set Sun's JDK as the default version of Java used by applications on your system. You will then be able to start Eclipse and activate the CDT update site. ∎

Your "Available Software" dialog should now resemble the one shown in Figure 23-2. Select the checkboxes for "CDT Main Features" and "CDT Optional Features," and click Next. If there are any problems or missing dependencies in the selected software, the subsequent "Install Details" dialog will report them and prevent you from continuing by graying out the Next button. If any problems are reported, you'll have to click Back to return to the previous dialog and deselect the software associated with the problem. For example, in some versions of Eclipse, I have had to deselect the "Eclipse Mylyn Bridge for CDT" and "Eclipse C/C++ Remote Launch" software in the CDT Optional Features list. If you had to deselect software packages, you can then click Next again, and should see a selectable Next button on the "Install Details" dialog. Click Next, accept the license agreements on the next page (after reading them all, of course), and click Finish. You'll be ready to work with C or C++ applications in Eclipse as soon as the download and installation processes finish and you restart Eclipse.

Creating a New Source Project in Eclipse

After starting Eclipse, you create new projects or project components by selecting File ⇨ New, and selecting the appropriate item from this menu. To create and work with an application in Eclipse, you must first create a project to hold your source code. Eclipse provides wizards to simplify creating projects of different types. Wizards are sets of graphical screens that walk you through the process of creating a specific type of project, making sure that you don't miss any of the steps in the process.

Selecting File ⇨ New ⇨ Project displays the "Wizard Selection" dialog shown in Figure 23-3.

FIGURE 23-3

Selecting a Project Creation wizard in Eclipse

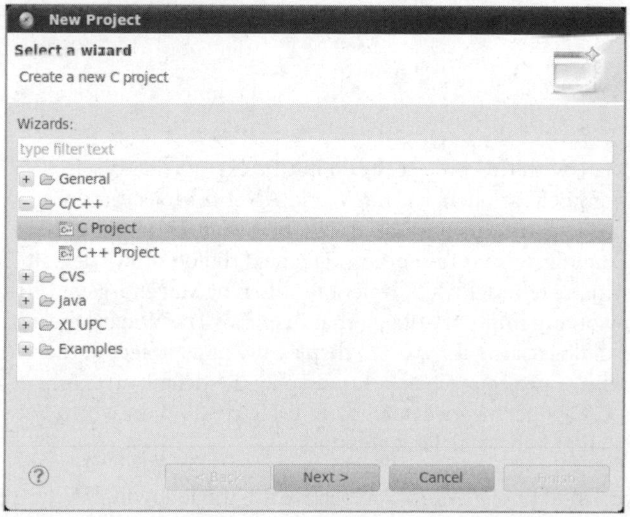

Because I'm creating a C source project in this section, I've expanded the C/C++ entry and have selected the C Project Wizard. Click Next to proceed to the Wizard for this particular type of project. The dialog shown in Figure 23-4 appears.

FIGURE 23-4

Specifying the name of your project in Eclipse

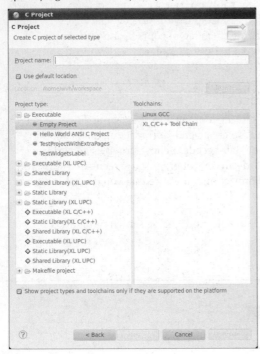

Enter the name that you want to associate with this project (**hello** in this example) and select "Executable ➪ Empty Project." (Although Eclipse offers a Hello World ANSI C Project, it does too much of the work for you for the purposes of this tutorial.) Make sure that the Linux GCC compiler is selected in the right pane, and click Next to proceed. The next dialog shows default Configurations for your application, which are roughly equivalent to different Make targets. Click Finish in this dialog, and Finish in any other temporary dialog that displays. The Wizard creates my new "hello" project and displays a dialog asking if I want to display my new project in the C/C++ Perspective that is associated with C projects. Click Yes to display the default structure and content of the project in Eclipse's C/C++ perspective, as shown in Figure 23-5, in which I've expanded the contents of the project to highlight its default contents.

The default views and editors displayed in Eclipse's C/C++ Perspective are the following:

- **Navigator:** The view at the left, which enables you to navigate through and work with your project and the files and other resources that it contains

- **Editor:** The pane at the top center, which differs based on the open resources in the Navigator view

- **Console:** The bottom-right view, in which messages about interactions with Eclipse are displayed. This view also provides a Problems tab that identifies any errors or warning associated with the current project, and a Properties tab that enables you to examine any properties associated with the current project.

- **Outline:** The view at the right, which shows an outline of the files and functions referenced and defined in the active project

FIGURE 23-5

A newly created project in Eclipse

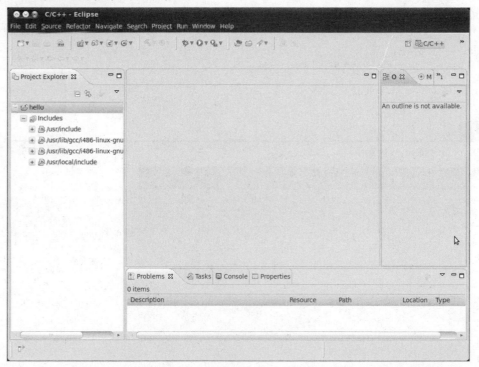

One thing missing from my sample C project is any C files, so I'll use the File ➪ New ➪ Source File menu command to create one, which displays the dialog shown in Figure 23-6. You can also create new resources for a project by right-clicking on the name of the project and selecting the type of item that you want to create from the pop-up menu's New submenu.

Creating a new source file in a project (the file hello.c in this example) and clicking Finish opens the new file in the type of editor associated with that source file, as shown in Figure 23-7.

FIGURE 23-6

Creating a new C source file in Eclipse

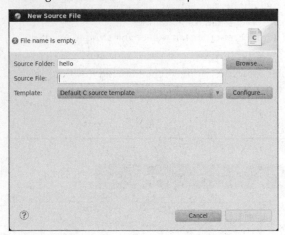

FIGURE 23-7

A new source file in an editor in Eclipse

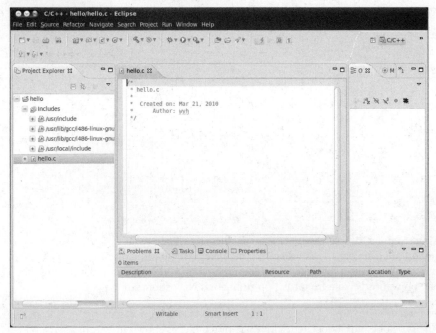

Eclipse provides many keyboard shortcuts to simplify moving around in its editors. You can see the list of current key bindings for the workbench by selecting Window ⇨ Preferences, and selecting General ⇨ Keys in the dialog that displays, as shown in Figure 23-8.

FIGURE 23-8

Viewing current key bindings in Eclipse

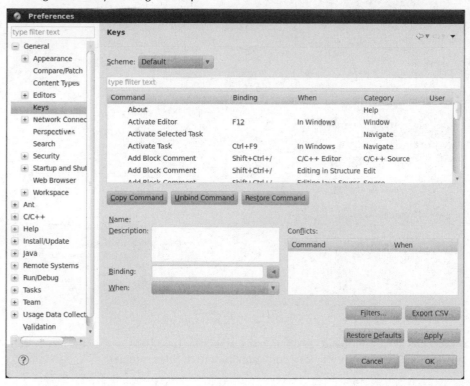

If your fingers have already been trained to use a specific set of editor commands (as mine have been trained by the Emacs text editor), you can select different sets of key bindings by clicking the Scheme dropdown in the dialog shown in Figure 23-8, which displays a list of available key bindings. From this tab, you can select key bindings with the Scheme dropdown menu, as shown in Figure 23-9. Click OK to close this dialog and return to the C/C++ perspective.

FIGURE 23-9

Customizing key bindings in Eclipse

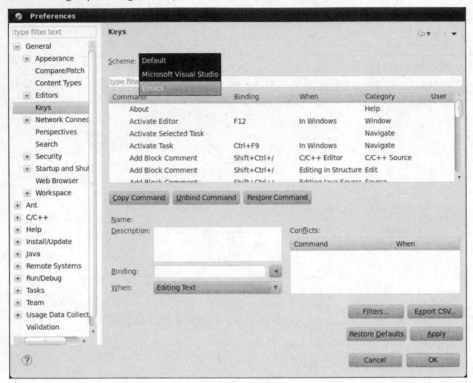

Now that you know what commands to use to move around in the editor, type in the source code for your application (the familiar "Hello, world!" application, in this example):

```
#include <stdio.h>
int main(void)
{
    printf("Hello, world!\n");
    return 0;
}
```

As you enter your source code, you'll notice that Eclipse automatically indents new lines, matches brackets and parentheses, and does the sort of code highlighting that you'd expect in a modern IDE. As you enter your code, you'll also notice that the Outline view to the left of the editor updates to identify any external references in your code, any functions that you have defined (including main), and so on. Figure 23-10 shows Eclipse after entering a complete "Hello, World!" program.

FIGURE 23-10

A sample application and its outline in Eclipse

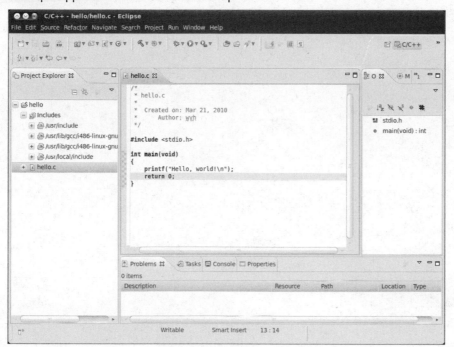

At this point, select File ⇨ Save to save your application. As part of the save process, Eclipse analyzes your code and identifies any possible problems that it sees. Common problems are missing newlines at end-of-file, missing return values, and so on.

Now it's time to build the project. Select Project ⇨ Build Project (or right-click on the project and select Build Configurations ⇨ Build ⇨ All from the pop-up menu). If you're lucky, you will not see any error or warning messages in the Console view's Problems tab, located below the Editor.

The final step in this example is to actually run the application and see its output. To do this, select one of the Run commands from the Run menu. Eclipse enables you to define multiple Build and Run configurations, enabling you (for example) to define sets of compilation and execution parameters for debugging your application, executing it normally, and so on. (The default Build configuration is to build for debugging, with symbols present, and so on.) In this case, I'll select the default way of running the application, which is as a stand-alone, local C/C++ application by selecting Run ⇨ Run As ⇨ Run Local C/C++ Application, which displays the dialog shown in Figure 23-11. This dialog enables you to select which of the available binaries will be used to run this program — selecting a binary displays an associated Qualifier that identifies whether this is s debugging, standard, or other type of binary.

FIGURE 23-11

Selecting a binary to run in Eclipse

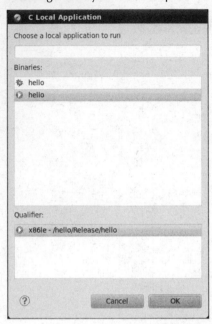

Select either binary and click OK. Eclipse runs the application and refreshes the Console view, displaying the Console tab in which the output from the sample application displays, as shown at the bottom of Figure 23-12.

To simplify running your sample application, you could create special Run configurations that would execute the application in Eclipse's other default Build configuration, which is called *Release* and enables you to build the application without debugging symbols, and so on, which is somewhat outside the scope of this simple tutorial. You've created a project, a source module, watched Eclipse do its magic, and even executed the application — not bad for 10 minutes or so from creation to execution.

Importing an Existing Source Project into Eclipse

Creating new projects in Eclipse is one thing, but you can also take advantage of the capabilities of Eclipse in existing projects by importing them into Eclipse. This example shows how to do just that, using one of my favorite open source applications as an example, which is the pop-3check application, which enables you to list the headings for any mail that is pending for you on a remote POP mail server. I often use this as a quick, command-line way of seeing if anything interesting has come in without risking being sucked into the black hole of actually reading all of my incoming mail. The pop3check application was written by Steven Radack and Simon Liddington, and is available from http://sourceforge.net/projects/pop3check.

FIGURE 23-12

Running the sample application in Eclipse

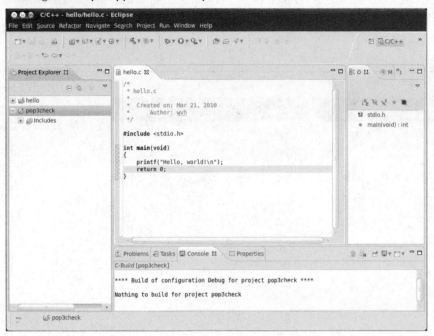

In my opinion, the easiest way to import an existing project into Eclipse is as a tarball that contains the source. This enables you to import a pristine version of the source code and also provides a convenient way for you to keep track of exactly what was in the project when you moved it into Eclipse, by archiving the tarball.

Preparatory to beginning the import process, cd to the top level of your source project directory and clean the project to remove object code, backup files, and any other items that you don't actually want to import. You'll want to generate a source tarball for your project from the top level of its source code directory so that the files that comprise your project are imported into the top level of your Eclipse project rather than being created in a subdirectory, which would happen if you imported a vanilla tarball that you retrieved from the Web or created as a backup of your project. In my case, I prepare the tarball with commands like the following:

```
$ cd pop3check-0.100.3
$ make clean
$ tar czf ../pop3check.tgz *
```

Tarball in hand, start Eclipse using the Applications ➪ Programming ➪ Eclipse command, and create an Eclipse project that corresponds to the source project that you are importing by using File ➪ New ➪ Project wizard selector. Since we are importing a complete project that contains a Makefile, you'll need to create a project that understands how to use Makefiles. Select the C

839

Project wizard as in the previous example, and select Makefile Project ⇨ Empty Project to create an empty, Makefile-based project. Make sure that Linux GCC is slected in the Toolchains list, and click Finish to create the new project. The new project is displayed in Eclipse beneath your other project(s), as shown in Figure 23-13.

FIGURE 23-13

The new pop3check project in Eclipse

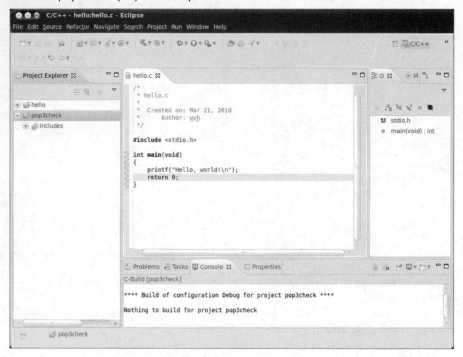

Next, to import the tarball you prepared earlier, right-click on the name of the project and select Import. This displays the dialog shown in Figure 23-14.

Because you're importing from a tarball, expand the General section, select the Archive File entry, and click Next. The dialog shown in Figure 23-15 displays, in which you've browsed for and selected the tarball that you prepared earlier.

You'll note that this dialog shows an expanded view of the tarball, which enables you to verify that it contains everything you need and that Eclipse can open it successfully. Click Finish to begin the import process. Once the import completes, the contents of the imported tarball are added to the selected project, as shown in Figure 23-16.

FIGURE 23-14

Specifying how to import an existing project into Eclipse

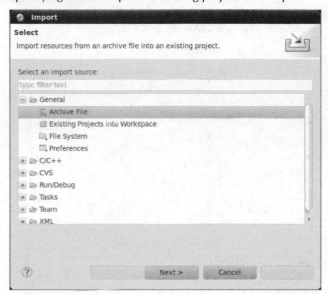

FIGURE 23-15

Selecting the tarball for importing into Eclipse

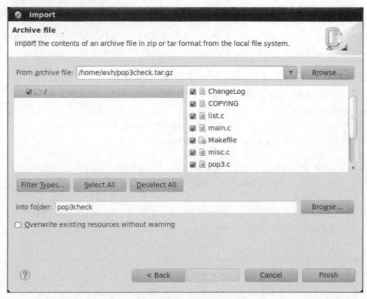

FIGURE 23-16

An imported project in Eclipse

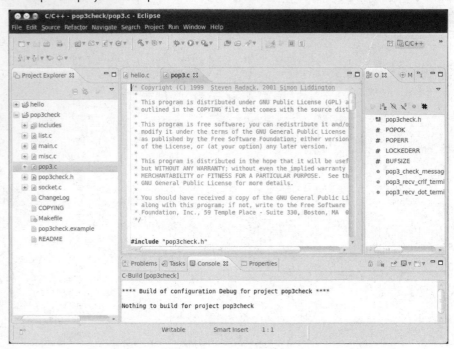

After importing a project into Eclipse, it's a good idea to verify that the Makefile uses the build targets that Eclipse expects to find, which are `all` and `check`. To check the Makefile, double-click its name in the Navigator view, which displays the Makefile in an editor, as shown in Figure 23-17.

In this case, the default target is `pop3check`, which you could simply change to `all` in order to simplify things. However, since this example is an existing open source project, you may not want to have to change things that you don't have to in the source files. You can tell Eclipse about other build targets by right-clicking on the Makefile in the project Explorer Panel and selecting Make Targets ➪ Create, which displays a dialog like the one shown in Figure 23-18.

This dialog enables you to define a new build target, `pop3check`, which in this case is simply an alias for the `pop3check` target in the imported Makefile. After entering this target name, click OK to close this dialog. This information is saved in the Eclipse project, not in any updates to the Makefile. You can then build the project by right-clicking in the Makefile window and selecting Make Targets ➪ Build from the pop-up menu to display the dialog shown in Figure 23-19.

FIGURE 23-17

Examining the Makefile for an imported make project

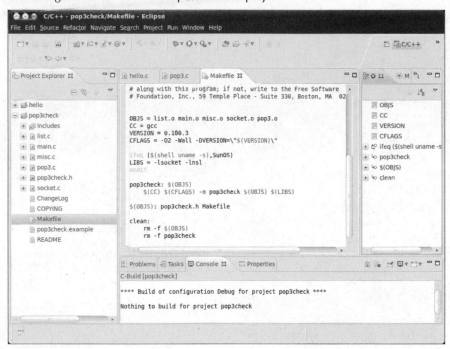

FIGURE 23-18

Defining a custom make target for an imported project

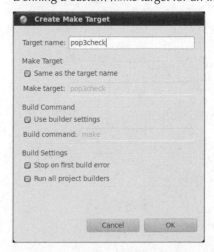

FIGURE 23-19

Building a custom make target in Eclipse

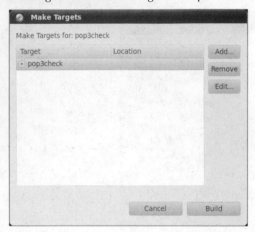

Make sure that your new Make target is selected, and click Build. The newly imported project should build correctly and successfully, as shown in the console tab at the bottom of Figure 23-20.

FIGURE 23-20

Console output from a build of an imported project in Eclipse

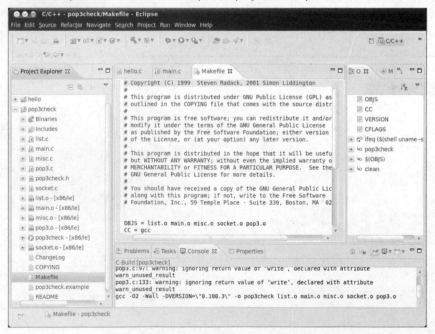

As you might expect, your mileage may vary when importing existing source projects into Eclipse, but the ease with which you can do so makes it easy for you to move your existing application development efforts into Eclipse so that you can take advantage of its many capabilities and the ease-of-use that a modern IDE like Eclipse provides.

Getting More Information about Eclipse

Eclipse is a powerful, full-featured IDE, which means that the examples in the previous two sections can only scratch the surface of its capabilities and bells and whistles. For more detailed information about using Eclipse, see one of the many books on using Eclipse that are available, or visit some of the following resources on the Web:

- `www.eclipse.org`: home page of the Eclipse mothership
- `www.eclipse.org/documentation`: Eclipse documentation site
- `http://planeteclipse.org/planet`: Planet Eclipse, frequented by Eclipse developers, contributors, hackers, and users
- `www.eclipseplugincentral.com`: Eclipse Plug-in Central, from which you can download many free Eclipse plug-ins

The next section talks about source code control software, highlighting Subversion. As an example of the wide range of free plug-ins available for Eclipse, the following are two free Subversion plug-ins for Eclipse:

- Subversive Plug-in at `www.polarion.org`
- Subclipse Plug-in at `http://subclipse.tigris.org`

Not only do these plug-ins provide an easy way to work with Subversion repositories in Eclipse, but they also provide a great example of how all of this open source stuff tends to fit together nicely.

Source Code Control Software

If you've ever accidentally deleted a source file that you were working on, lost the software version of the great American novel when your system crashed and scrambled its disks, or worked on a joint project with someone who was thoughtful enough to overwrite all of your new code, you might have wished that you'd been using a source code control system once you finished swearing. A source code control system, popularly known as an *SCCS*, is a software package that manages a repository of source code, tracking changes to existing code, managing different versions of that code (often known as *branches*), and providing a mechanism for recovering any version of any file in the repository at any point in time.

If I had to count the number of times that an SCCS had saved my bacon when doing development, I would quickly run out of fingers and toes. This doesn't necessarily mean that I'm sloppy.

When multiple developers work on the same sets of files, conflicts between their changes are bound to occur. An SCCS provides a mechanism for identifying and resolving conflicting sets of changes (known as *merges*). Similarly, a source code control system facilitates experimentation with code by providing a safety net that you can use to fall back to versions of files that you know to be working, just in case your latest bright idea didn't turn out to be very illuminating after all.

Caution

One common misconception is that an SCCS is a replacement for backups. Not really true. An SCCS may be a replacement for backing up your own files, because you can check them in and retrieve them later if your machine bursts into flames. However, the SCCS repository itself must be backed up regularly — if anything, a central repository used across a project or enterprise provides a single, critical point of failure. ∎

The next two sections discuss the most common source code control systems for Linux, the Concurrent Versioning System (CVS) and the Subversion Project. I used CVS for years, but am purposely giving it short shrift here — Subversion and other popular source code control systems such as Git and Mercurial are all more modern and powerful source code control systems, and you're doing your software projects (and your co-workers) a disservice if you're not using one of them. All of them are based on modern protocols; are more easily integrated into Web browsers, integrated development environments, and graphical computer interfaces; and are actively under development. Alas, poor CVS, I knew thee well. . . .

If you're just reading this section because you're looking for a recommendation for a source code control system, skip to the section on Subversion. Source control systems such as Git and Mercurial are gaining in popularity and offer many advantages, but Subversion is kid-tested and mother-approved without the musty smell of ancient history that accompanies CVS.

The Concurrent Versioning System (CVS)

My humorous comments about CVS in the previous section are meant to be just that, and should not be taken to mean that CVS is not a time-tested, stable SCCS. CVS has been in use and under development for years and is still often used to provide access to the source code for open software projects over the Internet. That said, most projects that I'm aware of which have traditionally depended on CVS are moving elsewhere, and that's a trend that I believe will continue, if not accelerate. However, if you're a CVS fanatic or your current projects already depend on CVS, you can use your favorite Package Management tool to install CVS, and then see sites such as the following for information about setting up and Web-enabling CVS repositories:

- `www.faqs.org/docs/ldev/0130091154_198.htm`: The Linux Development FAQ's section on CVS
- `www.flexwiki.com/default.aspx/FlexWiki/ConfiguringCVS.html`: A nice wiki that provides a lot of good information about understanding and using CVS

CVS is a fine system, and I've used it extensively at many companies. However, I feel that if you're going to set up an SCCS from scratch on your Ubuntu system, you may as well use something from this century.

Installing and Using Subversion

Subversion (http://subversion.apache.org) is an extremely popular source code control system. Aside from its power and rich command set, much of Subversion's popularity lies in the fact that it is based on WebDAV (Web Distributed Authoring and Versioning), a Web-based protocol that enables you to view and access Subversion repositories in any Web browser. This includes the ability to drag-and-drop files from your Web browser to your desktop to check them out, and vice versa to check them in. As you'll see in the next few sections, setting up a Subversion repository and integrating it into your Web server is quite easy to do, just as Subversion is easy to use from the desktop or the command line.

Tip

Another common way of setting up Subversion is to enable access to its repositories through SSH (Secure Shell). For a great explanation of setting up Subversion in this way, see www.startupcto.com/server-tech/subversion/setting-up-svn. Though it discusses installing Subversion in this fashion on CentOS rather than Ubuntu, the instructions are distribution-independent after the initial installation step. ∎

Installing Subversion

You can install Subversion using any of the commands described in Chapter 19. When installing Subversion, I generally install the following packages, not all of which are required. My rationale for each follows the name of the package in this list:

- libapache2-svn **(Optional):** This package is necessary only if you want to provide a Subversion repository that users can access through your Web server. Selecting this item causes the Apache2 Web server and related files to be installed on your system. I always find it handy to be able to access my repository over the Web, it's easy to configure everything at once, and the extra disk space that Apache2 consumes is always worth it to me. However, you can always add this in later. See Chapter 29, "Setting Up a Web Server," for information about manually installing different versions of the Apache Web server.

- rapidsvn, esvn, or kdesvn **(Optional):** Graphical clients for Subversion. Only necessary if you want to use a graphical client. The rapidsvn client is quite popular and is a GNOME client. The esvn client uses the Qt graphical interface and, therefore, doesn't have much baggage in either the GNOME or KDE desktops. The kdesvn client is a KDE client and, therefore, requires that the KDE libraries be installed on your system, but it is the only Subversion client that accepts command-line arguments. The kdesvn client can, therefore, be handy to use if you want to integrate a graphical Subversion client into Firefox to handle svn: URLs. See the sidebar entitled "Handling svn: URLs in Firefox" later in this chapter, for more information about doing this.

- subversion **(Mandatory):** This is the core Subversion package and provides everything you need to use Subversion from the command line on your local system.

Tip

You may also find it handy to install the `subversion-tools` **package when installing Subversion. This package provides a few tools for sharing Subversion repositories between users and doing more sophisticated imports of existing source code directories into Subversion. However, if you have not already installed a mail server on your system, selecting this package for installation causes the** `sendmail` **mail server and related files to be scheduled for installation on your system. I prefer the Postfix mailer, so I always install and configure a mail system before installing Subversion on a system that is also a real mail server. In other cases in which the Subversion server is separate from my mail server, I just accept that fact of some lost disk space. See Chapter 30, "Setting Up a Mail Server," for general information about the different mail servers that are available on Ubuntu. ∎**

Once the installation completes, you're ready to set up your repository and, if you installed the `libapache2-svn` package, configure Apache2 to support Subversion.

See Chapter 19 for more detailed information on installing applications.

Setting Up a Subversion Repository

Creating a Subversion repository is done with the `svnadmin create` command, which creates the directory structure that makes up a Subversion repository. This command takes one argument, which is the name of the directory in which you want your Subversion repository to be created.

One important thing to remember when creating a Subversion repository is that, because Subversion depends on WebDAV, which depends on the HTTP protocol, your Subversion repository must be owned by the user and group that is used for communication via this protocol. On Ubuntu, this is the www-data user and the www-data group.

Tip

If you are creating a Subversion repository named *svn* **and plan to export it through a Web server by that name, you must not create it in your Web server's** `DocRoot` **directory. As you'll see later in this section, you specify the full pathname to the Subversion repository in Apache's Subversion configuration file. Trying to use a repository named** *svn* **that is located in your Web server's** `DocRoot` **directory will result in the error** `301 Moved Permanently (http://server-name)`**, which isn't exactly intuitive. ∎**

For example, to create a Subversion repository in the directory /var/svn, you would execute the following command:

```
$ sudo-u www-data svnadmin create /var/svn
```

After supplying your password, the `svnadmin create` command creates your repository and populates it with the subdirectories it requires, all owned by the proper user and group. You can verify this by listing the contents of the specified directory, as in the following example:

```
$ ls -l /var/svn
total 28
drwxr-xr-x 2 www-data www-data 4096 2010-01-29 12:31 conf
```

```
drwxr-xr-x 2 www-data www-data 4096 2010-01-29 12:31 dav
drwxr-sr-x 5 www-data www-data 4096 2010-01-29 12:31 db
-r--r--r-- 1 www-data www-data    2 2010-01-29 12:31 format
drwxr-xr-x 2 www-data www-data 4096 2010-01-29 12:31 hooks
drwxr-xr-x 2 www-data www-data 4096 2010-01-29 12:31 locks
-rw-r--r-- 1 www-data www-data  229 2010-01-29 12:31 README.txt
```

Of course, an empty Subversion repository isn't all that exciting. The next section explains how to add an existing project to your repository so that you actually have some source code to control.

Importing Projects into a Subversion Repository

A Subversion repository is simply a catcher's mitt for the files and directories that make up different projects. You can simply check your existing files directly into a Subversion repository, but it's far better to check files in using a separate directory hierarchy for each project.

To check a project directory into Subversion, first remove all non-source files such as object files, intermediate files, binaries, and so on from that directory. Next, you simply import the project into Subversion using Subversion's svn import command, as in the following example in which you import a project that contains the canonical C program, "Hello, World!":

```
$ svn import hello file:///var/svn/hello  m "Creating hello project"
Authentication realm: <http://192.168.6.90:80> Subversion Repository
Password for 'wvh':
Adding         hello/hello.c
```

The arguments to the svn import command are the project that you want to import, the Subversion URL of the location in the repository where you want the project to be created, and the -m (message) option, followed by a string that contains the initial check-in message for the project, enclosed within quotation marks. The -m option is optional, of course, but it saves time because you would otherwise have to enter this message in a text editor that the svn command would start for you.

Once you've created a project or checked any files into Subversion, you can use the svn list command to display the contents of the repository, as in the following example, which uses the -R option to this command to recursively display the contents of the repository:

```
$ svn list -R file:///var/svn
hello/
hello/hello.c
```

You'll notice that this example uses a URL beginning with file:///, which provides access to a local repository. This is necessary at this point because you haven't started a Subversion server, so all URLs must be specified relative to the current filesystem. Trying to access your Subversion repository using any Web-based URL would cause an error message to be displayed at this point, either svn: PROPFIND of '/svn': could not connect to server (if you do not have a Web server running) or svn: PROPFIND of '/svn': 405 Method Not Allowed (if you have a Web server running, but no Subversion repository is available). The next section explains the two Subversion servers that are provided for use on Ubuntu systems and how to configure them to make your repository available from other machines.

Setting Up a Subversion Server

Although Subversion is based on WebDAV and, therefore, uses the HTTP protocol for basic communications between clients and servers, you can access a local Subversion repository (i.e., one that is physically located on the same machine that you are using) without running a Subversion server. However, you will need to be running a Subversion server on machines whose repositories you want to access from other systems. There are two common types of Subversion servers:

- **Apache2:** An Apache Web server with integrated support for Subversion. Support for Subversion and WebDAV is easily added to an Apache or Apache2 Web server, which enables you to access your Subversion repository over the Web using URLs like `http://host-name/repository` or `https://host-name/repository` (if you configure SSL support into Apache2 and Subversion). The examples in this chapter discuss Apache2 integration and configuration because Apache2 is the more modern and powerful Apache Web server.

- **Svnserve:** A stand-alone Subversion server that enables you to access your Subversion repository over the Web using URLs like `svn://host-name/repository`. The `svnserve` binary is installed as part of the Subversion package.

These two servers are not mutually exclusive and can easily run on the same machine at the same time, providing access to the same repository if correctly configured. The next two sections explain how to configure each of these to provide access to the sample repository that you set up and populated in previous sections.

Configuring Apache2 for Subversion Support

Configuring the Apache2 Web server to support Subversion is quite easy, only requiring that you install and integrate the right Apache module, configure that module, and create the authentication file that will control write access to the repository.

Installing the Apache2 Web server's support for Subversion was described earlier in this chapter in the section, "Installing Subversion," and is done by installing the `libapache2-svn` package using the Synaptic Package Manager or the `apt-get` utility. The Apache2 Web server's support for Subversion integration with Apache2 is loaded by the file `/etc/apache2/mods-available/dav_svn.load`. The configuration file for this module is the file `/etc/apache2/mods-available/dav_svn.conf`.

After installing the Apache2 Web server's support for Subversion, edit this file using `sudo` and your favorite text editor. Your configuration options are the following:

1. Update the `<Location /svn>` element if you want to make your repository available through any URL other than `http://Web-server/svn`.

2. Uncomment the DAV svn entry to enable the repository.

3. Edit the SVNPath entry to identify the full pathname of your Subversion repository in the server's directory structure.

4. To use basic HTTP authentication (which I will use in this example), uncomment the following three lines:

```
AuthType Basic
AuthName "Subversion Repository"
AuthUserFile /etc/apache2/dav_svn.passwd
```

5. Modify the pathname in the AuthUserFile entry to identify the HTTP password file that you want to use for HTTP authentication.

6. Purge any existing HTTP password file for Subversion and create the HTTP password file using the following commands, where *user-name* is the name of the first user for whom you want to create a password entry:

```
$ sudo rm -f /etc/apache2/dav_svn.passwd
$ sudo htpasswd2 -c /etc/apache2/dav_svn.passwd user-name
New password:
Re-type new password:
```

7. Add any other users to the HTTP password file using the following command:

```
$ sudo htpasswd2 /etc/apache2/dav_svn.passwd user-name
```

After editing this file, a sample dav_svn.conf file looks like the following example (I've removed the comments to make things easier to read):

```
<Location /svn>
  DAV svn
  SVNPath /var/svn
  AuthType Basic
  AuthName "Subversion Repository"
  AuthUserFile /etc/apache2/dav_svn.passwd
  <LimitExcept GET PROPFIND OPTIONS REPORT>
    Require valid-user
  </LimitExcept>
</Location>
```

At this point, all you have to do is restart the Apache2 Web server, which you can do using the sudo /etc/init.d/apache2 restart command, and your repository will be available from other machines through the URL http://Web-server/svn. See "Checking Files out of a Subversion Repository" later in this section, for information about using this URL to check out the files for your projects.

Configuring the svnserve Server

As mentioned earlier, Subversion's svnserve server enables Subversion clients to use URLs that use the svn protocol directly rather than the HTTP protocol. The svnserve server is installed as a part of the basic Subversion package.

You can start the svnserve server manually or through an Internet services daemon such as inetd or xinetd. The svnserve server doesn't require any special configuration because you identify the root of your Subversion repository on the command line or in the configuration files for any Internet services daemon that you want to use. To start the svnserve daemon from the command line to provide access to the repository you created earlier in this chapter, you would simply execute the following command:

```
$ sudo -u www-data /usr/bin/svnserve -r /var -d
```

This starts the svnserve server as the user www-data, uses the -r option to identify the root of the Subversion repository as /var, and uses the -d option to start the svnserve process as a daemon that runs in the background.

As mentioned previously, you can also configure an Internet services daemon to handle incoming requests for svn: URLs on demand, rather than starting the svnserve daemon manually each time that you log in or explicitly add it to your Ubuntu system's startup files. Internet services daemons wait for incoming requests for services on certain ports and start associated daemons on demand, rather than having the daemons always running. Ubuntu provides two Internet services daemons, inetd and xinetd. The inetd daemon is the original Internet services daemon, while the xinetd daemon is a more modern and flexible Internet services daemon. Neither of these is installed by default on a basic Ubuntu system, so you will have to manually install whichever one you choose (I suggest xinetd) using the Synaptic Package Manager or apt-get.

If you install the xinetd Internet services daemon, you will also have to create the file /etc/xinetd.d/svn, which is the configuration file that tells the xinetd daemon what to do when an incoming svn request is received on port 3690, as defined in the file /etc/services. An /etc/xinetd.d/svn file that provides access to the repository that you created earlier in this chapter would look like the following:

```
service svn
{
    disable = no
    socket_type = stream
    protocol = tcp
    wait = no
    user = www-data
    server = /usr/bin/svnserve
    server_args = -i -r /var
}
```

After creating this file, you must restart the xinetd daemon using a command like the following:

```
$ sudo /etc/init.d/xinetd restart
```

Handling svn: URLs in Firefox

Trying to access a URL that begins with `svn:` in Firefox will display a dialog with the message "Firefox doesn't know how to handle this address because the protocol (svn) isn't associated with any program." If you want to be able to handle these URLs in Firefox, you'll need to create a small wrapper script that invokes your favorite graphical Subversion client with that URL as an argument. For example, I use the following script to automatically start the `kdesvn` client (the only Subversion client that accepts command-line arguments at the moment) when I click on an `svn:` URL:

```
!#/bin/bash
/usr/bin/kdesvn "$1"
```

After saving this script in a file and making it executable, I modified Firefox to call it when I click on an `svn:` URL by doing the following:

1. Type **about:config** in the Firefox location bar, and press Return.
2. Right-click in the Preference Name window and select New ⇨ String.
3. Enter **network.protocol-handler.app.svn** as the name of the string. Click OK.
4. Enter the full pathname of the script as the value of the string.

This isn't especially exciting, but it does prevent occasional frustration when clicking on `svn:` URLs. It would be nice if `esvn` or `rapidsvn` took command-line arguments, because `kdesvn` is a KDE application and installs a ton of KDE libraries if you haven't already installed other KDE applications on your Ubuntu system. One of these days…

Checking Files Out of a Subversion Repository

Now that you've configured one (or two) Subversion server(s), you can access the sample repository from any machine that can reach your server. Sample checkout commands that would retrieve the entire Hello project are the following:

- `svn co file:///var/svn/hello`: This is the standard command to retrieve the Hello project. You can use this command only from the machine on which the Subversion repository is located.

- `svn co http://192.168.6.90/svn/hello`: This command retrieves the Hello project using the HTTP protocol, and it will work only if you have a Web server running on the host where the Subversion repository is located, as described in the section entitled "Configuring Apache2 for Subversion Support."

- `svn co svn://192.168.6.90/svn/hello`: This command retrieves the Hello project using the SVN protocol, and it will work only if you have the Subversion server running on the host where the Subversion repository is located, as described in the section entitled "Configuring the svnserve Server."

Executing any of these commands will create a directory named `hello` in your current working directory and will populate that directory with the file `hello.c`. Congratulations—you're using Subversion!

Committing Changes to a Subversion Repository

Once you have checked files out of your Subversion repository and modified them, you'll want to check them back into the repository from which they came—providing one true location for the latest and greatest version of your source code and being able to track changes to it is the whole point of source code control in the first place.

Subversion makes it very easy to check modified files back in because it automatically keeps track of version information and the repository from which checked-out files came in the first place. If you do a long listing (`ls -al`) of any directory that you've checked out of Subversion, you will see a directory named `.svn` that holds this information.

Because Subversion maintains this information for you, all you have to do to check a file back into Subversion is to use the `svn ci` (check-in) command, as in the following example, which checks in a new, improved version of the file `hello.c` and shows the output from the `svn` command's check-in operation:

```
$ svn ci hello.c -m "Added comment"
Sending        hello.c
Transmitting file data .
Committed revision 7.
```

The `-m` option enables you to specify your check-in message on the command line. If you do not use this option, the `svn` command will automatically start a text editor in which you can enter a check-in message and will proceed with the check-in once you exit the editor.

Getting More Information about Subversion

Subversion is a powerful source code control system, with many more commands and options than I've needed to discuss in the previous few sections. Some great web sites for additional information about Subversion are the following:

- **Subversion Book** (`http://svnbook.red-bean.com`): An online version of the O'Reilly book *Version Control with Subversion*. Although this is available online for your convenience, it's always nice to buy a copy (`http://svnbook.red-bean.com/buy/p`), because we all understand that authors like to be compensated for their work other than through "good vibes" and "thank you" messages.

- **Subversion FAQ** (`http://subversion.apache.org/faq.html`): The Subversion FAQ, which is a great source of answers to common questions and general information about Subversion

- **Subversion home page** (`http://subversion.apache.org`): This is the home page for Subversion, with as much information as you'd expect from the Subversion mothership.

- **Subversion IRC:** If you need answers *now* and are a fan of Internet Relay Chat, a dedicated channel for Subversion users is available at http://irc.freenode.net, channel #svn.

- **Subversion Mailing Lists:** The tigris.org folks provide a variety of mailing lists for Subversion information. The announce@subversion.apache.org mailing list is a low-traffic, read-only list to which release and update announcements are posted. The dev@subversion.apache.org list is a mailing list for Subversion developers. The users@subversion.apache.org list is a high-traffic list for Subversion users where you can ask questions and help out other Subversion users. To subscribe to any of these lists, send mail to listname-subscribe@subversion.apache.org and follow the instructions that you receive in the response mail that you receive. These mailing lists are moderated, so there may be a delay before any posts that you make actually appear on the lists.

Many other Subversion-related pages and sites are available on the Web; a simple Google or Clusty search for Subversion will keep you knee-deep in reading material for weeks. The Indian *Linux for You* magazine (www.linuxforu.com) published a nice article on Subversion, which I couldn't find in the archives on their site, but is available from the authors' site at www.stylesen.org/walk_through_subversion_16_linux_you_april_2009. This same publication has a good article on security in Subversion (though in an older version, by now) at www.linuxforu.com/previews/subversion-16-security-improvements-illustrated/.

Summary

You don't have to build your own Linux applications anymore unless you want to — providing a precompiled, integrated set of Linux applications, libraries, and a kernel is the whole point of a Linux distribution. However, you may sometimes want to build your own, bleeding-edge versions of existing software to get the latest and greatest features, or you may be a developer and want to write some of your own tools (hopefully open source) because that's what you do. This chapter explained how to install the tools that you'll need to compile most C and C++ applications on an Ubuntu system, including related software such as the make build tool and various libraries. The chapter also explored many of the most popular IDEs available for Linux systems, focusing on the popular, powerful, and open source Eclipse IDE. The chapter concluded by discussing popular source code control systems, highlighting Subversion, and explaining how to set up your own repositories and servers and how to access those remotely.

The next chapter discusses how to use virtual machines to experiment with other operating systems or set up dedicated servers for specific purposes. Virtual machines are a great way to experiment with different operating systems and Linux distributions, and are also a great way of enabling yourself to run Microsoft Windows tools occasionally without wasting hardware on a part-time operating system.

Using Virtual Machines and Emulators

IN THIS CHAPTER

Introducing virtualization

Using VirtualBox

Using KVM

Using QEMU

Virtualization is the logical separation of the request for a service from the physical resources that actually provide that service, and is also one of today's hottest IT topics. The primary reasons for the popularity of virtualization today are the increasing speed and capabilities of today's off-the-shelf processors, falling hardware prices, and the ubiquity of networks that offer the capability to connect almost anything to anything else. These combine to provide higher-performance and higher-capability systems at a lower cost, providing plenty of CPU cycles and processor capabilities to handle any extra layer of abstraction that virtualization might introduce.

The loudest virtualization-related buzz surrounds different approaches to two topics, namely, virtual storage and virtual machines:

- **Virtual storage:** Virtual storage, as the name suggests, prevents users and system administrators from having to know the physical devices upon which their data is stored because you access that storage through logical device, disk, or volume names. The physical hardware that supports these logical or virtual disks can be located on separate disk drives, storage devices, or even on physically distinct computer systems. Common virtual storage mechanisms such as logical volumes were introduced in Chapter 4, "Basic Linux System Concepts."

- **Virtual machines:** Virtual machines enable multiple complete operating systems to run simultaneously on the same physical computing hardware. Virtual machines must use the same instruction set as the system on which the virtual machines are running (which is typically referred to as the *host system*). In other words, you can only run x86-based operating systems on a machine with an x86-compatible processor. Virtual machines are often confused with *emulators*, which do approximately the same thing, but enable a single physical computer system to run operating systems and applications that require different processors and instruction sets by *emulating* those processors. Emulators are compiled for the instruction set of the machine on which they are running, but simulate an entire physical execution environment including the processor and hardware subsystems. Emulators running on x86-based systems can therefore run operating systems and applications that are compiled for either x86-based systems or for systems that use other types of processors, such as ARM, MIPS, PowerPC, and SPARC processors.

This chapter provides an introduction to different types of virtual machine technologies and discusses the different types of virtual machines and emulators that are available for Ubuntu systems, usually as packages in the Ubuntu repositories.

Note

As mentioned previously, *virtualization* is a hot buzzword. To get as much software as possible on the bandwagon, you'll often hear remote desktop connection technologies such as VNC and RDP, discussed in Chapter 25, "Connecting to Other Systems," referred to as *desktop virtualization* technologies because they provide the ability to display a graphical desktop from one computer system on another computer system or smart display device. ∎

Overview of Virtualization and Emulation

As discussed in the introduction to this chapter, virtualization is a hot term in computing today. The next few sections explore some of the reasons to consider virtualization (using it as *résumé fodder* is not discussed), and the different types of virtual machines that are in use today (and which of these are available as packages for Ubuntu systems), and make some recommendations on which virtual machine technology to adopt based on what you want to accomplish.

Why Virtualize?

The most obvious reason for wanting to run a virtual machine is so that you can run multiple operating systems at the same time on a single physical computer system. For example, suppose that you want to run Linux but occasionally need to run Microsoft Word. You can configure your system to dual-boot so that you can run either Linux or Windows, but that isn't very useful if you depend on your Linux system to read mail, browse the Web, and so on. Because you can run only one operating system at a time, dual-booting can be time-consuming and irritating. You could also run some Windows programs using WINE on your Linux system — *WINE* is a Linux-based

Windows API that supports Windows applications. However, you might encounter problems with WINE, and then what can you do?

Assuming that you have sufficient disk space, installing Windows as a virtual machine is probably your most convenient, robust, and long-term solution. Why waste hardware on Windows? Being able to run Windows while running Linux will enable you to use the Linux applications that you prefer while still being able to work on Microsoft Word documents that may have Windows-specific features (such as extensive Visual Basic macros, etc.).

Virtualization is more popular now than ever, for many reasons. Some of the most important reasons are the following:

- The power and performance of commodity x86 hardware continue to increase. Processors are faster than ever and support more memory than ever, and the latest multi-core processors literally enable single systems to perform multiple tasks simultaneously. Most modern systems can easily run a primary operating system and at least one virtual machine without taking a significant performance hit.

- The integration of direct support for hardware-level virtualization in the latest generations of Intel and AMD processors, motherboards, and related firmware makes virtualization on commodity hardware both easier and more powerful than ever before.

- A wide variety of virtualization products for both desktop and server systems running on commodity x86 hardware are available for free and are easily installed on your Ubuntu systems.

In general, the following are some common cases in which virtual machines are used:

- Dependency on a specific piece of software (described at the beginning of this section), where you need to use a software product that only runs (or runs best) on another operating system

- Running legacy software, where you depend on a software product that only runs on a specific version of a specific operating system

- Software system test and quality assurance environments, where you need to be able to test a specific software product on many different operating systems or versions of an operating system

- Low-level development environments, where developers may want or need to work with specific versions of tools, an operating system kernel, and a specific operating system distribution

Virtualization is not a new concept and has been in use for years. However, for the reasons discussed in this section, virtualization is both more available and easier to run than ever before.

The next section highlights different approaches to virtualization and details which virtualization packages use them, and which of these are available for your Ubuntu system.

Types of Virtual Machines

Virtual machines can work in many different ways. The differences between these approaches to virtualization can be subtle, but are always significant in terms of the capabilities that they provide and the hardware and software requirements for the underlying system. The most common approaches to virtual machines today are the following:

- **Guest OS:** Each virtual server runs as a separate operating system instance within a virtualization application that itself runs on an instance of a specific operating system. Parallels Workstation, VirtualBox, VMware Workstation, and VMware GSX Server are the most common examples of this approach to virtualization. The Ubuntu repositories include packages for the open source version of VirtualBox and also include the packages for Sun's version of VirtualBox, which is free for personal or individual use. A free version of the VMware Server, VMware Player, and VMware ESXi are all available for free download from the VMware web site.

- **System-level or operating system virtualization:** Multiple, logically distinct system environments that are running on a single instance of an operating system kernel. System-level virtualization is based on the change root (chroot) concept that is available on all modern UNIX-like systems, and which gives each virtual machine a portion of the parent system's root filesystem as the root filesystem for the virtual machine, as well as its own set of processes that execute relative to that root filesystem. Linux virtualization solutions such as FreeVPS, Linux VServer, OpenVZ, and Virtuozzo are all examples of system-level virtualization. The kernel and user-space administrative utilities for OpenVZ are provided in the Ubuntu repositories.

- **Parallel virtual machine:** Some number of physical or virtual systems are organized into a single virtual machine using clustering software such as PVM (`www.csm.ornl.gov/pvm/pvm_home.html`). The resulting cluster is capable of performing complex CPU and data-intensive calculations in a cooperative fashion. The PVM packages are available from the Ubuntu repositories, but are not discussed in more detail in this chapter because clustering is an advanced, specialized technology that requires its own book.

- **Paravirtualization:** Device drivers in the virtual machines are modified so that they *know* that they are running in a virtual machine environment and can optimize device access for that model. This can significantly reduce execution overhead and increase disk and network I/O. Paravirtualization is typically used in virtualization environments that also use a virtual machine monitor (known as a *hypervisor*), which runs on top of your machine's hardware, manages protected or privileged CPU operations that are requested by any virtual machine, and also manages the hardware access requests that are made by any virtual machine. The most popular examples of hypervisor-based virtualization in use today are Citrix Xen, Microsoft's Hyper-V, and VMware's ESXi product, all of which run an administrative operating system on top of the hypervisor, as do the virtual machines themselves. This administrative operating system can communicate with the hypervisor and is used to manage the virtual machine instances and the resources that are allocated to them. Virtualization technologies such as the Kernel-based Virtual Machine (KVM), wherein the Linux kernel that is running on the host system is equivalent to the hypervisor, are also actively working on paravirtualized device drivers.

- **Kernel-level virtualization:** Does not technically require a hypervisor, but instead runs a separate version of the Linux kernel and an associated virtual machine as a user-space process on the physical host. This provides an easy way to run multiple virtual machines on a single host, but only enables you to run Linux virtual machines, and then only those that have been compiled with support for the appropriate kernel-level virtualization technique. Examples of this are User-Mode Linux (UML), which has been supported in the mainline Linux kernel for quite a while, and KVM, which was introduced in the 2.6.20 mainline Linux kernel. UML does not require any separate administrative software in order to execute or manage its virtual machines, which can be executed from the Linux command line. KVM uses device drivers in the host's kernel for communication between the main Linux kernel and the virtual machines and uses a slightly modified QEMU process as the display and execution container for its virtual machines. In many ways, KVM's kernel-level virtualization is a specialized version of Full virtualization, wherein the Linux kernel serves as the hypervisor, but I think that UML and KVM are unique enough to merit their own class of server virtualization. The Ubuntu kernel includes KVM modules, and the user-space component of KVM is available in the Ubuntu repositories.

- **Hardware virtualization:** Very similar to both paravirtualization and Full virtualization, hardware virtualization uses a hypervisor, but is available only on systems that provide hardware support for virtualization. Hypervisor-based systems such as Xen and VMware ESXi and kernel-level virtualization technologies such as KVM can take advantage of the hardware support for virtualization that is provided on the latest generation of Intel (Intel VT, AKA Vanderpool) and AMD (AMD-V, AKA Pacifica) processors. Virtual machines in a hardware virtualization environment can run unmodified operating systems because the hypervisor can use the hardware's support for virtualization to handle privileged and protected operations and hardware access requests, and to communicate with and manage the virtual machines. Both Xen and KVM are available in the Ubuntu repositories.

Each of these approaches to virtualization has its own advantages and disadvantages. As mentioned previously, depending on your hardware, a single virtual machine technology can actually support more than one of these approaches to virtual machines. On Intel VT and AMD-V processors, Xen supports both paravirtualization and hardware virtualization. On these same processors, KVM supports both kernel-level and hardware virtualization.

What Kinds of Virtualization Can I Use?

With the exception of hardware virtualization, all of the virtualization techniques described in the previous section can be used on any x86-compatible system with a Pentium or better processor. I'd recommend using at least a Pentium IV or equivalent, and would also recommend using a 64-bit processor because those are modern, powerful, and often provide hardware support for virtualization.

If your system is using a processor that has hardware support for virtualization, such as the Intel VT and AMD SVM processors, you can run unmodified operating systems as virtual machines under virtualization technologies like KVM and Xen. Hardware support for virtualization enables you to install and run operating systems such as Microsoft Windows by installing it in a virtual machine just as you would on a new physical system. (You can also, of course, use any vanilla Linux installation disk and install any standard Linux distribution as a virtual machine, without modification.) At the time of this writing, processors that provide hardware support for virtualization are as follows:

- **Intel VT (Virtualization Technology, aka Vanderpool):** Selected Pentium 4 and Pentium D, Xeon 5000 and later, Xeon LV, Core Duo, Core 2 Duo, Core 2 Quad, and Quad-Core processors

- **AMD-V/SVM (Virtualization/Secure Virtual Machine, aka Pacifica):** AMD Athlon 64 (family "F" and "G") socket AM2, Athlon 64 X2 (family "F" and "G"), Turion 64 X2, newer Opteron, all Phenom, and all newer processors

To determine whether the processor in a given system supports virtualization, you can check the flags entry in the file /proc/cpuinfo, which you can do with a command like the following:

```
cat /proc/cpuinfo | grep flags
```

Depending on whether you are using an AMD or Intel processor, the output of this command is very different:

```
AMD flags :   fpu tsc msr pae mce cx8 apic mtrr mca cmov  \
              pat pse36 clflush mmx fxsr sse sse2 syscall \
              nx mmxext fxsr_opt lm 3dnowext 3dnow up pni \
              cx16 lahf_lm svm cr8_legacy

Intel flags : fpu vme de pse tsc msr pae mce cx8 apic sep  \
              mtrr pge mca cmov pat pse36 clflush dts acpi \
              mmx fxsr sse sse2 ss ht tm pbe syscall nx lm \
              constant_tsc arch_perfmon pebs bts rep_good  \
              pni monitor ds_cpl vmx est tm2 ssse3 cx16    \
              xtpr lahf_lm
```

If you are using an Intel CPU, you would look for the field vmx in the flags field. If you are using an AMD CPU, you would look for the field svm in the flags field. The following command is an easy way to do this in one step:

```
# egrep '(vmx|svm)' /proc/cpuinfo
```

If you see any output from this command, your system supports hardware virtualization. Congrats!

Selecting a Virtualization Technology

The key to selecting a virtualization technology boils down to how much work you want to do and what you want to use the virtual machines for:

- Guest OS solutions such as VirtualBox and the free VMware Server are the easiest to install and understand, and they require limited changes to your system aside from installing them in the first place. The kernel drivers for VirtualBox are built when you install VirtualBox, as they are for VMware Workstation. Of these two, VirtualBox is the easier to use and manage, but VMware is more of an industry standard than VirtualBox, and any experience that you get using the VMware Server may be useful both at home and at work.

- Hypervisor solutions such as Xen can provide higher performance and more flexible administration than other approaches to virtualization, but require additional administrative overhead. Your system's boot configuration is different when booting a hypervisor and loading the domain Xen kernel. You must use specialized tools (xm, virt_manager, etc.) to configure and manage your virtual machines.

- Kernel-level virtual machines such as KVM are simpler to administer than hypervisor-based virtual machines, but do not provide the same level of administrative granularity of memory use, execution priority, and so on.

Recommendations? If you simply want to run the occasional Windows application, use VirtualBox. If you want to experiment with more sophisticated virtualization technologies from a desktop system, try KVM. If you want a full-blown, enterprise-ready virtualization environment and are willing to do a bit of learning, go for Xen (which unfortunately isn't discussed in this chapter, but there are lots of great books available on Xen, including one by this author [*Professional Xen Virtualization*, Wrox, 2008, ISBN: 0470138114]). If you need to run virtual Windows machines and have an Intel VT or AMD-V processor, you can use either KVM or Xen to run virtual machines that take advantage of the hardware support for virtualization that is provided by these processors.

Popular Emulation Software for Linux

The best-known emulation package for most systems is not a desktop computer emulator at all — it's the Multi-Arcade Machine Emulator (MAME; www.mame.net), which enables you to play a variety of ancient arcade video games directly from images of their Read-Only Memory

(ROM) chips. I love this package—arcade video games were my original motivation for getting interested in computers. Although system administration turned out to be more fun for me, playing some ancient video game via MAME is incredibly fun, and the MAME technology is simply amazing. There are some legal issues with playing many of the traditional game ROMs because they are still technically owned by the original manufacturers—you should investigate these before downloading any game ROMS from the hundreds of sites that offer them on the Web. However, the copyright to many of them has been lost, and I do actually have a Centipede arcade game in my living room, so I don't feel too bad about things. A variety of MAME packages are available in the Ubuntu archives—I typically just install the basic xmame-x package, which contains the binaries for the vanilla X Window System version of MAME. The xmame-sdl package is slightly more modern, but takes over your screen by default, which can be disconcerting (and which Compiz doesn't always recover from well). If you want to simplify the process of figuring out where to put your ROM images from the MAME documentation, front-ends to this package such as gmameui (for GNOME systems) can be very handy.

If you actually want to do real work with an emulator, the most useful emulation technology in Linux circles is QEMU, which can emulate many different hardware platforms and associated hardware. Not only is QEMU great as a stand-alone emulator, but also open source virtualization packages such as Xen, VirtualBox, and KVM make heavy use of some of the code from QEMU to avoid reinventing the wheel regarding console emulation, graphics emulation, and so on.

A huge number of emulators are available today, especially on Linux, where many people want to revisit the software glories of their youth (or at least the systems that they ran on). Rather than trying to coax a 20-year personal computer from a defunct vendor back to life, writing an emulator can be entertaining, is useful to others who are also interested in that hardware, and provides a fun technical challenge. A quick search for *Linux Emulators* on the Internet returns hundreds of results. Two especially nice summary pages are Zophar's page of UNIX/Linux Emulators at www.zophar.net/linux.html, and the Using Linux summary at www.usinglinux.org/emulators/.

Managing Virtual and Emulated Machines

As discussed later in this chapter, virtualization packages such as VirtualBox and VMware Server provide a graphical virtualization console that makes it easy to configure, manage, and switch between the virtual machines that you have configured and may be running using these technologies. However, these management consoles only work for virtual machines of the associated type. Many software packages are under development to provide a single management, creation, and execution framework for virtual machines that have been created with multiple virtualization technologies. The best known of these is the Virtual Machine Manager, and is available in the Ubuntu repositories as the virt-manager package. For more information about the Virtual Machine Manager, see its home page at http://virt-manager.et.redhat.com.

This chapter focuses on the manual configuration, creation, and management of different types of virtual machines, rather than using a graphical management package. The primary reasons for this are the following:

- The Virtual Machine Manager only supports KVM, QEMU, and Xen virtual machines, but other virtualization technologies such as VirtualBox or VMware may be better suited to your needs.

- If you are planning to use a virtualization technology such as KVM or Xen in a server environment, a graphical user interface may not be available, in which case you cannot use the Virtual Machine Manager.

- Like most graphical tools, the Virtual Machine Manager is designed to simplify configuring, executing, managing, and monitoring its subject domain, in this case, virtual machines. If you're just getting started with virtualization and plan to use it in a SOHO or enterprise environment, it's important to understand the system-level configuration changes and underlying procedures associated with virtualization, especially networking configuration.

The Virtual Machine Manager is a great package that can be extremely useful. However, in my opinion, understanding what's going on under the covers and focusing on the creation and management tools associated with specific virtualization technologies provide a better foundation for getting started with virtualization. My apologies if that disappoints you.

Some other virtualization management tools that are available in the Ubuntu repositories are the xenman package, for managing Xen virtual machines, and packages such as qemuctl and qemu-launcher, for managing QEMU virtual machines.

Getting More Information about Virtualization

The Ubuntu web site provides some general information about virtualization on Ubuntu, Canonical's partners in the commercial virtualization space, and so on. The sections of this chapter that discuss specific virtualization solutions will provide pointers to additional information about that particular solution. You can get additional, general information about virtualization on Ubuntu systems at the following locations:

- **Ubuntu Virtualization Overview** (www.ubuntu.com/products/whatisubuntu/serveredition/technologies/virtualization): This is Canonical's corporate description of basic virtualization options for Ubuntu. Unfortunately, this doesn't mention things like VirtualBox and Xen! Luckily, the community documentation page that it points to does (the Ubuntu Community Virtualization Overview page in this list).

- **Ubuntu Community Virtualization Overview** (https://help.ubuntu.com/community/Virtualisation): The Ubuntu community documentation "home page" for information about different virtualization solutions on Ubuntu

If you are just generally interested in virtualization and would like to obtain additional information, there are a variety of sites that provide general-purpose information about virtualization and emulation on commodity hardware. The following are some of my favorites:

- **IBM developerWorks:** "Virtual Linux: An Overview of Virtualization Methods, Architectures, and Implementations" (`www.ibm.com/developerworks/linux/library/l-linuxvirt/`): This is a great article if you are interested in general information about virtualization on Linux systems. IBM's developerWorks always provides a huge amount of detailed, technically accurate information. This article provides a good overview and explanation of virtualization on Linux, along with links to many other sites.

- **Linux Virtualization Wiki** (`http://virt.kernelnewbies.org`): A nice site that provides a good overview of virtualization on Linux and more detailed discussions of various Linux virtualization technologies. It also provides a good introduction to various tools that are available for managing Xen virtual machines, and a good overview of the Xen (and other) virtualization support that is available in various x86 Linux distributions (and in other operating systems, such as OpenSolaris).

- **SearchServerVirtualization.com** (`http://searchservervirtualization.techtarget.com/`): A great TechTarget site that provides a tremendous amount of information about server virtualization, related storage virtualization topics, and so on. One of the advantages of this site is that many vendors make white papers and commercial announcements available there, which make it quite useful for keeping track of the pulse of commercial virtualization offerings.

- **TheFreeCountry.com** (`www.thefreecountry.com/emulators/index.shtml`): "Free Emulators and Virtual Machines" is a nice summary of free emulation and virtualization software for Intel x86-based (and compatible) machines. This is a great resource, but remember that *free* does not necessarily mean *open source*.

- **Wikipedia** (`www.wikipedia.com`): Big surprise here. Wikipedia has extensive articles about Xen (`http://en.wikipedia.org/wiki/Xen`), virtualization in general (`http://en.wikipedia.org/wiki/Virtualization`), emulation (`http://en.wikipedia.org/wiki/Emulation`), and most of the other terms and players in today's virtualization market. The Wikipedia is a great source of information, as always — although you should always corroborate anything that you read there because it is publicly editable, and anyone can add anything that they want there.

Installing and Using VirtualBox

VirtualBox (`www.virtualbox.org`) is an open source Guest OS virtualization package that runs on and hosts 32-bit and 64-bit operating systems such as Linux, *BSD, Solaris, and Microsoft Windows systems. VirtualBox itself runs on Linux, Mac OS X (Intel only), Solaris, and Microsoft Windows systems. VirtualBox is an open source application that was originally developed by

InnoTek Systemberatung GmbH (www.innotek.de/), a software company based in Stuttgart, Germany, which was purchased by Sun Microsystems (www.sun.com). VirtualBox leverages the open source QEMU emulator for some of its basic console and input device support, as do other open source Linux virtualization packages.

VirtualBox comes in both a commercial and an Open Source Edition (OSE) release. Precompiled commercial binaries are free for personal use or for evaluation purposes according to the terms of the VirtualBox Personal Use and Evaluation License (PUEL), whereas OSE sources and binaries are freely available under the terms of the GPL. Packages for the open source edition of VirtualBox are available in the Ubuntu repositories, along with the loadable kernel module that it uses (vboxdrv). This section discusses the VirtualBox OSE, although the personal commercial version has some nice features that the OSE does not, such as the USB device and filesystem support, and the ability to seamlessly run applications from Windows virtual machines on your Linux desktop. (You can download the version of the commercial edition that is free for personal use from Sun at www.sun.com/software/products/virtualbox/get.jsp.)

For more information about VirtualBox, see:

- **VirtualBox home page** (www.virtualbox.org): The home page for VirtualBox, which provides access to downloads of the latest (and beta) versions, the official VirtualBox documentation and related wikis, and so on. A variety of forums where you can ask questions, exchange tips and tricks, and so on, are available at http://forums.virtualbox.org/.

- **Oracle's Sun VirtualBox page** (www.sun.com/software/products/virtualbox/index.jsp): The page for VirtualBox at Sun Microsystems, the corporate overlords of commercial VirtualBox support

- **Community Ubuntu documentation for VirtualBox** (https://help.ubuntu.com/community/VirtualBox): Information about using VirtualBox on Ubuntu systems

VirtualBox Overview

VirtualBox provides both command-line and graphical tools for creating, administering, and managing virtual machines. Its graphical administrative environment is much like those provided by tools such as Parallels Workstation, VMware Workstation and Server, and even Microsoft's Virtual PC, enabling you to create and customize virtual machine configurations.

The emulation and display environment used by VirtualBox is very similar to that used by VMware and others, although the key to release the cursor from being captured is different (and configurable). Internally, VirtualBox uses a kernel module called vboxdrv to communicate with and manage virtual machines and associated resources through the VirtualBox device node /dev/vboxdrv. This node must be publicly writable or all users who want to run VirtualBox must be members of the vboxusers group. (The latter is the default mechanism.) VirtualBox includes a built-in Dynamic Host Configuration Protocol (DHCP) server and Network Address

Translation (NAT) support to simplify connectivity between multiple machines, whether physical or virtual, while also making it possible to segregate and manage virtual machine network traffic.

VirtualBox is stable and quite responsive and includes several nice features. One of these is the ability to specify the amount of video memory through a slider, which makes it possible to run more graphics-intense applications inside VirtualBox. Another is its built-in support for the VirtualBox Remote Desktop Protocol (RDP), which enables you to use a standard RDP client to connect to virtual machines running inside VirtualBox (analogous to VMware's support for remote connections and administration). VirtualBox also supports virtual channels between local devices and RDP-connected virtual machines, enabling you to connect USB devices locally but attach them to remote virtual machines. VirtualBox also provides a nice snapshot feature, which makes it easy to capture the state of a virtual machine at any point, for easy rollback. This is great if you want to experiment with installing certain applications for short-term use, but don't want to do so permanently — just take a snapshot, install and experiment with the applications that you're curious about, and then fall back to a previous snapshot.

The next few sections explain how to create a virtual machine in VirtualBox OSE, install an operating system, configure networking for your virtual machines on both your host system and in the virtual machines, and start and stop virtual machines.

Installing VirtualBox

As mentioned previously, packages for the Open Source Edition (OSE) version of VirtualBox are provided in the Ubuntu repositories and can be installed on any Ubuntu Desktop system. VirtualBox requires a graphical user interface and thus isn't really suitable for installation on a standard Ubuntu Server system unless you've also installed a graphical user interface there. VirtualBox is an excellent virtualization package for desktop computer users, but isn't really oriented toward heavy-duty virtual machine deployment in an enterprise environment — Xen, KVM, or VMware are better choices there, in my opinion.

To install VirtualBox on an Ubuntu Desktop system, use your favorite Package Management software, as described in Chapter 19, "Adding, Removing, and Updating Software." You will want to install the `virtualbox-ose` and `virtualbox-ose-source` packages. The former contains the actual VirtualBox binaries and related files, and the latter is a package from which the loadable kernel module that is used by VirtualBox is built. The latter will keep your VirtualBox installation working across Ubuntu kernel upgrades.

Note
Installing VirtualBox as a specific user should automatically add that user to the vboxusers group. Members of this group have write access to the `/dev/vboxdrv` device that is used by VirtualBox for communication between the kernel and virtual machines. If you want other users of your Ubuntu system to be able to use VirtualBox, you must manually add them to this group, which you can do with the command `sudo adduser USERNAME vboxusers`. ∎

Once VirtualBox is installed, the real fun begins. Proceed to the next section for information on creating a virtual machine in VirtualBox.

Tip

If you are going to be creating Ubuntu virtual machines, you can either follow the instructions in the next two sections for creating a virtual machine and installing an operating system in it, or you can use the `ubuntu-vm-builder` script to create a virtual machine (of type vbox) and automatically install Ubuntu into it. You must install the `ubuntu-vm-builder` in order to use this script, but it can be quite handy if you're oriented toward (or interested in) building virtual machines from the command line. After installing the package, see the man page for the `ubuntu-vm-builder` command or its online help (`ubuntu-vm-builder --help`) for more information. ■

Creating a Virtual Machine in VirtualBox

You can start VirtualBox on an Ubuntu system by selecting the Applications ➪ Accessories ➪ VirtualBox OSE menu command (sometimes located on the Applications ➪ System Tools menu) or on either system by executing the `virtualbox` command from any command-line environment such as an xterm or GNOME Terminal window. When you first start VirtualBox, you'll see a screen like the one shown in Figure 24-1.

As the panel at the right of this screen states, this screen is largely empty because you haven't created any virtual machines yet. Once you create a virtual machine, the screen will look like the one shown in Figure 24-2, where the virtual machines that are available are listed in the left pane, and information about the currently selected virtual machine displays in the set of tabs at the right.

FIGURE 24-1

Starting VirtualBox for the first time

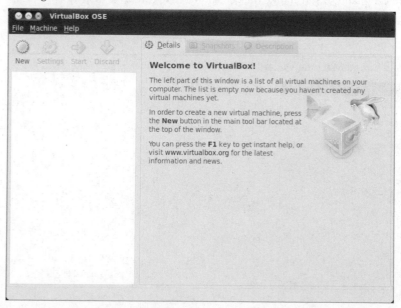

FIGURE 24-2

Starting VirtualBox after creating a virtual machine

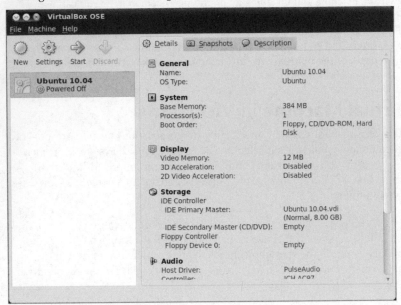

To create a new virtual machine, click the New icon in the VirtualBox toolbar or select the Machine ➪ New menu command. A screen like the one shown in Figure 24-3 displays.

FIGURE 24-3

The Welcome screen for the New Virtual Machine Wizard

Click Next to proceed. A screen like the one shown in Figure 24-4 displays.

FIGURE 24-4

Providing name and type information for a new virtual machine

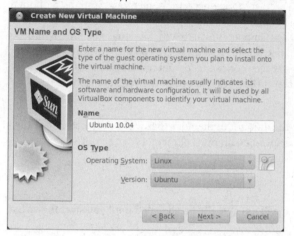

Enter the name that you want to associate with your new virtual machine in the Name field, and select the type of operating system that you are installing from the dropdown OS Type list. Click Next to proceed. A screen like the one shown in Figure 24-5 displays.

FIGURE 24-5

Specifying the amount of memory for a new virtual machine

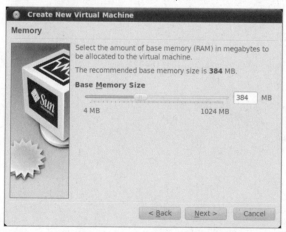

This screen enables you to specify the amount of memory that will be allocated to the virtual machine. This is the amount of physical memory that the virtual machine will believe that it has. You can change this later by modifying the settings for your virtual machine, so accepting the default suggestion (usually 256 MB) is fine unless you know in advance that you will want more or less memory. For example, systems with graphical interfaces on which you will also be running server processes (such as a Web server, etc.) may need more memory. Systems without a graphical interface will usually require less memory, unless they are running heavily used server processes. As you might expect, any memory that you associate with a virtual machine will be allocated from the amount of memory available on the system where you are running VirtualBox, and will therefore be unavailable to the host system once the virtual machine is started. I typically accept the defaults and adjust them later if the performance of the virtual machine is unacceptable.

After optionally using the slider to change the amount of memory that will be allocated to your virtual machine, click Next to associate the specified amount of memory with your virtual machine and display the screen shown in Figure 24-6.

Note
The amount of memory that you specify on this screen will not actually be allocated until you start the virtual machine. ∎

FIGURE 24-6

Specifying the hard disk image for a new virtual machine

Because you are creating a new virtual machine, you will probably want to create a new virtual hard disk for its use. A *virtual disk* is a file on some storage device that the host system (the one on which you're running VirtualBox) can access. By default, new virtual disks are created in the ~/.VirtualBox/VDI directory, located in your home directory, and have the file extension .vmi.

Click Next to begin the Create New Virtual Disk Wizard, which makes it easy to create a new virtual disk. The Virtual Disk Wizard's Welcome screen displays, as shown in Figure 24-7.

FIGURE 24-7

The Create New Virtual Disk Wizard

Note

When creating a virtual machine in VirtualBox, you can also select an existing VirtualBox or VMware hard disk for its use by clicking Existing and navigating to the disk image in the Virtual Disk Manager that displays. In most cases, you won't already have a disk image, so this section focuses on creating new virtual disks. ■

Click Next to proceed. The dialog shown in Figure 24-8 displays.

FIGURE 24-8

Specifying the type of virtual disk to create

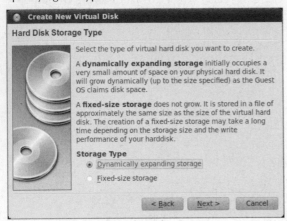

This dialog provides two options for the type of virtual disk that you want to create, either a dynamically expanding image or a fixed-size image. The differences between these two are as follows:

- **Fixed-size image:** All of the disk space required on your host system for the virtual disk is immediately allocated when you create the new virtual disk, based on the disk size that you will specify in a subsequent dialog.

- **Dynamically expanding image:** *Dynamically expanding images* initially use the minimum amount of disk space on the host system that is required to hold the files that you've installed in your virtual machine, plus some extra space required to hold information about the filesystem(s) that the virtual disk image contains. For example, the 20-GB dynamically expanding disk image for a Microsoft Windows 2003 Server system actually uses only 2 GB after a complete, default system is initially installed. As you install additional applications and as the virtual machine creates and expands additional files for caching, logging, and so on, the dynamically expanding image will continue to grow, up to the maximum size that you will specify in a subsequent dialog.

These two different types of disk images have some performance implications for your virtual machine and the host system:

- **Fixed-size image:** Using a fixed-size disk image will result in slightly higher performance for your virtual machine and the host system because neither of them needs to allocate additional space for the disk and to do the housekeeping required to accurately track the disk blocks on the host system that are actually allocated to the virtual machine. If you know that you will be installing large applications or creating/downloading large files in a virtual machine, you may as well pre-allocate all of the disk space because you're probably going to need it eventually. On the down side, your host system will have less storage remaining after allocating the entire disk, and your backups and any virtual machine snapshots that you create will be larger because they must back up or snapshot the entire disk image.

- **Dynamically expanding image:** Using a dynamically expanding disk image results in slightly lower performance for both your host system and the virtual machine because they will have to dynamically allocate new space to the virtual disk image as it is required, and will also have to perform the housekeeping associated with that allocation. Your host system must always have enough disk space available for the maximum size of the virtual disk image — running out of disk space when trying to expand a virtual disk image can seriously corrupt the virtual disk image, which could render the virtual disk unusable, meaning that you could lose all of the data that it contains. On the plus side, dynamically expanding images require substantially less storage on the host system, consume less space in your backups, and will require less space for any snapshots that you create of your virtual machines.

I recommend using a dynamically expanding image because it requires less space for the disk itself, snapshots of the virtual machine, and in the backups that you do of your host system. (You *are* doing backups, right?) The performance impact of using a dynamically expanding disk is relatively small, and I only use VirtualBox to enable me to run the occasional Windows application or for testing other Linux distributions, neither of which is a situation in which optimal performance is critical. As I've mentioned before, I typically use Xen for mission-critical virtual machines in which performance is critical. Your mileage may vary.

Click the radio button beside the type of disk image that you want to create, and click Next to proceed. The dialog shown in Figure 24-9 displays.

FIGURE 24-9

Specifying the name and size of a new virtual disk

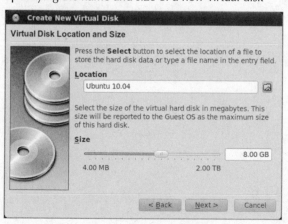

875

The name of a virtual disk image is initially set to the name that you specified for your virtual machine, but you can change this by entering a new name if you want. I rarely change the name of the disk image because using the same names for both makes it easy to see which disk image goes with which virtual machine if you explore the ~/.VirtualBox folder. The default size of the disk image for a virtual machine is typically set to 8 GB, which is enough for experimentation but probably not if you plan to install a large number of applications and/or do a significant amount of real work in your virtual machine. For example, I tend to use 20-GB disk images for Windows systems to reduce the chance that I'll run out of space some day (and because disk space is cheap nowadays). If you're using dynamically expanding images, you won't lose all of that disk space on your host system immediately, although you should really have that much available just in case the virtual machine actually needs it.

After making any changes that you want to the name or maximum size of your virtual disk image, click Next to proceed. A Summary dialog like the one shown in Figure 24-10 displays.

Click Finish to proceed. The dialog shown in Figure 24-6 re-displays, this time displaying the name and location of your new virtual disk as the Boot Hard Disk for your system. Click Next to proceed. The Summary dialog shown in Figure 24-11 displays.

This dialog summarizes the name, type, memory allocation, and virtual disk image for the new virtual machine that you are creating. Assuming that you've specified the values that you actually want to use in the preceding dialogs, nothing on this dialog should be a big surprise. You can change these settings later anyway, so you may as well proceed. Click Finish to proceed. The main VirtualBox window re-displays, showing an entry for your new virtual machine in the left column.

FIGURE 24-10

Summary information about a new virtual disk

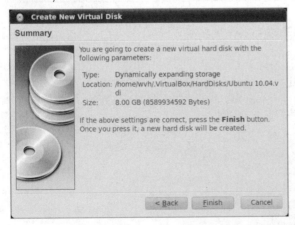

FIGURE 24-11

Summary information about a new virtual machine

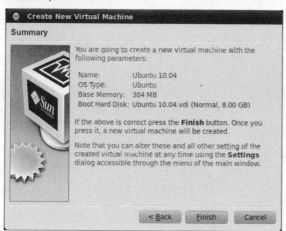

At this point, you've created a virtual machine, but it doesn't actually contain an operating system or any applications. If you're using a dynamically expanding disk, its virtual disk image has been created, but is using less than 100 KB of storage. To actually run the virtual machine, you must install your operating system of choice, as described in the next section.

Installing an Operating System in a Virtual Machine

VirtualBox provides a helpful First Run Wizard to walk you through the steps of installing an operating system in a new virtual machine. To install your operating system of choice into a new virtual machine, you simply start the virtual machine by making sure that its entry is selected in the left-hand VirtualBox pane and then clicking the Start button above that pane. This displays a VirtualBox window that is the console for your new virtual machine and also displays the Welcome screen for the First Run Wizard, which isn't very interesting. To get to a useful screen, click Next. This displays the dialog shown in Figure 24-12.

This dialog enables you to boot from a CD/DVD-ROM drive or a floppy disk to start the installation process for the operating system for your virtual machine. After selecting either of these as the Media Type, you can identify the source of that media, either a physical device or an image file in the bottom of the dialog. If you are booting from an image file rather than a physical device, you can click the Browse button beside the Image File entry to browse for the location of your disk or floppy image. Once you've selected the Media Type and Media Source, click Next to proceed. The Summary dialog shown in Figure 24-13 displays.

FIGURE 24-12

Specifying the installation media for a new virtual machine

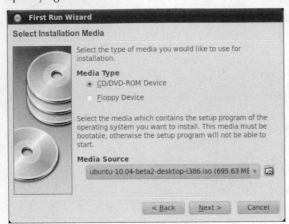

FIGURE 24-13

The installation media summary for a new virtual machine

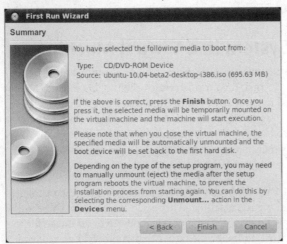

Beyond simply summarizing the boot information for your new virtual machine, this dialog points out that you may need to use the Devices ➪ Unmount command to manually unmount your boot media if a reboot occurs during installation. This is a good thing to remember if you find that your virtual machine is booting from the installation media again after a reboot.

To proceed, click Finish. The "First Run" dialog closes, and your new virtual machine should start to boot from the specified installation media.

To interact with the virtual machine during the installation process (and beyond), you will need to click inside the VirtualBox window so that the virtual machine has the input focus for your mouse and keyboard. The first time you do that, you will see a dialog like the one shown in Figure 24-14.

FIGURE 24-14

VirtualBox keyboard/mouse focus explanation dialog

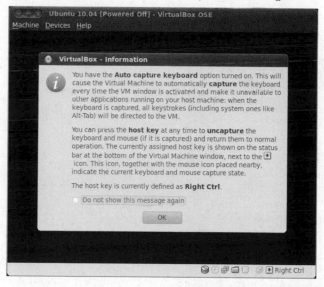

The "Auto capture keyboard" option makes it easy to interact with a virtual machine by sending all mouse and keyboard events directly to the virtual machine rather than the host system. However, some keyboard commands, such as the Ctrl+Alt+Delete required for initiating Windows logins, might accidentally shut down your host system, so you should send this sequence by selecting the "Insert Ctrl-Alt-Delete command from a virtual machine's Machine menu." Capturing keyboard input also makes interacting with the virtual machine more precise because the cursor can't leave the boundary of the virtual machine window while you're in this mode. To release the mouse and cursor from your virtual machine, press the right Control (Ctrl) key. (You can change this key binding later if you want.) As a handy reminder, the key to release keyboard capture is also displayed in the lower-right corner of a VirtualBox virtual machine window.

After the first time you see this warning dialog, you'll probably want to disable it in the future, which you can do by checking the "Do not show this message again" option before clicking OK to close this dialog.

At this point, the installation of your virtual machine begins, using the standard installation screens for the operating system that you are installing, just as if you were installing the operating system on a physical machine, as shown in Figure 24-15.

FIGURE 24-15

Installing an operating system in a virtual machine

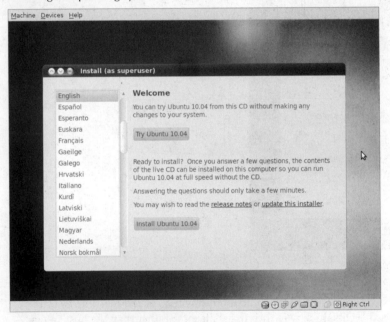

Once the installation process completes, your virtual machine will typically reboot. If necessary, remove the installation media as discussed earlier in this section and shown in Figure 24-13. You can now use your new virtual machine — congratulations!

Installing VirtualBox Guest Additions

The open source edition of VirtualBox provides enhanced drivers for better video resolution and better control of mouse interaction in Windows and Linux virtual machines once a virtual machine of either of those types has been installed. These drivers are known as the *VirtualBox Guest Additions* — if you're familiar with VMware, these are equivalent to VMware's Guest Tools.

Note

The Windows drivers in the Guest Additions package are precompiled. Installing the Linux drivers from this package requires that the GNU C Compiler (gcc) and the header files for the Linux kernel be installed in your virtual machine. See Chapter 23, "Software Development on Ubuntu," for information about installing these in an Ubuntu virtual machine (which is the same as installing them on a physical Ubuntu system). If you're running some other Linux distribution in your virtual machine, use that system's Package Management tools to install the gcc and kernel headers packages for that distribution. ■

To install the Guest Additions into a virtual machine, select the Devices ➪ Install Guest Additions menu entry in a virtual machine window. You will see a dialog to the effect that the Guest Additions CD image couldn't be found on your machine, and would you like to download it over the Internet? Click Yes. If you see a confirmation dialog for the download ("are you sure"), you should also click Yes there, and you will see a download progress bar appear in the bottom-left corner of the virtual machine window as the image is downloaded.

Once the ISO image for the Guest Additions is downloaded, VirtualBox displays a dialog asking if you want to mount the ISO image as a CD drive. Click Yes.

If your virtual machine is running some version of Windows, the Autorun.inf script on the CD will automatically install the Guest Additions for you when the CD is mounted. If you are running Linux, you will have to start a Terminal window (xterm, GNOME Terminal, Konsole, etc.), cd to the mounted image, and run the VBoxLinuxAdditions.run script via sudo to build and install the enhanced drivers.

Once you've installed the drivers, you can unmount the ISO image by using the standard mechanism for your operating system, or by selecting the Devices ➪ Unmount CD/DVD-ROM menu command from the virtual machine window.

Starting and Stopping Virtual Machines

Once you've created one or more virtual machines and installed an operating system in each, you can start any virtual machine by selecting its entry in the left pane of the VirtualBox window and clicking the Start icon.

After you're finished using a virtual machine, you can shut it down in one of two ways:

- By invoking the standard shutdown process for the virtual operating system that your virtual machine is running. When the shutdown process completes, the virtual machine window closes, and only the standard VirtualBox dialog will be displayed (unless you are running other virtual machines in other virtual machine windows).

- By clicking the Close box in the upper-right corner of the virtual machine window or selecting the Machine ⇨ Close menu command from the virtual machine window. Both of these display the dialog shown in Figure 24-16, which enables you to shut the virtual machine down in various ways.

Different ways of closing a virtual machine

The three options in this dialog do the following:

- **Save the machine state:** Saves the memory and disk state of the virtual machine to a file that will be used the next time that you start the virtual machine. Starting from a saved state is much faster than actually booting a virtual machine. However, you cannot edit the settings for a virtual machine if you have a saved state file because the state information for the virtual machine depends on the settings that were active when the machine's state was saved. In order to modify any settings for a virtual machine that has a saved state file, you must either start the virtual machine from the saved state file and then shut it down normally, or you must discard the saved state information by right-clicking on the virtual machine in the left pane of the main VirtualBox window and then selecting the Discard command from the context-sensitive menu. If you discard saved state information, you will lose any changes that were not written to your virtual machine's disk. If you have the time, it's definitely a better idea to start the virtual machine and shut it down normally rather than simply punting the saved state file.

- **Send the shutdown signal:** Begins a standard shutdown in the virtual machine's operating system. This option is provided if you accidentally clicked Close but have the time to do an orderly shutdown.

- **Power off the machine:** Immediately turns off the virtual machine without doing a clean shutdown. This is usually a bad idea because all operating systems need to ensure internal consistency before shutting down, but may be necessary in emergencies. However, if you've taken snapshots (described later in this section), the dialog shown in Figure 24-16 provides another option, shown in Figure 24-17, which enables you to fall back to the current snapshot, using it as a saved state file for this virtual machine. (Don't worry, I'll talk about snapshots in a few more paragraphs!)

FIGURE 24-17

Reverting to a snapshot during power-off

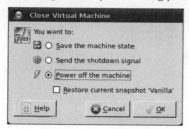

To proceed, select the way in which you want to shut down the virtual machine, and click OK.

In general, I prefer saving the state of a virtual machine to the other virtual machine shutdown options. However, these files can use significant amounts of disk space and can therefore require significant amounts of space in your backups (as well as increasing the time that it takes to do backups). You *are* doing backups, right?

An interesting capability that virtual machines introduce is the ability to take a snapshot of the state of a virtual machine and then undo any changes that you've made to your system by falling back to the previous state of the virtual machine. VirtualBox snapshots work slightly differently than you might think. When you create a snapshot using the Machine ⇨ Take Snapshot menu command from a virtual machine window, you actually continue to run in the snapshot. Once you've taken a snapshot, you can fall back to any previous snapshot by selecting the Snapshots tab for that virtual machine in the main VirtualBox window, right-clicking on the snapshot that contains the changes that you want to undo, and selecting the "Discard Snapshot" command from the context-sensitive menu that displays, as shown in Figure 24-18.

Selecting this command deletes the current snapshot. The next time that you start your virtual machine, it will start with the previous snapshot or, if no snapshot is available, with the default state of your virtual machine.

FIGURE 24-18

Deleting a snapshot to return to a previous state

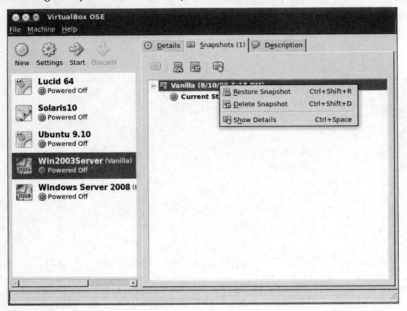

Networking and VirtualBox

VirtualBox includes an internal DHCP server and built-in support for NAT (Network Address Translation) that enables your virtual machines to automatically obtain IP addresses on a private Internet subnet. Virtual machines that you create in VirtualBox automatically use NAT networking to reach external networks such as the Internet. Unfortunately, such communications are handled by VirtualBox rather than through standard networking infrastructure. This means that, by default, you can't use standard network commands from your host system to reach your virtual machines, and you also can't reach the host machine from your virtual machines. Bogus! Luckily, VirtualBox supports other networking mechanisms, specifically Bridged networking, that eliminate these hassles by enabling your virtual machines to communicate with other hosts and networks by using a virtual network interface on the host system, rather than through VirtualBox itself. This enables communication between your virtual machines and any other system, including your host system, which also enables any other system that can reach your host system to reach your virtual machines. As a plus, it isn't hard at all to set this up.

Tip

You can also use port mapping to map ports on your host system to the ports associated with various services on your virtual machine, which will enable other systems to contact your virtual machine, but this doesn't help with access from the virtual machine to your host system. But, it's better than nothing. For more information about port mapping in VirtualBox, see the sidebar, "Remapping Ports for VirtualBox VM Access," at the end of this section. ■

VirtualBox's Bridging support is implemented in software on your Linux host. Bridging is a networking technique used to connect multiple network segments by forwarding packets from one to the other. In this context, bridging enables you to enable communication between multiple physical and virtual network interfaces by connecting them to a software bridge that you set up on your Ubuntu system. The network devices that are attached to this bridge consist of your system's primary network interface and one virtual network interface for each of your virtual machines. The bridge therefore sees any network traffic that the physical interface that is attached to it would originally have seen, and can route traffic to any other device on the bridge. This includes both connection traffic and infrastructure-related traffic such as DHCP requests, which therefore enables your virtual machines to get IP configuration information from a DHCP server on your local network, giving them standard addresses, standard DNS configurations, and any other bells and whistles that you've set up in your network's DHCP server. Of course, you can also give your virtual machines static addresses on your local network and supply other network configuration information as you would on any other host with a static IP address. It's all up to you!

Note

Bridging is not supported by many of the drivers for wireless network interfaces. If you want to use virtual machines on a laptop that uses (or only has) a wireless interface and need to be able to communicate between your laptop and your virtual machine(s), it's easier to install and use the VMware Server than VirtualBox. You can selectively remap selected ports to enable interaction between a VirtualBox virtual machine that uses NAT and its host machine, but this is a pain. (See the sidebar at the end of this section for specific information about how to do that.) ■

Thanks to the cleverness of the Linux, Ubuntu, and VirtualBox folks, setting up a bridge and virtual network interfaces on your host system does not require a certificate from Cisco, the ability to recite the seven layers of the OSI networking model, or the sacrifice of any form of poultry. Let's just do it! I'll present these instructions as a series of steps to make it easier to follow along (and to highlight the fact that there are not that many steps):

1. Use your favorite Package Management application to install the `bridge-utils` and `uml-utilities` packages on your system. The `bridge-utils` package contains the commands that are used to create bridges, attach devices to bridges, show status information, and so on. The `uml-utilities` package contains the utilities that are used to create and manage Linux virtual Point-to-Point (TUN) and Ethernet (TAP) network devices. (The *uml* stands for "User-Mode Linux," which is a mechanism for running

instances of the Linux operating system as a process on a Linux machine, which was mentioned earlier in this chapter in the section entitled "Overview of Virtualization and Emulation.")For example, you could install these packages using aptitude from a terminal window by using the following command:

```
sudo aptitude -y install bridge-utils uml-utilities
```

2. Modify your /etc/network/interfaces file to add an entry for a bridge, and connect the network device that is associated with your system's physical network interface to it. You should also comment out any existing entry for that network device. The following is a sample entry for a bridge named br0 to which the network device eth0 is attached:

```
auto eth0
    iface eth0 inet manual
  up ifconfig $IFACE 0.0.0.0 up
  up ip link set $IFACE promisc on
  down ip link set $IFACE promisc off
  down ifconfig $IFACE down

    auto br0
    iface br0 inet dhcp
      bridge_ports eth0
  bridge_fd 0
bridge_maxwait 0
      metric 0
```

The first section defines eth0 as a TCP/IP network device that is automatically started when the network is brought up, but which is manually configured to have a static IP address of 0.0.0.0, and which is also put into *promiscuous mode*. Promiscuous mode is a special mode in which a network interface can receive all traffic on the network, even if it is not addressed to that specific card or interface. Comment out any existing entries for your network device (eth0, in the example used in this section)! The second entry says that the br0 is automatically started when the network is brought up, is an IP bridge (because of the bridge_ports entry) that should get its configuration via DHCP, that no delay should be imposed when forwarding packets across the bridge (the bridge_fd entry), that the bridge should immediately enter forwarding mode as soon as it comes up (the bridge_maxwait entry), and that this interface should be considered a high-priority interface that can immediately reach a default gateway (the metric entry).

Tip

Unfortunately, Ubuntu systems don't provide a man page that describes the settings that you can use to define bridge settings in an /etc/network/interfaces file. For more information about the settings I've used (and the many others that I did not), see the man page for the bridge-utils-interface additions, which you can find on the NET at locations such as http://web.iesrodeira.com/cgi-bin/man/man2html?bridge-utils-interfaces+5. ■

3. Modify the rule file that is used when devices associated with VirtualBox are created during your system's boot process, adding a rule that specifies that the TUN/TAP virtual network device /dev/net/tun will be writable by anyone in the vboxusers group. You will want to add the following entry to the end of the /etc/udev/rules.d/ 99-virtualbox-ose.rules file. The following should be entered on a single line, without the \ character:

```
KERNEL=="vboxdrv", NAME="vboxdrv", OWNER="root", MODE="0660"
```

4. If you are using Network Manager or WiCD to manage your network interfaces, make sure that it does not automatically try to activate or connect eth0.

5. Reboot your system. When your system comes back up, you can use the brctl show command to verify that a bridge has been created and that the right physical and virtual network devices are attached to it. The output associated with the example that I've used in this section looks like the following:

```
$ brctl show
bridge name bridge id            STP enabled interfaces
br0          8000.0019d1239f01   no          eth0
```

You should also verify that routing is set up correctly by executing the route -n command — you should see only a few entries, all related to the bridge.

6. Start VirtualBox and update the network configuration information for each of your virtual machines. To do this:

   a. Select a virtual machine in the left pane, and click the Settings icon in the VirtualBox toolbar. The Settings dialog displays, showing the current configuration of the specified virtual machine. Click the Network entry in the left pane to display a dialog like the one shown in Figure 24-19.

Note

The Settings icon is available only for systems that have been shut down cleanly and that do not have snapshots or saved state information. You must delete your snapshots and saved state information before you can modify any of the settings for a virtual machine. ∎

   b. Click the down arrow beside the "Attached to" entry and select "Bridged Adapter" from the drop-down list. Click the Name drop-down and select the name of the bridge that you created earlier (br0, if you're following along exactly). The dialog should look like that shown in Figure 24-20.

   c. Click OK to save the updated network configuration information.

FIGURE 24-19

Default network settings for a virtual machine

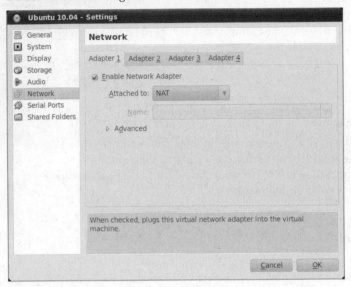

FIGURE 24-20

Host Interface setup for a virtual machine

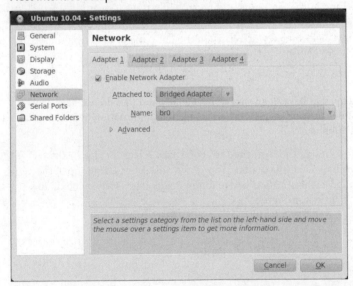

After updating all of your virtual machines, any virtual machine that you start will now be a true citizen of your local network. Not too shabby!

Remapping Ports for VirtualBox VM Access

Port forwarding is a technique in which one system forwards requests on certain network ports to another system. Nowadays, port forwarding is probably most commonly used on home gateways to forward requests from an external gateway to a specific system on an internal network. VirtualBox provides built-in support for port forwarding to enable external systems (or your host system) to contact services on your virtual machine directly, without having to make the virtual machine a full-fledged participant in your local network.

You use the VBoxManage command to set up port forwarding, which must be done when the virtual machine is not actually running. Doing this requires three commands for each service that you want to be able to contact on the virtual machine, as in the following example, which enables external access to an SSH server that is running on an old virtual machine named *Ubuntu-Hardy*:

```
VBoxManage setextradata "Ubuntu-Hardy" \
    "VBoxInternal/Devices/pcnet/0/LUN#0/Config/ssh/Protocol" TCP
VBoxManage setextradata "Ubuntu-Hardy" \
    "VBoxInternal/Devices/pcnet/0/LUN#0/Config/ssh/GuestPort" 22
VBoxManage setextradata "Ubuntu-Hardy" \
    "VBoxInternal/Devices/pcnet/0/LUN#0/Config/ssh/HostPort" 2222
```

(These commands would normally be typed on a single line—the backslash in each is present only for formatting purposes in this book.)

The first of these commands identifies the networking protocol that you are forwarding. The second identifies the port on the virtual machine to which requests on a specific port on your host should be forwarded. The third identifies the port on your host system that external systems should use in order to contact the service associated with this rule. The name of this rule is the field after the Config entry and before the keyword for the rule—in this case, the name of the rule is ssh.

Once you've entered commands like the one shown in this example, the rule is permanently defined in the VirtualBox configuration information for the specified virtual machine, in this case *Ubuntu-Hardy*. After you start the virtual machine, any host on your network can reach the SSH service on your virtual machine by using a command like ssh host-system -p 2222.

When setting up port forwarding in VirtualBox, you need to identify the port on the virtual machine where a given service is running (which you can do by consulting the /etc/services file), and select a port on your host system where no existing service is running. You should always use a port whose port number is greater than 1,024 on your host system because port numbers less than 1,024 are typically reserved for services that may actually be running on a physical system.

In the future, if you don't remember which rules you've set up, you can list any port-forwarding rules that you've defined for a specific virtual machine by using a command such as VBoxManage getextradata Ubuntu-Hardy enumerate.

Fixing Virtual Machine Boot/Installation Problems

As mentioned earlier in this section, any user who wants to run VirtualBox must be a member of the vboxusers group. This is usually done automatically for the user who installs VirtualBox, but other users will not be able to run VirtualBox until they are added to the vboxusers group with a command like `sudo adduser` *USERNAME* `vboxusers`.

Even if the current user is a member of this group, a related problem that you may encounter is a dialog to the effect that the `/dev/vboxdrv` device was not accessible by the current user. This device should always be owned by the root user and the vboxusers group, and should be set to mode 0660 so that anyone in the vboxusers group can read/write it. You can change this manually with the following commands:

```
sudo chown root.vboxusers /dev/vboxdrv
sudo chmod 0660 /dev/vboxdrv
```

Another common problem, especially if you're experimenting with multiple virtualization technologies, is that different virtualization solutions don't always play well with each other. For example, at the time of this writing, you would see an error dialog like the one shown in Figure 24-21 if you attempted to start a VirtualBox virtual machine on a system where the loadable kernel modules for the KVM virtual machine were loaded into the kernel.

FIGURE 24-21

An error dialog about conflicting virtualization solutions

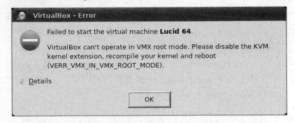

Fortunately, this dialog is somewhat misleading, telling you that you have to recompile your kernel. What is this, the Twentieth Century? To resolve this particular problem, all you have to do is remove the loadable kernel modules that VirtualBox is complaining about, using a command like the following:

```
sudo /sbin/rmmod kvm-intel kvm-amd kvm
```

Your system will be using only one of the kvm_amd and kvm_intel modules (because you probably have only one type of processor in your system), and will therefore complain about one of them. However, after running this command, you should be able to close the VirtualBox virtual machine window, click the Start icon in the VirtualBox window, and proceed with installing the operating system in the virtual machine. If you see a message in the virtual machine window about not being able to find any bootable media, use the Devices ➪ Mount menu command to remount the installation media for use by the virtual machine, and select the virtual machine window's Machine ➪ Reset command to restart the boot process.

Tip

If the loadable kernel modules for another virtualization technology are being automatically loaded when your system boots, the startup script for that technology is probably being run during system startup. Check the symbolic links in the /etc/rc2.d directory — you can remove the symbolic link to the "other" virtualization technology (such as KVM, in this example) to prevent its kernel modules from being loaded the next time that you boot your system. ■

Installing and Using KVM

Many Linux virtualization devotees were surprised when Linux Torvalds accepted patches that incorporated a largely unknown virtualization technology called Kernel-based Virtual Machines (KVM) from a largely unknown company (www.qumranet.com/) that was then in stealth mode. I certainly was. These patches were incorporated into the 2.6.20 release of the mainline Linux kernel. However surprising its appearance was, there are good precedents for an in-kernel virtualization technology such as KVM, most notably User-Mode Linux (UML), a mechanism for running an instance of Linux as a process on another Linux system. UML has been supported in the mainline Linux kernel for years. Like UML, KVM supports the creation and execution of virtual Linux systems running as a separate process on a Linux system. KVM currently requires a processor that supports Intel Virtualization Technology (VT) or AMD Secure Virtual Machine (SVM/AMD-V) (the same processors required for running unmodified Guest OS systems under Xen).

One of the primary reasons for the inclusion of KVM into the mainline kernel (aside from its bright, shiny, and clean implementation, of course) was the fact that KVM does not require a hypervisor and therefore is a pure Linux solution — Linux is still the operating system that is running on the bare metal, as opposed to hypervisor-based solutions such as Xen and various VMware products. Internally, KVM works through a device node called /dev/kvm, which is created and managed by CPU-specific loadable kernel modules, intel_kvm.ko and amd_kvm.ko, one of which is loaded as kvm.ko. Opening this device creates a new virtual machine, which can then be managed through ioctl() calls that perform operations such as creating a virtual CPU, allocating memory, intercepting privileged calls, and so on. KVM also requires a user-space application (based on QEMU, which is discussed later in this chapter) to view and interact with each virtual machine.

KVM currently supports 32- and 64-bit Linux virtual machines, 32-bit Windows virtual machines, OpenSolaris, and most *BSD operating systems. Work on support for 64-bit Windows virtual machines is in progress.

For more information about KVM, see the following:

- **Qumranet's KVM wiki** (`www.linux-kvm.org/page/Main_Page`): Provides overview information and documentation/HOWTOs for using KVM on various Linux distributions.

- **Ubuntu Kernel Virtual Machine** (`https://help.ubuntu.com/community/KVM`): Ubuntu community documentation on installing and using KVM, creating virtual machines of different types, and so on

- **KVM on Ubuntu** (`www.michaeldolan.com/1030`): One user's experience with installing and using KVM on Ubuntu 7.10. This is a nice hands-on reference, although it doesn't go into any detail about network setup.

Installing KVM and Related Packages

The software required to use KVM is located in a single package, the `qemu-kvm` package. You can install this package using your favorite package management tool, as described in Chapter 19. The `qemu-kvm` package does not include the kernel modules that must be loaded in order to run a virtual machine under KVM — the `kvm.ko` and `kvm-processor.ko` modules (where processor is either `amd` or `intel`) are always provided and installed as part of the standard Ubuntu Linux kernel image. However, these kernel modules are not loaded by default on a standard Ubuntu or Kubuntu system — the `qemu-kvm` package includes the `/etc/init.d/kvm` startup and shutdown script, which loads the `kvm` module and the appropriate module for your processor.

The `qemu-kvm` package depends on several other packages, such as the bridge utilities (`bridge-utilities`), IP routing (`iproute`), SDL (Simple DirectMedia Layer) video (`libsdl1.2debian`), and VGA BIOS (`vgabios`) packages, as well as some more standard system packages for sound, compression, and so on.

Once the `qemu-kvm` package is installed, it's quite easy to create a virtual machine and associated disk, install your operating system of choice, and run the virtual machine. The next few sections explain how to manually create a filesystem image for a KVM virtual machine, and how to manually install an operating system into it.

Creating a Disk for a KVM Virtual Machine

In order to create and use a KVM virtual machine, you must first create a virtual hard disk for use by that virtual machine. This virtual hard disk can be an existing logical volume or physical partition on your system, or a file in any filesystem that your system can access. Using a file as a virtual disk for your machine has two primary advantages:

- File-based virtual machines can easily be moved or cloned to another computer system that supports KVM by simply copying the file to the other machine.

- KVM inherits QEMU's support for a variety of clever disk formats, including the dynamically expanding QEMU-Copy-On-Write disk format. As explained in more detail later in this section, dynamically expanding disk formats enable you to create disk image files that initially only require enough space for the operating system itself, but that can expand as you create and add new files.

If you already have a free partition that you want to use with your virtual machine, you can just skip to the next section. No special formatting or allocation is required because the partition already exists and will be formatted during operating system installation, just like when installing that operating system on a physical machine. The rest of this section focuses on using KVM with file-based disk images.

You can create a virtual disk image in many different ways, my favorite of which are the following:

- By using the standard Linux/UNIX dd command to create a pre-allocated file of a specified size, as in the following example, which creates a 10-GB file called kvm_disk_image.img:

```
dd if=/dev/zero of=kvm_disk_image.img bs=1G count=10
```

- By using the qemu-img command to create a disk image in either raw (pre-allocated) or qcow (QEMU's copy-on-write format, which creates a dynamically expanding disk image). Because KVM and QEMU are quite intertwined, taking advantage of disk formats that were introduced by QEMU makes sense. The following is an example of using the qemu-img command to create a 10-GB file called kvm_disk_image.img:

```
qemu-img create -f qcow kvm_disk_image.img 10G
```

A qcow disk will start out very small, like any dynamically expanding disk image, but will expand as you install an operating system and create files in the virtual disk. I suggest using pre-allocated disks for any critical, production virtual machines that you create (so that you don't have to worry about running out of disk space whenever the disk needs to expand), but dynamically expanding disks are fine for personal use or if you don't have much disk space and are willing to take the chance that you'll always have the disk space that you need.

Installing an Operating System in a Virtual Machine

After creating a disk image, starting the virtual machine so that you can install an operating system in your disk image is quite easy. When starting a virtual machine, you must identify the disk image, volume, or partition that it should use as its primary hard drive; any other devices (such as a CD-ROM drive) that you will need during installation; the amount of memory that you want to allocate to it; and the device to boot from if that is a drive other than the virtual machine's primary hard drive. Many other command-line options are available (of course) — because KVM depends on QEMU, see the online reference for the qemu command for a complete list, which you can do by executing the man qemu command from any xterm, GNOME Terminal, or Konsole window.

As an example of booting a virtual machine to install a new operating system, the following command will start a kvm process using an image file named winxp.img as the primary boot drive, allow access to /dev/cdrom on your host system as the CD-ROM drive for the virtual machine, allocate 512 MB of memory to the virtual machine, and boot from the CD-ROM drive:

```
kvm -hda winxp.img -cdrom /dev/cdrom -m 512 -boot d &
```

This command starts KVM using an SDL (Simple DirectMedia Layer) window as a console for the virtual machine, as shown in Figure 24-22.

FIGURE 24-22

Installing a KVM virtual machine using an SDL console

Tip

Once you click inside an SDL KVM window, its QEMU underpinnings automatically capture the cursor, binding it to that window so that all mouse and keyboard events go directly to the virtual machine rather than to the host system. To release the cursor so that it is available to the host system and can move outside the boundaries of a KVM window, press [Left Ctrl]+[Left Alt] (hold down the left Ctrl key and press the left Alt key). ■

Virtual machines created via the kvm command can also use a VNC console rather than an SDL console, as in the following example:

```
kvm -hda winxp.img -cdrom /dev/cdrom -m 512 -boot d -vnc :1 &
```

This command starts KVM using a VNC console that you can access as HOSTNAME:1 or IP-ADDRESS:1 from the local system or any other system that can access the host system over the network. Figure 24-23 shows the VNC console for a KVM virtual machine in one of the VNC clients that are available for Ubuntu.

Installing a KVM virtual machine using a VNC console

You do not need to use the sudo command to install or start a KVM virtual machine as long as you are a member of the kvm group (which is required to run KVM in the first place) and that you are using KVM's default networking model (i.e., the networking model that is used when you do not specify a networking model). This networking model is known as *User Networking*. For more information about different ways of networking KVM virtual machines, see the section "Networking for KVM," later in this chapter.

After entering a command such as either of these, the virtual machine will boot from the host system's CD-ROM drive, where you have presumably inserted the boot media for the operating system that you want to install. Once you connect to the SDL or VNC console, the installation process for that operating system is exactly the same as it would be if you were installing that operating system on a physical machine.

Starting a KVM Virtual Machine

Once you've installed an operating system in your virtual machine, you can start that virtual machine at any time using a somewhat simpler version of commands like the one shown in the previous section. The primary difference between booting a virtual machine in order to install an operating system and booting a virtual machine in order to run a virtual machine on which an operating system has already been installed is the boot device. If you simply do not specify the -boot option, the virtual machine will boot from its primary root filesystem, as in the following commands:

```
sudo kvm -hda winxp.img -cdrom /dev/cdrom -m 512 &
sudo kvm -hda winxp.img -cdrom /dev/cdrom -m 512 -vnc :1 &
```

Either of the previous commands will start a KVM process using an image file named winxp.img as the primary boot drive, allow access to /dev/cdrom on your host system as the CD-ROM drive for the virtual machine, and allocate 512 MB of memory to the virtual machine. The first of these commands starts KVM using an SDL window as a console for the virtual machine. The second of these starts KVM using a VNC console that you can access as HOSTNAME:1 or IP-ADDRESS:1 from the local system or any other system that can access the host system over the network.

Networking for KVM

At this point, you probably won't be surprised to read that KVM's support for networking heavily leverages the networking support that is provided in QEMU. So, with yet another tip of the hat to Fabrice Bellard ("Mr. QEMU"), let's summarize the various networking approaches that are available in KVM:

- **User Networking:** KVM/QEMU provides a DHCP service for virtual machines and serves as a packet forwarder/receiver for packets sent from the Guest OS to an external network. This provides a fairly slow network connection but requires absolutely no configuration. By default, this networking mode does not support inbound network connections to the virtual machine, but you can use the -redir option when starting a virtual machine to map a port on the host system to a single port on the virtual machine. User Networking is the default networking mode for KVM/QEMU if no other networking mode is specified.

- **Public or private virtual bridge via TUN/TAP:** Uses a TAP device for each virtual machine, connecting them to a virtual bridge that is created and managed using the brctl utility. If the host also belongs to the bridge (i.e., the bridge is public), this mode makes it easy for you to create virtual machines with IP addresses on the same network as the host, and therefore enables bidirectional communication between host, virtual machines, and other hosts.

- **TUN/TAP and iptables:** Associates each virtual machine with a TAP device, and uses iptables kernel packet routing rules to route traffic between an external network and each virtual machine.

- **Virtual distributed Ethernet (VDE) via TUN/TAP:** Creates a virtual Ethernet and associated switch using a single TAP device on the host. This makes it easy for you to put all of your virtual machines on a single virtual Ethernet.

This section focuses on User Networking and Public Bridging because these are the most common networking mechanisms used with KVM and QEMU. For more information about iptables, see www.netfilter.org or Ubuntu-specific information such as http://ubuntuforums .org/showthread.php?t=111972. For more information about VDE, see http://wiki .virtualsquare.org/index.php/VDE, or the QEMU-oriented information at http:// alien.slackbook.org/dokuwiki/doku.php?id=slackware:vde.

Note
When specifying networking options for KVM or QEMU, you ordinarily use the -net option twice. The first option identifies the network interface card (and optionally, the device bus and VLAN) that you want to use, which defaults to an emulated PCI Realtek 8139 network interface card in KVM. The second option identifies the networking model that you want to use, which defaults to user (User Networking). The exception to the "two -net options" rule is when you want to indicate that no networking is supported, which is done by specifying -net none on the command line when you start a virtual machine. ■

Using KVM with User Networking

As summarized in the previous section, the default networking mode used by KVM/QEMU is called *User Networking*, in which KVM/QEMU serves as a packet forwarder/receiver for packets sent from the Guest OS to an external network, and also includes a DHCP server that will automatically assign an IP address to the virtual machine (on the 10.0.2.X subnet). User Networking is somewhat slow and does not support all networking protocols (no ICMP, e.g.). For this reason, some standard commands, such as ping, will not work outbound from the virtual machine. The biggest drawback of User Networking is that it does not support inbound connections. However, if your primary reason for running a virtual machine is to enable you to occasionally run some proprietary software (some Microsoft Office component, e.g.), the lack of inbound connections doesn't matter, and KVM/QEMU's User Networking is probably all you need. User Networking is active by default, but you can also explicitly specify it on the command line by using the -net nic -net user command-line options.

The User Networking support provided by KVM/QEMU doesn't prevent inbound communication to your virtual machines; it just doesn't provide full support for it. KVM and QEMU provide two mechanisms for extending the connectivity of your virtual machines when using User Networking:

- -redir protocol:host-port:guest-ip:guest-port: Enables you to re-direct incoming connections from a port on the host system to a port on a virtual machine. protocol is one of tcp or udp, host-port is the network port on the host system that should be directed to guest-port on the virtual machine, and guest-ip is the IP address of the virtual machine if it is not the default value (10.0.2. that is assigned by the internal KVM/QEMU DHCP server). This option and associated value must be provided on the command line when you start the virtual machine. You can specify the -redir option multiple times on the command line to re-direct multiple ports to the virtual machine.

- -smb /full/path/to/directory: Uses an internal KVM/QEMU SMB server to export the specified directory as a share named qemu, which the virtual machine can then mount as \\GATEWAY-IP\qemu. GATEWAY-IP is the IP address of the networking re-direct inside KVM/QEMU, and is 10.0.2.2 for Windows XP and Vista virtual machines, although it may differ for other versions of Windows.

While the -redir option always works, I've had problems getting the -smb option working with different versions of KVM and QEMU. A much simpler solution is to run Samba on your Ubuntu host and then configure a share named qemu in your /etc/samba/smb.conf file that looks something like the following:

```
[qemu]
   comment = Windows File Share for KVM/QEMU
   path = /full/path/to/directory
   browseable = yes
   read-only = no
   public = yes
```

After restarting Samba, you will then be able to mount the qemu share as \\GATEWAY-IP\qemu from within the virtual machine. I've had problems accessing other shares in the host environment from virtual machines, but this approach has always worked for me.

Using KVM with a Virtual Bridge

If you need to access your KVM/QEMU virtual machines from external systems and want them to be full-fledged participants on the same network as the host system on which they are running, the combination of a virtual bridge and TUN/TAP that is supported by KVM/QEMU is exactly what you need.

The steps for setting up a virtual bridge and creating a TAP device for each of your KVM/QEMU virtual machines are as follows:

1. Use your favorite Package Management application to install the `bridge-utils` and `uml-utilities` packages on your system. The `bridge-utils` package contains the commands that are used to create bridges, attach devices to bridges, show status information, and so on. The `uml-utilities` package contains the utilities that are used to create and manage Linux virtual Point-to-Point (TUN) and Ethernet (TAP) network devices. For example, you could install these packages using `aptitude` from a Terminal window by using the following command:

```
sudo aptitude -y install bridge-utils uml-utilities
```

2. Modify your `/etc/network/interfaces` file to add an entry for a bridge and connect the network device that is associated with your system's physical network interface to it. You should also comment out any existing entry for that network device. The following is a sample entry for a bridge named `br0` to which the network device `eth0` is attached:

```
auto eth0
    iface eth0 inet manual
  up ifconfig $IFACE 0.0.0.0 up
  up ip link set $IFACE promisc on
  down ip link set $IFACE promisc off
  down ifconfig $IFACE down

    auto br0
    iface br0 inet dhcp
       bridge_ports eth0
  bridge_fd 0
bridge_maxwait 0
     metric 0
```

The first section defines `eth0` as a TCP/IP network device that is automatically started when the network is brought up, but which is manually configured to have a a static IP address of 0.0.0.0, and which is also put into *promiscuous mode*. Promiscuous mode is a special mode in which a network interface can receive all traffic on the network, even if it is not addressed to that specific card or interface. Comment out any existing entries for your network device (`eth0`, in the example used in this section)! The second entry says that the `br0` is automatically started when the network is brought up, is an IP bridge (because of the `bridge_ports` entry) that should get its configuration via DHCP, that no delay should be imposed when forwarding packets across the bridge (the `bridge_fd` entry), that the bridge should immediately enter forwarding mode as soon as it comes up (the `bridge_maxwait` entry), and that this interface should be considered a high-priority interface that can immediately reach a default gateway (the metric entry).

Tip

Unfortunately, Ubuntu systems don't provide a man page that describes the settings that you can use to define bridge settings in an `/etc/network/interfaces` file. For more information about the settings I've used (and the many others that I did not), see the man page for the `bridge-utils-interface` additions, which you can find on the NET at locations such as `http://web.iesrodeira.com/cgi-bin/man/man2html?bridge-utils-interfaces+5`. ∎

3. Modify the rule file that is used when devices associated with KVM are created during your system's boot process, adding a rule that specifies that the TUN/TAP virtual network device `/dev/net/tun` will be writable by anyone in the kvm group. You will want to add the following entry to the end of the `/etc/udev/rules.d/45-kvm.rules` file. Enter this on a single line, with no \:

```
KERNEL=="tun", NAME="net/%k", OWNER="root", \
    GROUP="kvm", MODE="0660"
```

Note

I've seen problems with `udev` correctly setting ownership and permissions on tun/tap devices. To eliminate the chance of that, you can add the following entires to your `/etc/rc.local` file (before the "exit" entry!):

```
chown root:kvm /dev/net/tun
chmod 0660 /dev/net/tun ∎
```

4. Make sure that you can access the tap0 virtual network device by executing the following command:

```
sudo tunctl -u YOUR-USER-NAME
```

Reboot your system. When your system comes back up, you can use the `brctl show` command to verify that a bridge has been created and that the right physical and virtual network devices are attached to it. The output associated with the example that I'm using looks like the following:

```
$ brctl show
bridge name bridge id              STP enabled interfaces
br0          8000.0019d1239f01     no          eth0
```

You can also verify that routing is set up correctly by executing the `route -n` command—you should see only a few entries, all related to the bridge.

5. Start your virtual machines using a command like the following:

```
sudo kvm -hda kvm_disk_image.img -m 512 -net nic -net
tap,ifname=tap0
```

After entering your password, kvm will start your virtual machines, and the boot process will create a tap device for the virtual machine and execute the `/etc/kvm/kvm-ifup` script to attach it to the bridge. If your virtual machine gets its network configuration information from DHCP, it will get that information from a DHCP server on the same network as your host, not from KVM/QEMU's internal DHCP server.

Installing and Using QEMU

QEMU (`http://bellard.org/qemu`) is an amazingly powerful open source CPU emulator by Fabrice Bellard and a host of others. QEMU can emulate a huge variety of architectures, processors, and related peripheral hardware. QEMU can run operating systems and software that are compiled for platforms including 32- and 64-bit x86, 32- and 64-bit PowerPC, Motorola 68000, 32- and 64-bit SPARC, SH, MIPS, and ARM. QEMU virtualizes a complete hardware environment for each of these processors/architectures, including the CPU and peripheral devices like one or more serial ports, network interfaces, a PCI bus, VGA graphics adapters, sound hardware, disk drives, USB components, and more. This enables you to run unmodified guest operating systems for any of these architectures/processors in QEMU. For example, Figure 24-24 shows an xterm window in which QEMU has booted a ARM kernel and is therefore also running operating system binaries that have been compiled for the ARM platform.

If you are only planning to use QEMU to emulate a 32-bit or 64-bit x86 system, QEMU is installed as part fo the `qemu-kvm` package that was discussed in the previous section. If you did not install KVM, you must install the qemu-kvm package in order to install the QEMU application. If you want to use QEMU to emulate any other processor or architecture, you must also install the `qemu-kvm-extras` package.

An ARM kernel and root filesystem running under QEMU

QEMU's hardware emulation is so exceptional that significant parts of QEMU are used to support serial connections, graphics hardware, disk images, and so on in the full virtualization implementations of virtualization packages such as Xen and KVM. In fact, KVM works so closely with QEMU that I'm not going to go into much detail in this section — almost everything in the KVM portions of this chapter also applies to QEMU. For example, you can use QEMU to run virtual machines that were created under KVM — the only difference is that they will not be able to do hardware virtualization under QEMU, and will therefore execute solely through software emulation. Still, not too shabby!

For additional information about QEMU, see:

- **Fabrice Bellard's QEMU page** (`http://bellard.org/qemu/`): The QEMU page hosted by Fabrice Bellard, the primary author of QEMU

- **QEMU home page** (`http://qemu.org`): The best starting point for downloads, documentation, or general information about QEMU

- **QEMU user documentation** (`http://wiki.qemu.org/Qemu-doc.html`): The primary documentation for QEMU

- **QEMU developers mailing list** (`qemu-devel@nongnu.org`): You can subscribe to the mailing list at `http://mail.freesoftware.fsf.org/mailman/listinfo/qemu-devel`.

- **QEMU users forum** (http://qemu-forum.ipi.fi/): A great collection of forums discussing QEMU, recent patches, the use of QEMU on different platforms, and so on

- **QEMU IRC Chat** (#qemu channel on freenode.com): A great real-time way of asking questions about QEMU (and hopefully, getting answers as well)

- **QEMU Wiki** (http://qemu.kidsquid.com/moin.cgi): An unofficial wiki that provides a good deal of HOWTO information on using QEMU, QEMU networking setup, and so on

- **Information on converting disk images to/from QEMU** (http://en.wikibooks.org/wiki/QEMU/Images)

- **Information on QEMU networking** (www.h7.dion.ne.jp/~qemu-win/HowToNetwork-en.html and http://en.wikibooks.org/wiki/QEMU/Networking)

Summary

This chapter provided an overview of virtual machine technologies, explaining the differences between them and the advantages (and disadvantages) of each, and highlighting which are available for Ubuntu systems. It also compared emulation with virtualization and introduced popular emulation packages that are available for Ubuntu systems. Subsequent sections discussed installing and using VirtualBox and KVM, and provided an overview of QEMU.

The next chapter explores how you can connect to other machines on your network. Whether you need a command-line login session or a remote graphical console to execute commands directly on a remote machine, or simply need to transfer files back and forth between multiple machines, most of the tools you'll need are installed by default on Ubuntu Desktop systems. Anything else that you may need is only a few clicks and a download away in the Ubuntu repositories.

## CHAPTER 25

Connecting to Other Systems

Not too long ago, networking meant either talking with groups of friends or sending e-mail and surfing the Web from your home computer. Today's multi-computer households can provide much more than that, often featuring home or SOHO (small office/home office) networks of computers that share files and peripherals (such as printers and scanners); they are often centrally administered, and provide access to multiple people who want or need it. Although networked access to shared resources such as file servers and printers has been common in enterprise and home Windows networking environments for a long time, this is now a common requirement for the modern, enlightened household.

This chapter discusses various command-line and graphical solutions provided by Ubuntu Linux for directly connecting to remote systems, either by logging on to them directly or by obtaining remote, graphical access to a desktop session. This chapter doesn't explore connecting to remote file servers and file sharing—that's discussed in Chapter 26, "File Transfer and Sharing."

IN THIS CHAPTER

Establishing secure connections to other systems

Enabling incoming connections to your machine

Accessing remote systems graphically

Establishing Secure Connections to Other Systems

The traditional UNIX application that establishes a terminal connection (a command-line, login connection) to a remote machine over the network is known as *telnet*. The `telnet` application connects to a `telnet` daemon running on a remote system and creates a login session once the proper authentication credentials have been exchanged. Unfortunately, authentication information and all other data exchanged between a `telnet` client and a server are exchanged in the clear, meaning that it is readily visible to anyone with access to your network, a packet sniffer, and sufficient curiosity or other motivation. There are ways around this, of course: You can use `telnet` through an encrypted virtual private network (VPN) or tunnel, or install a version of `telnet` that uses Kerberos authentication, but why cling to an old application and protocol when there are newer, more secure alternatives available? (If you're still fascinated with `telnet`, search the Web for information about Linux VPNs or see Chapter 27, "Managing Users, Groups, and Authentication," for information about installing Kerberos on your system, which includes a Kerberized version of `telnet`.)

Tip

The `telnet` client is installed as a part of a default Ubuntu installation because you may need the `telnet` client to connect to older systems or systems that simply do not support more sophisticated remote connections, but a `telnet` server is not officially supported by Ubuntu. If you must, you can still explicitly install the `telnet` server—known as `telnetd`—from a "universe" repository by using your favorite package management software. ■

If you're an old-time UNIX fan, you may remember the Berkeley r-command suite, which provided commands such as `rsh` and `rcp`. These commands had the same security problems as the older `telnet` commands, namely, that they transmitted passwords and other information in the clear. Although these commands appear to be available on Ubuntu Linux systems, they are mapped to the corresponding SSH commands (`ssh` and `scp`, respectively) using the *alternatives* system that is discussed in Chapter 19, "Adding, Removing, and Updating Software."

Logging In to Remote Systems Using ssh

The newer, more modern and secure replacement for `telnet` is `ssh`, the secure shell application, which uses SSH, the Secure Shell protocol. The `ssh` application is installed as part of a default Ubuntu Linux installation, along with other applications that use the same protocol and authentication information, and shares much of the same command-line syntax, such as `sftp` (a secure File Transfer Protocol application) and `scp` (secure copy). Using `ssh`, you can establish a remote login session on any machine that is running an `ssh` daemon. An `ssh` daemon must be running on the remote system. If you try to connect to the remote system and see a message like the following, either an `ssh` daemon is not running on that system or it is running on some port other than the default port 22:

```
$ ssh ulaptop
ssh: connect to host ulaptop port 22: Connection refused
```

The remainder of this section discusses how to use `ssh` to connect to remote systems that are actually running an `ssh` daemon. For information on how to enable the `ssh` daemon on Ubuntu systems, see the next section.

Using `ssh` to connect to a remote system as the current user is as simple as typing the `ssh` `hostname` command, where `hostname` is the name or IP address of the host to which you want to connect. The first time that you attempt to connect to a remote system that you have never connected to before, you will see a message like the following:

```
$ ssh ulaptop
The authenticity of host 'ulaptop (192.168.6.90)' can't be established.
RSA key fingerprint is 07:e6:3a:50:4b:6d:e6:d8:f1:80:c6:b2:da:02:a3:da.
Are you sure you want to continue connecting (yes/no)?
```

To continue connecting to this system, type **yes** and press Return. The ssh utility adds the RSA key for the remote system to its list of known hosts (to prevent another machine from impersonating the remote machine in the future) and prompts you for your password, as in the following example:

```
Warning: Permanently added 'ulaptop' (RSA) to the list of known hosts.
wvh@ulaptop's password:
```

Note

If you're curious, *RSA* stands for Rivest, Shamir, and Adleman, the developers of the type of public key encryption technology that is used by default by the OpenSSH implementation of the SSH protocol. For more information about public key infrastructure (PKI) and related encryption technologies, see a web site such as Wikipedia's PKI information at http://en.wikipedia.org/wiki/Public_key_infrastructure. ∎

At the Password prompt, enter your password on the remote system and press Return. Assuming that you typed the correct password, you'll see a successful login message from the remote system, and that system's prompt will display, as in the following example:

```
Linux ubuntu32 2.6.24-19-386 #1 SMP Fri Jul 11 16:43:33 UTC 2008

The programs included with the Ubuntu system are free software;
the exact distribution terms for each program are described in the
individual files in /usr/share/doc/*/copyright.

Ubuntu comes with ABSOLUTELY NO WARRANTY, to the extent permitted
    by applicable law.
Last login: Wed May 1 20:15:16 2008
wvh@ubuntu32:~$
```

Once you've established an ssh connection to a remote machine, you can do anything from this login prompt that you could do from a physical connection to that machine, including starting graphical applications that display on your local system if you set the DISPLAY environment variable correctly, as discussed in the section of Chapter 5, "Using the GNOME Desktop," entitled, "What's a Desktop? Graphical Environments for Linux." When you're done working on the remote system, you can log out by pressing Ctrl+D or by typing the exit command.

All of this is well and good assuming that you have the same login name on all of the systems that you want to connect to, or that you always want to connect as yourself. Luckily, the ssh command provides an easy way to connect to another system as another user by using a command such as ssh user@host, where user is the name of the user that you want to log in as, and host is the name of the host to which you want to connect as that user. For example, the command ssh joeuser@ulaptop would use ssh to connect to the remote host ulaptop as the user `joeuser`. Assuming that you know this user's password, you can log in there as the specified user and perform any actions that the user is authorized to perform.

The `ssh` command has many other options, few of which you'll probably ever need to use. For complete information on the `ssh` command, see the online reference information for the command that is available through the `man ssh` command.

Enabling Incoming SSH Connections to Your System

As mentioned previously in this chapter, an `ssh` daemon must be running on your system if you want to be able to connect to it remotely using any command that requires the SSH protocol. The standard version of the SSH server that is available for Ubuntu systems is the OpenSSH server (`www.openssh.org`), an open source SSH server that is actively maintained by the people who also support the OpenBSD project (`www.openbsd.org`), an open source UNIX-like operating system (inspired by the original Berkeley UNIX distributions) that is well known for its focus on system security. The OpenSSH server is not installed by default as part of a standard Ubuntu installation but (like everything else in Ubuntu) is easy enough to add using any of the package management tools described in Chapter 19.

To install the OpenSSH server, use your favorite software installation package to install the `openssh-server` package. I prefer using the graphical Synaptic Package Manager on Ubuntu systems, but feel free to use the command-line package management tools if you prefer.

As part of installing the OpenSSH server, Ubuntu adds a script to the system startup process that can automatically start the server when you boot your system. Older versions of Ubuntu provided a graphical System Administration Services that made it easy to see the services that were installed on your system and the system run levels at which they are started. To see this on a Ubuntu 10.04 system, you must install a package such as the Boot-Up Manager application (by installing the bum package) or my favorite, sysv-rc-conf (from a package with the same name) using your favorite package management software. The sysv-rc-conf application provides a very simple interface for activating or deactivating services at system startup and various run levels. Figure 25-1 shows sysv-rc-conf running in a GNOME Terminal window, after activating SSH to start at run levels 2 and above.

Should you ever want to stop enabling remote logins to your system via SSH, you can simply run sysv-rc-sonf again, scroll down to the SSH entry shown in Figure 25-1, and deselect the checkboxes for run levels such as 2, the main run level for Ubuntu desktop systems.

Tip

The `dropbear` **package is an attractive alternative to the OpenSSH server, supporting most of the features of the OpenSSH server but using substantially fewer system resources. I typically use** `dropbear` **on laptops, netbooks (small-format, network-oriented portable computers), mobile Internet devices (tablet-like portable computers designed for Internet access), and any other limited-resource systems where I want to support secure, incoming SSH connections.** `dropbear` **is started and stopped by the** `/etc/init.d/dropbear` **startup script and is not integrated with the Services window shown in Figure 25-1. ∎**

FIGURE 25-1

Verifying the state of the SSH server in the sysv-rc-conf application

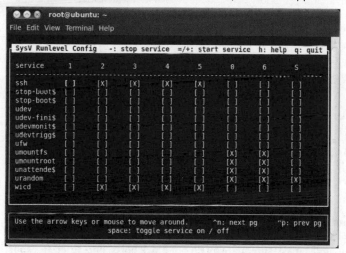

Connecting to Other Systems Using VNC

If you have multiple computer systems on a single network, getting up and going to the console of a specific machine to run a program there quickly becomes old. You'd think there would be a way that a graphical computer system could connect to another graphical computer system over the network and display what you would see on that machine's screen inside a window on the first machine. Actually, there is, and it's included in the standard Ubuntu distribution by default.

Virtual Network Computing (VNC) makes it easy for you to work on multiple graphical computer systems by enabling you to export their graphical displays across a network to another machine. VNC is a cross-platform technology originally developed by Olivetti Research Labs in Cambridge, England, which was later acquired by AT&T. A VNC server runs on one computer system and exports a system desktop that can be accessed by a VNC client running on another system. VNC servers are typically password-protected, which makes VNC an optimal environment for accessing and running graphical administrative and monitoring applications remotely. VNC servers export their virtual displays via network ports starting at 5900 plus the number of the graphical displays that they are exporting. For example, a VNC server running on the X Window System display :1 will use port 5901.

VNC is released under the GPL, and many of the original VNC developers now work for a company called RealVNC (www.realvnc.com), which distributes and supports a commercial VNC implementation but also makes the source code for its version of the VNC server and client freely available, as required by the GPL. The latest generation of their VNC client is named vnc4viewer and is available in the Ubuntu repositories but is not installed by default. Another extremely popular VNC implementation is TightVNC (www.tightvnc.com), an optimized VNC client and server, which is also available for Ubuntu systems but is also not installed by default.

Ubuntu systems provide graphical VNC clients that are installed by default as part of a standard desktop installation. The Ubuntu client that is installed by default is vinagre, and don't worry—a menu entry is provided for this application so that you don't have to try to remember its name. Using these applications is discussed later in this chapter.

Configuring a VNC Server

Before trying to use a VNC client to connect to a remote system, you must have a VNC server to connect to. This section explains how to enable the VNC server that is installed by default on Ubuntu systems.

Tip

Regardless of the platform on which you are running a VNC server, you must make sure that the network ports that it uses are not being blocked by other network software. For example, if your system does packet filtering or your network uses a firewall, you must make sure that you do not block ports 590*x* (used to export VNC server displays), 6000 (used to communicate with Linux or Unix X Window System servers), or 580*x* (used to communicate with a VNC server over the Web). ■

Enabling and Configuring Ubuntu's Vino VNC Server

Connecting to an Ubuntu system on your local network is quite simple—the software that you need to connect to the current graphical console is already installed. This is a GNOME-specific VNC server called vino (the actual executable is called vino-server), which was created by Mark McLoughlin. Little other information about vino is available beyond an updated proposal for Vino at http://www.gnome.org/~markmc/remote-desktop-2.html and the minimal information in /usr/share/doc/vino on your Ubuntu system. However (luckily), in my experience it "just works," and therefore I guess we don't really need to know much more.

Note

Vino works differently from traditional VNC servers, in that once it is enabled, the GNOME session manager automatically starts it for you whenever you log in. It can therefore export only the display of a user that is currently logged in, unlike more standard VNC servers that typically display a system's login screen and therefore support remote access to your system by random users. I discuss the high points of more traditional VNC servers later in this section, in the sidebar "How Traditional VNC Servers Work." ■

To make sure that the vino VNC server is enabled for you, select the System ➪ Preferences ➪ Remote Desktop menu item, which displays the dialog shown in Figure 25-2. To enable remote access to your desktop, select the Sharing section's "Allow other users to view your desktop" checkbox. This enables remote users to view the desktop but not to actually do anything there—you must select the "Allow other users to control your desktop" checkbox to enable a remote VNC client to control the mouse and use keyboard shortcuts.

FIGURE 25-2

Configuring the vino VNC server on an Ubuntu system

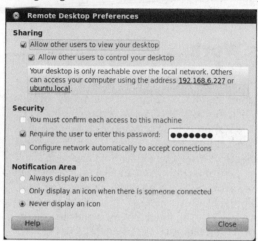

When configuring the vino server, always set a remote desktop password in the Security section of the dialog shown in Figure 25-2. To do this, select the "Require the user to enter this password" checkbox, and enter a password. You can optionally select the "You must confirm each access to this machine" checkbox, which displays the dialog shown in Figure 25-3 on your desktop when someone tries to connect to it using a VNC client.

FIGURE 25-3

A remote connection request on an Ubuntu desktop

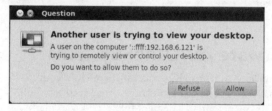

In general, I don't recommend enabling this option, first, because it largely defeats the purpose of supporting remote VNC connections in the first place; and second, because access to your VNC server should always be password-protected anyway, so only people to whom you've given the password should be able to access your desktop via VNC.

Once you've enabled remote access using the Remote Desktop Preferences dialog, the GNOME desktop starts the `vino-server` process and will start it automatically for you whenever you start a GNOME login session on this Ubuntu system.

How Traditional VNC Servers Work

Typically, VNC servers are started by a system daemon such as `inetd` or `xinetd`, or by a shell or Perl script called `vncserver`, and export their own displays rather than the desktop of the currently logged-in user. These mechanisms provide some additional flexibility in your VNC server environment. VNC servers that are started by the `inted` or `xinetd` daemons in response to incoming connection requests can start multiple servers that provide different desktop sizes and resolutions, which is very convenient if your system has a 21-inch monitor and you want to connect to it from a laptop without having to scroll all over the place. If you start a VNC server using the `vncserver` script, you can also take advantage of user-specific startup scripts that identify the window manager and any X applications that your VNC server should start. The VNC server's startup script is usually the file `~/.vnc/xstartup`. If this directory and the startup file do not exist the first time that you start a VNC server, the directory is created and the startup script is cloned from the default X Window System startup file `/etc/X11/xinit/xinitrc`.

Exporting a graphical console that is independent of any physical one and using a startup script to do so enables traditional VNC servers to follow the same somewhat convoluted chain of X Window startup files that are normally used: `~/.xinitrc`, `~/.Xclients` on some systems, `/etc/X11/xinit/xinitrc`, `/etc/X11/Xsession`, and so on. These startup files can launch various desktop environments and window managers by using environment variable settings, and also provide a last resort of starting the `twm` window manager when no other window manager can be found.

VNC servers that follow this more traditional model and are available for Ubuntu systems include the `vnc4server` and `tightvncserver` packages, which you can install using your favorite package management utility. However, if you install one of these on an Ubuntu system, you should uninstall the `vino` VNC server.

VNC Client and Server Software for Other Systems

If you still use other operating systems, you may want to use VNC to access them from your Ubuntu desktop, or access your Ubuntu desktop from the desktops of those other systems. This is no problem at all thanks to the fact that VNC is open source. The next two sections explain how to get VNC client and server software for popular platforms such as Mac OS X and Microsoft Windows.

VNC Servers and Clients for Mac OS X

A variety of VNC servers and clients are available for Mac OS X. Mac OS X has included a built-in VNC server since Mac OS X 10.4 (Tiger), but older Mac OS X releases required that you install one yourself. My favorite VNC server for pre-Tiger Mac OS X systems is the OSXvnc server, which is available at `http://sourceforge.net/projects/osxvnc`. You can download this as a Mac disk image (`.dmg`) file that will mount automatically and start the installer. The OSXvnc server displays its own configuration dialog when you start it—you configure the built-in VNC server using the System Preferences application's Sharing applet.

As far as VNC clients for Mac OS X go, my favorite is called "Chicken of the VNC." It's a small, fast VNC client with a funny name—and how can you beat that combination? The latest version of the Chicken of the VNC client is available from the project's SourceForge site at `http://sourceforge.net/projects/cotvnc`.

VNC Clients and Servers for Windows

TightVNC is a small, highly optimized VNC client and server. TightVNC makes efficient use of network bandwidth through some clever tricks using JPEG compression for the display and differentiating between local cursor movement and cursor movement that needs to be communicated back to the VNC server. TightVNC also provides security features that RealVNC does not, including automatic SSH tunneling for security purposes. Although RealVNC clients and servers are available for Windows, I really like TightVNC and therefore recommend using it. Both stable and bleeding edge (i.e., versions that are actively under development) versions of TightVNC are downloadable from `www.tightvnc.com/download.html` or from their SourceForge site at `http://sourceforge.net/projects/vnc-tight`.

The downloadable EXE file from either of these sites provides both the VNC client and server. After downloading and installing the executables, you can start the VNC server from the standard menus. The VNC server's administrative dialog supports standard configuration options such as setting a password that you will need to use to connect to the VNC server, automatically starting the VNC server when you log in, and displaying an icon for the VNC server in the system tray when the VNC server is running. The icon is extremely convenient because it lets you know when a server is running and also because you can get instant access to the configuration dialog by clicking on the icon.

Using Ubuntu's Remote Desktop Viewer

Once a VNC server is running on one of your systems, you can connect to it from any Ubuntu system by selecting the Applications ⇨ Internet ⇨ Remote Desktop Viewer menu command to start Ubuntu's graphical VNC client. If you want, you can also start this application from any terminal window by executing the `vinagre` command. This displays a window like the one shown in Figure 25-4.

FIGURE 25-4

Ubuntu's Remote Desktop Viewer application, vinagre

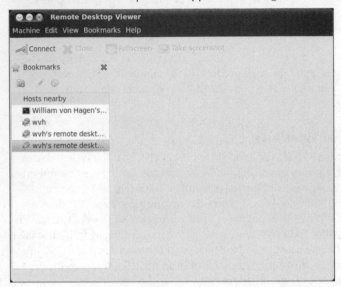

Once this window displays, click the Connect icon to display a dialog like the one shown in Figure 25-5. Enter the name or IP address of the system that you want to connect to and (optionally) specify the number of the port on which its VNC server is running.

FIGURE 25-5

Identifying the system to connect to in vinagre

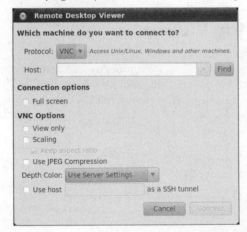

After entering this information, click the Connect button to connect to the VNC server on the specified system. If the remote system requires a password, a dialog displays in which you can enter that password. Once you have successfully connected to the remote system, a VNC connection to the specified system opens in a new tab in the window shown in Figure 25-4, as shown in Figure 25-6.

Viewing another Ubuntu system in the Remote Desktop Viewer

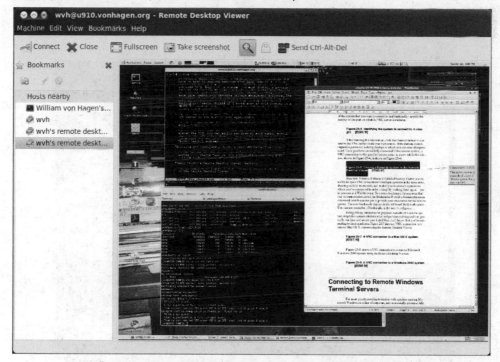

Two nice features of Ubuntu's Remote Desktop Viewer are its ability to open VNC connections to multiple systems at the same time, showing each in its own tab, and its ability to bookmark systems to which you've connected in order to simplify visiting them again—just as you can in a Web browser. To create a bookmark for a system that you've connected to, select the Bookmarks ⇨ Add to bookmarks menu command, which enables you to provide your own name for the remote system. The new bookmark displays in the left-hand Bookmarks pane. You can see examples of bookmarks in the next two figures.

Being able to connect to the graphical console of a remote system simplifies system administration and problem solving and can generally confuse and amaze your kids if they don't know that you're connecting to their machines. Figure 25-7 shows a VNC connection to a remote Mac OS X system using the Remote Desktop Viewer.

FIGURE 25-7

A VNC connection to a Mac OS X system

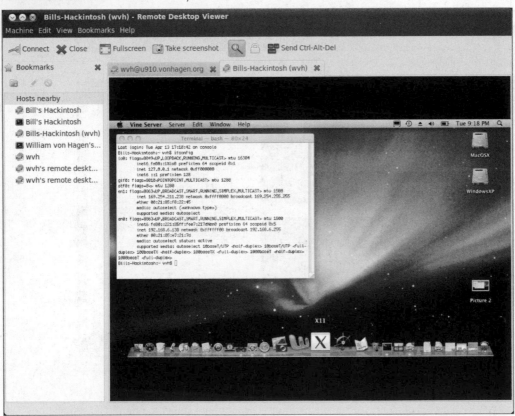

Figure 25-8 shows a VNC connection to a remote Microsoft Windows 2000 system using the Remote Desktop Viewer.

FIGURE 25-8

A VNC connection to a Windows XP system

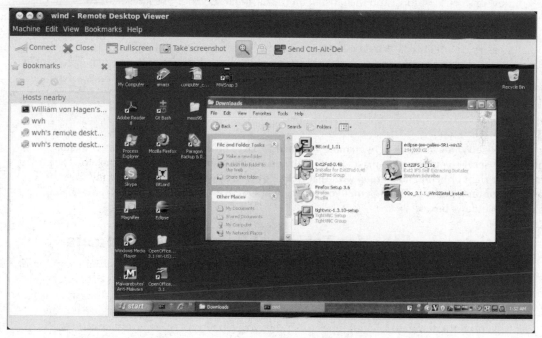

Connecting to Remote Windows Terminal Servers

For most people, needing to interact with systems running Microsoft Windows is a fact of corporate, and occasionally personal, life. In the home networking environment, most Windows connectivity can be handled quite nicely using the VNC server and client discussed earlier in this chapter, but if you need to connect to a remote Windows system at work or your home computing budget is a bit higher than mine, you may need to access Windows systems that are running a Windows Terminal Server.

If you need to give users occasional, personal access to a Windows system but want to minimize costs and administrative hassles rather than install one machine per user, a good solution is to install Windows Terminal Services on a reasonably robust Windows system, and purchase a small pool of Client Access Licenses that are distributed by the server, as needed. Remote clients can then attach to the Terminal Services server and run virtual Windows sessions in a window on their desktops. You then install on the terminal server or in shares defined in your user profiles the software that people need to use, and any remote user connected to the server can access it to run the necessary software. Fortunately, remote access to Windows Terminal Services doesn't even require a Windows system anymore. Ubuntu users can easily access Windows Terminal Servers using rdesktop or the Terminal Server Client (tsclient), two open source software packages that speak the Remote Desktop Protocol (RDP) used by Windows Terminal Services.

Tip

If you centralize Windows services by running Terminal Services on a Microsoft Windows Domain Controller or server, you'll need to make sure that the users who want to connect to it have the "Log in Locally" user right or belong to a group with that right. Otherwise, users will receive the message: "The local policy of this system does not permit you to log on interactively," and you may still have to give everyone a Windows box. ∎

Using rdesktop for Terminal Server Connections

The rdesktop package (www.rdesktop.org) is a remote desktop package for Linux and most other UNIX and UNIX-like systems that run the X Window System. The rdesktop package is installed by default on Ubuntu Linux systems and provides an excellent, high-power client with a few really cool features as described in this section. The rdesktop package is available from the standard Ubuntu repositories, but you can always get the latest version of its source code and installable packages for other types of systems from its SourceForge site at http://sourceforge.net/projects/rdesktop.

You must start rdesktop from a GNOME or xterm terminal, although you can certainly add it to your menus as explained in Chapter 5. The simplest rdesktop command line that you can use to connect to a remote system running Windows Terminal Services is rdesktop host, where host is the name or IP address of the system running Windows Terminal Services. A window displays on your desktop, showing the standard Windows login screen for the version of Windows that is hosting Windows Terminal Services as shown in Figure 25-9.

After you specify the domain that you want to log in to (if necessary) and log in, your rdesktop window displays the standard Windows desktop for the version of Windows that you are connecting to as shown in Figure 25-10.

FIGURE 25-9

A Windows Terminal Services login prompt in rdesktop

The rdesktop application provides you with several options that can simplify access to Windows Terminal Services. Some of my favorites are the following:

- -d: The domain that you want to authenticate to
- -f: Full-screen mode. This displays rdesktop in a decoration-free window that takes over your desktop. You can toggle decorations (and therefore window controls) by pressing Ctrl+Alt+Enter.
- -p: Your password in the remote domain
- -u: The name of the user that you want to log in as

FIGURE 25-10

A Windows 2008 Server desktop in rdesktop

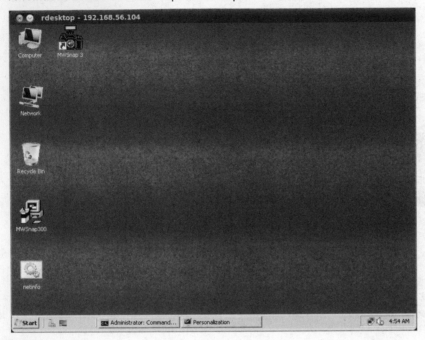

If the system running Windows Terminal Services is running Windows XP or a newer version of Windows, one especially handy option not listed in the previous section is the `-r` option, which lets you directly map resources on your Linux system to your Windows Terminal Services connection. This is especially useful when you want to map a local print queue to a virtual printer in your Windows Terminal session, or when you want to access a local drive in your terminal session. The syntax for these is `-r printer:local-queue-name` and `-r disk:share-name=/device/path`, respectively. For example, to attach PRN1 to a local print queue named *SuperScript-660i*, you would add `-r printer:SuperScript-660i` to your command-line options when executing the `rdesktop` command.

Similarly, to map your local CD-ROM drive to a share called *cdrom*, you would add `-r disk:cdrom=/dev/cdrom` to the `rdesktop` command line. If you still use floppies, you could map your local floppy drive to a share called *floppy* by adding `-r disk:floppy=/dev/fd0` to your `rdesktop` command line.

Note
The name that you specify as the share must consist of eight characters or fewer. ∎

Using Ubuntu's tsclient for Terminal Server Connections

In case you don't like rdesktop for some reason, Ubuntu also provides another Windows Terminal Server Client as part of a default Ubuntu installation. This is the tsclient (Terminal Services Client) application (http://gnomepro.com/tsclient). The tsclient application is a GNOME-centric Terminal Server Client that provides some optimization and also enables you to save information about a terminal server connection in a file that you can quickly and easily reload instead of manually specifying all of your settings each time that you want to connect. Although the latest version of tsclient for Ubuntu is always available from the Ubuntu repositories, you can get the latest source code and packages for other GNOME-based systems at the tsclient SourceForge project site at http://sourceforge.net/projects/ts-client.

To start the tsclient application, select Applications ⇨ Internet ⇨ Terminal Server Client, which displays the dialog shown in Figure 25-11.

FIGURE 25-11

The tsclient startup screen

If you enter only the name or IP address of the terminal server that you want to connect to and click Connect (or press Enter on your keyboard), the standard Windows Terminal Server login screen for the version of Windows that you are connecting to displays in a new `tsclient` window, and you can log in normally. Once you log in, a standard Windows desktop displays, as shown in Figure 25-12.

FIGURE 25-12

A Microsoft Windows terminal server session shown in tsclient

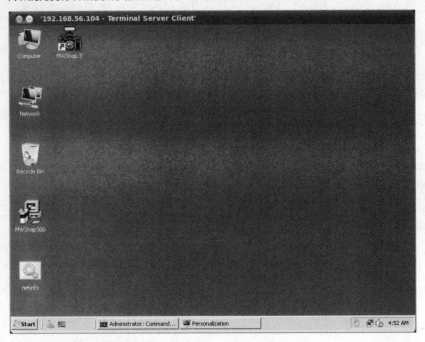

You can also customize your connection to a Windows Terminal Server by setting options that are available on tabs in the `tsclient` dialog. For example, the Local Resources tab enables you to make resources on your Ubuntu system available to your Windows Terminal Server session. Similarly, the Display tab lets you specify the size of the window used to connect to the terminal server, which can be very handy when connecting to a terminal server from a system with a smaller screen, such as a laptop.

To simplify future connections to terminal servers that you may contact frequently, you can fill out all of the particulars for a connection in the dialog shown in Figure 25-11, click "Save As," and enter the name that you want to associate with this connection. The `tsclient` application will save all of this information (except for your password) in a file by that name with the .rdp extension and store it in the directory ~/.tsclient in your home directory. In the future, you can select one of these files after starting tsclient, enter your password, and quickly establish a connection to the indicated terminal server.

Using Other Remote Connection Software

Although it is not supplied as part of a default Ubuntu Linux installation, another popular software package for graphically connecting to remote systems is the free version of NoMachine NX, known as FreeNX. This package (named freenx) is not provided in the Ubuntu repositories and is not installed by default on a standard Ubuntu system, primarily because its Linux clients are KDE-based, and therefore install many KDE libraries. However, versions of FreeNX are available from some of the additional, user-supported repositories listed in Chapter 19. See that chapter for additional information.

FreeNX is a free, GPL implementation of NoMachine's NX (NoMachine NX) Server (www .nomachine.com). NoMachine has developed a compression technology that substantially reduces the size of X Window System communications and adds other performance improvements through caching and general protocol optimization. The NX client applications for Linux are included in the freenx package—the clients for Microsoft Windows, Mac OS X, and Solaris are available as free downloads from the NoMachine site. The free and commercial versions of the NX server differ primarily in terms of capabilities (and, of course, cost). FreeNX provides all of the core capabilities of the commercial NX server for remote connections, but does not currently include the SMB and printing (Common Unix Printing System) support provided by the commercial NX server.

If you're already a VNC fan, NX is definitely worth a look for its superb compression technologies and associated performance improvements, and also because it inherently uses SSH for secure communications between client and server. FreeNX is effectively equivalent to VNC and also supports Linux Terminal Server (www.ltsp.org), Windows Terminal Server, Citrix Metaframe, and standard X Window System XDMCP (X Display Manager Control Protocol) connections. However, it is not part of any official Ubuntu repository from Canonical, so you won't be able to get support from them if you encounter any problems. (You may still get free sympathy, however.)

Summary

Networking is a given in today's academic, business, and even home computing environments. The need to access more and different systems goes hand-in-hand with that. This chapter discussed secure command-line mechanisms for connecting to remote Linux and UNIX systems and explained how to install the SSH server on your system so that people can securely connect to your Ubuntu system. I then explored the excellent VNC (Virtual Network Computing) clients and servers that enable you to remotely connect to the consoles of graphical systems such as Microsoft Windows, Mac OS X, Linux, and UNIX systems. The chapter concluded by discussing mechanisms for connecting to a Microsoft Windows Terminal Server from your Ubuntu system, and then introduced the popular NX and FreeNX software that enables you to securely connect to just about any remote graphical console service.

The next chapter discusses the related topic of connecting to remote file servers to access files that are stored on them, and explains how to share files from your Ubuntu system so that other systems on your network can quickly and easily access them. Music server, anyone?

File Transfer and Sharing

IN THIS CHAPTER

Transferring files between systems

Sharing files with Windows systems

Sharing files with Linux and UNIX systems

Sharing files Peer-to-Peer

Using BitTorrent

Sooner or later, you're going to want to copy a file to or from another computer system. In the old days before networking and e-mail (which you may not even remember), this usually involved writing a copy of the file to removable media of some sort, such as a floppy disk, carrying that floppy from one system to the other, and then copying the file from the floppy disk to the other system. This was known as *sneaker net* — you just can't beat that nerd humor!

Today, thanks to the fact that networking is almost ubiquitous and that most businesses and many homes have their own networks, electronic file transfer is an important capability. As you'd expect, there are many ways to transfer or copy files between systems, ranging from Point-to-Point (PPP) file transfers to the Peer-to-Peer (P2P) file transfers much beloved of the music and film industries. In Point-to-Point file transfers, you explicitly copy a file from one system to another, and you therefore know the addresses or identities of both hosts. In Peer-to-Peer file transfer, groups of systems share files with each other without necessarily knowing or caring about the specific systems from which they are getting the files or to which they are sending them. In Peer-to-Peer file transfers, somebody obviously has to know what hosts are sharing what files, but this is usually built into the software — more about that later in this chapter.

The first section of this chapter discusses popular Point-to-Point file transfer solutions that are built into your Ubuntu Linux system. The second section of this chapter, "Peer-to-Peer File Sharing on Ubuntu," discusses various P2P solutions that are easily installed and used on your system.

Note

You may have noticed by now that I am not a lawyer and that I have significant disdain for industry groups that try to suppress technologies just because they can be used to do something that may be illegal. Heck, I could conceivably club someone to death with my laptop, but does that mean that we should outlaw laptops? There is absolutely nothing inherently illegal about Peer-to-Peer file sharing. P2P is a great way to efficiently share and transfer large files among multiple systems, with everyone sharing part of the load. What you do with it is your business. Explaining how you can use it is mine. ■

Transferring Files to Other Systems

As noted in the introduction to this chapter, this section discusses how to copy files between systems in cases in which you know the identities of the machines involved in the transfer. Common examples of this sort of file transfer are, "I need to copy this file from my laptop to the machine on my desk," "I want to put this file on our home media server, so we can play it from any machine in the house," or "I need to put this spreadsheet on the corporate file server so that my boss can see that I'm actually working from home." In each of these cases, you have authorized access to the machines at both ends of the transfer and you know their names, whether by fully qualified hostname (`www.vonhagen.org`), IP address (`74.86.122.100`), or their local hostname on your network (`laptop`, `server1`, etc.). You'll also know the name of the directory in which the file that you're looking for is located, and the name of the Windows share in which that file is located for SMB/CIFS file transfers.

In addition to having authorized access to the system that you're transferring files to, the appropriate service already must be running on the remote system, holding up a sort of electronic catcher's mitt that can receive the files that you're transferring there. This chapter focuses on the client side of file transfers—transferring files to something that's ready to receive them, and doing anything you need to do to enable your local machine to reach them. This chapter doesn't discuss how to set up shared directories on Microsoft Windows or Linux systems. For information on sharing Linux directories so that you can reach them directly from a PC running Microsoft Windows, Mac OS X, or Linux, see Chapter 35, "Setting Up a Samba Server." For information on sharing Linux directories via NFS so that you can reach them directly from a PC running Mac OS X or Linux, see Chapter 34, "Setting Up an NFS Server." (You can also contact NFS Servers from Microsoft Windows but only by installing special software that doesn't come with Windows by default.) Information about setting up an FTP server is provided as a sidebar later in this chapter, because I received a few requests for information on that topic from readers of the first edition of this book.

Tip

Another common file transfer scenario is, "My brother would really like a copy of this file." In that case, I'd suggest just attaching the file to an e-mail message and sending it to him, as long as the file in question is under the size of any quota that is imposed by the recipient's e-mail server and the e-mail server doesn't block files with specific extensions (you can always change the file extension). You don't know the name of his machine or its IP address, and you probably don't have direct access to the machine anyway. ■

Creating Permanent Desktop
Icons for Services and Locations

The traditional way to connect to remote services in the graphical GNOME desktop environment used by Ubuntu Linux is to use the Nautilus File Manager. Using Nautilus to connect to FTP, SSH (Secure FTP), SMB/CIFS, and other servers creates a temporary icon for those servers that is automatically removed when you log out. You can also bookmark these servers, which is permanent but only visible from the Places menu or within Nautilus.

The easiest way to create a quick connection to a remote system from your Ubuntu system is to create a desktop shortcut to the remote location. You can create a Launcher for a remote location by right-clicking on the desktop, selecting Launcher from the context-sensitive menu, and selecting Location as the Type of that launcher. The dialog will now look like the one shown in Figure 26-1.

FIGURE 26-1

Creating a desktop launcher for a location in GNOME

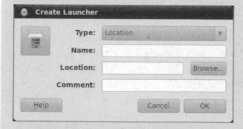

Enter some memorable text as the name of the location and identify the remote server by entering a URL of the form PROTOCOL://USER@HOST/SHARE/DIRECTORY. Replace PROTOCOL with ftp, smb, or ssh; replace USER with the name of the user that you want to connect as (you can leave out the USER@ portion of the URL if you are connecting to an anonymous FTP server); and specify the hostname or IP address of the system that you want to connect to. When connecting to a shared Windows directory, you must also specify the name of the SHARE that you want to connect to. Finally, you can specify a DIRECTORY path on the host or SHARE that you want to connect to, relative to the SHARE, login directory, or anonymous FTP directory.

Click Save to save the new launcher. Double-clicking on the desktop icon for that launcher will display an authentication dialog for the remote service if authentication is required. Entering the correct password will then display the remote location in Nautilus. (SSH connections are displayed as Secure FTP connections.)

If you're a fan of desktop icons for remote services, rather than selecting a menu item on Ubuntu systems, creating a desktop launcher/link is "the right thing to do" because these items persist after you log out and log back in again.

Using FTP

FTP in uppercase letters stands for "File Transfer Protocol," and is the oldest existing way of transferring files over a network, using the standard TCP/IP protocol that is the basis of the Internet. In lowercase letters, *ftp* is the name of a command-line program that you can run to connect to a remote FTP server so that you can transfer a file in either direction. As I'll explain in this section, Ubuntu makes it easy to transfer files using FTP in a variety of ways: The GNOME desktop provides built-in support for FTP connections, Ubuntu comes with the command-line ftp client, and the Ubuntu repositories provide stand-alone, graphical FTP applications if neither of the previous solutions meets your needs.

Tip

If you need to access files from an FTP server and aren't interested in using a GNOME-specific or command-line FTP client approach, you can simply connect to the FTP server using your favorite Web browser. For example, if the files that you're looking for are on an FTP server on a host named xen.vonhagen.org, you can try connecting to that host from your browser by specifying a URL of the form ftp://*USERNAME*@xen.vonhagen.org, where *USERNAME* is the account that you want to use to connect to the FTP server. If the FTP server supports anonymous connections, you can connect anonymously using a URL of the form ftp://xen.vonhagen.org. ∎

FTP is an old protocol, and the commands that you need to know are simple, even from the command line. You may never need to use ftp from the command line at all, because many equivalent command-line tools exist, such as wget and curl, which use newer protocols such as HTTP to retrieve files by directly specifying their URLs. In general, I prefer to err on the side of caution in this book — if you don't need certain information, that's fine and you can skip over it. However, if you did need to use FTP and information about it wasn't present in the book, both of us would be unhappy.

Note

FTP is as old as TCP/IP networking. If you're wondering why I'm even bothering to talk about FTP, the reason is that it may be the only mechanism that you can use to transfer relatively large files. Many mail servers enforce a size limit of 10 MB on attachments, which is a trivial size for archive files, video files, and so on. If you can't access a shared directory that contains the files that you need to download or upload and they aren't available for P2P download as a torrent, FTP is the tried-and-true solution that you'll probably need to use. ∎

Connecting to an FTP Server from the GNOME Desktop

Ubuntu's Places menu provides the Connect to Server command, which makes it easy to create an icon on your desktop for an FTP server, and then to connect to that share using the Nautilus File Manager. Selecting Places ⇨ Connect to Server displays the dialog shown in Figure 26-2.

FIGURE 26-2

Defining a connection to a Public FTP server

The default selection, Public FTP, is not the one that you want to use if the FTP server that you want to connect to requires authentication (a specific username and password), which is usually the case. (I'll explain how to do that later in this section.) As you might suspect, *Public FTP servers* are servers that do not require authentication and are traditionally known as *anonymous FTP servers*. However, if you are actually connecting to an anonymous FTP server, you must at least enter the name or IP address of the FTP server that you want to connect to. You need to specify a specific port only if the remote FTP server is running on a nonstandard TCP/IP port, and you need to specify the name of a remote directory only if you want to automatically connect to some directory other than the default one that the FTP server associates with the anonymous user. If you are, indeed, trying to connect to an anonymous FTP server, click Connect to create a desktop icon for that FTP server and to attempt to connect to it.

Tip

If you expect to connect to the same anonymous (or authenticated) FTP server multiple times, you can click the "Add bookmark" checkbox and enter the name of a bookmark that will be added to the Network section of your GNOME desktop's Places menu after you successfully connect to the FTP server for the first time. ∎

To specify that you want to connect to an FTP server that requires authentication, click the Service type menu at the top of this dialog and select the FTP (with login) entry to display the dialog shown in Figure 26-3.

As with an anonymous FTP server, you must at least enter the name or IP address of the FTP server that you want to connect to. You can also identify the name of the user that you want to connect as, but this is optional — if you don't specify one, you'll be prompted for that information when you actually connect. As with the Public FTP server, you need to specify a specific port only if the remote FTP server is running on a nonstandard TCP/IP port, and you need to specify the name of a remote directory only if you want to automatically connect to some directory other than the default one that the FTP server associates with any user that you've specified. Click Connect to create a desktop icon for that FTP server and to attempt to connect to it.

FIGURE 26-3

Defining a connection to an FTP server that requires authentication

When connecting to an authenticating FTP server, you will see a dialog that prompts you for any required information that you have not specified yet, as shown in Figure 26-4. This figure shows the dialog in which you only specified the name of the FTP server that you want to connect to, and did not specify a user name.

FIGURE 26-4

Completing the login information for an FTP server

If you are connecting to an FTP server that requires authentication and didn't specify the name of a user to connect as, the dialog shown in Figure 26-4 still gives you the opportunity to connect anonymously. However, to actually log in, select the "Connect as user" radio button and enter the login name and password of the user that you want to connect as.

Once you enter the correct username and log in (or successfully connect to an anonymous FTP server), a Nautilus File Manager window appears, which displays the contents of the default directory associated with the user that you are logged in as, as shown in Figure 26-5.

Once the Nautilus File Manager appears, you can copy files in either direction using the standard Nautilus and GNOME desktop conventions, as discussed in Chapter 5, "Using the GNOME Desktop."

FIGURE 26-5

A connection to an FTP server in the Nautilus File Manager

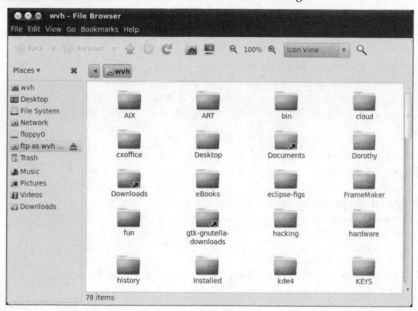

Once you are done accessing the FTP server, close the Nautilus File Manager window. Right-click on the icon for the FTP server and select "Unmount Volume" from the pop-up menu to sever the connection and discard the icon. The icons for FTP servers are transient and are also removed automatically when you log out. (See the sidebar earlier in this chapter — "Creating Permanent Desktop Icons for Services and Locations" — for information on how to create a permanent desktop icon if you want one.) To preserve a shortcut to an FTP server in GNOME, create a bookmark for it when you initiate the connection. This bookmark will be displayed in the Network section of the Places menu.

Tip

To remove a bookmark for an FTP server that you no longer plan to connect to, select the Places ➪ Network menu item from the GNOME desktop. This displays your network bookmarks in Nautilus. You can then select the Bookmarks ➪ Edit Bookmarks menu command; select any bookmark and click Remove to delete it. You can also do this from within any existing Nautilus window. ■

Connecting to an FTP Server from the Command Line

You can also connect to a remote FTP server by typing the `ftp` command and the name or IP address of the server from any Ubuntu command line, such as the GNOME Terminal or xterm. The following example connects to an FTP server running on a system whose IP address is 192.168.6.64:

```
$ ftp 192.168.6.64
Connected to 192.168.6.64.
```

```
220-Welcome to Pure-FTPd.
220-You are user number 2 of 10 allowed.
220-This is a private system - No anonymous login
220-IPv6 connections are also welcome on this server.
220 You will be disconnected after 15 minutes of inactivity.
Name (192.168.6.64:wvh):
```

When you connect to an FTP server from the command line, you see some information about the FTP server and the system that it is running on, and the remote system eventually prompts you for the login that you want to use to connect to it. (How much information an FTP server displays about itself depends on the specific FTP server software that it is running and how the FTP server was configured.)

As you'll see from the last line of the previous example, an FTP server's login prompt usually tries to provide some defaults. In this case, I was logged in as the user wvh on the system from which I initiated the FTP connection. If that is the login name that you want to use to connect to the remote FTP server, you can simply press Return to accept the default. If you want to connect as another user, type that user's login name and press Return, as in the following example in which I specify the username vonhagen:

```
Name (192.168.6.64:wvh): vonhagen
331 User vonhagen OK. Password required
Password:
```

Tip

You can usually log in on an anonymous FTP server from the command line by entering the login name anonymous and supplying your e-mail address as the password. ■

After entering your login name, the remote FTP server prompts you for the password for the specified user on the FTP server. Enter that password and press Return. If you've entered a valid username and password, you'll see a confirmation message, some optional information about the remote FTP server, and the ftp> prompt from the remote machine, telling you that it's ready to do something, as in the following example:

```
230 Login successful
Remote system type is UNIX.
Using binary mode to transfer files.
ftp>
```

All FTP servers support numerous commands, which you can see at any time by typing a question mark and pressing Return, as in the following example:

```
ftp> ?
Commands may be abbreviated.  Commands are:
!         debug       mdir      qc          send
$         dir         mget      sendport    site
account   disconnect  mkdir     put         size
append    exit        mls       pwd         status
ascii     form        mode      quit        struct
bell      get         modtime   quote       system
```

```
binary      glob       mput       recv        sunique
bye         hash       newer      reget       tenex
case        help       nmap       rstatus     tick
cd          idle       nlist      rhelp       trace
cdup        image      ntrans     rename      type
chmod       lcd        open       reset       user
close       ls         prompt     restart     umask
cr          macdef     passive    rmdir       verbose
delete      mdelete    proxy      runique     ?
ftp>
```

Because the chances are good that you'll never use most of these (and you can get a complete explanation of them from the online man page for the ftp command by using the man ftp command from any command line), I'll just discuss the most basic set of commands required to find and retrieve a file on a remote machine.

All FTP servers export a directory hierarchy, just like any directory on a Linux system. Therefore, you can use familiar commands like pwd to find out the name of the current directory, cd to change to a specified directory, and so on. If you've logged in to an FTP server as a specific user, chances are good that you'll initially find yourself in the system's standard file transfer directory (called /pub) or in that user's home directory.

Once you've navigated to the directory to which you want to transfer a file or from which you want to retrieve one, you issue either the put command (to send a file to the FTP server) or the get command (to retrieve a file from the FTP server). Before actually transferring a file, you should make sure that the file transfer will take place in the appropriate mode. Most FTP servers automatically set the transfer mode so that you can retrieve binary files, such as graphics, archive files (file formats such as .zip, .tgz, .bz2, .tar, .pax, etc.), music files, and so on. Just in case, I like to always make sure that the file transfer will take place in binary mode by issuing the bin command, as in the following example:

```
ftp> bin
200 TYPE is now 8-bit binary
ftp>
```

If you do not transfer files in binary mode, they will be transferred as ASCII files, which will corrupt any binary file that you transfer and prevent you from opening it correctly. If you transfer a file and then can't view, play, or de-archive it, you may have overlooked this step.

By default, when you send or retrieve a file, the FTP command doesn't display any status information until the transfer completes. Personally, I like a bit of feedback just to know that something is actually happening and therefore always use the FTP server's hash command, which causes the server to display a hash mark (#) for each kilobyte of data that it transfers. Typing the hash command once activates this feature; typing it a second time deactivates the feature. The following example shows hashing being activated before an FTP file transfer:

```
ftp> hash
Hash mark printing on (1024 bytes/hash mark).
ftp>
```

Now you're finally ready to actually send or retrieve a file. Sending a file to the remote machine is as easy as typing the put command followed by the name of the file that you want to transfer to the FTP server, as in the following example:

```
ftp> put JDSC-0.5.9a.zip
local: JDSC-0.5.9a.zip remote: JDSC-0.5.9a.zip
200 PORT command successful
150 Connecting to port 39972
###############################################################################
###############################################################################
###############################################################################
###############################################################################
###############################################################################
###############################################################################
###############################################################################
###################
226-File successfully transferred
226 0.202 seconds (measured here), 2.36 Mbytes per second
499668 bytes sent in 0.19 secs (2526.9 kB/s)
ftp>
```

Retrieving a file from the FTP server is equally easy: Type the get command followed by the name of the file that you want to retrieve from the FTP server, as in the following example:

```
ftp> get JDSC-0.5.9a.zip
local: JDSC-0.5.9a.zip remote: JDSC-0.5.9a.zip
200 PORT command successful
150-Connecting to port 35431
150 488.0 kbytes to download
###############################################################################
###############################################################################
###############################################################################
###############################################################################
###############################################################################
###############################################################################
###############################################################################
###################
226-File successfully transferred
226 0.105 seconds (measured here), 4.53 Mbytes per second
499668 bytes received in 0.12 secs (4217.0 kB/s)
ftp>
```

Tip

When sending or retrieving a file, you can give it a different name on the FTP server or your local machine (respectively), by specifying the new filename after the name of the one that you want to send or retrieve. ∎

Once the file transfer is complete, you can terminate your connection to the FTP server and exit from the ftp command by typing the quit command, as in the following example:

```
ftp> quit
```

It doesn't get much simpler than that! The nice thing about learning to use the standard command-line ftp utility is that it is available on most systems (even from the Microsoft Windows command line), and the commands are essentially the same everywhere. Learn once, use many, I always say.

Connecting to an FTP Server Using Graphical Clients

If you need to use FTP but would prefer a stand-alone graphical FTP client application, two popular ones are available from the Ubuntu repositories:

- **gtk-gftp:** If you are using a standard GNOME-based Ubuntu system, you'll probably want to install gftp-gtk, a GNOME FTP client that uses the GTK graphical interface. Installing this package will create an entry on the Applications ⇨ Internet menu called *gFTP*. This command makes it easy to graphically transfer files using FTP and also enables you to bookmark FTP settings (hostname, username, password, etc.) just as you would do in your favorite Web browser. Figure 26-6 shows the gftp-gtk application displaying the contents of a remote FTP server (the right pane) and a local directory (in the left pane) to or from which you can drag-and-drop files to transfer them.

FIGURE 26-6

Using the gftp-gtk graphical FTP client

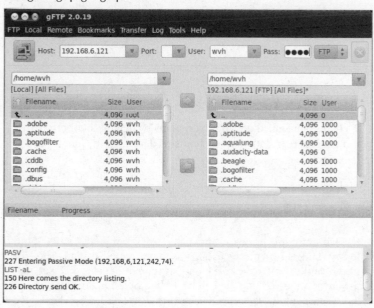

- **FileZilla** (http://filezilla-project.org): Is a graphical non-GNOME FTP client that uses a platform-independent set of widgets. FileZilla provides a relatively lightweight graphical FTP client for Ubuntu systems and, because it is not GNOME-based, can also be used on other desktop systems if you have to use those at work or elsewhere. Figure 26-7 shows the FileZilla application displaying the contents of a remote FTP server (the right pane) and a local directory (in the left pane) to or from which you can drag-and-drop files to transfer them.

FIGURE 26-7

Using the FileZilla graphical FTP client

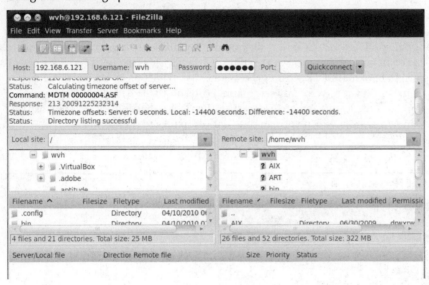

Neither of these graphical FTP clients is installed on Ubuntu systems by default, but both of them are easy to install using any of the software installation mechanisms described in Chapter 19, "Adding, Removing, and Updating Software."

Setting Up an FTP Server

Many FTP servers are available in the Ubuntu repositories: ftpd, inetutils-ftpd, krb5-ftpd, muddleftpd, proftpd, pure-ftpd, pyftpd, twoftpd, vsftpd, wu-ftpd, and wzdftpd. The FTP protocol has been around for a long time, and people have had plenty of time to develop FTP servers! I'm not going to compare and contrast each of these, since they all have their own feature sets and fan clubs, and, frankly, because I don't think many people will care. Of these, my favorite is Pure-FTPd, which is available as the pure-ftpd package in the Ubuntu repositories. Why? It's easy to install, lightweight, trivial to configure, secure, fully internationalized, and runs in several modes, depending on the kind of FTP server that you want to run.

After installing the `pure-ftpd` package using any of the software installation mechanisms discussed in Chapter 19, Pure-FTPd is ready to use in its default configuration. Any user with an account on the system where you installed Pure-FTPd can now connect to their home directory and transfer files to/from there via FTP. By default, Pure-FTPd disables anonymous connections—to enable anonymous connections, modify the file `/etc/pure-ftpd/conf/NoAnonymous` to contain the word *no* (by default, it contains the word *yes*, which means that anonymous users are not allowed). Next, create a user named `ftp` on your system whose home directory is the directory that you want anonymous users to be able to access. (See Chapter 27, "Managing Users, Groups, and Authentication," for information on creating users.) Finally, restart the Pure-FTPd server using the command `/etc/init.d/pure-ftpd restart`. Voilà! Anonymous users are now supported.

Pure-FTPd has an amazing number of command-line options that control how it is started and all of its different modes of operations, all of which you can specify in the `/etc/init.d/pure-ftpd startup/shutdown` script. Pure-FTPd makes it easy to set up virtual FTP servers, IP-address-specific FTP servers, upload and download quotas, and much more. It also comes with a variety of administrative commands, my favorite of which is the `pure-ftpwho` command, which displays information about all current FTP users and what they're doing.

If you're more comfortable administering your FTP server graphically, you can install the PureAdmin application (the `pureadmin` package) on Ubuntu systems.

Accessing Shares on Windows Systems

Your Ubuntu Linux systems can easily access shared directories on Microsoft Windows systems (commonly known as *shares*) thanks to one of the most popular and useful open source software packages ever created, Samba (`www.samba.org`). Samba was originally written by Andrew Tridgell, who has received numerous awards and accolades for it. Tridgell still works on it today, although thousands of others have contributed to Samba, and it is now a team effort. See Chapter 35 for a bit more background information on Samba.

Samba takes its name from the SMB (Server Message Block) protocol that is the original underlying protocol used for networked file sharing on Microsoft Windows systems. Tridgell created Samba in a massive feat of reverse engineering the protocol and how it worked, because Microsoft's specifications for SMB weren't publicly available. Today, thanks largely to Tridgell and Samba, Microsoft has opened up the SMB specification, which is now part of its larger CIFS (Common Internet File System) specification.

You can also use Samba to share files from a Linux system so that specified directories look like Windows shares and Windows users can access them. This requires that you set up a Samba server, which is explained in Chapter 35. This section focuses on accessing a shared Windows directory from the desktop of your Ubuntu Linux system and copying files to or from that Windows share.

Locating Windows Shares

If you're unsure of the shared directories and associated servers that are available on your local network, you can quickly list them all using the smbtree command, which will prompt you for your Windows password, as in the following example:

```
$ smbtree
Password:
WVH
    \\YM901252              YM901252
        \\YM901252\ADMIN$    IPC Service (YM901252)
        \\YM901252\IPC$      IPC Service (YM901252)
        \\YM901252\disk1
    \\HD-HTGLOB5
        \\HD-HTGLOB5\info      TeraStation utilities
        \\HD-HTGLOB5\share     TeraStation folder
        \\HD-HTGLOB5\capture   TeraStation folder
        \\HD-HTGLOB5\IPC$      IPC Service (HD-HTGLOB5)
        \\HD-HTGLOB5\ADMIN$    IPC Service (HD-HTGLOB5)
    \\XEN                    Samba Ubuntu Server
        \\XEN\wvh              Home Directories
        \\XEN\brother          Brother Hl-2070N - hl1250 Driver
        \\XEN\Silentwriter     Office Silentwriter
        \\XEN\Stylus_200       Epson Stylus Photo R200
        \\XEN\IPC$             IPC Service (Samba Ubuntu Server)
    \\UBUNTU                 Desktop Ubuntu
        \\UBUNTU\wvh           Home Directories
        \\UBUNTU\PDF           PDF
        \\UBUNTU\IPC$          IPC Service (Desktop Ubuntu)
        \\UBUNTU\print$        Printer Drivers
    \\WINSERVER              Windows 2000 LAN Mgr
        \\WINSERVER\IPC$       Remote IPC
        \\WINSERVER\print$     Printer Drivers
        \\WINSERVER\wvh        Home Directory
        \\WINSERVER\office     Shared Enterprise Data
```

If you're unsure of the shares that a specific Windows (or Samba) server exports, you can also list them by using the smbclient command, which will prompt you for your Windows password, as in the following example:

```
$ smbclient -L 192.168.6.2
Password:
Domain=[WINSERVER] OS=[Windows 5.1] Server=[Windows 2000 LAN Mgr]
        Sharename      Type      Comment
        ---------      ----      -------
        IPC$           IPC       Remote IPC
        print$         Disk      Printer Drivers
        wvh            Disk      Home Directory
        office         Disk      Shared Enterprise Data
Domain=[WINSERVER] OS=[Windows 5.1] Server=[Windows 2000 LAN Mgr]
```

```
Server              Comment
---------           -------
Workgroup           Master
---------           -------
                    HD-HTGLOB5
WVH                 YM901252
```

You can use the information from either of these examples to identify the name of the share that you want to mount and the server from which that directory is being shared. You will need this information to mount that share on your Ubuntu system using any of the mechanisms described in the next few sections.

Mounting Windows Shares at Boot Time

If you know that you will frequently need to access files and directories in a Windows share, the easiest way to make that share permanently available is to add it to the list of filesystems that your Ubuntu system mounts when that system boots. The section of Chapter 4, "Basic Linux System Concepts," entitled "Automatically Mounting Filesystems at Boot Time" explains the format of the text file that contains the list of filesystems that your system knows about and that can be mounted at boot time. This section explains the specific entries that are necessary when mounting a networked Windows shared directory at boot time.

If you know the name and associated server for the Windows share that you want to mount, you have all of the information that you need to mount that share on your Ubuntu system. If not, you can use the information from either of the examples in the previous section to get the share and server name. To mount that share on your system each time that you start your system, add an entry for the Windows share that you want to mount to the file /etc/fstab. For example, to mount the office share shown in the previous example on the directory /mnt/office (which must already exist), I would create an /etc/fstab entry like the following:

```
//192.168.6.2   /mnt/office  cifs \
    auto,credentials=/etc/cifs.login,uid=0,gid=users  0  0
```

(This entry would appear on a single line in the /etc/fstab file—the backslash is only present for formatting purposes.)

The only unique portions of this entry are the mount options, which have the following meanings:

- auto: Automatically mount the filesystem when the system boots.
- credentials=/etc/cifs.login: Identifies the name of a file that contains the username and password to authenticate with when mounting the filesystem. Because the /etc/fstab file is usually publicly readable, you do not want to embed this information in that file for security reasons. You should put this information in a separate file and change that file so that it can only be read by root (sudo chmod g-r,o-r /etc/cifs.login). This file should contain two lines of the following form:

```
username=USERNAME
password=PASSWORD
```

- USERNAME: This is the name of the user that you want to use to mount the Windows share on the remote host, and PASSWORD is that user's password.

- uid=0: Use User ID 0 when mounting the filesystem.

- gid=users: All files on the Windows share will be assigned to the group users. This enables users of your systems that belong to this group (with their Windows login names) to write to files that they can access on the remote system.

Caution

Some versions of the kernel support for CIFS filesystems still have some issues. If you are unable to mount CIFS shares from remote systems or cannot see files in these shares after mounting them, you must add the noserverino keyword to the list of mount options in the /etc/fstab entry for those shares. ■

Mounting a Windows share via the /etc/fstab file will make that share available to all users of your system, enforcing file access security through the users entry in the /etc/group file and Windows permission settings on the files and directories in the share, which is fine for multi-user server systems. For personal desktop Linux systems, you may prefer to require that users of each system manually mount the Windows shares that they themselves need, which will enable you to leverage their personal security settings more precisely on the Windows server. The next two sections discuss how users can mount Windows shares themselves on their Ubuntu desktop systems.

Connecting to Windows Shares from the GNOME Desktop

Ubuntu's Places menu provides the "Connect to Server" command, which makes it easy to create an icon on your desktop for a Windows share and connect to that share using the Nautilus File Manager. Selecting Places ➪ Connect to Server displays the dialog shown earlier in Figure 26-2. To specify that you want to connect to an FTP server that requires authentication, click the "Service type" menu at the top of this dialog and select the Windows share entry to display the dialog shown in Figure 26-8.

FIGURE 26-8

Identifying a Windows share to connect to

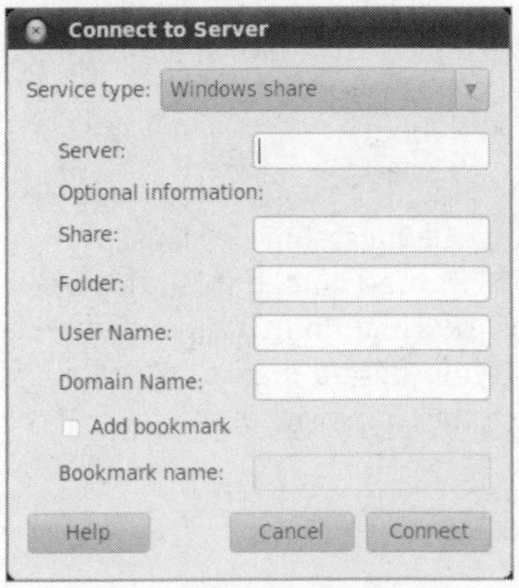

940

You must at least enter the name or IP address of the Windows server that hosts the share that you want to connect to. If you are going to access this directory frequently, you can create a permanent entry for it on the Places menu by checking "Add Bookmark" and entering a name for the bookmark on the Places menu. You can also identify the name of the user that you want to connect as, the name of the Windows domain or workgroup that you want to connect as, and the share that you want to connect to, but all of this is optional — you'll be prompted for anything that you don't specify here when you attempt to connect. Click Connect to create a desktop icon for the Windows share that you have defined.

Simply creating a desktop icon for a Windows share doesn't actually establish the connection. To do that, double-click on the appropriate desktop icon to open it. You will see a dialog that prompts you for any required information that you have not specified yet, as shown in Figure 26-9.

FIGURE 26-9

Completing authentication information for a Windows share

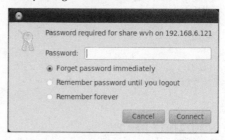

Once you enter any remaining information about the share that you want to connect to and the server upon which it resides, a Nautilus File Manager window appears that displays the contents of the default directory associated with the user that you are logged in as, as shown in Figure 26-10.

Once the Nautilus File Manager displays, copying files in either direction uses the standard Nautilus and GNOME desktop conventions, as discussed in Chapter 5.

Once you are done accessing the Windows share, close the Nautilus File Manager window. To discard the desktop icon, right-click on the icon for the Windows share and select "Unmount Volume" from the pop-up menu to sever the connection and discard the icon. Desktop icons for SMB shares will be automatically removed when you log out. If you want to create a permanent desktop icon, see the sidebar entitled "Creating Permanent Desktop Icons for Services and Locations," earlier in this chapter, for more information.

FIGURE 26-10

A connection to a Windows share in the Nautilus File Manager

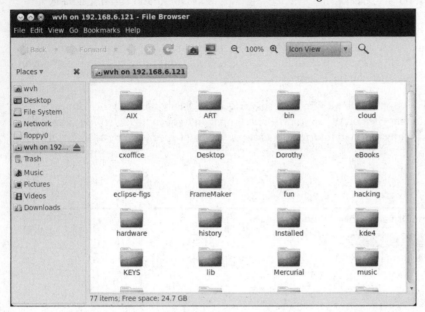

Connecting to Windows Shares from the Command Line

While many people find using the command line to be a throwback to the 1980s and serial terminals, command-line commands are eminently portable, working fine from your Terminal emulator of choice (a GNOME Terminal, xterm, etc.) on Ubuntu and even non-Ubuntu Linux distributions.

To mount a Windows share from the command line on any Ubuntu system, execute a command like the following:

```
sudo mount -t cifs //192.168.6.64/wvh /mnt/wvh \
    -o username=wvh,password=yeahright,rw
```

(This command would ordinarily be typed on a single line — the backslash in this command is only present for formatting purposes.)

This command mounts the Windows or Samba share wvh from the host 192.168.6.64 on the directory /mnt/wvh in read-write mode (rw), authenticating as the user wvh with the password yeahright. The mounted share will be available on this directory until it is unmounted, which you can do via the following command:

```
sudo umount /mnt/wvh
```

Note that this command isn't unmount, but umount. Why type that extra *n* if you don't have to?

Caution

Some versions of the kernel support for CIFS filesystems still have some issues. If you are unable to mount CIFS shares from remote systems or cannot see files in these shares after mounting them, you must add the noserverino **keyword to the** mount **command that you use to mount those shares.** ■

Accessing NFS Directories from Linux Systems

Long before Microsoft Windows, UNIX systems were sharing files over networks using Network File System (NFS), which was originally developed by Sun Microsystems, Inc. in the early 1980s. Sun was smart enough to release the specifications for NFS to the known universe, and every other UNIX system manufacturer with any common sense since then has also implemented support for NFS on their UNIX and UNIX-like systems. Today, most of those vendors are gone and even Sun's long-term future is cloudy, but NFS lives on as the default network filesystem and file sharing mechanism that you can find on any UNIX or UNIX-like system, such as Linux and Mac OS X.

Unfortunately, a whizzy graphical mechanism for mounting NFS filesystems isn't currently supported by the GNOME desktop's "Connect to Server" tool so you'll have to mount remote NFS filesystems manually, using the command line. And you may have thought you could get away with not reading Chapter 11, "Using Command-Line Tools"! Luckily, mounting filesystems from the command line is extremely easy to do. (The mechanism by which you export a filesystem from your local system via NFS is similarly easy, and is explained in Chapter 34.)

NFS filesystems are identified by the name or IP address of the NFS server on which they live, a colon, and the name of the directory that the server is exporting. For example, 192.228.6.64:/home/wvh identifies the directory /home/wvh that is being exported by the NFS server whose IP address is 192.228.6.64. NFS filesystems are mounted on directories on your local Ubuntu system just like any other filesystem (as explained in Chapter 4).

To mount the remote NFS filesystem that I just mentioned, you therefore need to create a mountpoint for it. I always create these in the directory /mnt so that they're easily identified as temporarily mounted devices. For example, the following command creates a mountpoint called /mnt/nfs:

```
$ sudo mkdir /mnt/nfs
Password:
```

After providing your password, the mountpoint exists, so you can now mount the NFS directory using the standard Linux mount command, as in the following example:

```
$ sudo mount -t nfs 192.228.6.64:/home/wvh /mnt/nfs
```

At this point, you can verify that the directory is successfully mounted either by listing that directory or by simply using the df command, as in the following example:

```
$ df
Filesystem          1K-blocks      Used Available Use% Mounted on
/dev/hda1           77299808   40359464  33013660  56% /
varrun                257968        136    257832   1% /var/run
varlock               257968          4    257964   1% /var/lock
```

```
udev                      257968        96     257872   1% /dev
devshm                    257968         0     257968   0% /dev/shm
192.228.6.64:/home/wvh
                       220010496 151044928   8965568  95% /mnt/nfs
```

The mounted directory is now available so that you can access the files that it contains and create new files there. Of course, because NFS filesystems are Linux (or UNIX) directories, you must have sufficient permissions to read and write files there. In most NFS environments, user identities are synchronized across systems so that you appear to be the same user on both the remote and local systems. If this is not the case, you can always use the sudo command (if necessary) to copy files or directories to the NFS filesystem, as in the following example:

```
$ sudo cp resume.xml /mnt/nfs
```

Synchronizing user identities across multiple systems and understanding how Linux systems recognize users in general is discussed in Chapter 27.

Once you're done accessing the files in an NFS filesystem, you can unmount it using the standard Linux umount command, as in the following example:

```
$ sudo umount /mnt/nfs
```

Tip

If you want to automatically mount an NFS filesystem on your system, you should create an entry for it (filesystem type nfs) in your /etc/fstab file, as described in the section of Chapter 34 entitled "Mounting NFS Directories on Clients." ■

Peer-to-Peer File Sharing on Ubuntu

Let's say that you have a tarball or ISO of the greatest open source software package ever, everyone who hears about it wants a copy, and you want to make it freely available to all users. The classic solution to this problem was for you to put it on your FTP or, more recently, Web server, and then to advertise its existence to the known universe. Regardless of how fast your servers are, how many you have, and how fast your connection to the Internet is, it's easy to spot the problem with this approach: Eventually too many people show up to download the file, consuming all of the resources on your site until new people who've just heard about your whizzy software package can't get to it anymore, the delivery of your files to the people who are already in the process of downloading them slows to a crawl, and your servers fall over from the load. It's the downloading equivalent of being mentioned on Slashdot (www.slashdot.org).

The key to this problem is that there is only one place to get the magic files and everyone who wants them has to get them there. The entire load for grabbing these magic files is dumped on that single site, which turns it from a one-stop-shopping experience into a huge bottleneck. Even if you have an arsenal of replicated servers serving up your files and you have the world's best load-balancing software managing the traffic, your resources are finite, while the load may be effectively infinite.

Peer-to-Peer (P2P) file sharing is an impressively cool solution to this problem. As mentioned in the introduction to this chapter, Peer-to-Peer (P2P) file sharing differs from traditional Point-to-Point file transfers in that P2P file transfers are essentially a community effort, a cooperative distribution network in which systems (peers) share files with each other without the user having to know which specific systems are involved in the transfer. Obviously, somebody has to know what hosts are sharing what files, or else no host would know where to get anything from, but there are some cool solutions to this problem. The legal Achilles heel of the pioneering P2P mechanism, Napster, was that it used a central database to track which peers were offering which files. Some legal idiots decided that this meant that Napster was effectively condoning all of the P2P traffic on the network, some of which involved sharing audio files that users might otherwise have had to pay for. They, therefore, forced Napster to shut down its central server, which effectively decapitated the original Napster network. Alas, poor Napster v1, I knew thee well.

Fortunately, performing a computer science autopsy of this "legal" fiasco has helped the second wave of P2P solutions come up with some great work-arounds. These primarily revolve around peers dynamically monitoring and querying other peers or a network in its entirety to find out who has the files that you're looking for. The key to the success of the next wave of P2P solutions has been, and will continue to be, the effective anonymity of which peer is sharing what with whom. Without directly querying each and every peer, you can never get a complete picture of a modern, anonymous P2P network, which is a good thing.

Today, there are many popular P2P protocols, file-sharing networks, protocols, and clients. Some of the most popular are the following:

- **BitTorrent**: `www.bittorrent.com`
- **eDonkey2000**: `www.edonkey2000.com`. This protocol and associated site has been killed by the RIAA, but the eDonkey network lives on. See `http://en.wikipedia.org/wiki/EDonkey2000`.
- **FastTrack (essentially Kazaa)**: `www.kazaa.com`
- **Freenet**: `http://freenet.sourceforge.net`
- **Gnutella**: `www.gnutellaforums.com`

The next two sections explain how to be part of the free speech revolution by installing and using P2P clients such as `gtk-gnutella`, a popular Linux client for the Gnutella file-sharing network, and `transmission`, a simple but complete Linux client for BitTorrent downloads. As in the rest of this chapter, these sections focus on using client software to retrieve files, not on how to explicitly publish files from your system—you're sharing them while this is happening, of course, but the focus here is on retrieving them.

Installing and Using gtk-gnutella

The Gnutella network (not to be confused with Nutella, the yummy European hazelnut and chocolate spread) is a widespread, immensely popular P2P network. Many people do not realize that popular P2P applications such as LimeWire and BearShare are actually just Gnutella clients. One of the coolest things about Gnutella clients is their search feature, which I'll explain later and which makes it easy to query the entire network for shared files that match your search terms. As explained in the introduction to this section, the search feature does not consult a single central-ized database because that would make it too easy to terminate Gnutella traffic. Instead, it uses a very cool friend-of-a-friend mechanism. Your query initially goes to a single Gnutella node, which passes on your original query to the other nodes it knows about, each of which passes on your original query to the other nodes it knows about, until much of the Gnutella network is buzzing with your search request.

Installing gtk-gnutella

Because not everyone wants or needs to do P2P file sharing, the gtk-gnutella client isn't installed by default on an Ubuntu Linux system. To install gtk-gnutella, use any of the Package Management tools discussed in Chapter 19 to install the gtk-gnutella package and any of its dependencies.

Using gtk-gnutella

Installing gtk-gnutella as described in the previous section creates a menu item on the Applications ➪ Internet menu. To start gtk-gnutella, click the Gtk-Gnutella item on this menu, which starts the application and displays a window like the one shown in Figure 26-11.

FIGURE 26-11

The gtk-gnutella startup window

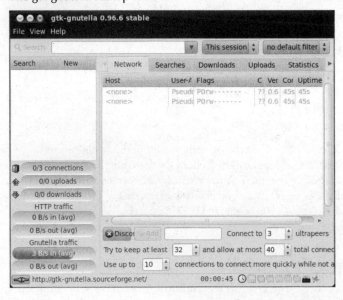

The first time that you start gtk-gnutella, it will create the `gtk-gnutella-downloads` directory in your home directory, which is where it will store the files that it downloads. This directory contains three subdirectories: `complete`, which is where successfully downloaded files are stored when a download completes; `incomplete`, which is where in-progress downloads are stored; and `corrupt`, which is where downloaded files that do not match Gnutella's official checksum for the files are stored. Files in the `corrupt` directory are probably bad, but just in case…

Note

When you start gtk-gnutella, you may also see a dialog entitled "Ancient version detected!" that notes that the version of gtk-gnutella that is provided in the Ubuntu repositories isn't the latest version and points you to gtk-gnutella's SourceForge site for the latest version. Although this is true, I wouldn't bother to get the latest version from SourceForge unless you're actually having a problem with the version that is provided in the Ubuntu repositories. Not only will you have to build it yourself, but you won't be able to automatically upgrade it as you would if you used the standard version from the Ubuntu repositories and a new version were released there. ■

Aside from the standard menu bar, the most interesting parts of the gtk-gnutella screen shown in Figure 26-11 are the following:

- **Graphical summary area (lower left):** An area that displays status information about the number of connected clients, the number of uploads and downloads in progress, the local HTTP (Web) traffic that the application sees, and the amount of Gnutella traffic it sees passing by on the network at the moment

- **Details window (upper left):** A window containing collapsible/expandable entries that enable you to get detailed information about any of the items that it lists: the state of the network, active and completed uploads, active and queued downloads, and the state of any searches that you have initiated

- **Search bar (upper left, just below the menu bar):** Enables you to search for files whose names match a specific sequence of characters

- **Connection Status window (middle right):** Shows the status of any active connections, the results of a search when performing a search, and the status of any active downloads when you view active or queued downloads. The type of information displayed in this window depends on the item selected in the control window

- **Control window (bottom right):** Enables you to control the number of connections that are supported to and from your machine

The interesting parts of gtk-gnutella are actually searching for something, seeing what matches you find, and then downloading the result. So let's first start a search. To demonstrate that there is plenty of legal and useful content out there, search for *Linux ISO*. To do this, put the cursor in the search field of the search bar, enter **Linux ISO**, and press Return. The search begins, with any matches for the search string displaying in the Connection Status (now a Search Results) window. Once search results are displayed, you can see summary information about any of them by positioning the cursor over its name.

Tip

If you do not see results after a while, you may actually need to get a newer version of gtk-gnutella because the Gnutella network often bans sufficiently old versions from accessing the network. You can find the latest versions of gtk-gnutella for i386 and 64-bit systems at `http://archive.ubuntu.com/ubuntu/pool/universe/g/gtk-gnutella`, and manually install these using the `dpkg -i PACKAGENAME` command. ∎

Once you've spotted a file that you want to download, you can select it for downloading by right-clicking on its name and selecting "Download selected files" from the pop-up menu.

Once you've started a download, you can view its status at any time by selecting the Downloads ⇨ Active entry in the details window. If the download is not listed there, it is queued, and you can select the Downloads ⇨ Queue entry in the details windows to see what it is waiting for.

Many systems in the Gnutella network offer many files for downloading and will therefore match search requests, but may already be delivering as many downloads as they have been configured to deliver by their operators. You may have to wait a while for a download to move from queued to active status. Frankly, if I find several matches for a specific file that I'm looking for, I often begin downloading more than one of them to ensure that I can get the file as quickly as possible. Once one of them actually begins to download, you can terminate the others so that you don't waste Gnutella bandwidth.

Tip

If you have problems getting gtk-gnutella to successfully locate or download files, make sure that any firewall that you are running does not block the ports that are used by the version of Gnutella. If you are seeing performance problems and are behind a configurable gateway or router, you may want to forward those ports from your external Internet interface directly to the host on which you are running your BitTorrent client. See the gtk-gnutella FAQ at `http://gtk-gnutella.sourceforge.net/en/?page=faq` for more information. A general discussion of port forwarding on a variety of routers is available at `www.portforward.com/routers.htm`. ∎

Using BitTorrent

BitTorrent, originally written by Bram Cohen, has been around for a few years and is an incredibly popular protocol and tool for P2P file sharing. Bram's original BitTorrent software is GPL and was written in Python. Frankly, I still primarily use the command-line version of BitTorrent (`btdown-loadheadless.py`) because "it just works." Don't worry, I'm not going to make you follow my lead here — although you can easily install the command-line version of the Python BitTorrent software by installing the `bittorrent` package. Instead, easy-to-use graphical BitTorrent clients are preinstalled on both Ubuntu systems, which are what I'll focus on in this section.

The special sauce in the BitTorrent P2P mechanism is the use of torrent files, which provide information about the files that are to be distributed as part of a *torrent* (the generic BitTorrent term for each collection of files that are shared as a group), and the use of a computer system that tracks the current activity related to a torrent (known to BitTorrent devotees as a *tracker*). Unlike Napster's old use of a central server, a BitTorrent tracker doesn't know anything about the contents of a torrent but simply knows what peers are currently involved in downloading, uploading, and sharing a particular torrent. The tracker initially choreographs communications between any peers interested in a specific torrent—once peers are communicating with each other, the tracker is no longer necessary. As you'd expect, when initiating a torrent, at least one peer must provide a complete set of the files in the torrent, which is known as *seeding* in BitTorrent vernacular.

One interesting optimization in BitTorrent is that peers retrieve and share the files in a torrent in a random sequence of chunks. This means that, while many peers may be in the process of downloading the collection of files that make up a torrent, it's normal to expect that no two of them are sharing the same portions of those files. This makes torrents quite durable—even if the tracker and the host that is seeding a torrent go away, it's quite possible that all of the peers together have a complete set of the files in the torrent—they all just have to trade missing chunks with each other. This is known as a *distributed copy* in BitTorrent terms.

BitTorrent is a great piece of software, an impressive protocol, an excellent software distribution mechanism, and a good example of how P2P file sharing can help guarantee the free sharing of data of any kind over the NET. It is also free.

Tip

If you have problems getting any BitTorrent client to work, make sure that any firewall that you are running does not block TCP ports 6881–6999, which are the ports that are used by the current version of BitTorrent. If you are seeing performance problems and are behind a configurable gateway or router, you may want to forward those ports from your external Internet interface directly to the host on which you are running your BitTorrent client. Michael Ingram has a great article on solving slow downloading problems and configuring specific routers and gateways at `www.slyck.com/news.php?story=493`. A general discussion of port forwarding on a variety of routers is available at `www.portforward.com/routers.htm`. ■

Using Transmission on Ubuntu Systems

Because Transmission is installed as part of a basic Ubuntu distribution, you don't have to do anything special to access or configure it. To start Transmission, select the Applications ↪ Internet ↪ Transmission BitTorrent Client menu command. This will display an initial dialog that explains the implications of using a file-sharing client like Transmission. Click "I Accept" to indicate that you understand this. The dialog shown in Figure 26-12 displays.

FIGURE 26-12

The initial Transmission dialog

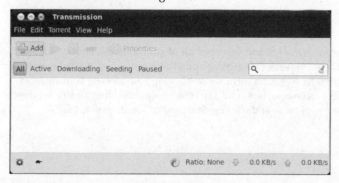

Click the Add icon (or select the File ⇨ Add File menu command) and use the Browse dialog to navigate to the directory that contains the torrent files that you have downloaded, select one, and click Add to begin downloading and sharing its contents. A summary dialog about the contents of this torrent displays. Review the contents of the torrent and deselect any file that you do not want to download. Click Add to begin downloading the selected files from the torrent. The Transmission dialog will show the status of your download, as shown in Figure 26-13.

FIGURE 26-13

Downloading in progress in Transmission

The information under the name of the torrent but above the progress bar gives the amount of the torrent that you've currently downloaded, the complete size of the files in the torrent, and the percentage of the files in the torrent that you've currently downloaded. The number of peers from which you're downloading portions of the torrent displays below the progress bar.

Once you have downloaded the complete set of files that are found in a torrent, Transmission will begin to seed the torrent, which means that you are offering the files in the torrent to other people who are trying to download it. It's generally good form to seed a torrent until the amount of data that other users have downloaded from your seed matches the size of the torrent (as long as other people are trying to download the torrent — there's no need to wait forever). File sharing does, indeed, mean sharing, and, as Mr. Rogers always said, "It's nice to share." Who would have thought that he was a BitTorrent fan?

Tip

If you're in the middle of downloading or seeding a torrent and you need all of your network bandwidth for some higher-priority task like transferring a file from work or watching something critical on YouTube, you can temporarily suspend BitTorrent activity by selecting each torrent and clicking Pause in the Transmission toolbar. When you're done with whatever was more important, you can resume downloading and/or seeding by selecting each paused torrent that you want to resume and clicking Start in the Transmission toolbar.

Transmission enables you to download and seed multiple torrents at the same time. By default, the Transmission dialog shows the status of all torrents, regardless of whether you're downloading or seeding them. To restrict the torrents shown in Transmission to those that are in a specific state, you can click any of the buttons above the Status window. Clicking Active shows all non-paused torrents. Clicking Downloading shows all torrents that you are still downloading, while clicking Seeding shows all torrents whose downloads have completed but that you are providing to other people. As you might guess, clicking Paused only shows torrents that you have explicitly paused. ∎

Happy file sharing! If you find the Transmission interface too minimal for your tastes, a variety of other graphical BitTorrent clients are available in the Ubuntu repositories. Some of the best known of these are `azureus`, a Java-based client that also includes a tracker and can therefore be used to seed torrents; `bittornado-gui`, a fast and powerful but relatively lightweight client; and `qtorrent`, a graphical client that uses the QT graphical interface.

Finding Torrents

At this point, I hope that you're thinking, "Well, BitTorrent sounds like the best thing since sliced bread, but where do I get these torrents from?" Because BitTorrent doesn't provide the same sort of search features as P2P networks such as Gnutella, you have to have a torrent file to actually use it. You may have noticed that the torrent I used as an example in Figure 26-13 is a live recording by the Grateful Dead, who are well known for allowing fans to freely share their live concert recordings. A quick search on the NET for *Grateful Dead* and *torrent* turns up zillions of hits, but that's hardly the most efficient search mechanism when looking for a live recording by your favorite band or some other freely available downloads.

Luckily, many sites provide search engines that are specifically designed for finding torrents. Some of my favorites are the following:

- **btjunkie:** `http://btjunkie.org`
- **isoHunt:** `http://isohunt.com`
- **Torrent Scan:** `www.torrentscan.com`

When getting started, you may also want to visit `http://netforbeginners.about.com/od/peersharing/a/torrent_search.htm`, which provides a user-submitted list of popular BitTorrent search engines.

Because BitTorrent is such an efficient P2P mechanism, many Linux distributions (including Ubuntu) provide torrents for their most recent distributions as well as supporting the standard, slow Web-based downloads. BitTorrent is a fast way of downloading the CD or DVD image (ISO file) for your favorite Linux distribution — which is Ubuntu, I hope. You can find links to sites that provide torrents for the latest Ubuntu releases at `www.ubuntu.com/download`.

Getting More Information about BitTorrent

Because this is a general-purpose book about the Ubuntu Linux distribution and not a BitTorrent bible, this section has only scratched the surface of available information about BitTorrent. I'm betting that once you've started to use BitTorrent, you'll have additional questions or will simply want to know more. Some great sources of dedicated information about BitTorrent are the following:

- **Bit Torrent Page:** `http://wiki.etree.org/index.php?page=BitTorrent`. A great collection of links to BitTorrent information on the Web from a popular file-sharing site for legal, lossless audio recordings

- **BitTorrent FAQ Guide Help:** `www.vladd44.com/torrent`. A useful guide to using BitTorrent and resolving common problems

- **Brian Dessent's FAQ:** `www.dessent.net/btfaq`. Although somewhat dated in parts, this FAQ provides a good deal of useful information.

Summary

Business and academic environments typically provide file servers where centralized collections of corporate documents, project directories, and even supported software are stored. Many networked home computing environments do the same thing to provide a central location for family photos, music, and documents. This chapter began by explaining how to access remote file servers running on Microsoft Windows, Mac OS X, and Linux systems using software such as FTP and how to mount shared folders and network directories using Samba and NFS. This chapter concluded by discussing Peer-to-Peer (P2P) file sharing on Ubuntu, the most popular and resource-friendly mechanism for sharing files that is in common use today.

The next chapter continues with system-related topics, discussing how to create and manage users and groups on your Ubuntu system, and why this is important. It also discusses advanced topics such as configuring and using Kerberos authentication, used in many of today's security-conscious networked environments.

Part III

Ubuntu for System Administrators

IN THIS PART

Chapter 27
Managing Users, Groups, and Authentication

Chapter 28
Backing Up and Restoring Files

Chapter 29
Setting Up a Web Server

Chapter 30
Setting Up a Mail Server

Chapter 31
Setting Up a DHCP Server

Managing Users, Groups, and Authentication

IN THIS CHAPTER

Creating users and groups

Understanding standard Linux authentication

Configuring the `sudo` **command**

Installing and using Kerberos

lthough many people install and use Ubuntu as the operating system on a truly personal computer, Linux is designed and implemented as a multi-user computer system from the ground up. Even if you're the only user of an Ubuntu system, that system still has multiple user and group accounts and runs many processes using the rights granted to those accounts. Similarly, the login process seems simple, but actually invokes several user and group checks under the hood, as do other commands that require specific permissions.

This chapter explains how to manage users and groups on Ubuntu systems. Chapter 4, "Basic Linux System Concepts," provides a basic introduction to the general Linux concepts of users, groups, file permissions, and performing privileged operations. The following is a quick review:

- The section of Chapter 4 entitled "Basic Concepts: Users and Groups" provides an overview of how users and groups work on Ubuntu and other UNIX-like systems, explaining the content and organization of the system files that hold user and group information.

- The section of Chapter 4 entitled "File and Directory Permissions under Linux" introduced file and directory permissions and explained what the cryptic permission entries in a long file listing actually mean.

- The section of Chapter 4 entitled "Performing Privileged Operations in Ubuntu" explained how Ubuntu handles the execution of privileged commands, which is a slight departure from how some other Linux and UNIX-like systems work.

This chapter delves into related topics in more detail. The information in this chapter ranges from a hands-on discussion of how to create and modify user and group accounts using graphical tools to more detailed discussions of how users and groups actually interact with your Ubuntu system and the files and directories that it contains. The first section discusses the graphical and command-line tools used to create and manage user and group accounts. The following section explains how authentication works when a user logs in, which should be of interest to Ubuntu system administrators in enterprise or academic environments that may require changes to the standard authentication process to support custom authentication mechanisms. This chapter also discusses the details of how Ubuntu systems handle the execution of privileged commands, which is a slight departure from how other Linux and UNIX-like systems work. The final section in this chapter discusses how to install and use Kerberos, a secure network-oriented authentication mechanism that is used in many large enterprise and academic environments because of the high level of security that it provides.

Note

Ironically, Kerberos, an open source project, is also the authentication mechanism that underlies authentication in Microsoft's most secure environments, such as Active Directory, Windows Server 2003, Windows Server 2008, and so on. ∎

Creating and Managing Users and Groups

Users and groups are primarily ways of granting different permissions to different individuals or sets of individuals, respectively. These permissions include the ability to read, write, and access specific files and directories; the ability to access specific devices in different ways; and the ability to read or write to and from special-purpose resources such as filesystems, portions of memory, and kernel resources.

Tip

The following sections focus on the graphical tools for user and group creation that are provided on Ubuntu systems. Command-line tools for quick user and group creation, modification, and removal are also available on all Ubuntu systems. For more information about these tools, see the online reference information for the adduser, useradd, userdel, usermod, groupadd, groupdel, and groupmod commands. I prefer to use the graphical tools when creating single users to take advantage of capabilities such as their default privilege settings and associated group memberships. The command-line tools are quite useful in scripts, but they are also well documented, and I don't see much point in simply recreating that documentation here. One tip, though—when you're using these commands to add users to existing groups, either use the adduser command (adduser user-name group-name) or make sure that you specify the -a option when using the usermod command (usermod -a -G group-name user-name). Forgetting to use the -a option with usermod will make the specified user-name a member of group-name and only that group—it will remove user-name from all other groups. I can personally attest to the fact that it is painful to remember and add back all of the other group memberships that most desktop users require. ∎

Managing Users and Groups on Ubuntu Systems

Ubuntu provides a convenient graphical tool for creating users, creating groups, and adding users to groups. Select the System ⇨ Administration ⇨ Users and Groups menu entry to execute this tool. The dialog shown in Figure 27-1 appears.

FIGURE 27-1

Ubuntu's Users and Groups tool

In order to do anything other than simply see the lists of users and groups in this tool and view their properties, you must click Unlock, enter your password in the dialog that appears (or select another user with administrative privileges and enter his or her password), and click Authenticate to proceed. This enables the Add User button on the Users Settings dialog and the Add Group button on the Groups Settings dialog, and also enables you to edit the properties of any existing user or group.

Tip

For information about using the Users and Groups tool beyond what is discussed in the next few sections, see its online manual, which you can access at any time by clicking Help on any panel of the main Users and Groups dialog. ∎

Creating New Users

To add a new user using the Users and Groups tool, click Add. After entering your password, the Create New User dialog displays, as shown in Figure 27-2.

FIGURE 27-2

The Create New User dialog

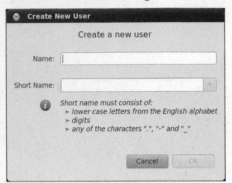

This dialog enables you to specify the Full Name and Short Name of the new user. The Short Name is the name that the new user will use to log in on your system. As you enter the new user's full name, the Create New user dialog will derive a suggested Short Name from the user's Full Name — if you don't like the suggested Short Name, simply backspace over it and enter a Short Name that you like better. Once you're done entering this information, click OK to proceed.

A dialog displays in which you can enter a password for the new user, have the system generate one for you, or specify that the user does not need to specify a password to log in. I always specify a password here (which you must type twice to verify that you're entering it correctly). A generated password is easy to forget, and enabling a user to log in without specifying a password is a poor security practice. After entering and verifying the password, click OK to proceed. The new account is created, and is selected when the dialog shown in Figure 27-1 redisplays.

To customize or correct the newly created account, you can click the Change buttons to the right of any of the entries for the new account. To customize the capabilities of the new account, click "Advanced Settings" to display the Change Advanced User Settings dialog. Click the User Privileges tab to display the dialog shown in Figure 27-3.

FIGURE 27-3

The User Privileges tab

This dialog enables you to give the new user administrative privileges and the ability to access various devices on the system. After checking the privileges that are specified on this tab and making any changes that you want to make, click the Advanced tab to display the dialog shown in Figure 27-4.

FIGURE 27-4

The Advanced tab of the New user account dialog

The fields on this dialog enable you to change the user's home directory, the shell that is started for them when they log in, or their User ID. Though you'll rarely want to change these values, one handy option on this dialog is the "Disable this account" checkbox, which you may want to use if you want to prevent a user from logging in temporarily, but you don't want to actually delete their account.

Once you've finished customizing the new user's account, click OK to save your changes and return to the Users Settings dialog.

Managing Existing Users

In addition to simplifying the creation of new accounts, the Users and Groups tool also simplifies updating (or deleting) an existing account. To update or delete an existing account, start the Users and Groups tool by selecting the System ➪ Administration ➪ Users and Groups menu entry to execute this tool. The dialog shown in Figure 27-1 displays.

Note

The most common administrative task performed after an account has been created is to add that account to other groups or remove it from groups of which it is currently a member. This is not done by modifying the settings for the account using the dialogs described in this section, but by using the procedures described later in this chapter in the section entitled "Managing Existing Groups." ■

To modify or delete an existing account, scroll through the list of available accounts and select the account that you want to update or delete.

To delete the selected account, click Delete. After you verify that you have the privileges to do this by entering your password, the Users Settings tool displays a dialog that requests confirmation that you actually want to delete the account, and provides various options for what to do with the user's files. You can delete the account and keep their files on the system, delete the account and all of the files in the user's home directory, or click Don't Remove Account to cancel deleting the user's account.

To modify an existing account, click the Change button to the right of the basic account information for the selected account, or click Advanced Setting to customize permissions, general account information, and so on.

Creating New Groups

Creating a new system group is usually done as a part of the installation process for any software that requires a group that does not yet exist on your Ubuntu system. *System groups* is the term used to refer to groups that are created to support a specific software subsystem or application, such as groups that control access to printers, databases, and various types of hardware. On Ubuntu Linux systems, the convention is to assign IDs less than 1,000 to system groups.

You may want to create your own groups to do things like identify project members, to limit access to selected directories to a group, or to use a group to limit the people who can execute selected binaries. Ubuntu's Users and Groups tool provides a graphical interface to simplify both group creation and group management (the latter is discussed in the next section). To start this tool, select the System ⇨ Administration ⇨ Users and Groups menu entry to execute this tool. The dialog shown in Figure 27-1 appears. To access the group-oriented portions of this tool, click the Manage Groups button, which displays a dialog like the one shown in Figure 27-5.

FIGURE 27-5

The Groups dialog in the Users and Groups tool

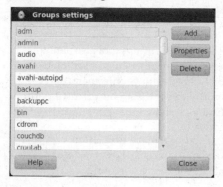

To create a new group, click Add. A dialog displays that prompts you for your password. After you enter your password and press return, the dialog shown in Figure 27-6 appears.

FIGURE 27-6

The New group dialog

Enter the name of the new group that you want to create in the Group name box. Next, you can optionally modify the group number associated with this group.

At this point, you can also add selected users to the group that you are creating by clicking the checkbox to the left of their names in the Group Members list. If you change your mind about adding a specific user to your new group, simply deselect the checkbox beside their name in the Group Members list.

Once you are finished changing settings and adding members to your new group, click OK to create that group and return to the Groups settings dialog of the Users and Groups application. If you are finished creating or modifying groups, you can click Close to exit the Groups settings dialog and return to the Users Settings dialog. To completely exit the Users and Groups application, click Close on the Users Settings dialog.

Managing Existing Groups

In addition to simplifying the creation of new groups, the Users and Groups tool also simplifies adding and removing users from those groups. To update groups' memberships, start the Users and Groups tool by selecting the System ➪ Administration ➪ Users and Groups menu entry to execute this tool. The dialog shown in Figure 27-1 appears. To access the group-oriented portions of this tool, click the Manage Groups button to display the dialog shown in Figure 27-5.

In this dialog, click the name of the group that you want to add or remove users from, and click Properties. This displays a dialog that is essentially identical to the dialog shown in Figure 27-6 except that you cannot change the name of the group, only its members or group ID.

Tip

You should rarely, if ever, use the Group settings dialog to change group IDs. Changing the group ID in this dialog changes the entry for this group in the file /etc/group but does not change the group ID of any files that may happen to already be owned by that group. This could prevent any per-group protections that are already in use from working correctly, preventing users that should be authorized from accessing files or directories associated with their group. ■

To add a user to an existing group, click the checkbox to the left of that user's username in the scrollable list at the bottom of this dialog. Similarly, to remove a user from an existing group, deselect the checkbox beside that user's username in the scrollable list of Group Members.

Any membership, name, or group ID changes that you make in this dialog are not written to the /etc/group file (and updated in the /etc/passwd file, if necessary) until you click OK. You can click Cancel at any time to discard your changes. Clicking either of these buttons returns you to the Groups settings dialog. Once you have finished making any changes to group memberships or other properties, click OK to close the Groups settings dialog and return to the Users Settings dialog. To completely exit the Users and Groups tool, click Close.

PAMs and the Linux Authentication Process

Many different Linux and UNIX applications require authentication or special privileges of one type or another to access special devices or files, or to start processes as a specific user and group. In the early days of Linux/UNIX, each authentication-aware application was compiled with hard-wired information about the authentication mechanism that it required. Changing or enhancing a system's authentication mechanism, therefore, required that all such applications be updated and recompiled, which is tedious at best even if you have the source code for all of the relevant applications on your system.

To resolve this problem, the folks at Sun Microsystems developed the idea of Pluggable Authentication Modules (PAMs), which provide a flexible and dynamic mechanism for authenticating any application or service that uses them. This model has since been adopted by most Linux and UNIX-like operating systems, including Ubuntu Linux. Applications or services compiled with the Linux-PAM library use text-format configuration files to identify and describe their authentication requirements and the specific shared library modules used to implement them. The PAM model lets you modify the authentication requirements of existing applications by simply adding entries to the PAM configuration file that is used by a specific application or service. Applications that use PAMs are typically referred to as *PAM-aware applications*, and PAMs are usually simply referred to as *PAM modules*.

PAMs satisfy different parts of the authentication requirements for PAM-aware applications, much like reusable code and libraries do for applications in general. For example, a PAM-aware version of the login program can invoke several PAMs that check things such as whether the user logging in as root is on a terminal listed as a secure terminal, whether users are allowed to log in on the system at the moment, and other similar, authentication requirements. Because PAMs are shared library modules, a PAM-aware version of the ssh command can reuse the same "are users allowed to log in on the system now" PAM module as the PAM-aware version of login, but can then apply other rules that are more relevant to ssh than to login.

The files that describe the sequence of PAMs associated with specific applications or services are located in the directory /etc/pam.d. The shared-library PAM modules themselves are stored in the directory /lib/security. In older PAM implementations, the PAM modules used by all applications on a system were defined in a central configuration file, /etc/pam.conf. This file is still used, but only as a fallback if no PAM configuration file for a specific application is found in /etc/pam.d.

Many different PAM libraries are available in the Ubuntu repositories, some of which are installed by default and many that are associated with specific authentication mechanisms such as Lightweight Directory Access Protocol (LDAP) or Kerberos. Searching the repository for packages that match the string *libpam* and extracting the names of unique package names shows that there are (currently) 48 PAM-related packages on an Ubuntu system, as the following command shows:

```
$ apt-file search libpam | sed -e 's;:.*;;' | grep libpam | \
  grep -v dev | sort | uniq |  wc -l
48
```

Note

The apt-file command is not installed by default on Ubuntu systems, but can easily be installed using your favorite package management software. Installing the apt-file command is recommended in the discussion of useful package management utilities in Chapter 19, "Adding, Removing, and Updating Software." ■

The PAM modules used by specific, nonstandard authentication mechanisms are identified as requirements for the packages that provide the applications and daemons associated with those authentication mechanisms and are, therefore, only installed when those authentication mechanisms are installed.

PAM Configuration Files for Applications and Services

The PAM configuration files in /etc/pam.d have the same name as the PAM-aware application or service that they are associated with and define the sequence of PAM modules invoked, in order, during the authentication and validation process for that application or service. In addition to PAM rules and related statements, the files in /etc/pam.d can contain blank lines (which are ignored) and comments—any characters on a line that follow the traditional hash mark (#) are interpreted as a comment.

Each non-comment line in one of the files in /etc/pam.d either is an @include statement that includes (inserts) the contents of another PAM definition file at this point or is an actual PAM rule for how a specific PAM module is used as part of the authentication process for the associated application or service. Included files are used to simplify PAM configuration files, enabling a common set of PAM rules to be included by other PAM configuration files. Each PAM rule can consist of four fields separated by white space, the first three of which are mandatory. These fields have the following meaning and content:

- module-type: The type of PAM module defined on that line. A module's type defines how a specific PAM module is used during the authentication process. Valid values are the following:

  - auth: Identifies modules that verify user identity or that system requirements have been met. Common system requirements are that a service can be started at the current time (e.g., that /etc/nologin does not exist when a user is trying to log in), that an acceptable device is being used (the device is listed in the file /etc/securetty), that the user is already the root user, and so on.

- account: Identifies modules that verify that the user can be authenticated based on system requirements such as having a valid account that is able to log in at the current time (based on per-account policies, not general system constraints), has access to the requested application or service, and so on.

- password: Identifies modules that verify that a user can authenticate to the system.

- session: Identifies modules associated with tasks that must be done before the associated service or application is activated, or just before the termination of that service or application. Modules of this type typically perform system functions such as mounting directories, logging audit trail information, or guaranteeing that system resources are available.

- control-flag: The control-flag specifies the implications of different return values from the specified PAM module. Valid values are the following:

  - optional: Indicates that success of the PAM module is not critical to the application or service unless this PAM is the only PAM for a specified module type. If it is, its success or failure determines the success or failure of the specified module type.

  - required: Indicates that success of the PAM module is mandatory for the specified module type. The failure of any PAM marked as required for a specific module type (such as all modules labeled as auth) is reported only after all required PAMs for that module type have been executed.

  - requisite: Indicates that failure of the PAM module immediately returns failure to the associated application or service.

  - sufficient: Indicates that success of the PAM module satisfies the authentication requirements of this module type. If no previous required PAM has failed, no other PAMs for the associated module type are executed after a module labeled as sufficient has succeeded. Failure of a PAM identified as sufficient is ignored as long as any subsequent modules that are identified as required for that module type return success. If a previous required PAM has failed, the success of a PAM marked as sufficient is ignored.

- module-name: The name of the PAM module associated with this entry. By default, PAM modules are located in /lib/security, but this field can also identify modules located in other directories by specifying the absolute path and filename of a PAM module.

- arguments: Optional, module-specific arguments.

The next section provides an example of the structure and organization of a PAM configuration file by examining the PAM configuration file used by the login process on Ubuntu systems.

Example: PAMs Used by the Login Process

To see how a PAM file actually works, let's look at an actual example. The configuration file for the PAMs used by the login program is the file /etc/pam.d/login. After removing blank lines and comments, the meaningful parts of this file on an Ubuntu system are the following:

```
 1:  auth       requisite   pam_securetty.so
 2:  auth       requisite   pam_nologin.so
 3:  session    required    pam_selinux.so close
 4:  session    required    pam_env.so readenv=1
 5:  session    required    pam_env.so readenv=1 envfile=/etc/default/locale
 6:  @include   common-auth
 7:  auth       optional    pam_group.so
 8:  session    required    pam_limits.so
 9:  session    optional    pam_lastlog.so
10:  session    optional    pam_motd.so
11:  session    optional    pam_mail.so standard
12:  @include   common-account
13:  @include   common-session
14:  @include   common-password
15:  session    required    pam_selinux.so open
```

Note

The actual /etc/pam.d/login file does not include line numbers (and cannot). I've added the line numbers to make it easier to match up the PAM entries with the explanations that follow. ∎

The respective lines of this sequence of PAMs do the following:

1. Invokes the PAM module pam_securetty.so to check whether the user is logged in on a secure terminal as defined in the file /etc/securetty. This check must succeed, but is not sufficient to enable a user to log in.

2. Invokes the pam_nologin.so PAM module to check whether logins are allowed on the system at the current time, which is usually done by checking for the file /etc/nologin. If this file is present, the system is in a maintenance state or in the process of being shut down, and logins are disabled. This check must succeed (i.e., the file must not exist), but it is not sufficient to enable a user to log in.

3. Invokes the pam_selinux.so PAM module to terminate any SELinux security context that might be active. If SELinux is not installed, this module simply returns success.

4. Invokes the pam_env.so module, which reads a list of environment variables to set or unset from the file /etc/security/pam.conf (which does not contain any non-commented entries on an Ubuntu system and is therefore somewhat meaningless). This PAM must succeed (i.e., be able to read its configuration file) but is not sufficient to enable a user to log in.

5. Invokes the pam_env.so module again, which in this case reads a list of environment variables to set or unset from the file /etc/default/locale, which sets the LANG environment variable on Ubuntu systems. This PAM must succeed (i.e., be able to read its configuration file), but is not sufficient to enable a user to log in.

6. Includes the contents of the file /etc/pam.d/common-auth, which provides a common set of PAM rules for system authentication. On Ubuntu systems that use standard /etc/passwd and /etc/shadow password authentication, this file contains the following PAM rules:

```
auth [success=1 default=ignore] pam_unix.so nullok_secure
auth    requisite                pam_deny.so
auth    required                 pam_permit.so
```

The first rule invokes the pam_unix.so to verify that the user has a valid entry in the /etc/shadow file. The nullok_secure argument indicates that null (empty) passwords are acceptable on this system when coming from the terminals listed in /etc/securetty. This PAM must succeed but is not sufficient to enable a user to log in. If this rule succeeds, the other rules in this file are not invoked. If the first rule fails, the second rule immediately returns failure to prevent authentication. The third rule puts a positive return value on the auth stack if no value is already present there, but should not be reached.

On Ubuntu systems where other authentication mechanisms, such as LDAP, Kerberos, or fingerprint swiping have been installed, this file would invoke the PAMs specific to checking authentication as required by those services.

7. Invokes the pam_group.so module, which verifies that the user is a member of one or more groups and that a group with the numeric identifier for the user's login group actually exists in the /etc/group file. This PAM module is executed but is optional—its success or failure does not matter unless it was the only auth module for the login service (which it is not), and it is therefore not sufficient to enable a user to log in.

8. Invokes the pam_limits.so module to set user limits specified in the configuration file /etc/security/limits.conf (which does not contain any non-commented entries on an Ubuntu system and is therefore somewhat meaningless). This PAM must succeed (i.e., be able to read its configuration file) but is not sufficient to enable a user to log in.

9. Invokes the pam_lastlog.so module to add an entry for the user to the file /var/log/lastlog, adding an entry when opening a session and terminating that entry when a session is closed. This PAM module is executed but is optional—its success or failure does not matter unless it was the only session module for the login service (which it is not), and it is therefore not sufficient to enable a user to log in.

10. Invokes the pam_motd.so module to display the contents of the /etc/motd file on the login console. This PAM module is executed but is optional—its success or failure does not matter unless it was the only session module for the login service (which it is not), and it is therefore not sufficient to enable a user to log in.

11. Invokes the pam_mail.so module to examine the user's mail directory and display a message if there is any pending mail. This PAM module is executed but is optional—its success or failure does not matter unless it was the only session module for the login service (which it is not), and it is therefore not sufficient to enable a user to log in.

12. Includes the contents of the file /etc/pam.d/common-account, which provides a common set of PAM rules for verifying that the user has a valid account on the system. On Ubuntu systems that use standard /etc/passwd and /etc/shadow password authentication, this file contains the following PAM rules:

```
account [success=1 default=ignore]    pam_unix.so
account requisite                      pam_deny.so
account required                       pam_permit.so
```

The first rule invokes the pam_unix.so module to perform the traditional Linux authentication mechanism check that the user's account is not marked as expired in the file /etc/shadow. This PAM sets the account stack value to 1 upon success but is not sufficient to enable a user to log in. If this rule succeeds, the other rules in this file are not invoked. If the first rule fails, the second rule immediately returns failure to prevent authentication. The third rule puts a positive return value on the auth stack if no value is already present there, but should not be reached.

On Ubuntu systems where other authentication mechanisms, such as LDAP, Kerberos, or fingerprint swiping, have been installed, this file would invoke the PAMs specific to verifying accounts as required by those services.

13. Includes the contents of the file /etc/pam.d/common-session, which provides a common set of PAM rules for interactive and noninteractive login sessions. On Ubuntu systems that use standard /etc/passwd and /etc/shadow password authentication, this file contains the following PAM rules:

```
session [default=1]    pam_permit.so
session requisite       pam_deny.so
session required        pam_permit.so
session required        pam_unix.so
session optional        pam_ck_connector.so nox11
```

The first rule invokes the pam_permit.so module to permit session access to the system and sets the session stack value to 1 if no value has previously been set. If the first rule fails, the second rule immediately returns failure to prevent session authentication. If this rule fails for some reason, the third rule puts a positive return value on the auth stack if no value is already present there, but should not be reached. The fourth rule invokes the pam_unix.so module to create a log entry to the syslog service identifying the beginning of a user's login session on the current system. This PAM must succeed but is not sufficient to enable a user to log in. The last rule invokes the pam_ck_connector.so module to register a non-X11 login session with the ConsoleKit daemon, meaning that the daemon recognizes that a login on the physical console has occurred.

14. Includes the contents of the file /etc/pam.d/common-password, which provides a common set of PAM rules for actually checking a password. On Ubuntu systems that

use standard /etc/passwd and /etc/shadow password authentication, this file contains the following PAM rules:

```
password   [success=1 default=ignore]   pam_unix.so obscure sha512
password   requisite                    pam_deny.so
password   required                     pam_permit.so
```

This rule invokes the pam_unix.so module to check /etc/passwd for a valid user and test the password for that user against the encrypted password entry found in the file /etc/shadow. The obscure argument specifies that, when changing a password, certain checks will be performed, such as verifying that the new password is not a palindrome or rotated version of the old password, that the new password does not differ from the old one simply in terms of case, and that the new password is not "too similar" to the old one. (I personally have never looked at the code to see how similarity is determined, but its rules seem to be fairly obscure.) The sha512 option specifies the encryption algorithm that will be used to encrypt the password. This PAM must succeed but is not sufficient by itself to enable a user to log in. If this rule succeeds, the other rules in this file are not invoked. If the first rule fails, the second rule immediately returns failure to prevent authentication. The third rule puts a positive return value on the password stack if no value is already present there, but should not be reached.

15. Invokes the pam_selinux.so module with the open parameter to open a new SELinux security context for the new login session.

Note

Some other password checking and password-strength checking PAMs are listed in the file /etc/pam.d/common-password but are commented out. You may want to uncomment these and comment out the original pam_unix.so entry if, for example, you want to take advantage of the dictionary checks performed by the pam_cracklib.so module, which are irritating but ensure that a password is not a word that is commonly found in a dictionary. ∎

Once all of the PAMs specified in the /etc/pam.d/login file (and files that it included) have completed successfully, the login process continues, the user's login shell is created, and any other startup actions specified in the user's login configuration files are executed.

The PAM authentication process can be complex and conducive to migraine headaches. Even though it is a pain, security is one of any sysadmin's most important responsibilities. You will rarely, if ever, want to muck with the PAM configuration files on a home Linux system, but you may want to modify them (and should certainly understand them) when using Ubuntu in an enterprise or academic environment. If it's any consolation, think how complex the code to implement all of this would have been without the flexibility that PAMs provide.

Configuration Files for Various PAMs

The text-format files in /etc/pam.d control the PAMs associated with each authentication-aware application or service. As mentioned when exploring the /etc/pam.d/login file in the previous section, some of these PAMs use optional configuration files to further refine their behavior. The configuration files for individual PAMs are located in the directory /etc/security. Although these files must exist, they do not need to contain any useful information—they are there in case you want to take advantage of the advanced configuration options that they provide. Here is a list of the files in this directory that are found on an Ubuntu system:

- access.conf: Provides fine-grained access control for logins and is used by the pam_access.so module.

- group.conf: Provides per-session group membership control and is used by the pam_group.so module.

- limits.conf: Provides a per-user mechanism for setting system resource limits; used by the pam_limits.so module.

- namespace.conf: Defines the directories that will be polyinstantiated if the pam_namespace.so module is being used to support the SELinux Multi Level Security (MLS) policy. Polyinstantiated directories are typically system temporary directories and user home directories. Polyinstantiation and namespaces mean that different users who are viewing a shared resource will each see different contents based on username, role, security level, and so on.

- namespace.init: Contains a shell script that will be executed if the pam_namespace.so module is being used to support the SELinux Multi Level Security (MLS) policy. This default script provided on Ubuntu systems guarantees that the contents of the /etc/skel directory will be copied to polyinstantiated home directories when a new user account is created.

- opasswd: Contains a list of hashes of recently used passwords for various users to prevent password reuse. This file really isn't a PAM configuration file per se, but is used by PAMs such as pam_cracklib.so. This file is only used if you add the remember=N option to the pam_unix.so configuration line in the /etc/pam.d/common-password file, where N is the number of previous password hashes that you want the system to remember for each user.

- pam_env.conf: Provides a mechanism for setting environment variables to specific values; used by the pam_env.so module.

- time.conf: Provides a mechanism for imposing general or user-specific time restrictions for system services and applications; used by the pam_time.so module.

If you install other authentication systems and their associated PAMs, other configuration files associated with those PAMs may also be installed in /etc/security. This section only lists the default configuration files provided by a standard Ubuntu installation.

What if PAM Configuration Files Are Missing?

PAMs provide a very powerful mechanism for authenticating various applications and making sure that only the right users are running them from the right devices. It is, therefore, easy to see that the correct configuration of application-specific PAMs is very important. But what if an application uses PAMs and you forget to create its PAM configuration file or that file is somehow accidentally deleted? To cover these cases, the Linux-PAM library provides a default configuration file for any applications and services that do not have their own configuration files. This is the file /etc/pam.d/other, which has the following valid entries on a standard Ubuntu system:

```
@include common-auth
@include common-account
@include common-password
@include common-session
```

The contents of each of these included files was discussed earlier in this chapter, in the section entitled "Example: PAMs Used by the Login Process." On Ubuntu systems, by default, the /etc/pam.d/other PAM configuration file provides a reasonable set of defaults for verifying that random applications are at least being executed by someone who can successfully log in and authenticate himself or herself to the system, and guarantees that various log entries for that user are created.

Tip

Because a missing PAM configuration file generally indicates a misconfigured system or that someone has imported a PAM-aware binary without thinking things through, you can use the /etc/pam.d/other file to disallow access and impose extremely paranoid security, by changing it to contain the following entries:

```
auth       required   pam_deny.so
auth       required   pam_warn.so
account    required   pam_deny.so
account    required   pam_warn.so
password   required   pam_deny.so
password   required   pam_warn.so
session    required   pam_deny.so
session    required   pam_warn.so
```

Because subsequent required entries for a given module type are still executed, each module-type entry first executes the pam_deny.so PAM, which denies access to the requested service, and then also executes the pam_warn.so PAM, which enters a warning message to the system log. These log entries will help you identify the problem if a cranky user hasn't already surfaced and asked why they can no longer run some obscure binary that they've imported. ■

Customizing the sudo Command

As introduced in the section of Chapter 4 entitled "Performing Privileged Operations," Ubuntu does not use the traditional root account to perform privileged operations but instead enables users who are members of the admin group to perform all privileged operations by specifying their own passwords. The rationale for why the root account (and its traditional friend, the sudo command) are disabled on these systems is discussed in the official online Ubuntu documentation at https://help.ubuntu.com/community/RootSudo. To save you a Web lookup, this is basically viewed as a security improvement, which it certainly can be. Regardless of whether you like this approach, hate it, or are simply puzzled by it, that's the way that Ubuntu Linux works.

Tip

The page at `https://help.ubuntu.com/community/RootSudo` explains how to change an Ubuntu system to reenable the traditional root account. Although this is possible, I strongly suggest that you do not do this unless you have an excellent, site-specific reason to do so and are willing to have your Ubuntu system(s) be fundamentally different from all other Ubuntu systems. ∎

This section explains the internals of the `sudo` command and its configuration file, and discusses how to grant administrative privileges to other users in various forms.

The following list highlights some of the ways in which the `sudo` command works and should be used on Ubuntu systems:

- `sudo` is a command that enables you to execute privileged command-line utilities, such as `apt-get`, `aptitude`, `dpkg`, and so on. If you want to execute graphical commands with administrative privileges on a standard Ubuntu system, you should use the `gksudo` command instead.

- The problem with running graphical applications using `sudo` rather than `gksudo` is that they may change the ownership of the `.ICEauthority` file in your home directory, which many KDE, GNOME, and Standard X Window System applications use to track the applications that are authorized to access a specific X Window System display. If you accidentally use `sudo` to start a graphical application and cannot execute subsequent graphical apps, you can remove the `.ICEauthority` file in your home directory by using the command `sudo rm .ICEauthority`, and then use `gksudo` to start your graphical applications.

- Once you have executed the `sudo` or `gksudo` commands to run any privileged commands, your authorization is stored for 15 minutes so that you don't have to provide your password over and over for each privileged command that you want to execute. During this time, you must still supply the `sudo` or `gksudo` commands, but you will not be prompted for a password. After 15 minutes, using `sudo` or `gksudo` again will result in your being prompted for a password, and the cycle repeats. For the paranoid, the `sudo` command provides a -k option that prevents the temporary storage of authentication information, so that you have to type your password every time.

Tip

If you are really lazy (as I have been known to be), a quick hack for using `sudo` is to use the `sudo` command to execute the bash shell by executing the command `sudo -s`. After supplying your password, this will give you a root shell in which you no longer have to specify the `sudo`, `gksudo`, or `kdesu` commands to execute privileged operations. This is convenient but is bad form and will generate verbal abuse from any other Ubuntu fans that see you doing this. Please be clandestine if you should ever want to do this. ∎

The operation of the sudo command is controlled by the file /etc/sudoers, which is a text file that cannot be viewed by mere mortals for security reasons. To view this file, you should therefore use the visudo command to display it, using a command like the following:

```
$ sudo visudo
```

The visudo command is a special version of the vi command that ensures that only one person is modifying the /etc/sudoers file at a time. You therefore do not need to identify the file /etc/sudoers as an argument—the visudo command knows what file it is designed to edit. You can, of course, open this file in any text editor, but you won't get the protection against simultaneous edits that the visudo command provides.

As you will see, the /etc/sudoers file can contain blank lines (which are ignored) and comments—any characters on a line that follow the traditional hash mark (#) are interpreted as a comment. The meaningful entries in the /etc/sudoers file on a standard Ubuntu system are the following:

```
Defaults    env_reset
root      ALL=(ALL) ALL
%admin    ALL=(ALL) ALL
```

The first of these lines specifies settings that identify default options for how the sudo command behaves. The only option in the Ubuntu /etc/sudoers file is the following:

- env_reset: Resets the environment to only contain the LOGNAME, SHELL, USER, USERNAME, and SUDO_* environment variables. This prevents the propagation of other environment variables to privileged environments.

One option that you may want to change in the /etc/sudoers file is the default period of time for which sudo or gksudo caches the credentials of the root user so that you don't have to enter your password again within a set period of time. By default, these commands cache credential for 15 minutes, which many administrators view as being too long. To explicitly set this cache period (known as the *time-out period*), modify (or add) the Defaults entry in your /etc/sudoers file to look like the following:

```
Defaults    env_reset, timestampt_timeout=XX
```

Change *XX* to be the number of minutes for which you want your privileges to be cached without requiring you to enter your password again. To require all users to always enter a password when entering any of these commands, set *XX* to 0.

The next two lines are the really interesting ones. The following entry states that root can do anything and execute any command on the system:

```
root    ALL=(ALL) ALL
```

Fixing a Broken sudo Command

Installing some versions of Ubuntu in Expert mode uses the standard root mechanism, which can leave your system in a state where normal users cannot use the `sudo` command to execute privileged commands. Similarly, even on a normal Ubuntu system, somehow losing the contents of your `/etc/group` or `/etc/sudoers` files can leave anyone unable to perform any privileged operation. In the latter case, you can reboot your system, press the Escape key to see the GRUB boot menus, and select the Recovery Mode entry from the GRUB menu. This will reboot your system and bring up a root shell.

Once you are logged in as `root` on your Ubuntu system, check to see that your `/etc/group` file contains the admin group and that any users who you want to be able to perform administrative operations are indeed members of that group. If you do not have an admin group, you can add it using the Users and Groups tool explained earlier in this chapter or by a command-line command (as the root user) such as the following:

```
# addgroup --system admin
```

Next, make sure that the `/etc/sudoers` file contains the entry that grants administrative privileges to the admin group, which is:

```
%admin ALL=(ALL) ALL
```

If this entry is not present in your `/etc/sudoers` command, you can use the `visudo` command to edit that file and add the entry.

After making sure that the admin group exists and is referenced in the `/etc/sudoers` file, all you have to do is add any user that you want to be able to run protected applications to the admin group. You can do this by using the Users and Groups tool discussed earlier in this chapter or from the command line by using a command such as the following:

```
# adduser djf admin
```

This command would add the user `djf` to the admin group, enabling them to run privileged operations using `sudo` and `gksudo` (or `kdesu`) in the future.

The following line states that all members of the admin group (as defined in the `/etc/group` file) can also do anything (i.e., run any command as `root`):

```
%admin ALL=(ALL) ALL
```

To enable other users to perform privileged operations, all you have to do is add them to the admin group in the `/etc/group` file using the Users and Groups utility (as explained earlier in this chapter) or by using the `sudo` command to execute a command-line utility such as `adduser`, as in the following example:

```
$ sudo adduser djf admin
```

This command would add the user djf to the admin group and enable that user to execute any commands using sudo or gksudo.

Configuring Kerberos Authentication

Kerberos is a distributed authentication and communication service that was originally developed at the Massachusetts Institute of Technology (MIT). Kerberos provides secure authentication and communication for client/server applications by using strong cryptography to enable clients to prove their identity to servers over the network.

Kerberos works by exchanging encrypted security information between clients (which can be users or machines), the Kerberos Authentication Server, and the resource you are trying to access. The information that is initially exchanged when attempting to prove one's identity is known as a *ticket*. The information used to encrypt tickets and subsequent communications is known as a *key*. Once the identity of a client is verified, that client is granted a Kerberos token that can be used to verify their identity to any Kerberos-aware service. For security reasons, Kerberos tokens are timestamped so that they automatically expire unless renewed by a user or service. The primary system for granting tickets (and which houses the master copy of the Kerberos database) is known as the Kerberos Key Distribution Center (KDC).

The timestamps contained within Kerberos tokens (and tickets) can only be verified if the time and data are synchronized across Kerberos clients and servers. Kerberos authentication will fail if client and server clocks become skewed by more than 5 minutes. You should always run an NTP (Network Time Protocol) daemon on all Kerberos servers and NTP clients on all Kerberos clients to guarantee that their clocks remain in sync.

Kerberos uses the term *realm* to differentiate between authentication and Internet domains. A *Kerberos realm* is a set of machines that rely on a specific Kerberos server for authentication and that, therefore, trust that server. In Kerberos configuration files, your realm is typically identified in uppercase characters in order to differentiate it from any similar DNS domain with which it is associated.

MIT's Kerberos implementation is only one of several. Several alternate Kerberos implementations have been created over the years, usually to get around U.S. export restrictions that have since been lifted. This section focuses on vanilla Kerberos from MIT as provided in the Ubuntu repositories.

Installing Kerberos Client and Server Commands

Using Kerberos requires that you either build and install it yourself from scratch or that a few basic packages are already installed on your systems. If you need to build it yourself, you can download the latest version from MIT at http://web.mit.edu/kerberos/www. However, building Kerberos is rarely necessary on Ubuntu systems because the Ubuntu repositories already provide an up-to-date version of the Kerberos packages that you'll need on the system that acts as your Kerberos server and on any clients of that Kerberos server. To install Kerberos, you must install the following packages using your favorite package management tool:

- `krb5-admin-server`: You must install this package on all Kerberos server and slave server systems. This package provides the programs that must be installed on a Kerberos 5 server or server replica.

- `krb5-config`: This package provides a template configuration file for Kerberos and associated documentation, and is automatically installed for you when you install the `krb5-admin-server` or `krb5-user` packages.

- `krb5-kdc`: This package provides the Kerberos Key Distribution Center (KDC) binaries, related utilities, a template configuration file, and associated documentation, and is automatically installed for you when you install the `krb5-admin-server` package.

- `krb5-user`: You must install this package on all client systems. This package provides basic Kerberos programs (`kinit`, `klist`, `kdestroy`, `kpasswd`) as well as Kerberized versions of the `telnet` and `ftp` applications.

- `libpam-krb5`: You must install this package on all Kerberos client and server systems in order to install the Kerberos PAM so that you can integrate Kerberos into the PAM authentication process on those systems.

- `ntp`: As mentioned in the introduction to this section, you should install a Network Time Protocol (NTP) server on your Kerberos server so that its timekeeping is accurate. The tickets used to authenticate clients with the Kerberos service are timestamped, and it is therefore extremely important that the clocks on the Kerberos server and all clients be synchronized.

- `ntpdate`: As mentioned in the introduction to this section, you should install a Network Time Protocol (NTP) client on all of your Kerberos client systems so that their timekeeping is accurate. The `ntpdate` client is installed by default on all Ubuntu desktop systems—I'm just listing it here to make sure that you understand that it must be available on your system and should synchronize with the NTP server on your Kerberos server.

Installing the `krb5-admin-server` package displays a warning message that explains that you must actually configure it for your site before you can use Kerberos authentication. No big surprise there—read on!

Configuring NTP on Servers and Clients

Before configuring and starting your Kerberos server, you should first make sure that your Kerberos server has the correct time. You should also configure each client of that Kerberos server to get its time information from the Kerberos server before starting any Kerberos client. You can configure the client to use the Kerberos server's time server when you install and configure the Kerberos software on the client system or beforehand—the instructions for client NTP configuration are provided in this section to help ensure that you don't forget this step.

Configuring an NTP Server

Installing the `ntp` package on the system that will be your Kerberos server automatically configures your server to consult the time server at `ntp.ubuntu.com`. In case this host goes down or is otherwise unavailable, you may want to configure your time server to be able to consult one or more other time servers from the pool of public NTP servers that is available on the Internet. For a list of public NTP servers and information about using them, see `http://support.ntp.org/bin/view/Servers/WebHome`.

The configuration information for an NTP server is stored in the configuration file `/etc/ntp.conf`. Edit this file in your text editor of choice, search for the default `ntp.ubuntu.com` entry, and add lines like the following after that entry:

```
server north-america.pool.ntp.org
server pool.ntp.org
```

If you are not located in North America, you would change the first line to be the name of a time server that is more appropriate for your geographic location, as explained at `http://support.ntp.org/bin/view/Servers/NTPPoolServers`.

After entering entries for additional time servers, save the file, exit your text editor, and restart the NTP server using a command like the following:

```
/etc/init.d/ntp restart
```

This will restart your time server with the new configuration entries.

Configuring an NTP Client

As mentioned previously, the `ntpdate` NTP client software is installed by default on all Ubuntu desktop systems. When installing Kerberos on a client system, you should make sure that the NTP client software on each client system gets its time synchronization information from your NTP server. This ensures that the timestamps on Kerberos tickets are synchronized throughout your site.

Unlike most system services, the `ntpdate` client is actually run whenever you bring up an Ethernet interface. The script `/etc/network/ifup.d/ntpdate` is executed whenever you bring up an Ethernet interface. This script runs the `/usr/sbin/ntpdate-debian` script, which, in turn, executes the `/usr/sbin/ntpdate` program with the time servers that are specified in the `/etc/default/ntpdate` configuration file used for the `ntpdate` application on Ubuntu Linux desktop systems.

By default, the `/etc/default/ntpdate` configuration file used on Ubuntu systems tells the `ntpdate` client to look for information in the same configuration file as that used by the NTP server, which is the file `/etc/ntp.conf`. Unfortunately, this file is not present on client systems unless you have also installed the NTP server software on those systems, which is unnecessary. For that reason, we'll modify the /etc/default/ntpdate configuration file to ignore this file and explicitly reference your NTP server. To do so:

1. Change the line that defines the NTPDATE_USE_NTP_CONF variable to set the value of this variable to No, so that the ntpdate client will not attempt to consult the file /etc/ntp.conf for the list of time servers to use, since this file is not present on your system unless you have also installed the NTP server package on that system.

2. Add the IP address for your ntp server at the beginning of the list of time servers that is defined in the NTPSERVERS variable. This entry should be separated from the default value of ntp.ubuntu.com by a space.

After editing this file, "the right thing" will happen whenever the system (or you) brings up an Ethernet interface, but that won't synchronize your clock for you at the moment, since your Ethernet interface(s) are presumably already up. To do this, run the /usr/sbin/ntpdate-debian application manually from a command line to synchronize your system's clock with your NTP server.

Tip

If your client systems run for a long time (i.e., days or weeks), it is possible that their clocks may become skewed from the time server, because the ntpdate application (or, more properly, the ntpdate-debian script) runs only when you bring up an Ethernet interface. This means that your clock is not regularly synced with the NTP server, which can therefore pose a problem for the timestamps in your Kerberos tickets. To eliminate this potential problem, you can simply set up a regularly scheduled CRON job to sync your system's clock with the time server at a specified interval. I find daily synchronization to suffice, so I simply use the sudo command to execute my favorite text editor and create the file /etc/cron.daily/ntpdate-debian with the following contents:

```
/usr/sbin/ntpdate-debian
```

After creating this file, make sure that it is executable by executing the following command:

```
sudo chmod 755 /etc/cron.daily/ntpdate-debian
```

Your system will now automatically synchronize with the time servers that you identified in the file /etc/default/ntpdate. ∎

Setting Up a Kerberos Server

Installing the Kerberos admin server package (krb5-admin-server) and its dependencies on your server displays some basic configuration information and prompts you for the name or IP address of the Kerberos servers for your realm. Unfortunately, the information that it requests is insufficient to actually start and use Kerberos in your domain, so this section walks you through the steps that you'll need to perform to actually begin using Kerberos on a server.

After installing the krb5-admin-server and its dependencies on the system that you want to become your Kerberos server, do the following:

1. Edit the file /etc/krb5.conf using your favorite text editor and do the following:

    1a. In the [libdefaults] section, modify the default_realm entry so that it is set to the name of your realm (in uppercase letters). In my case, where I use the realm VONHAGEN.ORG, this entry looks like the following:

    ```
    default_realm = VONHAGEN.ORG
    ```

    1b. In the [realms] section, add an entry that identifies the hostnames or IP addresses of your primary Kerberos server (i.e., the system on which the primary Kerberos admin daemon is running) and your primary Key Distribution Center. The entry for this on my primary Kerberos server looks like the following:

    ```
    VONHAGEN.ORG = {
            kdc = 192.168.6.140
            admin_server = 192.168.6.140
            }
    ```

    1c. In the [domain_realm] section, add entries to identify the hosts that the KDC should recognize as being members of your realm. These are essentially masks for the domain(s) or subdomain(s) containing the hosts that will be contacting the Kerberos server. You should enter two values for each domain or subdomain. For example, for hosts in the vonhagen.org domain, my entries in this section would look like the following:

    ```
    vonhagen.org  = VONHAGEN.ORG
    .vonhagen.org = VONHAGEN.ORG
    ```

    1d. Unless you need to maintain compatibility with any existing Kerberos servers in your environment, set both the krb4_convert and krb4_get_tickets variables in the [login] section to false. The entry for this on my primary Kerberos server looks like the following:

    ```
    krb4_convert = false
    krb4_get_tickets = false
    ```

Note

The default krb5.conf file that is installed on Ubuntu systems contains numerous entries for sites at CMU, MIT, Stanford, and other sites where Kerberos is popular. You should remove these before going into production with your Kerberos installation, but they initially serve as good examples for the types of customizations that you are making. ∎

2. Next, edit the configuration file for your Key Distribution Center, `/etc/krb5kdc/kdc.conf`, to include your realm. In the realms section, change the name of the example domain to the name of your Kerberos realm, as in the following example:

```
[realms]
    VONHAGEN.ORG = {
    ...
```

3. Execute the `/usr/sbin/krb5_newrealm` command to initialize the realm, entering a master keyphrase for the realm when prompted to do so. (This command runs the `krb5_util` command with specific options to create various configuration and data files that will be used by the Kerberos administration daemon.)

4. Next, create an administrative principal so that you can do remote administration by executing the following command:

```
kadmin.local -q "addprinc admin/admin"
```

After entering your password, the administrative principal for your Kerberos domain will have been created.

5. Next, start an interactive `kadmin` session (using the admin principal and the `kadmin.local` application), and add principals for your server (the host the `kdc` and `kadmin` servers are running on) and the first client system that you will be testing it with, your username, and the first client that you want to test with, as in the following example:

```
# kadmin.local -p admin/admin
kadmin.local: addprinc -randkey host/server.local.network
kadmin.local: addprinc -randkey host/workstation.local.network
kadmin.local: addprinc username
```

In these examples, replace `server` with the name of your server, `workstation` with the name of the client workstation, and `local.network` with the name of your realm. In my case, these would read something like `kerberos.wvh.org` and `ubuntu.wvh.org` because I tend to use `kerberos` as the hostname of my Kerberos servers. The add principal commands for the server and workstation principals use random keys when they are created (specified by the `-randkey` option) because no one will ever log in as those hosts, but you want them to exist as entities in the Kerberos database. You will be prompted for your password after creating a principal for your login—a random key won't do there, because you will actually want to be able to log in at some point.

Tip
When setting up `kerberos` for the first time and defining the principal for the user that you will be using for testing purposes, I suggest that you initially set the password for your user principal to something other than your standard Ubuntu password. This enables you to make sure that the authentication process on your client systems is actually using Kerberos—after doing so, you can delete your existing principal (using the `kadmin` command's `delprinc` command) and then create another with your standard password. ∎

Before exiting the `kadmin.local` command, create a keytab entry for your Kerberos server. The keytab files provide default information about a host, such as the encryptions protocol that it uses (I typically use the defaults):

```
kadmin.local: ktadd host/server.local.network
```

As you did previously, replace `server` with the name of your server and `local.network` with the name of your realm. In my case, this entry would read something like `kerberos.wvh.org`. You can then exit from the interactive command environment provided by the `kadmin.local` command by issuing the `quit` command:

```
kadmin.local: quit
```

6. That's it for your server. As a matter of good form, I generally restart the `kadmin` daemon and the KDC server at this point, to verify that they will start correctly when I next boot the system. The commands to do this are the following:

```
/etc/init.d/krb5-admin-server restart
/etc/init.d/krb5-kdc restart
```

Now, off to the client to configure it to use Kerberos and your server!

Setting Up a Kerberos Client

When installing the `krb5-user` and `libpam-krb5` packages, you will be prompted for the name of your Kerberos server and the name of your KDC server, which you can enter as hostnames or IP addresses. Entering IP addresses is safest because it eliminates the chance that DNS problems could prevent you from locating your Kerberos servers, but your clients obviously won't know how to find your Kerberos servers if you change their IP addresses. I typically resolve this by entering hostnames for the Kerberos and KDC servers and making sure that the IP addresses of these hostnames are listed in my `/etc/hosts` file. I then make sure that the `/etc/nsswitch.conf` file on each client uses both `dns` and files (in that order) in the hosts entry, which gives me both the flexibility of DNS and a fallback IP address if DNS is unavailable.

After entering these packages, use your favorite text editor to edit the file `/etc/pam.d/common-auth`, adding the following line after the line that invokes `pam_unix.so`:

```
auth sufficient   pam_krb5.so use_first_pass forwardable
```

Make sure that this entry does not contain any typos! After saving this file, you can now test that Kerberos is working by using the `kinit` command, which attempts to get Kerberos tokens for the specified user (in this case, `wvh`):

```
kinit wvh
```

You'll be prompted for your password and should not see any errors. You can verify that this actually worked by executing the `klist` command, which provides information about the Kerberos tokens held by the current user and (if all is well) will return something like the following:

```
# klist
Ticket cache: FILE:/tmp/krb5cc_1000_eYJHEN
Default principal: wvh@VONHAGEN.ORG

Valid starting       Expires              Service principal
10/22/08 05:52:52   10/22/08 15:52:52    krbtgt/VONHAGEN.ORG@VONHAGEN.ORG
renew until 10/23/08 05:52:52

Kerberos 4 ticket cache: /tmp/tkt0
klist: You have no tickets cached
```

If the `kinit` command returns an error or does not grant valid tickets, you can enable debugging during the Kerberos authentication process to attempt to identify (and then resolve) the problem. To activate debugging, edit the file `/etc/pam.d/common-auth`, using your favorite text editor and add the keyword *debug* to the end of the Kerberos entry, which should then look like the following:

```
auth    sufficient    pam_krb5.so use_first_pass forwardable debug
```

You can then execute the `kinit` command again and monitor `/var/log/auth.log`, which should contain information that will help you understand why Kerberos is not working.

Once you can successfully execute the `kinit` command and see tokens using the `klist` commands, use the `ssh` command to try to log in on your Kerberos server via its loopback address as a final test. If this works, you can then log out of the SSH connection, completely log out of your client, and log back in with your Kerberos password. Congratulations—you're using Kerberos!

Kerberos can be very useful as a centralized authentication mechanism, although you will have to create Kerberos principals for every user on your network (i.e., in your Kerberos realm) before they can log in on any client system that you have configured to use Kerberos authentication. As configured in this section, Kerberos requires that all of your users have local accounts (because the Kerberos authentication check in `/etc/pam.d/common-auth` follows the standard `pam_unix.so` authentication check).

Summary

This chapter started off by explaining the concepts of login users and protection groups on Ubuntu systems. It explained how Linux systems use Pluggable Authentication Modules to verify a user's identity and that a user is authorized to log in at a specific time and perform other authentication-related tasks when logging in on an Ubuntu system. It explained the basics of file and directory protection using Users and Groups on Ubuntu systems, and then discussed how users perform tasks that require system privileges on Ubuntu systems using the sudo command. The last section of the chapter explained how to install and configure Kerberos authentication on your system to provide a centralized, network-oriented authentication mechanism.

The next chapter discusses how to back up and restore files on Ubuntu systems in a variety of local and network-oriented mechanisms. Backups are probably the definitive mundane system administration task, even when automated. However, should your hard drive crash or you accidentally delete your thesis, the geneological research you've been working on for a decade, all of your e-mail, or your entire music collection, your backups will quickly become your best and most loyal friend.

Backing Up and Restoring Files

Backups are spare copies of the files and directories that are found on a computer system, written to and stored on removable media that is preferably stored somewhere other than on your computer. Doing backups is a time-consuming, but absolutely mandatory, task if you place any value at all on the files, e-mail, and other data that you have stored on your computer.

Backups are exactly like auto insurance policies — well, almost exactly, because they're not a legal requirement to own a computer system (in most states). You rarely need them, and you hope that you never do. They are usually just time-consuming and expensive (your time has some value, right?). However, one rainy night when you discover that you've just accidentally deleted your home directory or when a user comes to you and says that they've accidentally deleted your company's personnel records, payroll data, or the source code for your company's products, you'd better have a good answer. The right answer, of course, is, "I'll restore that from backups immediately."

It's hard to think of anything that so thoroughly combines the mundane and mandatory as backing up your data. It's boring. It's time-consuming. And, of course, it's critical. This chapter is oriented toward you as a systems administrator, regardless of how many systems you're responsible for. As system administrators, our responsibility is to provide secure, well-maintained, and rigorously backed-up systems for the benefit of the users of the computer systems we're responsible for. You should feel even more responsible if you're only supporting a user community of one (yourself), because you won't even have anyone else to blame if a catastrophe occurs. Even if you're a community of one, I'm sure that you feel that whatever you do on your computer system is important. Backups keep it safe.

IN THIS CHAPTER

Backups 101

Doing local backups to removable media

Using rsync for remote backups

Using backuppc for site-wide backups

Linux time machines

Backing up and Mirroring to the Cloud

This chapter explains a variety of solutions for creating backups on Ubuntu Linux systems, ranging from command-line solutions to some impressive graphical tools. It also covers the flip side of making backups — restoring files from them — which is what makes backups worthwhile in the first place.

Backups 101

Before discussing the different tools used to create backups, it's useful to review some of the basic issues and approaches in backing up any kind of computer system. Although you may already be totally familiar with these concepts and occasionally mumble backup and restore commands in your sleep, providing a clear picture of what you're trying to accomplish in doing backups and how backup systems are usually designed provides a firm foundation for discussing the various tools discussed later in this chapter. Since I have no way of knowing whether you're reading this book because you're using Ubuntu on your home computer or because you're deploying Ubuntu throughout your business, I'm going to err on the side of caution and discuss many topics that are overkill for a home computing environment but are mandatory in multi-system business or academic environments.

Why Do Backups?

In an ideal world, backups would not be necessary. Computer hardware and software would always work correctly, users would never make mistakes, and I'd be a rock star. Unfortunately, in the real world, things are different. Computer system administrators and other members of an MIS/IT department do backups for many reasons, helping protect you against the following types of problems:

- Natural disasters such as fires, floods, and earthquakes that destroy computer systems
- Hardware failures in disk drives or other storage media that make it impossible to access the data that they contain
- System software problems such as filesystem corruption that might cause files and directories to be deleted during filesystem consistency checks
- Software failures such as programs that crash and corrupt or delete the files that you're working on
- Pilot error, aka the accidental deletion of important files and directories

Note

Many people tend to confuse RAID (Redundant Array of Inexpensive Disks) arrays with backups. They are not the same thing at all. RAID arrays can be a valuable asset in keeping your existing data online and available in the face of disk failures, but they do not protect against any of the problems identified in the previous list. All of the drives in a RAID array will burn evenly in case of a fire or other natural disaster. ∎

In addition to protecting you against these sorts of problems accessing the data that they, you, and any other users of your systems require, there are a variety of procedural and business reasons to back up the data on your computer systems. Complete and accurate backups provide:

- A complete historical record of your personal, corporate, or organizational business and financial data. Sadly enough, this includes serving as a source of information that you, your company, or your organization may someday need to defend itself or to prove its case in a lawsuit or other legal proceedings.

- A source of historical information about research projects and software development

- A way of preserving data that you do not need to make continuously available online but that you may need to refer to someday. This includes things like projects that you've completed, the home directories of users who are no longer using your systems, and so on.

A Few Words about Backup Media

Backups take a significant amount of time and require a significant investment in both media and backup devices. Nowadays, even home computer systems store tens or hundreds of gigabytes of information, which means that you either need to have fast, high-capacity backup devices, or you must prepare yourself for a laborious day or two of loading CDs or DVDs, mounting backup hard drives, and so on. Other, more historical solutions such as Zip disks, Jazz disks, LS-120 disks, magnetic tapes, and so on provide such a small amount of storage that they're really only useful for backing up individual files, directories, or sets of system configuration files, and are therefore not discussed in this chapter.

CD-Rs, DVD-Rs, and USB sticks (AKA "thumb drives") are eminently suitable for backups of home computer systems because they are inexpensive and typically provide enough storage for backing up the selected files and directories that compose most home backups. For home use, I prefer CD-R and DVD-R media over their rewritable brethren because of the cost difference and the fact that rewritable CDs and DVDs are only good for a limited number of writes. On the other hand, CD-Rs and DVD-Rs are rarely appropriate for enterprise backups because even DVD-Rs are not large enough to back up complete systems, it's tricky to split backups across DVD-R media, and DVD-Rs are relatively slow to write to. They can be useful when restoring a system because of their portability—you can take them directly to the system you're restoring without having to move a tape drive, do a network restore, and so on. However, I personally prefer removable hard drives in enterprise or academic environments.

Another modern alternative to using physical devices for backups is to back up your data to one of the many cloud-based backup solutions that are available today, including Ubuntu's own Ubuntu One. These are perfectly suited to backing up critical files and directories, liberate you from having to provide your own backup media, and inherently deliver the benefits of off-site storage. In my opinion, cloud-based backup solutions are less suitable for academic or enterprise backups for reasons including security and the difficulty of and time required for doing complete system restores (AKA "bare-metal" restores) from remote storage that requires network access.

A final issue concerning backups is the need for off-site storage of all or specific sets of your backups. The history of personal, business, and academic computing is littered with horror stories about people who did backups religiously but stored them in a box beside the computer. After a fire or natural disaster, all that the administrators of those systems were left with were poor excuses and unemployment benefits. Off-site storage is critical to your ability to recover from a true physical catastrophe, but it also raises another issue — the need for appropriate security in the storage location you select.

For the same reasons that you wouldn't leave the door to your house propped open and then go on vacation and wouldn't put a system that didn't use passwords on the Internet, you shouldn't store your backups in an insecure location. This is especially important if you are in charge of computer systems that are being used for business. Wherever you store your company's current and historical backup media should have a level of security comparable to wherever your computers are in the first place. Although your local cat burglar might not actively target a stack of CDs or removable disks, or a storage locker full of backup tapes, any competitors you have would probably be ecstatic to be able to read and analyze the complete contents of your company's computer systems. Why not just save everybody time and mail them your source code and customer lists?

Different Types of Backups

Now that I've discussed why to do backups and some of the basic issues related to storing them, let's review the strategy behind actually doing backups. As mentioned previously, backups take time and have associated costs such as backup media, but there are a variety of ways to manage and minimize those costs.

There are three basic types of backups:

- **Archive backups:** Provide a complete snapshot of the contents of a filesystem at a given time.
- **Incremental backups:** Reflect the changes to the contents of a filesystem since a previous backup.
- **Spot backups:** Provide a snapshot of specific files or the contents of one or more important directories at a given time.

Note
Spot backups are the most common type of backups done by home computer users because writing a copy of your current projects, mail folders, or even your entire home directory to a few CD-Rs or DVD-Rs is relatively fast and cheap. There isn't all that much to say about this approach, because it can easily be done using drag-and-drop, so the rest of this section focuses on the classic backup models of archives and incremental backups. I'll discuss some techniques for doing spot backups later in this chapter. ■

Archive backups, often referred to as *archives* or *full backups*, are the ultimate source for restoring data because they usually contain a copy of every file and directory on a specific filesystem or under a certain directory on your computer at the time that the backup was done. In an ideal world, it would be great to be able to do daily archive backups simply because this would guarantee that no one could ever lose more than a day's work, regardless of the type of calamity that occurred to your computer system. Unfortunately, archive backups have some drawbacks:

- They take the maximum amount of time that backups could require because they make a copy of every file and directory on every filesystem on all of your computer systems.

- The volume of data that is preserved by an archive backup means that they use the maximum amount of space on your backup media.

- Producing the largest possible volume of backup media maximizes the amount of storage space required to store it and makes your record keeping as complex (and as critical) as it possibly could be.

- Archives are best done when no one is working on a computer system. This reduces the amount of time that it takes to do the backups (because they're not competing with anyone for computer time) and also guarantees the consistency of the files and directories that are being copied to your backup media, because nothing can be changing. This may not be a big point in a home computing environment, but in a business environment, making sure that no one is using a computer system so that you can do an archive backup is often impractical (as on systems that run 24x7 services such as Web servers, database systems, etc.) or, best case, reduces the availability of a computer system to the company and your customers.

Although the advantages of archive backups as a complete record of everything are significant, these kinds of issues keep archives from being a reasonable approach to daily backups for any home computer, business, or organization. You could always do them less often than daily, but reducing the frequency of your backups increases your exposure to losing a significant amount of data if your disks fail or your computer bursts into flames.

Enter incremental backups. As mentioned before, *incremental backups* are backups that contain a copy of all of the files and directories that have changed on a computer system since some previous backup was done. If a problem occurs and you need to restore files and directories from backups, you can restore an accurate picture of those files and directories by first restoring from an archive backup, followed by restoring from some number of incremental backups up through your most recent ones, which should restore whatever you've backed up to the date of your most recent incremental backups. When combined with archives, incremental backups provide the following advantages:

- They help minimize the amount of disk space or other backup media required to do backups. Archives usually require large quantities of most types of backup media, while incrementals inherently require less because they aren't preserving as much data.

- They can be done more quickly, because they are copying less data than an archive backup would.

- The backup media to which incremental backups are written require less storage space than archive backups because there's less of it.

- Even in business and academic environments, incremental backups can be done while the computer systems and filesystems you're backing up are available for use.

Another nice feature of incremental backups is that they record changes to the files and directories on your computer systems since some previous backups, which are not necessarily archives. In corporate environments, most systems administrators organize their backup media and associated procedures in a way similar to the following:

- Archives are done infrequently, perhaps every six months or so, or just before any point at which major changes to your filesystems or computer systems are being made.

- Monthly incremental backups are made of all changes since the previous archive. If your budget and backup storage capabilities are sufficient, you usually keep the monthly incremental backups around until you do another archive backup, at which point you can reuse them.

- Weekly incremental backups are made of all changes since the previous monthly backup. You can reuse these each month, after you do the new monthly backups.

- Daily backups are made of all changes since the previous weekly backup. You can reuse these each week, after you do the new weekly backups. Some installations even just do dailies since a previous daily or the daily done on some previous day of the week.

No backup system can make it possible to restore any version of any file on a computer system. Even if you were lucky or compulsive enough to be doing daily archives of all of your computer systems, files that exist for less than a day can't be restored, and it isn't possible to restore a version of a file that is less than a day old. Sorry. When designing a backup schedule and the relationships between archive and various incremental backups, you have to decide the granularity with which you might need to restore lost files. For example, the general schedule of archives, monthlies, weeklies, and dailies doesn't guarantee that you can restore a version of a file that is newer than the previous archive. For example:

- If the file was deleted one day before the first set of monthly backups was done based on the archive, it would be present on the archive and on the weekly backups for a maximum of one month. At that point, the weekly tape containing that file would be overwritten and the newest version of the file that could be restored would be the version from the archive.

- If the file was deleted one day after the first set of monthly backups was done based on the archive, it would be present on the archive and on the first monthly backup for a maximum of seven months. A new archive would be done at that point, and the monthly tape wouldn't be overwritten until one month after the new archive. At that point, the monthly tape containing that file would be overwritten and the newest version of the file that could be restored would be the version from the most recent archive.

Selecting a backup strategy is essentially a calculation of how long it will take someone to notice the absence of one or more files and request a restore, taking into account the level of service that you need to provide and the cost of various levels of service in terms of media, backup time, and storage/management overhead. Sometimes you will notice missing files immediately, such as when you accidentally delete the great American novel that you're actively working on. Other problems, such as lost files because of gradual disk failures or filesystem corruption, may not surface for a while.

Almost all backup systems generally provide automatic support for doing incremental backups since a previous incremental or archive backup. The Linux dump program, which I'll discuss in the section entitled "Local Backup and Restore Software for Linux," assigns different numbers to different backup "levels" and keeps track of which levels of backups have been done based on the name of the device on which the filesystem is located.

A final issue to consider when doing backups and restoring files is when to do them, and what privileges are required. It's generally fastest to do backups during off-peak hours when system usage is generally at a minimum, so that the backups can complete as quickly as possible, and when people are less likely to be modifying the files that you're backing up. In an enterprise environment, this may mean that you'll want to have a graveyard shift of operators. In this case, you'll need to think about how to make sure that operators have the right set of privileges. Being able to back up user files that may be heavily protected or using a backup system that accesses the filesystem at the filesystem level generally requires root privileges. Many people use programs such as sudo (which is already our friend on Ubuntu systems) or set s-bits on privileged binaries such as backup and restore programs so that they don't have to give the administrative password to the operators or part-time staff that generally do backups at off-peak hours. See the section of Chapter 27, "Managing Users, Groups, and Authentication," entitled "Customizing the sudo Command" for some suggestions on how to assign different privileges to different groups of individuals on your Ubuntu system.

Verifying and Testing Backups

Just doing backups isn't a guarantee that you're safe from problems, unless you're also sure that the backups you're making are readable and that files can easily be restored from them. Although it's less common today, there's always the chance that the heads in a tape drive may be out of alignment. This means either that you can only read the tapes back in on the same tape drive that you wrote them on, or that they can't be read at all. You should always verify that you can read and restore files from backups using another device than the one on which they were made. You don't have to check every tape every day, but random spot checks are important for peace of mind and for job security. Similarly, tapes can just stretch or wear out from use — be prepared to replace the media used to do various types of incremental backups after some set amount of time. Nobody appreciates WORN backup media — "write once, read never" — even though its storage capacity is apparently infinite.

One of the problems inherent to backups is that every type of computer media has a shelf life of some period of time, depending on the type of media, the environment in which it is stored, and how lucky you are. No backup media has infinite shelf life. For example, backup tapes can last for years, but they can also be unreadable after a much shorter period of time. Long-lived media such as write-once CD-Rs and DVD-Rs are attractive because of their supposed longevity, but they have other problems, as mentioned earlier in the sidebar entitled "A Few Words about Backup Media." Media such as these may only be suited for certain types of backups, depending on whether your backup software writes to the backup device as a filesystem or as a raw storage device. Also, no one yet knows exactly how long those types of media will last, but they certainly take up less room than almost any kind of tape or stack of hard drives. In addition to spot-checking the backup media that you are currently using, you should always make a point to spot-check old archives every few years to make sure that they're still useful.

Tip

Aside from the fact that backups can be subject to the vagaries of the device on which they're written, having those devices available when you need to restore backups is an important point to consider. It's a well-known nerd fact that many government and military sites have huge collections of backup data written on devices that don't exist anymore, such as super-low-speed tape drives and 1-inch or 7-track tapes. Even if the devices exist, the data is often not recoverable, because it's written in some ancient, twisted backup format, word size, and so on. When you retire a computer system, deciding if you'll ever need to restore any of its archive data is an easily overlooked issue. If you're lucky, you'll be able to read in the old archives on your new system and write them back out to some newer backup media by using some newer backup format. If you're not, you've just acquired a huge number of large, awkward paperweights that will remind you of this issue forever. ∎

Deciding What to Back Up

Aside from cost-saving issues like using higher-density media such as CD-ROMs for archive purposes, another way to reduce the number of old backups that you have to keep around, as well as minimize the time it takes to do them, is to treat different filesystems differently when you're backing them up. For example, system software changes very infrequently, so you may only want to back up the partitions holding your operating system when you do an archive. Similarly, even locally developed application software changes relatively infrequently, so you may only want to back that up weekly. I can count on one hand, with one finger, the number of times that I've needed to restore an old version of an application. On the other hand, you may not be so lucky.

Keeping backups of your operating system and its default applications is important, and is certainly critical to restoring or rebuilding an entire system should you ever need to do so (which is known in backup circles as a *bare-metal restore*). In terms of backups (and thanks to the excellence of the package management software available for Ubuntu systems), you can usually just preserve your original installation media (or even re-retrieve it over the net) if it is ever necessary to completely restore the system software for your Ubuntu system. However, if your systems run a custom kernel or use special loadable kernel modules, you should always make sure that you have a backup of your current configuration and all of the configuration files in directories such as /etc that describe the state of your system. You'll be glad you did if the disk on which your finely tuned and heavily tweaked version of an operating system bursts into flames late one night.

The issues in the first few sections of this chapter often give system administrators and system managers migraines. Losing critical data is just as painful if you're only supporting yourself. Thinking about, designing, and implementing reasonable backup policies, schedules, and disaster recovery plans is an important task no matter how many people will be affected by a problem. Backups are like insurance policies—you hope that you never need to use them, but if you do, they had better be available.

Backup Software for Linux

Many backup utilities are available for Ubuntu systems. Most of these are traditional command-line utilities that can either create archive files or write to your backup media of choice in various formats, but some interesting open source graphical solutions are also beginning to appear.

The next few sections discuss the most common open source utilities that are used to do backups on Linux systems, grouping them into sections based on whether they create local backup files or are inherently network-aware. As discussed in the previous section, off-site storage of backups is an important requirement of a good backup strategy. In today's networked environments, off-site storage can be achieved in two basic ways: either by writing to local backup media and then physically transporting that media to another location, or by using a network-aware backup mechanism to store backups on systems that are physically located elsewhere.

Commercial Backup Solutions for Linux

Commercial application vendors have also been moving into the Linux backup space, because of the popularity of Linux in server environments. In my opinion, commercial backup solutions for Linux are unnecessary in the home computing environment, but are well worth considering if you are using Ubuntu in a multi-system enterprise or academic computing environment. Before you scoff at using commercial software for backups on a free, open source operating system, consider just how critical backups are to the computers that you maintain. This book doesn't cover commercial backup solutions, but you may want to investigate the following vendors if you need or want a commercial, supported backup solution:

- **Arkeia**: Arkeia's Network Backup and Smart Backup applications are well-known cross-platform packages that also support backing up Microsoft Windows systems and have been bundled with a variety of commercial Linux distributions such as Red Hat, SUSE, and Mandrake. For more information, see `www.knox-software.com`.

- **Lone Star**: Lone Star's LONE-TAR software has been providing backup solutions for UNIX and Linux systems for more than a decade. They also offer an X Window System interface, LTX, for LONE-TAR. For more information, see `www.cactus.com`.

- **Microlite**: Microlite's BackupEDGE and RecoverEDGE software is a nice high-performance package that supports local and remote backups and provides some interesting bare-metal restore capabilities. For more information, see `www.microlite.com`.

- **Storix**: Storix's System Backup Administrator is a graphical tool for Linux (and AIX) backups that also supports Microsoft Windows backups via SMB network access and features some interesting bare-metal restore capabilities for Linux systems. For more information, see `www.storix.com`.

- **Symantec/Veritas**: Veritas's Backup Exec software, now owned by Symantec, is a well-known backup solution for Microsoft Windows systems that is also supposedly available for Linux. For more information, see `www.symantec.com/enterprise/veritas`.

- **TOLIS Group**: The BRU Backup and Restore suite is a well-known, and well-respected, client/server backup solution that provides backup solutions across Linux, UNIX, Mac OS X, and Microsoft Windows platforms, and has recently ventured into the virtualization space through a partnership with Parallels. For more information, see `www.tolisgroup.com`.

None of these vendors explicitly states that they support Ubuntu, but they all advertise Linux support, and I'm sure that they'd at least be happy to discuss Ubuntu support with you.

Local Backup and Restore Software for Linux

The roots of the core set of Linux utilities lie in UNIX, so it's not surprising that versions of all of the classic UNIX backup utilities are available with all Linux distributions. Some of them are starting to show their age, but these utilities have been used for years and guarantee the portability of your backups from any Linux system to any other.

The classic Linux/UNIX backup utilities available in the Ubuntu distributions are the following, in alphabetical order:

- cpio: The cpio utility (copy input to output) was designed for doing backups, taking a list of the files to be archived from standard input, and writing the archive to standard output or to a backup device using shell re-direction. The cpio utility can be used with filesystems of any type because it works at the filesystem level and, therefore, has no built-in understanding of filesystem data structures.

- dd: The original UNIX backup utility is called dd, which stands for *dump device*, and it does exactly that, reading data from one device and writing it to another. The dd utility doesn't know anything about filesystems, dump levels, or previous runs of the program — it's simply reading data from one source and writing to another, although you can manipulate the data in between the two to do popular party tricks like converting ASCII to EBCDIC. The dd utility copies the complete contents of a device, such as a disk partition to a tape drive, for backup purposes.

  It wasn't really designed to do backups, although there are situations in which dd is the perfect tool: For example, dd is the tool for you if you want to copy one partition to another when a disk is failing, make on-disk copies of the partitions on a standard boot disk for easy cloning, or use an application that reads and writes directly to and from raw disk partitions that you can only backup and restore as all or nothing. Because dd reads directly from devices and, therefore, doesn't recognize the concept of a filesystem, individual file restores are impossible from a partition archive created with dd without restoring the entire partition and selecting the files that you want.

- dump/restore: The dump and restore utilities were designed as a pair of utilities for backup purposes and have existed for UNIX since version 6. Although cpio and tar combine the ability to write archives with the ability to extract files and directories from them and dd can't extract anything except an entire backup, the dump program only creates backups, and the restore program only extracts files and directories from them. Both dump and restore work at the filesystem data structure level and, therefore, can only be used to back up and restore ext2 and ext3 filesystems (at the moment, at least). However, the dump/restore programs can accurately backup and restore any type of file that is found in ext2 and ext3 filesystems, including device-special files and sparse files (without exploding their contents and removing their *sparseness*). The dump/restore utilities can only be used to back up entire filesystems, although they have built-in support for doing incremental backups, keeping a record of which filesystems have been backed up and which level of backups has been performed for those filesystems.

All of this information is tracked in an easily understood text file named /etc/dumpdates. Archives created with the dump utility can automatically span multiple tapes or other media if the devices support end-of-media detection, but can also span cartridge or magnetic tape media by using command-line options that tell dump the length or capacity of the tape. The most entertaining feature of the restore program is the ability to execute it in interactive mode, in which case it reads the information from the tape necessary to create a virtual directory hierarchy for the archived filesystem that it contains. You can then use standard commands such as cd to explore the list of the files on the tape and mark specific files and directories to be restored.

Note

The dump/restore programs are not installed as part of a default Ubuntu distribution but can easily be installed using apt-get (both are located in the dump package). ■

- tar: Probably the most widely used and well-known UNIX backup utility, the tar command (tape archiver) takes a list of files and/or directories to be backed up and archives those files to an output device or to standard output. The GNU version of tar, once known as gtar to differentiate it from the version of tar that came with the UNIX operating system (back when anyone cared), is yet another amazing piece of work from the Free Software Foundation.

  GNU tar provides capabilities far and above the abilities of classic UNIX tar, including the built-in ability to read from compressed tar archives created with gzip, support for incremental backups, support for multivolume archives, and much more. The tar program is filesystem-independent and accesses files and directories without needing to know their low-level data structures. The tar program is far and away the most popular free archiving utility available for Linux and is used to archive almost every free software package. The DEB and RPM archive formats actually contain tar files that are compressed using the gzip utility, and files with the extension .tgz or .tar.gz (also gzipped tar files) are commonly used to distribute most Linux source code.

The utilities discussed in this section all create local archive files or write their archives to local storage devices. Of course, when you're using a network-aware operating system such as Ubuntu Linux, the term *local storage devices* actually includes anything that appears to be local to your system, which therefore includes network storage that is mounted on a directory of the system that you are using. Common examples of this are NFS-mounted directories or directories that are mounted on your Linux system via Samba. Directories that are mounted over the network enable you to integrate remote storage with local backup commands in ways such as the following:

- Back up remote directories to local archives by mounting the remote directories on your local system and including them in the backups that you do.
- Write your backup files to remote storage by creating your backup archives in remote directories that are mounted on your system as local directories.

Both of these scenarios provide ways of satisfying the basic off-site requirement of backups through the use of network-mounted directories.

Network-Oriented Backup Software for Linux

The utilities discussed in the previous section all create local archive files or write their archives to local storage devices (or storage that appears to be local). The backup utilities discussed in this section are slightly different — they are inherently network-aware and therefore enable you to create and manage local backups of the contents of remote systems.

The following are some of the more commonly used, network-aware backup applications that are available for Ubuntu systems. There are many more, which you can find by using your package manager's search capability to search for the term *backup*. The following are my personal favorites:

- **Amanda:** The Advanced Maryland Automated Network Disk Archiver is an open source distributed backup system that was originally developed for UNIX systems at the University of Maryland in the early 1990s. Amanda makes it quite easy to back up any number of client workstations to a central backup server, supports Windows Microsoft backups via Samba, and provides a complete backup management system for your Ubuntu system. Amanda supports multiple sets of backups with distinct configurations, supports disk and tape backups, tracks backup levels and dates on its client systems, produces detailed reports that are automatically delivered via e-mail, and keeps extensive logs that make it easy to diagnose and correct the reason(s) behind most problems. Communication between Amanda clients and servers is encrypted to heighten security. Amanda is not installed by default on Ubuntu systems but is available in the Ubuntu repositories and can easily be installed using your favorite package management software. Amanda consists of two packages, `amanda-server` and `amanda-client`. Amanda's home web site is at `www.amanda.org`.

- **BackupPC:** BackupPC is a nice backup system that provides a Web-based interface that enables you to back up remote systems using `smbclient`, `tar`, or `rsync`. Figure 28-1 shows the web page of a sample BackupPC server. BackupPC creates backups of your remote systems that are stored and managed on your BackupPC server, and also enables authorized users to restore their own files from these archives, removing the number one source of migraines for system administrators. Configuration data for each client system is stored on the BackupPC server, which enables you to back up different types of systems using different commands or protocols, and to easily identify which remote directories or filesystems you want to back up. One especially nice feature of BackupPC is that it uses standard Linux commands on the server to create backups and, therefore, doesn't require the installation of any software on client systems, although some client-side configuration may be necessary for certain backup commands.

  BackupPC's home page is located at `http://backuppc.sourceforge.net`. See "Installing and Using BackupPC," later in this chapter for more information about installing, setting up, and using BackupPC.

FIGURE 28-1

A BackupPC server's home page

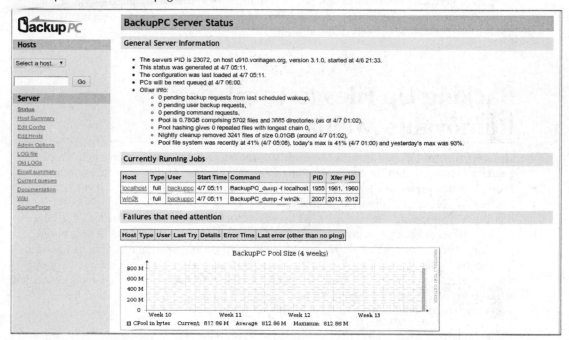

Note

BackupPC works fine in any modern graphical Web browser, including FireFox, Konqueror, Opera, Sea Monkey, Mac OS X's Safari, and even Microsoft's Internet Explorer. ∎

- **Bacula:** Bacula is an extremely powerful set of programs that provides a scalable network backup and restore system that supports Linux, UNIX, and Microsoft Windows systems. Its power and flexibility easily match that of Amanda, but it is more flexible in terms of how and where backups are stored. Bacula is not installed by default on Ubuntu systems, but it is available in the Ubuntu repositories and can easily be installed using Synaptic, apt-get, or aptitude. Bacula is quite powerful, but can be complex—if you're interested in exploring Bacula, you may want to start by installing the bacula-doc package and reading its documentation to determine if it is right for your environment. Bacula's home page is www.bacula.org.

- **rsync:** rsync (remote sync) is a command-line file and directory synchronization program that makes it easy to copy files and directories from one host to another. When both a local and remote copy of a file or directory hierarchy exist, rsync is able to leverage built-in features that help reduce the amount of data that needs to be transmitted to ensure that the local and remote copies of those files and directories are identical. The remote-update protocol used by the rsync utility enables rsync to transfer only the differences between two sets of files and directories. The rsync program is automatically installed as part of a default Ubuntu installation, but requires some configuration on the remote systems that you want to copy to your local host.

Backing Up Files to Local, Removable Media

The section of this chapter entitled "Backups 101" introduced the basic concepts of backups, many of which may seem impractical for home use. Whether or not they are really impractical depends on the problems that you want to be able to solve using your backups. If you're mostly interested in protecting yourself against disk failures or the accidental deletion of critical files that you're working on, you may not need to worry about doing archive and incremental backups — doing spot backups of important files and directories to a CD-R or DVD-R may suffice. Similarly, if you don't need to be able to restore any file from any point in time, but just need to have recent copies of your files, then spot backups of the directories that you want to back up may be sufficient, done with whatever frequency you're comfortable with. If you're not concerned about losing all of your data if your house or apartment is destroyed, then you don't have to worry about things like storing backups off-site.

The bottom line is that I can't tell you what you're comfortable with — that's up to you, and defines your backup strategy. The next few sections highlight how you can use some of the utilities mentioned earlier in this chapter (and even the standard Linux cp command) to create backup copies of important files.

Archiving and Restoring Files Using tar

The tar program is one of the oldest and most classic Linux/UNIX utilities. Although it can write to a backup device, such as a tape drive, the tar command is most commonly used to create archive files, such as source code, that can easily be shared with others. Archive files created using the tar command typically have the .tar file extension. The GNU tar command, which is the version of tar found on Ubuntu and all other Linux systems, provides built-in compression capabilities, being able to automatically compress tar archives on the fly. Compressed tar archives typically have either the file extension .tgz, indicating that they are compressed (and can be uncompressed) using the gzip application, or the file extension .tar.bz2, indicating that they are compressed (and can be uncompressed) using the bzip2 application. Archive files produced using the tar utility are typically referred to as *tarballs*.

Tip

For home use, the most popular backup method is simply dragging and dropping directories to CD-R or DVD-R media to create spot backups of those directories. The second most popular way of backing up your system is to use hard drives that you can attach to your system via USB or FireWire ports. On the plus side, unless you're using a really small removable hard drive, this gives you a larger pool of available storage for backups than a CD or DVD, and enables you to either store more backups of important files and directories or create a single copy of each important directory on removable storage, which you can then just update each time you do backups. On the minus side, a removable hard drive is much more expensive than CD-R or DVD-R disks and is more of a pain to store off-site and retrieve each time you do backups. ∎

Note

Because of its age, you have to be kind when passing arguments to the `tar` command, because in some cases they must be specified in a particular order. ∎

Creating an archive file using `tar` is easy. For example, to create a tarball called `home_dir_backup.tgz` that contains all of the directories in `/home`, you could use commands like the following:

```
$ cd /home
$ sudo tar czvf /tmp/home_dir_backup.tgz *
```

Note

Note that you want to write the backup file somewhere other than the directory that you are backing up. Creating a backup file in the directory that you're working in would cause the `tar` command to back up the file that it was creating, which would both not work correctly and waste tremendous amounts of space. ∎

The `tar` options in the preceding command have the following meanings:

- c: Create a new archive file. If a file by the specified name already exists, it will be over-written, and its original contents will be lost.

- z: Compress the archive file using the same techniques used by the `gzip` application.

- v: Be verbose, displaying the name of every file added to the archive file as it is added.

- f: Write the output of the `tar` command to the file whose name appears as the next argument on the command line. In this example, the output of the `tar` command would be written to the file `/tmp/home_dir_backup.tgz`.

After a significant amount of output, the file `/tmp/home_dir_backup.tgz` will be created, containing a complete recursive copy of all files and directories under `/home`. You can then copy this file to backup media such as a CD or DVD, or to a removable hard drive.

After you've created a tarball of a given set of directories, you can easily create another tarball that only contains files and directories that have changed since a specific date (such as the date on which the first tarball was created), using commands like the following:

```
$ cd /home
$ sudo tar czvf /tmp/home_dir_backup.tgz * --newer "2006-06-23"
```

This command produces extremely verbose output, even if you drop the v option, which is puzzling at first. This is an artifact of the format used in tar files. Even when used with the --newer option, the tar file header must contain the complete directory structure in which it is looking for files newer than the specified date. This is necessary so that the tar command can create extracted files in the right directory location. In other words, if you use the tar command to extract the entire contents of a tarball created using the --newer option, it will create an empty directory hierarchy that only contains files that are newer than the date that was specified when the tarball was created.

Creating tarballs isn't much fun without being able to retrieve files from them. You can extract various things from a tarball:

- Its entire contents. For example, the following command would extract the entire contents of the tarball home_dir_backup.tgz, creating the necessary directory structure under the directory in which you executed the command:

  ```
  $ sudo tar zxvf home_dir_backup.tgz
  ```

- One or more directories, which recursively extracts the complete contents of those directories. For example, the following command would extract the directory Ubuntu_Bible, and all the subdirectories and files that it contains, from the tarball home_dir_backup.tgz, creating the necessary directory structure under the directory in which you executed the command:

  ```
  $ sudo tar zxvf home_dir_backup.tgz Ubuntu_Bible
  ```

- One or more specific files, which extracts only those files but creates all of the directories necessary to extract those files in their original location. For example, the following command would create the directory Ubuntu_Bible and extract the file chap22.txt from the tarball home_dir_backup.tgz, creating the Ubuntu_Bible directory under the directory in which you executed the command:

  ```
  $ sudo tar zxvf home_dir_backup.tgz Ubuntu_Bible/chap22.txt
  ```

For more detailed information on the tar command, see its online reference information (man tar). As one of the oldest Linux/UNIX commands, it has accumulated a huge number of command-line options over the years, many of which you will probably never use. However, command-line options are like bullets — you can never have too many.

Making an Up-to-Date Copy of a Local Directory Using cp

If you're only backing up a few directories and are primarily concerned with keeping copies of the files that you are actively working on, it's often simplest to just keep copies of those directories on removable media. The traditional Linux/UNIX cp command provides options that make it easy to create a copy of a specified directory and then to subsequently update only files that have been updated or that do not already exist in the copy. For example, to back up all of the directories in /home to a removable drive mounted at /media/LACIE (LACIE is a popular manufacturer of prepackaged USB hard drives), you could use a command like the following:

```
$ sudo cp -dpRuvx /home /media/LACIE/home
```

The cp options in this command have the following meanings:

- d: Don't dereference symbolic links, that is, copy them as symbolic links instead of copying what they point to.
- p: Preserve modes and ownership of the original files in the copies.
- R: Copy the specified directory recursively.
- u: Copy files only if the original file is newer than an existing copy or if no copy exists.
- v: Display information about each file that is copied. (You may not want to use this option, but it's interesting, at least the first few times you do this.)
- x: Don't follow mountpoints to other filesystems.

After running this command, you will have a copy of every directory under /home on your system in the directory /media/LACIE/home. You can then detach your removable drive and store it somewhere safe (preferably off-site). Any time that you want to update your backup, retrieve the drive and update this copy at any time by simply rerunning this command.

Making an Up-to-Date Copy of a Remote Directory Using rsync

As mentioned earlier, rsync is a commonly used command-line utility that enables you to push or pull files to or from remote systems. The rsync program must be configured on the remote systems before you can push or pull files or directories to or from those systems.

To use rsync on an Ubuntu system, you must first enable it so that the system starts rsync as a background process, and then also modify the rsync configuration file to add entries for specific directories that you want to be able to read from and write to remotely. To enable rsync, edit the file /etc/defaults/rsync using your favorite text editor and a command like the following:

```
$ sudo emacs /etc/default/rsync
```

In the line that begins with RSYNC_ENABLE, change false to true, and then save the updated file. Next, create the rsync configuration file before actually starting the rsync daemon.

Note

Most Linux systems use an Internet service manager such as inetd or xinetd to manage incoming requests for on-demand services such as ftp, tftp, rsync, and vnc. These Internet service managers automatically start the appropriate daemon when an incoming request is received. Although these Internet service managers are available in the Ubuntu repositories, they are not installed by default. On Ubuntu systems, a specific system startup file that starts rsync in daemon mode is provided as /etc/init.d/rsync. If you subsequently install xinetd and want to use it to manage rsync requests, you will want to disable this file and create the file /etc/xinetd.d/rsync to make sure that the rsync service is enabled on your system. ■

The /etc/defaults/rsync file just determines whether rsync is enabled or not. The actual configuration information for rsync itself is stored in the file /etc/rsyncd.conf, which does not exist by default on an Ubuntu system. To create this file, use your favorite text editor and a command like the following:

```
$ sudo emacs /etc/rsyncd.conf
```

A minimal rsync configuration file that contains a definition remotely synchronizing the directories under /home on your system would look something like the following:

```
uid = root
transfer logging = true
log format = %h %o %f %l %b
log file = /var/log/rsyncd.log
hosts allow = 192.168.6.255/3

[homes]
    path = /home
    comment = Home Directories
    auth users = wvh
    secrets file = /etc/rsyncd.secrets
```

The first section of this file sets parameters for how the rsync daemon runs. In order, the rsync daemon runs as root (uid), logs all transfers (transfer logging), uses a specific log file format (log format) and log file (log file), and allows access from any host whose IP address is on the 192.168.6.*x* subnet (hosts allow). The second section of this file identifies a synchronizable entity known as home that maps to the directory /home on that system. Synchronization to or from this directory is done as the user wvh, whose password must be supplied in the file /etc/rsyncd.secrets.

After saving this file, use the sudo command and your favorite text editor to create the file /etc/rsyncd.secrets, with a command like the following:

```
$ sudo emacs /etc/rsyncd.secrets
```

This file should contain an entry for each auth users entry in the /etc/rsync.conf file, in this case, wvh. Each entry in this file contains the name of a user, a colon, and the plaintext password for that user, as in the following example:

```
wvh:hellothere
```

Next, save this file and make sure that it is readable only by the root user on your system using a command like the following:

```
$ sudo chmod 600 /etc/rsyncd.secrets
```

You can now start the rsync daemon using the following command:

```
$ sudo /etc/init.d/rsync restart
```

You can now create a local copy of the /home directory on your system using a command like the following, where system-name-or-addr is the name or IP address of the system on which you just configured the rsync daemon:

```
$ rsync -Havz system-name-or-addr::homes /media/LACIE/home
```

The arguments to the rsync command in this example have the following meaning:

- H: Preserve hard links if these exist in any directories that are being copied.
- a: Use archive mode, which preserves ownership, symbolic links, device files, and so on, and is essentially a shortcut that saves you specifying several other options.
- v: Be verbose, identifying each file that is copied or considered for copying. (You may not want to use this option, but it's interesting, at least the first few times you run rsync.)
- z: Use compression when transferring files, which improves throughput.

If you have problems using rsync, you should check the /var/log/rsyncd.log file (on the system that you are trying to retrieve files from) for error messages and hints for resolving them. If you are not using the verbose option on the host where you are retrieving these files, you may want to use it to see if you can identify (and resolve) any other errors that the host that is trying to retrieve files is reporting.

Note
The rsync configuration file created in this section is just a minimal example, and is not particularly secure. For details about all of the options available in an rsync configuration file and information about making rsync more secure, see the man page for the rsyncd.conf file (man rsyncd.conf). ■

Installing and Using BackupPC

This section explains how to install, configure, and use the BackupPC package to back up a variety of hosts on your local network to a central Ubuntu server. Introduced earlier in this chapter, BackupPC is a great application that is both easy to use for a system administrator and empowering for any authorized user. Any authorized user can initiate backups of the machines that they have admin rights to and can also restore files from existing backups of those machines, all using a convenient Web interface.

If you have more than one machine on your home network, or if you're working in a multi-machine enterprise or academic environment, the BackupPC software is well worth a look. Its Web-based interface is easy to set up and use; various types of supported backups are easy to configure, initiate, and monitor; it can back up your Linux, UNIX, Windows, and Mac OS X systems; and the fact that it doesn't require that you install any special software on the systems that you want to back up makes BackupPC a great package.

BackupPC supports four different backup mechanisms (known in the BackupPC documentation as *backup transports*) to enable you to back up different types of systems. These are the following:

- rsync: Backup and restore via rsync via rsh or ssh. This is a good choice for backing up Linux, UNIX, or Mac OS X systems, and you can also use it to back up Microsoft Windows systems that support rsync, such as those running the Cygwin Linux emulation environment.

- rsyncd: Backup and restore via the rsync daemon on the client system. This is the best choice for Linux, UNIX, and Mac OS X systems that are running an rsync daemon. You can also use this mechanism to back up Microsoft Windows systems that support rsyncd, such as those running the Cygwin Linux emulation environment.

- smb: Backup and restore using the smbclient and the SMB protocol on the backuppc server. This is the best (and easiest) choice to use when backing up Microsoft Windows systems using backuppc, and you can also use it to back up Mac OS X systems or Linux and UNIX systems that are running a Samba server.

- tar: Backup and restore via tar, tar over ssh, rsh, or nfs. This is an option for Linux, UNIX, and Mac OS X systems. You can also use this mechanism to back up Microsoft Windows systems that support tar, ssh, rsh, and/or nfs, such as those running the Cygwin Linux emulation environment.

A default backup transport value for all backups is set in the primary BackupPC configuration file, /etc/backuppc/config.pl. The specific mechanism used to back up any particular host can be identified in that host's configuration file, as discussed later in the sections entitled "Defining a Backup Using rsyncd" and "Defining a Backup Using SMB."

Note

Although backuppc does a great job of backing up systems running Microsoft Windows and Mac OS X, you should be aware of a few issues. First, backuppc is not suitable for backing up Windows systems so that you can do a bare-metal restore. backuppc uses the smbclient application on your Ubuntu system to back up Windows disks, so it doesn't back up Windows ACLs and can't open files that are locked by a Windows client that is currently running (such as, most commonly, things like Outlook mailboxes). Similarly, backuppc doesn't preserve Mac OS file attributes. See http://backuppc.sourceforge.net/faq/limitations.html for a list of current limitations in using backuppc. It's a surprisingly short document! ∎

For additional information about BackupPC, you can join various mailing lists that are available through the SourceForge BackupPC site. These lists are the following:

- **backuppc-announce:** A low-traffic list where announcements of new versions are posted (http://lists.sourceforge.net/lists/listinfo/backuppc-announce)
- **backuppc-devel:** The mailing list for BackupPC developers (http://lists .sourceforge.net/lists/listinfo/backuppc-devel)
- **backuppc-users:** The standard mailing list where you can ask and answer questions about using BackupPC (http://lists.sourceforge.net/lists/listinfo/ backuppc-users)

Installing and Configuring BackupPC

Special-purpose backup solutions such as BackupPC aren't installed as part of a default Ubuntu installation because they're probably overkill for most people. However, the various package management tools provided on Ubuntu systems make it easy to install BackupPC (located in the backuppc package) and the other software packages that it requires.

Because BackupPC uses a Web-based interface, it requires that you have installed (and config-ured) a Web server on your system, preferably Apache2. Similarly, because BackupPC can send e-mail notifications for various backup-related events, it requires a Mail Transfer Agent (MTA). If one is not already installed on your system, installing the backuppc package will install exim, which isn't my personal choice as far as MTAs go. If you're going to install BackupPC, I'd suggest installing (and configuring) Postfix first, as described in Chapter 30, "Setting Up a Mail Server." After doing so, BackupPC will detect that an MTA is installed on your system and will no longer try to install exim to satisfy dependencies.

Once the backuppc package has been installed on your system, your package management soft-ware will run its configuration script. During this phase, the various package managers ask which Web server configuration you're using so that they can configure backuppc appropriately, and automatically run a script that sets up the initial account that you will use to access backuppc via that Web server. This process appears as a dialog like the one shown in Figure 28-2, which tells you the initial password for the Web-based BackupPC interface.

This dialog is, of course, different for each package management tool — Figure 28-2 shows the screen that you would see if installing the backuppc package using the aptitude package man-agement tool. See Chapter 19, "Adding, Removing, and Updating Software," for more information about the various package management utilities that are available for Ubuntu systems.

Once you see a dialog like the one shown in Figure 28-2, write down the password for the backuppc interface and press Return or click Forward to proceed. Unless you're good at remem-bering passwords like *b3j2Bynf*, I'd suggest immediately changing the default password to one of your standard administrative passwords, which you can do via a command like the following (which the dialog in Figure 28-2 also explains):

```
sudo htpasswd /etc/backuppc/htpasswd backuppc
```

FIGURE 28-2

The initial password for the backuppc package

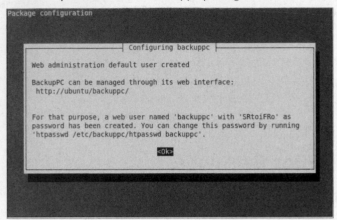

```
Package configuration
                    ┤ Configuring backuppc ├
   Web administration default user created

   BackupPC can be managed through its web interface:
    http://ubuntu/backuppc/


   For that purpose, a web user named 'backuppc' with 'SRtoiFRo' as
   password has been created. You can change this password by running
   'htpasswd /etc/backuppc/htpasswd backuppc'.

                          <Ok>
```

Once the remainder of the installation and configuration process completes, you're almost ready to back up the system you're using and the other systems on your network. While installing backuppc is supposed to integrate it with your Web server, that doesn't actually seem to be the case. To integrate backuppc with your Apache Web server, do the following:

1. Copy the file /etc/backuppc/backuppc.conf to the directory /etc/apache2/ sites-available giving it the name backuppc.

2. Create a symbolic link from the file /etc/apache2/sites-available/backuppc .conf to a file in the directory /etc/apache2/sites-enabled. I usually name this symbolic link backuppc so that it's clear exactly what site/application is enabled. You can do this by executing the following commands:

   ```
   cd /etc/apache2/sites-enabled
   sudo ln -s ../sites-available/backuppc.conf backuppc
   ```

3. Restart Apache using a command like the following:

   ```
   sudo /etc/init.d/apache2 reload
   ```

You should now be able to connect to the BackupPC Web interface via the /backuppc URL relative to your Web server as the user backuppc with whatever your current BackupPC password is (in other words, something like www.vonhagen.org/backuppc). This will display a screen like the one shown in Figure 28-1.

On Ubuntu systems, BackupPC stores its configuration information in two locations: General `backuppc` configuration information and passwords are stored in files in the directory `/etc/backuppc`. Backup files themselves and host-specific backup configuration information are stored in subdirectories of `/var/lib/backuppc`.

Tip

Backups of a single system take a significant amount of space, which is only compounded when you begin to back up other hosts to a central backup server. If you didn't specify using logical volumes when you installed your Ubuntu system, you may want to add a new disk to your system before starting to use BackupPC and format that disk as a logical volume. You can then copy the default contents of `/var/lib/backuppc` to the new disk (preserving file permissions and ownership) and mount that disk on the directory `/var/lib/backuppc` on the system that you are using for backups. When you need more space to store backups in the future, this will enable you to add other disks to your system and add their space to the logical volume used to store backups. BackupPC also provides an archive capability that enables you to migrate old backups to other hosts for archival purposes, freeing up disk space on your primary backup server. Although not discussed in this book, setting up archive hosts is discussed in the BackupPC documentation — which is great, by the way! ■

Identifying Hosts to Back Up

Each host that you want to back up must be identified in the file `/etc/backuppc/hosts`. Like all BackupPC configuration files, this file is easy to update. Any characters in any lines in this file that follow a hash mark are comments that help explain the meaning of the various fields used in the file. A minimal `backuppc` configuration file looks like the following:

```
host            dhcp    user            moreUsers
localhost       0       backuppc
```

The first non-comment line in `/etc/backuppc/hosts` defines the names of the various fields in each line and should therefore not be modified. (This is the line beginning with the word `host` in the example.) All other lines represent entries for hosts that will be backed up. The first actual host entry, for `localhost`, is a special entry used for backing up system configuration information on the `backuppc` server and should not be changed.

The fields in each entry that define a host have the following meanings:

- The first field identifies a particular machine, by hostname, IP address, or NetBios name.

- The second field should be set to 0 for any host whose name can be determined by DNS, the local hosts file, or an nmblookup broadcast. This field can be set to 1 to identify systems whose names must be discovered by probing a range of DHCP addresses, as is the case in some environments where DHCP and WINS are not fully integrated. Setting this field to 1 requires changes in the host-specific configuration file's `$Conf{DHCPAddressRanges}` variable to define the base IP address and range of IP addresses that should be probed.

- The third field identifies the name of the person who is primarily responsible for backing up that host. This primary user will receive e-mail about the status of any backup that is attempted. I tend to leave this as the backuppc user, so that this user maintains an e-mail record of all backup attempts, but you can set this to a specific user if you wish.

- The fourth field (which is optional) consists of one or more users who also have administrative rights to initiate backups or restore files for this machine. The names of multiple users must be separated by a comma.

As an example, the hosts file on one of my backuppc servers looks like the following:

```
host            dhcp    user        moreUsers
localhost       0       backuppc
192.168.6.64    0       backuppc    wvh
64bit           0       backuppc    wvh,djf
64x2            0       backuppc    juser
win2k           0       backuppc    wvh,djf
```

Tip

The backuppc program checks the timestamp on the /etc/backuppc/hosts files each time the backuppc process wakes up, and reloads this file automatically if the file has been updated. For this reason, you should not save changes to the hosts file until you have created the host-specific configuration files, as described in the examples in the next two sections. If the backuppc process reloads the hosts file before you have created the host-specific configuration data and another authorized user initiates a backup of this system, you will either back up the wrong thing or a backup failure will occur. You can always make changes to the hosts file and leave them commented out (by putting a # as the first character on the line) until you have completed the host-specific configuration. ■

Defining a Backup Using rsyncd

The section earlier in this chapter entitled "Making an Up-to-Date Copy of a Remote Directory Using rsync" explained how to set up rsync in daemon mode on an Ubuntu system and how to define synchronization entries that can be remotely accessed via rsync. The sample rsync configuration file created in that section defined a synchronization entry called homes that would enable an authorized user to synchronize the contents of all directories under /home on a sample Ubuntu system. We'll use that same configuration file in the example in this section.

The previous section showed how to define entries in the /etc/backuppc/hosts file for the various hosts that you want to back up via backuppc. The first step in host-specific configuration is to use the sudo command to create a directory to hold host-specific configuration data, logs, and so on. Throughout this section, I'll use the sample host entry 64bit, which I defined in the section entitled "Identifying Hosts to Back Up" as an example.

The first step in host-specific configuration is to use the sudo command to create the directory /var/lib/backuppc/pc/64bit, as in the following command:

```
sudo mkdir /var/lib/backuppc/pc/64bit
```

Next, use the sudo command and your favorite text editor to create a host-specific configuration file named config.pl in that directory, using a command like the following:

```
sudo emacs /var/lib/backuppc/pc/64bit/config.pl
```

The contents of this file should be something like the following:

```
$Conf{XferMethod} = 'rsyncd';
$Conf{Compresslevel} = '3';
$Conf{RsyncShareName} = 'homes';
$Conf{RsyncdUserName} = 'wvh';
$Conf{RsyncdPasswd} = 'hellothere';
```

The first line identifies the backup mechanism used for this host as rsyncd, which overrides the default backup mechanism specified in the generic /etc/backuppc/config.pl file. The second line sets the compression level for this host's backups to level 3, which provides a good trade-off between the CPU load and time required to do compression and the amount of compression that you actually get. The last three entries in this file correspond to the synchronization entry in the sample rsyncd.conf and associated rsyncd.secrets file created in "Making an Up-to-Date Copy of a Remote Directory Using rsync" earlier in this chapter.

Tip

When using BackupPC to do automated backups, I like to create a separate authorized user to use rsync for backup purposes, so that the system logs show who actually requested a remote sync operation. To do this, you would add this user (I usually use backuppc) to the auth users entry in the remote host's /etc/rsyncd.conf file and create an appropriate username/password pair in the remote host's /etc/rsyncd.secrets file. You would then modify the host-specific backuppc configuration file to use this username and password. I didn't do this here for simplicity's sake, but doing this would provide more accurate log data on the client system. ∎

If the remote system uses an rsync binary other than the default /usr/bin/rsync or the rsync program is listening on a port other than the standard port (873), you should add correct definitions for these to the host-specific configuration file. The default settings for the associated configuration parameters are the following:

```
$Conf{RsyncdClientPort} = 873;
$Conf{RsyncClientPath} = '/usr/bin/rsync';
```

Next, change the ownership and group of the /var/lib/backuppc/pc/64bit directory to backuppc and change the protection of the configuration file /var/lib/backuppc/pc/64bit/config.pl so that it is not publicly readable (because it contains password information) using the following commands:

```
sudo chmod -Rv backuppc:backuppc /var/lib/backuppc/pc/64bit
sudo chmod 600 /var/lib/backuppc/pc/64bit/config.pl
```

The last step in creating a host-specific backup definition for backuppc is to cause the backuppc process to reread its configuration data, which you can do by explicitly reloading the configuration file, by explicitly restarting the backuppc process, or by sending the associated process a hang-up (HUP) signal. You can force backuppc to reload the configuration file by using the following command:

```
sudo /etc/init.d/backuppc reload
```

The definition for your backup host can now be selected via the BackupPC Web interface. At this point, you can follow the instructions in the section entitled "Starting Backups in BackupPC" to back up this host.

The example in this section only backs up the home directories of users on the remote machine. To recursively back up other directories, you would simply create other synchronization entities for those directories in the remote host's /etc/rsyncd.conf file and then add entries for those synchronization entities to the host-specific configuration file. For example, to back up synchronization entries named /, homes, and /boot, you would change the host-specific RsyncShareName entry to look like the following:

```
$Conf{RsyncShareName} = ['/', 'homes', '/boot'];
```

If you back up multiple filesystems or synchronization points, you may create a custom set of arguments to the rsync command in the host-specific configuration file. This enables you to add options such as --one-file-system, which causes backuppc to back up each filesystem separately, simplifying restores. You can also add options to exclude certain directories from the backups, which you will certainly want to do if you are backing up a remote system's root directory (/), as in the following examples:

```
$Conf{RsyncArgs} = [
        # original arguments here
        '--one-file-system',
        '--exclude', '/dev',
        '--exclude', '/proc',
        '--exclude', '/media',
        '--exclude', '/mnt',
        '--exclude', '/lost+found',
];
```

These settings would prevent backups of /dev, which contains device nodes and is dynamically populated at boot time on modern Linux systems; /proc, which is the mountpoint for an in-memory filesystem that contains transient data; directories such as /media and /mnt on which removable media is often temporarily mounted; and /lost+found, which is a directory used during filesystem consistency checking. You can also exclude directories from rsync backups using the BackupFilesExclude directive, as in the following example:

```
$Conf{BackupFilesExclude} = ['/dev', '/proc', '/media', '/mnt', '/lost+found'];
```

The backuppc program reads the configuration settings in /etc/backuppc/config.pl first, and then loads host-specific configuration settings, which enables the /etc/backuppc/config .pl file to provide default settings for all backups. After you have used backuppc for a while and are comfortable with various settings, you may want to consider modifying the default settings in the /etc/backuppc/config.pl file for configuration variables such as $Conf{RsyncArgs}, $Conf{BackupFilesExclude}, and $Conf{CompressLevel}, to minimize the number of entries that you have to create in each of your host-specific configuration files.

Defining a Backup Using SMB

The section of this chapter entitled "Identifying Hosts to Back Up" showed how to define entries in the /etc/backuppc/hosts file for the various hosts that you want to back up via backuppc. The first step in host-specific configuration is to use the sudo command to create a directory to hold host-specific configuration data, logs, and so on. Throughout this section, I'll use the sample host entry win2k from the sample hosts file as an example. As you might gather from its name, this is indeed a system running Microsoft Windows 2000. There's no escaping from the Borg.

The first step in host-specific configuration is to use the sudo command to create the directory /var/lib/backuppc/pc/win2k, as in the following command:

```
$ sudo mkdir /var/lib/backuppc/pc/win2k
```

Next, use the sudo command and your favorite text editor to create a host-specific configuration file named config.pl in that directory, using a command like the following:

```
$ sudo emacs /var/lib/backuppc/pc/win2k/config.pl
```

The contents of this file should be something like the following:

```
$Conf{XferMethod} = 'smb';
$Conf{CompressLevel} = '3';
$Conf{SmbShareName} = ['wvh', 'djf'];
$Conf{SmbShareUserName} = 'backuppc';
$Conf{SmbSharePasswd} = 'hellothere';
```

The first line identifies the backup mechanism used for this host as smb, which overrides the default backup mechanism specified in the generic /etc/backuppc/config.pl file. The second line sets the compression level for this host's backups to level 3, which provides a good trade-off between the CPU load and time required to do compression and the amount of compression that you actually get. The last three entries in this file define the Windows shares that you want to back up, the name of an authorized user who has access to these shares, and the password for that user.

Tip

When using backuppc to back up Microsoft Windows systems, you should create a Windows user that you will only use to do backups and then add this user to the standard Windows Backup Operators group. This prevents you from having to put your Windows administrator password in the backuppc configuration files. Even though you'll protect those files so that randoms can't read them, the fewer places where you write down a password, the better, especially one with the keys to your entire Windows kingdom. ∎

Next, change the ownership and group of the /var/lib/backuppc/pc/win2k directory to backuppc and change the protection of the configuration file /var/lib/backuppc/pc/win2k/config.pl so that it is not publicly readable (because it contains password information) using the following commands:

```
sudo chmod -Rv backuppc:backuppc /var/lib/backuppc/pc/win2k
sudo chmod 600 /var/lib/backuppc/pc/win2k/config.pl
```

The last step in creating a host-specific backup definition for backuppc is to cause the backuppc process to reread its configuration data, which you can do by explicitly reloading the configuration file, by explicitly restarting the backuppc process, or by sending the associated process a hang-up (HUP) signal. You can force BackupPC to reload its configuration file by using the following command:

```
sudo /etc/init.d/backuppc reload
```

The definition for your backup host can now be selected via the backuppc Web interface. At this point, you can follow the instructions in the section entitled "Starting Backups in backuppc" to back up this host.

The example in this section only backs up shares that correspond to the home directories of selected users on the remote machine. As mentioned earlier in this chapter, backuppc backups do not support bare-metal restores of Windows systems, and I therefore typically don't back up shares such as C$, which is a default Windows share that represents your system's boot drive. You may find it useful to do so to make sure that you have backup copies of drivers, the registry, and so on, but I find it simpler to start from scratch when reinstalling Windows. Windows systems accumulate so much crap in their filesystems over time that doing a fresh installation from your distribution media often frees up a surprising amount of space. If you have several identical systems, restoring partition images created with Norton Ghost or the Linux partimage or g4u utilities is always the fastest way to rebuild a Windows system without having to locate the drivers for every device that you will ever want to use with your rebuilt system and reinstalling all of your favorite applications.

Tip

The backuppc program reads the configuration settings in /etc/backuppc/config.pl first and then loads host-specific configuration settings, which enables the /etc/backuppc/config.pl file to provide default settings for all backups. After you have used backuppc for a while and are comfortable with various settings, you may want to consider modifying the default settings in the /etc/backuppc/config.pl file for configuration variables, such as $Conf{CompressLevel}, to minimize the number of entries that you have to create in each of your host-specific configuration files. ∎

Starting Backups in BackupPC

Thanks to BackupPC's Web orientation, starting backups, viewing the status of those backups, and checking the backup history for any host are impressively easy. To start a backup in BackupPC, connect to the BackupPC Web interface, using the URL `http://hostname/backuppc`, where `hostname` is the name of the host on which the `backuppc` server is running. A dialog appears in which you are prompted for the login and password of an authorized user. Once you enter the user/password combination for a user listed in the file `/etc/backuppc/htpasswd`, the BackupPC server's home page appears, as shown (long ago) in Figure 28-1. Once this screen appears, click the "Select a host" dropdown box and select one of the hosts from the list that appears. Selecting the name of any host takes you to a summary page for that host, which provides status information, lists authorized users who can back up and restore files to this host using BackupPC, and enables you to browse existing backups for that host in order to locate and restore files, as shown in Figure 28-3.

FIGURE 28-3

A per-host page in the BackupPC Web interface

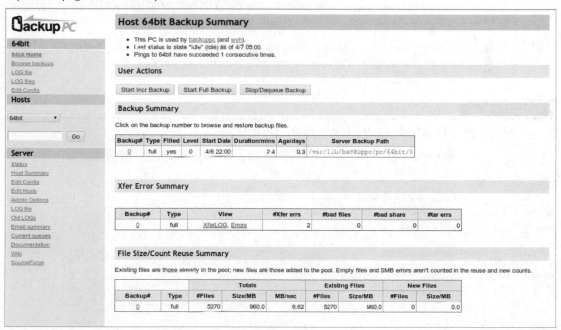

Note

Each system's home page displays the subject of the last e-mail sent to the owner of this host. E-mail is only sent occasionally, so seeing a historical problem report does not mean that the problem is still occurring. ∎

Once this page appears, you can scroll down on the page to see additional status information about available backups, any transfer errors that occurred during backups, and other tables that show the status of the pool where backup files are archived and the extent to which existing backups have been compressed to save disk space.

To start a backup, click either "Start Full Backup" to start a full (archive) backup of the system, or "Start Incr Backup" to start an incremental backup containing files that have changed since the last full backup. A confirmation page appears.

Clicking "Start Full Backup" (or "Start Incr Backup" for an incremental backup) queues the backup and displays a link that you can click to return to the main page for that host to monitor the state of the backup.

Restoring from Backups in BackupPC

Thanks to BackupPC's Web orientation and the fact that its backups are stored online on the backup server, restoring files from BackupPC backups can be done online, by any authorized user whose name is associated with that host in the /etc/backuppc/hosts file. BackupPC enables you to browse through online backups, interactively select the files and directories that you want to restore, and restore them in various ways.

To begin restoring files or directories, click the name of the full or incremental backup in which they are located. A screen like the one shown in Figure 28-4 appears.

FIGURE 28-4

Restoring files and directories in the backuppc Web interface

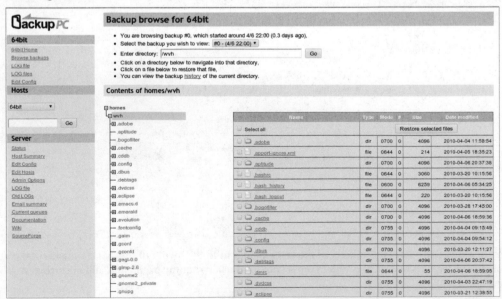

The bottom of the screen shown in Figure 28-4 displays a hierarchical listing of the files and directories that are contained in the full or incremental backup that you selected. If you selected an incremental backup, the contents of that incremental backup are overlaid on the contents of the previous full backup to give you an accurate snapshot of the contents of your system when the backup was done. You can drill down into the backup by selecting directories from the tree view at the left, or you can drill down into individual directories by selecting from the view of the current directory shown at the right of the main window.

To mark files and directories for restoration, select the checkbox beside their names. Once you have selected all of the files and directories that you want to restore, scroll to the bottom of the Restore page and click "Restore selected files." A page that enables you to specify how you want to restore those files appears, as shown in Figure 28-5.

FIGURE 28-5

Specifying the restore method in BackupPC's Web interface

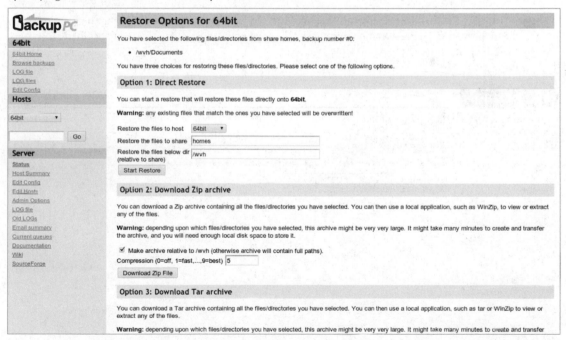

You have three options when restoring files using the BackupPC Web interface:

- **Direct restore:** Selecting this option restores files directly to the host from which they were backed up. When doing a direct restore, you have the option of restoring files in the locations from which they were originally backed up, or into a subdirectory that

BackupPC will create for you if it does not already exist. (The latter is almost always a good idea so that you don't accidentally overwrite any files that you don't actually mean to.) To select this option, enter the name of any subdirectory that you want to use (I usually specify one called `tmp`) and click "Start restore."

- **Download Zip archive:** Selecting this option restores the selected files and directories into a .zip-format archive that you can download to your desktop and manually extract the contents of. When selecting this option, you can optionally specify the compression level used in the .zip file, which can be important if you are restoring large numbers of files. To select this option, click "Download Zip file."

- **Download Tar archive:** Selecting this option restores the selected files and directories into a `tar`-format archive that you can download to your desktop and manually extract the contents of. To select this option, click "Download Tar file."

If you selected the Direct restore option, `backuppc` displays a confirmation screen like the one shown in Figure 28-6.

This lists the files and directories that you selected for restoration and confirms the location to which they will be restored, including the name of any subdirectory that you specified. To proceed, click Restore.

FIGURE 28-6

Confirming a restore directly to a remote system

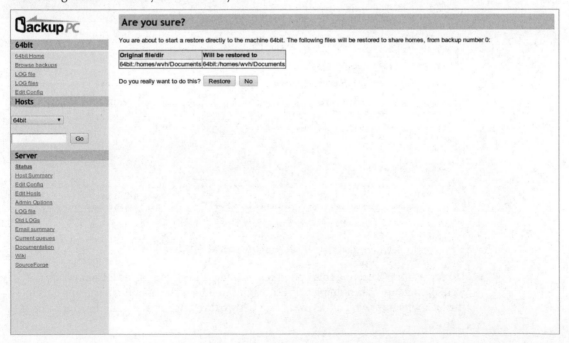

If you selected the Zip or Tar archive options, the BackupPC application displays your Web browser's standard file download dialog after the archive file has been created.

As you can see from this section (and the preceding sections), BackupPC provides a powerful, flexible interface for backing up and restoring files on many different systems to a single `backuppc` server. All you need are a few configuration files and sufficient disk space, and lost files (and the lost time that is usually associated with them) can be a thing of the past.

Backing Up and Mirroring to the Cloud with Ubuntu One

One of today's hottest buzzphrases is "cloud computing," which is the common name for a variety of ways of delivering hosted services that depend on the Internet (the "cloud"). Cloud computing encompasses a number of different hosted service models, including:

- Infrastructure-as-a-Service (IaaS), where you use, configure, and access virtual computer systems over the Internet

- Storage-as-a-Service (SaaS), where you store file and folder on remote storage over the Internet. The best known platform-independent examples of this are Amazon's Simple Storage Service (S3, `http://aws.amazon.com/s3`), DropBox (`https://www.dropbox.com`), and Canonical's Ubuntu One (`https://one.ubuntu.com`).

- Software-as-a-Service (the most common meaning of SaaS), where you access software over the Internet rather than installing it on your local computer system. The best known example of this type of software at the enterprise level is Salesforce.com. The best known free example of this at the personal (and business) levels is Google Apps (`www.google.com/apps`).

There are plenty of other cloud computing business models, but these are the basics. Frankly, I find the idea of storing my critical data on someone else's machine somewhere on the Internet and accessing that data via remote applications to be completely scary. Believe it or not, I occasionally work on documents, spreadsheets, presentations, listen to music, and watch videos in locations where I may not have access to the Internet. I'm also not sure that "my network connection was down" is going to fly as an excuse for missed homework assignments any more than "my dog ate my homework" did when I was a kid. Similarly, storing personal data on remote systems may introduce privacy issues, meaning that government or specific three-letter-acronym agencies may have the right to examine your data if they decide to investigate the company that is hosting your cloud data for any reason. You should always read the fine print regarding personal data protection before hosting data on someone else's system!

Regardless of how you feel about cloud computing (or whether you care at all), Storage-as-a-Service is inherently useful as a way of accessing your files from multiple computer systems without transferring them back and forth between each system on which you want to use them. Even if you don't want to use the cloud as a primary storage device for the files that you're working on, Storage-as-a-Service is amazingly useful as an excellent approach to doing backups. It inherently satisfies one of the most fundamental requirements for backup media, which is storing backup data off-site so that a local catastrophe doesn't wipe out both your computer and your backups. Canonical's Ubuntu One Storage-as-a-service offering is especially easy for Ubuntu users to take advantage of for two reasons:

- It offers 2GB of free storage to any Ubuntu user.
- The software that it uses is built into the Ubuntu Linux distribution.

Ubuntu One isn't purely a backup mechanism because its focus is actually on mirroring the contents of a given folder to any machine on which you use it. However, if you only use it on one or a small number of machines, it is a fine personal backup solution for critical files, as long as you remember to copy them into the Ubuntu One folder in your home directory (or simply work on them there).

Installing Ubuntu One on your Ubuntu system is as easy as using your favorite package management software to install the `ubuntuone-client-gnome` package on your desktop Ubuntu system, which also installs the underlying `ubuntuone-client` package. Installing these packages will create an Ubuntu One folder in your home directory, and will also install an Ubuntu One applet in your GNOME panel.

In order to actually use Ubuntu One, you'll have to create an account with Canonical's Launchpad site, which you can do from the page at `https://one.ubuntu.com/plans`. This page lists the available Ubuntu One plans: 2GB of free storage or 50GB of non-free storage (currently $10.00 US per month). Launchpad is Canonical's central site for interacting with Ubuntu and Canonical, reporting bugs, and so on. Once you have a Launchpad account, you can return to your computer system and use the Ubuntu One applet to connect to Ubuntu One using your Launchpad login and password. The first time you connect to Ubuntu One from any computer system that you use, you'll have to authorize access to your Ubuntu One account from that computer, which is easy to do using the Ubuntu One web page.

At this point, any files that you put in the Ubuntu One folder in your home directory will automatically be mirrored to your Ubuntu One account. To access them from any other Ubuntu system, simply right-click on the Ubuntu One applet, select Connect to authorize that machine to Ubuntu One, and the files in your Ubuntu One folder will automatically be synchronized to the computer that you're using. You can access your files via the web through `https://one.ubuntu.com/files`.

Ubuntu also provides a command-line tool called u1sync (that's u, the numeral one, and the word "sync") to automatically synchronize file and directories to directories other than your Ubuntu One directory. In order to use this tool, you must install the `ubuntuone-client-tools` package.

Once you've installed this tool, you can identify directories that you want to sync to/from your Ubuntu One account by executing the `u1sync --init DIRECTORY` command, where DIRECTORY is the name of a directory that you want to be a mirror of your Ubuntu One folder. Executing this command will display a dialog requesting that you grant access to your GNOME keyring (where GNOME stored authorization information). Click Always Allow. You can then synchronize that directory with your Ubuntu one folder, uploading files by using the `ulsync --action=upload` command, downloading them to a machine using the `ulsync --action=download` command, synchronizing using the `ulsync --action=sync` command, and so on. See the man page for the `ulsync` command for more details.

For more information about Ubuntu One, see the UbuntuOne Wiki topic at `https://wiki .ubuntu.com/UbuntuOne`.

Linux Time Machines

Apple's Mac OS X is a great computing environment — it provides an easy-to-use graphical interface on top of a powerful, UNIX-like operating system. Remind you of anything? Apple has always provided innovative, user-friendly software, and with the release of Mac OS X 10.5, aka *Leopard*, they introduced an impressively friendly and powerful backup package known as *Time Machine*. Time Machine automatically tracks changes to the files and directories on your system and backs up multiple snapshots of your system to an external (or networked) storage device. Should you accidentally delete a file or directory or simply want to consult an older version, you can explore those snapshots graphically and examine or restore a version of that data from any point in Time Machine's archives.

As the saying goes, "Imitation is the sincerest form of flattery" (Charles Colton, 1820). Not to be outdone by mere commercial software, Linux-based packages that provide equivalent functionality have begun to appear, most of which are graphical wrappers over the `rsync` utility (discussed earlier in this chapter), with various bells and whistles to make it easy to browse "snapshots," identify available versions of specific files, extract specific versions of those files, and so on. These sorts of utilities put an impressively useful face on traditional backups, and Apple deserves major kudos from conceptualizing and automating backups to the point where they are actually user-friendly. Like Mac OS X's Time Machine software, similar Linux backup mechanisms are best used with a networked resource or, in a single-system environment, an external drive. These backups can't protect against catastrophic problems, such as a fire or similar tragedy, unless you also "back up the backups" to an off-site location. If I had a nickel for every time that someone lost both their computer systems and their backups in a fire because they were stored side-by-side, I'd have a bunch of singed, smoky nickels. Don't add one to my collection.

The following are well worth a look to do snapshot-style backups on Ubuntu systems:

- **Back In Time:** Back In Time is a really nice GTK-based package that provides a nice, date-oriented snapshot browser and a single-button restore mechanism. Figure 28-7 shows the Back In Time snapshot browsing and restore interface. Back In Time is my favorite of the Linux Time Machine reimplementations, is the Time Machine-like solution that I personally use, and is the one that I'd recommend in Ubuntu-only environments. Back In Time is available as an Ubuntu DEB package through its home page at `www.le-web.org/back-in-time`.

FIGURE 28-7

Back In Time's user interface and snapshot browser

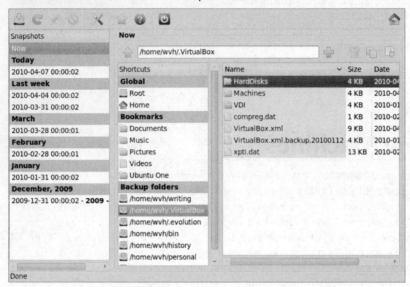

- **FlyBack:** Originally a Google Summer of Code project, FlyBack is the least active of the Linux Time Machine-like applications that I'm aware of, but works fine. FlyBack is installed from Subversion or a tarball, which is not exactly "grandfather-friendly," but it's worth a look and offers some handy features in its configuration interface, such as the ability to automatically identify networked filesystems as possible snapshot storage locations. For more information about FlyBack, see `http://code.google.com/p/flyback` and `http://flyback-project.org`.

- **TimeVault:** Under development by the folks at Canonical, TimeVault is GNOME-focused, integrated with Nautilus on Ubuntu systems, and provides a great snapshot browser and restore interface. TimeVault is available as an Ubuntu DEB package from its project page at `https://launchpad.net`. See `https://wiki.ubuntu.com/TimeVault` for more information about TimeVault.

At the time that this book was updated, none of these solutions was available through the Ubuntu repositories, but I'm sure that's just a matter of time.

Summary

This chapter discussed backups, which are the most time-consuming, boring, and valuable things that you need to do with your personal computer system. Ubuntu is knee deep in excellent software that you can use to do various types of backups, ranging from backing up to files that you can store on removable media or simply move to other systems. It then discussed doing simple backups over the network and concluded by discussing BackupPC, an excellent open source backup application for doing regular, networked backups of multiple systems to a central backup server. The chapter concluded by highlighting some Linux backup packages that provide functionality similar to that of Apple's much-loved Time Machine backup/restore software.

Chapter 29, "Setting Up a Web Server," discusses how to set up the Apache 2 Web server on your Ubuntu system. The chapter begins by providing a bit of background information about the Web and Web servers, and then explains the details of installing, configuring, and monitoring Apache 2, the latest and greatest Web server from the legendary Apache project.

Setting Up a Web Server

M ost of the significant advances in computing technology have what is known as a *killer app* (killer application)—one significantly unique, powerful, and compelling type of application that draws people to that technology in droves and makes it a part of the computing landscape for the foreseeable future. For personal computers in general, that application was the spreadsheet. For the Apple Macintosh, that application was desktop publishing. And for the Internet, that application was the World Wide Web. Sure, everyone loved e-mail, but the World Wide Web has turned the Internet into a seething pool of e-commerce, personal and technical information, social networking, and who knows what else in the future.

Chapter 8, "Surfing the Web with Firefox," explained how to use Firefox, the world's best Web browser, to surf the Web. This section explains the flip side of surfing the Web, which is how to set up a Web server so that you can deliver web pages and other content over the Web to anyone who has access to your server. Most businesses and academic environments today have both externally available and internal-only Web servers. Many people even set up Web servers on their home networks to facilitate Web-based scheduling, document sharing, a central repository for photos, and just about anything else that you can think of.

This chapter begins with a bit of background on the Web, how Web servers work, and a history of Apache, the most popular Web server in existence. Subsequent sections explain how to install Apache, how to configure it, where Web content lives in an Apache server, how to extend and customize the Apache Web server, and how to troubleshoot connectivity or permissions problems.

IN THIS CHAPTER

WWW 101

Introduction to Apache

Installing Apache

Configuring Apache

Troubleshooting your Web server

World Wide Web 101

There are many excellent books about the World Wide Web and HTML, and this book isn't designed to be one of them. However, if you are new to the Web, this section provides some quick history and a sampling of Web buzzwords so that I won't surprise you by using new terms at random.

In 1989, what has become the World Wide Web first entered the world in the mind of Tim Berners-Lee at CERN (Conseil Européenne pour la Recherche Nucléaire), the European Laboratory for Particle Physics near Geneva, Switzerland. The term *World Wide Web* wasn't actually coined until 1990, when Tim Berners-Lee and Robert Cailliau submitted an official project proposal for developing the World Wide Web. They suggested a new way of sharing information between researchers at CERN who used different types of terminals and workstations. The unique aspect of their information-sharing model was that the servers would host information and deliver it to clients in a device-independent form, and it would be the responsibility of each client to display (officially known as *render*) that information. Web clients and servers would communicate using a language (protocol) known as *HTTP*, which stands for the "HyperText Transfer Protocol."

Note

Hypertext is just text with embedded links to other text in it. The most common examples of hypertext outside of the World Wide Web are various types of online help files, where you navigate from one help topic to another by clicking on keywords or other highlighted text. The most basic form of hypertext used on the Web is HTML, the HyperText Markup Language, which is a structured hypertext format that I talk about a little later in this section. ∎

On the World Wide Web, the servers are Web servers and the clients are typically browsers, such as Firefox, Opera, SeaMonkey, Netscape, Microsoft Internet Explorer, Apple's Safari, and many others, running on your machine. To retrieve a web page or other web resource, you enter its address as a Uniform Resource Identifier (URI) in your browser by either typing it in or clicking on a link that contains a reference to that URI. Your browser contacts the appropriate Web server, which uses that URI to locate the resource that you requested and returns that resource as a stream of hypertext information that your browser displays appropriately, and you're off and running!

Today's browsers can understand many protocols beyond HTTP, including FTP (File Transfer Protocol, used to send and receive files), file (used to deliver plaintext files), POP (Post Office Protocol, used to send and receive electronic mail), and NNTP (Network News Transfer Protocol, used to send and receive Usenet News postings). Which protocol you use to retrieve a specific web resource is encoded into the URI, and is referred to as a *scheme* in Web nerd terms. A URI specifies three basic things:

```
scheme://host/pathname
```

The *scheme* is one of http, ftp, file, and many more, and specifies how to contact the server running on *host*, which the Web server then uses to determine how to act on your request. The *pathname* is an optional part of the URI that identifies a location used by the server to locate or generate information to return to you.

Web pages consist of a static or dynamically generated text document that can contain text, links to other web pages or sites, embedded graphics in a variety of formats, references to included documents such as style sheets, and much more. These text documents are created using a structured markup language called *HTML*, the HyperText Markup Language. (Markup languages are introduced and discussed in Chapter 13, "Creating and Publishing Documents.") A structured markup language is a markup language that enforces a certain hierarchy where different elements of the document can appear only in certain contexts. Using a structured markup language can be useful to guarantee that, for example, a heading can never appear in the middle of a paragraph. Like documents in other modern markup languages, HTML documents consist of logical elements that identify the type of each element — it is the browser's responsibility to identify each element and determine how to display (render) it. Using a device-independent markup language simplifies developing tools that render web pages in different ways, convert the information in web pages to other structured formats (and vice versa), and so on.

You Say URL, I Say URI...

As you may have noticed in the other chapters of this book, different Web-aware applications often use different terms from what you and I might simply think of as "web addresses." *URL* (Uniform Resource Locator) is the traditional acronym and term for a web address, but the acronym and term *URI* (Uniform Resource Identifier) is actually more technically correct. Another acronym and term that you may come across is *URN* (Universal Resource Name).

The relationship between these acronyms is the following: a *URI* is any way to identify a web resource. A *URL* is a URI that explicitly provides the location of a resource and the protocol used to retrieve it. A *URN* is a URI that simply provides the name of a resource and may or may not tell you how to retrieve it or where it is located.

The bottom line is that most people think of and use the terms *URI*, *URL*, and *web address* interchangeably. If you want to pick one to use, *URI* is the right term to use.

Introduction to Web Servers and Apache

As mentioned in the previous section, the flip side of a Web browser is the Web server, the application that actually locates and delivers content from a specified URI to the browser. What does a Web server have to do? At the most basic level, it simply has to deliver HTML and other content in response to incoming requests. However, to be useful in a modern Web-oriented environment, a Web server has to do several things. The most important of these are the following:

- Be flexible and configurable to make it easy to add new capabilities and web sites, and support increasing demand without recompilation and/or reinstallation.

- Support authentication to limit users who can access specific pages and web sites.

- Support applications that dynamically generate web pages, such as Perl and PHP, to support a customizable and personal user experience.

- Maintain logs that can track requests for various pages so that you can both identify problems and figure out the popularity of various pages and web sites.

- Support encrypted communications between the browser and server, to guarantee and validate the security of those communications.

The order of importance of these various requirements depends on whether you are a systems administrator or an e-commerce merchant, but all modern Web servers must provide at least these capabilities.

Many different Web servers are available today, depending on your hardware platform, the software requirements of third-party software that a web site depends on, your fealty to a particular operating system vendor, and whether or not you are willing to run open source software, get additional power, and save money.

As you might expect, the first Web server in the world went online at CERN, along with the first Web browser. These were written and ran on NeXT workstations, not exactly the world's most popular platform (sadly enough). The first test of a Web server outside of Europe was made using a server running at the Stanford Linear Accelerator Center (SLAC) in the United States.

The development focus of Web servers that ran on more popular machines was initially the NCSA (National Center for Supercomputing Applications) Web server, known as *NCSA httpd* (HTTP Daemon). Their development of a freely available Web server paralleled their development of the NCSA browser, known as *Mosaic*. (See Chapter 8 for information about Mosaic and its place in Web browser history.) When one of the primary developers of NCSA httpd (Rob McCool) left the NCSA, a group of NCSA httpd fans, maintainers, and developers formed to maintain and support a set of patches for NCSA httpd. This patched server eventually came to be known as the *Apache* Web server. Although the official Apache web site used to claim that the name *Apache* was chosen because of their respect for the endurance and fighting skills of the Apache Indians, most people (myself included) think that this was a joke, and that the name was chosen because the Web server initially consisted of many patches—in other words, it was "*a patchy* Web server."

Although some Linux distributions still provide Apache 1.*x* servers as an installation option, the Ubuntu repositories only provide the apache2 Web server package because its code base and configuration mechanisms are much improved over earlier versions of Apache. Apache 2.*x* is a far superior Web server and where future Apache extension development is going to take place. Any references to Apache in this chapter should be taken to refer to the Apache 2.x Web server.

Today, Apache Web servers installed at sites across the Internet deliver more Web content than any other Web server. I forget the name of the second most popular Web server, but it only runs on a single operating system (which is not Linux) and therefore loses conceptually as well as numerically.

Installing Apache

The latest version of the Apache 2.x Web server for Ubuntu systems is provided in the apache2 package in the Ubuntu repositories. You can use any of the package management tools discussed in Chapter 19, "Adding, Removing, and Updating Software," to install that package. When installing Apache from the command line using aptitude, I suggest that you use the -r option so that recommended packages are also installed. Regardless of whether you're using a command-line or graphical tool, I suggest that you install both the apache2 and apache2-doc packages.

Note

If you installed your system from an Ubuntu server CD and chose the "Install a LAMP server" option, the Apache 2 Web server was installed as part of your LAMP (Linux, Apache, MySQL, and Perl/PHP) server installation. You can therefore ignore this installation section and move on to the rest of the chapter (although you may want to install the Apache2 documentation). ∎

Apache 2 File Locations

This section provides a quick overview of the default locations of the configuration files, binaries, and content associated with the Apache 2 Web server on your Ubuntu system:

- /etc/apache2: A directory containing the configuration files for the Apache 2 Web server. The primary configuration file in this directory is the file apache2.conf.

- /etc/apache2/conf.d: A directory containing local configuration directives for Apache 2, such as those associated with third-party or locally installed packages

- /etc/apache2/envvars: A file containing environment variables that you want to set in the environment used by the apache2ctl script to manage an Apache 2 Web server

- /etc/apache2/mods-available: A directory containing available Apache 2 modules and their configuration files

- /etc/apache2/mods-enabled: A directory containing symbolic links to actively enable Apache 2 modules and their configuration files, located in the /etc/apache2/mods-available directory. This is analogous to the use of symbolic links to start various processes from the scripts in /etc/init.d at different run levels.

- `/etc/apache2/sites-available`: A directory containing files that define the web sites supported by this server
- `/etc/default/apache2`: A configuration file that determines whether the Apache 2 should automatically start at boot time
- `/etc/init.d/apache2`: A shell script that uses the `apache2ctl` utility to start and stop an Apache 2 Web server
- `/etc/mime.types`: The default MIME (Multipurpose Internet Mail Extensions) file types and the extensions associated with them.
- `/usr/lib/cgi-bin`: The location in which any CGI-BIN (Common Gateway Interface scripts) for a default Apache 2 Web server will be installed
- `/usr/sbin/apache2`: The actual executable for the Apache 2 Web server
- `/usr/sbin/apache2ctl`: An administrative shell script that simplifies starting, stopping, restarting, and monitoring the status of a running Apache 2 Web server
- `/usr/share/apache2-doc`: A directory that contains the actual Apache 2 manual (in the `manual` subdirectory). This directory is present only if you've installed the `apache2-doc` package (as suggested earlier).
- `/usr/share/apache2/error`: A directory containing the default error responses delivered
- `/usr/share/apache2/icons`: A directory containing the default set of icons used by an Apache 2 Web server. This directory is mapped to the directory `/icons` in your Apache server's primary configuration file.
- `/var/log/apache2/access.log`: The default access log file for an Apache 2 Web server. This log file tracks any attempts to access this Web server, the hosts that they came from, and so on.
- `/var/log/apache2/error.log`: The default error log file for an Apache 2 Web server. This log file tracks internal Web server problems, attempts to retrieve nonexistent files, and so on.
- `/var/run/apache2/apache2.pid`: A text file used by Apache 2 to record its process ID when it starts. This file is used when terminating or restarting the Apache 2 server using the `/etc/init.d/apache2` script.
- `/var/www/apache2-default`: A directory containing the default home page for this Web server. Note that the default Apache 2 Web server does not display the content of this directory correctly—I'll use that as an example of configuring a web site in the next section.

Some of these directories, most specifically the `/etc/apache2` configuration directory, contain other files that are included or referenced by other files in that same directory.

Configuring Apache

As mentioned in the previous section, the configuration files for the Apache 2 Web server are located in the directory /etc/apache2. Configuration files for web sites that are available in an Apache 2 Web server are located in the directory /etc/apache2/sites-available. To actually support a site from your Web server, you must create a configuration file for that Web server in /etc/apache2/site-available, and then create symbolic links to that configuration file in the /etc/apache2/sites-available directory.

The only web site that is provided out-of-the-box with a standard Apache 2 installation is its default web site, which displays the web page shown in Figure 29-1.

FIGURE 29-1

The default page for a newly installed Apache 2 Web server

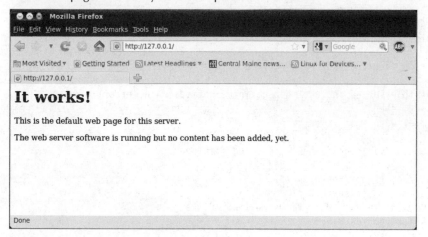

Note

If you are creating a new web site and want it to be your Web server's default page, you can simply put your content in the /var/www directory, where things would work fine immediately. ∎

The following is a listing of the file /etc/apache2/sites-available/default, which activates the site on this server. (I've added line numbers to make it easier to refer to different entries—they do not actually appear in the file!)

```
1. <VirtualHost *:80>
2. ServerAdmin webmaster@localhost
```

```
3.
4.     DocumentRoot /var/www
5.     <Directory />
6.         Options FollowSymLinks
7.         AllowOverride None
8.     </Directory>
9.     <Directory /var/www/>
10.        Options Indexes FollowSymLinks MultiViews
11.        AllowOverride None
12.        Order allow,deny
13.        allow from all
14.     </Directory>
15.
16.     ScriptAlias /cgi-bin/ /usr/lib/cgi-bin/
17.     <Directory "/usr/lib/cgi-bin">
18.        AllowOverride None
19.        Options +ExecCGI -MultiViews +SymLinksIfOwnerMatch
20.        Order allow,deny
21.        Allow from all
22.     </Directory>
23.
24.  ErrorLog /var/log/apache2/error.log
25.
26.  # Possible values include: debug, info, notice, warn, error, crit,
27.  # alert, emerg.
28.  LogLevel warn
29.
30.  CustomLog /var/log/apache2/access.log combined
31.
32.  Alias /doc/ "/usr/share/doc/"
33.  <Directory "/usr/share/doc/">
34.        Options Indexes MultiViews FollowSymLinks
35.        AllowOverride None
36.        Order deny,allow
37.        Deny from all
38.        Allow from 127.0.0.0/255.0.0.0 ::1/128
39. </Directory>
40.
41. </VirtualHost>
```

The first thing that I want to change here is line 2, which sends any mail directed to the Webmaster for this site to webmaster@localhost, which probably doesn't exist on your machine. You can either set up a local alias for Webmaster in your mail server configuration (see Chapter 30, "Setting Up a Mail Server," for more information) or simply change this to an explicit site-wide address that you've already assigned somewhere. I would change this to webmaster@vonhagen.org.

Suppose next that you also wanted to make the Apache documentation explicitly available through the URI /manual/. Although there is no such directory, it's easy enough to make an entry in the server's configuration file defining a re-direct to an existing directory. So let's make one. Inside the VirtualHost block, create something like the entry for the /doc/ directory that's shown in lines 32 through 39, but simplify it a bit:

```
1. Alias /manual/ "/usr/share/doc/apache2-doc/manual/"
2. <Directory "/usr/share/doc/apache2-doc/manual/">
3.   Order deny,allow
4.   Deny from all
5.   Allow from 192.168.6 127.0.0.1
6. </Directory>
```

Note

Again, the line numbers are not actually present in the file — I'm just using them in the example to make it easier to refer to specific lines. ■

Line 1 defines an alias called /manual/ that actually points to the directory /usr/share/doc/ apache2-doc/manual/, which is where Apache's online manual lives. The rest of the lines define who has access to that directory and under what circumstances. Line 2 defines the beginning of directives related to the directory /usr/share/doc/apache2-doc/manual/, and line 6 identifies the end of a block of directives for a specific directory. Lines 3, 4, and 5 specify how authentication works. Line 3 says that any statements denying access to the directory are processed before any that allow access to the directory. Line 4 denies all access to that directory, while line 5 allows access to that directory from any host whose first three octets are 192.168.6 (the subnet on which this Web server is running), and from the loopback address for the host. After adding these changes to the file (they must come before the </VirtualHost> directive shown in line 39 of the previous example because they are part of the definition for this host on this Web server), you can restart the Web server using the same command as before:

```
$ sudo /etc/init.d/apache2 restart
```

Because the startup script for Apache simply runs the apache2ctl utility (Apache's main administrative utility), you could also restart the Apache server by executing the following command:

```
$ sudo apache2ctl restart
```

Visiting the same URI as before and trying to access the Apache documentation hyperlink now shows the page shown in Figure 29-2.

FIGURE 29-2

The Apache documentation after updating the default server's config file

You may note that there is no equivalent to line 34 of the original server configuration file in the new entry that we created. This is because there was no need to provide these directory browsing options because I knew that the directory contained HTML files, so that the following options were not necessary:

- **Indexes:** Shows an index of the directory if no index.html file is present.
- **MultiViews:** Enables content negotiation, where the browser tries to find the best match for a request. In my case, I only want to see the docs in my default language, locale, and character set, so no negotiation is necessary.
- **FollowSymlinks:** Enables the Web server to follow symbolic links. Because I know that there are no symbolic links in this directory, there's no need to specify that they should be followed.

The Apache documentation is really quite good and explains all of the site configuration directives that I don't have space to describe here.

Troubleshooting

As in any debugging or troubleshooting exercise, log files are your friends. Lines 24, 28, and 30 in the original server configuration file shown earlier in this chapter identify the log files used by this server, and the level of logging that occurs. Line 24 identifies the name of the error log file as /var/log/apache2/error.log. Line 28 sets the logging level to warn (warnings), which is slightly more useful than only logging errors, but is not as useful as debug when actually debugging a new site or server. Line 30 tells the server to create a single log file named /var/log/apache2/access.log that will log all access requests to the server in NCSA combined log format.

The following Apache log files are exceptionally useful for debugging purposes:

- access.log: Shows all attempts to access the server, listing the IP address of the host that attempted access, a timestamp, the actual request that was made, and information about the browser that the request was received from.

- error.log: Shows all errors of level warning or above (i.e., more serious) that the server encountered when trying to process an access request. This includes pages that can't be found, directories to which access was denied, and so on.

Apache 2's logging levels are very useful in controlling the amount and type of information that appears in the Apache logs. These levels are as follows:

- **emerg:** Reports only emergency conditions that make the Web server unstable.

- **alert:** Logs situations requiring immediate action and that may identify problems in the host system.

- **crit:** Logs critical errors that may indicate security, server, or system problems.

- **error:** Reports noncritical errors that indicate missing pages, bad server configuration directives, and general error conditions.

- **warn:** Logs messages that warn of noncritical problems or internal conditions that should be investigated.

- **notice:** Reports normal but significant conditions that should still be looked into.

- **info:** Logs informational messages that may help you identify potential problems or suggest possible reconfigurations.

- **debug:** Logs pretty much every state change on the system, such as every file open, every server activity during initialization and operation, and so on

You should never set the log levels lower than crit on any production Web server. I generally find that warn is the best choice for production servers, and I use notice, info, or debug only when a server is actually having performance or responsiveness problems. Also, don't forget that you actually have to look at the log files for them to be useful.

More Information

You can find many excellent sources of information about Apache 2 on the Internet and in books in which the sole focus is Apache 2. The following are some of my favorite resources:

- `http://httpd.apache.org/docs/2.0/`: It doesn't get much more definitive than the actual Apache 2 docs. However, in addition to reference material, the Apache 2 docs include several tutorials and how-to style articles that provide practical, hands-on information.

- *Apache Server 2 Bible*, 2nd Edition, by Mohammed J. Kabir (Wiley, 2002; ISBN: 0-7645-4821-2)

- *Hardening Apache* by Tony Mobily (Apress, 2004; ISBN: 978-1590593783)

Your favorite search engine, such as Google or Clusty, can help you find information about specific error conditions, warning messages, specific server configurations, and so on.

Summary

This chapter discussed how to install and configure the Apache 2 Web server, one of the most commonly used applications on any networked Linux system. A Web server is not only useful for delivering web pages, but also provides the foundation of Web-oriented applications that are often used for system administration and monitoring tasks.

The next chapter continues the server-oriented theme of this chapter by discussing the mail servers that are available for Linux systems. The majority of the chapter discusses how to install and configure the Postfix mail server, a powerful, flexible, and easy-to-configure mail server that is a popular alternative to the traditional Linux sendmail server. The next chapter also explains how to install and integrate related software, such as anti-spam and virus-scanning software.

Setting Up a Mail Server

A s discussed in the introduction to Chapter 29, "Setting Up a Web Server," most of the significant advances in computing technology have what is known as a *killer app* (killer application) — one significantly unique, powerful, and compelling type of application that draws people to that technology in droves and makes it a part of the computing landscape for the foreseeable future. For the Internet, this application was the World Wide Web, but for networking in general, this application is probably e-mail. I can't deny that the Internet is the world's biggest and most powerful network, but many businesses already depended on e-mail long before they had access to the Internet.

E-mail can be a tremendous time sink, but it is the lifeblood of much business and personal communication nowadays. Some of the many advantages of e-mail for business communication are that it is asynchronous (you can send mail to anyone at your company at any time, and they can read it as soon as they have the chance) and location-independent (you can send mail to anyone at any location where your company has an office). Personal e-mail allows us to stay in touch with friends and family regardless of where they are. However, all of this requires a reliable transport mechanism (the Internet or your corporate network) and reliable software that handles mail transfer between computers and mail delivery into your mailbox, and provides the ability to read, store, and reply to e-mail.

Chapter 7, "Managing E-Mail and Personal Information with Evolution" discusses the e-mail capabilities of Evolution, a powerful piece of personal information management software that is installed as part of every non-server Ubuntu installation. This chapter explains how to install and configure Postfix, an equally powerful piece of software that handles mail transfer; how to integrate Postfix with various mail delivery packages; and how to extend its capabilities to filter out the spam that drives many people

IN THIS CHAPTER

Reviewing Linux mail servers

Installing Postfix, spam-checking, and virus-scanning packages

Configuring Postfix

Adding POP3 support to your mail server

Adding spam filtering

Adding virus scanning

crazy nowadays. However, before I get into the details, the first section discusses how e-mail works, defines some basic terminology and required software components, provides an overview of available Linux mail servers, and discusses some good reasons for running your own mail server. If you're an experienced sysadmin or are feeling lucky, feel free to skip ahead to the installation, configuration, and antivirus and spam filtering sections.

Introduction to Mail Servers

The components of an e-mail system can be confusing, so I usually generalize them as the difference between receiving and retrieving — my mail server receives e-mail for me, and my e-mail client lets me retrieve my e-mail from there to read it, archive or delete it, and so on. However, in official mailer-speak, there are actually three components involved in a mail system:

- **Mail Transfer Agent (MTA):** A program that handles transferring e-mail from one computer to another, using the Simple Mail Transfer Protocol (SMTP). Well-known examples of MTAs are Microsoft Exchange, Sendmail, Postfix, qmail, and exim. MTAs are often referred to as "mail servers," which can be confusing because this is also the term commonly used to identify the host on which an MTA runs.

- **Mail Delivery Agent (MDA):** A program that actually delivers the e-mail received by an MTA into my personal mailbox and can often do both preprocessing, such as spam filtering and virus detection, and auto-responder tasks, such as sending "I'm on vacation" mail. The MDA also often handles the presentation of mail from the mailbox to the user, supporting protocols such as the Post Office Protocol (POP and POP3) and the Internet Message Access Protocol (IMAP) on the host where mail is stored. Common examples of MDAs on Linux systems are procmail, Qpopper, Cyrus, pop3d, Courier IMAP, and /bin/mail. MDAs can be directly integrated into an MTA, as is the case with Microsoft Exchange and often with Linux MTAs when mail is read directly from a traditional UNIX-style mail file.

- **Mail User Agent (MUA):** A program that lets you send mail and read the messages in your personal mailbox using protocols such as POP, POP3, and IMAP. Most MUAs also provide support for composing and managing mail messages. Common examples of MUAs are Evolution, Microsoft Outlook, Mutt, KMail, Alpine, and Thunderbird.

In most cases, users never see the MDA because it is integrated with the MTA, either by the software vendor or by the system administrator. Similarly, most users could care less about the MTA and use the term *mail server* to identify the host on which whatever MTA they are using runs. Although the MUA is the most important component of a mail system from the user point of view, the MTA is the most important component from a mail system's and system administrator's point of view because it both performs the actual transfer of mail from one computer to another and identifies the MDA and any other applications involved in pre-processing mail on its way to the user's mailbox.

Popular Linux Mail Transfer Agents

As you might expect, several MTAs are available for Linux systems. Although this chapter focuses on installing and configuring Postfix, other Linux MTAs all have their devotees. For this reason, it's nice to know a bit about each of the most popular ones so that you can feel that you made an informed decision by following the suggestions in this chapter and going with Postfix. The next few sections provide an overview of the most popular Linux MTAs and some of the features, benefits, and downsides of each.

exim

exim is a popular, fast, and flexible MTA written by Philip Hazel at the University of Cambridge; it was originally written as a replacement for a popular, older MTA known as *smail*. exim is very popular with system administrators who also run mailing lists such as Mailman, because it can be configured to automatically look for addresses that are actually mailing lists before delivering mail to end users. It supports an extensive set of features for checking incoming mail for problems without the external applications that most other MTAs require. exim is the default MTA used on Linux distributions such as Debian.

For more information about exim, see:

- **exim home page:** www.exim.org
- **exim documentation and FAQs:** www.exim.org/docs.html

Postfix

Postfix is a popular, scalable, and secure MTA written by Witse Venema while working at IBM. Postfix was originally known as *VMailer* and was even marketed by IBM as *Secure Mailer*. In 1999, its name became *Postfix*, and the rest is history. Postfix is the MTA that is installed when you specify that you want to install a mail server when installing an Ubuntu Server distribution.

Postfix is reliable, fast, and easy to administer. Its configuration file is easy to read and edit, although you still have to know the many options that you can set and their possible values. It is a drop-in replacement for Sendmail, with the exception that it requires tasks to run as a special Postfix user and group for security reasons.

For more information about Postfix, see:

- **Postfix home page:** www.postfix.org
- **Postfix resources and FAQs:** www.seaglass.com/postfix
- **Postfix Shrine:** www.arschkrebs.de/postfix/

qmail

qmail is an extremely fast, secure, and scalable MTA written by Dan Bernstein, a Computer Science professor at the University of Illinois at Chicago who is well known for his interest in cryptography and security. This focus manifests itself in qmail—since 1997, there has been a standing reward of $500 for anyone who finds a verifiable security hole in the latest version of qmail. It has never been claimed.

qmail is extremely fast, secure, and scalable. Unfortunately, it is also encumbered by strange licensing requirements (e.g., you cannot re-distribute modified qmail source code without the direct approval of your changes by the author), it is not compatible with the Linux Filesystem Hierarchy Standard (it lives under /var), and its initial configuration and the irritations associated with adding new users are responsible for at least some portion of my gray hair. However, the licensing issues have primarily been responsible for its lack of widespread adoption by the open source community, because it isn't open source. As such, several qmail patches are available to add various capabilities, but it is simply tedious to always have to apply a variety of patches.

For more information about qmail, see:

- **Dan Bernstein's qmail page:** http://cr.yp.to/qmail.html
- **Life with qmail:** www.lifewithqmail.org
- **qmail home page:** www.qmail.org

Sendmail

Sendmail is the most common mail transfer agent in use on Linux and UNIX systems today. Note that I did not say "the most popular" — Sendmail comes as the default MTA for most UNIX and many Linux distributions, and therefore is often used "because it's there." If Sendmail is used on many existing systems in your organization, it's also difficult to argue for using a different MTA on any new box, based on the "don't fix it if it's not broken" approach to system administration.

Sendmail was written by Eric Allman, whose delivermail program was the original ARPANET mail delivery system provided with 4.0 BSD UNIX and early versions of 4.1 BSD. However, as the ARPANET grew, and then eventually became the Internet, delivermail proved to be too inflexible, largely because it used compiled-in configuration information. Sendmail was developed to use an external configuration file and was first delivered with later versions of BSD 4.1. Sendmail's configuration syntax is both tremendously rich and fiendishly arcane, and is the biggest argument against Sendmail. The configuration files actually used by Sendmail are generated from the configuration file maintained by a system administrator using the m4 macro processor, which makes them tremendously painful to debug and maintain. Sendmail configuration questions are tremendously popular during the interview process for system administrators.

On the positive side, no Internet mailer is more mature than Sendmail because it has been in active use for more than 20 years. It scales well and can be integrated with most of the popular anti-spam and antivirus packages that are available. Sendmail has a somewhat undeserved reputation for security problems, which largely is because it is the biggest and oldest target.

For more information about Sendmail, see:

- **Open Source Sendmail home page:** www.sendmail.org
- **Sendmail, Inc.:** www.sendmail.com (where Eric Allman is CTO)

Why Run Your Own Mail Server?

There are several good reasons to run your own mail server, but doing so also introduces both additional responsibilities and internal costs. All domain hosting companies and ISPs will manage a mail server for a domain, giving you some amount of control over its configuration. For example, you are usually given access to a Web-based control panel that enables you to create some number of e-mail accounts and mail aliases. However, this does not give you any control over the internals of the mail server. The following are some of the best reasons for wanting to run and manage your own mail server:

- **No limitation on the number of users or aliases:** Most ISPs and domain hosting companies provide a certain number of each, and then impose additional charges for higher numbers.

- **No limitation on the number of domains that can be served by a single mail server:** Most ISPs and hosting companies charge for each domain and require that you administer each domain separately. You can configure a single mailer to support all of your domains, sharing a central configuration across multiple domains.

- **The ability to use a different mail server from the one that is provided by your ISP or domain hosting company:** You can select the MTA and MDA combination that best suits your requirements, not the convenience of your ISP or domain hosting company.

- **The ability to integrate centralized spam and antivirus checking that is under your control and that you can fine-tune at no cost:** You can select the spam and antivirus software that you want to use, rather than the one that your ISP or domain hosting company selected.

- **Easy integration of additional capabilities such as mailing lists that may not be supported by your ISP or domain hosting company:** Not all MTAs and MDAs are created equal — you can select the combination that best suits your requirements, rather than the one that your ISP or domain hosting company selected.

Although deciding to run your own mail server provides several benefits, it introduces several costs and responsibilities that you must be prepared for. Some of the more important of these are the following:

- **Security becomes your concern and responsibility:** When an ISP or domain hosting firm manages your mail server, its security is their responsibility. When you manage your own mail server, you are directly responsible for its security, which is especially important if you run an IMAP mail server, where all of your personal, SMB, or enterprise mail is permanently stored on the mail server.

- **You will need to make sure that any host on the Internet can always contact your mail server:** Beyond being responsible for the uptime of the machine that hosts the mail server, you will need to make sure that the MX records for all domains that it supports correctly identify the mail server. It will either have to have a fixed IP address or it will need to be correctly identified by a dynamic DNS system that is always available.

- **You will become responsible for all of your mail server's system administration:** In addition to ensuring that it is configured correctly (no open relays, please), you will be responsible for ensuring that a mail server is always available at the location identified by your domain's MX record, that backups are done, that the system and all of the software that you depend on are always kept up-to-date, and that spam filtering and antivirus checking are always up-to-date and correctly configured, and much more.

It's easy to overlook incidental costs when setting up your own mail server. When everything works correctly, as it does most of the time, things are great. But when something breaks, *you* are the one in the hot seat.

Installing Postfix and Friends

This section explains how to install the packages necessary for a simple Postfix mail server that automatically scans messages for spam and viruses and that users can access via the POP3 protocol. Postfix and related packages are installed in different ways depending on whether you are running a system installed from an Ubuntu Server CD or an Ubuntu Desktop CD. If you are installing an Ubuntu Server distribution, installing a mail server is a suggested option during the installation process, but this installs only the core Postfix package, not all of the other packages that I suggest that you install. (If you do not install a mail server when initially installing an Ubuntu Server distribution, you can always subsequently install Postfix and related packages using apt-get or aptitude.) Otherwise, you can use any of the tools discussed in Chapter 19, "Adding, Removing, and Updating Software," (apt-get, aptitude, or the Synaptic Package Manager) to manually install Postfix and related packages. Ubuntu enables you to do things your way.

Packages to Install

In alphabetical order, the packages that I suggest you install are the following:

- clamav: An antivirus package that scans incoming mail for attachments that contain a virus and quarantines those messages so that people don't accidentally invoke the problematic attachment
- mailx: A package that contains a simple command-line tool for sending mail, which is used by many system utilities, but (in our case) is extremely useful for quick mail server tests
- mailscanner: A package that scans incoming mail using a variety of spam detection techniques and discards any matching mail
- postfix: The Postfix mailer and all related utilities and configuration files

- `postfix-doc`: Documentation for the Postfix mailer, installed in `/usr/share/doc/postfix` and `/usr/share/doc/postfix-doc`

- `postgrey`: A greylisting implementation for use with Postfix. Greylisting causes incoming mail requests to be rejected the first time that they arrive, but accepted when the remote mail system tries to deliver them a second time. Many spammers try to deliver mail only once, so this simple utility can significantly reduce the amount of spam that your site receives.

- `qpopper`: A package that enables users to read their mail remotely, using the POP/POP3 protocol that is supported by most MUAs

You don't have to install all of these now, of course, but I'm going to assume that these are all installed in subsequent sections of this chapter.

Although the way in which you install applications is up to you, I suggest that you use Aptitude to take advantage of its ability to install recommended packages as well as the basic packages required to run and support the Postfix mail server and related applications on your Ubuntu system. Synaptic and Aptitude will install all required packages but will not get you all of the bells and whistles associated with some of the recommended packages for Postfix. To install the Postfix mail server and related applications from the command line using Aptitude, execute the following command:

```
$ sudo aptitude -y -r install postfix postfix-doc postgrey \
      mailscanner mailx qpopper clamav
```

Installing all of these packages, their dependencies, and recommended packages will require around 65 MB of disk space. After being prompted for your password, installation will begin without confirmation (because of the -y option), and away we go!

Built-In Postfix Configuration Models

Regardless of whether you are installing Postfix and friends from the command line or graphically, you will be required to select a default configuration model during the installation process. Five different configuration models are built into the Postfix package, each of which sets up the Postfix configuration files in a certain basic way. The following are the configuration models:

- **Internet site:** Mail will be sent and received directly from this machine via SMTP using Postfix. This is the default choice, and is probably the right choice if you are configuring an incoming and outgoing mail server for your domain and you have a direct connection to the Internet.

- **Internet site using smarthost:** This machine either receives mail directly from the Internet or from another machine using a utility such as `fetchmail`, but sends mail through another mail server. This is probably the right choice if you want to run a home, Small Office, Home Office (SOHO), or Small or Medium Business (SMB) network with its own mail server but want to leverage your ISP or domain hosting company's existing mail server.

- **Local delivery only:** The machine only delivers mail locally, and does not send mail over any network. This is the right choice if you are setting up a system on which you want system status messages to be delivered by local e-mail, or a system shared by multiple users who need to exchange mail only between themselves.

- **No configuration:** The installation process will not modify the generic Postfix configuration files. You will have to make extensive manual modifications to them to get Postfix to work correctly on your system.

- **Satellite system:** This machine does not receive mail and forwards all outgoing mail to another mail server for actual delivery.

If you are setting up a system that doesn't match any of the pre-supplied configurations, it's probably best to select the default value, *Internet Site*, because this will provide a reasonable template that you can then customize to match your exact requirements.

During the installation process, you will see a screen like the one shown in Figure 30-1 if you are installing Postfix and friends via `aptitude`. (You'll see a similar screen if you're using Synaptic or Adept, but — of course — it will be graphical.)

FIGURE 30-1

Available Postfix configuration models

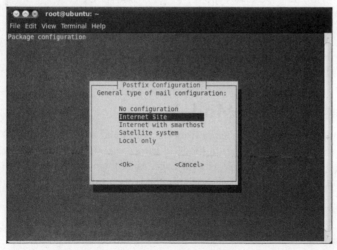

This screen displays the different configuration models that are built into the Postfix package. In most cases, you will want to select the default configuration model, Internet Site, by pressing Tab to move the cursor to the OK option and then pressing Return. You can also use the up/down arrows to select another configuration model, press Tab to move the cursor to the OK option, and press Return to accept the highlighted choice. The screen in Figure 30-2 displays this.

Note

If you simply press Return without tabbing to the OK option, you'll see another screen that provides some additional information about these options. If you continue on from that screen, the screen shown in Figure 30-1 re-displays. ∎

FIGURE 30-2

Specifying the name of your mail host in text mode

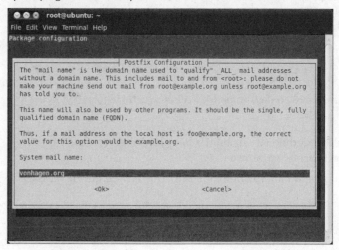

This screen (or its graphical equivalent) enables you to specify the name of this host as any external hosts will look for it, which should therefore be a fully qualified hostname that includes the name of your domain. By default, the actual name of the system is displayed. Use the left/right arrow and Delete keys if you need to make any changes to the name of this host. Press Return to accept the name on this screen. The remainder of the configuration process will continue with no further questions.

Configuring Postfix

As installed by default, your Postfix mail server is almost ready for prime time. It will already work fine locally, which you can test by using the command-line mail utility (which is provided by the `mailx` package that you installed in the previous section). To make your mail server able to accept incoming requests from and send mail to other hosts on a network, you will need to extend its capabilities somewhat. Similarly, the Postfix server by itself does local mail delivery, which is fine if all of your users want to log in on your mail server and read their mail there. Unfortunately, that is both poor security practice and a hassle for everyone. So you'll need to do a bit of fine-tuning to make our new Postfix mail server more usable for and by everyone.

The next section explores the default Postfix configuration file that was installed and configured in the previous section. Subsequent sections address how to make your Postfix server work on your network and how to configure your mail server so that it accepts incoming POP mail requests.

Note

As discussed in Chapter 7 and mentioned earlier in this chapter, POP and IMAP are the primary protocols used for remote systems to read e-mail on a mail server. The key difference between them is that POP is designed to store e-mail on the client, while IMAP is designed to store e-mail on the server. Each model has its advantages, but I believe that most people are more familiar with the POP model, so I'm going to focus on that in this chapter. ■

Postfix Configuration Files

The Ubuntu Postfix mail server uses three configuration files, all of which are installed in the directory /etc/postfix:

- dynamicmaps.cf: Identifies additional capabilities to be loaded at run time based on the type of operation that is being performed.
- main.cf: Contains configuration information for Postfix that is used during message processing.
- master.cf: Contains parameters used when the Postfix master program runs other programs from /usr/lib/postfix.

Postfix can also use standard mailer configuration files such as /etc/aliases (which allows e-mail addressed to one user to be automatically delivered to another), but this is not a Postfix-specific configuration file.

The main.cf configuration file is the only Postfix configuration file that most users will ever have to modify. As installed on an Ubuntu system, the main.cf configuration file for a system following the Internet site model looks like the following (I've removed some irrelevant comments and white space):

```
#myorigin = /etc/mailname
smtpd_banner = $myhostname ESMTP $mail_name (Ubuntu)
biff = no
append_dot_mydomain = no
#delay_warning_time = 4h
smtpd_tls_cert_file=/etc/ssl/certs/ssl-cert-snakeoil.pem
smtpd_tls_key_file=/etc/ssl/private/ssl-cert-snakeoil.key
smtpd_use_tls=yes
smtpd_tls_session_cache_database = \
    btree:${queue_directory}/smtpd_scache
smtp_tls_session_cache_database = \
    btree:${queue_directory}/smtp_scache
```

```
myhostname = ubuntu.vonhagen.org
alias_maps = hash:/etc/aliases
alias_database - hash:/etc/aliases
myorigin = /etc/mailname
mydestination = mail.vonhagen.org, ubuntu.vonhagen.org,
                localhost.vonhagen.org, localhost
relayhost =
mynetworks = 127.0.0.0/8 [::ffff:127:0.0.0]/104
mailbox_size_limit = 0
recipient_delimiter = +
inet_interfaces = all
html_directory = /usr/share/doc/postfix/html
```

In order, these configuration variables do the following:

- myorigin: An option for Debian and derivative distributions (such as Ubuntu) that enables you to use the first line of the text file /etc/mailname as the name of the mailer. This is actually set later in the default file.

- smtpd_banner: Sets the value of the banner that is displayed when an SMTP connection is established. In this case, the banner is constructed by using the value of other variables set in the configuration file.

- biff: Determines whether the local e-mail notification service (biff) should be used for each user with new mail each time Postfix processes the incoming mail queue. In this case, it is disabled because biff notifications can cause a performance drain, and are relevant only on the machine that houses the mail files. Users who use local mail files can enable this for themselves.

- append_dot_mydomain: Determines whether Postfix should append a domain name to mail sent to user@host. Nowadays, this is usually handled by the MUA, so this is disabled.

- delay_warning_time: Uncommenting this parameter would specify the period of time after which users would be notified if mail that they had sent had not yet been delivered. After all, the remote site could be using Microsoft Exchange, and might be down.

- smtpd_tls_cert_file: Identifies the full pathname of the file on this system that holds the certificate used by this machine when sending messages using TLS (Transport Layer Security).

- smtpd_tls_key_file: Identifies the full pathname of the file on this system that holds the RSA private key for the Postfix SMTP client when sending messages using TLS (Transport Layer Security).

- smtpd_use_tls: Determines whether this Postfix server should use TLS when a remote SMTP server announces STARTTLS support. If the remote server does not announce STARTTLS support, the message is sent in the clear.

- `smtpd_tls_session_cache_database`: Identifies the organization and location of the SMTP server TLS session cache used by the `tlsmgr` daemon.

- `smtp_tls_session_cache_database`: Identifies the organization and location of the SMTP client TLS session cache used by the `tlsmgr` daemon.

- `myhostname`: Identifies the actual Internet hostname of this system. By default, this value is the value returned by `gethostname()`.

- `alias_maps`: Identifies the organization and full pathname of the aliases file used for local mail delivery.

- `alias_database`: Identifies the organization and full pathname of the aliases file used for local mail delivery, and which is updated using the traditional `newaliases` command. This is often the same file as that identified by the `alias_maps` parameter, but need not be.

- `myorigin`: Identifies the name of the host or domain that local mail is assumed to come from and is sent to. On Ubuntu systems, it is the name of a file containing whatever you specified as the mail name when installing Postfix. This is suitable for single-domain installations, but insufficient for Postfix mail servers that support multiple domains.

- `mydestination`: A list of domains for which mail is delivered via local mail delivery. I specified `ubuntu.vonhagen.org` as the name of my host when I installed Postfix — in most cases, *mail.domain-name* (i.e., `mail.vonhagen.org`, in my case) would be the standard name to use for a mail server to help keep your sysadmins sane and make it easy to locate/identify your domain's mail server.

- `relayhost`: If outgoing mail must be sent to another mail server for delivery, this parameter identifies that mail server; otherwise, it is empty.

- `mynetworks`: Identifies the networks or specific hosts from which this mail server will send mail. This information is specified in both IPv4 and IPv6 formats. In this case, the mail server will only send mail from the loopback network, which is a problem. This is discussed in the following section, "Identifying Trusted Hosts and Domains."

- `mailbox_size_limit`: Identifies the maximum size of any mailbox on the system. In this case, 0 means that there is no limit.

- `recipient_delimiter`: Identifies the separator used internally by the Postfix server between usernames and addresses.

- `inet_interfaces`: Identifies the network interfaces on which the machine can receive mail. In this case, the Postfix server will listen on all network interfaces.

- `html_directory`: Identifies the location of HTML files that describe how to install and configure a Postfix server and various Postfix features.

A complete list of Postfix configuration parameters and possible values is available in the files section of the online reference information for the `postconf` command (`man 5 postconf`) or online at locations such as `www.postfix.org/postconf.5.html`.

Identifying Trusted Hosts and Domains

The main.cf configuration file in the previous section requires only one change to be a fully functional network mail server — the mynetworks parameter must be adjusted to add at least the local network. As installed by default, an Ubuntu Postfix server will listen for incoming requests on all network interfaces, but will only allow hosts on its loopback network to send e-mail through it.

The value of the mynetworks parameter can be a single host, an IP address and netmask to indicate a range of hosts or a subnet, or any number of comma-separated hosts or IP addresses and associated netmasks. The value of the mynetworks parameter in the main.cf file sets what is known as the *relay policy* for the host. A value must be present, or your mail server becomes what is known as an *open relay*, a mail server through which anyone can send e-mail. Open relays are favorite targets for spammers because they can abuse them indefinitely.

In this case, my mail server handles mail for all of the systems on my SOHO office, all of which are in the 192.168.6.* address family, so I would change the value of the mynetworks parameter to the following:

```
mynetworks = 127.0.0.0/8, 192.168.6.0/8
```

I then either restart the Postfix server (using sudo /etc/init.d/postfix restart) or use the sudo postfix reload command to cause the active Postfix daemon to pick up my changes to the configuration file. All hosts on my network can now send mail through the Postfix mail server.

Rewriting Addresses in Outgoing Mail

Although all hosts on the local network can now send mail through the mail server, many MUAs send mail using the fully qualified domain name of the host from which the mail was sent. This means that mail from me (wvh) on the host 64bit.vonhagen.org goes out with an e-mail address of wvh@64bit.vonhagen.org. Although I don't particularly care about this, I probably don't have a mailbox there, and therefore people can't reply to such mail.

To correct this problem, you can use the Postfix configuration parameter masquerade_domains to identify domains for which Postfix should rewrite outgoing mail addresses so that they simply appear to be from user@domain. In this case, mail from wvh@64bit.vonhagen.org would go out simply as wvh@vonhagen.org, which is my actual e-mail address. In this case, I would add the masquerade_domains setting to my main.cf file:

```
masquerade_domains = vonhagen.org
```

I then either restart the Postfix server (using sudo /etc/init.d/postfix restart) or use the sudo postfix reload command to cause the active Postfix daemon to pick up my changes to the configuration file. All hosts on my network can now send mail through the Postfix mail server without identifying the specific host from which the mail originated.

Accepting Mail for an Entire Domain

As mentioned earlier, the `mydestination` parameter identifies what mail the host will deliver locally. The default Postfix configuration file accepts mail for `localhost.localdomain`, `localhost`, the actual hostname of the machine, and whatever you specified as the mail name of the machine on the configuration screen shown in Figure 30-2 (if that differs from the actual hostname of your machine). To make your new Postfix mail server a valid final destination for all mail for your domain, you must add the name of your domain to the list of destinations in your `main.cf` file. Because I specified `ubuntu.vonhagen.org` as my mail name, my `mydestination` parameter currently looks like the following:

```
mydestination = ubuntu.vonhagen.org, ubuntu,
                localhost.vonhagen.org, localhost
```

I can either add my domain name to this list or set Postfix's `mydomain` parameter to the name of my domain and then leverage the value of that parameter to provide this information. I would add the `mydomain` parameter setting and then update the value of the `mydestination` parameter, which together would look like the following:

```
mydomain = vonhagen.org
mydestination = ubuntu.vonhagen.org, ubuntu,
                localhost.vonhagen.org, localhost, $mydomain
```

As with other configuration file changes, I would then either restart the Postfix server (using `sudo /etc/init.d/postfix restart`) or use the `sudo postfix reload` command to cause the active Postfix daemon to pick up my changes to the configuration file.

Tip
When you make the changes suggested in this section, you may also want to change the value of the `myorigin` parameter so that it is set to $mydomain. During installation, `myorigin` was set to whatever you specified as the mail name of the machine, which is useful because that value was also used in the value for your `mydestination` parameter, which would correctly handle the case in which someone sends mail to root@ubuntu.vonhagen.org. However, after installation, it is more useful to have `myorigin` be the same as the value of `mydomain`. ∎

Activating Qpopper for POP/POP3 Support

Qpopper (`www.eudora.com/products/unsupported/qpopper/index.html`) is a popular, free POP/POP3 server from the folks at Qualcomm, who both sell and give away the popular PC and Macintosh MUA, Eudora. I like Qpopper because it supports the vanilla Linux/UNIX mbox format that Postfix uses by default on Ubuntu. (When using the mbox mailbox format, all messages are stored in a single file, and each message begins with the string "From user@domain," followed by the timestamp for the message.) I suggested that you install Qpopper in the section on installing Postfix—if you didn't and want to activate POP3 support on your new mail server, please install it now and then proceed with this section.

Note

As mentioned before, POP/POP3 and IMAP are alternative protocols for accessing your e-mail, and both can be used with Postfix as long as you install an appropriate server for that protocol on your mail server. Qpopper is fast, lightweight, and well-supported. However, if you want to support both POP/POP3 and IMAP, the Cyrus IMAP (http://asg.Web.cmu.edu/cyrus/) and Courier IMAP (www.courier-mta .org/imap/) packages are popular and are both available in the Ubuntu repositories. However, configuring the Cyrus IMAP server can be tricky, and the Courier IMAP server supports only the Linux/UNIX maildir mailbox format, where each message is stored in a separate file, which is not the default behavior of Postfix on Ubuntu. Hence Qpopper, which is fast, easy, and "just works." ∎

Ubuntu's Qpopper package provides a ready-to-run Qpopper daemon that is suitable for use with the inetd or xinetd Internet services daemons that are discussed in the section of Chapter 23, "Software Development on Ubuntu," entitled "Configuring the svnserve Server." Both of these start various network services in response to specific types of incoming requests. If you have not already installed one of these, I suggest that you install the xinetd services daemon. You can then integrate Qpopper with xinetd by creating the following file with your favorite text editor and saving it as /etc/xinetd.d/pop3:

```
service pop3
{
    port            = 110
    socket_type     = stream
    protocol        = tcp
    wait            = no
    user            = root
    server          = /usr/sbin/in.qpopper
}
```

You can then restart the xinetd Internet services daemon using the command sudo /etc/ init.d/xinetd restart, and Qpopper will be working correctly on your system. You can test that Qpopper is responding correctly to incoming POP/POP3 requests by configuring your MUA to point at your new mail server using the POP/POP3 protocol and checking your mail, or you can do so from the command line by using the telnet command to connect to port 100 (the POP/POP3 port) and seeing if you can log in, as in the following example:

```
$ telnet ubuntu.vonhagen.org 110
Trying 192.168.6.182...
Connected to 192.168.6.182.
Escape character is '^]'.
+OK Qpopper (version 4.0.5) at mail starting. <28861.1153954154@ulive>
user wvh
+OK Password required for wvh.
pass *********************
+OK wvh has 1 visible message (0 hidden) in 696 octets.
```

```
quit
+OK Pop server at ulive signing off.
Connection closed by foreign host.
```

As you can see, Qpopper responded correctly to my request on the POP/POP3 port, accepted my username and password, and listed the amount of pending mail that I have. Success!

Adding Spam Filtering and Virus Scanning to Postfix

Now that you have a running mail server and are receiving incoming connections from other mail servers, you will quickly find that an incredible amount of the mail that you receive is spam (also known as *UCE*, Unsolicited Commercial E-mail). Some of that mail is going to contain virus-laden attachments. You may also, unfortunately, receive a virus from a friend who forwards you something that they thought was cute, but that actually contains a virus payload. If you're lucky, whoever was hosting your mail before you switched to your own mail server was filtering much of this out, and you may not even have known how bad things are in e-mail land. Now that you're hosting your own mail server, you will quickly see that spam and virus-laden mail is an epidemic. No wonder it takes so long for me to connect to Amazon.com from the office some days....

Aside from the fact that you're now aware of the spam/virus epidemic, it is also now your responsibility to do something about it because you're responsible for your mail server. Luckily, there are some great ways to configure Postfix to automatically handle much of this for you. If you installed all of the packages that I suggested back in the section "Installing Postfix and Friends," you've already installed the Postgrey greylisting service and MailScanner. MailScanner scans incoming mail and rejects the spam that it can identify, and then it can invoke other packages, such as SpamAssassin (http://spamassassin.apache.org), another package that does an even better job of spam detection, and ClamAV (www.clamav.net), which is an excellent open source antivirus package. All that remains to do now is to integrate these packages and Postfix.

At this point, you may be wondering why you should bother with an antivirus package on Linux because Linux systems are essentially virus-free. I suggest that you integrate an antivirus package as a matter of course because some of the users of your mail server may also want to read mail on the Microsoft Windows machines that they otherwise use for playing games. More seriously, you may be setting up a mail server in a SOHO, SMB, or enterprise environment in which many of your users need to use Microsoft Windows systems. Either way, installing an antivirus package when you configure your mail server is preventative medicine. It costs you nothing, and if it saves one person the agony of getting a virus on his or her system and having to try to remove it, you're way ahead.

The next three sections discuss various levels of spam and antivirus protection. The first discusses greylisting as implemented by the postgrey package. The second discusses some simple

Postfix parameters that you can add to your `main.cf` configuration file that will reject much incoming spam immediately, saving MailScanner the trouble of checking it. The third section then explains how to integrate MailScanner with Postfix and ClamAV with MailScanner to identify as much spam as possible that comes from correctly configured mail servers, and to check for viruses at the same time.

Greylisting via Postgrey

In the section on "Installing Postfix and Friends," I suggested that you install `postgrey`, which is a greylisting application that was designed to work with Postfix. That package is set up and started automatically and requires no other mandatory configuration — if you installed it when you installed and started Postfix, it's already working for you.

As mentioned in the installation section, *greylisting* is a cool technique wherein your mail server rejects all incoming mail the first time that a remote mail server tries to deliver it to you. Most spammers try only once and then move on — they can't afford to endlessly retry sending mail to hosts that have already rejected it once. All real mail servers that are sending real mail will try to deliver the mail again, at which point your Postfix server will actually talk to them. At that point, the other techniques described in this section kick in.

Note

If you're interested, the term *greylisting* is related to two other techniques for avoiding spam. The term *blacklisting* refers to the practice of refusing to accept mail from hosts that are on a list of known or suspicious hosts. The term *whitelisting* refers to the practice of accepting mail only from a short list of known hosts, specific people, and so on. It's a shame that we all have to resort to these sorts of techniques to protect ourselves from idiot spammers, but that's the reality of the Internet today. ∎

Although Postgrey requires no specific manual configuration, there are several command-line options that are not active by default but that you may want to take advantage of. The Postgrey service also has several features that you may want to take advantage of to customize how greylisting is done on your system. You can whitelist specific sites by adding them to the various whitelist files in `/etc/postgrey`. For example, the file `/etc/postgrey/whitelist_clients` identifies sites for which no greylisting will be done — all incoming mail from these sites will be accepted immediately. Similarly, the file `/etc/postgrey/whitelist_recipients` identifies users of your mail server that do not want greylisting — in other words, users for whom incoming mail will be accepted immediately, regardless of the site from which it originates. You should read the online man page for Postgrey using the `man postgrey` command to see if there are options that you want to take advantage of to fine-tune how the Postgrey service works on your system.

Adding Postfix Parameters to Reject Bogus Mail

As mentioned in the section "Postfix Configuration Files," a tremendous number of Postfix configuration parameters are available, relatively few of which are actually set in the default `main.cf` configuration file installed with the Ubuntu Postfix package. In general, that's a good sign, letting you know that the defaults are typically correct. However, several of these parameters provide additional capabilities that can help your Postfix mail server reject spam out of hand by checking for things that do not conform to Internet electronic mail standards (as defined in the RFCs). Although the next section, "Integrating MailScanner, SpamAssassin, and ClamAV with Postfix," explains how to scan the content of incoming e-mail for spam, scanning incoming mail takes some amount of time, which reduces the overall performance of your system slightly. Any mail that you can reject before you even have to scan it is therefore a win for everyone.

Adding the following block of commands to your Postfix main.cf configuration file can be very effective in reducing spam. (Note that the line numbers are present to make it easy for me to refer to different lines — they should not be present in your main.cf file!)

```
1    smtpd_delay_reject = yes
2    smtpd_helo_required = yes
3    smtpd_helo_restrictions =
4        permit_mynetworks,
5        reject_invalid_hostname,
6        reject_non_fqdn_hostname,
7        permit
8    smtpd_data_restrictions =
9        reject_unauth_pipelining,
10       permit
11   smtpd_sender_restrictions =
12       permit_mynetworks,
13       reject_non_fqdn_sender,
14       reject_unknown_sender_domain,
15       permit
16   smtpd_recipient_restrictions =
17       permit_mynetworks,
18       reject_unknown_recipient_domain,
19       reject_unauth_destination,
20       permit
```

Line 1 is required to use any of the subsequent blocks of restrictions, telling your Postfix server to wait until it receives certain commands from the remote mail server (i.e., a remote SMTP daemon that is a client of your mail server) before rejecting mail based on the rule chains that follow. The smtpd_delay_reject phrase is required because some SMTP servers misbehave if you reject mail before they've had the chance to waste at least some of your time. Line 2 rejects mail from any mail server that fails to correctly identify itself using the HELO or EHLO phrases required by the SMTP RFC. This saves you from having to check any of the subsequent rules.

Lines 3 through 7, 8 through 10, 11 through 15, and 16 through 20 are chains of rules that are applied to different portions of your mail server's interaction with a remote mail server:

- Lines 3 through 7 identify restrictions on the HELO or EHLO commands that are used by a remote mail server to identify itself to your Postfix mail server. Line 4 immediately permits connections from any mail server listed in the Postfix mynetworks parameter. Line 5 rejects connections from remote mail servers that identify themselves using a malformed hostname. Line 6 rejects connections from remote mail servers that do not identify themselves using a fully qualified hostname. Line 7 says that your mail server will accept HELO or EHLO commands from mail servers that have not failed the previous tests, and allows you to move on to the next set of tests.

- Lines 8 through 10 identify restrictions on the way in which the remote mail servers send commands to your mail server. Line 9 tells your server to reject connections that send commands to your mail server too quickly, or at least before your mailer has told the remote mail servers that it can accept a fast stream of SMTP messages. Many bulk e-mailers automatically do this to try to speed up deliveries — after all, they have a zillion targets to send mail to, so they can't afford to waste time (except for yours). Line 10 says that your mail server will accept additional data from mail servers that have not failed the previous tests, and allows you to move on to the next set of tests.

- Lines 11 through 15 identify restrictions on the sender of the e-mail that your server is receiving (identified using the SMTP MAIL FROM command). Line 12 immediately permits connections from any mail server listed in the Postfix mynetworks parameter. Line 13 rejects mail from any sender whose name is not identified using a fully qualified hostname. (Note that mail from your local network may use a short hostname, but we've already permitted mail from them.) Line 14 rejects mail from senders with unknown domains. Line 15 says that your mail server will accept mail from senders that have not failed the previous tests, and allows you to move on to the next set of tests.

- Lines 16 through 20 identify restrictions on the recipient of the e-mail your server is receiving (identified using the SMTP RCPT TO command). Line 17 immediately permits connections from any mail server listed in the Postfix mynetworks parameter. Line 18 rejects mail where the current mail server is not the final target of the mail and that target is not a valid domain. Line 19 rejects incoming mail if the recipient is not in the domains serviced by the current mail server (identified in the mynetworks parameter) or is not in the domains that your mail server will relay mail to (identified in the relayhost parameter). This prevents your mail server from being used as an open relay. Line 20 says that your mail server will accept mail for recipients that have not failed the previous tests, and allows your mail server to move on to actually processing and delivering the incoming mail.

Postfix provides many other checks that I haven't used here, such as checks that test whether the incoming mail is from a mail server that is known to be a source of spam (i.e., is on a blacklist). In my experience, this type of lookup is slow, and these lists are often wrong. For example, some sites that support these blacklists identify any IP addresses that are dynamically assigned by providers such as Comcast as sources of spam. Although this may sometimes be the case, it often is not — for example, Comcast is my ISP, and I promise that I don't send spam.

The sample commands shown in this section should significantly reduce the amount of incoming spam that you receive. Once you've had the chance to experiment with this, you may want to try adding other, similar commands. For a complete list of other checks that you can do to reject incoming spam, see the files section of the online reference information for postconf command (man 5 postconf) for more information, which is also available online at locations such as www.postfix.org/postconf.5.html.

Integrating MailScanner, SpamAssassin, and ClamAV with Postfix

MailScanner is a fast, powerful tool that scans incoming mail for spam and can optionally be configured to scan incoming mail for viruses. The Ubuntu MailScanner package requires that the SpamAssassin package (discussed in the section of Chapter 7 entitled "Automatically Checking for Junk Mail") be installed on your system so that it can invoke the SpamAssassin package after performing its own spam checks, to maximize the chances that it will catch and flag incoming spam.

Note

The MailScanner package always claims that it is scanning for viruses even if it is not. This is because its configuration file contains a setting for the virus scanner that you want to use, which by default is set to none. Don't worry; I'll explain how to fix that. ∎

I suggested that you install MailScanner and the ClamAV virus-scanning package in the section of this chapter entitled "Installing Postfix and Friends." If you didn't, please go back and see that section for information on how to install those packages.

Once installed, it is remarkably easy to add MailScanner to the Postfix food chain:

1. Add the following line to the end of your Postfix `main.cf` configuration file (`/etc/postfix/main.cf`):

   ```
   header_checks = regexp:/etc/postfix/header_checks
   ```

2. Use your favorite text editor to create the file `/etc/postfix/header_checks` with the following contents:

   ```
   /^Received:/ HOLD
   ```

   This line tells Postfix to scan every incoming message for instances of the string "Received:" at the beginning of a line and to move any matching messages (which will be all of them) to a HOLD queue. The HOLD queue is a temporary staging area that you'll use for scanning the incoming mail. Save this file and proceed to the next step.

3. Using your favorite text editor, bring up the MailScanner configuration file (`/etc/MailScanner/MailScanner.conf`) so that you can configure MailScanner to work correctly with Postfix as installed on your Ubuntu system. (By default, the Ubuntu MailScanner package is configured as it would be on a Debian system and is therefore configured for use with the exim mail server.)

4. Find the `Run As User` entries, remove the hash mark at the beginning of the line that says `Run As User = postfix`, and make sure that there is a hash mark at the beginning

of any other line that begins with Run As User. These entries should now look something like the following:

```
# Run As User = mail
Run As User = postfix
# Run As User = Debian-exim
```

5. Find the Run As Group entries, remove the hash mark at the beginning of the line that says Run As Group = postfix, and make sure that there is a hash mark at the beginning of any other line that begins with Run As Group. These entries should now look something like the following:

```
# Run As Group = mail
Run As Group = postfix
# Run As Group = Debian-exim
```

6. Find the Incoming Queue Dir entry and change its value to /var/spool/postfix/hold. This entry should now look like the following:

```
Incoming Queue Dir = /var/spool/postfix/hold
```

7. Find the Outgoing Queue Dir entry and change its value to /var/spool/postfix/incoming. This entry should now look like the following:

```
Outgoing Queue Dir = /var/spool/postfix/incoming
```

8. Find the MTA entry and change its value to postfix. This entry should now look like the following:

```
MTA = postfix
```

9. Find the Virus Scanners entry and set its value to clamav. This entry should now look like the following:

```
Virus Scanners = clamav
```

10. Save the /etc/MailScanner/MailScanner.conf file, and proceed to the next step.

11. Use the following commands to ensure that the Postfix user and group own MailScanner's working directory and the directory where it stores (quarantines) files that are suspected of containing viruses, so that the Postfix mail server can write to these directories:

```
sudo chown -R postfix:postfix /var/spool/MailScanner
```

12. Using your favorite text editor, modify the file `/etc/default/mailscanner` and remove the hash mark at the beginning of the line containing the `run_mailscanner` variable. This line should look like the following:

```
run_mailscanner=1
```

Enabling this variable will cause your system to automatically start MailScanner the next time you boot your system. Save the file, and exit from the text editor.

Now, start MailScanner for the first time by using the following command:

```
sudo check_mailscanner
```

Now either restart the Postfix server (using `sudo /etc/init.d/postfix restart`) or use the `sudo postfix reload` command to cause the active Postfix daemon to pick up your changes to the configuration file.

To test that MailScanner is correctly integrated with your mail server, send yourself a piece of mail through your mail server. If MailScanner is working correctly (and the mail was not spam and did not contain a virus), you should see the following banner at the bottom of the message:

```
This message has been scanned for viruses and
dangerous content by MailScanner, and is
believed to be clean.
```

Congratulations! You are now doing a decent amount of spam filtering and are also checking for viruses in any mail received by your mail server!

Tip

As mentioned previously, SpamAssassin is preconfigured for use with MailScanner and comes with several rules that it uses to test whether incoming messages should be marked as spam. You can obtain many other sets of rules for use with SpamAssassin that extend the basic capabilities that it provides. After you're comfortable with the fact that things are actually working correctly, you may want to add some of these other rule sets. Sites such as the Exit0.us SpamAssassin Wiki (`www.exit0.us/`) and the SpamAssassin Rules Emporium forums (`www.rulesemporium.com/forums/`) or a mailing list (`http://lists.maddoc.net/mailman/listinfo/sare-users`) are great sources for additional rules that you may find useful. However, remember that every additional rule that you add increases the amount of time that it takes to check each piece of incoming mail. Don't get carried away, or your mail server may be able to process only one or two incoming messages per day. ∎

More Information

This chapter provides a thorough explanation of setting up a simple Postfix mail server on your Ubuntu system. If you are going to run your own mail server, you should purchase one of the various Postfix books that are available so that you have an exhaustive, dedicated resource at your fingertips if anything ever goes wrong. The following are some of my favorites:

- *Postfix* by Richard Blum (Sams, 2001; ISBN: 0672321149): I have used this book for years, and it has always been an excellent basic reference for me, although it is the oldest and therefore is missing all of the configuration parameters that have been added since 2001.

- *Postfix: The Definitive Guide* by Kyle D. Dent (O'Reilly Media, 2003; ISBN: 0596002122): Another typically thorough guide from O'Reilly, with a Foreword by Witse Venema (creator of Postfix), who also reviewed the book as it was being written.

- *The Book of Postfix: State-of-the-Art Message Transport* by Ralf Hildebrandt and Patrick Koetter (No Starch Press, 2005; ISBN: 1593270011): Ralf Hildebrandt is a well-known Postfix expert and advocate — his Postfix Shrine web site was mentioned earlier as an excellent Postfix resource (more useful if you happen to speak German). Don't worry, monolinguals: the book is even better, and it's in English.

As with all hi-tech topics nowadays, your favorite search engine (www.clusty.com or www.google.com are two popular ones) is your best friend when looking for immediate help with a specific configuration problem, error message, or general Postfix problem.

Summary

E-mail is one of the killer applications of today's Internet, and running your own mail server is standard operating procedure in many enterprise and academic environments and is getting more and more common for home users. The complete control that running your own mail server provides can be a valuable asset in almost any environment, reducing if not eliminating spam and malicious system attacks through e-mail viruses and Trojans.

This chapter provided background information about the most popular Linux mail systems in use today, and then focused on installing and configuring the Postfix mail server. This chapter also explained how to integrate add-on services such as spam filtering and virus detection into a standard Postfix installation. Postfix is a powerful and easily configured mail server, with which a variety of additional open source services can be easily but tightly integrated.

Chapter 31, "Setting Up a DHCP Server," discusses how to install and configure a Dynamic Host Control Protocol Server (DHCP), which enables you to manage and monitor the distribution of IP addresses to client computer systems on your network. Dynamically assigning e-mail addresses enables you to serve a large pool of client systems with a relatively small set of IP addresses, and also simplifies the process to ensure that all client computer systems share the same network configuration data. Using DHCP also simplifies updating basic network information on client systems because this information is stored and updated centrally and can easily be pushed to all clients by the DHCP server.

Setting Up a DHCP Server

IN THIS CHAPTER

Overviewing DHCP

Configuring a DHCP server from the command line

Configuring a DHCP server graphically

Troubleshooting DHCP

A long time ago when even I was young, the Internet (or the *ARPANET* as it was called in those days) was a small place with a limited number of hosts, all of which had fixed IP addresses and names that were maintained in a file that everyone shared with everyone else, and then added their own local modifications for any private, local hosts and networks. However, as the ARPANET grew and more and more hosts became networked, maintaining all of this information in a single file became not only impractical, but also silly. This led to a flexible, software-based service known as the *Domain Name System* (DNS), which provided a flexible mechanism for identifying the hostname associated with an IP address, and vice versa. (For more information about DNS, see Chapter 32, "Setting Up a DNS Server.")

Why begin a chapter on DHCP (Dynamic Host Configuration Protocol) by discussing DNS? Because DHCP and its predecessors were largely developed to address similar sorts of scalability and flexibility by providing a similarly flexible service that could dynamically provide various types of network-related information. When few hosts at a site are networked and those hosts are all located on the same subnet, assigning them static IP addresses and statically maintaining other IP-related information such as name-server identities is reasonable. However, as the number of hosts on a network grows and hosts are added more and more frequently, requiring that someone from IT manually install and configure each host's networking quickly becomes impractical. Similarly, networked laptops are frequently used in multiple locations, each of which may require a different network configuration.

This chapter provides a bit of background information on DHCP and its predecessors, the types of problems that they were developed to solve, and then explains how to set up your own DHCP server and some of the issues to consider when doing so. This chapter focuses on DHCP servers for traditional IPv4 networks.

Overview of DHCP

DHCP stands for "Dynamic Host Configuration Protocol." But what does that mean for the users of a network? It means that when everything is working correctly, you should be able to connect your computer to the data jack on the wall with an Ethernet cable, and the University's computer will recognize your computer and allow it to join the network.

DHCP is used to provide network configuration information to the computer systems on a network that are configured to retrieve information dynamically. These systems, known as DHCP clients, locate a system running a software service known as a *DHCP server* and obtain network configuration information from that system.

DHCP was created by the Dynamic Host Configuration Working Group of the Internet Engineering Task Force (IETF). It was originally created to satisfy the requirements of Internet Request for Comments (RFC) document 1531, which begat RFC 1533 (which begat RFC 2132), which begat RFC 1534, which begat RFC 1541, which begat RFC 2131, and so on. As with all Internet RFCs, reading these documents can provide some fascinating insights into the thought processes that led to the development of many of the concepts and services that we all take for granted on today's networks and the Internet in general. You can access the IETF's RFC archive through the URL www.ietf.org/rfc.html, or find those same RFCs at a somewhat easier-to-browse site at www.faqs.org/rfcs. Some of these are true classics, such as RFCs 1149, 2549, and so on.

DHCP is based on an earlier protocol for retrieving the information required to boot specific hosts known as *BOOTP*, and maintains some backward compatibility with BOOTP—hosts that require BOOTP (such as some embedded systems) can retrieve the required information from a correctly configured DHCP server. The key difference between the two is that BOOTP was designed to provide specific responses to requests from specific hosts, whereas DHCP is a much more flexible system that responds to requests from essentially random clients. DHCP also provides a configurable mechanism for reallocating IP addresses to hosts that already have them and recovering network addresses that are no longer in use through its concept of *limited-duration leases*.

A DHCP client locates and retrieves network configuration information from a DHCP server through the following series of events. (For simplicity's sake, this example ignores routing DHCP requests through relay agents.)

1. A client broadcasts a DHCP discover message to the address 255.255.255.255. This broadcast includes information that uniquely identifies the client, such as its Media Access Control (MAC) address.

2. Any DHCP servers that receive the offer return an appropriate IP address by broadcasting a DHCP offer message. The IP address that is offered is based on the network interface and subnet from which the request was received, and is either a pre-allocated IP address that is associated with a specific MAC address, or one from the set of available addresses that this server can offer on the designated subnet. (The set of IP addresses that a specific DHCP server can provide is typically known as the *pool of addresses* for that server.) IP addresses that cannot be issued by a DHCP server are those that are already in use or those that are reserved for use by clients with specific MAC addresses.

   When broadcasting an offer message, the server temporarily reserves this address so that it does not offer it twice. The information returned to the client also includes information about any other configuration services that the DHCP server can provide for the client.

3. The DHCP client selects the best offer that it has received based on the type and number of services offered and broadcasts a request that identifies the IP address of the server whose offer it wants to accept. This broadcast enables all other DHCP servers to drop any addresses that they may have temporarily reserved and move on.

4. The DHCP server identified in the second broadcast message allocates the IP address that it has reserved for the client and enters that IP address into its database of allocated IP addresses, along with a timestamp identifying when it was allocated and an identifier for the time period for which assigned IP addresses are valid (the *lease period*). The DHCP server then sends an ACK (Acknowledge) response back to the client that contains all of the network configuration information that it can provide.

5. The DHCP client uses the configuration information sent to it by the DHCP server to configure its network interfaces, DNS servers, and so on, and continues booting. The client also notes the duration of the lease period and begins a countdown timer that will notify the DHCP server when the lease expires, asking for an extension. When this occurs, and if the extension request adheres to the DHCP server's lease policy, the DHCP server extends the lease.

When a DHCP server issues a lease for an IP address, it either begins a timer or simply polls to verify that the lease period for a specific IP address has not expired and that the address is still in use. Most DHCP clients notify a DHCP server that they no longer need an IP address as part of their orderly shutdown process. DHCP clients that "terminate abnormally" (i.e., *crash*) don't have time to do this, but any IP address that they allocated will automatically be freed for reuse by the DHCP server some period of time after the lease expires.

As you can see from this explanation, DHCP is an extremely clever and powerful mechanism that serves both the needs of hosts that require specific configuration settings (and which are therefore identified in the DHCP server's configuration information) and the requirements of random clients that just happen to appear on the subnet that a DHCP server is monitoring.

Note

The flip side of flexibility is the ease with which the wrong thing can happen. For example, DHCP servers that are misconfigured or started by accident may provide DHCP clients with completely incorrect information. In my experience, the most common cause of DHCP problems is "randoms" starting invalid DHCP servers on networks that already have an official DHCP server. In enterprise environments, few things can make a sysadmin crankier than someone starting a misconfigured DHCP server on their network(s). This is easy enough to do, especially on multi-homed systems (systems with multiple Ethernet interfaces) where you might have forgotten to identify the Ethernet interface that you wanted your DHCP server to listen on. ∎

Now that we're all one with the concept of DHCP servers and the types of information that they provide, let's install and configure one.

Installing a DHCP Server

Most server processes aren't installed as part of a default Ubuntu installation because not everybody needs (or wants) to run servers. However, as with all software packages on Ubuntu systems, the Package Management software discussed in Chapter 19, "Adding, Removing, and Updating Software," makes it easy to install a DHCP server. The DHCP server that I suggest installing is the Institutional Service Component's (ISC) v3 server, which is found in the package `dhcp3-server`. This is the latest and greatest DHCP server available and is certainly the one that provides the most functionality.

If your system has a GUI, I also suggest that you install the `gadmin-dhcpd` package, which provides an easy-to-use graphical interface that simplifies configuring and customizing a DHCP server. Installing a graphical DHCP server configuration tool is, of course, optional, but these tools can be quite convenient if you are new to DHCP configuration: They prevent most syntax errors because they create the DHCP configuration file based on fields that you fill in. They can also be useful if you are simply not a fan of using a text editor for everything. Another solution is to install a Web-based system configuration tool such as `webmin` if you are also running a Web server on the system on which your DHCP server is running. For more information about `webmin`, see Chapter 29, "Setting Up a Web Server."

If your system obtains its address through DHCP, packages such as `dhcp3-client` and `dhcp3-common` will already be installed on your system. The former contains the DHCP client that enables a system to get a DHCP address and related files, and the latter contains documentation, sample files, and utilities that are shared by all of the ISC DHCP packages. Be very careful when installing a new DHCP server in this scenario because this means that another DHCP server must already be running somewhere on your network. Your system will get its IP address earlier in the system startup process than when your DHCP server is started, but this is still a potentially dangerous thing to do.

Tip

If you are also running a DNS server, you may also want to install the `autodns-dhcp` package, which can automatically update a DNS server with information about systems whose IP information was newly assigned via DHCP. ∎

Alternate DHCP Servers

The Ubuntu repositories provide several DHCP servers in addition to the one that I suggested installing. One or the other of these may be better suited to your network configuration. Also, thanks to the fact that DHCP is, indeed, a standard, all DHCP servers use the same configuration commands. They may use different configuration files, but the commands that these files contain are the same across all DHCP servers. The following are optional DHCP servers available for Ubuntu systems:

- dnsmasq: A small-footprint DNS server (and proxy) that can also act as a DHCP server. I don't recommend this package as your primary DHCP server unless you have a specific reason not to use BIND, which is the standard, and most popular, DNS server. However, with its DHCP server support disabled, dnsmasq can be quite useful on laptops because of its DNS caching capabilities. See Chapter 32 for more information about BIND.

- udhcpd: A very small-footprint DHCP server designed primarily for use in embedded systems. You may want to install this DHCP server if memory or storage resource minimization is critical.

- wide-dhcpv6-server: A DHCP server for IPv6 hosts, this DHCP server requires that you use an IPv6 DHCP client such as wide-dhcpv6-client on any IPv6 systems that you want to configure using DHCP.

The DHCP server that you want to use is up to you. I suggest the dhcpd3-server package because it corresponds to the latest and greatest DHCP server available from the ISC. Your mileage may vary (or your environment may suggest or mandate a different DHCP server).

When running a DHCP server on a system that is itself a client of some other DHCP server, you must make sure that your new DHCP server hands out a different range of IP addresses from the existing DHCP server (and I hope that you're the sysadmin of that network!), is restricted to a different Ethernet interface from the one that your system uses to obtain its IP address, is restricted to specific hardware addresses, or all of the above. It's somewhat unusual to run a DHCP server on a system that itself gets its address via DHCP unless that system has multiple Ethernet interfaces and thus serves as a gateway or router between multiple networks. Most servers have fixed IP addresses so that you can always contact them even if services such as DNS are unavailable. As mentioned previously, setting up a DHCP server that hands out addresses on a network that you are not responsible for is usually bad form, at best.

Managing a DHCP Server from the Command Line

There are always a few people who would rather fight than switch, which in this case means that they would rather create a DHCP server configuration file with a text editor than use a whizzy graphical tool. That's fine — using a text editor is probably faster if you know what you're doing (or are willing to accept the consequences). The next few sections explain how to manually create DHCP server's configuration file and discuss some of the more important options that you may need to add to a DHCP server's configuration file to maximize its usability in your environment.

Creating DHCP Configuration Files Using a Text Editor

This section explains the basics of a DHCP configuration file and the most common set of entries that you will need to put in your configuration file to serve a specific range of IP addresses via a shiny new DHCP server.

Tip

The file /etc/dhcp3/dhcpd.conf is the configuration file used by the dhcpd3 server that I suggested installing in the previous sidebar. If you installed another DHCP server, shame on you — but I'm sure that you had your reasons, and its configuration file is probably /etc/dhcpd.conf, which is the traditional location for a DHCP server's configuration file. An easy way to verify the configuration file used by your DHCP server is the following command, where *server-name* is the name of the executable for your DHCP server:

```
strings $(which server-name) | grep dhcpd.conf
```

This will display several strings, one of which will be the full pathname of your DHCP server's configuration file. This works for all of the DHCP servers that I've used — you may find that you need to be slightly more creative with the arguments to the grep command, but you'll certainly find your config file with some similar command. ∎

To configure DHCP for your network, you need to add at least the following section (referred to by DHCP config file fans as a *stanza*) to your DHCP server's configuration file:

```
1: option domain-name "your.domain.name";
2: option domain-name-servers nameserver1-address, nameserver2-address,... ;
3: option routers router-address;
4: option subnet-mask 255.255.255.0;
5: subnet subnet-address netmask netmask-for-that-subnet  {
6:   range full-start-address full-end-address;
7: }
```

Note

The actual configuration file used by your DHCP server does not include line numbers (and cannot). I've added the line numbers to make it easier to match up entries in this sample file with the explanations that follow. ∎

This example provides an extremely minimal DHCP server configuration file that is useful, but which leverages many of the default values provided by the DHCP server. Each line of this stanza has the following meaning:

1. The name of the domain to which any host that receives an IP address from this server should belong. Replace *your.domain.name* with the name of your domain. This

configuration file entry is a global setting for the DHCP server and will apply to all subnet entries that it contains (unless they specifically override this value). On Linux systems, this domain is written to the file /etc/resolv.conf without preserving any existing entries. See Chapter 32 for more information about the /etc/resolv.conf file.

2. The name(s) of any DNS servers that any host that receives an IP address from this server should use to do DNS lookups. Replace *nameserver1-address*, *nameserver2-address*, and so on with the IP addresses of your DNS servers. If you are not running your own DNS server, you can use any DNS servers that your ISP provides, or one of the public DNS servers from sites such as OpenDNS.com (http://opendns.com/). This configuration file entry is a global setting for the DHCP server and will apply to all subnet entries that it contains (unless they specifically override this value). On Linux systems, these name servers are added to the file /etc/resolv.conf without preserving any existing entries. See Chapter 32 for more information about the /etc/resolv.conf file.

3. The third line identifies the IP address of the system through which requests for any host that is not found on the local network should be sent. Replace *router-address* with the IP address of your router. This configuration file entry is a global setting for the DHCP server and will apply to all subnet entries that it contains (unless they specifically override this value).

4. The fourth line specifies the default subnet mask to use on computers that get their IP addresses from this DHCP server. This is typically 255.255.255.0, but may differ depending on the configuration of your network. This configuration file entry is a global setting for the DHCP server and will apply to all subnet entries that it contains (unless they specifically override this value).

Note

Each global setting line in the host section ends with a semicolon. ∎

5. The fifth line identifies the subnet on which the DHCP server should hand out IP addresses. This is expressed by identifying the base address of a network, using zeroes for IP address fields that the DNS server can provide, and by specifying the subnet mask used to derive IP addresses on that network. Replace *subnet-address* with the base address of the network on which you will be handing out IP addresses, and replace *netmask-for-that-subnet* with the appropriate netmask.

6. The sixth line identifies the range of IP addresses that the DHCP server can issue to clients. Replace *full-start-address* with the first IP address that you want your DHCP server to provide, and replace *full-end-address* with the last IP address that you want your DHCP server to provide.

7. The final line terminates the entry for the specified subnet.

After making these changes to your DHCP server's configuration file, you must start (or restart) the DHCP server. If the DHCP server is running and you installed the DHCP server that I recommended, you can kill and restart it by using the following command:

```
$ sudo /etc/rc.d/init.d/dhcp3-server restart
```

All other DHCP servers provide similar start/restart configuration scripts — if you installed another DHCP server, check its control files in /etc/init.d for the name of the script that you need to execute and any additional arguments that you may need to supply.

Specifying Additional DHCP Server Configuration File Entries

In addition to the DHCP configuration statements discussed in the previous section, you can specify several other options in your DHCP server's configuration file. Using these other options can provide your DHCP server with additional configuration information, which enables it to forward this information to any of its clients.

Additional global dhcpd.conf statements that you may find useful are the following. An example of a dhcpd.conf file that uses these statements is given following the list, to clarify the context in which each statement can be used:

- default-lease-time: This DHCP server configuration option enables you to specify the default period of time for which a lease will be valid. The time period is specified as an integer number of seconds.

- ddns-update-style: This declaration is used if your site uses a DNS (Domain Name Server) server that can be automatically updated as addresses are assigned by the DHCP server and you installed the autodns-dhcp package on your DHCP server to integrate the two. If your site does not use a DNS server that accepts updates from a DHCP server, you should set this parameter to None to avoid potential performance problems.

- ip-forwarding: If, for example, you don't want a DHCP client to be able to forward IP requests to other networks, you may want to set this parameter to off. This option is sometimes used on local-only IP networks.

- max-lease-time: This DHCP server configuration option enables you to specify the maximum period of time for which a lease will be valid. The time period is specified as an integer number of seconds.

You can also use DHCP to provide specific IP addresses to specific hosts within a subnet group, where a host is identified by MAC address. This is done using the host declaration within a subnet group. An example of this, an associated, host-specific command, is the following:

```
authoritative;
option domain-name "vonhagen.org";
option domain-name-servers 192.168.6.1, 208.67.222.222;
option routers 192.168.6.1;
option ddns-update-style interim;
option default-lease-time 28800;
option max-lease-time 86400;
option ip-forwarding off;
subnet 192.168.6.0 netmask 255.255.255.0  {
    range 192.168.6.160  192.168.6.190
```

```
host dorothy {
    hardware ethernet 00:1E:0C:1D:75:1D;
    fixed_address 192.168.6.69;
    option host_name "dorothy" ;
  }
}
```

Note that the example for the specific host named dorothy overrides any default values specified earlier in the file.

Picking the Right Lease Period

The lease time for your server's DHCP clients is a delicate balance between usability and serviceability. You want clients that have been configured via DHCP to keep that configuration as long as they need that information, but you also want to maximize the availability of DHCP configuration to other clients on your network. This is especially (and primarily) important on networks where the number of potential users exceeds the number of available IP addresses.

Identifying any conceivable patterns in how users access and use your DHCP server will help determine a usable lease period. For example, if you know that the number of possible clients exceeds the number of available IP addresses, it's in your best interest to keep the lease period as short as possible. On the other hand, you want to minimize network traffic and the load on your DHCP server. If you have many more users than IP addresses and mobile users frequently connect to your network, you will want to keep the lease time as short as possible. However, if systems typically appear on your network for a certain period of time (30 minutes, an hour, etc.), you will want to set the lease time to that period to minimize lease refresh requests.

Another consideration is the amount of time required to recover from network problems or hardware failures on the DHCP server. For example, if your DHCP server were to crash and burn, the lease period would define the maximum amount of time that DHCP clients would maintain their current network configuration.

Finally, consider the *silly user* factor. If clients of your DHCP server are setting up network services that they expect others to be able to access for a significant amount of time, you may need to make sure that your DHCP leases are valid for at least that period of time. Even though DHCP leases are supposed to be renewed when they are actively in use, this may not happen for one reason or another. As we all learned in Cub Scouts, Brownies, or similar groups, "Be prepared." If users report problems, you can always fix things and report a success story, but sometimes no comments are the best comments of all.

Managing a DHCP Server Graphically

As you might expect, the Ubuntu repository provides an excellent GTK utility for graphically configuring a DHCP server. You should have installed this package (gadmin-dhcpd) as part of the instructions for installing a DHCP server in the section of this chapter entitled "Installing a DHCP Server."

Installing the `gadmin-dhcpd` package creates a GADMIN-DHCPD entry on the Applications ⇨ System Tools menu, which you can select to start Ubuntu's graphical DHCP server configuration tool. Unfortunately, the first time you start this utility, you'll need to specify the location of the DHCP server configuration and leases files. Start the `gadmin-dhcpd` command from a GNOME Terminal, xterm, or other Ubuntu command-line interface using the following command:

```
$ gksudo gdhcpd /etc/dhcp3/dhcpd.conf /var/lib/dhcp3/dhcpd.leases
```

After you supply your password, the `gadmin-dhcpd` utility starts, as shown in Figure 31-1.

FIGURE 31-1

Starting the gadmin-dhcpd configuration utility

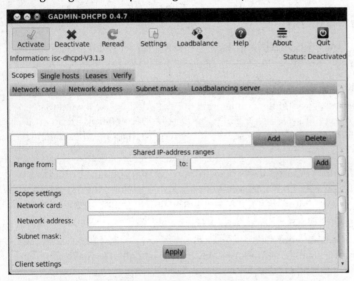

The first thing to do is to identify the scope for this DHCP server, which is the Ethernet interface that this DHCP will listen on, the possible range of IP addresses that it will deliver, and the subnet mask that it will use. To do this, enter these values in the fields shown in Figure 31-2, which identify a DHCP server running on Ethernet interface `eth0` of the host that will hand out IP addresses on the `192.168.6.0` subnet using a subnet mask of `255.255.255.0`.

Note

A *scope* is a way of identifying the complete range of possible IP addresses for a network. A scope typically defines a single physical subnet on your network to which DHCP services are offered. Scopes provide the primary way for a DHCP server to manage distributing and managing a specific range of IP addresses and delivering them (and other network configuration parameters) to clients on that subnet. ∎

FIGURE 31-2

Identifying the DHCP server's Ethernet information

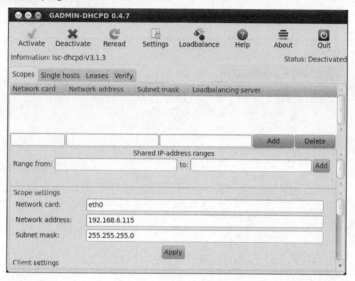

Once you have entered this information, click Apply to define that interface/server/netmask combination. An entry for that server displays on the Scopes tab, as shown in Figure 31-3.

FIGURE 31-3

Successful addition of a DHCP server scope

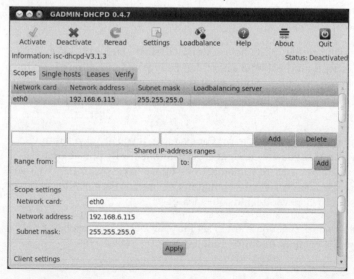

Next, enter the range of IP addresses that you want this DHCP server to offer to clients, as shown in Figure 31-4.

FIGURE 31-4

Identifying a range of DHCP addresses to serve

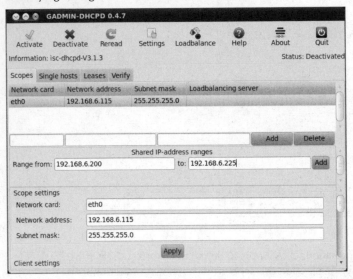

After entering these values, click Add to define this range. The defined range displays in the primary gadmin-dhcpd dialog, as shown in Figure 31-5.

Finally, click Settings to examine the default settings associated with your DHCP server. The dialog shown in Figure 31-6 displays.

Change any of the values on this screen that reflect how your DHCP server should behave. If you are configuring a DHCP server other than the dhcp3 server that I suggested installing earlier in this chapter, you may need to change the name of the DHCP server's configuration file and the path to the file in which DHCP leases are stored to reflect the appropriate locations for that DHCP server.

You may also want to change general configuration items. For example, if you are also running a DHCP server and the DHCP server that you are configuring can automatically update that server, you should change the value of the DDNS (Dynamic DNS) update style parameter to either ad-hoc or interim (ad hoc has been deprecated and should not be used; interim allows your DHCP server to update a DNS server whenever it hands out a lease).

Once you have verified any global values that you want to set for your DHCP server, click Apply to close this dialog and return to the primary gadmin-dhcpd dialog.

FIGURE 31-5

A defined range of DHCP addresses to serve

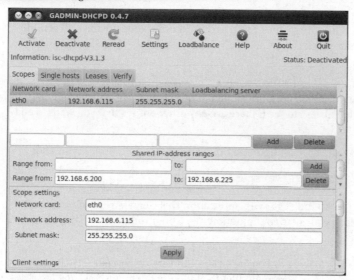

FIGURE 31-6

General DHCP server settings

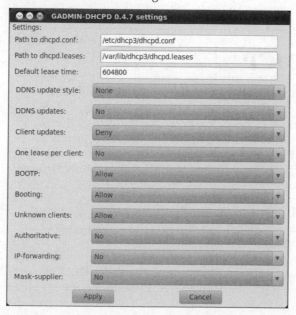

If you are finished defining ranges of DHCP addresses that you want your DHCP server to offer to clients, click Quit to exit the gadmin-dhcpd configuration utility. Your DHCP server is configured — all that remains is to start it! Though you can start your DHCP server by clicking Activate in the gadmin-dhcpd configuration utility, this is a one-time start of the utility. It's generally a better idea to start it using the standard system startup scripts in order to test what will actually occur when you restart your computer system.

Tip

Before starting your DHCP server, you may want to check the section of this chapter entitled "Specifying Additional DHCP Server Configuration File Entries" to see if there are any other entries that you want to add to your DHCP server's configuration file. ∎

To start your DHCP server using the new configuration file, execute the following command:

```
$ sudo /etc/init.d/dhcpd3-server restart
```

This terminates any version of the dhcpd3-server application that may be running and forces the process to restart, which reads your new configuration file. Congratulations — you're running a DHCP server.

At this point, you should check the file /var/log/messages to verify that your DHCP server started correctly. You can do this using a command like the following, which shows the last 100 lines in this file (just in case):

```
$ sudo tail -100 /var/.log/messages
```

If the DHCP server did not start correctly or clients cannot successfully connect to the DHCP server, see the following section for some debugging and troubleshooting tips.

Troubleshooting DHCP

The most common cause of DHCP problems is that the server did not start correctly or has already handed out all of the leases that are available to it. By default, any startup, status, and error messages from a DHCP server are written to the log file /var/log/messages. If your DHCP server does not start correctly, this file is the first place to look. If you have manually created your DHCP server's configuration file, missing semicolons or other syntax errors will cause the DHCP server to exit or, worst case, start up in some mode other than the one that you intended.

If a client computer is unable to contact a DHCP server, it usually assigns itself an IP address like 169.x.x.x, which traditionally means that your computer can't connect to the network. If any client system gets an address in this range, the first things to check are the obvious ones: Is the client computer actually connected to a port on your local network? And is the Ethernet interface that is connected configured as a DHCP client? On Ubuntu systems, you can check the configuration of your Ethernet interface(s) by selecting the System ⇨ Administration ⇨ Networking menu item and supplying your password. You should also check the /var/log/messages file on your DHCP server to see if the DHCP request from that client was received but rejected for some reason.

On multi-homed systems, a very common problem is that a DHCP server is listening on the wrong Ethernet interface and is therefore not receiving DHCP client requests on that subnet. Starting a DHCP server on a specific Ethernet interface is done by identifying the name of that Ethernet interface on the command line that starts the DHCP server, which is typically in a file with a name like /etc/init.d/dhcpd. The name of this file may be different depending on the DHCP server that you are using.

A final suggestion is to explicitly force the client to release any lease that it may believe it currently has. The dhclient3 -r command (or dhclient -r command, if you are running a v2 DHCP client) forces the client to explicitly release any leases that it believes that it has. The DHCP client then exits — you can restart it by executing a command like the following:

```
$ sudo /etc/init.d/networking restart
```

This restarts all of the networking-related processes on your system, starting the DHCP client as part of that sequence if your system is, indeed, configured as a DHCP client.

Summary

Being able to dynamically assign and centrally manage client IP address and network configuration information dramatically simplifies life for many system administrators. This chapter explained how to install a Dynamic Host Configuration Protocol (DHCP) server on your Ubuntu system, using either command-line or graphical software management tools. It then explained how to configure your DHCP server either from the command line or user-friendly graphical tools. The chapter concluded by discussing potential problems that you may encounter when using and configuring DHCP, and provided ways to diagnose and correct them.

Chapter 32 discusses how to set up your own Domain Name System (DNS) server. A DNS server maps hostnames to IP addresses (and vice versa) and is often a necessity on corporate or academic networks where you must manage your own hostnames and internal IP addresses.

Setting Up a DNS Server

IN THIS CHAPTER

Overviewing DNS and BIND

Overviewing BIND
   configuration files

Creating zone files

Creating reverse lookup files

Troubleshooting DNS

As I mentioned in Chapter 31, "Setting Up a DHCP Server," a long time ago when even I was young, the Internet (or the *ARPANET* as it was called in those days) was a small place with a limited number of hosts, all of which had fixed IP addresses. The mappings between those IP addresses and the actual names of those hosts were maintained in a central text file. Yes, that's right, a single text file. Everyone shared this text file (HOSTS.TXT) with everyone else by retrieving it from the Stanford Research Institute's Network Information Center (the one true NIC) every so often, and then adding their own modifications for any private local hosts and networks. However, as the ARPANET grew and more and more hosts became networked, maintaining all of this information in a single file became not only impractical, but silly.

Not only was this file long (and getting longer), but also its format was only specified by convention rather than explicit decree. Luckily, the Internet/ARPANET was created by smart people, so many improvements to this model occurred in the early 1980s. For example, in March of 1982, the hosts table definition was updated with the Department of Defense Internet Host Table Specification (RFC 810). Shortly thereafter, a server function to provide individual hostname/address translations was described in Request For Comment 811, which introduced the idea of dynamically providing and maintaining host information. RFC 819, "The Domain Naming Convention for Internet User Applications," woke everyone up, and RFC 830, "A Distributed System for Internet Name Service," suggested the one true concept of a distributed system of name servers, each serving its local domain. From 1982 to 1983 was a busy time for the fundamental concepts that we all take for granted today (and may not even be aware of).

Tip

Once the appropriate RFCs came out and people had the chance to think about them, implementation was the next step. By November 1983, the concept and schedule for actually implementing DNS were developed and published in RFC 881, "The Domain Names Plan and Schedule"; RFC 882, "Domain Names — Concepts and Facilities"; and RFC 883, "Domain Names — Implementation and Specification." ∎

In response to these RFCs, the clever folks at the University of California at Berkeley (UCB) created a software package called *BIND*, for "Berkeley Internet Name Daemon." Amusingly enough, this was first written as a graduate student project. BIND was eventually taken over and maintained first by the University's Computer Systems Research Group (CSRG), and then by Digital Equipment Corporation (DEC) for a while, and then eventually by the Internet Systems Consortium (www.isc.org), which still maintains BIND today. Many other DNS-related RFCs (973, 1035, etc.) have been published on DNS since the original flurry, some enhancing existing RFCs and some replacing them with newer, more modern and more specific, content. As mentioned in Chapter 31, you can find Internet RFCs at sites such as www.ietf.org/rfc.html or the somewhat easier-to-browse site at www.faqs.org/rfcs.

Note

References to BIND throughout the rest of this chapter should be taken to mean BIND version 9, which is the version that I suggest (and describe) installing and using. ∎

DNS was primarily designed to address the scalability problems that prompted the migration of hostname/IP address mappings from a central file to a flexible mechanism that can be queried and that returns results. This has some great additional benefits for local subnets in today's ubiquitous networking universe, where private networks can support their own DNS servers that satisfy local, private requests while forwarding requests for external host information to higher-level name servers. These local name servers can also cache retrieved requests, reducing the number of external network requests that your name servers have to issue over time. Many sites run name servers that only serve to cache external requests, and are therefore known as *caching-only name servers*.

The remainder of this chapter provides an overview of how DNS works, how to install the latest version of the BIND name server on your Ubuntu system, how to create the text files required for a basic BIND installation and integrate them into your BIND server, how to restart and test a BIND server, and how to diagnose many common DNS problems.

Note

BIND and DNS are rich, complex topics about which many entire books have been written. The last section of this chapter provides pointers to some more detailed, dedicated DNS and BIND resources that you can find online. If you are going to be setting up and managing complex or commercial DNS servers, I'd suggest that you pay a quick visit to any brick-and-mortar or online bookseller for dedicated DNS and BIND reference material that you will always have at your fingertips regardless of the state of your network. Two of my favorites are *DNS and BIND*, 5th ed. by Cricket Liu and Paul Albitz (O'Reilly Media, 2006; ISBN: 978-0596100575 — make sure you get the latest edition!), and *Pro DNS and BIND* by Ron Aitchison (Apress, 2005; ISBN: 978-1590594940). You can find the latter online at www.netwidget.net/books/apress/dns, but you should still buy a copy. ∎

Overview of DNS and BIND

DNS gives your network an entry point into a hierarchical collection of hostname and IP address servers on an intranet or the Internet itself. All of the hosts on your network can query one or more local DNS servers for local hostname and IP address information. Requests for hostname and IP address information outside the administrative domain of your DNS servers are automatically passed up the DNS food chain until some DNS server can authoritatively give you the information you're looking for.

A common DNS misconception is that a system needs to run a DNS server to participate in DNS. This is not the case. Systems can be pure DNS clients without running a name server process. The client-side portion of the DNS system is known as a *resolver*, which is configured through the file /etc/resolv.conf (which I'll discuss later in this section). Whether a system participates in DNS at all is configured through your system's Name Service Switch file, /etc/nsswitch .conf, which is also discussed in detail later in this section.

Most hosts have traditional sources of hostname/IP address information, such as /etc/hosts files, as well as DNS servers. When an application needs to contact a specific host by name, your system goes through the following process:

1. It first checks the /etc/nsswitch.conf file's hosts entry to determine how your system is configured to resolve hostnames and IP addresses. The /etc/nsswitch (Name Service Switch) identifies the sequence in which files and network resources should be consulted to find a variety of information, including hostname/IP address information. The hosts entry generally looks something like the following:

```
hosts:    files dns [NOTFOUND=return] nis nisplus
```

The system on which this entry is used first looks in the /etc/hosts file for host information and then consults DNS. If the host is not found after querying DNS servers, the hostname/IP address lookup fails. Items in a hosts entry after [NOTFOUND=return] are not consulted, but are often left on this line as a reminder that they are valid values for hostname/IP address information. In this example, the NIS and NIS+ information services would not be consulted.

Tip

Some older applications still consult another configuration file called /etc/host.conf. This file provides similar information to that provided in /etc/nssiwtch.conf files about the order in which an /etc/hosts file and DNS should be consulted using the following entry:

```
order hosts,bind
```

The resolver functions in most recent versions of glibc use /etc/nsswitch.conf. However, if you have changed your /etc/nsswitch.conf file and some specific application is consulting /etc/hosts and DNS in the wrong order, check your /etc/host.conf file. You may also want to report the problem to the current maintainer of the program that you were running. ■

2. Assuming the hostname or IP address of a specific host is not found in the `/etc/hosts` file, a system that is configured to consult DNS checks the contents of the text file `/etc/resolv.conf` to identify the DNS name servers that it should consult, in order. This file also often contains information such as the default domain that should be supplied when looking up non-fully qualified hostnames. For example, the `/etc/resolv.conf` file on one of my Ubuntu systems looks like the following:

```
domain vonhagen.org
nameserver 0.0.0.0
nameserver 192.168.6.64
nameserver 208.67.222.222
nameserver 208.67.220.22
```

In this example, non-fully qualified hostnames such as `64bit` are assumed to be within the domain `vonhagen.org`. The name servers are queried in order until one responds or a maximum number of connection failures and associated retries have elapsed, in which case the query fails. The name servers `208.67.222.222` and `208.67.220.22` are public name servers from the folks at `OpenDNS.com`, who provide public name servers and related services, and are well worth checking out! For a list of publicly available DNS servers all over the world, see `www.dnsserverlist.org`.

Tip

A name server specification of `0.0.0.0` is actually a shortcut for querying a local name server using the first IP address that was assigned to the local system. This is the loopback address, which is usually `127.0.0.1`, but is not guaranteed to be. Using the shortcut `0.0.0.0` causes your request to be sent to an IP address that is known to be valid for the current host, whatever it may be. ■

3. When a DNS server responds, it first tries to resolve the query itself. DNS servers are configured through many specially formatted text files that are discussed in the next section. These files identify any DNS zones, which are essentially analogous to a domain or subdomain that the server can provide authoritative information for. If the hostname or IP address request is in a zone that the DNS server is authoritative for or it is already present in the server's cache of previously answered requests, the DNS server will reply directly to the request. If the request is in a subdomain that the DNS server knows an authoritative source of information for, it will forward the request to that DNS server for resolution. That DNS server will then reply to the client.

4. If the first DNS server that responds cannot resolve the request in one way or another, it queries one of the Internet's top-level name servers (known as *root servers*) to identify the name server that it believes is responsible for the domain or the range of IP addresses that contains the IP address for which the application is looking for hostname information.

5. The root name server returns a pointer to the appropriate name server, which your system then queries for hostname or IP address information. If this name server is not actually authoritative for the domain or IP address that you are querying, it may forward the query to other name servers — this hierarchy continues until a name server is found that is actually authoritative for the domain or IP address that you are querying. This

forwarding is generally invisible to you and most often occurs when querying hosts on subdomains rather than top-level domains.

This combination of local, root, and hierarchical name servers is elegant in its simplicity. When your host finally receives the hostname or IP address that it is looking for, it typically caches that value so that subsequent requests for the same information won't have to go any further than the local name server.

BIND is generally configured in one of four ways:

- As a master server that is an authoritative source of DNS information for one or more zones, which generally map to a domain or subdomain

- As a slave server that is an authoritative source of DNS information for one or more zones, but periodically retrieves and synchronizes this information from a master server rather than being the actual repository for that information

- As a caching-only server that is not authoritative for any zone, but that caches the results from DNS queries to minimize network traffic and expedite answering multiple requests for the same DNS information. Most Ubuntu Server systems will run at least a caching-only name server for these reasons.

- As a resolver-only client that does not run a DNS Server but whose DNS resolver is configured to consult name servers through its /etc/resolv.conf file

Most desktop systems do not need to actually run a name server and will work fine as resolver-only clients. However, if you spend a vast amount of time surfing the Web or work on a heavily loaded network, you may want to upgrade your system to running a caching-only client. DNS servers do not consume a vast amount of system resources, but they do require memory, process slots, and so on. If a system that you are configuring or using does not need to provide host information for a zone (which would mandate running a DNS server), only the user(s) of a system can determine which of the caching-only or resolver-only configurations works best for that host.

Installing a DNS Server

Although every Ubuntu system provides the basic client-side commands for querying and dynamically mapping hostnames to IP addresses, an actual DNS server is not installed as part of a default Ubuntu installation. Let's face it — not everybody needs to run a DNS server, and for small, home networks, maintaining your /etc/hosts files isn't that big of an issue if you have only a few machines. However, if you want to run your own name server (which you will probably want to do if you are responsible for an enterprise network or a SOHO network with a relatively large number of hosts), the package management utilities provided on Ubuntu systems make it easy to install the BIND DNS server by installing the bind9 package. See Chapter 19, "Adding, Removing, and Updating Software," for more information about installing software on Ubuntu systems.

Tip

As always with server packages such as BIND, I suggest that you install BIND using `aptitude` from the command line. This will enable you to use the `-r` option to automatically install the packages that are recommended for use with BIND. They don't use much disk space, and having more tools is always better! ∎

After installing the `bind9` package and friends, setting up your own DNS server is a simple matter of creating a few configuration files, as explained in the next section.

Overview of BIND Configuration Files

The `/etc/nsswitch.conf` and `/etc/resolv.conf` files reflect your system's general approach to resolving hostname and IP address queries. The primary configuration file for the BIND name server, `named.conf`, is found in the directory `/etc/bind` on Ubuntu systems.

As delivered on Ubuntu systems, the `/etc/bind/named.conf` file primarily consists of statements that load other BIND configuration files, providing a simple, hierarchical structure for your BIND configuration files. The files that an Ubuntu BIND server loads fall into several categories:

- Configuration files for the BIND server process, `named`. BIND installations load a general, site-independent configuration file and a separate, site-specific configuration file. This simplifies future updates by making it easier to identify files that may have changed in the BIND installation on a specific system.

- Zone files that define the mapping of hostnames in that DNS zone to IP addresses

- Reverse lookup files that define the mapping of IP addresses in a numeric DNS zone to hostnames

As a specific example, the default `/etc/bind/named.conf` file on a BIND server loads the following files. These are listed in alphabetical order to simplify finding a file in this list rather than in the order that they are actually loaded:

- `/etc/bind/db.0`: Contains reverse lookup information that resolves the broadcast addresses `0.*`.

- `/etc/bind/db.127`: Contains reverse lookup information that resolves the loopback addresses `127.*`.

- `/etc/bind/db.255`: Contains reverse lookup information that resolves the broadcast addresses `255.*`.

- `/etc/bind/db.empty`: Contains a shared file that is used for each of the non-routable IP address families specified by RFC 1918, "Address Allocation for Private Internets" (`www.faqs.org/rfcs/rfc1918.html`).

- `/etc/bind/db.local`: Contains hostname to IP address information for the local loopback interface, `127.0.0.1`.

- `/etc/bind/db.root`: Contains hostname to IP address information for the root name servers.

- `/etc/bind/named.conf.local`: Contains zone entries that identify any zones and IP addresses for which this BIND server is a source of authoritative information. This file is a local, host-specific supplement to the file `/etc/named.conf`.

- `/etc/bind/named.conf.options`: Defines the basic options with which the local BIND server has been configured.

- `/etc/bind/zones.rfc1918`: Provides reverse lookup information for each of the non-routable IP families specified by RFC 1918, "Address Allocation for Private Internets" (`www.faqs.org/rfcs/rfc1918.html`). This file is not loaded by Ubuntu BIND servers by default, but can be loaded in your `/etc/bind/named.conf.local` file to reduce the time spent trying to resolve IP addresses in non-routable networks.

In most cases, you will modify only the `/etc/bin/named.conf.local` file for your BIND server. In this file, you will add entries for files that define the zones and IP address ranges for which your BIND server can provide authoritative DNS information.

Tip

The `/etc/bin/named.conf.options` file for BIND servers running on Ubuntu systems configures those servers to use `/var/cache/bind` as their default working directory. All temporary DNS data is stored in that directory. For this reason, all pathnames in the `/etc/bin/named.conf.local` file either should be the full pathnames of files located in non-transient directories in your filesystem, such as `/etc/bind`, or will be interpreted as files that are to be found in `/var/cache/bin`. ∎

A sample `/etc/bin/named.conf.local` file from one of my DNS servers looks like the following:

```
zone "vonhagen.org" {
type master;
file "/etc/bind/vonhagen.zone";
check-names warn;
};

zone "168.192.in-addr.arpa" {
type master;
file "/etc/bind/168.192.in-addr.arpa";
};

include "/etc/bind/zones.rfc1918.local";
```

As you can see, this DNS server is a master server for the zone `vonhagen.org`, which uses IP addresses in the `192.168.*` family. Information about the zone `vonhagen.org` is provided in the file `/etc/bind/vonhagen.zone`. Reverse lookup information for IP addresses in the `192.168.*` family is provided in the file `/etc/bin/168.192.in-addr.arpa`. As discussed previously, full pathnames must be provided for any files not found in `/var/cache/bind`, which is the default BIND server's default directory. This file also loads a local copy of the default /etc/ bin/zones.rfc1918 file, which I have edited to remove null responses for the zone "168.192 .in-addr.arpa" that I use locally.

The next section explains how to create the zone and reverse lookup files for any local systems for which your BIND server will provide authoritative information.

Creating DNS Zone and Reverse Lookup Files

As installed on Ubuntu systems, BIND is a caching-only name server that is appropriate for use on local servers or heavily network-dependent systems to help minimize the amount of external DNS traffic by caching DNS lookups so that subsequent requests for that same information can be provided from the cache rather than by repeating an external DNS request.

Many people want to run their own DNS servers to provide DNS information for the hosts that they are responsible for on their home, enterprise, or academic networks. As discussed earlier in this chapter, DNS information for each set of hosts and associated range of IP addresses is specified in a zone file, one that identifies the IP address associated with a specific hostname (known as name to IP address lookups), and one for reverse lookups that identifies the hostname that corresponds to a specific IP address. The next few sections discuss mandatory entries that are commonly used in both types of files, the format and content of a zone file, and the format and content of reverse lookup files.

Note
The files that I am calling *zone* and *reverse lookup* share the same format and are both examples of zone files. I refer to them separately because it's convenient to think of them that way. They contain different types of records and serve different logical purposes in the context of a DNS server. ■

Using Common Entries for Zone and Reverse Lookup Files: SOA and $TTL

The beginning of both zone and reverse lookup files contains variable settings for the BIND name server process (/usr/sbin/named) and an entry that sets basic variables for each zone or range of IP addresses for which your name server provides authoritative information.

A zone file typically begins with a TTL (Time To Live) entry that provides a default value for any record in the zone file. A TTL value determines how long remote DNS servers can cache any information about that resource that they have retrieved from your DNS server. The default TTL value is preceded with a dollar sign to indicate that you are setting a BIND server variable, and takes a time value expressed in seconds (the default), minutes, hours, or days. The sample TTL value that I generally use is 1 day (1d) because I frequently add, rename, or change hosts on my networks. This setting therefore looks like the following:

```
$TTL 1d
```

The most important entry in a zone or reverse lookup file is the Start of Authority (SOA) record, which defines global parameters for a zone or range of IP addresses. The format of an SOA record is defined in RFC 1035 (www.faqs.org/rfcs/rfc1035.html). A sample SOA record looks like the following:

```
@ 1d IN SOA ubuntu32.vonhagen.org. wvh.vonhagen.org. (
      2008090102 ; Serial
      21600      ; Refresh
      1800       ; Retry
      604800     ; Expiration
      900        ; Negative Cache TTL
)
```

Tip

One confusing thing about the SOA record (and, frankly, about many other DNS configuration file entries) is that many of the fields have default values and are therefore often omitted if the values that you specify are the same as the defaults. Personally, I find the practice of omitting values to be both lazy and the most common cause of DNS problems. The parser for DNS files is quite finicky (to use the technical term), and you will eventually burn yourself or one of your fellow sysadmins by leaving fields out. It's not as if any of the values in an SOA or other records in a zone or reverse lookup file are all that long or require all that much typing. Do everybody a favor — specify all of them. ∎

The fields in an SOA record are as follows:

1. The first field identifies the root name of the zone associated with this SOA record. The @ symbol is a shortcut for this name, which is specified in the zone declaration in the BIND configuration file (in this case, the file /etc/bind/named.conf.local). You may occasionally see people put an actual zone name here — I prefer to use the @ symbol because it more clearly differentiates the SOA record from other records in a zone or reverse lookup file.

2. The second field is the TTL value to this record. Even though I always put a default value at the beginning of a zone file, I simply repeat that value here to be more precise. This field is technically optional — if it is not specified, the default TTL for the server or an internal default value will be used.

3. The third field identifies the record class of the SOA record. An IN entry identifies this as a DNS resource of the *Internet* class. This field is technically optional because IN is the default class type for any resource record in a zone or reverse lookup file, but I prefer to explicitly provide a class value for readability and clarity purposes. Other possible record classes are HS (Hesiod) and CH (Chaos), which are types of records that only MIT staff or Lisp machine fans will recognize.

4. The fourth field identifies the name of the name server that provides authoritative information for this zone or IP address range. This name looks like a standard hostname, but usually ends with a period, which is the way in which the DNS configuration file parser identifies fully qualified Internet information. Names that do not end with a period are assumed to be local names to which the root name for the zone or IP range should be appended. For example, if the name of your name server is `ns1`, the root name for this domain is `vonhagen.org`, and the IP address of your name server is identified in the zone or reverse lookup file, then either the entries `ns1` or `ns1.vonhagen.org` are acceptable in this field. However, the entry `ns.vonhagen.org` is completely wrong because it does not end with a period, and the DNS parser therefore replaces it with `ns1.vonhagen.org.vonhagen.org`, which probably doesn't exist in your domain. Forgetting the period here is a common problem when creating zone or reverse lookup files.

5. The fifth field is the e-mail address of someone who is responsible for this zone or IP address range. As with other Internet names in a hosts or zone file, this entry usually ends with a period to indicate that it is a fully qualified Internet name. The @ sign that is traditionally used in an e-mail address is invalid here because the DNS parser uses that as a shortcut for the root name of the zone or reverse lookup range, and is replaced with a period. Again, forgetting the period here is a common problem when creating zone or reverse lookup files. However, it's harder to see this problem because you simply don't get mail sent from the BIND user. If you see several e-mail failures for this user, check the syntax of the SOA records for your BIND server.

6. The sixth field is actually a set of five parameters, separated by white space and enclosed within one set of parentheses. Many people, including myself, use semicolons (a comment character) to append text descriptions of each field that make it easier to see what each value means during future updates. The following are the five values that you must supply:

- **Serial number:** This is an unsigned integer that should be changed each time you modify a zone or reverse lookup file. This value is usually constructed by concatenating the four digits for the current year, two digits for the current month, two digits for the current day, and two final digits for a version number between 01 and 99. This makes it easy to decipher when the file was last modified and allows up to 99 revisions per day, which should hold just about anyone.

- **Refresh interval:** Identifies the amount of time in seconds after which a slave DNS server will update its zone and reverse lookup information from the master server for that zone.

- **Retry:** Identifies the time interval in seconds after which a slave DNS server whose refresh interval has expired but has failed to contact its master server will try to recontact that master server. This value should obviously be much smaller than the refresh interval.

- **Expiration:** Identifies the time interval between successful refreshes after which the zone data maintained by a slave server is no longer considered authoritative.

Slave servers stop responding to DNS requests if this time period has passed and the master server still cannot be contacted.

- **Negative cache TTL:** The amount of time that a negative response, such as a non-existent domain response, will be cached by the DNS server. Versions of BIND prior to version 9 used this value to represent the default TTL for a zone or reverse lookup file, which is now specified using $TTL (as described earlier).

The next sections describe how to create zone and reverse lookup files that use these common features.

Creating Zone Files

A basic zone file consists of four blocks of information:

- The $TTL and SOA statements described in the previous section
- An entry that defines the name server for that zone
- An entry that defines the mail server for that zone
- Entries for all of the hosts in that zone that map hostnames to their associated IP addresses and that identify any aliases (CNAMEs) that are associated with those hosts

A name server entry looks like the following:

```
@              . IN   NS    ubuntu32.vonhagen.org.
```

This entry identifies the root name of the zone using the same @ symbol shortcut as was used in the SOA record, the fact that this is an Internet class record (IN), the specific type (NS, for "name server"), and the hostname of the name server. The IP address of the name server is typically provided later in the zone file if it is in the same domain or subdomain. As with other Internet name entries in this file, the name of the name server must end with a period or the zone name will be appended to it. I use the @ shortcut to refer to the root domain in NS records because, frankly, this makes it easier for me to use a generic template for all of my zone files.

A mail server entry is very similar to a name server entry except that it uses the MX (Mail Exchanger) record type to identify a mail server, and you can optionally precede the name of the name server with a numeric weight that allows you to identify higher-priority mail servers. Lower values have higher priority. This is meaningless when you have only one mail server, but providing a value makes it easier for you to remember that this feature is available as your network and number of mail servers expand. A sample mail server entry looks like the following:

```
@              IN    MX    10 mail.vonhagen.org.
```

The IP address of the mail server is typically provided later in the zone file if it is in the same domain or subdomain. As with other Internet name entries in this file, the name of the mail server must end with a period or the zone name will be appended to it. I also use the @ shortcut to refer to the root domain in MX records because, again, this makes it easier for me to use a generic template for all of my zone files.

After the name server and mail server records, the rest of a simple zone file typically consists of address (A) and canonical name (CNAME) records for hosts in the zone. Address records look like the following:

```
64bit          IN    A      192.168.6.64
64x2           IN    A      192.168.6.80
ubuntu32       IN    A      192.168.6.90
```

Note that no period follows the short names because I want the root name of the zone to be appended to them. No trailing period is necessary after the IP address.

Canonical name records look like the following and identify aliases for a host:

```
dualcore       IN    CNAME 64x2
```

No period follows the canonical name or the name of the host that this record provides an alias for. CNAME records require two DNS lookups, one for the name of the alias and a second to find out the IP address of the host that this is an alias for, and so should be used sparingly. CNAME records are most commonly used to map generic server names such as www, ftp, and so on to a specific machine.

A sample, complete zone file for the domain vonhagen.org on one of my local name servers looks like the following:

```
$TTL 1d

@ 1d IN SOA ubuntu32.vonhagen.org. wvh.vonhagen.org. (
     2008090108 ; Serial
     21600      ; Refresh
     1800       ; Retry
     604800     ; Expire
     900        ; Negative Cache TTL
)

@              IN    NS    ubuntu32.vonhagen.org.
@              IN    MX    10 mail.vonhagen.org.

64bit          IN    A     192.168.6.64
64x2           IN    A     192.168.6.80
ubuntu32       IN    A     192.168.6.90
mail           IN    A     207.44.142.34

dualcore       IN    CNAME 64x2.vonhagen.org.
www            IN    CNAME mail.vonhagen.org.
ftp            IN    CNAME:mail.vonhagen.org.
```

The entries for the mail, www, and ftp hosts are somewhat unique in this file and merit some additional explanation and an associated apology. Because I use an ISP that already provides a public name server that is authoritative for the domain vonhagen.org, I added entries for the IP addresses of specific external hosts to my zone file so that I could find them internally while using this server as an authoritative source for my domain. People on external systems would still use the public authoritative name server for my domain, while internally, I could still find the right hosts for a few external systems. There are other, more complex but standard ways of doing this via delegation, but this hack let me keep my zone file simple while still doing the right thing.

Creating a zone file is half the DNS battle. Once you've created a zone file, you have to create a parallel file that identifies how a name server can deduce the hostname from an IP address, which is known as a *reverse lookup file*. These files are discussed in the next section.

Creating Reverse Lookup Files

A basic reverse lookup file, sometimes also referred to as a *reverse map file*, consists of three blocks of information:

- The $TTL and SOA statements described earlier in this chapter
- An entry that defines the name server for that zone
- Entries for all of the IP addresses in that zone and the hostnames that they point to

A name server entry looks exactly the same in a reverse lookup file as it does in a standard zone file:

```
@            . IN   NS   ubuntu32.vonhagen.org.
```

This entry identifies the root name of the zone using the same @ symbol shortcut as was used in the SOA record, the fact that this is an Internet class record (IN), the specific type (NS, for "name server"), and the hostname of the name server. The IP address of the name server is typically provided later in the zone file if it is in the same domain or subdomain. As with other Internet name entries in this file, the name of the name server must end with a period or the zone name will be appended to it. I use the @ shortcut to refer to the root domain in NS records because, frankly, this makes it easier for me to use a generic template for all of my zone files.

After the name server record, the rest of a simple reverse lookup file typically consists of pointer (PTR) records, each of which identifies the hostname associated with a specific IP address in the range that this file describes. Completely qualified PTR records for IP addresses of the form *AAA .BBB.CCC.DDD* have the following format:

```
DDD.CCC.BBB.AAA.in-addr.arpa. IN  PTR   hostname.domain.tld.
```

The entries in the first field that correspond to an IP address are backward from the actual IP address because this file tells how to map IP addresses back to hostnames, and you therefore want to start with the least significant portion of the IP address, which most easily and uniquely identifies a specific PTR record. All PTR records must include the extension .in-addr.arpa., either explicitly or by having it appended to the entry in the first field.

Sample pointer records from one of my reverse lookup files look like the following:

```
64.6     IN  PTR     64bit.vonhagen.org.
80.6     IN  PTR     64x2.vonhagen.org.
90.6     IN  PTR     ubuntu32.vonhagen.org.
```

Although the entries in the first field represent portions of an IP address, these entries are handled just like names, in the sense that because they are not terminated with a period, the root name of the zone (in this case, 168.192.in-addr.arpa) is appended to them. The hostnames are terminated with a period to identify them as fully qualified domain names.

A sample, complete reverse lookup file for IP addresses in the family below 192.168, which are defined in the file 168.192.in-addr.arpa on one of my local name servers, looks like the following:

```
$TTL 1d

@ 1d IN SOA ubuntu32.vonhagen.org. wvh.vonhagen.org. (
       2008090108 ; Serial
       21600      ; Refresh
       1800       ; Retry
       604800     ; Expire
       900        ; Negative Cache TTL
)

@        IN  NS      ubuntu32.vonhagen.org.

64.6     IN  PTR     64bit.vonhagen.org.
80.6     IN  PTR     64x2.vonhagen.org.
90.6     IN  PTR     ubuntu32.vonhagen.org.
```

Creating a reverse lookup file is the second half of the DNS battle. All that remains is to incorporate them into the BIND configuration for your name server, as described in the next section.

Incorporating Zone and Reverse Lookup Files with BIND

The previous two sections explained how to create zone and reverse lookup files. The files created in the previous two sections are vonhagen.zone, the zone file for the domain vonhagen.org, and the reverse lookup file 168.192.in-addr.arpa, which maps IP addresses under 192.168 to the hostnames in the vonhagen.org domain that they are associated with. To actually use the files you've created, you simply need to add them to the /etc/bin/named.conf.local file for the name server that you want to serve as an authoritative source for this information. The /etc/bin/named.conf.local file on this server looks like the following:

```
zone "vonhagen.org" {
type master;
file "/etc/bind/vonhagen.zone";
check-names warn;
};

zone "168.192.in-addr.arpa" {
type master;
file "/etc/bind/168.192.in-addr.arpa";
};

include "/etc/bind/zones.rfc1918.local";
```

These entries include each of these files and identify this server as the master server for the zone vonhagen.org, which uses IP addresses in the 192.168.* family. Information about the zone vonhagen.org is provided in the file /etc/bind/vonhagen.zone. Reverse lookup information for IP addresses in the 192.168.* family is provided in the file /etc/bin/168.192 .in-addr.arpa. The entries that identify these files use full pathnames because these files are stored in /etc/bind, not the server's default directory of /var/cache/bind as defined in the server's /etc/bin/named.options file. As mentioned previously, this /etc/bind/ named.conf.local file also loads a local copy of the default /etc/bin/zones.rfc1918 file, which I have edited to remove null responses for the zone "168.192.in-addr.arpa", because valid values for this range of non-routable IP addresses are explicitly provided in the file /etc/ bin/168.192.in-addr.arpa.

After updating your /etc/bin/named.conf.local file, all that remains is to reload this infor-mation into the name server and test the name server, as described in the next section.

Restarting and Testing Your Name Server

The DNS server startup file for BIND 9 is the file /etc/init.d/bind9. Although this startup script provides reload and force-reload options, these options use a name server control utility (rndc) that may not be correctly configured (yet) on your system. For this reason, I tend to sim-ply restart the BIND daemon using a familiar command like the following:

```
$ sudo /etc/init.d/bind9 restart
```

After supplying your password, you will see the familiar shutdown and startup messages from the script. You should then verify that the name server started correctly by checking for it in a process listing, using a command like the following:

```
$ ps alxww | grep named
```

If your configuration and zone files are valid, you will see a named process running on your sys-tem. Congratulations—you're running a DNS server! If not, proceed to the next section for some debugging tips and then return to this section to complete your testing.

Next, add an entry for your new DNS server to the file /etc/resolv.conf. On the system where you are actually running the DNS server, you can add an entry like the following as the first name server entry in that system's /etc/resolv.conf file:

```
nameserver 0.0.0.0
```

As mentioned previously, a name server specification of 0.0.0.0 is just a shortcut for querying a local name server using the first IP address that was assigned to the local system. This is the loopback address, which is usually 127.0.0.1, but is not guaranteed to be. Using the shortcut 0.0.0.0 causes your request to be sent to an IP address that is known to be valid for the current host, whatever it may be.

Once you're sure that your name server is working correctly, you add the actual IP address of the host on which the name server is running to the /etc/resolv.conf file on all of your other systems.

Now it's time to test the DNS server. You can use several commands for testing a DNS server. The most common of these are the following:

- dig: The recommended tool for DNS testing nowadays, its output takes a bit of getting used to because of the richness of the information that it returns.

- host: The simplest tool for initial DNS testing

- nslookup: Officially deprecated, this command is still found everywhere and is quite useful. Unfortunately, one of these days, the nslookup command will stop displaying a warning that it is deprecated and will simply go away.

All of these commands are easy to use to test your new name server. The following is some sample output from each of these commands on the sample name server that I've configured in this chapter:

```
$ host 64bit
64bit.vonhagen.org has address 192.168.6.64

$ nslookup 64bit
Server:        127.0.0.1
Address:       127.0.0.1#53

Name:   64bit.vonhagen.org
Address: 192.168.6.64


$ dig 64bit.vonhagen.org
; <<>> DiG 9.3.2 <<>> 64bit.vonhagen.org
;; global options:  printcmd
;; Got answer:
;; ->>HEADER<<- opcode: QUERY, status: NOERROR, id: 47870
;; flags: qr aa rd ra; QUERY: 1, ANSWER: 1, AUTHORITY: 1, ADDITIONAL: 1
```

```
;; QUESTION SECTION:
;64bit.vonhagen.org.            IN      A

;; ANSWER SECTION:
64bit.vonhagen.org.    86400  IN      A       192.168.6.64

;; AUTHORITY SECTION:
vonhagen.org.          86400  IN      NS      ubuntu32.vonhagen.org.

;; ADDITIONAL SECTION:
ubuntu32.vonhagen.org. 86400  IN      A       192.168.6.90

;; Query time: 1 msec
;; SERVER: 127.0.0.1#53(127.0.0.1)
;; WHEN: Wed Dec  5 01:18:21 2008
;; MSG SIZE  rcvd: 91
```

The output of the host and nslookup commands is straightforward. The output of the dig command is the most verbose and useful for debugging purposes because it actually identifies the query that was sent to DNS, identifies the answer that it received, and lists the name server that was identified as being authoritative for the domain in which a host is located. For complete information on the dig command and its many options, see the online reference information for this command (man dig).

Tip

If you are running a DNS server on a host whose IP address is assigned by a DHCP server (usually through a reserved MAC Address to IP Address mapping), the /etc/dhcp3/dhclient-script will overwrite your existing resolv.conf entries with the list that is maintained by the DHCP server each time that it checks or renews your lease. The best solution is to add your new DNS server to the official list maintained by the DHCP server. If you don't want to do this for some reason, you can add a line like the following to the file /etc/dhcp3/dhclient.conf:

```
prepend domain-name-servers 0.0.0.0;
```

This would put the name for the local host's DNS server as the first entry in your /etc/resolv.config file. Alternately, you can simply comment out the make_resolv_conf() function in the script file /etc/dhcp3/dhclient-script to prevent your system's /etc/resolv.conf file from being updated in the first place, but this cancels out some of the dynamic aspects of DHCP. ■

Troubleshooting DNS

One nice feature of BIND 9 is that the named process will not start if there are fatal errors in any of your configuration files. This can be quite irritating until you resolve them, but it does help prevent you from accidentally starting a mangled BIND server. Also, the definition of a fatal error is somewhat flexible. Syntax and parser errors that prevent all of your configuration files from being read correctly are fatal errors, whereas others that seem equally important, such as missing files or missing or mangled records in a configuration file, are not.

If your BIND server does not start correctly, the first place to look for information is the system log file on your Ubuntu system, /var/log/syslog. By default, BIND logs a variety of events to this file when you start or stop the named process, when events such as file reloads occur while the named process is running, and so on. A sample section of the /var/log/syslog file showing BIND messages is as follows (I've removed the timestamp and host identification information that would normally begin each line):

```
named[19897]: starting BIND 9.3.2 -u bind
named[19897]: found 1 CPU, using 1 worker thread
named[19897]: loading configuration from '/etc/bind/named.conf'
named[19897]: /etc/bind/named.conf:60: missing ';' before end of file
named[19897]: loading configuration: failure
named[19897]: exiting (due to fatal error)
```

In this case, you can see that there is a missing semicolon on line 60 of my named.conf file. After correcting one error in a configuration file, you usually want to check the configuration file again, to make sure that you've eliminated all of the errors, not just one. The Ubuntu bind package includes a utility called named-checkconf that does just this. Running this utility provides an easy way of checking the syntax of a BIND configuration file without restarting the named process over and over, checking the log each time, fixing one problem or the other, and so on.

The following is another common message that you may see in /var/log/syslog:

```
named[20222]: zone vonhagen.org/IN: loading master file: file not found
```

Oddly enough, the fact that the zone file vonhagen.zone could not be found is not a fatal error, so the BIND server is running—it just isn't providing any name information for the vonhagen .org domain. Aside from syntax errors in the filename, the most common cause of this error message is forgetting to provide the full pathname for an included file. As mentioned previously, BIND on Ubuntu systems is configured to use the directory /var/cache/bind as its working directory. It will look for any files without full pathnames in this directory instead of looking in /etc/bind.

The named-checkconf file checks the syntax of your /etc/bind/named.conf file and other configuration files that it includes—it does not validate the contents or syntax of your zone files. Luckily, Ubuntu's bind package includes another utility, named-checkzone, that does just that. Although it provides several options, the most common way of using the named-checkzone utility is to simply provide its two mandatory arguments: the name of the zone that a file describes, and the name of the file that describes that zone. This can be either a standard zone file or a reverse lookup file because both of these are different types of zone files that have different logical purposes and contents. Some sample error output from running this utility follows:

```
$ named-checkzone vonhagen.org vonhagen.zone
dns_rdata_fromtext: vonhagen.zone:8: near '@': extra input text
zone vonhagen.org/IN: loading master file vonhagen.zone: extra input text

# named-checkzone 168.192.in-addr.arpa  168.192.in-addr.arpa
168.192.in-addr.arpa:11: unknown RR type 'ubuntu32.vonhagen.org.'
zone 168.192.in-addr.arpa/IN: loading master file: unknown class/type
```

Don't worry — I mangled copies of these files to illustrate common errors! The ones shown earlier in this chapter are still valid.

The first error, "extra input text," indicates a parser error when trying to read one of the records in this file — in this case, the SOA record. To generate this error message, I removed the closing parenthesis from the SOA record, which causes the parser to continue on to the next line and report that it found extra, unexpected text in the next line, which began with an @ symbol.

The second errors, "unknown RR type 'ubuntu32.vonhagen.org'" and "unknown class/type," are somewhat more insidious. These also indicate parser errors in reading one of the resource records, in this case on line 11. This is the name server declaration in my reverse lookup file. As I mentioned earlier in this chapter, the DNS file parser is very finicky. Although it is clever about using default values whenever possible, you still have to be very careful about how you use white space in the file. In this case, I had removed the leading @ symbol and deleted all of the white space at the beginning of this record, so that the IN declaration was at the beginning of the line. Because it appeared at the beginning of the lines, without any white space preceding it, this was interpreted as the root name of my name server entry, the NS entry was used as the record class, and the name of my name server, ubuntu32.vonhagen.org, was interpreted as a record type specification. Attempting to resolve this problem also displayed the message "zone 168.192.in-addr.arpa/IN: has no NS records" in the file /var/log/syslog, which was caused by a similar parser error that I stumbled over en route to a valid name server entry.

Trying to resolve parser errors in zone files can be frustrating. Worst case, you can fall back to providing an explicit value for every possible field, verifying that the file works correctly, and then simplifying the file until it looks the way that you want it to. Examples, such as those provided earlier in this chapter, are always useful for the purpose of comparison.

Parser and syntax errors can prevent your configuration files from being read at all or from being interpreted correctly. However, once these files are read and interpreted correctly, they may still not work correctly. The most common problem with any zone file is forgetting to append a period to what you intended to be a fully qualified domain name or putting a superfluous period at the end of a name that you meant to be concatenated with the root name for a zone. Names that do not end with a period are assumed to be local names to which the root name for the zone or IP range should be appended. For example, if the name of your name server is ns1, the root name for this domain is vonhagen.org, and the IP address of your name server is identified in the zone or reverse lookup file, then either the entries ns1 or ns1.vonhagen.org. are acceptable as the name of the name server. The first is a short name that does not end with a period, which means that the root name of the zone will be appended to it. The second is a fully qualified domain name that ends with a period, so nothing will be appended to it. However, the entry ns.vonhagen.org is completely wrong because it does not end with a period, and the DNS parser therefore replaces it with ns1.vonhagen.org.vonhagen.org, which probably doesn't exist in your domain.

This section has presented some of my *favorite* errors in BIND configuration and zone files, and some ways to identify and resolve them. You will undoubtedly see other error messages — unfortunately, this is part of the baptismal process of configuring and starting a BIND DNS server. Be prepared: First, don't panic, and second, have a browser open with your favorite search engine preloaded.

Getting More Information about DNS and BIND

As mentioned previously, DNS and BIND are rich, complex topics about which many entire books have been written. This chapter provided an overview of DNS and BIND and explained simple BIND configuration and troubleshooting. For additional information, see one of the books mentioned earlier or consult one of the following online resources:

- **BIND 9 Administrator Reference Manual** (`www.net.cmu.edu/groups/netdev/docs/bind9/Bv9ARM.html`): This is a copy of the official *BIND 9 Administrator's Manual*, done by the BIND folks.

- **Pro DNS and BIND** (`www.netwidget.net/books/apress/dns`): This is an online copy of one of the DNS/BIND books mentioned earlier in this chapter.

- **DNS Resources Directory** (`www.dns.net/dnsrd`): This is a directory site that provides links to a huge collection of other BIND resources.

If you'll pardon the expression, these resources can help you resolve almost any DNS problem.

Summary

This chapter explained how a name server maps hostnames to IP addresses in a flexible, distributed fashion, and explained how to set up your own name server for the hosts on your local network, while still leveraging the other zillion name servers on the Internet. In real life, you would want to set up more than one name server on a local network of any significant size, to protect against the failure of any single system, but this chapter focused on setting up a single name server for smaller networks.

Chapter 33, "Setting Up a Print Server," continues our exploration of important system servers by explaining how to install and configure a Print server. Unless you have more money and surface area than most people, you will want to attach printers to a small number of systems on your network and point your other systems to those Print servers for printing purposes. Not only does this save money and simplify administration, but it also helps minimize the number of places that you have to explore to find missing printouts.

Setting Up a Print Server

I f you have a single system and a single printer, setting up and configuring printing is quite straightforward, and was explained in the section "Adding a Printer" in Chapter 20, "Adding Hardware and Attaching Peripherals." However, in today's more complex networked environments, the chances are that you want to access a printer on one system from many other systems, including machines that may run operating systems other than Linux for some legacy software or game-playing reason.

This chapter explains how to set up and tweak connectivity from other computer systems so that your printer is available to everyone else. It concludes by providing some troubleshooting tips and discussions of common problems, as well as additional sources of information.

Tip

Hacking the Ubuntu printing system's configuration files and using unauthenticated printing as described in this chapter is really suitable only for home, SOHO (Small Office, Home Office), or SMB (Small and Medium Business) environments that are firewalled from the outside world, and in which you hopefully trust everyone. If you have Microsoft Windows systems in your network environment, you may simply want to set up a Samba Server on the system to which your printer is attached. This will leverage your existing Windows authentication mechanisms (depending on how you configure Samba) and will also work with Apple's Mac OS X systems because of its built-in support for Windows printing and SMB. Setting up a Samba Server is discussed in Chapter 35, "Setting Up a Samba Server." ■

Linux and UNIX Printing History

Today's printers are typically high-quality laser or inkjet printers, often capable of color printing and near-photographic quality. The original UNIX printing system, known as *Line Printer Daemon* (LPD), was designed to queue and print jobs that were intended for huge, text-only line printers. As more sophisticated printers were developed that were capable of higher-quality printouts (such as the original Xerox x9700, Canon-CX, and Imagen-300 laser printers), the original LPD print system continued to be used, but required that the jobs that you were printing be preprocessed so that they contained the special commands that the printer used internally to produce higher-quality printouts. This quickly became tedious because it required users to know to which printer they wanted to print to use the appropriate preformatting commands. Eventually, the LPD system was updated and a similar printing system known as *LP* was developed, which encapsulated the knowledge about the formats required by specific printers. LP implemented the necessary preformatting commands internally by automatically executing them as filters (aka *print drivers*) that performed the right formatting and other printer-specific commands before sending the jobs to the target printer. Other updated printing systems, such as lprng ("lpr, Next Generation," based on the name of the print command used by the LPD system) have also flourished — both LPD and lprng are available in the Ubuntu repositories if you need them for compatibility reasons (or because they are the devil that you already know).

The evolution of multiple printing systems for UNIX systems led to incompatibilities between the different print systems, requiring recompilation of the filters for specific printers on different UNIX systems (if you could get the source code at all), and so on. Eventually, a company known as Easy Software Products began developing a more generalized printing system for UNIX, Linux, and other UNIX-like systems known as the *Common UNIX Printing System* (CUPS). The original version of CUPS used the standard networked LPD protocol, but quickly switched to using a new standard, the Internet Printing Protocol (IPP), which non-UNIX/Linux systems such as Windows can use to print to CUPS printers. Easy Software Products also had the foresight to make the CUPS source code freely available under the GPL so that it could be compiled for multiple operating systems and thus become a true, cross-system standard popularized by zillions of users and system administrators. And this strategy has worked — today, CUPS is used in every major Linux distribution and most other UNIX-like systems.

Most Linux distributions, including Ubuntu, provide their own utilities for setting up printers and doing some basic configuration of the printing subsystem. Ubuntu uses the GNOME printer configuration tool, which was described in the section "Adding a Printer" in Chapter 20. However, in addition to standardizing how printing works across many Linux systems, CUPS added one especially nice gift for system administrators: a built-in administrative tool for CUPS configuration that is easily accessed through any Web browser via port 631. In this chapter, however, I am focusing on using the standard Ubuntu/GNOME printer configuration tools as much as possible.

Enabling Remote Hosts to Access Your CUPS Print Server

As distributed with most Linux distributions (including Ubuntu releases prior to 6.06), CUPS servers listen for incoming requests on port 631 of your host's external IP address. With Ubuntu 6.06 and later distributions, the CUPS server only listens for requests on your host's loopback interface, 127.0.0.1, which effectively eliminates any hope of network printing. Luckily, this is easy enough to correct.

Note

To avoid having to show the complete documentation for the CUPS configuration file, the print server described in this chapter is a simple print server without any special authentication requirements. This may be unsuitable for WAN enterprise or academic environments. ■

To enable network printing on your Ubuntu system, you must remove this restriction. You can do this by editing the printer's configuration file `/etc/cups/cupsd.conf` manually or by using the graphical configuration applet that is provided on your Ubuntu system. This is the same utility that you use to add a printer, select a default printer, and so on — you're just using additional menus to do more advanced administrative tasks.

Tip

After enabling remote hosts to print to the printers that are provided by your print server, you may still need to configure a printer on remote Linux systems. Whether or not this is necessary depends on the capabilities of the remote Linux system. Most newer Linux distributions support some form of automatic printer discovery. If you can't see the printers on your print server from another Linux system, you will need to configure the printer manually.

When manually configuring remote printing from another Linux system to your Ubuntu print server, you need to use an Internet Printing Protocol URI of the following form:

```
ipp://hostname/printers/queuename
```

For example, if I were setting up a connection to the CUPS printer named *SuperScript-660i* **running on the host** `ubuntu32.vonhagen.org`**, I would supply the URI** `ipp://ubuntu32.vonhagen.org/printers/SuperScript-660i`**. Depending on the type of other Linux systems that you are using, you may have to specify the IP address and queue name separately. In that case, the queue name would be** `printers/queuename`**.** ■

Enabling Remote Printing on Ubuntu Systems

On Ubuntu systems, start the printer configuration applet by selecting the System ⇨ Administration ⇨ Printing menu command. A dialog like the one shown in Figure 33-1 displays.

FIGURE 33-1

Starting the printer configuration applet

This dialog initially shows the printers that you have specifically configured on your system. Select the Server ➪ Settings menu command to display the dialog shown in Figure 33-2.

FIGURE 33-2

Configuring printer settings

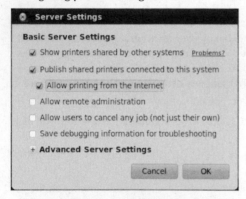

To enable other hosts to see the printers that are exported by this print server, click the "Publish shared printers connected to this system" checkbox. To enable other hosts to actually print to these printers, select the "Allow printing from the Internet" checkbox that is available once you activate the "Publish shared printers..." checkbox.

To enable this system to see printers that are shared by other print servers on your network, click the "Show printers shared by other systems" checkbox. You will certainly want to do this if you are sharing printers that are directly connected to any Microsoft Windows or Mac OS X systems that are also on your network.

Tip

If you want to be able to administer this print server from other hosts on your network, select the "Allow remote administration" checkbox on this dialog. I'd generally recommend against this unless you trust all users with administrative privileges on their systems (which is at least one user on each of your Ubuntu systems) to administer, configure, and reconfigure your print servers. ∎

Click OK to proceed. To ensure that the new settings are picked up by the CUPS daemon that is running as the print server on your system, restart the CUPS daemon on your system using the following command:

```
$ sudo /etc/init.d/cups restart
```

At this point, other systems on your local network should be able to see any printers that are attached to your system when browsing the list of available printers. If you selected the "Show printers shared by other systems" checkbox, you should be able to see other printers on your local network, as shown in Figure 33-3.

FIGURE 33-3

The printer applet showing printers shared by other systems

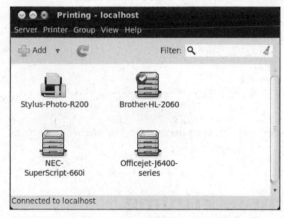

To verify that other systems on your network can connect to your print server, you can connect to its Web interface using port 631 and the actual IP address of your system. As mentioned earlier, the default behavior of an Ubuntu 6.06 and later system is to accept only connections from your system's loopback IP address, which is the host localhost and the IP address 127.0.0.1. To demonstrate that other IP addresses can contact your print server, you can try to contact its Web interface using your system's actual (i.e., non-loopback) IP address. If the CUPS server is indeed listening on that port on your print server's external Ethernet interface, you will see a page like the one shown in Figure 33-4.

FIGURE 33-4

The CUPS server's Web interface

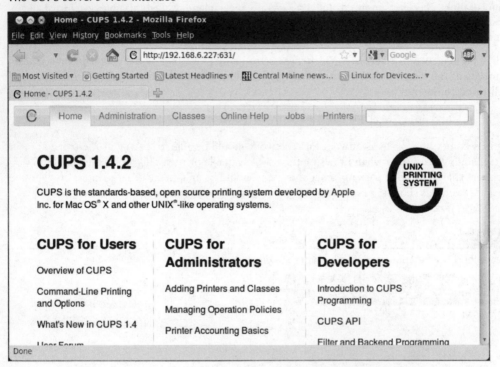

You should now be able to go to any of the other hosts on your network and create printer entries there. Adding a printer on an Ubuntu system is discussed in Chapter 20.

Troubleshooting Remote Printing

This section summarizes a few common sources of diagnostic information and potential problems that you may need to try, depending on the version of CUPS that you are running and whether or not you have typed every URI correctly.

Checking the CUPS Log Files

CUPS print servers maintain three log files that provide a variety of information about attempts to access or use them. These log files, stored in the directory /var/log/cups, are as follows:

- access_log: Contains log messages for each remote host that attempts to access the CUPS print server.

- `error_log`: Contains log messages that record any errors encountered or produced by the CUPS print server.

- `page_log`: Contains log messages for every page printed by a CUPS server. These log messages also summarize information about the host from which the print job was received, the name of the printer being used, and so on.

Of these, the `access_log` and `error_log` files are the most useful for diagnostic purposes. Examining the end of these files after encountering a print failure usually shows useful, meaningful error messages. The `access_log` file will identify the IP address of the systems that have connected to your print server. This can help you verify that the remote system is actually connecting to the print server. Once you've established this, check the `error_log` file for tips about why the job may not have printed.

Accessing Controls for Portions of the CUPS Web Interface

The default CUPS configuration on Ubuntu systems tends to change with different releases, reflecting both enhancements and current security concerns. It's almost certain that the CUPS print server will be updated at some point while you are using this and subsequent releases of Ubuntu. If remote printing works fine but then ceases to work, you may need to add your remote hosts (or your entire network) to the list of acceptable locations in the CUPS daemon's primary configuration file, `/etc/cups/cupsd.conf`. The list of valid locations for incoming print jobs is stored inside the `<Location />` `</Location>` stanza. If printing suddenly stops working, make sure that this stanza contains an entry that either enables access by default or explicitly allows access from the printer from all hosts on the local network. For example, the following is a restrictive version of this stanza that denies access from anywhere other than `localhost` or any hosts on the `192.168.6.*` network:

```
<Location />
   Order Deny,Allow
   Deny From All
   Allow From localhost
   Allow From 192.168.6.*
</Location>
```

The CUPS configuration file that is provided as part of a standard Ubuntu installation at the time of this writing allows access from anywhere (once you've changed CUPS to actually listen on your print server's external Ethernet interface, as described earlier in this chapter). However, changes to the default configuration file are common, and it's pretty depressing to have printing cease to function after a system "update." For example, different portions of the CUPS administrative interface each have their own `<Location>` entries. If you cannot access them from your system, try adding an `Allow` entry for a specific host (rather than from an entire subnet, as described previously).

Similarly, most administrative functions on modern CUPS servers require that you contact them using SSL (i.e., a URI that begins with *https*). You can either disable this requirement by commenting out the lines in your cupsd.conf file that contain the word *Encryption* or use SSL. When using SSL, you may need to create an exception for the default SSL certificate used on Ubuntu systems because this is a self-signed certificate that is not guaranteed by any recognized certificate authority. You will also have to do this on every system that you want to use to contact the CUPS server's Web-based interface. Your browser will walk you through the steps to create an exception for your print server's certificate.

Handling Preformatted Print Jobs

Another common update-related problem may arise if you receive an update that changes how CUPS handles different types of incoming print jobs. If you are printing from a remote system, such as a Microsoft Windows or Apple Mac OS X system, that system preformats the print jobs before sending them to the print server. If printing suddenly stops after an update and you see error messages in the error_log file about enabling raw input, make sure that the following entry is present in the file /etc/cups/mime.types and is not preceded by a hash mark (#):

```
application/octet-stream
```

The hash mark is a comment character in CUPS configuration files. This entry must be present for preformatted print jobs to be received via HTTP and sent to the printer.

After making any changes to any CUPS configuration file, you need to restart the CUPS daemon on your system using the following command:

```
$ sudo /etc/init.d/cupsys restart
```

Getting More Information About CUPS

As you have probably guessed, CUPS configuration is either extremely rich and powerful or extremely irritating — and usually both. The CUPS configuration file /etc/cups/cupsd.conf has so many possible options that it makes even the command-line gcc, ls, and tar commands jealous. If you try to do anything serious with CUPS beyond the simple print server described in this chapter, you will want more information. The following are some excellent sources of additional information about CUPS:

- www.cups.org/documentation.php: The online documentation for CUPS that is available from Easy Software, Inc.

- www.linuxprinting.org: Specializing in help with printing on GNU/Linux systems, this site features a very useful database of printers that are known to work with Linux (www.linuxprinting.org/printer_list.cgi) and a good deal of useful information about CUPS, including a great CUPS troubleshooting tutorial. (I left out the URL for the latter intentionally because it would line-wrap into the next chapter.)

- *CUPS: Common UNIX Printing System* by Michael R. Sweet (SAMS, 2002; ISBN: 0672321963): Michael Sweet is one of the owners of Easy Software, Inc., and thus, this is a pretty definitive book, not just for CUPS, but also for the Internet printing protocol. Unfortunately, the book is a bit old now, but it is still an excellent resource, and my copy is a valuable asset.

As with other Ubuntu topics, you should also be able to get a significant amount of useful information from the online Ubuntu Forums discussed in Chapter 1 of this book, "The Ubuntu Linux Project."

Summary

Centralizing print services on one or a small number of computer systems is a good idea for almost any network. This chapter provided a bit of background about printing on UNIX and Linux systems, and then discussed how to install and configure CUPS, the Common UNIX Printing System. Most modern personal computer systems, including Microsoft Windows or Mac OS X systems that you may still have lying around, can easily print to a CUPS server that is running on your Ubuntu system.

The next chapter explains how to share directories over a network using NFS, the Network File System, which is the standard distributed filesystem mechanism for all UNIX and Linux systems. Sharing a central repository of project files, documents, and code over a network in a work environment is important from many standpoints, including increasing efficiency, minimizing confusion, and minimizing the size of your backups. Today, it is just as important in many home environments, enabling everyone on your home network to share access to your household's music collection, vacation photos, and any other files that you want your housemates, spouse, or children to be able to see.

Setting Up an NFS Server

IN THIS CHAPTER

Overview of NFS

Installing an NFS server

Configuring an NFS server

Mounting NFS filesystems

Debugging NFS problems

S haring groups of files that multiple people need access to is standard operating procedure in business today and, thanks to home networking, is getting to be Standard Operating Procedure for home use as well. Providing centralized access to a collection of audio materials that you've extracted from your CD collection or the vacation photos from your most recent trips is just as important to the home user as providing centralized access to your procedure manuals and software source repository is to the business user or Small Office, Home Office (SOHO) developer. Luckily, Linux systems provide several ways of sharing directories over a network, some oriented primarily toward Linux and other UNIX-like systems, including Apple's Mac OS X, and others oriented more toward Microsoft Windows systems (which Linux and Mac OS X systems can also access, of course). This chapter discusses how to set up one of your Ubuntu Linux systems so that other systems can access its directories over the network using NFS, the Network File System, which is popularly used on Linux and UNIX-like systems. (For information on setting up your Ubuntu system to share directories with Microsoft Windows systems, see Chapter 35, "Setting Up a Samba Server.")

Sun Microsystems' Network File System, better known simply as *NFS*, is the most common networked filesystem in use on UNIX and UNIX-like systems today, largely because it is available and free for every UNIX and UNIX-like system I've seen since 1990 or so (including Mac OS X), and is also available for Microsoft Windows. Microsoft Windows networked filesystems that use CIFS (SMB) may be a close second. However, because NFS was designed for systems whose filenames are case-sensitive and understand UNIX-style permissions, NFS is still a superior choice for UNIX-like systems such as Linux.

This chapter provides an overview of NFS, discusses different versions of NFS and their capabilities, and discusses the various applications associated with NFS. Beyond this background material, this chapter focuses on explaining how to set up your Ubuntu system to be an NFS file server — accessing NFS file servers from other systems is explained in Chapter 26. NFS is commonly used with Kerberos, a networked authentication protocol that provides secure authentication in any networked environment by exchanging encrypted keys. Setting up Kerberos authentication is discussed in Chapter 27.

Overview of the Network File System

The *Network File System* (NFS) is a network filesystem that provides transparent access to files residing on remote disks. Network filesystems are often commonly referred to as *distributed filesystems* because the files and directories that they provide access to may be physically located on many different computer systems that are distributed throughout your home, academic environment, or business. Developed at Sun Microsystems in the early 1980s, the NFS protocol has been revised and enhanced several times between then and now, and is available on all Linux, UNIX, and UNIX-like systems (including Mac OS X), and even for Windows systems from many third-party software vendors. The specifications for NFS have been publicly available since shortly after it was first released, making NFS a de facto standard for distributed filesystems.

NFS is the most common distributed filesystem in use today, largely because it is free and available for almost every type of modern computer system. NFS enables file servers to export centralized sets of files and directories to multiple client systems. Good examples of files and directories that you may want to store in a centralized location but make simultaneously available to multiple computer systems are users' home directories, site-wide sets of software development tools, and centralized data resources such as mail queues and the directories used to store Internet news bulletin boards.

The following are some common scenarios for using NFS:

- **Sharing common sets of data files:** Sharing files that everyone on your network wants to access, whether they are audio files, business data, or research data, is the most common use of any type of networked filesystem.

- **Explicitly sharing home directories:** Suppose that the home directories for all of your users are stored in the directory /export/home on your NFS file server, which is automatically mounted as /home on all of your UNIX and UNIX-like systems at boot time. Users can then log in on any NFS client system and instantly see their home directory, which would be transparently made available to them over the network. If you want to have a local /home directory for some users and an NFS-mounted home directory for others, you could mount /export/home from your NFS server elsewhere (perhaps /home/remote or something similarly evocative) and manually configure specific users to have home directories located in this other directory.

Tip

An alternative to the previous bullet is to automatically mount networked home directories using an exported NFS directory that is managed by an NFS automount daemon known as autofs on Linux systems. Whenever access to a directory managed by an automount daemon is requested by a client, the daemon automatically mounts that directory on the client system. Automounting simplifies the contents of your server's /etc/ exports file by enabling you to export only the parent directory of all home directories on the server, and letting the automounter manage that directory (and therefore its subdirectories) on each client. See the sidebar later in this chapter for general information on automounting, a complete discussion of which is outside the scope of this chapter. ■

- **Sharing specific sets of binaries across systems:** Suppose that you want to make a specific set of GNU tools available on all of the systems in your computing environment, but also want to centralize them on an NFS server for ease of maintenance and updating. To ensure that configuration files were portable across all of your systems, you might want to make these binaries available in the directory /usr/gnu regardless of the type of system that you were using. You could simply build binaries for each type of system that you support, configuring them to be found as /usr/gnu but actually storing them in directories with names such as /export/gnu/ubuntu, /export/ gnu/solaris8, and so on. You would then configure each client of a specified type to mount the appropriate exported directory for that system type as /usr/gnu. For example, /export/gnu/ubuntu would be mounted as /usr/gnu on Ubuntu systems, /export/gnu/solaris8 would be mounted as /usr/gnu on Solaris systems, and so on. You could then simply put /usr/gnu/bin in your path and the legendary "right thing" would happen regardless of the type of system that you logged in on.

As you'll see in this chapter, NFS is easy to install and easy to configure, and provides a flexible networked filesystem that any Ubuntu, other Linux, UNIX, or UNIX-like system can quickly and easily access. In some cases, it's easy to trip over a few administrative gotchas, but Ubuntu provides powerful and easy-to-use tools that simplify configuring NFS file servers to "do the right thing."

How NFS Works

If you simply want to use NFS and aren't too concerned about what's going on under the hood, you can skip this section. However, this section provides the details of many internal NFS operations because some enquiring minds do, indeed, want to know and because, frankly, it's just plain interesting to see some of the hoops that NFS clients and servers have to use to successfully communicate between different types of computer systems, often with different types of processors. So, if you're interested, read on, Macduff!

The underlying network communication method used by NFS is known as *Remote Procedure Calls* (RPCs), which can use either the lower-level User Datagram Protocol (UDP) as their network transport mechanism (NFS version 2) or TCP (NFS version 3 and later). For this reason, both UDP and TCP entries for port 2049, the port used by the NFS daemon, are present in the Linux

/etc/services file. UDP minimizes transmission delays because it does not attempt to do sequencing or flow control and does not provide delivery guarantees — it simply sends packets to a specific port on a given host, where some other process is waiting for input. TCP provides the delivery guarantees that UDP cannot, and should therefore be used whenever possible.

The design and implementation of RPCs make NFS platform-independent, interoperable between different computer systems, and easily ported to many computing architectures and operating systems. RPCs are a client/server communication method that involves issuing RPC calls with various parameters on client systems, which are actually executed on the server. The client doesn't need to know whether the procedure call is being executed locally or remotely — it receives the results of an RPC in exactly the same way that it would receive the results of a local procedure call.

The way in which RPCs are implemented is extremely clever. RPCs work by using a technique known as *marshalling*, which essentially means packaging up all of the arguments to the remote procedure call on the client into a mutually agreed-upon format. This mutually agreed-upon format, known as *eXternal Data Representation* (XDR), provides a sort of "computer Esperanto" that enables systems with different architectures and byte-orders to safely exchange data with each other. The client's RPC subsystem then ships the resulting, system-independent packet to the appropriate server. The server's RPC subsystem receives the packet and unmarshalls it to extract the arguments to the procedure call in its native format. The RPC subsystem executes the procedure call locally, marshalls the results into a return packet, and sends this packet back to the client. When this packet is received by the client, its RPC subsystem unmarshalls the packet and sends the results to the program that invoked the RPC, returning this data in exactly the same fashion as any local procedure call. Marshalling and unmarshalling, plus the use of the common XDR data representation, make it possible for different types of systems to transparently communicate and execute functions on each other.

RPC communications are used for all NFS-related communications, including communications related to the authentication services used by NFS (the Network Information System, NIS or NIS+), file locks, NFS mount requests, status information, and requests made to the NFS automount daemon. To enable applications to contact so many different services without requiring that each communicate through a specific, well-known port, NFS lets those services dynamically bind to any available port as long as they register with its central coordination service, the portmapper daemon. The portmapper always runs on port 111 of any host that supports RPC communications and serves as an electronic version of directory assistance. Servers register RPC-related services with the portmapper, identifying the port that the service is actually listening on. Clients then contact the portmapper at its well-known port to determine the port that is actually being used by the service that they are looking for.

Communication failures occur with any networked communication mechanism, and RPCs are no exception. As mentioned at the beginning of this section, UDP does not provide delivery guarantees or packet sequencing. Therefore, when a response to an RPC call is not received within a specific period of time, systems will resend RPC packets. This introduces the possibility that a remote system may execute a specific function twice, based on the same input data. Because this can happen, all NFS operations are *idempotent*, which means that they can be executed any number of times and still return the same result — an NFS operation cannot change any of the data that it depends on. Even though NFS versions 3 and later use TCP as their network transport mechanism, the idea of idempotent requests is still part of the NFS protocol to guarantee compatibility with NFS version 2 implementations.

As another way of dealing with potential communication and system failures, NFS servers are stateless, meaning that they do not retain information about each other across system restarts. If a server crashes while a client is attempting to make an RPC to it, the client continues to retry the RPC until the server comes back up or until the number of retries exceeds its configured limit, at which time the operation aborts. Stateless operation makes the NFS protocol much simpler because it does not have to worry about maintaining consistency between client and server data. The client is always right, even after rebooting, because it does not maintain any data at that point.

Although stateless operation simplifies things, it is also extremely noisy, inefficient, and slow. When data from a client is saved back to a server, the server must write it synchronously, not returning control to the client until all of the data has been saved to the server's disk. As described in the next section, "Comparing Different Versions of NFS," newer versions of NFS do some limited write caching on clients to return control to the client applications as quickly as possible. This caching is done by the client's rpciod process (RPC Input/Output daemon), which stores pending writes to NFS servers in the hopes that it can bundle groups of them together and thus optimize the client's use of the network. In the current standard version of NFS (NFS version 4), cached client writes are still essentially dangerous because they are only stored in memory and will therefore be lost if the client crashes before the write completes.

In a totally stateless environment, a server crash would make it difficult to save data that was being modified on a client back to the server once it were available again. The server would have no way of knowing what file the modified data belonged to because it had no persistent information about its clients. To resolve the problem, NFS clients obtain file handles from a server whenever they open a file. *File handles* are data structures that identify both the server and the file that they are associated with. If a server crashes, clients retry their write operations until the server is available again or their time-out periods are exceeded. If the server comes back up in time, it receives the modified data and the file handle from the client, and can use the file handle to figure out which file the modified data should be written to.

NFS 4 provides client-side caching, which can significantly improve performance by reducing the number of calls that need to be made to an NFS 4 server in order to retrieve data, and which further helps prevent data loss if a server is unavailable for a short period of time. However, this is not sufficient to insulate NFS clients from performance problems if they must execute binaries located on an NFS server as part of the client's reboot process. If the server is unavailable, the client cannot boot. For this reason, most NFS clients must contain a full set of system binaries, and typically only share user-oriented binaries and data via NFS.

Comparing Different Versions of NFS

NFS has been around almost since the beginning of UNIX workstation time, appearing on early Sun Microsystems workstations in the early 1980s. This section provides an overview of the differences between the four different versions of NFS, both for historical reasons, and to illustrate that NFS is by no means a done deal. NFS 4 resolves the biggest limitations of NFS 3, most notably adding real client-side data caching that survives reboots. The most common versions of NFS used on systems today are NFS versions 4 and 3, which are the versions that this chapter focuses on. You will probably want to use NFS 4 whenever possible, but may still need to use NFS 3.

The following list identifies the four versions of NFS and highlights the primary features of each:

- **Version 1:** The original NFS protocol specification was used only internally at Sun during the development of NFS, and I have never been able to find any documentation on the original specification. This would only be of historical interest.

- **Version 2:** NFS version 2 was the first version of the NFS protocol that was released for public consumption. Version 2 used UDP exclusively as its transport mechanism and defined the 18 basic RPCs that made up the original public NFS protocol. Version 2 was a 32-bit implementation of the protocol and therefore imposed a maximum file size limitation of 2 GB on files in NFS and used a 32-byte file handle. NFS version 2 also limited data transfer sizes to 8 KB.

- **Version 3:** NFS version 3 addressed many of the shortcomings and ambiguities present in the NFS version 2 specification and took advantage of many of the technological advances in the 10+ years between the version 2 and 3 specifications. Version 3 added TCP as a network transport mechanism, making it the default if both the client and server support it; increased the maximum data transfer size between client and server to 64 KB; and was a full 64-bit implementation, thereby effectively removing file size limitations. All of these were made possible by improvements in networking technology and system architecture after NFS version 2 was released. Version 3 also added a few new RPCs to those in the original version 2 specification and removed two that had never been used (or implemented in any NFS version that I've ever seen). To improve performance by decreasing network traffic, version 3 introduced the notion of bundling writes from the client to the server and also automatically returned file attributes with each RPC call, rather than requiring a separate request for this information as NFS version 2 had done.

- **Version 4:** Much of the NFS version 4 protocol is designed to position NFS for use in Internet and World Wide Web environments by increasing persistence, performance, and security. Version 4 adds persistent, client-side caching to reduce network traffic and decrease the chance of data loss in a reboot, and adds support for ACLs and extended file attributes in NFS filesystems. Version 4 also adds an improved, standard API for increased security through a general RPC security mechanism known as *Remote Procedure Call Security - Generic Security Services* (RPCSEC_GSS). This mandates the use of the Generic Security Services Application Programming Interface (GSS-API, specified in RFC 2203) to select between available security mechanisms provided by clients and servers.

The version of the NFS server that is shipped with Ubuntu provides support for NFS versions 4, 3, and 2.

NFS Users and Authentication

NFS uses the user ID (UID) and group ID (GID) of each user from a system's password file (/etc/passwd) to determine who can write to and access exported files and directories, based on the UID and GID that own those directories on the file server. This means that all of your users should have the same UID and GID on all systems to which NFS directories such as home directories are exported.

In small networks, it is often sufficient to make sure that you create the same users and groups on all of your systems, or to make sure that the password and group files on your file server contain the correct entries for all of the users and groups who will access any directory that it exports.

In larger networks, this is impractical, so you will want to consider network-oriented authentication mechanisms, such as Kerberos, which is discussed in Chapter 27, or the traditional Network Information System (NIS), which was developed by Sun Microsystems specifically for use with NFS. Unfortunately, discussing NIS installation and setup on Linux systems is usually a history lesson rather than something that modern sysadmins actually do, so it is outside the scope of this chapter. If you need to use NIS on Linux, you can find a variety of excellent information about it online in documents such as the NIS HOWTO (www.linux-nis.org/nis-howto/), which is even available in multiple languages. NIS was great in its day and can still be quite useful in networks of heterogeneous and aging UNIX systems, but it's not the way to go in a modern networked environment comprising Linux systems, Mac OS X systems, and the occasional Microsoft Windows system.

Installing an NFS Server

You can use the Synaptic Package Manager, the Adept Package Manager, or the command-line package management utilities described in Chapter 19 to install the packages required to run and monitor an NFS server on your Ubuntu system. You must install both the nfs-common and nfs-kernel-server packages on any system where you want to run an NFS server—only the nfs-common package is required on a system on which you only want to mount NFS file-systems. (Installing the nfs-kernel-server package on a server will automatically install the nfs-common package as a requirement.) Once the installation completes, you're ready to configure your server to share data from your system with any system that supports NFS.

Tip
If you are going to want to use Kerberos as the authentication mechanism for your NFS server (and your computing environment in general), see the section of Chapter 27 entitled "Configuring Kerberbos Authentication." This chapter focuses on setting up an NFS server in small networks where common user and group IDs can be manually maintained, although Kerberos requirements or alternatives are explained wherever possible. ∎

Configuring an NFS Server

Older releases of Ubuntu have provided various graphical tools for NFS server configuration, but, frankly, a text editor is the best tool for NFS server (and client) setup. This section therefore focuses on configuring an NFS server from the command line because that method works on all Ubuntu desktop and Ubuntu Server systems.

As described in the next few sections, configuring an NFS server is a relatively simple process, consisting of setting some parameters in two configuration files that identify the services that should be started, and defining the directories that you want to export in a text file called /etc/exports.

Given that the NFS kernel server in the Ubuntu repositories supports NFS versions 2, 3, and 4, you should usually configure a new NFS server as an NFS 4 server, as is done in the next few sections. As long as the /etc/exports file explicitly defines all exported directories, NFS 4 servers can still respond to mount requests from NFS clients that support only NFS 2 or NFS 3. The primary differences between configuring an NFS 4 server and configuring NFS 2 or 3 servers are:

- NFS 4 servers export directories using a pseudo-filesystem, which is just a directory that you create with specific protections on your NFS 4 server and define specially in your /etc/exports file.

- NFS 4 adds new configuration options for the exported directories that are listed in the /etc/exports file.

The next few sections explain each of these steps, highlighting differences between NFS servers that expect common UID and GID values, and those that use a networked authentication mechanism such as Kerberos.

Note
The parameter settings in the NFS configuration files discussed in the next two sections have no values by default. An NFS server will attempt to infer the correct settings for these when it starts. However, to ensure compatibility with mount requests from clients that can only speak older versions of the NFS protocol, I find it useful to explicitly specify values for these parameters. This ensures that services that are only required by older NFS clients are also started, and also helps in debugging, because you know exactly what services are supposed to be started. ∎

Configuring Common NFS Options

Options for the common NFS services for an NFS server are set in the file /etc/default/ nfs-common, which you can edit using your favorite text editor. Each of the following options is defined in a setting that looks like *setting=value*, where *value* is either yes or no. You should set the following options:

- NEED_STATD: Set this to yes to ensure that the rpc.statd daemon, required by NFS 2 and NFS 3 clients, is started. This server supports the NSM (Network Status Monitor)

RPC protocol, which implements a reboot notification service (letting clients know when the NFS server has been rebooted), which is used by the NFS file locking service, `rpc.lockd`, to handle existing locks after a reboot. You can set this to `no` in a pure NFS 4 environment to avoid starting an unnecessary server, but I recommend against that unless you can guarantee that no client that speaks only the NFS 2 or NFS 3 protocol will ever need to mount directories from this NFS server.

- `STATDOPTS`: Enables you to pass arguments to the `rpc.statd` daemon when it starts. The most common of these are the `-p listen-port` and `-o send-port` options, which you can use to define specific ports for the status daemon to listen and send on. This can be useful if you are using a port-based firewall or if you want to use ports other than the defaults as a security measure. Unless this is the case, you should usually not provide a value for this option.

- `NEED_IDMAPD`: Set this to `yes` to ensure that the `rpc.idmapd` daemon, required by NFS 4 clients, is started. This server supports UID/GID mappings to specific user and group names.

- `NEED_GSSD`: Set this to `no` to ensure that the `rpc.gssd` daemon, which is required for Kerberos authentication support, is not started. If you are using Kerberos authentication with NFS, you should set this to `yes` to ensure that this daemon is started.

After setting these values, save this file and restart the services associated with basic NFS support by executing the command `sudo /etc/init.d/nfs-common restart`.

Note
When run in start or restart modes, this startup script creates and mounts an in-memory pipe filesystem called `rpc_pipefs`, used for inter-process communication by RPC-based server processes such as `rpc.idmapd` or `rpc.gssd`, mounting it on the directory `/var/lib/nfs/rpc_pipefs`. Although this filesystem will be listed in output from the `mount` command, you will not see this filesystem in your `/etc/fstab` file because the filesystem is created and mounted by the `nfs-common` script to limit NFS-related changes to files that are provided by other packages. ∎

Configuring NFS Kernel Server Options

Options for the common NFS services for an NFS server are set in the file `/etc/default/nfs-kernel-server`, which you can edit using your favorite text editor. Each of the following options is defined in a setting that looks like *setting=value*, where *value* is one of `yes` or `no`. The options that you should set are the following:

- `RPCNFSDCOUNT`: Set this to a specific numeric value to identify the number of NFS daemon instances that you want to start. The default value, 8, is usually sufficient, although you may want to increase this value if your NFS server is serving files to a large number of clients.

- RPCNFSDPRIORITY: Set this to a specific numeric value to start the NFS daemon at a specific priority. The numeric values to which you can set this option are the same as those used by the nice command. The default value, 0, is usually sufficient, although you may want to increase this value if your NFS server is serving files to a large number of clients and you want to ensure that it runs at a higher priority than other processes on the server.

- RPCMOUNTDOPTS: Enables you to pass arguments to the rpc.mountd daemon when it starts. The most common of these are the -p listen-port and -o send-port options, which you can use to define specific ports for the NFS mount daemon to listen and send on. This can be useful if you are using a port-based firewall or if you want to use ports other than the defaults as a security measure. Unless this is the case, you should usually not provide a value for this option.

- NEED_SVCGSSD: Set this to no to ensure that the rpc.svcgssd daemon, which is required for Kerberos authentication support, is not started. If you are using Kerberos authentication with NFS, you should set this to yes to ensure that this daemon is started.

- RPCSVCGSSDOPTS: Enables you to pass arguments to the rpc.svcgssd daemon when it starts. Most of the options for this daemon change the location or verbosity of its output, which you will only want to change if you are having authentication problems and want additional information about what it's doing internally. You should rarely need to provide a value for this option.

After setting these values, save this file and restart the services associated with the NFS server by executing the command sudo /etc/init.d/nfs-kernel-server restart.

Note
When run in start or restart modes, this startup script also creates and mounts an in-memory nfsd filesystem that is used for inter-process communication by instances of the NFS daemon, mounting it on the direct/ var/lib/nfs/rpc_pipefs. Although this filesystem will be listed in output from the mount command, you will not see this filesystem in your /etc/fstab file because the filesystem is created and mounted by the nfs-kernel-server script to limit NFS-related changes to files that are provided by other packages. ■

Setting Up the Pseudo-Filesystem and Exported Directories

As mentioned previously, NFS 4 differs from earlier versions of NFS by exporting a pseudo-filesystem in which the directories that you want to export are mounted using the mount command's --bind option. The pseudo-filesystem is uniquely identified by a special fsid=0 parameter that you must specify in the /etc/exports options for that filesystem. Your /etc/ exports file should contain entries for the pseudo-filesystem and for each directory that is mounted in it.

Tip

If you are exporting only a single directory, such as the mountpoint for a large shared filesystem, you can simply export that filesystem and use the fsid=0 option to identify it as the top-level filesystem that you are exporting. However, this is relatively inflexible. If there is any chance that you will be exporting multiple directories/filesystems from an NFS server, it's smarter to set up your NFS server using a pseudo-filesystem from the beginning. ∎

The pseudo-filesystem used by an NFS 4 server is just a directory with special permissions, in which the directories that you want to export via NFS have been mounted. I typically use the directory /export on an NFS server as my pseudo-filesystem, but you can use any directory that you want. This directory should be created and its mode set using commands like the following:

```
sudo mkdir /export
sudo chmod a+rwxt /export
```

For each directory that you want to export via NFS, create a mountpoint for that directory under the directory that you just created and use the mount command's --bind option to mount the directory that you want to export there. For example, if you wanted to export the /home directory from your NFS server, you would execute the following commands:

```
sudo mkdir /export/home
sudo mount --bind /home /export/home
```

After repeating this process for each directory or mounted filesystem that you want to export, the next step in setting up your NFS server is to create appropriate entries for each of these in the file /etc/exports, as described in the next section.

Defining Exported Directories in /etc/exports

The file that contains information about each of the directories that is being exported by an NFS server is a text file named /etc/exports. Entries in this file have the following form:

```
full-path-name-of-exported-directory      hosts(export-options)
```

Each non-commented entry in the /etc/exports file is referred to as an *export specification*. The following are examples from one of my /etc/exports files:

```
/export       192.168.1.0/24(rw,fsid=0,insecure,no_subtree_check,async)
/export/users 192.168.1.0/24(rw,insecure,no_subtree_check,async)
```

The full-path-name-of-exported-directory field identifies the directory that is being exported. As shown in the previous example, your /etc/exports file should contain one export specification for your NFS pseudo-filesystem and one entry for each directory that is mounted in that pseudo-filesystem.

The hosts entry identifies the hosts that can access a specific exported directory. Hosts can be specified by IP address, IP address and netmask, hostname, or subnet to state that only those hosts can access a specific directory exported by NFS. An entry such as 192.168.6.61 would limit access to a specific NFS directory from that host, while entries such as 192.168.6.*, 192.168.6.0, or 192.168.6.0/24 would limit access to a specific NFS directory to hosts on the 192.168.6 subnet. You can also grant access to an NFS server from any host that can access it by using an asterisk as the host specification.

The export-options identify specific characteristics of whether the exported directory is read-only or both readable and writable, how the UIDs and GIDs of incoming users should be mapped to users on the NFS server, how write and status requests should be processed, and so on. As you'd expect, many mount options are available. The pseudo-filesystem in which all of the directories that you are exporting are mounted must be identified using the fsid=0 export option, as shown in the previous example. The following are some of the more commonly used mount options:

- all_squash: Maps all NFS read or write requests to a specific user, usually "anonymous." This option is often used for public resources such as directories of USENET news, public FTP and download areas, and so on. All files written to an NFS directory that is exported with the all_squash mount option will be assigned the UID and GID of the user anonymous or some other UID and GID specified using the anonuid and anongid mount options. The default is no_all_squash, which preserves all UIDs and GIDs.

- async: Enables the NFS server to return control to the client before a write has completed, increasing performance. The default behavior when this option is not specified is synchronous writes, which are safer but which block the client until the write completes.

- insecure: Enables access to NFS directories by NFS clients that are running on non-standard NFS network ports. By default, this option is off, and NFS requests must originate from ports where the port number is less than 1024. The insecure option may be necessary to enable access from random PC and Macintosh NFS clients. If you need to use this option, you should limit machines using the NFS option to a home network or secure corporate intranet. You should not use this option on any machines that are accessible from over the Internet because it introduces potential security problems.

- no_subtree_check: Prevents NFS from having to verify that a file requested through NFS is both in the filesystem from which the directory was exported on the NFS server and hierarchically under the directory that is being exported via NFS, known as a *subtree check*. Performing this check can cause problems when files in the NFS directory are renamed. This check is usually disabled in filesystems with significant read/write activity by specifying the no_subtree_check mount option.

- no_root_squash: Lets root users on client workstations have the same privileges as the root user on the NFS file server. This option is off by default.

- ro: Exports directories that you don't want users to be able to write to because it is read-only. The default is rw, which enables read/write access.

- `sec=method1:method2:etc`: Enables you to provide a colon-separated list of security mechanisms that clients must supply in order to connect to the specified exported directory. Listed security mechanisms are tried in the order that they are specified. The default value is `sys`, which means no security.

- `sync`: Forces writes to the NFS server to be done synchronously, where the client waits for the writes to complete before returning control to the user. This is the default — as explained in the previous section, you can also specify asynchronous operation (`async`), which is slightly faster.

See the man page for `/etc/exports` (by using the `man 5 exports` command) for complete information on the options that are available in this file.

Once you have created an entry for a new exported directory in your `/etc/exports` file, you can export that directory by rerunning the `exportfs` command with the `-r` option, which tells the NFS server to reread the `/etc/exports` file and make any necessary changes to the list of directories that are exported by that NFS server.

Mounting NFS Directories on Clients

Many different export options are available for entries in an `/etc/exports` file export specification on an NFS server, but their number pales beside the number of mount options that you can specify when mounting an NFS filesystem from a client system. Mounting a directory from an NFS server can be done in several ways:

- By using the `mount` command from the command line, as in the following example, which mounts the entire pseudo-filesystem that is being exported from the NFS server `server` on the directory `/mnt`, using the mount options specified in `mount-options`. This pseudo-filesystem includes all of the entries that were mounted within it:

  ```
  sudo mount -t nfs4 -o mount-options server:/ /mnt
  ```

- By using the `mount` command from the command line, as in the following example, which mounts the `/home` subdirectory that is being exported from the NFS server `server` on the directory `/mnt`, using the mount options specified in `mount-options`:

  ```
  sudo mount -t nfs4 -o mount-options server:/home /mnt
  ```

- By creating an entry for that filesystem in the file `/etc/fstab`, and then mounting it by executing the `mount` command for that filesystem. The following is a sample `/etc/fstab` entry for the entire pseudo-filesystem that is being exported from the NFS server `server` on the directory `/mnt`, using the mount options specified in `mount-options`:

  ```
  server:/   /mnt nfs4 mount-options  0  0
  ```

Tip

Adding an entry to the /etc/fstab file is the best way to ensure that an NFS filesystem will always be mounted whenever the system is booted. You can maintain /etc/fstab entries for one or more NFS filesystems that you do not want to mount automatically by adding the noauto option to the *mount-options* string. Manually executing the mount command only mounts the filesystem until the system reboots or until you manually unmount it using the umount command. (There is no "n" after the initial "u" in umount, honest!) ∎

After executing any of the commands in this list, you should be able to access the specified NFS filesystem through the specified mountpoint. Access to these filesystems and their subdirectories will follow the authentication model that you are using: either standard UID/GID mappings or the authorization rights provided by an authentication model such as Kerberos.

One huge difference between mounting NFS 4 and NFS 2 or 3 exported directories is that NFS 4 filesystems are identified relative to the pseudo-filesystem that the NFS server is exporting, whereas NFS 2 or 3 filesystems required that you specify the full name of the directory that is being exported. For example, the NFS 2 or 3 equivalent of the third bullet in the previous list is the following:

```
sudo mount -t nfs -o mount-options server:/export/home /mnt
```

The filesystem type is nfs, rather than nfs4, and you must supply the full pathname of the exported filesystem. Your mount options specification should also include the string nfsvers=3 to mount the exported directory in NFS 3 mode.

As mentioned previously, many mount options can be specified in a mount-options string when mounting NFS filesystems manually or in /etc/fstab entries. The mount-options string is a comma-separated sequence of mount options (and associated values, if required). The following are some of the most common:

- hard: Retry indefinitely if an NFS file operation times out. You cannot specify both hard and soft options.

- intr: Allows signals to interrupt NFS file operations that time out.

- ro: Mounts the NFS filesystem in read-only mode, regardless of how it is being exported by the NFS server.

- *rsize=number*: *number*: Specifies the size of the read buffer that the client should try to use when reading data from the NFS server.

- rw: Mounts the NFS filesystem in read-write mode if it being exported in read/write mode from the NFS server.

- soft: Reports an I/O error to the calling program when an NFS file operation times out. You cannot specify both the soft and hard options.

- *timeo=number*: *number*: Specifies the number of tenths of a second to wait before retransmitting when an RPC time-out occurs.

- *wsize=number*: *number*: Specifies the size of the write buffer that the client should try to use when writing back to the NFS server.

See the man page for the nfs command (by executing the command man 5 nfs from any command-line environment) for a complete list of mount options for NFS filesystems.

Automounting NFS Home Directories

Automounting is the process of automatically mounting NFS filesystems in response to requests for access to those filesystems. Automounting is controlled by an automount daemon that runs on the client system. In addition to automatically mounting filesystems in response to requests for access to them, an automount daemon can also automatically unmount volumes once they have not been used for a specified period of time.

Using an automount daemon prevents you from having to mount shared NFS directories that you are not actually using at the moment. Mounting all NFS directories on all clients at all times causes a reasonable amount of network traffic, much of which is extraneous if those directories are not actually being used. Using the NFS automount daemon helps keep NFS-related network traffic to a minimum.

The automount daemon is called autofs and is available in the autofs package. The autofs automounter daemon is configured through the file /etc/auto.master or through NIS maps with the same name. Because the autofs daemon is part of the kernel, it is faster and the automounter of choice for many Linux distributions (such as Ubuntu). Both of these packages are available in the Ubuntu repositories, but discussing all of the nuances of automounting is outside the scope of this chapter.

Debugging NFS Problems

If you encounter problems mounting an NFS filesystem or accessing the files that it contains, there are a number of ways to try to resolve these problems. The next few sections provide suggestions to help you identify and resolve the problems.

Verifying RPC Services

If you are having problems mounting an NFS filesystem, the first thing to check is to use the rpcinfo command to probe the NFS server that you are trying to contact to verify that it is running both the right NFS services and the right versions of those services. The -p option probes the specified host, or the current system if no hostname or IP address is provided. The following example probes the portmapper on the NFS server at the IP address 192.168.6.143:

```
$ rpcinfo -p 192.168.6.143
   program vers proto   port
   100000    2   tcp    111  portmapper
   100000    2   udp    111  portmapper
   100024    1   udp  33264  status
   100024    1   tcp  37575  status
```

```
100003    2    udp    2049    nfs
100003    3    udp    2049    nfs
100003    4    udp    2049    nfs
100021    1    udp    56344   nlockmgr
100021    3    udp    56344   nlockmgr
100021    4    udp    56344   nlockmgr
100003    2    tcp    2049    nfs
100003    3    tcp    2049    nfs
100003    4    tcp    2049    nfs
100021    1    tcp    50947   nlockmgr
100021    3    tcp    50947   nlockmgr
100021    4    tcp    50947   nlockmgr
100005    1    udp    54674   mountd
100005    1    tcp    33465   mountd
100005    2    udp    54674   mountd
100005    2    tcp    33465   mountd
100005    3    udp    54674   mountd
100005    3    tcp    33465   mountd
100005    1    tcp    33465   mountd
100005    2    udp    54674   mountd
100005    2    tcp    33465   mountd
100005    3    udp    54674   mountd
100005    3    tcp    33465   mountd
```

This output shows that NFS versions 3 and 4 are both supported by the NFS server and the Lock Manager. In this case, the right services seem to be available on the server. You should also verify that the required processes are running on both the NFS server and the client system by using the ps command with your favorite options for listing system processes, as in the following example from an NFS 4 server:

```
$ ps -ef | egrep '(rpc|nfs)'
root    16447   2   0 Jul20 ?        00:00:00 [rpciod/0]
statd   17308   1   0 Jul20 ?        00:00:00 /sbin/rpc.statd
root    17316   1   0 Jul20 ?        00:00:00 /usr/sbin/rpc.idmapd
root    17345   2   0 Jul20 ?        00:00:00 [nfsd4]
root    17346   2   0 Jul20 ?        00:00:00 [nfsd]
root    17347   2   0 Jul20 ?        00:00:00 [nfsd]
root    17348   2   0 Jul20 ?        00:00:00 [nfsd]
root    17349   2   0 Jul20 ?        00:00:00 [nfsd]
root    17350   2   0 Jul20 ?        00:00:00 [nfsd]
root    17351   2   0 Jul20 ?        00:00:00 [nfsd]
root    17352   2   0 Jul20 ?        00:00:00 [nfsd]
root    17353   2   0 Jul20 ?        00:00:00 [nfsd]
root    17357   1   0 Jul20 ?        00:00:00 /usr/sbin/rpc.mountd
root    17415   2   0 Jul20 ?        00:00:00 [nfsv4-svc]
root    17828 945   0 05:47 tty1     00:00:00 egrep (rpc|nfs)
```

An NFS 4 server should be running at least the rpc.idmapd, rpc.mountd, and nfsd processes. An NFS 4 client should be running at least the rpc.idmapd process.

Verifying Filesystem Export

The kernel-nfs-server package includes utilities called exportfs and showmount that you can use to list the directories that an NFS server is currently exporting from your system and verify that the correct filesystems are being exported. The following is an example of using the exportfs command's -v to display a verbose listing of the filesystems that are being exported:

```
$ exportfs -v
/export/users  192.168.6.0/24(rw,async,wdelay,nohide,\
    insecure,no_root_squash,no_subtree_check)
/export/pub    192.168.6.0/24(rw,async,wdelay,\
    insecure,root_squash,all_squash,no_subtree_check)
/export        192.168.6.0/24(rw,async,wdelay,insecure,\
    root_squash,no_subtree_check,fsid=0)
```

(Entries for each exported directory would appear on a single line in actual output.)

The following is an equivalent example of using the showmount command:

```
$ showmount -e
Export list for userver:
/export       192.168.6.0/24
/export/pub   192.168.6.0/24
/export/users 192.168.6.0/24
```

If the right processes are running and the right filesystems are being exported, it may be necessary to bring out the big guns to help diagnose your problem—activating RPC debugging, as described in the next section.

For complete information about the exportfs and showmount utilities, see their online reference information, which is available by typing **man exportfs** or **man showmount** from any Ubuntu command line, such as an xterm or the GNOME Terminal application.

Debugging NFS Operations

If you are having problems mounting or accessing NFS directories, you can generate tracing information in the system log (/var/log/messages) by activating various RPC debugging options. The easiest way to activate these is to write a specific debugging mask to the files in the /proc filesystem that are associated with these debugging options. These files are the following:

- /proc/sys/sunrpc/nfs_debug: Controls tracing for the NFS client. The tracing output is generated in the system log on the host where the NFS client is running—the host that is attempting to mount or access an NFS directory. The debugging values that are available are listed in /usr/include/linux/nfs_fs.h.

- /proc/sys/sunrpc/nfsd_debug: Controls tracing for the NFS daemon. The tracing output is generated in the system log on the host where the NFS daemon is running—the host that is exporting the NFS directory. The debugging values that are available are listed in /usr/include/linux/nfsd/debug.h.

- `/proc/sys/sunrpc/nlm_debug`: Controls tracing for the Network Lock Manager. The tracing output is generated in the system log on the host where the NFS Lock Manager is running—the host that is exporting the NFS directory. The debugging values that are available are listed in `/usr/include/linux/lockd/debug.h`.

- `/proc/sys/sunrpc/rpc_debug`: Controls tracing for the underlying RPC layer used by all NFS client/server communications. The debugging values that are available are listed in `/usr/include/linux/sunrpc/debug.h`.

You can write decimal numbers that represent a bitmask that enables different types of tracing to these files by using the `sysctl` command or by simply writing to the appropriate file. For example, the following two commands activate all possible debugging for the NFS client:

```
# echo 65535 > /proc/sys/sunrpc/nfs_debug
# sysctl -w sunrpc.nfs_debug=65535
```

If you can think in terms of bitmasks, you can consult the appropriate kernel header files from the previous list. Personally, I typically find the NFS client and NFS server output to be most useful, and therefore begin with a value of 1023 because this activates most of the useful debugging for each without truly becoming overwhelming. I often test both the client and the NFS server on the system that is running the NFS server by first starting NFS server process, and then attempting to mount one of its exported directories somewhere else on the same host. Once things work locally, you can move on to try to get them working from a remote client.

Getting More Information about NFS

Not surprisingly, the Web provides many excellent sources of additional information about NFS. For more information, consult any of the following:

- **NFS:** FAQ (`http://nfs.sourceforge.net`)
- **NFS-HOWTO:** `http://nfs.sourceforge.net/nfs-howto`
- **NFS4 on Ubuntu:** `http://help.ubuntu.com/community/NFSv4Howto`

Summary

This chapter explained NFS, the Network File System, which is the de facto standard for sharing directories between UNIX-like systems over a network. NFS is simple, lightweight, and fast—and its implementation has been freely available for almost any UNIX-like system since the mid-1980s. After a bit of background, this chapter explained how to install and configure an NFS server on your Ubuntu desktop or server systems.

Although NFS implementations for Microsoft Windows systems exist, most of them cost money, and thus they aren't an out-of-the-box alternative for people who have heterogeneous networks comprised of systems running Linux, Mac OS X, and Microsoft Windows. (Mac OS X systems, with their Mach and BSD underpinnings, natively support NFS.) Interestingly enough, the most "standard" way of sharing files between all of these types of systems is by using a package known as Samba, which allows Ubuntu and other UNIX-like systems to share directories and filesystems over a network using the proprietary Server Message Block (SMB) protocol used by Microsoft Windows systems (and from which Samba takes its name). Chapter 35 explains how to quickly and easily set up Samba so that everyone on your home network can access files stored on your Ubuntu systems, regardless of what operating system those other machines are running, and (of course) at no cost.

Setting Up a Samba Server

L ike it or not, Microsoft Windows systems are everywhere. This chapter discusses the various ways in which software available on Linux systems makes it easy to integrate Linux and Windows filesystems in both directions, and provides features such as automatic printer sharing as freebies along the way.

You'd have to have been living in a cave for the last five or so years not to have heard of Samba, arguably one of the most popular applications ever written for Linux and UNIX-like systems. In a nutshell, *Samba* is a set of applications that was originally developed to provide support for Microsoft's networking protocols on Linux systems, but which has been ported to just about every other network-aware operating system.

A huge number of books are available that are dedicated to discussing Samba, explaining every nuance of its configuration files, installation, and use. My goal in this chapter is not to embed another one inside a book on Ubuntu, but rather to provide some interesting background information about Windows networking and Samba, and then to explain how to use Samba to share directories and printers on your Ubuntu system so that Microsoft Windows users in your home, academic, or business computing environment can access them.

IN THIS CHAPTER

Installing a Samba server

Sharing directories with Windows systems

Sharing printers with Windows systems

Overview of Microsoft Windows File Sharing

Networking and related technologies such as routing are probably responsible for more acronyms than any other aspect of the computer industry.

MS-DOS and Microsoft Windows networking have contributed their share, largely because of the ubiquity of these operating systems in modern computing environments. Because of the popularity of DOS systems (yesterday) and Windows systems (today), today's Windows systems provide support for almost everyone's networking protocols. Frankly, Windows does an admirable job of continuing to make forward progress while still maintaining backward compatibility with almost every ancient DOS application and networking protocol. Windows systems still support the Internet Packet Exchange (IPX) and Sequenced Packet Exchange (SPX) networking protocols used by Novell to provide the first PC file servers. However, more relevant for our discussion here are the networking protocols and attendant acronyms that were developed by Microsoft and used to provide file and resource sharing over PC networks without requiring the involvement of any third parties, thank you very much.

The *Basic Input and Output System* used by PCs to interact with local devices is best known by its initials as the PC's *BIOS*. As networks began to appear, Microsoft extended the capabilities of the BIOS to support accessing and sharing information over a network, naming the related protocols the Network BIOS, or as it's more popularly known, *NetBIOS*. Just as the BIOS provides the basic functions that support all system input and output, the NetBIOS provides the basic functions that let you use and administer network services. NetBIOS commands and functions must be exchanged between networked systems and therefore require a lower-level network transport mechanism to move network packets from one host to another. The lower-level transport protocols that are still in common use in PC networking today are IPX, NetBEUI (Network Basic Extended User Interface), and TCP/IP (Transmission Control Protocol/Internet Protocol). Interestingly, the *internet* in the full names of both IPX and TCP/IP refers to "inter-network communications," not "the Internet" as we know it today.

Modern Windows systems send their NetBIOS requests by using TCP/IP as a transport protocol. On top of the NetBIOS level, Windows networking provides a higher-level interface for network services known as the *Server Message Block* (SMB) protocol, which is a networking protocol that can be easily used by applications. SMB is a connection-oriented protocol rather than a broadcast protocol, meaning that it depends on establishing connections to specific networked services provided by other networked hosts rather than simply broadcasting its availability. Once a connection is established, SMB provides four basic types of functions:

- Session functions that negotiate and establish networked connections between machines (often referred to as *virtual circuits*), authenticate, and verify the access privileges that each party has with the other
- File functions that enable applications to open, close, read, and write remote files, shared directories, and so on
- Printer functions that enable applications to spool output to remote output devices
- Message functions that enable applications to send and receive control, status, and informational messages between different systems on the network

SMB became an Open Group standard for networking interoperability in the early 1990s. Samba takes its name from SMB, the addition of two vowels making it easily pronounced and somewhat softer than simply being *YAA* ("Yet Another Acronym").

In recent developments, an enhanced version of the SMB protocol called *CIFS* (Common Internet File System) was submitted by Microsoft to the IETF (Internet Engineering Task Force), an open association of people who are interested in the architecture of Internet communication and the smooth operation of the Internet. CIFS has been approved as a standard and extends the capabilities of SMB by expanding its focus to sharing resources using even more open, cross-platform standards such as HTTP URLs (HyperText Transfer Protocol Uniform Resource Locators) and DNS (the Domain Name System used to map hostnames to IP addresses and vice versa).

Introducing Samba

When you get right down to it, more data is probably stored on Windows systems than on any other type of computer system. All of those 10-GB home and office systems add up to a tremendous number of Windows filesystems holding a staggering amount of data. Samba gives Linux users transparent access to Windows filesystems but is more commonly used to give Windows users transparent access to Linux, UNIX, and UNIX-like systems. Samba does this by providing a network interface that is compatible with the networked file and printer-sharing protocols used between Windows systems. To a Windows system, a Linux system running Samba looks exactly like a random Windows system that is sharing filesystems across the network. This enables Windows users to take advantage of the speed, power, and capacity of Linux systems without even realizing that they are accessing Linux filesystems.

Samba is a free and impressive interface for Linux, UNIX, and other types of systems to any other networked device that can communicate using the SMB protocol, most notably Windows systems that provide networked access to files, directories, and printers. Samba enables Windows users to access Linux filesystems and resources just like any other Windows shared filesystem or networked resource. For example, with Samba running on a Linux system on your network, Windows users can mount their Linux home directories as networked Windows drives and automatically print to Linux printers just like any other networking Windows printer. Samba, which was originally authored by Andrew Tridgell, is one of the most impressive pieces of interoperability software ever developed.

Samba includes both client and server software — in other words, client software that enables users to communicate from Linux machines to SMB hosts on your network, and server software that provides an SMB interface for your Linux machine. Using the Samba client software is discussed in Chapter 26, "File Transfer and Sharing." This chapter focuses on explaining how to install and set up a Samba server.

A Samba server actually consists of two processes, both of which can be started from the command line or automatically by integrating them into your system's startup procedure. These processes are smbd, the Samba daemon that provides file sharing and print services to Windows clients, and nmbd, the NetBIOS name server that maps the NetBIOS names used by Windows SMB requests to the IP addresses used by Linux systems. The Samba daemon is configured by modifying its configuration file, /etc/samba/smb.conf. On Ubuntu systems, the easiest and most standard way to configure specific directories that you want to export via Samba is to manually modify the Samba configuration file, as discussed later in the section, "Samba Server Configuration Essentials."

Interoperability between Linux and Windows systems requires much more than just Samba. While Samba provides support for networked Windows filesystems, the Linux kernel provides built-in support for the protocols used to access physical Windows filesystems such as FAT and NTFS, enabling Linux users to mount Windows filesystems via entries in /etc/fstab, just like any other filesystem resource.

Note

The Ubuntu repositories provide both the current version of Samba and preliminary packages for the next version of Samba, Samba 4. This chapter focuses on the current version of Samba (Samba 3.x) because it is completely stable. Although Samba 4 will deliver improvements in performance, power, and flexibility, it isn't ready for prime-time use at the moment. Stay tuned! ■

Installing the Samba Server and Friends

Samba client packages are installed by default on Ubuntu desktop systems, making it easy for any Ubuntu system to contact and access SMB/CIFS shared directories from Microsoft Windows systems or Samba servers. To install the packages required to run and monitor a Samba server so that you can share directories from your Ubuntu system, you must install the samba package using your favorite package management tool: Synaptic, Adept, aptitude, or apt-get. See Chapter 19, "Adding, Removing, and Updating Software," for more detailed information on installing and using these package-management tools.

When installing the samba package, you may also want to install the samba-doc and samba-doc-pdf packages, which provide HTML and PDF versions, respectively, of all of the official Samba project documentation, plus HTML and PDF copies of the first edition of a book entitled *Samba-3 by Example: Practical Exercises in Successful Samba Deployment* (Prentice Hall, 2005, ISBN: 013188221X) by one of the leaders of the Samba project, John H. Terpstra. (The first edition of this book is now GPL — newer editions are available in print.)

Samba Server Configuration Essentials

While graphical utilities for configuring Samba exist, they are in a state of flux on Ubuntu systems. Previous releases of Ubuntu included a Shared Folders tool that enabled you to identify the Linux directories that you wanted to export via NFS or Samba, but that tool is no longer part of Ubuntu. A tool called system-config-samba, originally developed for the Red Hat Linux distribution, is available for Ubuntu systems but doesn't provide access to all of the configuration options that you will want to use in most cases. As a graphical tool, it also cannot be used on Ubuntu Server systems unless you also install a window manager or desktop environment.

Therefore, this chapter focuses on doing Samba server configuration in the aging but tried-and-true Linux way — by editing configuration files using a text editor. Samba's configuration file is /etc/samba/smb.conf. The Samba configuration file contains many helpful comments, which are lines beginning with a hash mark. It also contains many sample, inactive configuration commands, which are lines beginning with a semicolon. These indicate configuration commands that you may want to activate by removing the leading semicolon.

As you'll see in the next few sections, editing the file /etc/samba/smb.conf to configure Samba is actually quite simple but is also somewhat inelegant when compared to the rest of the system administrative environment provided by Ubuntu Linux.

Note

Web-based system administration tools such as swat **(Samba Web Administration Tool) and** webmin **(a more generalized Web-based administrative environment) are available from the Ubuntu repositories but require special configuration before they'll work correctly in Ubuntu. Rather than taking the conceptual detour of explaining how to use these tools, I'll continue to wait for a desktop solution for Samba setup and configuration on desktop Ubuntu systems. ∎**

The next few sections focus on specific entries in the Samba configuration file that you may need to update to use Samba in your environment, instead of discussing the Samba configuration file in its entirety. Between the official Samba documentation, the online documentation that is provided as part of the samba-doc and samba-doc-pdf packages, and the many books available on Samba, there's no shortage of detailed information about every nuance of Samba — the rest of this chapter focuses on getting things to work, as quickly and as easily as possible.

Identifying Your Workgroup or Domain

The Samba configuration file is divided into several sections, each identified by a section name enclosed within square brackets. The entries related to the network identity of your Samba server and how you authenticate to it are located in the [global] section of the Samba configuration file /etc/samba/smb.conf.

The key entry that you must set to define how your Ubuntu Server interacts with Windows systems is the workgroup entry, which identifies the workgroup or Windows domain to which your Samba server belongs. On a sample system of mine, this entry looks like this:

```
[global]
    workgroup = WVH
```

This entry identifies my machine as belonging to the Windows workgroup or domain named *WVH*. In this Small Office Home Office (SOHO) example, it's a workgroup, but that is essentially transparent — the key thing here is that your Samba server is either a member of the workgroup/domain that you are already using at your site, or a primary domain controller that defines the domain that you want it to host.

Note

If you want your Samba server to function as a domain controller (PDC) for a Windows domain, you must also change the value of the domain master setting in the [Domains] section of the Samba configuration file to yes and make sure that the entry is not commented out. In this case, the entry would look something like the following:

```
domain master = auto
```

This means that the Samba server will serve as a primary domain controller for your domain if no other domain controller can be located, which will be the case if your Samba server is hosting the domain. ∎

This chapter explains how to use Samba as part of a workgroup, which is the typical way that Samba is used on a home or SOHO network. For information about setting up a complete Windows domain, make sure that you installed the samba-doc as suggested in the section of this chapter, "Installing the Samba Server and Friends," and consult the online copy of *Samba-3 by Example* that is provided in the directory /usr/share/doc/samba-doc/htmldocs/ Samba3-ByExample.

Note

Windows 7 systems do a better job of enforcing security than any earlier release of Microsoft Windows. If you want your Windows 7 system to join a Samba domain controller, you'll have to be running Samba 3.3.4 or later (Ubuntu 10.04 provides Samba 3.4.6 or better) and do a few registry hacks on your Windows 7 system. See the excellent tutorial at www.linuxplanet.com/linuxplanet/tutorials/6911/2/ for detailed information. ∎

Because this example shows a small workgroup, you will probably also want to activate the entries that tell Samba not to function as a WINS (the Windows NetBIOS name service, discussed earlier in this chapter), but to instead use your system's Domain Name Server to look up Windows hostnames, which should look like the following:

```
wins support = no
dns proxy = yes
name resolve order = lmhosts host wins bcast
```

The last entry tells Samba that clients will first look in their local lmhosts file for name information (on Windows systems), will then check information in the file /etc/hosts on the Samba server, will then check WINS (which, in this case, is proxied to the local DNS server), and will finally use a broadcast to search for the right host. This combination covers the hostname lookup bases for every Samba server configuration that I've ever set up or used.

Finally, you must define the security model that will be used to identify authenticated users of the Samba server. To do this, uncomment the following entry in the Samba configuration file:

```
security = user
```

This completes the core modifications to the Samba configuration file that are necessary for Samba to be able to share files with the specified workgroup or domain. That wasn't so bad, was it?

Configuring Samba Authentication

In the workgroup configuration that we are using as an example in this chapter, Samba comes preconfigured to perform the type of authentication required by workgroup members. However, to be able to access shared resources, you must be able to authenticate to the Samba server. Samba maintains its own authentication information — to add login and password information about a user, you must use the smbpasswd command. When adding information about a user, you must use the -a option, followed by the name of the user that you want to add. The smbpasswd command will prompt you for a password and will then prompt you for that password again to ensure that you have typed the password correctly. The following is a sample transcript of adding the user wvh:

```
$ sudo smbpasswd -a wvh
Password:
New SMB password:
Retype new SMB password:
```

The first password prompt is from the sudo application, asking for my Ubuntu password so that I can perform this privileged operation. The second two are for entering and verifying the Samba password for the user wvh.

Note

The suggested security level in the Samba configuration file, security = user, requires that Samba users must also exist in the password file on the Ubuntu system, or you will receive an error message and the smbpasswd command will fail. For information about other security models and their implications, see the file /usr/share/doc/samba-doc/htmldocs/ServerType.html from the samba-doc package. ∎

Sharing Printers and Home Directories Using Samba

After setting up the workgroup and creating a user, the next thing to consider is the general resources on the Ubuntu system that you want to make available to all users of Windows systems that connect to your Samba server. The most common examples of these are printers and users' home directories.

The entries in the [global] section of a Samba configuration file that are relevant to printers and printing on Ubuntu are the following, which you should make sure are not commented out (i.e., preceded by a semicolon):

```
load printers = yes
printing = cups
printcap name = cups
```

Later in the Samba configuration file, the [printers] and [print$] sections provide information about how your Windows system will interact with the Samba server. You won't need to change any of these, but for your reference, these entries are as follows:

```
[printers]
    comment = All Printers
```

```
        browseable = no
        path = /tmp
        printable = yes
        guest ok = no
        read only = yes
        create mode = 0700
[print$]
        comment = Printer Drivers
        path = /var/lib/samba/printers
        browseable = yes
        read only = yes
        guest ok = no
```

The [printers] section identifies how the Samba server will handle requests for printer identification and incoming print requests from Windows clients, while the [print$] section maps the traditional Windows print$ share name to a directory on your Linux system where you can put the print drivers for specific printers so that your Windows clients can locate and load them if they are not already available on a client system.

Aside from printers, the most natural resource for users to want to access from their Windows systems is their Ubuntu home directories. This provides an easy way to use your home directory on a Samba server as a centralized place to store files, but also enables you to automatically back up files from your Windows system to the Samba server and enables you to leverage any standard backups that you are doing on the Samba server. (See Chapter 28, "Backing Up and Restoring Files," for more information about backing up files on your Ubuntu system.)

Happily, Samba's configuration file is already set up to support sharing home directories by default, as long as your Linux and Windows usernames match. The following is the section of the Samba configuration file that supports this:

```
[homes]
        comment = Home Directories
        browseable = no
        read only = yes
        create mask = 0700
        directory mask = 0700
```

As you can see from this configuration file excerpt, home directories are shared by default but are not writable from Windows clients. This is pretty inconvenient, so you will want to change the read only entry in this section of the configuration file to no, as in the following example:

```
        read only = no
```

This enables users to both read and write files in their home directories.

Tip

If your Windows and Ubuntu users happen to have different logins, you can associate the two by creating appropriate entries in the file /etc/samba/smbusers. Entries in this file have the form UnixLogin = WindowsLogin. For example, to map the Ubuntu user wvh to the Windows user bill.vonhagen, I would create the following entry in the /etc/samba/smbusers file:

```
wvh = bill.vonhagen
```

If your Windows login names contain one or more spaces, you must enclose them within quotation marks in this file.

In practice, I suggest keeping logins the same across Ubuntu and Samba systems, but this file can be used if you have different naming conventions for the users of different types of systems. ■

Verifying the Samba Configuration File

After making any changes to your Samba configuration file, you should verify that you haven't accidentally violated the syntax of the file. If a Samba configuration file contains any invalid entries, Samba displays an error message and will not load. This could be extremely discouraging, were it not for the fact that the Samba server package also provides a utility that tests the validity of a Samba configuration file and identifies the exact location of any errors that it finds. This utility is testparm, which you can run with no arguments to test the default Samba configuration file /etc/samba/smb.conf. The output from a run of the testparm utility looks like the following:

```
$ testparm
Load smb config files from /etc/samba/smb.conf
Processing section "[homes]"
Processing section "[printers]"
Processing section "[print$]"
Loaded services file OK.
WARNING: passdb expand explicit = yes is deprecated
Server role: ROLE_STANDALONE
Press enter to see a dump of your service definitions
```

As shown in the preceding example, after displaying some general information, the testparm utility prompts you to press Enter on your keyboard to see detailed information about the services that your Samba server has been configured to provide. The following is an example of this detailed information:

```
[global]
        workgroup = WVH
        server string = %h server (Samba, Ubuntu)
        obey pam restrictions = Yes
        passdb backend = tdbsam, guest
        syslog = 0
        log file = /var/log/samba/log.%m
        max log size = 1000
```

```
                name resolve order = lmhosts host wins bcast
                printcap name = cups
                panic action = /usr/share/samba/panic-action %d
                invalid users = root
                printing = cups
                print command =
                lpq command = %p
                lprm command =

[homes]
                comment = Home Directories
                read only = No
                create mask = 0700
                directory mask = 0700
                browseable = No

[printers]
                comment = All Printers
                path = /tmp
                create mask = 0700
                printable = Yes
                browseable = No

[print$]
                comment = Printer Drivers
                path = /var/lib/samba/printers
```

Depending on the version of Samba installed on your Ubuntu system and the changes that you have made to your Samba configuration file, your output may differ slightly.

The testparm utility only checks the Samba configuration file — it does not consult the running Samba service for information about how it is configured and the services that it provides. To do this, you can use the smbclient utility, as described in the next section.

Testing Samba Availability and Services

The Samba applications suite includes an application called smbclient, which is a command-line client for contacting and browsing Samba servers. You can also use this utility to test if your Samba server is up and running, and to list the services that it is providing.

If you have made any changes to your Samba configuration file, you should restart your Samba server before attempting to verify the services that it provides. To do this, execute the following command:

```
/etc/init.d/samba restart
```

This command shuts down any instance of the Samba server that is currently running and then starts the Samba server again, which forces it to read your updated configuration file.

Once you have done this, you can query your Samba server by using the `smbclient` application, as discussed in Chapter 26, to verify that your Samba server is working. Once it's clear that the Samba server is working and is correctly configured to allow users to access user-specific resources, it's time to add some system-wide resources that all authenticated users will be able to take advantage of.

Sharing Other Directories via Samba

Samba's configuration file makes it easy to access your home directory on a Samba server because that's probably the directory that you will want to access most frequently from a Windows system. As mentioned earlier, being able to access your Linux home directory from a Windows system provides a convenient mechanism for backing up critical Windows files by copying them to your Linux home directory (which you're certainly backing up, right?). Of course, if you are using a Samba server as a domain controller and using Samba's network logon mechanism to actually use Samba directories as your Windows home directories, things are even easier.

At some point, however, you will certainly want to export other directories from your Samba server so that all users can have access to them. For example, I always share the /opt2 directory that contains my online audio collection, which I should point out was either legally ripped from CDs that I own or consists of freely downloadable live recordings. To do this, I add the following entries to the end of my /etc/samba/smb.conf file:

```
[opt2]
    path = /opt2
    comment = Music
    available = yes
    browseable = no
    public = yes
    read only = yes
```

These entries enable all users on my network to browse for and access this share. Adding these entries to the standard Samba configuration file ensures that the newly defined share opt2 will always be available as soon as the Samba daemon is started (or restarted) on the Ubuntu system that is acting as a Samba server.

Getting More Information about Samba

Not surprisingly, the Web is an excellent source of additional information about Samba. Somewhat surprisingly, the Samba project itself provides some excellent documentation, as well as an online version of a great book about the current version of Samba, which is Samba version 3. As suggested earlier, you can install your own copies of the Samba documentation by installing the samba-doc and `samba-doc-pdf` packages when you install the Samba server. For more information, consult any of the following:

- `www.samba.org`: The main site for the Samba project, where you can find the latest tips, tricks, and source code

- `/usr/share/doc/samba-doc/htmldocs/Samba3-HOWTO`: A directory containing a HOWTO file in HTML format that explains how to install and configure Samba version 3 and answers many common questions. (You'll want to open the file `index.html` in this directory from your Web browser.) The HTML version of this document is provided in the `samba-doc` package.

- `/usr/share/doc/samba-doc/htmldocs/Samba3-ByExample`: A directory containing an HTML version of an excellent, hands-on book about Samba 3. This book was written by John Terpstra, one of the leaders of the Samba project, and explains how to install and configure Samba 3 for a complete spectrum of networked environments, from smaller SOHO environments (as discussed in this chapter) to enterprise environments with thousands of users. (You'll want to open the file `index.html` in this directory from your Web browser.) The HTML version of this document is provided in the `samba-doc` package. You'll probably also want to buy a paper copy of John's book — it's definitive, complete, and battery-free.

Summary

This chapter explained how to install and set up a Samba server to enable your Ubuntu system to export directories so that they can be accessed by users who are still stuck on Microsoft Windows systems. The combination of Samba utilities and the SMB/CIFS support that is built into the Linux kernel also provides the ability to access Windows shares from Ubuntu systems, all of which is available by default on those systems, as explained in Chapter 26.

Samba is probably the best example of the value that open source software can bring to modern computing, enabling seamless data sharing between UNIX-like and Microsoft Windows systems thanks to a fantastic combination of reverse engineering and insightful development.

What's on the CD-ROM?

This appendix provides you with information on the contents of the CD that accompanies this book.

System Requirements

Make sure that your computer meets the minimum system requirements listed in this section. If your computer doesn't match up to most of these requirements, you may have a problem using the contents of the CD.

For Linux or Windows Systems:

- PC with a Pentium processor running at 300 MHz or faster; for best performance, we recommend a Pentium IV or AMD equivalent running at 700 MHz or better

- At least 384 MB of total RAM installed on your computer; for best performance, we recommend at least 512 MB

- Ethernet network interface card (NIC) or modem with a speed of at least 28,800 bps

- A CD-ROM drive

- A VGA graphics card that is capable of at least 1024x768 resolution

- At least 4 GB of available disk space if installing Ubuntu Linux

If your system does not satisfy these requirements, you may still be able to install Ubuntu Linux on your system by either installing the Ubuntu Server

IN THIS APPENDIX

System Requirements

Using the CD with Windows and Linux Systems

What's on the CD

Troubleshooting

edition or by downloading, burning, and using the Ubuntu Alternate Install CD. Both of these options are discussed in Chapter 3.

Using the CD with Windows

To install Ubuntu Linux from the CD to your hard drive without changing the partitions on your disk, follow these steps:

1. Insert the DVD into your computer's CD-ROM drive.

   A window will appear, giving you the opportunity to install Ubuntu Linux on your Windows system by using the Wubi Installer.

   For more information using Wubi, see Chapter 2.

If you do not have autorun enabled or if the autorun window does not appear, follow the steps below to access the CD.

1. Click Start ⇨ Run.
2. In the dialog box that appears, type *d*:\wubi.exe, where *d* is the letter of your CD-ROM drive.
3. Choose the "Install inside Windows" option, as described in Chapter 2.

Using the CD with Linux

Note

The CD that is included with this book is a beta version of the Ubuntu Linux distribution for 32-bit x86 systems, and should not be installed on 64-bit systems. To install or test-drive Ubuntu Linux on a 64-bit x86 system, you must obtain and burn a copy of the Ubuntu CD for 64-bit systems. See the instructions in Chapter 2 for information on obtaining and burning a CD that contains the 64-bit version of Ubuntu Linux. To use the special-purpose versions of Ubuntu that are discussed in Chapter 3, you must download and install the associated CDs. See the instructions in Chapter 3 for information on obtaining and burning CDs that contain these special-purpose versions of Ubuntu Linux. ∎

To install or test-drive Ubuntu Linux from the CD to your hard drive, follow these steps:

1. Insert the CD into your computer's DVD-ROM drive.
2. Reboot your computer system, booting from the CD-ROM. If your system is not already configured to boot from a CD before booting from the hard drive, you may need to

modify your computer's BIOS settings in order to give precedence to booting from the CD-ROM drive.

3. Press Return or wait 30 seconds to boot into Ubuntu Linux.

4. Experiment with Ubuntu Linux or follow the instructions in Chapter 2 to permanently install Ubuntu Linux on your computer system. If your system already contains an operating system that you want to preserve and has sufficient disk space for both that operating system and Ubuntu , the Ubuntu Linux installer will offer to re-partition your disk without removing your existing data.

5. To remove the CD from your CD-ROM drive, select System ➪ Quit, and select Shut Down from the menu that displays. Remove the CD-ROM from your computer's CD-ROM drive when prompted to do so.

What's on the CD?

The CD that is included with this book provides a version of Ubuntu Linux from Canonical, Ltd. that you can either test-drive or install on a 32-bit x86-compatible computer system. You can install it on a new system or as an alternate operating system on an existing computer system. You can install it as an alternate operating system by either re-parititioning your disk to provide a partition where Ubuntu Linux can be installed directly, or as an alternate operating system on an existing Microsoft Windows system that has at least 4 GB of free space without re-partitioning.

Shareware programs are fully functional, trial versions of copyrighted programs. If you like particular programs, register with their authors for a nominal fee and receive licenses, enhanced versions, and technical support.

Freeware programs are copyrighted games, applications, and utilities that are free for personal use. Unlike shareware, these programs do not require a fee or provide technical support.

GNU software is governed by its own license, which is included inside the folder of the GNU product. See the GNU license for more details.

Trial, demo, or evaluation versions are usually limited either by time or functionality (such as being unable to save projects). Some trial versions are very sensitive to system date changes. If you alter your computer's date, the programs will "time-out" and will no longer be functional.

Troubleshooting

If you have problems installing or running Ubuntu Linux on a particular computer system, consult the Ubuntu Forums at http://www.ubuntuforums.org/.

Customer Care

If you have trouble with the CD-ROM, please call the Wiley Product Technical Support phone number at (800) 762-2974. Outside the United States, call 1(317) 572-3994. You can also contact Wiley Product Technical Support at http://support.wiley.com. John Wiley & Sons will provide technical support only for installation and other general quality control items. For technical support on the applications themselves, consult the program's vendor or author.

To place additional orders or to request information about other Wiley products, please call (877) 762-2974.

Index

SYMBOLS & NUMBERS

( ), vi, 433
".", ls, 395
"..", ls, 395–396
#
  /etc/apt/sources.list, 675
  FTP, 933
  IRC channels, 386
  PAMs, 965
$, vi, 433
*
  bash shell wildcard, 418
  executable, 394
+, Emacs, 446
-
  command line, 397
  permissions, 124, 413
.
  files, 395
  ls, 395
/
  backups, 1010
  directory, 394
  Linux filesystem, 82, 106, 107
  partitions mount point, 89
:, PATH, 424
;, SOA, 1084
=, OpenOffice.org Calc, 504
>, output re-direction, 420
?, bash shell wildcard, 418
@
  MX, 1085–1086
  SOA, 1083
  symbolic link, 396
[], bash shell wildcard, 418
\, command-line utilities, 197
^
  Emacs, 446
  vi, 433
{ }
  bash shell wildcard, 418
  vi, 433
|, bash shell commands, 420–421
~, home directory, 423
0.0.0.0, 1078
.123, 519
802.11, IEEE standard, 801, 814

A

a, rsync, 1003
-a
  ls, 395
  usermod, 956
AAC. *See* Advanced Audio Coding
AbiWord, 15, 497
About GNOME, System menu, 140
About Ubuntu, System menu, 140
About.com, 536
ABR. *See* average bit rate
Absolute Beginner Talk, ubuntuforums.org, 24
Accelerated Indirect GLX (AIGLX), 192
Access Control, printers configuration options, 725
access.conf, 970
accessibility, 9
  GNOME, 165–166
access.log, 1033
access_log, 1100
Accessories, Application menu, 138
account, 965
ACK, DHCP, 1061
acx, 817
ad hoc networks, 800
Add to Panel, 152–155
add-ons
  Eclipse, 829–831
  Firefox, 306–314
address books, 257–267
  Microsoft Windows migration, 320–321

adduser, 956
Adept Package Manager, 691–692
    GUI, 695
    NFS, 1111
Adium X, 374, 386
Adjust Colors, F-Spot, 652
Administration, System menu, 139
Administrator, Users and Groups tool, 958
Advanced Audio Coding (AAC), 560, 576–577
Advanced linux Sound Architecture (ALSA), 573
Advanced Maryland Automated Network Disk Archiver
        (Amanda), 996
Advanced Shell Scripting Guide, 423
AIFF. *See* Audio Interchange File Format
AIGLX. *See* Accelerated Indirect GLX
AIM. *See* AOL Instant messenger
aircrack-ng.org, 774
AisleRiot Solitaire, 619
Aitchison, Ron, 1076
ALAC. *See* Apple Lossless Audio Codec
alarms, Evolution Calendar, 270–271
Albitz, Paul, 1076
alert, 1033
aliases, 426, 587
aliasing, 533
alias_maps, 1046
Alias/Wavefront PIX, 546
alien, 714–717
Allman, Eric, 1038
all_squash, 1116
Almquist shell, 400
.alpha, 546
.als, 546
ALSA. *See* Advanced linux Sound Architecture
Alternate Install CD, 62–63
    command-line system, 96, 100
    Desktop system installation, 97–98
    install options, 95–100
    LTSP, 96, 100
    OEM installation, 98–99
Amanda. *See* Advanced Maryland Automated Network Disk
        Archiver
Amazon, Simple Storage Service, 1017
AMD, V/SVM, 861–862, 891
America Online (AOL), 356
angelfire.com, 557
Animations, Compiz Appearance Preferences, 194
anonymous FTP servers, 929

.ansi, 546
anti-aliasing, 532
antivirus, 1039
AOL. *See* America Online
AOL Instant messenger (AIM), 360
Apache, 1023–1057
    backuppc, 1006
    debugging, 1032–1033
    Subversion server, 850–853
Apache Server 2 Bible (Kabir), 1034
apache2ctl, 1028, 1030
apache2-doc, 1027
APE, 560
Appearance Preferences, Compiz, 193–196
append_dot_mydomain, Postfix, 1045
Apple Lossless Audio Codec (ALAC), 560
Apple's iChat (AIM), 358
applets
    Add to Panel, 153–154
    GNOME, 134, 179–181
    panels, 153–155
applications, 6
    language, 469
    PAM-aware, 963
Application description pane, Software Center, 670
Application launchers, 154
    GNOME, 134
Application menu, GNOME, 134, 138
Applixware, 498
AppSocket/HP JetDirect, printer connection options, 727
apt-cache, 686
apt-file, 688, 690, 964
apt-file list package, 688, 690
apt-get, 117, 671–672, 677, 690–695
    Bacula, 997
    build-time dependencies, 694–695
    development software installation, 820
    dlocate, 689
    dump, 995
    restore, 995
    smart upgrade, 692–693
    sudo, 690, 972
    Synaptic Package Manager, 690, 703
apt-get build-dep package, 821
apt-get dist-upgrade, 692, 703
apt-get install, 690
apt-get remove, 690–691
apt-get source package, 821

apt-get update, 681, 691
apt-get upgrade, 692
aptitude, 117, 667, 671–672
   apt-get, 690, 691
   Bacula, 997
   colors, 697–698
   development software installation, 820
   dlocate, 689
   Emacs, 686
   GNOME Terminal, 696
   installation, 696
   menus, 697–698
   Package Management, 685, 699
   Postfix, 1041
   show xemacs21, 687
   software, 695–700
   sudo, 972
   Synaptic Package Manager, 703
   user interface, 696–698
   vt100, 697
   --with-recommends, 699
aptitude install, 696
apt-key, 680, 681
Aquamarine, 192
arcade games, 635–640
archive backups, 988–989
arguments, command line, 393
arguments, PAMs, 965
Arkeia, 993
ARM
   Canonical, 32
   processors, 19–20
armagetronad.net, 639
ARPANET, 1038, 1059, 1075
Art of Computer Programming (Knuth), 462
ASCII Art, 546, 683
async, 120, 1116
ATI graphics chip, 192
Atlantik, 629–633
Atomic Tanks, 635–636
Audio Interchange File Format (AIFF), 560
audodns-dhcp, 1062
auth, 964
authentication. *See also* Kerberos; Pluggable Authentication
      Modules
   e-mail, 228
   FTP, 930
   Linux filesystem, 123

   Samba, 1131
   shares, 941
Authentication tab, Software Sources tool, 680
AuthUserFile, 851
auto
   eth1, 785
   /mnt/office, 939
   mount, 120
Auto Color, F-Spot, 652
autocmd, 439
autocompletion, address books, 258
Autodesk FLIC animation, 546
autofs, 1107
automatic presentations, 524
automount, 1108, 1119
Avant Window Navigator (AWN), 209–214
average bit rate (ABR), 560
AVI, 352
AWN. *See* Avant Window Navigator
azureus, 951

B

b
   permissions, 124
   vi, 433
Baby N Connector (BNC), 765
Back In Time, 1019
background
   bash shell, 421
   desktop, 162–163
   OpenOffice.org Impress, 523–524
backports components, 673
backups, 985–1021
   archive, 988–989
   bookmarks, 303
   cloud computing, 1017–1019
   directories, 985–1021
      cp, 1000–1001
      rsync, 1001–1003
   DVD, 589–590, 987, 998
   Evolution, 223–224
   files, 985–1021
   incremental, 989–990
   local storage devices, 994–996
   Mac OS X, 1019–1020
   Microsoft Windows migration, 322, 351–353
   privileges, 991

RAID, 986
removable media, 998–1003
SCCS, 846
SMB, 1011–1012
software, 992–997
spot, 988
sudo, 991
verifying/testing, 991–992
backup transports, 1004
BackupFilesExclude, rsync, 1010
BackupPC, 996
    DHCP, 1007
    hosts, 1007–1008
    installation, 1003–1016
    mailing lists, 1004
    MTA, 1005
    restore, 1014–1015
    rsyncd, 1008–1010
backuppc
    Apache Web server, 1006
    /etc/backuppc/config.pl, 1012
    /etc/backuppc/hosts, 1008
    hostname, 1012
    Microsoft Windows, 1011
    passwords, 1005
    smbclient, 1005
backuppc-announce, 1005
backuppc-devel, 1005
backuppc.sourceforge.net, 996
backuppc-users, 1004
bacula.org, 997
bare-metal restore, 992
BASE, 551
base station, 800
bash shell
    aliases, 426
    background, 421
    command line, 415–426
    configuration files, 423–424
    environment variables, 424–425
    job control, 421–422
    Tab key, 417–418
    wildcards, 418–420
~/.bash_profile, 423
.bashrc, 395
~/.bashrc, 414, 423, 587
Basic Input and Output System (BIOS), 1127
    boot order, 33, 63

EIDE/ATA, 740–741
hard disks, 743–744
USB flash memory stick, 53
Basic Service Set (BBS), 800
Battle for Wesnoth, 639
BBS. *See* Basic Service Set
BBSs. *See* bulletin-board systems
BCC. *See* blind carbon copy
BCM43xx, 817
Beagle, 173
Bellard, Fabrice, 896, 902
Berkeley Internet Name Daemon (BIND), 1076–1079
    configuration files, 1080–1082
    reverse lookup files, 1088–1089
    zone files, 1088–1089
Berkeley r-command suite, 906
Berkeley Standard Distribution (BSD), 428
Bernstein, Dan, 1037
Beryl, 191–192
bg, 422
BGA. *See* British Go Association
Bibble, 551
bibblelabs.com, 551
biff, 1045
/bin, 107
binary packages, 672, 821, 1107
/bin/ash, 400
/bin/bash, 400
/bin/csh, 400
BIND. *See* Berkeley Internet Name Daemon
bind9, 1079–1080
BIND 9 Administrator's Manual, 1094
/bin/dash, 400
/bin/ksh, 400
/bin/nash, 400
/bin/pdksh, 400–401
/bin/sh, 399, 401
/bin/tcsh, 401
/bin/zsh, 401
BIOS. *See* Basic Input and Output System
.bitmap, 547
bitmaps (BMP), 532, 547
bittornado-gui, 951
BitTorrent, 560–561, 565, 945, 948–952
blacklisting, 1051
blender.org, 17, 557
blind carbon copy (BCC), 236, 267

blogs, 23
Blum, Richard, 1057
BMP. *See* bitmaps
BNC. *See* Baby N Connector
board games, 619–622
Bogofilter, 248
The Book of Postfix: State-of-the-Art Message Transport
        (Hildenbrandt and Koetter), 1057
bookmarks
    backups, 303
    Firefox, 284, 296–306
    HTML, 303
    Microsoft Windows migration, 345–351
    URL, 296
bool, 198
boot
    command line, 392
    Desktop CD, 32–36, 746
    drive, 740
    GRUB, 45, 745–746
    hard disks, 743–746
    mounting filesystems, 118–121
    order, BIOS, 33, 63
    process, server installation, 90–91
    shares, 939–940
    USB flash memory stick, 53, 54
    virtual machines, 890–891
/boot
    Linux filesystem, 82
    partitions, 87–88, 746
Boot Device Priority, hard disks, 743–744
Boot from first hard disk, Alternate Install CD, 96
Boot me, server installation, 64–65
BOOTP, DHCP, 1060
Bourne, Stephen, 399
branches, 845
Brasero, 594–596
brctl, 897
brctl show, 886
Breezy Badger, 10
bridge_fd, 885
bridge_maxwait, 885
bridge_ports, 885
bridge-utils, 885, 899
bridging, 884
    /etc/network/interfaces, 899
    Network Manager, 900
British Go Association (BGA), 629

Broadband Ethernet, 764
Broadcom, 817
BSD. *See* Berkeley Standard Distribution
btjunkie.org, 951
Buddy List, Pidgin, 376–383
build-dep, 694–695
build-essential, 820–821
build-time dependencies, apt-get, 694–695
bulletin-board systems (BBSs), 356
burning, 561
    CD, 590–606
        ISO, 672
        k3b, 599–606
    DVD, 590–606
        Brasero, 595–596
        k3b, 599–606
        Nautilus CD/DVD Creator, 596–599
.bw, 547
.bz2, 546
Bzip archive, 546

C

c
    dpkg, 683
    permissions, 124
    tar, 999
c$, vi, 434
-c, gcc, 822
.c, 546
\C-, 454
C compiler, GCC, 822–823
C Development Toolkit (CDT), 830
C source code, 546
ca, 782
cache
    BIND, 1079
    negative cache TTL, 1085
    Package Management, 680
cactus.com, 993
Cairo-Dock, 214–215
Calc. *See* OpenOffice.org Calc
CalDAV, 274–275
CALs. *See* client access licenses
cameras. *See* digital cameras
Cancel, Evolution, 234
Canonical
    ARM, 32

components, 672–673
    MPEG, 576
    paid support, 27
carbon copy (CC), 234, 236
card games, 618–620
`cardctl`, 758
`caspar-rw`, 52
CBR. *See* constant bit rate
CC. *See* carbon copy
CCSM. *See* CompizConfig Settings Manager
CD. *See* compact disc
cd, 407, 933
`--cd`, 782
CD Database (CDDB), 561, 586
CDDB. *See* CD Database
CD/DVD Creator, Nautilus File Manager, 571–572, 596–599
CD-R. *See* compact disc/recordable
CD-RW. *See* compact disc/rewritable
CDT. *See* C Development Toolkit
CE. *See* consumer electronics
`.cel`, 547
Centos, 668
`cert`, 782
CGI. *See* Common Gateway Interface
`cgoban`, 628
CH, 1083
chains, 792
changing permissions in symbolic mode, 412
channels, IRC, 386
checksum, 563
Chess, 620, 624–627
`chgrp`, 414
Chicken of the VNC, 913
`chmod`, 414
`chown`, 414
`chsh`, 401
CIFS. *See* Common Internet File System
`cinepaint.org`, 17, 557
Citrix, 860
`clamav`, 1040
`clamav.net`, 1050, 1054–1056
Claws, 15
client access licenses (CALs), 100
clip art, 532
cloud computing, 91, 1017–1019
cloud controller system, UEC installation, 93
Cloud Server, 64

`clusty.com`, 1057
CMYK. *See* Cyan, Magenta, Yellow, Black
CNAME, 1086
codec. *See* compressor/decompressor
CodeWeavers, 655
Colloquy, 386
colors, 532
    `aptitude`, 697–698
    GIMP, 540
color depth, 533
Color Lines, 620
color space, 533
Colored XHTML, 546
columns, spreadsheets, 500, 511–512
command line, 391–426
    Alternate Install CD, 96, 100
    `apt-cache`, 686
    bash shell, 415–426
    boot, 392
    development software installation, 820
    DHCP, 1063–1067
    directories, 408–414
    DVD backups, 589–590
    files, 408–414
    FTP, 931–935
    GNOME Terminal application, 401–403
    groups, 956
    hard disks, 752–757
    ID3, 655
    LaTeX, 464
    Nautilus File Manager, 392
    partitions, 752–757
    permissions, 412–414
    shares, 942–943
    shells, 399–406
    `sudo`, 972
    TeX, 464
    users, 956
    vi, 430, 436–437
    vim, 439
    wireless networks, 811–813
    X Window System, 392, 403–406
Comma-Separated Value (CSV), 320, 518–519
Common Gateway Interface (CGI), 1028
Common Internet File System (CIFS), 114–115, 937, 940, 943, 1105, 1128
Common Unix Printing System (CUPS), 923, 1096
    log files, 1100–1102

compact disc (CD), 21–22, 561
  adding drives, 738–757
  aliases, 587
  backups, 987, 998
  burning, 590–606
    Brasero, 590–596
    ISO, 672
    k3b, 599–606
  compatibility, 593
  contents of, 1137–1139
  Copy, k3b, 604–606
  Free DB, 580
  ISO, 595
  Microsoft Windows, 1138
  multimedia, 570–573, 579–583
  playing, 579–583
  Rhythmbox, 580–581
    ripping, 583–585
  ripping, 583–589
    ID3, 655
    k3b, 585–588
  special-purpose systems, 62
  troubleshooting, 1139
compact disc/recordable (CD-R), 561
compact disc/rewritable (CD-RW), 561
CompactFlash, 665
Compiz, 189–219
CompizConfig Settings Manager (CCSM), 201–208
components, repositories, 672–681
compositing, Compiz, 189–219
compressor/decompressor (codec), 561, 676
CompuServe, 356
Computer Systems Research Group (CSRG), 1076
Concurrent Versioning System (CVS), 846
$Conf{BackupFilesExclude}, 1010
$Conf{CompressLevel}, 1010, 1012
$Conf{DHCPAddressRanges}, 1007
Config, 888
--config, 782
~/.config/compiz/compiz-manager, 193
Configuration dialog, printers, 724–725
Conflicts, DEB packages, 698
Connect to Server, 928–931
Connectiva Linux, 701
consistency checker, /etc/fstab, 121
Console, Eclipse, 833
constant bit rate (CBR), 561
consumer electronics (CE), 641–666
  customization, 645–648
  default actions, 643–645
  filesystem, 641
  Nautilus File Manager, 645
contacts
  adding/editing, 262–264
  customization, 257–261
  e-mail, 257–267
Contact List
  BCC, 267
  Empathy, 361, 369–372
  Evolution, 265–267
Content Scramble System (CSS), 581
Contents menu, F-Spot, 652
context-sensitive menus, 140–141
  Firefox, 286–287
  gnome-panel, 150–151
  Inkscape, 556
  Nautilus File Manager, 169
  OpenOffice.org Calc, 502–503
  OpenOffice.org Draw, 553
  OpenOffice.org Impress, 526
  OpenOffice.org Writer, 471–472
control-flag, 965
Conversation window, Pidgin, 378–379
convert, 546
cookies, 294, 342
Coordinated Universal Time (UTC), 79, 98
Copy
  CD, k3b, 604–606
  digital audio players, 658
  DVD, k3b, 604–606
  F-Spot, 650
  Rhythmbox, 658
Copy and Paste
  Emacs, 452
  OpenOffice.org Calc, 506–507
  vi, 435–436
CorelDraw, 531
Coulouris, George, 428
Courier IMAP, 1049
courier.mta.org, 1049
cp, 408–410, 1000–1001
cpio, 994
Create as, GNOME Partition Editor, 750
Create Commons, 532
creativecommons.org, 532
credentials=/etc/cifs.login, /mnt/office, 939

C

crit, 1033
C-shell, 400
CSRG. *See* Computer Systems Research Group
CSS. *See* Content Scramble System
CSV. *See* Comma-Separated Value
Cub 2: Sauerbraten, 639
Cube Gears, 208
CUPS. *See* Common Unix Printing System
CUPS: Common UNIX Printing System (Sweet), 1103
cups.org, 1102
curl, 928
currency data type, OpenOffice.org Calc, 516–517
cursor
    Emacs, 451–452
    vi, 432–433
    virtual machines, 894
customization
    CE, 645–648
    contacts, 257–261
    Emacs, 453–456
    GNOME, 146–166
    menus, 141–146
    mouse, 146–148
    OpenOffice.org Writer, 472–473
    panels, 149–155
    sudo, 972–975
    vim, 439–441
CVS. *See* Concurrent Versioning System
cw, vi, 434
Cyan, Magenta, Yellow, Black (CMYK), 532, 540
Cyrus IMAP, 1049

D

d
    cp, 1001
    permissions, 124
-d, rdesktop, 919
3D Chess, 627
DAE. *See* digital audio extraction
DansGuardian, 16
Dapper Drake, 10
Dasher, 165
DAT. *See* digital audio tape
Data Interchange Format (.dif), 519
data partitions, 82
Datagram Protocol (UDP), 765
DAV svn, 851

.dbt, 519
DBX, 336
/dcc chat nickname, 386
DCIM, 665
.dcm, 546
dd, 590, 994
DDNS. *See* Dynamic DNS
ddns-update-style, 1066
DEB packages, 12, 698–699
    alien, 714
    TimeVault, 1020
debfoster, 718
debhelper, 714
Debian, 7, 11–12
    Almquist shell, 400
    software, 668
debootstrap, 892
deborphan, 718
debug, 1033
debugging
    Apache 2.x, 1032–1033
    NFS, 1119–1122
    power management, 160
DEC. *See* Digital Equipment Corporation
default actions, CE, 643–645
default presentations, 524
default-lease-time, 1066
default_realm, 979
defaults, mount, 120
delay_warning_time, 1045
Delete
    digital audio player, 658
    Evolution, 234
    vi, 434
delprinc, 980
Dent, Kyle D., 1057
Desaturate, F-Spot, 652
Deskbar applet, 153
    GNOME, 179–181
desktop. *See also* GNOME desktop
    background, 162–163
    search applications, GNOME, 173–181
    users, 14–17
        GNOME, 129–187
        installation CD, 21
        Users and Groups tool, 958
    virtualization, 858

Desktop CD
    64-bit, 32
    boot, 32–36, 746
    disks, 49–51
    Examples folder, 47–49
    games, 618
    installation, 31–32, 37–47
    persistence, 52–56
    USB flash memory stick, 52–56
Desktop Cube/RotateCube, 208
Desktop Size, CCSM, 204
Desktop system installation
    Alternate Install CD, 97–98
    Text-mode, 97–98
Desktop Wall, Compiz Appearance Preferences, 195
Detect Duplicates, F-Spot, 650
dev, mount, 120
/dev, 107, 1010
/dev/cdrom, 589, 894
/dev/dvd, 589
developerWorks, 865
device drivers, 721
    printers, 728
    wireless networks, 813–818
Device Independent (DVI), 463
Device Manager, 760–761
    GNOME, 569–570
DeviceChooser, PulseAudio, 577–578
Devices
    Network Tools, 788
    printer connection options, 726
/dev/sdc, 746
/dev/sdX, 741
/dev/vboxdrv, 868
df, 752
dhclient, 1073
DHCP. See Dynamic Host Configuration Protocol
dhcp3-client, 1062
dhcp3-common, 1062
dhcp.conf, 1066
dhcpd3, 1063–1067
Dia, 554, 557
dial-up connections, 786
.dicom, 546
.dif. See Data Interchange Format
diff.gz, 693
digital audio extraction (DAE), 561

digital audio players, 654–665
    Copy, 658
    default actions, 643–645
    Delete, 658
    disconnecting, 659
    GNOME, 657
    playlists, 658–659
    Rhythmbox, 656–659
digital audio tape (DAT), 561
digital cameras
    default actions, 643
    F-Spot, 648–654
    import, 649–652
    JPEG, 544
    megapixels, 544
Digital Equipment Corporation (DEC), 1076
Digital Image and Communications in Medicine Image, 546
Digital Millennium Copyright Act (DMCA), 561
Digital Rights Management (DRM), 562
digital signal processing (DSP), 562
digital video disc (DVD), 562
    adding drives, 738–757
    backups, 589–590, 987, 998
    burning, 590–606
        Brasero, 595–596
        k3b, 599–606
    Copy, 604–606
    encryption, 581
    ISO, 590
    multimedia, 570–573, 579–583
    playing, 579–583
    Totem, 581–583
digital video recorder (DVR), 641
direct restore, 1015–1016
Direct Video Express (DivX), 314
directories, 106–108. See also home directories
    backups, 985–1021
    command line, 408–414
    /etc/fstab, 119
    export, 1114–1117
    GNOME, 106
    iPod, 661–662
    k3b, 587
    Microsoft Windows migration, 351–353
    mount, 1117–1119
    Nautilus CD/DVD Creator, 597
    Nautilus File Manager, 170–172

permissions, 124–125
root, 106
Samba, 1135
disc-at-once, 561
Disk Manager, 746
DISPLAY, 130, 907
display, 131
Display Settings, CCSM, 203
distributed copy, BitTorrent, 949
distrowatch.com, 28
dithering, 533
DivX. *See* Direct Video Express
DKMS. *See* Dynamic Kernel Module Support
dlocate, 689
DMCA. *See* Digital Millennium Copyright Act
dmesg, 752
DNS. *See* Domain Name System
DNS and BIND (Liu and Albitz), 1076
DNS Resources Directory, 1094
dnsmasq, 1063
dns.net/dnsrd, 1094
DOC, 353
dockable dialogs, GIMP, 538–539
docks, 214–216
DocRoot, 848
docs.scribus.net, 497
documents, 461–498
frames, 486
HTML, 462
LaTeX, 462–466
markup language, 462–466
OpenOffice.org Writer, 466–486
publishing, 461–498
Scribus, 486–497
TeX, 462–466
Document Converter
OpenOffice.org Calc, 519–521
OpenOffice.org Impress, 528–529
OpenOffice.org Writer, 468, 483–486
templates, 520–521
Domain Controller, Microsoft Windows, 918
Domain Name System (DNS), 767, 1059, 1075–1103
DHCP, 1062, 1093
installation, 1079–1080
IP address, 1065, 1093
Kerberos, 981
mail servers, 1040

manual configuration, 784
restarting/testing, 1089–1091
reverse lookup files, 1082–1089
RFCs, 1075–1076
troubleshooting, 1091–1094
zone files, 1082–1089
[domain-realm], 979
[Domains], 1130
DOOM, 636
Download Tar file, restore, 1016
Download Zip file, restore, 1016
dpkg, 667, 671–672, 682–690
alien, 714
ASCII Art, 683
Emacs, 684–685
-L, 687–688
-l, 682, 683
-l emacs, 684
--search, 688–689
sudo, 972
dpkg-dev, 714
Draw. *See* OpenOffice.org Draw
Drawer applet, 153
DriverLoader, 818
DRM. *See* Digital Rights Management
dropbear, 908
dropbox.com, 1017
DSC, 694
dselect, 671–672
DSL, 766
DSP. *See* digital signal processing
dual-band cards, 801
dual-boot, 45–46, 79, 858
dump, 121, 994, 995
DVD. *See* digital video disc
DVI. *See* Device Independent
DVR. *See* digital video recorder
dynamic addresses, 767
Dynamic DNS (DDNS), 1070
Dynamic Host Configuration Protocol (DHCP), 767,
1059–1073
BackupPC, 1007
DNS, 1062, 1093
IP address, 1061, 1065, 1093
scope, 1068–1069
text editor, 1064–1066
VirtualBox, 867, 883
Dynamic Kernel Module Support (DKMS), 722

dynamically expanding images, virtual disks, 874
`dynamicmaps.cf`, 1044

E

`e`, `fdisk`, 754
`-e`, `xterm`, 406
E17, 15
E Pierce, 548
EAP. *See* Extensible Authentication Protocol
EasyPeasy, 18
EasyTAG, 352
`echo`, 424–425
Eclipse, 825–845
    Makefiles, 841
    new source project, 831–838
    plug-ins, 845
    tarball, 840–841
    updates, 829–831
`.eclipse`, 827–828
`ed`, text editor, 456
Edgy Eft, 10
Edit pane, OpenOffice.org Impress, 526
Editing Macros (Emacs), 358, 428–429
    `aptitude`, 686
    buffer, 447
    Copy and Paste, 452
    cursor, 451–452
    customization, 453–456
    `dpkg`, 684–685
    keyboard, 446–447
    modeless editors, 446
    wildcards, 684–685
    window, 447
    X Window System, 442
    `xterm`, 443
Editor, Eclipse, 829, 832
editor for mortals (em), 428
`edonkey2000.com`, 945
Edubuntu, 7, 15
EHLO, 1052–1053
EIDE/ATA. *See* Enhanced Integrated Drive Electronics/
    Advanced Technology Attachment
`eject`, 665
em. *See* editor for mortals
ema, bash shell, 418
Emacs. *See* Editing Macros
`emacs`, 422

`emacspeak`, 166
e-mail, 1035–1057
    authentication, 228
    contacts, 257–267
    Evolution, 221–279
    filters, 244–249
    folders, 240–244
    HTML, 237–239
    mailing lists, 265–267
    Microsoft Windows migration, 323–339
    panels, 228
    receiving, 223
    search folders, 242–244
    sending, 230–231, 235–240
    SOA, 1084
    undeleting, 240
    Web-based, 249–256
embedded devices, 641
`embraceubuntu.com`, 28
Emerald, 191–192, 216–219
`emerg`, 1033
Empathy, 357
    Contact List, 361, 369–372
    groups, 371–372
    IM, 361–373
    IRC, 387
    MeMenu, 361–362
    Past Conversations, 372–373
    Pidgin, 362–364
    user accounts, 362–369
emulators, 857–903
enabled components, 674–675
encapsulated Postscript, 546
encryption
    DVD, 581
    server installation, 75–76
    SSL, 252–254
    wireless networks, 806
Enhanced Integrated Drive Electronics/Advanced
    Technology Attachment (EIDE/ATA), 739–741
`enlightenment.org`, 15
environment variables, 424–425
`.eps`, 546
EQ. *See* equalize
equalize (EQ), 562, 602
`error`, 1033
`error.log`, 1033
`error_log`, 1101

Escape sequence, 447
EsoundD, 574
ESS. *See* Extended Service Set
esvn, 847, 853
ESXi, 860
/etc, 107, 746
/etc/aliases, 1044
/etc/apache2, 1027
/etc/apache2/conf.d, 1027
/etc/apache2/mods-available, 1027
/etc/apache2/mods-enabled, 1027
/etc/apache2/sites-available, 1028
/etc/apache2/sites-available/default,
    1029–1030
/etc/apt/sources.list, 674–675
  apt-cache, 686
  apt-get, 691
  apt-get upgrade, 692
  Software Sources tool, 676–678
  Synaptic Package Manager, 701
  Update Manager, 713
  Wicd, 803–804
/etc/backuppc, 1006
/etc/backuppc/config.pl, 1004, 1009, 1011
/etc/backuppc/hosts, 1007–1008
/etc/bash.bashrc, 423
/etc/bind, 1092
/etc/bind/db.0, 1080
/etc/bind/db.127, 1080
/etc/bind/db.255, 1080
/etc/bind/db.empty, 1080
/etc/bind/db.local, 1080
/etc/bind/db.root, 1081
/etc/bind/named.conf, 1092
/etc/bind/named.conf.local, 1081
/etc/bind/named.conf.options, 1081
/etc/bind/zones.rfc1918, 1081
/etc/bin/named.conf.local, 1089
/etc/cups/cupsd.conf, 1097
/etc/cups/mime.types, 1102
/etc/default/apache2, 1028
/etc/default/mailscanner, 1056
/etc/default/nfs-common, 1112
/etc/default/nfs-kernel-server, 1113
/etc/default/ntpdate, 977
/etc/defaults/rsync, 1002
/etc/dhcpd.conf, 1063–1067
/etc/dhcp3/dhclient.conf, 1093

/etc/dhcp3/dhclient-script, 1093, 1094
/etc/dhcp3/dhcph.conf, 1063–1067
/etc/dump-dates, 995
/etc/exports, 115–117
/etc/fstab, 115, 117, 118–121, 939
  GRUB, 745
  /mnt, 1117
  mount, 1113
  nfs, 944
  NFS filesystem, 1118
  noserverino, 940
  Samba, 1128
/etc/group, 122–123, 962, 967
/etc/host.conf, 1077
/etc/hosts, 981, 1077–1078
/etc/init.d, 1027, 1066
/etc/init.d/apache2, 1028
/etc/init.d/dhcpd, 1073
/etc/init.d/freepops, 255
/etc/init.d/rsync, 1001
/etc/init.d/samba restart, 1134
/etc/krb5kdc/kdc.conf, 980
/etc/mime.types, 1028
/etc/modules, 816
/etc/motd, 967
/etc/network/interfaces, 783, 885, 899
/etc/nsswitch.conf, 1077
/etc/pam, 963
/etc/pam.conf, 963
/etc/pam.d, 965
/etc/pam.d/common-account, 968
/etc/pam.d/common-auth, 967, 982
/etc/pam.d/common-password, 969
/etc/pam.d/common-session, 968
/etc/pam.d/login, 965
/etc/passwd, 122–123, 401, 962, 968, 969
/etc/postgrey, 1051
/etc/profile, 423
/etc/rc2.d, 891
/etc/resolv.conf, 1065, 1077, 1094
/etc/rsyncd.conf, 1002
/etc/rsyncd.secrets, 1009
/etc/samba/smb.conf, 1128, 1135
/etc/samba/smbusers, 1133
/etc/securetty, 966, 967
/etc/security/limits.conf, 967
/etc/services, 796, 888, 1107–1108
/etc/shadow, 967–969

/etc/skel, 970
/etc/sudoers, 125, 972
/etc/vbox/interfaces, 885
/etc/vimrc, 439
/etc/X11/xinit/xinitrc, 912
/etc/X11/Xsession, 912
eth1, 785
Ethernet, 764–765
    VDE, 897
    wireless networks, 802
Eucalyptus, 64, 91
eudora.com, 1048–1050
events, Evolution Calendar, 269–272
Evolution
    authentication, 228
    backups, 223–224
    Calendar, 267–278
    Contact List, 265–267
    contacts, 257–267
    e-mail, 221–279
    filters, 244–249
    folders, 240–244
    forums, 278
    Gmail, 249–254
    GNOME desktop, 222–223
    HTML, 237–239
    import, 334–335
    IRC, 278
    mailing lists, 265–267, 279
    panels, 228
    PIM, 221–279
    Preferences, 236–240
    receiving, 223
    search folders, 242–244
    sending, 230–231, 235–240
    Setup Assistant, 223–232
    Thunderbird, 328, 332–335
    undeleting, 240
    versions, 224
    Web-based e-mail, 249–256
    wiki, 279
ex, text editor, 456
Examples folder, Desktop CD, 47–49
Excel, 519
exec, mount, 120
exim.org, 1037
Expo, Compiz Appearance Preferences, 195
export
    F-Spot, 653–654

NFS
    directories, 1114–1117
    filesystem, 1121
exportfs, 1121
/export/home, 1106
export-options, 1116
.exrc, 439
ext2 filesystem, 112–113, 757
ext3 filesystem, 113, 757
ext4 filesystem, 86
Extended Service Set (ESS), 800
Extensible Authentication Protocol (EAP), 802
extensions. See add-ons
eXternal Data Representation (XDR), 1108
Extra, Compiz Appearance Preferences, 195

F

f, tar, 999
-F, ls, 394
-f, rdesktop, 919
fanaticattack.com, 623, 683
faqs.org, 846, 1060
FastTrack, 945
Favorites, Internet Explorer, 296, 321
-fcp, 626
fdisk, 115–116, 753–757
Fedora, 6, 668
Feisty Fawn, 10
Feldman, Stu, 823
fetchmail, 1041
ffmpeg.org, 600
FFP. See FLAC footprint
FidoNet, 356
file:///, 849
files, 106–108
    ., 395
    backups, 985–1021
    command line, 408–414
    Microsoft Windows migration, 342, 351–353
    Nautilus File Manager, 170–172
    OpenOffice.org Writer, 468–469
    passwords, 122
    paths, 106
    permissions, 124–125
    reverse lookup, 1082–1089
    sharing, 944–952
        Microsoft Windows, 1125–1127
        NFS, 106

text, 427–459
Torrent, 565
transfer, 926–944
zone, 1082–1089
32-bit File Allocation Table (FAT32), 49
file handles, 1109
File Name, Rhythmbox, 585
File Transfer Protocol (FTP), 52, 928–937, 1024
   authentication, 930
   command line, 931–935
   GNOME desktop, 928–931
   hash, 933
   IP address, 929
   Nautilus File Manager, 929–931
   repositories, 936–937
   TCP/IP, 928
/file/ntp.conf, 977
filesystems, 109. *See also specific filesystems*
   CE, 641
   command line, 393
   directories, /etc/fstab, 119
   formats, 757
   GNOME Partition Editor, 750
   iPod, 665
   mounting, 115–122
   Nautilus File Manager, 170
   network, 114–115
   NFS
      /etc/fstab, 1118
      export, 1121
   partitions, 115–122
   removable media, 121–122
   type, 117
   types, /etc/fstab, 119–120
FileZilla, 935–936
filters
   e-mail, 244–249
   packets, 791
   spam, 1050–1056
Find bar, F-Spot, 651
Firebird, 282
Firefox, 281–317, 284
   GNOME desktop, 283
   Internet Explorer, 339–351
   Microsoft Windows migration, 339–351
   mouse, 286–287
   passwords, 295–296
   personas, 306–314

Plugin Finder Service, 288–289, 316
Safari, 339–351
tabbed browsing, 287–288
URL, 283, 853
user interface, 284–289
Xubuntu, 17
firewalls, 790–798
   NFS, 796–797
   Package Management, 793
First Run Wizard, VirtualBox, 877
.fit, 546
.fits, 546
Five or More, 620
FLAC. *See* Free Lossless Audio Codec
FLAC footprint (FFP), 562
Flash, 533, 551
.flc, 546
Flexible Image Transport System, 546
flexwiki.com, 846
.fli, 546
Flickr, 653–654
float, 198
fluendo.com, 576–577
Fluxbuntu, 15
Flyback, 1020
FOAF. *See* Friend of a Friend
Focus & Raise Behavior, CCSM, 204
forums, 23–24
   Evolution, 278
   QEMU, 902
   SpamAssassin, 1056
Forward/backward buttons, Evolution, 234
Four-in-a-Row, 622
frames
   documents, 486
   graphics, 491–493
   Scribus, 489–497
   text, 489–496
frameworks, GStreamer, 574
Free Lossless Audio Codec (FLAC), 562, 588, 600
Free Software Foundation (FSF), 4
freechess.org, 624
FreeDB, 562, 580, 586
freenet.sourceforge.net, 945
freenx, 923
FreePOPs!, 254–256
freeradius.org, 775
FreeVPS, 860

freeware, 1139
Fridge, 26
Friend of a Friend (FOAF), 23
Frozen Bubble, 636–637
fsck, 112–114, 121
FSF. *See* Free Software Foundation
fsid=0, 1115, 1116
F-Spot, digital cameras, 648–654
ftoc, 588
FTP. *See* File Transfer Protocol
ftp, 1001
    FTP, 934
    zone files, 1087
full backups. *See* archive backups
full stop, 395
fundamental mode, 454

G

-g, gcc, 822
0G, vi, 433
1G, vi, 433
gadmin-dhcpd, 1062, 1067–1072
GAIM. *See* GTK+AOL Instant Messenger
games, 617–640
    Application menu, 138
    arcade, 635–640
    Atlantik, 629–633
    Atomic Tanks, 635–636
    board, 620–622
    cards, 618–620
    Chess, 624–627
    Desktop CD, 618
    DOOM, 636
    Frozen Bubble, 636–637
    Go, 627–629
    Metal Blob Solid, 637–638
    Monopoly, 629–633
    Scrabble, 633–635
    Tux Racer, 638–639
    video, 622–623
gateways, 766
.gbr, 546
GCC. *See* GNU Compiler Collection
gcc, 714, 819, 822, 881
GCompris, 15
GConf. *See* GNOME Configuration Editor
gconf-editor, 198–201

gconftool-2, 196–201
gedit, text files, 456–458
gegl.org, 540
General
    CCSM, 203
    Evolution Calendar, 268
geographic location, 37–38, 67, 98
get, 934
Getting to Grips with LaTeX, 466
Geubuntu, 15
Ghost, Norton, 1012
GID. *See* group ID
gid=users, 940
gid=value, 120
GIF. *See* Graphics Interchange Format
Gigabit Ethernet, 765
.gih, 546
GIMP. *See* GNU Image Manipulation Program
gimp, 536–537
GIMP Brush, 546
GIMP Compressed XJT, 546
GIMP pattern, 546
gimp.org, 548
GIMPshop, 548
gksudo, 972
[global], 1129, 1131
Gmail, 249–254
gmameui, 863
GNOME. *See* GNU Network Object Model Environment
GNOME Art, 164
GNOME Configuration Editor (GConf), Compiz, 196–201
GNOME desktop
    command line, 392
    Evolution, 222–223
    Firefox, 283
    FTP, 928–931
    Places menu, 572
    shares, 940–942
    themes, 163–164
GNOME Do, 215–216
GNOME Format, 746
GNOME Office Suite, 497
GNOME Partition Editor, 746–751
GNOME Terminal, 401–403
    aptitude, 696
gnome-device-manager, 569
GNOME-Look.org, 164
gnome-panel, 149–152

gnome-ppp, 786
gnome-screenshot, 541
gnome-volume-manager, 121–122
gnome-volume-manager-gthumb, 648
gnome-wm, 185
GNU, 4
GNU Chess, 624–625
GNU Compiler Collection (GCC), 819, 821–823
GNU Image Manipulation Program (GIMP), 5, 536–551
    CMYK, 540
    colors, 540
    dockable dialogs, 538–539
    keyboard, 548
    screenshots, 541–544
    Separate+, 540
    Xubuntu, 17
GNU Network Object Model Environment (GNOME), 9, 14
    accessibility, 165–166
    application windows, 135–136
    customization, 146–166
    Deskbar applet, 179–181
    desktop search applications, 173–181
    desktop users, 129–187
    Device Manager, 569–570
    digital audio players, 657
    directories, 106
    keyboard shortcuts, 166–167
    language, 469
    menus, 136–146
    mouse, 132–133
    Nautilus File Manager, 167–173
    Network Tools, 786–789
    printers, 1096
    TimeVault, 1020
    Tracker, 173–181
    Ubuntu One, 1018
    vim, 441
    window managers, 181–186
GNU Paint, 557–558
gnuchess-book, 626
gnuchessx, 626
gnumeric, 670
gnu.org, 557–558, 825
gnushogi, 627
Gnutella, 945–948
Go, 628–629
Gobuntu, 7, 15–16

Google, 174
    Calendar, 274–275
    FlyBack, 1020
    Gmail, 249–254
    IM, 359, 360
    Picasa, 550–551
    Talk, 361, 388
Gosling, James, 428–429
gparted, 747
gpg, 680
Grand Unified Boot Loader (GRUB), 118, 739
    boot, 45, 745–746
    /etc/fstab, 745
    server installation, 78–79
graphics, 531–558
    Application menu, 138
    Compiz, 189–219
    frames, 491–493
    GIMP, 536–551
    OpenOffice.org Draw, 551–553
    photo editing, 548–551
graphical user interface (GUI), 106, 129. *See also* GNOME
    Adept Package Manager, 695
    DHCP, 1062
    LaTeX, 464
    Synaptic Package Manager, 695
    vi, 441
Graphics Interchange Format (GIF), 533, 546
graphicsoft.about.com, 536
grayscale, 533
grep, 685
greylisting, 1051
groups, 956–963
    Empathy, 371–372
    Linux filesystem, 122–124
group ID (GID), 1111
groupadd, 956
group.conf, 970
groupdel, 956
groupmod, 956
group-name, 956
GRUB. *See* Grand Unified Boot Loader
GStreamer, 574–577
    SHN, 615
    Sound Converter, 613
gThumb, 648
GTK, 1067–1072
GTK+, 701

GTK+AOL Instant Messenger (GAIM), 373, 374
gtkatlantik, 630–631
gtk-gftp, 935
gtk-gnutella, –945–948
gtkpod, 659–665
gtk-window-decorator, 192
g4u, 1012
Guest Additions, VirtualBox, 881
Guest OS, 860, 862–863
gufw, 794, 796
GUI. *See* graphical user interface
Gutsy Gibbon, 10
.gz, 546
Gzip archive, 546

H

H
   dpkg, 683
   rsync, 1003
h, dpkg, 682, 683
.h, 546
Haley, Chuck, 428
halftone, 533
hang-up (HUP), 1009, 1012
happypenguin.org, 623
hard, 1118
hard disks. *See also* partitions
   adding, 738–757
   BIOS, 743–744
   boot, 743–746
   Boot Device Priority, 743–744
   command line, 752–757
   Desktop CD, 49–51
   EIDE/ATA, 739–741
   formatting, 746–757
   GNOME Partition Editor, 746–751
   installation, 39–41
   KVM, 893–894
   Linux filesystem, 109–110
   partitions, 746–757
   PATA, 742
   SATA, 742
   SCSI, 742–743
   virtual machines, 872–876
hard links, 396
Hardening Apache (Mobily), 1034
hardware, 721–761

   networks, 768–786
   requirements, 20–21
   sound, 569–570
   virtualization, 861
Hardy Heron, 10
hasbro.com, 629
hash, 933
Haugland, Solveig, 553
Hazel, Philip, 1037
hd, 752
Heliodor, 192
hello, 824
HELO, 1052–1053
-help, 397
--help, 398
help.ubuntu.com, 26
The Hessling Editor (THE), 456
Hibernate, 159–160
:hide, 439
Hildebrandt, Ralf, 1057
history, 416–417
HISTSIZE, 416
Hoary Hedgehog, 10
/home, 82, 108
home directories
   NFS, 1106–1107
      automounting, 1119
      Samba, 1131–1133
home page, Firefox, 291–292, 344
home_dir_backup.tgz, 1000
/home/music, 584
home/remote, 1106
host, 131, 918, 1066–1067
Host Interface, VirtualBox, 884
hostname, 1013
hostname:directory, 118
HOSTS.TXT, 1075
23hq, 653
HS, 1083
HSV. *See* hue, saturation, brightness
.htm, 546
HTML. *See* HyperText Markup Language
HTML table, 546
html_directory, 1046
HTTP, Subversion, 850
hubs, 765
hue, saturation, brightness (HSV), 533
100-BaseT, 765

HUP. *See* hang-up

HyperText Markup Language (HTML), 237–239, 303, 462, 546, 1024

Hyper-V, 860

hypervisor, 860, 863

I

`i`, `dpkg`, 683

`-I`, `gcc`, 822

i386, 19

    `gtk-gnutella`, 948

IaaS. *See* Infrastructure-as-a-Service

`iab`, 440

Iagno, 620

`ibm.com`, 865

IBSS. *See* Independent Basic Service Sets

iCal, 274–275

ICCCM. *See* Inter-Client Communication Conventions Manual

`.ICEauthority`, 972

IceWM, 183–184, 186

`.ico`, 547

`.icon`, 547

ICQ, 357, 358, 360

`-ics`, 626

ID3, 562, 655, 661

idempotent, 1108

IDEs. *See* integrated development environments

`id3tool`, 655

`id3v2`, 655

IEEE. *See* Institute of Electrical and Electronics Engineers

IETF. *See* Internet Engineering Task Force

`ietf.org`, 1060

`iface`, 785

`ifconfig`, 392

`ifconfig interface-name`, 787

`ifuse`, 660

IGS. *See* Internet Go Server

Illustrator, 531

IM. *See* instant messaging

`.im1`, 547

`.im8`, 547

`.im24`, 547

`.im32`, 547

Image tab, Scribus, 493

IMAP. *See* Internet Message Access Protocol

import

    Eclipse, 838–845

    Evolution, 334–335

    F-Spot, 649–652

    LaTeX, 464

    OpenOffice.org Calc, 517–521

    OpenOffice.org Draw, 554

    OpenOffice.org Impress, 528–529

    OpenOffice.org Writer, 483–486

    photographs, 649–652

    Rhythmbox, 607

    Subversion repository, 849

Impress. *See* OpenOffice.org Impress

`IN`, zone files, 1085

`Incoming Queue Dir`, 1055

incremental backups, 989–990

Independent Basic Service Sets (IBSS), 800

InDesign, 477

    Scribus, 486

Indexes, Apache Web server, 1032

`inet`, 783–785

`inetd`, 852, 1001

`inet_interfaces`, 1046

`info`, 399, 422, 1033

infrastructure wireless networks, 800

Infrastructure-as-a-Service (IaaS), 1017

Ingram, Michael, 949

`--init DIRECTORY`, 1018

`inkscape.org`, 551, 554–557

Ink/Toner Levels, printers configuration options, 725

input re-direction, 421

`insecure`, 1116

installation, 31–60

    Apache Web server, 1027

    `apt-get`, 690

    `aptitude`, 696

    BackupPC, 1003–1016

    command-line system, 100

    Desktop CD, 31–32, 37–47

    development software, 820–825

    DHCP, 1062–1063

    disks, 39–41

    DNS, 1079–1080

    Eclipse, 827

    Enterprise Cloud, 91–95

    Eucalyptus, 64

    firewalls, 790–798

    geographic location, 37–38

    `gtkpod`, 659

    Kerberos, 976

keyboard, 38
KVM, 891–893
Live CD, 31–32
ndiswrapper, 814
NFS, 1111
OEM, Alternate Install CD, 98–99
OpenOffice.org Writer, 468–469
partitions, 39–40, 43–45
passwords, 42
Postfix, 1040–1043
QEMU, 900–902
requirements, 19–21
Samba, 1128
Scribus, 487
software, 668–670
special-purpose systems, 61–101
Subversion, 847–855
Synaptic Package Manager, 706–711
user account, 41–42
virtual machines, 890–891
VirtualBox, 866–868
Wicd, 803–804
Wubi, 56–59
install-css, 581
instant messaging (IM), 355–390, 359
    Empathy, 361–373
    IRC, 385–388
    Mac OS X, 359
    Pidgin, 373–387
    security, 358
Institute of Electrical and Electronics Engineers (IEEE),
        800–801
int, 198
integrated development environments (IDEs), 820,
        825–845
Intel VT, 861–862, 891
Inter-Client Communication Conventions Manual
        (ICCCM), 184–185
intergofed.org, 629
International Standards Organization (ISO), 562
    burning CD, 672
    CD, 595
    DVD, 590
    k3b, 602–604
internationalization, 9
Internet Engineering Task Force (IETF), 1060
Internet Explorer, 282, 297, 321, 339–351
Internet Go Server (IGS), 628

Internet Message Access Protocol (IMAP), 226–230
    Gmail, 250–254
    Postfix, 1049
    Thunderbird, 326
Internet Packet Exchange (IPX), 1127
Internet Printing Protocol (IPP), 727
Internet Protocol (IP), 766, 780. See also IP address
Internet radio, 606–612
Internet Relay Chat (IRC), 25, 356–357, 385–388
    Empathy, 387
    Evolution, 278
    passwords, 386
    Subversion, 855
Internet Scrabble Club, 633
Internet service provider (ISP), 221, 763
    mail servers, 1039
Internet Systems Consortium, 1076
InterPress, 535
intr, 1118
Intrepid Ibez, 10
IP. See Internet Protocol
IP address, 766–767
    DHCP, 1061, 1065, 1093
    DNS, 1065, 1093
    /etc/hosts, 1077–1078
    FTP, 929
    Kerberos, 981
    localhost, 1099
    mail servers, 1040
    Pidgin, 376
    reverse lookup files, 1087–1088
    scope, 1068–1069
    SOA, 1084
    UEC installation, 92, 94
    wired network, 770–771
    zone files, 1085–1086
ipchains, 792
ip-forwarding, 1066
ipfw, 792
iPhones, 660
iPod, 654–665
IPod touch, 660
IPP. See Internet Printing Protocol
iproute, 892
iptables, 791–792
IPX. See Internet Packet Exchange
IRC. See Internet Relay Chat
IRChelp.org, 388

I

IRC.org, 388
isc.org, 1076
isc.ro, 633
Islamiccal, 16
ISO. *See* International Standards Organization
isohunt.com, 951
Isolinux, 672
ISP. *See* Internet service provider
iTunes, 655
iwconfig, 811
iwfwadmin, 792
iwlist, 808, 811–813

J

Jabber, 358–359, 360
jackaudio.org, 574
jaggies, 533
Jaunty Jackalope, 10
Java, 292, 635
JavaScript, 292
JavaScript Object Notation (JSON), 303
JDuplicate, 635
jedit, text editor, 456
JeOS. *See* Just Enough Operating System
JFS filesystem, 113, 757
Job Options, printers configuration options, 725
/join #channel, 386
Joint Photographic Experts Group (JPEG), 533, 544–546
Joy, Bill, 428
.jpe, 546
JPEG. *See* Joint Photographic Experts Group
.jpg, 5467
JSON. *See* JavaScript Object Notation
jumpers, 740
Junk, Evolution, 234, 241
junk mail, 244–249
Just Enough Operating System (JeOS), 19
    server installation, 66

K

-k, 415
K Development Environment (KDE), 131
    Edutainment, 15
    k3b, 585
    Kubuntu, 16
Kabir, Mohammed J., 1034

kadmin, 980
kadmin.local, 980–981
Karbon14, 554
Karmic Koala, 10
kazaa.com, 945
Kazehakase, 15
k3b, 589
    burning CD/DVD, 599–606
    CD Copy, 604–606
    CDDB, 586
    directories, 587
    DVD Copy, 604–606
    EQ, 602
    FLAC, 600
    ISO, 602–604
    KDE, 585
    MP3, 586
    OGG, 586
    ripping CD, 585–588
    WAV, 586
KDC. *See* Key Distribution Center
KDE. *See* K Development Environment
kdesvn, 847, 853
KDevelop, 826
Kerberos, 975–982
    KDC, 975
    NFS, 1112–1113
    PAMs, 963
kernel, 6
    PCI cards, 802
    virtualization, 860–861
kernel headers, 881
Kernel-based Virtual Machine (KVM), 860–861, 863
    hard disks, 891–896
    networks, 896–900
    User Networking, 896–898
    Virtual Bridge, 898–900
    Virtual Machine Manager, 864
kernel-nfs-server, 1121
key, 782
key bindings
    CCSM, 204
    Eclipse, 835–836
    Emacs, 453–454
Key Distribution Center (KDC), Kerberos, 975
keyboard
    accessibility, 165

Emacs, 446–447
GIMP, 548
GNOME, 166–167
installation, 38
server installation, 68
Totem, 582–583
VirtualBox, 878–879
kill, 422
kinit, 981, 982
Kino, 17
KISS CEL, 546
klist, 982
Klondike, 619
Klotski, 621
Knuth, Donald, 462, 466
Koetter, Patrick, 1057
Korn shell, 400
kppp, 786
krb5-admin-server, 976, 978–979
krb5.conf, 979
krb5-config, 976
krb4_convert, 979
krb5-kdc, 976
krb5-user, 976, 981
Kubuntu, 7, 16, 18
KVM. *See* Kernel-based Virtual Machine
kvm.ko, 892

L

-L, dpkg, 687–688
-l
   dpkg, 682, 683
   fdisk, 753
   ls, 394
-l emacs, 684
Label, GNOME Partition Editor, 750
LAMP. *See* Linux, Apache, MySQL, and Perl
Lamport, Leslie, 462, 466
Landscape, 76
language, 66, 468–469
LANs. *See* local area networks
laptop users, 14–17
LaTeX, 462–466
LaTeX: A Document Preparation System (Lamport), 466
launchpad.net, 17, 1020
layers, 534
Layers and Brushes window, GIMP, 538

layhands.com, 623
Layouts pane, OpenOffice.org Impress, 526
LDAP. *See* Lightweight Directory Access Protocol
LEAP. *See* Lightweight Extensible Authentication Protocol
lease period, DHCP, 1061, 1067
/leave #channel, 386
Lempel-Ziv-Welch (LZW), 533
Lesser General Public License (LGPL), 467
Letter Wizard, OpenOffice.org Writer, 473–477
LGPL. *See* Lesser General Public License
/lib, 107
libapache2-svn, 847
[libdefaults], 979
libpam, 963
libpam-krb5, 976, 981
libpurple, 374
Library, Firefox, 301–303
Library Location, Rhythmbox, 584
Library Structure, Rhythmbox, 585
libsdl1.2debian, 892
/lib/security, 963
license
   CALs, 100
   codec, 676
   LGPL, 467
   PUEL, 866
   SISSL, 467
Licq, 388
Liddington, Simon, 838
lifewithqmail.org, 1038
Lightweight Directory Access Protocol (LDAP), 123, 259–261, 963
Lightweight Extensible Authentication Protocol (LEAP), 775
Lightweight, Productive, Agile, Efficient (LPAE), 15
lil8nux.net, 9
LiLo. *See* Linux Loader
limited-duration leases, 1060
limits.conf, 970
Line Printer Daemon (LPD), 1096
lines per inch (LPI), 535
Link Text Frames, Scribus, 495
LinkSys, 817
Linux Alternatives Project, 353
Linux, Apache, MySQL, and Perl (LAMP), 19, 1027
Linux Application Finder, 353
Linux distribution, 5–7

Linux filesystem, 109–115
    authentication, 123
    groups, 122–126
    permissions, 122–126
Linux Loader (LiLo), 118
Linux Shell Scripting Tutorial, 423
Linux Standard Base (LSB), 108, 715
Linux Terminal Server Project (LTSP), 19, 96, 100
Linux Virtualization Wiki, 865
linuxant.com, 818
linuxdevcenter.com, 824
linuxforu.com, 855
linux-nis.org, 1111
linuxprinting.org, 723, 1102–1103
list, 198
/list, 386
Liu, Cricket, 1076
Live Bookmarks, 290, 303–306
live.gnome.org/Dia, 557–558
live.gnome.org/GnomeOffice, 497
loadable kernel modules, 721
local area networks (LANs), 800
local filesystems, 112–114
local storage devices, backups, 994–996
local time, 98
localhost, 1007, 1048, 1099
localhost.localdomain, 1048
localization, 9
local.network, 981
<Location/>, 1101
<Location/svn>, 850
Lock to Panel, 153
logical partitions, 84
Logical Volume Management (LVM), 22, 71
logical volumes, 109–112
Lone Star, 993
Long Term Support (LTS), 11
Lookup, Network Tools, 788
lossless formats, 534, 562
lossy formats, 534, 562
lost+found, 1010
Lotus 1-2-3, 519
LPAE. See Lightweight, Productive, Agile, Efficient
LPD. See Line Printer Daemon
LPI. See lines per inch
ls
    command line, 393–397
    wc -l, 420

ls -al, 854
LSB. See Linux Standard Base
lspci, 567–568
lsusb, 722
LTS. See Long Term Support
LTSP. See Linux Terminal Server Project
Lucid Lynx, 10, 804
LVM. See Logical Volume Management
lyx, 464–465
lyx.org, 465
LZW. See Lempel-Ziv-Welch

M

-m, Subversion, 849
\M-, Emacs key bindings, 454
M4A, 562
MAC. See Media Access Control
Mac OS X
    backups, 1019–1020
    IM, 359
    NFS, 1106
    VNC, 912–913
macros, LaTeX, 462
Mahjongg, 621
mail, 1087
Mail Delivery Agent (MDA), 223, 1036
Mail Exchanger (MX), 1085–1086
mail servers, 1035–1057, 1040
Mail Transfer Agent (MTA), 223, 1005, 1036
Mail User Agent (MUA), 223, 1036
mailbox_size_limit, 1046
mailing lists, 25–26
    BackupPC, 1004
    e-mail, 265–267
    Evolution, 279
    mail servers, 1039
    Subversion, 855
Mailman, 265
mailscanner, 1040, 1054–1056
mailto URL, 223
mailx, 1040
Main window
    Firefox, 286
    GIMP, 538
main.cf, 1044, 1051
Makefiles, 823–825
    Eclipse, 841
    pop3check, 842

make_resolv_conf(), 1094
makeuseof.com, 623
MAME. *See* Multi-Arcade Machine Emulator
mame.net, 863
man, 398, 399
man ftp, 933
man qemu, 894
managed networks, 800
Manager, PulseAudio, 577
Mandriva, 668, 701
Mann, Tim, 624
/manual/, 1030
map, 440
markup language, 462–466
Mashey, John, 399
.mask, 546
master, 740
    BIND, 1079
Master Boot Record (MBR), 22
master.cf, 1044
.matte, 546
Mattessich, Richard, 500
max, 84
max-lease-time, 1066
MBR. *See* Master Boot Record
McCool, Rob, 1026
McNealy, Scott, 467
MD5, 563
MDA. *See* Mail Delivery Agent
Media Access Control (MAC), 802, 1060–1061
/media/cdrom, 815
medibuntu.org, 17, 676
Meebo, 374, 388
meetings, Evolution Calendar, 272–274
megapixels, 534, 544
MeMenu, Empathy, 361–362
memory. *See also* USB flash memory stick
    cards, 665
    partitions, 88
    Test, 96
    virtual machines, 871–872
Menu Catalog, 142
menus. *See also specific menus*
    aptitude, 697–698
    context-sensitive, 140–141
        Firefox, 286–287
        gnome-panel, 150–151
        Inkscape, 556

Nautilus File Manager, 169
Nautilus File System, 169
    OpenOffice.org Calc, 502–503
    OpenOffice.org Draw, 553
    OpenOffice.org Impress, 526
    OpenOffice.org Writer, 471–472
customization, 141–146
    Firefox, 284, 286–287
    F-Spot, 651
    GNOME, 134, 136–146
    Inkscape, 555
    OpenOffice.org Calc, 502
    OpenOffice.org Draw, 552
    OpenOffice.org Impress, 525
    OpenOffice.org Writer, 470
    panels, 137–140
mepis.org, 17
merges, 845
Metacity, 191–192
metadata, 534
Metal Blob Solid, 637–638
Microlite, 993
microlite.com, 993
Microsoft Live/Hotmail, 359, 360
Microsoft Windows
    backuppc, 1011
    CD, 1138
    CIFS, 1105
    Domain Controller, 918
    file sharing, 1125–1127
    migration, 319–354
    shares, 937–943
    VNC, 913
    Windows Terminal Server, 917–923
    wireless device drivers, 814–816
MID. *See* mobile Internet device
millions of colors, 533
MIME. *See* Multipurpose Internet Mail Extensions
Mines, 621
Minibar, 16
Miranda, 386
mIRC, 386
~/.mission-control, 362
mkfs, 753, 757
mkswap, 753
MLS. *See* Multi Level Security
.mng, 547
MNG animation, 547

/mnt, 1117
/mnt/office, 939
mobile Internet device (MID), 18
Mobily, Tony, 1034
MockLisp, 429
modal editor, 430
modeless editors, 429, 446
modems, 786
module-name, 965
module-type, 964
Monitor Preferences, 148–149
monkeysaudio.com, 560
monochrome, 533, 534
monopd, 632
monoped, 630
Monopoly, 629–633
Mosaic, 282
Motion Picture Association of America (MPAA), 563
Motion Picture Experts Group (MPEG), 563
    Canonical, 576
    Fluendo, 576–577
Motor, 826
mount
    /etc/fstab, 120–121, 1113
    NFS directories, 1117–1119
    noserverino, 943
    -t, 117
mount points
    Linux filesystem, 109–110
    partitions, 86–87
    /, 89
mount-options, 1117, 1118
mouse
    accessibility, 165
    customization, 146–148
    Firefox, 286–287
    GNOME, 132–133
    VirtualBox, 878–879
Move Window, Compiz Appearance Preferences, 195
Mozilla, 282
~/.mozilla/firefox, 343
MP3. *See* MPEG-1 Audio Layer 3
MP3 CD, 563
MPAA. *See* Motion Picture Association of America
MPEG. *See* Motion Picture Experts Group
MPEG-4, 563
MPEG-1 Audio Layer 3 (MP3), 352, 563
    Fluendo, 576–577
    ID3 tags, 655

k3b, 586, 600
playlists, 658–659
Rhythmbox, 585
MPG, 352
MrPostman, 254
/msg, 386
MTA. *See* Mail Transfer Agent
MUA. *See* Mail User Agent
Multi Level Security (MLS), 970
Multi-Arcade Machine Emulator (MAME), 863
multi-homed systems, 767
multimedia, 559–616
    Brasero, 590–596
    CD, 570–573, 579–583
        burning, 590–606
        ripping, 583–589
    DVD, 570–573, 579–583
        burning, 590–606
    GNOME Device Manager, 569–570
    k3b, 585–588
    Medibuntu, 17
    Nautilus CD/DVD Creator, 596–599
    PulseAudio, 577–579
    Rhythmbox, 580–581, 606–612
    Totem, 581–583
    Ubuntu Studio, 17
Multiplan, 519
multi-protocol clients, 359
Multipurpose Internet Mail Extensions (MIME), 173, 1028
multiverse components, 673
MultiViews, Apache Web server, 1032
~/Music, 587
music players. *See* digital audio players
Muslims, 16
mv, 410
MX. *See* Mail Exchanger
mydestination, 1046, 1048
mydomain, 1048
myhostname, 1046
mynetworks, 1046, 1053
myorigin, 1045, 1046, 1048
Mythbuntu, 16
MythTV, 16, 694–695

N

n
    dpkg, 683
    fdisk, 754

Name Service Switch, 1077
named-checkconf, 1092
named.conf, 1080
namespace.conf, 970
namespace.init, 970
nano, text editor, 456
NAS. *See* Network Audio System
NAT. *See* Native Address Translation; Network Address
    Translation
National Center for Supercomputing Applications (NCSA),
    1026
Native Address Translation (NAT), 764
Nautilus File Manager, 146, 170–172
    CD/DVD Creator, 571–572
        burning, 596–599
    CE, 645
    command line, 392
    FTP, 929–931
    GNOME, 167–173
    shares, 941–942
    TimeVault, 1020
nautilus-file-management-properties, 646
Navigation toolbar, Firefox, 284
Navigator, Eclipse, 832
NCP. *See* Novell Core Protocol
NCSA. *See* National Center for Supercomputing
    Applications
ndisgtk, 814–816
ndiswraper, 803
ndiswrapper, 809, 813–814, 816–818
    ndiswrapper modules, 814
ndiswrapper-utils, 814
NEED_GSSD, 1113
NEED_IDMAPD, 1113
NEED_STATD, 1112–1113
NEED_SVCGSSD, 1114
negative cache TTL, 1085
-net, 897
NetBeans, 826
NetBEUI. *See* Network Basic Extended User Interface
netbook users, 18
Netfilter, 791–792
netpbm.sourceforge.net, 546
Netscape, 282
Netstat, 788
netwidget.net, 1076, 1094
networks
    DHCP, 1062

filesystems, 114–115
hardware, 768–786
KVM, 896–900
QEMU, 902
remote systems, 905–924
security, 763–798
VirtualBox, 883–889
VPNs, 777–783
wired, 770–773
wireless, 773–776
Network Address Translation (NAT), 767, 790
    VirtualBox, 867, 883
Network Audio System (NAS), 574
Network Basic Extended User Interface (NetBEUI), 1127
Network Connections, Network Manager, 769–770
Network File System (NFS), 114, 943–944, 1105–1123
    Adept Package Manager, 1111
    file sharing, 106
    filesystem
        /etc/fstab, 1118
        export, 1121
    firewalls, 796–797
    GID, 1111
    home directories, 1106–1107, 1119
    pseudo-filesystem, 1114–1117
    Synaptic Package Manager, 1111
    UID, 1111
    versions, 1109–1110
Network Information Center (NIC), 1075
Network Information System (NIS), 1108, 1111
Network Manager, 768–786
    bridging, 900
    Network Connections, 769–770
    VirtualBox, 885
    Wicd, 804
Network Printer, printer connection options, 727
Network Status Monitor (NSM), 1112–1113
Network Time Protocol (NTP), 975, 976
Network Tools, GNOME, 786–789
network-admin, 392
network-manager, 885
New Document
    OpenOffice.org Writer, 480–481
    Scribus, 487–488
New Mail notifications, Pidgin, 374
New Size, GNOME Partition Editor, 750
New users, Users and Groups tool, 957–958
--newer, 999

newgrp, 124
NFS. *See* Network File System
nfs, 944
nfs-common, 1111
nfs-kernel-server, 1111
nfs.sourceforge.net, 1122
Nibbles, 622–623
NIC. *See* Network Information Center
/nick, 386
NIS. *See* Network Information System
nm-applet, 769
nmbd, 1128
NNGS. *See* No Name Go Server
No Name Go Server (NNGS), 628
no_all_squash, 1116
noatime, 120
noauto, 120
nodev, 120
noise reduction, 563
NoMachine NX, 923
nomachine.com, 923
non-routable IP address, 766
Normal
    Alternate Install CD, 96
    Compiz Appearance Preferences, 194
    vi, 430
normalize, 563
    Brasero, 594
normalize-audio, 602
no_root_check, NFS, 1116
no_root_squash, NFS, 1116
Norton, Ghost, 1012
noserverino
    CIFS, 940, 943
    /etc/fstab, 940
    mount, 943
no_subtree_check, 1116
Not Junk, Evolution, 234
notice, 1033
Notification area
    GNOME, 134
    Power Management Preferences, 160
nouser, mount, 120
Novell, 6
Novell Core Protocol (NCP), 115
NSM. *See* Network Status Monitor
NT File System (NTFS), 49
NTFS. *See* NT File System

NTP. *See* Network Time Protocol
ntp, 976, 977
ntpdate, 976–978, 977
NTPDATE_USE_NTP_CONF, 978
NTPSERVERS, 978
nullok_secure, 967
NVIDIA graphics chip, 192

O

-o send-port, 1113, 1114
ODF. *See* OpenDocument Format
.odg, 551
odm, 468
.ods, 519
odt, 468
OEM. *See* Original Equipment Manufacturers
Office, Application menu, 138
OGG. *See* Ogg Vorbis
Ogg Vorbis (OGG), 563
    ID3 tags, 655
    k3b, 586, 600
    otoc, 588
Oikarinen, Jarkko, 356
ol2mbox. *See* Outlook to mbox
On Battery Power tab, Power Management Preferences,
        158–159
On The Web, 274–275
--one-file-system, rsync, 1010
one.ubuntu.com, 1017–1018
online calendars, Evolution Calendar, 274–276
:only, vim, 439
oocalc, 501
oodraw, 551
oooauthors.org, 553
oowriter, 469
OOXML. *See* Open Office XML
opasswd, 970
Open Clip Art Library, 532
Open Graphics Library (OpenGL), 189, 191–192
Open Office XML (OOXML), 467
open relay, 1047
Open Sound System (OSS), 573
Open Source Edition (OSE), VirtualBox, 866, 885–886
OpenBSD, 908
openbsd.org, 908
openclipart.org, 532
OpenDNS, 1065

opendns.com, 1065
OpenDocument Drawing, 551, 554
OpenDocument Format (ODF), 467
OpenGL. *See* Open Graphics Library
OpenJDK, 830
OpenOffice, 15
OpenOffice.org Calc, 501–521
    cells, data types, 515–517
    context-sensitive menus, 502–503
    Copy and Paste, 506–507
    currency data type, 516–517
    Document Converter, 519–521
    format, 519
    Formula bar, 504
    functions, 514–515
    import, 517–521
    menus, 502
    OpenOffice.org Writer, 503
    row and column headings, 502
    selection box, 505
    toolbars, 502
OpenOffice.org Draw, 551–553
    context-sensitive menus, 553
    import, 554
    menus, 552
    rulers, 553
    Styles and Formatting window, 553
    toolbars, 552
OpenOffice.org Impress
    background, 523–524
    context-sensitive menus, 526
    Document Converter, 528–529
    Edit pane, 526
    import, 528–529
    Layouts pane, 526
    menus, 525
    OpenOffice.org Writer, 526
    Presentation Wizard, 522–525
    presentations, 522–529
    Preview pane, 526, 528
    Styles and Formatting window, 526
    toolbars, 525
OpenOffice.org Writer, 466–486
    context-sensitive menus, 471–472
    customization, 472–473
    Document Converter, 468, 483–486
    file extensions, 468
    files, 468–469
    import, 483–486
    installation, 468–469
    language, 468–469
    Letter Wizard, 473–477
    menus, 470
    New Document, 480–481
    ODF, 467
    OpenOffice.org Calc, 503
    OpenOffice.org Impress, 526
    paragraphs, 477–480
    rulers, 470
    styles, 477–480
    Styles and Formatting window, 471, 477–480
    templates, 476, 480–483
    toolbars, 470
    User Data, 472–473
    wizards, 473–477
openprinting.org, 723, 728–729
OpenSSH server, 908
openssh-server, 908
OpenVPN, 777–783
OpenVZ, 860
operating system
    KVM, 894–896
    virtual machines, 877–880, 894–896
OPML. *See* Outline Processor Markup Language
/opt, 82, 108
optional, PAMs control-flag, 965
Orca, 165
Original Equipment Manufacturers (OEM), 22, 65, 96, 98–99
Orville Write, 356
OSE. *See* Open Source Edition
OSS. *See* Open Sound System
OSXvnc server, 913
Other Community Discussions, ubuntuforums.org, 24
otoc, 588
ott, 468
Outbox, Evolution folder, 241
Outgoing Queue Dir, 1055
Outline, Eclipse, 833
Outline Processor Markup Language (OPML), 23
Outlook, 320–321
    readpst, 337–339
Outlook Express
    readdbx, 336–337
    Thunderbird, 324–326
Outlook to mbox (ol2mbox), 337–338

output re-direction, 420–421
owner, mount, 120

P

p
  bash shell, 417
  cp, 1001
  dpkg, 683
  fdisk, 754
-p
  gcc, 822
  rdesktop, 919
-p listen-port, 1114
  NFS, 1113
Pacifica, 861–862
package
  apt-file, 688, 690
  apt-get build-dep package, 821
Package Management. *See also* Adept Package Manager; Red
      Hat Package Manager; Synaptic Package Manager
  apt-file, 964
  aptitude, 685, 699
  bridge-utils, 885
  cache, 680
  CVS, 846
  dlocate, 689
  firewalls, 793
  GStreamer, 575–576
  gtkpod, 659
  shntool, 615
  software, 670–672
  uml-utilities, 885
packets, 766
  filters, 791
padevchooser, 577
page_log, CUPS, 1101
PageMaker, 477
  Scribus, 486
Paint Shop Pro, 531
pair, 198
Palette, Inkscape, 556
PAM modules, 964
pam_access.so, 970
PAM-aware applications, 963
pam_cracklib.so, 970
pam_deny.so, 971
pam_env.conf, 970
pam_env.so, 966

pam_group, 967
pam_group.so, 970
pam_lastlog.so, 967
pam_limits.so, 967, 970
pam_mail.so, 967
pam_motd.so, 967
pam_namespace.so, 970
pam_nologin.so, 966
pam_permit.so, 968
PAMs. *See* Pluggable Authentication Modules
pam_securetty.so, 966
pam_selinux.so, 967, 969
pam_time.so, 970
pam_unix.so, 967, 969, 982
pam_warn.so, 971
Panel Properties, gnome-panel, 151–152
panels
  applets, 153–155
  customization, 149–155
  e-mail, 228
  GNOME, 134
  menus, 137–140
Pantone Matching System (PMS), 534
paprefs, 577
paragraphs, OpenOffice.org Writer, 477–480
Parallel Advanced Technology Attachment (PATA), 742
  SCSI, 746
parallel virtual machine, 860
partimage, 1012
partitions
  /boot, 87–88, 746
  command line, 752–757
  data, 82
  /etc, 746
  fdisk, 753–757
  filesystems, 115–122
  hard disks, 746–757
  installation, 39–40, 43–45
  Linux filesystem, 109–110
  logical, 84
  max, 84
  memory, 88
  mkfs, 753
  mkswap, 753
  mount points, 86–87
    /, 89
  physical, 84
  server installation, 70–72
    manual, 81–90

swap, 82, 88
USB flash memory stick, 54
partner components, 673
password, PAMs, 965
passwords
    backuppc, 1005
    files, 122
    Firefox, 295–296
    installation, 42
    iPod, 665
    IRC, 386
    Kerberos, 980
    Microsoft Windows migration, 342
    Pidgin, 374
    remote systems, 907
    Samba, 1131
    server installation, 74–75
        boot process, 90
    Subversion, 851
    sudo, 972
    Wicd, 804–805
Past Conversations, Empathy, 372–373
.pat, 546
PATA. See Parallel Advanced Technology Attachment
PATH, 415, 424–425
paths, files, 106
pavucontrol, 577
pavumeter, 577
.pbm, 547
.pcc, 547
pccardctl, 758
PCI cards, 759–760
    kernel, 802
PCL. See Printer Control Language
PCM. See Pulse Code Modulation
PCMCIA. See Personal Computer Memory Card
        International Association
.pcx, 547
PDA. See personal digital assistant
PDF, 353
Peer-to-Peer (P2P), 563, 800, 925, 944–952
PenDriveLinux.com, 53
permissions
    command line, 412–414
    directories, 124–125
    files, 124–125
    Linux filesystem, 122–126
persistence, Desktop CD, 52–56

Personal Computer Memory Card International Association
        (PCMCIA), 758
    LinkSys, 817
    wireless networks, 802
personal digital assistant (PDA), 641
Personal Information, contacts, 262–263
Personal Information Manager (PIM)
    calendar, 267–278
    Evolution, 221–279
Personal Storage Table (PST), 320–321, 337–339
Personal Use and Evaluation License (PUEL), VirtualBox,
        866
personas, Firefox, 304–314
perspective, Eclipse, 829
.pgm, 547
Phoenix, 282
photo editing, 548–551
photographs. See F-Spot
Photos, 652
Photoshop, 531, 540, 546, 548
Photoshop Express, 550–551
    Flash, 551
physical partitions, 84
physical volumes, 111
Picasa, 550–551, 653
pico, text editor, 456
Pida. See Python Integrated Development Application
Pidgin, 259, 357, 359
    Buddy List, 376–383
    Conversation window, 378–379
    Empathy, 362–364
    IM, 373–387
    IP address, 376
    passwords, 374
    user accounts, 374–376
PIM. See Personal Information Manager
Ping, Network Tools, 788
PiTiVi, 17
.pix, 546
pixels, 532, 534
pixels per inch (PPI), 535
PKG, 715
PKI. See public key infrastructure
Places menu, GNOME, 134, 139, 572
Planet Ubuntu, 23
planeteclipse.org, 845
plasticbugs.com, 548
--play white|black, 627

playlist.m3u, 588

playlists
    digital audio players, 658–659
    gtkpod, 662–664
    iPod, 656, 659, 662–664
    MP3, 658–659
    Rhythmbox, 609, 656

Pluggable Authentication Modules (PAMs), 123, 962–971
    Kerberos, 963
    LDAP, 963
    repositories, 963

Plugin Finder Service, Firefox, 288–289, 315–316

plug-ins
    Eclipse, 829, 845
    Firefox, 314–317
    GStreamer, 575–577
    k3b, 600
    Rhythmbox, 657

PMS. See Pantone Matching System

PNG. See Portable Network Graphics

.png, 547

.pnm, 547

Pocket Excel, 519

podcasts, Rhythmbox, 610–612

Point-to-Point Protocol (PPP), 786, 925

Point-to-Point Tunneling Protocol (PPTP), 777

polarion.org, 845

Policies, printers configuration options, 724–725

Polypaudio, 577

pool of addresses, 1061

POP. See Post Office Protocol

pop3check, 838, 840
    Makefiles, 842

popd, 407

pop-up blocking, Firefox, 288–289, 292

ports
    virtual machines, 884
    VirtualBox, 888
    VNC, 910

port forwarding, 888

Port Scan, Network Tools, 788

Portable AnyMap (PNM), 547

Portable BitMap (PBM), 547

Portable GrayMap (PGM), 547

Portable Network Graphics (PNG), 533, 535, 553

Portable PixMap (PPM), 547

portmapper, 1108, 1119

Post Office Protocol (POP), 226–229
    FreePOPs!, 256
    Gmail, 250–254
    Postfix, 1041
    Qpopper, 1048–1050
    Thunderbird, 326
    Yahoo! mail, 256

postconf, 1053

Postfix, 1005, 1035–1057
    ClamAV, 1054–1056
    IMAP, 1049
    installation, 1040–1043
    localhost, 1048
    localhost.localdomain, 1048
    mailscanner, 1054–1056
    main.cf, 1051
    Pop, 1049
    SMTP, 1051, 1053
    spam, 1051–1053
    SpamAssassin, 1054–1056
    trusted hosts, 1047

Postfix (Blum), 1057

Postfix: The Definitive Guide (Dent and Venema), 1057

postfix-doc, 1041

postgresql, 699–700

postgrey, 1041, 1050, 1051

PostScript, 535, 547

Power Management Preferences, 157–161

PowerPC (PPC), 20, 32

PowerPoint, 528–529

P2P. See Peer-to-Peer

PPC. See PowerPC

PPI. See pixels per inch

.ppm, 547

PPP. See Point-to-Point Protocol

PPT, 353

PPTP. See Point-to-Point Tunneling Protocol

Pre-Depends, DEB packages, 698

Preferences
    Evolution, 236–240
    Firefox, 290
    F-Spot, 652
    PulseAudio, 577–579
    Synaptic Package Manager, 702–704
    System menu, 139
    Wicd, 808–809

Preferred Format, Rhythmbox, 585

prepress, 535

Presentation Wizard, OpenOffice.org Impress, 522–525
presentations
    automatic, 524
    default, 524
    OpenOffice.org Impress, 522–529
preshared key mode (PSK), 802
Preview pane, OpenOffice.org Impress, 526, 528
Print, Evolution, 234
[print$], 1131–1132
printenv, 424–425
Printer Control Language (PCL), 534
Printer Options, printers configuration options, 725
printers, 722–731, 1095–1103
    Configuration dialog, 724–725
    device drivers, 728
    GNOME, 1096
    naming, 731
    Samba, 1131–1133
[printers], 1131–1132
Printing utility, 723
privacy, Firefox, 293–296
privileges
    backups, 991
    Linux filesystem, 125–126
    User Privileges, Users and Groups tool, 958–959
Pro DNS and BIND (Aitchison), 1076
/proc, 107, 1010
process colors, 532
process identifier, 422
/proc/filesystems, 119–120
/proc/partitions, 116
/proc/sys/sunrpc/nfsd_debug, 1121
/proc/sys/sunrpc/nfs_debug, 1121
/proc/sys/sunrpc/nlm_debug, 1122
/proc/sys/sunrpc/rpc_debug, 1122
Prodigy, 356
Project Creation Wizard, Eclipse, 831–838
Properties dialog, Synaptic Package Manager, 705–706
Properties menu, Scribus, 493
ProTools, 17
Provide PPD file, printer identification options, 730
.psd, 546, 547
pseudo-filesystem, 1114–1117
Psi, 388
PSK. *See* preshared key mode
PST. *See* Personal Storage Table
/pub, 933
Public FTP, 929

public key infrastructure (PKI), 907
publishing
    documents, 461–498
    Evolution Calendar, 276–278
PUEL. *See* Personal Use and Evaluation License
pull format, 25
Pulse Code Modulation (PCM), 564
PulseAudio, 574, 577–579
    DeviceChooser, 577–578
    Manager, 577
    Preferences, 577–579
    Volume Control, 577
    Volume Unit Meter, 577
pulseaudio.org, 574
Pure-FTPd, 936–937
--purge, 690–691
Purple, Pidgin, 374, 376
~/.purple, 376
push format, 25
pushd, 407
Put computer to sleep when inactive for, Power
    Management Preferences, 158
Put display to sleep when inactive for, Power Management
    Preferences, 158
PVM, 860
pwd, 407, 933
.pxl, 519
PyScrabble, 633
pyscrabble-server, 633
Python Integrated Development Application (Pida), 826

Q

:q!, vi, 432
QEMU, 863–864
    forums, 902
    installation, 900–902
    KVM, 893
    networks, 902
    Virtual Machine Manager, 864
    wiki, 902
qemuctl, 865
qemulauncher, 865
qmail, 1037–1038
qmail.org, 1038
Qpopper
    POP, 1048–1050
    Postfix, 1041

Q

Quackle, 635
Quadrapassel, 623
Quark XPress, 486
Quattro Pro, 519
Quick Search, Synaptic Package Manager, 704–706
QuickTime, 315, 533
quit, 934
/quit, 386
qumranet.com, 891

R

R
    cp, 1001
    dpkg, 683
r
    dpkg, 683
    permissions, 125, 413
-R, gconftool-2, 197
-r
    cp, 408–409
    dhclient, 1073
    svnserve, 852
Radack, Steven, 838
RADIUS. *See* Remote Authentication Dial-In User Service
radscan.com, 574
RAID. *See* Redundant Arrays of Inexpensive Disks
rapidsvn, 847, 853
raster graphics, 535
raster images, 532
rcp, 906
RCPT TO, SMTP, 1053
rdesktop
    host, 918
    Windows Terminal Server, 918–920
RDP. *See* Remote Desktop Protocol
readdbx, 336–337
readline library, 416
readpst, 337–339
RealAudio, 564
real.com, 564
Really Simple Syndication (RSS), 23, 303
realm, Kerberos authentication, 975
[realms], 979
RealPlayer, 314
RealVNC, 909, 913
realvnc.com, 909
recipient_delimiter, 1046
Recoll, 174

Recommends, DEB packages, 699
recurring appointments, Evolution Calendar, 271–272
red, green, blue (RGB), 534, 535
    GIMP, 540
Red Hat, 6, 668
Red Hat Package Manager (RPM), 668, 715
    alien, 715, 716
-redir, 896–898
-redir protocol:host-port:guest-ip:guest-port, 898
Redundant Arrays of Inexpensive Disks (RAID), 22
    backups, 986
    SATA, 742
refresh interval, SOA, 1084
Reiser4 filesystem, 113
Reiser, Hans, 113
ReiserFS filesystem, 113, 757
relay policy, 1047
relayhost, 1053
    Postfix, 1046
release schedule, 10–11
remote, 782
Remote Authentication Dial-In User Service (RADIUS), 775
Remote Desktop Protocol (RDP), 918
    VirtualBox, 867
Remote Desktop Viewer, 913–917
remote hosts, CUPS, 1097–1100
remote printing, troubleshooting, 1100–1102
Remote Procedure Calls (RPCs), 1107–1109
remote systems
    networks, 905–924
    passwords, 907
    ssh, 906–909
    VNC, 909–917
    Windows Terminal Server, 917–923
removable media
    backups, 998–1003
    filesystems, 121–122
    multimedia, 571
Reply, Evolution, 234
Reply to All, Evolution, 234
repositories, 668
    components, 672–681
    FTP, 936–937
    PAMs, 963
    Software Sources tool, 676–681
    Subversion, 848–855
    Update Manager, 713

Requests for Comment (RFCs), 766, 1060
    DNS, 1075–1076
`required`, PAMs `control-flag`, 965
`requisite`, PAMs `control-flag`, 965
Rescue a broken system, Alternate Install CD, 96
Resize Info, Compiz Appearance Preferences, 195
resolution, 535
`resolv.conf`, 1093
resolvers, 1077
    BIND, 1079
restore
    BackupPC, 1013–1016
    direct, 1015
    Download Tar file, 1015
    Download Zip file, 1015
    `tar`, 1015
`restore`, 994, 995
restricted components, 673
reverse lookup files
    BIND, 1088–1089
    DNS, 1082–1089
    IP address, 1087–1088
RFCs. *See* Requests for Comment
RGB. *See* red, green, blue
`.rgb`, 547
Rhythmbox, 575
    audio files, 606–612
    CD, 580–581
        ripping, 583–585
    Copy, 658
    digital audio players, 656–659
    File Name, 585
    Folder Hierarchy, 585
    ID3 tags, 655
    import, 607
    Internet radio, 606–612
    iPod, 656
    Library Location, 584
    Library Structure, 585
    MP3, 585
    playlists, 656
    plug-ins, 657
    podcasts, 610–612
    Preferred Format, 585
Rich Site Summary (RSS), 23
Rich Text Format (RTF), 483
Ring Switcher, 208

ripping, 564
    CD, 583–589
        ID3, 655
        k3b, 585–588
        Rhythmbox, 583–585
Rivest, Shamir, Adelman (RSA), 907
`rm -r`, 411
`rmdir`, 411
`rndc`, 1089
`ro`
    `mount`, 120
    NFS, 1116, 1118
Roberts, Andrew, 466
Robots, 623
`root`, 125
root directory, 106
Rosetta, 9
Round to Cylinders, GNOME Partition Editor, 750
`route -n`, 886
routers, 765–766
row and column headings, OpenOffice.org Calc, 502
rows, spreadsheets, 500
`RPCMOUNTDOPTS`, 1114
`RPCNFSDCOUNT`, 1113
`RPCNFSDPRIORITY`, 1114
`rpc_pipefs`, 1113
RPCs. *See* Remote Procedure Calls
`rpc.statd`, 1113
`rpc.svcgssd`, 1114
`RPCSVCGSSDOPTS`, 1114
RPM. *See* Red Hat Package Manager
RSA. *See* Rivest, Shamir, Adelman
`rsh`, 906
`rsize=number: number`, 1118
RSS. *See* Really Simple Syndication
`rsync`
    `BackupFilesExclude`, 1010
    BackupPC, 1004
    backups, 997
    directories backups, 1001–1003
    `--one-file-system`, 1010
    uid, 1002
`rsyncd`
    BackupPC, 1004, 1008–1010
    `/etc/backuppc/config.pl`, 1009
`RsyncShareName`, 1010
RTF. *See* Rich Text Format

rulers
  Inkscape, 556
  OpenOffice.org Draw, 552
  OpenOffice.org Writer, 470
Rules Emporium forum, SpamAssassin, 1056
run_mailscanner, 1056
rw, 942
  mount, 120
  NFS, 1116, 1118

S

-S, dlocate, 689
-s, Wobbly Windows, 197
SaaS. *See* Software-as-a-Service
sabaytonlinux.org, 17
Sabily, 16
Safari, 339–351
Samba, 115, 937, 995, 1125–1136
  authentication, 1131
  configuration, 1128–1135
  directories sharing, 1135
  /etc/fstab, 1128
  home directories, 1131–1133
  installation, 1128
  passwords, 1131
  printers, 1131–1133
  security, 1131
  sharing, 1131–1133
  testparm, 1133–1134
  WINS, 1130
  workgroups, 1129–1130
Samba-3 by Example: Practical Exercises in Successful Samba Deployment (Terpstra), 1128
Samba Web Administration Tool (swat), 1129
samba-doc, 1130
samba-doc-pdf, 1129
samba.org, 937, 1136
SamePlace, 389
SANE. *See* Scanner Access Now Easy
sane-project.org, 731
SATA. *See* Serial Advanced Technology Attachment
SATDOPTS, 1113
sauerbraten.org, 639
SBCL. *See* Steel Bank Common Lisp
/sbin, 107
/sbin/mount.type, 117
Scalable Vector Graphics (SVG), 547, 551, 553–554

Scale, GIMP, 545
Scale to Frame Size, Scribus, 494
Scanner Access Now Easy (SANE), 731
scanners, 731–738
ScatterChat, 374, 389
SCCS. *See* source code control software
schemes, 1024
scope
  DHCP, 1068–1069
  IP addresses, 1068–1069
scp. *See* secure copy
Scrabble, 633–635
screen, 131
screen burn, 155–156
screen resolution, 148–149
screensaver, 155–157
screenshots, GIMP, 541–544
Scribus
  documents, 486–497
  frames, 489–497
  InDesign, 486
  installation, 487
  New Document, 487–488
  PageMaker, 486
  Quark XPress, 486
  Story Editor, 489–490
  templates, 487–489
scribus, 487
Scribus Documentation Site, 497
Scribus Wiki, 497
scribus-doc, 487
scribus.net, 486
scribus-template, 487
script kiddies, 764
scrollbars, Inkscape, 556
SCSI. *See* Small Computer System Interface
SD. *See* Secure Digital
sd, 752
.sdc, 519
SDL, KVM, 894–895
SDL. *See* Simple DirectMedia Layer
seamonkey-project.org, 283
search
  Emacs, 452–453
  folders, 242–244
  Synaptic Package Manager, 704–706
  vi, 436–437
--search, dpkg, 688–689

Search field, Software Center, 670
Search for a print driver to download, printer identification options, 728, 730
Search toolbar, Firefox, 286
searchservervirtualiztion.techtarget.com, 865
sec=method1:method2:etc, NFS, 1117
secure copy (scp), 52, 906
Secure Digital (SD), memory cards, 665
Secure Hash Algorithm (SHA), 564
Secure Shell (SSH), 794–795, 906
    Subversion, 847
Secure Sockets Layer (SSL)
    CUPS, 1102
    encryption, 252–254
security. *See also* authentication; passwords; permissions
    IM, 358
    mail servers, 1039
    networks, 763–798
    Samba, 1131
security = user, 1131
seeding, BitTorrent, 949
Select printer from database, printer identification options, 730
selection box, OpenOffice.org Calc, 505
Sendmail, 1038–1039
sendmail, 848
sendmail.org, 1039
Send/Receive, Evolution, 233
Sensei Library, 629
Sent, Evolution folder, 241
Separate+, GIMP, 510
Sepia Tone, F-Spot, 652
sequence numbers, command line, 417
Sequenced Packet Exchange (SPX), 1127
Serial Advanced Technology Attachment (SATA), 742
    IDE drives, 744
    name changes, 744
    SCSI, 746
serial number, SOA, 1084
Serial Port #1, printer connection options, 726–727
Serial Port #2, printer connection options, 727
servers. *See also specific server types*
    installation
        boot process, 90–91
        partitions, 70–72
    users, 18–19
        installation CD, 21–22, 63–91
Server Install CD, 63–91

configurations, 65–66
Server Message Block (SMB), 114–115, 937, 1127
    backups, 1011–1012
    sudo, 1011
Service Set Identifier (SSID), 774, 802
session, PAMs, 965
set
    environment variable, 424–425
    vim, 440
Settings, VirtualBox, 887
sftp, 906
.sgi, 547
SHA. *See* Secure Hash Algorithm
sha512, 969
shares
    authentication, 941
    boot, 939–940
    command line, 942–943
    GNOME desktop, 940–942
    Microsoft Windows, 937–943
    Nautilus File Manager, 941–942
shareware, 1139
sharing
    binaries, 1107
    directories, Samba, 1135
    files, 944–952
        Microsoft Windows, 1125–1127
        NFS, 106
        Samba, 1131–1133
shell script, 400
shells, 399–406
Shift Switcher, Compiz Appearance Preferences, 195
SHN. *See* Shorten codec
shntool, 615
Shockwave, 533
Shogi, 627
Shorten codec (SHN), 564
    GStreamer, 615
    stoc, 588
Show Desktop button, GNOME, 134
show xemacs21, 687
showmount, 1121
Shutdown, Power Management Preferences, 160
shutter, 541
Shuttleworth, Mark, 7
sidebars, Firefox, 288
Silicon Graphics IRIS, 547
Simple DirectMedia Layer (SDL), 892

Simple Mail Transport Protocol (SMTP), 221, 230
    Gmail, 254
    Postfix, 1041, 1051, 1053
    RCPT TO, 1053
Simple Scan, 731–734
Simple Storage Service, Amazon, 1017
single namespace, 109
SISSL. *See* Sun Industry Standards Source License
16-bit, GIMP, 540
64-bit, 20
    Desktop CD, 32
    `gtk-gnutella`, 948
    PST, 338
skin, 564
`SKIP_CHECKS=yes, ~/.config/compiz/compiz-`
      `manager`, 193
Slackware, 715
slave, 740
    BIND, 1079
SLP, 715
Small Computer System Interface (SCSI), 731, 742–743
    PATA, 746
    SATA, 746
smart upgrade
    `apt-get`, 692–693
    Synaptic Package Manager, 703
`smarthost`, 1041
smartphones, 7
SMB. *See* Server Message Block
`smb`, 1004
`smbclient`, 938, 1004, 1134–1135
`smbd`, 1128
`-smb/full/path/to/directory`, 898
`smbpasswd`, 1131
`smbtree`, 938
SMTP. *See* Simple Mail Transport Protocol
`smtpd_banner`, 1045
`smtpd_delay_reject`, 1051
`smtpd_tls_cert_file`, 1045
`smtpd_tls_key_file`, 1045
`smtpd_tls_session_cache_database`, 1046
`smtpd_use_tls`, 1045
`smtp_tls_session_cache_database`, 1046
SmugMug, 653
Snapping Windows, Compiz Appearance Preferences, 195
sneaker net, 925
`S28NetworkManager`, 783
SOA. *See* Start of Authority

`soft`, 1118
Soft Focus, F-Spot, 652
software, 667–719
    `aptitude`, 695–700
    backups, 992–997
    Debian, 668
    development, 819–855
    installation, 668
        Software Center, 669–670
    Package Management, 670–672
    Synaptic Package Manager, 700–713
    Update Manager, 713–714
Software Category pane, Software Center, 670
Software Center, software installation, 669–670
Software Sources tool
    Authentication tab, 680
    `/etc/apt/sources.list`, 676–678
    repositories, 676–681
    Third-Party Software tab, 677–679
    Updates tab, 679
Software-as-a-Service (SaaS), 1017
`software-center`, 669, 671
Solid-State Drive (SSD), 109
Solitaire, 619
sound
    APIs, 573
    daemons, 573
    devices, 566–568
    hardware, 569–570
    levels, 568
    servers, 573–574
Sound & Video, Application menu, 138
Sound Converter, 613–615
    GStreamer, 613
    WAV, 615
Sound Effects, Sound Preferences, 569
Sound Preferences, 566–567
    Sound Effects, 569
`soundconverter`, 613
source code
    `apt-get`, 693–694
    binary packages, 821
source code control software (SCCS), 845–855
    backups, 846
source packages, 672
SourceForge, 336
`sourceforge.net`, 913
`sox.sourceforge.net`, 600

spam, 244–249
    filters, 1050–1056
    mail servers, 1039
    Postfix, 1051–1053
SpamAssassin, 248, 1050
    MailScanner, 1056
    Postfix, 1054–1056
    Rules Emporium forum, 1056
spamassassin.apache.org, 1050
special effects, Compiz, 193–208
special-purpose systems
    CDs, 62
    installation, 61–101
Spin down hard disks when possible, Power Management
        Preferences, 158
:split, vim, 439
spot backups, 988
spreadsheets, 500. See also OpenOffice.org Calc
SPX. See Sequenced Packet Exchange
Spyglass, 282
SSD. See Solid-State Drive
SSH. See Secure Shell
ssh, 888
    remote systems, 906–909
    xterm, 406
ssh hostname, 906
SSID. See Service Set Identifier
SSL. See Secure Sockets Layer
stair-stepping, 535
Stallman, Richard, 4, 428
Stampede, 715
standards, 5
stanzas, DHCP, 1064
StarOffice, 467, 498
Start of Authority (SOA), 1083
startx, 184
static addresses, 767
Static Application Switcher, Compiz Appearance
        Preferences, 195
Status bar
    Firefox, 286
    Inkscape, 556
Steel Bank Common Lisp (SBCL), 826
Steele, Guy, 428
stemming, 174
Stick Notes applet, 153
stoc, SHN, 588
Storage-as-a-Service (SaaS), 1017

Storix, 993
storix.com, 993
Story Editor, Scribus, 489–490
streaming, 564
Strigi, 174
string, 198
stw, 468
styles, OpenOffice.org Writer, 477–480
Styles and Formatting window
    OpenOffice.org Draw, 553
    OpenOffice.org Impress, 526
    OpenOffice.org Writer, 471, 477–480
su, 125–126
Subclipse Plug-in, 845
subclipse.tigris.org, 845
subdirectories, 106
submenus, 137
subtractive primary colors, 532
Subversion
    FlyBack, 1020
    HTTP, 850
    installation, 847–855
    IRC, 855
    -m, 849
    mailing lists, 855
    passwords, 851
    repositories, 848–855
    server, 850–853
    SSH, 847
subversion, 847
Subversion Book, 854
Subversion FAQ, 854
subversion.apache.org, 847, 854
subversion-tools, 848
Subversive Plug-in, 845
sudo, 125–126
    alien, 714
    apt-get, 690, 972
    aptitude, 972
    backups, 991
    chgrp, 414
    chown, 414
    command line, 972
    customization, 972–975
    dpkg, 972
    fdisk, 754
    gksudo, 972
    .ICEauthority, 972

passwords, 972
SMB, 1011
sudo adduser, 868
sudo aptitude update, 804
sudo postfix reload, 1047
sudo/etc/init.d/postfix restart, 1047
sudo/etc/init.d/xinetd restart, 1049
Sudoku, 621–622
sufficient, PAMs control-flag, 965
--suggest, 699
Suggests, DEB packages, 699
suid, 120
sum, 504
Sun Industry Standards Source License (SISSL), 467
Sun Microsystems, 467
Sun Rasterfile, 547
Super Video CD (SVCD), 564
SuperScript-660i, 1097
superusers, 125
support, 22–27
SUSE, 6
Suspend, Power Management Preferences, 159
SVCD. See Super Video CD
SVG. See Scalable Vector graphics
.svg, 547
:sview, 439
svn, 849
svn ci, 854
svn co file:///var/svn/hello, 853
svn co http://192.168.6.90/svn/hello, 853
svn co svn://192.168.6.90/svn/hello, 853
svn list, 849
svnadmin create, 848
svnbook.red-bean.com, 854
SVNPath, 851
svnserve, 852
swap partitions, 82, 88
/etc/fstab, 119
swapon/dev/sda2, 757
swat. See Samba Web Administration Tool
swatch book, 534
Sweet, Michael R., 1103
Swell Foop, 623
SWF, 352
S20wicd, 783
switches, 765
sxg, 468
sxw, 468

.sylk, 519
Symantec, 993
symantec.com, 993
symbolic links, 396
symbolic mode, changing permissions in, 412
Synaptic Package Manager, 117, 667, 671, 672, 691–692
apt-get, 690, 703
apt-get dist-upgrade, 703
aptitude, 703
Bacula, 997
development software installation, 820
/etc/apt/sources.list, 701
GTK+, 701
GUI, 695
installation, 706–711
NFS, 1111
Postfix, 1041
Preferences, 702–704
Properties dialog, 705–706
Quick Search, 704–706
removing packages, 711–713
search, 704–706
smart upgrade, 703
software, 700–713
Terminal window, 710–711
window managers, 705
sync, 1117
Synserve, Subversion server, 850–853
/sys, 107
system groups, 124
System menu, GNOME, 134, 139–140
System Monitor applet, 153
system requirements, 1137–1138
system sounds, 568–569
system-config-samba, 1128

T

-t
mkfs, 757
mount, 117
Tab key, bash shell, 417–418
tabbed browsing, Firefox, 287–288
tabs, Firefox, 284
Tag, F-Spot, 650
Tagged Image File Format (TIFF), 535, 547
Tali, 619
talk, 356

tar, 715, 998–999
    BackupPC, 1004
    backups, 995
    restore, 1015
tarball, 1000
    Eclipse, 840–841
    FlyBack, 1020
TarGA, 547
tar.gz, apt.get, 694
Tavmjong Bah, 557
TCP/IP. *See* Transmission Control Protocol/Internet
        Protocol
TECO. *See* Text Editor and Corrector
telnet, 905–906, 1049
    Kerberos authentication, 906
    VPN, 906
telnetd, 906
templates
    Document Converter, 520–521
    Evolution folder, 241
    OpenOffice.org Writer, 476, 480–483
    Scribus, 487–489
10/100 Ethernet, 765
10-baseT, 765
TENEX C-shell, 401
Terminal window, Synaptic Package Manager, 710–711
Terpstra, John H., 1128, 1136
Test memory, Alternate Install CD, 96
testparm, Samba, 1133–1134
Tetravex, 622
TeX, 462–466
    command line, 464
    TRIP, 462
TeX Live, 462
TeXbook (Knuth), 466
texlive, 462
texlive-doc, 462
TeXmacs, LaTeX, 464–465
texmacs.org, 465
text
    editors
        DHCP, 1064–1066
        text files, 428–429
    files, 427–459
        Emacs, 442–456
        gedit, 456–458
        text editors, 428–429
        vi, 430–442
    frames, 489–496

.text, 546
Text Editor and Corrector (TECO), 428
Text Processing Using LaTeX, 466
Text-mode, Desktop system installation, 97–98
tftp, 1001
.tga, 547
TGZ, 715
THE. *See* The Hessling Editor
thefreecountry.com, 865
Theme Manager, Emerald, 217–219
themes
    Firefox, 306–314
    GNOME desktop, 163–164
Third-Party Software tab, Software Sources tool, 677–679
32-bit
    FAT32, 49
    PST, 338
Thompson, Ken, 399, 428
1000-BaseT, 765
Thunderbird, 255, 283, 324–335
.tif, 547
TIFF. *See* Tagged Image File Format
tightvnc.com, 910, 913
tightvncserver, 912
Time Machine, 1019–1020
Time To Live (TTL), 1082, 1083
time zone, server installation, 68–69
time.conf, 970
timeo=number: number, 1118
time-out period, 972
TimeVault, 1020–1021
tim-mann.org, 624
Tinyproxy, 16
title bar, 136
TiVo, 641
tldp.org, 825
TLS. *See* Transport Layer Security
/tmp, 82, 107
TOLIS Group, 993
tolisgroup.com, 993
Tool Options, GIMP, 539–540
toolbars
    F-Spot, 651
    Inkscape, 556
    OpenOffice.org Calc, 502
    OpenOffice.org Draw, 552
    OpenOffice.org Impress, 525
    OpenOffice.org Writer, 470

Toolbox window
    GIMP, 538
    Inkscape, 556
Torcs, 640
torcs.sourceforge.net, 640
Torrent files, 565
torrentscan.com, 951
Torvalds, Linus, 4
Totem, 581–583
Traceroute, 788
track-at-once, 564
Tracker, 173–181
tracker-search-tool, 174
tracker-stats, 179
tracker-status, 179
tracker-utils, 174, 179
transcode, 564
translucency, 190
Transmission Control Protocol/Internet Protocol (TCP/IP),
        764–765, 783–785, 885, 928, 1127
transparency, 190
Transport Layer Security (TLS), 775, 1045–1046
Trash
    Evolution folder, 241
    GNOME, 135
Tridgell, Andrew, 937
Trillian, 386
troubleshooting
    CD, 1139
    Device Manager, 760–761
    DHCP, 1072–1073
    DNS, 1091–1094
    remote printing, 1100–1102
True Audio codec (TTA), 564–565
true-audio.com, 565
trusted hosts, Postfix, 1047
tsclient, 921–923
TTA. See True Audio codec
TTL. See Time To Live
tug.org/texlive, 462
TUN/TAP, 897
Tutorial: Getting Started with Scribus, 497
tutorialsforopenoffice.org, 486
Tux Racer, 638–639
Tux4Kids, 15
.txt, 546
type, 117
--type, 197–198

U

u
    cp, 1001
    dpkg, 683
-u, rdesktop, 919
Ubuntu Community Virtualization Overview, 865
Ubuntu Enterprise Cloud (UEC), 64, 91–95
Ubuntu Foundation, 11
Ubuntu Manifesto, 8–10
Ubuntu Marketplace, 28
Ubuntu Mobile Internet Device Edition, 18
Ubuntu Netbook Remix (UNR), 18
Ubuntu One, 1017–1019
Ubuntu Server Edition, 18–19
Ubuntu Software Center, 668–670
Ubuntu Studio, 17, 557
Ubuntu Virtualization Overview, 865
ubuntuforums.org, 23–24
ubuntuguide.org, 29
ubuntu-restricted-extras, 575, 591
ubuntustudio.org, 557
ubuntu-vm-builder, 868
    KVM, 892–893
ubuntu-women.org, 29
ubuntux.org, 29
udhcpd, 1063
UDP. See Datagram Protocol; User Datagram Protocol
UEC. See Ubuntu Enterprise Cloud
ufw. See Uncomplicated Firewall
UID. See user ID
uid, rsync, 1002
uid=0, /mnt/office, 940
uid=value, mount, 121
ulsync --action=download, 1019
ulsync --action=upload, 1019
UltraSPARC, 20, 32
umask, 414
UML. See User-Mode Linux
uml-utilities, 899
    Package Management, 885
umount, 942
Uncomplicated Firewall (ufw), 793
Undisclosed Recipients, Contact List, 266
Undo
    F-Spot, 653
    vi, 437
Uniform Resource Identifier (URI), 1024–1025
    printer connection options, 727

Uniform Resource Locator (URL), 223
    bookmarks, 296
    Firefox, 283, 853
    URI, 1025
Uniform Resource Name (URN), 1025
Universal Unique Identifiers (UUIDs), 745
universe component, 673
Unix-to-Unix Calling Program (UUCP), 763
unmount, 942
Unprivileged, Users and Groups tool, 958
UNR. *See* Ubuntu Netbook Remix
unzip, 815
updates, 11
    Eclipse, 829–831
    server installation, 76–77
Update Manager, software, 713–714
update-alternatives --config java, 830
update-grub, 739, 746
update-manager, 671
Updates tab, Software Sources tool, 679
uplink port, 766
URI. *See* Uniform Resource Identifier
URL. *See* Uniform Resource Locator
URN. *See* Uniform Resource Name
usage message, 398
USB flash memory stick
    backups, 987
    BIOS, 53
    boot, 53, 54
    Desktop CD, 52–56
    partitions, 54
    reformatting, 55–56
Usenet, 26
users, 956–963
    command line, 956
user accounts
    Empathy, 362–369
    installation, 41–42
    Linux filesystem, 122–124
    Pidgin, 374–376
    server installation, 73
User Data, OpenOffice.org Writer, 472–473
User Datagram Protocol (UDP), 1107–1108
user ID (UID), 1111
user interface. *See also* graphical user interface
    aptitude, 696–698
    Eclipse, 828
    Firefox, 284–289
    XUL, 283

User Networking, KVM, 896–898
User Privileges, Users and Groups tool, 958–959
useradd, 956
userdel, 956
usermod, 956
User-Mode Linux (UML), 861
username, server installation, 74
    boot process, 90
USERNAME, 940
user-name, 956
Users and Groups tool, 957–963
/user/sbin/apache2ctl, 1028
/user/share/doc/apache2-, 1030
usinglinux.org, 864
/usr, 82, 108
/usr/bin/ar, 688
/usr/bin/rsync, 1009
/usr/local, 82, 407
/usr/share/apache2/error, 1028
/usr/shared/doc/3dchess/3dc-rules.html, 627
/usr/skin/krb5_newrealm, 980
UTC. *See* Coordinated Universal Time
UUCP. *See* Unix-to-Unix Calling Program
UUIDs. *See* Universal Unique Identifiers

V

v
    cp, 1001
    rsync, 1003
    tar, 999
/var, 108
variable bit rate (VBR), 565
/var/lib/backuppc, 1006–1007
/var/lib/backuppc/win2k, 1011
/var/lib/nfs/rpc_pipefs, 1113
/var/log/apache2/error.log, 1028
/var/log/cups, 1100–1101
/var/log/lastlog, 967
/var/log/messages, 1072
/var/log/syslog, 1091
/var/run/apache2/apache2.pid, 1028
/var/spool/postfix/hold, 1055
/var/spool/postfix/incoming, 1055
/var/svn, 848
/var/www, 1029
/var/www/apache2-default, 1028
vboxdrv, 866
VBR. *See* variable bit rate

V

vCards, 264
VCDs. *See* Video CDs
VDE. *See* virtual distributed Ethernet
vector graphics, 535
Venema, Wietse, 1037, 1057
Veritas, 993
versions, 8, 14–19
    Evolution, 224
    NFS, 1109–1110
    vim, 441
vfolders, 242
vgabios, 892
vi, 431–441
video burn, 156
Video CDs (VCDs), 564, 565
video games, 622–623
vim, 430
    command line, 439–441
    customization, 439–441
.vimrc, 439, 441
vim-tiny, 441
vinagre, 910, 913–914
vino-server, 910
virt.kernelnewbies.org, 865
virt_manager, 863, 864
Virtual Bridge, KVM, 898–900
virtual desktops, Compiz, 193
Virtual Disk Manager, 872
virtual disks, 872–876
virtual distributed Ethernet (VDE), 897
virtual folders, 242
Virtual Machine Manager, 864–865
virtual machines, 857–903
    boot, 890–891
    cursor, 894
    hard disks, 872–876
    installation, 890–891
    memory, 871–872
    operating system, 877–880, 894–896
    ports, 884
    starting/stopping, 881–883
    types, 859–861
    VirtualBox, 868–877
Virtual Network Computing (VNC), 909–917
virtual private networks (VPNs), 777–783, 906
virtual storage, 857
VirtualBox, 862–863
    DHCP, 867, 883

/etc/network/interfaces, 885
Guest Additions, 881
Host Interface, 884
NAT, 883
Network Manager, 885
networks, 883–889
OSE, 885–886
ports, 888
Settings, 887
TCP/IP, 885
virtual machines, 867–880
virtualbox, 868
~/.VirtualBox, 875
virtualbox-ose, 868
virtualization, 7, 857–903
Virtualization Technology (VT), Intel, 891
Virtualization/Secure Virtual Machine (V/SVM), 861–862,
    891
Virtuozzo, 860
virus scanning, 1050–1056
vistasource.com, 498
VMWare, 860, 862–863
VNC. *See* Virtual Network Computing
vnc, 1001
vnc4server, 912
vnc4viewer, 910
~.vnc/xstartup, 912
Voice over IP (VoIP), 357
VoIP. *See* Voice over IP
Volume Control, PulseAudio, 577
Volume Control applet, 153
Volume Unit Meter, PulseAudio, 577
VPN Concentrator (VPNC), 777
VPNC. *See* VPN Concentrator
VPNs. *See* virtual private networks
VServer, 860
:vsplit, 439
V/SVM. *See* Virtualization/Secure Virtual Machine
VT. *See* Virtualization Technology
vt100, 697

W

w
    permissions, 125, 413
    vi, 433
:w, vi, 432
Walrus, 64

warn, 1033
Warty Warthog, 10
Water Effect, 208
WAV, 565, 586, 600, 615
WAvPack, 565
.wb1, 519
.wb2, 519
.wb3, 519
wc -l, ls, 420
Weather, Evolution Calendar, 274–275
Weather Report applet, 154
Web Distributed Authoring and Versioning (WebDAV), 847
Web servers, 1023–1057
Web-based e-mail, Evolution, 249–256
WebCal, 274–276
WebDAV. *See* Web Distributed Authoring and Versioning
webmaster@localhost, 1030
webmin, 1129
WEP. *See* Wired Equivalent Privacy
wesnoth.org, 639
wget, 928
What You *See* Is What You Get (WYSIWYG), 464
which, 689
whitelisting, 1051
/who #channel, 386
Whois, 788
Wicd, 768, 776, 803–810
wide-dhcpv6-server, 1063
Wi-Fi Protected Access (WPA), 775, 802
wiki
    Evolution, 279
    KVM, 892
    Linux Virtualization Wiki, 865
    QEMU, 902
    Ubuntu One, 1017
wiki.scribus.net, 497
wiki.ubuntu.com, 26
wildcards
    bash shell, 418–420
    Emacs, 684–685
Window Decorations, Compiz Appearance Preferences, 195
Window list, GNOME, 134
window managers
    GNOME, 181–186
    Synaptic Package Manager, 705
windowmaker.info, 701
Windows BMP, 547
Windows Media Audio (WMA), 565, 576–577, 600

Windows Media Player, 314
Windows Media Video (WMV), 565, 576–577
Windows Terminal Server, 917–923
Windows Terminal Services, 921–923
Windows-based Ubuntu Installer (Wubi), 56–59
Windowsprinter via SAMBA, 727
WINE, 655, 858
WINGS toolkit, 701
Win-modems, 786
WINS, 1007, 1130
Wired Equivalent Privacy (WEP), 774, 802
wireless networks, 773–776, 799–818
    command line, 811–813
    device drivers, Microsoft Windows, 814–816
    encryption, 806
    Ethernet, 802
    PCMCIA, 802
wireless-essid, 785
wireless-tools, 811
--with-recommends, 554, 699
Wixson, Kevin, 557
.wk1, 519
.wks, 519
WMA. *See* Windows Media Audio
WMV. *See* Windows Media Video
Wobbly Windows, 195, 197, 208
WordBiz, 633
w3.org, 553
workgroups, Samba, 1129–1130
workspace
    Compiz, 193
    Eclipse, 829
    GNOME, 134–135
wormux.org, 640
WPA. *See* Wi-Fi Protected Access
:wq, 432
write, 356
Writer. *See* OpenOffice.org Writer
wsize=number: number, 1118
Wubi. *See* Windows-based Ubuntu Installer
wvh, 942
www, 1087
www-data, 852
WYSIWYG. *See* What You See Is What You Get

X

X, dpkg, 683

X

x
   cp, 1001
   permissions, 125, 413
:x, vi, 432
X Bitmap, 547
X Display Manager Control Protocol (XDMCP), 923
X Pixmap, 547
X Window System, 130, 181–185
   command line, 392, 403–406
   Emacs, 442
   OpenGL, 191–192
xaraxtreme.org, 558
Xbase, 519
.xbm, 547
xboard, 625–626
.xcf, 546
.xcfbz2, 546
.xcfgz, 546
xchat-gnome, 387
xcompmgr, 191
XDMCP. *See* X Display Manager Control Protocol
XDR. *See* eXternal Data Representation
XEmacs, 445–446
xemacs, 685
Xen, 860, 863, 864
xenman, 865
Xfce, Xubuntu, 17
XFS filesystem, 113, 757
Xfvwm, 191–192
.xhtml, 546
Ximian, 221
xinetd, 852, 1001
xinit, 184
.xjt, 546
.xjtbz2, 546
.xjtgz, 546
.xls, 353, 519
.xlsx, 519
.xlt, 519

.xlw, 519
xm, 863
xmame-sdl, 863
xmame-x, 863
.xml, 519, 554
XML User Interface Language (XUL), 283
XMMS, 655
.xpm, 547
XSane Image Scanner, 732, 734–738
.xsession, 183–185
xterm
   -e, 406
   Emacs, 443
   ssh, 406
   vi, 431
Xubuntu, 7, 17
XUL. *See* XML User Interface Language
.xwd, 547

Y

Yahoo!, 359, 360
   mail, 256
Yoshinori Yamakawa, 540
YPOPs!, 254

Z

z
   rsync, 1003
   tar, 999
Z shell, 401
Zekr, 16
zone files, 1082–1089
Zoomr, 653
zophar.net, 864
ZQ, 432
Zsoft PCX, 547
ZZ, 432

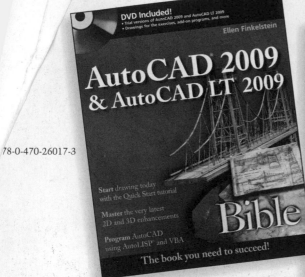
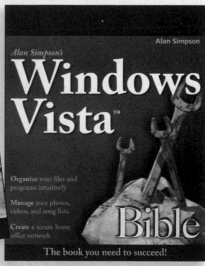